T0305199

STABLE PARETIAN
MODELS IN FINANCE

WILEY

SERIES IN FINANCIAL ECONOMICS
AND QUANTITATIVE ANALYSIS

Series Editor: Stephen Hall, *London Business School,* UK

Editorial Board: Robert F. Engle, *University of California, USA*
John Flemming, *European Bank, UK*
Lawrence R. Klein, *University of Pennsylvania, USA*
Helmut Lütkepohl, *Humboldt University, Germany*

Further titles in preparation
Proposals will be welcomed by the Series Editor

STABLE PARETIAN
MODELS IN FINANCE

Svetlozar Rachev
University of California, USA

and

Stefan Mittnik
University of Kiel, Germany

JOHN WILEY & SONS LTD.
Chichester · New York · Weinheim · Brisbane · Singapore · Toronto

Copyright © 2000 by John Wiley & Sons Ltd,
Baffins Lane, Chichester,
West Sussex PO19 1UD, England

National   01243 779777
International (+44) 1243 779777

e-mail (for orders and customer service enquiries:

cs-books@wiley.co.uk
Visit our Home Page on http://www.wiley.co.uk
or http://www.wiley.com

Other Wiley Editorial Offices

John Wiley & Sons, Inc., 605 Third Avenue,
New York, NY 10158-0012, USA

Wiley-VCH GmbH, Pappelallee 3,
D-69469 Weinheim, Germany

Jacaranda Wiley Ltd, 33 Park Road, Milton,
Queensland 4064, Australia

John Wiley & Sons (Asia) Pte Ltd, 2 Clementi Loop #02-01,
Jin Xing Distripark, Singapore 129809

John Wiley & Sons (Canada) Ltd, 22 Worcester Road,
Rexdale, Ontario M9W 1L1, Canada

British Library Cataloguing in Publication Data

A catalogue record for this book is available from the British Library

ISBN 0-471-95314-8

Produced from PS files supplied by the authors
Printed and bound by CPI Antony Rowe, Eastbourne
This book is printed on acid-free paper responsibly manufactured from sustainable forestry,
in which at least two trees are planted for each one used for paper production.

TO OUR PARENTS

Contents

Series Preface

This series aims to publish books which give authoritative accounts of major new topics in financial economics and general quantitative analysis. The coverage of the series includes both macro and micro economics and its aim is to be of interest to practitioners and policy-makers as well as the wider academic community.

The development of new techniques and ideas in econometrics has been rapid in recent years and these developments are now being applied to a wide range of areas and markets. Our hope is that this series will provide a rapid and effective means of communicating these ideas to a wide international audience and that in turn will contribute to the growth of knowledge, the exchange of scientific information and techniques and the development of cooperation in the field of economics.

Stephen Hall
London Business School, UK and
Imperial College, UK

Foreword

The adoption of stable modeling in finance and econometrics is undoubtedly one of the most interesting and promising ideas which has arisen in these fields. It is now widely accepted that classical models for the description of the dynamics of financial and economic variables suffer from major structural weaknesses, as they fail to explain important features of the empirical data. Therefore, the search for new more powerful models is a fundamental and fascinating topic of research. In this book, Rachev and Mittnik, two of the most prominent experts in so-called Stable Finance, present a wealth of convincing arguments to support the claim that stable models offer the right approach to the subject. Their monograph, which collects a large part of the authors' work in stable financial modeling, brings together innovative insights as well as new elegant explanations of financial and economic phenomena.

While alternative models based on other non-Gaussian distributions are to be found in the literature, the stable assumption has unique distinctive characteristics that make it an ideal candidate. The central limit theorem provides a theoretically sound explanation for its emergence: whenever a financial variable can be regarded as the result of many microscopic effects, it can be described by a stable law, as this is the only possible limit in distribution of the sum of i.i.d. random variables. Moreover, stable laws can account naturally for asymmetries and heavy tails.

On the other hand, an argument frequently invoked against stable models is that infinite variance is unverifiable. In my opinion, models with infinite variance do not have to be rejected a priori. There is no reason to assume that the "determinants" of observable financial variables have finite variance. Moreover, from an empirical point of view, in many situations stable models offer a better description of the data. Similar reasoning would induce us to reject distributions with infinite support. How could we justify the assumption that an infinitely large shock is possible, even if very unlikely? Another objection to the stable assumption is that the estimated index of stability of real data sets tends to increase with the time horizon. This observation actually implies that returns are not independent, and/or not identically distributed, and/or not stable, but it does not automatically rule out that stable processes may underlie generating models. On the contrary, the stable models introduced in this book can exhibit sophisticated dependence structures. The authors do not limit themselves to an account of their contributions, but exhibit a sharp critical sense towards their proposals, raising interesting questions and stimulating topics for further research.

In addition to their many desirable properties, stable models are also highly versatile. They have many possible applications, ranging from equilibrium asset pricing to risk management. Moreover, with the current availability of computational power, stable models do not present serious numerical difficulties and should quickly repay the time and effort spent in their implementation. Rachev and Mittnik guide the more practically oriented readers through the subtleties of the computational aspects, explaining how to implement with relative ease the powerful models they present.

The book explains in a lucid and understandable manner how to extend a wide range of financial paradigms to the stable case, presenting both new theoretical results and empirical applications. The material covered is truly impressive in its breadth and quality, and will be of great interest to researchers and advanced graduate students, as well as practitioners looking for state-of-the-art models with a better fit to real data.

EDUARDO S. SCHWARTZ

California Chair in Real Estate and
Professor of Finance
Anderson School of Management
University of California, Los Angeles
September 1999

Preface

"...some scholars now believe that stock prices have been more volatile (with Black Monday and Terrible Tuesday, October 19-20, 1987, being prime examples) that any existing theory would suggest."
– William F. Sharpe and Gordon J. Alexander: Investment, Prentice Hall 1992, Preface.

"Most of the models assume that stock options follow a log-normal distribution, in fact, I found out that the actual price distributions of virtually all financial markets tend to have fatter tails than suggested by the log-normal distribution."
–Blair Hull (The New Market Wizzards, by Jack D. Schwager, Hupper/Collins 1992, p.337)

Most of the concepts in theoretical and empirical finance that have been developed over the past decades rest upon the assumption that asset returns follow a normal distribution. By now, there is, however, ample empirical evidence that many—if not most—financial return series are heavy–tailed and, possibly, skewed. This is not only of concern to financial theorists, but also to practitioners who are, in view of the frequency of sharp market down turns, troubled by the "...compelling evidence that something is rotten in the foundation of the statistical edifice..." used, for example, to produce probability estimates for financial risk assessment.[1]

---

[1] Richard Hoppe, "It's time we buried Value–at–Risk," *Risk Professional*, Issue 1/5, July/August 1999, p. 16.

In this book we investigate the consequences of relaxing the normality assumption and develop generalizations of prevalent concepts in modern theoretical and empirical finance that can accommodate heavy–tailed returns. New non–Gaussian approaches to issues like security pricing, portfolio management, risk analysis, and empirical analysis are presented. The results are of interest to researchers and graduate students working in financial economics and those practitioners, who want to base their financial models and decisions on more realistic and more reliable distributional assumptions.

The material in this book builds upon Benoit Mandelbrot's fundamental work in the 1960s which strongly rejected normality as a distributional model for asset returns. Examining various time series on commodity returns and interest rates, he conjectured that financial return processes behave like non–Gaussian stable processes. To distinguish between Gaussian and non–Gaussian stable distributions, the latter are often referred to as "stable Paretian" (emphasizing the fact that the tails of the non–Gaussian stable density have Pareto power–type decay) or "Lévy stable" (due to the seminal work of Paul Lévy introducing and characterizing the class of non–Gaussian stable laws).

Mandelbrot's contributions give rise to a new probabilistic foundation for financial theory and empirics, and are of similar importance as the fundamental contributions of Louis Bachelier (1900) and Paul Samuelson (1955). His early investigations on asset returns were carried further by Eugene Fama and Richard Roll, among others, and led to a consolidation of the Stable Paretian Hypothesis. In the 1970s, however, closer empirical scrutiny of the "stability" of fitted Stable Paretian distributions also produced evidence that was not consistent with the Stable Paretian Hypothesis. In particular, it was often reported that fitted characteristic exponents (or tail–indices) do not to remain constant under temporal aggregation. Partly in response to these empirical "inconsistencies", various alternatives to the stable law have been proposed in the literature. Among the candidates considered were, for example, fat–tailed distributions being only in the domain of attraction of a stable Paretian law, finite mixtures of normal distributions, the Student t–distribution, or the hyperbolic distribution.

A major drawback of all these alternative models is their lack of *stability*. As has been stressed by Mandelbrot and will be argued in this book, the stability property is highly desirable for asset returns. This is particularly evident in the context of portfolio analysis and risk management. Only for stable distributed returns do we have the property that linear combinations of different return series (e.g., portfolios) follow again a stable distribution. Indeed, the Gaussian law shares this feature, but it is only one particular member of a large and flexible class of distributions, which also allows for skewness and heavy–tailedness.

Recent critique of Mandelbrot's Stable Paretian Hypothesis centers around the claim that asset return distributions are not as heavy–tailed as the non–Gaussian stable law suggests. Studies that come to such conclusions are typically based on tail–index estimates obtained with the Hill estimator. This estimator is, however, highly unreliable for testing the stable hypothesis, because sample sizes beyond 100,000 are required to obtain reasonably accurate estimates. More importantly, the Mandelbrot Stable Paretian Hypothesis is interpreted too narrowly, if one focuses solely on the *marginal* distribution of return processes. In our view, the hypothesis involves more than simply fitting marginal asset–return distributions. Stable Paretian laws describe the fundamental "building blocks" (e.g., innovations) that drive asset return processes. In addition to describing these "building blocks", a complete model should be rich enough to encompass relevant stylized facts, such as

- non–Gaussian, heavy–tailed and skewed distributions

- volatility clustering (ARCH–effects)

- temporal dependence of the tail behavior

- short– and long–range dependence

An attractive feature of stable models—not shared by other distributional models—is that they allow us to generalize Gaussian–based financial theories and, thus, to build a coherent and more general framework for financial modeling. The generalizations are only possible because of specific probabilistic properties that are unique to (Gaussian and non–Gaussian) stable laws, namely, the stability property, the Central Limit Theorem, and the Invariance Principle for Lévy–stable processes.

In this book we focus on topics of particular relevance in theoretical and empirical finance. Specifically, we address the following issues:

- modeling asset return processes (Chapters 1-7)

- portfolio analysis and risk management (Chapters 8-10)

- derivative pricing (Chapters 11-13)

- econometrics in the presence of heavy–tailed innovations (Chapters 14-15)

Writing this book has been a challenging task. We have greatly benefited from research collaborations—some of which have lasted over many years—with Benny Cheng, David Chenyao, Toker Doganoglu, Bertrand Gamrowski, Joe Gani, Simon Hurst, Rajeeva Karandikar, Irina Khindanova, Jeong-Ryeol Kim, Lev Klebanov, Tom Kozubowski, Carlo Marinelli, Mark Paolella, Vygantas Paulauskas, Eckhard Platen, Sascha Rieken, Ludger Rüschendorf, Gennady Samorodnitsky, and Huang Xin. We thank all of them for fruitful interactions and hope there will be more.

The completion of the book would not have been possible without Thomas Plum, who was not only responsible for technical typing but also instrumental in assembling, organizing and editing the manuscript.

Support from the National Science Foundation, the German Science Foundation (DFG) and the Alexander–von–Humboldt Foundation is gratefully acknowledged.

All errors are our own responsibility. We encourage the readers to alert us to shortcomings and look forward to receiving comments and suggestions.

Svetlozar Rachev, Santa Barbara, Karlsruhe
Stefan Mittnik, Kiel
August 1999

1

Introduction

1.1 Stable Models in Finance

Financial investment decisions are almost exclusively based on the expected return and risk associated with available investment opportunities. The distributional form of returns on financial assets has important implications for theoretical and empirical analyses in economics and finance. For example, asset, portfolio and option pricing theories are typically based on distributional assumptions. In empirical tests, statistical inference concerning, for example, the efficient market hypothesis, the excess volatility question or option pricing models may be sensitive to the distributional assumptions for the returns of the underlying assets.

The work of Mandelbrot (1962, 1963a,b, 1967) and Fama (1965a) has sparked considerable interest in studying the empirical distribution of returns on common stocks as well as other financial assets.[1] While earlier theories, building on Bachelier's (1900) original theory on speculation, had been based on the normal distribution, the excess kurtosis found in Mandelbrot's and Fama's investigations led them to reject the normal assumption and propose the *stable Paretian distribution* as a statistical model for asset returns. In subsequent years a number of empirical investigations supported this conjecture (see, for example, Teichmoeller (1971); Officer (1972), Mittnik, Rachev and

---

[1]For example, distributional aspects of returns on treasury bills (Roll (1970); DuMouchel (1983)), commodity futures (Clark (1973); Dusak (1973)) and foreign exchange (Westerfield (1977); McFarland et al. (1978, 1987); Calderson-Ressel and Ben-Horim (1982); So (1987)) have been studied.

Paolella (1997). As a consequence of this empirical evidence and the fact that the attractive theoretical properties, the stable Paretian assumption enjoyed quite some popularity among financial modelers (see, for example, Mandelbrot (1997), Mittnik and Rachev (1993a,b); Chobanov, Mateev, Mittnik and Rachev (1996), Adler et al. (1998) and the references therein).

Detailed accounts of properties of stable distributed random variables can be found in Samorodnitsky and Taqqu (1994) and Janicki and Weron (1994). An important desirable property is the fact that stable Paretian distributions have *domains of attraction*. In general, any decision (inference) based on observed data is a functional on the space of distributions that govern the data. In practice one cannot expect that observed data follow *exactly* the "ideal" distribution specified by the modeler. The distributional model represents only an approximation of the distribution underlying the observed data. This problem gives rise to the crucial question of what is the domain of applicability of the specified model. Could it happen that slight perturbations in the data give rise to substantially different distributional outcomes and, thus, different conclusions? Loosely speaking, any distribution in the domain of attraction of a specified stable distribution will have properties which are close to those of the stable distribution. Consequently, decisions will, in principle, not be affected by adopting an "idealizing" stable distribution as the distributional model instead of the true distribution. Moreover, it is possible to check whether or not a distribution is in the domain of attraction of a stable distribution by examining only the tails of the distribution, because only they specify the domain-of-attraction properties of the distribution. Thus, the continuity (stability) of the adopted model is valid for any distribution with the appropriate tail.

A second attractive aspect of the stable Paretian assumption is the *stability property*. This is desirable because it implies that each stable distribution has an "index of stability" (shape parameter), which remains the same regardless of the scale adopted. The index of stability plays the role of the "compound" parameter that governs the main properties of the underlying distribution. When using stable distributions, we need not be concerned with the question: which of the parameters is most relevant. The index of stability can be regarded as an overall parameter, which can be employed for inference and decision making.

There are alternative probabilistic schemes that give rise to *stability*. They are summarized in Table 1.1, where X_i stands for the return on an asset in period $t_0 + i$. We assume that $X_1, X_2, \ldots$ are i.i.d. real-valued r.v.'s. We write

$$X_1 \stackrel{d}{=} a_n(X_1 \circ X_2 \circ \cdots \circ X_n) + b_n, \tag{1.1}$$

where $\stackrel{d}{=}$ denotes equality in distribution; $\circ$ stands for summation, min, max, or multiplication; n is a deterministic or random integer; $a_n > 0$; and $b_n \in \mathbf{R}$. The standard nonrandom summation scheme, i.e., $\circ$ stands for $+$ and n is a deterministic integer, produces the stable Paretian distribution. The maximum and minimum schemes lead to extreme-value distributions. The multiplication scheme yields the multiplication-stable distribution of which the log-normal is the basic example.

Table 1.1   Stable Probabilistic Schemes.

Scheme	Stability Property[a]
Summation	$X_1 \overset{d}{=} a_n(X_1 + \cdots + X_n) + b_n$
Maximum	$X_1 \overset{d}{=} a_n \max_{1 \leq i \leq n} X_i + b_n$
Minimum	$X_1 \overset{d}{=} a_n \min_{1 \leq i \leq n} X_i + b_n$
Multiplication	$X_1 \overset{d}{=} A_n(X_1 X_2 \cdots X_n)^{C_n}$
Geometric Summation	$X_1 \overset{d}{=} a(p)(X_1 + \cdots + X_{T(p)}) + b(p)$
Geometric Maximum	$X_1 \overset{d}{=} a(p) \max_{1 \leq i \leq T(p)} X_i + b(p)$
Geometric Minimum	$X_1 \overset{d}{=} a(p) \min_{1 \leq i \leq T(p)} X_i + b(p)$
Geometric Multiplication	$X_1 \overset{d}{=} A(p)(X_1 X_2 \cdots X_{T(p)})^{C(p)}$

[a] Notation "$X_1 \overset{d}{=}$" stands for "equality in distribution."
(Adapted from: Mittnik, Rachev and Paolella (1998))

In the geometric schemes, where n is random, we set $n = T(p)$, with $T(p)$ representing a geometrically distributed random variable with parameter $p \in (0,1)$ independent of X_i, i.e.,

$$P(T(p) = k) = (1-p)^{k-1}p, \qquad k = 1, 2, \dots . \tag{1.2}$$

In (1.2), $T(p)$ could be interpreted as the moment at which the probabilistic structure governing the asset returns breaks down. Such a *breakdown* could, for example, be due to new information affecting future fundamentals of the underlying asset in a presently unknown manner. Thus, the stability properties of random variables X_i are only preserved up to period $T(p)$, the moment of the breakdown.

In this book we will focus on the non-Gaussian stable Paretian case and discuss possible consequences of the stable Paretian assumption for financial modeling. We shall consider implications for both financial theory and empirical finance. Before doing so, we present additional empirical evidence comparing Gaussian and non-Gaussian stable assumptions. Our empirical analyses go beyond those typically found in the literature. The latter focus almost exclusively on the unconditional distribution of asset returns. Here we examine, in addition, conditional homoskedastic (i.e., constant–conditional–volatility) and heteroskedastic (i.e., varying–conditional–volatility) distributions. The *conditional* distributions are of interest, because asset returns typically exhibit temporal dependence.

If financial modeling involves information on past market movements, it is not the *unconditional* return distribution which is of interest, but the *conditional* distribution, which is conditioned on information contained in past return data, or a more general information set. The class of autoregressive moving average (ARMA) models is a natural candidate for conditioning on the past of a return series. These models have the property that the conditional distribution is homoskedastic. In view of the fact that financial markets frequently exhibit volatility clusters, the homoskedasticity assumption may be too restrictive. As a consequence, conditional heteroskedastic models, such as Engle's (Engle (1982)) autoregressive conditional heteroskedastic (ARCH) models and the generalization (GARCH) of Bollerslev (Bollerslev (1986)), possibly in combination with an ARMA model, referred to as an ARMA–GARCH model, are common in empirical finance. It turns out that ARCH-type models driven by normally distributed innovations imply unconditional distributions which themselves possess heavier tails. Thus, in this respect, GARCH models and α–stable distributions might be viewed as competing hypotheses.

However, many studies have shown that GARCH-filtered residuals are themselves heavy-tailed, so that α-stable distributed innovations ("building blocks") would be a reasonable distributed assumption.

1.2   An Empirical Application

As an illustration of stable modeling of financial returns, we report on[2] three time series whose behavior is rather typical for financial return data:

(i)   The daily AMEX Composite index from September 1, 1988 to July 28, 1994, with sample size $n = 1810$.

(ii) The daily AMEX OIL index from September 1, 1988 to July 28, 1994, with sample size $n = 1810$.

(iii) The daily DM/US\$ exchange rate from January 2, 1973 to July 28, 1994, with $n = 5401$.

The levels and returns[3] of each series are shown in Figure 1.1.

Table 1.2 summarizes the basic statistical properties of the three return series. A negative skewness statistic indicates that the distribution is skewed to the left, i.e., compared to the right tail, the left tail is elongated. The kurtosis statistic reflects the peakedness of the center compared to that of the normal distribution, so that a value near three would be indicative of normality. Although formal tests could, in principle, be conducted, it should

---

[2]In this exposition, we follow the results in Mittnik, Rachev and Paolella (1998).
[3]We use the standard convention and define the return r_t in period t by $r_t = (\ln P_t - \ln P_{t-1}) \times 100$, where P_t is the price of the asset at time t.

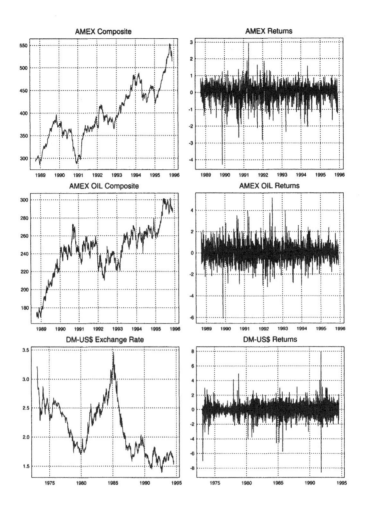

Fig. 1.1 Levels and Returns of Time Series.(Adapted from: Mittnik, Rachev and Paolella (1998))

be kept in mind that under the non-Gaussian stable hypothesis, second and higher moments do not exist, rendering such tests useless. The numbers in Table 1.2 are fairly typical for daily asset return data and indicate considerable deviation from normality. Formal tests confirm this as well.

To obtain conditional models, we estimate both ARMA and ARMA–GARCH models under normal and α–stable assumptions, employing (approximate) conditional maximum-likelihood (ML) estimation. The ML estimation is *conditional*, in the sense that, when estimating, for example, an ARMA(p, q) model, we condition on the first p realizations of the sample, $r_p, r_{p-1}, \ldots, r_1$, and set innovations $\varepsilon_p, \varepsilon_{p-1}, \ldots, \varepsilon_{p-q+1}$ to their unconditional mean $\mathbf{E}(\varepsilon_t) = 0$. The estimation of all α–stable models is *approximate* in the sense that the α–stable density function, $S_{\alpha,\beta}(\delta, c)$ (also denoted by $S_\alpha(c, \beta, \delta)$, see Samorodnitsky and Taqqu (1994)), is approximated via fast Fourier transformation (FFT) of the α–stable characteristic function (ch.f.),

$$\int_{-\infty}^{\infty} e^{itx} dH(x) = \begin{cases} \exp\{-c^\alpha |t|^\alpha [1 - i\beta \mathrm{sign}(t) \tan \frac{\pi\alpha}{2}] + i\delta t\}, & \text{if } \alpha \neq 1, \\ \exp\{-c|t|[1 + i\beta \frac{2}{\pi} \mathrm{sign}(t) \ln |t|] + i\delta t\}, & \text{if } \alpha = 1, \end{cases} \quad (1.3)$$

where H is the distribution function corresponding to $S_{\alpha,\beta}(\delta, c)$; α $(0 < \alpha \leq 2)$ is the *index of stability*; and β $(-1 \leq \beta \leq 1)$; δ $(\delta \in \mathbf{R})$ and c $(c > 0)$ are the *skewness*, *location* and *scale* parameters, respectively (see Figure 1.2 and Figure 1.3, and also Section 2.1 for a detailed exposition of the theory of stable laws).

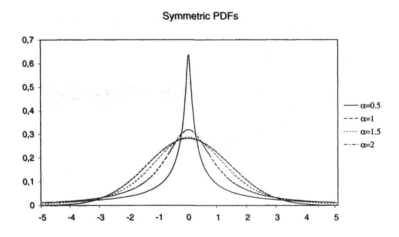

Fig. 1.2 Probability density functions for standard symmetric α–stable random variables with different values of α. (Adapted from: Marinelli, Rachev and Roll (1999))

In our ML estimation we essentially follow DuMouchel (1973), but numerically approximate the α–stable density by an FFT of the ch.f. rather than some series expansion (see further Section 3.7). Considering, for example, the unconditional case, the ML estimate of $\theta = (\alpha, \beta, c, \delta)$ is obtained by

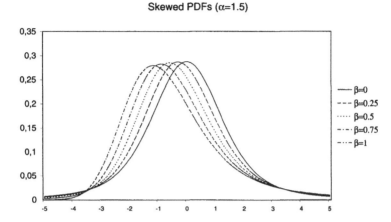

Fig. 1.3 Probability density functions for standard skewed α–stable random variables with different values of β. (Adapted from: Marinelli, Rachev and Roll (1999))

maximizing the logarithm of the likelihood function

$$L(\theta) = \prod_{t=1}^{T} S_{\alpha,\beta}\left(\frac{r_t - \delta}{c}\right) c^{-1}.$$

For details on our α–stable ML estimation we refer to Mittnik, Rachev, Doganoglu and Chenyao (1996) and Mittnik and Rachev (1994) (see also Chapter 3).

We employ two criteria for comparing candidate distributions. The first is the maximized likelihood value obtained from the (conditional) ML estimation. The ML value may be viewed as an overall measure of goodness of fit and allow us to judge which candidate is more likely to have generated the

Table 1.2 Statistical Properties of Returns.

	Mean	Std.Dev.	Skewness	Kurtosis
AMEX	0.0311	0.5173	-0.8916	8.120
AMEX OIL	0.0283	0.8488	0.1369	6.637
DM/US$	-0.0132	0.7353	-0.3210	13.63

(Adapted from: Mittnik, Rachev and Paolella (1998))

data. The second criterion is the Kolmogorov distance (KD)

$$\rho = \sup_{x \in \mathbf{R}} |F_s(x) - \hat{F}(x)|,$$

where $F_s(x)$ denotes the empirical sample distribution and $\hat{F}(x)$ is the estimated distribution function. It is a robust measure in the sense that it focuses only on the maximum deviation between the sample and fitted distributions. Note that the ML value of nested models will necessarily increase as they become more general. This may not be the case with the KD value.

ML estimation of the three unconditional return distributions led to the estimates given in Table 1.3, where the parameter labels correspond to ch.f. (1.3). Note that the scale for the normal case is given by the standard deviation and not by parameter c in (1.3), so that the entries cannot be compared directly. For each asset, the estimated shape parameter of the α– stable distribution is well below $\alpha = 2$, the Gaussian case. The standard deviations of $\hat{\alpha}$ suggest that the normal hypothesis is inappropriate for all three assets. This is supported by the goodness-of-fit measures reported in Table 1.4. Both the maximum log–likelihood values and the Kolmogorov distances clearly indicate that, in all three cases, the α–stable distribution dominates that of the normal.

To provide a visual impression, Figure 1.4 shows the empirical densities obtained via kernel density estimation (dashed lines), along with fitted normal distributions (left panels) and fitted α–stable distributions (right panels). The graphs are consistent with the goodness-of-fit measures reported in Table 1.4. For all three cases, the α–stable model provides a much closer approximation to the empirical densities.

The unconditional results ignore possible temporal dependencies in the return series. Typically serial dependence in time series is modeled by ARMA structures. Such models allow conditioning of the process mean on past realizations, and have been proven successful for the short-term prediction of time series.

A peculiar feature of ARMA models is that the conditional (prediction error) variances are, in fact, independent of past realizations; i.e., they are conditionally homoskedastic. The assumption of conditional homoskedasticity is commonly violated in financial data, where we typically observe volatility clusters, implying that a large absolute return is often followed by more large absolute returns, which more or less slowly decay. Such behavior can be captured by ARCH or GARCH models (see Engle (1982) and Bollerslev (1986)). They express the conditional variance as an explicit function of past information and permit conditional heteroskedasticity.

Let us consider first the homoskedastic case, before moving to the more interesting conditional heteroskedastic case.

Table 1.3 Estimates of Unconditional Distributions[a].

| | | Parameters | | |
	Index	Location	Scale	Skewness
AMEX:				
Normal	2	0.0311	0.5173	0
	—	(0.0121)	(0.0081)	—
α-stable	1.728	0.0171	0.2996	-0.5860
	(0.0386)	(0.0142)	(0.0059)	(0.0898)
AMEX OIL:				
Normal	2	0.0283	0.8488	0
	—	(0.0200)	(0.0122)	—
α-stable	1.776	0.0345	0.5132	0.1873
	(0.0358)	(0.0214)	(0.0123)	(0.1241)
DM/US$:				
Normal	2	-0.0132	0.7353	0
	—	(0.0136)	(0.0070)	—
α-stable	1.727	-0.0100	0.4189	-0.0127
	(0.0232)	(0.0087)	0.0061)	(0.0149)

[a] Standard deviations are given in parentheses.
(Adapted from: Mittnik, Rachev and Paolella (1998))

An ARMA model of autoregressive order p and moving average order q is of the form

$$r_t = \mu + \sum_{i=1}^{p} a_i r_{t-i} + \varepsilon_t + \sum_{j=1}^{q} b_j \varepsilon_{t-j}, \qquad (1.4)$$

where $\{\varepsilon_t\}$ is a white noise process. To specify the orders p and q in (1.4), we followed standard Box–Jenkins identification techniques (see, for example, Box and Jenkins (1976), Wei (1990), Brockwell and Davis (1991), or Johnston (1984)) and inspected sample autocorrelation functions (SACFs) and sample partial autocorrelation functions (SPACFs) of the return series, as shown in Figure 1.5. The exponentially decaying SACF and the single large spike in the SPACF corresponding to the AMEX series strongly suggest the appropriateness of an AR(1) structure. The correlograms for the other two series are not as easy to interpret. Both the SACF and SPACF for the AMEX Oil returns exhibit two relatively large spikes at lags 1 and 4, possibly suggesting either a subset AR(4) or MA(4), with the second and third coefficients restricted to zero. We opt for the subset AR(4), as it resulted in a higher likelihood value,

Table 1.4   Goodness of Fit of Unconditional Distributions.

	log-like		KD	
	Normal	Stable	Normal	Stable
AMEX	-1374	-1255	7.07	1.93
AMEX OIL	-2270	-2194	5.57	1.85
DM/US$	-6001	-5597	5.86	2.07

(Adapted from: Mittnik, Rachev and Paolella (1998))

both under the normal and stable Paretian assumption for the innovation process. The correlograms for the DM-US$ return series exhibit a less clear pattern, with a relatively large negative first order component, along with small, though persistent, positive correlation occurring for the next few lag times. Within the linear ARMA class of models, it appears that a parsimonious parameterization is restricted to either an AR(1) or an MA(1) model. As with the AMEX Oil series, a better fit was achieved using an AR(1) model[4].

These findings, led us to the following specifications for the conditional homoskedastic models:

   (i) AMEX: AR(1);

  (ii) AMEX OIL: Subset AR(4) with $a_2 \equiv a_3 \equiv 0$;

 (iii) DM/US$: AR(1)

Conditional ML estimation was used to estimate both the normal and stable ARMA(p, q) models, whereby we took the first p values of the return series

---

[4]It should be noted that we used Gaussian asymptotic confidence intervals to determine the significance of SACF and SPACF spikes. Recall that, although the SACF provides a consistent estimate of the theoretical ACF in the presence of α-stable data, it is not asymptotically normally distributed (see Davis and Resnick (1986)). Brockwell and Davis (Brockwell and Davis (1991), pp. 540-2) provide examples, however, showing that with Cauchy data (i.e., symmetric 1-stable), the usual variance bounds obtained from Bartlett's formula are close to the true ones, the latter being somewhat smaller, so that standard identification rules might still be approximately applicable.

Arguably more disturbing is the fact that the presence of ARCH invalidates the standard asymptotic theory of the SACF, so that inference from Figure 1.5 is potentially misleading (see Diebold (1986) and Bera, Higgins and Lee (1992)). For two of the series however, namely AMEX and AMEX OIL, the SACFs and PACFs depicted in Figure 1.5 were qualitatively the same as those obtained by using the GARCH filtered residuals, as detailed in the next subsection. Those for the DM-US$ did in fact differ somewhat, although not decisively so.

For the DM-US$ return series with the GARCH component removed, there was less evidence of an AR(1) component. This is also reflected in the estimates in Table 1.7, showing that a_1 is insignificant. It was decided to keep this term, because the likelihood ratio test is, in fact, significant, and the remaining parameters change insignificantly when it is omitted.

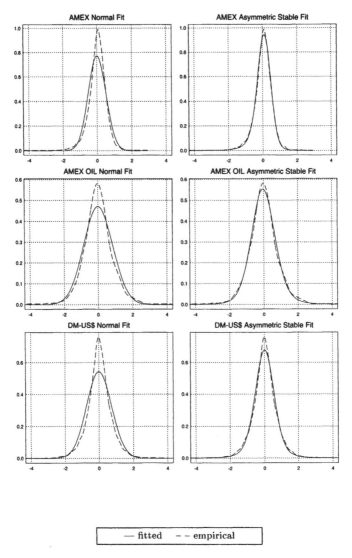

Fig. 1.4 Fitted Unconditional Normal and Stable Densities.(Adapted from: Mittnik, Rachev and Paolella (1998))

to be fixed. The parameter estimates of the fitted conditional distributions are reported in Table 1.5. Comparing the results to those of the fitted uncon- . ditional distributions, we see little differences in the parameters common to both, with two exceptions, both of which pertain to the AMEX data. Firstly, the location parameter μ for the conditional model has changed considerably,

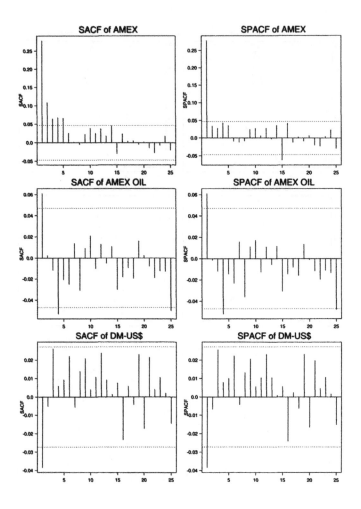

Fig. 1.5   Sample Correlation Functions of Returns.(Adapted from: Mittnik, Rachev and Paolella (1998))

which is not surprising in light of the relatively strong AR(1) component. Secondly, the skewness parameter for the α-stable parameterization has also changed quite a bit. One should keep in mind, however, that, as α increases towards 2, the effect of the skewness parameter diminishes. For α near 1.8, even a skewness component of -0.8 is very mild, so that the large change is somewhat illusory.

Table 1.5   Estimates of Conditional Homoskedastic Distributions[a].

	ARMA Parameters[b]		Index	Distribution Parameters	Skewness
	μ	a_1 a_4		Scale	
AMEX:					
Normal	0.0219	0.2781	2	0.4966	0
	(0.0111)	(0.0224)	—	(0.0078)	—
α-stable	0.0045	0.2490	1.796	0.2970	-0.8146
	(0.0121)	(0.0210)	(0.0287)	(0.0058)	(0.0018)
AMEX OIL:					
Normal	0.0283	0.0607	2	0.8448	0
	(0.0198)	(0.0234)	—	(0.0130)	—
		-0.0527			
		(0.0230)			
α-stable	0.0346	0.0543	1.778	0.5110	0.1837
	(0.0211)	(0.0232)	(0.0363)	(0.0119)	(0.1300)
		-0.0495			
		(0.0363)			
DM-US\$:					
Normal	-0.0137	-0.0385	2	0.7347	0
	(0.0100)	(0.0134)	—	(0.0070)	—
α-stable	-0.0103	-0.0157	1.727	0.4188	-0.0138
	(0.0087)	(0.0128)	(0.0229)	(0.0060)	(0.0160)

[a] Standard deviations are given in parentheses.
[b] The fourth-order AR parameter applies only to AMEX-OIL returns.
(Adapted from: Mittnik, Rachev and Paolella (1998))

Table 1.6 reports the goodness of fit of the estimated ARMA–based conditional distributions. For the AMEX and AMEX OIL series, we observe a significant increase in the likelihood, for both the normal and Paretian stable models. For the DM-US\$ series, the additional AR(1) component adds very little, particularly in the stable case. With the exception of the normal case for the AMEX series, the KD values remain virtually unchanged. Analogous to the results for the unconditional distributions, both the maximum log–likelihood values and the KDs again indicate the dominance of the α–stable distributions over the normal. (The detailed analysis of this approach and possible extensions are given in Chapter 6.)

Table 1.6 Goodness of Fit of Conditional Homoskedastic Distributions.

	log-like		KD	
	Normal	Stable	Normal	Stable
AMEX	-1300	-1187	5.99	1.79
AMEX OIL	-2257	-2181	5.12	1.91
DM-US\$	-5997	-5596	5.84	2.15

(Adapted from: Mittnik, Rachev and Paolella (1998))

An ARCH or GARCH model[5] extends the mean equation, here (1.4), by assuming that

$$\varepsilon_t = c_t u_t, \tag{1.5}$$

where, in the normal case, $u_t \sim N(0,1)$ and

$$c_t^2 = \omega + \sum_{i=1}^{r} \alpha_i \varepsilon_{t-i}^2 + \sum_{i=1}^{s} \beta_i c_{t-i}^2, \qquad c_t > 0. \tag{1.6}$$

Panorska, Mittnik and Rachev (1996a) and Mittnik, Rachev and Paolella (1996) proposed the stable GARCH model and derived necessary and sufficient conditions for stationarity. The model takes the form

$$c_t = \omega + \sum_{i=1}^{r} \alpha_i |\varepsilon_{t-i}| + \sum_{i=1}^{s} \beta_i c_{t-i}, \qquad c_t > 0, \tag{1.7}$$

where u_t is α–stable with $\alpha > 1$.

A standard approach to detecting GARCH-dependencies in a time series, y_t, is to compute the SACF of the squared series, y_t^2. Figure 1.6 shows the SACF and PACF of the squared returns. For the AMEX Composite and the DM-US\$ exchange rate, standard Box-Jenkins methodology would suggest the need for a mixed model, i.e., one with r and s both greater than zero. As is common in financial GARCH modeling (see, for example, Bollerslev, Chou and Kroner (1992)), it was found that $r = s = 1$ was adequate in capturing the correlation structure for these two squared series. The AMEX OIL squared returns exhibit an ARCH(1) structure.

For each series, the conditional mean was modeled with the same ARMA parameterization as used in the homoskedastic case. We specified the following conditional heteroskedastic models for the three return series:

(i) AMEX: AR(1)-GARCH(1,1);

---

[5]More extensive analysis of non-Gaussian ARCH and GARCH model will be provided in Chapter 6.

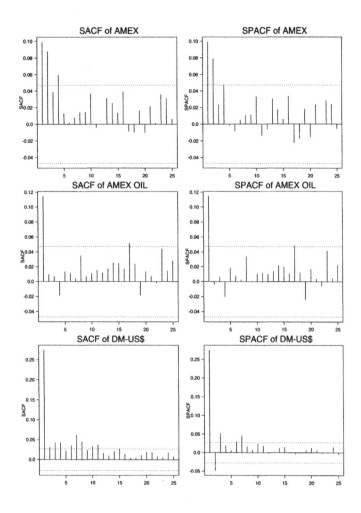

Fig. 1.6 Sample Correlation Functions of Squared Returns.(Adapted from: Mittnik, Rachev and Paolella (1998))

(ii) AMEX OIL: Subset AR(4)-GARCH(1,0)

(iii) DM/US$: AR(1)-GARCH(1,1)

The parameters in the ARMA and GARCH equations of a model were jointly estimated via conditional ML, where we assumed that the scaled innovations, $u_t = \varepsilon_t/c_t$, are either i.i.d. normal or i.i.d. α–stable and c_t satisfies

GARCH recursions (1.6) or (1.7), respectively. The parameter estimates are reported in Table 1.7. We observe that the estimates of stable index α, which correspond now to the scaled innovations, u_t, are larger than those for the distributions in Tables 1.3 and 1.5. This is what one expects, as ARCH/GARCH components absorb a portion of the excess kurtosis of the unconditional distribution.

Table 1.7 Estimates of Conditional Heteroskedastic Distributions[a].

	ARMA Parameters[b]		GARCH Parameters			Distribution Parameters	
	μ	a_1 a_4	ω	α_1	β_1	Index	Skewness
AMEX:							
Normal	0.0326	0.2904	0.0856	0.1484	0.5079	2	0
	(0.0115)	(0.0261)	(0.0202)	(0.0312)	(0.0992)	—	—
α-stable	0.0279	0.2545	0.0403	0.0844	0.7664	1.852	-0.815
	(0.0122)	(0.0170)	(0.0055)	(0.0100)	(0.0225)	(0.028)	(0.145)
AMEX OIL:							
Normal	0.0249	0.0729	0.6602	0.0702	0	2	0
	(0.0217)	(0.0255)	(0.0252)	(0.0237)	—	—	—
		-0.0496					
		(0.0230)					
α-stable	0.0305	0.0532	0.4825	0.0484	0	1.782	0.1432
	(0.0231)	(0.0237)	(0.0120)	(0.0102)	—	(0.015)	(0.0200)
		-0.0475					
		(0.0243)					
DM/US\$:							
Normal	-0.0044	0	0.0078	0.0944	0.9052	2	0
	(0.0004)	—	(0.0003)	(0.0023)	(0.0011)	—	—
α-stable	-0.0139	0	0.0073	0.0860	0.8816	1.827	-0.0510
	(0.0069)	—	(0.0017)	(0.0062)	(0.0093)	(0.019)	(0.0138)

[a] Standard deviations are given in parentheses.
[b] The fourth-order AR parameter applies only to AMEX-OIL returns.
(Adapted from: Mittnik, Rachev and Paolella (1998))

Table 1.8 reports the goodness of fit of the estimated ARMA–GARCH–based conditional heteroskedastic distributions. Allowing for GARCH components clearly improves the fits of all models in terms of the log–likelihood values. The KD values decrease for all three series using the normal assumption, but increase slightly for two of the three under the stable assumption.

Figure 1.7 shows the SACFs corresponding to both the ARMA–GARCH residuals themselves (left panels) and their squares (right panels).[6] One sees

---

[6]The associated SPACFs were qualitatively similar and are not shown.

Table 1.8 Goodness of Fit of Conditional Heteroskedastic Distributions.

| | log-like | | KD | |
	Normal	Stable	Normal	Stable
AMEX	-1257	-1149	4.53	2.77
AMEX OIL	-2245	-2178	4.86	2.03
DM/US$	-5476	-5183	4.81	1.29

(Adapted from: Mittnik, Rachev and Paolella (1998))

that the parsimoniously parameterized ARMA–GARCH models are capable of extracting the majority of the outstanding serial correlation exhibited by both the mean and variance of the asset returns.

Similar to Figure 1.4, Figure 1.8 shows the kernel and fitted densities of the residuals corresponding to both the normal and α-stable conditional heteroskedastic models. As with the previous fits, the results demonstrate, again, the clear dominance of the α–stable distribution over the normal, even after having removed the GARCH component. Especially for the DM-US$ exchange rate series we see that for both the normal and α–stable cases, the conditional heteroskedastic model significantly outperforms its unconditional counterpart. Thus, a combination of fat-tailed innovations and a GARCH structure appears necessary to successfully account for the excess kurtosis in some series. This agrees with the findings in Bollerslev (1986), who proposed the use of the Student's t distribution in conjunction with GARCH models (see Chapter 6).

1.3 Overview

In the book we shall extensively study the theoretical aspects of stable models in finance. In this section we highlight particular topics treated in this book, namely risk and portfolio management, option valuation, and asset pricing.

Univariate models are used to capture the marginal distribution of an *individual asset* or index. Univariate stable fits of asset or index returns are reported in Mittnik and Rachev (1993a), Mittnik, Rachev and Chenyao (1996) and Chobanov, Mateev, Mittnik and Rachev (1996a) and references therein. These fits demonstrate that the normal assumption is inappropriate for returns computed on a weekly or daily basis or for even higher frequencies. From these estimated stable distributions, one can obtain more realistic *risk assessments*. Especially, the question of how frequently one can expect the occurrence of large price movements or stock market crashes can be assessed more realistically with the stable Paretian than with the normal assumption (see, for example, Gamrowski and Rachev (1996), Hols and de Vries (1991) and Jansen and de Vries (1983)).

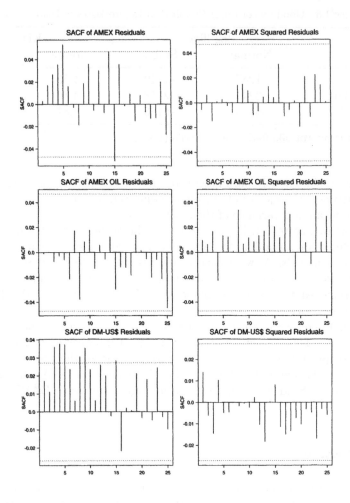

Fig. 1.7 SACFs of Conditional Heteroskedastic Residuals.(Adapted from: Mittnik, Rachev and Paolella (1998))

A second issue which typically involves univariate models is the problem of *option valuation*. The question of pricing options under stable assumptions is rather complex and has been addressed in Karandikar and Rachev (1995), Janicki and Weron (1994) and Hurst, Platen and Rachev (1995). For results on the *generalized binomial model* and the *generalized Mandelbrot–Taylor model* (cf. Mandelbrot and Taylor (1967)) we refer to Rachev and Samarodnitsky

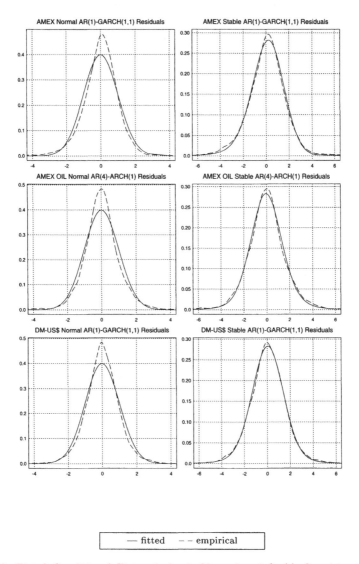

Fig. 1.8 Fitted Conditional Heteroskedastic Normal and Stable Densities.(Adapted from: Mittnik, Rachev and Paolella (1998))

(1993) and Karandikar and Rachev (1995). Option pricing for infinitely divisible returns, which encompasses the stable hypothesis as a particular case, is treated in Rachev and Rüschendorf (1994a).

The crucial feature of the Mandelbrot–Taylor Model is that the return process $(W(T))_{T \geq 0}$, is measured in relation to the transaction volume and not physical or calendar time. Transaction volume is assumed to follow Brownian motion with zero drift and variance v^2. The cumulative volume $(T(t))_{t \geq 0}$, i.e., the number of transactions up to calendar time t, is assumed to follow a positive, increasing in time $\frac{\alpha}{2}$-stable process, $1 < \alpha < 2$, with scale parameter $\nu > 0$. The subordinated process $Z(t) = W(T(t))$, see Figures 1.9, 1.10 and 1.11, representing the return process with respect to calendar time, is then an α-stable Lévy motion with ch.f.

$$\mathbf{E}e^{i\theta Z(t)} = e^{-t|\sigma\theta|^\alpha}, \tag{1.8}$$

where $\sigma^\alpha = \nu(v^2/2)^{\alpha/2}/\cos(\frac{\pi\alpha}{4})$.

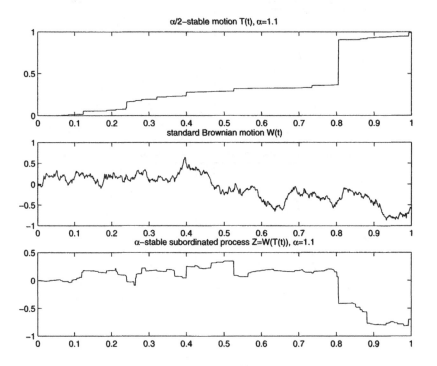

Fig. 1.9 Simulated paths of an $\alpha/2$–stable subordinator $T(t)$, of a standard Brownian motion $W(t)$, and of the corresponding subordinated α–stable Lévy motion $Z(t) = W(T(t))$ ($\alpha = 1.1$). (Adapted from: Marinelli, Rachev and Roll (1999))

A discrete version of the Mandelbrot–Taylor model and various alternative approaches to derivative pricing are considered in Rachev and Samorodnit-sky (1993), Karandikar and Rachev (1995), Hurst, Platen and Rachev (1995a), Hurst, Platen and Rachev (1995b), and Mittnik and Rachev (1997), see Chapters 11, 12 and 13.

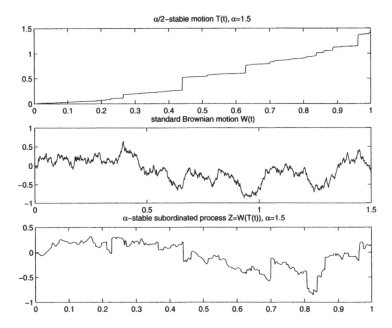

Fig. 1.10   Same as previous figure, but with $\alpha = 1.5$. (Adapted from: Marinelli, Rachev and Roll (1999))

While much work has been devoted to investigate the univariate distribution of individual asset return series, *multivariate distributions* of sets of assets have rarely been studied. Some results in this area can be found in Press (1972a,b), Press (1982) (Chapter 12), Ziemba (1974), Mittnik and Rachev (1991); (see also the discussion in Mittnik and Rachev (1993b)). The lack of multivariate modeling efforts is somewhat surprising, given that modern portfolio management and asset–pricing theories involve distributional properties of sets of investment opportunities (see Chapters 8 and 10). In portfolio theory, for example, the Markowitz model assumes that returns of alternative investments have a joint multivariate distribution whose relevant properties are described by its mean vector and covariance matrix. In fact, the optimal composition of an investor's portfolio depends crucially on the covariances between the individual returns. The evaluation of the risk of a *portfolio of assets* with α-stable distributed returns involves multivariate models. This issue has been addressed in Rachev and Xin (1993), Cheng and Rachev (1995) and Gamrowski and Rachev (1995b). The problem of how to determine the dependence structure in a portfolio of stable distributed assets corresponds to that of deriving the covariance structure in a multivariate normal portfolio.

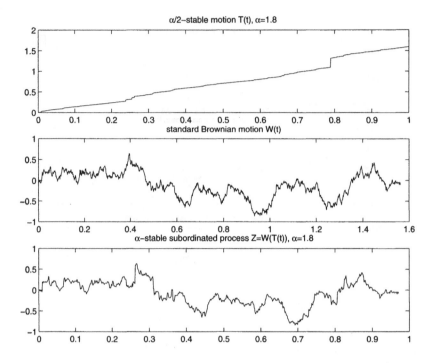

Fig. 1.11 Same as previous figure, but with $\alpha = 1.8$. (Adapted from: Marinelli, Rachev and Roll (1999))

This issue has been considered in Lee, Rachev and Samorodnitsky (1990) and Lee, Rachev and Samorodnitsky (1993), see Chapters 7 and 8.

The implications of having a portfolio with multivariate stable Paretian returns have been investigated in Gamrowski and Rachev (1994a), Gamrowski and Rachev (1994b) and Gamrowski and Rachev (1995a). Below, we shall focus on the Capital Asset Pricing Model (CAPM)—in particular the issue of computing the so–called beta coefficient—and the Arbitrage Pricing Theory (APT). We will also address question of testing the CAPM and APT.

The *Capital Asset Pricing Model (CAPM)* was introduced by Sharpe (1964) and Lintner (1965). It states that, given certain market assumptions, the mean return of asset i is given by

$$\mathbf{E}(R_i) = \rho_0 + \beta_{im}(\mathbf{E}(R_m) - \rho_0), \tag{1.9}$$

where ρ_0 represents the return of the riskless asset; R_m is the random return of the market portfolio (i.e., the portfolio of all marketed assets) and β_{im}— known as the "beta" of asset i—is $\mathrm{cov}(R_i; R_m)/\mathrm{var}(R_m)$.

The CAPM was the first attempt to explain the asset return behavior (with one factor) and has experienced considerable theoretical developments in the last thirty years. Merton (1973b) added a temporal dimension to CAPM by modeling asset returns by a diffusion process; and Chamberlain (1983) showed that the hypothesis of normality could be replaced with the weaker one of finite variance. But neither the CAPM nor its extensions seemed satisfactory when tested empirically (see, for example, Affleck-Graves and Mac Donald (1990) and Blume and Friend (1973)). All these studies assumed square integrability or, more strongly, normality of asset returns. If this is not the case, the statistical test may suffer from inconsistency.

Fama (1970) established a CAPM for symmetric stable Paretian[7] returns. It is of the form

$$R_i = \rho_i + b_i \delta + \epsilon_i \tag{1.10}$$

where δ and ϵ_i are independent and symmetric α-stable Paretian. Fama showed that in this case, the "beta" coefficient in (1.9) is given by

$$\beta_{im} = \frac{1}{\sigma(R_m)} \frac{\partial \sigma(R_m)}{\partial(\lambda_{im})}, \tag{1.11}$$

where $R_m = \Sigma_i \lambda_{im} R_i$, with $\Sigma_i \lambda_{im} = 1$, represents the return of the market portfolio; and $\sigma(\cdot)$ is the scale parameter of the return under consideration. Ross (1978) also claimed that a CAPM-like formula would still hold for stable-distributed returns when the restriction for independence of δ and ϵ_i is not satisfied. However, he does not provide an expression for beta analogous to the classical beta in the Gaussian case. In fact, with stable Paretian returns, it is not possible to compute beta in this fashion or to conduct straightforward tests of the CAPM.

In Gamrowski and Rachev (1994a,b) a testable version of the stable CAPM is provided in terms of the "covariation", $[R_i, R_m]_\alpha$, between R_i and R_m and the "variation" of R_m, $[R_m, R_m]_\alpha$.[8] Then, analogous to the normal case, one obtains

$$\beta_{im} = \frac{[R_i, R_m]_\alpha}{[R_m, R_m]_\alpha}.$$

For details, see Gamrowski and Rachev (1995a,b) and Mittnik and Rachev (1997a,b,c).

In response to the CAPM's empirical failures, Ross (1976) suggested a linear multi-factor pricing model, the so-called *Arbitrage Pricing Theory (APT)*. The APT implies that if the return of asset i, R_i, is of the form $(R_i) = \rho_0 + \beta_{i1}\delta_1 + \cdots + \beta_{ik}\delta_k + \epsilon_i$ (here the δ_j's are the *factors* and the ϵ_i's are the

---

[7] As in Fama (1970), we assume $1 < \alpha < 2$ from now on. As we have pointed out, $\alpha \leq 1$ does not seem to be encountered in financial return data.

[8] For a systematic treatment of variation and covariation we refer to Samorodnitsky and Taqqu (1994) and the references therein.

idiosyncratic risks), then, under usual assumptions, the mean return of the *i*-th asset is

$$\mathbf{E}(R_i) = \rho_0 + \beta_{i1}\rho_1 + \cdots + \beta_{ik}\rho_k,$$ (1.12)

where ρ_j is the *risk premium* linked to factor δ_j. The idea of the APT is that the mean return is not tied to its total variance, but only to that portion of the variance that is due to the market, because the idiosyncratic part can be diversified.

The Arbitrage Pricing Theory (APT) can be viewed as a multi-index generalization of the CAPM. Connor (1984) treats the APT for situations where asset returns are defined in normed vector spaces. Without going into details, it should be noted that there are two versions of the APT for α-stable distributed returns, a so-called equilibrium and an asymptotic version. Connor (1984) provides the proof for the former, while Gamrowski and Rachev (1994a,b) for the latter.

The difficulty in testing the APT empirically is the determination of the risk factors. In the Gaussian case, a maximum likelihood based approach to multi–factor analysis can be adopted. Unfortunately, this approach cannot be generalized to stable Paretian laws. Gamrowski and Rachev (1994a) and Gamrowski and Rachev (1994b) developed a method for this case (see Chapter 9).

In the last part of the book (Chapters 14 and 15) we focus on aspects of empirical modeling under the stable Paretian assumption—in particular, implications for inference when disturbances are stable Paretian. Specifically, we shall address the problems of testing for structural breaks, outliers, and unit roots and cointegration in time series.

2

Univariate Stable Distributions

It is well known that asset returns are not normally distributed, but this information has been downplayed or rationalized away over the years to maintain the traditional hypothesis that asset prices follow the geometric Brownian motion, which implies that asset prices are log-normally distributed. The analysis of the frequency distributions of returns shows however, that this is not the case. There are observed far too many large up-and-down changes at all frequencies for the normal curve to be fitted to these data.

As discussed in the Introduction, in a search for satisfactory descriptive models for financial return data, the α-stable laws as a model for financial returns distribution was proposed: The class of α-stable (Paretian) distributions represents a generalization of the normal distribution in the sense that it allows for both asymmetries and fat tails. In addition to a location and scale parameter, the α-stable distribution with characteristic function (1.3) is characterized by the tail-index or shape parameter $\alpha \in (0, 2]$ and the skewness parameter $\beta \in [-1, 1]$. If $\alpha = 2$, the α-stable distribution coincides with the normal distribution; if $\alpha \in (0, 2)$, it is fat tailed and has only moments of orders less than α. The tail thickness increases as α decreases. If $\alpha < 2$ and $\beta \neq 0$, the distribution is asymmetric and the skewness increases as β moves away from 0 to $\pm$ 1.

In the economics and finance literature *stable* distributions are virtually exclusively associated with *stable Paretian* distributions. In this book we adopt a more fundamental view and extend the concept of stability to a variety of probabilistic schemes, giving rise to "alternative stable distributions".

The objective of this chapter is to reconsider the problem of specifying parametric distributions suitable for modeling asset returns. By considering a variety of probabilistic schemes (see Table 1.1) we extend Mandelbrot's stability concept which arises from a specific scheme, the nonrandom summation scheme. The alternative schemes lead to a wide range of distributions that are stable with respect to their underlying scheme.

To keep the size of the chapter within reasonable bounds, its focus is very specific. There are a number of interesting theoretical and empirical issues as well as implications for financial modeling that could be pursued. Here, we confine ourselves to the univariate case; multivariate processes will be treated in Chapter 7.

2.1   Definitions and Main Properties of Univariate Stable Distributions

2.1.1   Stable Paretian or Summation-stable Distributions

In the 1960's Benoit Mandelbrot and Eugene Fama argued strongly in favor of the stable Paretian distribution as a model for the unconditional distribution of asset returns. A substantial body of subsequent empirical studies supported this position.

As mentioned in the Introduction, there are several reasons for the popularity of the stable Paretian distribution for modeling asset returns:

(i) Stable Paretian distributions are leptokurtic; i.e., compared to the normal distribution they are typically fat-tailed and more peaked around the center, a phenomenon which is commonly observed with asset-return data. Mandelbrot (1963b, 1977, 1997) and Fama (1965a), for example, argue that the high probability of large changes in stock returns makes statistical techniques based on the asymptotic theory of finite-variance distributions, such as the normal distribution, inapplicable.

(ii) Stable Paretian distributions have domains of attraction. The CLT for normalized sums of i.i.d. random variables determines the domain of attraction of each stable law.

(iii) Stable Paretian distributions belong to their own domain of attraction (i.e., stability with respect to the summation of i.i.d. random variables). The set of stable Paretian distributions is stable with respect to the n-fold convolution and scaling.

(iv) The family of stable Paretian distributions is fairly flexible, given that it is characterized by four parameters.

It is for these reasons that the stable Paretian distribution has frequently been viewed as the major competitor for the normal distribution in portfolio analysis[1].

To define α-stable laws, suppose $X_1, X_2, \ldots$ are independently and identically, real-valued random variables (r.v.'s) with common distribution function (d.f.) H. We assume that H is nondegenerate.

Definition 2.1 (See, for example, Zolotarev, 1986a, B.24; Samorodnitsky and Taqqu, 1994). The d.f. H is said to be *stable*, if there exist constants $a_n > 0$ and $b_n \in \mathbf{R}$, such that for any n

$$a_n(X_1 + \ldots + X_n) + b_n \stackrel{d}{=} X_1. \tag{2.1}$$

D.f. H is said to be *strictly stable* if (2.1) holds with $b_n = 0$. A stable d.f. is called *symmetric* if $H(x) = 1 - H(-x)$.

Note that a symmetric stable H is also strictly stable.

Property 2.1 (*Explicit representation of characteristic function*): The d.f. H is stable, if there are parameters $0 < \alpha \leq 2$, $-1 \leq \beta \leq 1$, $c \geq 0$, and $\delta \in \mathbf{R}$ such that the characteristic function (ch.f.) of H has the following form:

$$\int e^{itx} dH(x) = \begin{cases} \exp\{-c^\alpha |t|^\alpha [1 - i\beta \mathrm{sign}(t) \tan \frac{\pi\alpha}{2}] + i\delta t\}, & \text{if } \alpha \neq 1 , \\ \exp\{-c|t|[1 + i\beta \frac{2}{\pi} \mathrm{sign}(t) \ln |t|] + i\delta t\}, & \text{if } \alpha = 1 , \end{cases} \tag{2.2}$$

where $\mathrm{sign}(t)$ is 1 if $t > 0$, 0 if $t = 0$, and -1 if $t < 0$.[2]

The characteristic exponent α is the *index of stability* and can also be interpreted as a *shape* parameter; β is the *skewness* parameter; δ is a *location* parameter; and c is the *scale* parameter. H is called stable Paretian or α-*stable* and is usually denoted by $S_\alpha = S_\alpha(c, \beta, \delta)$. When $\beta = 1$, the d.f. H (or the stable r.v. with d.f. H is said to be totally right skewed. If also $0 < \alpha < 1$, and $\delta = 0$, then X has the positive real line as its support, in which case it has the Laplace transform $\mathbf{E}[\exp(-\theta X)] = \exp(-\omega(c\theta)^\alpha)$, where $\omega = (\cos \frac{\pi\alpha}{2})^{-1}$.

Property 2.2 (*Domain of attraction of stable Paretian distributions*): D.f. H is in the domain of attraction of the α-stable distribution S_α, if for any

---

[1]For a variety of applications of stable laws we refer to the works of McCulloch (1985,1994a,b,c,1997a - d), Bidarkota and McCulloch (1996) and the references therein.
[2]Note that there is some confusion in the literature concerning the sign of skewness parameter β. For example, Holt and Crow (1973) define the sign of β incorrectly for the case $\alpha \neq 1$. See also Hall (1981).

sequence $X_1, X_2,...$ of i.i.d. r.v.'s with common d.f. H there are sequences of constants $a_n > 0$ and $b_n \in \mathbf{R}$ such that

$$Z_n := a_n(X_1 + ... + X_n) - b_n \overset{d}{\to} Y_\alpha, \qquad (2.3)$$

where Y_α is an S_α-distributed r.v.[3]

It follows from Definition 2.1, that S_α belongs to its own domain of attraction. Relation (2.1) states that if X_k is assumed to be α-stable distributed then, under certain normalizations, the sum $X_1 + \cdots + X_n$ has the same distribution. On the other hand, (2.3) states that if the d.f. of X_k belongs to the domain of attraction of S_α the normalized sum Z_n is asymptotically S_α-distributed.

An important issue is the closeness of d.f.'s $F_{Z_n}(x) = P(Z_n \leq x)$ and $S_\alpha(x) = P(Y_\alpha \leq x)$, because the rate of convergence can be very slow (see DuMouchel, 1983, and Rachev, 1991). To measure closeness we employ the *uniform (Kolmogorov) distance* ρ in the space of r.v.'s, i.e.,

$$\rho(X', X'') := \rho(F_{X'}, F_{X''}) := \sup_{x \in \mathbf{R}} |F_{X'}(x) - F_{X''}(x)|, \qquad (2.4)$$

where X' and X'' are any real-valued r.v.'s. It is clear that the distance $\rho(Z_n, Y_\alpha)$, where Z_n and Y_α are as defined in (2.3), should depend on the closeness of $H(x) = P(X_1 \leq x)$ and S_α. Without great loss of generality assume that $a_n = n^{-1/\alpha}$, $b_n = 0$ and that S_α has parameters $c = 1$ and $\delta = 0$.[4]

The next property represents a refinement of the estimates used by Du-Mouchel (1971), who used Cramér's (1963) result to get an estimate of $\rho(Z_n, Y_\alpha)$. Define the "smoothing metrics"

$$\nu_r(X', X'') = \sup_{h>0} h^r \nu(X' + hY_\alpha, X'' + hY_\alpha), \qquad (2.5)$$

where Y_α is an S_α-distributed r.v. (independent of X' and X''), and ν is the *total variation distance*

$$\nu(X', X'') = \int ||F_{X'} - F_{X''}||(dx) = 2 \sup_{\text{Events } A} |P(X' \in A) - P(X'' \in A)|, \qquad (2.6)$$

see Rachev and Yukich (1989,1991).[5] Assuming that

$$\int_{-\infty}^{+\infty} x^j d(F_{X'}(x) - F_{X''}(x)) = 0, \qquad \text{for all } j = 0, 1, \ldots, s, \qquad (2.7)$$

---

[3] Notation "$\overset{d}{\to}$" stands for "convergence in distribution."

[4] The restriction $a_n = n^{-1/\alpha}$ corresponds to the condition that H belongs to the *normal domain of attraction of S_α*. See Feller (1971, Sec. XVII.6).

[5] Here $F_{X'}$ is the d.f. of X'; and $||F_{X'} - F_{X''}|| = (F_{X'} - F_{X''})^+ + (F_{X'} - F_{X''})^-$ comes from the Hahn decomposition; see, for example, Billingsley (1986, p. 441). The set $A < \mathbf{R}$ is an *event*, if it is Borel measurable; the family of all events forms the Borel σ-field $\mathcal{B}(\mathbf{R})$ on $\mathbf{R}$.

where s is an integer and $r - s =: q \in (0, 1]$, we have

$$\nu_r(X', X'') \le c_r \kappa_r(X', X''), \tag{2.8}$$

where c_r is an absolute constant, and κ_r is the *absolute pseudomoment* of order $r > 0$, i.e.,

$$\kappa_r(X', X'') = \int_{-\infty}^{+\infty} |x|^r \|F_{X'}(x) - F_{X''}\|(dx) = 0. \tag{2.9}$$

Property 2.3 Let $r > \alpha$ and $n \ge 1$. Then,

$$\rho(Z_n, Y_\alpha) \le c_\alpha [\nu_r n^{1-r/\alpha} + \max(\rho, \nu_1, \nu_r) n^{-1/\alpha}], \tag{2.10}$$

where c_α is an absolute constant, $\nu_r := \nu_r(Y_\alpha, X_1)$, $\nu_1 := \nu_1(Y_\alpha, X_1)$ and $\rho := \rho(Y_\alpha, X_1)$.[6]

DuMouchel (1971) considered also the deviation of Z_n from Y_α in terms of the total variation distance ν. A more precise estimate is given by the following property.[7]

Property 2.4 Let $r > \alpha$, $a := (2^{r/\alpha} A)^{-1}$ and $A = 2(2^{r\alpha} + 3^{r/\alpha})$. If

$$\tau_0 := \tau_0(X_1, Y_\alpha) := \max[\nu(X_1, Y_\alpha), \nu_r(X_1, Y_\alpha)] \le a, \tag{2.11}$$

then, for any $n \ge 1$,

$$\nu(Z_n, Y_\alpha) \le A \tau_0 n^{1-r/\alpha} \le 2^{-r/\alpha} n^{1-r/\alpha}. \tag{2.12}$$

Estimates (2.10) and (2.12) show that if an S_α-distribution with $\beta \in [-1, 1]$, $c = 1$, $\delta = 0$ is to be approximated by means of the n-fold convolution $F_{Z_n}(x) = F^{*n}(n^{1/\alpha} x)$, then a good choice for F will be a distribution with exactly the same tail as S_α, i.e.,

$$\lim_{x \to \infty} x^\alpha (1 - S_\alpha(x)) = C_\alpha \frac{1 + \beta}{2} c^\alpha = \lim_{x \to \infty} x^\alpha (1 - F(x)),$$

$$\lim_{x \to \infty} x^\alpha S_\alpha(-x) = C_\alpha \frac{1 - \beta}{2} c^\alpha = \lim_{x \to \infty} x^\alpha F(-x),$$

where $C_\alpha = (1 - \alpha)/[\Gamma(2 - \alpha)\cos(\pi\alpha/2)]$, if $\alpha \ne 1$, and $C_1 = -2/\pi$.

---

[6]This follows from Rachev and Yukich (1989,1991) with some additional, but straightforward, arguments.
[7]See Rachev and Yukich (1989) and Rachev (1991). Note that they consider the case $\beta = 0$, but the method can be carried out without changes for any $\beta \in (-1, 1)$.

2.1.2 Max-stable and Min-stable Distributions

Suppose $X, X_1, X_2, \ldots$ are i.i.d. r.v.'s with common d.f. H and let

$$M_n := \max(X_1, \ldots, X_n). \qquad (2.13)$$

Definition 2.2 (See, for example, Galambos, 1978, and Leadbetter et al., 1983.) Distribution $\mathcal{M}$ is called *max-stable*, if

$$a_n M_n + b_n \overset{d}{\to} Y, \qquad (2.14)$$

where Y is a r.v. with d.f. $\mathcal{M}$; and $a_n > 0$ and $b_n \in \mathbf{R}$ are suitable normalizing constants. The set of all d.f.'s, H, for which (2.14) holds is called the *max-domain* of attraction of the max-stable distribution $\mathcal{M}$.

Gnedenko (1943) proved that there exists a location parameter, $b \in \mathbf{R}$, and a scale parameter, $a > 0$, such that the max-stable distribution $\mathcal{M}$ admits one of the following three parametric forms:

Property 2.5 *(Explicit representation of $\mathcal{M}$)*:
(a) max-stable distribution of Type I:

$$\mathcal{M}(x) = \exp\{-e^{-ax+b}\}, \quad x \in \mathbf{R}; \qquad (2.15)$$

(b) max-stable distribution of Type II:

$$\mathcal{M}(x) = \begin{cases} 0, & \text{if } x \le b/a \\ \exp\{-(ax-b)^{-\alpha}\}, & \text{if } x > b/a, \end{cases} \quad \text{for some } \alpha > 0; \qquad (2.16)$$

(c) max-stable distribution of Type III:

$$\mathcal{M}(x) = \begin{cases} \exp\{-(-ax+b)^{\alpha}\}, & \text{if } x \le b/a, \quad \text{for some } \alpha > 0, \\ 1, & \text{if } x > b/a. \end{cases} \qquad (2.17)$$

Property 2.6 *(Stability property)*: Suppose $X, X_1, X_2, \ldots$ are i.i.d. r.v.'s with common max-stable distribution $\mathcal{M}$, then
(a) $\max(X_1, \ldots, X_n) - \frac{1}{a}\ln n \overset{d}{=} X$, if $\mathcal{M}$ is of Type I;
(b) $n^{-1/\alpha}\max(X_1, \ldots, X_n) + \frac{b}{a}(1 - n^{-1/\alpha}) \overset{d}{=} X$, if $\mathcal{M}$ is of Type II;
(c) $n^{1/\alpha}\max(X_1, \ldots, X_n) + \frac{b}{a}(1 - n^{1/\alpha}) \overset{d}{=} X$, if $\mathcal{M}$ is of Type III.

The proof of Property 2.6 is obvious. Also, one can easily see that it is enough to study the properties of $\mathcal{M}(x)$ for $a = 1$ and $b = 0$; i.e., $\mathcal{M}$ is one of the three extreme-value distributions:

$$\Lambda(x) = \exp\{-e^{-x}\}, \quad x \in \mathbf{R}; \qquad (2.18)$$

$$\varphi_\alpha(x) = \begin{cases} \exp\{-x^{-\alpha}\}, & x > 0, \\ 0, & x \le 0; \end{cases} \qquad (2.19)$$

$$\psi_\alpha(x) = \begin{cases} \exp\{-(-x)^{\alpha}\}, & x \le 0, \\ 1, & x > 0. \end{cases} \qquad (2.20)$$

As in the previous subsection, the uniform rate of convergence in (2.14) is of interest. Here consider the rate-of-convergence problem in (2.14) for three cases:

Case 1: $a_n = 1$, $b_n = \ln n$;
Case 2: $a_n = n^{-1/\alpha}$, $b_n = 0$;
Case 3: $a_n = n^{1/\alpha}, b_n = 0$.

The three normalizing constants correspond to the stability relationships (a)–(c) in Property 2.6 with $a = 1$ and $b = 0$. We can reduce all cases to the simplest one, namely $a_n = n^{-1}$ and $b_n = 0$, because the uniform distance $\rho(X, Y)$, see (2.4), is invariant with respect to monotone transformations; and, for $x > 0$, one can choose $\theta_1(x) := x^{1/\alpha}$, $\theta_2(x) := -x^{-1/\alpha}$, and $\theta_3(x) := \ln x$, such that

$$\varphi_\alpha(\theta_1(x)) = \psi_\alpha(\theta_2(x)) = \Lambda(\theta_3(x)) = \varphi_1(x). \tag{2.21}$$

Property 2.7 (See Omey and Rachev (1989)) Suppose $X, X_1, X_2, \ldots$ are non-negative r.v.'s and Y is a φ_1-distributed r.v. Assume that the weighted Kolmogorov distance is finite, i.e.,

$$\rho_s(X, Y) = \sup_{x \geq 0} x^s |F_X(x) - \varphi_1(x)| < \infty, \tag{2.22}$$

for some $s > 1$. Then,

$$\lim_{n \to \infty} \sup n^{s-1} \rho(n^{-1} M_n, Y) = B_s \rho_s(X, Y), \tag{2.23}$$

where $B_s = (s/e)^s$.

Tail condition (2.22) for the distribution of X is necessary for the uniform rate $O(n^{1-s})$. One cannot improve (2.23) without making further assumptions. For related results see also Smith (1982), de Haan and Rachev (1989), Resnick (1987a,b), Omey (1988), and Rachev (1991).

Because the minimum

$$m_n := \min(X_1, X_2, \ldots, X_n) \tag{2.24}$$

is equivalent to $m_n := -\max(-X_1, -X_2, \ldots, -X_n)$, all results concerning stability, domains of attraction, explicit representations, and uniform rate of convergence are analogous to those of maxima. Here, we consider only the explicit parametric form of the *min-stable distribution*, m.

Property 2.8 Let $m_n = \min(X_1, X_2, \ldots, X_n)$, where $X_1, X_2, \ldots, X_n$ are i.i.d. r.v.'s. If, for some constants $c_n > 0$ and $d_n \in \mathbf{R}$,

$$c_n m_n + d_n \overset{d}{\to} Z, \tag{2.25}$$

where Z is a r.v. with nondegenerate d.f. m, then m is one of the three following extreme types of the min-stable distribution:

$$\text{Type I}: \quad m(x) \;=\; 1 - \exp\{-e^{ax-b}\}, \quad x \in \mathbf{R} ; \tag{2.26}$$

$$\text{Type II}: \quad m(x) \;=\; \begin{cases} 0, & \text{if } x \le b/a. \\ 1 - \exp\{-(ax - b)^{\alpha}\}, & \text{if } x > b/a ; \end{cases} \tag{2.27}$$

$$\text{Type III}: \quad m(x) \;=\; \begin{cases} 1 - \exp\{-(-ax + b)^{-\alpha}\}, & \text{if } x \le b/a , \\ 1, & \text{if } x > b/a ; \end{cases} \tag{2.28}$$

with $a > 0$, $b \in \mathbf{R}$, and $\alpha > 0$.

The d.f. of Type II leads to the well-known *Weibull* distribution with parameters $\lambda > 0$ and $\alpha > 0$, i.e.,

$$W(x) = \begin{cases} 0, & \text{if } x \le 0 , \\ 1 - \exp\{-\lambda x^{\alpha}\}, & \text{if } x > 0 . \end{cases} \tag{2.29}$$

As will be seen in Chapter 4, the Weibull distribution also appears to be appropriate for modeling return data.[8]

2.1.3 *Multiplication-stable Distributions*

Let S be a stable-Paretian distributed r.v. with probability density function (p.d.f.) g. Then, random variable $X = \exp\{S\}$ has p.d.f.

$$m_g(x) = \begin{cases} \frac{g(\ln x)}{x}, & x > 0 , \\ 0, & x \le 0 . \end{cases} \tag{2.30}$$

Definition 2.3 (*Explicit representations*): Each stable Paretian distribution with p.d.f. g determines three $(\alpha, multiplication)$-*stable*—in short, $(\alpha, \mathcal{M})$-*stable*—distributions, namely,

(a) log-stable density:

$$m_{g,1}(x) = m_g(|x|)I\{x > 0\}, \quad x \in \mathbf{R}; \tag{2.31}$$

(b) negative log-stable density:

$$m_{g,2}(x) = m_g(|x|)I\{x < 0\}, \quad x \in \mathbf{R}; \tag{2.32}$$

(c) symmetric log-stable density:

$$m_{g,3}(x) = \frac{1}{2}m_g(|x|), \quad x \in \mathbf{R}. \tag{2.33}$$

---

[8] Jansen and de Vries (1983) use max-stable distributions to investigate the tail behavior of stock returns; see also the recent monograph Embrechts, Klüppelberg and Mikosch (1997).

The corresponding analogues of these three distributions for the standard normal distribution are the log-normal, negative log-normal, and symmetric log-normal distribution, respectively. The latter, for example, has the p.d.f.

$$\frac{1}{2|x|\sqrt{2\pi}}\frac{1}{2\sigma^2}(\ln|x-\mu|)^2. \tag{2.34}$$

$(\alpha, \mathcal{M})$-stable distributions are weak limits of the distributions of the normalized product $Y_n = X_1 X_2 \ldots X_n$ of the i.i.d. r.v.'s X_i. In the following we will only investigate the properties of the log-stable density $m_{g,1}(x) =: m_g(x)$, $x > 0$. The other two types of log-stable densities can be dealt with in a similar fashion.

Property 2.9 (*Stability property*): Let $X_1, X_2, \ldots$ be i.i.d. non-negative random variables with common $(\alpha, \mathcal{M})$-stable p.d.f. m_g, then there exist constants $A_n > 0$ and $B_n > 0$, such that, for any n,

$$A_n(X_1 X_2 \ldots X_n)^{B_n} \stackrel{d}{=} X_1.$$

For example, if g is a stable density with parameters α, β, δ, and $c = 1$, then

$$A_n = \exp\{-\delta(n^{1-1/\alpha} - 1)\}, \quad B_n = n^{-1/\alpha}.$$

Property 2.10 (*Domain of attraction of $(\alpha, \mathcal{M})$- stable distributions*): The distribution function H is in the normal domain of attraction of $(\alpha, \mathcal{M})$-stable distribution (2.31), if for any sequence $X_1, X_2, \ldots$ of i.i.d. non-negative r.v.'s with common d.f. H there is a sequence of constants $\{A_n\}$, such that

$$W_n := A_n(X_1 X_2 \ldots X_n)^{n^{-1/\alpha}} \stackrel{d}{\to} M_\alpha, \tag{2.35}$$

where M_α is a random variable with the log-stable density m_g.

To investigate the rate-of-convergence in (2.35), we use the *log-absolute pseudomoment of order r* given by

$$\ell_r := \ell_r(X_1, M_\alpha) := \int_0^\infty |\log x|^r \|F_{X_1}(x) - F_{M_\alpha}(x)\| dx, \tag{2.36}$$

where $\| \cdot \|$ is as defined in (2.6). Moreover, we use the Kolmogorov distance

$$\rho := \rho(X_1, M_\alpha) := \sup_{x \geq 0} |F_{X_1}(x) - F_{M_\alpha}(x)|, \tag{2.37}$$

(recall (2.4)) and the total variation distance $\nu := \nu(X_1, M_\alpha)$ (see (2.6)).

Property 2.11 Let $r > \alpha$ and $n \geq 1$. Then,

$$\rho(W_n, M_\alpha) \leq c_\alpha[\ell_r n^{1-1/\alpha} + \max(\rho, \ell_1, \ell_r) n^{-1/\alpha}], \qquad (2.38)$$

where c_α is as in (2.10).

Property 2.12 Let constants a and A be as defined in Property 2.1.4 and $r > \alpha$. If

$$\tau := \tau(X_1, M_\alpha) := \max\{\nu(X_1, Y_\alpha), \ell_r(X_1, Y_\alpha)\} \leq a, \qquad (2.39)$$

then, for any $n \geq 1$,

$$\nu(W_n, M_\alpha) \leq A\tau_0 n^{1-r/\alpha} \leq 2^{-r/\alpha} n^{1-r/\alpha}. \qquad (2.40)$$

The proofs of Properties 2.11 and 2.12 follow directly from Properties 2.3 and 2.4.[9]

2.2   Univariate Geometric Stable Distributions

In this section we consider the *geometric* analogues of the summation-stable, multiplication-stable, max-stable, and min-stable distributions. The motivation underlying these geometric analogues is to enable us to model processes that may, with some small probability, change in each period. In the context of asset returns we can, for example, think of major, unexpected news events, which could—with some small probability—occur in any period and drastically affect investors' behavior and, hence, the overall market.

To state this formally, let X_i denote the r.v. at period $t = t_0 + i$. R.v.'s $\{X_i\}$ are assumed to be i.i.d. with d.f.

$$H(u) = P(X_i \leq u), \quad u \in \mathbf{R}. \qquad (2.41)$$

With probability $p \in (0, 1)$ an investor may expect in any period the occurrence of an event altering the characteristics of the underlying asset-return process. Let $T(p)$ denote the period in which such an event is expected to occur. $T(p)$ is assumed to be independent of $\{X_i\}$ and to have a *geometric distribution* of the form

$$P\{T(p) = k\} = (1 - p)^{k-1} p, \quad k = 1, 2, \dots . \qquad (2.42)$$

The time until random period $T(p)$ may be viewed as the time for which an investor assumes the market fundamentals to remain unchanged and correspond to the investment horizon.

In the following we replace the deterministic variable n in the probabilistic schemes considered in Section 2.1 by the geometric random variable $T(p)$ and investigate their properties given the geometric randomization.

---

[9]For somewhat different limit results for multiplication-stable distributions see Grigorevski (1980) and Zolotarev (1986b, p. 97).

2.2.1 Geometric Summation-stable Distributions

The *geometric sum*

$$G_p = \sum_{i=1}^{T(p)} X_i \tag{2.43}$$

represents the accumulation of the X_i's up to the event at time $t_0 + T(p)$, i.e., the total return of an asset over that period. This scheme has some resemblance with Clark's (1973) subordinated stochastic process model. In his model, *operational time* is random, whereas *calendar time* is fixed; i.e., the number of X_i's per unit of calendar time is random. In the geometric-summation model, operational time is nonrandom (i.e., the number of X_i's per unit of calendar time is fixed), but the length of the time intervals are random (i.e. $T(p)$ is a random variable).

Definition 2.4 D.f. H is said to be strictly geometric-stable with respect to the summation scheme—in short, *strictly (geo,sum)-stable* — if, for any $p \in (0,1)$, there exist constants $a = a(p) > 0$, such that

$$aG_p \overset{d}{=} X_1. \tag{2.44}$$

If $f(t)$ is the ch.f. of H (i.e., $f(t) := \mathbf{E}\exp\{itX_1\}$) then, by (2.44) it follows that $f(t)$ satisfies

$$f(t) = \frac{pf(at)}{1 - (1-p)f(at)}, \tag{2.45}$$

see Klebanov et al. (1984, 1986). In this case, setting $\varphi(t) := \exp\{1 - 1/f(t)\}$ in (2.45), we have

$$\varphi(t) = [\varphi(at)]^{1/p}, \quad p \in (0,1); \tag{2.46}$$

i.e., φ is the ch.f. of a strictly stable distribution (see Section 3.1). This gives rise to the following result of Klebanov et al. (1984).[10]

Property 2.13 *(Explicit representation of ch.f. of strictly (geo,sum)-stable distributions)*: A nondegenerate d.f. $\mathcal{G} = \mathcal{G}_p$ is strictly (geo,sum)-stable if and only if its ch.f., f, has the form

$$f(t) = \left[1 + \lambda|t|^\alpha \exp\left\{-i\frac{\pi}{2}\theta\alpha \ \text{sign}(t)\right\}\right]^{-1}, \tag{2.47}$$

where $0 < \alpha \le 2$, $|\theta| \le \theta_\alpha = \min(1, \frac{2}{\alpha} - 1)$, and $\lambda > 0$.

---

[10]For more general results concerning non-strictly (geo,sum)-stable distributions, we refer to Mittnik and Rachev (1993a), Rachev and Samorodnitsky (1994), Kozubowski (1994b), Panorska (1999), Kozubowski and Panorska (1999a), and Klebanov and Rachev (1996a).

If $\alpha = 2$ and $\theta = 0$, $\mathcal{G}$ is a symmetric Laplace distribution; i.e.,

$$\mathcal{G}(t) = \frac{\lambda}{2} \int_{-\infty}^{t} e^{-\lambda |u|} du \,. \tag{2.48}$$

The Laplace distribution plays among the (geo,sum)-stable distributions a role that is analogous to that of the normal distribution in the class of the stable Paretian distributions. The exponential distribution $\mathcal{G}(t) = 1 - e^{-\lambda t}$, $t > 0$, is a strictly (geo,sum)-stable distribution and plays the role of the discrete distribution in the class of stable Paretian distributions. For $0 < \alpha < 2$, stable Paretian and (geo,sum)-stable distributions have one and the same tail behavior (see Mittnik and Rachev, 1993a).

Property 2.14 *(Domain of attraction)*: D.f. H is in the domain of attraction of the strictly (geo,sum)-stable distribution $\mathcal{G}$ if, for any sequence $X_1, X_2, \ldots$ of i.i.d. r.v.'s with common d.f. H and geometric r.v. $T(p)$ (independent of $\{X_i\}$), there exist constants $a(p) > 0$ such that, as $p = 1/\mathbf{E}T(p) \to 0$,

$$Z_p = a(p) \sum_{i=1}^{T(p)} X_i \overset{d}{\to} Y, \tag{2.49}$$

where Y is $\mathcal{G}_p$-distributed.

The study of the domain of attraction of geometric stable distributions was initiated in the pioneering works of Robbins (1948a,b), Rényi (1956) and Gnedenko and Fahim (1969). One way of determining F_Y, the d.f. of Y, is based on approximation $F_Y \approx F_{Z_p}$. To this end we measure the closeness between F_{Z_p} and F_Y in terms of the Lévy metric

$$
\begin{aligned}
L(Z_p, Y) \quad &:= \quad L(F_{Z_p}, F_Y) \\
&= \quad \inf\{\varepsilon > 0 \colon F_{Z_p}(x-\varepsilon) - \varepsilon \le F_Y(x) \le F_{Z_p}(x+\varepsilon) + \varepsilon, \\
&\qquad \text{for all } x \in \mathbf{R}\} \,,
\end{aligned}
\tag{2.50}
$$

which metrizes the convergence in distribution. We would like to estimate $L(Z_p, Y)$ in terms of the difference pseudomoments of order s, i.e.,

$$\kappa_s := \kappa_s(X_1, Y) = s \int_{-\infty}^{+\infty} |x|^{s-1} |F_{X_1}(x) - F_Y(x)| dx. \tag{2.51}$$

Obviously, we have $\kappa_s(X_1, Y) \le \mathbf{E}|X_1|^s + \mathbf{E}|Y|^s$, but $\kappa_s(X_1, Y)$ may be finite even when $\mathbf{E}|X_1|^s + \mathbf{E}|Y|^s = +\infty$. For given $s > 0$, define the integer m and the real number $p \ge 1$ by $s = m + 1/p$.

Property 2.15 *(Approximating strictly (geo,sum)-stable distributions)*: Suppose for some $s > 0$

$$\infty > \bar{\kappa}_s := \begin{cases} \kappa_1, & \text{if } s < 1 \,, \\ \kappa_s, & \text{if } s \ge 1 \,, \end{cases} \tag{2.52}$$

$$\int x^j d(F_{X_1} - F_Y)(x) = 0, \quad \text{for } j = 0, 1, \ldots, \tag{2.53}$$

and

$$A(p) := \frac{a(p)^s}{p} \to 0 \quad \text{as } p \to 0. \tag{2.54}$$

Then,

$$L(Z_p, Y) \leq (A(p))^{1/(s+1)} \kappa_1(X_1, Y)^{1/(s+1)p}, \quad \text{if } 0 < s \leq 1, \tag{2.55}$$

$$L(Z_p, Y) \leq \left(4A(p) \frac{\Gamma(1 + \frac{1}{p})}{\Gamma(1 + s)} \kappa_s(X_1, Y) \right)^{1/(s+1)}, \quad \text{if } 1 < s \leq 2, \tag{2.56}$$

and

$$L(Z_p, Y) \leq \left(C(s) A(p) \frac{\Gamma(1 + \frac{1}{p})}{\Gamma(1 + s)} \kappa_s(X_1, Y) \right)^{1/(s+1)}, \quad \text{if } s > 2, \tag{2.57}$$

where $C(s)$ is a constant, whose determination is described in Mittnik and Rachev (1993a).

In particular, from Property 2.15 it follows—given that some "tail" conditions on F_{X_1} (see (2.52)), some "moment" conditions (see (2.53)), and some normalizing conditions (see (2.54)) are met—that, as $p \to 0$, the Lévy distance $L(Z_p, Y)$ goes to zero with a rate determined by (2.55)–(2.57). In the special, but important, case of $\alpha = 1$ and Y being exponentially distributed, we have a refined analogue to Property 2.15:

Property 2.16 Let $\{X_i\}_{i \geq 1}$ be non-negative i.i.d. r.v.'s with $\mathbf{E}X_i = 1/\lambda$ and let Y be an exponentially distributed r.v. with parameter λ. Then, (Rényi theorem)

$$Z_p := p \sum_{i=1}^{T(p)} X_i \xrightarrow{d} Y, \quad \text{as } p \to 0.$$

Moreover, if $\mathbf{E}X_i^s < \infty$, for some $1 < s \leq 2$, then

$$\rho(Z_p, Y) = \sup_{x \geq 0} |F_{Z_p}(x) - (1 - e^{-\lambda x})| \leq C_\lambda p^{s-1} \mathbf{E}X_1^s,$$

where C_λ is an absolute constant.[11]

Property 2.16 leads straightforwardly to the characterization of the *Weibull distribution with parameter $\lambda > 0$ and $\alpha > 0$*, i.e.,

$$W(x) = \begin{cases} 1 - e^{-\lambda x^\alpha}, & x > 0, \\ 0, & x \leq 0, \end{cases}$$

---

[11]This is Theorem 4 in Kalashnikov and (1985).

as a limiting distribution for geometric sums of i.i.d. r.v.'s.

Property 2.17 Let $\{X_i\}_{i\geq 1}$ be non-negative r.v.'s, $\mathbf{E}X_i^\alpha = 1/\lambda$ ($\alpha > 0$, $\lambda > 0$) and let Y be Weibull distributed with parameters λ and α. Then,

$$Z_{p,\alpha} = p^{1/\alpha} \left(\sum_{i=1}^{T(p)} X_i^\alpha \right)^{1/\alpha} \to Y, \quad \text{as } p \to 0. \tag{2.58}$$

Moreover, if $\mathbf{E}X_i^s < \infty$, for some $s \in (\alpha, 2\alpha]$, then

$$\rho(Z_{p,\alpha}, Y) = \sup_{x \geq 0} \left| F_{Z_{p,\alpha}}(x) - (1 - e^{-\lambda x^\alpha}) \right| \leq C_\lambda p^{\frac{s}{\alpha}-1} \mathbf{E}X_1^s, \tag{2.59}$$

where C_λ is the same constant as in Property 2.16.

Properties 2.8 and 2.17 show that the Weibull distribution is "double stable" in the sense that it arises as the limit distribution of two probabilistic schemes, namely the minimum and the geometric random summation scheme for i.i.d. r.v.'s; see Mittnik and Rachev (1993a) for the fit of Weibull laws to various asset return series

This gives rise to the following well-known characterization of the Weibull distribution:

Property 2.18 If $X_1, X_2, \ldots$ are i.i.d. r.v.'s with Weibull distribution with parameters λ and α, then

$$n^{1/\alpha} \min_{1 \leq i \leq n} X_i \stackrel{d}{=} X_1, \quad n = 1, 2, \ldots, \tag{2.60}$$

and

$$p \sum_{i=1}^{T(p)} X_i^\alpha \stackrel{d}{=} X_1^\alpha, \quad 0 < p < 1. \tag{2.61}$$

The symmetric Weibull distribution, which naturally arises from the Laplace law (see (2.51)), may be viewed as a member of the geometric sum-stable family which has thin tails.

Next, we address the *theory of geometric stable laws with heavy tails.*[12]

Let us recall the definition of geometric (summation-)stable random variables and their domains of attractions (see Klebanov et al., 1984; Mittnik and Rachev, 1989; Kruglov et al., 1990).

---

[12]For more results we refer to the doctoral thesis by Tomasz Kozubowski (1992), Kozubowski and Rachev (1994, 1999a,b), Rachev and Samorodnitsky (1994), Kozubowski (1994a,b), Klebanov and Rachev (1996a).

Definition 2.5 A random variable with distribution function G is said to be geometric stable with respect to the summation scheme (in short, (geo+)-stable), if there exists a sequence of i.i.d. random variables $X_1, X_2, \ldots,$ a geometric random variable $T(p)$, independent of all X_i, and constants $a = a(p) > 0$ and $b = b(p) \in \mathbf{R}$, such that

$$a(p) \sum_{i=1}^{T(p)} [X_i + b(p)] \overset{w}{\to} Y, \qquad \text{as } p \to 0. \tag{2.62}$$

Definition 2.6 If, in (2.62), $b(p) = 0$, then Y is called strictly geometric stable.

Definition 2.7 *(Domains of attraction)* Distribution H belongs to the domain of attraction of (geo+)-stable distribution G, i.e., $H \in D(G)$, if (2.62) holds with $X_i \sim H$ and $Y \sim G$.[13]

Geometric stable distributions can be characterized in terms of their ch.f.[14]

Theorem 2.1 Y is (geo+)-stable if and only if its ch.f., $\psi(t)$, has the form

$$\psi(t) = \frac{1}{1 - \log \phi(t)} = \int_{-\infty}^{\infty} [\phi(t)]^z e^{-z} dz, \tag{2.63}$$

where $\phi(t)$ is the ch.f. of some α-stable Paretian distribution.

Several representations of the ch.f. of stable Paretian (in short, α-stable) laws exist (see Hall, 1981). Adopting a representation due to Zolotarev (see, for example, Devroye, 1986), we have the following representation for the ch.f. of (geo+)-stable distributions:

$$\psi(t) = \frac{1}{1 + |\sigma t|^\alpha w_B(t, \alpha, \beta) - i\mu t}, \tag{2.64}$$

where

$$w_B(t, \alpha, \beta) = \begin{cases} \exp\{-i\beta \frac{\pi}{2} K(\alpha) \mathrm{sign}(t)\} , & \text{if } \alpha \neq 1 \\ 1 + i\beta \frac{2}{\pi} \mathrm{sign}(t) \log |t|, & \text{if } \alpha = 1 , \end{cases}$$

with $K(\alpha) = \min(\alpha, 2 - \alpha)$, $0 < \alpha \leq 2$, $-1 \leq \beta \leq 1$, $-\infty < \mu < \infty$, and $\sigma \geq 0$.

Random variable Y is (geo+)-stable with parameters $(\alpha, \beta, \sigma, \mu)$ with distribution function $GS(x, \alpha, \beta, \sigma, \mu)$ and density $gs(x, \alpha, \beta, \sigma, \mu)$, if its ch.f. is defined by (2.64). Parameter α, called the index parameter, describes the overall characteristics of the distribution; β is the skewness parameter; σ is the scale parameter; and μ is the location parameter. Analogous to the case of strictly stable α-stable distributions, we say Y is *strictly* geometric stable, if, for $\alpha \neq 1$, we have $\mu = 0$ or, for $\alpha = 1$, we have $\beta = 0$. If $\mu = 0$

---

[13]Here, "$\sim$" means "distributed as".
[14]For proofs of Theorems 2.1 - 2.5 we refer to (1992).

and $\sigma = 1$, the distribution is said to be in *standard* form with distribution function $GS(x, \alpha, \beta)$ and density $gs(x, \alpha, \beta)$.

Let the distribution function and density of the standard α-stable distribution $S_\alpha(1, \beta, 0)$ be denoted by $S(x, \alpha, \beta)$, $\kappa \in \mathbf{R}$ and $s(x, \alpha, \beta)$, respectively. Then, Theorem 2.1 gives rise to the following representation of (geo+)-stable laws.

Corollary 2.1 If $\sigma \neq 0$, (geo+)-stable distributions are absolutely continuous with distribution function

$$GS(x, \alpha, \beta, \mu, \sigma) = \begin{cases} \int_0^\infty S\left(\frac{x - \mu z}{\sigma z^{1/\alpha}}, \alpha, \beta\right) e^{-z} dz, & \text{if } \alpha \neq 1, \\ \int_0^\infty S\left(\frac{x - z\sigma\beta\frac{2}{\pi}\log(\sigma z) - \mu z}{\sigma z}, \alpha, \beta\right) e^{-z} dz, & \text{if } \alpha = 1, \end{cases}$$

and density

$$gs(x, \alpha, \beta, \mu, \sigma) = \begin{cases} \int_0^\infty \frac{1}{\sigma z^{1/\alpha}} s\left(\frac{x - \mu z}{\sigma z^{1/\alpha}}, \alpha, \beta\right) e^{-z} dz, & \text{if } \alpha \neq 1, \\ \int_0^\infty \frac{1}{\sigma z} s\left(\frac{x - z\sigma\beta\frac{2}{\pi}\log(\sigma z) - \mu z}{\sigma z}, \alpha, \beta\right) e^{-z} dz, & \text{if } \alpha = 1. \end{cases}$$

Corollary 2.1 can be restated in terms of random variables.

Corollary 2.2 [15] Let $Y \sim GS(x, \alpha, \beta, \mu, \sigma)$ ((geo+)-stable), $X \sim S(x, \alpha, \beta)$ (standard α-stable), $Z \sim \exp(1)$ (exponential distribution with mean 1); and let X and Z be independent. Then,

$$Y \stackrel{d}{=} \begin{cases} \mu Z + Z^{1/\alpha}\sigma X, & \text{if } \alpha \neq 1 \\ \mu Z + Z\sigma X + \sigma Z\beta\frac{2}{\pi}\log(Z\sigma), & \text{if } \alpha = 1. \end{cases}$$

Theorem 2.2 For any admissible quadruple $(\alpha, \beta, \sigma, \mu)$ with $\sigma \neq 0$, we have
$GS(-x, \alpha, \beta, \sigma, \mu) = 1 - GS(x, \alpha, -\beta, \sigma, -\mu)$
and $gs(-x, \alpha, \beta, \sigma, \mu) = gs(x, \alpha, -\beta, \sigma, -\mu)$.

This result allows us to investigate the properties of (geo+)-stable laws by considering only the case of $x > 0$.

As is well known, densities of α-stable laws are uniformly bounded (see Zolotarev, 1986a). The following theorem establishes a similar result for (geo+)-stable laws with $\alpha > 1$.

Theorem 2.3 Let Y be a (geo+)-stable r.v. with density $gs(x, \alpha, \beta, \sigma, \mu)$ and $\alpha > 1$ and $\sigma > 0$. Then, for any x,

$$gs(x, \alpha, \beta, \sigma, \mu) \leq \frac{\Gamma(1/\alpha)\Gamma(1 - 1/\alpha)}{\alpha\sigma\pi\cos^{1/\alpha}\gamma},$$

where $\gamma = \beta\frac{\pi}{2}\min(\alpha, 2 - \alpha)$.

---

[15] Corollary 2.2 is not only useful for deriving theoretical properties, but also for generating (geo+)-stable pseudo-random numbers (see Kozubowski, 1992).

While densities of (geo+)-stable laws are uniformly bounded for $\alpha > 1$, they are unbounded for $0 < \alpha < 1$.

Next, we describe the asymptotic behavior of density and distribution functions of standard (geo+)-stable laws at ∞.

Theorem 2.4 For $\alpha \neq 1$ and $x > 0$, the standard (geo+)-stable density can be expanded as

$$gs(x, \alpha, \beta) = \sum_{j=1}^{n} c_j x^{-j\alpha-1} + C_{n+1}^*(x), \qquad n = 1, 2, \ldots,$$

where $c_j = (-1)^{j-1}\Gamma(j\alpha + 1)\sin[j(\alpha\pi/2 + \gamma)]/\pi$, with $\gamma = \beta\frac{\pi}{2}\min(\alpha, 2 - \alpha)$; and $|C_{n+1}^*(x)| \leq \Gamma(\alpha(n+1)+1)(x\cos\theta)^{-[\alpha(n+1)+1]}/\pi$, with $\theta = \max(0, \pi/2 + (\gamma - \pi/2)/\alpha)$.

Theorem 2.5 For $\alpha \neq 1$ and $x > 0$, the standard (geo+)-stable distribution function can be expanded as

$$1 - GS(x, \alpha, \beta) = \sum_{j=1}^{n} d_j x^{-j\alpha-1} + D_{n+1}^*(x), \qquad n = 1, 2, \ldots,$$

where $d_j = (-1)^{j-1}\Gamma(j\alpha)\sin[j(\alpha\pi/2 + \gamma)]/\pi$; and

$$|D_{n+1}^*(x)| \leq \frac{\Gamma(\alpha(n+1))}{\pi(x\cos\theta)^{\alpha(n+1)}},$$

with γ and θ being defined as in Theorem 2.4.

Next, we consider the case $1 < \alpha < 2$. While Corollary 2.1 provides a representation of the geo–stable density in terms of the corresponding α–stable density, the next theorem provides a direct integral representation for the geo-stable density giving rise to a fast–convergent integral representation. Analogous to Property 2.13, the ch.f. of a geo-stable distribution can be represented as

$$f(t) = f(t; \alpha, \theta, \lambda, \mu) = \frac{1}{1 + \lambda|t|^\alpha \exp\{-i\frac{\pi}{2}\alpha\theta\text{signt}\} - i\mu t},$$

where $1 < \alpha < 2$; $|\theta| \leq \theta_\alpha = \min(1, 2/\alpha - 1)$; $\lambda > 0$; and $\mu \in \mathbf{R}$. Although α can, in general, take any value in $(0, 2]$, we consider $1 < \alpha < 2$, because $f(t)$ has infinite first moments for $\alpha \leq 1$, which does not seem to be a likely situation with asset return data. The case $\alpha = 2$ corresponds to the well–known Laplace distribution given by (2.48).

Applying the inversion formula to $f(t)$ we obtain the geo-stable density

$$p(x) = p(x; \alpha, \theta, \lambda, \mu) = \frac{1}{2\pi} \int_{-\infty}^{\infty} e^{-itx} f(t) dt.$$

The standard Fourier–inversion approach leads to a representation for $p(x)$ with slowly convergent integrals. In the next theorem we present representations of geo-stable densities with fast convergent integrals. They are similar to a representation given by Linnik in the context of so–called Linnik distributions (see Linnik, 1960; and Kotz, Ostrovskii and Hayfavi, 1995).

The integral representations given below should be useful for deriving a maximum likelihood estimator for the parameter of geo-stable distributions[16].

Theorem 2.6 For $1 < \alpha < 2$ and $x \neq 0$ the density of geo-stable distribution $p(x)$ can be represented by

$$p(x) = \frac{\lambda \sin(\frac{\pi}{2}\alpha(1 + \theta\mathrm{sign}x))}{\pi}$$

$$\times \int_0^\infty \frac{v^\alpha e^{-vx} dv}{\left|1 - \mu v\mathrm{sign}x + \lambda v^\alpha \exp\{\frac{i\pi}{2}\alpha(1 + \theta\mathrm{sign}x)\}\right|^2}, \quad x \in \mathbf{R}\backslash\{0\}.$$

Proof: Let $x < 0$ and split $p(x)$ into two integrals, i.e.,

$$I_1(x) := \int_0^\infty e^{-itx} f(t)dt$$

and $I_2(x) = 2\pi p(x) - I_1(x)$. In the complex t–plane consider the region

$$Q_R = \{t = u + iv \colon |t| \leq R, u \geq 0, v \geq 0\}, \quad R > 1,$$

and define

$$t^\alpha = |t|^\alpha e^{i\alpha\varphi}, \quad 0 < \varphi = \arg t < \frac{\pi}{2}.$$

Function

$$\delta(t, x) = \frac{e^{-itx}}{1 + \lambda t^\alpha \exp\{-i\frac{\pi}{2}\alpha\theta\} - i\mu t}$$

is continuous in Q_R and analytic in the interior of Q_R. Denote by $q(R)$ the boundary of Q_R and by $C(R)$ the curve $\{t = u + iv \colon |t| = R, u \geq 0, v \geq 0\}$. According to the Cauchy Theorem we have

$$\int_{q(R)} \delta(t; x)dt = 0.$$

Therefore,

$$\int_0^R \delta(t; x)dt + \int_{C(R)} \delta(t; x)dt - i \int_0^R \frac{e^{vx}}{1 + \lambda v^\alpha \exp\{i\frac{\pi}{2}\alpha(1 - \theta)\} + \mu v} dv = 0.$$

---

[16]The rest of the results in this section are due to Klebanov, Melamed, Mittnik and Rachev (1995).

The integral over $C(R)$ tends to zero as R tends to infinity. Hence,

$$I_1(x) = i \int_0^\infty \frac{e^{vx}}{1 + \lambda v^\alpha \exp\{i\frac{\pi}{2}\alpha(1-\theta)\} + \mu v} dv.$$

Then, because $x < 0$ and $1 < \alpha < 2$, $I_1(x)$ is an exponentially convergent integral.

To obtain an analogous representation for

$$I_2(x) = \int_0^\infty \frac{e^{itx}}{1 + \lambda |t|^\alpha \exp\{i\frac{\pi}{2}\alpha\theta\} + i\mu t} dt,$$

consider now region

$$P_R = \{t = u + iv \colon |t| \leq R, u \geq 0, v \leq 0\}, \qquad R > 1,$$

in the complex t-plane and define

$$t^\alpha = |t|^\alpha e^{i\alpha\varphi - 2\pi i}, \qquad \frac{3\pi}{2} < \varphi = \arg t < 2\pi.$$

Applying to function $I_2(x)$ and set P_R arguments similar to those used in deriving the integral representation for $I_1(x)$ leads to representation

$$I_2(x) = -i \int_0^\infty \frac{e^{vx}}{1 + \lambda v^\alpha \exp\{i\frac{\pi}{2}\alpha(\theta - 1)\} + \mu v} dv$$

Combining the representations for $I_1(x)$ and $I_2(x)$ we obtain

$$p(x) = \frac{\lambda \sin(\frac{\pi}{2}\alpha(1-\theta))}{\pi} \int_0^\infty \frac{v^\alpha e^{vx} dv}{|1 + \mu v + \lambda v^\alpha \exp\{\frac{i\pi}{2}\alpha(1-\theta)\}|^2}, \qquad x < 0.$$

Proceeding in a similarly fashion to derive the corresponding representations for $x > 0$, we obtain

$$p(x) = \frac{\lambda \sin(\frac{\pi}{2}\alpha(1+\theta))}{\pi} \int_0^\infty \frac{v^\alpha e^{-vx} dv}{|1 - \mu v + \lambda v^\alpha \exp\{\frac{i\pi}{2}\alpha(1+\theta)\}|^2}, \qquad x > 0.$$

$\square$

Using Theorem 2.4 the following asymptotic expansions of $p(x)$ for both $x \to \infty$ and $x \to -\infty$ can be derived.

Theorem 2.7 The geo–stable density has asymptotic expansion

$$p(x) \sim \frac{1}{\pi} \sum_{n=0}^\infty \sum_{k=0}^n \frac{(-1)^k n!}{k!(n-k)!} \mu^k \lambda^{n-k} \frac{\Gamma((n-k)\alpha + k + 1)}{x^{(n-k)\alpha + k + 1}} \sin \frac{\pi\alpha(1+\theta)(n-k)}{2},$$

for $x \to \infty$;

$$p(x) \sim \frac{1}{\pi} \sum_{n=0}^{\infty} \sum_{k=0}^{n} \frac{kn!}{k!(n-k)!} \mu^k \lambda^{n-k} \frac{\Gamma((n-k)\alpha+k+1)}{x^{(n-k)\alpha+k+1}} \sin \frac{\pi\alpha(1-\theta)(n-k)}{2},$$

for $x \to -\infty$.

Direct differentiation provides asymptotic expansions of the derivatives of $p(x)$. It follows from Theorem 2.4 that density $p(x)$ is a completely monotone function for both semiaxes $(-\infty, 0)$ and $(0, \infty)$. Consequently, $p(x)$ is infinitely differentiable for $x \neq 0$. However, at $x = 0$ we have

$$\lim_{x \to +0} (-1)^k p^{(k)}(x) = +\infty, \qquad k = 1, 2, \ldots .$$

This implies that $\lim_{x \to +0} p'(x) = -\infty$. In fact,

$$p'(x) \sim -\frac{\lambda \Gamma(-\alpha)}{\pi x^{2-\alpha} \sin(\frac{\pi}{2}\alpha(1+\theta))}$$

as $x \to +0$. Therefore, density $p(x)$ satisfies the Hölder condition with exponent $\alpha - 1$. This shows that one has to deal with the so-called singular case of Ibragimov and Khasminskii (1979).

2.2.2   Geometric Max-stable and Min-stable Distributions

Let $\{X_i\}$ be i.i.d. r.v.'s with $H(x) := \mathrm{P}(X_i \leq x)$ which are independent of the geometrically distributed r.v. $T(p)$ (see (2.42)). Define the random maximum

$$\xi_p = \max_{t_0+1 \leq t \leq t_0+T(p)} X_t, \tag{2.65}$$

and let $F_{\xi_p}(u)$ be the d.f. of ξ_p. If X_i represents the return on an asset during period $t_0 + i$, r.v. ξ_p in (2.65) describes the maximum return up to an event occurring at time $t_0 + T(p)$.

Definition 2.8 D.f. H is said to be a *strictly geometric max-stable* (in short, *strictly (geo,max)-stable*), if for any $p \in (0,1)$ there exist constants $a = a(p) > 0$ such that

$$a\xi_p \overset{d}{=} X_1.$$

The following three properties can be proved by straightforward calculation.

Property 2.19 *(Stability)*: Suppose all X_t $(t \geq t_0)$ have one and the same distribution, $G_{a,\alpha}$ $(a > 0, \alpha > 0)$, defined by

$$G_{a,\alpha}(x) = \begin{cases} \frac{x^\alpha}{a+x^\alpha}, & \text{if } x > 0, \\ 0, & \text{if } x \leq 0. \end{cases} \tag{2.66}$$

Then, the normalized maximum return

$$p^{\bar{\alpha}}\xi = [\mathbf{E}T(p)]^{-\bar{\alpha}} \max_{t_0+1\leq t\leq t_0+T(p)} X_t, \tag{2.67}$$

where $\bar{\alpha} = 1/\alpha$, will also have this distribution for any $p \in (0,1)$, namely

$$G_{a,\alpha}(x) = P(p^{\bar{\alpha}} \max_{t_0+1\leq t\leq t_0+T(p)} X_t \leq x). \tag{2.68}$$

Remark 2.1 The corresponding statement for the stable Paretian model is as follows (cf. Section 2.2.1). Given that r.v.'s X_t $(t \geq t_0)$ are i.i.d. stable Paretian with d.f. S_α and ch.f.

$$\mathbf{E}\exp\{iuX_t\} = \exp\{-|cu|^\alpha\},$$

then the normalized averages

$$T^{-\bar{\alpha}} \sum_{t=t_0+1}^{t_0+T} X_t \tag{2.69}$$

have the same α-stable distribution, S_α, for any fixed (i.e., nonrandom) T. A comparison of (2.67) and (2.69) reveals the "duality" between the random max-stable model (2.67) and the stable Paretian model (2.69). Instead of summing up X_t up to the fixed moment T as in (2.69), in (2.67) we focus on the maximum of X_t up to the random moment $T(p)$. Moreover, instead of the normalizing constant $T^{-\bar{\alpha}} = \mathbf{E}T^{-\bar{\alpha}}$ in (2.69), we have $[\mathbf{E}T(\rho)]^{-\bar{\alpha}}$ in (2.67).

The next property is an extension of Property 2.19.

Property 2.20 *(Characterization of strictly (geo,max)-stable distributions)*: D.f. H is strictly (geo,max)-stable if and only if $H(x) = G_{a,\alpha}(x)$, or

$$H(x) = G_{a,\alpha}^{(-)}(x) := \begin{cases} \frac{1}{1+a(-x)^\alpha}, & \text{if } x \leq 0, \\ 1, & \text{if } x > 0. \end{cases} \tag{2.70}$$

Because $G_{a,\alpha}(x)$ and $G_{a,\alpha}^{(-)}(x)$ are somewhat symmetric, we consider only $G_{a,\alpha}(x)$.

The next property states the necessary and sufficient condition for the random maxima ξ_p to have distribution $G_{a,\alpha}(x)$ as limiting distribution as p approaches zero.

Property 2.21 *((Geo,max)-stable domain of attraction)*: Let $\{X_i\}$ be i.i.d. r.v.'s with common d.f. $H(x) = P\{X_i \leq x\}$; and let ξ_p be defined by (2.65). Then,

$$F_p(x) := F_{\xi_p}(xp^{-\bar{\alpha}}) \longrightarrow G_{z,\alpha}(x), \quad \text{as } p \to 0, \text{ for any } x \in \mathbf{R}, \tag{2.71}$$

if and only if

$$u^\alpha [1 - H(u)] \longrightarrow a, \quad \text{as } u \to \infty. \tag{2.72}$$

Remark 2.2 Property 2.21 states that the tail condition (2.72) is necessary and sufficient for H to be in the (random) maxima domain of attraction of $G_{a,\alpha}$.[17]

Next, we address the question of how close distributions F_p and $G_{a,\alpha}$ are. To measure closeness, we introduce the following metric in the space of distribution functions. For any two distribution functions F_1 and F_2 on $\mathbf{R}$ define

$$\rho_r(F_1, F_2) = \sup_{x \in \mathbf{R}} |x|^r |F_1(x) - F_2(x)|, \quad r > 0. \tag{2.73}$$

The following property provides a precise estimate of the rate of convergence in (2.67) in terms of metric ρ_r.

Property 2.22 Assume that $\{X_i\}$ and F_p are defined as in Property 2.21; and let

$$\rho_r(H, G_{a,\alpha}) < \infty, \tag{2.74}$$

for some $r > \alpha$. Then, for any $p \in (0, 1)$,

$$\rho_r(F_p, G_{a,\alpha}) \leq p^{\bar{\alpha}r - 1} \rho_r(H, G_{a,\alpha}). \tag{2.75}$$

Remark 2.3 (i) It can be shown that condition (2.74) is necessary and sufficient for estimate (2.75); i.e., it cannot be improved upon without additional assumptions.

(ii) Property 2.22 states that if $r = 2\alpha$, then

$$\rho_r(F_p, G_{a,\alpha}) \leq p\rho_r(H, G_{a,\alpha}).$$

(iii) The corresponding result for the stable Paretian model is as follows (see Section 2.1). Let χ_r and θ_r $(0 < r < 2)$ represent metrics in the distribution-functions space given by

$$\chi_r(F_1, F_2) = \sup_{u \in \mathbf{R}} |u|^r \left| \int_{-\infty}^{\infty} e^{iux} d(F_1(x) - F_2(x)) \right| \tag{2.76}$$

and

$$\theta_r(F_1, F_2) = \begin{cases} \left(\int_{-\infty}^{\infty} \left| \int_{-\infty}^{x} F_1(u) - F_2(u) du \right|^{\frac{1}{r-1}} dx \right)^{r-1}, & \text{if } 1 < r \leq 2, \\ \left(\int_{-\infty}^{\infty} |F_1(u) - F_2(u)|^{\frac{1}{r}} du \right)^r, & \text{if } 0 < r \leq 1. \end{cases} \tag{2.77}$$

---

[17]The corresponding tail condition for α-stable distribution S_α is referred to as the Pareto-Doeblin-Gnedenko condition in Mandelbrot (1963a,b).

Then, for any $0 < \alpha < r \leq 2$,

$$\chi_r(F_\alpha, S_\alpha) \leq T^{1-r\bar{\alpha}}\chi_r(H, S_\alpha), \qquad (2.78)$$

where F_α is the d.f. of sum (2.69) and H is the d.f. of X_t specified in (2.70), we have (see Zolotarev, 1983; and Maejima and Rachev, 1987)

$$\theta_r(F_\alpha, S_\alpha) \leq T^{1-r\bar{\alpha}}\theta_r(H, S_\alpha). \qquad (2.79)$$

The next property characterizes the uniform departure of F_p from $G_{a,\alpha}$. For simplicity, we consider only the case of $a = \alpha = 1$. Let $t_0 = 0$, $X = X_0$ and $M(p) = p\max(X_1, \ldots, X_{T(p)})$; and let U be a r.v. with d.f.

$$G(x) = \frac{x}{1+x}, \quad x \geq 0. \qquad (2.80)$$

Then, by Property 2.21, the tail condition

$$\lim_{x \to \infty} x\bar{H}(x) = 1, \quad \bar{H} = 1 - H, \qquad (2.81)$$

is necessary and sufficient for the uniform convergence

$$\rho(M(p), U) \longrightarrow 0, \quad \text{as } p \to \infty, \qquad (2.82)$$

where $\rho(X, Y) = \sup_{x \in \mathbf{R}} |F_X(x) - F_Y(x)|$ is the uniform (Kolmogorov) distance in the space of distribution functions.

Further, we are interested in the right order estimates

$$\rho(M(p), U) = O(p^{r-1}), \quad 1 < r \leq 2, \qquad (2.83)$$

in terms of the weighted Kolmogorov distance

$$\rho_s = \rho_s(X_1, U) = \sup_{x \geq 0} x^s |H(x) - G(x)|, \quad s > 0. \qquad (2.84)$$

Defining

$$A := A(H) := \inf\left\{ a > 0: \sup_{\nu \geq a} \frac{1}{\nu\bar{H}(\nu)} \leq \frac{1}{\bar{H}(a)} \right\} \qquad (2.85)$$

and assuming that (2.81) holds, we have

$$A < \infty. \qquad (2.86)$$

Condition

$$B(H) := \sup_{\nu \geq 0} H^2(\nu)/\nu\bar{H}(\nu) < \infty \qquad (2.87)$$

is slightly stronger than (2.86). Note that $B(G) = 1 < \infty$. Expression (2.87) can be regarded as a condition for the "closeness" of H and G at 0 and ∞.

Property 2.23 (i) Let $r \in (1,2]$, $\rho = \rho(X,U)$, $\rho_1 = \rho_1(X,U)$, and $\rho_r = \rho_r(X,U)$. Then,

$$\rho(M(p),U) \leq p(\rho + \rho_1)[2 + B(F)] + p^{r-1}\rho_r B(F)C(r),$$

where $C(r) := (2-r)^{r-2}(r-1)^{1-r}$.
   (ii) If $r = 2$, then

$$\rho(M(p),U) \leq 2p(\rho + \rho_1 + \rho_2)\left(1 + \frac{1}{\bar{H}(A)}\right).$$

Remark 2.4 The corresponding result for the stable Paretian distribution is reported in Rachev and Yukich (1989,1991), providing a quantitative estimate of the following version of (2.78). If $\theta_r(H,S_\alpha) < \infty$, and $\alpha < r \leq 2$, then

$$\rho(F_\alpha, S_\alpha) = O(n^{1-r/\alpha}).$$

As in Section 2.1.2, we also consider the geometric-minimum scheme

$$Y_p = \min(X_1, \ldots, X_{T(p)}) \tag{2.88}$$

by making use of the "symmetry" between the maximum and minimum of i.i.d. r.v.'s.

Property 2.24 Let $X_1, X_2, \ldots$ be i.i.d. r.v.'s with common nondegenerate d.f. H; and let $T(p)$ be independent of $\{X_i\}$. Then, there exist constants $c(p)$ and $0 < p < 1$, such that[18]

$$c(p)Y_p \overset{d}{=} X_1, \tag{2.89}$$

for any $0 < p < 1$, if and only if H is either of the form

$$H_1(x) := 1 - G_{a,\alpha}(-x) = \begin{cases} \frac{a}{a+(-x)^\alpha}, & \text{if } x \leq 0, \\ 1, & \text{if } x > 0, \end{cases} \tag{2.90}$$

or

$$H_2(x) := 1 - G_{a,\alpha}^{(-1)}(-x) = G_{a,\bar{\alpha}}(x) = \begin{cases} 0, & \text{if } x \leq 0, \\ \frac{ax^\alpha}{1+ax^\alpha}, & \text{if } x > 0. \end{cases} \tag{2.91}$$

---

[18]I.e., H is strictly geometric min-stable.

2.2.3   Geometric multiplication-stable distributions

Using the same notation as in Section 2.1.3, define

$$\tilde{G}_p = \exp\{G_p\} = \prod_{i=1}^{T(p)} \exp\{X_i\}. \tag{2.92}$$

In the context of asset-return modeling, X_i with d.f. H (see (2.41)) would represent the positive return (or, the absolute value of the negative return) in period $t_0 + i$, and G_p, defined by (2.43), represents the total return up to time $t_0 + T(p)$. We write $\tilde{X}_i = \exp\{X_i\}$ and let $\tilde{H}$ be the d.f. of $\tilde{X}_i$.

Definition 2.9 Each (geo,sum)-stable distributed r.v., X, determines the r.v.

$$\tilde{X} = \exp\{X\}, \tag{2.93}$$

which is called *geometric stable* w.r.t. the multiplication scheme or, in short *(geo,mult.)-stable*.

Let $\tilde{H}$ be the d.f. of the (geo,mult)-stable r.v. $\tilde{X}$. If r.v. X in (2.93) has the symmetric Laplace distribution function $H = \mathcal{G}$ given by (2.48), then the p.d.f. of $\tilde{H}$ is given by

$$\tilde{H}'(x) := \frac{\partial}{\partial x}\tilde{H}'(x) \;\; = \;\; \begin{cases} H'(\ln x)\frac{1}{x} = \frac{1}{2\lambda x}\exp\{-\lambda|\ln x|\}, & x > 0, \\ 0, & x \le 0, \end{cases}$$

$$= \begin{cases} \frac{1}{2\lambda}x^{-\lambda-1}, & x \ge 1, \\ \frac{1}{2\lambda}x^{\lambda-1}, & 0 < x < 1, \\ 0, & 0 \le x, \end{cases}$$

which can be regarded as the p.d.f. form the family of a *symmetric Pareto distribution* with parameter $\lambda > 0$. The two-parameter symmetric Pareto distribution $\tilde{H} = M_{\lambda,x_0}$ has a similar p.d.f., namely

$$\tilde{H}'_{\lambda,x_0}(x) := \begin{cases} \mu x^{-\lambda-1}, & \text{if } x \ge x_0, \\ \mu x^{\lambda-1}, & \text{if } 0 < x < x_0, \\ 0, & \text{if } x \le 0, \end{cases} \tag{2.94}$$

where $\mu := \lambda(x_0^{-\lambda} + x_0^{\lambda})^{-1}$ and $\lambda > 0$.

Similarly, if X has the shifted exponential distribution

$$H(t) = F_X(t) = \begin{cases} 1 - \exp\{-\lambda(t - t_0)\}, & \text{if } t \ge t_0, \\ 0, & \text{if } t < t_0, \end{cases} \tag{2.95}$$

then,

$$\tilde{M}(x) = F_{\tilde{X}}(x) = \begin{cases} 1 - \mu x^{-\lambda}, & \text{if } x \ge x_0 := e^{t_0}, \ \mu := e^{\lambda t_0}, \\ 0, \text{if } x < x_0, \end{cases} \tag{2.96}$$

is the well-known classical form of the *Pareto distribution*. Clearly, one can derive the "stability" properties of (geo,mult)-stable distributions, $\tilde{M}$, by simply setting $X_i = \ln \tilde{X}_i$ in Properties 2.14–2.17.

2.3 A Contaminated Geometric Stable Law

As it was shown in Mittnik and Rachev (1993a), the double (or two-sided) Weibull distribution yields good empirical fits and the Laplace (or double–exponential) distribution is also a strong candidate, given that it is a restricted version of the double Weibull distribution. If the data are generated by more than one scheme or if outliers are present, a mixture distribution can be a reasonable modeling strategy. This idea motivated the work of Boness et al. (1974), who considered mixtures of normals, and DuMouchel (1973a,b), who considered a mixture of a stable Paretian and a normal distribution.

Following the general Central Limit Theorem, see Gnedenko (1970), the Laplace distribution could be viewed as the "normal" distribution within the geometric stable scheme, while the double Weibull plays a role similar to the stable Paretian distribution. For this reason and in view of the empirical findings, a Laplace–Weibull mixture seems to be an interesting candidate for modeling asset returns. We refer to such a mixture as contaminated Laplace distribution and write

$$\Lambda_\pi(x) = \pi\Lambda(x) + (1 - \pi)W(x), \quad 0 < \pi < 1, \tag{2.97}$$

where Λ is the Laplace d.f. with parameter $\lambda > 0$; W is a symmetric (double) Weibull distribution with parameters $\mu > 0$ and $\gamma > 1$. Note that $\Lambda_\pi(x)$ can resemble unimodal (as $\pi \to 1$), bimodal (as $\pi \to 0$) or multimodal (for different parameter combinations) distributions and provides a high degree of flexibility.

Suppose $X^{(1)}, \ldots, X^{(T)}$ represent a sequence of asset returns until the geometrically distributed period $T = T(p)$, where $p \in (0, 1)$ represents the probability that a fundamental change of the return process occurs in any given period. We assume that the $X^{(i)}$'s are i.i.d. with distribution Λ_π and consider the total normalized change $\sqrt{p}\sum_{i=1}^T X^{(i)}$. To compare it with the Laplace distribution, we use a bound of the deviation between the distribution of $\sqrt{p}\sum_{i=1}^T X^{(i)}$ and $X = F_U$ in terms of the *Khinchin metric*

$$\chi(X, Y) = \sup_{\chi \geq 0} \left| \int_x^\infty [F_X(x) - F_Y(x)]dx \right|.$$

Theorem 2.8 Let the means and the variances of $X^{(i)}$ and U match; i.e. $x^{(i)}$ and U have equal first and second moments. Then,

$$\chi\left(\sqrt{p}\sum_{i=1}^T X^{(i)}, U\right)$$

$$\leq (1 - \pi)\left[\sqrt{p}\tilde{\chi} + qp^{\frac{r}{2}-1}\tilde{\kappa}_r \frac{1}{(r-1)}\left(\frac{\lambda}{2}\right)^{r-1}\left[\Gamma\left(1 + \frac{1}{p}\right)\right]^\beta\right], \tag{2.98}$$

where

$$\tilde{\chi} := \sup_{x \in \mathbf{R}} \left| \int_{-\infty}^x (\Lambda(t) - W(t))dt \right|$$

and

$$\tilde{\kappa}_r := r \int_{-\infty}^{+\infty} |x|^{r-1} |\Lambda(x) - W(x)| dx.$$

One can use the Khinchin metric to obtain bounds similar to (2.98) for the mixture case.

Theorem 2.9 Let $F_{X^{(i)}} = \pi F_U + (1 - \pi) F_V$, where U is geometric stable with index $\alpha \in (0,1)$. Then,

$$\chi \left(p^{\frac{1}{\alpha}} \sum_{i=1}^{T} X^{(i)}, U \right) \le p^{\frac{1}{\alpha}-1} (1 - \pi) \chi(V, U). \tag{2.99}$$

This follows from the "idealness" of χ (see Rachev 1991c, Chapter 14, for the properties of *ideal metrics*). Cases $1 \le \alpha < 2$ and $\alpha = 2$ can be treated analogously. See also Rachev and SenGupta (1993).

2.4   Distributions Arising in the General Random Summation Scheme

2.4.1   The Random Summation Scheme

In this section a general theory of a random number of r.v.'s is developed.[19] A description of all random variables ν admitting an analogue to the Gaussian distribution under ν-summation, namely, the summation of a random number ν of random terms, is given.

The study of sums of a random number of variables originated in Robbins (1948) and was developed further by Dobrushin (1955) and Gnedenko and his students (Gnedenko, 1967; Gnedenko and Fakhim, 1969; Gnedenko, 1983a,b).This research is partially summarized in Kruglov and Korolev (1990).

In the classical scheme infinitely divisible distributions can be defined in two ways. In the *first definition* a random variable, Y, is called *infinitely divisible* if for any integer $n \ge 2$ there exist i.i.d. r.v.'s $X_1^{(n)}, \cdots, X_n^{(n)}$ for which $Y \overset{d}{=} X_1^{(n)} + \cdots + X_n^{(n)}$ (here $\overset{d}{=}$ denotes equality of distributions). The *second definition* consists in the fact that only infinitely divisible distributions are limits of increasing sums of independent r.v.'s in triangular arrays provided that the terms are infinitely small.

In the classical, nonrandom scheme both definitions are equivalent. However, for sums of a random number of random variables this is no longer the case. The results of Robbins, Dobrushin, Gnedenko, and others are generalizations of the second definition, see the review in Mittnik and Rachev (1993a,b).

---

[19]The results in this section are due to Klebanov and Rachev (1996a).

Klebanov et al. (1984a) generalized the first definition to the case where the number of terms is geometric infinitely divisible and gave the definition of geometrically stable distributions.

An attempt to investigate more general summations than the geometric sums was made in Klebanov et al. (1985, 1987), and Klebanov and Rachev (1996a). In this section, following Klebanov and Rachev (1996a), we present a general theory of summation of a random number of random variables generalizing the first definition of infinite divisibility. All random variables, ν, admitting an analogue of the Gaussian distribution under the summation of ν random terms are described. For these summations all ν-infinitely divisible distributions (i.e., infinitely divisible in the sense of the first definition) are characteristic. This allows us to introduce the concept of ν-*accompanying infinitely divisible distributions*, to obtain finite estimates of the rate of approximation of the distributions of ν-sums using the ν-accompanying infinitely divisible and geometrically stable distributions; to obtain estimates of their approximation, which cannot be improved upon; and their domains of attraction.

2.4.2 ν-Gaussian Random Variables

Let $X_1, X_2, \cdots$ be a sequence of i.i.d. r.v.'s. and assume that $\{\nu_p, p \in \Delta\}$, $\Delta \subset (0,1)$ is a family of nonnegative integer-valued r.v.'s independent of $\{X_j, j \geq 1\}$. It is then assumed that there exists $\mathbf{E}\nu_p$ and that $\mathbf{E}\nu_p = 1/p$ for all $p \in \Delta$. We study the distributions of sums $S_p = \sum_{j=1}^{\nu_p} X_j, p \in \Delta$.

Definition 2.10 Random variable Y is called ν-*infinitely divisible*, if for any $p \in \Delta$ there exists a sequence of i.i.d. r.v.'s, $\{X_j^{(p)}, j \geq 1\}$, independent of ν_p, such that

$$Y \stackrel{d}{=} \sum_{j=1}^{\nu_p} X_j^{(p)}. \tag{2.100}$$

Definition 2.11 A random variable X_1 is called ν-*strictly Gaussian*, if $\mathbf{E}X_1 = 0, \mathbf{E}X_1^2 < \infty$, and for all $p \in \Delta$

$$X_1 \stackrel{d}{=} p^{1/2} \sum_{j=1}^{\nu_p} X_j, \tag{2.101}$$

where $\{X_j, j \geq 1\}$ is a sequence of i.i.d. r.v.'s independent of $\{\nu_p, p \in \Delta\}$.

Distributions of ν-infinitely divisible (ν-strictly stable, ν-strictly Gaussian) r.v.'s are called ν-infinitely divisible (ν-strictly stable, ν-strictly Gaussian) distributions.

The first question of interest is how to describe families $\{\nu_p, p \in \Delta\}$ for which ν-strictly Gaussian random variables exist. Recall first that if $P^{(1)}$ and

$P^{(2)}$ are the *generating functions*[20] (gf) of two r.v.'s taking natural values, then their superposition $P^{(1)} \circ P^{(2)}(z) := P^{(1)}(P^{(2)}(z))$, is also a gf of some r.v. that takes natural values.

Let P_p denote the gf of r.v. ν_p and $\mathcal{P}$ a semigroup with operation of superposition $\circ$ generated by family $\{P_p, p \in \Delta\}$.

Theorem 2.10 For a ν-strictly Gaussian random variable, X_1, to exist it is necessary and sufficient that semigroup **P** be commutative.

Proof: Let $f(t)$ be the ch.f of X_1. Then, (2.101) is equivalent to the system of equalities

$$f(t) = P_p(f(p^{1/2}t)), \; p \in \Delta, \tag{2.102}$$

fulfilled for all real t (the equations of the system are indexed by parameter $p \in \Delta$).

Let us consider (2.102) only for $t \geq 0$. Let $\varphi(t) = f(\sqrt{t})$. Since $\mathbf{E}X_1 = 0$ and $EX_1^2 < \infty$, function $f(t)$ is twice continuously differentiable and $f'(0) = 0, f''(0) \neq 0$. Therefore, $\varphi(t)$ is differentiable for $t \in (0, \infty)$ and $\varphi'(+0) \neq 0$. It is easy to see that if $f(t)$ satisfies (2.102), then $\varphi(t)$ satisfies the system

$$\varphi(t) = P_p(\varphi(pt)), p \in \Delta \tag{2.103}$$

for $t \geq 0$ and, conversely, if $\varphi(t)$ satisfies (2.103), then $f(t) = \varphi(t^2)$ satisfies (2.102). This implies that if $f(t)$ does exist then it is symmetric.

Let us choose an arbitrary $p_0 \in \Delta$. For simplicity's sake, let us denote the gf of ν_{p_0} by $P(z)$. From (2.103) it follows that

$$\varphi(t) = P(\varphi(p_0 t)) \tag{2.104}$$

Equation (2.104) is the Poincare equation.[21] Note that (2.104) also occurs in the theory of branching processes (see, for example, Harris (1963)). It is well-known that (2.104) has a unique and differentiable solution with initial values $\varphi(0) = 1, \varphi'(0) = -\alpha, \alpha \geq 0$ is an arbitrary constant. This solution is the Laplace transform of probability solution $A(z)$ concentrated on the n on-negative semiaxis R_+. Thus,

$$\varphi(t) = \int_0^\infty e^{-tx} dA(x) \tag{2.105}$$

and $\varphi(t)$ is determined to within a scale parameter. Clearly, if $\varphi'(0) = -a \neq 0$, then A is not degenete at zero.

It is clear that the solution of the *overdetermined* system (2.103) (if it exists) must satisfy (2.104), that is, it must coincide with (2.105). Of course,

---

[20] $P(t)$ is the generating function of a r.v. X if $P(t) = \mathbf{E}t^x$.
[21] Poincare (1890) was interested in the existence and uniqueness of the analytic solution of (2.104).

for (2.103) to have a solution, it is necessary and sufficient that the solution of (2.104) be independent of the choice $p_0 \in \Delta$. In other words, for $p \in \Delta, p \neq p_0$ equations

$$\varphi_p(t) = P_p(\varphi_p(pt)) \quad p \text{ is fixed}, \tag{2.106}$$

and (2.104) must have the same solutions with initial values $\varphi(0) = \varphi_p(0) = 1, \varphi'(0) = \varphi_p(0) = -a, a > 0$.

Let us show that (2.104) and (2.106) have the same solution if and only if P_p and P commute, that is,

$$P_p \circ P = P \circ P_p. \tag{2.107}$$

Suppose first that (2.107) holds. Let $\varphi(t)$ be a solution of (2.104) with the desired initial values. Consider function $P_p(\varphi(tp))$. Using (2.104) and (2.107), we write $P_p(\varphi(tp)) = P_p(P(\varphi(tp_0p))) = P(P_p(\varphi(tp_0p)))$. Thus, $P_p(\varphi(tp))$ satisfies (2.104). In addition,

$$P_p(\varphi(tp))|_{t=0} = P_p(\varphi(0)) = P_p(1) = 1,$$

$$\frac{d}{dt}P_p(\varphi(tp))|_{t=0} = P_p'(\varphi(tp))\varphi'(tp)p|_{t=0} = \frac{1}{p}\varphi'(0)p = -a.$$

Consequently, $\varphi(t)$ an $P_p(\varphi(tp))$ satisfy (2.104) and have the same initial values. By virtue of the uniqueness of the solution of (2.104) satisfying specified initial values, we obtain $\varphi(t) = P_p(\varphi(tp))$. Making use of the symmetry between p and p_0', we obtain that under (2.107) equations (2.104) and (2.106) have the same solution.

Assume now that (2.104) and (2.106) have the same solution. Then $P_p(P(\varphi(pp_0t))) = P_p(\varphi(pt)) = \varphi(t)$. Changing the places of the arguments we get $P(P_p(\varphi(pp_0t))) = P(\varphi(p_0t)) = \varphi(t)$, and therefore $P(P_p(\varphi(pp_0t))) = P_p(P(\varphi(pp_0t)))$. However, for $\varphi'(0) = -a \neq 0$ we see from (2.105) that $\varphi(t)$ is the Laplace transform of distribution function $A(x)$ which is not degenerate at zero, that is, the values of $\varphi(t)$ for $t > 0$ fill interval $(0,1]$. Consequently, $P(P_p(z)) = P_p(P(z))$ for $z \in (0,1]$, and by virtue of the analyticity of the generating function in the unit circle this implies (2.107).

Let us return to (2.102). It follows from (2.105) that $f(t)$ must have the form $f(t) = \int_0^\infty e^{-t^2x}dA(x)$. In addition, (2.102) is consistent if and only if (2..4.4) is consistent, that is, if and only if (2.107) is fulfilled for any $p, p_0 \in \Delta$. The latter is clearly equivalent to the commutativity of $\mathcal{P}$.   □

Theorem 2.10 differs from the corresponding result of Klebanov, Manija and Melamed (1985) in that they assumed the existence of limit $\lim_{p\to 0} P\{p\nu_p < x\}$ for all $x \geq 0$, and as result, our proof differs substantially from the corresponding proof in Klebanov, Manija and Melamed (1985).

Remark 2.5 If $\mathcal{P}$ is commutative, then (see the proof of Theorem 2.10), the characteristic function of a ν-strictly Gaussian distribution has form $f(t) =$

$\varphi(at^2)$, where $a > 0$ is a parameter and $\varphi(t)$ is a solution of (2.104) satisfying the conditions $\varphi(0) = -\varphi'(0) = 1$.

Corollary 2.3 The semigroup $\mathcal{P}$ is commutative if and only if for $z > 0$,

$$P_p(z) = \varphi(\frac{1}{p}\varphi^{-1}(z)), p \in \Delta,$$

where $\varphi(t)$ is a differentiable solution of (2.104) and $\varphi(0) = -\varphi'(0) = 1$.

Proof. As the proof of Theorem 2.10 implies, the commutativity of $\mathcal{P}$ is equivalent to (2.103) with initial values $\varphi(0) = 1, \varphi'(0) = -a$ (we fix $a = 1$) having a solution independent of p_0. Thus, the commutativity of $\mathcal{P}$ is equivalent to $\varphi(t) = P_p(\varphi(pt))$ for all p with φ independent of p. Since φ is invertible for $t > 0$ and is non-negative, the last equality can be rewritten in the form $P_p(z) = \varphi(\frac{1}{p}\varphi^{-1}(z)), z > 0$. $\square$

Let us turn to examples of families of random variables $\{\nu_p, p \in \Delta\}$ admitting ν-strictly Gaussian laws.

Example 2.1 *(The classical scheme of summation)* Let $\nu_p = \frac{1}{p}$ with probability 1 and $p \in \Delta = \{1/n, n \in \mathcal{N}\}$. Clearly, $P_p(z) = z^{1/p}$ and $P_{p_1} \circ P_{p_2}(z) = z^{1/(p_1 p_2)} = P_{p_2} \circ P_{p_1}(z)$. By virtue of Theorem 2.4, there exists a ν-strictly Gaussian distribution. Of course we are dealing with the classical scheme and ν-strictly Gaussian distributions coincide with ordinary Gaussian one.

Example 2.2 *(The geometric summation scheme)* Let ν_p be a geometric random variable with parameter p: $P\{\nu_p = \kappa\} = p(1-p)^{\kappa-1}, \kappa \in \mathcal{N}$. We have $P_p(z) = pz/(1-(1-p)z)$. It is easy to see that $P_{p_1} \circ P_{p_2}(z) = \frac{p_1 p_2 z}{1-(1-p_1 p_2)z} = P_{p_2} \circ P_{p_1}(z)$. Therefore, there exists a ν-strictly Gaussian distribution. Equation (2.104) has the form (for $p_0 \in (0,1)$)

$$\varphi(t) = \frac{p_0 \varphi(p_0 t)}{1 - (p_0)\varphi(p_0 t)}. \tag{2.108}$$

As is well known (see Azlarov, Dzhamirzaev and Sultanov (1972), and Kakosyan, Klebanov and Melamed (1984)) the Laplace transforms of the exponential distribution are solutions of form (2.105) of this equation, that is, $\varphi_a(t) = 1/(1 + at)$. In particular, $\varphi(t) = 1/(1 + t)$ is the unique solution of (2.108) provided that $\varphi(0) = -\varphi'(0) = 1$. Therefore, ν-strictly Gaussian distributions are Laplace distributions with characteristic functions

$$f(t) = 1/(1 + at^2), \qquad a > 0. \tag{2.109}$$

Example 2.3 *(The ν-summation scheme)* Let ν be a r.v. taking natural values and having $\mathbf{E}\nu > 1$. Denote $p_0 = 1/\mathbf{E}\nu$ and let $P(z)$ be the gf ν. Let

$$P_{p_0}(z) = P(z), P_{p_0^2}(z) = P(P(z)) = P^{o2}(z), \cdots, P_{p_0^n}(z) = P^{on}(z), \tag{2.110}$$

and suppose that $\Delta = \{p_0^n, n \in \mathcal{N}\}$. Assume that $\{\nu_p, p \in \Delta\}$ is a family of rv's with gf's (2.110). Clearly $\mathcal{P}$ is commutative since it is a semigroup of degrees in the sense of superposition of function $P(z)$. The system (2.103) has form

$$\varphi(t) = P(\varphi(p_0 t)) = P^{o2}(\varphi(p_0^2 t)) = \cdots = P^{on}(\varphi(p_0^n t)) = \cdots .$$

It coincides with (2.104): $\varphi(t) = P(\varphi(p_0 t))$.

Example 2.3 shows that a summation generated by *only* one random variable ν is equivalent to a summation related to the family $\{\nu_p, p \in \Delta\}, \Delta = \{p_0^n, n \in \mathcal{N}\}$. Note that this circumstance has a more general character: instead of $\{\nu_p, p \in \Delta\}$ (for generic Δ) we can consider a family of all r.v.'s ν whose gf's belong to $\mathcal{P}$. This is reflected neither on the existence of ν-Gaussian distributions nor on the form of their characteristic functions. Everywhere below (unless otherwise stipulated) we assume $\{\nu_p, p \in \Delta\}$ to be such that $\{P_p, p \in \Delta\} = \mathcal{P}$, with $\mathcal{P}$ being commutative semigroup.

A solution of (2.104) given by (2.105), differentiable on $[0, \infty)$, and satisfying the conditions $\varphi(0) = -\varphi'(0) = 1$ will be called *standard*.

2.4.3 ν-Infinitely Divisible Random Variables

Let us turn to the description of ν-infinitely divisible laws (see Definition 2.10). A part of the results set forth here has been announced in Klebanov, Manija and Melamed (1985, 1987).

We start with an analog of the de Finetti's theorem (see, for example, Lucas (1969)).

Theorem 2.11 Let φ be a standard solution of (2.104). A r.v. with ch.f. $g(t)$ is ν-infinitely divisible if and only if

$$g(t) = \lim_{m \to \infty} \varphi(\alpha_m [1 - g_m(t)]), \qquad (2.111)$$

where α_m is a positive constant and $g_m(t)$ is a ch.f.

Proof.

(i) We first show that if $h(t)$ is a ch.f. and α is a positive constant, then

$$\Psi_\alpha(t) = \varphi(\alpha[1 - h(t)]) \qquad (2.112)$$

is a ch.f. Indeed, since $\{\nu_p, p \in \Delta\}$ satisfies $\{P_p, p \in \Delta\} = \mathcal{P}$, then 0 is the limit point of set Δ. Therefore, for $\alpha > 0$ and sufficiently small $p \in \Delta$, $h_\alpha(t) = (1 - \alpha p) + \alpha p h(t)$ is a ch.f. Consequently, $\varphi\left(\frac{1}{p}\varphi^{-1}\{(1 - \alpha p) + \alpha p h(t)\}\right)$ is a ch.f. (this is the ch.f. of $\sum_{j=1}^{\nu_p} X_j$, where X_j are i.i.d. with ch.f. $h_\alpha(t)$). However, $\varphi(\alpha[1 - h(t)]) = $

$\lim_{p\to 0} \varphi\left(\frac{1}{p}\varphi^{-1}\{(1-\alpha p)+\alpha p h(t)\}\right)$, which proves the assertion of part (i).

(ii) For any $\alpha > 0$ and ch.f. $h(t)$, function (2.112) is ν-infinitely divisible. Indeed, for all $p \in \Delta$ function $\Psi_\alpha(t)$ is a ch.f. of $\sum_{j=1}^{\nu_p} X_j$, if $\{X_j, j \geq 1\}$ is a sequence of i.i.d. variables with ch.f. $\Psi_{\alpha p}(t)$.

(iii) The function (2.111) is ν-infinitely divisible. This follows from (ii) and the fact that the limit of ν-infinitely divisible ch.f.'s is also a ν-infinitely divisible function.

(iv) Any ν-infinitely divisible ch.f. $g(t)$ can be written in the form of 2.111. Indeed, if $g(t)$ is a ν-infinitely divisible ch.f., then for any $p \in \Delta$ there exists a ch.f. $g_p(t)$ such that $g(t) = \varphi\left(\frac{1}{p}\varphi^{-1}g_p(t)\right)$. Hence, $g_p(t) = \varphi(p\varphi^{-1}g(t))$, that is, $\varphi(p\varphi^{-1}g(t))$ is a ch.f.. Therefore, by (ii), $\varphi\left(\frac{1}{p}(1-g_p(t))\right) = \varphi\left(\frac{1}{p}(1-\varphi(p\varphi^{-1}g(t)))\right)$ is a ν-infinitely divisible ch.f.. Finally, $g(t) = \lim_{p\to 0}\varphi\left(\frac{1}{p}[1-\varphi(p\varphi^{-1}g(t))]\right)$, which proves (iv).

$\square$

Theorem 2.12 Let φ be a standard solution of (2.104). A ch.f. g is ν-infinitely divisible if and only if

$$g(t) = \varphi(-\log f(t)), \qquad (2.113)$$

where $f(t)$ is an infinitely divisible ch.f. (in the classical scheme).

The proof of this theorem follows directly from a comparison of Theorem 2.11 and de Finetti's theorem.

Theorem 2.12 leads to analogs of the Lévy and Lévy-Khinchin representations for ν-infinitely divisible characteristic functions, and furthermore, it serves as a basis for the definition of such concepts as ν-strictly stable, ν-stable, and ν-semistable characteristic functions (random variables). Let us give precise formulations.

Corollary 2.4 *(Analogue to the canonic Lévy-Khinchin representation)* A function $g(t)$ is ν-infinitely divisible ch.f. if and only if it can be represented in the form of

$$g(t) = \varphi\left[ita - \int_{-\infty}^{\infty}\left[e^{itx} - 1 - \frac{itx}{1+x^2}\right]\frac{1+x^2}{x^2}d\theta(x)\right],$$

where a is a real number, $\theta(x)$ is a nondecreasing bounded function under the condition that $\theta(-\infty) = 0$, and φ is the standard solution of (2.104). This representation is unique (of course for a fixed family $\{\nu_p, p \in \dot{\Delta}\}$).

Corollary 2.5 *(Analogue to the canonic Lévy representation)* A function $g(t)$ is a ν-infinitely divisible ch.f. if and only if it can be represented as

$$
g(t) = \varphi \left[ita + \frac{\sigma^2 t^2}{2} - \int_{-\infty}^{-0} \left[e^{itx} - 1 - \frac{itx}{1+x^2} \right] dM(x) \right.
$$

$$
\left. - \int_{+0}^{\infty} \left[e^{itx} - 1 - \frac{itx}{1+x^2} \right] dN(x) \right],
$$

where φ is a solution of (2.104), a is a real number, σ is a non-negative number, and functions $M(x)$ and $N(x)$ satisfy the conditions:

(i) $M(x)$ and $N(x)$ do not decrease on intervals $(-\infty, 0)$ and $(0, +\infty)$, respectively;

(ii) $M(-\infty) = N(0) = 0$;

(iii) integrals $\int_{-\epsilon}^{0} x^2 dM(x)$ and $\int_{0}^{\epsilon} x^2 dN(x)$ are finite for any $\epsilon > 0$.

This representation is unique.

Remark 2.4.2. If the standard solution of (2.104) φ is a Laplace transform of an infinitely divisible distribution, then ν-infinitely divisible distributions are infinitely divisible (in the regular sense), see Feller (1971), Section XIII.7.

Definition 2.12 A function $g(t)$ is called a ν-stable (correspondingly, ν-strictly stable, ν-semistable) *characteristic function with exponent* α if it admits representation (2.113) in which φ is a standard solution of (2.104) and $f(t)$ is the ch.f. of a stable (correspondingly, strictly stable, semistable) law with exponent α.

However, care should be exercised when using Definition 2.12. We illustrate this with an example comparing ν-strictly stable and ν-semistable ch.f.'s.

Let $X_1, X_2, \ldots$ be a sequence of i.i.d. symmetric r.v.'s. Assume that for some $\alpha \in (0, 2)$ and for all $p \in \Delta$

$$
X_1 \stackrel{d}{=} p^{1/\alpha} \sum_{j=1}^{\nu_p} X_j \tag{2.114}
$$

is fulfilled. (Such a r.v. X_1 was called ν-strictly stable in Klebanov et al. 1987.) From (2.114) it apparently follows that X_1 is ν-infinitely divisible. Consequently, we have $g(t) = \varphi(-\log f(t))$, $P_p(z) = \varphi(\frac{1}{p}\varphi(-\log f(p^{1/\alpha}t)))$, that is,

$$
f(t) = f^{1/p}(p^{1/\alpha}t), \quad p \in \Delta. \tag{2.115}
$$

If $\Delta \supset \{1/n : n \in \mathbf{N}\}$, then it clearly follows form (2.115) that $f(t)$ is a strictly stable and, consequently, $g(t)$ is a ν-strictly stable ch.f. in the sense of Definition 2.12. However, if $\Delta = \{p_0^n : n \in \mathbf{N}\}$ for a specific $p_0 \in (0,1)$, then $f(t)$ is a semistable ch.f. and, hence $g(t)$ is a ν-semistable ch.f. in the sense of Definition 2.12. (But is the sense of the definition of Klebanov et al. (1987) $g(t)$ is a ν-strictly stable ch.f.). It should be noted that (2.114) is indeed a full analog of the classical definition of strictly stable laws.

2.4.4   Accompanying Laws

Let us now introduce the concept of accompanying ν-infinitely divisible laws (characteristic functions, random variable). In the classical scheme (i.e., when $\nu_p = 1/p$ a.s., $p \in \{1/n : n \in \mathbf{N}\}$) the concept of an accompanying infinitely divisible distribution is due to Gnedenko (1938). It proved to be rather useful when approximating distributions of sums of a large (but not random) number of random terms (see, for example, Arak and Zaitsev (1988)).

Definition 2.13 Let $X_1, \ldots, X_n, \ldots$ be a sequence of i.i.d. r.v.'s with ch.f. $f(t)$. Assume that $\varphi(t)$ is a standard solution to (2.104). Let $S_p = \sum_{j=1}^{\nu_p} X_j$. A r.v. Y_p with ch.f.

$$\Psi_p(t; f) = \varphi\left(\frac{1}{p}[1 - f(t)]\right) \tag{2.116}$$

is called an *accompanying divisible r.v. for sum* S_p. Its distribution function (correspondingly, c.f.) is said to be accompanying ν-infinitely divisible for the d.f. (correspondingly, the c.f.) of S_p. For the sake of brevity, we speak of a *ν-accompanying r.v. (ν-accompanying distribution)*.[22]

Let us now investigate whether distributions of sums S_p can be approximated with a ν-accompanying distribution. First, let us check whether this is possible in terms of the uniform metric χ_0; if X and Y are r.v.'s with ch.f.'s $f_X(t)$ and $f_Y(t)$, respectively, then

$$\chi_0(X, Y) := \sup_t |f_X(t) - f_Y(t)|. \tag{2.117}$$

For its properties see, Zolotarev (1986b), Kakosyan et al. (1988), Rachev (1991). Denote by $\mathcal{F}_+$ the class of all r.v.'s with non-negative ch.f.'s.

---

[22]In the classical case our definition differs somewhat from the one given in Gnedenko (1938), who admits, in addition, centering and normalization of f, that is, Gnedenko would have $\Psi_p(t, f; a_p, b_p) = \varphi(\frac{1}{p}[1 - f(a_p t)e^{ib_p t}])$. Everywhere below we will use the definition corresponding to (2.116).

Theorem 2.13 Let $X_1, X_2, \ldots$ be a sequence of i.i.d. r.v.'s, $X_1 \in \mathcal{F}_+$. Suppose that $S_p = \sum_{j=1}^{\nu_p} X_j$ and Y_p is a ν-accompanying r.v. for S_p. Then

$$\sup_{X_1 \in \mathcal{F}_+} \chi_0(S_p, Y_p) \to 0 \quad \text{as } p \to 0, p \in \Delta. \tag{2.118}$$

In other words, Theorem 2.13 asserts that for sufficiently small p the distributions of S_p and ν-accompanying variable Y_p are close regardless of what the distribution of terms $X_j \in \mathcal{F}_+$ is, that is, the closeness of S_p and Y_p is uniform with respect to the distributions of $X_j \in \mathcal{F}_+$.

Proof. We have

$$
\begin{aligned}
\sup_{X_1 \in \mathcal{F}_+} \chi_0(S_p, Y_p) &= \sup_{X_1 \in \mathcal{F}_+} \sup_t \left| \varphi\left(\frac{1}{p}\varphi^{-1} f_{X_1}(t)\right) - \varphi\left(\frac{1}{p}[1 - f_{X_1}(t)]\right) \right| \\
&= \sup_{z \in [0,1]} \left| \varphi\left(\frac{1}{p}\varphi^{-1}(z)\right) - \varphi\left(\frac{1}{p}(1-z)\right) \right| \\
&= \sup_{u \in [0,\infty)} \left| \varphi\left(\frac{u}{p}\right) - \varphi\left(\frac{1}{p}(1 - \varphi(u))\right) \right| \\
&= \max \left[\sup_{u \in [\sqrt{p},\infty)} \left| \varphi\left(\frac{u}{p} - \varphi\left(\frac{1}{p}(1 - \varphi(u))\right)\right) \right|, \right. \\
&\qquad\qquad \left. \sup_{u \in [0,\sqrt{p}]} \left| \varphi\left(\frac{1}{p}(1 - \varphi(u))\right) \right| \right]
\end{aligned}
$$

For $u \geq \sqrt{p}$, it is clear that, as $p \to 0$, $\varphi(\frac{u}{p}) \to 0$, $\varphi(\frac{1}{p}[1 - \varphi(u)]) \to 0$. Therefore, as $p \to 0$, $\sup_{u \in [\sqrt{p},\infty)} |\varphi(\frac{u}{p} - \varphi(\frac{1}{p}[1 - \varphi(u)]))| \to 0$. For $u \leq \sqrt{p}$, denoting $\nu = \frac{u}{p}$, we obtain

$$
\begin{aligned}
&\sup_{u \in [0,\sqrt{p}]} \left| \varphi\left(\frac{u}{p}\right) - \varphi\left(\frac{1}{p}[1 - \varphi(u)]\right) \right| \\
&= \sup_{v \in [0,1/\sqrt{p}]} \left| \varphi(v) - \varphi\left(-\frac{\varphi(pv) - \varphi(0)}{pv}v\right) \right| \\
&\to 0,
\end{aligned}
$$

as $p \to 0$ because $(\varphi(pv) - \varphi(0))/(pv) \to \varphi'(0) = -1$ as $p \to 0$ uniformly with respect to $v \in [0, 1/\sqrt{p}]$. $\qquad\square$

Note that, generally speaking, the constraint $X_1 \in \mathcal{F}_+$ cannot be waived. Namely, if we consider a sequence of i.i.d. r.v.'s taking values 1 or -1 with probability $1/2$ each a.s. ($p \in \{1/n, n \in \mathbf{N}\}$), then it is easy to calculate that $\chi_0(S_p, Y_p)$ does not vanish as $p \to 0$.

The condition of non-negativity of the c.f. can be replaced by the condition of non-negativity of random variable X_1. However, the approximation of S_p by means of $Y - p$ will be attained in terms of a different metric.

Let X, Y be non-negative random variables with Laplace transforms $l_X(u)$, $l_Y(u)$, respectively, and let

$$\chi_{0,l}(X,Y) := \sup_{u \geq 0} |l_X(u) - l_Y(u)|. \qquad (2.119)$$

In contrast to metric (2.117), convergence in metric $\chi_{0,l}$ is equivalent to the weak convergence of distributions of random variables, in the class $\mathcal{X}_+$ of all non-negative random variables.

Note that if S_p is the sum of a random number ν_p of i.i.d. r.v.'s from $\mathcal{X}_+$ with Laplace transforms $l(u)$, then it is easy to see that the Laplace transform of a ν-accompanying random variable Y_p is equal to $\Psi_p(u;l) = \varphi\left(\frac{1}{p}[1 - l(u)]\right)$.

Theorem 2.14 Let $X_1, X_2, \ldots$, be a sequence of i.i.d. r.v.'s, $X_1 \in \mathcal{X}_+$. Suppose that $S_p \sum_{j=1}^{\nu_p} X_j$ and Y_p is a ν-accompanying r.v. for S_p. Then

$\sup_{X_1 \in \mathcal{X}_+} \chi_{0,l}(S_p, Y_p) \to 0$,   as $p \to 0$, $p \in \Delta$.

The proof is completely analogous to the proof of Theorem 2.13.

Now we can obtain an analogue to the Poisson theorem for the Bernoulli scheme with a random number of trials.

Corollary 2.6 Let $(X_n, p)_{n \in \mathbb{N}}$ be a sequence of i.i.d. r.v.'s taking only two values: 1 with probability α_p or 0 with probability $1 - \alpha_p$. Assume that α_p depends only on p so that $\lim_{p \to 0} \frac{\alpha_p}{p} = \lambda \neq 0$ exists. Then, the distribution of sum[23] $S_p = \sum_{j=1}^{\nu_p} X_{j,p}$ converges as $p \to 0$ to a limiting distribution with Laplace transform $\varphi(\lambda(1 - e^{-u}))$, where φ is a standard solution of (2.104).

Proof. It is clear that the Laplace transform of random variable $X_{1,p}$ is equal to $l_p(u) = 1 - \alpha_p + \alpha_p e^{-u}$. The ν-accompanying random variable Y_p has Laplace transform

$$\begin{aligned}
\Psi_p(u;l) &= \varphi\left(\frac{1}{p}(1 - l_p(u))\right) \\
&= \varphi\left[\frac{\alpha p}{p}(1 - e^{-u})\right] \\
&\to \varphi\left[\lambda(1 - e^{-u})\right], \quad \text{as } p \to 0.
\end{aligned}$$

---

[23] Note that S_p is the number of success in the Bernoulli scheme with a random number of trials ν_p.

The assertion of the corollary now follows from Theorem 2.14.   □

Note that under the condition $P\{p\nu_p < x\} \to A(x)$ as $p \to 0$, the assertion of Corollary 2.6 follows from Gnedenko's transfer theorem (see Gnedenko (1983)).

2.4.5   Approximation of Random Sums

The problems of approximating distributions of sums of large nonrandom number of random terms with accompanying infinitely divisible distributions have been studied rather at length (see the bibliography in Arak and Zaitsev (1988)).

Here, we consider the problem of such an approximation for the case where the number of the terms in S_p has a geometric distribution.

Let ν_p be a geometric r.v. with parameter $p \in (0,1)$, that is,

$$P\{\nu_p = \kappa\} = p(1-p)^{\kappa-1}, \quad \kappa \in \mathbf{N}. \tag{2.120}$$

We consider the following three metrics in the set of all real-valued random variables on $\mathcal{X}$:

- $\chi_0(X,Y)$ — a metric defined on $\mathcal{X}$ by (2.117);

- $\rho(X,Y)$ — uniform distance (or Kolmogorov distance) defined as
  $$[\rho(X,Y) := \sup_x |F_X(x) - F_Y(x)|,]$$
  where F_X, F_Y are the df's of X, Y, respectively;

- $\sigma(X,Y)$ — the total variation distance defined by
  $$[\sigma(X,Y) := \sup_{A \in \mathcal{A}} |P\{X \in A\} - P\{Y \in A\}|,]$$
  where $\mathcal{A}$ is the Borel σ-field on $\mathbf{R}$ (for their properties, see for example Zolotarev (1986b), Rachev (1991), p. 476, 477).

These metrics are notable in that they are invariant under linear transformations of random variables. Topologically, metric χ_0 is strictly stronger than uniform distance, ρ, and strictly weaker than the total variation distance σ.

As was noted in Example 2.2, function $\varphi(t) = \frac{1}{1+t}$, which is the standard solution of 2.104, corresponds to random variable (2.120). This and (2.116) imply that a ν-accompanying (we call it *geometrically accompanying*) r.v. Y_p has ch.f. $\Psi_p(t; f) = \frac{1}{1-(f(t)-1)/p}$. In general, in the case under consideration (i.e., for (2.120)), we speak of *geometrically infinitely divisible, geometrically stable*, and so on, variables (or distributions).

Theorem 2.15 Let $S_p = \sum_{j=1}^{\nu_p} X_j$, where $\{X_j : j \geq 1\}$, be a sequence of i.i.d. r.v.'s, and suppose that ν_p has distribution (2.120). Assume that Y_p is a geometrically accompanying r.v. Then,

$$\sup_{X_1 \in \mathcal{X}} \chi_0(S_p, Y_p) = \frac{p}{1 - (p/2)^2}, \quad p \in (0,1).$$

Proof. The ch.f. $f_p(t)$ of $S - p$ has the form $f_p(t) = \frac{pf(t)}{1-(1-p)f(t)}$, where $f(t)$ is the ch.f. of X_1. Therefore,

$$
\begin{aligned}
\chi_0(S_p, Y_p) &= \sup_t \left| \frac{pf(t)}{1 - (1-p)f(t)} - \frac{1}{1 - p^{-1}(f(t) - 1)} \right| \\
&\leq p \sup \left\{ \left| \frac{(z-2)^2}{1 - (1-p)z(1+p-z)} \right| : z \in \mathcal{C}, |z| \leq 1 \right\} \\
&= p \sup_\theta \left\{ \frac{4\sin^2 \frac{\theta}{2}}{(16(1-p^2)\sin^4 \frac{\theta}{2} + 8p^2 \sin^2 \frac{\theta}{2} + p^4)^{1/2}} \right\} \\
&\leq \frac{p}{1 - \left(\frac{p}{2}\right)^2},
\end{aligned}
$$

recalling that the maximum of the moduls of a function analytic in $|z| \leq 1$ is attained on $|z| = 1$. Thus,

$$
\sup_{X_1 \in \mathcal{X}} \chi_0(S_p, Y_p) \leq \frac{p}{1 - \left(\frac{p}{2}\right)^2}. \tag{2.121}
$$

To obtain the lower estimate of $\sup_{X_1 \in \mathcal{X}} \chi_0(S_p, Y_p)$, we consider the case of degenerate terms $X_j = 1$. Then, $f(t) = e^{it}$, $f_p(t) = pe^{it}/(1 - (1-p)e^{it})$ and the ν-accompanying ch.f. has form $\Psi_p(t; f) = \frac{1}{1 - (e^{it}-1)/p}$. Direct calculations easily lead to $\chi_0(S_p, Y_p) = \frac{p}{1-\left(\frac{p}{2}\right)^2}$. This implies that

$$
\sup_{X_1 \in \mathcal{X}} \chi_0(S_p, Y_p) \geq \frac{p}{1 - \left(\frac{p}{2}\right)^2}. \tag{2.122}
$$

The desired result follows from (2.121) and (2.122). □

The proof of Theorem 2.15 shows that the approximization of the distribution of S_p with geometrically accompanying laws in metric χ_0 is worst for the case when there are degenerate terms in this sum.

Note that in the classical scheme of summation (i.e., $\nu_p = 1/p$ a.s.) a result analogous to Theorem 2.15 is impossible. This follows, for example, from an investigation of the symmetric binomial distribution (in this case X_j takes the values -1 or 1 with probability $1/2$ each).

Let us now turn to the class of uniform distance ρ and the total variation distance σ.

Theorem 2.16 Let ν_p have distribution (2.120). Then

$$
\sup_{X_1 \in \mathcal{X}} \sigma(S_p, Y_p) = \sup_{X_1 \in \mathcal{X}} \rho(S_p, Y_p) = \frac{p}{1+p} + (1+p)^{-(n_0+1)} - (1-p)^{n_0}, \tag{2.123}
$$

where

$$
n_0 = \left[\left(\ln \frac{1-p}{1+p} \right) / \ln \left(1 - p^2\right) \right]. \tag{2.124}
$$

(Here $[x]$ denotes the integer part of x.)

Proof. For any $X_1 \in \mathcal{X}$

$$
\begin{aligned}
\rho(S_p, Y_p) \ &\leq \ \sigma(S_p, Y_p) \\
&= \ \sup_{A \in \mathcal{A}} \left| \sum_{n=1}^{\infty} P\left(\sum_{j=1}^{n} X_j \in A \right) p(1-p)^{n-1} \right. \\
&\qquad \left. - \sum_{n=1}^{\infty} p(1+p)^{n+1} P\left(\sum_{j=1}^{n} X_j \in A \right) - \frac{p}{1+p} \right| \\
&= \ \sup_{A \in \mathcal{A}} \left| \sum_{n=1}^{\infty} P\left(\sum_{j=1}^{n} X_j \in A \right) (1-p)^{n-1} - (1+p)^{-1(n+1)} \right. \\
&\qquad \left. - \frac{1}{p+1} \right|.
\end{aligned}
$$

It is easy to see that $(1-p)^{n-1} \geq (1+p)^{-(n+1)}$ for all $n \leq n_0$ where n_0 is defined by (2.124) while for $n \geq n_0$ the inverse inequality is fulfilled. We then find

$$
\begin{aligned}
\sigma(S_p, Y_p) \ &\leq \ p \max \left\{ \sum_{n=1}^{n_0} \left((1-p)^{n-1} - \frac{1}{(1+p)^{n+1}} \right), \right. \\
&\qquad \left. \sum_{n=n_0+1}^{\infty} \left(\frac{1}{(1+p)^{n+1}} - (1-p)^{n-1} + \frac{1}{1+p} \right) \right\} \\
&= \ \frac{p}{1+p} + \frac{1}{(1+p)^{n_0+1}} - (1-p)^{n_0}.
\end{aligned}
$$

Thus, $\sup_{X_1 \in \mathcal{X}} \rho(S_p, Y_p) \leq \sup_{X_1 \in \mathcal{X}} \sigma(S_p, Y_p) \leq \frac{p}{1+p} + \frac{1}{(1+p)^{n_0+1}} - (1-p)^{n_0}$. To see the equality, consider the degenerate case $X_j = 1$, where we have

$$
\begin{aligned}
\rho(S_p, Y_p) \ &\geq \ |P(\nu_p \geq n_0) - P(Y_p \geq n_0)| \\
&= \ \sum_{n=n_0+1}^{\infty} \left(\frac{p}{(1+p)^{n+1}} - p(1-p)^{n-1} \right) + \frac{p}{1+p} \\
&= \ \frac{p}{1+p} + \frac{1}{(1+p)^{n_0+1}} - (1-p)^{n_0}.
\end{aligned}
$$

$\square$

Theorems 2.15 and 2.16 provide the estimates of the rate-of-convergence for the analogue to the Poisson theorem in the Bernoulli scheme with a geometrically distributed number of trials.

Corollary 2.7 Let $(X_{n,p})_{n\in\mathbb{N}}$ be a sequence of i.i.d. r.v.'s taking only values: 1 with probability $\alpha = \lambda p$ or 0 with probability $1-\alpha$, where λ=const. Denote by μ_λ a r.v. with geometric distribution: $P(\mu_\lambda = \kappa) = \frac{\lambda^\kappa}{(1+\lambda)^{\kappa+1}}$, $\kappa = 0,1,\ldots$. Then, for all $p \in (0,1)$ we have

$$\chi_0(S_p, \mu_\lambda) \leq \frac{p}{1 - \left(\frac{p}{2}\right)^2}$$

and

$$\sigma(S_p, \mu_\lambda) \leq \frac{p}{1+p} + \frac{1}{(1+p)^{n_0+1}} - (1-p)^{n_0},$$

where n_0 is defined by (2.124).

The above corollary follows from Theorems 2.15 and 2.16, since μ_λ is a geometrically accompanying variable for $S_p = \sum_{j=1}^{\nu_p} X_{j,p}$.

Theorems 2.15 and 2.16 offer the exact estimates of approximations of sums of a geometric number of random variables with geometrically accompanying laws. However, the question can also be posed as to how to approximate with geometrically infinitely divisible distributions. Although a complete investigation of this problem is beyond the scope of the book, we will show that for χ_0 such an approximation cannot lead to a substantial improvement compared to the result of Theorem 2.15.

Theorem 2.17 For the class $\mathcal{G}$ of all geometrically infinitely divisible rv's, the following inequality holds:

$$\sup_{X-1\in\mathcal{X}} \chi_0(S_p, \mathcal{G}) \geq \frac{p}{2-p}.$$

Proof. Theorem 2.11 implies that every geometrically infinitely divisible ch.f. $g(t)$ can be represented as

$$g(t) = \lim_{m\to\infty} \frac{1}{1 - \alpha_m(g_m(t) - 1)}, \tag{2.125}$$

where $\{\alpha_m, m \geq 1\}$ is a sequence of positive numbers and $\{g_m(t), m \geq 1\}$ is a sequence of ch.f.'s. From (2.125) we can see that $Re\ g(t) \geq 0$ for all real t. Suppose that the ch.f. of X_1 is $f(t) = \cos(t)$. Then, the ch.f. $f_p(t)$ of $S_p = \sum_{j=1}^{\nu_p} X_j$ is equal to $f_p(t) = \frac{p\cos(t)}{1-(1-p)\cos(t)}$. We finally have $\chi_0(S_p, \mathcal{G}) = \inf_{g\in\mathcal{G}} \sup_t |f_p(t) - g(t)| \geq \inf_{g\in\mathcal{G}} |f_p(\pi) - g(\pi)| \geq \frac{p}{2-p}$. $\square$

2.4.6   Random Sums of Random Vectors

To treat the multivariate case, let $(X_n)_{n\in\mathbb{N}}$ be a sequence of i.i.d. random vectors in $\mathbf{R}^S$. We consider the same families $\{\nu_p, p \in \Delta\}$ as before. It is assumed that semigroup **P** is commutative. Virtually all the results set fourth above are also valid (with obvious changes) in this case. This follows from the Cramer-Wold Device for Theorems 2.10 - 2.14, while for the remaining theorems the arguments given in their proofs remain valid. Let us note only certain changes:

(i) The ch.f. of a ν-strictly Gaussian s-variate distribution has the form

$$f(t) = \varphi((At, t)), \qquad (2.126)$$

where A is a symmetric, positive definite matrix, and φ is a standard solution to (2.104).

(ii) Let φ be a standard solution to (2.104). A ch.f. $g(t_1, \ldots, t_s)$ is a ν-infinitely divisible ch.f. of an s-dimensional r.v. if and only if

$$g(t) = \varphi(-\log f(t)), \quad t \in \mathbf{R}^s, \qquad (2.127)$$

where $f(t)$ is an infinitely divisible ch.f.

(iii) Let $(X_n)_{n\in\mathbf{N}}$ be a sequence of i.i.d. s-dimensional r.v.'s with ch.f. $f(t_1, \ldots, t_s)$. Assume that φ is a standard solution of (2.104). Let $S_p = \sum_{j=1}^{\nu_p} X_j$.

An s-dimensional r.v. Y_p with ch.f.

$$\Psi_p(t; f) = \varphi\left(\frac{1}{p}[1 - f(t)]\right)$$

is called an accompanying ν-infinitely divisible s-dimensional random vector for S_p. For the sake of brevity we will speak of ν-accompanying random vectors.

Note that the assertions of Theorems 2.15 and 2.16 are generally independent of the dimension, s, (in the formulations of these theorems one only needs to speak of random vectors rather than of random variables).

2.4.7 Domains of Attraction of Multivariate Geometrically Stable Laws

To study domains of attraction for a geometric summation of independent random vectors, let $\nu_p (p \in (0, 1))$ be a geometric random variable as defined in (2.120); and let $(X_n)_{n\in\mathbf{N}}$ be a sequence of i.i.d. s-dimensional r.v.'s independent of ν_p. If for some constants $b_p \in \mathbf{R}^s$ and non-singular $s \times s$ matrices A_p the d.f.'s of sums

$$\tilde{S}_p = A_p^{-1} \sum_{j=1}^{\nu_p} (X_j - b_p) \qquad (2.128)$$

weakly converge, as $p \to 0$, to some s-dimensional d.f. V, then we say that the df of vector X_1 is *weakly geometrically attracted to V*. The collection of all d.f.'s weakly geometrically attracted to V is called *the domain of geometric attraction* of V and is denoted by $\text{reg}_g(V)$.

We now describe the relationship between domains of geometric attraction and domains of attraction in the classical sense (denoted by $\text{reg} V$).

Theorem 2.18 The domain of geometric attraction of a law V with ch.f. $h(t)$, $t \in \mathbf{R}^s$ coincidences with the (classical) domain of attraction of $\tilde{V}$ with ch.f.

$$\tilde{h}(t) = \exp\{1 - 1/h(t)\}, \quad t \in \mathbf{R}^s. \tag{2.129}$$

Proof. Let X_1 be weakly geometrically attracted to V. This means that ch.f. $f_p(t)$ ($t \in \mathbf{R}^s$) of (2.128) converges to $h(t)$, as $p \to 0$. However, Theorem 2.15 implies that $\chi_0(\tilde{S}_p, \tilde{Y}_p) \to 0$, as $p \to 0$, where $\tilde{Y}_p$ is a random vector with ch.f.

$$\Psi_p(t; f) = \frac{1}{1 - \frac{\exp^{i(b_p, A_p t)} f(A_p t) - 1}{p}},$$

which tends to $h(t)$, as $p \to 0$. Choosing $p = 1/n$, $n \in \mathbf{N}$, we see that $n(e^{i(b_{1/n}, A_{1/n}t)} f(A_{1/n}t) - 1) \to 1 - \frac{1}{h(t)}$ as $n \to \infty$. This clearly implies that the normalized sum $A_{1/n}^{-1} \sum\limits_{j=1}^{n} (X_j - b_{1/n})$ converges to a distribution with ch.f. (2.129) when $n \to \infty$. Thus, X_1 is weakly attracted to $\tilde{V}$ and consequently, $\text{reg}_g(V) \subset \text{reg}(\tilde{V})$.

Repeating the argument in reverse order, we obtain the inverse inclusion $\text{reg}(V) \supset \text{reg}_g(\tilde{V})$. □

Of course, the same result can also be obtained if, instead of normalization by matrices A_p^{-1} we use in (2.128) a scalar normalization of A_p^{-1}. Neither the formulation nor the proof will be changed by this.

2.4.8   Bounds For Random Sums

As we have seen in Section 2.4.7, the key to proving Theorem 2.18 is Theorem 2.15. Therefore, to study domains of ν-attraction we must investigate the possibility of generalizing Theorem 2.15 to sums $S_p = \sum\limits_{1}^{\nu_p} X_j$, where ν_p does not necessarily have geometric distribution (2.120).

As has been noted above, if $\nu_p = 1/p$, $p \in \{1/n : n \in \mathbf{N}\}$, then $\sup_{X_1 \in \mathcal{X}} \chi_0(S_p, Y_p)$ does not tend to zero as $p \to 0$. Therefore, nontrivial estimates of

$$\delta_p = \sup_{X_1 \in \mathcal{X}} \chi_0(S_p, Y_p) \tag{2.130}$$

are far from possible for all families $\{\nu_p, p \in \Delta\}$ with commutative **P**. Below, we calculate the estimate of δ_p and establish the conditions under which $\delta_p \to 0$ as $p \to 0$.

Theorem 2.19 Let $l_p(t)$ be the ch.f. of a r.v. ν_p and $\varphi(z)$ a standard solution of (2.104). Then, (2.130) can be by:

$$\delta_p = \sup_{0 \le \theta < 2\pi} \left| l_p(\theta) - \varphi\left(\frac{1}{p}[1 - e^{i\theta}]\right) \right|. \tag{2.131}$$

Proof. If $(X_n)_{n \in \mathbb{N}}$ is a sequence of i.i.d. r.v.'s (or vectors) independent of ν_p and with ch.f. $f(t)$, then $P_p(f(t))$ is the ch.f. of $S_p = \sum_{j=1}^{\nu_p} X_j$. The ν-accompanying variable Y_p has ch.f. $\varphi(\frac{1}{p}[1 - f(t)])$. Since for real t we have $[f(t)| \le 1$, $P_p(z)$ is analytic in $|z| < 1$, and $\varphi(u)$ is analytic in the half-plane $Re u > 0$, then

$$
\begin{aligned}
\chi_0(S_p, Y_p) &= \sup_{t \in \mathbf{R}} \left| P_p(f(t)) - \varphi\left(\frac{1}{p}(1 - f(t))\right) \right| \\
&\le \sup_{z \in C, |z| \le 1} \left| P_p(z) - \varphi\left(\frac{1}{p}(1 - z)\right) \right| \\
&= \sup_{|z| = 1} \left| P_p(z) - \varphi\left(\frac{1}{p}(1 - z)\right) \right| \\
&= \sup_{\theta \in [0, 2\pi)} \left| P_p(e^{i\theta}) - \varphi\left(\frac{1}{p}(1 - e^{i\theta})\right) \right|. \tag{2.132}
\end{aligned}
$$

We have used the fact that the maximum of the modulus of a function analytic in a domain is attained on its boundary. However, $P_p(e^{i\theta}) = l_p(\theta)$. In addition, it is clear that $|P_p(e^{i\theta}) - \varphi(\frac{1}{p}(1 - e^{i\theta}))|$ is equal to $\chi_0(S_p, Y_p)$, when the X_j's have a degenerate distribution concentrated at 1. Consequently, an equality is attained in (2.132) and (2.132) coincidences with (2.131). □

Theorem 2.15 shows that in the case of the geometric variable ν_p (cf. (2.120)) $\delta_p = \frac{p}{1 - (\frac{p}{2})^2}$ is fulfilled.

Let us now give an estimate for δ_p for the r.v. ν_p from Example 2.1. Recall that in this case $\nu_p = 1/p$; $p \in \{1/n, n \in \mathbf{N}\}$ and we are dealing with the classical scheme. In the case under consideration

$$
\begin{aligned}
\delta_{1/n} &= \sup_{\theta \in [0, 2\pi)} \left| e^{in\theta} - \exp\{-n(1 - e^{i\theta})\} \right| \\
&= \sup_{\theta \in [0, 2\pi)} \left(1 + e^{-2n(1 - \cos\theta)} - 2\cos(n\theta - n\sin\theta)e^{-n(1 - \cos\theta)} \right)^{1/2} \\
&\ge 1 - e^{-2n},
\end{aligned}
$$

and equality is attained for even n. Thus, $\delta_{1/n} \to 1 \ne 0$ as $n \to \infty$ (i.e. as $p \to 0$), which is consistent with what has been said above regarding $\delta_{1/n}$ not tending to zero.

Unfortunately, we do not know the necessary and sufficient conditions for $\delta_p \to 0$ (cf. (2.131)) as $p \to 0$. However, we can separately give the necessary or sufficient conditions for such convergence.

Let us assume that

(A) $A(x) = \lim_{p \to 0} P\{p\nu_p < x\}$ is absolutely continuous for $x > 0$;

(B) $\frac{1}{p} \sum_{\kappa=1}^{\infty} |P\{\nu_p = \kappa\} - P\{\nu_p = \kappa + 1\}| \le C$ for all $p \in \Delta$, where $C > 0$ is a constant.

Theorem 2.20 Under Conditions (A) and (B)

$$\lim_{p \to 0} \delta_p = 0. \tag{2.133}$$

is fulfilled for (2.131).

Proof. Choose an arbitrary but fixed $\epsilon > 0$. Since function $A(x)$ is absolutely continuous (see Condition (A)), we have $\lim_{t \to \infty} \int_0^\infty e^{itx} dA(x) = 0$. Therefore, there exists a $v_0 > 0$, such that $|\int_0^\infty e^{itx} dA(x)| < \epsilon$ for all $t \ge v_0$.

Let us first consider the difference $l_p(\theta) - \varphi(\frac{1}{p}(1 - e^{i\theta}))$ for $\theta \in [0, v_0 p]$. Let $\theta = vp$, $v \in [0, v_0]$. We have: $l_p(vp) = \mathbf{E} \exp(iv(p\nu_p))$ is the ch.f. of $p\nu_p$, therefore $l_p(vp) \to \int_0^\infty e^{ivx} dA(x)$ as $p \to 0$, moreover, the convergence is uniform with respect to $v \in [0, v_0]$. On the other hand, $\lim_{p \to 0} \frac{1 - e^{ivp}}{p} = -iv$ and, consequently, $\lim_{p \to 0} \varphi\left[\frac{1 - e^{ivp}}{p}\right] = \varphi(-iv) = \int_0^\infty e^{ivx} dA(x)$, and the convergence is also uniform with respect to $v \in [0, v_0]$. In summary,

$$\lim_{p \to 0} \left(l_p(vp) - \varphi\left(\frac{1 - e^{ivp}}{p}\right) \right) = 0 \tag{2.134}$$

uniformly on $v \in [0, v_0]$. The case $\theta \in [2\pi - v_0 p, 2\pi)$ is handled in exactly the same fashion.

Without loss of generality, we can assume that $2C/v_0 < \epsilon$, where C is the constant in Condition (B).

Suppose now that $\theta \in [v_0 p, 2\pi - v_0 p]$. Consider first $l_p(\theta)$. Denoting $B_m = \sum_{\kappa=1}^{m} e^{i\theta\kappa}$ and applying the Abel transform, we find $l_p(\theta = \sum_{\kappa=1}^{\infty} P\{\nu_p = \kappa\} e^{i\theta\kappa} = -\sum_{\kappa=1}^{\infty} (P\{\nu_p = \kappa+1\} - P\{\nu_p = \kappa\}) B_\kappa$. However, $B_m = \sum_{\kappa=1}^{m} e^{i\theta\kappa} = e^{i\theta} \frac{(1 - e^{i\theta m})}{(1 - e^{i\theta})}$. Therefore, $|B_\kappa| \le |\sin(\frac{\theta}{2})|^{-1}$, $k \in \mathbf{N}$. From this and Condition (B) we find that $|l_p(\theta)| \le Cp |\sin(\frac{\theta}{2}|^{-1}$. This way, we have for $\theta \in [v_0 p, 2\pi - v_0 p]$

$$|l_p(\theta)| \le \frac{2C}{v_0} \le \epsilon. \tag{2.135}$$

For the same values of θ we consider $\varphi\left(\frac{1 - e^{i\theta}}{p}\right)$. Since $\varphi(u)$ is the Laplace transform of $A(x)$,

$$\varphi\left(\frac{(1 - e^{i\theta})}{p}\right) = \int_0^\infty e^{-\frac{2x \sin^2 \frac{\theta}{2}}{p}} \cos\left(\frac{x \sin \theta}{p}\right) dA(x)$$

$$-i\int_0^\infty e^{-\frac{2x\sin^2\frac{\theta}{2}}{p}}\sin\left(\frac{x\sin\theta}{p}\right)dA(x).$$

Therefore, it is clear that

$$\left|\varphi\left(\frac{1-e^{i\theta}}{p}\right)\right| \le \left|\int_0^\infty e^{\frac{ix(\sin\theta)}{p}}dA(x)\right| \le \epsilon, \tag{2.136}$$

since $\frac{|\sin\theta|}{p} \ge v_0$. The desired now follows from (2.134), (2.135) and (2.136).
$\square$

Corollary 2.8 Suppose that for all $p \in \Delta$ and $\kappa \in \mathbf{N}$ we have $P\{\nu_p = \kappa\} \ge P\{\nu_p = \kappa + 1\}$. If $A(x)$ from condition (A) has density bounded in some neighbourhood of the point $x = 0$, then (2.133) is true.
Proof. We have

$$\sum_{\kappa=1}^\infty |P\{\nu_p = \kappa\} - P\{\nu_p = \kappa + 1\}| \le P\{\nu_p = 1\} \le P\{\nu_p \le 1\} = P\{p\nu_p \le p\}.$$

However, since $A(x) = \lim_{p\to 0} P\{p\nu_p < x\}$ has bounded density in a neighbourhood of $x = 0$, we have $p\{p\nu_p \le p\} \le Cp$. The desired now follows from Theorem 2.20.
$\square$

The necessary conditions (2.133) are given by the following assertion.

Theorem 2.21 Let the family $\{\nu_p, p \in \Delta\}$ be such that for some $n \ge 1$ and $r \ge 2$ independent of p

$$\sum_{\kappa=1}^n P\{\nu_p = \kappa\} + \sum_{\kappa=1}^\infty P\{\nu_p = n + \kappa r\} = 1 \tag{2.137}$$

for all $p \in \Delta$, is fulfilled. Then (2.133) does not hold.
Proof. For the sake of brevity denote $a_\kappa(p) = P\{\nu_p = \kappa\}$, $\kappa \in \mathbf{N}$. We have $P_p(e^{i\theta}) = \sum_{\kappa=1}^n a_\kappa(p)\exp(i\theta\kappa) + \sum_{\kappa=1}^\infty a_{\kappa r+n}(p)\exp(i\theta(\kappa r + n))$. Letting here $\theta = 2\pi/r$, we find $P_p(\exp(\frac{i2\pi}{r})) = \exp(\frac{i2\pi n}{r}) + \sum_{\kappa=1}^{n-1} a_\kappa(p)(\exp(\frac{i2\pi\kappa}{r}) - \exp(\frac{i2\pi n}{r}))$. Since $a_\kappa(p) \to 0$ has $p \to 0$ because $p\nu_p$ as a proper limiting distribution, then

$$P_p\left(\exp\left(\frac{i2\pi}{r}\right)\right) \to \exp\left(\frac{2\pi in}{r}\right), \quad \text{as } p \to 0. \tag{2.138}$$

However, it is easy to see that as $p \to 0$

$$\varphi\left(\frac{1-\exp\left(\frac{2\pi i}{r}\right)}{p}\right) \to 0, \tag{2.139}$$

since $Re\left(1 - \exp\left(\frac{2\pi i}{r}\right)\right) > 0$ and $\varphi(z)$ is the Laplace transform of $A(x)$. From a comparison of (2.138) and (2.139), we see that, as $p \to 0$, $\delta_p \geq |P_p(\exp\frac{2\pi i}{r})) - \varphi\left(\frac{1-\exp(\frac{2\pi i}{r})}{p}\right)| \to 1$, which implies the desired. $\qquad\square$

Example 2.4 Suppose that for every $m \in \mathbf{N}$, $\{\nu_{p,m} : p \in (0,1)\}$ is a family of r.v.'s such that
$$P\{\nu_{p,m} = 1\} = p^{1/m},$$

$$P\{\nu_{p,m} = 1 + \kappa m\} = \left(\prod_{j=0}^{\kappa-1}\left(\frac{1}{m}\right)\right)p^{1/m}\frac{(1-p)^\kappa}{\kappa!}, \quad \kappa \in \mathbf{N}. \qquad (2.140)$$

It is easy to see that $\mathbf{E}\nu_{p,m} = \frac{1}{p}$, $P_{p,m}(z) = p^{1/m}\frac{z}{(1-(1-p)z^m)^{1/m}}$. In this case the standard solution of (2.104) has the following form, $\varphi_m(t) = (1+mt)^{-1/m}$. It is easy to see that in this case $\mathcal{P}$ is commutative. Theorem 2.21 implies that for $m > 1$ relation (2.133) does not hold. For $m = 1$ the assumptions of Corollary 2.8 are fulfilled but, of course, in this case we are dealing with a geometric r.v., that is, Theorem 2.15 is applicable.

For an even m the r.v. $\nu_{p,m}$ with distribution (2.140) is an example of a case where we may not be able at all to approximate the distributions of sums S_p with ν-infinitely divisible distributions in metric χ_0. Indeed, let $\mathcal{G}_\nu$ be the class of all ν-infinitely divisible r.v.'s. Then ($\nu_{p,m}$ has distribution (2.140) with even m)
$$\sup_{X_1 \in \mathcal{X}} \chi_0(S_p, \mathcal{G}_\nu) \geq 1.$$

Indeed, suppose that X_1 has ch.f. $\cos t$. Then the ch.f. of S_p is
$$f_{p,m}(t) = \frac{p^{1/m}\cos t}{(1 - (1-p)\cos^m t)^{1/m}}.$$

Clearly, $f_{p,m}(\pi) = -1$. On the other hand, any ν-infinitely divisible ch.f. has form $g(t) = \lim_{\kappa\to\infty}(1 + m(\alpha_\kappa(1 - g_\kappa(t)))^{-1/m}$, where $\alpha_k > 0$ and $g_\kappa(t)$ is a ch.f. It is easy to see that $\text{Reg}(t) \geq 0$. Therefore, if U has ch.f. $g(t)$, then
$$\inf_{g\in\mathcal{G}}\sup_{X_1\in\mathcal{X}} \chi_0(S_p, U) \geq \sup_t |f_{p,m}(t) - g(t)| \geq |f_{p,m}(\pi) - g(\pi)| \geq 1.$$

We have thus shown the desired estimate.

2.4.9 The Domain of Attraction for ν-Stable Random Vectors

We can now obtain an analog of the result of Section 2.4.7 for generic "ν-sums".

Let $\{\nu_p, p \in \Delta\}$ be a family of random variable taking natural values and such that $\mathcal{P}$ is commutative. Assume that $(X_n)_{n\in\mathbf{N}}$ is a sequence of i.i.d.

s-dimensional r.v.'s independent of ν_p. If for some choice of $b_p \in \mathbf{R}^s$ and non-singular $s \times s$ matrices A_p the d.f.'s of sums $\tilde{S}_p = A_p^{-1} \sum_{j=1}^{\nu_p}(X_j - b_p)$ weakly converges as $p \to 0$ to some d.f. V, then, we say that the d.f. of X_1 is weakly ν-attracted to V. The collection of all the df's weakly ν-attracted to V is called the domain of ν-attraction of V.

Theorem 2.22 Let (2.133) be fulfilled. Then the domain of ν-attraction of law V with ch.f. $H(t)$, $t \in \mathbf{R}^s$ coincides with the (classic) domain of attraction of law $\tilde{V}_\nu$ with ch.f. $\tilde{h}_\nu(t) = \exp\{-\varphi^{-1}(h(t))\}$, where φ is a standard solution of (2.104).

The proof of this is analogous to the proof of Theorem 2.18 and is therefore omitted.

Naturally, the same result also holds if instead of normalization with matrices scalar normalization is used in $\tilde{S}_p$.

If, however, (2.133) is not fulfilled, then the problem of describing the domain of ν-attraction remains unsolved.

We can also try to solve the problem of describing the domains of attraction for arbitrary summations by using approximation with the ν-accompanying law of the distribution of S_p not in metric χ_0 but in some other metric, for example, σ of ρ. For this we need an analog of Theorem 2.16 for the case of arbitrary families $\{\nu_p, p \in \Delta\}$ with commutative semigroup $\mathcal{P}$.

In the sequel we assume that $A(x) = \lim_{p \to 0} P\{p\nu_p \le x\}$, cf. condition (A) in Theorem 2.20. Let $a_\kappa(p) = P\{\nu_p = \kappa\}$, $\kappa \in \mathbf{N}$ and $b_\kappa(p) = \frac{1}{\kappa!p^\kappa}\int_0^\infty x^\kappa e^{-x/p}dA(x)$, $\kappa = 0,1,\ldots..$ As before, $S_p = \sum_{j=1}^{\nu_p} X_j$ and Y_p is a ν-accompanying random variable for S_p.

Theorem 2.23 Assume that $a_\kappa(p)$ and $b_\kappa(p)$ are such that for any $p \in \Delta$ there exists a natural number $n_0 = n_0(p)$ such that

$$a_\kappa(p) - b_\kappa(p) \ge 0, \quad \kappa = 1,\ldots,n_0. \tag{2.141}$$

Let

$$K_p = \{\kappa : \kappa \ge 1, a_\kappa(p) - b_\kappa(p) \ge 0\}. \tag{2.142}$$

Then,

$$\sum_{\kappa=1}^{n_0}[a_\kappa(p) - b_\kappa(p)] \le \sup_{X_1 \in \mathcal{X}} \rho(S_p, Y_p)$$
$$\le \sup_{X_1 \in \mathcal{X}} \sigma(S_p, Y_p)$$
$$\le \sum_{\kappa \in K_p}[a_\kappa(p) - b_\kappa(p)].$$

Before proving this theorem let us note that (2.141) can be replaced by the requirement that $b_\kappa(p) - a_\kappa(p) \ge 0$ for $\kappa = 1,\ldots,n_0$. Then $a_\kappa(p)$ and $b_\kappa(p)$ must be switched in (2.142) and (2.143).

Proof of Theorem 2.23. We have

$$
\begin{aligned}
\varphi\left(\frac{1-z}{p}\right) &= \int_0^\infty \exp\left(-\frac{(1-z)x}{p}\right) dA(x) \\
&= \int_0^\infty e^{-x/p} \sum_{\kappa=0}^\infty \frac{z^\kappa x^\kappa}{\kappa! p^\kappa} dA(x) \\
&= \sum_{\kappa=0}^\infty b_k(p) z^\kappa.
\end{aligned}
$$

Therefore, $\varphi\left(\frac{1-f(t)}{p}\right) = \sum_{\kappa=0}^\infty b_k(p) f^\kappa(t)$. This representation implies that for any $X_1 \in \mathcal{X}$

$$
\begin{aligned}
\rho(S_p, Y_p) &\leq \sigma(S_p, Y_p) \\
&= \sup_{A \in \mathcal{A}} \left| \sum_{n=1}^\infty P\left\{ \sum_{j=1}^n X_j \in A \right\} [a_n(p) - b_n(p)] - b_0(p) \right|.
\end{aligned}
$$

Taking into account (2.142), we find that

$$
\sigma(S_p, Y_p) = \max\left(\sum_{\kappa \in K_p} [a_\kappa(p) - b_\kappa(p)], (b_0(p) + \sum_{\kappa \notin K_p} [b_\kappa(p) - a_\kappa(p)]) \right).
$$
(2.143)

However, $\sum_{n=1}^\infty a_\kappa(p) = \sum_{n=1}^\infty b_\kappa(p) = 1$. Therefore,

$$
\left[b_0(p) + \sum_{\kappa \notin K_p} (b_\kappa(p) - a_\kappa(p)) \right) = \sum_{\kappa \in K_p} (a_\kappa(p) - b_\kappa(p)); \right],
$$

and from (2.143) we find

$$
\left[\sup_{X_1 \in \mathcal{X}} \rho(S_p, Y_p) \leq \sup_{X_1 \in \mathcal{X}} \sigma(S_p, Y_p) \leq \sum_{\kappa \in K_p} (a_\kappa(p) - b_\kappa(p)). \right]
$$

This proves the upper bound. To prove the lower bound, consider the degenerate r.v.'s $X_j = 1$. For these variables

$$
\rho(S_p, Y_p) = \sup_{x \in \mathbf{R}} |P\{\nu_p \leq x\} - P\{1 \leq Y_p \leq x\}| \geq \sum_{\kappa=1}^{n_0} (a_\kappa(p) - b_\kappa(p)),
$$

producing the lower bound in (2.143) and concluding the proof.   □

Corollary 2.9 Assume that $K_p = \{1, 2, \ldots, n_0\}$ or, in other words, $a_\kappa(p) - b_\kappa(p) \geq 0$, for $1 \leq \kappa \leq n_0$, and $a_\kappa(p) - b_\kappa(p) < 0$, for $\kappa > n_0$. Then,

$$\sup_{X_1 \in \mathcal{X}} \rho(S_p, Y_p) = \sup_{X_1 \in \mathcal{X}} \sigma(S_p, Y_p) = \sum_{\kappa=1}^{n_0} [a_\kappa(p) - b_\kappa(p)]. \tag{2.144}$$

The proof is obvious, since in this case the upper and lower bounds in (2.143) coincide.

Let us consider some examples.

Example 2.5 Let $\nu_p = 1/p = n$ with probability 1. In this case $A(u)$ is the function of a degenerate distribution concentrated at $u = 1$. Then,

$$b_\kappa(p) = b_k\left(\frac{1}{n}\right) = \frac{n^\kappa e^{-n}}{\kappa!};$$

and $a_\kappa(p) = a_\kappa(1/n) = 0$, for $\kappa \neq n$, and $a_\kappa(1/n) = 1$, for $\kappa = n$. Therefore, we obtain from Theorem 2.23

$$e^{-n} \sum_{\kappa=1}^{n} \frac{n^\kappa}{\kappa!} \leq \sup_{X_1 \in \mathcal{X}} \rho(S_{1/n}, Y_{1/n}) \leq \sup_{X_1 \in \mathcal{X}} \sigma((S_{1/n}, Y_{1/n}) \leq 1 - e^{-n} \frac{n^n}{n!}.$$

If $n \to \infty$, then it is easy to verify that

$$\frac{1}{2} \leq \underline{\lim}_{n \to \infty} \sup_{X_1 \in \mathcal{X}} \rho(S_{1/n}, Y_{1/n}) \leq \overline{\lim}_{n \to \infty} \sup_{X_1 \in \mathcal{X}} \rho(S_{1/n}, Y_{1/n}) \leq 1.$$

Thus, $\rho(S_{1/n}, Y_{1/n})$ and $\sigma(S_{1/n}, Y_{1/n})$ do not tend to zero as $n \to \infty$.[24]

Example 2.6 Suppose now that ν_p is a geometric r.v. with distribution (2.120). In this case, $A(u) = 1 - e^{-u}(u \geq 0)$. It is easy to show that $b_\kappa(p) = \frac{p}{(1+p)^{\kappa+1}}$, $\kappa = 0, 1, \ldots$, and (2.120) implies that $a_\kappa(p) = p(1-p)^{\kappa-1}$, $\kappa \in \mathbf{N}$. Clearly, we are under the hypotheses of Corollary 2.9. The verification of this is, in essence, the content of Theorem 2.16, which leads to (2.123) and (2.124) coinciding with (2.144).

Corollary 2.10 Assume that the hypotheses of Theorem 2.23 are fulfilled and

$$\lim_{p \to 0} \sum_{\kappa \in K_p} (a_\kappa(p) - b_\kappa(p)) = 0.$$

Then, the domain of ν-attraction of V with $h(t)$ coincides with the classic domain of attraction $\tilde{V}_\nu$,

$$\tilde{h}_\nu(t) = \exp\{-\varphi^{-1}(h(t))\},$$

---

[24]The difference between the result of Example 2.5 and Theorem 2.23 and that in Arak and Zaitsev (1988) is is due to the difference in the definition of accompanying law. They use centralization and normalization, which we do not. Regarding this See Footnote 22 on p. 59.

where, as before, φ is the standard solution of (2.104).
The proof is analogous to the proof of Theorem 2.18.

2.4.10   Rate of Convergence

Here, we consider a certain special metric and investigate the problem of approximating S_p with accompanying variable Y_p in this metric. We then consider only some subclasses of class $\mathcal{X}$ of all random vectors. More precisely, our estimate will turn out to be uniform in only some subclass of $\mathcal{X}$.

Let X be an s-dimensional r.v. with a non-singular distribution F (i.e., F is not concentrated on any proper subspace of R^S).

Assume that $r > 0$ and consider ball $B(r) = \{x : x \in \mathbf{R}^S, \|x\| < r\}$. It is known that F is uniquely determined by the probabilities with which X occurs in the shifted balls $B_y(r) = B(r) - y$, $y \in \mathbf{R}^S$ (see Sapogov (1974)). Therefore, if Y is another random vector in $\mathbf{R}^S$, then

$$d_r(X,Y) = \sup_{y \in \mathbf{R}^S} |P\{X \in B_y(r)\} - P\{Y \in B_y(r)\}|. \qquad (2.145)$$

is a metric in the space of random variables. (Note that (2.145) is a metric even without the assumption that F is a non-degenerate distribution).

Suppose that for $t > 0$, $\chi(t) = \int_{\|x\| \leq 1/t} d(F(x) * F(-x))$, where $F(x) * F(-x)$ is the symmetrization of F. If $Q_F^0(r)$ is a spheric concentration function, that is, $Q_F^0(r) = \sup_{u \in \mathbf{R}^S} P\{X \in B_y(r)\}$, then we know that (see Hengartner and Theodorescu (1973))

$$Q_{F^{*n}}^0(r) \leq \mathcal{A}(s) \left(\sup_{u \geq r} u^{-2} \chi(u)^{-s/2} \right) n^{-s/2}, \qquad (2.146)$$

where F^{*n} is an n-fold convolution of F and $\mathcal{A}(s)$ is a positive variable dependent on the dimension of the space (i.e., only on s).

Theorem 2.24 Suppose that $A(x) = \lim_{p \to 0} P\{p\nu_p < x\}$, and $a_\kappa(p)$ and $b_\kappa(p)$ are defined as in Theorem 2.23 and K_p by (2.142). Assume that $(X_n)_{n \in \mathbf{N}}$ is a sequence of i.i.d. s-dimensional r.v.'s with non-singular distributions. Then,

$$d_r(S_p, Y_p) \leq \mathcal{A}(s) \left(\sup_{u \geq r} u^{-2} \chi(u) \right)^{-s/2} \qquad (2.147)$$

$$\times \max \left\{ \sum_{\kappa \in K_p} [a_\kappa(p) - b_\kappa(p)] \kappa^{-s/2}, \sum_{\kappa \notin K_p} [b_\kappa(p) - a_\kappa(p)] \kappa^{-s/2} + b_0(p) \right\},$$

where $S_p = \sum_{j=1}^{\nu_p} X_j$ and Y_p is a ν-accompanying r.v.

Proof. As in Theorem 2.23, we can write

$$d_r(S_p, Y_p) \le \sup_{y \in \mathbf{R}^s} |P\{S_p \in B_y(r)\} - P\{Y_p \in B_y(r)\}|$$

$$\le \sup_{y \in \mathbf{R}^s} \max \left\{ \sum_{\kappa \in K_p} (a_\kappa(p) - b_\kappa(p)) P \left\{ \sum_{j=1}^{\kappa} X_j \in B_y(r) \right\}, \right.$$

$$\left. \sum_{\kappa \notin K_p} [b_\kappa(p) - a_\kappa(p)] P \left\{ \sum_{j=1}^{\kappa} X_j \in B_y(r) \right\} + b_0(p) \right\} \quad (2.148)$$

However, (2.146) implies that

$$P \left\{ \sum_{\kappa=1}^{\kappa} X_j \in B_y(r) \right\} \le A(s) \left(\sup_{u \ge r} u^{-2} \chi(u) \right)^{-s/2} n^{-s/2}.$$

After substituting the last estimate into (2.148) we arrive at (2.147).   □

Corollary 2.11 If in the hypotheses of Theorem 2.24 $s > 2$, then

$$d_r(S_p, Y_p) \le A(s) \left(\sup_{u \ge r} u^{-2} \chi(u) \right)^{-s/2} \cdot \sum_{\kappa=1}^{\infty} \kappa^{-s/2} \max_\kappa |a_\kappa(p) - b_\kappa(p)|.$$

Example 2.7 Let ν_p be the degenerate r.v. $\nu_p = 1/p = n$ a.s., $p \in \{1/n : n \in \mathbf{N}\}$. As in Example 2.6, we have $b_\kappa(p) = \frac{n^\kappa e^{-n}}{\kappa!}$, $a_\kappa(p) = 0$, for $k \ne n$, and $a_n(1/n) = 1$. Theorem 2.24 implies that

$$d_r(S_p, Y_p) \le \max \left\{ \left(1 - \frac{n^n}{n!} e^{-n} \right) n^{-s/2}, e^{-n} + \sum_{\kappa \ne n}^{\infty} \frac{n^\kappa}{\kappa!} e^{-n} \kappa^{-s/2} \right\}$$

$$\times A(s) \left(\sup_{u \ge r} u^{-2} \chi(u) \right)^{-s/2}.$$

Of course the last inequality can be made cruder into the form

$$d_r(S_p, Y_p) \le \left(\sum_{\kappa=1}^{\infty} \frac{1}{\kappa^{s/2}} \frac{n^\kappa}{\kappa!} e^{-n} + e^{-n} \right) A(s) (\sup_{u \ge r} u^{-2} \chi(u))^{-s/2}. \quad (2.149)$$

Then,

$$e^{-n} \sum_{\kappa=1}^{\infty} \frac{1}{\kappa^{s/2}} \frac{n^\kappa}{\kappa!} \le \left(\sum_{\kappa=1}^{\infty} \frac{1}{\kappa^s} \frac{n^\kappa}{\kappa!} e^{-n} \right)^{1/2} \le \frac{C}{n^{s/2}},$$

where C is an absolute constant. Thus, (2.149) implies

$$d_r(S_p, Y_p) \le A(s)(\sup_{u \ge r} u^{-2} \chi(u))^{-s/2} C n^{-s/2}. \quad (2.150)$$

Note that (2.150) is remarkable in that the rate-of-convergence of distributions $S_{1/n}$ and $Y_{1/n}$ grows as dimension s of random vector X_1 increases.

2.5 Stable and Geo-stable Central Pre-limit Theorems and Their Applications

There is a considerable debate in the literature concerning the applicability of α-stable distributions as they appear in Lévy's central limit theorems (see Properties 2.1 and 2.2 in Section 2.1.1). A serious drawback of Lévy's approach is that, in practice, one can never know whether the underlying distribution is heavy tailed, or just has a long but truncated tail. Limit theorems for stable laws are not robust with respect to truncation of the tail or with respect to any change from "light" to "heavy" tail, or conversely. In this section we present a "pre-limiting" approach that helps to overcome this drawback of Lévy-type central limit theorems[25].

Based on finite samples, one can never justify the specification of a particular tail behavior. Hence, one cannot justify the applicability of classical limit theorems in probability theory. In this section we attempt to show that instead of relying on limit theorems, one may use the so-called pre-limit theorems explained later. The applicability of our prelimit theorem relies not on the tail but on the "central section" ("body") of the distributions. Thus, instead of a limiting behavior (when n, the number of i.i.d. observations tends to infinity), pre-limit theorems should provide an approximation for distribution functions in case n is "large" but not too "large".

More than a hundred years ago Vilfredo Pareto (1897) observed that the number of people in the population whose income exceeds a given level, x, can be satisfactorily approximated by $Cx^{-\alpha}$ for some C and $\alpha > 0$ (see Arnold (1983), DuMouchel (1983) for more details). Later Mandelbrot (Mandelbrot (1959), (1960)) argued that stable laws should provide the appropriate model for income distributions and claimed:

(i) the distribution of the size of income for different (but sufficiently long) time periods must be of the same type; in other words, the distribution of the income follows a stable law (Lévy's stable law);

(ii) the tails of the Gaussian law are too thin to describe the distribution of the income in typical situations.

Because the variance of any non-Gaussian stable law is infinite, an essential condition for a non-Gaussian stable limit distribution for sums of random incomes is that the summands have *heavy* tails, in the sense that the variance of the summands must be infinite. On the other hand, it is obvious that the incomes are always bounded random variables. Thus, in practice, the underlying distribution *cannot* be heavy tailed. *Does this mean that we have to reject the Pareto-stable model??*

---

[25]The results in thes section are due to Klebanov, Rachev and Szekely (1999), and Klebanov, Rachev and Safarian (1999).

We can see the same problem in a more general situation. Given i.i.d. r.v.'s $X_j, j \geq 1$, the limiting behavior of the normalized partial sums $S_n = n^{-1/\alpha}(X_1 + \ldots + X_n)$ depends on the tail behavior of X. Both the proper normalization, $n^{-1/\alpha}$, and the corresponding limiting law are extremely sensitive to a tail truncation. However, in this sense, the problem of limiting distributions for sums of i.i.d. r.v.'s is *ill-posed*. Below, we present a "well-posed" version of the problem and provide a solution in the form of a *pre-limit theorem*.

Let c and γ be two positive constants and consider the following semi-distance between the r.v.'s X and Y:[26]

$$d_{c,\gamma}(X,Y) = \sup_{|t| \geq c} \frac{|f_X(t) - f_Y(t)|}{|t|^\gamma}.$$

Observe that in the case $c = 0$, $d_{c,\gamma}(X,Y)$ defines a well-known probability distance in the space of all r.v.'s for which $d_{0,\gamma}(X,Y)$ is finite, see Zolotarev (1986), Rachev (1991). Next, recall that Y is a strictly α-stable r.v., if for every positive integer n

$$Y_1 \stackrel{d}{=} U_n := \frac{Y_1 + \ldots + Y_n}{n^{1/\alpha}},$$

where $\stackrel{d}{=}$ stands for equality in distribution; and $Y_j, j \geq 1$, are i.i.d. $Y_j \stackrel{d}{=} Y$, see Zolotarev (1983c), Lukacs (1970). Let $X, X_j, j \geq 1$, be a sequence of i.i.d. r.v.'s such that $d_{0,\gamma}(X,Y)$ is finite for some strictly stable random variable Y. Suppose that $Y, Y_j, j \geq 1$, are i.i.d. strictly α-stable random variables, and $\gamma > \alpha$. Then,

$$
\begin{aligned}
d_{0,\gamma}(S_n, Y) &= d_{0,\gamma}(S_n, U_n) \\
&= \sup_t \frac{|f_X^n(t/n^{1/\alpha}) - f_Y^n(t/n^{1/\alpha})|}{|t|^\gamma} \\
&\leq n \sup_t \frac{|f_X(t/n^{1/\alpha}) - f_Y(t/n^{1/\alpha})|}{|t|^\gamma} \\
&= \frac{1}{n^{\gamma/\alpha-1}} d_{0,\gamma}(X,Y),
\end{aligned}
$$

see Zolotarev (1983). From this we can see that $d_{0,\gamma}(S_n, Y)$ tends to zero as n tends to infinity; that is, we have convergence (in $d_{0,\gamma}$) of the normalized sums of X_j to a strictly α-stable random variable, Y, provided that $d_{0,\gamma}(X,Y) < \infty$. However, *any* truncation of the tail of the distribution of X leads to $d_{0,\gamma}(X,Y) = \infty$. Our goal is to analyze the closeness of the sum S_n to a strictly α-stable random variable, Y, without the assumption on the finiteness of $d_{0,\gamma}(X,Y)$, restricting our assumptions to bounds in terms of $d_{c,\gamma}(X,Y)$

---

[26]Here and in what follows $F_Y(x)$ and $f_Y(t)$ stand for the cdf and the c.f. of X, respectively.

with $c > 0$. This leads to a general type of a *central pre-limit theorem* with no assumption on the tail behavior of the underlying random variables.

The following Central Pre-Limit Theorem specifies the closeness of the sum S_n to a strictly α-stable r.v. Y in terms of the following Kolmogorov metric (see Kolmogorov (1953) and Rachev (1991)) for any cdf's F and G,

$$k_h(F, G) := \sup_{x \in \mathbf{R}} |F * h(x) - G * h(x)|,$$

where $*$ stands for convolution, and the "smoothing" $h(x)$ is a fixed cdf with a bounded continuous density function, $\sup_x |h'(x)| \leq c(h) < \infty$. Metric k_h metrizes the weak convergence in the space of cdf's (see Kolmogorov (1953)).

Theorem 2.25 *(Central Pre-Limit Theorem)* Let $X, X_j, j \geq 1$, be i.i.d. r.v.'s and $S_n = n^{-1/\alpha} \sum_{j=1}^{n} X_j$. Suppose that Y is a strictly α-stable r.v. Let $\gamma > \alpha$ and $\Delta > \delta$ be arbitrary, given positive constants; and let $n \leq (\frac{\Delta}{\delta})^\alpha$ be an arbitrary positive integer. Then,

$$k_h(F_{S_n}, F_Y) \leq \inf_{a>0} \left(\sqrt{2\pi} \frac{d_{\delta,\gamma}(X, Y)(2a)^\gamma}{n^{\frac{\gamma}{\alpha}-1}\gamma} + 2\frac{c(h)}{a} + 2\Delta a \right).$$

Remark 2.6 If $\Delta \to 0$ and, furthermore, $\Delta/\delta \to \infty$, then we can choose a large enough n, so that the right-hand-side of the above bound is sufficiently small; that is, we obtain the classical limit theorem for weak convergence to an α-stable law. This result, of course, includes the central limit theorem for weak distance.

Proof. See Klebanov, Rachev and Szekely (1998) $\qquad\qquad\qquad$ □

Thus, the cdf of the normalized sums of i.i.d. r.v.'s is close to the corresponding α-stable distribution for 'mid-size values' of n.

Theorem 2.25 shows that for 'mid-size values' of n the closeness of S_n to a strictly α-stable r.v. depends on the 'center part' ('body') of the distribution of X.

Next suppose $X, X_j, j \geq 1$, are i.i.d. r.v.'s and let $\{\nu_p, \ p \in \Delta \subset (0, 1)\}$ be a family of positive integer-valued r.v.'s independent of the sequence of X's. Suppose that $\{\nu_p\}$ is such that there exists a ν-*strictly stable r.v.* Y, that is

$$Y \stackrel{d}{=} p^{1/\alpha} \sum_{j=1}^{\nu_p} Y_j,$$

where $Y, Y_j, j \geq 1$, are i.i.d. r.v.'s independent of ν_p, and $E\nu_p = 1/p$.

Bunge (1996) and Klebanov and Rachev (1996a), see Section 2.4, independently obtained general conditions guaranteeing the existence to analogues of strictly stable distributions for sums of a random number of i.i.d. r.v.'s. For this type of a random summation model we can derive an analogue to Theorem 2.25.

Theorem 2.26 Let $X, X_j, j \geq 1$, be i.i.d. r.v.'s; and let $\tilde{S}_p = p^{1/\alpha} \sum_{j=1}^{\nu_p} X_j$. Suppose that $\tilde{Y}$ is a strictly ν-stable r.v. Let $\gamma > \alpha$ and $\Delta > \delta$ be arbitrary given positive constants; and let $p \geq (\frac{\delta}{\Delta})^\alpha$ be an arbitrary positive number from $(0, 1)$. Then, the following inequality holds:

$$k_h(F_{\tilde{S}_p}, F_{\tilde{Y}}) \leq \inf_{a>0} \left(p^{\frac{\gamma}{\alpha}-1} \sqrt{2\pi} \frac{d_{\delta,\gamma}(X, \tilde{Y})(2a)^\gamma}{\gamma} + 2\frac{c(h)}{a} + 2\Delta a \right).$$

Proof. See Klebanov, Rachev and Szekely (1998)   □

Remark 2.7 Consider now our first example concerning Pareto-stable laws. Following the Mandelbrot (1960) model for asset returns we view a daily asset return as a sum of a random number of tick-by-tick returns observed during the day. Following Klebanov and Rachev (1996a), Mittnik and Rachev (1993a) and Mittnik and Rachev (1993b) we can assume that the total number of tick-by-tick returns during the day has a geometric distribution with a large expected value. In fact, the limiting distribution for geometric sums of random variables (when the expected value of the total number tends to infinity) is geo-stable (see Klebanov, Maniya, Melamed (1984)). Then, according to Theorem 2.26 the d.f. of daily returns is approximately geo-stable (in fact, it is ν-stable with a geometrically distributed ν).

Remark 2.8 Note that this new type of "pre-limit" theorems provides the theoretical basis for modeling asset return distribution by the so called truncated Lévy flights. Empirical evidence for the good fit of Lévy flights to financial returns was reported in Cont, Potters and Bouchaud (1997).

We conclude by presenting two results on *local pre-limiting theorems*, whose proofs are given in Klebanov, Rachev and Safarian (1999).

Consider a distribution function, $h(x)$, with bounded (by a constant $c(h)$) continuous d.f. We use metric $k_h(f, g)$ between two densities f and g,

$$k_h(f, g) = \sup_{x \in \mathbf{R}} |f * h(x) - g * h(x)|,$$

where $*$ stands again for convolution between corresponding functions, to formulate the "pre-limit" analogue of the classical local limit theorem.[27]

Theorem 2.27 *(Local Pre-Limit Theorem)* Let $X, X_j, j \geq 1$ be i.i.d. r.v.'s having bounded density function with respect to the Lebesgue measure, and $S_n = n^{-1/\alpha} \sum_{j=1}^n X_j$. Suppose that Y is a strictly α-stable random variable; and let $\gamma > \alpha$, $\Delta > \delta > 0$ and $n(\frac{\Delta}{\delta})^\alpha$ be positive integer not greater than

---

[27]If we compare the fit of a density rather than cdf, the local prelimit and limit theorems may be of greater relevance than the classical limit theorems.

$(\frac{\Delta}{\delta})^\alpha$. Then,

$$k_h(p_{S_n}, p_Y) \leq \inf_{a>0} \left(\sqrt{2\pi} \frac{d_{\delta,\gamma}(X,Y)(2a)^{\gamma+1}}{n^{\frac{\gamma}{\alpha}-1}(\gamma+1)} + 2\frac{c(h)}{a} + 2c(h)\Delta a \right),$$

where p_{S_n} and p_Y are the density functions of S_n and Y, respectively.

Theorem 2.28 *(Local Pre-Limit Theorem for Random Sums)* Let $X, X_j, j \geq 1$ be i.i.d. r.v.'s having bounded density function with respect to the Lebesgue measure. Let $\tilde{S}_\tau = \tau^{1/\alpha} \sum_{j=1}^{\nu_\tau} X_j$ and suppose that $\tilde{Y}$ is a strictly ν-stable r.v. Let $\gamma > \alpha$, $\Delta > \delta > 0$, and $\tau \in [(\frac{\Delta}{\delta})^\alpha, 1)$. Then, the inequality:

$$k_h(p_{\tilde{S}_\tau}, p_{\tilde{Y}}) \leq \inf_{a>0} \left(\tau^{\frac{\gamma}{\alpha}-1} \sqrt{2\pi} \frac{d_{\delta,\gamma}(X,\tilde{Y})(2a)^\gamma}{\gamma} + 2\frac{c(h)}{a} + 2\Delta a \right)$$

holds.

3

Identification, Estimation and Goodness of Fit

In this chapter we address issues that are of concern in practical work. We discuss visual identification and estimation techniques for the stable distributions considered in the previous chapter. Because implementability and computational complexity are important issues in empirical applications, we first discuss simple regression-type techniques for estimating the parameters of the majority of the alternative distributions considered. In this context, we address the potential use of linear transformations, leading to certain linear relationships, for the purpose of identifying a particular stable distribution with visual means, i.e., without prior estimation. The estimates obtained with the implied regression-type estimators could serve as final estimates or as starting values in maximum likelihood or other nonlinear estimation procedures. Tail estimators for the index of stability (heavy-tailedness) are discussed in the last section of this chapter.

3.1 Regression-type Estimators

Throughout this chapter let N denote the size of the whole sample if the distribution under consideration is defined over $\mathbf{R}$, or the number of observations that are associated with the domain over which the distribution is defined—usually the positive or negative half-line.

Various procedures for estimating the parameters of the stable Paretian distribution with the ch.f. given by (2.2) have been proposed in the literature (see McCulloch, 1986). DuMouchel (1971, 1973b) suggests a maximum likelihood method, whose implementation is a nontrivial task. For this reason, we mention here a variety of alternative (not necessarily regression-type) estimation procedures for the stable Paretian distribution. Paulson et al. (1975) fit the Fourier transform of the data to the sample ch.f. Alternative procedures such as the method-of-moments approach by Press (1972b) or the regression-type estimation proposed by Koutrouvelis (1980, 1981) are based on the sample ch.f. All these procedures are rather complex and require some arbitrary choices along the way. The quantile procedures of Fama and Roll (1968, 1971) and the modified version of McCulloch (1986), based on tabulated functions of predetermined order statistics, are commonly used in empirical work.

There are only few systematic comparisons of these estimations techniques. Akgiray and Lamoureux (1989), comparing in a simulation study the iterative regression-type estimator of Koutrouvelis (1980, 1981) and McCulloch's (1986) quantile estimator, find evidence in favor of the regression-type estimator. Chen (1991), comparing his maximum likelihood estimator with the McCulloch's quantile estimator, strongly recommends the maximum likelihood estimator.

Given the parameter estimates, the actual construction of the stable Paretian d.f. is nontrivial. Zolotarev (1986a) gives a procedure involving proper integral representations. Tabulated values of the distribution function can be used in empirical work. For special values of the characteristic exponent α and the skewness parameter β, Fama and Roll (1968) and DuMouchel (1971) report such tables. A tabulation of various density functions can be found in Holt and Crow (1973).

We now turn to regression-type estimators for the other stable distributions. To simplify matters, we express—where possible—the regression-type estimators in terms of linear relationship

$$Y_i^* = \beta_0 + \beta_1 X_i^*, \qquad i = 1, \ldots, N, \tag{3.1}$$

where Y_i^* represents a transformation of Y_i, the value of the sample distribution function that corresponds to observation X_i, and X_i^* is the corresponding transformation of X_i. The particular transformations producing Y_i^* and X_i^* depend on distribution in question.

It follows from (2.15) that the d.f. of the *max-stable distribution of Type I* can be transformed into $\mathcal{M}(x) = \exp\{-e^{-ax+b}\}$, $x \in \mathbf{R}$; linear form (3.1) by defining

$$
\begin{aligned}
Y_i^* &:= \ln(-\ln Y_i), \quad Y_i \in (0,1], & (3.2) \\
X_i^* &:= -X_i, \quad X_i \in \mathbf{R}, & (3.3) \\
\beta_0 &:= b, & (3.4) \\
\beta_1 &:= a. & (3.5)
\end{aligned}
$$

Fitting (3.1) we obtain the parameter estimates of the max-stable distribution of Type I. The fitted distribution, denoted by $\hat{G}$, is computed from $\hat{Y}_i^* =$

$\hat{\beta}_0 + \hat{\beta}_1 X_i^*$ by

$$\hat{G}_i = \exp\{-e^{\hat{Y}_i^*}\}. \tag{3.6}$$

Because the ordinary-least-squares fit of (3.1) provides us with the best fit (in the least-squares sense) for the transformed sample distribution function, but not the underlying sample distribution function, it is preferable to use weighted least squares. For the max-stable distribution of Type I the weights, w_i $(i = 1, \ldots N)$, are specified by the derivative of (3.6), i.e.,

$$w_i = \exp\{Y_i^* - e^{Y_i^*}\}, \ i = 1, \ldots, N. \tag{3.7}$$

Restricting ourselves to the case where $b = 0$, the *max-stable distribution of Type II* can be estimated by separately fitting line (3.1) to the positive and negative half-lines. Defining

$$Y_i^* \ := \ \ln(-\ln Y_i), \quad Y_i \in (0, 1], \tag{3.8}$$

$$X_i^* \ := \ \begin{cases} -\ln X_i, & \text{if } X_i > 0 \\ -\ln |X_i|, & \text{if } X_i < 0, \end{cases} \tag{3.9}$$

$$\beta_0 \ := \ -\alpha \ln a, \tag{3.10}$$

$$\beta_1 \ := \ \alpha, \tag{3.11}$$

the estimated d.f. is, as in the case of Type I, given by

$$\hat{G}_i = \exp\{-e^{\hat{Y}_i^*}\} \tag{3.12}$$

and the weights are

$$w_i = \exp\{Y_i^* - e^{Y_i^*}\}. \tag{3.13}$$

It follows from (3.10) and (3.11) that $\hat{\alpha} = \hat{\beta}_1$ and $\hat{a} = \exp\{-\hat{\beta}_0/\hat{\beta}_1\}$. The regression-type estimation of the *max-stable distribution of Type III* is, in principle, the same as for Type II, assuming again $b = 0$.

Analogous to the max-stable distributions, the *min-stable* distributions given by

Type I: $m(x) \ = \ 1 - exp\{-e^{ax-b}\}, \ x \in \mathbf{R}$

Type II: $m(x) \ = \ \begin{cases} 0, & \text{if } x \le b/a \\ 1 - exp\{-(ax-b)^{\alpha}\}, & \text{if } x > b/a \, ; \end{cases}$

Type III: $m(x) \ = \ \begin{cases} 1 - exp\{-(ax-b)^{-\alpha}\}, & \text{if } x \le b/a \\ 1, & \text{if } x > b/a; a > 0, b \in \mathbf{R}, \text{ and } \alpha > 0 \, , \end{cases}$

can be estimated by fitting (3.1). For the *min-stable distribution of Type I*, define

$$Y_i^* \ := \ \ln(-\ln(1 - Y_i)), \quad Y_i \in (0, 1) \tag{3.14}$$

$$X_i^* \ := \ X_i, \quad X_i \in \mathbf{R}, \tag{3.15}$$

$$\beta_0 \ := \ -b, \tag{3.16}$$

$$\beta_1 \ := \ a. \tag{3.17}$$

Note that the observation $X_{max} := \max\limits_{1 \leq i \leq N} X_i$ has to be omitted, because the corresponding $Y_{max} = 1$, for which Y_i^* is not defined. From $\hat{Y}_i^* = \hat{\beta}_0 + \hat{\beta}_1 X_i^*$ we obtain the estimated d.f. by

$$\hat{G}_i = 1 - \exp\{-e^{\hat{Y}_i^*}\}. \tag{3.18}$$

As for the max-stable distribution, the weights for the weighted-least-squares estimation are of the form

$$w_i = \exp\{Y_i^* - e^{Y_i^*}\}. \tag{3.19}$$

For the *min-stable distribution of Type II*, setting $b = 0$, we have

$$Y_i^* := \ln(-\ln(1 - Y_i)), \quad Y_i \in (0,1), \tag{3.20}$$

$$X_i^* := \begin{cases} \ln X_i, & \text{if } X_i > 0 \\ \ln |X_i|, & \text{if } X_i < 0, \end{cases} \tag{3.21}$$

$$\beta_0 := \alpha \ln a, \tag{3.22}$$

$$\beta_1 := \alpha, \tag{3.23}$$

$$\hat{G}_i = 1 - \exp\{-e^{\hat{Y}_i^*}\}, \tag{3.24}$$

$$w_i = \exp\{Y_i^* - e^{Y_i^*}\}. \tag{3.25}$$

The parameters of the *min-stable distribution of Type III* are in principle estimated as described by (3.20–3.25).

The explicit representation for the density of *(geo,sum)-stable* distributions is only known for some special cases, namely the Laplace and exponential distributions. Because the exponential distribution is a special case of the min-stable distribution of Type II with $\alpha = 1$, we consider only the Laplace distribution given by (2.48):

$$\mathcal{G}(t) = \frac{\lambda}{2} \int_{-\infty}^{t} e^{-\lambda|u|} du,$$

In Chapter 4 we shall fit

$$\mathcal{G}(x) = \begin{cases} \dfrac{1}{2} e^{\lambda(x-x_0)}, & 0 < x \leq x_0 \\ 1 - \dfrac{1}{2} e^{-\lambda(x-x_0)}, & x > x_0 \end{cases} \tag{3.26}$$

for the positive half-line. (The d.f. for the negative half-line is defined analogously.) Because the functional form of $\mathcal{G}(x)$ changes at x_0, a regression-type estimation is not directly applicable. Noting, however, that x_0 corresponds to the median, i.e., $x_0 = X_{med}$, we can fit (3.1) by defining

$$Y_i^* := \begin{cases} \ln 2Y_i, & \text{if } < Y_i \leq \frac{1}{2} \\ \ln(2 - 2Y_i), & \text{if } \frac{1}{2} < Y_i \leq 1, \end{cases} \tag{3.27}$$

$$X_i^* := \begin{cases} X_i - X_{\mathrm{med}}, & \text{if } -\infty < X_i \le X_{\mathrm{med}} \\ X_{\mathrm{med}} - X_i, & \text{if } X_i > X_{\mathrm{med}}, \end{cases} \tag{3.28}$$

$$\beta_0 := 0, \tag{3.29}$$

$$\beta_1 := \lambda. \tag{3.30}$$

The estimated Laplace d.f. is derived from

$$\hat{G}_i = \begin{cases} \frac{1}{2} e^{\hat{Y}_i^*}, & \text{if } X_i \le X_{\mathrm{med}} \\ 1 - \frac{1}{2} e^{\hat{Y}_i^*}, & \text{if } X_i > X_{\mathrm{med}}, \end{cases} \tag{3.31}$$

and the weights are of the form

$$w_i = \frac{1}{2} e^{Y_i^*}. \tag{3.32}$$

The *(geo,max)-stable* and *(geo,min)-stable* distributions are identical (compare Properties 2.20 and 2.21). In Chapter 4 we fit a distribution of the form (2.66)

$$G_{a,\alpha} = \begin{cases} \frac{x^\alpha}{a + x^\alpha}, & \text{if } x > 0 \\ 0, & \text{if } x \le 0. \end{cases}$$

to each half-line. To fit a relationship of the form (3.1), define

$$Y_i^* := \ln \frac{1 - Y_i}{Y_i}, \quad Y_i \in (0,1), \tag{3.33}$$

$$X_i^* := -\ln X_i, \quad X_i > 0, \tag{3.34}$$

$$\beta_0 := \ln a, \tag{3.35}$$

$$\beta_1 := \alpha. \tag{3.36}$$

The estimated d.f. and the least-squares weights are obtained by

$$\hat{G}_i = \frac{1}{1 + e^{\hat{Y}_i^*}}, \tag{3.37}$$

$$w_i = \frac{e^{Y_i^*}}{(1 + e^{Y_i^*})^2}. \tag{3.38}$$

Finally, for the *(geo,multiplication)-stable distribution* we fit (for the positive half-line) a d.f. of the type

$$H(x) = \begin{cases} \frac{\mu}{\lambda} x^\lambda, & 0 < x \le x_0 \\ 1 - \frac{\mu}{\lambda} x^{-\lambda}, & x > x_0, \end{cases} \tag{3.39}$$

where $\mu = \lambda (x_0^{-\lambda} + x_0^\lambda)^{-1}$. As with the Laplace distribution, a change in the functional form occurs at x_0. Here, x_0 corresponds to the mode of the distribution, i.e., $x_0 = X_{\mathrm{mod}}$, and can be estimated from the sample density function and, subsequently, improved either iteratively or via grid search. For the regression-type estimation define

$$Y_i^* := \begin{cases} \ln Y_i, & 0 < X_i \le X_{\text{mod}} \\ \ln(1 - Y_i), & X_i > X_{\text{mod}}, \end{cases} \tag{3.40}$$

$$X_i^* := \begin{cases} \ln X_i, & 0 < X_i \le X_{\text{mod}} \\ -\ln X_i, & X_i > X_{\text{mod}}, \end{cases} \tag{3.41}$$

$$\beta_0 := \ln \frac{\mu}{\lambda}, \tag{3.42}$$

$$\beta_1 := \lambda. \tag{3.43}$$

The fitted d.f. is derived from

$$\hat{G}_i = \begin{cases} e^{\hat{Y}_i^*}, & 0 < X_i \le X_{\text{mod}} \\ 1 - e^{\hat{Y}_i^*}, & X_i > X_{\text{mod}} \end{cases} \tag{3.44}$$

and the weights are determined by

$$w_i = e^{Y_i}. \tag{3.45}$$

Note again that the observation which corresponds to max X_i has to be omitted from the estimation. From the estimates $\hat{\beta}_0$ and $\hat{\beta}_1 = \hat{\lambda}$ we can derive $\hat{\mu}$ by $\hat{\mu} = \hat{\beta}_1 \exp\{\hat{\beta}_0\}$. From $\mu = \lambda(X_{\text{mod}}^{-\lambda} + X_{\text{mod}}^{\lambda})$, it is evident that the X_{mod}-estimate could be improved iteratively, solving the quadratic equation $\lambda z^2 - \mu z + \lambda = 0$ in each iteration, where $X_{\text{mod}} = z^{1/\lambda}$.

The class of *multiplication-stable* distributions has not been mentioned here. Below we consider the basic example, namely the *log-normal* distribution. In the empirical application below, we fit the *log-normal* for the positive and the *negative log-normal* for the negative half-line.

3.2   Visual Identification

The linear relationships of the regression-type estimators derived in the previous section give rise to graphic techniques for evaluating the appropriateness of a distribution for a given data set by visually assessing the linearity of a set of points in the (X^*, Y^*)-plane. A plot of the transformed sample distribution, Y_i^*, against the corresponding transformed value of the observations, X_i^*, should approximate a straight line. Any systematic deviations from a straight line are an indication that the proposed distribution is inadequate.

Table 3.1 summarizes the necessary transformations for the stable distributions for which such linear relationships are specified.

Table 3.1 Linear Relationships for Visual Identification.

Distribution	Y_i^*	X_i^{*a}
max:		
Type I	$\ln(-\ln Y_i)$, $Y_i \in (0,1]$	$-X_i$, $X_i \in \mathbf{R}$
Type II,III	$\ln(-\ln Y_i)$, $Y_i \in (0,1]$	$-\ln X_i$, $X_i > 0$ $-\ln|X_i|$, $X_i < 0$
min:		
Type I	$\ln(-\ln(1-Y_i))$, $Y_i \in (0,1)$	X_i, $X_i \in \mathbf{R}$
Type II,III	$\ln(-\ln(1-Y_i))$, $Y_i \in (0,1)$	$-\ln X_i$, $X_i > 0$ $-\ln|X_i|$, $X_i < 0$
(geo,sum):		
Laplace	$\ln 2Y_i$, $Y_i \in (0,.5]$	$X_i - X_{\text{med}}^+$, $0 < X_i \leq X_{\text{med}}^+$ $-(X_i - X_{\text{med}}^-)$, $X_{\text{med}}^- \leq X_i < 0$
	$\ln(2 - 2Y_i)$, $Y_i \in (.5,1]$	$X_{\text{med}}^+ - X_i$, $X_i > X_{\text{med}}^+$ $-(X_{\text{med}}^- - X_i)$, $X_i < X_{\text{med}}^-$
exponential	min-stable Type II,III with $\alpha = 1$	
Weibull	see min-stable Type II,III	
(geo,max)	$\ln\frac{1-Y_i}{Y_i}$, $Y_i \in (0,1)$	$-\ln X_i$, $X_i > 0$ $-\ln|X_i|$, $X_i < 0$
(geo,min)	see (geo,max)-stable	
(geo,mult.)	$\ln Y_i$,	$\ln X_i$, $0 < X_i \leq X_{\text{mod}}^+$ $\ln|X_i|$, $X_{\text{mod}}^- \leq X_i < 0$
	$\ln(1 - Y_i)$	$-\ln X_i$, $X_i > X_{\text{mod}}^+$ $-\ln|X_i|$, $X_i < X_{\text{mod}}^-$

[a] Superscripts "+" and "−" refer to positive and negative X_i's, respectively. Subscripts "med" and "mod" refer to the median and mode, respectively.

The visual identification techniques described here allow us to judge the appropriateness of a candidate distribution by examining to what extent there are systematic deviations from linearity. In order to judge the severity of any deviations, their statistical significance has to be assessed.

The identification is based on linear-regression relationship

$$Y_i^* = \beta_0 + \beta_1 X_i^* + u_i, \qquad i = 1, \ldots, N, \qquad (3.46)$$

where, depending on the distribution under consideration, the transformed distribution-function values Y_i^*, transformed quantiles X_i^* and parameters β_0 and β_1 are defined above. Plotting Y_i^*'s and $\hat{Y}_i^*$'s, i.e., actual and fitted values, against X_i^*'s allows us to assess the appropriateness of a candidate distribution. Using the standard prediction interval for regressions, a confidence band can be approximated by

$$Y_i^* \pm t_{\alpha/2}\hat{\sigma}_u \sqrt{1 + \frac{1}{N} + \frac{(X_i^* - \bar{X}^*)^2}{\sum_{j=1}^{N}(X_j^* - \bar{X}^*)^2}}, \qquad (3.47)$$

where $t_{\alpha/2}$ is the $100 \times (1 - \alpha/2)\%$ critical value of the t distribution with $N - 2$ degrees of freedom; $\hat{\sigma}_u$ is the estimated residual standard deviation; $\bar{X}^*$ denotes the sample mean of the X_i^*'s; and N is the sample size of regression (3.46).

If the transformed distribution-function values deviate systematically from linearity, residuals u_i will be positively autocorrelated.[1] OLS estimates $\hat{\beta}_0$ and $\hat{\beta}_1$ are unbiased but not efficient—a fact which may not be too much of a concern in the visual-identification stage. However, $\hat{\sigma}_u^2$ will be biased and is likely to be underestimated. Therefore, confidence bands constructed from (3.47) may be too conservative.

3.3   Maximum Likelihood Estimation

Maximum likelihood estimators of the distributions considered here are discussed extensively in the statistics literature (see, for example, Kalbfleisch and Prentice, 1980; Cohen and Whitten, 1988). An exception is the stable Paretian distribution, for which researchers typically do not use maximum likelihood estimators. DuMouchel (1971) presents an algorithm for obtaining maximum likelihood estimates of the parameters of the (asymmetric) stable Paretian distribution which is rather burdensome computationally. A similar but more straightforward algorithm is presented in Chen (1991).

Next we briefly summarize the maximum likelihood estimation (for details see, for example, Rockette et al., 1974; Kalbfleisch and Prentice, 1980, or

---

[1]The Durbin-Watson statistic should also be useful in comparing candidate distributions.

Cohen and Whitten, 1988).[2] Given N observations, $X = (X_1, \ldots, X_N)'$, for the, say, positive half line, the log-likelihood function is of the form

$$\ell(\alpha, \lambda; X) = N \ln \lambda + N \ln \alpha + (\alpha - 1) \sum_{i=1}^{N} \ln X_i - \lambda \sum_{i=1}^{N} X_i^{\alpha}, \qquad (3.48)$$

which can be maximized using, for example, a Newton-Raphson algorithm. It follows from the first-order condition,

$$\lambda = N \left(\sum_{i=1}^{N} X_i^{\alpha} \right)^{-1}, \qquad (3.49)$$

that the optimization problem can be reduced to finding the value for α which maximizes the concentrated likelihood

$$\ell^*(\alpha; X) = \ln \alpha + \alpha c - \ln \left(\sum_{i=1}^{N} X_i^{\alpha} \right), \qquad (3.50)$$

where $c = N^{-1} \sum_{i=1}^{N} \ln X_i$. The information matrix evaluated at the maximum likelihood estimates, denoted by $I(\hat{\alpha}, \hat{\lambda})$, is given by

$$I(\hat{\alpha}, \hat{\lambda}) = \begin{bmatrix} N\hat{\alpha}^{-2} & \sum_{i=1}^{N} X_i^{\hat{\alpha}} \ln X_i \\ \sum_{i=1}^{N} X_i^{\hat{\alpha}} \ln X_i & N\hat{\lambda}^{-2} \end{bmatrix}. \qquad (3.51)$$

It can be shown that, under fairly mild conditions, the maximum likelihood estimates $\hat{\alpha}$ and $\hat{\lambda}$ are consistent and have asymptotically a multivariate normal distribution with mean $(\alpha, \lambda)'$. Moreover, the covariance of the estimated parameters is given by the inverse of $EI(\alpha, \lambda)$ and can be replaced by $I^{-1}(\hat{\alpha}, \hat{\lambda})$. Starting values for the parameters are provided by regression-type estimator (3.14).

3.4   Efficient Estimators for the Parameters of Paretian-stable and Geometric Laws

In this section estimators for the vectors of parameters of Paretian-stable and geometric stable laws are constructed based on the modified method of

---

[2]See Hirose (1991) for a Monte Carlo comparison of alternative estimators, including the maximum likelihood estimator, for the three-parameter Weibull distribution (i.e., $b \neq 0$).

scoring.[3] The estimators are consistent, asymptotically normal, and asymptotically efficient in the class of estimators with partial information on the distribution.

We start with estimators for the vector $\tilde{\theta} = (\alpha, \beta, \gamma, \lambda)$ of parameters of a stable law with a distribution function (d.f.) $F(x; \tilde{\theta})$, whose characteristic function (ch.f.) is given by

$$\varphi(t; \tilde{\theta}) = \left\{ \begin{array}{ll} \exp\{\lambda[it\gamma - |t|^\alpha + it(|t|^{\alpha-1} - 1)\beta \tan(\frac{\pi}{2}\alpha)]\} & \text{if } \alpha \neq 1 , \\ \exp\{\lambda(it\gamma - |t| - i\frac{2}{\pi}\beta t \ln|t|)\} & \text{if } \alpha = 1 . \end{array} \right. \quad (3.52)$$

Here $0 < \alpha \leq 2, -1 \leq \beta \leq 1, \gamma \in \mathcal{R}$, and $\lambda > 0$. $\varphi(t; \tilde{\theta})$ is continuous with reference to $\tilde{\theta}$. For the construction of the estimator, we utilize *the modified method of scoring* (MMS) (This representation of α-stable ch.f. is slightly different from that in (2.1.2), see also Zolotarev (1986a) Introduction.) The constructed estimators exploit the available information on $F(x, \tilde{\theta})$ to the utmost.

Let $x_1, \ldots, x_n$ be a random sample of size n from a population with the d.f. $F(x; \tilde{\theta})$ and ch.f. given by (3.52).

φ depends on an unknown vector parameter, $\tilde{\theta} = (\theta_1, \theta_2, \theta_3, \theta_4) = (\alpha, \beta, \gamma, \lambda)$ where $0 < \alpha \leq 2$, $-1 \leq \beta \leq 1$, $-A < \gamma < A$, $0 < \lambda < B$ for some $A > 0$ and $B > 0$. The constants A and B are assumed to be known.

We now construct the estimator of $\tilde{\theta}$. Let t_j, $j = 1, \ldots, k$, be k positive numbers. Let L be a linear space spanned by elements 1, and $\xi = ((\cos(t_j x_1), \sin(t_j x_1))'$, $j = 1, 2, \ldots, k)$. Let $\mathcal{A} = \mathcal{A}(\tilde{\theta}) = \|a_{pq}^{(r\ell)}\|$ be the matrix with elements,

$$
\begin{aligned}
a_{pq}^{(11)} &= \frac{1}{2}\left[Re\varphi(t_p - t_q; \tilde{\theta}) + Re\varphi(t_p + t_q; \tilde{\theta})\right] \\
&\quad - Re\varphi(t_p; \tilde{\theta})Re\varphi(t_q; \tilde{\theta}) , \\
a_{pq}^{(12)} &= a_{pq}^{(21)}\frac{1}{2}\left[Im\varphi(t_p + t_q; \tilde{\theta}) + Im\varphi(t_p - t_q; \tilde{\theta})\right] \\
&\quad - Im\varphi(t_q; \tilde{\theta})Re\varphi(t_p; \tilde{\theta}), \\
a_{pq}^{(22)} &= \frac{1}{2}\left[Re\varphi(t_p - t_q; \tilde{\theta}) - Re\varphi(t_p + t_q; \tilde{\theta})\right] \\
&\quad - Im\varphi(t_p; \tilde{\theta})Im\varphi(t_q; \tilde{\theta}), \quad p, q = 1, \cdots, k.
\end{aligned}
\quad (3.53)
$$

[3]The results in this section are due to Klebanov and Melamed (1984) and Klebanov, Melamed and Rachev (1994).

In fact, $\mathcal{A}$ is $2k \times 2k$ matrix of the form:

$$
\begin{pmatrix}
a_{11}^{(11)} & a_{12}^{(11)} & \cdots & a_{1q}^{(11)} & a_{11}^{(12)} & a_{12}^{(12)} & \cdots & a_{1q}^{(12)} \\
\vdots & \vdots & \vdots & \vdots & \vdots & \vdots & \vdots & \vdots \\
a_{p1}^{(11)} & a_{p2}^{(11)} & \cdots & a_{pq}^{(11)} & a_{p1}^{(12)} & a_{p2}^{(12)} & \cdots & a_{pq}^{(12)} \\
a_{11}^{(21)} & a_{12}^{(21)} & \cdots & a_{1q}^{(21)} & a_{11}^{(22)} & a_{12}^{(22)} & \cdots & a_{1q}^{(22)} \\
\vdots & \vdots & \vdots & \vdots & \vdots & \vdots & \vdots & \vdots \\
a_{p1}^{(21)} & a_{p2}^{(21)} & \cdots & a_{pq}^{(21)} & a_{p1}^{(22)} & a_{p2}^{(22)} & \cdots & a_{pq}^{(22)}
\end{pmatrix}
$$

Let

$$
\begin{aligned}
E_{\tilde{\theta}}\zeta' &= \Big(E_{\tilde{\theta}}\cos(t_1 x_1), E_{\tilde{\theta}}\sin(t_1 x_1), \ldots, E_{\tilde{\theta}}\cos(t_k x_1), E_{\tilde{\theta}}\sin(t_k x_1)\Big) \quad (3.54) \\
&= \Big(Re\big(\varphi(t_1;\tilde{\theta})\big), Im\big(\varphi(t_1;\tilde{\theta})\big), \ldots, Re\big(\varphi(t_k;\tilde{\theta})\big), Im\big(\varphi(t_k,\tilde{\theta})\big)\Big),
\end{aligned}
$$

where expectation is w.r.t. unknown parameter $\tilde{\theta}$. Define next the $(2k+2) \times (2k+2)$ matrix

$$
\Lambda^{(a,b)}(\tilde{\theta}) = \begin{pmatrix}
0 & 0 & \frac{\partial}{\partial\theta_a}E_{\tilde{\theta}}\zeta' \\
0 & 1 & O' \\
\frac{\partial}{\partial\theta_1}E_{\tilde{\theta}}\zeta & O & \mathcal{A}
\end{pmatrix}, \quad a,b = 1,2,3,4 \quad (3.55)
$$

where O is the null column vector of dimension $2k$ and $\Lambda_{0,j}^{(a)}(\tilde{\theta})$ is a cofactor of the element in the first line and (j+1)st column of the matrix $\Lambda^{(aa)}(\tilde{\theta})$.

The matrix $I(\tilde{\theta}; L) = \|I_{ab}(\tilde{\theta})\|$ with elements given by

$$
I_{ab}(\tilde{\theta}) = -\frac{\det \Lambda^{(ab)}(\tilde{\theta})}{\det \mathcal{A}}, \quad a,b = 1,2,3,4 \quad (3.56)
$$

is the matrix of Fisher information on $\tilde{\theta}$ contained in the linear space L (see Kagan (1976)). It is clear that $\det \mathcal{A} > 0$ when $F(x;\tilde{\theta})$ has more then k points of growth. This follows from the fact that $\det \mathcal{A}$ is Gram's determinant of the linearly independent system $\breve{1}, \zeta' - E_{\tilde{\theta}}\zeta'$.

Consider $\varphi_n(t) = \frac{1}{n}\sum_{j=1}^{n} e^{itx_j}$ the empirical ch.f., and let

$$
\xi' = (\xi_j, j = 1, \ldots, 2k),
$$

where

$$
\xi_j = \begin{cases} Re\left(\varphi_n(t_j)\right) & j = 1, \ldots, k \\ Im\left(\varphi_n(t_{j-k})\right) & j = k+1, \ldots, 2k . \end{cases} \quad (3.57)
$$

We introduce the *vector score function* $\mathcal{J}_n(\tilde{\theta})$ (see Kagan(1976)) with the components

$$
J_n^{(a)}(\tilde{\theta}) = -n\sum_{j=1}^{2k} \frac{\Lambda_{0,j+1}^{(a)}(\tilde{\theta})}{\det \mathcal{A}(\tilde{\theta})}(\xi_j - E_{\tilde{\theta}}\xi_j), \quad a = 1,2,3,4. \quad (3.58)
$$

Let $\tilde{\theta}^* = (\theta_1^*, \theta_2^*, \theta_3^*, \theta_4^*)$ be a $\sqrt{n}$-consistent estimator of $\tilde{\theta}$. The process of constructing such an estimator will be described later on. Consider now the corresponding MMS estimator of $\tilde{\theta}$ given by

$$\tilde{\theta} = \tilde{\theta}^* - \left(\frac{1}{n} \frac{\partial \mathcal{J}_n(\tilde{\theta})}{\partial \tilde{\theta}} \bigg|_{\tilde{\theta}=\tilde{\theta}^*} \right)^{-1} \left(\frac{1}{n} \mathcal{J}_n(\tilde{\theta}^*) \right), \qquad (3.59)$$

where $\left(\frac{\partial \mathcal{J}_n(\tilde{\theta})}{\partial \tilde{\theta}} \bigg|_{\tilde{\theta}=\tilde{\theta}^*} \right)^{-1}$ is the matrix reciprocal of $\left\| \frac{\partial J_n^{(a)}(\tilde{\theta})}{\partial \theta_b} \right\|$, $a,b = 1,2,3,4$.

Summarizing and applying (Kagan (1976)) we have the following limiting result.

Theorem 3.1 Let the d.f. $F(x;\tilde{\theta})$ have more than k points of growth. Let $t_1,\ldots,t_k$ be positive numbers such that (i) the functions $\varphi(t_j;\tilde{\theta})$, $j = 1,\ldots,k$, $\varphi(t_p + t_q;\tilde{\theta})$, $p \neq q$, $p,q = 1,\ldots,k$ are continuous w.r.t. $\tilde{\theta}$ and $\varphi(t_j;\tilde{\theta})$, $j = 1,\ldots,k$, have continuous w.r.t. $\tilde{\theta}$ partial derivatives of the first and second order; (ii) $\det I(\tilde{\theta};C) \neq 0$.

Then $\tilde{\theta} \xrightarrow{p} \tilde{\theta}$ as $n \to \infty$, and the random vector $\sqrt{n}\left(\tilde{\theta} - \tilde{\theta}\right)$ is asymptotically normal $\mathcal{N}(O, I^{-1}(\tilde{\theta};C))$.

The ch.f. (3.52) has continuous partial derivatives w.r.t. $\tilde{\theta}$ up to the second order:

$$\frac{\partial \varphi(t;\tilde{\theta})}{\partial \alpha} = \begin{cases} \exp\{\lambda[it\gamma - |t|^\alpha + it(|t|^{\alpha-1} - 1)\beta \tan(\frac{\pi}{2} - \alpha)]\} \cdot \{-\lambda|t|^\alpha \ell n|t| \\ \quad +i\lambda\beta t\{|t|^{\alpha-1}(\ell n|t| \cdot \tan(\frac{\pi}{2}\alpha) + \frac{\pi}{2}\cos^{-2}(\frac{\pi}{2}\alpha)) - \frac{\pi}{2}\cos^{-2}(\frac{\pi}{2}\alpha)\}\}, \\ \hfill \text{if } \alpha \neq 1, \\[6pt] \exp\{\lambda(it\gamma - |t| - i\frac{2}{\pi}\beta t\ell n|t|)\} \cdot [-\lambda\ell n|t|(|t| + i\beta t \cdot \frac{1}{\pi}\ell n|t|)], \\ \hfill \text{if } \alpha = 1; \end{cases}$$

$$\frac{\partial^2 \varphi(t;\tilde{\theta})}{\partial \alpha^2} = \begin{cases} \exp\{\lambda[it\gamma - |t|^\alpha + it(|t|^{\alpha-1} - 1)\beta \tan(\frac{\pi}{2}\alpha)]\} \cdot [\{-\lambda|t|^\alpha \ell n|t| \\ \quad +i\lambda\beta t[|t|^{\alpha-1}(\ell n|t| \cdot \tan(\frac{\pi}{2}\alpha) + \frac{\pi}{2}\cos^{-2}(\frac{\pi}{2}\alpha)) \\ \quad -\frac{\pi}{2}\cos^{-2}(\frac{\pi}{2}\alpha)]\}^2 - \lambda|t|^\alpha \ell n^2|t| + i\lambda\beta t\{|t|^{\alpha-1}(\ell n^2|t| \cdot \tan(\frac{\pi}{2}\alpha) \\ \quad +2\pi\ell n|t|/(1 + \cos\pi\alpha) + 2\pi^2\sin\pi\alpha/(3 + 4\cos\pi\alpha + \cos 2\pi\alpha)) \\ \quad -2\pi^2\sin\pi\alpha/(3 + 4\cos\pi\alpha + \cos 2\pi\alpha)\}], \hfill \text{if } \alpha \neq 1, \\[6pt] \exp\{\lambda(it\gamma - |t| - i\frac{2}{\pi}\beta t\ell n|t|)\} \cdot [\lambda^2\ell n^2|t|(|t| + i\beta t \cdot \frac{1}{\pi}\ell n|t|)^2 \\ \quad -\lambda|t|\ell n^2|t| + i\lambda\beta t \cdot \frac{1}{3\pi}(\pi^2\ell n|t| - 2\ell n^3|t|)], \hfill \text{if } \alpha = 1. \end{cases}$$

Let us now construct an auxiliary $\sqrt{n}$-consistent estimator of $\tilde{\theta}$. We first choose a $t_0 > 0$ such that $|\lambda\gamma t_0 + \lambda t_0(t_0^{\alpha-1} - 1)\beta \tan(\frac{\pi}{2}\alpha)| < \frac{\pi}{2}$ for all $0 < \alpha \leq 2$, $-1 \leq \beta \leq 1$, $-A < \gamma < A$, $0 < \lambda < B$.

Let $0 < \varepsilon < A$. Then since

$$\lim_{\alpha \to 1} \left| (t^{\alpha-1} - 1) \tan\left(\frac{\pi}{2}\alpha\right) \right| = \frac{2}{\pi}|\ell nt| \qquad \text{for } t > 0,$$

there exists a $\delta > 0$ such that for all $0 < \alpha \le 2$ and $|\alpha - 1| < \delta$ we have

$$\left| (t^{\alpha-1} - 1) \tan \frac{\pi}{2}\alpha \right| < \frac{2}{\pi}|\ell nt| + \varepsilon.$$

One can verify now that

$$t_0^{(1)} = \max \left\{ t : 0 < t < 1, \ 2ABt + Bt|\ln t| < \frac{\pi}{2} \right\}$$

satisfies the inequality

$$\left| \lambda \gamma t + \lambda t \left(t^{\alpha-1} - 1 \right) \beta \tan \left(\frac{\pi}{2}\alpha \right) \right| < \frac{\pi}{2} \tag{3.60}$$

on the set where $\Theta_1 = \{\alpha \in (1-\delta, 1+\delta), \beta \in [-1,1], \gamma \in (-A, A), \lambda \in (0, B)\}$. Similarly, we choose $t_0^{(2)}$ such that,

$$0 < t_0^{(2)} < \min \left\{ \left(\frac{\pi}{4B \tan \left(\frac{\pi}{2}(1 - \delta) \right)} \right)^{\frac{1}{1-\delta}}, \frac{\pi}{4AB} \right\}.$$

$t_0^{(2)}$ satisfies (3.60) on the set $\Theta_2 = \{\alpha \in (0, 1-\delta), \beta \in [-1,1], \gamma \in (-A, A), \lambda \in (0, B)\}$. We now choose $t_0^{(3)} > 0$, such that

$$0 < t_0^{(3)} < \frac{\pi}{2 \left[AB + B \tan \left(\frac{\pi}{2}(1-\delta) \right) \right]}$$

and $t_0^{(3)}$ satisfies (3.60) on the set $\Theta_3 = \{\alpha \in (1 + \delta, 2), \beta \in [-1,1], \gamma \in (-A, A), \lambda \in (0, B)\}$.

Define $t_0 = \min \left(t_0^{(1)}, t_0^{(2)}, t_0^{(3)} \right)$. Let $\tau_1, \tau_2 \in (0, t_0)$. Using the method-of-moments estimators for Paretian-stable distribution parameters, described in Fielitz and Roselle (1981), we construct $\tilde{\theta}^*$ as,

$$\alpha^* = \ln \left(\frac{\ln \left(|\varphi_n(\tau_1)| \right)}{\ln \left(|\varphi_n(\tau_2)| \right)} \right) / \ln \left(\frac{\tau_1}{\tau_2} \right) \tag{3.61}$$

$$\lambda^* = \exp \left\{ [\ln \tau_1 \cdot \ln \left(- \ln |\varphi_n(\tau_2)| \right) - \ln \tau_2 \cdot \ln \left(- \ln |\varphi_n(\tau_1)| \right)] / \ln \frac{\tau_1}{\tau_2} \right\} \tag{3.62}$$

$$\beta^* = \frac{\frac{1}{\tau_1} \arctan \left(Im \left(\varphi_n(\tau_1) \right) / Re \left(\varphi_n(\tau_1) \right) \right)}{\left(\tau_1^{\alpha^*-1} - \tau_2^{\alpha^*-1} \right) \lambda^* \tan \left(\frac{\pi}{2}\alpha^* \right)}$$

$$- \frac{\frac{1}{\tau_2} \arctan \left(Im \left(\varphi_n(\tau_2) \right) / Re \left(\varphi_n(\tau_2) \right) \right)}{\left(\tau_1^{\alpha^*-1} - \tau_2^{\alpha^*-1} \right) \lambda^* \tan \left(\frac{\pi}{2}\alpha^* \right)} \tag{3.63}$$

$$\gamma^* = \frac{\left(\tau_1^{\alpha^*-1} - 1 \right) \frac{1}{\tau_2} \arctan \left(Im \left(\varphi_n(\tau_2) \right) / Re \left(\varphi_n(\tau_2) \right) \right)}{\left(\tau_1^{\alpha^*-1} - \tau_2^{\alpha^*-1} \right) \lambda^*}$$

$$- \frac{\left(\tau_2^{\alpha^*-1} - 1 \right) \arctan \frac{Im(\varphi_n(\tau_1))}{Re(\varphi_n(\tau_1))}}{\left(\tau_1^{\alpha^*-1} - \tau_2^{\alpha^*-1} \right) \lambda^*} \tag{3.64}$$

It can be seen that the random vector $\sqrt{n}(\theta^* - \tilde{\theta})$ is asymptotically normal. Hence, θ^* is the $\sqrt{n}$-consistent estimator of $\tilde{\theta}$. Thus, the following assertion holds.

Corollary 3.1 Let $t_1, \ldots, t_k$ be positive numbers such that $\det I(\tilde{\theta} : \mathcal{L}) \neq 0$. Then the MMS estimator $\tilde{\theta}$ defined by relations (3.59), (3.4.9) possesses the following properties:

- (i) $\tilde{\theta} \xrightarrow{p} \tilde{\theta}$ as $n \to \infty$;

- (ii) the random vector $\sqrt{n}(\tilde{\theta} - \tilde{\theta})$ is asymptotically normal $\mathcal{N}(0, I^{-1}(\tilde{\theta}; \mathcal{L}))$.

Remark 3.1 Since the covariance matrix of the limit law for the vector $\sqrt{n}(\tilde{\theta} - \tilde{\theta})$ coincides with the informational bound in the Rao-Cramer inequality for estimators belonging to a linear space, then $\tilde{\theta}$ is asymptotically efficient in the class of $\tilde{\theta}$ parameter estimators belonging to $\mathcal{L}$.

Remark 3.2 The ch.f. of stable law is often represented in forms other than the one given by (3.52). We list two of them below:

A.
$$\varphi_A.(t; \tilde{\theta}_A.) = \exp\{\lambda_A.(it\gamma_A. - |t|^{\alpha_A.} + itw_A.(t; \alpha_A., \beta_A.)\}, \tag{3.65}$$

where
$$w_A.(t; \alpha_A., \beta_A.) = \begin{cases} |t|^{\alpha_A.-1}\beta_A.\tan\left(\frac{\pi}{2}\alpha_A.\right), & \text{if } \alpha_A. \neq 1, \\ -\beta_A.\frac{2}{\pi}\ln|t|, & \text{if } \alpha_A. = 1. \end{cases}$$

B.
$$\varphi_B.(t; \tilde{\theta}_B.) = \exp\{\lambda_B.(it\gamma_B. - |t|^{\alpha_B.} \cdot w_B.(t; \alpha_B., \beta_B.))\}, \tag{3.66}$$

where
$$w_B.(t; \alpha_B., \beta_B) = \begin{cases} \exp\left(-i\frac{\pi}{2}\beta_B K(\alpha_B.)signt\right), & \text{if } \alpha_B. \neq 1, \\ \frac{\pi}{2} + i\beta_B.\ln|t| \cdot signt, & \text{if } \alpha_B. = 1, \end{cases}$$
$$K(\alpha_B.) = \alpha_B. - 1 + sign(1 - \alpha_B.),$$

$\tilde{\theta}_u = (\alpha_u, \beta_u, \gamma_u, \lambda_u)$, $0 < \alpha_u \leq 2$, $-1 \leq \beta_u \leq 1$, $-\infty < \gamma_u < \infty$, $0 < \lambda_u < \infty$, $u = A, B$.

By making use of the relations between the parameters in various forms, (Zolotarev, 1986a, Introduction) based on the constructed MMS estimator $\tilde{\theta}$ we write down the estimators for $\tilde{\theta}_B$ and $\tilde{\theta}_B$ (under the condition that the range of variation of these parametric vectors is identical to the one we have):

$$\tilde{\theta}_A = \left(\hat{\alpha}_A, \hat{\beta}_A, \hat{\gamma}_A, \hat{\lambda}_A\right) : \hat{\alpha}_A = \hat{\theta}_1, \hat{\beta}_A = \hat{\theta}_2,$$
$$\hat{\gamma}_A = \hat{\theta}_3 - \hat{\theta}_2 + \tan\left(\frac{\pi}{2}\hat{\theta}_1\right), \hat{\lambda}_A = \hat{\theta}_4;$$

$$\tilde{\theta}_{\mathbf{B}} = \left(\hat{\alpha}_{\mathbf{B}}, \hat{\beta}_{\mathbf{B}}, \hat{\gamma}_{\mathbf{B}}, \hat{\lambda}_{\mathbf{B}}\right) : \hat{\alpha}_{\mathbf{B}} = \hat{\theta}_1, \hat{\beta}_{\mathbf{B}}$$

$$= 2\arctan\left(\hat{\theta}_2 \tan\left(\frac{\pi}{2}\hat{\theta}_1\right)\right) / \left(\pi K\left(\hat{\theta}_1\right)\right),$$

$$\hat{\gamma}_{\mathbf{B}} = \left(\hat{\theta}_3 - \hat{\theta}_2 \tan\left(\frac{\pi}{2}\hat{\theta}_1\right)\right) \cos\left[\arctan\left(\hat{\theta}_2 + \tan\left(\frac{\pi}{2}\hat{\theta}_1\right)\right)\right],$$

$$\hat{\lambda}_{\mathbf{B}} = \hat{\theta}_4 / \cos\left[\arctan\left(\hat{\theta}_2 \tan\left(\frac{\pi}{2}\hat{\theta}_1\right)\right)\right].$$

Hence, it is clear that when the problem of estimating $\tilde{\theta}$ for the forms (**A**) or (**B**) is considered, one must ensure that consistent estimators can be constructed only if it is known that $\alpha = 1$ or $\alpha \neq 1$.

The rest of the section will be divoted to MMS-estimators for the parameters of strictly laws. The ch.f. of strictly geo stable distribution has the form:

$$\varphi(t) = \varphi(t; \tilde{\theta}) = \frac{1}{1 + \lambda|t|^\alpha exp\{-i\frac{\pi}{2}\beta\alpha signt\}} \tag{3.67}$$

where $\tilde{\vartheta} = (\alpha, \beta, \lambda)$ satisfies the conditions:

$$0 < \alpha \leq 2, -\beta_\alpha \leq \beta \leq \beta_\alpha(\beta_\alpha := min(1, \frac{2}{\alpha} - 1)), \lambda > 0 \tag{3.68}$$

We denote the ch.f. of strictly geo-stable law with ch.f. (3.67) by $F(x; \tilde{\vartheta}.$ We assume that the vector of parameters ϑ belongs to a compact set Θ.

We next follow the same construction as we did for estimating the parameters of Paretian-stable law. We however describe a slightly more general situation. Consider a random sample $x_1, \cdots, x_n$ depending on an unknown vector parameter $\tilde{\vartheta} \in \Theta \subset \mathcal{R}^s, s > 1$ Choose now k positive numbers $t_j, j = 1, \cdots, k$. Consider as before the linear space $\mathcal{L}$, spanned by the elements $1, \zeta = (cost_j x_i, sint_j; x_1, j = 1, \cdot, k)$, and let $\mathbf{A} = \mathbf{A}(\tilde{\vartheta})$ be the matrix with elements defined as in (3.54):

$$a_{pq}^{(11)} = \frac{1}{2}\left[Re\varphi(t_p - t_q; \tilde{\vartheta}) + Re\varphi(t_p + t_q; \tilde{\vartheta})\right] - Re\varphi(t_p; \tilde{\vartheta})Re\varphi(t_q; \tilde{\vartheta}),$$

$$a_{pq}^{(12)} = a_{pq}^{(21)}\frac{1}{2}\left[Im\varphi(t_p + t_q; \tilde{\vartheta}) + Im\varphi(t_p - t_q; \tilde{\vartheta})\right]$$
$$- Im\varphi(t_q; \tilde{\vartheta})Re\varphi(t_p; \tilde{\vartheta}), \tag{3.69}$$

$$a_{pq}^{(22)} = \frac{1}{2}\left[Re\varphi(t_p - t_q; \tilde{\vartheta}) - Re\varphi(t_p + t_q; \tilde{\vartheta})\right]$$
$$- Im\varphi(t_p; \tilde{\vartheta})Im\varphi(t_q; \tilde{\vartheta}), p, q = 1, \cdots, k.$$

where $\varphi(t; \tilde{\vartheta}$ is the ch.f. of $F(x; \tilde{\vartheta}.$ Following (3.55) let

$$E_\vartheta\zeta = (Re\varphi(t_j; \tilde{\vartheta}), Im\varphi(t_j; \tilde{\vartheta}), j = 1, \cdots, k), \tag{3.70}$$

and

$$\Lambda^{(a,b)}(\tilde{\theta}) = \begin{pmatrix} 0 & 0 & \frac{\partial}{\partial\vartheta_a}E_{\tilde{\vartheta}}\zeta^T \\ 0 & 1 & O^T \\ \frac{\partial}{\partial\vartheta_l}E_{\tilde{\vartheta}}\zeta & O & \mathcal{A}(\vartheta) \end{pmatrix}, \quad r, l = 1, \ldots, s$$

Similarly to (3.55) define $\Lambda_{0,j}^{(r)}(\tilde{\vartheta})$ to be a cofactor of the element in the first line and $(j+1)$ -st column of the matrix and, $\Lambda^{(r,r)}(\vartheta) = \Lambda^{(r)}(\vartheta)$. Define next the Fischer Information matrix $\mathbf{1}(\vartheta; \mathcal{L}) = \|I_{rl}(\vartheta)\|$ with elements $I_{rl}(\vartheta) = -det\Lambda^{(r,l)}(\vartheta)/det\mathbf{A}(\vartheta)$, $r, l = 1, \cdots, s$. Be the empirical ch.f., and define $\xi = (\xi_j, j = 1, \cdots, 2k)$ as we already did in (3.57). Next set the vector score function $\frac{1}{n}\mathbf{J}_n(\tilde{\vartheta})$ with components

$$\frac{1}{\sqrt{n}}J_n^{(p)}(\tilde{\vartheta}) = -\sum_{j=1}^{2k} \frac{\Lambda_{0,j+1}^{(r)}(\tilde{\vartheta})}{det\mathbf{A}(\tilde{\vartheta})}\sqrt{n}(\xi_j - E_{\tilde{\vartheta}}\xi_j), \qquad (3.71)$$

$r = 1, \cdots, s$. Let $\tilde{\vartheta}^*$ be some $\sqrt{n}$ consistent estimator of $\tilde{\vartheta}$. Consider the MMS-estimator of the vector parameter $\tilde{\vartheta}$

$$\hat{\vartheta} = \vartheta^* - \left(\frac{1}{n}\frac{\partial \mathbf{J}_n(\vartheta)}{\partial \tilde{\vartheta}}\bigg|_{\tilde{\vartheta}=\tilde{\vartheta}^*}\right)^{-1}\left(\frac{1}{n}\mathbf{J}_n(\tilde{\vartheta}^*)\right), \qquad (3.72)$$

where $\left(\frac{1}{n}\frac{\partial \mathbf{J}_n(\vartheta)}{\partial \tilde{\vartheta}}\bigg|_{\tilde{\vartheta}=\tilde{\vartheta}^*}\right)^{-1}$ is the matrix reciprocal to $\left\|\frac{\partial J_n^{(r)}(\tilde{\vartheta})}{\partial \vartheta_t}\right\|_{r,t=1,\cdots,s}$ in which instead of $\tilde{\vartheta}$ the estimator $\tilde{\vartheta}^*$ is substituted. Let $\mu_{min} = \mu_{min}(\tilde{\vartheta}) = min\{\mu; det(\mathbf{1}(\tilde{\vartheta}; \mathcal{L}) - \mu\mathbf{1}) = 0\}$, where $\mathbf{1}$ is the unit vector of appropriate dimension. Let $\mathcal{F}_o$ be a set of d.f.'s $F(x; \vartheta)$ with more than k points of growth and such that there are constants $C_j = C_j(\vartheta) > 0, j = 1, 2$ and $inf_{F \in \mathcal{F}_o}\mu_{min}(\vartheta) \geq C_1, inf_{F \in \mathcal{F}_o}det\mathbf{A}(\vartheta) \geq C_2$,

Theorem 3.2 *(see Kagan (1976), Klebanov and Melamed (1984), Klebanov, Manija and Melamed (1986))* Let $F \in \mathcal{F}_l$ and assume that
   (i) the functions $\varphi(t_j; \vartheta), j = 1, \cdots, k, \varphi(t_p \pm t_q; \vartheta), p \neq q, p, q = 1, \cdots$, are continuous w.r.t. ϑ and $\varphi(t_j; \vartheta), j = 1, \cdots, k$, have continuous w.r.t. ϑ partial derivatives up to the second order and furthermore,
   (ii) $det\mathbf{1}(\vartheta; \mathcal{L}) \neq 0$.
   Then $\hat{\vartheta} \xrightarrow{P} \vartheta$ and the random vector $\sqrt{n}(\hat{\vartheta} - \vartheta)$ is asymptotically normal $N(\mathbf{0}, \mathbf{1}^{-1}(\vartheta; \mathcal{L}))$. If, moreover, the estimator ϑ^* is $\sqrt{n}$-consistent uniformly w.r.t $\mathcal{F}_0$,then the convergence of $\sqrt{n}(\hat{\vartheta} - \vartheta)$ to the limiting normal d.f. is uniform in $\mathcal{F}_o$.

Let us apply the obtained results to study the properties of estimators of a parameter vector $\vartheta = (\alpha, \beta, \lambda)$ of the geo-strictly geo-stable law ch.f. (3.67). Let $h_o(z) = \frac{1}{1-z}$, and so $h_o^{-1}(n) = 1 - \frac{1}{n}$. Next set $\psi_n(t) = h_o^{-1}(\varphi_n(t))$ and choose $\tau_j > 0$ such that $Re\varphi_n(\tau_j) \neq 0, Im\varphi_n(\tau_j) \neq 0, j = 1, 2, 3, 4$. We now construct the MMS-estimator $\hat{\theta}$, based on the auxiliary estimator $\hat{\theta}^*$ with components

$$\alpha^* = ln\frac{|\varphi_n(\tau_1)|}{|\varphi_n(\tau_2)|}/\vartheta\frac{\tau_1}{\tau_2},$$

$$\lambda^* = |\varphi_n(\tau_3)/\tau_3^{\alpha^*}|,$$

$$\beta^* = -\frac{2}{\pi\alpha^*} arctg \frac{I_m\varphi_n(\tau_4)}{Re\varphi_n(\tau_4)}.$$

With the help of (3.72) we construct the MMS-estimator $\hat{\vartheta}$. The estimator $\hat{\vartheta}$, in general, takes values from a larger set than (3.68). Therefore, let us introduce a new estimator $\bar{\theta} = (\bar{\alpha}, \bar{\beta}, \bar{\lambda})$ with components

$$\bar{\alpha} = \begin{cases} 0, \hat{\alpha} \leq 0 \\ \hat{\alpha}, 0 < \hat{\alpha} < 2, \\ 2, \hat{\alpha} \geq 2, \end{cases} \qquad \bar{\beta} = \begin{cases} -1, \hat{\beta} \leq 1, \\ \hat{\beta}, -1 < \beta < 1, \\ 1, \hat{\beta} \geq 1, \end{cases} \qquad \bar{\lambda} = \hat{\lambda}. \quad (3.73)$$

The asymptotic behavior of $\bar{\vartheta}$ is described by the following assertion.

Theorem 3.3 Let the positive numbers $t_1, \cdots, t_k$ such that $\det \mathbf{1}(\vartheta; \mathcal{L})$. Then the estimator $\bar{\vartheta}$ defined by (3.73) enjoys the properties:

(i) $\bar{\vartheta} \xrightarrow{P} \vartheta$

(ii) $\sqrt{n}(\bar{\vartheta} - \vartheta)$ is asymptotically normal $\mathbf{N}(0, 1)^{-1}(\vartheta; \mathcal{L})$.

(iii) the convergence of the law of $\sqrt{n}(\hat{\vartheta} - \vartheta)$ is uniform in $\mathcal{F}_0$.

Remark 3.3 In the case of a strictly geo-random variable with $0 < \alpha < 1$ the constructed estimator $\hat{\vartheta}$ is not asymptotically efficient for the normalization $\sqrt{n}$ is not exact in this case. Since in all known examples of asset returns data the distribution tails are always thinner enough to allow the existence of a finite first moment, we can, without loss of generality, assume that $\alpha > 1$ in applying theorem 3.3.

For the proof of Theorem 3.3 we refer to Klebanov, Manija and Melamed (1986).

3.5 Statistical Inference for Laplace–Weibull Mixture Models

In this section we consider inference on mixture distributions that incorporate members from both geometric stable and alternative stable laws. In section 2.3 we have already discussed a "contaminated" geometric stable law leading to mixture distributions. Here we address estimation of mixture models and statistical inference. In the next section we summarize an empirical application to real-estate prices in Paris. "Stability" properties and rate-of-convergence issues are discussed in some detail in an appendix at the end of chapter 7[4]. We use the notations from section 2.3. The pdf of mixture model

---

[4]The material in this chapter is based on Rachev and SenGupta (1992, 1993).

$\Lambda_\pi(x) = \pi\Lambda(x) + (1-\pi)W(x)$, see (2.97), is

$$
\begin{aligned}
p(x; \pi, \lambda, \mu, \gamma) &:= p(x; \underline{\psi}) \\
&= \pi f_1(x; \lambda) + (1-\pi)f_2(x; \mu, \gamma), 0 \leq \pi \leq 1,
\end{aligned}
$$

where

$$f_1(x; \lambda) = \frac{\lambda}{2}\exp\{-\lambda|x|\}, \qquad \lambda > 0, \tag{3.74}$$

and

$$f_2(x; \mu, \gamma) = \frac{\gamma\mu}{2}|x|^{\gamma-1}\exp\{-\mu|x|^\gamma\}, \quad \gamma > 1, \ \mu > 0. \tag{3.75}$$

Suppose random sample $X_1, \ldots, X_n$ from the above distribution is observed. There does not exist any nontrivial sufficient statistic for $\underline{\psi}$. Also, because $f_2(\cdot)$ is not a member of the exponential family, the standard approach of obtaining the maximum likelihood estimator cannot be used. However, the general EM algorithm can be employed. The resulting estimating equations at the $(m+1)$st stage are

$$\pi_j^{(m+1)} = \frac{1}{n}\sum_{i=1}^n \omega_{ij}(\underline{\psi}^{(m)}), \quad j = 1, 2, \quad \pi_1 \equiv \pi, \ \pi_2 \equiv 1 - \pi,$$

$$\omega_{ij}(\underline{\psi}^{(m)}) = \pi_j^{(m)}\frac{f_j(x_s)}{P(x; \psi^{(m)})} \tag{3.76}$$

$$\frac{1}{\lambda^{(m+1)}} = \frac{1}{n\pi_1^{(m+1)-1}}\sum_{i=1}^n \omega_{ij}(\underline{\psi}^{(m)})|x_i|, \tag{3.77}$$

$$\frac{1}{\gamma^{(m+1)}} - \left[\sum \omega_{i2}(\psi^{(m)})\ln|x_i|\right]\left[\frac{|x_i|\gamma^{(m+1)}}{\sum \omega_{i2}(\psi^{(m)})|x_i|\gamma^{(m+1)}} - \frac{1}{n\pi_2^{(m+1)-1}}\right] = 0 \tag{3.78}$$

$$\frac{1}{\mu^{(m+1)}} = \frac{1}{n\pi_2^{(m+1)-1}}\sum_{i=1}^n \omega_{i2}(\underline{\psi}^{(m)})|x_i|\gamma^{(m)}. \tag{3.79}$$

As can be done when solving the likelihood equations for the parameters of a Weibull distribution, (3.78) is written in terms of $\gamma^{(m+1)}$ as the only unknown parameter at the $(m+1)$st stage. An iterative method can then be employed to solve for $\gamma^{(m+1)}$. Once $\gamma^{(m+1)}$ is given, $\mu^{(m+1)}$ can be obtained from (3.79). Hence, at each stage we need to iteratively solve for $\gamma^{(\cdot)}$ and $\mu^{(\cdot)}$.

In Model (3.75) Laplace density $f_1(x; \lambda)$ is to be understood as the main underlying density with Weibull density $f_2(x; \mu, \gamma)$ as a possible contaminant. One wants to test H_0: Absence of mixture (i.e., $p \equiv f_1$) against H_1: Presence of Mixture distribution for X. The test needs to be derived depending on whether one of the crucial parameters $\pi \in [0, 1]$ and $\gamma \geq 1$ can be considered as a nuisance parameter or if both need to be represented in the parametric

formulation of H_0. This leads to interesting and diverse situations. Considering the four possible cases for λ and μ, namely:
(i) λ and μ both known,
(ii) $\mu = \mu_0$ known, λ unknown,
(iii) $\lambda = \lambda_0$ unknown, μ unknown, and
(iv) λ and μ both unknown,
a variety of tests can be established.

Case 1: $\gamma = \gamma_0 > 1$ known. For all cases (i)-(iv), H_0 and H_1 above reduce to H_{01}: $\pi = 1$ and H_1: $\pi < 1$ respectively.
(i) Let $\mu = \mu_0$ and $\lambda = \lambda_0$ be known. Considering appropriate one-sided derivative the locally most powerful (LMP) test given by,

$$\omega : \sum_{i=1}^{n} \left. \frac{\partial \ln p(x_i, \psi)}{\partial \pi} \right|_{\pi=1} > c_0$$

reduces to

$$\omega : T^* = \frac{1}{\sqrt{n}} \sum_{i=1}^{n} [(\gamma_0 - 1) \ln |x_i| - \mu_0 |x_i|^{\gamma_0} + \lambda_0 |x_i|] > C. \qquad (3.80)$$

Note that T^* is easily to computed and asymptotically normally distributed under both H_0 and H_1.
(ii) Though λ is a nuisance parameter, unfortunately here and also for (iii) below, no reduction is available through similarity or invariance. There does not even exist any nontrivial sufficient statistic. Nevertheless, it can be shown that all the five conditions for the validity of Neyman's C_α test hold, provided $\gamma \leq K < \infty$. Let

$$T^* = \left[\sum \frac{\partial \ln p(x_i, \psi)}{\partial \pi} - a_1^0 \sum \frac{\partial \ln p(x_i, \psi)}{\partial \lambda} \right]_{\pi=1}. \qquad (3.81)$$

Unfortunately, because λ and π are not orthogonal, a_1^0, the regression coefficient of the first term on the second, does not vanish.
Define $Z_n^* = \hat{T}^*/\hat{\sigma}_0(T^*)$, where $\sigma_0(T^*)$ is the standard deviation of T^* computed under H_0, and $\hat{T}^*$ and $\hat{\sigma}_0(T^*)$ are computed by replacing the unknown parameter λ in T^* and σ_0 by any root-n consistent estimator, e.g., the maximum likelihood estimator, under H_0. Then, the test becomes,

$$\omega : Z^* > C_1. \qquad (3.82)$$

For any sequence $\pi^* = \{\pi_n\}$ such that $\pi_n \sqrt{n} \to \tau$, the asymptotic value of the power of the test is given by

$$1 - \frac{1}{\sqrt{2\pi}} \int_{-\infty}^{\tau_a} \exp\left\{ -\frac{1}{2}(t - \sigma_0\tau)^2 \right\} dt.$$

Among all tests Z_n^{**} for H_0: $\pi = 1$ with asymptotic level of significance α, for whatever sequence of alternatives $\pi_n > 0$ with $\pi_n \to \pi_0 = 1$, and whatever fixed $\lambda > 0$,

$$\underline{\lim}[\text{Power}\{Z_n^*(\pi_n, \lambda)\} - \text{Power}\{Z_n^{**}(\pi_n, \lambda)\}] \geq 0.$$

Test Z_n^* is in this sense an asymptotically locally most powerful test.

(iii) Because nuisance parameter μ is present only under H_{11}, Neyman's C_α test fails to be applicable here—the requirement of a root-n consistent estimator of μ under H_{01} is meaningless. Consider, however, T^* from (i) and rewrite it as $T^*(\mu_0)$. Let $T^*(\mu)$ be standardized such that $S(\mu) = \{T^*(\mu) - E(T^*(\mu)]/[(T^*(\mu))]^{1/2}$ has asymptotically a standard normal distribution under H_{01}. We rejected H_{01} for large values of $S(\mu_0)$. Assume that $\mu \in [L, U]$. Then, $S(\mu)$ is continuous on $[L, U]$ with a continuous derivative (except possibly for a finite number of jumps in the derivative) and forms a Gaussian process. Then we reject H_0 for large values of

$$M = \sup\{S(\mu) : L \leq \mu \leq U\}. \tag{3.83}$$

To obtain the cut-off points, use bound

$$P\{\sup S(\mu) \geq c : L \leq \mu \leq U\} \leq \phi(-c) + \exp\left\{-\frac{1}{2}c^2\right\} \int_L^U [-\rho_{11}(\mu)]^{1/2} d\mu/2\pi,$$

where ϕ denotes the normal cdf $\rho_{11}(\mu) = [\partial^2 \rho(\phi, \mu)/\partial\phi^2]_{\phi=\mu}$, $\rho(\phi, \mu) = \text{corr}\{S(\phi), S(\mu)\}$. An estimate of the significance probability is given by

$$\Phi(-M) + V \exp\left\{-\frac{1}{2}M^2\right\} \bigg/ (8\pi)^{1/2},$$

where M denotes the maximum of $S(\mu)$ and V the total variation,

$$\begin{aligned} V &= \int_L^U |T(\mu)| d\mu \\ &= |S(\mu_1) - S(L)| + \sum_{i=1}^{n-1} |S(\mu_{i+1}) - S(\mu_i)| + |S(U) - S(\mu_n)|, \end{aligned}$$

$T(\mu) \equiv \partial S(\mu)/\partial\mu$, with $\mu_1, \ldots, \mu_n$ ($n < \infty$) being the successive turning points of $S(\mu)$.

(iv) No statistical test is known for this situation. We propose to combine approaches (ii) and (iii) above. Consider the C_α-test statistic $\hat{T}^* \equiv \hat{T}^*(\gamma_0, \mu_0, \hat{\lambda})$ from (ii). Letting $S^*(\mu) = \hat{T}^*(\gamma_0, \mu, \hat{\lambda})$ we can proceed exactly as in (iii) above with $S(\mu)$ being replaced by $S^*(\mu)$.

Case 2: $\pi \in (0, 1)$ known. H_0 and H_1 reduce to H_{02}: $\gamma = 1$ and H_{12}: $\gamma > 1$ provided that $\lambda = \mu$. Thus, knowledge of λ and/or μ needs to be incorporated in the hypotheses.

(i) Here the common value of $\lambda = \mu$ is known and, say, equal to 1. Then, H_{02} reduces to $H_{02}^1: \gamma = 1$.

$$\omega : \sum_{i=1}^{n} \left. \frac{\partial \ln p(x_i, \Psi)}{\partial \gamma} \right|_{\gamma=1} > c_0,$$

i.e.,

$$\omega : T_1 \equiv \sum_{i=1}^{n} \ln |x_i| (1 - |x_i|) > C. \qquad (3.84)$$

T is simple in form; and it is easy to simulate its null distribution, to get the percentage points. Further, $T/\sqrt{n}$ is asymptotically normally distributed under both H_0 and H_1.

(ii) $\mu = \mu_0$ known, λ unknown and (iii) $\lambda = \lambda_0$ known, μ unknown. H_0 now becomes the multiparameter hypothesis $H_{02}^2(H_{02}^3): \gamma = 1, \lambda = \mu_0 \ (\mu = \lambda_0)$. An optimal multiparameter test can be obtained by using the locally most mean powerful unbiased (LMMPU). The test is given by

$$\omega : T_2 \equiv \sum_{t=1}^{2} \ddot{L}_{tt}(x, \psi_0) - cL(x, \psi_0) - \sum_{t=1}^{2} c_t \dot{L}_t(x, \psi_0) \geq 0, \qquad (3.85)$$

where $L \equiv \prod_{i=1}^{n} p(x_1, \psi)$, $\psi = (\gamma, \lambda)$, $\psi_0 = (1, \mu_0)$ for case (ii) and $(1, \lambda_0)$ for case (iii) and c, c_1 and c_2 are to be determined from

$$\int_{\omega} L(x, \psi_0) = \alpha$$

and

$$\int_{\omega} \dot{L}_t(x, \psi_0) = 0, \quad t = 1, 2.$$

Note that $\sqrt{n}T_2$ can be explicitly computed and, is asymptotically normally distributed under both H_0 and H_1. This test is locally optimal for all sample sizes in the sense that among all locally unbiased tests it maximizes at ψ_0, the mean curvature of the power hypersurface. Further, this LMMPU test, φ possesses the property that for any other locally unbiased test φ^*, there exists an $r_0 > 0$ (depending on φ^*) such that

$$\int_{S_r} \beta_\varphi(\psi) d\psi > \int_{S_r} \beta_{\varphi^*}(\psi) d\psi, \quad r < r_0, \ S_r = \{\psi : |\psi - \psi_0| < r\},$$

where β_ξ is the power function of the test ξ. One could also use other multiparameter tests for testing simultaneously the hypotheses $\gamma = 1$ and $\mu = \lambda \ (\lambda = \mu_0)$; e.g., a step-down test could be used. Then, however, the exact level of significance any optimality property of such a test is not known.

(iv) Both λ and μ are unknown. H_0 now becomes $H_{02}^4: \gamma = 1$, $\mu = \lambda$, which is a composite hypothesis; and, hence, the previous optimal LMP test can no longer be used. Standard multiparameter large-sample tests (e.g., likelihood ratio, Wald's or Rao's tests, which are all asymptotically equivalent) can be explored. However, the test statistics need not have closed forms. For example, for the likelihood ratio test, even the maximum likelihood estimator of p is not available in closed form.

Case 3: Both π and γ are unknown, but $\pi \in [L, U] \subset (0, 1)$. The testing problem is still identifiable and H_0 reduces to $H_{03}: \gamma = 1$, provided that $\lambda = \mu$. This is exactly the same situation as in Case 2 above with π being an additional nuisance parameter. Thus, the same approaches as for Case 2 (i)-(iv) can be used here with the modification described in Case 1 (iii) now applied to π. For example, T_1 and T_2 of (3.83) and (3.84), which now become functions of the unknown π, should be replaced by

$$\tilde{S}_1 = \sup\{S(\pi): L \leq \pi \leq U\}$$

and

$$\tilde{S}_2 = \sup\{S_2(\pi): L \leq \pi \leq U\},$$

respectively, where $S_1(\pi)$ and $S_2(\pi)$ are standardized versions of $T_1(\pi)$ and $T_2(\pi)$.

Case 4: Both π and γ are unknown, $\pi \in [0, 1]$.

(i)(a). Suppose $\gamma > 1$ but γ is otherwise unknown. This greatly simplifies the situation. Further, let H_0 specify $H_0: p = f_1(\lambda_0)$, λ_0 given, i.e., $H_0 \equiv H_{04}^1: \pi = 1, \lambda = \lambda_0$. This reduces to a case of "strongly identifiable" mixtures and is easier to handle. For example, one may use the likelihood ratio test to test the single hypothesis H_{04}^1. However, even under this special case, the classical distribution theory of the log likelihood ratio statistic does not hold. We no longer have asymptotically a χ^2 distribution. Rather the likelihood ratio statistic is distributed as a certain functional $W^2 I_{\{W > 0\}}$, where $W = \sup\{T(\mu, \gamma)\}$ and $T(\cdot)$ is a Gaussian process with zero mean and covariance kernel depending on the true value λ_0 under H_0. If $\mu = \mu_0$ is known, we simply replace $T(\mu, \gamma)$ by $T(\mu_0, \gamma)$.

(i)(b). Suppose $\lambda = \mu$ but the common value is unknown. This results greatly simplifies the situation. H_0 reduces to

$$H_0 \equiv \overline{H}_{04} = \overline{H}_{04}^{1(1)} \cup \overline{H}_{04}^{1(2)} \cup (\overline{H}_{04}^{1(1)} \cap \overline{H}_{04}^{1(2)}),$$

where $\overline{H}_{04}^{1(1)}: \pi = 1$ and $\overline{H}_{04}^{1(2)}: \gamma = 1$. Note that $\overline{H}_{04}^{1(1)}$ and $\overline{H}_{04}^{1(2)}$ can be tested by suitably modifying the methods already discussed above, because the value of λ (and hence $\mu = \lambda$) can be easily estimated under $\overline{H}_{04}^{1(1)}$ and $\overline{H}_{04}^{1(2)}$; while the nuisance parameter $\lambda(\pi)$ may be dealt with as in Case 1 (iv). However, we now also need to test $\overline{H}_{04}^{1(1)} \cap \overline{H}_{04}^{1(2)}$, i.e., the multiparameter composite hypotheses $\pi = 1$ and $\gamma = 1$ with the nuisance parameter $\lambda = \mu$. This calls for a multiparameter generalization of Neyman's C_α test.

(ii) and (iii). Both of these cases require modification of $\overline{H}_{04}^{1(2)}$ and can be dealt with analogously. For (ii) ((iii)) we have $\overline{H}_{04}^{2(2)}$ ($\overline{H}_{04}^{3(2)}$): $\gamma = 1, \lambda = \mu_0$

$(\mu = \lambda_0)$. Treating π as known, the LMMPU test for this hypothesis can be derived. This can then be used to construct $T^*(\pi)$ from which a test can be obtained as in Case 1 (iii).

(iv). All parameters π, γ, μ, and λ are unknown and no constraint (assumption) is imposed on the usual parameter space. We now face the problem of nonidentifiability. H_0 is represented by $H_0 \equiv H_{04}^4$: $H_{04}^{4(1)} \cup H_{04}^{4(2)} \cup (H_{04}^{4(1)} \cap H_{04}^{4(2)})$, where $H_{04}^{4(1)}$: $\pi = 1$, $H_{04}^{4(2)}$: $\gamma = 1$ and $\mu = \lambda$.

A simple ad hoc test based on the pivotal parametric product (P^3),

$$P^3 = (\pi - 1)\{(\gamma - 1)^2 + (\mu - \lambda)^2\},$$

is now described. Observe that H_{04}^4 holds if and only if $P^3 = 0$ and under alternative H_1 we have $P^3 < 0$. We propose rejecting H_0 ($\equiv H_{04}^4$) for small values of $\hat{P}^3$, where $\hat{P}^3$ is obtained from P^3 by replacing the parameters by their consistent estimators (in case efficient estimators are not easily available). The cut-off points need to be determined by simulation. In many cases, tests based on P^3's are L-optimal. However, it has not yet been able to establish this property for testing Laplace-Weibull mixtures.

Rachev and SenGupta (1993) summarize an empirical investigation of monthly changes in prices of apartments in Paris using Laplace-Weibull mixtures. They examined average prices of one–bedroom apartments over the period 1984-89, i.e., 60 months. Employing the EM algorithm described above they estimated the parameters π, x, λ and μ and obtained the results shown here in

Table 3.2 EM–Estimates for the parameters of (3.75).
for certain apartments in Paris:
$\psi = (\pi, \gamma, \lambda, \mu)'$, $\hat{\psi} = (\hat{\pi}, \hat{\gamma}, \hat{\lambda}, \hat{\mu})'$

	$n = 70$		$n = 173$	
	ϵ	$\hat{\psi}$	ϵ	$\hat{\psi}$
π	0.01	0.85	0.001	0.852
γ	0.01	5.00	0.001	5.070
λ	0.10	8.00	0.010	7.970
μ	0.10	45.00	0.010	45.390

Table 3.2 shows the estimates of the parameters; number of iterations needed for convergence n and the preassigned value e such that the iteration terminates if the absolute difference between two successive estimates is smaller than this value. Using several different sets of starting values they found that in all cases the algorithm converged to almost the same estimates. They also simulated 60 observations from (3.75) with the parameters being assigned the values of the corresponding estimators for $n = 173$. They show a

Q–Q plot exhibiting almost a straight line and report that the quantile plots for observed and simulated data sets were fairly close.

3.6   Tail Estimation of the Stable Index α

A number of recent studies have used the Hill estimator (see Hill (1975)) to measure the tail thickness of financial data and inferred from its estimates the maximum moments of the data (see, for example, Koedijk, Schafgans and de Vries (1990), Jansen and deVries (1983), Phillips (1993)). Assuming the right tail of a distribution is asymptotically Pareto, i.e., for large x, $1 - F(x) \approx cx^{-\alpha_P}$ ($\alpha_P > 0$, $c > 0$), the Hill estimator attempts to measure tail thickness α_P[5]. Given a sample of n observations, $X_1, X_2, \ldots, X_n$, the Hill estimator is given by

$$\hat{\alpha}_{\text{Hill}} = \frac{1}{(1/k) \sum_{j=1}^{k} \ln\left(X_{n+1-j:n}\right) - \ln X_{n-k:n}} \qquad (3.86)$$

with standard error

$$\widehat{STD}\left(\hat{\alpha}_{\text{Hill}}\right) = \frac{k\hat{\alpha}_{\text{Hill}}}{(k-1)(k-2)^{1/2}}, \qquad k > 2,$$

where $X_{j:n}$ denotes the jth order statistic of sample $X_1, \ldots, X_n$.

If the right tail of the distribution is asymptotically Pareto, i.e., for large x, $1 - F(x) \approx cx^{-\alpha_P}$, then, given an appropriate choice of k, $\hat{\alpha}_{\text{Hill}}$ provides an estimate of Pareto tail index, α_p. Recall that the Pareto distribution possesses absolute moments of order less than α_P. Because for $0 < \alpha < 2$ the Pareto distribution is in the domain of attraction of the α-stable Paretian law, i.e., the right and left tails are of Pareto type with tail index α, the Hill estimator is also commonly used to estimate the stable index α.

Moreover, it was shown by Mason (1982) that the Hill estimator is consistent for distributions in the (max-) domain of attraction of the (max-) type extreme value distributions $e^{-x^{-\alpha}}$. These include, among others, the Student's t, Pareto and stable Paretian distributions. Goldie and Smith (1987) proved its asymptotic normality, i.e., $\left(\hat{\alpha}_{\text{Hill}}^{-1} - \alpha^{-1}\right)k^{1/2} \sim \text{N}\left(0, \hat{\alpha}^{-2}\right)$, for large values of n and $k = k(n)$, so that standard inference procedures can be used (see, for example, Koedijk, Schafgans and de Vries (1990), and Lux (1995)). The rate at which $k(n)$ increases to infinity is specified in the main result of Goldie and Smith (1987); see also Hall (1982) and Hall and Welsh (1984). Further details and references regarding the consistency of the Hill estimator

---

[5]The results in this section are due to Mittnik and Rachev (1995) and Mittnik, Paolella and Rachev (1998b).

can be found in Dekkers, Einmahl and de Haan (1989) and Dekkers and de Haan (1993).

Integer k indicates where the tail area of the empirical distribution is considered to "start". The choice of k involves a tradeoff, because it must be sufficiently small so that $X_{n-k:n}$ is in the tail of the distribution; but if too small, the estimator will lack precision. This is illustrated in Figure 3.1, which shows the behavior of $\hat{\alpha}_{\text{Hill}}$ and $\hat{\alpha}_{\text{Hill}} \pm 2\widehat{STD}\left(\hat{\alpha}_{\text{Hill}}\right)$, for $k = 20, 40, \ldots, 980$, with $n = 1,000$ observations generated from a Pareto distribution with $\alpha_p = 1.7$. We see that a large range of k-values yield estimates very close to the true value of 1.7, indicated by the solid line, but there is low precision for small k's.

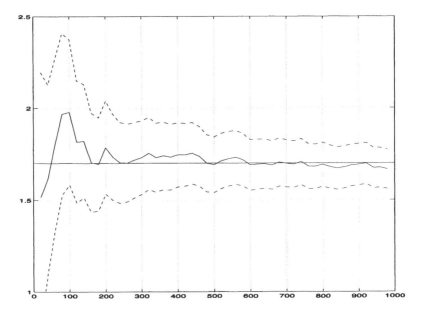

Fig. 3.1 Hill Estimates for Pareto Sample with $\alpha = 1.7$ and $n = 1000$.(Adapted from: Mittnik, Paolella and Rachev (1998b))

Figure 3.2 differs from Figure 3.1 in that the data come from an α-stable distribution with index $\alpha = 1.7$. Here, the Hill estimator performs quite differently. As in the Pareto case, r^{th} moments of an α-stable distribution exist only for $r < \alpha$. We see that for all $k < n/3$, which would be reasonably deemed to lie in the tail of the distribution, one would falsely conclude that $\alpha > 2$, which erroneously implies the existence of finite variance and, hence, the rejection of the stable Paretian hypothesis.

There are numerous examples in the literature where the Hill estimator delivers tail-index estimates which are greater than 2, causing authors to reject the α-stable hypothesis. As an example, based on simulation evidence,

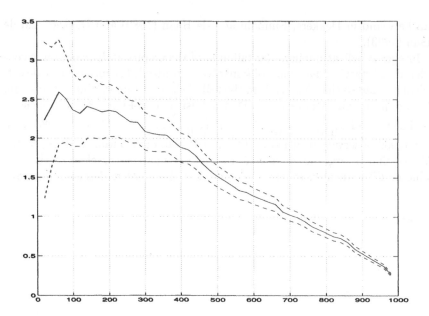

Fig. 3.2 Hill Estimates for α-stable Sample with $\alpha = 1.7$ and $n = 1000$.(Adapted from: Mittnik, Paolella and Rachev (1998b))

as well as the recommendation of DuMouchel (1983), Loretan and Phillips not exceeding 10 percent of the sample size and conclude that tail indexes of returns on certain stocks and foreign exchange rates lie between 2.5 and 4.0. Their simulations, however, involved values of the tail index α between 0.5 and 100, and thus not α-stable samples in particular. In another applied paper, Lux (1995, p. 15) claims that, based on "...the Monte Carlo simulations of other authors", taking k to be approximately 15% of sample size is appropriate for α-stable data with index α between 1 and 2. Using k values of 15%, 10%, 5%, and 2.5%, he reports the resulting Hill estimates for various German stock returns, and concludes that in all cases, $\alpha > 2$, and thus the α-stable hypothesis can be rejected. In light of Figure 3.2, it is clear that the Hill estimator with k between 2.5 and 15 percent of the sample size will severely overestimate α and lead to false conclusions when applied to α-stable data.

An alternative tail index estimator, proposed by Pickands (1975), takes the form

$$\hat{\alpha}_{\text{Pick}} = \frac{\ln 2}{\ln\left(X_{n-k+1:n} - X_{n-2k+1:n}\right) - \ln\left(X_{n-2k+1:n} - X_{n-4k+1:n}\right)}, \ 4k < n.$$

More recently it has been discussed in Drees (1996), and Rosen and Weissman (1996). The Pickands estimator is based on the assumption that for a large value, u, the conditional probability of X_i given that $X_i \geq u$ is of the form

$$P(X_i \geq u + x \mid X_i \geq u) = \frac{1 - F(u + x)}{1 - F(u)} \approx \left(1 + \frac{x}{a\alpha}\right)^{-\alpha},$$

for $\alpha > 0$, $a > 0$, and $x > 0$.

Because the Pickands estimator performs poorly in estimating the tail index for α-stable data, Mittnik and Rachev (1996a) introduced a series of possible modifications of the Pickands tail index estimator based on the Bergström expansion. Bergström (1952) (see also Janicki and Weron, 1994) gives the following asymptotic expansion of the standard symmetric α–stable distribution function, $S_\alpha(x)$,

$$S_\alpha(x) = 1 + \frac{1}{\pi} \sum_{m=1}^{\infty} (-1)^m \frac{\Gamma(\alpha m)}{m!} x^{-\alpha m} \sin \frac{\alpha m \pi}{2}, \qquad \text{as } x \to \infty. \qquad (3.87)$$

Given the sample $X_1, \ldots, X_n$, Mittnik and Rachev (1996a) use (3.87) and propose a tail estimator for the stable index by truncating the infinite sum

$$\frac{j-1}{n} = \frac{1}{\pi} \sum_{m=1}^{\infty} (-1)^{m+1} \frac{\Gamma(\hat{\alpha} m)}{m!} X_{n-j+1:n}^{-\hat{\alpha} m} \sin \frac{\hat{\alpha} m \pi}{2}. \qquad (3.88)$$

Truncation of (3.88) at $m = 1$ leads, for $j = k$ and $j = 2k$, to

$$\frac{k-1}{n} \approx c_\alpha X_{n-k+1:n}^{-\hat{\alpha}}, \qquad \frac{2k-1}{n} \approx c_\alpha X_{n-2k+1:n}^{-\hat{\alpha}},$$

which, for $k \to \infty$ and $k/n \to \infty$, implies

$$\hat{\alpha}_{\text{UP}} = \frac{\ln 2}{\ln X_{n-k+1:n} - \ln X_{n-2k+1:n}}. \qquad (3.89)$$

Estimator (3.89) is sometimes referred to as the unconditional Pickands tail estimator. In our setting, the stable law has "unconditionally" the series representation (3.87), which, when truncated after the first term, gives "unconditional" Pareto tails and leads to the estimator, $\hat{\alpha}_{\text{UP}}$. As such, the Pareto-type estimator $\hat{\alpha}_{\text{UP}}$ might be preferred to the original Pickands estimator, $\hat{\alpha}_{\text{Pick}}$. Simulation results indeed confirmed that, under the stable assumption, $\hat{\alpha}_{\text{Pick}}$ yields very poor estimates of index α, relative to $\hat{\alpha}_{\text{UP}}$.

The new tail estimator investigated here is obtained by truncating (3.88) at $m = 2$ and finding $\hat{\alpha}, \hat{c}_1$, and $\hat{c}_2$ as the solution to

$$\frac{jk-1}{n} \approx c_1 X_{n-jk+1:n}^{-\alpha} + c_2 X_{n-jk+1:n}^{-2\alpha}, \qquad j = 1, 2, 3, 4. \qquad (3.90)$$

System (3.90) consists of four approximate equations with three unknowns, but, because c_1 and c_2 enter linearly, can be straightforwardly reduced to a system of two equations with only α being unknown. That is, defining

$$\mathbf{X}_1 = \left[\begin{array}{cc} X_{n-k+1:n}^{-\alpha} & X_{n-k+1:n}^{-2\alpha} \\ X_{n-2k+1:n}^{-\alpha} & X_{n-2k+1:n}^{-2\alpha} \end{array} \right], \quad \mathbf{X}_2 = \left[\begin{array}{cc} X_{n-3k+1:n}^{-\alpha} & X_{n-3k+1:n}^{-2\alpha} \\ X_{n-4k+1:n}^{-\alpha} & X_{n-4k+1:n}^{-2\alpha} \end{array} \right],$$

$$\text{(3.91)}$$

$$\kappa_1 = \left[\begin{array}{c} k-1 \\ 2k-1 \end{array} \right], \quad \text{and} \quad \kappa_2 = \left[\begin{array}{c} 3k-1 \\ 4k-1 \end{array} \right], \qquad (3.92)$$

solving the first two equations for c_1 and c_2, and substituting into the last two equations of (3.90), we have the following nonlinear two-equation system

$$\kappa_2 \approx \mathbf{X}_2 \mathbf{X}_1^{-1} \kappa_1. \qquad (3.93)$$

Expressions (3.90) and, hence, (3.93) differ from those of Mittnik and Rachev (1996a). In (3.90) they used exponent β instead of 2α, as implied by infinite series (3.88), to obtain a better approximation after truncation. In simulations, we found that restricting β to $\beta = 2\alpha$ adds numerical stability with virtually no loss in accuracy.

We found that estimating α via nonlinear least squares from

$$\kappa_2 = \mathbf{X}_2 \mathbf{X}_1^{-1} \kappa_1 + \epsilon \qquad (3.94)$$

yields very reliable estimates. We refer to the estimator implied by (3.93) as the *modified unconditional Pickands estimator*, denoted by $\hat{\alpha}_{\text{MUP}}$.

A further modification we considered was to extend (3.91) and (3.94) to include $r > 2$ equations, to obtain more smoothing for the α-estimate. For $r > 2$, there will be a tradeoff between the potential reduction in variance through additional overfitting, and possibly adding bias resulting from moving farther away from the tail. Simulations suggested that in terms of the MSE of $\hat{\alpha}$, there is little appreciable advantage in taking $r > 2$. Therefore, we consider only the case $r = 2$ below.

The third modification we considered stems from noting that the choice of κ_1 and κ_2 is rather arbitrary. We investigated the performance of the estimator using different choices for κ_1 and κ_2. It was found that the values as given in (3.92) worked the best, yielding a modest but consistent reduction in variance over other values tried.

These possible modifications notwithstanding, estimator $\hat{\alpha}_{\text{MUP}}$ still remains somewhat inoperational without guidance as to the choice of k. This issue, which has traditionally thwarted effective use of the Hill estimator, is addressed in the next section.

As noted earlier, Figure 3.2 clearly shows the dependence of $\hat{\alpha}_{\text{Hill}}$ on k when the underlying sample is drawn from a stable Paretian distribution. With such data, the $\hat{\alpha}_{\text{UP}}$ estimator displays precisely the same behavior, except that it has a noticeably higher variance than $\hat{\alpha}_{\text{Hill}}$. Ideally, for α-*stable data*, estimator $\hat{\alpha}_{\text{MUP}}$ would behave as either $\hat{\alpha}_{\text{Hill}}$ or $\hat{\alpha}_{\text{UP}}$ do with Pareto data. However, $\hat{\alpha}_{\text{MUP}}$ also varies with k. Despite this, it will be seen to possess several decisive numerical advantages over both $\hat{\alpha}_{\text{Hill}}$ and $\hat{\alpha}_{\text{UP}}$. As all three estimators under consideration do in fact recover the true α for some value of k, one might postulate that an optimal choice of k, in terms of a function in n and α, could be found for each estimator. We denote these functions by $k_{\text{Hill}}(n, \alpha)$, $k_{\text{UP}}(n, \alpha)$, and $k_{\text{MUP}}(n, \alpha)$, for the respective estimators. If these functions are "not too dependent" on α, they could be applied in practice, where α is unknown. Determination and discussion of these k functions is considered next.

Although the asymptotic properties of the Hill estimator are well known, little can be said about its small sample performance. As noted, with α-stable data, both $\hat{\alpha}_{\text{Hill}}$ and $\hat{\alpha}_{\text{UP}}$ do not display anything resembling their asymptotic behavior—even for sample sizes in excess of 10,000. Simulation experiments, on the other hand, can provide an easy and accurate way to assess any desired characteristic of the estimators; in our case, we wish to model the optimal choice of k for a given sample size, n, and stable Paretian index, α. In fact, small scale simulations of this sort have already been conducted by Koedijk and Kool (1992) for Student's t data. These authors considered the 3 sample sizes $N = 107, 215$, and 431, as required for a specific example, and $\alpha = 1, 2, 3, 4$, where α corresponds to the degrees of freedom of the t distribution.

For 12 sample sizes (between 100 and 10,000) and 11 values of α (between 1 and 2), we simulated 1200 samples of symmetric α stable random variates and computed the three estimators $\hat{\alpha}_{\text{Hill}}$, $\hat{\alpha}_{\text{UP}}$ and $\hat{\alpha}_{\text{MUP}}$ using their appropriate ranges of k. We only considered α-values between 1 and 2 because values below 1 do not seem to be of much relevance in practice. The algorithm of Chambers et al. (1976), as implemented in Splus, Version 3.1, was used to generate the samples.

Figure 3.3 gives an idea of the performance of the three estimators. The solid curve in each panel plots for each k the $\hat{\alpha}$–values when averaged over the 1200 realizations, along with ± 2 times the corresponding sample or Monte Carlo standard errors. For each estimator we see that the magnitude of the standard error is inversely proportional to k, as would be expected. Observe how the top panel, corresponding to the Hill estimator, resembles a smoothed version of Figure 3.2. From the bottom panel, one sees that the MUP estimator gives rise to appropriate α-estimates for two k-values, the first of which occurs for very small k (i.e., very far in the tail) where the estimator exhibits a high variance;[6] the second "crossing" possesses a much lower variance, and is the one we make use of.

For all the (n, α)-combinations considered, there always existed a small neighborhood of k values which was virtually linear, and "crossed" the true value of α. Using linear interpolation, the optimal values of k were computed, and presented in Table 3.3 for each of the three estimators. For example, either from Table 3.3 or Figure 3.3, these values are seen to be 425, 170, and

---

[6]Contrary to what the depicted standard errors suggest, the estimator is, in fact, always positive, but highly skewed in this k region.

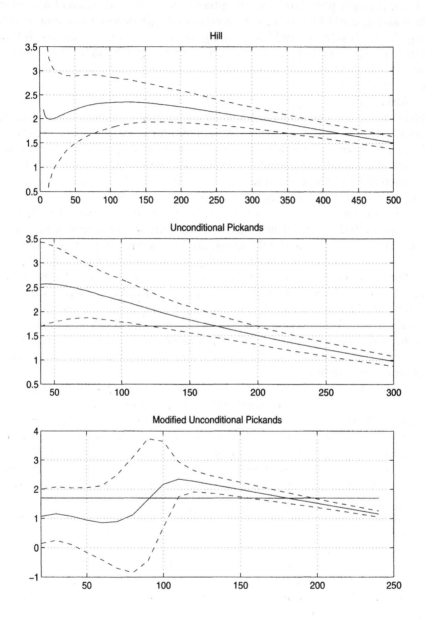

Fig. 3.3 Monte Carlo Performance of Estimators for $n = 1000$ and $\alpha = 1.7$.(Adapted from: Mittnik, Paolella and Rachev (1998b))

181, for the Hill, unconditional Pickands, and MUP, respectively. Table 3.4 shows their corresponding Monte Carlo standard errors, multiplied by 1000.

One striking result reported in Table 3.3 is that the values of $k_{\text{Hill}}(n, \alpha)$ estimates are much larger than expected, particularly for a *tail* estimator. Regarding the standard deviations, we see that both the MUP and Hill estimators clearly dominate the UP estimator. It appears that for $1.0 \leq \alpha \leq 1.3$, the MUP estimator possesses a lower standard error than Hill; but for larger α, Hill would indeed be preferred, when the correct value of k (and, hence, that of α itself) is known. Certainly in practice, the true value of α is not known, so that this result is only of theoretical interest. The most important finding is that $k_{\text{MUP}}(n, \alpha)$, the optimal k for the MUP estimator, is far less dependent on α than is the case with either the Hill or Pickands estimator.

The last column in Table 3.3 indicates the range (maximum minus minimum k value) which k/n takes on for the values of α between 1.0 and 1.95. We see that for larger sample sizes, the range for the MUP estimator is almost 10 times smaller than that of the unconditional Pickands, and almost 20 times smaller than that of the Hill estimator. Also noteworthy is that the range for MUP is almost exactly linear in n, the sample size, whereas for both Hill and Pickands, the range is somewhat nonlinear in n, and increases as a percentage of n as n increases.

Of secondary interest is the nature of the dependency of k on α. For all three estimators, k depends nonlinearly on α. Given a particular sample size, $k_{\text{MUP}}(n, \alpha)$, peaks somewhere between $1.3 < \alpha < 1.4$ and is, to some extent, symmetric over the range $\alpha \in [1.0, 1.95]$. Indeed, k for $\alpha = 1.0$ and $\alpha = 1.95$ are almost identical. $k_{\text{Hill}}(n, \alpha)$ on the other hand reaches its maximum between 1.9 and 1.95, and appears to change with sample size. As α decreases to 1.0, k decreases substantially. Although $k_{\text{UP}}(n, \alpha)$ peaks at approximately $\alpha = 1.6$, it is highly skewed, dropping off dramatically as $\alpha \to 1.0$.

Without further apriori knowledge about α—except that it lies in the interval $[1, 1.95]$—Table 3.3 could be used to deliver a plausible *range* of k–values for each of the three estimators, given sample size n. For example, for the Hill estimator with $n = 1000$ the minimum value for k to be considered is 121 and corresponds to $\alpha = 1.0$. Likewise, the maximum k–value is 439; it corresponds to $\alpha = 1.9$. Hence, for the Hill estimator, k–values ranging from 121 and 439 would have to be used, whereas for $\hat{\alpha}_{\text{UP}}$ and $\hat{\alpha}_{\text{MUP}}$, k–ranges 58 to 171 and 171 to 187, respectively, would be necessary. Notice that the range corresponding to the MUP estimator is substantially smaller than those of Hill and unconditional Pickands. In view of these k–ranges one would expect that the performance of the MUP estimator will be appreciably better. Figure 3.4 illustrates this by showing the "cloud" of α–estimates for each of the three estimators for α equal to 1.3 and 1.7. Sample size $n = 1000$ was used, so that the k–ranges in the plot correspond to the aforementioned values. For case $\alpha = 1.3$, Hill delivers estimates between about 1.0 and 1.8, whereas MUP stays between 1.2 and 1.6. The unconditional Pickands estimator, with its

Table 3.3 Optimal k/n Ratio for Tail Estimators.

n	Est.	1.0	1.1	1.2	1.3	1.4	α 1.5	1.6	1.7	1.8	1.9	1.95	Range
	Hill	.23	.29	.35	.37	.39	.41	.42	.43	.44	.44	.44	.21
100	UP	.12	.14	.16	.17	.18	.18	.18	.18	.18	.17	.17	.06
	MUP	.20	.20	.21	.20	.20	.20	.20	.19	.19	.19	.18	.03
	Hill	.168	.240	.324	.348	.380	.408	.420	.424	.432	.440	.440	.272
250	UP	.080	.116	.148	.156	.168	.172	.176	.172	.172	.168	.164	.096
	MUP	.184	.188	.192	.192	.192	.192	.188	.184	.180	.180	.176	.016
	Hill	.140	.214	.308	.348	.378	.404	.418	.424	.432	.440	.438	.300
500	UP	.072	.102	.134	.154	.164	.170	.172	.170	.168	.168	.164	.100
	MUP	.178	.182	.188	.188	.188	.188	.186	.182	.178	.176	.172	.016
	Hill	.121	.197	.295	.342	.378	.402	.417	.425	.431	.439	.438	.318
1000	UP	.058	.090	.126	.150	.164	.169	.171	.170	.167	.166	.162	.113
	MUP	.173	.181	.186	.187	.187	.186	.184	.181	.177	.174	.171	.016
	Hill	.0907	.1947	.2927	.3413	.3767	.4007	.4160	.4247	.4313	.4387	.4380	.3480
1500	UP	.0480	.0900	.1267	.1493	.1620	.1680	.1700	.1693	.1673	.1653	.1620	.1220
	MUP	.1727	.1807	.1853	.1867	.1867	.1860	.1833	.1800	.1767	.1740	.1707	.0160
	Hill	.0715	.1845	.2880	.3405	.3765	.3995	.4160	.4245	.4315	.4380	.4380	.3665
2000	UP	.0370	.0835	.1260	.1485	.1615	.1680	.1700	.1690	.1670	.1650	.1620	.1330
	MUP	.1710	.1800	.1845	.1865	.1865	.1855	.1830	.1800	.1770	.1735	.1710	.0155
	Hill	.0660	.1808	.2860	.3408	.3764	.3992	.4156	.4244	.4312	.4380	.4384	.3724
2500	UP	.0356	.0872	.1252	.1488	.1620	.1672	.1696	.1688	.1668	.1648	.1620	.1340
	MUP	.1708	.1796	.1840	.1864	.1864	.1848	.1832	.1800	.1764	.1732	.1708	.0156
	Hill	.0627	.1793	.2843	.3403	.3763	.3990	.4157	.4243	.4317	.4377	.4380	.3753
3000	UP	.0323	.0860	.1253	.1480	.1617	.1670	.1697	.1687	.1670	.1647	.1620	.1374
	MUP	.1703	.1793	.1843	.1863	.1863	.1850	.1830	.1797	.1767	.1733	.1707	.0160
	Hill	.0703	.1795	.2815	.3392	.3760	.3980	.4142	.4242	.4315	.4375	.4380	.3677
4000	UP	.0335	.0825	.1250	.1485	.1610	.1670	.1693	.1688	.1670	.1645	.1618	.1358
	MUP	.1698	.1792	.1848	.1860	.1852	.1848	.1828	.1798	.1765	.1732	.1705	.0162
	Hill	.0660	.1768	.2814	.3390	.3750	.3980	.4140	.4240	.4318	.4372	.4382	.3722
5000	UP	.0302	.0804	.1250	.1482	.1610	.1674	.1692	.1686	.1670	.1644	.1618	.1390
	MUP	.1696	.1792	.1840	.1860	.1860	.1846	.1824	.1796	.1764	.1730	.1706	.0164
	Hill	.0597	.1727	.2810	.3388	.3748	.3982	.4140	.4240	.4318	.4373	.4382	.3785
6000	UP	.0275	.0797	.1243	.1482	.1610	.1673	.1692	.1685	.1668	.1645	.1618	.1417
	MUP	.1695	.1790	.1840	.1860	.1857	.1847	.1828	.1795	.1767	.1730	.1705	.0165
	Hill	.0400	.1671	.2801	.3385	.3747	.3981	.4139	.4239	.4317	.4373	.4381	.3981
10000	UP	.0245	.0778	.1240	.1479	.1607	.1674	.1692	.1686	.1668	.1644	.1617	.1447
	MUP	.1693	.1788	.1839	.1858	.1858	.1846	.1825	.1795	.1764	.1729	.1704	.0165

(Adapted from: Mittnik, Paolella and Rachev (1998b))

Table 3.4 Standard Errors of Tail Estimators (multiplied by 1000).

n	Est.	1.0	1.1	1.2	1.3	1.4	α 1.5	1.6	1.7	1.8	1.9	1.95
	Hill	219	205	201	217	219	230	233	258	267	280	282
100	UP	328	331	296	314	347	366	380	454	455	458	480
	MUP	181	197	217	222	240	255	297	309	318	330	372
	Hill	159	139	129	142	139	147	148	159	162	166	179
250	UP	240	216	202	213	209	225	225	252	271	268	295
	MUP	123	131	131	143	153	162	171	186	199	211	223
	Hill	119	103	95	99	97	104	102	110	118	120	131
500	UP	169	155	151	145	149	148	164	168	188	190	198
	MUP	87	95	96	99	110	114	124	133	146	155	160
	Hill	89	79	69	69	70	73	73	76	82	86	90
1000	UP	137	113	109	105	104	111	119	119	131	133	140
	MUP	65	65	66	71	75	81	87	91	99	109	111
	Hill	86	64	58	56	56	59	62	62	67	71	72
1500	UP	121	93	90	83	85	88	95	98	106	113	116
	MUP	53	53	56	57	62	65	70	74	81	88	91
	Hill	84	56	50	50	49	50	54	55	58	62	62
2000	UP	122	85	77	74	74	74	80	87	92	97	98
	MUP	46	45	49	51	54	54	61	65	70	78	77
	Hill	79	52	45	44	44	45	48	50	51	54	57
2500	UP	109	73	68	64	65	66	71	80	80	84	88
	MUP	41	42	42	45	47	52	54	58	62	67	72
	Hill	74	48	41	40	41	41	44	45	47	50	51
3000	UP	102	70	64	59	61	63	67	71	74	77	80
	MUP	37	37	39	42	44	46	50	54	56	61	64
	Hill	61	42	35	35	35	36	37	39	41	43	45
4000	UP	89	63	55	51	52	54	54	62	64	68	70
	MUP	32	32	32	35	39	40	42	47	48	54	57
	Hill	58	37	32	31	31	32	34	34	37	39	40
5000	UP	84	57	50	44	44	48	50	55	59	60	63
	MUP	29	29	30	31	34	35	38	41	45	48	51
	Hill	55	34	30	29	28	29	31	32	34	35	37
6000	UP	77	52	45	41	42	45	46	49	51	55	59
	MUP	26	27	28	29	31	33	35	38	40	44	48
	Hill	54	27	23	22	22	23	24	24	26	26	29
10000	UP	64	41	35	31	33	35	36	38	41	43	47
	MUP	20	20	21	22	24	26	27	29	32	34	38

(Adapted from: Mittnik, Paolella and Rachev (1998b))

higher variance, provides virtually no guidance to a reasonable estimator of α. For case $\alpha = 1.7$, both Hill and unconditional Pickands deliver estimates, which are very often well above 2.0, erroneously disqualifying the α-stable as a candidate distribution, as has often been done in empirical studies referred to in the Introduction. The vast majority of the MUP estimates, on the other hand, are comfortably between 1.5 and 2.0. Clearly, even with the correct range of k, both Hill and Pickands are seen to be poor estimators of the tail index for α-stable data.

Rather than deriving $\hat{\alpha}$'s for each k in the k-range and computing some form of average, we consider using the estimate of α delivered from just a single value of k, which depends only of the sample size, n. An inspection of Table 3.3 shows a near linear relationship between the sample size and the "optimal" k-value for the MUP estimator. Note that Hill and UP do not exhibit this linear relationship. Thus, for the MUP estimator, we fit a linear model relating k and n, choosing the values of k to be the average of the row entries in Table 3.3. Doing so, we obtain twelve (k, n) pairs, for which an OLS regression yields

$$k_{\text{MUP}}(n) \approx 1.70 + 0.179n \qquad (3.95)$$

with an R^2-value of 0.9999, justifying the linearity assumption.

Figure 3.5 shows a boxplot of the MUP estimates from 1000 replications with $n = 1000$, using the choice of k dictated from (3.95). We see that the estimator performs acceptably well for $\alpha \leq 1.7$, but tends to slightly underestimate α-values near two. Although this bias remains even for larger sample sizes, it still delivers reasonable estimates for sample sizes as small as 100.

To investigate the extent to which the normal approximation is adequate in finite samples, the estimator was computed for 1000 replications of α-stable data with $\alpha = 1.7$ and sample sizes $n = 100, 250, 500, 1000, 2500$, and 5000. For each of the 6 sample sizes, the p-values associated with the Lagrange multiplier test of normality (see Jarque and Bera, 1987; and Deb and Sefton, 1996) are presented in Table 3.5. The p-values steadily increase as n increases; and for $n = 5000$, the normal assumption cannot be rejected at the 0.05 level. Although the asymptotic properties of the MUP estimator remain to be investigated, asymptotic normality appears to be a reasonable assumption.

Table 3.5 (Asymptotic) p–values for the Normality Test of the MUP Estimator.

Sample Size	100	250	500	1000	2500	5000
p-value	0	0	5×10^{-12}	0.010	0.023	0.137

Figure 3.6 provides a visual impression of a kernel density estimate (dashed lines) along with the superimposed fitted normal curve (solid line) of the simulated MUP estimates for $n = 1000$. Although for this case, the p-value of the Lagrange multiplier test was only 0.010, we see that for $n = 1000$,

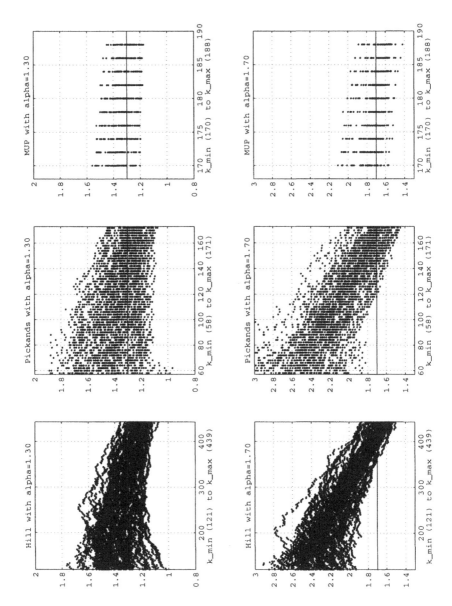

Fig. 3.4   Cloud Plot of Estimators Using $n = 1000$. (Adapted from: Mittnik, Paolella and Rachev (1998b))

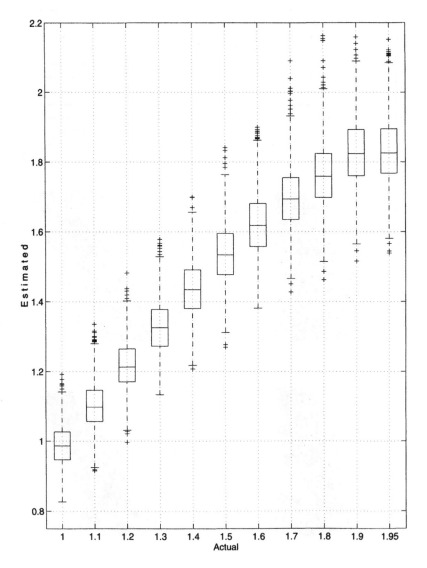

Fig. 3.5 Performance of the MUP Estimator over $1 \leq \alpha \leq 1.95$ Using $n = 1000$.(Adapted from: Mittnik, Paolella and Rachev (1998b))

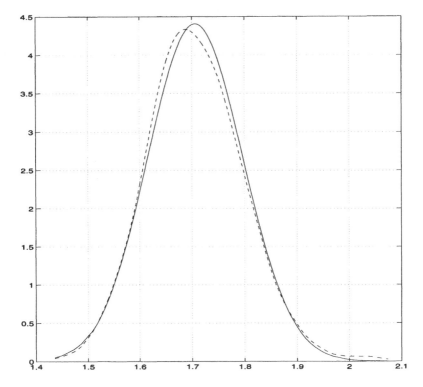

Fig. 3.6 Kernel (- - -) and Fitted Normal (—) Density of the MUP Estimator for
$\alpha = 1.7$ and $n = 1000$.
(Adapted from: Mittnik, Paolella and Rachev (1998b))

the normal approximation appears adequate for standard inference. Thus,
the error bounds in Table 3.4 could be used in conjunction with the $\hat{\alpha}_{MUP}$
estimator for establishing approximate confidence intervals and hypothesis
testing.

3.7 FFT-approximation and ML-Estimation of stable Paretian laws

A major reason for the limited use of stable distributions in applied work is
due to the facts that there are, in general, no closed-form expressions for its
probability density function and that numerical approximations are nontrivial
and computationally demanding, see Section 1.1 and 3.4. Therefore, maximum likelihood (ML) estimation of stable Paretian models is rather difficult
and time consuming. In this section, we study the problem of ML estima-

tion using Fast Fourier Transform (FFT) to approximate the stable density functions[7].

The first Fourier Transform (FFT) for the parameters of stable densities were described by DuMouchel (1971), see also Zolotarev (1986a). Following Zolotarev's (1966, 1986a) – representations, Brorsen and Yang (1990) and Nolan (1997a) developed ML-estimation algorithms based on numerical approximation and integration of stable non-Gaussian densities. These algorithms are very burdensome from a computational viewpoint. As a consequence, maximum likelihood (ML) estimation algorithm based on such approximations are difficult to implement and—especially for the large high-frequency data sets encountered in finance—time consuming in their execution.

Because of the computational complexity, there are few Monte Carlo studies in the literature comparing ML estimation with alternative approaches, such as the widely used quantile-based estimator of McCulloch (1986). Calder and Davis (1998) perform a Monte Carlo study of the estimation of several ARMA models with symmetric stable disturbances comparing the least squares, least absolute deviation and ML estimators of the ARMA parameters. However, they focus solely on the ARMA parameter estimates and do not analyze distributional parameter estimates. Brorsen and Yang (1990), for example, report results from a Monte Carlo experiment based on *one* replication for *one* particular parameter setting. Hence, it is not clear whether or not the performance of the ML estimator justifies the high burden it carries.

Next we shall address this issue. We start with numerical approximatiion of the stable density. Recall first the stable characteristic function (ch.f.):

$$\varphi(t, \alpha, \beta, c, \mu) = \exp\left\{i\mu t - |ct|^\alpha \left[1 - i\beta \frac{t}{|t|}\omega(|t|, \alpha)\right]\right\}, \qquad (3.96)$$

where $0 < \alpha \leq 2$, $-1 \leq \beta \leq 1$, $c > 0$, $\mu \in \mathbf{R}$, and

$$\omega(|t|, \alpha) = \left\{ \begin{array}{ll} \tan \frac{\pi\alpha}{2}, & \text{for} \quad \alpha \neq 1, \\ -\frac{2}{\pi} \log |t|, & \text{for} \quad \alpha = 1. \end{array} \right.$$

As before we denote the stable Paretian distribution by $S_\alpha(\beta, \mu, c)$ or, in short, S_α. If $\beta = 0$, $S_\alpha(0, \mu, c)$ is symmetric; if $\alpha = 2$, the cf reduces to $\varphi(t) = \exp\{i\mu t - c^2 t^2\}$, which is that of the normal distribution with mean μ and variance $2c^2$; and $S_1(0, \mu, c)$ coincides with the Cauchy distribution with median μ and semi-interquartile range c. Defining

$$z = \frac{x - \mu}{c}, \qquad (3.97)$$

---

[7]The results in this section are due to Mittnik, Rachev, Doganoglu and Chenyao (1999), Mittnik, Doganoglu, Chenyao (1999), and Doganoglu, Mittnik (1998).

the S_α pdf $f(x; \alpha, \beta, c, \mu)$ can be standardized such that

$$f(x; \alpha, \beta, c, \mu) = \frac{1}{c} f(z; \alpha, \beta, 1, 0). \tag{3.98}$$

Then, for $c = 1$, $\mu = 0$ and $\alpha \neq 1$, the cf becomes

$$\varphi(t) = \exp\left\{ -|t|^\alpha + i\beta t|t|^{\alpha-1} \tan \frac{\pi\alpha}{2} \right\}. \tag{3.99}$$

An approach to approximating the S_α probability density function (p.d.f.) by applying FFT to cf (3.96) has been considered by DuMouchel (1971). However, he combined it with Bergtröm's (1952) series expansion. The ML estimation procedure presented here avoids any series approximation or direct integration. It is solely based on a computationally efficient Fast Fourier Transforms (FFT)-based pdf approximation which has been proposed in Chen (1991) and detailed in Mittnik, Doganoglu and Chenyao (1999).[8]

To briefly summarize the FFT-based approximation, recall that the pdf can be written in terms of the ch.f. as

$$f(x; \alpha, \beta, c, \mu) = \frac{1}{2\pi} \int\limits_{-\infty}^{\infty} e^{-ixt} \varphi(t; \alpha, \beta, c, \mu) dt. \tag{3.100}$$

The integral in (3.100) can be calculated for N equally-spaced points with distance h, such that $x_k = \left(k - 1 - \frac{N}{2}\right) h$, $k = 1, \ldots, N$. Setting $t = 2\pi\omega$, (3.100) implies

$$f\left(\left(k - 1 - \frac{N}{2}\right) h\right) = \int\limits_{-\infty}^{\infty} \varphi(2\pi\omega) e^{-i2\pi\omega(k-1-\frac{N}{2})h} d\omega. \tag{3.101}$$

The integral in can be approximated by

$$f\left(\left(k - 1 - \frac{N}{2}\right) h\right) \approx s \sum_{n=1}^{N} \varphi\left(2\pi s \left(n - 1 - \frac{N}{2}\right)\right) e^{-i2\pi(n-1-\frac{N}{2})(k-1-\frac{N}{2})hs} \tag{3.102}$$

or, setting $s = (hN)^{-1}$,

$$f\left(\left(k - 1 - \frac{N}{2}\right) h\right) \approx s(-1)^{k-1-\frac{N}{2}}$$
$$\times \sum_{n=1}^{N} (-1)^{n-1} \varphi\left(2\pi s \left(n - 1 - \frac{N}{2}\right)\right) e^{-\frac{i2\pi(n-1)(k-1)}{N}}. \tag{3.103}$$

---

[8] Doganoglu and Mittnik (1999) present a polynomial approximation for asymmetric stable Paretian densities for $1.2 \leq \alpha \leq 2$ which could be used alternatively for calculating the p.d.f. values.

The sum in (3.103) can be efficiently computed by applying FFT to sequence

$$(-1)^{n-1}\varphi\left(2\pi s\left(n-1-\frac{N}{2}\right)\right), \quad n=1,\ldots,N.$$

Normalizing the kth element of this sequence by $s(-1)^{k-1-\frac{N}{2}}$, we obtain the p.d.f. value for each grid point. By substituting (3.99) into (3.103), with $t = 2\pi s(n-1-N/2)$, standardized pdf values can be calculated and, via (3.98) and (3.97), transformed to any desired parameter combination.

To balance accuracy and CPU time for different stable parameter settings, the tuning parameters N (the number of summands for integral approximation) and h (grid spacing) should be set in accordance with the desired accuracy level. Because N is expressed in terms of a power of 2, say $N = 2^q$, accuracy is determined by the choice of q and h. The accuracy of the approximation in 3.103 improves when the integration limits are large. The size of the region, over which the integration is performed, is equal to $2\pi/h$ and does not depend on q. Therefore, h should be sufficiently small. Another reason for choosing a small value for h, is to attain accuracy in the interpolation step, when pdf values are calculated for unevenly spaced samples.

Recall that $s = (hN)^{-1}$ is the spacing in frequency domain. Because the cf contains oscillating terms, q should be large enough so that the approximation involves a sufficient number of points. The smaller h, the larger q has to be, thus increasing the computational burden. For the standardized distribution, most of the probability mass is concentrated in the interval $(-4, 4)$.[9] For financial data empirical studies show that typically $1.6 < \alpha < 1.9$. In these cases, suitable choices for h and q are possible without introducing an unreasonable computational burden. Our experiments, together with those reported in the next section, suggest that, for this range of α values, setting $h = 0.01$ and $q = 13$ leads to fast and sufficiently accurate approximations.

We compare the accuracy of the FFT-based approach with that of the Direct Numerical Integration (DNI) method. To perform the comparisons, we compute $S_\alpha(\beta, 0, 1)$ pdf values for $\alpha \in \{1.25, 1.50, 1.75\}$, $\beta \in \{0, \pm0.5, \pm1.0\}$ and $x \in \{0, 0.1, \ldots, 4.8, 4.9\}$. For the FFT-based method we set $h = 0.01$ and $q = 13, 16$. The pdf values for DNI method were generated with the executable Fortran program provided by Nolan.[10]

We used two distance measures to assess the proximity of the pdf values generated by the two algorithms. The first, denoted by D_1, is the *mean absolute deviation* of the vectors of the pdf values; the second, denoted by D_2, is the *maximum absolute deviation*. Letting y and z be two vectors of length

---

[9]For example, for $\alpha = 1.5$ and $\beta = 0$, the interval (-4.4) contains 94% of the probability mass.

[10]The program was downloaded from: http://www.cas.american.edu/~jpnolan.

Table 3.6 Difference Measures of DNI and FFT-based algorithms.

| | | | q | | |
| | | 13 | | 16 | |
α	β	$D_1 \times 10^{-5}$	$D_2 \times 10^{-5}$	$D_1 \times 10^{-5}$	$D_2 \times 10^{-5}$
	-1.0	4.502	5.4	0.346	0.7
	-0.5	4.680	5.7	0.378	0.9
1.25	0.0	4.864	6.5	0.330	1.7
	0.5	5.114	6.8	0.310	1.9
	1.0	5.000	5.7	0.270	0.9
	-1.0	1.290	1.8	0.242	0.6
	-0.5	1.292	1.9	0.202	0.6
1.50	0.0	1.340	2.4	0.162	1.1
	0.5	1.484	2.6	0.184	1.2
	1.0	1.476	2.5	0.112	1.1
	-1.0	0.260	0.3	0.002	0.1
	-0.5	0.260	0.3	0.000	0.0
1.75	0.0	0.276	0.3	0.000	0.0
	0.5	0.278	0.3	0.002	0.1
	1.0	0.298	0.4	0.002	0.1

(Adapted from: Mittnik, Doganoglu and Chenyao (1999))

K, then, D_1 and D_2 are given by

$$D_1 = \frac{1}{K} \sum_{i=1}^{K} |y_i - z_i|$$

and

$$D_2 = \max_{i=1,\dots,K} |y_i - z_i|,$$

respectively. Since Nolan's program reports the pdf values with six significant digits, we rounded our values to same number of digits.

The distance measures are presented in Table 3.6. Note that all entries in this table are multiplied by 10^{-5}. The results show that deviations between pdf values generated by the two methods can be found only in the last (i,e, sixth) digit. In fact, the magnitude of the differences suggests that the difference is partly due to rounding. As expected, the difference becomes smaller if q is larger. In addition, as α gets larger, even the approximation with $q = 13$ is sufficiently accurate. Note also that both D_1 and D_2 behave similiarly. Hence, both measures lead to the same conclusions.

We also compared both the DNI and the FFT-based method with the tabulated pdf values in Holt and Crow (1973). Obviously, one has the difficulty of choosing a benchmark in this situation, because all the results are based on approximations. The Holt-Crow tables report pdf values only up to the 4 digits and comparisons reveal that all three pdf values are in virtual agreement, justifying the use of either algorithm in empirical work.

Concerning the computational efficiency of the algorithms, there is no clear answer; it certainly depends on the particular application. The advantage of DNI is that, it is possible to calculate the pdf value for a specified x-value, while the FFT method intrinsically requires calculation of a set of pdf values, to obtain desired accuracy.

To assess computational efficiency of two methods, it is possible to make some approximate order-of-complexity calculations. Let us assume that pdf values for K irregularly-spaced x-values need to be generated. The proposed algorithm involves two steps to perform this task. First, pdf values for N evenly spaced x-values are generated; in the second step, the desired pdf values are computed via linear interpolation. The number of operations required for the first step is of order $N \log_2 N$. For the second step, at most N comparisons and K arithmetic operations are required. In total, the order of computational complexity of the algorithm will be $N \log_2 N$ for large N.

Because we are not aware of the exact computational implementation of the DNI performed in Nolan (1996), we can estimate its complexity only in a crude fashion. With DNI, one has to evaluate an integral for each of the K points. The limits of integration for each point are adaptively chosen according to the accuracy required. This leads to a varying number of operations for each of the integrations. Assuming that, on average, one needs I operations to evaluate each integral, the computation of K pdf values will be of order KI operations.[11]

One has to compare the order-of-complexity figures discussed above, to decide which algorithm will be more efficient for a particular application. For example, for $K = 1000$, the FFT-based method with $N = 2^{13}$ (i.e., $q = 13$), the order of complexity is given by $N \log_2 N = 2^{13} \log_2 2^{13} = 106496 \approx 10^5$. For the DNI method, with $I = 1000$, if we assume that the pdf values are accurately computed,[12] then the order of complexity will amount to $KI = 10^6$. Thus, for this example, one should expect the FFT-based method to be about ten times faster than DNI. However, it has to be re-emphasized that these numbers are very crude estimates.

Although the FFT-based approximation represents a significant improvement over the existing approximation methods as far as the computational complexity is concerned, it is still rather burdensome in situations requiring a large number of pdf evaluations. This is, for example, the case in iterative

---

[11]We strongly stress that this is only a crude estimate.

[12]For calculating the pdf values for small α's one will need more than 1000 points for the integral to converge. Similiarly, the computation of the pdf value for a large x-values requires I to be much larger, since the frequency of the oscillatory terms in the cf is proportional to x.

maximum–likelihood estimation procedures. Especially in applications in finance applications, where we encounter large sample sizes or, possibly, the need for fast on-line estimation, it is highly desirable to employ even faster pdf-evaluation routines. The polynomial approximation presented in this section accomplishes this.

Rather than working with standardized z-values (see (3.97)), we shift the arguments of the pdf by $\beta \tan \frac{\pi \alpha}{2}$ (see Samorodnitsky and Taqqu, 1994) and define

$$y := y(\alpha, \beta) := z - \beta \tan \frac{\pi \alpha}{2}. \tag{3.104}$$

This transformation locates the distribution such that for every α and β most of the probability mass lies in an interval around zero.

In designing the polynomial approximation procedure we use the fact that

$$f(-y; \alpha, \beta, c, \mu) = f(x; \alpha, -\beta, c, \mu), \tag{3.105}$$

which allows us to restrict our analysis to $\beta \in [0, 1]$.

For $\alpha = 2$, the stable Paretian density reduces to the normal density, whose exponential functional form admits a polynomial expansion in positive powers of y. On the other hand, for $\beta = 0$, as α moves towards 1, the pdf approaches the Cauchy density. In general, as $|y| \to \infty$ the tail behavior of the stable Paretian family can be approximated by $\kappa |y|^{-\alpha-1}$, where κ is a function of α and β. Thus, we can employ polynomials in negative powers of y for the tails; while polynomials in positive powers of y are employed for the region around the mode.

A straightforward approximation approach is to adopt the (finite) series expansion

$$f(y; \alpha, \beta, 1, 0) \approx \sum_{k=k_1}^{k_K} \sum_{l=l_1}^{l_L} \sum_{m=m_1}^{m_M} c_{klm} \alpha^k \beta^l y^m. \tag{3.106}$$

Given coefficients c_{klm}, (3.106) would allow us to easily calculate the pdf values for any (y, α, β)-combination. Coefficients c_{klm} can be obtained by constructing a linear system of equations from (3.106) with pdf values of relevant (y, α, β)-combinations being computed with the FFT-based procedure.

To express this system of linear equations compactly in matrix form, namely $p \approx Zc$, we specify a grid of N y-values, denoted by $N \times 1$ vector $\mathbf{y}$, for each (α_i, β_j)-combination of interest and denote the corresponding $N \times 1$ vector of FFT-approximated pdf values by $f_{ij} := f(\mathbf{y}; \alpha_i, \beta_j)$. Then, let $Y_{ij} := Y(\alpha_i, \beta_j)$ denote the $N \times M$ matrix whose typical (m, n)–element, $y_{m,n}(\alpha_i, \beta_j)$, corresponds to the nth grid value of y raised to power m,[13] i.e.,

$$Y_{ij} := \begin{bmatrix} y_1^{m_1}(\alpha_i, \beta_j) & \cdots & y_N^{m_1}(\alpha_i, \beta_j) \\ \vdots & & \vdots \\ y_1^{m_M}(\alpha_i, \beta_j) & \cdots & y_N^{m_M}(\alpha_i, \beta_j) \end{bmatrix}, \quad \begin{array}{l} i = 1, \ldots, T_\alpha, \\ j = 1, \ldots, T_\beta. \end{array}$$

---

[13] Note that, due to transformation (3.104), the entries in Y_{ij} depend on α_i and β_j.

Also, let a_i be a $1 \times K$ vector with powers of α_i,

$$a_i = [\alpha_i^0 \ \alpha_i^1 \ \dots \ \alpha_i^K] \qquad i = 1, \dots, T_\alpha; \qquad (3.107)$$

and let b_j be a $1 \times L$ vector containing powers of β_j,

$$b_j = [\beta_j^0 \ \beta_j^1 \ \dots \ \beta_j^L] \qquad j = 1, \dots, T_\beta. \qquad (3.108)$$

Then, (3.106) gives rise to

$$f_{ij} \approx Y_{ij} [I_M \otimes (a_i \otimes b_j)] c = Z_{ij} c, \qquad (3.109)$$

where c is the $KLM \times 1$ vector collecting coefficients c_{klm}; I_M denotes the $M \times M$ identity matrix; and $Z_{ij} := Y_{ij} [I_M \otimes (a_i \otimes b_j)]$. Combining the $T :=$ $T_\alpha T_\beta$ (α_i, β_j)-combinations and stacking the vectors and matrices in (3.109) appropriately, we obtain

$$f \approx Zc, \qquad (3.110)$$

where

$$f := [f'_{1,1} \dots f'_{T_\alpha,1} \ f'_{1,2} \dots f'_{T_\alpha,T_\beta}]'$$

denotes the $NT \times 1$ vector of stacked pdf values and

$$Z := [Z'_{1,1} \dots Z'_{T_\alpha,1} \ Z'_{1,2} \dots Z'_{T_\alpha,T_\beta}]'$$

the $NT \times KLM$ matrix with elements $\alpha_i^k \beta_j^l y_n^m (\alpha_i, \beta_j)$.

If the system of linear equations in (3.110) is overidentified (i.e., $NT >$ KLM), coefficient vector c could be derived by least squares methods. However, in practice, matrix Z tends to be large and ill-conditioned. This makes a direct derivation of coefficients c_{klm} via (3.110) rather infeasible—even when using stepwise methods.

To circumvent this problem, we derive coefficients c_{klm} in a two-stage procedure. In the first stage we fit a polynomial in y to the pdf values of a given (α_i, β_j)-combination, i.e.,

$$f_{ij} \approx Y_{ij} d(\alpha_i, \beta_j), \qquad i = 1, \dots, T_\alpha, \quad j = 1, \dots, T_\beta, \qquad (3.111)$$

where f_{ij} and Y_{ij} are defined as before; and $d(\alpha_i, \beta_j)$ is an $M \times 1$ vector of polynomial coefficients. Let $d_m(\alpha_i, \beta_j)$, $m = 1, \dots, M$, denote the mth entry of vector $d(\alpha_i, \beta_j)$. Then, as follows from (3.106), $d_m(\alpha_i, \beta_j)$ corresponds to the "coefficient" $c_{klm} \alpha_i^k \beta_j^l$ of monomial y^m. Next, we collect all $T = T_\alpha T_\beta$ $d_m(\cdot, \cdot)$–elements in $T_\alpha \times T_\beta$ matrix D_m, i.e.,

$$D_m := \begin{bmatrix} d_m(\alpha_1, \beta_1) & \dots & d_m(\alpha_1, \beta_{T_\beta}) \\ \vdots & & \vdots \\ d_m(\alpha_{T_\alpha}, \beta_1) & \dots & d_m(\alpha_{T_\alpha}, \beta_{T_\beta}) \end{bmatrix}, \quad m = m_1, \dots, m_M.$$

Then, in the second stage, we fit a polynomial function in α and β to the surface implied by D_m. Again, this can be done by an expansion of the form

$$d_m(\alpha_i, \beta_j) \approx \sum_{k=k_1}^{k_K} \sum_{l=l_1}^{l_L} \bar{c}_{klm} \alpha_i^k \beta_j^l, \quad i = 1, \ldots, T_\alpha, \quad j = 1, \ldots, T_\beta. \quad (3.112)$$

and approximating the coefficients $\bar{c}_{klm}$ by least squares. In matrix notation, (3.112) can be written as

$$\text{vec}(D_m) \approx (A \otimes B)\bar{c}_m, \quad m = m_1, \ldots, m_M, \quad (3.113)$$

where $A = (a_{ik})$ and $B = (b_{jl})$ are $T_\alpha \times K$ and $T_\beta \times L$ matrices with typical elements α_i^k and β_j^l, respectively, or, using the vector notation defined in (3.107) and (3.108),

$$A = \begin{bmatrix} a_1 \\ \vdots \\ a_{T_\alpha} \end{bmatrix} \quad \text{and} \quad B = \begin{bmatrix} b_1 \\ \vdots \\ b_{T_\beta} \end{bmatrix}.$$

Vector $\bar{c}_m$ is of dimension $KL \times 1$ and contains the coefficients to be derived in the second stage. Given coefficients $\bar{c}_{klm}$, pdf approximations are computed by evaluating $d_m(\alpha_i, \beta_j)$ via (3.112) and substitution into (3.111).

Least-squares techniques can be used to fit the coefficients $d_m(\alpha_i, \beta_j)$ and $\bar{c}_{klm}$ in each of the steps. In our experiments, this two-stage approximation procedure did not suffer from the numerical problems encountered in the direct polynomial approximation (3.106).

Rather than constructing one global approximation which is valid for all $y \in \mathbf{R}$, one may, as will be be done in the illustrative application below, specify different approximation schemes for different y-regions, in order to obtain a more parsimonious approximation. In this case one could be interested in having polynomial approximations that are continuously differentiable up to a certain degree. This can be accomplished by increasing the polynomial degrees accordingly and imposing appropriate restrictions when estimating the coefficients via least squares.

Employing the two-stage procedure we construct approximations for the stable Paretian density for $z \in [-10, 10]$, $\alpha \in [1.1, 2)$ and $\beta \in [-1, 1]$.[14] We have used an FFT grid which is implied by $N = 2^{16}$ and $h = 0.01$ (see Section 2).

Initial experiments indicated that high-order polynomials in α and β would be necessary to obtain reasonable approximations. Therefore, the y-range was divided into several subregions: a left tail region (L), a left center region (LC), a center region (C), a right center region (RC), and a right tail region (R). For

---

[14]Because of relationship (3.105), the calibration can be restricted to $\beta \in [0, 1]$. The approximation for $|y| > 10$ will be discussed later.

the center region, C, experiments suggested a polynomial in positive powers of y; for the left and right center regions, LC and RC, we used either a polynomial in positive powers of y or a mixed (positive and negative) power polynomial; for both the left and right tails, L and R, we used polynomials in negative powers of y. It turned out that the cutoff points for these regions have to be moved as α and β change, indicating that it is advantageous to partition the (α, β)-parameter space rather than using a single—potentially very complex—approximation for the whole (α, β)-space. Obviously, there is some degree of arbitrariness in the choice of these regions.

Table 3.7 presents the values of the tuning parameters and the specific partitions for the y-range and (α, β)-space.[15] It turned out that different regions of the (α, β)-space required different y-polynomial degrees, m_1 and m_M, to obtain approximations of similar accuracy. For the expansions in α and β we specified polynomials of identical degrees, i.e., in (3.112) we set $K = L$. Clearly, these tuning parameters were derived by limited trial-and-error experiments, mainly to illustrate the approximation procedure. We do not claim that they are optimal choices.

The approximation involves 11998 coefficients over all regions. The memory required to store them as a binary file in MATLAB is about 95KB. Obviously, execution time depends on the hardware configuration and the particular implementation of the algorithm. Compared to the FFT-based approximation the computational burden is reduced to about one tenth.[16]

To assess the performance of the approximation we use two measures. The first, denoted by D_1, is the *probability–weighted absolute deviation* of the polynomial approximation, denoted by $\tilde{f}_i$, and the FFT-based pdf values, f_i, i.e.,

$$D_1 = h \sum_{i=1}^{N} f_i |f_i - \tilde{f}_i|.$$

where h is the step size used in this calculation.[17] The second, denoted by D_2, is the *maximum absolute deviation*, i.e.,

$$D_2 = \max_{i=1,\dots,N} |f_i - \tilde{f}_i|.$$

---

[15]It turned out that no separate RC region was needed for $1.1 \leq \alpha \leq 1.4$.

[16]The following information may provide some indication of the execution time. The evaluation of 1000 pdf-values takes about one tenth of a second on a 300MHz Pentium II PC with 64MB RAM, when using an executable version of our MATLAB program that has not been optimized for speed.

[17]Multiplication by the step size h makes D_1 an approximation of

$$E(|f(\mathbf{y}, \alpha_i, \beta_j) - \tilde{f}(\mathbf{y}, \alpha_i, \beta_j)|) = \int_{-\infty}^{\infty} |f(\mathbf{y}, \alpha_i, \beta_j) - \tilde{f}(\mathbf{y}, \alpha_i, \beta_j)| f(\mathbf{y}, \alpha_i, \beta_j) dy.$$

Table 3.7 Tuning Parameters Settings for Two–Step Approximation.[a]

	α			
	1.1–1.4		1.4–1.7	1.7–2.0
	β 0.0–0.5	β 0.5–1.0	β 0.0–1.0	β 0.0–1.0
y-region: L	[-10,-3)	[-10,-3)	[-10,-3.1)	[-10,-4)
$\{m_1, m_M\}$	{-11,0}	{-11,0}	{-10,0}	{-10,0}
K	6	6	5	5
y-region: LC	[-3,-1.3)	[-3,-1.3)	[-3.1,-1.6)	[-4,-2)
$\{m_1, m_M\}$	{-2,11}	{-2,11}	{0,11}	{-2,11}
K	6	6	7	5
y-region: C	[-1.3,1.3]	[-1.3,1.3]	[-1.6,1.6]	[-2,2]
$\{m_1, m_M\}$	{0,17}	{0,17}	{0,17}	{0,17}
K	7	7	7	5
y-region: RC	NA	NA	(1.6,3.1]	(2,4]
$\{m_1, m_M\}$	NA	NA	{0,11}	{-2,9}
K	NA	NA	5	5
y-region: R	(1.3,10]	(1.3,10]	(3.1,10]	(4,10]
$\{m_1, m_M\}$	{-12,2}	{-12,2}	{-10,0}	{-10,0}
K	6	6	5	5

[a]The entries indicate the summation limits in polynomial approximation (3.106) (or equivalently (3.111) and (3.112)) which are associated with each of the five y–regions. Notation $\{m_1, m_M\}$ indicates that we use an y-polynomial of the form $\sum_{i=m_1}^{m_M} d_i y^i$ with m_1 possibly being negative. K refers to the degrees of the (α,β)–polynomial expansion in (3.112). The same degrees for α and β were used in each of the cases.

(Adapted from: Doganoglu and Mittnik (1998))

The tuning parameters reported in Table 3.7 were chosen such that the order of the maximum absolute approximation error measure, D_2, did not exceed 10^{-6}.

Figures 3.7 and 3.8 give a visual impression of how the approximations perform in terms of quantities D_1 and D_2 for different (α,β)-combinations.[18] As can be seen, there is only little systematic structure in the approximation errors. However, for larger α–values the average error tends to be smaller; and for large β–values there is an increase approximation errors. The pdf values we obtain match the four-decimal values reported in Holt and Crow (1973).

[18]These figures are based on the following grid of parameter values $\alpha = [1.125, 1.175, \ldots, 1.975, 1.999]$, $\beta = [0.025, 0.075, \ldots, 0.975, .999]$ and $z = [-10, -9.99, \ldots, 9.99, 10]$.

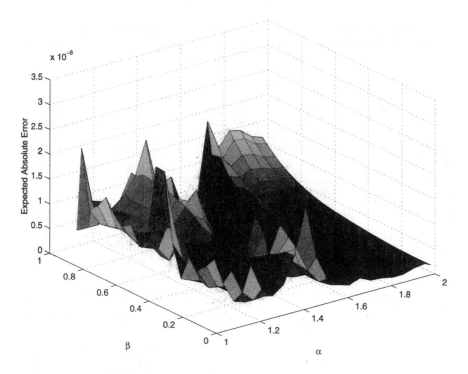

Fig. 3.7 Probability–Weighted Absolute Approximation Error.   (Adapted from: Doganoglu and Mittnik (1998))

The approximation procedure described so far was limited—after transformation (3.104)—to $z \in [-10, 10]$.[19] For the extreme tails outside this region, one may either use the Bergström series expansion, or a direct numerical integration method. In preliminary experiments we used the Bergström expansion up to term 15 as given in McCulloch (1996b), i.e.,

$$f(y; \alpha, \beta, 1, 0) \approx \sum_{k=0}^{15} s_k |y|^{-\alpha k - 1} \qquad (3.114)$$

with

$$s_k = \frac{-(-c^*)^k \Gamma(k\alpha)\alpha \sin\left[\frac{k\pi\alpha}{2}(1+\theta)\right]}{\pi(k-1)!},$$

where, in terms of the original parameters,

$$c^* = \left(1 + \beta^2 \tan^2 \frac{\pi\alpha}{2}\right)^{-\frac{1}{2\alpha}}$$

[19]This is, in fact, the practically relevant range. For example, for $\alpha = 1.2(1.9)$ and $\beta = 0$ it contains about 96.4%(99.9%) of the probability mass.

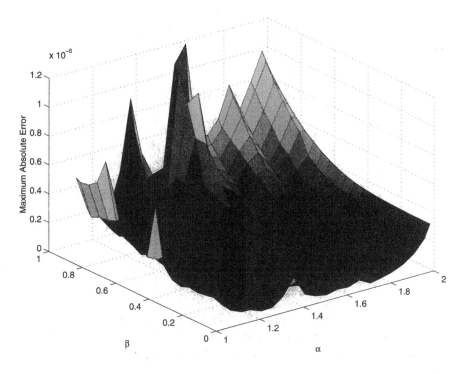

Fig. 3.8 Maximum Absolute Approximation Error. (Adapted from: Doganoglu and Mittnik (1998))

and

$$\theta = \frac{2}{\pi \alpha} \tan^{-1}\left(\beta \tan \frac{\pi \alpha}{2}\right).$$

For $\alpha > 1.2$, the deviations between the pdf values calculated by (3.114) and the FFT-based pdf values are also of the order of 10^{-6}. While for lower α–values, the tail approximation yields gross errors due to the explosion of the summands in (3.114). Other tail approximations (cf. Nikias and Shao, 1995, pp. 16) can be employed to overcome this problem.

The two-step polynomial-based procedure reduces the computational burden by a factor of about ten when compared to the FFT-based approximation.

We next develop the ML-estimation procedure based on the FFT-p.d.f. approximation. Let $X = (X_1, \ldots, X_T)$ be a vector of i.i.d. stable Paretian random variables, i.e., $X_i \overset{i.i.d.}{\sim} S_\alpha(\beta, c, \mu)$; and let $x = (x_1, \ldots, x_T)$ denote the corresponding vector of observations. Defining $\theta = (\alpha, \beta, c, \mu)'$, the ML estimate of θ is obtained by maximizing the log-likelihood function

$$\ell(\theta, x) = \sum_{i=1}^{T} \log f(x_i; \theta) \tag{3.115}$$

with respect to the unknown parameter vector θ.

DuMouchel (1973b) investigates the theoretical properties of the ML estimator for θ and shows its asymptotic normality under certain regularity conditions; i.e.,

$$\sqrt{T}(\hat{\theta} - \theta_0) \overset{d}{\to} N(0, I^{-1}(\theta_0)), \tag{3.116}$$

where "$\overset{d}{\to}$" stands for convergence in distribution and I denotes the Fisher information matrix

$$I(\theta_0) = -\mathrm{E}\left(\frac{\partial^2 \ell(\theta; X)}{\partial\theta\partial\theta'}\right), \tag{3.117}$$

which can be approximated either by using the Hessian matrix arising in the maximization or, as in Nolan (1997a), by numerical integration.

In our ML estimation algorithm we maximize log-likelihood function (3.115) numerically. Rather than employing constrained optimization, we estimate a transformed version of θ, say $\tilde{\theta} = (\tilde{\alpha}, \tilde{\beta}, \tilde{c}, \mu)'$, such that $\theta = h(\tilde{\theta})$. The transformation can take the form

$$\alpha = \frac{2}{1 + \tilde{\alpha}^2}, \qquad \beta = \frac{2 - \tilde{\beta}^2}{2 + \tilde{\beta}^2}, \qquad c = \tilde{c}^2. \tag{3.118}$$

In many applications it is assumed that first moments of X_i exist. Then, one may restrict $\alpha \in (1, 2]$ by adopting the transformation $\alpha = 1 + \frac{1}{1 + \tilde{\alpha}^2}$. With the parameter transformations in place and defining the gradient $\nabla_{\tilde{\theta}} h = \partial h/\partial \tilde{\theta}'$, (3.116) becomes

$$\sqrt{T}(\hat{\theta} - \theta_0) \overset{d}{\to} N\left(0, \nabla_{\tilde{\theta}} h I^{-1}(\tilde{\theta}_0)\nabla_{\tilde{\theta}} h'\right). \tag{3.119}$$

To investigate the performance of the FFT-based ML procedure and to compare it to that of the widely used quantile estimator of McCulloch (1986), we conduct a Monte Carlo study; for brevity, we denote both approaches by MLE and MCE, respectively. In their study, Brorsen and Yang (1990) restrict themselves to the *symmetric* case, and, as mentioned earlier, consider only one parameter setting and one replication. In Mittnik, Rachev, Doganoglu, and Chenyao (1999) our analysis is based on twelve different parameter combinations, namely $\alpha = 1.4, 1.6, 1.8, 1.9$ and $\beta = 0, 0.5, 0.9$ (in each case we set, without loss of generality, $c = 1$ and $\mu = 0$) and three sample sizes, $T = 250, 500, 1000$. For each of the 36 (α, β, T)-combinations we perform 400 replications. The pseudo-random stable Paretian variates were generated with the algorithm of Weron (1996).

In order to examine to what extent the MLE is capable of improving upon quantile-based MCE, we use the latter for obtaining starting values for the MLE iterations. Experimentation shows that the MLE procedure is rather robust with respect to the chosen starting values, so that Monte Carlo results should also be valid when starting values are determined by other intitial estimators, by grid search or by trial and error. In the estimation routine, the FFT tuning parameters in this section are initially set to $N = 2^{12}$ and

$h = 0.01$, so that the grid, whose endpoints are $\pm Nh/2$, covers $[-20.48, 20.48]$. In case there are (centered and scaled) observations outside this initial grid, we first increase N up to 2^{16}, so that the interval becomes [-327.68,327.68], and then, in case this is not sufficient, the grid width, h.

The simulation results are summarized in form of box plots. Figures 3.9 – 3.11 show the results for the estimates of the characteristic exponent, α, for the three sample sizes 1000, 500 and 250, respectively.[20] The box plots indicate that both the MCE and MLE are practically median-unbiased. However, the dispersion of the MCE is considerably larger than for MLE. For example, for $\alpha = 1.6$ and $\alpha = 1.8$, a range which is highly relevant for financial modeling, the MLE yields interquartile ranges (IQRs) which are about half the size of those of the MCE. Also, the sizes of the MLE IQRs hardly change with α; while the MCE IQRs tend to increase as α increases.

The simulation results for the estimates of skewness parameter β are summarized in Figures 3.12 – 3.14. The results for both estimators reflect the fact that the role of β vanishes as α approaches two. For example, for $\alpha = 1.9$ changes in skewness due to variation in β can hardly be detected visually. As a consequence, for both estimators the IQRs increase as α approaches two. In fact, for $\alpha = 1.9$ their range covers the permissible interval $\beta \in [-1, 1]$—even for sample size $T = 1000$. For α-values below 1.9 the MLE IQRs are smaller, especially for the larger sample sizes. With respect to the median-bias both estimators are compatible.

One aspect of the MLE is that it can get trapped during the iterative maximization at the β boundaries ± 1. This happens quite frequently in our simulations when $\beta = 0.9$. Thus, for applied work, the optimization algorithm should be modified such that it may escape corner solutions more easily. This is particularly relevant when MCE estimates are routinely used as starting values, because they, too, often yield to corner solutions for $\hat{\beta}$.

Figures 3.15 – 3.17 and 3.18 – 3.20 indicate that both estimators perform equally well for the scale parameter, c, and the location parameter, μ. The median-biases of both estimators are negligible; the dispersions of the estimates are similar, but always somewhat smaller in the case of the MLE.

As may be expected from the box plots, the MLE clearly dominates the MCE also in terms of the mean squared errors (MSEs) of the estimates for the four parameters (not reported here). This is mainly due to the low dispersion of the former, because, as with the median-biases, the mean-biases of the two estimators are negligible.

The Monte Carlo experiments indicate that the quantile-based McCulloch estimator yields rather precise point estimates. However, quantile-based estimators suffer from the fact that they cannot be employed in more general and, in practical work, more relevant models, which relax the i.i.d. assumption for

---

[20]In financial applications, commonly conducted with daily data, a sample size of 1000 is typically on the lower side of the sample sizes reported in the literature.

the data. Such i.i.d. violations are typically due to varying location and/or scale.

The ML estimation is easily modified to allow such generalizations. For example, in case of a regression model (see Blattberg and Sargent (1971), and Brorsen and Preckel (1993))

$$y_i = x_i\gamma + \varepsilon_i, \qquad i = 1, \ldots, T, \qquad (3.120)$$

with regression-coefficient vector γ and $\varepsilon_i \overset{iid}{\sim} S_\alpha(\beta, c, 0)$, the log-likelihood function (3.115) becomes

$$\ell(\gamma, \theta; \varepsilon) = \sum_{i=1}^{T} \log f(\varepsilon_i; \gamma, \theta) \qquad (3.121)$$

with $\varepsilon_i = y_i - x_i\gamma$ and $\theta = (\alpha, \beta, c)'$.

In time series analysis one often finds that the conditional mean of a series exhibits ARMA behavior, possibly affected by additional exogenous variables (ARMAX). In Chapter 1, for example, we estimated ARMA models driven by asymmetric stable Paretian distributions for several stock-index series. Let an ARMAX model be given by

$$y_t = \nu + \sum_{i=1}^{p} a_i y_{t-i} + \sum_{i=1}^{q} b_i \varepsilon_{t-i} + \sum_{i=0}^{r} c_i' x_{t-i} + \varepsilon_t, \qquad (3.122)$$

where x_{t-i} represents a vector of (lagged) exogenous variables and $\varepsilon_i \overset{iid}{\sim} S_\alpha(\beta, c, 0)$. Defining $a = (a_1, \ldots, a_p)'$, $b = (b_1, \ldots, b_q)'$ and $C = (c_1, \ldots, c_r)$, the conditional log-likelihood function is given by

$$\ell(\nu, a, b, C, \theta; \varepsilon) = \sum_{t=p+1}^{T} \log(\varepsilon_t; \nu, a, b, C, \theta), \qquad (3.123)$$

with $\varepsilon_t = y_t - \nu - \sum_i a_i y_{t-i} - \sum_i b_i \varepsilon_{t-i} - \sum_i c_i' x_{t-i}$ and, as in the regression model, $\theta = (\alpha, \beta, c)'$. The resulting ML estimates are conditional in the sense that we condition on the first p realizations $y_p, \ldots, y_1$ and set $\varepsilon_p, \ldots, \varepsilon_{p-q+1}$ to 0. Stationarity conditions, requiring the roots of the autoregressive polynomial $1 - a_1 z - a_2 z^2 - \ldots - a_p z^p$ to be greater than one in magnitude, can be imposed in the usual way during ML estimation.

A further—and in financial modeling more important—generalization is to allow for time-varying dispersion (volatility) when conditioning on past realizations, modeled by GARCH models, see Chapter 1. Recall the general form of a GARCH-stable model:

$$y_t = \mu_t + c_t u_t, \qquad (3.124)$$

$$c_t^\delta = \omega_0 + \sum_{i=1}^{r} \omega_i |y_t - \mu_t|^\delta + \sum_{i=1}^{s} \rho_i c_{t-i}^\delta, \qquad (3.125)$$

where μ_t may reflect a time varying location (e.g., an ARMAX structure). To guarantee positivity of c_t, restrictions $\omega_0 > 0$, $\omega_i \geq 0$ and $\rho_i \geq 0$ are typically enforced.[21] Here, u_t is a standardized innovation, i.e., $u_t = (y_t - \mu_t)/c_t \overset{iid}{\sim} S_\alpha(\beta, 1, 0)$. If $X \sim S_\alpha(\beta, c, \mu)$, the standardized random variable $Z = (X - \mu)/c \sim S_\alpha(\beta, 1, 0)$ has pdf $\frac{1}{c} f(Z; \alpha, \beta, 1, 0)$. Therefore, the conditional log-likelihood function is of the form

$$\ell(\omega, \rho, \theta_\mu, \theta; u_t) = \sum_{t=r+1}^{T} \left[\log f(u_t; \omega, \rho, \varphi_\mu, \theta) - \log c_t \right], \qquad (3.126)$$

where $u_t = (y_t - \mu_t)/c_t$ with $c_t = (\omega_0 + \sum_i \omega_i |y_t - \mu_t|^\delta + \sum_i \rho_i c_{t-i}^\delta)^{-\delta}$; $\omega = (\omega_0, \dots, \omega_r)'$; $\rho = (\rho_0, \dots, \rho_s)'$; θ_μ reflects the parameters required to model the conditional location, μ_t; and $\theta = (\alpha, \beta)'$.

It turns out[22] that the condition for stationarity for the conditional volatility equation of conventional GARCH models with standard normal innovations, namely

$$\sum_{i=1}^{r} \omega_i + \sum_{i=1}^{s} \rho_i \leq 1, \qquad (3.127)$$

has to be modified to

$$\lambda_{\alpha,\beta,\delta} \sum_{i=1}^{r} \omega_i + \sum_{i=1}^{s} \rho_i \leq 1, \qquad (3.128)$$

where, assuming $\alpha > 1$ and $\alpha > \delta$,

$$\lambda_{\alpha,\beta,\delta} = E|u_t|^\delta = \frac{(2-\delta)(1-\delta)}{\Gamma(3-\delta)\cos\frac{\pi\delta}{2}} \Gamma\left(1 - \frac{\delta}{\alpha}\right) \left(1 + \tau_{\alpha,\beta}^2\right)^{\frac{1}{2\alpha}} \cos\left(\frac{\arctan \tau_{\alpha,\beta}}{\alpha}\right),$$

with $\tau_{\alpha,\beta} = \beta \tan(\pi\alpha/2)$ (see also Chapter 1). Note that, the stationarity condition for GARCH models driven by stable Paretian innovations is more restrictive than under normal assumptions.

In conclusion, our study shows that Monte Carlo simulations demonstrate that FFT-based MLE procedure performs accurately and possesses less dispersion than the widely used quantile-based estimator of McCulloch (1986). It should be pointed out that the McCulloch estimator performs remarkably well, while, due to being a noniterative estimator, requiring little computational effort. However, a drawback of the quantile estimator is that it cannot obviously be extended to more complex estimation problems, such as regressions with stable Paretian disturbances, or ARMA and GARCH driven by stable Paretian innovations. In contrast, the ML estimator is easily modified to for allow such extensions.

---

[21] Nelson and Cao (1992) show that these restrictions can be somewhat relaxed.
[22] see further Section 4.3

By making use of the FFT in the pdf evaluations, the MLE approach is remarkably fast compared to pdf calculations based on direct numerical integration (see Brorsen and Yang, 1990; or Nolan, 1997a).

It should be noted that our simulation results do not fully reflect the precision of the ML estimator. For speedy calculations we chose a rather coarse FFT grid and limited ourselves to linear interpolation. The adoption of finer grids and nonlinear interpolation or spline methods will lead to an even higher degree of precision. For practical implementation of the ML procedure we expect that an algorithm that starts with a coarse grid and linear interpolation and then, as it tends to converge, switches to finer grids and possibly nonlinear interpolation will provide a good compromise between computational speed and accuracy.

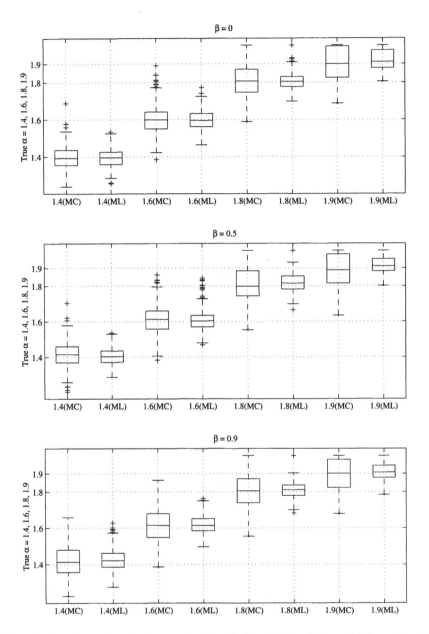

Fig. 3.9 Boxplots of α Estimates for Sample Size 1000. (Adapted from: Mittnik, Rachev, Doganoglu, and Chenyao (1999))

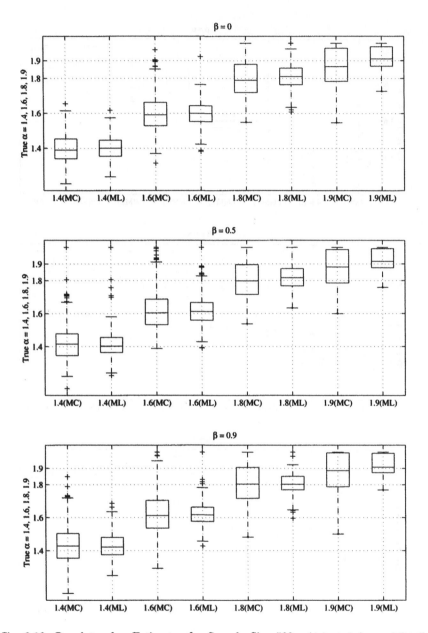

Fig. 3.10 Boxplots of α Estimates for Sample Size 500. (Adapted from: Mittnik, Rachev, Doganoglu, and Chenyao (1999))

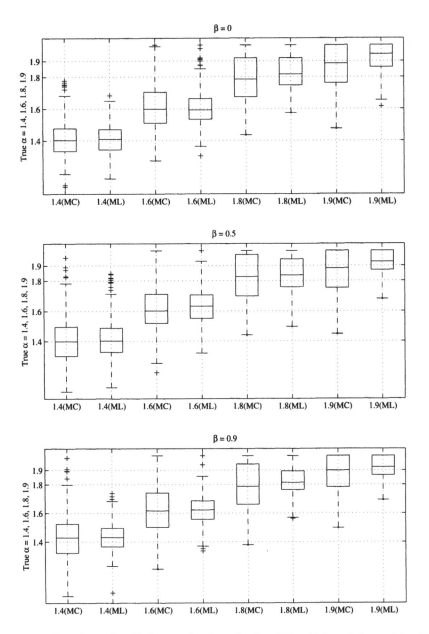

Fig. 3.11 Boxplots of α Estimates for Sample Size 250. (Adapted from: Mittnik, Rachev, Doganoglu, and Chenyao (1999))

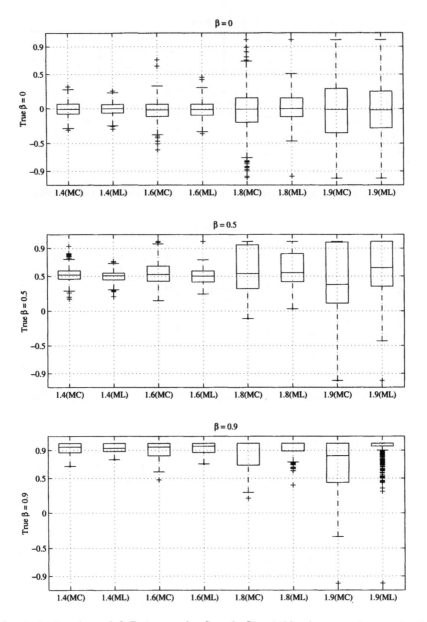

Fig. 3.12 Boxplots of β Estimates for Sample Size 1000. (Adapted from: Mittnik, Rachev, Doganoglu, and Chenyao (1999))

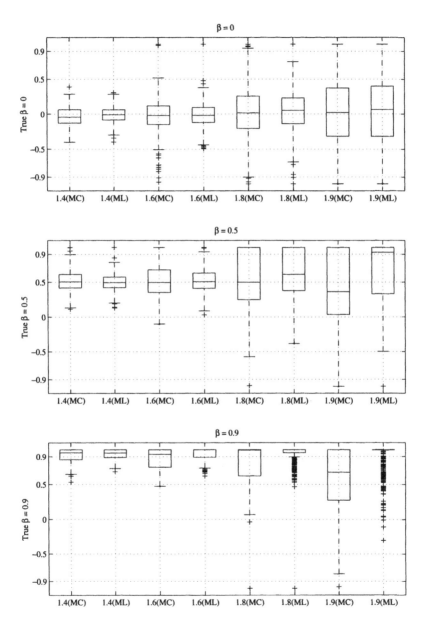

Fig. 3.13 Boxplots of β Estimates for Sample Size 500. (Adapted from: Mittnik, Rachev, Doganoglu, and Chenyao (1999))

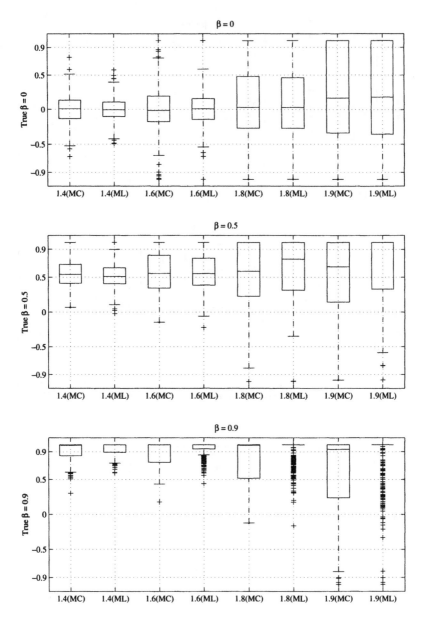

Fig. 3.14 Boxplots of β Estimates for Sample Size 250. (Adapted from: Mittnik, Rachev, Doganoglu, and Chenyao (1999))

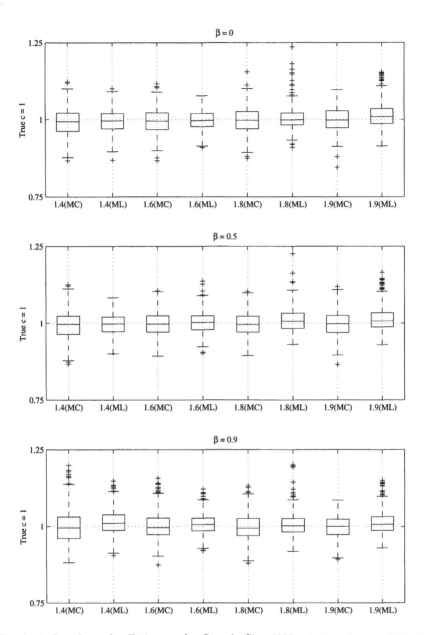

Fig. 3.15 Boxplots of c Estimates for Sample Size 1000. (Adapted from: Mittnik, Rachev, Doganoglu, and Chenyao (1999))

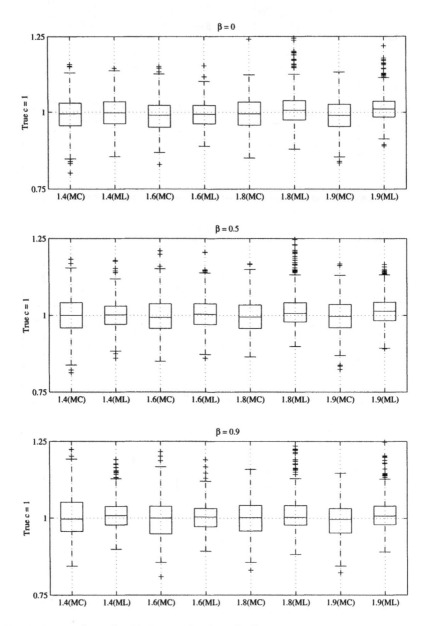

Fig. 3.16 Boxplots of c Estimates for Sample Size 500. (Adapted from: Mittnik, Rachev, Doganoglu, and Chenyao (1999))

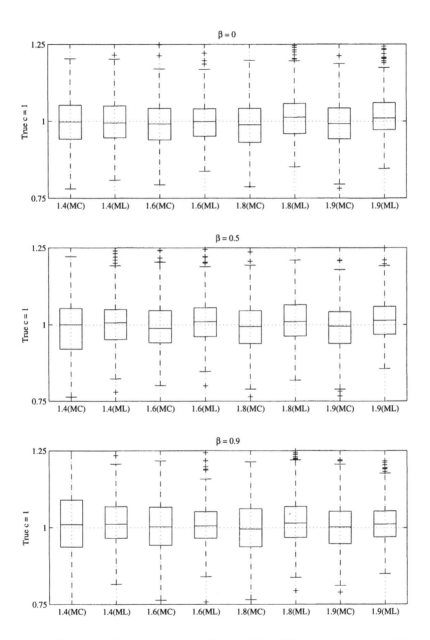

Fig. 3.17 Boxplots of c Estimates for Sample Size 250. (Adapted from: Mittnik, Rachev, Doganoglu, and Chenyao (1999))

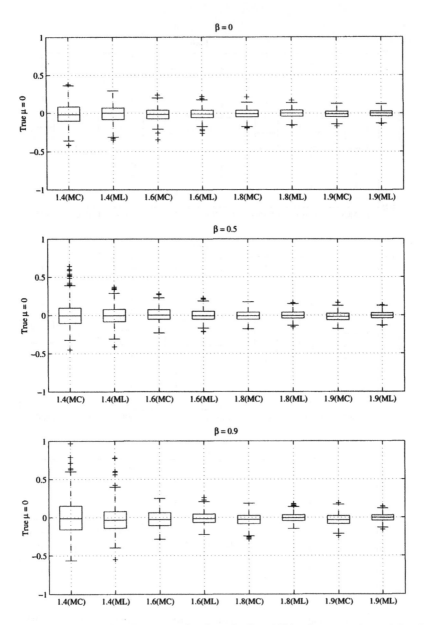

Fig. 3.18 Boxplots of μ Estimates for Sample Size 1000. (Adapted from: Mittnik, Rachev, Doganoglu, and Chenyao (1999))

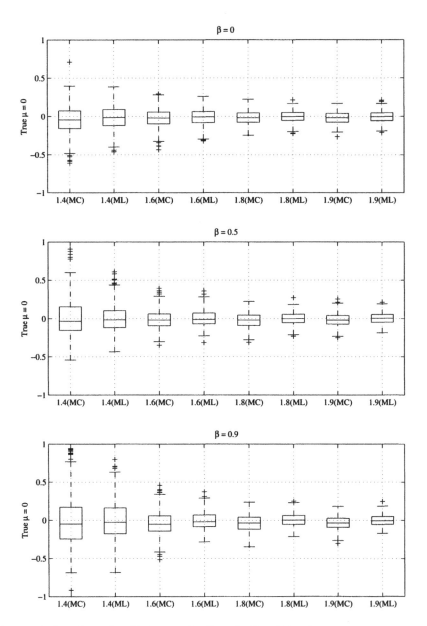

Fig. 3.19 Boxplots of μ Estimates for Sample Size 500. (Adapted from: Mittnik, Rachev, Doganoglu, and Chenyao (1999))

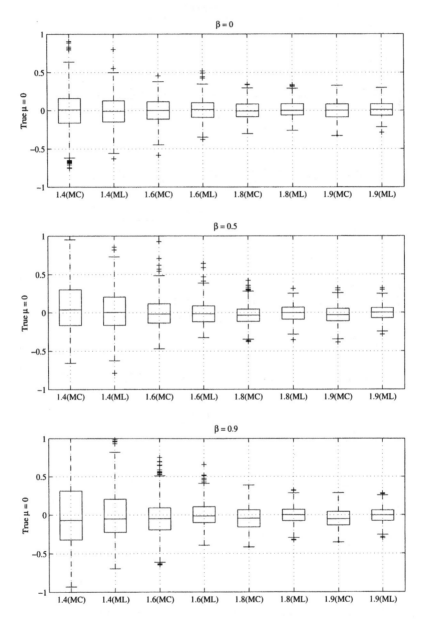

Fig. 3.20 Boxplots of μ Estimates for Sample Size 250. (Adapted from: Mittnik, Rachev, Doganoglu, and Chenyao (1999))

4

Empirical Comparison

In this chapter we compare the fit of various geometric-stable conditional and unconditional models [1].

4.1 Modeling the unconditional Distribution of Highly Volatile Exchange-rate Time Series

Several empirical studies have examined the distributional properties of exchange rate time series in recent years. As with stock returns, relative to the normal distribution, empirical distributions of exchange-rate returns are typically fat-tailed and more peaked around the origin. Various statistical distributions allowing for such features have been suggested in the literature. The stable Paretian distribution, the Student t distribution and the mixture-of-normals distribution have been used as alternatives to the prevailing normal assumption in finance.

As we have pointed out in Chapter 1, Stable Paretian distributions have several theoretical properties that are attractive in financial modeling. They are stable with respect to addition and scaling, implying that distributions of returns over periods of different lengths have the same *shape*; they have domains of attractions; and, being characterized by four parameters, they are fairly flexible in fitting empirical distributions. Despite these desirable properties, stable Paretian unconditional distributions have not been overly

---

[1] This section is based on Mittnik and Rachev (1993a,b), and Chobanov, Mateev, Mittnik and Rachev (1996).

successful in empirical modeling of financial asset returns. It should be noted, however, that almost all studies consider only *symmetric* stable Paretian distributions and/or use crude and unreliable estimation techniques.

In this chapter, we first examine the goodness of fit of the above candidate distributions for the Bulgarian lev/US dollar exchange rate by comparing the maximum likelihood values of estimated distributions. To estimate both the *symmetric* and *asymmetric* stable Paretian distribution, we use the maximum-likelihood estimation algorithm in Chen (1991). Secondly, we also consider certain members of the *random summation stable distributions*—specifically, we fit Laplace and (double) Weibull distributions.

Letting X_i, $i = 1, \ldots, n$, denote identically and independently distributed (iid) random variables, the schemes can be written as

$$X_1 \overset{d}{=} a_n(X_1 \circ X_2 \circ \cdots \circ X_n) + b_n, \qquad (4.1)$$

where $\overset{d}{=}$ denotes equality in distribution; operator $\circ$ stands for *summation, min, max,* or *multiplication* operations; n is a *deterministic* or *random* integer independent of the X_i's; $a_n > 0$; and $b_n \in \mathbf{R}$, see Chapter 1.

Letting r denote the (random) return on an asset, we say r is *stable under scheme (4.1)*, if, for some $\alpha_{pos}, \alpha_{neg} > 0$,

$$X_1 = \begin{cases} r^{\alpha_{pos}}, & r > 0, \\ -|r|^{\alpha_{neg}}, & r \leq 0, \end{cases}$$

satisfies relationship (4.1). The standard (deterministic) summation scheme, i.e., $\circ$ stands for $+$ and n is a deterministic integer, produces the well-known stable Paretian distribution; the maximum and minimum schemes lead to extreme-value distributions; and the multiplication scheme yields the multiplication stable distribution. If n is random and independent of the X_i's, we obtain *random* summation, maximum, minimum, and multiplication stable distributions, respectively. In the case of the random summation scheme, it can be shown analytically that the only possible choice for n is the class of geometric random variables with support on a general lattice. For this reason in chapters 1 and 2, we refer to this scheme as the *geometric summation scheme*.

We examine daily Bulgarian lev/US dollar exchange spot rates covering the period from February 1991 to February 1995, altogether 1021 observations. The returns, r_t, are computed by $r_t = 100 \times \log(R_t/R_{t-1})$, where R_t is the level of the exchange rate at time t. Level and return data, R_t and r_t, are shown in Figures 4.1 and 4.2.

We compare the goodness of fit of the stable Paretian, Laplace and Weibull distributions with that of alternatives commonly used in financial modeling. We consider both symmetric and asymmetric versions of these three distributions. The symmetric stable Paretian distribution is specified by setting the skewness parameter β (see Chapter 1). The symmetric (double) Weibull

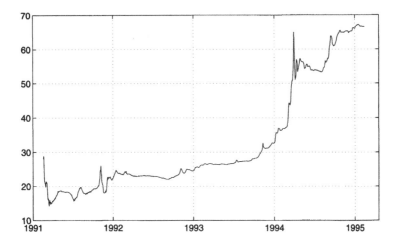

Fig. 4.1 Daily Lev-Dollar Exchange Rate. (Adapted from: Chobanov, Mateev, Mittnik, and Rachev (1996))

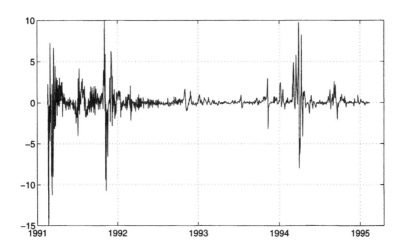

Fig. 4.2 Daily Returns on Lev-Dollar Exchange Rate. (Adapted from: Chobanov, Mateev, Mittnik, and Rachev (1996))

distribution is given by

$$\mathrm{P}(|r| < x) = F(x; \alpha, \lambda) = 1 - \exp\left\{-\lambda x^{\alpha}\right\}, \quad x > 0, \ \lambda > 0, \ \alpha > 0, \quad (4.2)$$

i.e., negative and positive returns are assumed to have the same distributional properties, and the asymmetric (double) Weibull distribution by modeling positive returns with

$$P(r_{pos} < x) = F(x; \alpha_{pos}, \lambda_{pos}) = 1 - \exp\{-\lambda_{pos} x^{\alpha_{pos}}\}, \qquad (4.3)$$
$$x > 0, \ \lambda_{pos} > 0, \ \alpha_{pos} > 0,$$

and the absolute values of negative returns with

$$P(|r_{neg}| < x) = F(x; \alpha_{neg}, \lambda_{neg}) = 1 - \exp\{-\lambda_{neg} x^{\alpha_{neg}}\}, \qquad (4.4)$$
$$x > 0, \ \lambda_{neg} > 0, \ \alpha_{neg} > 0.$$

For the symmetric and asymmetric Laplace distribution we have $\alpha = 1$ and $\alpha_{neg} = \alpha_{pos} = 1$ in (4.2), (4.3) and (4.4), respectively.

As alternative candidates we consider the simple normal distribution with density function

$$f(x; \mu, \sigma^2) = \frac{1}{\sqrt{2\pi}\sigma} \exp\left\{-\frac{(x-\mu)^2}{2\sigma^2}\right\}; \qquad (4.5)$$

the mixture of two normals with common mean, i.e.,

$$f(x; \mu, \sigma_1^2, \sigma_2^2, \rho) = \rho f(x; \mu, \sigma_1^2) + (1-\rho)f(x; \mu, \sigma_2^2), \qquad (4.6)$$

with mixing proportion ρ, $0 \le \rho \le 1$, and $\sigma_1^2 > \sigma_2^2$;[2] the asymmetric stable Paretian distribution with characteristic function (2.2); and the Student t distribution with density

$$f(x; \mu, H, n) = \frac{n^{n/2} H^{1/2}}{B(\frac{1}{2}, \frac{n}{2})} [n + H(x-\mu)^2]^{-(n+1)/2}, \qquad (4.7)$$

where $B(\cdot, \cdot)$ denotes the beta function $B(a, b) = \Gamma(a)\Gamma(b)/\Gamma(a+b)$; and μ, H, and n are the location, scale and degrees-of-freedom parameters, respectively.

We employ the log-likelihood values obtained from maximum-likelihood estimation to compare the goodness of fit of the distributions considered.[3] The maximum-likelihood value may be viewed as an overall measure of goodness of fit, allowing us to judge which of the candidate distributions is more likely to have generated the data. From a Bayesian viewpoint, given large samples and assuming equal prior probabilities for two candidates, the ratio of maximum likelihood values of two competing models represents the asymptotic posterior odds ratio of one candidate relative to the other (see Zellner (1971) and Blattberg and Gonedes (1974)).

Parameter estimates for successfully estimated distributions are shown in Table 4.1. It turned out that we could not obtain maximum-likelihood estimates for the Student t distribution. The estimation did not converge, because

---

[2]Using this convention, mixing proportion ρ reflects the portion of observations that is associated with the normal that has the higher variance.

[3]Note that this comparison does not take into account how many parameters we require to specify a distribution.

Table 4.1 Results of Maximum-Likelihood Estimation.

Distribution	Parameter Estimates				Log-lik
Normal:	μ	σ_1^2	σ_2^2	ρ	
simple	0.0839	1.5733	—	—	-1910.91
mixture	0.0485	3.3388	0.3415	0.2137	-1187.28
α-stable:	α	β	c	δ	
symmetric	0.9780	0	0.2413	0.0301	-1117.40
asymmetric	0.9535	0.1758	0.2385	-0.5426	-1110.96
Geo-sum stable:	α_{neg}	λ_{neg}	α_{pos}	λ_{pos}	
sym. Laplace	1	1.4463	1	1.4463	-1350.69
asym. Laplace	1	1.4832	1	1.4174	-1350.43
sym. Weibull	0.6851	1.6028	0.6851	1.6028	-1171.85
asym. Weibull	0.6384	1.7035	0.7344	1.5266	-1165.58

(Adapted from: Chobanov, Mateev, Mittnik, and Rachev (1996))

the degree-of-freedom parameter attempted to assume values below two, causing the maximum-likelihood estimation algorithm to fail. This failure is no surprise in view of the estimates of the stability index α for the stable Paretian distribution. Values below 2 imply that no second moments and values below 1 that no first moments exist. Hence, with α-estimates below one the degree-of-freedom parameter of the t distribution should be less than unity.

The maximum log-likelihood values of the estimated distributions are shown in the last column of Table 4.1. The asymmetric and the symmetric stable Paretian distributions achieve the best fit with maximum log-likelihood values of -1110.96 and -1117.40, respectively. They are followed by the asymmetric (-1165.58) and symmetric (-1171.85) Weibull distributions, the mixture of normals (-1187.28), and the asymmetric (-1350.43) and symmetric (-1350.69) Laplace distributions. The normal distribution has by far the poorest fit with a maximum log-likelihood value of -1910.91.

A visual comparison of empirical and estimated densities confirms the goodness-of-fit results—especially, the dismal fit of the normal distribution. Figure 4.3 shows substantial deviations between the empirical density (dotted curve) and the estimated normal density (solid curve). The mixture of normals fits considerably better, but has still problems in capturing the peakedness of the empirical distribution (see Figure 4.4). The symmetric and asymmetric stable Paretian distributions fit very well in the center and the tails (see Figures 4.5 for the asymmetric case). The Laplace distributions yield less reasonable fits with respect to both the peak and the tails. However, considering the symmetric Laplace distribution (see Figure 4.6), which involves only one parameter, the goodness of the fit, relative to the normal, is somewhat surprising. The Weibull distributions fit reasonably well (see Figure 4.7 for the asymmetric case). An exception is the exaggeration of the peak, which occurs, however, only in the narrow return range ± 0.05%—a range that is irrelevant for practical investment decisions.

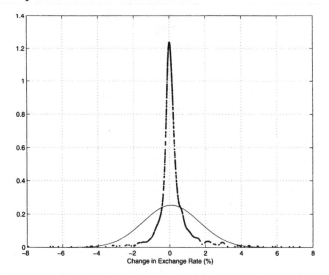

Fig. 4.3 Estimated Normal and Empirical Density for Bulgarian Lev. (Adapted from: Chobanov, Mateev, Mittnik, and Rachev (1996))

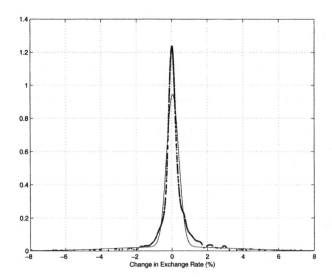

Fig. 4.4 Estimated Mixed Normal and Empirical Density for Bulgarian Lev. (Adapted from: Chobanov, Mateev, Mittnik, and Rachev (1996))

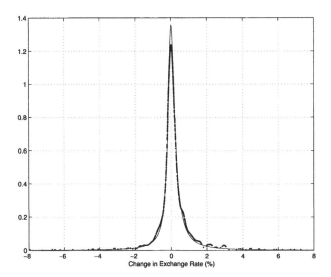

Fig. 4.5 Estimated Asymmetric Stable Paretian and Empirical Density for Bulgarian Lev. (Adapted from: Chobanov, Mateev, Mittnik, and Rachev (1996))

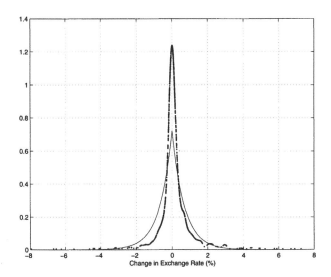

Fig. 4.6 Estimated Symmetric Laplace and Empirical Density for Bulgarian Lev. (Adapted from: Chobanov, Mateev, Mittnik, and Rachev (1996))

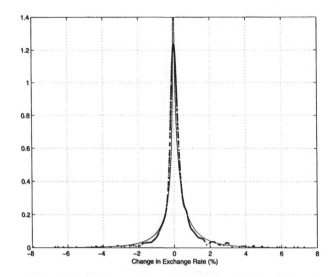

Fig. 4.7 Estimated Asymetric Weibull and Empirical Density for Bulgarian Lev. (Adapted from: Chobanov, Mateev, Mittnik, and Rachev (1996))

In conclusion we find that the asymmetric stable Paretian distribution dominates all other candidates. The symmetric stable Paretian distribution has the second best fit, but a likelihood-ratio test will reject the symmetry restriction $\beta = 0$.

All other distributions under consideration are thin-tailed and not quite as capable in capturing the distributional characteristics as the fat-tailed stable Paretian distribution. The goodness of fit, measured in terms of the maximum log-likelihood, and a visual comparison of empirical and estimated densities reveal their shortcomings. However, the Weibull, mixture of normals and, to some extent, the Laplace distributions are still reasonable, whereas the normal distribution—the model most widely adopted in financial modeling—appears to be very inappropriate for modeling highly volatile returns on exchange rates like that of the Bulgarian lev against the US dollar.

4.2   Unconditional Distributional Models for the Nikkei Index

In this and the next section we investigate alternative unconditional and conditional distributional models for the returns on Japan's Nikkei 225 stock market index [4]. Of the eight entertained distributions, the partially asymmetric Weibull, Student's t and asymmetric α-stable present themselves as the

---

[4]The results in Sections 4.2 and 4.3 are due to Mittnik, Rachev and Paolella (1998).

most viable candidates in terms of overall fit. However, the tails of the sample distribution are approximated best by the asymmetric α-stable distribution.

Letting r_t denote the return at time t, each of the entertained distributions are location and scale families; i.e., for general probability density function (pdf) $f_{\mu_t,\sigma_t}(r_t)$, we have a standardized counterpart with location zero and scale unity such that

$$f_{\mu_t,\sigma_t}(r_t) = f_{0,1}\left(\frac{r_t - \mu_t}{\sigma_t}\right). \tag{4.8}$$

The models we consider distinguish themselves with respect to two types of assumptions, namely assumptions concerning their dynamic behavior and those describing the distributional form $f_{\mu_t,\sigma_t}(\cdot)$. The dynamic properties of the models are characterized by the assumptions specifying the evolution of μ_t and σ_t over time. The unconditional distributional models assume that $\mu_t = \mu$ and $\sigma_t = \sigma$ are constants, implying that the returns, r_t, are i.i.d. with pdf $f_{0,1}((r_t - \mu)/\sigma)$ for all t. In the conditional homoskedastic case, μ_t is allowed to vary over time, but $\sigma_t = \sigma$ is still fixed, so that the mean–corrected returns are i.i.d. with pdf $f_{0,1}((r_t - \mu_t)/\sigma)$ [5].

Estimation of conditional ARMA–GARCH models under normal and non-normal distributional assumptions is conducted via *conditional* maximum-likelihood (ML) estimation. Specifically, the ML estimation is conditional in the sense that, when estimating, for example, an ARMA(p,q)–GARCH$(1,1)$ model, we condition on the first p realizations, $r_p, r_{p-1}, \ldots, r_1$, of the sample and set the required functionals $r_p - \hat{\mu}_p$ and $\hat{\sigma}_p$ to their unconditional values implied by the other parameters. Details are elaborated upon in Section 5.

In its standard version, GARCH models are assumed to be driven by normally distributed innovations, i.e., denoting the mean corrected returns by $\epsilon_t = r_t - \mu_t$, the normal distribution is the scale family given by

$$f_N(\epsilon_t; \sigma) = \frac{1}{\sqrt{2\pi}\sigma}\exp\left\{-\frac{1}{2}\left(\frac{\epsilon_t}{\sigma}\right)^2\right\}. \tag{4.9}$$

In the following five subsections, the other alternative distributions are discussed with some more detail.

(a) Laplace

Mittnik and Rachev (1993a) suggested the Laplace or double exponential distribution for modeling the unconditional distributions of asset returns. In

---

[5] Although more general models could be considered, below we confine ourselves to the class of ARMA models to capture the conditional expectation of r_t, $\mu_t = \mathrm{E}(r_t \mid r_{t-1}, r_{t-2}, \ldots)$. Finally, in the conditional heteroskedastic case, σ_t is permitted to have a GARCH structure, implying that the standardized, mean–corrected returns, $(r_t - \mu_t)/\sigma_t$, are i.i.d. with pdf $f_{0,1}((r_t - \mu_t)/\sigma_t)$.

the context of GARCH models it has been employed by Granger and Ding (1995) and González-Rivera (1997). The pdf of the Laplace distribution is given by

$$f_L\left(\epsilon_t;\sigma\right) = \frac{1}{2\sigma}\exp\left\{-\left|\frac{\epsilon_t}{\sigma}\right|\right\}. \tag{4.10}$$

(b) Double Weibull and Partially Asymmetric Weibull

The double, or two–sided Weibull, denoted DW, is a generalization of the Laplace distribution and was also proposed in Mittnik and Rachev (1993a) as a distributional model for asset returns. The pdf is given by

$$f_{DW}\left(\epsilon_t;\alpha,\sigma\right) = \frac{\alpha}{2\sigma}\left|\frac{\epsilon_t}{\sigma}\right|^{\alpha-1}\exp\left\{-\left|\frac{\epsilon_t}{\sigma}\right|^{\alpha}\right\}, \tag{4.11}$$

where $\alpha > 0$ and $\sigma > 0$. Denoting estimates of α and σ by $\hat{\alpha}$ and $\hat{\sigma}$, respectively, the estimated cumulative density function (cdf) is given by

$$\hat{F}\left(\epsilon_t\right) = \left\{ \begin{array}{ll} \frac{1}{2}\left[1 - F\left(-\epsilon_t;\hat{\alpha},\hat{\sigma}\right)\right], & \text{if } \epsilon_t \leq 0, \\ \frac{1}{2}\left[1 + F\left(\epsilon_t;\hat{\alpha},\hat{\sigma}\right)\right], & \text{if } \epsilon_t > 0, \end{array} \right. \tag{4.12}$$

where

$$F\left(x;\alpha,\sigma\right) := 1 - \exp\left\{-\left(\frac{x}{\sigma}\right)^{\alpha}\right\}, \quad \text{for } x \geq 0. \tag{4.13}$$

The double Weibull can be extended to cover the asymmetric case by

$$f_{AW}\left(\epsilon_t;\alpha^-,\alpha^+,\sigma^-,\sigma^+\right) = \left\{ \begin{array}{ll} \frac{1}{2}\frac{\alpha^-}{\sigma^-}\left|\frac{\epsilon_t}{\sigma^-}\right|^{\alpha^--1}\exp\left\{-\left|\frac{\epsilon_t}{\sigma^-}\right|^{\alpha^-}\right\}, & \text{if } \epsilon_t \leq 0, \\ \frac{1}{2}\frac{\alpha^+}{\sigma^+}\left(\frac{\epsilon_t}{\sigma^+}\right)^{\alpha^+-1}\exp\left\{-\left(\frac{\epsilon_t}{\sigma^+}\right)^{\alpha^+}\right\}, & \text{if } \epsilon_t > 0, \end{array} \right. \tag{4.14}$$

denoted AW, and all four parameters are strictly positive. The *partially asymmetric Weibull (PAW)* restricts $\sigma^- = \sigma^+ = \sigma$, but allows α to be different in each tail. Thus,

$$f_{PAW}\left(\epsilon_t;\alpha^-,\alpha^+,\sigma,\right) = \left\{ \begin{array}{ll} \frac{1}{2}\frac{\alpha^-}{\sigma}\left|\frac{\epsilon_t}{\sigma}\right|^{\alpha^--1}\exp\left\{-\left|\frac{\epsilon_t}{\sigma}\right|^{\alpha^-}\right\}, & \text{if } \epsilon_t \leq 0, \\ \frac{1}{2}\frac{\alpha^+}{\sigma}\left(\frac{\epsilon_t}{\sigma}\right)^{\alpha^+-1}\exp\left\{-\left(\frac{\epsilon_t}{\sigma}\right)^{\alpha^+}\right\}, & \text{if } \epsilon_t > 0. \end{array} \right. \tag{4.15}$$

The estimated cdf is now given by

$$\hat{F}\left(\epsilon_t\right) = \left\{ \begin{array}{ll} \frac{1}{2}\left[1 - F\left(-\epsilon_t;\hat{\alpha}^-,\hat{\sigma}^-\right)\right], & \text{if } \epsilon_t \leq 0, \\ \frac{1}{2}\left[1 + F\left(\epsilon_t;\hat{\alpha}^+,\hat{\sigma}^+\right)\right], & \text{if } \epsilon_t > 0. \end{array} \right. \tag{4.16}$$

The advantage of the PAW over its fully asymmetric counterpart, AW, is that it can still incorporate asymmetries in the innovations process, but, because σ enters as a genuine scale parameter, it is more suitable for GARCH modeling. There is one caveat regarding both the *AW* and PAW distributions – the likelihood functions stemming from (4.14) and (4.15) are only piecewise continuous in μ, i.e., the likelihood "jumps" for values of μ equal to observed sample points. Hence, maximum likelihood (ML) estimation entails numeric optimization over the parameter space for a fixed value of μ, and grid searching over the range of μ dictated by the sample values. Because of the amenable pdf forms, optimization with fixed μ is very fast, so that this is not a terrible hindrance, although standard errors, as usually returned from optimization algorithms which implement numeric gradients, are not reported for the intercept parameter. As absolute values are taken in the DW and Laplace cases, this idiosyncracy does not arise.

(c) Generalized Exponential

The pdf of the generalized exponential distribution (GED) is given by

$$f_{GED}\left(\epsilon_t; p, \sigma\right) = \frac{p}{2\sigma\Gamma\left(p^{-1}\right)} \exp\left\{-\left|\frac{\epsilon_t}{\sigma}\right|^p\right\} \quad p > 0.$$

It is symmetric and nests both the Normal ($p = 2$) and Laplace ($p = 1$). Some estimation issues of the GED with an added location parameter are taken up in Rahman and Gokhale (1996), where further references can also be found. Characterizing properties of the GED are studied in Rachev (1991, Sections 19.2 and 19.5).

(d) Student's t

The pdf of the (Student's) t distribution is

$$f_t\left(\epsilon_t; \alpha, \sigma\right) = \frac{K_\alpha}{\sigma}\left(1 + \frac{\epsilon_t^2}{\alpha\sigma^2}\right)^{-\frac{\alpha+1}{2}}, \quad K_\alpha = \frac{\alpha^{-1/2}}{B\left(\frac{1}{2}, \frac{\alpha}{2}\right)} = \frac{\Gamma\left(\frac{\alpha+1}{2}\right)\alpha^{-1/2}}{\sqrt{\pi}\Gamma\left(\frac{\alpha}{2}\right)}.$$

Zellner (1976) treated the linear regression model with multivariate t disturbances with fixed $\alpha > 2$, and showed that ordinary least squares estimators for β are still valid, as well as the standard t and F statistics. Singh (1988) derived a simple estimator for α and σ, valid when $\alpha > 4$. He proposed $\hat{\alpha} = 2\left(2\hat{a} - 3\right)\left(\hat{a} - 3\right)^{-1}$ where $\hat{a} = T\left(\sum_{t=1}^{T}\epsilon_t^4\right)\left(\sum_{t=1}^{T}\epsilon_t^2\right)^{-2}$ and

$$\tilde{\sigma}^2 = \frac{3\sum_{t=1}^{T}\epsilon_t^2}{\left(2\hat{a} - 3\right)\left(T - k + 2\right)}$$

as a minimum MSE estimator of σ^2. Lange et al. (1989) describe further applications of t distribution as a generalization of the normal, as well as issues in estimation, including use of the EM algorithm.

(e) α-stable

The α-stable, or, in short, $S_{\alpha,\beta}$, distribution, has, in general, no closed–form expression for its pdf, but can, instead, be expressed by its characteristic function (cf) $E\left(e^{i\epsilon_t \theta}\right)$ via

$$\log E\left(e^{i\epsilon_t \theta}\right) = \begin{cases} i\mu\theta - |\sigma\theta|^\alpha \left[1 - i\beta\mathrm{sgn}\left(\theta\right)\tan\frac{\pi\alpha}{2}\right], & \text{if } \alpha \neq 1, \\ i\mu\theta - |\sigma\theta| \left[1 + i\beta\frac{2}{\pi}\mathrm{sgn}\left(\theta\right)\log|\theta|\right], & \text{if } \alpha = 1, \end{cases}$$

for $\alpha \in (0,2]$, $\beta \in [-1,1]$, $\sigma > 0$, and $\mu \in \mathbf{R}$, see chapter 2. Recall that for positive (negative) β, the distribution is skewed to the right (left), and is symmetric for $\beta = 0$. Also, for $\alpha \neq 2$, we have

$$\beta = \lim_{x \to \infty} \frac{P\left(\epsilon_t > x\right) - P\left(\epsilon_t < -x\right)}{P\left(\epsilon_t > x\right) + P\left(\epsilon_t < -x\right)}. \tag{4.17}$$

For fixed $\beta \neq 0$, the α-stable distribution tends towards symmetry as α approaches 2, while for $\alpha = 2$, β vanishes from the cf.

Evaluation of the pdf, and, thus, the likelihood function of the α-stable distribution is nontrivial, because it lacks an analytic expression. The ML estimate of parameter vector θ is obtained by maximizing the logarithm of the likelihood function

$$L(\theta; r_1, \dots, r_T) = \prod_{t=1}^{T} S_{\alpha,\beta}\left(\frac{r_t - \mu_t}{\sigma_t}\right) \sigma_t^{-1}.$$

The estimation of α–stable models is *approximate* in the sense that the α–stable density function $S_{\alpha,\beta}\left((r_t - \mu_t)/\sigma_t\right)$ needs to be approximated. Our ML estimation essentially follows that of DuMouchel (1973a,b), but differs in that we numerically approximate the α–stable density via fast Fourier transform of the cf rather than some series expansion. As DuMouchel (1973a,b) shows, the resulting estimates are consistent and asymptotically normal with the asymptotic covariance matrix of $T^{1/2}(\hat{\theta} - \theta_0)$ being given by the inverse of the Fisher information matrix.

The standard errors of the estimates reported below are obtained by evaluating the Fisher information matrix at the ML point estimates. For details on our α–stable ML estimation we refer to Mittnik et al. (1996) and Mittnik and Rachev (1997).

Next we discuss the properties of Nikkei-returns data set we are going to examine. We shall study the weekly returns[6] from July 31, 1983 to April 9, 1995, with $T = 608$ observations.

We will see that the behavior of this series is rather typical for financial return data, in that it exhibits considerable kurtosis, a small but persistent autoregressive component, and volatility clustering. Figure 4.8 shows time series of the levels and returns on the index. From the latter plot, volatility clusters are clearly visible, suggesting the presence of conditional heteroskedasticity.

---

[6]We use the standard convention and define the return r_t in period t by $r_t = 100 \times (\ln P_t - \ln P_{t-1})$, where P_t is the index level at time t.

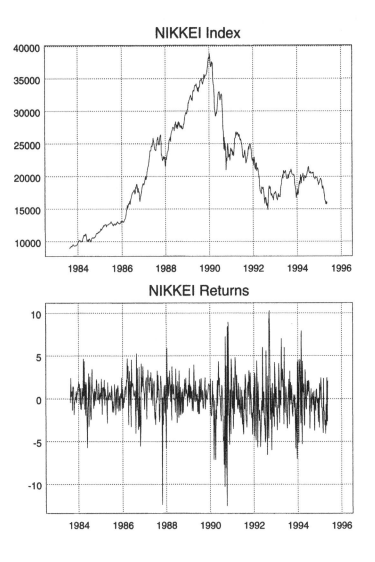

Fig. 4.8 Levels and Percent Returns of Nikkei 225 Index. (Adapted from: Mittnik, Paolella, Rachev (1998))

Table 4.2 summarizes basic statistical properties of the Nikkei return series. The mean return, 0.0958, is positive, but close to zero. The returns appear to be somewhat asymmetric, as reflected by a skewness estimate of -0.4539. Recall that a negative skewness statistic indicates that the distribution is skewed to the left, i.e., compared to the right tail, the left tail is elongated. The estimated kurtosis statistic of 6.196 reflects the peakedness of the center compared to that of the normal distribution; a value near three is indicative of normality, while a larger value indicates the presence of a higher central peak, as well as fatter tails.

Table 4.2   Statistical Properties of Returns.[a]

Mean	Std. Dev.	Skewness	Kurtosis	LM	$LM_{.95,608}$
0.0958	2.537	-0.4539	6.196	273.8	5.92

LM is the Lagrange multiplier test for normality,

$$T\left(\frac{\hat{\mu}_3^2}{6\hat{\mu}_2^3} + \frac{\left(\hat{\mu}_4/\hat{\mu}_2^2 - 3\right)^2}{24}\right),$$

where $\hat{\mu}_r = T^{-1}\sum_{i=1}^T \hat{\epsilon}_i^r$, the rth sample raw moment; and $LM_{.95,608}$ refers to the approximate 5% critical value for $T = 608$ observations.
(Adapted from: Mittnik, Paolella, Rachev (1998))

To formally test for normality, we use the Lagrange multiplier test of Jarque and Bera (1987) given by

$$LM = T\left(\frac{\hat{\mu}_3^2}{6\hat{\mu}_2^3} + \frac{\left(\hat{\mu}_4/\hat{\mu}_2^2 - 3\right)^2}{24}\right) \qquad (4.18)$$

where $\hat{\mu}_r = T^{-1}\sum_{i=1}^T \hat{\epsilon}_i^r$, the rth sample raw moment.[7] For the Nikkei return sample, we reject normality. The estimated value of LM is 273.8, which clearly exceeds critical values at any conventional significance level given by the asymptotically valid χ^2 distribution with two degrees of freedom.

One can visually judge the fitted density by graphically overlaying it with the nonparametric kernel density estimate for the sample. In doing so, one must somewhat subjectively specify the smoothing constant, h, required in kernel density estimation.[8] For the series considered here, with its sufficiently large sample size and clear unimodality, there is no discernable difference in the appearance of the kernel estimates for a large range of h, including the standard choices.

We employ three criteria for comparing the goodness of fit of the candidate distributions. The first is the maximum log-likelihood value obtained from the ML estimation. It may be viewed as an overall measure of goodness of fit

[7]To circumvent the inaccuracy of its asymptotic χ_2^2 distribution under the null of normality, Deb and Sefton (1996) provide refined 5% and 10% critical values for a range of sample sizes under 800. By fitting a spline function through their simulated points, critical values for $20 \leq T \leq 800$ can be accurately approximated.
[8]We follow the recommendation of Silverman (1986, pp. 45-47), and take $h = 1.06T^{-1/5}s_T$, when the data are believed to be approximately normally distributed; and $h = 0.79T^{-1/5}IQR$, when believed to be fatter tailed. Here, s_T denotes the sample standard deviation, and IQR the interquartile range.

and allows us to judge which candidate is more likely to have generated the data. From a Bayesian viewpoint, given large samples and assuming equal prior probabilities for two candidate distributions, the ratio of the maximum log likelihood values of two competing models represents the asymptotic posterior odds ratio of one candidate relative to the other (see Zellner, 1971; and Blattberg and Gonedes, 1974).

The second criterion is the Kolmogorov distance

$$\text{KD} = 100 \times \sup_{x \in \mathbf{R}} |F_s(x) - \hat{F}(x)|, \tag{4.19}$$

where $\hat{F}(x)$ denotes the cdf of the estimated parametric density, and $F_s(x)$ is the empirical sample distribution, i.e., $F_s(x) = T^{-1} \sum_{t=1}^{T} \mathcal{I}_{(-\infty, x]} \left(\frac{r_t - \hat{\mu}_t}{\hat{\sigma}_t} \right)$ where $\mathcal{I}(\cdot)$ is the indicator function. This statistic is discussed further in DeGroot (1986) and D'Agostino and Stephens (1986). It is a robust measure in the sense that it focuses only on the maximum deviation between the sample and fitted distributions.

The third is the Anderson-Darling statistic (Anderson and Darling, 1952; see also Press et al., 1991; and Tanaka, 1996), which weights the absolute deviations $|F_s(x) - \hat{F}(x)|$ by the reciprocal of the standard deviation of $F_s(x)$, $\sqrt{\hat{F}(x) \left(1 - \hat{F}(x) \right)}$, i.e.,

$$\text{AD}_0 = \sup_{x \in \mathbf{R}} \frac{|F_s(x) - \hat{F}(x)|}{\sqrt{\hat{F}(x) \left(1 - \hat{F}(x) \right)}}, \tag{4.20}$$

The use of this statistic allows discrepancies in the tails of the distribution to be appropriately weighted. On the other hand, KD emphasizes deviations around the median of the fitted distribution. In the next section, we will see that for the data set at hand, one or two values can be decisive for the AD_0 statistic. Instead of just the maximum discrepancy, is is also meaningful to look at the second (third) largest value, which we denote as AD_1 (AD_2). The AD_i statistics, $i = 1, 2$ prove particularly useful when, with respect to a given distribution, one or two extreme values appear incompatible. Note also that the ML values of encompassing models are non-decreasing as they become more general. This may not be the case with KD and AD_i statistics.

When comparing the goodness of fit, one has to keep the number of freely estimated parameters in mind. Ignoring the location parameter, which is estimated for all candidates, the normal and Laplace have only scale parameter σ. Along with σ, the DW, GED, t and $S_{\alpha,0}$ have one additional shape parameter, whereas the PAW and $S_{\alpha,\beta}$ have two, thereby allowing for asymmetry.

The empirical unconditional distribution reflects the statistical properties of the returns and can be used to specify the risk associated with the underlying asset. In practice, one is typically more interested in a conditional risk assessment. However, the unconditional sample distribution is of interest, because any dynamic model used for that purpose has to be compatible with the unconditional distributions of the data at hand.

Table 4.3 contains the various goodness–of–fit statistics for the eight fitted unconditional distributions. The second column shows that, among the distributions considered, the largest maximized log-likelihood value, $\mathcal{L}$, is achieved by the PAW (-1389.0) with values for the Student's t (-1392.2), $S_{\alpha,\beta}$ (-1393.2), GED (-1394.3), Laplace (-1395.5), and $S_{\alpha,0}$ (-1396.0) marginally lower. With an $\mathcal{L}$ value of -1428.3, the normal distribution fits relatively poorly. Notice that, compared to the normal, the other one-parameter candidate, the Laplace, fits remarkably well, even slightly outperforming the $S_{\alpha,0}$. Also, compared to its generalizations DW, PAW, and GED, the Laplace provides a surprisingly close fit.

Table 4.3 Goodness of Fit of Unconditional Distributions.[a]

	$\mathcal{L}$	KD	AD$_0$	AD$_1$	AD$_2$
Normal	-1428.3	6.89	4.92	2.81	1.07
		(543)	(2)	(1)	(3)
Laplace	-1395.5	4.57	0.127	0.125	0.125
		(543)	(543)	(546)	(548)
DW	-1393.8	4.65	0.120	0.118	0.118
		(543)	(543)	(546)	(542)
PAW	-1389.0	3.77	0.122	0.106	0.106
		(214)	(2)	(27)	(543)
GED	-1394.3	4.65	0.204	0.136	0.129
		(543)	(2)	(3)	(543)
t	-1392.2	3.77	0.107	0.104	0.103
		(543)	(543)	(542)	(546)
$S_{\alpha,0}$	-1396.0	3.70	0.124	0.123	0.120
		(235)	(20)	(63)	(69)
$S_{\alpha,\beta}$	-1393.2	3.00	0.085	0.084	0.081
		(235)	(69)	(63)	(76)

[a] $\mathcal{L}$ refers to the maximum log–likelihood value; KD is the Kolmogorov distance $100 \times \sup_{x \in \mathbf{R}} |F_s(x) - \hat{F}(x)|$; and AD$_i$, $i = 0, 1, 2$, is the Anderson-Darling statistic

$$\sup_{x \in \mathbf{R}} \frac{|F_s(x) - \hat{F}(x)|}{\sqrt{\hat{F}(x)\left(1 - \hat{F}(x)\right)}}$$

neglecting i extreme values (see Section 3). The numbers in parentheses, τ, indicate to which order statistic, $(r_{\tau:T} - \hat{\mu})/\hat{\sigma}$, the KD and AD$_i$ values correspond.

(Adapted from: Mittnik, Paolella, Rachev (1998))

With respect to the other goodness–of–fit criteria reported in Table 4.3, we see that $S_{\alpha,\beta}$ is preferred. In particular, a KD–value of 3.00 is achieved by the asymmetric α-stable fit, as compared to $S_{\alpha,0}$ (3.70), Student's t (3.77), PAW (3.77), Laplace (4.57), GED (4.65), and the normal (6.89). The values in parentheses indicate for which ordered cdf value the maximum occurred, i.e., values near 1 (608) refer to extremes in the left (right) tail. Commonly occurring were values 543 and 235, neither of which would be regarded as being in the tails.

Similarly, the AD_0 statistic favors $S_{\alpha,\beta}$, with a value of 0.085, as opposed to those of the t (0.107), DW (0.120), PAW (0.122), $S_{\alpha,0}$ (0.124), Laplace (0.127), GED (0.204) and normal (4.92). For the DW and Laplace, the 543rd ordered cdf value was again decisive, although for the normal, PAW, and GED, the 2nd value was, i.e., a value far in the left tail. The removal of two extreme values from the calculation results in dramatic improvement for the normal, for which $AD_2 = 1.07$. Likewise, $AD_2 = 0.129$ marks an improvement for the GED, although, with respect to AD_2, it is the worst fitting distribution outside of the normal. The AD_i values for the remaining distributions change little, indicating that, for the majority of the distributions considered here, there are no observations which are grossly inconsistent, and need to be labeled as "outliers".

To get a visual impression of the AD goodness–of–fit measure, Figure 4.9 plots the estimated standardized distances $\left[F_s(x) - \hat{F}(x) \right] / \sqrt{\hat{F}(x) \left(1 - \hat{F}(x) \right)}$ for the eight entertained distributions, with their corresponding lower and upper bounds indicated by the dashed lines.[9] Observe that the only distribution for which all absolute distances are less than 0.1 is the $S_{\alpha,\beta}$.

As an additional measure of the goodness-of-fit, we consider the estimated quantiles corresponding to several left and right tail values. For each estimated distribution we compute the quantile ξ_π as

$$\xi_\pi = \hat{\sigma} z_\pi + \hat{\mu} \tag{4.21}$$

where z_π is determined by $\pi = \Pr(Z \le z_\pi \mid \hat{\nu})$ and Z denotes a random variable from a density with location 0, scale 1, and (possibly) shape and skewness parameter(s) $\hat{\nu}$. Calculation of quantile values z_π for the normal and t distributions are available in most numerical software packages. For the PAW density,

$$z_\pi = \begin{cases} -(-\log 2\pi)^{1/\hat{\alpha}^-}, & \text{if } \pi \le 0.5, \\ \left[-\log\{2(1-\pi)\} \right]^{1/\hat{\alpha}^+}, & \text{if } \pi > 0.5, \end{cases} \tag{4.22}$$

with analogous expressions for the symmetric Weibull ($\hat{\alpha}^- = \hat{\alpha}^+ = \hat{\alpha}$) and Laplace ($\hat{\alpha}^- = \hat{\alpha}^+ = 1$). By numerically integrating the pdf of the GED distribution, quantile values can be solved for by using any standard root-finder. Similarly, the cdf of the $S_{\alpha,\beta}$ distribution can be evaluated by numerically integrating the integral expression given by Zolotarev (1986a) or McCulloch (1996).

---

[9]For graphical purposes, several of the extreme values for the normal have been clipped from view.

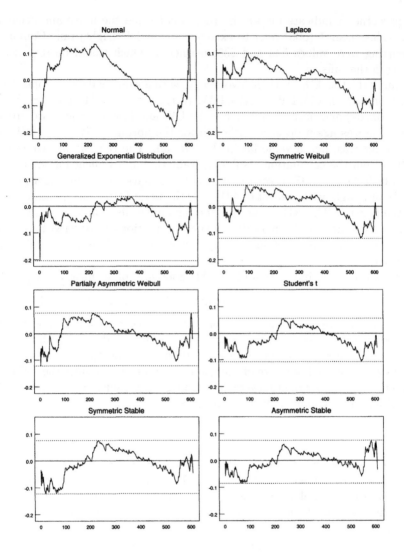

Fig. 4.9 Standardized cdf Deviations (Anderson–Darling) of Fitted Unconditional Densities. (Adapted from: Mittnik, Paolella, Rachev (1998))

Table 4.4 lists the ξ_π values for $\pi = 0.025,\ 0.05,\ 0.10,\ 0.20,\ 0.50,\ 0.80,\ 0.90$, and 0.975, for the eight estimated distributions, as well as the corresponding

Table 4.4 Quantile Fit of Estimated Unconditional Distributions.[a]

	Probability π								
	0.025	0.05	0.10	0.20	0.5	0.8	0.90	0.95	0.975
					Empirical				
	-5.526	-4.125	-2.980	-1.594	0.289	1.800	2.584	3.829	4.636
					Fitted				
Normal	-4.877	-4.077	-3.156	-2.039	0.096	2.231	3.347	4.269	5.068
Laplace	-5.173	-3.908	-2.644	-1.380	0.292	1.963	3.227	4.492	5.756
DW	-5.024	-3.872	-2.699	-1.495	0.229	1.952	3.156	4.329	5.481
PAW	-5.657	-4.206	-2.787	-1.411	0.252	1.944	3.010	4.014	4.979
GED	-5.016	-3.865	-2.685	-1.465	0.260	1.985	3.205	4.385	5.536
t	-4.893	-3.697	-2.591	-1.502	0.221	1.943	3.032	4.138	5.334
$S_{\alpha,0}$	-4.866	-3.651	-2.618	-1.580	0.185	1.950	2.987	4.021	5.235
$S_{\alpha,\beta}$	-5.657	-4.039	-2.775	-1.607	0.215	1.891	2.814	3.680	4.634

[a] Empirical values of ξ_π are given by $r_{t:T}$, $t = \lceil \pi \times T \rceil$. Estimated quantile $\hat{\xi}_\pi = \hat{\sigma} z_\pi + \hat{\mu}$, with z_π determined by $\pi = \Pr(Z \leq z_\pi \,|\hat{\nu})$ and Z denotes a random variable from a location-zero, scale-one density and (possibly) shape and skewness parameter(s) $\hat{\nu}$.

(Adapted from: Mittnik, Paolella, Rachev (1998))

empirical values from the returns.[10] In comparison to the other distributions, the $S_{\alpha,\beta}$ quantiles are considerably closer to the empirical counterparts, particularly so for the tail values. Here, the $S_{\alpha,\beta}$ dominates the t distribution; though the latter achieved a marginally better log-likelihood value. Observe that for $\pi = 0.05$ and 0.10, the normal assumption fairs reasonably well, whereas, for the remaining π values, it usually performs worst. It is also interesting to note that the median of the returns is captured best by the Laplace fit.[11]

The parameter estimates of the fitted unconditional distributions are shown in Table 4.5. Focusing on the distributions that are nested in terms of the shape parameter α, point and interval estimates suggest that the Laplace assumption, $\alpha = 1$, is marginally rejected by both the DW ($\hat{\alpha} = 1.063$) and PAW ($\hat{\alpha}^- = 0.9342$, $\hat{\alpha}^+ = 1.1533$). Against the GED alternative ($\hat{\alpha} = 1.1202$), there is little evidence to reject the Laplace. On the other hand, normality is strongly rejected by the GED, as well as by the symmetric ($\hat{\alpha} =$

[10] That is, the empirical ξ_π is given by $r_{t:T}$, the tth order statistic of the returns, and $t = \lceil \pi \times T \rceil$, with $\lceil \cdot \rceil$ denoting the "ceiling" function.
[11] Recall that, for fixed sample size, the variance of the empirical ξ_π increase as π approaches 0 and 1. As such, with $T = 608$, the common values $\pi = 0.01$ and 0.99 are not useful for comparative purposes. To illustrate, in the right tail, $\pi = 0.99$ corresponds to $r_{602:608} = 7.002$, while $r_{601:608} = 6.014$ and $r_{603:608} = 7.233$. Confidence intervals can, in fact, be derived for the ξ_π (see, for example, Mood et al., 1974), although we do not pursue this here.

1.705) and asymmetric ($\hat{\alpha} = 1.671$) stable Paretian distributions. For the latter, we find that symmetry (i.e., $\beta = 0$) is rejected with $\hat{\beta} = -0.3677$.

Table 4.5 Estimates of Unconditional Distributions.[a]

	Location	Scale	Shape[b]		Skew
Normal	0.0958	2.537	2		—
	(0.103)	(0.073)	—		—
Laplace	0.2917	1.824	1		—
	(0.104)	(0.073)	—		—
DW	0.2285	1.871	1.063		—
	(0.012)	(0.074)	(0.033)		—
PAW	0.2517	1.826	0.9342	1.153	—
	NA	(0.083)	(0.035)	(0.050)	—
GED	0.2599	2.1150	1.120		—
	(0.088)	(0.197)	(0.080)		—
t	0.2207	1.826	3.915		—
	(0.091)	(0.096)	(0.680)		—
$S_{\alpha,0}$	0.1847	1.455	1.705		0
	(0.085)	(0.500)	(0.031)		—
$S_{\alpha,\beta}$	0.0151	1.431	1.671		-0.3677
	(0.120)	(0.060)	(0.065)		(0.130)

[a]Standard deviations are given in parentheses.
[b]The "Shape" entry for PAW consists of pair $\left(\alpha^-, \alpha^+\right)$, see (4.15).
(Adapted from: Mittnik, Paolella, Rachev (1998))

Figure 4.10 shows the kernel pdf of the Nikkei returns (dashed lines) along with the fitted pdf for each of the eight distributions. Although only an informal graphical tool, the plots suggest that only the $S_{\alpha,\beta}$ distribution can acceptably fit both the tails *and* the center of the empirical return distribution.

4.3   Conditional Distributional Models for Nikkei Index

The unconditional results in the previous section ignore possible temporal dependencies in the return series. Traditionally, serial dependence in time series

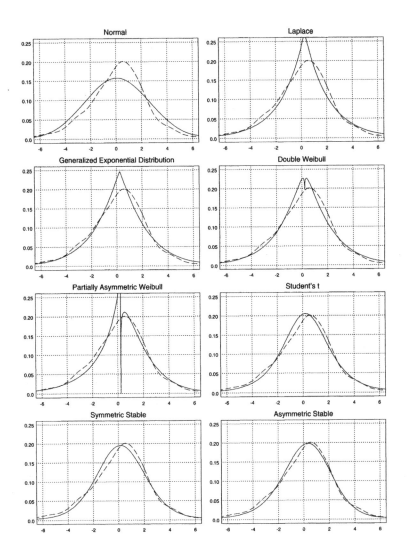

Fig. 4.10   Fitted Unconditional Densities of the Nikkei Returns. (Adapted from: Mittnik, Paolella, Rachev (1998))

has been modeled with ARMA structures. Such models allow conditioning of the process mean on past realizations, and have been proven successful for short-term prediction. An ARMA model of autoregressive order p and moving–average order q is of the form

$$r_t = a_0 + \sum_{i=1}^{p} a_i r_{t-i} + \epsilon_t + \sum_{j=1}^{q} b_j \epsilon_{t-j}, \qquad (4.23)$$

where ϵ_t is a white noise process. The unconditional distribution of ϵ_t corresponds to the conditional distribution of r_t conditioned on past returns.

As we have seen in Figure 4.8, the Nikkei returns exhibit volatility clusters. Such behavior can be captured by incorporating ARCH or GARCH structures (see Engle, 1982; and Bollerslev, 1986) which permit conditional heteroskedasticity by conditioning on past information. Below, we use ARMA-GARCH models to capture the conditional distribution of the Nikkei returns.

The ARMA–orders p and q in (4.23) were determined by inspection of the sample autocorrelation function (SACF) and sample partial autocorrelation function (SPACF) of the return series, shown in the top half of Figure 4.11. These are regarded as the standard univariate time–series "identification tools"—as advocated by Box and Jenkins (1976) (see also Brockwell and Davis, 1991; and Wei, 1990).

As is often the case in practice, no standard "textbook pattern" readily presents itself, rendering necessary a more subjective or "intuitive" judgement. With both a preference for parsimoniously parameterized models, and more emphasis placed on the short–run correlation spikes, we deemed the marginal significance of the two or three higher–order spikes, with no apparrant seasonal pattern, as unimportant. We considered instead either an AR(3) or MA(3) model, with the former yielding a higher likelihood value under all the innovation distributions considered here.[12]

Finally, it should be noted that we used normal asymptotic confidence intervals to determine the significance of SACF and SPACF spikes. The validity of this approach depends, among other things, on the existence of the fourth moment of the innovations. This is clearly violated under the assumption of α-stable innovations. Although the SACF provides a consistent estimate of the theoretical ACF in the presence of α-stable data, it is not asymptotically normally distributed (see Davis and Resnick, 1986).[13]

We model the GARCH structure of r_t by letting ϵ_t in (4.23) be of the form

$$\epsilon_t = \sigma_t u_t, \qquad (4.24)$$

where u_t denotes an i.i.d. location zero, scale unity random variable, and allowing the scale parameter σ to be time–varying according to the GARCH(r,s)

---

[12]Interestingly enough, inspection of the correlograms of the ARMA-GARCH filtered residuals, displayed in Figure 4.14 below, shows *no* significant spikes. This emphasizes the findings of Diebold (1986) and Bera, Higgins and Lee (1992), who show that the presence of ARCH structures invalidates the standard asymptotic theory of the sample correlograms.

[13]Brockwell and Davis (1991, pp. 540-2) provide examples, however, showing that with Cauchy (i.e., $S_{1,0}$) data, the usual variance bounds obtained from Bartlett's formula are close to the true ones; the latter being somewhat smaller, so that standard identification rules might still be approximately applicable.

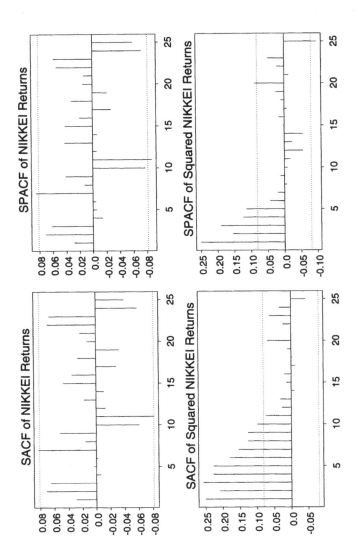

Fig. 4.11 Sample Correlograms of the Nikkei Returns.   (Adapted from: Mittnik,
Paolella, Rachev (1998))

equation

$$\sigma_t^2 = \omega + \sum_{i=1}^{r} \alpha_i \epsilon_{t-i}^2 + \sum_{i=1}^{s} \beta_i \sigma_{t-i}^2. \qquad (4.25)$$

For instance, in the normal case, $u_t \sim N(0,1)$, so that (4.25) represents the
conditional variance of the process at time t. For the Laplace, GED, t, and

PAW, scale parameter σ is not precisely the variance of the distribution,[14] but rather a multiple of it, so that the conditional volatility is not identical with the conditional variance.

For the α-stable case, for which the variance does not exist, (4.25) is meaningless in characterizing the heteroskedasticity of the data. Instead, Panorska, Mittnik and Rachev (1995) proposed the stable GARCH model by combining (4.24) with

$$\sigma_t = \omega + \sum_{i=1}^{r} \alpha_i |\epsilon_{t-i}| + \sum_{i=1}^{s} \beta_i \sigma_{t-i}, \qquad (4.26)$$

where u_t are i.i.d. realizations of an α-stable distributed random variable with $\alpha > 1$. Assumption $\alpha \in (1, 2]$, avoids a number of technical problems arising from the fact that $\alpha \leq 1$ implies such fat tails that u_t and, thus, σ_t and r_t, do not even possess first moments. However, the restriction does not seem to have practical relevance in empirical work, because the existence of first moments is hardly rejected in financial or economic time series. As α approaches 2, model (4.26) becomes the GARCH extension of the standard deviation ARCH model with normal innovations, as proposed by Taylor (1986) and Schwert (1989).

A standard approach to detecting GARCH-dependencies in time series r_t is to compute the SACF and SPACF of the squared series, r_t^2, as shown in the bottom half of Figure 4.11. Standard Box-Jenkins methodology would suggest the need for a mixed GARCH model, i.e., one with r and s both greater than zero. As is common in financial GARCH modeling (see, for example, Bollerslev, Chou and Kroner, 1992; and Bollerslev, Engle and Nelson, 1994), it was found that $r = s = 1$ was adequate in capturing the autocorrelation structure for the squared Nikkei returns.

Although other methods exist for estimation of the parameters in a joint ARMA-GARCH model, ML estimation possesses at least two noteworthy advantages (see Hsieh, 1989). Firstly, joint estimation of all model parameters, including the "nuisance" parameters characterizing the innovations distribution is possible; and, secondly, parameter constraints ensuring stationarity and nonnegativity of σ_t are more easily embedded in the estimation routine. Precise details of the latter constraint in general GARCH(r, s) models are provided by Nelson and Cao (1992). For the GARCH(1,1) model used here, the constraints, as originally proposed by Bollerslev (1986), namely that $\omega \geq 0$, $\alpha_1 > 0$, and $\beta_1 \geq 0$, have to hold. With GARCH models, conditional ML estimation is far more feasible than exact ML, particularly so when using nonnormal distributions.[15] In addition to conditioning on $\{r_0, r_{-1}, r_{-2}\}$, as required for the AR(3) structure, we need to specify values for ϵ_0^2 and σ_0^2.

---

[14]Calculations show that the variance of the Laplace, GED, Student's t and PAW distributions are given by 2, $\Gamma(3/\alpha)/\Gamma(1/\alpha)$, $\frac{\alpha}{\alpha-2}$ and $\frac{1}{2}\left[\Gamma\left(1 + \frac{2}{\alpha-}\right) + \Gamma\left(1 + \frac{2}{\alpha+}\right)\right]$, respectively, multiplied by σ^2.

[15]Diebold and Schuermann (1992) have considered exact ML estimation of an ARCH model with normal innovations.

We follow the suggestion of Nelson and Cao (1992), and use values set to the unconditional variance dictated by the GARCH parameters, provided the variance of ϵ_t exists, which we assume when using distributions other than the α-stable.

It follows from (4.25) that

$$\mathrm{E}\sigma_0^2 = \omega \left(1 - \lambda \sum_{i=1}^{r} \hat{\alpha}_i + \sum_{j=1}^{s} \hat{\beta}_j \right)^{-1}, \qquad (4.27)$$

where $\lambda := \mathrm{E}u_t^2$ depends on the particular distribution (e.g., for Student's t, $\lambda = \alpha/(\alpha - 2)$), and $\mathrm{E}\epsilon_0^2 = \lambda\mathrm{E}\sigma_0^2$. At the kth iteration in the iterative ML estimation, we set $\hat{\epsilon}_0^2$ and $\hat{\sigma}_0^2$ to their unconditional values, as implied by the parameter estimates at the $(k-1)^{\mathrm{st}}$ iteration.

For the α-stable cases, where $|\epsilon_t|$ is modeled in the GARCH structure, we take $\lambda = \lambda_{\alpha,\beta} := \mathrm{E}\,|u_t|$, where

$$\lambda_{\alpha,\beta} = \frac{2}{\pi}\Gamma\left(1 - \frac{1}{\alpha}\right)(1 + \tau_{\alpha,\beta}^2)^{\frac{1}{2\alpha}}\cos\left(\frac{1}{\alpha}\arctan\tau_{\alpha,\beta}\right), \qquad (4.28)$$

with $\tau_{\alpha,\beta} = \beta\tan\frac{\alpha\pi}{2}$. In the symmetric case, i.e., $\beta = 0$, (4.28) reduces to

$$\lambda_{\alpha,0} = \frac{2}{\pi}\Gamma\left(1 - \frac{1}{\alpha}\right), \qquad 1 < \alpha < 2. \qquad (4.29)$$

Panorska, Mittnik and Rachev (1995) derived the necessary and sufficient conditions for strict stationarity of (4.26), when driven by symmetric stable innovations. This was generalized by Mittnik, Paolella and Rachev (1997) to the asymmetric case, where the class of IGARCH processes with asymmetric α-stable innovations is considered in more detail.

The goodness–of–fit measures of the fitted conditional heteroskedastic models and their ML parameter estimates are reported in Tables 4.6 and 4.7, respectively. Compared to their unconditional $\mathcal{L}$ values from Table 4.3, for each distribution, the improvement in fit obtained by adding an AR-GARCH structure is substantial. As in the conditional case, the PAW achieves the largest likelihood value, with $\mathcal{L} = -1330.5$. In comparison, $\mathcal{L}$ values for the $S_{\alpha,\beta}$ (-1333.7), t (-1333.9), $S_{\alpha,0}$ (-1334.9), DW (-1335.3), GED (-1336.9), Laplace (-1344.2), and normal (-1352.5) are smaller.

Across nested models, likelihood ratio tests indicate significant differences. For example, comparing the DW and PAW, $\Lambda = -2\,(\mathcal{L}_{DW} - \mathcal{L}_{PAW}) = 9.6$, yielding the highly significant "p-value" $\mathrm{Pr}\,(X \geq \Lambda) = 0.0019$, where $X \sim \chi_1^2$, the asymptotic distribution of Λ. It should be kept in mind that this is not a test for asymmetry *per se*, as it is distribution dependent. Indeed, $\Lambda = -2\,(\mathcal{L}_{\alpha,0} - \mathcal{L}_{\alpha,\beta}) = 2.4$, with p-value 0.1213, so that under the α-stable assumption, symmetry cannot be adamantly rejected. Finally, p-values between Laplace and DW (2.5×10^{-5}), and Laplace and GED (1.3×10^{-4}),

Table 4.6 Goodness of Fit and Persistence of Volatility Measure of Conditional Heteroskedastic Distributions.[a]

	$\mathcal{L}$	KD	AD_0	AD_1	AD_2	$\hat{\lambda}\hat{\alpha}_1 + \hat{\beta}_1$
Normal	-1352.5	4.31	447.6	0.978	0.113	0.9505
		(514)	(1)	(2)	(561)	
Laplace	-1344.2	4.08	0.129	0.123	0.121	0.9710
		(182)	(579)	(578)	(577)	
DW	-1335.3	3.26	0.115	0.113	0.113	0.9761
		(195)	(587)	(570)	(586)	
PAW	-1330.5	3.84	0.202	0.197	0.195	0.9708
		(199)	(7)	(8)	(31)	
GED	-1336.9	4.29	1.015	0.132	0.124	0.9628
		(111)	(1)	(2)	(111)	
t	-1333.9	4.42	0.282	0.129	0.127	0.9581
		(109)	(1)	(109)	(110)	
$S_{\alpha,0}$	-1334.9	3.22	0.095	0.093	0.092	0.9490
		(503)	(12)	(45)	(48)	
$S_{\alpha,\beta}$	-1333.7	3.07	0.086	0.086	0.085	0.9468
		(494)	(85)	(87)	(84)	

[a]See Table 4.3 for explanations of $\mathcal{L}$, KD and AD. For $S_{\alpha,0}$ and $S_{\alpha,\beta}$, $\hat{\lambda}$ refers to $\lambda_{\alpha,\beta} = E|\epsilon_t|$; otherwise, $\hat{\lambda} = E\epsilon_t^2$, which depends on the particular distribution and its shape parameters. $\hat{\lambda}\hat{\alpha}_1 + \hat{\beta}_1$ is a measure of persistence of volatility, which, if equal to one, indicates an integrated GARCH model.
(Adapted from: Mittnik, Paolella, Rachev (1998))

are quite significant, indicating that, even against symmetric alternatives, the Laplace is not adequate for modeling the innovations driving the Nikkei return series.

Regarding the KD and AD statistics, once again, the $S_{\alpha,\beta}$ distributional assumption dominates, with both minimal KD-value 3.07 (as compared to $S_{\alpha,0}$, 3.22; DW, 3.26; PAW, 3.84; Laplace, 4.08; GED, 4.29; Normal, 4.31; and t, 4.42), and minimal AD_0-value ($S_{\alpha,\beta}$; 0.086, $S_{\alpha,0}$, 0.095; DW, 0.115; Laplace, 0.129; PAW, 0.202; t, 0.282; GED, 1.015; and Normal, 447.6). Rather alarming is the AD_0-value 447.6 for the normal. Even more interesting is that removal of the two largest "outliers" results in the normal tying the DW with the third best AD_2-value of 0.113. Whereas centrally located observations were decisive for the KD statistics of all eight distributions, with the exception of Laplace and DW, values from the left tail were critical for the AD_0, primarily, in fact, the smallest (most negative) value. For the Laplace and DW, values near the right tail were decisive (recall there are only 605 innovations under the conditional model).

Table 4.7 Estimates of Conditional Heteroskedastic Distributions.[a]

	\multicolumn{4}{c}{AR Parameters}				\multicolumn{3}{c}{GARCH Parameters}	\multicolumn{2}{c}{Distribution Parameters}	
	a_0	a_1	a_2	a_3	ω	α_1	β_1	Shape[b]	Skew
Normal	0.1699	0.0303	0.0624	0.0862	0.3073	0.1495	0.8010	2	—
	(0.084)	(0.043)	(0.047)	(0.042)	(0.104)	(0.025)	(0.032)	—	—
Laplace	0.2502	0.0455	0.1085	0.0729	0.1574	0.0848	0.8015	1	—
	(0.040)	(0.018)	(0.014)	(0.026)	(0.048)	(0.015)	(0.031)	—	—
DW	0.2765	0.0452	0.0454	0.0772	0.1400	0.1022	0.8117	1.1432	—
	(0.013)	(0.010)	(0.008)	(0.003)	(0.030)	(0.024)	(0.031)	(0.031)	—
PAW	0.2612	0.0369	0.0389	0.1082	0.1450	0.1023	0.8056	1.047 1.283	—
	NA	(0.011)	(0.011)	(0.039)	(0.033)	(0.025)	(0.030)	(0.050) (0.090)	—
GED	0.2449	0.0492	0.0892	0.0676	0.2485	0.1487	0.8048	1.252	—
	(0.041)	(0.041)	(0.043)	(0.041)	(0.043)	(0.030)	(0.028)	(0.025)	—
t	0.2375	0.0469	0.0586	0.0618	0.1849	0.1161	0.7972	7.183	—
	(0.044)	(0.040)	(0.042)	(0.040)	(0.073)	(0.025)	(0.041)	(1.730)	—
$S_{\alpha,0}$	0.2396	0.0597	0.0517	0.0580	0.0835	0.1167	0.8085	1.877	0
	(0.040)	(0.041)	(0.041)	(0.041)	(0.030)	(0.021)	(0.035)	(0.024)	—
$S_{\alpha,\beta}$	0.2003	0.0524	0.0492	0.0505	0.0850	0.1156	0.8075	1.881	-0.4813
	(0.041)	(0.039)	(0.041)	(0.037)	(0.029)	(0.022)	(0.036)	(0.027)	(0.013)

[a] Standard deviations are given in parentheses.
[b] The "Shape" entry for PAW consists of pair $\left(\alpha^-, \alpha^+\right)$, see (4.15).
(Adapted from: Mittnik, Paolella, Rachev (1998))

Similar to the unconditional case, Figure 4.12 plots the estimated standardized distances $\left[F_s(x) - \hat{F}(x)\right] / \sqrt{\hat{F}(x)\left(1 - \hat{F}(x)\right)}$ for the eight fitted conditional distributions, omitting extreme values for the normal and GED cases. Cursory inspection of the indicated bounds (dashed lines) again points to the superiority of the fit obtained using the $S_{\alpha,\beta}$ assumption.[16]

From Table 4.7, one notices that the shape parameters of all six relevant distributions have increased, as compared to those of the unconditional distributions reported in Table 4.5. This indicates that the GARCH–conditional distributions have thinner tails than the unconditional counterparts. This is what one expects, as ARCH/GARCH components are potentially responsible for some portion of the excess kurtosis in the unconditional distribution.

---

[16] Calculation and comparison of estimated quantile values could, in principle, also be conducted in the conditional case, using the filtered r_t values. However, their direct interpretation as measures of risk no longer holds.

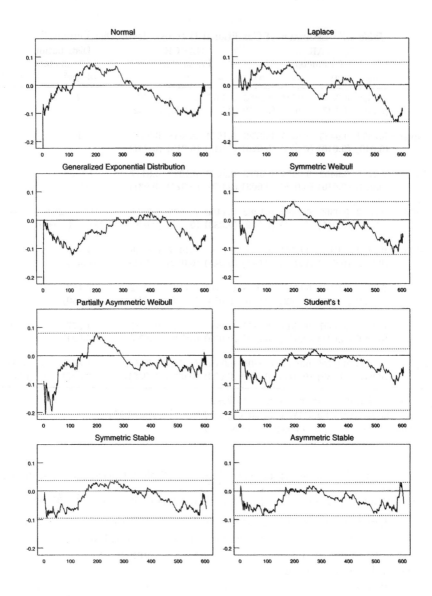

Fig. 4.12 Standardized cdf Deviations (Anderson–Darling) of Fitted Conditional Densities. (Adapted from: Mittnik, Paolella, Rachev (1998))

Of considerable interest is the persistence of volatility, i.e., to what extent does u_t, the shock at time t, remain influential for future σ_{t+i}, $i = 1, 2, \ldots$. For a GARCH model with *finite* variance innovations, conditional volatility is synonymous with a multiple of the conditional variance. For a GARCH(1,1)

Table 4.8 Statistical Properties of AR(3)-GARCH(1,1) Filtered Residuals Under Normality Assumption.[a]

Mean	Std. Dev.	Skewness	Kurtosis	LM	$LM_{.95,605}$
0.0453	1.0102	-0.7214	6.540	312.7	5.92

[a]See Table 4.2 for explanations.

(Adapted from: Mittnik, Paolella, Rachev (1998))

model, the persistence of volatility can be measured with the statistic $\lambda\alpha_1 + \beta_1$, where $\lambda = E\epsilon_t^2$ in the finite variance case, and $\lambda = E|\epsilon_t|$ for the α-stable infinite variance case, as discussed above. If strictly less than unity, this implies a conditional volatility equation where the impact of a shock dies out over time. If $\lambda\alpha_1 + \beta_1 = 1$, we have a so-called *integrated* GARCH or IGARCH model, which implies non-decaying effects of shocks on the conditional volatility (see Engle and Bollerslev, 1986).

From Table 4.6, the estimates of $\hat{\lambda}\hat{\alpha}_1 + \hat{\beta}_1$ are normal (0.9505), Laplace (0.9710), DW (0.9761), PAW (0.9708), GED (0.9628), and t (0.9581). For $S_{\alpha,0}$, $\lambda_{\hat{\alpha},0}\hat{\alpha}_1 + \hat{\beta}_1 = 0.9490$; for $S_{\alpha,\beta}$, $\lambda_{\hat{\alpha},\hat{\beta}}\hat{\alpha}_1 + \hat{\beta}_1 = 0.9468$. As each value is well away from the borderline value of unity, we conclude that the innovations driving the Nikkei index are not persistent in their effect on conditional volatility, but rather die out over time.

Similar to Figure 4.10, Figure 4.13 shows the kernel and fitted pdf's of the conditional AR–GARCH residuals across the eight distributions. It should be kept in mind that, with the GARCH component taken into account, the resulting plots refer to the standardized (location-zero, scale-one) distributions, and, hence, are not directly comparable with one another. Nevertheless, it is still visually clear that incorporation of the GARCH component improves the fit of all the distributions; and, by any criteria considered here, the normal distribution is still seen to be inadequate in modeling the underlying innovations of the Nikkei returns.

Table 4.8 is analogous to Table 4.2 and presents summary statistics of the AR-GARCH residuals assuming normal innovations. Note that the estimated standard deviation is very close to unity, which stems from the normalization induced by the GARCH structure. Compared to the rejection region $\{x : x \geq 5.92\}$, test statistic $LM = 312.7$ allows the null hypothesis of normality, once again, to be strongly rejected, which agrees with the visual impression from Figure 4.13.[17]

---

[17]The fact that the LM test statistic corresponding to the conditional case is in fact larger than that in the unconditional case, where $LM = 273.8$, is somewhat surprising. Although one would think that the GARCH term has removed excess kurtosis to pull the LM statistic "into the ballpark", the sheer magnitude of both statistics indicate that this is not the case, and that normality is still strongly rejected.

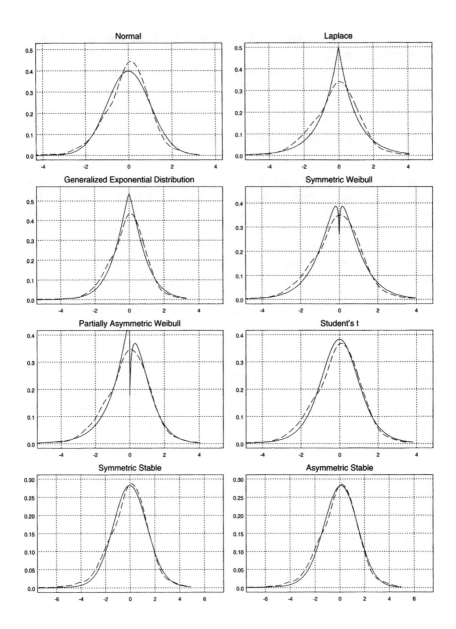

Fig. 4.13 Fitted Conditional Densities of the Nikkei Returns. (Adapted from: Mittnik, Paolella, Rachev (1998))

Finally, Figure 4.14 shows the correlograms of the ARMA–GARCH residuals themselves (top panels) and their squares (bottom panels), corresponding to the α-stable distribution.[18] One sees that the parsimoniously parameterized AR–GARCH model is capable of extracting the majority of the outstanding serial correlation exhibited by both the mean and variance of the Nikkei returns.

In conclusion, our empirical results show that simply assuming a fat–tailed unconditional distribution is not sufficient to capture the features of the Nikkei return data. In addition to the fat-tailed innovations, AR–GARCH structures are needed to successfully capture temporal dependencies in the returns on the Nikkei 225 index.

In terms of maximum obtained likelihood, the PAW, t, and $S_{\alpha,\beta}$ appear to be close competitors, with the former obtaining the largest likelihood value in both the unconditional and conditional cases. The $S_{\alpha,\beta}$ appears to be superior in terms of the cdf statistics KD and AD. Overall, the α-stable distribution presents itself as arguably the best candidate distribution, when one considers its desirable theoretical properties, its potential to model asymmetries, and its ability to fit the tails of the data exceptionally well.

These aspects make the asymmetric α-stable AR-GARCH model the most suitable candidate when attempting to assess the probability of large market moves or deriving value–at–risk type measures.

---

[18] The corresponding correlograms for the other seven distributions were qualitatively similar, and are not shown.

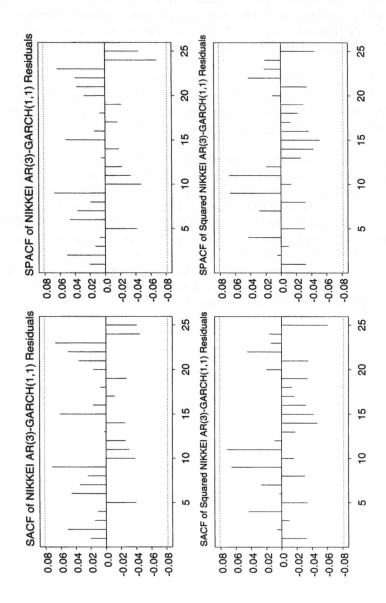

Fig. 4.14 Sample Correlograms of the Nikkei Residuals. (Adapted from: Mittnik, Paolella, Rachev (1998))

5

Subordinated, Fractional Stable and Stable ARIMA Processes

The literature on modeling asset–return processes can be broadly classified into two directions. The first direction deals with models for the unconditional return distribution. It began with the Gaussian model of Bachelier (1900), continued with stable Paretian model of Mandelbrot (1963a,b) and Fama (1965a) and has led to rather sophisticated families of distributions, which show a close fits to the data. Examples for the latter are the alternative stable distributions (Mittnik and Rachev, 1993a), hyperbolic distributions (Barndorff-Nielsen, 1994; Eberlein and Keller, 1994, 1995; and Küchler et al., 1994), the Student t distribution (Spanos, 1993), references given in the introduction. This direction has been at the center of this book, so far.

The second direction pursued in the literature has been concerned with modeling the dynamic structure of return processes, i.e., their evolution over time. Here much work has been done along the lines of processes with stationary and independent increments ("the random–walk hypothesis"), especially Brownian motion (Samuelson, 1965; for a recent discussion see also Föllmer and Schweizer, 1993) and jump processes (see Merton, 1989, Part 1, Sec. 3; and Section 5.1 below). This work focuses mainly on modeling the temporal movements of the first moment of returns. Such models are considered in this chapter.

Another large body of recent work on dynamic return modeling investigates the evolution of the variance (or volatility) of returns. The temporal dependence of these variances has led to the wide application of Engle's (1982) autoregressive conditional heteroskedasticity (ARCH) model and Bollerslev's (1986) generalization to GARCH models. These time series models can account, for example, for the heavy tails and the serial clustering properties of the financial return processes (see also the review Bollerslev, Chou and Kroner, 1992). ARCH–type models and their relationships to (unconditional) stable return–distribution models will be discussed in the subsequent chapter, among other things.

5.1   Subordinated Processes

5.1.1   An Overview of Some Subordinated Processes

The aim of this section is to provide several models for asset price dynamics which generalize the classical lognormal asset price model. In this first section we introduce an additional parameter to capture empirically observed anomalies that contradict the lognormality assumption. The method we use goes back to the seminal work of Mandelbrot and Taylor (1967).[1] It generalizes the classical lognormal asset price model using subordination. That is, we substitute the physical or calendar time in the well-known lognormal model by an *intrinsic* or *operational time* which, in a natural, way provides tail effects as observed in the market. This means mathematically, if $W = \{W(t), t \geq 0\}$ is a stochastic process and $T = \{T(t), t \geq 0\}$ is a non-negative stochastic process, then a new process $\{W(T(t)), t \geq 0\}$ may be formed which is said to be *subordinated* to W by the *intrinsic time process* T.[2]

We shall compare a number of subordinated processes as possible models for asset returns. The possible subordinated asset price models considered for the distribution of change in asset returns are: the classical lognormal model; the Mandelbrot Paretian stable model; the hyperbolic model; the log Students t model; the Clark model; and the log Laplace model. These models all have asset return processes subordinated to the *Wiener process* but they differ by their intrinsic time processes.

In the following section tests are performed on Standard&Poor's 500 composite index data to determine the "best" subordinated asset price model. These test include the Kolmogorow test and the Anderson and Darling test. The latter is well suited to test the tail behavior.

All of the models in this and next section have the asset price $S = \{S(t), t \geq 0\}$ modelled by a stochastic equation of the form

$$S(t) = S(t_0) \exp\{\mu(t - t_0) + \rho(T(t) - T(t_0)) + \sigma(W(T(t)) - W(T(t_0)))\} \quad (5.1)$$

for $0 \leq t_o < t < \infty$. The stochastic process $T = \{T(t), t \geq 0\}$, as already mentioned above, is called the *intrinsic time process* and has non-negative stationary independent increments. Intuitively it can be thought of as the cumu-

---

[1]The results in Section 5.1 are based on Hurst, Platen and Rachev (1995a,b).

[2]In Chapter 11 we shall derive non-arbitrage European call option prices by modeling the asset return process by processes subordinated to the Wiener process. An option pricing formula is derived which generalizes the Black and Scholes (1973) formula.

lative trading volume process which measures the cumulative volume of all the transactions up to physical time t. The stochastic process $W = \{W(u), u \geq 0\}$ represents the *noise process* which is introduced on the *intrinsic* time scale. It is assumed to be a standard Wiener process, which is independent of T. The process *subordinated* to the standard Wiener process W by the independent intrinsic process T is denoted by $Z = \{Z(t) = W(T(t)), t \geq 0\}$. It is used as the *driving process* in equation (5.1). We note that the process T plays the role of a stochastic internal time that is independent from the noise process W. Furthermore in equation (5.1) we have the *drift in the physical time scale* μ, the *drift in the intrinsic time scale* ρ and the *volatility* σ which are assumed to be constants.

In the following we combine the constant volatility σ into the subordinated process Z by using the Wiener process (Brownian motion) with increments $W(u+v) - W(u) \sim N(0, \sigma^2 v)$ for all $u, v \geq 0$, that are normally distributed with mean 0 and variance $\sigma^2 v$. Each model can then be characterized by either its intrinsic time process $T = \{T(t), t \geq 0\}$ or its subordinated driving process $Z = \{Z(t) = W(T(t)), t \geq 0\}$.

To formulate the relationship between the intrinsic time process T and the subordinated process Z we introduce the following notation. Consider the stochastic process with the stationary independent increments $X = \{X(t), t \geq 0\}$. For its increment $X(t+s) - X(t)$ where $s, t \geq 0$, we denote the corresponding distribution function (d.f.) by $F_{X,s}(\cdot)$; the ch.f. by

$$\phi_{X,s}(\theta) = \int_{\mathbf{R}} e^{i\theta x} dF_{X,s}(x) \tag{5.2}$$

for $\theta \in \mathbf{R}$; the density function by

$$f_{X,s}(x) = \frac{dF_{X,s}(x)}{dx} \tag{5.3}$$

for $x \in \mathbf{R}$ if this derivative exists; and the Laplace transform by

$$L_{X,s}(\gamma) = \int_0^\infty e^{-\gamma x} dF_{X,s}(x), \tag{5.4}$$

for $\gamma \geq 0$ if the increments of X are non-negative a.s.

The subordination approach explored here goes back to Bochner (1955), see also Feller (1966), Janicki and Weron (1994, pp. 33-34).

Let $W = \{W(t), t \geq 0\}$ be a Wiener process (as defined above) and $T = \{T(t), t \geq 0\}$ be a stochastic process with *non-negative* stationary independent increments, where W and T are independent processes. Then, $Z = \{Z(t) = W(T(t)), t \geq 0\}$ is also a stochastic process with stationary independent increments. Its increment $Z(t+s) - Z(t)$ has for all $s, t \geq 0$ the d.f.

$$F_{Z,s}(x) = \int_0^\infty \Phi\left(\frac{x}{\sigma\sqrt{u}}\right) dF_{T,s}(u), \tag{5.5}$$

where Φ is the standard normal d.f.; density function

$$f_{Z,s}(x) = \frac{1}{\sqrt{2\pi\sigma^2}} \int_0^\infty \frac{1}{\sqrt{u}} \exp\left\{-\frac{x^2}{2\sigma^2 u}\right\} dF_{T,s}(u), \qquad (5.6)$$

if it exists; and ch.f.

$$\phi_{Z,s}(\theta) = L_{T,s}\left(\frac{1}{2}\sigma^2\theta^2\right). \qquad (5.7)$$

Process T is called the *directing process* or *intrinsic time process*. Process Z is said to be *subordinated to W* using the intrinsic time process T.

For the proof that $Z = \{Z(t) = W(T(t)), t \geq 0\}$ is a process with stationary independent increments and distribution function given by equation (5.5), we refer to Feller (1966 pp. 333-336). Equations (5.6) and (5.7) follow directly from (5.5) with the definitions (5.3), (5.2) and (5.4).

Clark (1973) showed that for the subordinated process $Z = \{Z(t) = W(T(t)), t \geq 0\}$, the stationary increment $Z(t+s) - Z(t)$ has mean $\mu_{Z,s} = 0$, variance $\sigma_{Z,s}^2 = \mu_{T,s}\sigma^2$ and kurtosis $\kappa_{Z,s} = 3(1 + \sigma_{T,s}^2/\mu_{T,s}^2)$ for all $s \geq 0$, where $\mu_{T,s}$ and $\sigma_{T,s}^2$ are, respectively, the mean and variance of the stationary increment $T(t+s) - T(t)$ of the intrinsic time process T. It can also be shown that the stationary increments of Z are symmetric, i.e., the coefficient of skewness $\beta_{Z,s}$ is 0 for all $s \geq 0$. Consequently, all of our models are symmetric about the mean of zero. The models have finite variance if the intrinsic time process has finite mean of zero. The models have finite variance if the intrinsic time process has finite mean.

An important fact is that subordinated models with random intrinsic time are leptokurtic. This means that all of our subordinated models will have heavier tails and higher peaks around the mode of zero than the normal distribution. One can conclude from this discussion that just by introducing a random intrinsic time scale one ends up with a leptokurtic distribution for the increments of asset log-prices. On the other hand it is a very natural assumption to suppose that the intrinsic time driving an asset price evolution is a stochastic process.

Example 5.1 *(The Classical Lognormal Model)* Samuelson (1955) and Osborne (1959) proposed the asset log-price process to be modelled by a linear transformation of the Wiener process. (See also the discussion about the origin of this model in Cootner (1964).) For the subordinated process $Z = \{Z(t) = W(T(t)), t \geq 0\}$ to become a Wiener process W we require the intrinsic time process $T = \{T(t), t \geq 0\}$ to be deterministic physical time, that is $T(t) = t$ for all $t \geq 0$. Hence, the increment of Z has density

$$f_{Z,s}(x) = \frac{1}{\sqrt{2\pi\sigma^2 s}} \exp\left\{-\frac{x^2}{2\sigma^2 s}\right\}, \qquad (5.8)$$

ch.f.

$$\phi_{Z,s}(\theta) = \exp\left\{-\frac{1}{2}\sigma^2 s\theta^2\right\}, \qquad (5.9)$$

and d.f.

$$F_{Z,s}(x) = \Phi\left(\frac{x}{\sigma\sqrt{s}}\right), \tag{5.10}$$

where Φ is again the standard normal d.f. Note that the lognormal model is a one parameter model where the only parameter is σ.

Example 5.2 *(The Mandelbrot and Taylor Model)* Mandelbrot (1963a,b, 1967) proposed the asset log-prize process to be driven by a symmetric α-stable Lévy process, (see also Fama, 1963, 1965). For the subordinated process Z to become a symmetric α-stable Lévy process (Lévy motion) Mandelbrot and Taylor (1967) required the intrinsic time process T to be a maximal positively skewed $\alpha/2$-stable Lévy process. That is, they required T to have stationary independent increments

$$T(t + s) - T(t) \stackrel{d}{=} S_{\frac{\alpha}{2}}(cs^{\frac{\alpha}{2}}, 1, 0) \tag{5.11}$$

for all $s, t \geq 0$, $\alpha \in (0, 2)$ and $c > 0$. Recall that the first parameter $\alpha/2$ denotes the index of stability; the second parameter $cs^{\frac{\alpha}{2}}$ is a scale parameter; the third parameter represents the skewness and here obtains its maximal positive value of 1; and, finally, the fourth parameter is a location parameter and is set to 0.

The increment of T has ch.f.

$$\phi_{T,s}(\theta) = \exp\left\{-c^{\frac{\alpha}{2}}s|\theta|^{\frac{\alpha}{2}}\left(1 - i\tan\left(\frac{\pi\alpha}{4}\right)\mathrm{sign}(\theta)\right)\right\} \tag{5.12}$$

and Laplace transform

$$L_{T,s} = \exp\left\{-\frac{(c\gamma)^{\frac{\alpha}{2}}s}{\cos\left(\frac{\pi\alpha}{4}\right)}\right\}. \tag{5.13}$$

Using equations (5.7) and (5.13) the ch.f. of the increment of Z is

$$\phi_{Z,s}(\theta) \;=\; \exp\left\{-\frac{(\frac{1}{2}c\sigma^2\theta^2)^{\frac{\alpha}{2}}s}{\cos\left(\frac{\pi\alpha}{4}\right)}\right\} \tag{5.14}$$

$$\;=\; \exp\{-\varsigma^\alpha s|\theta|^\alpha\}, \tag{5.15}$$

where[3]

$$\varsigma = \frac{\sigma\sqrt{\frac{1}{2}c}}{\cos\left(\frac{\pi\alpha}{4}\right)^{\frac{1}{\alpha}}}. \tag{5.16}$$

One can easily show that equation (5.15) is the ch.f. of a symmetric α-stable Lévy process (α-stable motion) with *scale parameter* ς, see Samorodnitsky

---

[3] Mandelbrot and Taylor (1967) incorrectly have $\varsigma = \sigma\sqrt{\frac{1}{2}c}(1 + \tan(\frac{\pi\alpha}{4}))^{\frac{1}{\alpha}}$.

and Taqqu (1994). The subordinated process Z is therefore an α-stable motion. That is, Z has stationary independent increments $Z(t+s) - Z(t) \sim S_\alpha(\varsigma s^{\frac{1}{\alpha}}, 0, 0)$ for all $s, t \geq 0$.

Note that for the characterization of the intrinsic time process in the Mandelbrot and Taylor model we only need to specify the index of stability $\alpha \in (0, 2)$. Thus we need one additional parameter in comparison to the lognormal model. Furthermore, it can be shown that for $\alpha \to 2$ the intrinsic time process T asymptotically approaches physical time which leads us to the lognormal model.

Example 5.3 *(The Hyperbolic Model)* Barndorff-Nielsen (1994), Eberlein and Keller (1994, 1995) (see also Eberlein, 1992, and Küchler, Neumann, Sørensen and Streller, 1994) proposed the asset return process to be modelled by a process termed as "Hyperbolic Lévy motion". This process Z is subordinated to the Wiener process W (a Gaussian process) by an inverse Gaussian process T, hence, it is also referred to as a "Gaussian-Inverse Gaussian" process. As an inverse Gaussian process we require the intrinsic time process T to have stationary independent increments.

$$T(t+s) - T(t) \stackrel{d}{=} \textit{Inverse-Gaussian } (\alpha, \delta, s) \qquad (5.17)$$

for all $s, t \geq 0$ and given $\alpha, \delta > 0$, with probability density function

$$f_{T,s}(x) = \frac{\delta s}{\sqrt{2\pi}} x^{-\frac{3}{2}} \exp\left\{ -\frac{(\alpha x - \delta s)^2}{2x} \right\}, \quad x > 0. \qquad (5.18)$$

Their Laplace transform is

$$L_{T,s}(\gamma) = \exp\left\{ \alpha\delta s \left(1 - \sqrt{1 + \frac{2}{\alpha^2}\gamma} \right) \right\}. \qquad (5.19)$$

Using (5.6) and (5.18) the density function of the increment of Z follows as

$$
\begin{aligned}
f_{Z,s}(x) &= \frac{\delta s}{2\pi\sigma} \int_0^\infty u^{-2} \exp\left\{ -\frac{1}{2u}\left((\alpha u - \delta s)^2 + \frac{x^2}{\sigma^2} \right) \right\} du \qquad (5.20) \\
&= \frac{\alpha\delta s}{\pi} \exp\{\alpha\delta s\} \frac{1}{\sqrt{x^2 + (\sigma\delta s)^2}} K_1\left(\frac{\alpha}{\sigma}\sqrt{x^2 + (\sigma\delta s)^2} \right), (5.21)
\end{aligned}
$$

where $K_1(\cdot)$ denotes the modified Bessel function of the third kind with index 1, as derived in Barndorff-Nielsen (1977). Similarly, by using equations (5.5) and (5.18) the distribution function for the increments of Z obtains the form

$$F_{Z,s}(x) = \frac{\delta s}{\sqrt{2\pi}} \int_0^\infty u^{-\frac{2}{3}} \exp\left\{ -\frac{(\alpha u - \delta s)^2}{2u} \right\} \Phi\left(\frac{x}{\sigma\sqrt{u}} \right) du. \qquad (5.22)$$

Also, by using (5.7) and (5.19) the ch.f. of the increment of Z can be computed as

$$\phi_{Z,s}(\phi) = \exp\left\{\alpha\delta s\left(1 - \sqrt{1 + \frac{\sigma^2}{\alpha^2}\theta^2}\right)\right\}. \qquad (5.23)$$

If we re-parameterize, setting

$$\tilde{\alpha} = \frac{\alpha}{\sigma}, \quad \tilde{\delta} = \sigma\delta, \qquad (5.24)$$

the density of the increment of Z can also be written in the form

$$f_{Z,s}(x) = \frac{\tilde{\alpha}\tilde{\delta}s}{\pi}\exp\{\tilde{\alpha}\tilde{\delta}s\}\frac{1}{\sqrt{x^2 + (\tilde{\delta}s)^2}}K_1\left(\tilde{\alpha}\sqrt{x^2 + (\tilde{\delta}s)^2}\right); \qquad (5.25)$$

the d.f. as

$$F_{Z,s}(x) = \frac{\tilde{\delta}s}{\sqrt{2\pi}}\int_0^\infty u^{\frac{3}{2}}\exp\left\{-\frac{(\tilde{\alpha}u - \tilde{\delta}s)^2}{2u}\right\}\Phi\left(\frac{x}{\sqrt{u}}\right)du; \qquad (5.26)$$

and the ch.f. as

$$\phi_{Z,s}(\theta) = \exp\left\{\tilde{\alpha}\tilde{\delta}s\left(1 - \sqrt{1 + \frac{1}{\tilde{\alpha}^2}\theta^2}\right)\right\}. \qquad (5.27)$$

Density (5.25) and ch.f. (5.27) imply that the subordinated process Z is a process with stationary independent increments $Z(t+s) - Z(t)$ which have the *generalized hyperbolic* distribution with parameters $\lambda = -\frac{1}{2}$, $\alpha = \tilde{\alpha}$, $\beta = 0$, $\mu = 0$ and $\delta = \tilde{\delta}s$ in the parameterization of Barndorff-Nielsen (1978), see also, Eberlein and Keller (1995), and Küchler, Neumann, Sørensen and Streller (1994).

Example 5.4 *(The Log Students t-Model)* For the classical lognormal model, the Mandelbrot and Taylor model, and the Barndorff-Nielsen and Eberlein model, the probabilistic features of the stationary independent increments $Z(t + s) - Z(t)$ of the subordinated process Z for any time increment s can be characterized by simple analytic expressions. The following models, which will be the log Students t model, the Clark model and the log Laplace model, do not have similar simple general analytic expressions but on the basis of a time increment of unit length there still exists a compact mathematical characterization. This means that we confine ourselves to equal physical time increments for the characterization of these models.

These models do however have a more complex generalized analytic characterization of the increments of the subordinated process. By using the ch.f. property of infinitely divisible processes, namely

$$\phi_{X,s}(\theta) = \{\phi_{X,1}(\theta)\}^s, \qquad (5.28)$$

the models defined in terms of a time increment of unit length can be generalized to time increments of any length s. The resulting expressions turn out to be just more complex. For simplicity we restrict ourself to physical time increments of unit length.

Praetz (1972) and Blattberg and Gonedes (1974) proposed the asset logprice processes to be driven by a Students t process. For the subordinated process Z to become a Students t process we require the intrinsic time process T to have increments

$$T(t+1) - T(t) \stackrel{d}{=} \frac{\nu}{\chi_\nu^2} \tag{5.29}$$

for all $t \geq 0$ which relate to the inverse of random variables that are chi-square distributed with ν degrees of freedom. Then, the increment of T has density

$$f_{T,1}(x) = \frac{(\frac{1}{2}\nu)^{\frac{1}{2}\nu}}{\Gamma(\frac{1}{2}\nu)} x^{-\frac{1}{2}\nu-1} \exp\left\{-\frac{\nu}{2x}\right\}, \quad x > 0, \tag{5.30}$$

where $\Gamma(z) = \int_0^\infty x^{z-1} e^{\{-x\}} dx$ is the Gamma function. Using (5.6) and (5.30) the probability density function of the increment of Z becomes

$$f_{z,1}(x) = \frac{(\frac{1}{2}\nu)^{\frac{1}{2}\nu}}{\sqrt{2\pi\sigma^2}\Gamma(\frac{1}{2}\nu)} \int_0^\infty u^{-\frac{1}{2}\nu-\frac{3}{2}} \exp\left\{-\frac{1}{2u}\left(\frac{x^2}{\sigma^2} + \nu\right)\right\} du. \tag{5.31}$$

Now transforming the integral in equation (5.31) into a Gamma function by letting $y = \frac{1}{2u}(\frac{x^2}{\sigma^2} + \nu)$ we obtain

$$f_{Z,1}(x) = \frac{\Gamma(\frac{1}{2}(\nu+1))}{\sigma\sqrt{\pi\nu}\Gamma(\frac{1}{2}\nu)}\left(1 + \frac{x^2}{\sigma^2\nu}\right)^{-\frac{1}{2}(\nu+1)} \tag{5.32}$$

$$= \frac{1}{\sigma}f_\nu\left(\frac{x}{\sigma}\right), \tag{5.33}$$

where $f_\nu(\cdot)$ is the probability function of a random variable $\nu \stackrel{d}{=} t_\nu$, which has a Students t distribution with ν degrees of freedom.

The subordinated process Z is therefore the Students t process which has increments $Z(t+1) - Z(t) \stackrel{d}{=} \sigma t_\nu$ for all $t \geq 0$. This model has two parameters, where the second parameter, namely the degrees of freedom parameter ν.

Example 5.5 *(The Clark Model)* As an alternative of the Mandelbrot-Taylor logstable model Clark (1973) proposed the asset *price* process to be generated via the process Z subordinated to the Wiener process W by a lognormal process T. Because we are interested in the log-price process, we model the asset *log-price* process by the subordinated process Z. Therefore, we require the intrinsic time process T to have increments

$$T(t+1) - T(t) \stackrel{d}{=} \log N(\mu, \varphi^2) \tag{5.34}$$

for all $t \geq 0$ and $\mu \in \mathbf{R}$, $\varphi > 0$. Here, the increment of T has probability density function

$$f_{T,1}(x) = \frac{1}{\sqrt{2\pi\varphi^2}} x^{-1} \exp\left\{-\frac{1}{2}\left(\frac{\log x - \mu}{\varphi}\right)^2\right\}, \quad x > 0. \tag{5.35}$$

Using (5.6) and (5.35) the density of the increment of Z becomes

$$f_{Z,1}(x) = \frac{1}{2\pi\varphi} \int_0^\infty y^{-\frac{3}{2}} \exp\left\{-\frac{1}{2}\left(\frac{x^2}{y} + \left(\frac{\log y - \mu - \log\sigma^2}{\varphi}\right)^2\right)\right\} dy \tag{5.36}$$

by transforming the integral in equation (5.6) with $y = \sigma^2 u$. Similarly, by (5.5) and (5.35), transforming the integral in (5.5) by again writing $y = \sigma^2 u$, the d.f. of the increment of Z is obtained as

$$F_{Z,1}(x) = \frac{1}{\sqrt{2\pi\varphi^2}} \int_0^\infty y^{-1} \exp\left\{-\frac{1}{2}\left(\frac{\log y - \mu - \log\sigma^2}{\varphi}\right)^2\right\} \Phi\left(\frac{x}{\sqrt{y}}\right) dy. \tag{5.37}$$

If we re-parameterize by setting

$$\tilde{\mu} = \mu + \log\sigma^2, \tag{5.38}$$

then

$$f_{Z,1}(x) = \frac{1}{2\pi\varphi} \int_0^\infty u^{-\frac{3}{2}} \exp\left\{-\frac{1}{2}\left(\frac{x^2}{u} + \left(\frac{\log u - \tilde{\mu}}{\varphi}\right)^2\right)\right\} du \tag{5.39}$$

and the distribution function of the increment of Z has the form

$$F_{Z,1}(x) = \frac{1}{\sqrt{2\pi\varphi^2}} \int_0^\infty u^{-1} \exp\left\{-\frac{1}{2}\left(\frac{\log u - \tilde{\mu}}{\varphi}\right)^2\right\} \Phi\left(\frac{x}{\sqrt{u}}\right) du. \tag{5.40}$$

Therefore, the subordinated process Z therefore has increments $Z(t+1) - Z(t) \stackrel{d}{=} \sqrt{T}W$ for all $t \geq 0$, where $W \stackrel{d}{=} N(0,\sigma^2)$ and $T \stackrel{d}{=} \log N(\mu, \varphi^2)$, or, equivalently, when re-parameterized $W \stackrel{d}{=} N(0,1)$ and $T \stackrel{d}{=} \log N(\tilde{\mu}, \varphi^2)$. Note that we have the two parameters $\tilde{\mu}$ and φ in the Clark model.

Example 5.6 *(The Log Laplace Model)* In Mittnik and Rachev (1993a) (see Section 2.2.1) an the asset log-price process to be driven by the symmetric geometric-stable process is proposed. In particular, the symmetric Laplace process belongs to this class of processes playing the role of the Wiener process in the geometric summation scheme. For the subordinated process Z to become the symmetric Laplace process we require the intrinsic time process T to be a negative-exponential process with increments

$$T(t+1) - T(t) \stackrel{d}{=} \mathrm{Exp}(\lambda), \tag{5.41}$$

for all $t \geq 0$ and $\lambda > 0$. The increment of T has probability density function

$$f_{T,1}(x) = \lambda e^{-\lambda x}, \tag{5.42}$$

for $x > 0$, and Laplace transform

$$L_{T,1}(\gamma) = \frac{\lambda}{\lambda + \gamma}, \tag{5.43}$$

for $\gamma \geq 0$. Using (5.6) and (5.42) the density function of the increment of Z is

$$f_{Z,1}(z) = \frac{\lambda}{\sqrt{2\pi\sigma^2}} \int_0^\infty \frac{1}{\sqrt{u}} \exp\left\{ -\frac{z^2}{2\sigma^2 u} - \lambda u \right\} du \tag{5.44}$$

$$= \frac{\sqrt{\lambda}}{\sqrt{2}\sigma} \exp\left\{ -\frac{\sqrt{2\lambda}|z|}{\sigma} \right\}, \tag{5.45}$$

for $z \in \mathbf{R}$. With the definition of the distribution function given by (5.3) and (5.45) the distribution function of the increment of Z has the form

$$F_{Z,1}(z) = \begin{cases} \frac{1}{2} \exp\left\{ \frac{\sqrt{2\lambda}z}{\sigma} \right\}, & z < 0 \\ 1 - \frac{1}{2}\exp\left\{ -\frac{\sqrt{2\lambda}z}{\sigma} \right\}, & z \geq 0. \end{cases} \tag{5.46}$$

From (5.7) and (5.43) the c.f. of the increment of Z turns out to be

$$\phi_{Z,1}(\theta) = \frac{1}{1 + \frac{1}{2}\sigma^2\theta^2}, \tag{5.47}$$

for $\theta \in \mathbf{R}$.

With re-parameterization

$$\tilde{\sigma} = \frac{\sigma}{\sqrt{2\lambda}} \tag{5.48}$$

the probability density function of the increment of Z is

$$f_{Z,1}(z) = \frac{1}{2\tilde{\sigma}} \exp\left\{ -\frac{|z|}{\tilde{\sigma}} \right\}, \tag{5.49}$$

for $z \in \mathbf{R}$; the distribution function of Z can be written as

$$F_{Z,1}(z) = \begin{cases} \frac{1}{2} \exp\left\{ \frac{z}{\tilde{\sigma}} \right\}, & z < 0 \\ 1 - \frac{1}{2}\exp\left\{ -\frac{z}{\tilde{\sigma}} \right\}, & z \geq 0; \end{cases} \tag{5.50}$$

and the ch.f. has the form

$$\phi_{Z,1}(\theta) = \frac{1}{1 + \tilde{\sigma}^2\theta^2}, \tag{5.51}$$

for $\theta \in \mathbf{R}$. The subordinated process Z is therefore the symmetric Laplace process which has increments $Z(t + 1) - Z(t) \stackrel{d}{=} L(0, \tilde{\sigma})$, for all $t \geq 0$, that have mean 0 and variance $2\tilde{\sigma}^2$. Note that the Laplace model has only one parameter.

5.1.2   Empirical Comparison

Hurst, Platen and Rachev (1995a,b) (in short, HPR) examined the daily returns on the S&P 500 index from July 2, 1962 to December 31, 1991, a sample of 7421 observations.

Let $S(t)$ denote the asset price and $R(t)$ the return deserved on day t, i.e.,

$$R(t) = \log S(t) - \log S(t-1) \tag{5.52}$$

or equivalently

$$S(t) = S(t-1) \exp\{R(t)\}. \tag{5.53}$$

Table 5.1[4] displays some distributional properties of the S&P 500 daily returns, namely estimates for the mean $\hat{\mu}_1 = (\sum_{i=1}^{n} x_i)/n$, the kth moment about the mean $\hat{\mu}'_k = (\sum_{i=1}^{n} (x_i - \hat{\mu}'_1)^k)/(n-1)$ for $k = 2, 3, 4$, the skewness coefficient $\hat{\beta} = \hat{\mu}_3/\hat{\mu}_2^{3/2}$ and the kurtosis coefficient $\hat{\kappa} = \hat{\mu}_4/\hat{\mu}_2^2$. The estimate of the mean of the daily returns $\hat{\mu}_1$ is 2.71×10^{-4}, which equates to an effective annual return of 10.4%. The daily returns are slightly negatively skewed with an estimate of the coefficient of kurtosis $\hat{\kappa} = 64.83$. This value is significantly greater than 3, the value of the kurtosis when the distribution is normal, indicating that the daily returns of the S&P500 index are highly leptokurtic.

Table 5.1   Statistics of the S&P500 daily returns.

Statistic	Raw Data R	Normalized Data N
$\hat{\mu}_1$	0.0002709506	0
$\hat{\mu}'_2$	8.069187×10^{-5}	1
$\hat{\mu}'_3$	-1.644349×10^{6}	-2.268555
$\hat{\mu}'_4$	4.221392×10^{-7}	64.83300
$\hat{\beta}$	-2.268555	-2.268555
$\hat{\kappa}$	64.83300	64.83300

The types of models that HPR have considered are one parameter and two parameter models. The one-parameter models are the classical lognormal model (with parameter σ) and the log Laplace model (with parameter $\tilde{\sigma}$). The two-parameter models are the logstable model of Mandelbrot and Taylor (with parameters α and ς) and the Clark model (with parameters $\tilde{\mu}$ and φ).

Similar to Clark (1973), HPR estimated the parameters in all models by maximum likelihood estimators obtained from a *normalized* data N_i with

$$N_i = \frac{R(t_i) - \hat{\mu}_1}{\hat{c}_N}, \tag{5.54}$$

---

[4]For more complete exposition of the empirical results we refer to Hurst, Platen and Rachev (1995a,b).

where $\hat{\mu}_1$ and $\hat{c}_N$ are the estimated mean and standard deviation of the observed returns. For the daily returns of the S&P500 index we estimate $\hat{c}_N = 0.008982865$. The difference between the parameters for the normalized data N; and the raw data R_i can be seen in the equation between the variances:

$$\sigma^2_{W,\rho,R} = c^2_N \sigma^2_{W,\rho,N},\tag{5.55}$$

where $\sigma^2_{W,\rho,R}$ and $\sigma^2_{W,\rho,N}$ are the variances for the Wiener increments $W(t + \rho) - W(t)$, for all $t \geq 0$ and $\rho > 0$, for the raw and normalized data, respectively. The maximum likelihood parameter estimates for all the subordinated asset price models discussed in Section 5.1.1. are summarized in Table 5.2.

Table 5.2 The maximum likelihood parameter estimates for all of the models.

Model		Parameter Estimates	
Type	Name	Raw Data	Normalized Data
One parameter	lognormal	$\hat{\sigma} = 0.008982865$	$\hat{\sigma} = 1$
	log Laplace	$\hat{\hat{\sigma}} = 0.006162025$	$\hat{\hat{\sigma}} = 0.6859755$
Two parameter	Mandelbrot-Taylor	$\hat{\alpha} = 1.714$	$\hat{\alpha} = 1.714$
		$\hat{\varsigma} = 0.004950$	$\hat{\varsigma} = 0.551$
	Hyperbolic	$\hat{\hat{\alpha}} = 103.2767$	$\hat{\hat{\alpha}} = 0.927721$
		$\hat{\hat{\delta}} = 0.007667639$	$\hat{\hat{\delta}} = 0.853585$
	log Students t	$\hat{\nu} = 3.925560$	$\hat{\nu} = 3.925560$
		$\hat{\sigma} = 0.006159505$	$\hat{\sigma} = 0.6856949$
	Clark	$\hat{\hat{\mu}} = -9.948$	$\hat{\hat{\mu}} = -0.523$
		$\hat{\varphi} = 0.930$	$\hat{\varphi} = 0.930$

To use maximum likelihood estimation in the Clark model one needs probability density function (5.40) for increments $Z(t+1) - Z(t)$. Writing $u = \tan v$ the density is

$$\begin{aligned} f_{Z,1}(x) &= \frac{1}{2\pi\varphi} \int_0^{\frac{\pi}{2}} (\tan v)^{-\frac{3}{2}} \exp\left\{-\frac{1}{2}\left(\frac{x^2}{\tan v}\right.\right. \\ &\quad \left.\left. + \left(\frac{\log(\tan v) - \tilde{\mu}}{\varphi}\right)^2\right)\right\} (1 + \tan^2 v) dv. \end{aligned}\tag{5.56}$$

For the logstable model HPR used Zolotarev's (1966) integral representation for the probability density function, i.e.,

$$f_{Z,1}(x) = \frac{\alpha}{(\alpha - 1)\pi|x|} \int_0^{\frac{\pi}{2}} V_{\alpha,\varsigma}(x, \theta) \exp\{-V_{\alpha,\varsigma}(x, \theta)\} d\theta, \quad \text{if } \alpha > 1, \tag{5.57}$$

where

$$V_{\alpha,\varsigma}(x, \theta) = \left(\frac{|x| \cos(\theta)}{\varsigma \sin(\alpha\theta)}\right)^{\frac{\alpha}{\alpha - 1}} \frac{\cos((\alpha - 1)\theta)}{\cos(\theta)}.\tag{5.58}$$

The corresponding distribution function has the form

$$F_{Z,1}(x) = \begin{cases} 1 - \frac{1}{\pi} \int_0^{\frac{\pi}{2}} \exp\{-V_{\alpha,\varsigma}(x,\theta)\} d\theta, & \text{if } x \geq 0, \\ \frac{1}{\pi} \int_0^{\frac{\pi}{2}} \exp\{-V_{\alpha,\vartheta}(x,\theta)\} d\theta, & \text{if } x < 0, \end{cases} \qquad (5.59)$$

where $V_{\alpha,\vartheta}(x,\theta)$ is the same function as in equation (5.58).

HPR also used an alternative estimation method for the Mandelbrot-Taylor model. This method involves quantile estimation. The two parameters of the Mandelbrot-Taylor model were estimated by using a quantile method similar to the one described in McCulloch (1986). The quantile estimate (QE) of α is $\hat{\alpha} = 1.536155$ and that of ς is $\hat{\varsigma} = 0.510317$.

In HPR the *best model* is chosen to be the model whose distribution function $F_{Z,1}(x)$ is closest to the empirical distribution function $F_e(x)$ according to the Anderson and Darling (1952) statistics, which will be described below. The Kolmogorov distance (see Conover, 1980, Ch. 6)

$$K = \max_{x \in \mathbf{R}} |F_e(x) - F_{Z,1}(x)| \qquad (5.60)$$

could alternatively be used to decide which is a good model (see Chapter 2).

A short-coming of the Kolmogorov distance is that they are most sensitive around the median value, where $F_{Z,1}(x) = 0.5$, and less sensitive at the tails of the distribution, where $F_{Z,1}(x)$ is near 0 or 1. The reason for this is that under the null hypothesis the absolute difference $|F_e(x) - F_{Z,1}(x)|$ does not have a distribution that is dependent of x. Its variance is proportional to $F_{Z,1}(x)(1 - F_{Z,1}(x))$, which is largest at the median value and smallest at the tails of the distribution. To overcome this short-coming one can increase the power of the Kolmogorov statistic in the tails of the distribution by using the Anderson-Darling statistic (see Press et al., 1992, Sec. 14.3)

$$AD = \max_{x \in \mathbf{R}} \frac{|F_e(x) - F_{Z,1}(x)|}{\sqrt{F_{Z,1}(x)(1 - F_{Z,1}(x))}}. \qquad (5.61)$$

Table 5.3 summarizes the HPR-results on the values of the Kolmogorov and Anderson and Darling statistics for all models. The best models to fit the data near the *median* are the Clark model, the Barndorff-Nielsen model and the Mandelbrot and Fama logstable (quantile-estimated - QE), see Table 5.3. These models are followed by the log Students t model, the Mandelbrot and Fama logstable (maximum likelihood estimated - MLE) model and the log Laplace model. The lognormal model is clearly the worst model near the median value.

The best models to fit the data in the *tails of the distribution*, in particular the lower tail, are the Mandelbrot and Fama logstable (MLE & QE) model and the log Students t model.

Table 5.3 Goodness of fit the models.

Model		Test Statistic	
Type	Name	Kolmogorov	Anderson and Darling
One parameter	lognormal	0.06405479	5.746796×10^{67}
	log Laplace	0.02192405	23053.31
Two parameter	Mandelbrot-Taylor MLE	0.021289000	0.05580664
	Mandelbrot-Taylor QE	0.01290645	0.08718802
	Hyperbolic	0.01177449	247.1225
	log-t	0.01442057	0.09693746
	Clark	0.01157195	4.331836

5.2 Fractional Stable Processes

A crucial restriction in the Mandelbrot and Fama α-stable model[5] is the assumption that the returns are i.i.d. r.v.'s. This restriction can be relaxed by considering the more realistic model of self-similar processes.[6] An objective will be to "translate" the results for i.i.d. α-stable distributed r.v. driving the return process to "moving averages" as models for the financial return process.

Let return Y_k at time t_k be of the form

$$Y_k = \sum_{j \in \mathbf{Z}} c_j X_{k-j}, \quad \mathbf{Z} = \{0, \pm 1, \pm 2, \ldots\}, \tag{5.62}$$

where

$$c_j = \begin{cases} j^{-\beta-1}, & \text{if } j > 0 \\ 0, & \text{if } j = 0 \\ -|j|^{-\beta-1}, & \text{if } j < 0, \end{cases} \tag{5.63}$$

for some $\beta \in \left(\frac{1}{\alpha} - 1, \frac{1}{\alpha}\right)$ and $\alpha \in (0, 2)$; $\{X_j, \ j \in \mathbf{Z}\}$ is a sequence of i.i.d. r.v.'s belonging to the domain of attraction of a *strictly stable r.v. with index* α, whose ch.f. is given by

$$\mathbf{E}e^{i\theta X_k} = \exp\{-|\theta|^\alpha(A_1 + iA_2 \mathrm{sign}\theta)\}, \tag{5.64}$$

for some $A_1 > 0$, $A_2 \in \mathbf{R}$, with $|A_1^{-1} A_2| \leq \tan(\alpha\pi/2)$. From the representation of Y_k (5.62) it follows that the return at t_k depends on past returns

---

[5]See Section 2.1.1 in Chapter 2.

[6]For a recent account of the theory of self-similar processes (or so-called self-affine processes) we refer to Samorodnitsky and Taqqu (1994), Kono and Maejima (1991), Takenaka (1991), Evertsz and Mandelbrot (1992), Cioczek-Georges and Mandelbrot (1994b, 1995), Mandelbrot (1995a,b), Mori and Sato (1994), Cioczek-Georges, Mandelbrot, Samorodnitsky and Taqqu (1995) and the references therein.

and affects future returns. The nature of dependence of $\{Y_k\}$ is determined by the unknown parameters α and β, which have to be estimated. As for the usual α-stable approximation of i.i.d. r.v.'s in the domain of attraction of an α-stable distribution, we use the *fractional stable process* defined by Maejima (1983). For $t \in [0,1]$, we define

$$\Delta_n(t) \equiv |\beta| n^{-H} \left(\sum_{k=1}^{[nt]} Y_k + (nt - [nt]) Y_{[nt]+1} \right),$$

where $[a]$ is the integer part of a; summation $\sum_{k=1}^{0}$ is defined to be 0; and $H = 1/(\alpha - \beta)$. Consider two independent stable processes $\{Z_+(t), t \geq 0\}$ and $\{Z_-(t), t \geq 0\}$, both having ch.f.'s

$$\mathrm{E}\{e^{izZ_\pm(t)}\} = \exp\{-t|z|^\alpha(A_1 + iA_2 \operatorname{sign} z)\}. \tag{5.65}$$

Define the fractional stable process by

$$\Delta(t) = \int_{-\infty}^{+\infty} (|t-s|^{-\beta} - |s|^{-\beta}) dZ(s), \quad t \in [0,1],$$

where $\Delta(0) = 0$ a.s. and $Z(s) = Z_+(s)I[s \geq 0] - Z_-(-s+0)I[s < 0]$.

The fractional stable process $\Delta(\cdot)$, which was defined by Maejima (1983), is a *self-similar process* with parameter of self-similarity $H \in [0,1)$. Recalling briefly the definition of self-similar process we say $\{X(t), t \geq 0\}$ is a self-similar process (with parameter $H > 0$) having stationary increments, if $X(c\cdot) \stackrel{d}{=} c^H X(\cdot)$, for any $c > 0$, and $X(\cdot + b) - X(b) \stackrel{d}{=} X(\cdot) - X(0)$, for any $b > 0$. We refer to Samorodnitsky and Taqqu (1994), Janicki and Weron (1994) for a discussion of some basic properties of such processes.

The stationary sequence $\{Y_j\}_{j=1}^\infty$ is said to belong to the *domain of attraction of the self-similar process* $X(t)$ if, for some slowly varying function $L(\cdot)$,

$$n^{-H} L(n)^{-1} \sum_{j=1}^{[nt]} Y_j \stackrel{D}{\longrightarrow} X(t). \tag{5.66}$$

Here "$\stackrel{D}{\longrightarrow}$" stands for convergence of finite-dimensional distributions.

Many limit theorems of type (5.66) for strongly dependent random variables $\{Y_j\}$ have been obtained (see Samorodnitsky and Taqqu, 1994).

Theorem 5.1 *(Maejima (1983))* As $n \to \infty$,

$$\Delta_n(t) \stackrel{D}{\longrightarrow} \Delta(t). \tag{5.67}$$

To investigate the rate of convergence in (5.67), recall metric

$$\theta_r(X,Y) = \theta_r(F_X, F_Y)$$
$$= \left(\int_{-\infty}^{+\infty} \left| \int_{-\infty}^{x} F_X(u) - F_Y(u)du \right|^{\frac{1}{r-1}} \right)^{r-1}, \quad \text{for } 1 < r \le 2,$$

where $F_X(x) := P(X \le x)$, and

$$\theta_r(X,Y) = \left(\int_{-\infty}^{+\infty} |F_X(u) - F_Y(u)|^{1/r} du \right)^r, \quad \text{if } 0 < r < 1. \tag{5.68}$$

Then, clearly

$$\theta_r^{1/r}(X,Y) \le \int_{-\infty}^{+\infty} |F_X(u) - F_Y(u)| du \tag{5.69}$$

and, moreover, if $\int (F_X(x) - F_Y(x))dx = 0$ (i.e., $\mathbf{E}(X - Y) = 0$), then,

$$r\theta_r(X,Y) \le \int |x|^r |F_X(x) - F_Y(x)| dx \tag{5.70}$$

(see Maejima and Rachev (1987)). Let $\rho(X,Y) = \rho(F_X, F_Y) := \sup_x |F_X(x) - F_Y(x)|$ be the uniform distance between the d.f.'s F_X and F_Y.

In the remainder of this section, we shall apply metric θ_r to obtain the rate of convergence of (5.67) in terms of ρ. Let $\{X_j^*, j \in \mathbf{Z}\}$ be i.i.d. r.v.'s with c.f. (5.65); and let $\Delta_n^*(t)$ denote the counterpart of $\Delta_n(t)$ but defined with respect to $\{X_j^*, j \in \mathbf{Z}\}$. Note that by the stability property of α-stable distribution implies that for any fixed t $\Delta_n^*(t)$ is α-stable distributed.

Theorem 5.2 *(Maejima and Rachev (1987))*
(a) If $\theta_r(X_0, X_0^*) < \infty$ for some $r \in (\alpha, 2)$, then

$$\rho(\Delta_n(t), \Delta(t)) \le C_1 \theta_r(\Delta_n(t), \Delta_n^*(t))^{\frac{1}{1+r}} + \psi(n), \tag{5.71}$$

where

$$\psi(n) = \begin{cases} C_1 n^{-1}, & \text{for } \beta < 0, \\ C_2(n,t) n^{-H\alpha}, & \text{for } \beta > 0. \end{cases} \tag{5.72}$$

Here, C_1 depends only on α and β, $C_2(n,t) < C_3$ if $nt > C_4$, and C_3 and C_4 are constants depending on α and β.

(b) Quantity $\theta_r(\Delta_n(t), \Delta_n^*(t))$ can be estimated as follows. For each $t \in [0,1]$

$$\theta_s(\Delta_n(t), \Delta_n'(t)) \le Cn^Q D(n) \theta_s(X_0, X_0') , \tag{5.73}$$

where C is a positive constant depending on H, s and t ,

$$Q = -Hs + (s-1)^+ + \left\{ 2 - \left(1 - H + \frac{1}{\alpha} \right) s \right\}^+, \text{with}(a)^+ := max(0, a),$$

and

$$D(n) = \begin{cases} 1, & \text{if } H \neq 1/\alpha + 1 - 2/s, \\ \ln n, & \text{if } H = 1/\alpha + 1 - 2/s. \end{cases}$$

The above restrictions on α, H and s have the effect that $C < \infty$ and that Q, the exponent of n in (5.73), is negative.

Assuming that a return at time t has a α-stable distribution $\Delta(t)$ and that for $t_1 < t_2 < \ldots < t_k$ the joint distribution of the returns at $t_1, \ldots, t_k$ is distribution $(\Delta(t_1), \ldots, \Delta(t_k))$ is equivalent to assuming that returns follow a stable process. The statistical problem then is to estimate the parameters α and β in $\Delta(t)$. Note that one could easily extend the model by assuming that ch.f. (5.65) has the general form of the α-stable ch.f. Then, parameter β in (5.63) and the four parameters of the α-stable distribution need to be estimated.

5.3   ARMA and ARIMA Models with Infinite–Variance Innovations

In this section we briefly summarize some recent results on the estimation of ARMA and ARIMA processes with infinite variance.[7] Mikosch, Gadrich, Klüppelberg and Adler (1995) (hereafter, MGKA) considered a casual stationary, autoregressive, moving average process $\{X_t\}_{t\in\mathbf{Z}}$ satisfying the difference equation (see also Samorodnitsky and Taqqu (1994), Sec. 7.12)

$$X_t - \phi_1 X_{t-1} - \cdots - \phi_p X_{t-p} = Z_t + \theta_1 Z_{t-1} + \cdots + \theta_q Z_{t-q}, \qquad (5.74)$$

for $t \in \mathbf{Z} = \{0, \pm1, \pm2, \ldots\}$. In (5.74) the innovations $\{Z_t\}_{t\in\mathbf{Z}}$ consists of i.i.d. symmetric r.v.'s, in the domain of normal attraction of a symmetric stable distribution with index $\alpha \in (0,2)$ and scale parameter $\sigma_0 > 0$; i.e., as $n \to \infty$,

$$n^{-1/\alpha} \sum_{t=1}^{n} Z_t \xrightarrow{d} Y, \qquad (5.75)$$

where Z_0 has ch.f.

$$E e^{iuZ_0} = e^{-|\sigma_0 u|^\alpha}.$$

Process (5.74) is referred to as an infinite variance ARMA(p, q) process. MGKA determined estimators for

$$\beta = (\phi_1, \ldots, \phi_p, \theta_1, \ldots, \theta_q)'$$

[7]The results in this section are due to Mikosch, Gadrich, Klüppelberg and Adler (1995), Klüppelberg and Mikosch (1995a,b), (1996a,b,c), Davis (1996), Kokoszka and Taqqu (1995) and Kokoszka and Mikosch (1995). For more detailed analysis we refer to the proceedings Adler et al. (1998), and the monograph Embrechts et al. (1997).

and study their asymptotic properties. The MGKA method was based on the *sample periodogramm* of $\{X_t\}$, which is defined by

$$I_{n,X}(\lambda) = \left| n^{-1/\alpha} \sum_{t=1}^{n} X_t e^{-i\lambda t} \right|^2, \quad -\pi < \lambda < \pi. \tag{5.76}$$

Define now $(X_t)_{t \in \mathbf{Z}}$ as an infinite moving average

$$X_t = \sum_{j=0}^{\infty} \psi_j Z_{t-j}, \quad t \in \mathcal{Z}, \psi_0 := 1,$$

where ψ_j are specified, for a complex $z \in \mathbf{C}$ with norm $|z| \le 1$, by

$$1 + \psi_1 z + \psi_2 z^2 + \ldots := \psi(z) := \frac{\theta(z)}{\phi(z)}$$

with $\phi(z) = 1 - \phi_1 z - \cdots - \phi_p z^p$ and $\theta(z) = 1 + \theta_1 z + \cdots + \theta_q z^q$. Define the parameter space for β as

$$C := \{ \beta \in \mathbf{R}^{p+q} : \phi_p \ne 0, \theta_q \ne 0, \phi(z) \text{ and}$$
$$\theta(z) \text{ have no common zeros}, \phi(z)\theta(z) \ne 0 \text{ for } |z| \le 1 \}.$$

Next, define

(i) the "power transfer function" $g(\lambda, \beta)$ corresponding to $\beta \in \mathbf{C}$,

$$g(\lambda, \beta) := \left| \frac{\theta(e^{-i\lambda})}{\phi(e^{-i\lambda})} \right|^2 = |\psi(e^{-i\lambda})|^2;$$

(ii) the self-normalized periodogram $I_{n,X}$,

$$\tilde{I}_{n,X}(\lambda) = \frac{|\sum_{t=1}^{n} X_t e^{-i\lambda t}|^2}{\sum_{t=1}^{n} X_t^2}, \quad -\pi < \lambda \le \pi;$$

(iii) and objective functions

$$\sigma_n^2(\beta) = \int_{-\pi}^{\pi} \frac{\tilde{I}_{n,X}(\lambda)}{g(\lambda, \beta)} d\lambda,$$

and

$$\bar{\sigma}_n^2(\beta) = \frac{2\pi}{n} \sum_{j:\lambda_j = 2\pi j/n \in (-\pi,\pi]} \frac{\tilde{I}_{n,X}(\lambda_j)}{g(\lambda_j, \beta)}.$$

Suppose $\beta_0 \in \mathbf{C}$ is the true, but unknown, parameter vector. Then, two natural estimators of β_0 are given by[8]

$$\beta_n = \operatorname{argmin}_{\beta \in \mathbf{C}} \sigma_n^2(\beta),$$

and

$$\bar{\beta}_n = \operatorname{argmin}_{\beta \in \mathbf{C}} \bar{\sigma}_n^2(\beta) = \operatorname{argmin}_{\beta \in \mathbf{C}} \hat{\sigma}_n^2(\beta).$$

Theorem 5.3 *(MGKA (1995), Consistency of the β-estimators)* Under the above assumptions; we have as $n \to \infty$,

$$\beta_n \xrightarrow{p} \beta_0$$

and

$$\sigma_n^2(\beta_n) \xrightarrow{p} 2\pi \psi^{-2}(\beta_0).$$

The same limit relationship hold also for $\bar{\beta}_n$ and $\bar{\sigma}_n^2$.

Theorem 5.4 *(MGKA (1995): Asymptotic distribution of β_n and $\bar{\beta}_n$.)* Under the above assumptions we have

$$\left(\frac{n}{\ln n}\right)^{1/\alpha} (\beta_n - \beta_0) \xrightarrow{d} 4\pi W^{-1}(\beta_0) \frac{1}{Y_0} \sum_{k=1}^{\infty} Y_k b_k. \qquad (5.77)$$

In (5.77), $Y_0, Y_1, Y_2, \ldots$ are independent r.v.'s and

(i) Y_0 is positive $\frac{\alpha}{2}$-stable r.v. with Laplace transform

$$\mathbf{E} e^{-n Y_0} = e^{-(c_{Y_0} u)^{\alpha/2}}, \quad u \geq 0,$$

and $c_{Y_0} := C_{\alpha/2}^{-2/\alpha}$,

$$C_\alpha = \begin{cases} \frac{1-\alpha}{\Gamma(2-\alpha)\cos(\pi\alpha/2)}, & \text{if } \alpha \neq 1, \\ \frac{2}{\pi}, & \text{if } \alpha = 1; \end{cases}$$

---

[8]In the Gaussian case the estimator β_n is related to least squares and maximum likelihood estimators and is a standard estimator for ARMA processes with finite variance, see Whittle (1953), Hannan (1973), Fox and Taqqu (1986) and Dahlhaus (1989), Brockwell and Davis (1991). The Whittle estimator $\bar{\beta}_n$ in the Gaussian case (see, e.g. Brockwell and Davis, 1991, Sec. 10.8) is defined to be the value of β which minimizes

$$\hat{\sigma}_n^2(\beta) = \frac{1}{n} \sum_j \frac{I_{n,X}(\lambda_j)}{g(\lambda_j, \beta)},$$

where the sum is taken over all Fourier frequencies $\lambda_j = 2\pi j/n \in (-\pi, \pi]$; $I_{n,X}$ is given by (5.76); and

$$g(\lambda, \beta) := \frac{|1 + \sum_{k=1}^{q} \theta_k e^{-i\lambda k}|^2}{|1 - \sum_{k=1}^{p} \phi_k e^{-i\lambda k}|^2}, \quad -\pi < \lambda \leq \pi.$$

(ii) $Y_1, Y_2, \ldots$ are i.i.d. symmetric α-stable r.v.'s with ch.f.

$$\mathbf{E}e^{iuY_i} = e^{-|c_{Y_1} u|^{\alpha}}, \quad n \in \mathbf{R},$$

where $c_{Y_1} := C_{\alpha}^{-1/\alpha}$.

Furthermore, $W^{-1}(\beta_0)$ is the inverse of matrix

$$W(\beta_0) = \int_{-\pi}^{\pi} \left[\frac{\partial \ln g(\lambda, \beta_0)}{\partial \beta} \right] \left[\frac{\partial \ln g(\lambda, \beta_0)}{\partial \beta} \right]' d\lambda,$$

and; for $k \in \mathbf{N}$, b_k is the vector

$$b_k = \frac{1}{2\pi} \int_{-\pi}^{\pi} e^{-ik\lambda} g(\lambda, \beta_0) \frac{\partial g^{-1}(\lambda, \beta_0)}{\partial \beta} d\lambda, \qquad (5.78)$$

where g^{-1} denotes the reciprocal of g. Finally, (5.77) holds also with β_n being replaced by $\tilde{\beta}_n$.

Klüppelberg and Mikosch (1995-1996) studied the limit properties of the Whittle estimator when the underlying model is *not necessarily* an ARMA process. They consider a general linear model $X_t = \sum_{j=-\infty}^{\infty} \psi_j Z_{t-j}$ where the innovations Z_t belong to the domain of attraction of an α-stable law for $\alpha < 2$. Now the (X_t) is not necessarily a standard ARMA process of the form $\phi(B)X_t = \theta(B)Z_t$ but Klüppelberg and Mikosch (1994) fit an ARMA process of given orders to the data, $X_1, \ldots, X_n$, by estimating the coefficients of ϕ and θ.

In (5.77) the limiting distribution Y_1/Y_0 has heavy tails, in particular, $\mathbf{E}|Y_1/Y_0|^{\alpha} = \infty$. The explicit form of the distribution of Y_1/Y_0 can be determined by the following lemma.

Lemma 5.1 *(due to Klüppelberg and Mikosch)* Suppose that $\tilde{Y}_0$ and $\tilde{Y}_1$ are independent such that $\tilde{Y}_0$ is $S_{\alpha/2}(1, 1, 0)$ and $\tilde{Y}_1$ is $S_{\alpha}(1, 0, 0)$; i.e.; $\tilde{Y}_0$ is a positive standard $\alpha/2$-stable r.v. with Laplace transform

$$\mathbf{E}e^{-u\tilde{Y}_0} = e^{-u^{\alpha/2}}, \quad u \geq 0,$$

and $\tilde{Y}_1$ is a standard symmetric α-stable r.v. with ch.f.

$$\mathbf{E}e^{iu\tilde{Y}_1} = e^{-|u|^{\alpha}}, \quad u \in \mathbf{R}.$$

Then,

$$U = \frac{\tilde{Y}_1}{\tilde{Y}_0} \stackrel{d}{=} \epsilon |4Z(1, \rho)\gamma|^{1/\alpha},$$

where ϵ, $Z(1,\rho)$, and γ are independent r.v.'s, ϵ is a Rademacher variable, i.e.,

$$P(\epsilon = +1) = P(\epsilon = -1) = \frac{1}{2};$$

$Z(1,\rho)$ is a cut-off Cauchy variable with parameter $\rho = \alpha/2$, i.e.

$$P(Z(1,\rho) \le x) = \frac{G(x) - G(0)}{1 - G(0)},$$

where G is the d.f. of an $S_1(1, \alpha - 1, 0)$ r.v., i.e.,

$$\int_{\mathbf{R}} e^{itx} dG(x) = \exp\left\{ -|t| \left(1 + \frac{\alpha i(\alpha - 1)}{\pi} \operatorname{sign} t \right) \ln |t| \right\};$$

and γ is Gamma distributed with density $\pi^{-1/2} x^{-1/2} e^{-x}$.

It is somewhat surprising to notice that while for $ARMA(p, q)$ processes with finite variance, the Whittle estimate β_n is asymptotically normal with rate of convergence $\sqrt{n}$, in the stable case of Theorem 5.4 a considerably faster rate of convergence of order $(n/\ln n)^{1/\alpha}$, $\alpha < 2$, is obtained.

Davis (1995) considers two other estimates for $\beta = (\phi_1, \ldots, \phi_p, \theta_1, \ldots, \theta_q)'$,

(i) the Gauss-Newton-type estimator (see Brockwell and Davis, 1991, Sec. 8.11); and

(ii) an M-estimator.

For the Gauss-Newton estimator (i), Davis (1995) relaxed the assumption that innovations in (5.74) are in the normal domain of attraction, assuming that the d.f. F of Z_j is in the domain of attraction of α-stable law with $0 < \alpha < 2$, i.e., there exist constants $A_n > 0$ such that

$$\frac{1}{A_n} \sum_{i=1}^{n} Z_j \xrightarrow{d} Y,$$

where Y is an α-stable r.v..

His regularity assumptions in the setting of this section is of the form[9]

$$P(|Z_1| > x) = x^{-\alpha} L(x), \tag{5.79}$$

where $\alpha \in (0, 2)$ and $L(\cdot)$ is a slowly varying function at infinity;

$$\lim_{x \to \infty} \frac{P(Z_1 > x)}{P(|Z_1| > x)} = p \tag{5.80}$$

[9]Davis (1995) relaxed the symmetry assumption for Z_t replacing it with the condition that, if $\alpha > 1$, then $\mathbf{E} Z_t = 0$ while, if $\alpha = 1$, Z_t has a symmetric distribution.

for some $p \in [0, 1]$; and

$$\lim_{x \to \infty} \frac{P(|Z_1 Z_2| > x)}{P(|Z_1| > x)} = 2E|Z_1|^\alpha. \tag{5.81}$$

Now, if $\hat{\beta}_0 = (\hat{\beta}_{01}, \ldots, \hat{\beta}_{0,p+q})$ is an initial estimate of the true vector β_0, the *Gauss-Newton estimator*, $\hat{\beta}_G$, is given by

$$\hat{\beta}_G = \hat{\beta}_0 + \hat{\Delta}\beta, \tag{5.82}$$

where

$$\hat{\Delta}\beta = (D'D)^{-1} D' Z(\hat{\beta}_0) \tag{5.83}$$

with

$$Z_t(\hat{\beta}_0) = X_t - \phi_1 X_{t-1} - \cdots - \phi_p X_{t-p} - \theta_1 Z_{t-1}(\hat{\beta}_0) - \cdots - \theta_q Z_{t-q}(\hat{\beta}_0),$$

$$D_t = (D_{t,1}(\hat{\beta}_0), \ldots, D_{t,p+q}(\hat{\beta}_0))' \tag{5.84}$$

and

$$D_{t,i}(\beta) = -\frac{\partial Z_t(\beta)}{\partial \beta_i}, \quad i = 1, \ldots, p+q.$$

From a computational point of view, the Gauss-Newton estimator $\hat{\beta}_G$ is typically easier to calculate.

The asymptotic normality of $\hat{\beta}_G$ is shown in Davis (1996) by relying on the following results in Davis and Resnick (1985, 1986), who define

$$a_n = \inf\{x : P(|Z_1| > x) \le n^{-1}\} \tag{5.85}$$

and

$$b_n = \inf\{x : P(|Z_1 Z_2| > x) \le n^{-1}\}, \tag{5.86}$$

to show:

Lemma 5.2 *(Davis and Resnick (1985, 1986))* As $n \to \infty$,

$$\frac{b_n}{a_n} \to \begin{cases} \infty, & \text{if } E|Z_t|^\alpha = \infty, \\ (2\mathbf{E}|Z_t|^\alpha)^{-1/\alpha}, & \text{if } E|Z_t|^\alpha < \infty, \end{cases} \tag{5.87}$$

and, for any $h > 0$,

$$\left(a_n^{-2} \sum_{t=1}^n Z_t^2, b_n^{-1} \sum_{t=1}^n Z_t Z_{t+1}, \ldots, b_n^{-1} \sum_{t=1}^n Z_t Z_{t+h} \right) \overset{d}{\to} (S_0, S_1, \ldots, S_h),$$

$$\tag{5.88}$$

where S_0 is a positive $\alpha/2$-stable distributed random variable; and $S_1, \ldots, S_h$ are identically distributed α-stable distributed random variables. If $\mathbf{E}|Z_t|^\alpha = \infty$, then the S_j's are independent.

Theorem 5.5 *(Asymptotic distribution of the Gauss-Newton estimator $\hat{\beta}_G$;*
Davis (1996)) Let $\{X_t\}$ be the ARMA process defined in (5.74), where $\{Z_t\}$
is an i.i.d. sequence of random variables satisfying (5.79), (5.80) and (5.81).
Suppose that $\hat{\beta}_0$ is a preliminary estimate such that

$$\hat{\beta}_0 - \beta_0 = o_p(a_n^{-1/2}). \tag{5.89}$$

Then,

(i)

$$a_n^{-2}D'D \xrightarrow{d} W(\beta_0)S_0$$

and

(ii)

$$a_n^2 b_n^{-1}(\beta_G - \beta_0) \xrightarrow{d} W^{-1}(\beta_0)\sum_{k=1}^{\infty} c_k S_k/S_0,$$

where $S_0, S-1, S_2, \ldots$ are given in Lemma 5.2, $W(\beta)$ is matrix

$$W(\beta_0) = \frac{1}{4\pi}\int_{-\pi}^{\pi}\left[\frac{\partial \ln g(\lambda;\beta_0)}{\partial \beta}\right]\left[\frac{\partial \ln g(\lambda;\beta_0)}{\partial \beta}\right]' d\lambda; \tag{5.90}$$

and c_k is the vector

$$c_k = \frac{1}{2\pi}\int_{-\pi}^{\pi} e^{-ik\lambda}g(\lambda;\beta_0)\frac{\partial g^{-1}(\lambda;\beta_0)}{\partial \beta}d\lambda. \tag{5.91}$$

Davis (1996) studied two types of *M-estimators* of the parameters of the
ARMA(p, q) model

$$X_t = \phi_1 X_{t-1} + \ldots + \phi_p X_{t-p} + Z_t + \theta_1 Z_{t-1} + \ldots + \theta_q Z_{t-q}, \tag{5.92}$$

with Z_j satisfying the α-stable domain of attraction conditions (5.79) and
(5.80). The first M-estimator, β_M, minimizes the objective function

$$\sum_{t=1}^{n} \rho(Z_t(\beta)) \tag{5.93}$$

for some suitably chosen loss function $\rho(x)$, where, as before, $Z_t(\beta)$ is defined
as

$$Z_t(\beta) = X_t - \phi_1 X_{t-1} - \ldots - \phi_p X_{t-p} - \theta_1 Z_{t-1}(\beta) - \ldots - \theta_q Z_{t-q}(\beta). \tag{5.94}$$

The second, β_{LM}, minimizes the linearized version of (5.93) given by

$$\sum_{t=1}^{n} \rho(Z_t(\hat{\beta}_0) - \mathbf{D}'_t(\hat{\beta}_0))(\beta - \hat{\beta}_0), \tag{5.95}$$

where $\hat{\beta}_0$ is some initial parameter estimate.

The next theorem describes the asymptotic properties of both M-estimators. Let $\mathbf{u} = a_n(\beta - \beta_0)$, where a_n are normalizing constants in (5.85). Then, minimizing (5.93) and (5.95) is equivalent to minimizing

$$W_n(\mathbf{u}) = \sum_{t=1}^n \{\rho[Z_t(\beta_0 + a_n^{-1}\mathbf{u})) - \rho(Z_t(\beta_0)]\} \qquad (5.96)$$

and

$$U_n(\mathbf{u}) = \sum_{t=1}^n [\rho(Z_t(\hat{\beta}_0 - \mathbf{D}'_t(\hat{\beta}_0) = (\beta_0 - \hat{\beta}_0 + a_n^{-1}\mathbf{u})) - \rho(Z_t(\beta_0))]. \qquad (5.97)$$

The two processes $W_n(\cdot)$ and $U_n(\cdot)$ converge on the space $C(\mathbf{R}^{p+q})$ of continuous functions on $\mathbf{R}^{p+q}$ to the same limit processes defined by

$$
\begin{aligned}
W(\mathbf{u}) = \sum_{i=1}^\infty \sum_{k=1}^\infty [\rho(Z_{k,i} - (\psi_{1,i-1}u_1 + \cdots + \psi_{1,i-p}u_p + \psi_{2,i-1}u_{p+1} + \cdots \\
+ \psi_{2,i-q}u_{p+q})\delta\Gamma_k^{-1/\alpha}) - \rho(Z_{k,i})],
\end{aligned} \qquad (5.98)
$$

where coefficients $\{\psi_{1,j}\}$ and $\{\psi_{2,j}\}$ are the coefficients in the causal representation of the autoregressive processes

$$U_t = \theta^{-1}(B)X_t = \phi^{-1}(B)Z_t$$

and

$$V_t = \theta^{-1}(B)Z_t,$$

in terms of $\{Z_s, s \leq t\}$. For $\mathbf{Y}_t = (U_{t-1}, \ldots, U_{t-p}, V_{t-1}, \ldots, V_{t-q})'$,

$$
Y_{t,i} = \begin{cases}
\sum_{j=0}^\infty \psi_{1,j} Z_{t-j-i}, & i=1,\ldots,p \\
\sum_{j=0}^\infty \psi_{2,j} Z_{t-j+p-i}, & i=p+1,\ldots,p+q.
\end{cases}
$$

Further, the sequences of r.v. $\{Z_{k,i}\}$, $\{\delta_k\}$ and $\{\Gamma_k\}$, in (5.98), are defined as follows: the sequences are independent, with

(i) $\{Z_{k,i}\}$ – i.i.d. with d.f. F,

(ii) $\{\delta_k\}$ – i.i.d. with $p = P[\delta = 1] = 1 - P[\delta_k = -1]$ and $\Gamma_k = E_1 + \cdots + E_k$

where $\{E_k\}$ is a sequence of i.i.d. standard exponentials.

Theorem 5.6 *(Asymptotic properties of M-estimators; Davis (1996))* Suppose that $\{X_t\}$ is the ARMA(p,q) process (5.92) such that the distribution of the innovations satisfies (5.79) and (5.80) with $\alpha \in (0,2)$. Assume that the loss function $\rho(\cdot)$ is convex with influence function $\psi(x) = \rho'(x)$ satisfying

(a) ψ is Lipschitz of order τ; $|\psi(x) - \psi(y)| \leq C|(x-y|^\tau$, where $\tau > \max(\alpha - 1, 0)$ and C is a constant;

(b) $\mathbf{E}(|\psi(Z_1)|) < \infty$, if $\alpha < 1$;

(c) $\mathbf{E}(\psi(Z_1) = 0$ and $\mathrm{Var}\psi(Z_1)) < \infty$, if $\alpha \geq 1$.

Then, on $C(\mathbf{R}^{p+q})$,

$$W_n(\cdot) \xrightarrow{d} W(\cdot). \tag{5.99}$$

Moreover, if $W(\cdot)$ has a unique minimum $\hat{\mathbf{u}}$ a.s., then

$$a_n(\hat{\beta}_M^* - \beta_0) \xrightarrow{d} \hat{\mathbf{u}}, \tag{5.100}$$

where $\hat{\beta}_M^*$ is a sequence of local minima of (5.93). The limits in (5.99) and (5.100) are also valid with W_n being replaced by U_n and $\hat{\beta}_M^*$ by $\hat{\beta}_{LM}$, provided the initial estimate satisfies $\hat{\beta}_0 - \beta = o_p(a_n^{-1/2})$.

Kokoszka and Taqqu (1996) (see also Samorodnitsky and Taqqu, 1994, Sec. 7.13) discussed the estimation of the parameters of the fractional ARIMA time series $\{X_n\}$ defined by the equations

$$\phi(B)X_n = \theta(B)\Delta^{-d}Z_n, \tag{5.101}$$

where the innovations Z_n have *infinite variance* and where d is a positive fractional number; B and Δ denote the backward and differencing operator, respectively, i.e.,

$$B(X_n) = X_{n-1}, \; B^2(X_n) = X_{n-2}, \ldots$$

and

$$\Delta X_n = X_n - X_{n-1} = (1 - B)X_n,$$

with Δ^d (for $d = 1, 2, \ldots$) stands for the operator Δ iterated d times, and

$$\Delta^{-d} = (1 - B)^{-d} = \sum_{j=0}^{\infty} b_j(-d)B^j,$$

where $b_0(-d) := 1$ and

$$b_j(-d) = \frac{\Gamma(j + d)}{\Gamma(d)\Gamma(j + 1)}, \quad j = 1, 2, \ldots,$$

(see Samorodnitsky and Taqqu (1994, p.380f)). Because of the presence of the fractional d, times series (5.101) has not only infinite variance but also exhibits long-range dependence.[10] The problem is to estimate both d and

---

[10]For some details on *long-range dependence* (or *"long memory"*) see Samorodnitsky and Taqqu (1994) and Kokoszka and Taqqu (1995, 1996).

the coefficients of the polynomials ϕ and θ, by using a variant of Whittle's method.

The innovations Z_n in (5.101) are assumed to be i.i.d. *zero mean* and in the domain of attraction of an α-stable law with $1 < \alpha < 2$; i.e.,

$$P(|Z_n| > x) = x^{-\alpha} L(x), \text{ as } x \to \infty, \tag{5.102}$$

where L is a slowly varying function, and

$$P(Z_n > x)/P(|Z_n| > x) \to a, \ P(Z_n < -x)/P(|Z_n| > x) \to b, \tag{5.103}$$

where a and b are nonnegative numbers satisfying $a + b = 1$. Then, there is a unique moving average representation[11]

$$X_n = \sum_{j=0}^{\infty} c_j Z_{n-j} \tag{5.104}$$

satisfying (5.101), provided that the polynomials Φ and Θ have no zeros in the closed unit disk $D = \{z : |z| \le 1\}$ and no zeros in common; and that $d < 1 - \frac{1}{\alpha}$. The coefficients c_j are defined by

$$\sum_{j=0}^{\infty} c_j z^j = \frac{\theta(z)}{\phi(z)(1-z)^d}, \quad |z| < 1. \tag{5.105}$$

Define the vector of true parameters:

$$\beta_0 = (\phi_1, \ldots, \phi_p, \theta_1, \ldots, \theta_q, d),$$

where $\phi_1, \ldots, \phi_p$ and $\theta_1, \ldots, \theta_q$ are the coefficients of the autoregressive polynomial $\Phi(z) = 1 - \phi_1 z - \ldots - \phi_p z^p$ and the moving average polynomial $\Theta(z) = 1 + \theta_1 z + \ldots + \theta_q z^q$, respectively, and d is the differencing parameter in (5.101). Assume that d is positive and hence lies in the open interval $(0, 1 - \frac{1}{\alpha})$. The parameter space E is chosen to be a compact subset of

$$\left\{ (\phi_1, \ldots, \phi_p, \theta_1, \ldots, \theta_q, d) : \phi_p \ne 0, \theta_q \ne 0, \right.$$

$$n\phi(z) \text{and} \theta(z) \text{have no common zeros},$$

$$\left. \phi(z)\theta(z) \ne 0, \text{ for } |z| \le 1, \ d \in \left(0, 1 - \frac{1}{\alpha}\right) \right\}.$$

Process (5.104) is called a *fractional ARIMA* process or, in short, a *FARIMA-(p, d, q)* process. The elements of E are denoted by β (possibly with sub- and/or superscripts). The last coordinate of the vector β representing the

---

[11]This has been shown in Kokoszka and Taqqu (1996).

difference parameter d. The *sample autocovariance* and *autocorrelation functions* are defined respectively by

$$\gamma_n(h) = \frac{1}{n} \sum_{t=1}^{n-|h|} X_t X_{t+|h|} \tag{5.106}$$

and

$$\rho_n(h) = \left(\sum_{t=1}^{n} X_t^2\right)^{-1} \left(\sum_{t=1}^{n-|h|} X_t X_{t+|h|}\right) = (\gamma_n(0))^{-1} \gamma_n(h). \tag{5.107}$$

We set

$$\gamma(h) = \sum_{j=0}^{\infty} c_j c_{j+|h|}, \quad \rho(h) = (\gamma(0))^{-1} \gamma(h). \tag{5.108}$$

As before, the *self-normalized periodogram* is defined by

$$\tilde{I}_n(\lambda) = \left(\sum_{t=1}^{n} X_t^2\right)^{-1} \left|\sum_{t=1}^{n} X_t e^{-i\lambda t}\right|^2 = \sum_{|h|<n} \rho_n(h) e^{-i\lambda h}, \quad -\pi \le \lambda \le \pi. \tag{5.109}$$

For $\beta \in E$ the *power transfer function* is

$$g(\lambda, \beta) = \left|\frac{\theta(e^{-i\lambda}, \beta)}{\phi(e^{-i\lambda}, \beta)(1 - e^{-i\lambda})^{d(\beta)}}\right|^2 = \left|\sum_{j=0}^{\infty} c_j(\beta) e^{-i\lambda j}\right|^2. \tag{5.110}$$

Finally, as in Theorem 5.3, define the Whittle estimator β_n as the value of β minimizing

$$\sigma_n^2(\beta) = \int_{-\pi}^{\pi} \frac{\tilde{I}_n(\lambda)}{g(\lambda, \beta)} d\lambda, \quad \beta \in E. \tag{5.111}$$

Theorem 5.7 (*Consistency of the estimator; Kokoszka and Taqqu (1996)*)
As $n \to \infty$,

$$\beta_n \overset{p}{\to} \beta_0 \tag{5.112}$$

and

$$\sigma_n^2(\beta_n) \overset{p}{\to} \frac{2\pi}{\gamma(0)}. \tag{5.113}$$

The next theorem is an analogue of Theorem 5.4 in this more general setting. Define matrix $W(\beta_0)$ with entries

$$w_{ij} = \int_{-\pi}^{\pi} g(\lambda, \beta_0) \frac{\partial^2}{\partial \beta_i \partial \beta_j} g^{-1}(\lambda, \beta_0) d\lambda, \quad i, j = 1, \dots, p+q+1, \tag{5.114}$$

and vectors b_k, $k \in \mathbf{Z}$, whose jth element is

$$(b_k)_j = \frac{1}{2\pi} \int\limits_{-\pi}^{\pi} e^{-ik\lambda} g(\lambda, \beta_0) \frac{\partial}{\partial \beta_j} g^{-1}(\lambda, \beta_0) d\lambda, \quad j = 1, \ldots, p+q+1. \quad (5.115)$$

Theorem 5.8 *(Asymptotic distribution of β_i; Kokoszka and Taqqu (1996))* If innovations Z_n are symmetric and satisfy the domain of attraction condition

$$\lim_{\lambda \to \infty} \lambda^\alpha P(|Z| > \lambda) = C_\alpha \sigma^\alpha, \quad (5.116)$$

where C_α is defined as in Theorem 5.4, then

$$\left(\frac{n}{\log n} \right)^{1/\alpha} (\beta_n - \beta_0) \xrightarrow{d} 4\pi W^{-1}(\beta_0) \sum_{k=1}^{\infty} \frac{Y_k}{Y_0} b_k,$$

where $Y_0, Y_1, \ldots$ are defined as in Theorem 5.4.

Next, we summarize the results in Kokoszka and Mikosch (1997) on functional limit theorems for integrated periodograms of the stationary process

$$X_t = \sum_{j=0}^{\infty} c_j Z_{t-j}, \quad t \in \mathbf{Z}, \quad (5.117)$$

with a noise sequence, $(Z_t)_{t \in \mathbf{Z}}$, of i.i.d. random variables, which may have finite of infinite variance.

The assumptions impose a slow hyperbolic decay on the real coefficients $(c_j)_{j \in \mathbf{N}}$, which is characteristic of *long memory* as well as exponential *short memory* decay.

Remark 5.1 *(Long memory or long-range dependence)* There seems to be no commonly accepted definition of long-range dependence. One finds at least five plausible definitions of processes with *long memory* (or *long-range dependence*) (see Beran, 1994; and also Samorodnitsky and Taqqu, 1994). If sequence (Z_t) has finite variance and covariance function $\gamma(h) = \text{cov}(X_t, X_{t+h})$, long memory is usually defined by $\sum_{k=0}^{\infty} |\gamma(h)| = \infty$. This is typically the case when the c_j in (5.117) are of the form $c_j = j^{d-1} L(j)$, where $0 < d < 1/2$ and L is a slowly varying function. Fractional ARIMA (FARIMA) processes, which are particular case of (5.117), exhibit long-range dependence. This is in contrast, to causal ARMA processes, where both the coefficients c_j and the covariances $\gamma(h)$ decay at an exponential rate, a phenomenon referred to as *short memory*.

To see that FARIMA exhibits long memory recall that finite variance FARIMA[12] sequence (X_t), for $d < 1/2$, is the unique solution to

$$\phi(B)(1 - B)^d X_t = \theta(B) Z_t, \quad t \in \mathbf{Z},$$

---

[12]The infinite variance case was given in (5.101).

Where polynomials

$$\phi(z) \ = \ 1 - \phi_1 z - \cdots - \phi_p z^p,$$
$$\theta(z) \ = \ 1 + \theta_1 z + \cdots + \theta_q z^q, \quad z \in \mathcal{C},$$

give vise to a causal, invertible ARMA process (i.e., $\phi(\cdot)$ and $\theta(\cdot)$ do not have common zeros and $\phi(z)\theta(z) \neq 0$ for $|z| \leq 1$). Samorodnitsky and Taqqu (1994, Sec. 7.13) showed that $c_j \sim cj^{d-1}$ as $j \to \infty$. If $d \in (0, 1/2)$, then sequence (c_j) is square summable, but not absolutely summable. Hence, the FARIMA process (X_t) exhibits long-range dependence.

Next, we specified the assumptions on i.i.d. noise (Z_t) and coefficients (c_j). The noise variable $Z \overset{d}{=} Z_t$ will be in the domain of normal attraction of a symmetric α-stable ($s\alpha s$) law with $\alpha \in (1, 2]$ (in short, $Z \in \text{DNA}(\alpha)$).

If Z is in the domain of normal attraction of the Gaussian law, i.e., $Z \in \text{DNA}(2)$, we assume that $\mathbf{E}Z = 0$. In the stable non-Gaussian case with $\alpha \in (1, 2)$, we assume that the Z_t's are symmetric. Then,

$$x^\alpha P(Z > x) \sim \frac{C_\alpha \sigma_\alpha^\alpha}{2}, \quad x \to \infty, \tag{5.118}$$

where C_α is defined in Theorem 5.4.

In the Gaussian case, $Z \in \text{DNA}(2)$, i.e., as $n \to \infty$,

$$\frac{1}{\sqrt{n}} \sum_{t=1}^{n} Z_t \overset{d}{\to} Y \overset{d}{=} N(0, \sigma^2),$$

square summability of sequence (c_j), i.e., $\sum_{j=0}^{\infty} c_j^2 < \infty$, is necessary and sufficient for the a.s. convergence of series (5.117). If $Z \in \text{DNA}(\alpha)$, $\alpha \in (1, 2)$, is symmetric, then a necessary and sufficient condition for the a.s. convergence of series (5.117) is α-summability, i.e.,

$$\sum_{j=0}^{\infty} |c_j|^\alpha < \infty. \tag{5.119}$$

Consider now the periodogram

$$I_{n,X}(\lambda) = a_n^{-1} \left| \sum_{t=1}^{n} X_t e^{i\lambda t} \right|^2, \quad \lambda \in [-\pi, \pi], n \geq 1, \tag{5.120}$$

with the normalizing sequence (a_n) defined by

$$a_n = \begin{cases} (n \ln n)^{1/\alpha}, & \text{if } \alpha < 2, \\ n^{1/2}, & \text{if } \alpha = 2, \end{cases} \tag{5.121}$$

and the transfer function

$$C(\lambda) = \sum_{j=0}^{\infty} c_j e^{-i\lambda j}, \quad \lambda \in [-\pi, \pi]. \tag{5.122}$$

For the next four theorems we assume that $0 < |C(\lambda)| < \infty$ with the possible exception of $C(0) = \infty$. Define the *integrated periodogram*[13]

$$K_n(\lambda) = \int_{-\pi}^{\lambda} \frac{I_{n,X}(x)}{|C(x)|^2} dx, \quad \lambda \in [-\pi, \pi], \tag{5.123}$$

and denote the *normalized sample autocovariances of the noise* by[14]

$$\gamma_{n,Z}(t) = a_n^{-1} \sum_{i=1}^{n-t} Z_i Z_{i+t}, \quad t = 0, \ldots, n, \ n \geq 1. \tag{5.124}$$

The approximation

$$K_n(\lambda) = \int_{-\pi}^{\lambda} \frac{I_{n,X}(x)}{|C(x)|^2} dx \approx \int_{-\pi}^{\lambda} \frac{I_{n,X}(x)|C(x)|^2}{|C(x)|^2} dx$$

$$= \int_{-\pi}^{\lambda} I_{n,Z}(x) dx$$

$$= (\lambda + \pi)\gamma_{n,Z}(0) + 2 \sum_{t=1}^{n-1} \frac{\sin(\lambda t)}{t} \gamma_{n,Z}(t), \tag{5.125}$$

indicates that the sequence of processes[15]

$$(K_n(\lambda) - \gamma_{n,Z}(0)(\lambda + \pi))_{\lambda \in [-\pi,\pi]} \tag{5.126}$$

---

[13]Bartlett (1954, 1955) proposed a discrete version of the process K_n for goodness-of-fit tests of stationary processes (see also Priestly, 1981).

[14]Under some regularity conditions, a finite vector of sample autocovariances $(\gamma_{n,Z}(h))_{h=1,\ldots,m}$ converges in distribution to a vector of i.i.d. random variables $(Y_h)_{h=1,\ldots,m}$. Brockwell and Davis (1991) showed that limiting vector (Y_h) consists of i.i.d. normals if $\sigma^2 = \mathbf{E}Z_1^2 < \infty$. Davis and Resnick (1985, 1986) showed that they are stable if Z_1 is in the domain of attraction of a non-Gaussian stable law.

[15]The centering in (5.126) by $\gamma_{n,Z}(0) = a_n^{-1} \sum_{t=1}^{n} Z_t^2$ depends on the unobservable noise (Z_t). If $EZ_1^2 < \infty$, one could replace $\gamma_{n,Z}(0)$ by $a_n^{-1}\sigma^2$. Since $a_n^{-1} \sum_{t=1}^{n}(Z_t^2 - \sigma^2)$ has a Gaussian limit distribution this will perturb the limiting process by an additional Gaussian random variable, see Anderson (1993). Kokoszka and Mikosch (1997) chose the random centered sequence

$$\left(K_n(\lambda) - K_n(\pi)\frac{\lambda + \pi}{2\pi}\right)_{\lambda \in [-\pi,\pi]}$$

with

$$K_n(\pi) \approx \int_{-\pi}^{\pi} I_{n,Z}(x) dx = 2\pi\gamma_{n,Z}(0)$$

(see the next two theorems). In the infinite variance case such a random centering sequence is necessary, since $\gamma_{n,Z}(h) = o_P(\gamma_{n,Z}(0))$ for $h \neq 0$ (see Davis and Resnick, 1985, 1986), i.e., K_n does not converge in distribution.

converges in distribution to process[16]

$$\left(2\sum_{t=1}^{\infty}\frac{\sin(\lambda t)}{t}Y_t\right)_{\lambda\in[-\pi,\pi]}. \tag{5.127}$$

The next two theorems consider the case of long-range dependence. Theorem 5.9 represents the case with innovations having finite variance, while Theorem 5.10 gives the heavy-tailed version. The results of these theorems are also valid for FARIMA processes.

Theorem 5.9 *(Kokoszka and Mikosch (1997))* Let (X_t) be the linear process

$$X_t = \sum_{j=0}^{\infty} c_j Z_{t-j}, \quad t \in \mathbf{Z}, \tag{5.128}$$

with coefficients (c_j) satisfying

$$c_j = L(j)j^{d-1}, \quad j \to \infty, \tag{5.129}$$

$$|C(\lambda)| > 0, \quad \lambda \in [-\pi, \pi] \setminus \{0\}, \tag{5.130}$$

$$\left|\frac{d}{d\lambda}\frac{1}{C(\lambda)}\right| \leq c(\epsilon)|\lambda|^{d-1-\epsilon}, \quad \lambda \in [-\pi, \pi] \setminus \{0\}, \tag{5.131}$$

for small values $\epsilon > 0$, where $d \in (0, 1/2)$; and L is a normalized slowly varying function.[17]

Suppose also that $\mathbf{E}|Z|^p < \infty$ for some $p > 2(1-d)^{-1}$, $\mathbf{E}Z = 0$ and $\mathbf{E}Z^2 = \sigma^2 > 0$. Then, the functional limit relation

$$\left(K_n(\lambda) - K_n(\pi)\frac{\lambda+\pi}{2\pi}\right)_{-\pi\leq\lambda\leq\pi} \xrightarrow{d} \sigma^2\left(2\sum_{t=1}^{\infty}\frac{\sin(\lambda t)}{t}Y_t\right)_{-\pi\leq\lambda\leq\pi} \tag{5.132}$$

holds in the space $\mathcal{C}[-\pi, \pi]$ of continuous functions on $[-\pi, \pi]$ with the standard sup-norm, where (Y_t) is a sequence of i.i.d. standard normals.

Theorem 5.10 *(Kokoszka and Mikosch (1997))* Let (X_t) be linear process (5.128) with coefficients (c_j) satisfying (5.129) and (5.130) for some $d \in (0, 1-$

---

[16]If $\sigma^2 < \infty$, the restriction of this limiting process on $[0, \pi]$ is a Brownian Bridge, see, e.g., Hida (1980).

[17]Recall that a positive measurable function L is a *slowly varying function* if $L(cx)/L(x) \to 1$ as $x \to \infty$ for every $c > 0$. In particular, for every $\epsilon > 0$,

$$\lim_{x\to\infty} x^{\epsilon}L(x) = \infty, \quad \lim_{x\to\infty} x^{-\epsilon}L(x) = 0.$$

Function L is a *normalized slowly varying function*, if L is positive, measurable and, for every $\epsilon > 0$, $x^{\epsilon}L(x)$ is ultimately increasing and $x^{-\epsilon}L(x)$ is ultimately decreasing (cf. Theorem 1.5.5 in Bingham, Goldie and Teugels, 1987).

$1/\alpha$). Assume that innovations Z_t are symmetric r.v.'s in DNA(α) for some $\alpha \in (1,2)$. Then, the limit relation

$$\left(K_n(\lambda) - K_n(\pi)\frac{\lambda + \pi}{2\pi}\right)_{-\pi \leq \lambda \leq \pi} \xrightarrow{d} \sigma_\alpha^2 C_\alpha^{2/\alpha}\left(2\sum_{t=1}^{\infty}\frac{\sin(\lambda t)}{t}Y_t\right)_{-\pi \leq \lambda \leq \pi}$$
(5.133)

hold in $\mathcal{C}[-\pi, \pi]$, where (Y_t) is a sequence of i.i.d. stable r.v.'s with ch.f. $\mathbf{E}e^{itY_1} = e^{-C_\alpha|t|^\alpha}$ and $C_\alpha = \left(\alpha \int_0^\infty (1 - \cos x)x^{-\alpha - 1}\right)^{-1}$.

The next two theorems present the analogues of Theorems 5.9 and 5.10 for the case short-range dependence. Again, the first theorem treats the finite variance case; while the second considers the case of heavy-tailed distributed innovations.

Theorem 5.11 *(Kokoszka and Mikosch (1997); see also Klüppelberg and Mikosch (1995b))* Let (X_t) be linear process (5.128) with the coefficients (c_j) satisfying (5.130) and

$$\sum_{j=1}^{\infty} j|c_j| < \infty.$$

Assume that $\mathbf{E}Z = 0$ and $0 < \mathbf{E}Z^2 = \sigma^2 < \infty$. Then, the functional limit relation (5.132) holds.

Theorem 5.12 *(Kokoszka and Mikosch (1997); see also Klüppelberg and Mikosch (1995a))* Let (X_t) be linear process (5.128) with the coefficients (c_j) satisfying (5.130) and

$$\sum_{j=1}^{\infty} j|c_j|^\delta < \infty$$

for some $\delta < 1$. Assume that innovations Z_t are symmetric r.v.'s in DNA(α) for some $1 < \alpha < 2$. Then, the functional limit relation (5.132) holds.

The next three corollaries provide the limiting distributions of some goodness-of-fit test statistic.

Corollary 5.1 *(Functional limit theorem for the integrated periodogram; Kokoszka and Mikosch (1997))* Under the assumptions of any of the Theorems 5.9 - 5.12 and setting $\alpha = 2$ in the finite variance case, the functional limit relation

$$\left(a_n n^{-2/\alpha} K_n(\pi), \left(K_n(\lambda) - \frac{\lambda + \pi}{2\pi}K_n(\pi)\right)_{\lambda \in [-\pi, \pi]}\right)$$

$$\xrightarrow{d} \left(Y_0, \left(2c_1\sum_{t=1}^{\infty}\frac{\sin(\lambda t)}{t}Y_t\right)_{\lambda \in [-\pi, \pi]}\right) = (Y_0, 2c_1 S) \qquad (5.134)$$

holds. Here, Y_0 and $(Y_t)_{t\geq 1}$ are independent; and $(Y_t)_{t\geq 1}$ is defined in the same way as in the corresponding theorems. Moreover, under the conditions of Theorems 5.9 and 5.11 $Y_0 = \sigma^2$ and $c_1 = \sigma^2$. Under the conditions of Theorems 5.10 and 5.12, Y_0 is a positive $\alpha/2$-stable random variable and $c_1 = \sigma_\alpha^2 C_\alpha^{2/\alpha}$.

As a result of the above functional limit theorem we have the following goodness-of-fit tests as a consequence of the invariance principle (the functional limit theorem):

Corollary 5.2 *(Kolmogorov-Smirnov tests for the integrated periodogram, Kokoszka and Mikosch (1997))*. Under the assumptions of Corollary 5.1 the relations

$$\sup_{-\pi\leq\lambda\leq\pi}\left|K_n(\lambda) - K_n(\pi)\frac{\lambda+\pi}{2\pi}\right| \overset{d}{\to} 2c_1 \sup_{-\pi\leq\lambda\leq\pi}|S(\lambda)|, \qquad (5.135)$$

$$\left(\frac{n}{\ln n}\right)^{1/\alpha}\sup_{-\pi\leq\lambda\leq\pi}\left|K_n(\lambda)/K_n(\pi) - \frac{\lambda+\pi}{2\pi}\right| \overset{d}{\to} 2c_1 \sup_{-\pi\leq\lambda\leq\pi}|S(\lambda)|/Y_0 \quad (5.136)$$

hold, where process S is defined by the right-hand side of (5.134),

$$S(\lambda) := \sum_{t=1}^{\infty}\frac{\sin(\lambda t)}{t}Y_t, \quad \lambda \in [-\pi, \pi].$$

Corollary 5.3 *(Cramér-Mises tests for the integrated periodogram, Kokoszka and Mikosch (1997))* Under the assumptions of Corollary 5.1 the relations

$$\int_{-\pi}^{\pi}\left(K_n(\lambda) - K_n(\pi)\frac{\lambda+\pi}{2\pi}\right)^2 d\lambda \overset{d}{\to} 4c_1^2\int_{-\pi}^{\pi}S^2(\lambda)d\lambda$$

$$\overset{d}{=} 4c_1^2\pi\sum_{t=1}^{\infty}\frac{Z_t^2}{t^2}, \quad (5.137)$$

$$\left(\frac{n}{\ln n}\right)^{2/\alpha}\int_{-\pi}^{\pi}\left(K_n(\lambda)/K_n(\pi) - \frac{\lambda+\pi}{2\pi}\right)^2 d\lambda \overset{d}{\to}$$

$$4c_1^2\int_{-\pi}^{\pi}S^2(\lambda)/Y_0^2 d\lambda \overset{d}{=} 4c_1^2\frac{\pi}{Y_0^2}\sum_{t=1}^{\infty}\frac{Z_t^2}{t^2}, \qquad (5.138)$$

holds.

Remark 5.2 (The limiting distributions of the test statistics). In the finite variance case the quantiles of the limits in (5.135)-(5.138) can be found as functionals of a Brownian Bridge, see Shorack and Wellner (1986). In the finite variance case some quantiles of the limit distributions can be found as described in Klüppelberg and Mikosch (1995a).

Klüppelberg and Mikosch (1995a,b), (1996a,b) studied some additional tests for the integrated periodogram which we briefly list. The framework is again

$$X_t = \sum_{j=-\infty}^{\infty} \psi_j Z_{t-j}, \quad t \in \mathbf{Z}, \tag{5.139}$$

but here $(Z_t)_{t \in \mathbf{Z}}$ is a noise sequence of i.i.d. symmetric α-stable r.v.'s for $\alpha \in (0,2)$, with ch.f.

$$\mathbf{E}e^{itZ_1} = e^{-\sigma|t|^{\alpha}}.$$

·The assumption

$$\sum_{j=-\infty}^{\infty} |j||\psi_j|^{\delta} < \infty, \quad \text{for some } \delta < \min(1,\alpha), \tag{5.140}$$

guarantees a.s. absolute convergence of (5.139). Suppose that $|\psi(\lambda)|^2$ is everywhere positive. Define

(i) the periodogram

$$I_{n,X}(\lambda) = n^{-2/\alpha} \left| \sum_{t=1}^{n} e^{-i\lambda t} X_t \right|^2, \quad \lambda \in [-\pi, \pi]; \tag{5.141}$$

(ii) the self-normalized periodogram

$$\tilde{I}_{n,X}(\lambda) = \frac{I_{n,X}(\lambda)}{\gamma_{n,X}^2}, \quad \lambda \in [-\pi, \pi], \tag{5.142}$$

with

$$\gamma_{n,X}^2 = n^{-2/\alpha} \sum_{t=1}^{n} X_t^2;$$

(iii) the smooth integrated periodogram

$$\int_{-\pi}^{\pi} I_{n,X}(\lambda) f(\lambda) d\lambda, \quad x \in [-\pi, \pi], \tag{5.143}$$

where f is a smooth weight function f;

(iv) the smooth self-normalized integrated periodogram

$$\int_{-\pi}^{\pi} \tilde{I}_{n,X}(\lambda) f(\lambda) d\lambda, \quad x \in [-\pi, \pi]; \tag{5.144}$$

(v) the power transfer function of the linear filter $(\psi_j)_{j\in Z}$,

$$|\psi(\lambda)|^2 = \left| \sum_{j=-\infty}^{\infty} \psi_j e^{-ij\lambda} \right|^2, \quad \lambda \in [-\pi, \pi]; \qquad (5.145)$$

(vi) the integrated periodogram

$$T_n = \frac{1}{2\pi} \int_{-\pi}^{\pi} \frac{I_{n,X}(\lambda)}{|\psi(\lambda)|^2} d\lambda. \qquad (5.146)$$

Theorem 5.13 Suppose that linear process $(X_t)_{t\in\mathbf{Z}}$ is given by (5.139) and (5.140); and let $\psi^2 := \sum_{j=-\infty}^{\infty} \psi_j^2$. Next, let "smoother" f be a non-negative 2π-periodic continuous function such that the Fourier coefficients of $f(\cdot)|\psi(\cdot)|^2$ are absolutely summable.

Define Y_0 to be an $\alpha/2$-stable positive r.v., which is independent of $(Z_t)_{t\in\mathbf{Z}}$ and has Laplace transform

$$\mathbf{E}e^{-rY_0} = \exp\{-\sigma K_\alpha r^{\alpha/2}\}, \qquad (5.147)$$

where $K_\alpha = E|N|^{\alpha/2}$ for an $N(0,2)$-r.v. Then, the functional limiting result

$$\left(\gamma_{n,X}^2, T_n, \int_{-\pi}^{x} I_{n,X}(\lambda)f(\lambda)d\lambda \right)_{-\pi \leq x \leq \pi} \xrightarrow{d} Y_0 \left(\psi^2, 1, \int_{-\pi}^{x} |\psi(\lambda)|^2 f(\lambda)d\lambda \right)_{-\pi \leq x \leq \pi} \qquad (5.148)$$

holds on $\mathbf{R} \times \mathbf{R} \times C[-\pi, \pi]$.

Corollary 5.4 Under the assumptions of Theorem 5.13 we have

$$\sup_{-\pi \leq x \leq \pi} \left| \sum_{-\pi}^{\pi} \left(\tilde{I}_{n,X}(\lambda) - \frac{|\psi(\lambda)|^2}{\psi^2} \right) f(\lambda)d\lambda \right| \xrightarrow{p} 0. \qquad (5.149)$$

Klüppelberg and Mikosch (1996a) provide tables for selected quantiles of the limit distribution of several test statistics derived from Theorem 5.13 and demonstrate a significant difference between the normal and the stable non-Gaussian cases.

5.4   Subordinated Models: Evidence for Heavy Tailed Distributions and Long–Range Dependence

In this and next section we study the probabilistic structure of high–frequency data in the setting of stochastic subordination[18], i.e. we model the high–frequency process in physical time as a compound process $Z(t) = S(T(t))$, where $S(t)$ is a stochastic process indexed on a stochastically "deformed" time scale represented by a process $T(t)$. In this setting, $T(t)$ models the market activity, which changes over time, as it is well known, and $S(t)$ is the process in market time.

We shall focus on the properties of heavy tailedness and long–range dependence, studying their scaling behavior with respect to the time lag, for all the processes involved in the setting of subordination.[19]

5.4.1   Self-similarity and stable processes

In this section, we will be interested in stochastic processes that are self-similar with index H and have stationary increments (H-s.s.s.i.).

For their importance in modeling, some results about the stationary increments of H-s.s.s.i. processes will be briefly reviewed.

Definition 5.1 The **R**-valued stochastic process $X(t)_{t\in\mathbf{R}}$ is said to be self-similar with index $H > 0$ if, for all $c > 0$, the finite-dimensional distributions of $X(ct)_{t\in\mathbf{R}}$ are identical to the finite-dimensional distributions of $c^H X(t)_{t\in\mathbf{R}}$.

We often adopt the simpler notation $X(ct)_{t\in\mathbf{R}} \stackrel{d}{=} c^H X(t)_{t\in\mathbf{R}}$.

As an example, a Brownian motion $X(t)_{t\in\mathbf{R}}$ is a Gaussian processes with mean 0 and autocovariance function

$$EX(t)X(s) = \min(t,s).$$

For all $c > 0$ and $t, s \in \mathbf{R}$ it holds

$$EX(ct)X(cs) = \min(ct, cs) = c\min(t,s) = E\left(c^{1/2}X(t)\right)\left(c^{1/2}X(s)\right),$$

i.e. Brownian motion is self-similar with index $H = 1/2$.

Another example of a self-similar process is the α-stable Lévy motion, i.e. a stochastic process $X(t)_{t\in\mathbf{R}_0^+}$ that satisfies the following conditions:

1. $X(0) = 0$ almost surely;

---

[18]See Section 5.1. The results in this and next section are due to Marinelli, Rachev and Roll (1999), see also Marinelli, Rachev, Roll and Göppl (1999).

[19]The ideas of scaling and self-similarity were originally introduced in connection with deterministic structures, like fractals. For a brief account of the notions of scaling and self-similarity from a probabilistic point of view, see Section 5.3.

2. $X(t)$ has independent increments;

3. $X(t) - X(s) \sim S_\alpha\left(|t - s|^{1/\alpha}, 0, 0\right)$ for some $\alpha \in]0, 2]$.

In fact, since this process has independent increments, it is sufficient to show that $X(ct) - X(cs) \overset{d}{=} c^H\left(X(t) - X(s)\right)$:

$$X(ct) - X(cs) \sim S_\alpha\left(c^{1/\alpha}|t - s|^{1/\alpha}, 0, 0\right) = c^{1/\alpha}S_\alpha\left(|t - s|^{1/\alpha}, 0, 0\right)$$

i.e. $X(ct) - X(cs) \overset{d}{=} c^H\left(X(t) - X(s)\right)$ with $H = 1/\alpha$.

Note that the increments of Lévy motions are stationary, and that a α-stable Lévy motion with $\alpha = 2$ is a Brownian motion.

Also note that a non-degenerate self-similar process $X(t)$ cannot be stationary: in fact we would have

$$X(t) \overset{d}{=} X(ct) \overset{d}{=} c^H X(t),$$

that leads to a contradiction because $\lim_{c \to \infty} c^H X(t) = \infty$. However, the following interesting proposition holds (for a proof see Samorodnitsky and Taqqu, Proposition 7.1.4).

Theorem 5.14 Let $X(t)_{t \in \mathbf{R}}$ be a self-similar process with index H. Then the process $Y(t)_{t \in \mathbf{R}}$ defined by

$$Y(t) = e^{-tH} X(e^t)$$

is stationary. Conversely, let $Y(t)_{t \in \mathbf{R}}$ be stationary. Then $X(t)_{t \in \mathbf{R}}$ defined by

$$X(t) = t^H Y(\log t)$$

is self-similar with index H.

An important role among self-similar processes is played by those having stationary increments (H-s.s.s.i.). It is customary to suppose, for instance, that returns are stationary. Formally, an $\mathbf{R}$ valued stochastic process $X(t)_{t \in \mathbf{R}}$ is said to have stationary increments if

$$\left(X(t + h) - X(t)\right)_{t \in \mathbf{R}} \overset{d}{=} \left(X(t) - X(0)\right)_{t \in \mathbf{R}}$$

for all $h \in \mathbf{R}$.

It is clear that, from the way they are defined, both Brownian motion and α-stable Lévy motion are self-similar with stationary increments. In particular, for Brownian motion it holds $H = 1/2$, while $H = 1/\alpha$ for Lévy motion.

There exists a general theorem which poses boundary conditions on the possible values of H depending on the existence of moments of $X(1)$ (see

Samorodnitsky and Taqqu (1994)). As a corollary, it can be proved that, for a non-degenerate α-stable H-s.s.s.i. process, it holds:

$$\alpha < 1 \implies H \in (0, 1/\alpha]$$
$$\alpha \geq 1 \implies H \in (0, 1].$$

Note that this is consistent with the value of $H = 1/\alpha$ we found for α-stable Lévy motion.

Moreover, it would be possible to show that for each permissible pair (H, α) we can find an α-stable H-s.s.s.i. process, and that for fixed α and H there are often several such processes. However, in the Gaussian case, i.e. for $\alpha = 2$, the only α-stable H-s.s.s.i. process is the fractional Brownian motion (FBM). This process has been widely applied in many fields, especially in the context of long–range dependence, and is the basic "building block" of the so-called Fractal Market Hypothesis (FMH), proposed by Mandelbrot and other researchers as a replacement of the Efficient Market Hypothesis (EMH): in particular, Mandelbrot suggests to model the price process as a FBM instead of a simple Brownian motion.

It can be shown that FBM is the only H-s.s.s.i. Gaussian process for $H \in (0, 1)$ (modulo multiplication by a constant), while for $H = 1$ all the H-s.s.s.i. Gaussian processes have the same autocovariance function, but can differ by their mean.

Definition 5.2 A fractional Brownian motion is a self-similar Gaussian process with index $H \in (0, 1]$ that has stationary increments.

A FBM is called standard if var $X(1) = 1$.

The following proposition gives a characterization of fractional Brownian motion.

Proposition 5.1 Let $H \in (0, 1)$ and $\sigma^2 = EX(1)^2$. The following statements are equivalent:

1. $X(t)_{t \in \mathbf{R}}$ is Gaussian and H-s.s.s.i.

2. $X(t)_{t \in \mathbf{R}}$ is a fractional Brownian motion with self-similarity index H.

3. $X(t)_{t \in \mathbf{R}}$ is Gaussian, has mean zero and autocovariance function

$$\Sigma(t_1, t_2) = \frac{1}{2} \sigma^2 \left(|t_1|^{2H} + |t_2|^{2H} - |t_1 - t_2|^{2H} \right).$$

Note that FBM reduces to Brownian motion when $H = 1/2$, and that for $H = 1$ it degenerates ($X(t) = tX(1)$ a.s. for all $t \in \mathbf{R}$).

In the more general setting of α-stable processes, as it is obvious to expect, there exist more than just one type of H-s.s.s.i. for an admissible pair (α, H). Remember that, as we have seen, possible values are $\alpha \in (0, 1)$, $H \in (0, 1/\alpha]$ and $\alpha \in (1, 2)$, $H \in (0, 1]$.

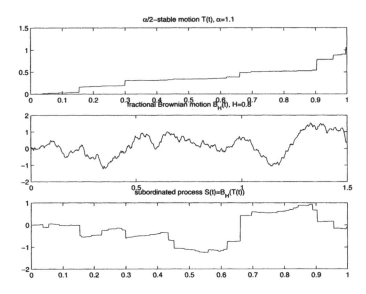

Fig. 5.1 Simulated paths of an $\alpha/2$–stable subordinator $T(t)$, of a fractional Brownian motion $B_H(t)$, and of the corresponding subordinated process $S(t) = B_H(T(t))$ ($\alpha = 1.1$, $H = 0.8$). (Adapted from: Marinelli, Rachev, Roll (1999))

The following two propositions outline what restrictions are imposed by the the properties of self-similarity and of stationary increments.

Proposition 5.2 Let $X(t)$ be an α-stable H-s.s.s.i. process. Then $X(0) = 0$ a.s. and, for any fixed $t \in \mathbf{R}$, it holds $X(t) \sim S_\alpha(\sigma_{X(t)}, \beta_{X(t)}, \mu_{X(t)})$ with

$$
\begin{aligned}
\sigma_{X(t)} &= |t|^H \sigma_{X(1)} \\
\beta_{X(t)} &= (t)\beta_{X(1)} \\
\mu_{X(t)} &= \begin{cases} |t|^H (\mathrm{sgn}\ t)\mu_{X(1)} & \text{for } \alpha \neq 1 \\ |t|^H (\mathrm{sgn}\ t)\left(\mu_{X(1)} - \frac{2}{\pi}|t|^H (\log |t|^H)\sigma_{X(1)}\beta_{X(1)}\right) & \text{for } \alpha = 1. \end{cases}
\end{aligned}
$$

Proposition 5.3 Let $X(t)$ be an α-stable H-s.s.s.i. process with $\alpha \in]0, 2[$. If $H \neq 1$, then $X(t)$ is strictly stable. Otherwise, if $H = 1$ and $\alpha \neq 1$, then there exists a constant μ such that $X(t) - \mu t$ is strictly stable.

5.4.2   The Mandelbrot's Multifractal Model of Asset Returns

The Multifractal Model of Asset Returns (MMAR) has been recently proposed by Mandelbrot, Fisher and Calvet (1997) and is based on the original ideas of Mandelbrot (1972, 1974) on multifractal measures. The main characteristic

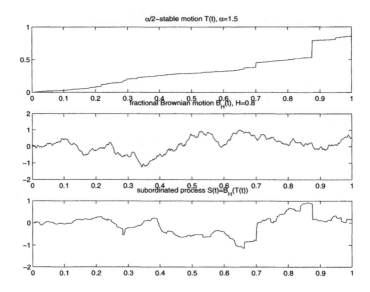

Fig. 5.2 Same as previous figure, but with $\alpha = 1.5$. (Adapted from: Marinelli, Rachev, Roll (1999))

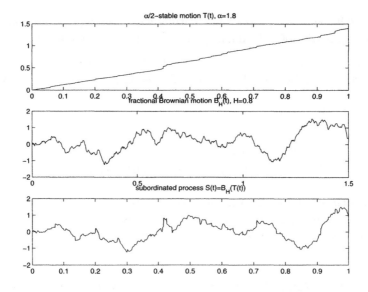

Fig. 5.3 Same as previous figure, but with $\alpha = 1.8$. (Adapted from: Marinelli, Rachev, Roll (1999))

of MMAR is multiscaling: this property can be regarded as a generalization of self-similarity for stochastic processes. While a self-similar process $X(t)$ with index H satisfies the relation

$$X(ct) \stackrel{d}{=} c^H X(t),$$

a multifractal process follows the more general scaling rule

$$X(ct) \stackrel{d}{=} M(c)X(t),$$

where $M(c)$ is a stochastic process independent of $X(t)$.

While this definition is intuitively more appealing, multifractal processes are actually defined in a slightly different way, that is as follows.

Definition 5.3 Let $X(t)_{t\in \mathbf{R}}$ be a stochastic process with stationary increments. Let T and Q be intervals in $\mathbf{R}$ such that $0 \in T$ and $[0,1] \subseteq Q$. If the moments of $X(t)$ satisfy the relation

$$E|X(t)|^q = c(q)t^{\tau(q)+1}$$

for all $t \in T$, where $c(\cdot)$ and $\tau(\cdot)$ are $\mathbf{R}$-valued functions defined on Q, then we say that $X(t)$ is a multifractal process.

The function $\tau : Q \to \mathbf{R}$ is called the *scaling function* of the multifractal process $X(t)$.

Note that a self-similar process $X(t)$ with index H is multifractal with scaling function $\tau(q) = Hq - 1$: in fact, since it holds $X(t) \stackrel{d}{=} t^H X(1)$, then

$$E|X(t)|^q \stackrel{d}{=} t^{Hq}E|X(1)|^q,$$

i.e. $E|X(t)|^q \stackrel{d}{=} c(q)t^{\tau(q)+1}$ with $c(q) = E|X(1)|^q$ and $\tau(q) = Hq - 1$.

It can also be shown that if the process $X(t)$ is such that $X(ct) \stackrel{d}{=} M(c)X(t)$ with $M(c)_{c\in]0,1]}$ an $\mathbf{R}^+$-valued stochastic process independent of $X(t)$, and we further assume that $M(c)$ satisfy the relation

$$M(ab) = M_1(a)M_2(b)$$

with M_1 and M_2 independent copies of M, then $X(t)$ satisfy the definition of multifractal process given above.

A constructive definition of the MMAR can now be given, on the basis of the following result (see Mandelbrot, Fisher and Calvet (1997)).

Theorem 5.15 Let $B_H(t)$ be a fractional Brownian motion with self-similarity index H, and $T(t)$ a multifractal process with continuous, non-decreasing paths and stationary increments, independent of $B_H(t)$. Then the subordinated process $X(t)$ defined by

$$X(t) = B_H \circ T(t) = B_H(T(t)) \tag{5.150}$$

is a multifractal process with scaling function $\tau_X(q) = \tau_T(Hq)$ and stationary increments.

If $S(t)_{t \in \mathbf{R}_0^+}$ is the asset price process and we define the normalized log price as

$$X(t) = \log S(t) - \log S(0),$$

the Multifractal Model of Asset Returns consist in the assumption that $L(t)$ is generated as in the previous theorem.

It is clear that the process $T(t)$ in (5.150) is regarded as the intrinsic time process that we introduced in the appendix on subordination. While we focused on stable subordinated processes, MMAR models the log price process as a fractional Brownian motion in the intrinsic time scale (see Figures 5.1-5.3), thus allowing the increments (i.e. the returns) to be dependent.

It can be shown that the intrinsic time process determines the existence of the moments of the price process $X(t)$, in the meaning that the q-th moment of $X(t)$ exists if and only if the process $T(t)$ admits moments of order Hq.

5.4.3   Long–range dependence

In finance, the study of long–range dependence has been a topic of research for a rather long time, although it is still a source of controversies whether stock market price models should include long memory or not (see, for example, Lo (1991), Cutland et al. (1995), and Baillie and King (1996) and section 5.3).

The long–range dependent stochastic processes provide an elegant explanation of the so–called Hurst effect. In brief, let $\{X_i\}_{i \geq 1}$ be an observed time series, $Y_n = \sum_{i=1}^{n} X_i$ its partial sums, $\overline{X}_n = \frac{1}{n} Y_n$, and $S_n^2 = \frac{1}{n} \sum_{i=1}^{n} (X_i - \overline{X}_n)^2$ its sample variance. Then, if we define the *rescaled adjusted range statistics* (often called simply *R/S–statistics*) as

$$R/S(n) = \frac{R_n}{S_n} = \frac{1}{S_n} \left(\max_{1 \leq t \leq n} \left(Y_t - t\overline{X}_n \right) - \min_{1 \leq t \leq n} \left(Y_t - t\overline{X}_n \right) \right), \quad (5.151)$$

Hurst (1951) showed that many empirical records satisfy the asymptotic relation

$$E\left(R/S(n) \right) \propto n^H$$

for $n \to \infty$, with typical values of the Hurst exponent H in the interval $(0.5, 1)$. However, if the observations are generated by a short–range dependent process, then it holds

$$E\left(R/S(n) \right) \propto n^{0.5}$$

for $n \to \infty$ (see Annis and Lloyd (1976)). This discrepancy is known as *Hurst effect*.

These empirical results led Mandelbrot and Wallis (1969) to the development of classical R/S–analysis, whose goal is to determine from an observed

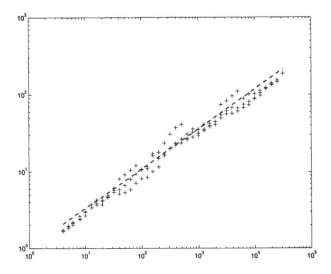

Fig. 5.4 Rescaled adjusted range plot for a standard Brownian motion. (Adapted from: Marinelli, Rachev, Roll (1999))

time series the value of the Hurst parameter of a generating long–range dependent stochastic process. In particular, let N be the sample size: we divide the sample in K blocks each of size N/K, and define $k_m = (m-1)\frac{N}{K}+1$ with $m = 1, \ldots, K$. Now we estimate $R_n(k_m)$ and $S_n(k_m)$ for each lag n such that $k_m + n \leq N$, i.e. we ignore all the data points before k_m. Note that for values of $n < N/K$ there are K different estimates of $R/S(n)$, while for n approaching N there are fewer estimates. The graphical R/S method consists then in the calculation of $R_n(k_m)$ and $S_n(k_m)$ for logarithmically spaced values of n, and hence plotting $R_n(k_m)/S_n(k_m)$ vs. n in logarithmic scale for all starting points k_m. The resulting graph is called *rescaled adjusted range plot*, or *pox plot of R/S*. An example of such a plot (for a standard Brownian motion, i.e. for a process with no long–range dependence) is given in Figure 5.4.

An appealing characteristic of the classical R/S method is its robustness against variations in the marginal distribution of the data, even if they have heavy tails with infinite variance. In fact, defining a long–range dependence parameter d by

$$d = H - 1/2$$

for finite variance processes, and by

$$d = H - 1/\alpha$$

for infinite variance processes, R/S analysis consistently provides an estimate of $H' = d + 1/2$, independently of the value of α.[20] Note that long–range dependence corresponds to $d > 0$, or equivalently to $H' > 1/2$, and that $H = H'$ for finite variance time series. A major drawback however is the lack of limiting results for the distribution for the underlying statistics (5.151). Moreover, R/S analysis is sensitive to the presence of short–range dependencies, and rather unreliable for small samples. On the other hand, it gives an explicit indication of the intensity of long–range dependence through the Hurst index H.

The modified R/S–statistics, due to Lo (1991), offers a more rigorous test for the presence of long–range dependent structures in the underlying generating process. Two striking differences in Lo's approach are the use of only one lag, namely $n = N$, and the adoption of a consistent estimator for the variance of the partial sums Y_n, given by:

$$S_N^2(q) = \frac{1}{N}\sum_{i=1}^{N}(X_i - \hat{\mu})^2 + \frac{2}{N}\sum_{j=1}^{q}\omega_j(q)\left(\sum_{i=j+1}^{N}(X_i - \hat{\mu})(X_{i-j} - \hat{\mu})\right) \quad (5.152)$$

where $\hat{\mu}$ is the sample mean of the observations $\{X_i : i = 1, \ldots, N\}$ and the weights $\omega_j(q)$ are defined as

$$\omega_j(q) = 1 - \frac{j}{q+1}$$

for $q < N$.
Note how the second term in (5.152) takes into account the fact that for dependent random variables, the variance of the partial sums also includes the autocovariances, up to a reasonable choice of the lag q.
The modified R/S–statistic then is defined as

$$V_N(q) = \frac{1}{\sqrt{N}}\frac{R_N}{S_N(q)}$$

with R as in (5.151).
If X_i has no long–range dependence, one can show (see Lo (1991)) that, for an appropriate choice of $q = q(N)$, it holds, as $N \to \infty$:

$$V_N(q) \xrightarrow{d} W_1 = \max_{t\in[0,1]} W_0(t) - \min_{t\in[0,1]} W_0(t),$$

where $W_0(t)$ is a standard Brownian bridge, i.e.

$$W_0(t) \stackrel{d}{=} B(t) - tB(1)$$

---

[20]See Taqqu and Teverovsky (1998).

with $B(t)$ standard Brownian motion.

Furthermore, since the distribution function of the random variable W_1 can be written as

$$F_{W_1}(x) = 1 - 2 \sum_{n=1}^{\infty} (4n^2 x^2 - 1) e^{-2n^2 x^2},$$

it follows that

$$P(W_1 \in [0.809, 1.862]) = 0.95. \tag{5.153}$$

Now let H_0 be the hypothesis that the data do not have long–range dependence, and H_1 the hypothesis that the data do have long–range dependence, i.e. they have an Hurst index $H \in (0.5, 1)$. Then the interval $[0.809, 1.862]$ represents the asymptotic 95% acceptance region for testing the null hypothesis H_0 against the alternative H_1.

Lo's test is insensitive to the presence of short–range dependence, in the sense that a time series displaying both short– and long–range dependence would result in a value of $V_N(q)$ falling outside the confidence interval (5.153). However, the modified R/S method does not provide an estimate of H, but simply checks if the data display long memory. One could also show (see Willinger et al. (1999)) that, as q increases, it holds

$$V_N(q) \simeq q^{1/2 - H},$$

so that, for large enough q, the statistic $V_N(q)$ will fall within the acceptance region of the null hypothesis H_0.

Due to this and other drawbacks, Willinger, Taqqu and Teverovsky (1999) suggest not to use Lo's test only when checking for the presence of long memory, but instead to rely on a wider spectrum of tests, especially when the modified R/S test rejects alternatives hypotheses favoring the absence of long–range dependence in the underlying process.

In the next section, we shall use a quantile-based algorithm based on the paper of McCulloch (1986) with some modifications: using the table of quantiles for stable distribution published by Nolan[21], we computed again the value of the functions ϕ and ψ on a set of (ν_α, ν_β) such that:

$$\alpha = \phi(\nu_\alpha, \nu_\beta)$$
$$\beta = \psi(\nu_\alpha, \nu_\beta)$$

where

$$\nu_\alpha = \frac{q_{0.95} - q_{0.05}}{q_{0.75} - q_{0.25}}$$
$$\nu_\beta = \frac{q_{0.95} + q_{0.05} - 2q_{0.5}}{q_{0.95} - q_{0.05}}.$$

---

[21]See http://www.cas.american.edu/~jpnolan/stable.html.

The estimation scheme, given a sample, is now clear: we calculate first the sample quantiles we need, and then, by interpolation we compute

$$\hat{\alpha} = \phi(\hat{\nu}_\alpha, \hat{\nu}_\beta)$$
$$\hat{\beta} = \psi(\hat{\nu}_\alpha, \hat{\nu}_\beta)$$

where $\hat{}$ indicates sample values, or estimated values for α and β.

When building the tables, we considered $\alpha \in \{2, 1.99, 1.95, 1.9, 1.8, \ldots, 0.4\}$ and $\beta \in \{0, 0.1, 0.2, \ldots, 1\}$. The improvements with respect to the tables in McCulloch (1986) should be clear, since the computed quantiles we used have higher accuracy and the value of the estimator functions ϕ and ψ are known on a finer grid of their arguments. Moreover, instead of using linear interpolation, we adopted bidimensional cubic interpolation, since this method, in contrast to linear interpolation, is smoother (continuous).

The estimation of σ and μ is analogous, and follows the same steps outlined in McCulloch (1986).

Carlo Marinelli provides[22] a MATLAB 5 routine implementing this estimation algorithm. The use interface is very simple: if the stable sample is saved in the column vector x, at the MATLAB prompt one just needs to type [alpha,beta,sigma,mu]=stable(x) in order to obtain estimates of a fitting $S_\alpha(\sigma, \beta, \mu)$-law. Roughly speaking, the complexity of this algorithm is $N \log N$, i.e. it is proportional to the time to sort the input vector (operation needed to calculate the sample quantiles).

5.5   The Heavy–Tailedness and Long–Range Dependence in the USD–CHF Exchange Rate Time Series

5.5.1   The high–frequency time series of USD–CHF exchange rate

In our example of high–frequency data we consider a set of 128400 measurements of the USD-CHF exchange rate starting from May 20th 1985 until May 20th 1987. The data set spans a total of 499 business days, with an average of 256.8 measurement per day and an average time between quotes of 126 seconds (2 minutes and 6 seconds).[23] It is necessary to filter the data in order to remove extreme outliers. In general, this procedure does not considerably alter the data set: in our case, it removes 0.007% of the data (9 measurements out of 128400).

The logarithmic levels of exchange rate (as defined below in Definition 5.4) after filtering are shown in Figure 5.5. Note that the time series is indexed using the notion of quote time, i.e. we plotted $\{x(t_i)\}_{i=1,\ldots,N}$ against $i =$

---

[22]See http://www.pstat.ucsb.edu/~carlo/stable.html.
[23]The market opens at 8 and closes at 17, so there are 9 hours a day of floor trading, see Marinelli, Rachev and Roll (1999).

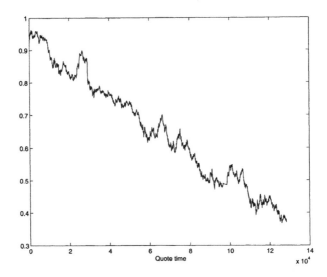

Fig. 5.5 Logarithmic levels of exchange rate in quote time, as modelled by the process $S(t)$. (Adapted from: Marinelli, Rachev, Roll (1999))

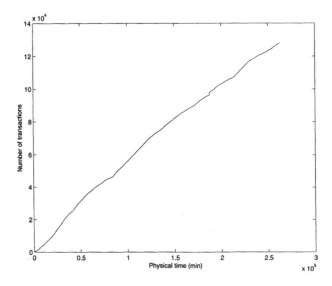

Fig. 5.6 The intrinsic time process $T(t)$, defined as the number of transactions up to time t. (Adapted from: Marinelli, Rachev, Roll (1999))

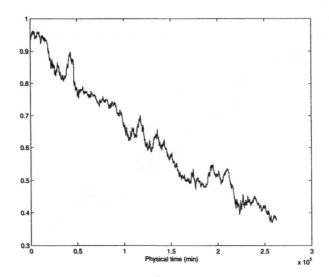

Fig. 5.7 Logarithmic levels of exchange rate in physical time, as modelled by the process $Z(t)$. (Adapted from: Marinelli, Rachev, Roll (1999))

$1,\ldots,N$. Note that $x(t_i)$ can be regarded as a sample path of the process $S(t)$. The (log) levels of exchange rate in physical time $Z(t) = S(T(t))$ are displayed in Figure 5.7, while Figure 5.6 is a plot of the market time process $T(t)$, as defined below.

We shall assume that all the time series to be defined over a set $T = \{t_i\}_{i=1,\ldots,N}$.

Definition 5.4 Let $p_{\text{bid}}(t_i)$ and $p_{\text{ask}}(t_i)$ be the bid price and ask price for a certain asset at time t_i. Then the (logarithmic) price at time t_i is defined as

$$x(t_i) = \frac{\log p_{\text{bid}}(t_i) + \log p_{\text{ask}}(t_i)}{2}. \tag{5.154}$$

The exchange rate at high frequency is similarly defined. Figure 5.5, as stated, represents $x(t_i)$ for USD–CHF exchange rate data.

This definition is motivated by the work of Petersen and Fialkovski (1994) who showed that the real transaction price tends to be comprised between the quoted bid/ask spread, and that (5.154) is a good approximation of the trading price.

Definition 5.5 The return (or change of price) at time t_i over the period Δt is defined as

$$r(t_i; \Delta t) = x(t_i) - x(t_i - \Delta t). \tag{5.155}$$

Note that $x(t_i - \Delta t)$ in (5.155) is defined by interpolation over the two adjacent values t_j and t_{j+1} such that $t_j < t_i - \Delta t \leq t_{j+1}$.

The change of price is often used instead of the price because it is the variable of interest for traders (whose aim is to maximize the short term investment return), its distribution is more symmetric than the price distribution and the process has a higher level of stationarity.

Definition 5.6 The volatility at time t_i with sampling period $N\Delta t$ is defined as

$$v(t_i; \Delta t, N) = \frac{1}{N} \sum_{j=1}^{N} |r(t_{i-j}; \Delta t)|$$

Definition 5.7 The relative spread at time t_i is defined as

$$s(t_i) = \log p_{\text{ask}}(t_i) - \log p_{\text{bid}}(t_i)$$

Sometimes the log spread is used, which is simply $\log s(t_i)$.

The relative spread is preferred to the nominal spread $p_{\text{ask}}(t_i) - p_{\text{bid}}(t_i)$ since it is dimensionless and therefore can be used to compare exchange rates between different currencies. Note that the variance of $s(t_i)$ is invariant under inversion of the rate.

Definition 5.8 The tick frequency at time t_i is defined as

$$f(t_i; \Delta t) = \frac{1}{\Delta t} \text{card}(x(t_j) \mid t_j \in (t_i - \Delta t, t_i])$$

Sometimes the log tick frequency, $\log f(t_i; \Delta t)$ is used.

The tick frequency can be considered a proxy of the transaction volume on the markets.

In the following, we shall make use of the notion of quote time, which can simply be viewed as the "change of variable" on the time axis defined by $t_i \rightarrow i$, that is we will reindex our measurements as taking place on $1, 2, \ldots, N$, where N is the number of measurements.

Under this new notion of time, the return is defined as

$$r_i = x_i - x_{i-1},$$

where x_i is the price at time t_i, i.e.

$$x_i = \frac{\log p_{\text{bid}}(t_i) + \log p_{\text{ask}}(t_i)}{2}.$$

Note how the notion of quote time is closely related to the idea of intrinsic time as modeled by a subordinator $T(t)$: in fact, if we define

$$T(t) = \{\text{Number of transactions up to time } t\},$$

then it holds $i = T(t_i)$, where i is the quote time corresponding to the physical time t_i. The return in quote time for our time series is shown in Figure 5.8.

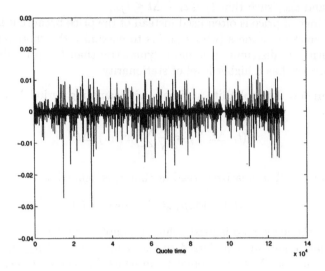

Fig. 5.8   1–quote returns. (Adapted from: Marinelli, Rachev, Roll (1999))

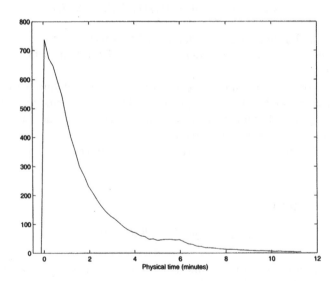

Fig. 5.9   Empirical PDF of the waiting times between two successive quotes. (Adapted from: Marinelli, Rachev, Roll (1999))

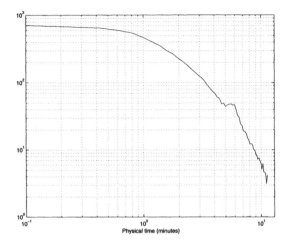

Fig. 5.10 Tail of the estimated PDF of the waiting times in logarithmic scale. (Adapted from: Marinelli, Rachev, Roll (1999))

The probability density function (PDF) of the waiting times between successive quotes is displayed in Figure 5.9. The tail of the estimated PDF in logarithmic scale (Figure 5.10), exhibits a power law behavior of the type $f(x) \sim x^{-1-\alpha}$ with different α for waiting times between 1 and 5 and between 6 and 10 minutes.

Recall the definition of the Hill's estimator $\hat{\alpha}$, for the tail index α: For a sample $X_1, \ldots, X_n$,

$$\hat{\alpha}_{k,n} = \hat{\alpha}_k = \left(\frac{1}{k} \sum_{j=1}^{k} \log X_{n+1-j:n} - \log X_{n-k:n} \right)^{-1},$$

where $X_{j:n}$ denotes the j-th order statistics of the sample. Figure 5.11 (left panel) represents $\hat{\alpha}_k$: it is clear that, approximately, $\alpha \in [2.3, 2.5)$, i.e. the waiting times between quotes seem to admit second moment. Moreover, a least–squares regression in the log–log plot of the farthest portion of the tail of the estimated density function (see Figure 5.11, right panel) gives an estimate of the tail index α as 2.36, in good agreement with the Hill estimate.

To estimate the Hurst exponent H of the tick–by–tick return series (see Figure 5.8), we shall fit the average absolute value of the returns over k quotes to a power law of the type $\beta_0 k^H$. To estimate β_0 and H, we use loglinear regression, i.e. we fit by ordinary least squares (OLS) the series $Y_k = \log \hat{E}|x(t+k) - x(t)|$ to the regressors $\gamma_0 + \gamma_1 \log k$, where $\hat{E}(\cdot)$ stands for sample mean. We obtain

$$\gamma_0 = 3 \cdot 10^{-4} \tag{5.156}$$

$$\gamma_1 = 0.5878, \tag{5.157}$$

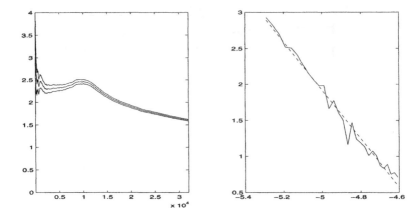

Fig. 5.11 Hill tail index estimator with 95% confidence bounds of the waiting times between quotes (left) and tail index estimation via OLS regression of the estimated PDF in logarithmic scale (right). (Adapted from: Marinelli, Rachev, Roll (1999))

implying an estimate of the Hurst exponent as $\hat{H} = \gamma_1 = 0.5878$. This value is consistent with many other studies in the literature (see for example Guillaume et al. (1997)).

A plot of $\log \hat{E}|x(t+k) - x(t)|$ versus k (dots) and of the regression line (solid) is shown in Figure 5.12 (bottom panel). The above panel is plot of $\hat{E}|x(t+k) - x(t)|$ (dots) and of the map $k \mapsto \gamma_0 k^{\alpha_1}$ (solid).

5.5.2 Statistical Analysis of the Price Process in Quote Time

In this section we investigate the probabilistic structure of the price process in quote time (i.e. in the intrinsic time scale) $S(t)$ (see Figure 5.5).
By estimating the probability density function (PDF) of the returns at the highest frequency, i.e. the 1-quote returns, we get a multimodal empirical PDF, as shown in the left panel of Figure 5.13. A gaussian PDF with the same mean and variance is superimposed for comparison. This bimodal behavior tends to disappear in the 2-quote return PDF, shown in the right panel.

Figure 5.14 shows the empirical density function of 3-quote returns, which does not display evident signs of multimodality (however, we cannot exclude this possibility, due to the smoothing effects of kernel density estimation). While it does not make sense to look for a stable fit for 1- and 2-quote returns, it might be interesting to see how adequately a stable distribution would model 3-quote returns. Using McCulloch's quantile based estimators, we find the following values for the parameters of a stable fit in the S parametrization:

$$\alpha = 1.842$$
$$\beta = -0.122$$

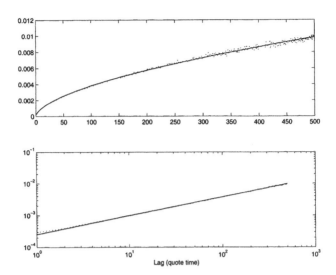

Fig. 5.12 Loglinear regression of absolute average returns. (Adapted from: Marinelli, Rachev, Roll (1999))

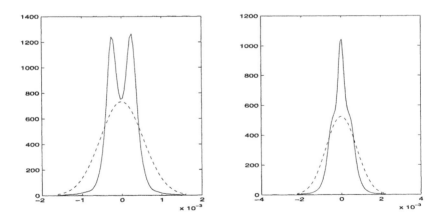

Fig. 5.13 Estimated PDFs of 1–quote and 2–quote returns (solid) and normal fits (dashed). (Adapted from: Marinelli, Rachev, Roll (1999))

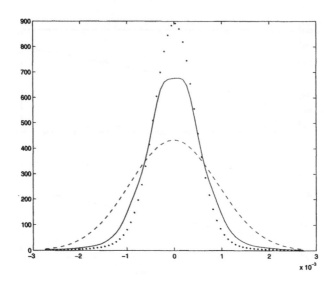

Fig. 5.14 Estimated PDF of 3–quote returns (solid), normal (dashed) and stable fit (dotted). (Adapted from: Marinelli, Rachev, Roll (1999))

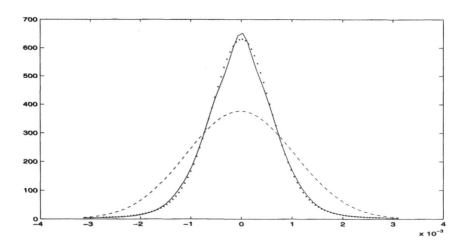

Fig. 5.15 Estimated PDF of 4–quote returns, normal (dashed) and stable fit (dotted). (Adapted from: Marinelli, Rachev, Roll (1999))

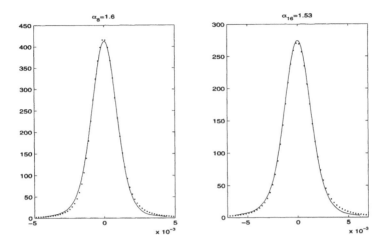

Fig. 5.16 Estimated PDF of 8–quote (left) and 16–quote (right) returns (solid) and stable fit (dotted). (Adapted from: Marinelli, Rachev, Roll (1999))

$$\sigma = 3.171\,10^{-4}$$
$$\mu = -5.719\,10^{-6}.$$

The dotted curve in Figure 5.14 is the numerically calculated PDF of a stable random variable with distribution $S_\alpha(\sigma, \beta, \mu)$ where the parameters are those estimated.

Note that if we suppose that the underlying stochastic process generating our return process is symmetric Lévy stable, then it would be self–similar with index $H = 1/\alpha = 0.543$, which differs for about 8% from our previous estimation, that was $H = 0.588$.

Let us continue our analysis a step further, i.e. at the frequency of 4 quotes: in Figure 5.15 we estimate the PDF of the 4-quote returns and plot a stable PDF with the fitted parameters given by:

$$\alpha = 1.716$$
$$\beta = 0.0436$$
$$\sigma = 4.518 \cdot 10^{-4}$$
$$\mu = 1.212 \cdot 10^{-5}.$$

The stable fit is exceptionally good, and note how α decreased, indicating thicker tail, and the skewness parameter β is close to zero, suggesting that returns in quote time (and more precisely, at this frequency) are nearly symmetric.

At higher sampling periods, stable laws still offer a very good fit to the distribution of returns in quote time, as evidenced in Figure 5.16, where the 8-quote and 16-quote returns are plotted together with their stable fits. Note

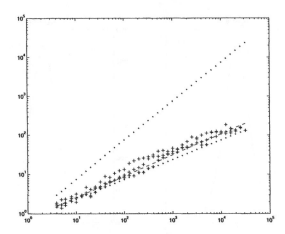

Fig. 5.17 Pox plot for 4–quote returns. Dotted lines corresponds to $H = 0.5$ and $H = 1$. (Adapted from: Marinelli, Rachev, Roll (1999))

how the estimated stability index α varies with the sampling period, decreasing from $\alpha = 1.71$ for 4-quote returns, to $\alpha = 1.6$ and $\alpha = 1.53$ for 8 and 16-quote returns, respectively.

A very recent hypothesis about the modeling of price movements with processes exhibiting different scaling behaviors is the Multifractal Model of Asset Returns[24] (MMAR) of Mandelbrot, Fisher and Calvet (1997): they consider, loosely speaking, self-similar stochastic processes with stochastic Hurst exponent, i.e. their theory takes into account relationships of the type

$$X(ct) \stackrel{d}{=} M(c)X(t)$$

where X and M are independent stochastic processes. Their theory however, in contrast to the Lévy-stable model, does not necessarily imply infinite variance of the returns, while it implies long memory (as the Fractional Brownian Motion model with $H > 1/2$ does).

For another study on multifractality of financial data, from the point of view of analogies between non–linear group theoretical methods developed in mathematical physics and scaling transformations of price processes, see Brachet, Taflin and Tcheou (1997).

We now turn to the analysis of long–range dependence in the price process in intrinsic time $S(t)$.

---

[24]For more details, see Section 5.4.2.

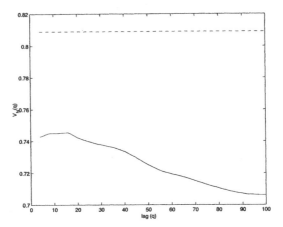

Fig. 5.18 Lo's modified R/S–statistic $V_N(q)$ as function of the lag q for 4–quote returns. The dashed line is the lower boundary of the confidence region for rejecting long memory. (Adapted from: Marinelli, Rachev, Roll (1999))

While classical R/S analysis for the price process in intrinsic time $S(t)$ results in a value of the parameter $H' = d + 1/2$[25] very close to 0.5 (see Figure 5.18), which distinguishes processes with independent increments, Lo's modified R/S–statistic suggests that long–range dependence structures must be present in $S(t)$ (see Figure 5.18): in fact, for choices of the truncation lag up to $q = 200$, the statistic $V_N(q)$ falls below the lower boundary of the confidence region for rejecting long memory. Note that Lo's test is insensitive to the presence of short–dependence structures, so it cannot be conjectured that the value of H' close to 0.5 comes from short–memory. However, given the low value of the estimated parameter H', it can be inferred that long memory in $S(t)$ is very weak.

Moreover, one should be aware of the inner limitation of Lo's test when applied to time series with infinite variance, as the returns in quote time appear to be, since the statistic $V_N(q)$ implicitly requires the existence of the second moment of the distribution generating the data. However, Lo's statistic falls inside the confidence region when calculated on simulated samples of a stable random variable with $\alpha = 1.5 - 1.9$, so it is reasonable to assume that the empirical evidence provided by the application of Lo's test to the increments of $S(t)$, and hence of $Z(t)$, as we shall see, is at least meaningful.

---

[25]Recall that for time series with infinite variance innovations, classical R/S analysis estimates $H' = d + 1/2$, not $H = d + 1/\alpha$. See Section 5.4.3 and Taqqu and Teverovsky (1998) for more details.

5.5.3   Statistical Analysis of the Market Time Process

As we have already seen, we define the market time (also called *trading time* or *intrinsic time*) as

$$T(t) = \{\text{Number of transactions up to time } t\},$$

and we model it as an increasing stochastic process taking values in $\mathbf{R}^+$.

A natural choice of underlying distributions for the increments of the intrinsic time process $T(t)$ is the family of infinitely divisible distributions.[26] Here we consider only exponential, Gamma, lognormal laws and stable subordinators (i.e. maximally skewed α-stable laws with $\alpha < 1$, together with Weibull law (which is not infinitely divisible, but as we will see, it provides a very good fit).

For 8–minute increments of $T(t)$ (corresponding approximately to a sampling period of 4 quotes), i.e. for

$$\Delta T_8(t) = T(t) - T(t-8),$$

we obtain the following descriptive statistical data

$$
\begin{aligned}
\hat{\mu} &= 3.896 \\
\hat{\sigma} &= 4.478 \\
\hat{\beta} &= 36.63 \\
\hat{\kappa} &= 2462,
\end{aligned}
$$

where μ is the mean, σ the standard deviation, β the skewness, and κ the kurtosis. Note how the high value of the sample kurtosis $\hat{\kappa}$ suggests that the increments of $T(t)$ have heavy tails, even if, according to the likelihood ratio test, we will find that the best fit is not heavy tailed. Table 5.4 shows the values of the parameter estimates and of the logarithmic likelihood for all the chosen fits, while Figure 5.19 displays the empirical PDF of the 8–minute increments of $T(t)$ and its two best fits. Both clearly indicate Weibull distribution as the best fit.

This result seems to be in contrast with the value of the sample kurtosis, since the Weibull law admits finite moments of every order. Moreover, Weibull law unfortunately does not belong to the class of infinitely divisible distributions. However, note that if $S(t)_{t \geq 0}$ is an α–stable process and $T(t)$ has Weibull distributed increments, then one can easily prove that the subordinated process $Z(t) = S(T(t))$ has marginal distributions that are in the domain of attraction of an α–stable law.

It is also noteworthy that the Gamma distribution as well offers a good fit: this is an interesting fact since the Gamma distribution is infinitely divisible, and a stable process subordinated to a process with Gamma distributed increments has ν–stable distributed increments (see Section 2.4).

---

[26]For the definition and basic properties of infinitely divisible laws, see Feller (1971), Section 6.3 or Janicki and Weron (1994), Section 4.4.

Table 5.4 Fits of the 8–minute increments of the market time process $T(t)$.

Distribution	Parameter estimates	$-\log \mathcal{L}$
Exponential	$\hat{\alpha} = 3.8962$	$7.7465 \cdot 10^4$
Gamma	$\hat{a} = 1.5128$ $\hat{b} = 2.5776$	$7.5948 \cdot 10^4$
Lognormal	$\hat{\mu} = 0.9944$ $\hat{\sigma} = 0.9695$	$7.8198 \cdot 10^4$
Stable	$\hat{\alpha} = 0.99$ $\hat{\beta} = 1$ $\hat{\sigma} = 1.3678$ $\hat{\mu} = -83.978$	$7.9247 \cdot 10^4$
Weibull	$\hat{a} = 0.1478$ $\hat{b} = 1.3357$	$7.5394 \cdot 10^4$

(Adapted from: Marinelli, Rachev, Roll (1999))

Moreover, due to the fact that the empirical kurtosis of the increments of $T(t)$ is very high, it would be advisable not to exclude a distribution with heavy tails.

Using classical R/S analysis[27], we have found an estimate of the Hurst exponent for the increments of $T(t)$ of around $H = 0.8$, significantly different from the theoretical values of $H = 0.5$ valid for processes with independent (or short–range dependent) increments. Figure 5.20 displays the rescaled adjusted range plot for the increments of $T(t)$, while Figure 5.4 displays the same plot for a process with no long memory.

Similarly, Lo's modified statistic $V_N(q)$ falls by far outside the acceptance region for the null hypothesis of no long–range dependence, as clearly evidenced in Figure 5.21.

Now we extend our analysis for time lags of 15 and 30 minutes, and 1, 2 and 4 hours. Table 5.4 report the likelihood values $(-\log \mathcal{L})$ for all the chosen parametrization and for the different time lags, while full tables with parameter estimates for all laws are deferred to Tables 5.15 – 5.20 in the Appendix.

It is evident how the Weibull law consistently gives the best fit, and how the Gamma distribution becomes a better fit with increasing lags, approaching the Weibull likelihood value.

As it is reasonable to expect, the intrinsic time process $T(t)$ displays strong long–range dependence also for time lags greater than 8 minutes. In partic-

---

[27]See Section 5.4.3.

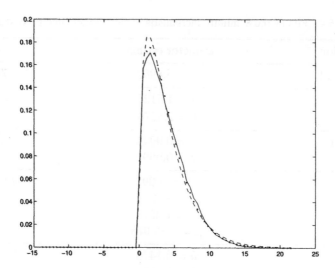

Fig. 5.19 Empirical PDF of 8–min. increments of $T(t)$ (solid line), with Weibull (dotted line) and Gamma fit (dashed line). (Adapted from: Marinelli, Rachev, Roll (1999))

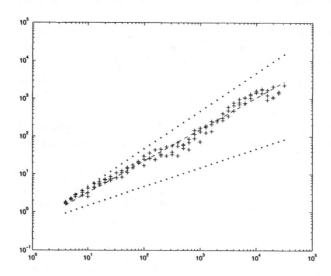

Fig. 5.20 Rescaled adjusted range plot for 8–min. increments of $T(t)$. Dotted lines corresponds to $H = 0.5$ and $H = 1$. The plot indicates the presence of long–range dependence with an estimated Hurst index $H = 0.85$. (Adapted from: Marinelli, Rachev, Roll (1999))

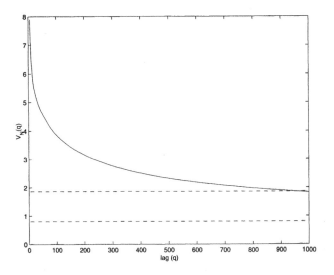

Fig. 5.21 Lo's statistic $V_N(q)$ for 8–minute increments of $T(t)$ keeps outside the confidence region (between dashed lines), thus accepting the hypothesis of long memory. (Adapted from: Marinelli, Rachev, Roll (1999))

Table 5.5 Negative log likelihood values (in multiples of 10^4) for the fits of the increments of $T(t)$ at different time lags: Weibull law consistently gives the lowest value of $-\log \mathcal{L}$, hence providing the best fit.

Distribution	15 m	30 m	1 h	2 h	4 h
Exponential	5.2319	3.2227	1.9144	1.1089	0.63027
Gamma	5.0827	3.0975	1.8195	1.0387	0.58103
Lognormal	5.2338	3.1752	1.8501	1.0462	0.58278
Stable	7.9247	–	–	–	–
Weibull	5.0351	3.0731	1.8035	1.0294	0.57685

(Adapted from: Marinelli, Rachev, Roll (1999))

Table 5.6 Estimates of the Hurst index H and the long memory parameter d for the increments of the market time process $T(t)$ for different time lags. Note that d sensibly differs from zero and hence strongly indicates the presence of long–range dependence.

Time lag	$\hat{H}$	$\hat{d}$
8 m	0.8551	0.3551
15 m	0.8596	0.3596
30 m	0.8606	0.3606
1 h	0.8959	0.3959
2 h	0.8791	0.3791
4 h	0.8635	0.3635

(Adapted from: Marinelli, Rachev, Roll (1999))

ular, the estimated values of the Hurst index H are comprised between 0.85 and 0.9. Table 5.6 reports the estimated Hurst indexes for the chosen lags.

Similarly, Lo's statistic $V_N(q)$ falls outside the confidence region of rejection of long memory for a large part of the lags q, as evidenced in Figure 5.21. In particular, Lo's test suggests that the increments of the market time process, i.e. the variations in trading activity, are dependent for choices of the time lag up to about 16–17 business days. Note that the value q beyond which $V_N(q)$ enters the confidence region decreases with increasing sampling period. This fact is expected, if we consider that the length of the time series decreases with increasing sampling period. Moreover, Lo's result requires that $q(N) = o(N^{1/4})$, and for all of our time series, $V_N(q)$ enters the confidence region for q well beyond $N^{1/4}$.

5.5.4   Statistical Analysis of the Price Process in Physical Time

We begin the analysis of the exchange rate process in physical time $Z(t) = S(T(t))$ (see Figure 5.7).

We now check what structure has the log price driving process in physical time $Z(t) = S \circ T(t) = S(T(t))$, analyzing the empirical distribution of its increments and looking for long–range dependence structures.

The increments of $Z(t)$ sampled with a period of 8 minutes are again well fit by a stable law with parameters

$$
\begin{aligned}
\alpha &= 1.3745 \\
\beta &= -0.0511 \\
\sigma &= 3.8352 \cdot 10^{-4} \\
\mu &= -1.9433 \cdot 10^{-5}.
\end{aligned}
$$

A plot of the empirical PDF of the 8–minute increments and its stable fit is displayed in Figure 5.23. Note that the stability index α is considerably

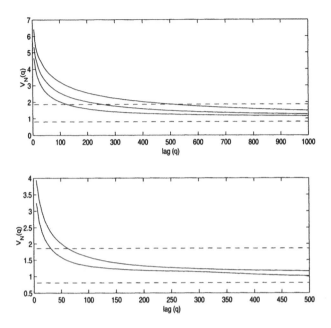

Fig. 5.22 Lo's statistic $V_N(q)$ vs. q for 15, 30 and 60–minute (above panel, right to left) and for 2 and 4–hour (bottom panel, right to left) increments of $T(t)$. In dashed lines, the boundaries of the confidence region for Lo's test. (Adapted from: Marinelli, Rachev, Roll (1999))

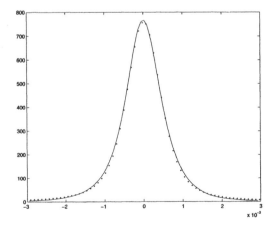

Fig. 5.23 Estimated PDF of 8–minute returns (solid) and stable fit (dotted). (Adapted from: Marinelli, Rachev, Roll (1999))

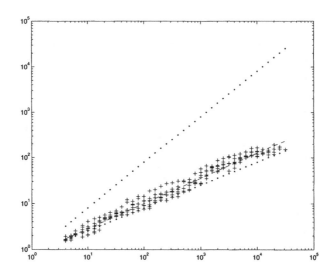

Fig. 5.24 Rescaled adjusted range plot of the 8–min. returns of $Z(t)$. (Adapted from: Marinelli, Rachev, Roll (1999))

different for the stable fits in intrinsic and physical time at comparable time scales (recall that 4 quotes corresponds to approximately 8 minutes).

The compound process $Z(t)$ "inherits" long–range dependence from $S(t)$ and $T(t)$. However, while $T(t)$ exhibits a large value of the Hurst index H, $Z(t)$ behaves in a way closer to $S(t)$, i.e. it exhibits weak long memory, but Lo's test rejects the hypothesis of *no* long–range dependence (see Figures 5.24 and 5.25).

We now extend the analysis of the probabilistic structure and of long memory for the increments of $Z(t)$ to different choices of the time lag. In particular, as we have already done for the market time process $T(t)$, we consider 15 and 30–minute returns, and 1, 2 and 4–hour returns. The estimated values of the stability index α and of the R/S parameter $H' = d + 1/2$ for the considered time lags are reported in Table 5.7. Note that the estimates of the stability index are quite similar for time lags from 8 minutes to 2 hours, while it differs rather substantially at a time lag of 4 hours.

The estimated PDFs of the returns at the different time lags, together with their stable fit, are displayed in Figures 5.27 to 5.29.

The estimated values of H' for $Z(t)$ as given in the table indicate that the price process in physical time exhibits long–range dependence, although its intensity is rather weak. However, values of H in the range 0.55-0.6 are often encountered in the literature (see for example Willinger, Taqqu and Teverovsky (1999)). In our case, Lo's test cannot reject the hypothesis of long memory in $Z(t)$, as it is shown in Figure 5.26. Note that for values of the lag q up to more than 350 (corresponding to almost 22 business days

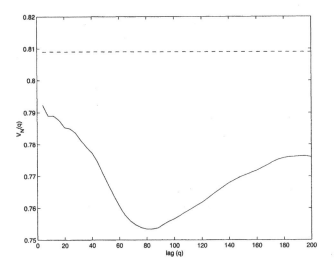

Fig. 5.25 Lo's modified R/S statistic $V_N(q)$ as function of the lag q for the 8–min. returns of $Z(t)$. The dashed line is the lower boundary of the confidence region for rejecting long memory. (Adapted from: Marinelli, Rachev, Roll (1999))

Table 5.7 Estimated stability index α, R/S parameter $H' = d+1/2$ and long memory parameter d for increments of $Z(t)$ at different time lags.

Time lag	$\hat{\alpha}$	$\hat{H}'$	$\hat{d}$
8 m	1.3745	0.5488	0.0488
15 m	1.3966	0.5467	0.0467
30 m	1.3860	0.5523	0.0523
1 h	1.3466	0.5747	0.0747
2 h	1.3865	0.5515	0.0515
4 h	1.4912	0.5528	0.0528

(Adapted from: Marinelli, Rachev, Roll (1999))

for 30–minute increments), the corresponding Lo's statistic falls outside the confidence region for rejecting long–range dependence.

As we have already pointed out, $S(t)$ has an R/S parameter H' rather close to the theoretical value of $H' = 0.5$ (although Lo's test again speaks in favor of long–memory in the data): therefore we could infer that the long–range dependence in $Z(t)$ comes from both $S(t)$ and $T(t)$, with the long memory parameter d of $Z(t)$ taking values closer to the corresponding parameter of $S(t)$.

In the following we show that the intrinsic time process $T(t)$ cannot be self–similar. In fact, note that if we suppose $T(t)$ to be self–similar with index H_T, and $S(t)$ self–similar with index H_S, then $Z(t)$ must be self–similar with index $H_Z = H_T H_S$. Namely, it holds:

$$Z(ct) = S(T(ct)) \overset{d}{=} S(c^{H_T} T(t)) \overset{d}{=} (c^{H_T})^{H_S} S(T(t)) = c^{H_T H_S} Z(t).$$

In our case, since $T(t)$ has finite variance innovations and a Hurst index H_T in the range 0.85–0.9, it also holds $H_Z < H_S$. Recall that our statistical analysis suggests that $Z(t)$ is a process with increments in the domain of attraction of a stable law. If we define, as an extension of the notation used for stable processes,

$$d_Z = H_Z - \frac{1}{\alpha_Z} ,$$

then we would also have

$$d_Z + \frac{1}{\alpha_Z} < d_S + \frac{1}{\alpha_S} .$$

However, as we have found that $\alpha_S > \alpha_Z$, we should also expect $d_Z < d_S$, i.e. long–range dependence in the return process in physical time should be weaker than in the return process in market time. Note that this is also the case if $S(t)$ and $Z(t)$ have the same index of stability α.

In our case, since H_T is in the range 0.85–0.9 and $H_S \approx 0.6$ (found by analyzing the scaling of the absolute increments), we should expect $Z(t)$, under the above mentioned hypothesis, to have a self–similarity index H_Z no greater than 0.55. Furthermore, the estimated stability indices α of the increments of $Z(t)$ are no greater than $\overline{\alpha} = 1.5$, hence

$$H_Z < \frac{1}{\overline{\alpha}} ,$$

which shows that the increments of $Z(t)$ are *negative* dependent, not long–range dependent. On the other hand, we have found that long memory should be present in the increments of $Z(t)$. Therefore, we are led to conclude that $T(t)$ is in fact not self–similar.

The daily increments of the market time process $T(t)$ are also very well described by a Weibull law, with the Gamma distribution as an almost equally good candidate, similarly as we have seen for intra–daily increments. Table 5.8 reports the likelihood values for both daily and weekly increments of $T(t)$.

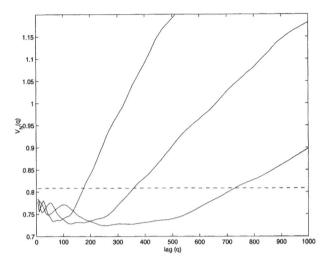

Fig. 5.26 Lo's statistic for 15, 30 and 60–minute increments of $Z(t)$ (right to left). (Adapted from: Marinelli, Rachev, Roll (1999))

Moreover, R/S analysis still gives an estimated value of the Hurst index $H = 0.85$ (see the pox plot in Figure 5.30, left panel), suggesting again the presence of long–range dependence structures in $T(t)$ that are persistent over different business days.

The increments of the return process in physical time $Z(t)$ display a probabilistic structure, even for a sampling period of 1 day, that is closely approximated by a stable law, as evidenced in Figure 5.31, top left panel. The fitting stable distribution in this case has a stable index $\alpha = 1.78$, which means that daily returns are less heavy tailed than returns over shorter periods.

Our analysis suggests that long–range dependence is still present also in daily returns, and the R/S method gives an estimate $H' = 0.54$, while Lo's test speaks in favor of the presence of long memory for choices of the lag $q < 20$ business days (see Figure 5.31, top right panel).

The most important feature of weekly data for the increments of the market time is that they still exhibit long–range dependence, with an estimated Hurst index $H = 0.8$ (see Figure 5.30, right panel). This suggests that long memory in the market time process $T(t)$ persists even over different weeks.

Another interesting feature of weekly increments of $T(t)$ is that there is no Weibull fit (the negative log likelihood value "explodes"), while the best fit becomes a Gamma distribution.

Similarly as we have seen above, we have found a very satisfactory stable fit of the weekly returns in physical time, with an estimated stability index $\alpha = 1.91$ (see Figure 5.31, bottom left panel). Note how α, a measure of the tail thickness, increases with increasing sampling periods, as intuition would

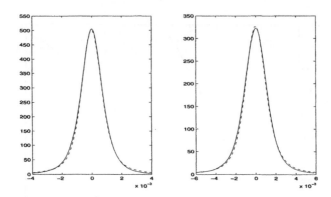

Fig. 5.27 Estimated PDF (solid) and stable fit (dashed) for 15 and 30–minute returns. (Adapted from: Marinelli, Rachev, Roll (1999))

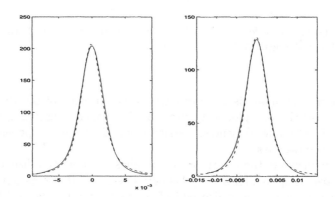

Fig. 5.28 Estimated PDF (solid) and stable fit (dashed) for 1 and 2–hour returns (Adapted from: Marinelli, Rachev, Roll (1999))

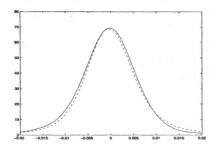

Fig. 5.29 Estimated PDF (solid) and stable fit (dashed) for 4–hour returns. (Adapted from: Marinelli, Rachev, Roll (1999))

Table 5.8 Fits of the daily and weekly increments of the market time process $T(t)$.

Distribution	1 day	1 week
Exponential	3262.5	843.93
Gamma	2994.5	781.96
Lognormal	3005.5	786.21
Weibull	2994.4	3748.5

(Adapted from: Marinelli, Rachev, Roll (1999))

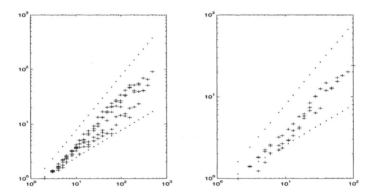

Fig. 5.30 Rescaled range plot for daily (left) and weekly (right) increments of the market time process $T(t)$. (Adapted from: Marinelli, Rachev, Roll (1999))

suggest. However, even returns cannot be approximated by a normal law, and do not admit second order moments.

On the other hand, long–range dependence in $Z(t)$ is very weak. In fact, we obtained an estimated $H' = 0.53$, and Lo's statistic $V_N(q)$ falls within the acceptance region of the hypothesis of no long memory for $q > 4$ (see Figure 5.31). However, note that this value corresponds to the value of $q = 20$ business days that we have found for daily returns. Moreover, while it is true that classical R/S analysis is sensitive to the presence of short–range dependence, that hence could be responsible for such a small value of H', we should also consider that Lo's results are asymptotic (see Willinger, Taqqu and Teverovsky (1999)), and we have about 100 weekly closing data, so the reliability of this test on such a small sample is rather uncertain.

Summarizing our findings, we see that a reasonable model for the description of exchange rates is a subordinated process $Z(t) = S(T(t))$, where

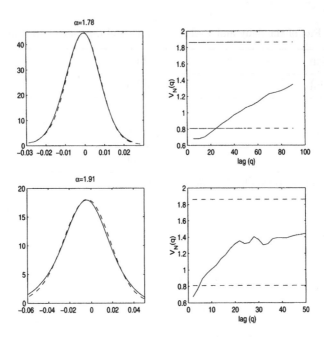

Fig. 5.31 Estimated density function (solid) and stable fit (dashed) of daily (top left) and weekly (bottom left) returns in physical time. Right portion: corresponding daily and weekly plots of the Lo's statistic $V_N(q)$. (Adapted from: Marinelli, Rachev, Roll (1999))

1. The price process in market time $S(t)$ is an α–stable Lévy motion, or more generally, $S(t)$ is a fractional stable motion with self–similarity index H slightly greater than $1/\alpha$.

2. The intrinsic time process $T(t)$ has Weibull (or Gamma) distributed, long–range dependent increments, with Hurst index H in the range 0.8–0.9.

3. The price process in physical time $Z(t)$ is a process with increments in the domain of attraction of stable law. Furthermore, the increments of $Z(t)$ are weakly long–range dependent.

Table 5.9   Fits of the 15-minute increments of the market time process $T(t)$.

Distribution	Parameter estimates	$-\log \mathcal{L}$
Exponential	$\hat{\alpha} = 7.3055$	$5.2319 \cdot 10^4$
Gamma	$\hat{a} = 1.7885$ $\hat{b} = 4.0847$	$5.0827 \cdot 10^4$
Lognormal	$\hat{\mu} = 1.68372$ $\hat{\sigma} = 0.89342$	$5.2338 \cdot 10^4$
Stable	$\hat{\alpha} = 0.99$ $\hat{\beta} = 1$ $\hat{\sigma} = 1.3678$ $\hat{\mu} = -83.978$	$7.9247 \cdot 10^4$
Weibull	$\hat{a} = 0.044085$ $\hat{b} = 1.50349$	$5.0351 \cdot 10^4$

(Adapted from: Marinelli, Rachev, Roll (1999))

Table 5.10   Fits of the 30-minute increments of the market time process $T(t)$.

Distribution	Parameter estimates	$-\log \mathcal{L}$
Exponential	$\hat{\alpha} = 14.611$	$3.2227 \cdot 10^4$
Gamma	$\hat{a} = 2.1885$ $\hat{b} = 6.6763$	$3.0975 \cdot 10^4$
Lognormal	$\hat{\mu} = 2.43623$ $\hat{\sigma} = 0.79643$	$3.1752 \cdot 10^4$
Weibull	$\hat{a} = 9.0368 \cdot 10^{-3}$ $\hat{b} = 1.692$	$3.0731 \cdot 10^4$

(Adapted from: Marinelli, Rachev, Roll (1999))

Table 5.11   Fits of the 1–hour increments of the market time process $T(t)$.

Distribution	Parameter estimates	$-\log \mathcal{L}$
Exponential	$\hat{\alpha} = 29.219$	$1.9144 \cdot 10^4$
Gamma	$\hat{a} = 2.7299$ $\hat{b} = 10.7033$	$1.8195 \cdot 10^4$
Lognormal	$\hat{\mu} = 3.18063$ $\hat{\sigma} = 0.68962$	$1.8501 \cdot 10^4$
Weibull	$\hat{a} = 1.2214 \cdot 10^{-3}$ $\hat{b} = 1.9264736$	$1.8035 \cdot 10^4$

(Adapted from: Marinelli, Rachev, Roll (1999))

5.6   The Heavy–Tailedness and Long–Range Dependence in the High–Frequency Deutsche Bank Price Record

In this section we study the probabilistic structure of the Deutsche Bank high–frequency price data in the setting of stochastic subordination[28], i.e. we model the log price process in physical time as a compound process $Z(t) = S(T(t))$, where $S(t)$ is a stochastic process indexed on a stochastically "deformed" time scale represented by a process $T(t)$[29]. In this setting, $T(t)$ models the market activity, which changes over time, as it is well known, and $S(t)$ is the stock (log) price process in market time.

We focus on the properties of heavy tailedness and long–range dependence[30], studying their behavior with respect to the time lag, for all the processes involved in the setting of subordination.

We consider the high–frequency Deutsche Bank price record registered at the Frankfurt Stock Exchange from May 1, 1996 to April 30, 1998. The data set consists of 66255 observations for a total of 498 business days, so we have an average of around 133 ticks per day. In the period of our records, the business hours of the Frankfurt Stock Market were from 10:30am to 1:30pm, while they were extended to 8:30am to 4:30pm only on July 1, 1998. We have therefore approximately 44 quotes an hour, or equivalently one quote every 1.35 minutes. Figure 5.32 displays the empirical paths of the processes $S(t)$, $T(t)$ and $Z(t)$ for our data set.

---

[28]See Section 5.4

[29]The results of this section are due to Marinelli, Rachev, Roll, Göppl (1999).

[30]See Beran (1994) for an introduction to the theory of long–range dependence and for a survey of the available statistical methods.

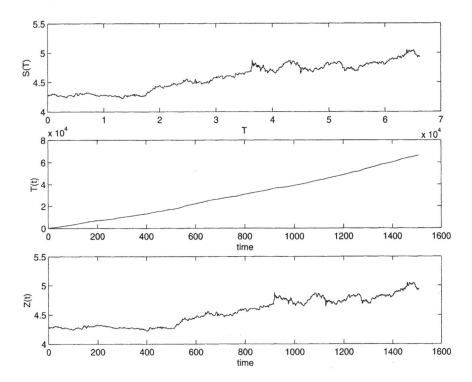

Fig. 5.32   Tick–by–tick logarithmic price levels, trace of the trading time $T(t)$, and log price levels in physical time for the Deutsche Bank stock, from top to bottom. Times are expressed in hours. (Adapted from: Marinelli, Rachev, Roll, Göppl (1999))

We have obtained this data set from the Karlsruher Kapitalmarktdaten-bank, which collects a great variety of financial data for the German market.[31]

As in Section 5.4 we define the market time (also called *trading time* or *intrinsic time*) as

$$T(t) = \{ \text{ Number of transactions up to time } t \},$$

and we model it as an increasing $\mathbf{R}_0^+$–valued stochastic process defined on $\mathbf{R}_0^+$, and such that $T(0) = 0$.

Recall that the tick frequency at time t is defined as

$$f(t; \Delta t) = \frac{1}{\Delta t} \text{card} \left\{ x(t_j) \, | \, t_j \in (t - \Delta t, t] \right\},$$

---

[31]See the Appendix at the end of this section for more details on the format of the data, and Lüdecke (1997) for informations on the data bank.

where t_j are the times at which the quotes are registered, and $x(t_j)$ are the corresponding prices. In the setting of subordination, it holds

$$f(t; \Delta t) = \frac{T(t) - T(t - \Delta t)}{\Delta t}.$$

For increments of $T(t)$ with a sampling period $\Delta t = 2$, 5, 15, 30 minutes, 1 hour and 1 day, i.e. for

$$\Delta T(t) = T(t) - T(t - \Delta t),$$

we obtain the following descriptive statistical data

	2 min	5 min	15 min	30 min	1 h	1 day
$\hat{\mu}$	1.4644	3.6612	10.9836	21.9671	43.9343	133.0422
$\hat{\sigma}$	1.0060	2.0881	5.1872	9.4774	17.4650	46.9927
$\hat{\beta}$	1.1231	0.8723	0.7652	0.7684	0.7332	0.6021
$\hat{\kappa}$	4.4089	3.9521	3.8329	4.0429	4.2443	4.0642

(Adapted from: Marinelli, Rachev, Roll, Göppl (1999))

where μ is the mean, σ the standard deviation, β the skewness, and κ the kurtosis. Note that the value of the sample kurtosis $\hat{\kappa}$ suggests that the increments of $T(t)$ have light tails.

Table 5.12 shows the values of the parameter estimates and of the logarithmic likelihood for all chosen fits of the 2–minute increments. Moreover, we report in Table 5.13 the likelihood values $(-\log \mathcal{L})$ of all parametrizations for time lags of 2, 5, 15, 30 minutes and 1 hour, while full tables with parameter estimates can be found in the Appendix of this section. Note that the Gamma distribution offers the best fit in all cases, except for $\Delta t = 5$ and 10 minutes, for which the Weibull distribution performs slightly better. Moreover, the Weibull distribution proves to be inadequate as a model for daily increments of $T(t)$. Figure 5.33 displays the empirical PDFs of the increments of $T(t)$ and their best two fits (i.e., Gamma and Weibull) for sampling periods from 2 to 30 minutes.

The probabilistic structure of the increments of $T(t)$, as we have already pointed out, is in agreement with the low value of their sample kurtosis, since both Gamma and Weibull laws admit finite moments of every order.

Moreover, due to the fact that the empirical kurtosis of the increments of $T(t)$ is very low, and that the family of stable subordinators performs poorly in comparison to the other fits, we are lead to exclude an underlying distribution with heavy tails.

It is evident, from both the likelihood scores and the empirical fits, how the Gamma law consistently provides an accurate fit.

The whole picture is then complicated by the fact that, as we show in the following, the increments of $T(t)$ cannot be assumed to be independent. In fact, both classical R/S analysis and Lo's modified R/S statistics favor the

Table 5.12   Fits of the 2–minute increments of the market time process $T(t)$.

Distribution	Parameter estimates	$-\log \mathcal{L}$
Exponential	$\hat{a} = 1.464434$	$6.2500 \cdot 10^4$
Gamma	$\hat{a} = 2.073898$ $\hat{b} = 0.706131$	$5.6772 \cdot 10^4$
Lognormal	$\hat{\mu} = 0.121410$ $\hat{\sigma} = 0.774806$	$5.8144 \cdot 10^4$
Stable	$\hat{\alpha} = 0.9993$ $\hat{\beta} = 1$ $\hat{\sigma} = 0.4684$ $\hat{\mu} = -399.326$	$6.1146 \cdot 10^4$
Weibull	$\hat{a} = 0.475704$ $\hat{b} = 1.519623$	$5.7065 \cdot 10^4$

(Adapted from: Marinelli, Rachev, Roll, Göppl (1999))

Table 5.13   Negative log likelihood values for the fits of the increments of $T(t)$ at time lags up to 1 hour.

Distribution	2 m	3 m	5 m	10 m	15 m	30 m	1 h
Exponential	62500	53895	41580	27061	20487	12334	7212
Gamma	56772	48989	37554	24163	18205	10937	6399
Lognormal	58144	50421	38668	24709	18529	11081	6453
Stable	61146	–	–	–	–	–	–
Weibull	57065	49006	37463	24138	18212	10964	6421

(Adapted from: Marinelli, Rachev, Roll, Göppl (1999))

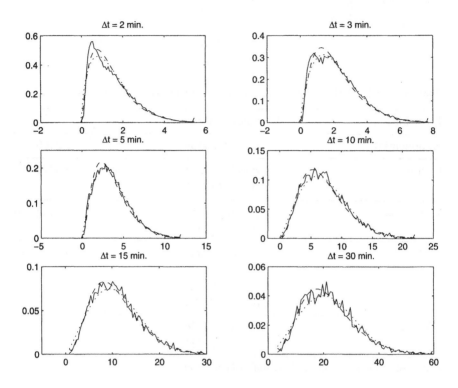

Fig. 5.33 Empirical PDF (solid) of the increments of the market times process $T(t)$ for different time lags, together with Gamma (dashed) and Weibull fit (dotted). (Adapted from: Marinelli, Rachev, Roll, Göppl (1999))

hypothesis that long–range dependence structures are present in the market time process $T(t)$.

Classical R/S analysis applied to the increments of $T(t)$ strongly evidences the presence of long memory in the data. In fact, the estimated Hurst index H belongs to the range $0.8 - 0.9$ for all considered time lags. In the following table, we summarize our findings:

	2 m	3 m	4 m	5 m	10 m	15 m	30 m	1 h	1 d
H	0.89	0.89	0.88	0.89	0.88	0.87	0.86	0.84	0.82

(Adapted from: Marinelli, Rachev, Roll, Göppl (1999))

Note that the intra–hourly estimates of H are almost equal, while they tend to slightly decrease at lower frequencies (i.e., for longer sampling periods), as it is reasonable to expect. Since R/S analysis is sensitive to the presence of short–range dependence, the small variation in H might also be seen as a "weakening" of the effects of short memory as the time lags increases.

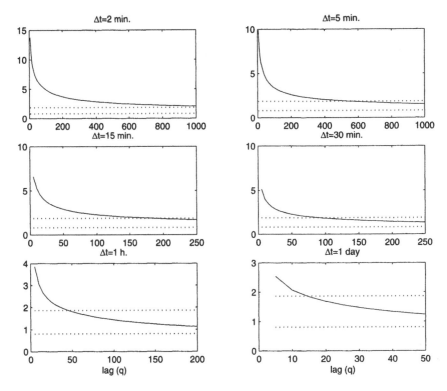

Fig. 5.34 Graphs of the Lo's statistic $V_N(q)$ against q (the lag) for the increments of $T(t)$ at different sampling periods. Between dotted lines is the 95% confidence region of Lo's test. (Adapted from: Marinelli, Rachev, Roll, Göppl (1999)

We have also applied Lo's test to the increments of $T(t)$, and a plot of the modified R/S statistic $V_N(q)$ against q for different choices of the sampling period is given in Figure 5.34. The values of the lag q beyond which $V_N(q)$ enters the confidence region of Lo's test are quite large compared to the sizes of the corresponding time series, so this behavior is not to be considered in contradiction with the estimates of H obtained through classical R/S analysis.

The plots also show a behavior of $V_N(q)$ consistent with that of fractional ARIMA (see Teverovsky, Taqqu and Willinger (1998)), which suggests, at a level of qualitative analysis, that the increments of $T(t)$ could possibly be generated by a FARIMA process with Gamma distributed innovations.

The 1–quote returns (i.e., in our setting, the increments of $S(t)$ with unit sampling period) are clearly not drawn from a stable random variable, as it can be inferred by the shape of their empirical PDF displayed in Figure 5.35.

The stable law offers a reasonably good fit of the central portion of the density, but unfortunately it cannot fully explain the shape of the empirical PDF.

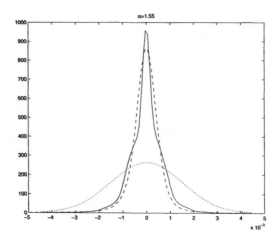

Fig. 5.35 Empirical PDF (solid) of the 1–quote returns, together with stable (dashed) and normal fit (dotted). (Adapted from: Marinelli, Rachev, Roll, Göppl (1999))

Table 5.14 Stable fits of the increments of $S(t)$ for different sampling periods.

Lag	$\hat{\alpha}$	$\hat{\beta}$	$\hat{\sigma}$	$\hat{\mu}$
1	1.55	$-9.91 \cdot 10^{-2}$	$3.64 \cdot 10^{-4}$	$-2.66 \cdot 10^{-5}$
2	1.54	$6.78 \cdot 10^{-2}$	$5.09 \cdot 10^{-4}$	$1.58 \cdot 10^{-5}$
4	1.46	$6.48 \cdot 10^{-2}$	$7.01 \cdot 10^{-4}$	$2.05 \cdot 10^{-5}$
8	1.31	$7.24 \cdot 10^{-2}$	$9.98 \cdot 10^{-4}$	$7.81 \cdot 10^{-5}$
16	1.22	$8.67 \cdot 10^{-2}$	$1.47 \cdot 10^{-3}$	$2.96 \cdot 10^{-4}$

(Adapted from: Marinelli, Rachev, Roll, Göppl (1999))

The estimated index of stability α is fairly "stationary" for sampling periods up to 4 quotes, while it decreases to approximately 1.3 and 1.2 for sampling periods of 8 and 16 quotes. However, there is no reason to believe that α would be constant for tick–by–tick data at the shortest time scales, nor that it would decrease for longer sampling periods. Moreover, we observed a similar phenomenon in the study of the tick–by–tick returns of the USD–CHF exchange rate, see Section 5.5. The variability of the index of stability α might be due to the fact that the increments of the process $S(t)$ are in fact not independent, or that they are not identically distributed, or that the underlying distribution is not purely stable, but instead could be a mixture with, speaking loosely, a dominant stable component.

The estimated values of the Hurst index for the increments of $S(t)$ at all considered sampling periods are very close to the theoretical value $H_0 = 0.5$ distinguishing processes with no long memory: namely, they are in the range

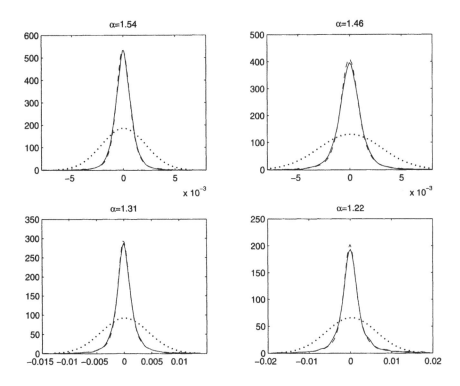

Fig. 5.36 Empirical PDF (solid) of the 2, 4, 8 and 16–quote returns (in left–right, top–down order), together with stable (dashed) and normal fit (dotted). (Adapted from: Marinelli, Rachev, Roll, Göppl (1999))

0.52 – 0.53. Recall that the classical R/S method is robust with respect to heavy–tailed time series: in fact, $R(n)$ asymptotically behaves like $n^H = n^{d+1/\alpha}$, and $S(n)$ like $n^{1/\alpha-1/2}$, hence $R/S(n)$ asymptotically behaves like $n^{d+1/2}$, independently of the value of α. What we actually estimate with the classical R/S method is therefore $d + 1/2$, and not the self–similarity index H. Since $d = 0$ distinguishes processes with no long memory, the obtained values suggest that long–range dependence, if at all present, has very weak intensity.

Moreover, Lo's modified R/S statistic $V_N(q)$ falls inside the acceptance region for rejecting long memory for all values of the lag q, even for very small ones, as evidenced in Figures 5.37 and 5.38. However, since Lo's $V_N(q)$ statistics implicitly requires the existence of the second moment of the distribution generating the data, Lo's test might not be robust with respect to heavy–tailed time series, even if a small simulation study suggests that it provides useful results when applied to stable noise (see Sections 5.4, 5.5).

On the basis of the fact that stable laws offers a very good fit of the increments of $S(t)$, and that there is strong evidence for rejecting the hypothesis

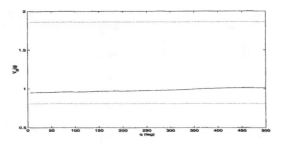

Fig. 5.37 Lo's statistic $V_N(q)$ versus q for the 1–quote increments of the tick–by–tick price record. (Adapted from: Marinelli, Rachev, Roll, Göppl (1999))

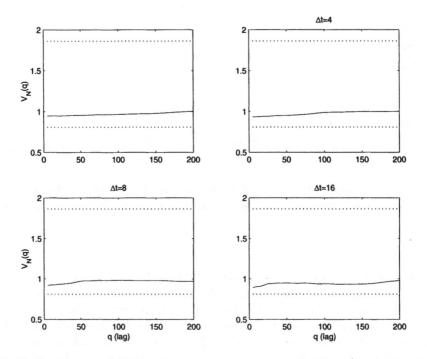

Fig. 5.38 Lo's statistic $V_N(q)$ versus q for the increments of the tick–by–tick price record: sampling periods of 2, 4, 8 and 16 quotes, in left to right, top–down order. (Adapted from: Marinelli, Rachev, Roll, Göppl (1999))

of long–range dependence in the underlying generating process, we are led to propose as a suitable model for the log price in market time, on a first level of approximation, an α–stable Lévy process. The clearest limitation of this model is that it does not allow the stability index α of the increments to change with respect to the time scale. A possible explanation of this behavior

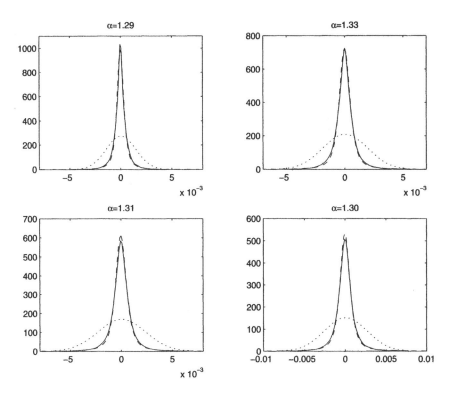

Fig. 5.39 Empirical PDF (solid) of the 2, 3, 4 and 5–minute returns (in left–right, top–down order), together with stable (dashed) and normal fit (dotted). (Adapted from: Marinelli, Rachev, Roll, Göppl (1999))

is that the there could be other components in the dynamics of tick–by–tick prices that "add up" to the stable component. Another suggestive hypothesis could be that the underlying process is in fact a GARCH process with stable innovations.

Next we study what probabilistic structure have the increments of the compound process $Z(t) = S \circ T(t) = S(T(t))$, which describes the log price in physical time. Since we have seen that $S(t)$ and $T(t)$ are properly approximated by, respectively, an α–stable Lévy process and a process with Gamma distributed increments, we would expect the subordinated process $Z(t)$ to have increments in the domain of attraction of stable laws.

As expected, the stable domain of attraction offers a good description of the increments of the compound process $Z(t) = S(T(t))$, as evidenced by Figures 5.39 and 5.40.

The estimated index of stability is close to 1.3 for time lags of 2, 3, 4 and 5 minutes, while it decreases to about 1.2 for lags of 10 and 15 minutes, and to about 1.15 for lags of 30 minutes and 1 hour. Similarly to our analysis of

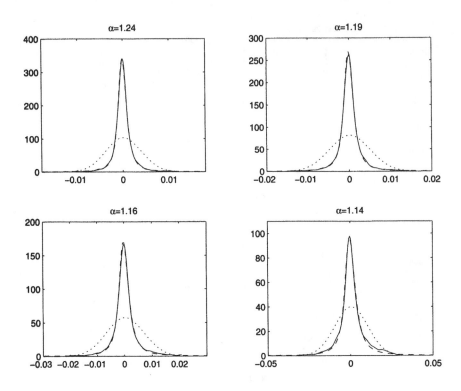

Fig. 5.40 Empirical PDF (solid) of the 10, 15, 30 and 60–minute returns (in left–right, top–down order), together with stable (dashed) and normal fit (dotted). (Adapted from: Marinelli, Rachev, Roll, Göppl (1999))

USD–CHF exchange rates, see Section 5.5 the estimated indices of stability α of $S(t)$ and $Z(t)$ are different. We conjecture that the increase in tail thickness from $S(t)$ to $Z(t)$ is induced by the long–range dependence structures of the intrinsic time process $T(t)$. Moreover, we cannot exclude the presence of explicit dependence between the processes $T(t)$ and $S(t)$, that in our setting are assumed to be independent.

The estimated Hurst index $H = d + 1/2$ is almost constantly equal to 0.58, and to 0.61 for daily returns. This indicates the possible presence of long–range dependence, although of weak intensity. On the other hand, Lo's test consistently favors the hypothesis of absence of long memory, as evidences by Figure 5.41. In essence, there is no conclusive evidence of presence or absence of dependece structures in the underlying generating process, but we can safely assert that long memory is weak, but stronger than that of $S(t)$. This is most likely due to the fact that $Z(t)$ "inherits" long range dependence structures from both $S(t)$ and $T(t)$, the latter of which was found to have strongly dependent increments.

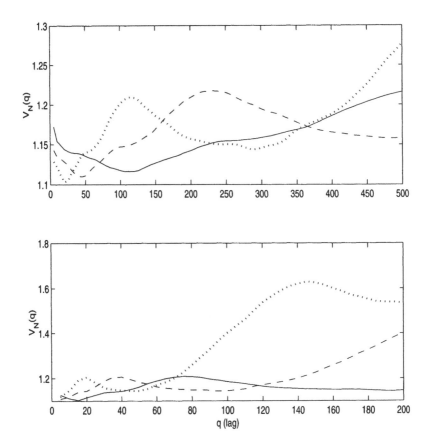

Fig. 5.41 Lo's statistic $V_N(q)$ versus q for the increments of the price record in physical time $Z(t)$. In the top panel, for sampling periods of 2, 5, and 10 minutes (solid, dashed, and dotted respectively). In the bottom panel, for sampling periods of 15, 30, and 60 minutes (same graphical conventions). (Adapted from: Marinelli, Rachev, Roll, Göppl (1999))

Concerning the daily retuns note that the estimated index of stability $\alpha = 1.64$ for daily returns is greater than the estimates at shorter time scales, an expected behavior that was observed in our previous study on exchange rates as well.

The classical R/S estimate $H = 0.61$ (corresponding to $d = 0.11$), however, is in line with the results obtained at higher frequencies, showing that long–range dependence, even if of weak intensity, is persistent over different business days.

Summarizing our empirical findings, we see that a reasonable model for the description of stock prices is an α-stable Lévy motion subordinated by a

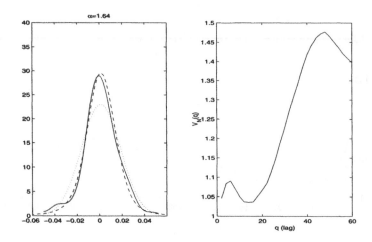

Fig. 5.42 Left panel: empirical PDF of the daily increments of $Z(t)$, with stable (dashed) and normal fit (dotted). Right panel: Lo's statistic $V_N(q)$ against q for the the daily increments of $Z(t)$. (Adapted from: Marinelli, Rachev, Roll, Göppl (1999))

long–range dependent intrinsic time process with Hurst index $H \approx 0.9$ and Gamma distributed increments.

In our study of high–frequency exchange rates, see Section 5.5, we obtained very similar results: in particular, we found $S(t)$ to be well approximated by an α–stable process, possibly fractionally stable, and the market time $T(t)$ to be a process with strongly dependent increments, well fit by the Gamma distribution (although it was outperformed by the Weibull law). These characteristics seem therefore to be of general nature, and not only peculiar features of the time series we have considered. We have not given formal explanations of why, for instance, the intrinsic time $T(t)$ has strong long range dependent increments, but we conjecture that, under the point of view of stochastic subordinated models, heavy tailedness comes from the price process in intrinsic time, and long–range dependence has its origin in the market time process.

Appendix

5.6.1 *The Karlsruher Kapitalmarktdatenbank*

The tick-by-tick data set we study is part of the database called "Fortlaufende Kurse + Umsatzdaten", available from the Karlsruher Kapitalmarktdaten-bank (KKMDB). More informations are available at the Internet URL

> http://finance.wiwi.uni-kalrsruhe.de/kkmdb.

Each record in the database consists of 7 fields, i.e.

1. Security code (e.g., 804010 in the case of Deutsche Bank).

2. The date.

3. The stock market where the record was registered (in our case, it is always the Frankfurt Stock Exchange).

4. The transaction time, in the format hh:mm:ss.ss.

5. A flag, taking a value of either E, V or S, where E denotes an opening price, V a variable intra–day price, and S a closing price.

6. The transaction price in DEM, with an accuracy of 4 decimal digits.

7. The transaction volume.

5.6.2   Tables

Table 5.15   Fits of the 3–minute increments of the market time process $T(t)$.

Distribution	Parameter estimates	$-\log \mathcal{L}$
Exponential	$\hat{\alpha} = 2.1967$	53896
Gamma	$\hat{a} = 2.3280$ $\hat{b} = 0.9436$	48989
Lognormal	$\hat{\mu} = 0.5570$ $\hat{\sigma} = 0.7377$	50421
Weibull	$\hat{a} = 0.2274$ $\hat{b} = 1.6444$	49006

(Adapted from: Marinelli, Rachev, Roll, Göppl (1999))

Table 5.16   Fits of the 5–minute increments of the market time process $T(t)$.

Distribution	Parameter estimates	$-\log \mathcal{L}$
Exponential	$\hat{\alpha} = 3.6611$	41581
Gamma	$\hat{a} = 2.7733$ $\hat{b} = 1.3201$	37555
Lognormal	$\hat{\mu} = 1.1068$ $\hat{\sigma} = 0.6778$	38668
Weibull	$\hat{a} = 0.07482$ $\hat{b} = 1.8296$	37463

(Adapted from: Marinelli, Rachev, Roll, Göppl (1999))

Table 5.17 Fits of the 10–minute increments of the market time process $T(t)$.

Distribution	Parameter estimates	$-\log \mathcal{L}$
Exponential	$\hat{\alpha} = 7.3224$	27062
Gamma	$\hat{a} = 3.5967$ $\hat{b} = 2.0358$	24163
Lognormal	$\hat{\mu} = 1.8455$ $\hat{\sigma} = 0.5866$	24710
Weibull	$\hat{a} = 0.01208$ $\hat{b} = 2.0898$	24138

(Adapted from: Marinelli, Rachev, Roll, Göppl (1999))

Table 5.18 Fits of the 15–minute increments of the market time process $T(t)$.

Distribution	Parameter estimates	$-\log \mathcal{L}$
Exponential	$\hat{\alpha} = 10.9836$	20487
Gamma	$\hat{a} = 4.1542$ $\hat{b} = 2.6439$	18205
Lognormal	$\hat{\mu} = 2.2712$ $\hat{\sigma} = 0.5389$	18529
Weibull	$\hat{a} = 3.554 \cdot 10^{-3}$ $\hat{b} = 2.2391$	18212

(Adapted from: Marinelli, Rachev, Roll, Göppl (1999))

Table 5.19   Fits of the 30–minute increments of the market time process $T(t)$.

Distribution	Parameter estimates	$-\log \mathcal{L}$
Exponential	$\hat{\alpha} = 21.9671$	12334
Gamma	$\hat{a} = 5.0868$ $\hat{b} = 4.3184$	10937
Lognormal	$\hat{\mu} = 2.9880$ $\hat{\sigma} = 0.4806$	11081
Weibull	$\hat{a} = 3.81 \cdot 10^{-4}$ $\hat{b} = 2.4525$	10964

(Adapted from: Marinelli, Rachev, Roll, Göppl (1999))

Table 5.20   Fits of the hourly increments of the market time process $T(t)$.

Distribution	Parameter estimates	$-\log \mathcal{L}$
Exponential	$\hat{\alpha} = 43.9343$	7212
Gamma	$\hat{a} = 6.0628$ $\hat{b} = 7.2465$	6399
Lognormal	$\hat{\mu} = 3.6980$ $\hat{\sigma} = 0.4330$	6453
Weibull	$\hat{a} = 3.122 \cdot 10^{-5}$ $\hat{b} = 2.6602$	6420

(Adapted from: Marinelli, Rachev, Roll, Göppl (1999))

6

ARCH–type and Shot Noise Processes

6.1   Relationship Between Unconditional Stable and ARCH-type Models

ARCH-type and stable models have similar implications for unconditional distributions. The latter, however, do not address the issue of temporal dependency.[1] In chapters 1 and 2 we presented several examples illustrating that a wide range of asset-price processes can be generated from i.i.d. random up and down movements and suitable operations, i.e., "∘", between consecutive returns.[2]

In this section, we discuss some of the relationships between unconditional stable and ARCH (Autoregressive Conditional Heteroskedasticity) models, see chapter 1 for the definition and the fit to financial data. The key observation will be that in the limit (as $n \to \infty$) an ARCH process has a Pareto tail and, in many cases, is in the domain of attraction of stable or geometric stable laws. To illustrate this, we follow de Haan et al. (1989) and consider the *random recursion*

$$S_n = A_n S_{n-1} + B_n, \qquad n \geq 0, \ S_0 \geq 0, \tag{6.1}$$

where $\{(A_n, B_n), n \in \mathbf{N}\}$ are i.i.d., nonnegative random pairs. Define the first-order ARCH process

$$\xi_n = X_n(\beta + \lambda \xi_{n-1}^2)^{1/2}, \qquad n \geq 1, \tag{6.2}$$

---

[1]For alternative autoregressive models infinite variance and Paretian stable ARMA processes see Chan and Tran (1989), Kokoszka and Taqqu (1994) and the references therein.
[2]We considered operations $+$, max, min, and multiplication. More generally, one can consider a "generalized convolution" (see , 1992).

where $\{X_n\}$ are i.i.d., standard normals, $\beta > 0$, and $\lambda \in (0,1)$.[3] Thus, $S_n = \xi_n^2$ satisfies (6.1) with $A_n = \lambda X_n^2$ and $B_n = \beta X_n^2$. Note that higher-order versions of ARCH model (6.2) can be handled by specifying higher-order recursions in (6.1) and applying techniques that are analogous to the ones discussed below.

Although it is constructed from normal variates, ARCH process ξ_n has Pareto-like tails. This is a consequence of the following result.

Theorem 6.1 *(de Haan et al., 1989)* Suppose (6.1) holds and there exists a $\kappa > 0$ such that the moment conditions

$$\mathbf{E}A_1^\kappa = 1, \quad \mathbf{E}A_1^\kappa \log^+ A_1 < \infty, \quad 0 < \mathbf{E}B_1^\kappa < \infty \quad (6.3)$$

hold. Moreover, suppose that $B_1/(1 - A_1)$ is nondegenerate and the conditional distribution of $\log A_1$ is nonlattice for $A_1 \neq 0$. Then:

(i) Equation $S_\infty \overset{d}{=} A_1 S_\infty + b_1$ (S_∞ and are (A_1, B_1) independent) has a solution unique in distribution given by $S_\infty \overset{d}{=} \sum_{j=1}^\infty B_j \prod_{i=1}^{j-1} A_i$.

(ii) If, in (6.1), $S_0 \overset{d}{=} S_\infty$, then process $\{S_n\}$ is stationary.

(iii) Regardless of the initialization of $\{S_n\}$, $S_n \overset{w}{\to} S_\infty$.

(iv) There exists a constant $c > 0$, such that, as $t \to \infty$, S_∞ has Pareto tails; i.e., $\mathrm{P}(S_\infty > t) \sim ct^{-\kappa}$.

For ARCH process $\{\xi_n^2\}$, with $A_1 = \lambda X_1^2$ and $B_1 = \beta X_1^2$, moment conditions (6.3) hold and κ is obtained by solving—for a given $\lambda \in (0,1)$—equation

$$\mathrm{E}(\lambda X_1^2)^\kappa = 1 \quad (6.4)$$

where $X_1 \sim \mathrm{N}(0,1)$. Evaluating (6.4) for selected λ-values we obtain

λ	0.1	0.2	0.3	0.4	0.5	0.6	0.7	0.8	0.9	0.99
κ	13.6	6.17	4.11	3.02	2.36	1.91	1.58	1.34	1.15	1.007

In particular, for $\lambda \geq 0.576$, we have $\kappa < 2$, implying that S_∞ is in the domain of attraction of the Paretian stable or, what is the same, a geometric-stable law with infinite variance.

The next two subsections describe the limiting results for S_n, as $n \to \infty$, and the characteristics of the set of S_∞, respectively.

---

[3]The recursion (6.1) can, in fact, be used to described general ARCH and GARCH models. In section 5.4 we will fit stable-Paretian GARCH into a multivariate version of (6.1) and analyze its properties.

6.1.1 Limit Results for S_n

We now show that the log of the cumulative-return process, $\log S_n$, is stable in the limit. Moreover, we present analogous results for the geometric summation-stable model.[4]

Rewriting recursion (6.1) as

$$S_n = \sum_{i=1}^{n} Y_i \prod_{j=1}^{i} Z_j, \quad n \in \mathbf{N}, \tag{6.5}$$

where $\{Y_n, Z_n\}_{n \in \mathbf{N}}$ is a sequence of random vectors in $\mathbf{R}^2$ and define stochastic process $\{S_n^*\}$ by

$$S_n^* = S_{n-1}^* Z_n + Y_n Z_n, \quad n \in \mathbf{N}, \tag{6.6}$$

with $S_0^* = 0$ and setting, in (6.1), $S_n = S_n^*$, $A_n = Z_n$ and $B_n = Y_n Z_n$, we see that (6.6) and (6.1) are equivalent.[5]

Next, we assume that there will be a "break" in (or change in characteristics of) process $\{S_n\}_{n \geq 1}$ at geometrically distributed random time $\tau = \tau(p)$, i.e., $P(\tau(p) = k) = (1-p)p^{k-1}$, $k = 1, 2, \ldots$. If this break is caused by a sequence of events occurring with high probability, i.e., $p \approx 1$, we obtain a negative binomial model, i.e., $\tau = \tau_1 + \cdots + \tau_r$, where times τ_i are i.i.d. geometric with mean $1/p$. For $p \to 1$, $r \to \infty$ and $r(1-p) \to \lambda > 0$, we obtain Poisson approximation $P(\tau = n + r) \approx e^{-\lambda}\lambda^n/n!$. This leads to a Poisson model for the time in which the break occurs. Assuming that times N_k are i.i.d. Poisson(λ) and $T_i = N_1 + \cdots + N_i$ represents the time of the ith break, we examine—in the framework of model (6.5)—the distributions of

$$S_{T_1} = \sum_{i=0}^{T_1} Y_i \prod_{j=0}^{i} Z_j, \quad S_{T_{k+1}} - S_{T_k} = \sum_{i=T_k+1}^{T_{k+1}} Y_i \prod_{j=0}^{i} Z_j, \quad k = 1, 2 \ldots, \tag{6.7}$$

where $\{(Y_n, Z_n)\}_{n \geq 0}$ is, unless stated otherwise, a sequence of nonnegative i.i.d. random vectors such that $P(Y_n > 0) > 0$ and $P(Z_n > 0) = 1$.[6]

To describe the limiting distribution of the cumulative return process S_n, define $\xi_n = \log Z_n$ and—provided it exists—$\nu = E\xi_n$, and assume that ξ_n belongs to the domain of attraction of α-stable r.v. η_α ($1 < \alpha \leq 2$). In other words, there exist $a_n > 0$ and $b_n \in \mathbf{R}$ such that $a_n \sum_{i=1}^{n} \xi_i + b_n \overset{w}{\to} \eta_\alpha$, $a_n = n^{-1/\alpha}L(n)$, where $L(n)$ is a slowly varying function.

---

[4]Proofs of results in this and the following subsections as well as additional references can be found in Rachev and Samorodnitsky (1995).

[5]Replacing, in (6.5) and (6.6), "summation" by "maximum" operation, i.e., $M_n = \bigvee_{i=1}^{n} Y_i \prod_{j=1}^{i} Z_j$, $n = 1, 2, \ldots$, and $M_n^* = \max(M_{n-1}^* Z_n, Y_n Z_n)$, $n = 1, 2, \ldots$, $M_0^* = 0$, we obtain models for the maximum scheme. Rachev and Samorodnitsky (1995) also provide limiting results for this scheme.

[6]The assumption that $\{(Y_n, Z_n)\}$ starts at $n = 0$ is made for the sake of simplicity.

Proposition 6.1 *(Characterization of the limiting cumulative return process)* Suppose that $\mathbf{E}\log(1+Z_n) < \infty$. Then:

(a) (Non-degenerate case; $S_n \overset{a.s.}{\to} \infty$ and in the limit the normalized $\log S_n$ is stable) If $\nu > 0$ and $\mathbf{E}\log(1+Y_n) < \infty$, then $a_n \log S_n + b_n \overset{w}{\to} \eta_\alpha$.

(b) (Degenerate case) If $\nu < 0$ and $\mathbf{E}\log(1+Y_n) < \infty$, then $a_n \log(S_\infty - S_n) + b_n \overset{w}{\to} \eta_\alpha$.

(c) (Critical case) Let $\nu = 0$ and assume, without loss of generality, that $b_n \equiv 0$. Also, suppose that sequences $\{Y_n\}_{n\geq 1}$ and $\{Z_n\}_{n\geq 1}$ are independent and that $\mathrm{P}(\log Y_1 > 1/a_n) = o(n^{-1})$ as $n \to \infty$. Then, $a_n \log S_n \overset{w}{\to} \sup_{0\leq t\leq 1} \mathcal{L}(t)$, $n \to \infty$, where $\mathcal{L}$ is a stable motion on $[0,1]$ with $\mathcal{L}(1) \overset{d}{=} \eta_\alpha$.

Note that the divergent case (b) implies that sequence S_n does not converge in distribution.

Next, we consider the geometric-summation model, where $\xi_n = \log Z_n$ belongs to the domain of attraction of a geometric α-stable r.v. G_α. I.e., there exist $a = a(p) > 0$ and $b = b(p) \in [0,1]$ such that $a\sum_{i=1}^{n}(\xi_i + b) \overset{w}{\to} G_\alpha$, as $p \to 0$. Here, $a(p) = p^{1/\alpha}L(1/p)$ and L is, again, a slowly varying function.

Proposition 6.2 Suppose that $\mathbf{E}\log(1+Z_n) < \infty$ and, as $p \to 0$, $a\sum_{i=1}^{n}(\xi_i + b) \overset{w}{\to} G_\alpha$. Then; we have

(a) If $\nu > 0$ and $\mathbf{E}\log(1+Y_n) < \infty$, then $a(\log S_\tau + \tau b) \overset{w}{\to} G_\alpha$, as $p \to 0$.

(b) If $\nu < 0$ and $\mathbf{E}\log(1+Y_n) < \infty$, then $a(\log \sum_{j\geq\tau+1} X_j + \tau b) \overset{w}{\to} G_\alpha$, as $p \to 0$, where $X_j = Y_j \prod_{i=i}^{j} Z_i$.

(c) Let $\nu = 0$ and $b_n \equiv 0$. Assume that sequences $\{Y_n\}_{n\in\mathbb{N}}$ and $\{Z_n\}_{n\in\mathbb{N}}$ are independent and that $\mathrm{P}(\log Y_1 > n^{1/\alpha})L^{-1}(n)) = o(n^{-1})$ as $n \to \infty$. Then, $a\log S_\tau \overset{w}{\to} \sup_{0\leq t\leq 1} \mathcal{G}(t)$, as $p \to 0$, where $\mathcal{G}(\cdot)$ is a geometric Lévy stable motion, i.e., the weak limit of $\mathcal{G}_p(t) = a\sum_{j=1}^{[\tau t]} \xi_j$, $0 \leq t \leq 1$, in the Skorohod space $\mathcal{D}[0,1]$.

Next, let us consider the cumulative return up to Poisson(λ) random moment $T = T(\lambda)$. Let sequence $\{Y_n, Z_n\}_{n\geq 0}$ be as before and independent of T and suppose that the ch.f. of $\xi_n = \log Z_n$ f_{ξ_n} satisfies condition $\lim_{u\to 0} |u|^{-\alpha}[1 - f_{\xi_n - a}(u)] = \mu$, for some $\mu > 0$, $a \in \mathbf{R}$ and $1 < \alpha \leq 2$. At least for $\alpha \neq 2$, this condition together with $a = \mathbf{E}\xi_n$ is equivalent to assuming that the ξ_i's are in the domain of attraction of an α-stable distribution (see Feller, 1971, p. 596).

Proposition 6.3 Suppose that $\mathbf{E}\log(1+Z_n) < \infty$ and that $\lim_{u\to 0} |u|^{-\alpha}[1 - f_{\xi_n - a}(u)] = \mu$ holds and let $S_T = \sum_{i=0}^{T} X_i = \sum_{i=0}^{T} Y_i \prod_{j=0}^{i} Z_j$. Then:

(a) If $\nu = \mathbf{E}\xi_n > 0$ and $\mathbf{E}\log(1+Y_n) < \infty$, then, as $\lambda \to \infty$, $\lambda^{-1/\alpha}(\log S_T - aT) \overset{w}{\to} Y_{(\alpha)}$, where $Y_{(\alpha)}$ is a α-symmetric stable r.v. with ch.f. $\exp\{-\mu|\theta|^\alpha\}$.

(b) If $\nu < 0$ and $\mathbf{E}\log(1+Y_n) < \infty$, then, as $\lambda \to \infty$, $\lambda^{-1/\alpha}(\log \sum_{j=T+1}^{\infty} X_j - aT) \overset{w}{\to} Y_{(\alpha)}$ and $\lambda^{-1/\alpha}(\log \sum_{j=T_1+1}^{T_k} X_j - aT_1) \overset{w}{\to} Y_{(\alpha)}$, where T_1 and T_k are as in (6.7).

(c) Let $\nu = 0$ and suppose that sequences $\{Y_n\}_{n\geq 0}$ and $\{Z_n\}_{n\geq 0}$ are independent and that $\mathrm{P}(\log Y_n > u) = o(n^{-\alpha})$ as $\lambda \to \infty$. Then, as $\lambda \to \infty$,

$\lambda^{-1/\alpha} \log S_T \overset{w}{\to} \sup_{0 \le t \le 1} \mathcal{L}(t)$, where $\mathcal{L}(\cdot)$ is a stable motion on $[0,1]$ with $\mathcal{L}(1) \overset{d}{=} Y_{(\alpha)}$.

6.1.2   Characteristics of Limiting Laws for S_n

Theorem 6.1 and the above discussion on ARCH allows us to characterize the respective classes of limiting laws of S_n and S_τ as n and τ approach infinity. To this end, note that distributional characterizations of S_n and S_τ are closely related to solutions of certain distributional equations. For example, if S_n (or S_n^*) converges in distribution, then the limiting (in distribution) r.v. S satisfies

$$S \overset{d}{=} (Y + S)Z, \qquad (6.8)$$

with $(Y, Z) \overset{d}{=} (Y_n, Z_n)$ and S and (Y, Z) on the right hand side of (6.8) are independent. In many cases the solution to (6.8) turns out to be an infinitely divisible r.v. The cumulative return up to the break at geometric time τ, S_τ satisfies

$$S_\tau \overset{d}{=} (Y + \delta S_\tau)Z, \qquad (6.9)$$

where, as before, $(Y, Z) \overset{d}{=} (Y_n, Z_n)$; δ is Bernoulli with success probability $1 - p$; and p, S, and (Y, Z) on the right hand side of (6.9) are independent.[7] If $Z \equiv 1$, then S_τ is said to be geometrically infinitely divisible (see Klebanov et al., 1984a).

Next, we characterize the set of laws of S which arise from any distribution of Z_n's in a given parametric family of distributions. In the following, we assume that sequences $\{Y_n\}_{n \in \mathbf{N}}$ and $\{Z_n\}_{n \in \mathbf{N}}$ are independent and limit ourselves to distributions of Z_n that are supported on $(0,1)$.

Rachev and Samorodnitsky (1995) show that S_n converges to a finite limit S if (and only if, in case $\mathbf{E} \log Z_n > -\infty$)

$$0 \le \mathbf{E} \log(1 + Y_n) < \infty. \qquad (6.10)$$

Relationship (6.10) implies that S satisfies (6.8). In our case, the converse is also true.

Let S_1 denote the class of laws of S, $L(S)$, such that for any $L(Z) \in \mathcal{Z}_1$ there exists $Y = Y(Z)$ satisfying (6.8). Here, $\mathcal{Z}_1$, consists of distributions on $(0,1)$ with densities $f_\alpha(z) = (1 + \alpha)z^\alpha$ with $0 < z < 1$ and $\alpha \ge 0$. A complete description of class S_1 is as follows.

Proposition 6.4 Class S_1 of laws L(S) solving $S \overset{d}{=} (Y + S)Z$ consists of all nonnegative infinitely divisible r.v.'s S with Laplace transform $\phi_S(\theta) = \exp\{-\int_0^\infty x^{-1}(1 - e^{-\theta x})M_S(dx)\}$ whose Lévy measure, M_S, is of the form

---

[7]See Rachev and Todorovich (1990) and Rachev and Samorodnitsky (1995) for some examples of distributions of S_τ.

$M_S(dx) = H(x)dx$, where $H(0) \in [0,1]$, H is non-increasing on $[0,\infty)$ and vanishing at ∞. The corresponding Y has distribution function $1 - H$.

Example 6.1 *(Rachev and Samorodnitsky, 1995)* Let Z be uniformly $(0,1)$-distributed and consider (6.8) with nonnegative Y and S. By (6.8), $\theta\phi_S(\theta) = \int_0^\theta \phi_S(x)\theta_Y(x)dx$, for all $\theta > 0$, where ϕ_X denotes the Laplace transform of nonnegative r.v. X. Differentiation yields $\theta_Y(\theta) = 1 + \theta\phi_S'(\theta)/\phi_S(\theta)$ and, thus, $\phi_S(\theta) = \exp\{-\int_0^\theta x^{-1}[1 - \theta_Y(x)]dx\}$. The latter implies that

$$\infty > \int_0^\theta \frac{1 - \phi_Y(x)}{x}dx = \int_0^\theta \left(\int_0^\infty \exp\{-xy\}[1 - F_Y(y)]dy\right)dx$$

$$= \int_0^\infty [1 - F_Y(y)]\frac{1 - \exp\{-y\theta\}}{y}dy,$$

so that $\int_1^\infty y^{-1}[1 - F_Y(y)]dy < \infty$ or $\int_1^\infty (\log y)F_Y(dy) < \infty$. Therefore, in distributional equation $S \overset{d}{=} (Y + S)Z$, with Z uniformly distributed, Y must satisfy $\mathbf{E}\log(1 + Y) < \infty$.

Note that if S is the solution of (6.8) with Y given and Z uniformly distributed, then, for any $\alpha > 0$, $S \overset{d}{=} (Y_\alpha + S)Z_\alpha$ (S, Y_α and Z_α are independent), where notation X_α, $0 < \alpha < 1$, stands for

$$X_\alpha := \begin{cases} 0, & \text{withprobability}1 - \alpha \\ X, & \text{withprobability}\alpha; \end{cases}$$

F_{Y_α} is the mixture $\alpha/(1 + \alpha)F_0 + 1/(1 + \alpha)F_Y$; and Z_α has density $f_{Z_\alpha}(z) = (1 + \alpha)z^\alpha$ with $0 \leq z \leq 1$.

Next, let S_2 represent the class of laws, $L(S)$, such that for every $L(z) \in \mathcal{Z}_2 \equiv \{\delta_z, 0 < z < 1\}$ there is a $Y = Y(Z)$ satisfying (6.8). It turns out that class S_2 coincides with class L of Khinchine (cf. Feller, 1971, Ch. XVII, Sec. 8) of nonnegative r.v.'s. A more explicit description of class S_2 than that in Feller (1971, Theorem XVII.8) is as follows.

Proposition 6.5 Class S_2 coincides with the family of all nonnegative, infinitely divisible r.v.'s with Laplace transform $\phi_S(t) = \exp\{-at - \int_0^\infty x^{-1}(1 - e^{-tx})M_S(dx)\}$, with $a \geq 0$ and Lévy measure, whose Radon-Nikodym derivative has a nonincreasing version.

For any $S \in S_2$ and $z \in (0,1)$, the corresponding Y in equation $S \overset{d}{=} (Y + S)z$ is nonnegative, infinitely divisible with Laplace transform $\phi_Y(t) = \exp\{-z^{-1}at(1 - z) - \int_0^\infty x^{-1}(1 - e^{-tx})M_Y(dx)\}$, where $\frac{dM_Y}{d\lambda}(x) = \frac{dM_S}{d\lambda}(zx) - \frac{dM_Y}{d\lambda}(x)$ with λ being the Lebesgue measure.

Remark 6.1 Note that $S_1 \subset S_2$.

Multivariate analogues of the above characterization are given in Rachev and Samorodnitsky (1995). Here, we consider one example.

Example 6.2 The Mandelbrot-Taylor model is a solution of $S \stackrel{d}{=} (Y + S)Z$, i.e., it is the limit of $S_n \stackrel{d}{=} (Y + S_{n-1})Z$, as $n \to \infty$. Here, S, Y, Z, S_n, and S_{n-1} are continuous random processes on $[0, T]$, and $(YZ)(t) \stackrel{def}{=} Y(t)Z(t)$, $t \in [0, T]$.

Any symmetric, α-stable process[8] on $[0, T]$ can be represented as a solution of $S \stackrel{d}{=} (Y + S)Z$, because, for any $z \in (0, 1)$ one can choose an α-stable $Y_{\bar{t}} = (Y(t_1), \ldots, Y(t_n))$ with spectral measure $\Gamma_{Y_{\bar{t}}}(d\bar{s}) = (1 - z^\alpha)z^{-\alpha}\Gamma_{S_{\bar{t}}}(d\bar{s})$, so that S satisfies $S \stackrel{d}{=} (Y + S)Z$ with $Z = z$ and Y having marginals $Y_{\bar{t}}$.

We conclude by pointing out that de Haan et al. (1989) study the extremal behavior of $S_n = A_n S_{n-1} + B_n$ (see (6.1)) and, in particular, the case of $S_n = \xi_n^2$, where ξ_n is ARCH model (6.2). For $0 < \lambda < 1$ in (6.2), they provide numerical values for the extremal index θ in limiting relation $\lim_{n\to\infty} P(n^{-1/\alpha} \bigvee_{i=1}^n \xi_i^2 \geq x) = \exp\{-c\theta x^{-\kappa}\}$, where c and κ are given in Theorem 6.1. Their results give a precise picture of the Pareto-tail behavior of the exceedances of ARCH models.

6.2 The Stable Paretian GARCH Model

6.2.1 The Framework

As we have pointed out in Section 6.1, ARCH models of a particular type, can be embedded into a recursion $S_n = A_n S_{t-1} + B_n$, $n \geq 0$ (see (6.1)). In this section, we investigate multidimensional version of this random models recursion and its relationship to stable ARCH and GARCH. We shall treat ARCH and GARCH models as a *very* special case of a recursion for the sequence of random vectors X_n:

$$X_{n+1} = A_n X_{n-1} + B_n, \quad n \in Z.$$

In chapter 1, we introduced a *stable GARCH(α, p, q)* process. In this section we shall give necessary and sufficient conditions for existence and uniqueness of a stationary solution of the stable GARCH equation, and discuss the issue of simulation of stationary stable GARCH processes.

We restrict ourselves to symmetric, strictly stable random variables, that is we assume $\beta = \mu = 0$, see (2.2) in Section 2.1. We denote symmetric α-stable random variable X with scale parameter σ by $S_\alpha S(\sigma)$, i.e. its ch.f. equals $\exp\{-|\sigma t|^\alpha\}$.

---

[8] Recall that $(S(t))_{t\in[0,T]}$ is a symmetric α-stable process, if the ch.f. of $S_{\bar{t}} = (S(t_1), \ldots, S(t_n))$, where $\bar{t} = (t_1, \ldots, t_n)$ with $0 < t_1 < \cdots < t_n \leq 1$, is $E \exp\{i(\theta, S_{\bar{t}})\} = \exp\{-\int_{R^n} |(\theta, \bar{s}|^\alpha \Gamma_{S_{\bar{t}}}(d\bar{s})\}$. Here, $\Gamma_{S_{\bar{t}}}(\cdot)$ denotes the (spectral) finite, symmetric measure of symmetric, α-stable random vector $S_{\bar{t}}$.

Recall first the definition of the stable GARCH process.

Definition 6.1 A sequence of random variables $\{Y_n, n \in Z\}$ is said to be a *stable GARCH(α, p, q)* process if:

1. $Y_n = \sigma_n S_n$, where S_n are i.i.d. r.v.'s distributed as $S_\alpha S(1)$, $1 < \alpha \le 2$,

2. there exist nonnegative constants $\alpha_i, i = 1, \ldots, q$ and $\beta_j, j = 1, \ldots, p$ and $\delta > 0$, such that

$$\sigma_n = \delta + \sum_{i=1}^{q} \alpha_i \mid Y_{n-i} \mid + \sum_{j=1}^{p} \beta_j \sigma_{n-j}, \ n \in Z. \qquad (6.11)$$

Our assumption that $1 < \alpha \le 2$ is not very restrictive in practice, because most of the financial time series have finite mean. For $\alpha=2$ we obtain a L_1 - version of the classical Gaussian GARCH(p, q) model.

To show the existence and uniqueness of strictly stationary solutions of equation (6.11), we use the results of Bougerol and Picard (1992b). Following their notation we define:

$B = [\delta, 0, \ldots, 0]' \in \mathbf{R}^{p+q-1}$

$X_n = [\sigma_{n+1}, \ldots, \sigma_{n-p+2}, \mid Y_n \mid, \ldots, \mid Y_{n-q+2} \mid] \in \mathbf{R}^{p+q-1}$,

$t_n = [\beta_1 + \alpha_1 \mid S_n \mid, \beta_2, \ldots, \beta_{p-1}] \in \mathbf{R}^{p-1}$,

$z_n = [\mid S_n \mid, 0, \ldots, 0] \in \mathbf{R}^{p-1}$,

$\alpha = [\alpha_2, \ldots, \alpha_{q-1}] \in \mathbf{R}^{q-2}$,

$$A_n = \begin{bmatrix} t_n & \beta_p & \alpha & \alpha_q \\ I_{p-1} & 0 & 0 & 0 \\ z_n & 0 & 0 & 0 \\ 0 & 0 & I_{q-2} & 0 \end{bmatrix} p+q-1 \times p+q-1, \qquad (6.12)$$

where I_{p-1} and I_{q-2} are identity matrices of size $p-1$ and $q-2$, respectively, and $[\prime]$ denotes the transpose of a vector. Then,

$$X_{n+1} = A_{n+1} X_n + B, \ n \in Z. \qquad (6.13)$$

Clearly, existence of solutions of (6.13) is equivalent to existence of solutions of (6.11). The major role in what follows is played by a Lyapunov exponent associated with matrices $\{A_n, n \in Z\}$. Let us recall the definition of the top Lyapunov exponent.

Let $\| \cdot \|$ be any norm on $\mathbf{R}^d$, and define an operator norm on the set $M(d)$ of $d \times d$ matrices by $\|M\| = \sup\{\|Mx\|/\|x\|, x \in \mathbf{R}^d, x \ne 0\}$, for any $M \in M(d)$. Then, the top Lyapunov exponent associated with the sequence $\{A_n, n \in Z\}$ of i.i.d. random matrices, is defined by

$$\gamma = \inf \mathbf{E} \left(\frac{1}{n+1} \log \|A_0 A_{-1} \ldots A_{-n}\| \right), \ n \in N,$$

when $\mathbf{E}(\log^{+} \|A_0\|) < \infty$ (where $\log^{+} x = \max(\log x, 0)$). It follows (see Bougerol and Picard, 1992a) that, almost surely,

$$\gamma = \lim_{n \to \infty} \frac{1}{n} \log \|A_0 A_{-1} \ldots A_{-n}\|.$$

Given that r.v.'s S_n are i.i.d. random matrices A_n defined in (6.12) are also i.i.d. Because $\gamma \leq \mathbf{E} \log \|A_0\|$ and $\mathbf{E} \log \|A_0\| < \infty$ (because $\mathbf{E} \mid S_0 \mid < \infty$), γ is well defined for the sequence $\{A_n, n \in Z\}$. Clearly, $\mathbf{E}(\log^{+} \|B\|) < \infty$. Thus, by Bougerol and Picard (1992a, Theorem 3.2), we have the following proposition:[9]

Proposition 6.6 The stable GARCH(α, p, q) process with $\delta > 0$, $p \geq 2$ and $q \geq 2$ has a stationary solution if the Lyapnnov exponent of $\{A_n, n \in Z\}$ is strictly negative. The series

$$X_n = B + \sum_{i=1}^{\infty} A_n A_{n-1} \ldots A_{n-i+1} B$$

converges almost surely for all n, and the process $\{X_n, n \in Z\}$ is the unique strictly stationary and ergodic solution of (6.13).

To obtain the conditions on the coefficients $\alpha_i, i = 1, \ldots, q$ and $\beta_j, j = 1, \ldots, p$ for the strictly stationary solution to exist, we consider the characteristic polynomial of $\mathbf{E}A_0$:

$$f(z) = \det(Iz - EA_0) = z^{p+q-1} \left(1 - a \sum_{i=1}^{q} \alpha_i z^{-i} - \sum_{j=1}^{p} \beta_j z^{-j} \right),$$

where $a = \mathbf{E} \mid S_1 \mid = \Gamma(1 - 1/\alpha) / \int_0^{\infty} u^{-2} \sin^2(u) du$. The (approximate) values of a for several values of α are presented in Table 6.1.

Following the argument of Bougerol and Picard (1992a, Corollary 2.2) we conclude:

Proposition 6.7 If $\delta > 0$ and $a \sum_{i=1}^{q} \alpha_i + \sum_{j=1}^{p} \leq 1$, then the stable GARCH($\alpha, p, q$) with $p \geq 2$ or $q \geq 2$, has a unique strictly stationary solution.

The case when $p = q = 1$ has to be treated separately, because then the matrices $\{A_n, n \in Z\}$ have zero columns and the results of Kesten and Spitzer (1984) do not apply. For stable GARCH($\alpha, 1, 1$) we can compute the largest Lyapunov exponent directly as follows:

$$\|A_0 A_{-1} \ldots A_{-n}\| = \Pi_{i=1}^{n} (\beta_1 + \alpha_1 \mid S_i \mid) \max(\beta_1 + \alpha_1 \mid S_0 \mid, 1, \mid S_0 \mid),$$

and by the Law of Large Numbers we obtain

---

[9]The results of this section are due to Panorska, Mittnik and Rachev (1995).

Table 6.1   Values of a corresponding to values of α.

α	1.05	1.1	1.15	1.2	1.25
a	13.0303	6.6883	4.5868	3.5436	2.9226
α	1.3	1.35	1.4	1.45	1.5
a	2.512	2.2211	2.0048	1.8379	1.7055
α	1.55	1.6	1.65	1.7	1.75
a	1.598	1.5091	1.4344	1.3709	1.3162
α	1.8	1.85	1.9	1.95	1.99
a	1.2687	1.2271	1.1903	1.1576	1.1340

$$
\begin{aligned}
\gamma \;=\; & 1/(n+1)[\log(\max(\beta_1 + \alpha_1 \mid S_0 \mid, 1, \mid S_0 \mid)) \\
& + \sum_{i=0}^{n} \log(\beta_1 + \alpha_1 \mid S_i \mid)] \xrightarrow{p} \mathbf{E}\log(\beta_1 + \alpha_1 \mid S_0 \mid).
\end{aligned}
$$

If $\mathbf{E}\log(\beta_1 + \alpha_1 \mid S_0 \mid) < 1$, then stable GARCH$(\alpha,1,1)$ has a strictly stationary solution. Using Jensen's inequality we obtain a stationarity condition $\beta_1 + a\alpha_1 < 1$ compatible with the result of Proposition 6.7.

Next, we consider the simulation of stable GARCH processes. For notational convenience, let $A \stackrel{d}{=} A_0$, then A_n's defined in (6.12) are i.i.d. copies of A and let $A^i = \prod_{n=1}^{i} A_n$, and $A^0 = I$. Under the assumptions of Proposition 6.6

$$
X \stackrel{d}{=} \sum_{i=0}^{\infty} A^i B \tag{6.14}
$$

is the unique stationary and ergodic solution of (6.13). The simulated version of X, denoted by $\hat{X}_{N,k}$ is determined by

$$
\hat{X}_{N,k} = \sum_{i=0}^{k} \hat{A}^i B, \tag{6.15}
$$

where k is the truncation level, and $\hat{A}$ is the empirical version of A, that is

$$
\hat{A} \stackrel{d}{=} \hat{A}_N = \begin{bmatrix} t_N & \beta_p & \alpha & \alpha_q \\ I_{p-1} & 0 & 0 & 0 \\ z_N & 0 & 0 & 0 \\ 0 & 0 & I_{q-2} & 0 \end{bmatrix} \tag{6.16}
$$

where $t_N = [\beta_1 + \alpha_1 \mid \hat{S}_N \mid, \beta_2, \ldots, \beta_{p-1}] \in \mathbf{R}^{p-1}$, and $z_N = [\mid \hat{S}_N \mid, 0, \ldots, 0] \in \mathbf{R}^{p-1}$, with $\hat{S}_N$ being the empirical version of S_0 based on N i.i.d. observations $S_1, \ldots, S_N$ of S_0. The problem we are faced with in stimulating $\hat{X}$ is to determine, for a given $\epsilon > 0$, the lower bounds for k and N, so that

$$\mathbf{E}\pi(X, \hat{X}_{N,k}) \leq \epsilon, \tag{6.17}$$

where π is the Prohorov metric[10] in the space of probability laws in $\mathbf{R}^d$, ($d = p + q - 1$), and $\mathbf{E} = \mathbf{E}_{(S_1^{(i)}, \ldots, S_N^{(i)})_{i \geq 0}}$ is the average with respect to independent samples $(S_1^{(i)}, \ldots, S_N^{(i)})_{i \geq 0}$ we use to determine the sample counterparts of $(S_i)_{i \geq 0}$. While π is chosen as the most natural metric metrizing the convergence in distribution in $\mathbf{R}^d$, other metrics can also be used in (6.17), which will be seen from the proof below.

Theorem 6.2 Suppose that $\| A \|_r = (\mathbf{E} \| A \|^r)^{1/r} < 1$ and, for $0 < \epsilon < 1 - \|A\|_r$, let $N = N(\epsilon)$ be large enough to satisfy

$$\mathbf{E} \| A - \hat{A}_N \|^r \leq \epsilon^r, \text{ for some } r \geq 1,$$

where $\hat{A}_N$ is chosen to be independent of A.
Choose k large enough so that

$$(\epsilon + \| A \|_r)^{k+1} \leq \epsilon.$$

Then,

$$\mathbf{E}\pi(X, \hat{X}_{N,k}) \leq 2\epsilon^{r/(r+1)} \frac{\delta^{r/(r+1)} + (E \| \hat{X} \|_r)^{r/(r+1)}}{(1 - \epsilon - \|A\|_r)^{r/(r+1)}}.$$

The following lemma gives the rate of convergence of the truncated stationary solution. The result is interesting and important in itself, but also illuminates possible improvements in Theorem 6.2. The proofs of the theorem and the next two lemmas are given in the next Section 6.2.2..

Lemma 6.1 Suppose that for some $r \geq 1$,

$$\| A \|_r := (\mathbf{E} \| A \|^r)^{1/r} < 1.$$

Then, the distribution of the truncated stationary solution $X_k^* = \sum_{i=0}^k A^i B$ converges exponentially fast to the distribution of $X = \sum_{i=0}^\infty A^i B$, as $k \to \infty$. More precisely, the bound:

$$\pi(X, X_k^*) \leq (\delta \| A \|_r^{k+1} / (1 - \| A \|_r))^{r/(r+1)}$$

[10]The metric π in the space of probability laws on R^d is defined by

$$\pi(X, X^*) = \inf\{\epsilon > 0 : P(X \in A) \leq P(X^* \in A^\epsilon) + \epsilon, \text{ for all closed sets } A \subset \mathbf{R}^d\},$$

where A^ϵ is an ϵ-neighborhood of A, i.e. $A^\epsilon := \{x : \| x - A \| < \epsilon\}$. Here and in what follows $\| \cdot \|$ is a norm in $\mathbf{R}^d$.

holds.

For the special case when $p = q = 1$, we have the following

Lemma 6.2 Suppose that $p = q = 1$, and that for some $r \geq 1$

$$\Delta_r := \beta_1^r + \alpha_1^r \mathbf{E} \mid S_0 \mid^r < 1.$$

Then, the distribution of $X_k^* = \sum_{i=0}^k A^i B$ converges exponentially fast to the distribution of $X = \sum_{i=0}^\infty A^i B$ as $k \to \infty$. Moreover,

$$\pi(X, X_k) \leq \epsilon_r :=$$

$$\delta^{r/(r+1)} 2^{(r-1)/(r+1)} (\Delta_r + 1 + \mathbf{E} \mid S_0 \mid^r)^{1/(r+1)} \Delta_r^{k/(r+1)} (1 - \Delta_r^{1/r})^{-r/(r+1)}.$$

6.2.2 Proofs of Results on Stable GARCH Processes

Proof of Lemma 6.1. First, we shall estimate the distance between X_k^* and X in terms of the Kantorovich L_r-minimal distance:

$$\hat{L}_r(X, Y) = \inf\{L_r(\tilde{X}, \tilde{Y}) : \tilde{X} \overset{d}{=} X, \tilde{Y} \overset{d}{=} Y\}, \text{ for } r \geq 1,$$

where the infimum is taken over the set of all joint distributions of $(\tilde{X}, \tilde{Y})$ with fixed marginals $P^{\tilde{X}} = P^X$ and $P^{\tilde{Y}} = P^Y$. Here,

$$L_r(\tilde{X}, \tilde{Y}) = (\mathbf{E} \parallel \tilde{X} - \tilde{Y} \parallel^r)^{1/r}.$$

Obviously, $\parallel B \parallel = \delta$, and therefore,

$$\hat{L}_r(X, X_k^*) \leq (\mathbf{E} \parallel (\sum_{i>k} A^i) B \parallel^r)^{1/r} \leq \sum_{i>k} (\mathbf{E} \parallel A^i \parallel^r \parallel B \parallel^r)^{1/r}$$

$$\leq \delta \sum_{i>k} (\mathbf{E} \parallel A_1 \times \cdots \times A_i \parallel^r)^{1/r}$$

$$\leq \delta \sum_{i>k} (\mathbf{E} \parallel A_1 \times \cdots \times A_{k+1} \parallel^r \cdot \parallel I \times A_{k+2} \times \cdots \times A_i \parallel^r)^{1/r}$$

$$\leq \delta (\mathbf{E} \parallel A^{k+1} \parallel^r)^{1/r} \sum_{i \geq 0} (\mathbf{E} \parallel A \parallel^{ir})^{1/r}$$

$$= \delta \parallel A \parallel_r^{k+1} \sum_{i \geq 0} \parallel A \parallel_r^i$$

$$\leq \delta \parallel A \parallel_r^{k+1} / (1 - \parallel A \parallel_r),$$

where $\parallel A \parallel_r := (\mathbf{E} \parallel A \parallel^r)^{1/r}$.

Since $\pi \leq (\hat{L}_r)^{r/(r+1)}$ (see for example Rachev (1991a), Lemma 8.2.1.)

$$\pi(X, X_k^*) \leq \left(\frac{\delta \parallel A \parallel_r^{k+1}}{1 - \parallel A \parallel_r}\right)^{r/(r+1)},$$

as required in Lemma 6.1. $\square$

Proof of Lemma 6.2 Following the arguments of Lemma 6.1, we have

$$\hat{L}_r(X, X_k^*) \le (\mathbf{E} \| (\sum_{i>k} A^i) B \|^r)^{1/r} = \delta(\mathbf{E} \| \sum_{i>k} A^i) \|^r)^{1/r}$$

$$= \delta(\mathbf{E} \| \sum_{i>k} A_0 A_1 \dots A_i \|^r)^{1/r} \le \delta \sum_{i \ge k} (\mathbf{E} \| A_0 A_1 \dots A_i \|^r)^{1/r}$$

$$= \delta \sum_{i \ge k} [\mathbf{E} \prod_{j=1}^{i} (\beta_1 + \alpha_1 | S_j |)^r (\beta_1 + \alpha_1 | S_0 \vee 1 \vee | S_0 |)^r]^{1/r}$$

$$= \delta \sum_{i \ge k} \prod_{j=1}^{i} [\mathbf{E}(\beta_1 + \alpha_1 | S_j |)^r \mathbf{E}((\beta_1 + \alpha_1 |S_0|) \vee 1 \vee |S_0|)^r]^{1/r}$$

$$\le \delta \sum_{i \ge k} \prod_{j=1}^{i} [2^{r-1}(\beta_1^r + \alpha_1^r \mathbf{E} | S_j |^r)(\beta_1^r + \alpha_1^r \mathbf{E}|S_o|^r + 1 + \mathbf{E}|S_0|^r)]^{1/r}$$

$$= \delta 2^{(r-1)/r}(\beta_1^r + 1 + (\alpha_1^r + 1)\mathbf{E} | S_0 |^r)^{1/r}(\beta_1^r + \alpha_1^r \mathbf{E} | S_0 |^r)^{k/r} \times$$
$$\times 1/(1 - (\beta_1^r + \alpha_1^r \mathbf{E} | S_0 |^r)^{1/r}).$$

Since $\pi \le L_r^{r/(r+1)}$, the required estimate follows. $\square$

Proof of Theorem 6.2. We will split the proof of Theorem 6.2 into two claims.

Proposition 6.8 Suppose that

$$\mathbf{E} \| \hat{A} \|_r < 1.$$

Then

$$\mathbf{E}\pi(\hat{X}_N, \hat{X}_{N,k}) \le \frac{\delta}{1 - E \| \hat{A} \|_r} (\mathbf{E} \| \hat{A} \|_r)^{k+1})^{r/(r+1)},$$

where $\hat{X}_N = \sum_{i=0}^{\infty} \hat{A}^i B$ and $\hat{X}_{N,k}$ is its truncated version.

Proof. As in Lemma 6.1,

$$\mathbf{E}\hat{L}_r(\hat{X}, \hat{X}_{N,k}) \le \delta(\mathbf{E} \| \hat{A} \|_r^{k+1} \sum_{i \ge 0} (\mathbf{E} \| \hat{A} \|_r)^i,$$

and since
$$\mathbf{E}\pi(\hat{X}, \hat{X}_{N,k}) \le \mathbf{E}\hat{L}_r(\hat{X}, \hat{X}_{N,k})^{r/(r+1)}$$
$$\le (\mathbf{E}\hat{L}_r(\hat{X}, \hat{X}_{N,k})^{r/(r+1)(r+1)/r})^{r/(r+1)} = (\mathbf{E}\hat{L}_r(\hat{X}, \hat{X}_{N,k}))^{r/(r+1)},$$
we obtain the required bound. $\square$
In the case $p = q = 1$ a more refined version of Proposition 6.8 can be derived.

Proposition 6.9 Suppose $p = q = 1$, and $\Delta_r := \beta_1^r + \alpha_1 E \mid S_0 \mid^r < 1$. Consider the empirical counterparts of X and X_k^*, namely

$$\hat{X}_N = \sum_{i=0}^{\infty} \hat{A}^i B \text{ and } \hat{X}_{N,k} = \sum_{i=0}^{k} \hat{A}^i B.$$

Then $E\pi(\hat{X}_N, \hat{X}_{N,k}) \leq \epsilon_r$, where ϵ_r is defined as in Lemma 6.2.

Proof. As in Proposition 6.8, we have
$$E_{(S_1,\ldots,S_N)\infty} \hat{L}_r(\hat{X}_N, \hat{X}_{N,k}) \leq \delta E_{(S_1,\ldots,S_N)\infty} (E \parallel \sum_{i>k} \hat{A}^i \parallel^r)^{1/r}$$

$$\leq \delta E_{(S_1,\ldots,S_N)\infty} \sum_{i>k} (E \parallel \hat{A}_0, \cdots, \hat{A}_i \parallel^r)^{1/r}$$

$$\leq \delta E_{(S_1,\ldots,S_N)\infty} 2^{(r-1)/r} (\beta_1^r + 1 + (\alpha_1^r + 1) E_{(S_1,\ldots,S_N)\infty} E \mid \hat{S}_0 \mid^r)^{1/r} \times$$
$$\times (\beta_1^r + \alpha_1^r E_{(S_1,\ldots,S_N)\infty} E \mid \hat{S}_0 \mid^r)^{k/r} 1/(1 - (\beta_1^r + \alpha_1^r E_{(S_1,\ldots,S_N)\infty} E \mid \hat{S}_0 \mid^r)^{1/r}).$$
Here, $\mid \hat{S}_0 \mid$ is the empirical version of S_0 that is,

$$E \mid \hat{S}_0 \mid^r = \int \mid x \mid^r d(1/N \sum_{j=1}^{N} I_{\{S_j \leq x\}}) = 1/N \sum_{j=1}^{N} \mid S_j \mid^r.$$

Therefore $E_{(S_1,\ldots,S_N)\infty} E \mid \hat{S}_0 \mid^r = E \mid S_0 \mid^r$. The same argument as in Proposition 6.8 completes the proof of Proposition 6.9   □

Finally, we must compare X and $\hat{X}_N$, the solutions of the equations

$$X \stackrel{d}{=} AX + B, \text{ with } A \text{ and } X \text{ independent}$$

and

$$\hat{X} \stackrel{d}{=} \hat{A}\hat{X} + B, \text{ with } \hat{A} \text{ and } \hat{X} \text{ independent.} \qquad (6.18)$$

Let $\hat{L}_r(A, A^*)$ be the rth minimal distance in the space of $d \times d$ matrices:

$$\hat{L}_r(A, A^*) := \inf\{\hat{L}_r(A_1, A_1^*) : A_1 \stackrel{d}{=} A, A_1^* \stackrel{d}{=} A^*\}, \qquad (6.19)$$

with $\hat{L}_r(A_1, A_1^*) := (E \parallel A_1 - A_1^* \parallel^r)^{1/r}$.
The next claim gives a bound for $E\pi(X, \hat{X})$ in terms of $E\hat{L}_r(A, A^*)$, where $E = E_{(S_1,\ldots,S_N)\infty}$ stands for the average with respect to the sample of stable observations determining $\hat{A}$ and $\hat{X}$, in (6.18).

Proposition 6.10 Suppose $E\hat{L}_r(A, \hat{A}) + \parallel A \parallel_r < 1$. Then for $\hat{X} = \hat{X}_N = \sum_{i=0}^{\infty} \hat{A}^i B$,

$$E\pi(X, \hat{X}) \leq \left[E \parallel \hat{X} \parallel_r E\hat{L}_r(A, \hat{A})/(1 - E\hat{L}_r(A, \hat{A}) - \parallel \hat{A} \parallel_r) \right]^{r/(r+1)}.$$

Proof. By the regularity property of the minimal metrics (see Rachev (1991a), Section3.2)

$\hat{L}_r(X,\hat{X}) = \hat{L}_r(AX + B, \hat{A}\hat{X} + B) \le \hat{L}_r(AX, \hat{A}\hat{X})$

$\le \hat{L}_r(AX, \hat{A}X) + \hat{L}_r(\hat{A}X, \hat{A}\hat{X}) \le \| X \|_r \hat{L}_r(A,\hat{A}) + \| \hat{A} \|_r \hat{L}_r(X,\hat{X}),$

where $\| X \|_r = (E \| X \|^r)^{1/r}$ and $\hat{L}_r(A,\hat{A})$ is defined in (6.19). Clearly;
$\hat{L}_r(A,\hat{A}) \le \hat{L}_r(A_1, \hat{A}_1)$ where A_1 and $\hat{A}_1$ are independent and $A_1 \stackrel{d}{=} A$,
$\hat{A}_1 \stackrel{d}{=} \hat{A}$. Hence
$\hat{L}_r(X,\hat{X}) \le (\hat{L}_r(X,\hat{X}) + \| \hat{X} \|_r)\hat{L}_r(A,\hat{A}) + \| A \|_r \hat{L}_r(X,\hat{X}),$
and therefore,

$$\mathbf{E}\hat{L}_r(X,\hat{X}) \le \| \hat{X} \|_r \hat{L}_r(A,\hat{A})/(1 - \hat{L}_r(A,\hat{A}) - \| A \|_r),$$

and the desired estimate follows:

$$\mathbf{E}\pi(X,\hat{X}) \le \left[\mathbf{E} \| \hat{X} \|_r \mathbf{E}\hat{L}_r(A,\hat{A})/(1 - \mathbf{E}\hat{L}_r(A,\hat{A}) - \| \hat{A} \|_r) \right]^{r/(r+1)}. \quad \square$$

Combining Proposition 6.8; for $\mathbf{E} \| \hat{A} \|_r < 1$,

$$\mathbf{E}\pi(\hat{X}_N, \hat{X}_{N,k}) \le \left(\frac{\delta}{1 - \mathbf{E} \| \hat{A} \|_r} (\mathbf{E} \| \hat{A} \|_r)^{k+1} \right)^{r/(r+1)},$$

and Proposition 6.10; for $\mathbf{E}\hat{L}_r(A,\hat{A}) + \| A \|_r < 1$,

$$\mathbf{E}\pi(X, \hat{X}_N) \le \left(\frac{\mathbf{E} \| \hat{X} \|_r \mathbf{E}\hat{L}_r(A,\hat{A})}{1 - \mathbf{E}\hat{L}_r(A,\hat{A}) - \| A \|_r} \right)^{r/(r+1)},$$

we have that
$$\mathbf{E}\pi(X, \hat{X}_{N,k}) \le \left(\frac{\delta}{1 - \mathbf{E} \| \hat{A} \|_r} \right)^{r/(r+1)} (\mathbf{E} \| \hat{A} \|_r)^{(k+1)r/(r+1)}$$

$$+ \left(\frac{\mathbf{E} \| \hat{X} \|_r}{1 - \mathbf{E}\hat{L}_r(A,\hat{A}) - \| A \|_r} \right)^{r/(r+1)} (\mathbf{E}\hat{L}_r(A,\hat{A}))^{r/(r+1)},$$

$$\le \left(\frac{\delta}{1 - \mathbf{E}\hat{L}_r(A,\hat{A}) - \| A \|_r} \right)^{r/(r+1)} (\mathbf{E}\hat{L}_r(A,\hat{A}) + \|A\|_r)^{(k+1)r/(r+1)}$$

$$+ \left(\frac{\mathbf{E} \| \hat{X} \|_r}{1 - \mathbf{E}\hat{L}_r(A,\hat{A}) - \| A \|_r} \right)^{r/(r+1)} (\mathbf{E}\hat{L}_r(A,\hat{A}))^{r((r+1)},$$

which proves Theorem 6.2. $\square$

6.2.3 *Asymmetric GARCH-stable Processes*

Generalizing the stable GARCH process to the asymmetric case, sequence $y_t, t \in \mathbf{Z}$, is said to be a stable Paretian Asymmetric GARCH process, in short, an $S_{\alpha,\beta}$GARCH process, if

$$y_t = \mu_t + c_t\varepsilon_t, \ \varepsilon_t \stackrel{iid}{\sim} S_{\alpha\beta}, \quad (6.20)$$

$$c_t = \alpha_0 + \sum_{i=1}^{r} \alpha_i |y_{t-i} - \mu_{t-i}| + \sum_{j=1}^{s} \beta_j c_{t-j}, \qquad (6.21)$$

where $S_{\alpha\beta}$ denotes the standard asymmetric stable Paretian distribution with stable index α, skewness parameter $\beta \in [-1, 1]$, zero location parameter, and unit scale parameter [11]. By letting $E(y_t) = \mu_t$ in (6.20) to be time-varying, we allow for a broad range of mean equations, including, for example, regression and/or ARMA structures.

In Liu and Brorsen (1995), hereafter LB, and Panorska, Mittnik and Rachev (1995), hereafter PMR, it is assumed that $\alpha \in (1, 2]$, to avoid a number of technical problems arising from the fact that $\alpha \le 1$ implies such fat tails that ε_t and, thus, y_t and c_t do not even possess first moments. However, the restriction does not seem to have practical relevance in empirical work, because the existence of first moments is hardly rejected in financial or economic time series.

LB state the conditional volatility equation (6.21) more generally as

$$|c_t|^\delta = \alpha_o + \sum_{i=1}^{r} \alpha_i |y_{t-i} - \mu_{t-i}|^\delta + \sum_{j=1}^{s} \beta_j |c_{t-j}|^\delta.$$

In their empirical applications, they experiment by setting δ equal to 1, 2, or the stable index, α. They find that the choice of δ does not affect the conclusions (LB, p. 275) and continue to work with $\delta = \alpha$. However, any choice of $\delta \ge \alpha$ has to be questioned, because it implies that the unconditional first moments of c_t and, thus, y_t are infinite for any $\alpha < 2$. This knife-edge specification does not only induce theoretical difficulties, but also leads to highly volatile c_t series in practical work. In view of this and the fact that the choice of δ does not seem to affect empirical conclusions in finite samples, we adopt specification (6.21), i.e., setting $\delta = 1$, when referring to $S_{\alpha,\beta}$GARCH processes. This, together with assumption $\alpha > 1$ and the restrictions on GARCH coefficients α_i and β_j (discussed in the next section) guarantees finite first moments for c_t.

Observe that, as α approaches 2, model (6.21) becomes the so-called absolute value GARCH model with normal innovations, originally proposed by Taylor (1986) and Schwert (1989). Nelson and Foster (1994) have shown that, compared to GARCH models in c_t^2, the absolute value GARCH model is a more efficient filter of the conditional variance in the presence of leptokurtic error distributions.

Bougerol and Picard (1992a) have shown that a mean-corrected GARCH(r, s) process driven by *normally* distributed innovations has a unique strictly stationary solution if

$$\sum_{i=1}^{r} \alpha_i + \sum_{j=1}^{s} \beta_j \le 1. \qquad (6.22)$$

[11]The results of this subsection are due to Mittnik, Paolella and Rachev (1998c).

The following result implies that condition (6.22) does not apply to $S_{\alpha,\beta}$ GARCH models with $\alpha < 2$.

Proposition: An $S_{\alpha,\beta}\text{GARCH}(r,s)$ process defined by (6.20) and (6.21) with $1 < \alpha < 2$ has a unique strictly stationary solution if $\alpha_i > 0, i = 0, \ldots, r$, $\beta_j > 0$, $j = 1, \ldots, s$, and

$$\lambda_{\alpha,\beta} \sum_{i=1}^{r} \alpha_i + \sum_{j=1}^{s} \beta_j \leq 1, \qquad (6.23)$$

where $\lambda_{\alpha,\beta} := E|\varepsilon_t|$ is given by

$$\lambda_{\alpha,\beta} = \begin{cases} \frac{2}{\pi}\Gamma\left(1 - \frac{1}{\alpha}\right)\left(1 + \tau_{\alpha,\beta}^2\right)^{\frac{1}{2\alpha}} \cos\left(\frac{1}{\alpha}\arctan\tau_{\alpha,\beta}\right), & \text{if} \quad 1 < \alpha < 2, \\ \sqrt{2/\pi}, & \text{if} \quad \alpha = 2, \end{cases} \qquad (6.24)$$

with $\tau_{\alpha,\beta} := \beta\tan\frac{\alpha\pi}{2}$. In the symmetric case, i.e., $\beta = 0$, (6.24) reduces to

$$\lambda_{\alpha,0} = \begin{cases} \frac{2}{\pi}\Gamma\left(1 - \frac{1}{\alpha}\right), & \text{if} \quad 1 < \alpha < 2, \quad \beta = 0, \\ \sqrt{2/\pi}, & \text{if} \quad \alpha = 2 \end{cases} \qquad (6.25)$$

The value of parameter $\lambda_{\alpha,\beta}$ defined by (6.24) or (6.25) depends on the stable index α and skewness β. Figure 6.1 shows how $\lambda_{\alpha,\beta}$ depends on the parameters α and β of the standard α-stable distribution. Values of $\lambda_{\alpha,\beta}$ for selected (α, β) combinations are reported in Table 6.2. For $\alpha < 2$ we have $\lambda_{\alpha,\beta} > 1$. This implies that stationarity condition (6.23) is more restrictive than in the normal case. Observe also that, in the normal case, $\lambda_{2,0} = \sqrt{2/\pi} < 1$, implying that $\sum_{i=1}^{r} \alpha_i + \sum_{j=1}^{s} \beta_j$ could be greater than one and not violate the stationarity condition.

Table 6.2 Selected Values of $\lambda_{\alpha,\beta}$

α	0	± 0.2	± 0.4	± 0.6	± 0.8	± 1.0
1.1	6.6882	7.0448	7.7422	8.5297	9.3472	10.1759
1.3	2.5120	2.5452	2.6341	2.7584	2.9027	3.0579
1.5	1.7055	1.7130	1.7346	1.7682	1.8111	1.8609
1.7	1.3709	1.3726	1.3777	1.3860	1.3973	1.4112
1.9	1.1903	1.1905	1.1909	1.1916	1.1927	1.1940

The β label spans the columns ± 0.2 through ± 1.0 above.

In case of normally distributed innovations for the variance–GARCH model, Engle and Bollerslev (1986) referred to GARCH processes satisfy-

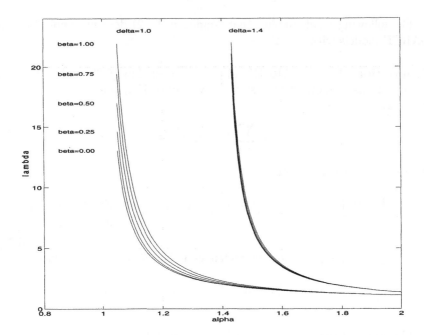

Fig. 6.1 Values of $\lambda_{\alpha,\beta}$.(Adapted from: Mittnik, Paolella and Rachev (1997))

ing the borderline condition

$$\sum_{i=1}^{r} \alpha_i + \sum_{j=1}^{s} \beta_j = 1 \tag{6.26}$$

as an *integrated* GARCH or IGARCH process. Condition (6.26) implies that the autoregressive polynomial $1 - (\alpha_1 + \beta_1)L - \cdots - (\alpha_n + \beta_n)L^n$ with $n = \max(r, s)$, when rewriting the GARCH process in an ARMA form in terms of ε_t^2, has a unit root. In the $S_{\alpha,\beta}$GARCH case the analogue to (6.26) is

$$\lambda_{\alpha,\beta} \sum_{i=1}^{r} \alpha_i + \sum_{j=1}^{s} \beta_j = 1, \tag{6.27}$$

giving rise to *integrated* $S_{\alpha,\beta}$GARCH or $S_{\alpha,\beta}$IGARCH processes. The implied autoregressive polynomial for the ARMA representation of $|c_t|$ is $1 - (\lambda_{\alpha,\beta}\alpha_1 + \beta_1)L - \cdots (\lambda_{\alpha,\beta}\alpha_n + \beta_n)L^n$, in which case we have persistence of the conditional volatility.

The GARCH(1,1) model is most commonly specified in empirical work. Stationarity of an $S_{\alpha,\beta}$GARCH(1,1) process requires $\lambda_{\alpha,\beta}\alpha_1 + \beta_1 \leq 1$. Thus, when estimating an $S_{\alpha,\beta}$IGARCH(1,1) model the restriction $\beta_1 = 1 - \lambda_{\alpha,\beta}\alpha_1$ needs to be imposed during estimation.

As an Emprical Application consider modeling returns[12] on the Bulgarian Lev – U.S. Dollar daily exchange rate series from February 19, 1991 to February 14, 1995, with 1022 observations, see Chapter 4. The mean equation was found to be adequately described using an autoregressive model of order 3, i.e.,

$$\mu_t = a_0 + \sum_{i=1}^{3} a_i r_{t-i} \tag{6.28}$$

and, as is common in practice, a GARCH specification with $r = s = 1$ was enough to capture the correlation in the absolute (and squared) returns.

From Figure 4.1 and 4.2, showing the exchange rate and percentage returns, extreme kurtosis, as well as volatility clustering, are clearly visible.

In addition to fitting the GARCH model with stable innovations, we consider four other specifications as well. Firstly, and to some extent, a benchmark, is the GARCH(1,1) model assuming Student's t innovations, i.e.,

$$y_t = \mu_t + c_t \varepsilon_t, \ \varepsilon_t \overset{iid}{\sim} t(\nu), \tag{6.29}$$

$$c_t^2 = \alpha_0 + \sum_{i=1}^{r} \alpha_i \left(y_{t-i} - \mu_{t-i}\right)^2 + \sum_{j=1}^{s} \beta_j c_{t-j}^2, \tag{6.30}$$

and $t(\nu)$ refers to the zero-mean t distribution with ν degrees of freedom and scale parameter c equal to one,

$$f_t\left(\varepsilon_t; \nu, c\right) = \frac{K_\nu}{c} \left(1 + \frac{\epsilon_t^2}{\nu c^2}\right)^{-\frac{\nu+1}{2}}, \quad K_\nu = \frac{\nu^{-1/2}}{B\left(\frac{1}{2}, \frac{\nu}{2}\right)} = \frac{\Gamma\left(\frac{\nu+1}{2}\right)\nu^{-1/2}}{\sqrt{\pi}\Gamma\left(\frac{\nu}{2}\right)}.$$

Assuming that $\nu > 2$, taking unconditional expectations of c_t^2 in (6.30) shows that $\mathrm{E}c_t^2$ exists if $\lambda_{\nu,2} \sum_{i=1}^{r} \alpha_i + \sum_{j=1}^{s} \beta_j < 1$, where $\lambda_{\nu,2} := \mathrm{E}\varepsilon_t^2 = \nu/(\nu - 2)$.

Secondly, we again assume the t distribution, but use absolute mean-corrected returns in the GARCH equation instead of their squares. In light of the previously mentioned finding of Nelson and Foster (1994), one would expect that, in the presence of severe kurtosis such as exhibited by the returns on the Lev, the absolute value GARCH-t model will "outperform" its variance-modeling counterpart. We will denote the former as $t_{|c|}$, and the latter as t_{c^2}. From (6.30) with $\nu > 1$, $\mathrm{E}|c_t|$ exists if $\lambda_{\nu,1} \sum_{i=1}^{r} \alpha_i + \sum_{j=1}^{s} \beta_j < 1$, where $\lambda_{\nu,1} := \mathrm{E}|\varepsilon_t| = \sqrt{\nu}\Gamma\left(\frac{\nu-1}{2}\right)/\sqrt{2}\Gamma\left(\frac{\nu}{2}\right)$.

With the generic value λ denoting either $\lambda_{\alpha,\beta}$, $\lambda_{\nu,1}$, or $\lambda_{\nu,2}$, we also consider the IGARCH(1,1) processes formed by restricting $\beta_1 = 1 - \lambda\alpha_1$, which results in persistence of the conditional volatility.

In addition to conditioning on $\{r_0, r_{-1}, r_{-2}\}$, as required for the AR(3) structure, we need to specify values for ε_0 and c_0. Following Nelson and Cao

---

[12]We use the standard convention and define the return r_t in period t by $r_t = 100 \times (\ln P_t - \ln P_{t-1})$, where P_t is the exchange rate at time t.

(1992), one could set them to their unconditional expected values, i.e., in the absolute value case,

$$\hat{c}_0 = \hat{\alpha}_0 / \left(1 - \lambda \hat{\alpha}_1 - \hat{\beta}_1\right), \tag{6.31}$$

with $\hat{\varepsilon}_0 = \lambda \hat{c}_0$, where λ denotes one of the aforementioned expected values, evaluated using the parameter estimates at the kth iteration of the numerical maximization of the log-likelihood function. In the IGARCH case, (6.31) will be invalid, so we instead *estimate* c_0 as an additional parameter of the model. We do this for all models considered here, as (6.31) will also be problematic for models which are close to being IGARCH.

Evaluation of the pdf, and, thus, the likelihood function of the $S_{\alpha,\beta}$ distribution is nontrivial, because it lacks an analytic expression. The ML estimate of parameter vector θ is obtained by maximizing the logarithm of the likelihood function

$$L(\theta; r_1, \ldots, r_T) = \prod_{t=1}^{T} S_{\alpha,\beta} \left(\frac{r_t - \mu_t}{c_t}\right) c_t^{-1}.$$

The estimation of α–stable models is *approximate* in the sense that the α–stable density function $S_{\alpha,\beta}\left((r_t - \mu_t)/c_t\right)$ needs to be approximated. Our ML estimation essentially follows that of DuMouchel (1973a,b), but differs in that we numerically approximate the α–stable density via fast Fourier transform of the cf rather than some series expansion. As DuMouchel (1973a,b) shows, the resulting estimates are consistent and asymptotically normal with the asymptotic covariance matrix of $T^{1/2}(\hat{\theta} - \theta_0)$ being given by the inverse of the Fisher information matrix. The standard errors of the estimates reported below are obtained by evaluating the Fisher information matrix at the ML point estimates. For details on our α–stable ML estimation we refer to Mittnik et al. (1996) and Mittnik and Rachev (1997).

We employ three criteria for comparing the goodness of fit of the candidate distributions. The first is the maximum log-likelihood value obtained from the ML estimation. It may be viewed as an overall measure of goodness of fit and allows us to judge which candidate is more likely to have generated the data. From a Bayesian viewpoint, given large samples and assuming equal prior probabilities for two candidate distributions, the ratio of the maximum log likelihood values of two competing models represents the asymptotic posterior odds ratio of one candidate relative to the other (see Zellner, 1971; and Blattberg and Gonedes, 1974).

The second criterion is the Kolmogorov distance

$$KD = 100 \times \sup_{x \in \mathbf{R}} |F_s(x) - \hat{F}(x)|, \tag{6.32}$$

where $\hat{F}(x)$ denotes the cdf of the estimated parametric density, and $F_s(x)$ is the empirical sample distribution, i.e., $F_s(x) = T^{-1} \sum_{t=1}^{T} \mathcal{I}_{(-\infty, x]} \left(\frac{r_t - \hat{\mu}_t}{\hat{c}_t}\right)$ where $\mathcal{I}(\cdot)$ is the indicator function. This statistic is discussed further in

DeGroot (1986) and D'Agostino and Stephens (1986). It is a robust measure in the sense that it focuses only on the maximum deviation between the sample and fitted distributions.

The third is the Anderson–Darling statistic (Anderson and Darling, 1952; see also Press et al., 1991; and Tanaka, 1996), which weights the absolute deviations $|F_s(x) - \hat{F}(x)|$ by the reciprocal of the standard deviation of $F_s(x)$, $\sqrt{\hat{F}(x)\left(1 - \hat{F}(x)\right)}$, i.e.,

$$AD = \sup_{x \in \mathbf{R}} \frac{|F_s(x) - \hat{F}(x)|}{\sqrt{\hat{F}(x)\left(1 - \hat{F}(x)\right)}}, \qquad (6.33)$$

The use of this statistic allows discrepancies in the tails of the distribution to be appropriately weighted. On the other hand, KD emphasizes deviations around the median of the fitted distribution.

Tables 6.3 and 6.4 displays the parameter estimates and goodness-of-fit measures of the various models, respectively. For all α-stable models, the skewness parameter β was insignificant, so that we restrict ourselves to the symmetric stable case. In this way, the t and α-stable cases are directly comparable in terms of number of estimated parameters. The entry $\lambda\alpha_1 + \beta_1$ in Table 6.3 refers to the appropriate measure of persistence in volatility, e.g., for the GARCH–t_{c^2} model, $\lambda_{\hat{\nu},2}\hat{\alpha}_1 + \hat{\beta}_1 = 1.1859$, implying that the variance process is explosive. For the GARCH–$t_{|c|}$ model, on the other hand, $\lambda_{\hat{\nu},1}\hat{\alpha}_1 + \hat{\beta}_1 = 0.7288$, quite far from the IGARCH border.

Comparing first the models with t innovations, we see that the maximized log-likelihood value, $\mathcal{L}$, of the t_{c^2} model is considerably larger than either that of $t_{|c|}$ or the IGARCH–t_{c^2}. Also, this model is favored by the KD and AD statistics. The value of this model is questionable, however, given its implication for both the conditional and unconditional variance. Both the restricted IGARCH form, and the absolute value GARCH–t do not appear to fit the data adequately, as is also evident from Figure 6.2, showing the overlayed kernel (– –) and fitted (—) conditional densities of the $(r_t - \hat{\mu}_t)/\hat{c}_t$.

Quite different results are obtained by the models corresponding to the $S_{\alpha,0}$ innovation assumption. Without any restriction on the parameters, the $S_{\alpha,0}$GARCH model is almost identical to its $S_{\alpha,0}$IGARCH counterpart, both of which obtain a value $\mathcal{L}$ strikingly close to the (arguably misspecified) unrestricted GARCH–t_{c^2} model. In addition, the KD and AD statistics slightly favor both $S_{\alpha,0}$ parameterizations. The kernel and fitted density plots of the two $S_{\alpha,0}$ models were virtually identical, so that Figure 6.2 only shows that one corresponding to $S_{\alpha,0}$IGARCH.

$$y_t = u_t + c_t \in_t, \quad \in_t iid \\ \sim S_{\alpha\beta}, \qquad (6.34)$$

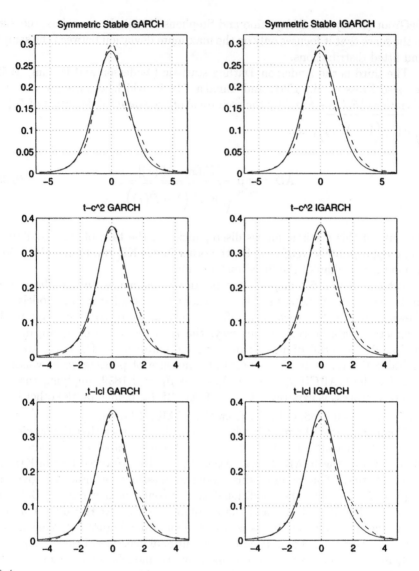

Fig. 6.2 Empirical (– –) and Fitted (—) Conditional Densities.(Adapted from: Mittnik, Paolella and Rachev (1997))

We consider modeling the Japanese Yen–U.S. Dollar daily exchange rate series from January 8, 1973 to July 28, 1994, yielding a total of 5,350 observations.

Table 6.3 Parameter Estimates[a]

| | GARCH | | | IGARCH | |
	t_{c^2}	$t_{|c|}$	$S_{\alpha,0}$	t_{c^2}	$S_{\alpha,0}$
a_0	0.0121	0.0192	0.0157	0.0168	0.0155
	(0.007)	(.)	(0.007)	(0.004)	(0.008)
a_1	0.2760	0.2693	0.2919	0.2689	0.2945
	(0.038)	(.)	(0.034)	(0.027)	(0.031)
a_2	0.1600	0.1214	0.1561	0.1583	0.1564
	(0.035)	(.)	(0.028)	(0.030)	(0.030)
a_3	0.0396	0.0570	0.0381	0.0464	0.0367
	(0.031)	(.)	(0.029)	(0.024)	(0.031)
α_0	3.449×10^{-3}	0.1046	9.242×10^{-3}	0.0322	9.878×10^{-3}
	(9.56×10^{-4})	(.	(2.32×10^{-3})	(0.004)	(2.53×10^{-3})
α_1	0.3394	0.3661	0.2578	0.2507	0.2527
	(0.051)	(.)	(0.016)	(0.026)	(0.029)
β_1	0.5538	0.2594	0.6709	0.6653	0.6723
	(0.038)	(.)	(0.020)	—	—
c_0	65.39	12.75	6.080	9.769	6.080
	(69.68)	(.)	(0.157)	(5.868)	(0.154)
$\lambda\alpha_1 + \beta_1$	1.1859	0.7288	1.0080	1.000	1.000
Shape	4.319	3.698	1.758	7.976	1.769
	(0.617)	(.)	(0.031)	(1.049)	(0.021)

[a] The model is given by $r_t = \mu_t + c_t \varepsilon_t$, with $\mu_t = a_0 + \sum_{i=1}^{3} a_i r_{t-i}$ and, for t_{c^2}, $c_t^2 = \alpha_0 + \alpha_1 (r_{t-1} - \mu_{t-1})^2 + \beta_1 c_{t-1}^2$; otherwise, $c_t = \alpha_0 + \alpha_1 |y_{t-1} - \mu_{t-1}| + \beta_1 c_{t-1}$. Numerically approximated Standard deviations are given in parentheses.

(Adapted from: Mittnik, Paolella and Rachev (1997))

Table 6.4   Goodness of Fit[a]

	GARCH			IGARCH	
	t_{c^2}	$t_{|c|}$	$S_{\alpha,0}$	t_{c^2}	$S_{\alpha,0}$
$\mathcal{L}$	-698.51	-794.18	-703.64	-736.78	-703.76
KD	4.19	5.21	3.85	8.61	4.00
AD	0.135	0.220	0.122	1.78	0.132

[a] $\mathcal{L}$ refers to the maximum log–likelihood value; KD is the Kolmogorov distance $100 \times \sup_{x \in \mathbf{R}} |F_s(x) - \hat{F}(x)|$; and AD is the Anderson-Darling statistic

$$\sup_{x \in \mathbf{R}} \frac{|F_s(x) - \hat{F}(x)|}{\sqrt{\hat{F}(x)\left(1 - \hat{F}(x)\right)}}.$$

(Adapted from: Mittnik, Paolella and Rachev (1997))

| α-stable | 0.0068 | -0.0047 | 0.0053 | 0.1286 | 0.8251 | 1.000[c] | 1.709 | -0.0769 |
| (Stationary) | (2.2E-4) | (9.3E-4) | (6.3E-5) | (0.0013) | (0.0015) | | (0.0016) | (0.0017) |

(Adapted from: Mittnik, Paolella and Rachev (1997))

Table 6.5   Parameter Estimates[a]

	Mean–Equation Parameters		Dispersion–Equation Parameters				Distribution Parameters	
	μ	a_1	α_0	α_1	β_1	$\lambda_{\alpha,\beta}$ $\alpha_1 + \beta_1$	Shape	Skewness
Normal	-0.0087	0.0276	0.0444	0.1116	0.7830	0.8946	2	—
	(0.0077)	(0.014)	(0.056)	(0.013)	(0.024)		—	—
Student's t	0.0053	-0.0019	0.0096	0.1757	0.6912	0.8669	3.998	—
	(0.0048)	(0.014)	(2.9×10^{-5})	(0.013)	(0.015)		(0.238)	—
α-stable	-3.61×10^{-6}	-4.05×10^{-5}	1.92×10^{-4}	0.1026	0.8734	1.016	1.682	-0.1898
	(2.8×10^{-4})	(0.0030)	(1.3×10^{-4})	(0.0066)	(0.0077)		(0.021)	(0.010)
IGARCH	0.0011	-6.3×10^{-4}	0.0017	0.0915	0.8783	1.0	1.738	-0.1931
	(0.014)	(0.014)	(0.0011)	(0.0083)	—		(0.0089)	(0.0077)

[a] Standard deviations are given in parentheses.
(Adapted from: Mittnik, Paolella and Rachev (1997))

Table 6.6 Parameter Estimates[a]

	Normal	Student's t	α-stable Unrestricted	Integrated
		Distributions		
μ	-0.0500 (0.0073)	0.0053 (0.0048)	-7.25×10^{-6} (4.67×10^{-5})	0.0011 (0.014)
a_1	0.0263 (0.014)	-0.0019 (0.014)	-5.278×10^{-4} (0.0020)	-6.3×10^{-4} (0.014)
α_0	0.0135 (5.9×10^{-4})	0.0096 (2.9×10^{-5})	1.302×10^{-4} (5.77×10^{-6})	0.0017 (0.0011)
α_1	0.1454 (0.0012)	0.1757 (0.013)	0.1103 (0.0073)	0.0915 (0.0083)
β_1	0.8545 (0.0012)	0.6912 (0.015)	0.8655 (0.0070)	0.8783 —
$\alpha_1 + \beta_1$ $\lambda_{\alpha,\beta}\alpha_1 + \beta_1$	0.9999 —	0.8669 —	0.976 1.019	0.9698 1.000
Shape	2 —	3.998 (0.238)	1.688 (0.005)	1.738 (0.0089)
Skewness	— —	— —	-0.1872 (0.008)	-0.1931 (0.0077)

[a]Numerically approximated Standard deviations are given in parentheses.
(Adapted from: Mittnik, Paolella and Rachev (1997))

Table 6.7 Goodness of Fit of Conditional Heteroskedastic Distributions[a]

	$\mathcal{L}$	KD	AD$_0$	AD$_1$	AD$_2$
Normal	-4681.0	7.79 (4527)	∞ (1)	∞ (2)	∞ (5348)
Student's t	-3805.1	1.80 (633)	0.634 (1)	0.078 (5347)	0.067 (5346)
$S_{\alpha,\beta}$ (GARCH)	-3742.1	2.17 (2521)	0.047 (1)	0.045 (5336)	0.045 (5337)
$S_{\alpha,\beta}$ (IGARCH)	-3760.0	2.92 (2686)	0.066 (631)	0.066 (632)	0.066 (630)

[a]$\mathcal{L}$ refers to the maximum log–likelihood value; KD is the Kolmogorov distance $100 \times \sup_{x \in \mathbf{R}} |F_s(x) - \hat{F}(x)|$; and AD$_i$, $i = 0, 1, 2$, is the Anderson-Darling statistic

$$\sup_{x \in \mathbf{R}} \frac{|F_s(x) - \hat{F}(x)|}{\sqrt{\hat{F}(x) \left(1 - \hat{F}(x)\right)}}$$

neglecting i extreme values. The numbers in parentheses, τ, indicate to which order statistic, $(r_{\tau:T} - \hat{\mu})/\hat{c}$, the KD and AD$_i$ values correspond.
(Adapted from: Mittnik, Paolella and Rachev (1997))

6.3 Numerical Solution of Stochastic Differential Equations with Applications to ARCH/GARCH Modeling

In this section we study numerical solutions of multi-dimensional stochastic differential equations (SDE's) of the Itô type, and adapt those such that their solutions serve as approximations of ARCH/GARCH-type processes.[13] These are SDE's, whose drift and diffusion may depend both on present and past time points. The methods employed are based on the evaluation of drift and diffusion coefficients over grid points. The grid combines the *time discretization* of the SDE[14] with the *discretization of the stochastic input*, here a Wiener process. This combination of time and chance discretization is necessary for a numerical solution of the Itô SDE.

A broad survey over various approximations of solutions for SDE's given in Platen (1981) and Kloeden and Platen (1992); in this approach the approximations are constructed via the stochastic Taylor expansion with respect to the mean squared supremum norm. The method considered there is the stochastic Euler method (see also Maruyama, 1955) and will be the basis of the method considered in this section. Simultaneously, with the time discretization we shall discretize the Wiener process. Then, we shall estimate the distance between the distribution of the exact solution and the distributions of the approximate solutions.[15]

The Discretization. Let H be an equidistant grid on an interval $[t_0, T]$ let H with grid points

$$t_0 = \hat{t}_0 < \hat{t}_1 < \cdots < \hat{t}_n = T$$

and step size h. H will be the minimal set of time points at which values are available for the method, and $\hat{h}$ will be the period between two neighbouring observations in the past which influence the present drift and diffusion coefficients at any time.

For any $t \in [t_0, T]$ define

$$i_h(t) := \max\{i : \hat{t}_i \leq t\}$$

as the number of time steps $\hat{h}$ one can go back to the past from t.

The SDE. Consider a stochastic differential equation (SDE) in integral form where grift and diffusion coefficients depend on the present state as well

---

[13]The results of this section are due to Gelbrich and Rachev (1995); see also Gelbrich (1989, 1995).

[14]The time discretization of the SDE amounts to the stochastic analogue of Euler's method.

[15]Kanagawa (1986) used a method derived from the stochastic Euler method by replacing the increments of the Wiener process by other "simpler" i.i.d. random variables: He uses L^p-Wasserstein metrics ($p \geq 2$) between the distributions of exact and approximate solutions, thus achieving convergence rates. (For a broad survey on probability metrics see Rachev (1991), on L^p-Wasserstein metrics see e.g. Givens and Shortt (1984) and Gelbrich (1989), (1990)). In this section, we use the same metrics, but generalize the method of Kanagawa.

as on the states at past time intervals which are multiples of $\hat{h}$:

$$x(t) \;\; = \;\; x_0 + \int_{t_0}^{t} b(x,s)ds + \int_{t_0}^{t} \sigma(x,s)dw(s) \tag{6.35}$$

$$= \;\; x_0 + \int_{t_0}^{t} b(x,s)ds + \sum_{j=1}^{q} \int_{t_0}^{t} \sigma_j(x,s)dw_j(s), \quad t \in [t_0,T], x_0 \in \mathbf{R}^d.$$

Here,

(i) $w = (w_1,\ldots,w_q)^T$ is a q-dimensional standard Wiener process, (q-dimensional Brownian motion), playing the role of the "market shots" if $x(t)$ is viewed as the process of multivariate asset returns.

(ii) the drift $b(x,s) := b^{i_h(s)}(x(s-\hat{h}), x(s-2\hat{h}),\ldots, x(s-i_h(s)\hat{h}))$, and

(iii) the diffusion

$\sigma(x,s) = (\sigma_1(x,s),\ldots,\sigma_q(x,s)) := \sigma^{i_H(s)}(x(s), x(s-\hat{h}), x(s-2\hat{h}),\ldots, x(s-i_H(s)\hat{h}))$.

The drift and the diffusion in (6.35) are continuous: for any $\nu = 0,\ldots, i_H(T)$, $b^\nu \in C(\mathbf{R}^{\nu d}; \mathbf{R}^d)$, and $\sigma^\nu \in C(\mathbf{R}^{\nu d}; \mathcal{L}(\mathbf{R}^q, \mathbf{R}^d))$, where $\sigma_j^\nu \in C(\mathbf{R}^{\nu d}; \mathbf{R})$, $j = 1,\ldots,q$, denote the columns of the matrix function $\sigma^\nu = (\sigma_1^\nu,\ldots,\sigma_q^\nu)$.

Here, $C(\mathbf{R}^{\nu d}; \mathbf{R}^d)$ is the space of continuous functions on $\mathbf{R}^{\nu d}$ into $\mathbf{R}^d$, $\mathcal{L}(\mathbf{R}^q; \mathbf{R}^d)$ is the space of $q \times d$-matrices determining the linear space of linear operators from $\mathbf{R}^q$ to $\mathbf{R}^d$, and finally $C(\mathbf{R}^\nu; \mathcal{L}(\mathbf{R}^q, \mathbf{R}^d))$ is the space of continuous functions from $\mathbf{R}^{\nu d}$ into $\mathcal{L}(\mathbf{R}^q, \mathbf{R}^d)$.[16]

Remark 6.2 The case with drift and diffticion, b and σ explicitly depending on t can be written in the form (6.35) by taking the time t as another component of x. A direct treatment of this case follows the same lines as in this section, see also Gelbrich (1989). Our present formulation (6.35) allows to relax eventually required second order differentiability with respect to t to first order differentiability which we assume here.

Remark 6.3 Let $p \in [1, \infty)$ and $\mathcal{M}_p(X) := \{\mu \in \mathcal{P}(X) : \int_X (d(x,0))^p d\mu(x) < \infty, \theta \in X\}$. Define the L^p-*Kantorovich metric* (or also called L^p-*Wasserstein metric*, see Rachev (1991)) W_p on $\mathcal{M}_p^{(}X)$ by

$$W_p(\mu,\nu) := \left[\inf \int_{X \times X} (d(x,y))^p d\eta(x,y)\right]^{1/p}$$

---

[16]In what follows, we shall denote by C the spaces of continuous functions and by $\mathcal{L}$ the spaces of linear mappings. By $\|\cdot\|$ we shall denote the Euclidean norm on $\mathbf{R}^n (n \in \mathbf{N})$ and the corresponding induced norm on a space $\mathcal{L}$. Furthermore, for any random variable ζ, (i.e. ζ is mapping a probability space $(\Omega, \mathcal{A}, P)$ into a separable metric space (X, d) with the Borel σ-algebra $\mathcal{B}(X)$), the notation $D(\zeta)$ will mean the distribution $P \circ \zeta^{-1}$ induced on X by ζ. $\mathcal{P}(X)$ will be the set of all Borel probability measures on X.

where the infimum is taken over all measures $\eta \in \mathcal{P}(X \times X)$ with fixed marginal distributions μ and ν ($\mu, \nu \in \mathcal{M}_p(X)$).

Applying the "minimality" property of W_p, Kanagawa (1986) states a convergence result for a sequence of approximations to the solution x of (6.35). The approximations were constructed over equidistant grids using both the stochastic Euler method and a substitution of the Wiener process increments between grid points by other i.i.d. r.v.'s, see also Janssen (1984). This joint "time and chance" discretization give rise to the construction of our approximate solution see equation (6.44) further on.

Remark 6.4 Our discretization method leading to an approximate (numerical) solution can be seen as a framework for embedding of ARCH and GARCH models into the SDE's given by (6.35).

Let us reformulate some ARCH/GARCH models in a form close to our formulation of the problem (6.35).

The Univariate ARCH/GARCH. Consider the equidistant grid $t_0 = \hat{t}_0 < \hat{t}_1 < \cdots < \hat{t}_{\hat{n}} = T$ with step size $\hat{h}$ on the time interval $[t_0, T]$. Define the *univariate ARCH model* as a discrete time stochastic process $(\epsilon_{\hat{t}_i})_{i=0,\ldots,\hat{n}}$ of the form

$$\epsilon_{\hat{t}_{i+1}} = \hat{\sigma}_{\hat{t}_i} \delta_{\hat{t}_i}$$

where $\hat{\sigma}_{\hat{t}_i}$ is a positive measurable function of the time points $\hat{t}_0, \hat{t}_1, \ldots, \hat{t}_i$ and the $\delta_{\hat{t}_i}$ are i.i.d. r.v.'s with zero mean and variance one, see Engle (1982) and Bollerslev et al. (1992).

In the linear ARCH(ψ) the variances $\sigma_{\hat{t}_i}$ depend on the squares of the past ψ values of the process:

$$\hat{\sigma}_{\hat{t}_i}^2 := \omega + \sum_{r=0}^{\psi-1} \alpha_r \epsilon_{\hat{t}_{i-r}}^2 .$$

In the more general *linear* GARCH(ϕ, ψ) $\hat{\sigma}_{\hat{t}_i}^2$ may also depend on the ϕ recent variances:

$$\hat{\sigma}_{\hat{t}_i}^2 := \omega + \sum_{r=0}^{\psi-1} \alpha_r \epsilon_{\hat{t}_{i-r}}^2 + \sum_{r=1}^{\phi} \beta_r \hat{\sigma}_{\hat{t}_{i-r}}^2 . \tag{6.36}$$

In these models it is assumed that $\omega > 0$, $\alpha_r \geq 0$, $\beta \geq 0$ for all r. Later we will embed this model (slightly modified) into the constructed approximation for the SDE (6.35).

The Multivariate GARCH. The multivariate ARCH and GARCH models reflect price changes (returns) in portfolios of d assets and is a process $(\epsilon_{\hat{t}_i})_{i=0,\ldots,\hat{n}} \subset \mathbf{R}^d$ with

$$\epsilon_{\hat{t}_{i+1}} = \Omega_{\hat{t}_i}^{1/2} \delta_{\hat{t}_i}$$

where the $\Omega_{\hat{t}_i}$ are defined positive definite $d \times d$ matrices and measurable functions of $\hat{t}_0, \ldots, \hat{t}_i$, and where $\delta_{\hat{t}_i}$ are i.i.d. r.v.'s with zero mean and have the d-dimensional unity matrix as covariance matrix.

In the multivariate *linear* GARCH(ϕ, ψ) we set

$$\text{vech}(\Omega_{\hat{t}_{i+1}}) := W + \sum_{r=0}^{\psi-1} A_r \text{vech}(\epsilon_{\hat{t}_{i-r}} \epsilon_{\hat{t}_{i-r}}^T) + \sum_{r=1}^{\psi} B_r \text{vech}(\Omega_{\hat{t}_{i-r}}).$$

Here,
(i) vech($\cdot$) puts the lower right triangle of a symmetric $d \times d$ matrix in the form of a vector in $\mathbf{R}^{1/2 \cdot d(d+1)}$,
(ii) $W \in \mathbf{R}^{1/2 \cdot d(d+1)}$, and
(iii) A_r and B_r are $(1/2 \cdot d(d+1)) \times (1/2 \cdot d(d+1))$ matrices
The process $(\epsilon_{\hat{t}_i})$ is designed to model stock price returns, and a model $(S_{\hat{t}_i})_{1,\dots,\hat{n}}$ of a d-dimensional price process is obtained by setting

$$\epsilon_{\hat{t}_i} = \ln(S_{\hat{t}_i} - \ln(S_{\hat{t}_{i-1}})),$$

the logarithms taken componentwise. Then the process

$$\Lambda_{\hat{t}_i} := \ln(S_{\hat{t}_i}) = S_{\hat{t}_0} + \sum_{r=1}^{i} \Lambda_{\hat{t}_r}$$

has independent increments whose covariance matrices $\Omega_{\hat{t}_r}$ depend on the prices at the times $\hat{t}_0, \dots, \hat{t}_r$.

Our discretization method (see (6.44) further on) will also produce processes with independent increments. Moreover, it will provide convergence of the numerical solution towards the solution of (6.35). The rate-of-convergence of our procedure in terms of the W_p-metrics will be close to the optimal rate. Compared with $(\ln(S_{\hat{t}_i}))_{i=0,\dots,\hat{n}}$, the discretization will go beyond the grid mentioned above and use (possibly) a finer grid for a better time discretization.

The Assumptions on the Drift and Diffusion. We use the following general assumptions concerning the SDE (5.8.1):

Assumption 1. There exists a constant $M > 0$ such that   (6.37)
for all $j = 1, \dots, q; \nu = 0, \dots, i_H(T)$ and $x_0, \dots, x_\nu \in \mathbf{R}^d$
$$\|b^\nu(x_0, \dots, x_\nu)\| \leq M(1 + \max_{0 \leq \rho \leq \nu} \|x_\rho\|) \quad \text{and}$$
$$\|\sigma_j^\nu(x_0, \dots, x_\nu)\| \leq M.$$

Assumption 2. There exists a constant $L > 0$ such that   (6.38)
for all $j = 1, \dots, q; \nu = 0, \dots, i_H(T)$ and $x_0, \dots, x_\nu, y_0, \dots, y_\nu \in \mathbf{R}^d$
$$\|b^\nu(x_0, \dots, x_\nu) - b^\nu(y_0, \dots, y_\nu)\| \leq L \max_{0 \leq \rho \leq \nu} \|x_\rho - y_\rho\| \quad \text{and}$$
$$\|\sigma_j^\nu(x_0, \dots, x_\nu) - \sigma_j^\nu(y_0, \dots, y_\nu)\| \leq L \max_{0 \leq \rho \leq \nu} \|x_\rho - y_\rho\|.$$

The regularity assumptions (6.37) and (6.38) secure the existence and unique-ness of the solution of (6.35).[17] The boundedness of σ_j in (6.37) and (6.38) seems to be essential for the proof of Theorem 6.5.

The Grid. Our approximate solutions are based on a "double grid":

(i) A *coarse* grid for the time discretization;

(ii) A *fine* grid which is a refinement of the coarse grid. It will serve for the chance discretization. It yields a lower convergence speed than the time discretization.

We combine both grids in a grid class $\mathcal{G}(m, \Lambda, \alpha, \beta)$, where $m : (0, T - t_0] \to [1, \infty)$ is a monotonously decreasing function and $\Lambda, \alpha, \beta > 0$ are constants. Each element G of $\mathcal{G}(m, \lambda, \alpha, \beta)$ consists of two kinds of grid points:

the *time discretization points* t_k, $k = 0, \ldots, n$, with   (6.39)

$$t_0 < t_1 < \ldots < t_n = T$$

and

the *chance discretization points* u_i^k, $i = 0, \ldots, m_k$,   (6.40)

$k = 0, \ldots, n - 1$, with $t_k = u_0^k < u_1^k < \ldots < u_{m_k}^k = t_{k+1}$, $k = 0, \ldots, n - 1$.

Now, G is a combination of a coarse subgrid consisting of all points t_k relevant for the pure time discretization and of a fine grid consisting of all points u_i^k needed for the discretization of the Wiener process. We set G to satisfy the following :[18]

$$t_k - t_{k-1} = \frac{T - t_0}{n} =: h \le 1 \text{ for all } k = 1, \ldots, n \text{ and } \hat{h}/h \in \mathbf{N}, \quad (6.41)$$

$$u_i^k - u_{i-1}^k = \frac{h}{m_k} \le \beta \frac{h}{m(h)} \quad (6.42)$$

for all $k = 0, \ldots, n - 1$, $i = 1, \ldots, m_k$, $1 \le m_k \le m(h)^\alpha$ for all $k = 0, \ldots, n - 1$. Finally for a grid G of $\mathcal{G}(m, \Lambda, \alpha, \beta)$ we define

$$[t]_G := t_k \quad \text{and} \quad i_G(t) := k, \quad \text{if} \quad t \in [t_k, t_k + 1), k = 0, \ldots, n - 1,$$

---

[17]Both the existence and the uniqueness of the SDE are defined in the strong sense, see for example Gikhman and and Skorokhod (1979).

[18]Condition (6.41) reads that the coarse grid is equidistant with stepsize h. Here, h is required to be bounded by 1 only for convenience, in order to write simpler upper bounds later. Also the coarse grid contains the master grid H. Condition (6.42) requires that each interval of the coarse subgrid is subdivided in an equidistant way by the points u_i^k moreover, both the number of the subdivisions and the step size of the full grid being bounded by functions of h. As an example, it is easy to see that all equidistant grids with the property

$$m_k = [m(h)], \quad k = 0, \ldots, n - 1,$$

belong to $\mathcal{G}(m, T - t_0, 1, 2)$.

and

$$[t]_G^* := u_i^k \quad \text{if} \quad t \in [u_i^k, u_{i+1}^k), \quad i = 1, \ldots, m_k, \quad k = 0, \ldots, n-1.$$

The Approximate (Numerical) Solution of the SDE. We construct the approximate solution of the SDE (6.35) in three steps.

The first step is a *pure time discretization* $(y^E(t))$ using the stochastic Euler method (see Maruyama, 1955). Here, only the coarse subgrid is involved:

$$y^E(t) = x_0 + \int_{t_0}^t b(y^E, [s]_G)ds + \sum_{j=1}^q \int_{t_0}^t \sigma_j(Y^E, [s]_G)dw_j(s) \quad \text{for all} \quad t \in [t_0, T],$$

(6.43)

In the second step we use a continuous and *piecewise linear interpolation* $(\tilde{y}^E(t))$ of the trajectories in (6.43) between the points of the whole fine grid;

$$\begin{cases} \tilde{y}^E \text{ be continuous, and linear in the intervals } [u_{i-1}^k, u_i^k], \\ i = 1, \ldots, m_k, k = 0, \ldots, n-1 \text{ with} \\ \tilde{y}^E(u_i^k) = y^E(u_i^k), i = 0, \ldots, m_k, k = 0, \ldots, n-1, \end{cases}$$

(6.44)

In the third step we replace the Wiener process increments over the fine grid by other set of i.i.d. r.v..'s (ξ_{js}^k). Namely, let $\mu \in \mathcal{P}(\mathbf{R})$ be a measure with mean value 0 and variance 1, and define

$$\{\xi_{js}^k : j = 1, \ldots, q; s = 1, \ldots, m_k; k = 0, \ldots, n-1\}$$

to be a family of i.i.d. r.v..'s with distribution $D(\xi_{11}^0) = \mu$.

Now we can define a *discretization method* $(z^E(t))$:

$$\begin{cases} z^E(u_0^0) = x_0, \\ z^E(u_i^k) = x_0 + \sum_{r=0}^{k-1} h_r b(z^E, t_r) + h_k \cdot \frac{i}{m_k} b(z^E, t_k) \\ + \sum_{j=1}^q \left[\sum_{r=0}^{k-1} \sqrt{\frac{h}{m_r}} \sigma_j(z^E, t_r) \sum_{s=1}^{m_r} \xi_{js}^r + \sqrt{\frac{h}{m_k}} \sigma_j(z^E, t_k) \sum_{s=1}^i \xi_{js}^k \right] \\ \text{for all } i = 1, \ldots, m_k; \quad k = 0, \ldots, n-1; \end{cases}$$

(6.45)

The trajectories of z^E are continuous, and between neighbouring grid points linear.

For this last step we require that the Wiener process w and the r.v.'s ξ_{ji}^k will have to be defined anew on a *common* probability space. This is indeed possible assuming that the initial probability space is "rich enough", see for example Rachev (1991).

The Discretization Method for the SDE and GARCH Type Models; the RBGARCH Model. To see how (6.45) can be interpreted as a type of an univariate GARCH(ψ, ϕ) model (6.36) we first note the one can write diffusion $\hat{\sigma}_{\hat{t}_\nu}$, $\nu = 0, \ldots, \hat{n}$ as the function

$$\hat{\sigma}_{\hat{t}_\nu} = \hat{\sigma}^\nu(\Lambda_{\hat{t}_\nu}, \Lambda_{\hat{t}_\nu - \hat{h}}, \ldots, \Lambda_{\hat{t}_\nu - \nu\hat{h}})$$

$$= [\omega_\nu + \sum_{k=0}^{\nu-1} \theta_{\nu,k}(\Lambda_{\hat{t}_\nu - k\hat{h}} - \Lambda_{\hat{t}_\nu - (k+1)\hat{h}})^2]^{1/2},$$

for some positive numbers ω_ν and $\theta_{\nu,k}$. This becomes clear by a recursive substitution using (6.35). Now all $\hat{\sigma}^\nu$ satisfy (6.37) (for σ_1^ν). To get the boundedness condition in (6.37) fulfilled we use instead of $\hat{\sigma}^\nu$ a function bounded by some number $B > 0$, namely

$$\bar{\sigma}^\nu. = (\hat{\sigma}^\nu \wedge B) \vee (-B).$$

This slight modification should nor be significant in practical applications.

Now our discretization model (6.45) has a form which is very close to the univariate linear GARCH(ψ, ϕ). We will call this version of the GARCH model *Refined Bounded G ARCH (RBGARCH)*:

$$(\text{RBGARCH}) \begin{cases} \Lambda^E(u_0^0) = \lambda(t_0), \text{ and} \\ \Lambda^E(u_i^k) = \lambda^E(t_k) \\ \quad + \sqrt{\dfrac{h}{m_k}} \bar{\sigma}^{i_H(t_k)} \Big(\Lambda^E(t_k), \Lambda^E(t - k - \hat{h}), \ldots, \\ \qquad \lambda^E(t_k - i_H(t_k)\hat{h}) \Big) \sum_{s=1}^{i} \xi_{js}^k \\ \text{for all } i = 1, \ldots, m_k; k = 0, \ldots n - 1. \end{cases}$$

Here, we define the values of Λ^E between the grid points by linear interpolation. Note that the increments of Λ^E may depend on all the so far passed time points in the coarse time discretization grid. In other words, with a finer time discretization more observations are needed for the whole approximation, but at each time point the diffusion coefficient still needs a restricted number of observations back in the past in time intervals with fixed length $\hat{h}$.

Next, the SDE corresponding to the RBGARCH method has the following form:

$$\Lambda(t) = \Lambda(t_0) + \int_{t_0}^{t} \bar{\sigma}^{i_H(s)}(\Lambda(s), \Lambda(s - \hat{h}), \Lambda(s - 2\hat{h}), \ldots, \Lambda(s - i_H(s)\hat{h}))dw(s),$$

(6.46)

for $t \in [t_0, T]$.

At the end of their section we shall see that Λ^E converges towards Λ in W_p-sense.[19] We call (6.46) *bounded continuous GARCH*.

---

[19] W_p-convergence implies weak convergence and the convergence of the L_p-moments; see Rachev (1991), Section 8.2.

Remark 6.5 It is our hope that the L^p-estimates of the closeness between the discrete model RBGARCH and the bounded continuous GARCH will provide us with the necessary tools to develop asset pricing models and contingency claim valuation theory based on (6.46) which is indeed a more realistic model for asset pricing then the log-Gaussian model.

We now state the main convergence results. Recall the three steps (6.43), (6.44), (6.45) of our discretization model. We investigate the convergence rates in each of the three steps. The bounds for the rate-of-convergence will be in terms of the norm $\mathbf{E}\sup_{t_0 \le t < T} \| \cdot \|^p$ for $C([t_0, T]; \mathbf{R}^d)$-valued r.v.'s.

According to the evolution of our method via (6.43), (6.44) and (6.45), each step will be represented by one convergence theorem, yielding then immediately the main result.[20]

The first theorem[21] gives rates-of-convergence of the solution of the approximate method in step 1 (6.44), to the solution of the SDE (6.35).

Theorem 6.3 Let $p \in [2, \infty)$ and the regularity assumptions on the drift and diffusion (6.37) and (6.43) hold. Then

$$\mathbf{E} \sup_{t_0 \le t \le T} \|x(t) - y^E(t)\|^p \le K \cdot h^{p/2}.$$

The proofs of this theorem and the rest of the results in this section will be given in Appendix 5.8.

The next theorem gives convergence rates for the L^p-norm of the difference between the solutions in the approximate methods (6.43) and (6.44):[22]

Theorem 6.4 Let $p \in [2, \infty)$. Then (6.37) and (6.38) imply

$$\mathbf{E} \sup_{t_0 \le t \le T} \|y^E(t) - \tilde{y}^E(t)\|^p \le K \left(\frac{h}{m(h)} \right)^{p/2} \left(1 + \ln \left(\frac{m(h)}{h} \right) \right)^{p/2}.$$

In the last discretization step the Wiener process increments shall be replaced by i.i.d. r.v.'s with a given distribution μ on $\mathbf{R}$.[23]

---

[20]The theorems in the sequel will be formulated for an arbitrary fixed grid G of the grid class $\mathcal{G}(n, \Lambda, \alpha, \beta)$. Therefore G fulfills (6.41) and (6.42).

Throughout the rest of the section we shall denote by K any constant depending only on p, the considered grid class, and on the data of the original SDE (6.35). This means, K does not depend on the particular grid. Moreover, K may have different values at different places.

[21]In the case when $p = 2$ and drift and diffusion are only dependent on the present state, this theorem was proved by Platen (1981). It was generalized to the case $p \in [2, \infty)$ in Gelbrich (1995), Theorem 2.6, using a quite similar technique.

[22]The solution in (6.43) behaves like the Wiener process between two neighbouring points t_{k-1} and t_k of the coarse subgrid of G. In our second step of the discretization method, the equation (6.44) provides a solution smoothened by linear interpolation with vertices in *all* gird points of G, in other words in all u_i^k.

[23]However, the corresponding estimates in Theorem 6.5 hold only in the weak sense, i.e. the Wiener process (and its increments between the points of G) and i.i.d. r.v.'s ξ_{ji}^k can be defined on a common probability space such that the estimates hold.

Theorem 6.5 Let $p \in [2, \infty)$ and (6.37) and (6.38) hold. Suppose that $\mu \in \mathcal{P}(\mathbf{R})$ satisfies the conditions:

$$\int_{-\infty}^{\infty} x d\mu(x) = 0,$$

$$\int_{-\infty}^{\infty} x^2 d\mu(x) = 1 \text{ and}$$

$$\int_{-\infty}^{\infty} e^{tx} d\mu(x) < \infty \text{ for all } t \text{ with } \|t\| \leq \tau, \text{ for some } \tau > 0.$$

Then one can define a q-dimensional standard Wiener process $(w(t))_{t \in [t_0, T]}$ and a set of i.i.d. r.v.'s $\{\xi_{ji}^k : j = 1, \ldots, q; i = 1, \ldots, m_k; k = 0, \ldots, n-1\}$ with distribution $D(\xi_{11}^0)$ μ on a common probability space, such that for the solutions in (6.44) and (6.45) with so defined variables the following bound holds:

$$\mathbf{E} \sup_{t_0 \leq t \leq T} \|\tilde{y}^E(t) - z^E(t)\|^p \leq K \left(\frac{1 + \ln m(h)}{\sqrt{m(h)}} \right)^p .$$

The preceding Theorems 6.3, 6.36 and 6.37 yield the main theorem which provides bounds for the L^p-norm of the differences between the exact solution x of the SDE (6.35) and the solution z^E of the approximate method defined in (6.45). Again, as in Theorem 6.5, this is a result in the weak sense.

Theorem 6.6 Suppose the conditions of Theorem 6.37 are satisfied. Then we can define a q-dimensional standard Wiener process $(w(t))_{t \in [t_0, T]}$ and a set of i.i.d. r.v.'s $\{\xi_{ji}^k : j = 1, \ldots, q; i = 1, \ldots, m_k; k = 0, \ldots, n-1\}$ with distribution $D(\xi_{11}^0) = \mu$ on a common probability space, such that

$$\mathbf{E} \sup_{t_0 \leq t \leq T} \|x(t) - z^E(t)\|^p \leq k \left\{ h^{p/2} + \left(\frac{1 + \ln m(h)}{\sqrt{m(h)}} \right)^p \right\},$$

where x is the solution of the SDE (6.35) and x^E is the solution of the discretization method (6.45).

We can reformulate Theorem 6.38 it as an estimate for the L^p-Wasserstein metric between the *distributions* of the exact solution and the solution of the discretized problem.

Corollary 6.1 Suppose the conditions of Theorem 6.5 are satisfied. Moreover, let $(w(t))_{t \in [t_0, T]}$ be a q-dimensional standard Wiener process and $\{\xi_{ji}^k : j = 1, \ldots, q; i = 1, \ldots, m_k; k = 0, \ldots, n-1\}$ a set of i.i.d. r.v.'s with distribution $D(\xi_{11}^0) = \mu$. Then for the SDE (6.35) and the method (6.45), with so constructed variables, the following bound holds:

$$W_p(D(x), D(z^E)) \le k \left\{ h^{1/2} + \frac{1 + \ln m(h)}{\sqrt{m(h)}} \right\}.$$

Remark 6.6 The bounds in Theorem 6.6 and Corollary 6.1 provide convergence rates in terms of the step-size h for any grid sequence in $\mathcal{G}(m, \Lambda, \alpha, \beta)$. These rates consist of two summands, one depending on h and the other depending on $m(h)$, representing the rates of time and chance discretization, respectively. Obviously it is not desirable that one of both summands converges faster than the other. Indeed, if the second summand goes faster to zero than the first, this would mean that $m(h)$ increases too fast. Then, because of (6.42), we would have too small step sizes of the whole *fine* grids, i.e. to have too many points u_i^k in relation to the t_k in each grid, which implies the use of the random number generator too often. On the other hand, if the first summand converges faster than the second, then $m(h)$ increases too slowly, i.e. the intervals $[t_k, t_{k+1}]$ do not have enough intermediate grid points u_i^k, such that the chance discretization does not keep up with the time discretization. Summarizing, it is desirable to tune the rates of both summands, i.e. to equal the powers of h in both summands. This means to choose $m(h)$ to be increasing like $1/h$. In this way we get the following two corollaries as direct consequences of Theorem 6.6 and Corollary 6.1.

Corollary 6.2 Suppose the conditions of Theorem 6.5 are satisfied. Assume also that $\max \left\{ \sup_{0 \le s \le 1} sm(s), \sup_{0 < s \le 1} \frac{1}{sm(s)} \right\} \le K$. Then we can construct the solutions in (6.35) and (6.45) on a common probability space as in Theorem 6.6, so that

$$\mathbf{E} \sup_{t_0 \le t \le T} \left\| x(t) - z^E(t) \right\|^p \le K \cdot h^{p/2} (1 - \ln h)^p.$$

Corollary 6.3 Under the assumptions in Corollary 6.2,

$$W_p(D(x), D(z^E)) \le K \cdot h^{1/2} (1 - \ln h).$$

Remark 6.7 So under the assumptions of Corollary 6.2, with a given grid sequence in $\mathcal{G}(m, \Lambda, \alpha, \beta)$ and using the metric W_p, we have the convergence rates:

(i) $O(h^{1/2}(1 - \ln h))$ with respect to the maximal step sizes h of the coarse subgrids;

(ii) $O((\frac{h}{m(h)})^{1/4}(1 - \ln \frac{h}{m(h)}))$ with respect to the maximal step sizes $\frac{h}{m(h)}$ of the whole fine grids;

(iii) $O(N^{-1/4}(1 + \ln N))$ with respect to the number N of all gridpoints of the whole fine grids.[24]

---

[24] (1986) deals with the method (6.45 in the case of $m(h) \equiv 1$ and equidistant grids. His method yields at most the convergence rate $O(N^{-1/6}(\ln N)^\epsilon)$, ($\epsilon > 1/2$). Kanagawa's

Remark 6.8 *(The rate-of-convergence of the discrete RBGARCH to the bounded continuous GARCH.)* Applying Corollary 6.3 to the discrete RB-GARCH and the solution of (6.46) (the bounded continuous GARCH), we get the following rate-of-convergence result

$$W_p(D(\Lambda), D(\Lambda^E)) = O(h^{1/2}(1 - \ln h)). \qquad (6.47)$$

According to (6.47) the distribution of the process Λ^E – obtained by RB-GARCH – and the solution Λ of the SDE (6.46) are closely related, where Λ can be referred to as the ideal, continuous model and Λ^E as its discrete approximation. Moreover, for the model RBGARCH we can estimate the approximation error in terms of the W_p-metric. The link of this model to the SDE (6.45) and its solution, the continuous martingale Λ, immediately allows the use of stochastic calculus and martingale theory to investigate (6.45) and Λ, and draw conclusions for the time discrete process Λ^E defined by the method RBGARCH.

6.4   Shot Noise Processes for Modeling Asset Returns

In this section we present G. Samorodnitsky's (1995) approach to modeling asset returns via non-Markov shot noise processes. The attractive feature of this type of model is that it captures four important empirically observed properties of return processes of the form

$$X(t) = \log \frac{S(t+1)}{S(t)}, \quad t \geq 0,$$

where $S(t)$ is the price asset at time t.

   1. *The marginal distribution of the return process $X(t)$ is heavy tailed:* This means that the tail probabilities are regularly varying at infinity, i.e.,

$$P(X(t) > \lambda) \sim \lambda^{-\alpha}L_1(\lambda) \,, \ P(X(t) < -\lambda) \sim \lambda^{-\alpha}L_2(\lambda), \quad \lambda > 0, \qquad (6.48)$$

for some $\alpha > 0$, where L_1 and L_2 are slowly varying functions.[25]

---

result does not follow from the results proved here and was proved using different tools and different assumptions. Our method yields a better order (essentially $N^{-1/4}$) than Kanagawa's method – we call it (K) – (essentially $N^{-1/6}$). Moreover, in our method one needs to compute the coefficients b and σ only in a small part of the N grid points, namely the points t_k of the coarse subgrids, whereas (K) requires the computation of the coefficients in all N grid points. This shows that our method has also a lower "cost" than (K) for the same N. If we take in the grids for our method and (K) the same numbers n of "expensive" grid points (i.e. points where b and σ have to be computed) or the same corresponding maximal step sizes h, then the orders of our method and (K) are essentially $n^{-1/2}$ and $n^{-1/6} = N^{-1/6}$, or $h^{1/2}$ and $h^{1/6}$, respectively.

[25] See the discussion in Mandelbrot (1963a,b), Fama (1965a), Blattberg and Gonedes (1974), Mittnik and Rachev (1993a,b), Akgiray and Booth (1988), Loretan and Phillips (1994) and

2. *The tails of the return distribution become thinner as the sampling intervals increase:* As it was reported, for example, in Akgiray and Booth (1988), daily returns appear to have heavier tails than weekly returns, which, in turn, appear to have heavier tails than monthly returns, etc. I.e., tail exponent α in (6.48) increases when we add high-frequency observations; see also Guillaume et al. (1994).

3. *Clustering and ARCH-GARCH effects:* Returns exhibit periods of high and low volatility as was already observed in Mandelbrot (1963a,b) (see also Bollerslev, Chou and Kroner, 1992).

4. *Long-range dependence:* This means that $X(t)$ and $X(t - s)$ are highly dependent, even for very large time lags, s. This is typically observed through the sample autocorrelation function of squared or absolute returns (see Bollerslev, Chou and Kroner, 1992, Guillaume et al. 1994).

Samorodnitsky (1995) proposed a class of continuous time shot models for return processes that arise naturally and intuitively, if one thinks of market activity being caused by new events. He assumed that events i, $i = 1, 2, \ldots$, arrive at (random) times, T_i, and have the (random) initial effect Z_i which then changes over time according to deterministic function $f(t)$, $t \geq 0$. R.v.'s $Z_1, Z_2, \ldots$ are assumed to be i.i.d. Because the effect of event i begins at the time of its arrival, T_i, one can think of the return at time t as the sum of the effects caused up t, i.e.,

$$X(t) = \sum_{T_i \leq t} Z_i f(t - T_i).$$

Such a model is a simplification of the general shot noise model[26] described usually as

$$X(t) = \sum_{T_i \leq t} W_i(t - T_i),$$

with i.i.d. stochastic processes $\{W_i(t), t \geq 0\}$. The deterministic nature of the dynamic effect of each event on the market leads to a simpler model, but even this leads to a very rich class of models, which can account for the four observed properties listed above. These processes are non-Markov moving averages; and many statistical problems associated with them are still open.

To give a general description of Samorodnitsky's model, consider the "*cluster Poisson shot noise process*"

$$X(t) = \sum_{i=1}^{\infty} Z_i f(t - T_i), \quad t \in \mathbf{R}, \tag{6.49}$$

McCulloch (1994a) about the range of α in (6.48). The Hill (1975) estimator is frequently used to estimate α. However, this estimator requires large samples to yield reliable results. Simulating, for examples, samples with $\alpha = 1.8$, the Hill estimator of α range from 1.5 to 4.5 for samples below 10,000. If the sample size exceeds 50,000, the estimator becomes reliable.

[26]Shot noise processes were used in risk theory (Klüppelberg and Mikosch, 1995a, in modeling earthquake aftershocks (Vere-Jones, 1970) and computer failure times (Lewis, 1964).

where $f : \mathbf{R} \to \mathbf{R}$ is a measurable function vanishing on the negative half-line; $Z_1, Z_2, \ldots$ are i.i.d. r.v. with a common d.f. F; and $T_1, T_2, \ldots$ constitute a *cluster Poisson process* independent of the sequence $Z_1, Z_2, \ldots$. Such a process is defined by three parameters; namely *cluster arrival rate* ρ, *cluster size probabilities* p_k, $k \geq 1$ and *displacement distribution* H. That is, cluster "centers" C_j, $j \geq 1$, arrive according to a time homogeneous Poisson process with rate ρ. The jth cluster is of size $K_j = k$ with probability p_k, $k \geq 1$; and the points in this cluster are located at $C_j + D_{ij}$, $i = 1, \ldots, K_j$. Array $\{D_{ij}, i \geq 1, j \geq 1\}$ is an array of i.i.d. random variables, which have common distribution H and are independent of both the Poisson arrivals $\{C_j, j \geq 1\}$ and the i.i.d. discrete r.v. $\{K_j, j \geq 1\}$ with probabilities p_k, $k \geq 1$.

The cluster Poisson shot noise process $(X(t), t \in \mathbf{R})$ is infinitely divisible, whenever it is well defined; i.e. whenever it is defined by a convergent sum. To understand its properties it is more convenient to regard this process as a stochastic integral,

$$X(t) = \int_{\mathbf{R}} f(t - s) M(ds), \quad t \in \mathbf{R}, \tag{6.50}$$

with respect to a cluster compound Poisson random measure M defined by

$$M(A) = \sum_{j=1}^{\infty} \sum_{i=1}^{K_j} Z_{ij} \mathbf{1}((C_j + D_{ij}) \in A), \tag{6.51}$$

where Z_{ij}, $i, j \geq 1$ is an i.i.d. array with the common distribution F. This form of representation of the cluster Poisson shot noise model shows that it is also a *moving average* with respect to the random measure M. Define the stochastic integral

$$I(f) = \int_{\mathbf{R}} f(s) M(ds)$$

by

$$I(f) = \lim_{R \to \infty} \int_{\mathbf{R}} f(s) M_R(ds) := \lim_{R \to \infty} I_R(f),$$

where

$$M_R(A) = \sum_{|C_j| \leq R} \sum_{i=1}^{K_j} Z_{ij} \mathbf{1} \left(C_j + D_{ij} \right) \in A \right).$$

Lemma 6.3 Suppose that

$$\int_{\mathbf{R}} \sum_{k=1}^{\infty} p_k \mathbf{E} \left(1 \wedge \left| \left(\sum_{i=1}^{k} Z_{i1} f(x + D_{i1}) \right) \right| \right) dx < \infty. \tag{6.52}$$

Then, the stochastic integral $I(f) = \int_{\mathbf{R}} f(s) M(ds)$ exists a.s. and is an infinitely divisible random variable with ch.f.

$$\mathbf{E} e^{i\theta I(f)} = \exp \left\{ -\rho \int_{\mathbf{R}} [1 - \varphi_K(\mathbf{E} e^{i\theta Z_{11} f(x + D_{11})})] dx \right\}, \tag{6.53}$$

where $\varphi_K(s) = \sum_{k=1}^{\infty} p_k s^k$, $|s| \leq 1$, is the generating function of the cluster of size K. Moreover, the Lévy measure of $I(f)$ is given by

$$\mu = \rho \sum_{k=1}^{\infty} p_k \mu_k, \tag{6.54}$$

where $\mu_k = (\text{Leb} \otimes P) \circ T_k^{-1}$, $k \geq 1$ and T_k is a map from $\mathbf{R} \times \Omega$ to $\mathbf{R}$ defined by

$$T_k(x, \omega) = \sum_{i=1}^{k} Z_{i1}(\omega) f(x + D_{i1}(\omega)), \quad yx \in R, \omega \in \Omega. \tag{6.55}$$

For the proof of this lemma and the rest of the statements in this section we refer to Samorodnitsky (1995).

If the compounding distribution F is symmetric, then the integrability condition (6.52) may be replaced by the weaker condition

$$\int_{\mathbf{R}} \sum_{k=1}^{\infty} p_k E \left(1 \wedge \left| \left(\sum_{i=1}^{k} Z_{i1} f(x + D_{i1}) \right) \right|^2 \right) dx < \infty. \tag{6.56}$$

The assumption of homogeneous arrivals for the underlying Poisson process clearly implies that, once the function f satisfies (6.52), the well defined stochastic process $\{X(t), t \geq 0\}$, given by (6.49), is a stationary process. Its second-order properties are described by the following lemma.

Lemma 6.4 Assume (6.48) holds, and that $\mathbf{E}K_1^2 < \infty$, $\mathbf{E}Z_{11}^2 < \infty$ and

$$\int_{R} f(y)^2 dy < \infty.$$

Then, the stochastic process $\{X(t), t \geq 0\}$ has a finite second moment; and its covariance function is given by

$$R(t) = \rho \mathbf{E}K_1 \mathbf{E}Z_{11}^2 \int_{\mathbf{R}} f(y) f(y + t) dy + \rho(\mathbf{E}K_1^2 - \mathbf{E}K_1)(\mathbf{E}Z_{11})^2 \delta(t), \tag{6.57}$$

where

$$\delta(t) \int_{\mathbf{R}} f(y + t) \left(\int_{\mathbf{R}^2} f(y + x_1 - x_2) H(dx_1) H(dx_2) \right) dy. \tag{6.58}$$

The next theorem shows that shot noise processes exhibit the four observed properties listed above. For simplicity, chose $F(x)$ to be a standard Laplace distribution, i.e., its density is given by

$$F'(x) = \frac{1}{2} e^{-|x|}, \quad x \in \mathbf{R}.$$

For a $\gamma > 0$, $d > 0$ and an integer $m \geq 1$ let

$$f_{\gamma,d,m}(s) = j^\gamma \cos \pi \frac{j}{m}, \tag{6.59}$$

$$\text{if} \quad s \in \left(j - (j+1)^{-(d+1)}, j + (j+1)^{-(d+1)} \right), \quad j \geq 1,$$

and $f_{\gamma,d,m}(s) = 0$ if s does not belong to any of the above intervals. Define

$$X_{\gamma,d,m}(t) = \int_{\mathbf{R}} f_{\gamma,d,m}(t-s) M(ds), \quad t \geq 0, \tag{6.60}$$

where M is a cluster compound Poisson random measure. The following theorem describes the properties of process $X_{\gamma,d,m}$.

Theorem 6.7 (i) Suppose that $\mathbf{E}K_1 < \infty$. Then, $X_{\gamma,d,m}$ is a well-defined stationary stochastic process.
(ii) Assume that

$$\mathbf{E}K_1^2 < \infty \tag{6.61}$$

and that the displacement distribution H has a density. Then,

$$P(X_{\gamma,d,m}(t) > \lambda) \sim c_{d,\gamma,m}^{(1)} \rho \mathbf{E}K_1 \lambda^{-d/\gamma}, \quad \lambda \to \infty, \tag{6.62}$$

where

$$c_{d,\gamma,m}^{(1)} = \frac{1}{2\gamma m} \Gamma(d/\gamma) \sum_{i=0}^{2m-1} \left| \cos\left(\pi \frac{i}{m} \right) \right|^{d/\gamma}.$$

(iii) Under the assumptions of (ii), if $\gamma > 1$, then,

$$P\left(\sum_{k=0}^{2m-1} X_{\gamma,d,m}(t+k) > \lambda \right) \sim \tag{6.63}$$

$$\begin{cases} c_{d,\gamma,m}^{(2)} \rho \mathbf{E}K_1 \lambda^{-(d+1)/\gamma}, & if \frac{d+1}{\gamma} < \frac{d}{\gamma-1}, \\ c_{d,\gamma,m}^{(3)} \rho \mathbf{E}K_1 \lambda^{-d/(\gamma-1)}, & if \frac{d+1}{\gamma} > \frac{d}{\gamma-1}, \\ (c_{d,\gamma,m}^{(2)} + c_{d,\gamma,m}^{(3)}) \rho \mathbf{E}K_1 \lambda^{-(d+1)/\gamma}, & if \frac{d+1}{\gamma} = \frac{d}{\gamma-1}, \end{cases}$$

and, if $\gamma \leq 1$, then,

$$P\left(\sum_{k=0}^{2m-1} X_{\gamma,d,m}(t+k) > \lambda \right) \sim c_{d,\gamma,m}^{(2)} \rho \mathbf{E}K_1 \lambda^{-(d+1)/\gamma} \tag{6.64}$$

as $\lambda \to \infty$. Here,

$$c_{d,\gamma,m}^{(2)} = \frac{1}{m} \Gamma\left((d+\gamma+1)/\gamma \right) \sum_{i=1}^{2m-1} \sum_{j=1}^{2m} \left| \sum_{k=0}^{i-1} \cos(\pi(j+k)/2m) \right|^{(d+1)/\gamma} > 0$$

and

$$c_{d,\gamma,m}^{(3)} = \frac{1}{\gamma - 1}(\gamma m)^{d/(\gamma-1)}\Gamma\left(d/(\gamma - 1)\right).$$

(iv) Assume that (6.61) holds and that

$$d > 2\gamma. \tag{6.65}$$

Then, process $X_{\gamma,d,m}$ has a finite variance, and its covariance function $R(n)$ satisfies, as $n \to \infty$,

$$R(n) \sim \kappa_{d,\gamma,m}\rho E K_1 n^{2\gamma-d} \sum_{i=1}^{2m} \cos(\pi i/m)\cos(\pi(i+n)/m) \tag{6.66}$$

in the sense that the product $n^{d-2\gamma}R(n)$ has at most $2m$ subsequential limits given by (6.66), all of which are finite, and some of which are positive. Here

$$\kappa_{d,\gamma,m} = 2m^{-1}\int_0^\infty x^\gamma(1+x)^{\gamma-d-1}ds.$$

As the theorem shows the probability tails of the process $X_{\gamma,d,m}$ are heavy, and the tail of $\sum_{k=0}^{2m-1} X_{\gamma,d,m}(k)$ is lighter than that $X_{\gamma,d,m}(0)$, which corresponds to the observed properties of financial returns. Moreover, the covariance function of $X_{\gamma,d,m}$ decays like a power, and not as exponential, function, and, if $2\gamma < d \leq 2\gamma + 1$, then

$$\sum_{n=1}^\infty |R(n)| = \infty,$$

that is, $X_{\gamma,d,m}$ exhibits long range dependence in its usual meaning (cf. Brockwell and Davis (1991)).

6.5 Conditionally Exponential Dependence Model for Financial Returns

In this section we propose a new model of the asset market based on the idea of local conditionally exponential dependence (CED) property of complex systems [27]. This idea has been applied recently in the context of universal dynamical behavior of physical systems (see Weron and Jurlewicz (1993) and Jurlewicz, Weron and Weron (1996)).

In ARCH and GARCH models, the effects of shocks on the conditional variance of a financial time series typically decay in an exponential manner

---

[27]The results in this section are due to Rachev, Weron and Weron (1997).

and are long lasting (Bollerslev, Chou and Kroner (1992) and Engle and Mezrich (1995)). For heavy tailed stable GARCH models see Panorska, Mittnik and Rachev (1995). The dependence in the CED model measured by the conditional return excess decays similarly as in ARCH models in an exponential way, but reflects both short as well as long range effects. This new probabilistic idea concerns systems in which the behavior of each individual entity strongly depends on its short- and long-range random interactions.

The model is a discrete time economy with a finite number of trading dates from time 0 to time T and its uncertainty has a global impact on the market index daily returns on the interval $[0, T]$. Let R_{iN} be the positive (or the absolute value of negative) part of the ith agent's return. The economy is populated by a finite, but a large number N of agents (investors) on the market whose beliefs satisfy the following assumptions.

Assumption 1. For the ith investor the following CED property holds:

$$\phi_{iN}(r|a, b) = P\left(R_{iN} \geq r \mid A_i = a, \, b_N^{-1} \max(B_1^i, \ldots, B_{i-1}^i, B_{i+1}^i, \ldots, B_N^i) = b\right)$$
$$(6.67)$$
$$= \exp(-[a \min(r, b)]^c),$$

where r, a, b are non-negative constants, b_N is a suitable, positive normalizing constant and $c \geq 1$. The range of the exponent c is justified by the reversion tendency of the market.

Assumption 2. We assume that there are N investors each with a different investment horizon ("short-range interaction") affected by a different information set ("long-range interaction") and $N \to \infty$. The investment horizon of the investor is reflected by the random variable A_i, while $\{B_j^i, j = 1, 2, \ldots, N, j \neq i\}$ reflect the information flow to this investor.

The probability that the return R_{iN} will be not less than r is conditioned by the value a taken by the random variable A_i and by the value b taken by the maximum of the set of random variables $\{B_j^i, j = 1, 2, \ldots, N, j \neq i\}$. Therefore (1) can be rewritten as follows:

$$\phi_{iN}(r \mid a, b) \equiv \begin{cases} 1 & for \quad r = 0 \\ \exp(-(ar)^c) & for \quad r < b \\ \exp(-(ab)^c) & for \quad r \geq b, \end{cases} \qquad (6.68)$$

i.e., the conditional return excess $\phi_{iN}(r \mid a, b)$ decays exponentially with a decay rate a and exponent c as r tends to the value b. Then it takes a constant value $\ll 1$. The basic statistical assumption is that

Assumption 3. The random variables $A_1, A_2, \ldots$ and $B_1^i, B_2^i, \ldots$ form independent sequences of non-negative, independent, identically distributed (iid) random variables. The variables $R_{1N}, \ldots, R_{NN}$ are also non-negative, iid for each N.

The assumption 3 can be partially justified by the following argument. Institutional trading is a major factor in the determination of security prices. If professional investment managers have similar beliefs, then the iid distributions assumption may hold as a first approximation. Professional managers are likely to have similar beliefs because they have access to a similar information sources. This uniformity of information over time would tend to generate similar beliefs.

Let us stress however, that the above relationship of each R_{iN} with A_i and $\max(B_1^i, \ldots, B_{i-1}^i, B_{i+1}^i, \ldots, B_N^i)$, see (1), incorporates the dependence on external conditions. Note that (1) precisely defines the meaning of random variables related by it. It does not hold for sets of any arbitrarily chosen variables. If R_{iN} has to denote a return, then $A_i = a$ has the sense of an individual risk aversion factor and

$$b_N^{-1} \max(B_1^i, \ldots, B_{i-1}^i, B_{i+1}^i, \ldots, B_N^i) = b$$

the sense of a submarket maximal risk factor given by

$$\phi_{iN}(r \mid b) = \int_0^\infty \phi_{iN}(r \mid a, b) dF_A(a),$$

where F_A is the common distribution function (but unknown !) of the sequence of random variables $\{A_i\}$. The cut-off at $r = b$ in (2) takes into the considerations unlimited returns with a small, but non-zero probability. Thus it may represent an arbitrage opportunity.

Theorem 1. Let the global behavior of the asset market be given by

$$\phi(r) = \lim_{N \to \infty} P(r_N \min(R_{1N}, \ldots R_{NN}) \geq r), \qquad (6.69)$$

where r_N is a suitable, positive normalizing constant. Under the above assumptions, the function $\phi(r)$, fulfills the following Global Return Equation (GRE):

$$\frac{d\phi}{dr}(r) = -\alpha\lambda(\lambda r)^{\alpha-1} \left(1 - \exp(-\frac{(\lambda r)^{-\alpha}}{k}) \right) \phi(r), \qquad (6.70)$$

where the parameters $\lambda > 0, k > 0$ and $\alpha = \alpha' c$ $(c > 1, 0 < \alpha' \leq 1)$ are determined by the limiting procedure in (3).

It is a straightforward result that the solution of eq. (4) has the following integral form

$$\phi(r) = \exp[-\frac{1}{k}\int_0^{k(\lambda r)^\alpha} (1 - \exp(-\frac{1}{x}))dx].\qquad(6.71)$$

Hence the function $\phi(r)$ monotonically decreases from $\phi(0) = 1$ to $\phi(\infty) = 0$.

Observe that (3) defines the return excess $P(\tilde{R} \geq r)$ of a system as a whole, where $\tilde{R}$ represents the global return. The derivative $f(r) = -\frac{d\phi}{dr}(r)$ represents the frequency distribution (probability density) of $\tilde{R}$. It is easy to check that the density $f(r)$ exhibits the two power-laws:

$$f(r) \propto \begin{cases} (\lambda r)^{\alpha-1} & \text{for} \quad \lambda r \ll 1, \\ (\lambda r)^{-\frac{\alpha}{k}-1} & \text{for} \quad \lambda r \gg 1. \end{cases}\qquad(6.72)$$

Hence, the global return (GR) distribution $F(r)$ is characterized by the 3 parameters α, λ, and k. Here α is the shape and λ the scale parameter, respectively. At this point let us stress the role of the parameter k. It decides how fast the information flow is spread out in the market; $k \to 0$ denotes the case when the long-range interaction is neglected. So, there are no unlimited returns on the market. If $k \to 0$, eq. (4) takes the form $\frac{d\phi}{dr}(r) = -\alpha(\lambda r)^{\alpha-1}\phi(r)$ with the solution $\phi(r) = \exp[-(\lambda r)^\alpha]$. Thus, in the case when $k \to 0$, the probability density of the global return obtains the well-known form of the Weibull density

$$f(r) = \alpha\lambda(\lambda r)^{\alpha-1} \exp(-(\lambda r)^\alpha),\qquad(6.73)$$

and the following specific cases are observed:

- if $\alpha' = 1$ (A_i is a non-random variate), then $\alpha = c$;

- if $\alpha = 1$, then $f(r) = \lambda\exp(-\lambda r)$ - the density of the global return has the exponential tail for $\lambda r \gg 1$;

- if $\alpha = 2$, then $f(r) = 2\lambda^2 r\exp(-(\lambda r)^2)$ - the density of the global return has the normal tail for $\lambda r \gg 1$.

In general, the parameter $0 < \alpha' \leq 1$ slows down, in comparison with an individual investor, the return rate $\alpha\lambda(\lambda r)^{\alpha-1}$ of the global market return distribution. Let us observe that the inclusion of unlimited returns ($k > 0$) changes essentially the tail of the density $f(r)$ for $\lambda r \gg 1$. Both solutions, eqs (6) and (7), have the same behavior for $\lambda r \ll 1$. Thus, the above discussion explains well the special role of the Weibull distribution in modeling of asset returns for markets with no arbitrage, see chapter 2. However, our model leads one step further introducing the new type of return distribution completely described by GRE (4). It exhibits the two power-laws property (6) of the density of the global returns, evident in the empirical data.

Notice that the form of $\phi(r)$ given by (5) does not indicate directly any commonly known probability distribution function. However, it can be shown its close relationship with a two–parameter Pareto distribution. Indeed, taking into account two terms in the series expansion of the exponential term $\exp x^{-1}$ in the integrand, one obtains the approximate form

$$\phi_a(r) = [1 + k(\lambda r)^\alpha]^{-\frac{1}{k}} = 1 - F_{\frac{1}{k},\alpha}(r)$$

of the solution of (4). So, the GR distribution $F(r) = 1 - \phi(r)$ can be approximated by the two–parameter Pareto distribution $F_{\frac{1}{k},\alpha}(r)$. Observe that $\lim\limits_{r\to 0}\frac{\phi(r)}{\phi_a(r)} = 1$ and $\lim\limits_{r\to\infty}\frac{\phi(r)}{\phi_a(r)} = \exp[-(1-\gamma)/k]$, where $\gamma = 0.577216...$ is the Euler gamma constant. Hence we have the following

Theorem 2. The GR distribution function $F(r)$ determined by the GRE (4) *is well approximated by the following two–parameter Pareto distribution function* $F_{\frac{1}{k},\alpha}(r) = 1 - [1 + k(\lambda r)^\alpha]^{-\frac{1}{k}}$

$$F(r) = \begin{cases} F_{\frac{1}{k},\alpha}(r) & \text{for} \quad \lambda r \ll 1, \\ e^{-(1-\gamma)/k)}F_{\frac{1}{k},\alpha}(r) & \text{for} \quad \lambda r \gg 1. \end{cases} \tag{6.74}$$

6.6   Proofs of the Results on Numerical Solution of Stochastic Differential Equations

Proof of Theorem 6.3. The proof Theorem 6.3 uses three lemmas which are stated below and proved in Gelbbrich (1995). The first one provides the multi-dimensional Hölder inequality in its continuous and discrete versions.

Lemma 6.5 *(Multi-dimensional Hölder's inequality)* a) Let $p \in [1,\infty)$, $s < t$, and let $g : [s,t] \to \mathbf{R}^d$, $g(u) = (g_1(u),\ldots,g_d(u))^T$ $(u \in [s,t])$, be a Borel measurable function such that $|g_i|^p$ is Lebesque integrable over $[s,t]$ for $i = 1,\ldots,d$. Then

$$\left\| \int\limits_s^t g(u)du \right\|^p \le (t-s)^{p-1} \int\limits_s^t \|g(u)\|^p du.$$

b) Let $p \in [1,\infty)$ and $a_i \in \mathbf{R}^d$ for all $i = 1,\ldots,r$. Then

$$\left\| \sum_{i=1}^r a_i \right\|^p \le r^{p-1} \sum_{i=1}^r \|a_i\|^p.$$

To show Theorem 6.3 we use multi-dimensional martingale inequalities which the following lemma contains in both continuous and discrete version.[28]

---

[28]The lemma is a consequence of a generalization of results in Ikeda and Watanabe (1981) and Jannssen (1984) to the multi-dimensional case and Lemma 6.5.

Lemma 6.6 *(Multivariate continuous and discrete martingale inequalities.)* Let $p \in [2, \infty)$. Then there exist constants C_p, $A_p > 0$ such that the following hold:

a) Let $(w(t), \mathcal{F}(t))_{t \in [\alpha, \beta]}$ be a one-dimensional standard Wiener process on a probability space $(\Omega, \mathcal{A}, O)$. Then for every function $g = (g_1, \ldots, g_d) :$ $[\alpha, \beta] \times \Omega \to \mathbf{R}^d$ with the properties

(i) $g(\cdot, \omega)$ is square-integrable over $[\alpha, \beta]$ for almost all $w \in \Omega$,

(ii) $g(u) = g(u, \cdot)$ is $\mathcal{F}(u)$-measurable for all $u \in [\alpha, \beta]$, we have

$$\mathbf{E} \sup_{\alpha \leq s \leq t} \left\| \int_\alpha^s g(u) d\omega(u) \right\|^p \leq [d(\beta - \alpha)]^{p/2-1} C_p \int_\alpha^t \mathbf{E} \|g(u)\|^p du,$$

for all $t \in [\alpha, \beta]$.

b) Let $(M_s, \mathcal{F}_s)_{s=0,\ldots,r}$ be an $\mathbf{R}^d$-valued martingale (i.e. each component is a martingale), and let $p \in [2, \infty)$. Then with $\Delta M_s := M_s - M_{s-1}$ we have

$$\mathbf{E} \max_{0 \leq s \leq r} \|M_s\|^p \leq A_p (dr)^{p/2-1} \mathbf{E} \sum_{s=1}^r \|\Delta M_s\|^p.$$

The next lemma states the classical Gronwall inequality with its continuous and discrete versions.

Lemma 6.7 *(Gronwall's inequalities)* a) Let $f : [t_0, T] \to [0, \infty)$ be a continuous function and c_1, c_2 be positive constants. If for all $t \in [t_0, T]$

$$f(t) \leq c_1 + c_2 \int_{t_0}^t f(s) ds$$

then

$$\sup_{t_0 \leq t \leq T} f(t) \leq c_1 e^{c_2(T - t_0)}$$

b) Let $a_0, \ldots, a_n$ and c_1, c_2 be non-negative real numbers. If for all $k = 0, \ldots, n$

$$a_k \leq c_1 + c_2 \frac{1}{n} \sum_{i=0}^{k-1} a_i$$

then

$$\max 0 \leq i \leq n a_i \leq c_1 e^{c_2}.$$

Proof of Theorem 6.3 We start showing the boundedness of the p-th moment of the solution on r SDE:

$$x(t) - x_0 = \int_{t_0}^t b(x, s) ds + \int_{t_0}^t \sigma(x, s) dw(s) \qquad (6.75)$$

$$= \int_{t_0}^{t} b(x,s)ds + \sum_{j=1}^{q} \int_{t_0}^{t} \sigma_j(x,s)dw_j(s), \quad t \in [t_0,T], x_0 \in \mathbf{R}^d,$$

(cf. (6.35)) Applying Lemmas 6.5 and 6.6 and the boundness condition (6.37) we get : for all $t \in [t_0,T]$,

$$\mathbf{E} \sup_{t_0 \leq s \leq t} \|x(s)\|^p$$

$$\leq K \left(\|x_0\|^p + \mathbf{E} \sup_{t_0 \leq s \leq t} (T_{t_0})^{p-1} \int_{t_0}^{s} \|b(x,u)\|^p du \right.$$

$$\left. + \sum_{j=1}^{q} \mathbf{E} \sup_{t_0 \leq s \leq t} \left\| \int_{t_0}^{s} \sigma_j(x;u)dw_j(u) \right\|^p \right)$$

$$\leq K \left(1 + \int_{t_0}^{t} \mathbf{E}\|b(x,u)\|^p du + \sum_{j=1}^{q} \int_{t_0}^{t} \mathbf{E}\|\sigma_j(x,u)\|^p du \right)$$

$$\leq K \left(1 + \int_{t_0}^{t} \mathbf{E} \sup_{t_0 \leq s \leq u} \|x(s)\|^p du \right).$$

Next, applying Lemma 6.7, we have

$$\mathbf{E} \sup_{t_0 \leq t \leq T} \|x(t)\|^p \leq K. \tag{6.76}$$

Recall our first step of the discretization procedure:

$$y^E(t) = x_0 + \int_{t_0}^{t} b(y^E, [s]_G)ds \tag{6.77}$$

$$+ \sum_{j=1}^{q} \int_{t_0}^{t} \sigma_j(y^E, [s]_G)dw_j(s) \quad \text{for all } t \in [t_0,T].$$

Consider the difference between $x(t)$ in (6.75) and $y^E(t)$ in (6.77):

$$x(t) - y^E(t) = \int_{t_0}^{t} [b(x,s) - b(x,[s]_G)]ds + \int_{t_0}^{t} [b(x,[s]_G) - b(y^E,[s]_G)]ds$$

$$+ \sum_{j=1}^{q} \left\{ \int_{t_0}^{t} [\sigma_j(x,s) - \sigma_j(x,[s]_G)]dw_j(s) \right. \tag{6.78}$$

$$+ \int_{t_0}^{t} [\sigma_j(x, [s]_G) - \sigma_j(y^E, [s]_G)]dw_j(s) \Bigg\}$$

$$=: \quad J_1(t) + J_2(t) + \sum_{j=1}^{q}\{J_{3j}(t) + J_{4j}(t)\} \quad t \in [t_0, T].$$

We now estimate the first two terms in the right-hand-side of (6.78). We apply Lemma 6.5 and the Lipschitz regularity condition (6.38):

$$\mathbf{E} \sup_{t_0 \leq r \leq t} \|J_1(r)\|^p \leq (T - t_0)^{p-1} L^p \int_{t_0}^{t} \mathbf{E} \sup_{t_0 \leq u \leq s} \|x(u) - x([u]_G)\|^p ds, \quad (6.79)$$

$$\mathbf{E} \sup_{t_0 \leq r \leq t} \|J_2(r)\|^p \leq (T - t_0)^{p-1} L^p \int_{t_0}^{t} \mathbf{E} \sup_{t_0 \leq u \leq s} \|x([u]_G) - y^E(u)\|^p ds$$

$$\leq K \int_{t_0}^{t} \mathbf{E} \sup_{t_0 \leq u \leq s} \|x([u]_G) - y^E(u)\|^p ds,$$

$$t \in [t_0, T]. \qquad (6.80)$$

Similarly we estimate the terms in the sum on the right of (6.78); this time we apply Lemma 6.6 and again (6.38) to get

$$\mathbf{E} \sup_{t_0 \leq r \leq t} \|J_{3j}(r)\|^p \leq K \int_{t_0}^{t} \mathbf{E} \sup_{t_0 \leq u \leq s} \|x(u) - x([u]_G)\|^p ds, \qquad (6.81)$$

$$\mathbf{E} \sup_{t_0 \leq r \leq t} \|J_{4j}(r)\|^p \leq K \int_{t_0}^{t} \mathbf{E} \sup_{t_0 \leq u \leq s} \|x([u]_G) - y^E([u]_G)\|^p ds$$

$$\leq K \int_{t_0}^{t} \mathbf{E} \sup_{t_0 \leq u \leq s} \|x(u) - y^E(u)\|^p ds. \qquad (6.82)$$

To get a bound for the right-hand-side of (6.81) we apply Lemmas 6.5, 6.6, the boundness condition (6.37) and bound (6.78):

$$\mathbf{E} \sup_{t_0 \leq u \leq s} \|x(u) - x([u]_G)\|^p \qquad (6.83)$$

$$\leq K \cdot \mathbf{E} \sup_{t_0 \leq u \leq s} \left\{ \left\| \int_{[u]_G}^{u} b(x, v)dv \right\|^p + \sum_{j=1}^{q} \left\| \int_{[u]_G}^{u} \sigma_j(x, v)dw_j(v) \right\|^p \right\}$$

$$\leq K \cdot \mathbf{E} \sup_{t_0 \leq u \leq s} \left\{ h^{p-1} \int\limits_{[u]_G}^{u} \|b(x,v)\|^p dv + \sum_{j=1}^{q} h^{p/2-1} \int\limits_{[u]_G}^{u} \|\sigma_j(x,v)\|^p dv \right\}$$

$$\leq K \left\{ h^{p/2} \left(1 + \mathbf{E} \sup_{t_0 \leq t \leq T} \|x(t)\|^p \right) \right\} \leq K \cdot h^{p/2}.$$

We now summarize our estimates in (6.78) - (6.83) to get

$$\mathbf{E} \sup_{t_0 \leq r \leq t} \|x(r) - y^E(r)\|^p \leq K \left[\mathbf{E} \sup_{t_0 \leq r \leq t} \|J_1(r)\|^p + \mathbf{E} \sup_{t_0 \leq r \leq t} \|J_2(r)\|^p \right.$$

$$\left. + \sum_{j=1}^{q} \left\{ \mathbf{E} \sup_{t_0 \leq r \leq t} \|J_{3j}(r)\|^p + \mathbf{E} \sup_{t_0 \leq r \leq t} \|J_{4j}(r)\|^p \right\} \right]$$

$$\leq K \left\{ \int_{t_0}^{t} \mathbf{E} \sup_{t_0 \leq u \leq s} \|x(u) - y^E(u)\|^p ds + H^{p/2} \right\}, \quad \text{for all } t \in [t_0, T]$$

The above bound together with the Gronwald Lemma 6.7 yields the desired inequality

$$\mathbf{E} \sup_{t_0 \leq t \leq T} \|x(t) - y^E(t)\|^p \leq K \cdot h^{p/2}. \tag{6.84}$$

completing the proof of Theorem 6.3.   □

Proof of Theorem 6.4. We need to show that

$$\mathbf{E} \sup_{t_0 \leq t \leq T} \|y^E(t) - \tilde{y}^E(t)\|^p \leq K \left(\frac{h}{m(h)} \right)^{p/2} \left(1 + \ln \left(\frac{m(h)}{h} \right) \right)^{p/2}, \tag{6.85}$$

where $y^E(t)$ is given by (6.77) and $\tilde{y}^E(t)$ is defined in the second step of our discretization method:

$$\begin{cases} \tilde{y}^E \text{ be continuous, and linear in the intervals } [u_{i-1}^k, u_i^k], i = 1, \ldots, m_k, \\ k = 0, \ldots, n-1, \\ \text{with } \tilde{y}^E(u_i^k), i = 0, \ldots, m_k, \ k = 0, \ldots, n-1 \end{cases} \tag{6.86}$$

cf. (6.44).

We start the proof of (6.85) with the following lemma:[29]

Lemma 6.8 Let $a_0 < a_1 < \ldots < a_r$ be a partition of $[a_0, a_r]$ with maximal step size $\Delta := \max_{0 \leq i \leq r-1}(a_{i+1} - a_i)$, and $(\tilde{w}(t))_{t \in [a_0, a_r]}$ be a one-dimensional standard Wiener process. Then

$$\mathbf{E} \max_{0 \leq i \leq r-1} \sup_{a_i \leq t \leq a_{i+1}} |\tilde{w}(t) - \tilde{w}(a_i)|^p \leq K \cdot \Delta^{p/2} (1 + \ln r)^{p/2}. \tag{6.87}$$

---

[29]The proof of Lemma 6.8 can be found in Gelbrich (1995), see Lemma 3.3. The proof of Theorem 6.4 follows the lines of the proof of Theorem 3.4 in Gelbrich (1995).

Now consider the process $\bar{y}^E$ with $\bar{y}^E(t_0) = x_0$, $\bar{y}^E(u_i^k) = \tilde{y}^E(u_i^k)$, $\bar{y}^E(t) = \bar{y}^E(u_{i-1}^k)$ for $t \in [u_{i-1}^k, u_i^k)$ $k = 0, \ldots, n-1; i = 1, \ldots, m_k)$. Then we have

$$
\mathbf{E} \sup_{t_0 \leq t \leq T} \left\| y^E(t) - \bar{y}^E(t) \right\|^p
$$

$$
\leq K \left\{ \mathbf{E} \sup_{t_0 \leq t \leq T} \left\| \int_{[t]_G^*}^t b(y^E, [t]_G) ds \right\|^p \right.
$$

$$
\left. + \sum_{j=1}^q \mathbf{E} \sup_{t_0 \leq t \leq T} \left\| \sigma_j(y^E, [t]_G) \int_{[t]_G^*}^t dw_j(s) \right\|^p \right\}
$$

$$
\leq K \left\{ \mathbf{E} \sup_{t_0 \leq t \leq T} \left[(t - [t]_G^*)^p M^p (1 + \sup_{t_0 \leq s \leq t} \| y^E([s]_G) \|^p) \right] \right.
$$

$$
\left. + M^p \sum_{j=1}^q \mathbf{E} \max_{0 \leq k \leq n-1, 0 \leq i \leq m_k-1} \sup_{u_i^k \leq t \leq u_{i+1}^k} |w_j(t) - w_j(u_i^k)|^p \right\}
$$

$$
\leq K \left\{ \max_{0 \leq k \leq n-1} \left(\frac{h}{m_k} \right)^p \left(1 + \mathbf{E} \sup_{t_0 \leq t \leq T} \| y^E(t) \|^p \right) \right.
$$

$$
\left. + \sum_{j=1}^q \max_{0 \leq k \leq n-1} \left(\frac{h}{m_k} \right)^{p/2} (1 + \ln(n \cdot m(h)^\alpha))^{p/2} \right\}
$$

$$
\leq K \left\{ 1 + \mathbf{E} \sup_{t_0 \leq t \leq T} \| y^E(t) \|^p \right\} \left(\frac{h}{m(h)} \right)^{p/2} (1 + \ln n + \ln m(h))^{p/2},
$$

here we have applied Lemma 6.5, the boundness condition (6.37), Lemma 6.8 and the assumptions on our grid:

$$
t_k - t_{k-1} = \frac{T - t_0}{n} =: h \leq 1 \text{ for all } k = 1, \ldots, n \text{ and } \hat{h}/h \in \mathbf{N}, \tag{6.88}
$$

$$
1 \leq m_k \leq m(h)^\alpha \text{ for all } k = 0, \ldots, n-1, \tag{6.89}
$$

$$
u_i^k - u_{i-1}^k = \frac{h}{m_k} \leq \beta \frac{h}{m(h)} \text{ for all } k = 0, \ldots, n-1, \, i = 1, \ldots, m_k, \tag{6.90}
$$

cf. (6.41) and (6.42).
By the Minkovski inequality

$$
\left(\mathbf{E} \sup_{t_0 \leq t \leq T} \| y^E(t) \|^p \right)^{1/p} \leq \left(\mathbf{E} \sup_{t_0 \leq t \leq T} \| x(t) - y^E(t) \|^p \right)^{1/p}
$$

$$
+ \left(\mathbf{E} \sup_{t_0 \leq t \leq T} \| x(t) \|^p \right)^{1/p}. \tag{6.91}
$$

The right-hand side is bounded of (6.91) (cf. (6.84) and (6.76)). Thus,

$$\mathbf{E} \sup_{t_0 \leq t \leq T} \left\| y^E(t) \right\|^p \leq K. \tag{6.92}$$

Applying (6.88) we have

$$\mathbf{E} \sup_{t_0 \leq t \leq T} \left\| y^E(t) - \bar{y}^E(t) \right\|^p \leq K \left(\frac{h}{m(h)} \right)^{p/2} (1 + \ln n + \ln m(h))^{p/2}$$

$$\leq K \left(\frac{h}{m(h)} \right)^{p/2} \left(1 + \ln \left(\frac{m(h)}{h} \right)^{p/2} \right). \tag{6.93}$$

To complete the estimate for $\mathbf{E} \sup_{t_0 \leq t \leq T} \left\| y^E(t) - \tilde{y}^E(t) \right\|^p$ we need a bound for $\mathbf{E} \sup_{t_0 \leq t \leq T} \left\| \bar{y}^E(t) - \tilde{y}^E(t) \right\|^p$. From the definition of $\bar{y}^E$ we get

$$\mathbf{E} \sup_{t_0 \leq t \leq T} \left\| \bar{y}^E(t) - \tilde{y}^E(t) \right\|^p$$

$$= \mathbf{E} \max_{0 \leq k \leq n-1, 0 \leq i \leq m_k - 1} \sup_{u_i^k \leq t \leq u_{i+1}^k} \left\| \bar{y}^E(t) - \tilde{y}^E(t) \right\|^p$$

$$= \mathbf{E} \max_{0 \leq k \leq n-1, 0 \leq i \leq m_k - 1} \left\| \tilde{y}^E(u_{i+1}^k) - \tilde{y}^E(u_i^k) \right\|^p$$

$$\leq \mathbf{E} \max_{0 \leq l \leq n-1, 0 \leq i \leq m_k - 1} \sup_{u_i^k \leq t \leq u_{i+1}^k} \left\| y^E(t) - y^E(u_i^k) \right\|^p$$

$$= \mathbf{E} \sup_{t_0 \leq t \leq T} \left\| y^E(t) - \bar{y}^E(t) \right\|^p. \tag{6.94}$$

Finally combining (6.93) and (6.94) we have

$$\mathbf{E} \sup_{t_0 \leq t \leq T} \left\| y^E(t) - \tilde{y}^E(t) \right\|^p \leq K \left\{ \mathbf{E} \sup_{t_0 \leq t \leq T} \left\| y^E(t) - \bar{y}^E(t) \right\|^p \right.$$

$$\left. + \mathbf{E} \sup_{t_0 \leq t \leq T} \sup_{t_0 \leq t \leq T} \left\| \bar{y}^E(t) - \tilde{y}^E(t) \right\|^p \right\}$$

$$\leq K \cdot \mathbf{E} \sup_{t_0 \leq t \leq T} \left\| y^E(t) - \bar{y}^E(t) \right\|^p$$

$$\leq K \left(\frac{h}{m(h)} \right)^{p/2} \left(1 + \ln \left(\frac{m(h)}{h} \right) \right)^{p/2},$$

which shows (6.85) and completes the proof of Theorem 6.4. $\square$

Proof of Theorem 6.5. We need to show that

$$\mathbf{E} \sup_{t_0 \leq t \leq T} \left\| \tilde{y}^E(t) - z^E(t) \right\|^p \leq K \left(\frac{1 + \ln m(h)}{\sqrt{m(h)}} \right)^p; \tag{6.95}$$

where $\tilde{y}^E(t)$ is defined by (6.86) and $z^E(t)$ describes the third step of our discretization procedure:

$$z^E(u_0^0) \;=\; x_0, \text{ and} \tag{6.96}$$

$$z^E(u_i^k) \;=\; x_0 + \sum_{r=0}^{k-1} h_r b(z^E, t_r) + h_k \cdot \frac{i}{m_k} b(z^E, t_k)$$

$$+ \; \sum_{j=1}^{q} \left[\sum_{r=0}^{k-1} \sqrt{\frac{h}{m_r}} \sigma_j(z^E, t_r) \sum_{s=1}^{m_r} \xi_{js}^r + \sqrt{\frac{h}{m_k}} \sigma_j(z^E, t_k) \sum_{s=1}^{i} \xi_{js}^k \right]$$

$$\text{for all } i = 1, \dots, m_k; \, k = 0, \dots, n-1; \tag{6.97}$$

cf. (6.45) and the assumptions of Theorem 6.5 we start the proof of (6.95) with the following lemma:[30]

Lemma 6.9 Let $\mu \in \mathcal{P}(\mathbf{R})$ have the following properties:

$$\int_{-\infty}^{\infty} x \, d\mu(x) = 0, \quad \int_{-\infty}^{\infty} x^2 d\mu(x) = 1 \;\; \text{and} \;\; \int_{-\infty}^{\infty} e^{tx} d\mu(x) < \infty$$

for all t with $\|t\| \le \tau, \tau > 0$.

Then there exist a q-dimensional standard Brownian motion $(w(t))_{t \in [t_0, T]}$ and a set $\{(\xi_{ji}^k) : j = 1, \dots, q \;\; k = 0, \dots, n-1; \; i = 1, \dots, m_k\}$ of i.i.d. r.v.'s with distribution $D(\xi_{11}^0) = \mu$, both on the same probability space, such that if $\Delta_i^k w_j := w_j(u_i^k) - w_j(u_{i-1}^k); \; j = 1, \dots, q; \; i = 1, \dots, m_k; \; k = 0, \dots, n-1$, the following three assertions hold:
a) For $k = 0, \dots, n-1, \; j = 1, \dots, q$,

$$\mathbf{E} \max_{0 \le i \le m_k} \left| \sum_{s=1}^{i} \xi_{js}^k - \sum_{s=1}^{i} \sqrt{\frac{m_k}{h}} \Delta_s^k w_j \right|^p \le K(1 + \ln m(h))^p.$$

b) For $j = 1, \dots, q$,

$$\mathbf{E} \max_{0 \le i \le m_k} \left| \sum_{s=1}^{i} \xi_{js}^k - \sum_{s=1}^{i} \sqrt{\frac{m_k}{h}} \Delta_s^k w_j \right|^p \le K(1 + \ln n + \ln m(h))^p.$$

---

[30]The proof of the lemma can be found in Gelbrich (1995) and uses the KMT-method, see Komlós, Major, and Tusnády (1975).

c) For $k = 1, \ldots, n - 1$,

ξ_{js}^r and $\Delta_s^r w_j$, $j = 1, \ldots, q$; $s = 1, \ldots, m_r$; $r = k, \ldots, n-1$
are independent of the σ-algebra $\mathcal{A}_k$ generated by
$\{\xi_{js}^r \Delta_s^r w_j : j = 1, \ldots, q; \ s = 1, \ldots, m_r; \ r = 0, \ldots, k-1\}$.

Let the common probability space, the Brownian motion $w(t)$ and r.v.'s ξ_{ji}^k are given by Lemma 6.9. Consider the approximation methods (6.86) and (6.96) defined in terms of the above w and ξ_{ji}^k.
Recall the assumptions on our grid (6.88) - (6.90) and denote

$$\Delta_k w_j := w_j(t_{k+1}) - w_j(t_k), \quad j = 1, \ldots, q; \quad k = 0, \ldots, n-1.$$

Consider the approximate solutions (6.86) and (6.87) only in the grid points t_k of the coarse subgrid of G. Then, applying Lemma 6.5

$$\mathbf{E} \max_{0 \le f \le k} \|\tilde{y}^E(t_f) - z^E(t_f)\|^p$$

$$\le K \left\{ \mathbf{E} \max_{0 \le f \le k} \left\| \sum_{r=0}^{f-1} h_r[b(\tilde{y}^E, t_r) - b(z^E, t_r)] \right\|^p \right.$$

$$\left. + \sum_{j=1}^q \mathbf{E} \max_{0 \le f \le k} \left\| \sum_{r=0}^{f-1} \left[\sigma_j(\tilde{y}^E, t_r)\Delta_r w_j - \sigma_j(z^E, t_r)\sqrt{\frac{h}{m-r}} \sum_{s=1}^{m_r} \xi_{js}^r \right] \right\|^p \right\}$$

$$=: K \left\{ D_1^E(k) + \sum_{j=1}^q D_{2j}^E(k) \right\}, \quad k = 0, \ldots, n. \tag{6.98}$$

We use the Lipschitz condition (6.43):

$$D_1^E \le k^{p-1} L^p \, \mathbf{E} \max_{0 \le f \le k} \sum_{r=0}^{f-1} h^p \max_{0 \le \rho \le i_H(t_r)} \|\tilde{y}^E(t_r - \rho\hat{h}) - z^E(t_r - \rho\hat{h})\|^p$$

$$\le K(nh)^p \frac{1}{n} \mathbf{E} \sum_{r=0}^{k-1} \max_{0 \le \rho \le i_H(t_r)} \|\tilde{y}^E(t_r - \rho\hat{h})\|^p$$

$$\le K \cdot \frac{1}{n} \sum_{r=0}^{k-1} \mathbf{E} \max 0 \le s \le r \|\tilde{y}^E(t_s) - z^E(t_s)\|^p, \quad k = 0, \ldots, n. \tag{6.99}$$

Moreover, for $j = 1, \ldots, q$, we get a bound for the second term in (6.98):

$$D_{2j}^E(k) \le K \left\{ \mathbf{E} \max_{0 \le f \le k} \left\| \sum_{r=0}^{f-1} [\sigma_j(\tilde{y}^E, t_r)\sigma_j(z^E, t_r)]\Delta_r w_j \right\|^p \right.$$

$$\left. + \mathbf{E} \max_{0 \le f \le k} \left\| \sum_{r=0}^{f-1} \sigma_j(z^E, t_r) \left[\Delta_r w_j - \sqrt{\frac{h}{m_r}} \sum_{s=1}^{m_r} \xi_{js}r \right] \right\|^p \right\}$$

$$=: K\{D_{2j1}^E(k) + D_{2j2}^E(k)\}. \tag{6.100}$$

To estimate now the terms in the right-hand-side of (6.100) observe that due to Lemma 6.9

$$M_{j1}(f) := \sum_{r=0}^{f-1} [\sigma_j(\tilde{y}^E, t_r)\sigma_j(z^E, t_r)]\Delta_r w_j$$

and

$$M_{j2}(f) := \sum_{r=0}^{f-1} \sigma_j(z^E, t_r)\left[\Delta_r w_j - \sqrt{\frac{h}{m_r}}\sum_{s=1}^{m_r} \xi_{js}^r\right], \quad f = 0, \ldots, n,$$

are d-dimensional martingales with respect to the filtration $(\mathcal{A}_f)_{f=0,\ldots,n}$. Now,

$$D_{2j1}^E(k) \leq K(dk)^{p/2-1} \sum_{r=0}^{k-1} \mathbf{E}\{\|\sigma_j(\tilde{y}^E, t_r) - \sigma_j(z^E, t_r)\|^p|\Delta_r w_j|^p\}$$

for all $j = 1, \ldots, q$ and $k = 0, \ldots, n$.
By the construction of the probability space in Lemma 6.9, the random variables $\sigma_j(\tilde{y}^E, t_r)$, $\sigma_j(z^E, t_r)$ are independent. Thus by the grid condition (6.88) and the Lipschitz condition (6.38), we get[31]

$$
\begin{aligned}
D_{2j1}^E(k) &\leq K \cdot n^{p/2-1} \sum_{r=0}^{k-1} \{\mathbf{E}\|\sigma_j(\tilde{y}^E, t_r) - \sigma_j(z^E, t_r)\|^p \mathbf{E}|\Delta_r w_j|^p\} \\
&\leq K \cdot n^{p/2-1} \sum_{r=0}^{k-1} \left\{h^{p/2}\mathbf{E}\left(\frac{1}{\sqrt{h}}|\Delta_r w_j|\right)^p \right. \\
&\qquad\qquad\qquad \left. \mathbf{E}\max_{0\leq\rho\leq i_H(t_r)}\|\tilde{y}^E(t_r - \rho\hat{h}) - z^E(t_r - \rho\hat{h})\|^p\right\} \\
&\leq K \cdot n^{p/2-1}h^{p/2}\sum_{r=0}^{k-1}\mathbf{E}\max_{0\leq\rho\leq i_H(t_r)}\|\tilde{y}^E(t_r - \rho\hat{h}) - z^E(t_r - \rho\hat{h})\|^p \\
&\leq K \cdot \frac{1}{n}\sum_{r=0}^{k-1}\max_{0\leq s\leq r}\|\tilde{y}^E(t_s) - z^E(t_s)\|^p.
\end{aligned}
\tag{6.101}
$$

We next bound the second term in the right-hand-side of (6.100). Applying the boundness condition (6.37), Lemma 6.9 and the grid conditions (6.88) and (6.90) we get

$$D - 2j2^E(k) \leq K \cdot (dk)^{p/2-1} \tag{6.102}$$

---

[31] Here we use that all $\frac{1}{\sqrt{h}}\Delta_r w_j$ are standard normals, and so, all $\mathbf{E}\left|\frac{1}{\sqrt{h}}\Delta_r w_j\right|^p$ are bounded by a constant depending on p only.

$$\cdot \sum_{r=0}^{k-1} \mathbf{E} \left\{ \|\sigma_j(z^E, t_r)\|^p \left| \Delta_r w_j - \sqrt{\frac{h}{m_r}} \sum_{s=1}^{m_r} \xi_{js}^r \right|^p \right\}$$

$$\leq K \cdot n^{p/2-1} \sum_{r=0}^{k-1} \left(\frac{h}{m_r} \right)^p \mathbf{E} \left| \sqrt{\frac{m_r}{h}} \Delta_r w_j - \sum_{s=1}^{m_r} \xi_{js}^r \right|^p$$

$$\leq K \cdot n^{p/2-1} \left(\frac{h}{m(h)} \right)^{p/2} k(1 + \ln m(h)) \right)^p$$

$$\leq K \left(\frac{nh}{m(h)} \right)^{p/2} (1 + \ln m(h))^p \leq K \left(\frac{1 + \ln m(h)}{\sqrt{m(h)}} \right)^p.$$

We now summarize our estimates in (6.98) - (6.102):

$$\mathbf{E} \max_{0 \leq f \leq k} \|\tilde{y}^E(t_f) - z^E(t_f)\|^p \qquad (6.103)$$

$$\leq K \left\{ \frac{1}{n} \sum_{r=0}^{k-1} \mathbf{E} \max_{0 \leq s \leq r} \|\tilde{y}^E(t_s) - z^E(t_s)\|^p + \left(\frac{1 + \ln m(h)}{\sqrt{m(h)}} \right)^p \right\}$$

for all $k = 1, \ldots, n$. Combining (6.103) with Lemma 6.9 we obtain

$$\mathbf{E} \max_{0 \leq f \leq n} \|\tilde{y}^E(t_f) - z^E(t_f)\|^p \leq K \left(\frac{1 + \ln m(h)}{\sqrt{m(h)}} \right)^p. \qquad (6.104)$$

We now pass to the second pair of the proof. Here we shall extend the bound (6.104) to the intermediate grid points u_i^k. To this end denote

$$\Delta_{i,0}^k w_j := w_j(u_i^k) - w_j(u_0^k), \qquad (6.105)$$
$$j = 1, \ldots, q, \ k = 0, \ldots, n-1, \ i = 1, \ldots, m_k.$$

Then we have

$$\mathbf{E} \max_{0 \leq k \leq n-1} \max_{0 \leq i \leq m_k} \|\tilde{y}^E(u_i^k) - z^E(u_i^k)\|^p$$

$$\leq K \left\{ \mathbf{E} \max_{0 \leq k \leq n-1} \|\tilde{y}^E(t_k) - z^E(t_k)\|^p \right.$$

$$+ \mathbf{E} \max_{0 \leq k \leq n-1} \max_{0 \leq i \leq m_k} \left\| h \cdot \frac{i}{m_k} (b(\tilde{y}^E, t_k) - b(z^E, t_k)) \right\|^p$$

$$+ \sum_{j=1}^{q} \mathbf{E} \max_{0 \leq k \leq n-1} \max_{0 \leq i \leq m_k} \left\| \sigma_j(\tilde{y}^E, t_k) \Delta_{i,0}^k w_j \right.$$

$$\left. - \sigma_j(z^E, t_k) \sqrt{\frac{h}{m_k}} \sum_{s=1}^{i} \xi_{js}^k \right\|^p \right\}$$

$$=: K \left\{ \mathbf{E} \max_{0 \leq k \leq n-1} \|\tilde{y}^E(t_k) - z^E(t_k)\|^p + D_4^E + \sum_{j=1}^{q} D_{5j}^E \right\}. \qquad (6.106)$$

Next we estimate each of the terms in (6.106). By the Lipschitz condition (6.38),

$$D_4^E \leq K \cdot h^p \mathbf{E} \max_{0 \leq k \leq n-1} \|\tilde{y}^E(t_k) - z^E(t_k)\|^p. \tag{6.107}$$

As for D_{5j}^E in (6.106) we have

$$
\begin{aligned}
D_{5j}^E \leq\ & K \left\{ \mathbf{E} \max_{0 \leq k \leq n-1} \max_{0 \leq i \leq m_k} \|[\sigma_j(\tilde{y}^E, t_k) - \sigma_j(z^E, t_k)]\Delta_{i,0}^k w_j\|^p \right. \\
& \left. + \mathbf{E} \max_{0 \leq k \leq n-1} \max_{0 \leq i \leq m_k} \left\| \sigma_j(z^E, t_k) \left[\Delta_{i,0}^k w_j - \sqrt{\frac{h}{m_k}} \sum_{s=1}^i \xi_{js}^k \right] \right\|^p \right\} \\
=:\ & K\{D_{5j1}^E + D_{5j2}^E\}, \quad j = 1, \ldots, q.
\end{aligned}
\tag{6.108}
$$

To estimate D_{5j1}^E, we use the inequality

$$h(1 + \ln n) \leq K \cdot h(1 + \ln \frac{\Lambda}{h}) \leq K \quad \text{for } h \in (0, T - t_0] \tag{6.109}$$

the Cauchy-Bonjakowski-Schwarz inequality, the conditions (6.38), (6.88), Lemma 6.8 and the bound (6.104). As result we get[32]

$$
\begin{aligned}
D_{5j1}^E \leq\ & \mathbf{E} \left\{ \left(\max_{0 \leq k \leq n-1} \|\sigma_j(\tilde{y}^E, t_k) - \sigma_j(z^E, t_k)\|^p \right) \right. \\
& \left. \cdot \left(\max_{0 \leq k \leq n-1} \max_{0 \leq i \leq m_k} |\Delta_{i,0}^k w_j|^p \right) \right\} \\
\leq\ & K \left(\mathbf{E} \max_{0 \leq k \leq n-1} \|\tilde{y}^E(t_k) - z^E(t_k)\|^{2p} \right)^{1/2} \\
& \cdot \left(\mathbf{E} \max_{0 \leq k \leq n-1} \max_{0 \leq i \leq m_k} |\Delta_{i,0}^k w_j|^{2p} \right)^{1/2} \\
\leq\ & K \left(\frac{1 + \ln m(h)}{\sqrt{m(h)}} \right)^p \left(\mathbf{E} \max_{0 \leq k \leq n-1} \sup_{t_k \leq t \leq t_{k+1}} |w_j(t) - w_j(t_k)|^{2p} \right)^{1/2} \\
\leq\ & K \left(\frac{1 + \ln m(h)}{\sqrt{m(h)}} \right)^p h^{p/2} (1 + \ln n)^{p/2} \\
\leq\ & K \left(\frac{1 + \ln m(h)}{\sqrt{m(h)}} \right)^p.
\end{aligned}
\tag{6.110}
$$

To estimate the term D_{5j1}^E, we use the bound

$$\frac{1 + \ln \gamma + \ln \delta}{\sqrt{\gamma \delta}}$$

---

[32]This estimate could be easily improved, but a better estimate than in (6.110) will not make a difference for the final bound (6.95).

$$\leq \frac{1 + \ln \gamma + \ln \delta + \ln \gamma \ln \delta}{\sqrt{\gamma \delta}} = \left(\frac{1 + \ln \gamma}{\sqrt{\gamma}}\right)\left(\frac{1 + \ln \delta}{\sqrt{\delta}}\right)$$

$$\leq \frac{2}{\sqrt{e}}\left(\frac{1 + \ln \delta}{\sqrt{\delta}}\right) \quad \text{for all real } \gamma, \delta \geq 1. \tag{6.111}$$

Combining (6.111) with the boundness condition (6.37), the grid condition (6.88), (6.90) and Lemma 6.9 yields

$$
\begin{aligned}
D_{5j2}^E &\leq K \cdot \mathbf{E}\left\{\max_{0 \leq k \leq n-1} \max_{0 \leq i \leq m_k} \left(\frac{h}{m_k}\right)^{p/2} \left\|\sqrt{\frac{m_k}{h}}\Delta_{i,0}^k w_j - \sum_{s=1}^{i} \xi_{js}^k\right\|^p\right\} \\
&\leq K\left(\left(\frac{h}{m(h)}\right)^{p/2}(1 + \ln n + \ln m(h))\right)^p \leq K\left(\frac{1 + \ln n + \ln m(h)}{\sqrt{n \cdot m(h)}}\right)^p \\
&\leq K\left(\frac{1 + \ln m(h)}{\sqrt{m(h)}}\right)^p. \tag{6.112}
\end{aligned}
$$

We now put together (6.106), (6.107), (6.110) and (6.112) to get

$$
\begin{aligned}
&\mathbf{E} \max_{0 \leq k \leq n-1} \max_{0 \leq i \leq m_k} \|\tilde{y}^E(u_i^k) - z^E(u_i^k)\|^p \\
&\leq K\left\{\mathbf{E} \max_{0 \leq k \leq n-1} \|\tilde{y}^E(t_k) - z^E(t_k)\|^p + \left(\frac{1 + \ln m(h)}{\sqrt{m(h)}}\right)^p\right\}, \tag{6.113}
\end{aligned}
$$

completing the second half of our proof. Now the estimates (6.104) and (6.113) we obtain the desired inequality (6.95). Theorem 6.5 is now proved.   □

Proof of Theorem 6.6. To show that

$$\mathbf{E} \sup_{t_0 \leq t \leq T} \|x(t) - z^E(t)\|^p \leq K\left\{h^{p/2} + \left(\frac{1 + \ln m(h)}{\sqrt{m(h)}}\right)^p\right\} \tag{6.114}$$

we use the inequality

$$\frac{h}{m(h)}\left(1 + \ln\left(\frac{m(h)}{h}\right)\right) \leq K\left(\frac{1 + \ln m(h)}{\sqrt{m(h)}}\right)^2. \tag{6.115}$$

To see (6.115) we apply the condition (6.37) together with (6.111) for $\gamma = \frac{1}{h} \geq 1$ and $\delta = m(h) \geq 1$. Now Theorems 6.3, 6.4 and 6.5 and the bound (6.115) yield (6.114) as desired.   □

Proof of Corollary 6.1. We need to show that

$$W_p(D(x), D(z^E)) \leq K\left\{h^{1/2} + \frac{1 + \ln m(h)}{\sqrt{m(h)}}\right\}. \tag{6.116}$$

For $p \in [2, \infty)$ the inequality (6.116) follows directly from Theorem 6.6, (see (6.114)). (To see that apply the inequality $a_1^p + a_2^p \le (a_1 + a_2)^p$ for $a_1, a_2 \ge 0$ and $p \in [2, \infty)$.) Then the assertions are also true for $p \in [1, 2)$, since $W_{p_1} \le W_{p_2}$ for $1 \le p_1 \le p_2 < \infty$ (see Givens and Shortt (1984) and Rachev (1991), Section 3.2). □

7

Multivariate Stable Models

7.1 Multivariate (α, +)-stable and Operator Stable Distributions

Suppose $X, X^{(1)}, X^{(2)}, \ldots$ are i.i.d., m-dimensional random vectors with common distribution function (d.f.) H.

Definition 7.1 The d.f. H is said to be *α-stable, (or more precisely, α, +)-stable)* $\alpha \in (0, 2]$, if for any positive numbers A and B there is a vector $a \in \mathbf{R}^d$ such that

$$AX^{(1)} + BX^{(2)} \stackrel{d}{=} (A^\alpha + B^\alpha)^{1/\alpha} X + a. \qquad (7.1)$$

H is called *strictly stable* if $a = 0$, and is said to be *symmetric stable* if $P(X \in A) = P(-X \in A)$ for any Borel set A of $\mathbf{R}^d$.

Given a random vector $X = (X_1, \ldots, X_d)$, then X has a strictly (symmetric) stable d.f. if and only if all linear combinations $Y = \sum_{k=1}^d b_k X_k$ have strictly (symmetric) stable distributions. Note that for $\alpha \in (0, 1)$ Marcus (1983) shows the existence of a *non-stable vector* $X = (X_1, X_2)$ in $\mathbf{R}^2$ such that all linear combinations of its components are α-stable random variables with $\alpha < 1$. However, for $\alpha > 1$, X is a stable (distributed) vector in $\mathbf{R}^d$ if and only if all linear combinations Y are α-stable (see the detailed discussion in Samorodnitsky and Taqqu, 1994).

Property 7.1 *(Explicit representation of the characteristic function):* H is α-stable if there exists a finite measure Γ on the unit sphere S_d of $\mathbf{R}^d$ and a vector G in $\mathbf{R}^d$ such that the characteristic function (ch.f.)

$$f_H(\theta) := \int_{\mathbf{R}^d} \exp\{i(\theta, x)\} dH(x) = \mathbf{E} \exp\{i(\theta, X)\} \qquad (7.2)$$

where $(\theta, x) := \sum_{i=1}^{d} \theta_i x_i$, is given by

$$f_H(\theta) = \exp\left\{-\int_{S_d} |(\theta, s)|^\alpha (1 - i\operatorname{sign}(\theta, s)) \tan \tfrac{\pi\alpha}{2} \Gamma(ds) + i(\theta, \mu)\right\},$$
$$\text{if } \alpha \neq 1 \qquad (7.3)$$

$$= \exp\left\{-\int_{S_d} |(\theta, s)|(1 + i\tfrac{2}{\pi}\operatorname{sign}(\theta, s)) \ln |\theta, s|)\Gamma(ds) + i(\theta, \mu)\right\},$$
$$\text{if } \alpha = 1. \qquad (7.4)$$

The pair (Γ, μ) is unique when $0 < \alpha < 2$. The proof is given in Külbs (1973).

The measure Γ is called *spectral measure* of the α-stable vector X. Specifically, if X is symmetric α-stable, i.e. $X \overset{d}{=} -X$, then it has ch.f. of the form

$$f_H(\theta) = \exp\{-\int_{S_d} |\theta_1 s_1 + \ldots + \theta_d s_d|^\alpha \Gamma(ds)\}$$

where Γ is a finite symmetric measure on the Borel subsets of the unit sphere S_d.

Note that an α-stable random vector X has independent components if and only if its spectral measure Γ is discrete and concentrated on the intersection of the axes with the unit sphere S_d. See Samorodnitsky and Taqqu (1994) for a review on properties of multivariate stable random vectors.

Definition 7.2 *(Esary, Proschan, and Walkup, 1967; Barlow and Proschan, 1975; Resnick, 1987a).* A random vector X in $\mathbf{R}^d$ is *(positively) associated*, if the covariance

$$\operatorname{cov}(f(X), g(X)) = \mathbf{E}\{(f(X) - \mathbf{E}f(X))(g(X) - \mathbf{E}g(X))\} \qquad (7.5)$$

is nonnegative for any functions $f, g \colon \mathbf{R}^d \to \mathbf{R}$ nondecreasing in each argument and such that (7.5) exists.

The concept of *association* was introduced by Esary, Proschan, and Walkup (1967) in reliability theory. In a completely different context, Fortuin, Kastelyn, and Ginibre (1971), considered the association concept in statistical physics. Association represents a strong form of positive dependence.

Pitt (1982), Joag-Dev, Perlman and Pitt (1983) show that nonnegatively correlated normal variables are associated. Inspired by their results , Lee, Rachev and Samorodnitsky (1990) derive the following theorem, see also Lee, Rachev and Samorodnitsky (1993) and Samorodnitsky and Taqqu (1994), Theorem 4.6.1.

Theorem 7.1 *(Lee, Rachev and Samorodnitsky, 1990)* X is (positively) associated if and only if its ch.f. (see (7.2)–(7.4)) has spectral measure Γ with

$$\Gamma(S_\alpha^-) = 0, \qquad (7.6)$$

where

$$S_d^- = \{(s_1, \ldots, s_d) \in S_d; \ s_i > 0, \ s_j < 0 \text{ forsome } i, j = 1, \ldots, d\}. \qquad (7.7)$$

Note that a result related to the sufficiency part of the above theorem was obtained by Resnick (1988) in terms of Poisson representation of an infinitely divisible random vector.

Remark 7.1 In the bivariate case ($d = 2$) Theorem 7.1 says that the spectral measure Γ is concentrated on the first and third quadrant, if and only if random pair X have positively associated components.

Given two assets with dependent returns, which are governed by a bivariate α-stable distribution ($\alpha < 2$), one could check whether the prices are associated by investigating the distribution of the mass of the spectral measure on S_2. If the measure is concentrated on S_2^+ (i.e. on the first and third quadrant), then the prices are (positively) associated. One possible statistical procedure for checking the "associativeness" consists of approximating Γ by

$$\Gamma_n(A) := \sum_{k=1}^n a_k \delta_{s_k}(A), \qquad n \geq 1$$

where $a_k > 0$, δ_{s_k} are the point measures

$$\delta_{s_k}(A) = \begin{cases} 1, & \dot{s}_k \in A \\ 0, & s_k \notin A, \end{cases} \qquad 1 \leq k \leq n,$$

and $s_k = \exp\{ik2\pi/n\}$. Roughly speaking, if $a_k \approx 0$ for all k such that $s_k \in S_2^-$, we can conclude that the prices of the two states are associated. To estimate a_k, a method based on the Press (1972a,b) could be used.

We list here some notions of dependence. A bivariate density function $f(x, y)$ of two arguments is said to be *totally positive of order 2* (abbreviated TP_2) if for all $x_1 < x_2$, and $y_1 < y_2$,

$$\begin{vmatrix} f(x_1, y_1) & f(x_1, y_2) \\ f(x_2, y_1) & f(x_2, y_2) \end{vmatrix} \geq 0.$$

A joint density function $f(x_1, \ldots, x_d)$ of d arguments is said to be TP_2 *in pairs* if $f(x_1, \ldots, x_i, \ldots, x_j, \ldots, x_d)$ is TP_2 in (x_i, x_j) for all $i \neq j$ and all fixed values of the remaining arguments. If a random vector has a TP_2-in-pairs density then it is associated. See Karlin (1968), Barlow and Proschan (1981), and Tong (1990) for a review. Random variables $X_1, \ldots, X_d$ are called *positive upper orthant dependent* (PUOD) if

$$P(X_1 > x_1, \ldots, X_d > x_d) \geq P(X_1 > x_1) \ldots P(X_d > x_d)$$

for any $x_1, \ldots, X_d$, and they are called *positive lower orthant dependent* (PLOD) if

$$P(X_1 \leq x_1, \ldots, X_d \leq x_d) \geq P(X_1 \leq x_1) \ldots P(X_n \leq x_d)$$

for any $x_1, \ldots, x_d$. That is, if $X_1, \ldots, X_d$ are PUOD or PLOD, then they are more likely to taken on larger values together or smaller values together. Lehmann (1966) shows that for the bivariate case, X_1, X_2 are PUOD if and only if they are PLOD; however, for higher dimensional cases, the equivalence no longer holds. It is also well known that association implies both PUOD and PLOD, but in general these implications cannot be reversed. For stable random variables, Lee, Samorodnitsky and Rachev (1990) show, as a result of Theorem 7.1 that PLOD or PUOD implies association.

Corollary 7.1 Let $X_1, \ldots, X_d$ be jointly α-stable. Then the notion of association is equivalent to PLOD or PUOD.

Following Alam and Saxena (1982) we call the random vector X *negatively associated* if for any $k = 1, \ldots, d-1$, and any functions $f: \mathbf{R}^k \to \mathbf{R}$, $g: \mathbf{R}^{d-k} \to \mathbf{R}$, which are nondecreasing in each argument, $\mathrm{cov}(f(X'), g(X'')) \leq 0$, whenever the covariance exists, where X' and X'' are any k and $d-k$ dimensional random vectors, respectively, representing a partition of $X = (X_1, \ldots, X_d)$ into two subsets of sizes k and $d-k$. In the normal case, negative association has been characterized by Joag-dev and Proschan (1983). Lee, Samorodnitsky and Rachev (1990) derive the following theorem, see also Samorodnitsky and Taqqu (1994), Theorem 4.6.3.

Theorem 7.2 *(Lee, Rachev and Samorodnitsky, 1990).* Let X be an α-stable distributed random vector, $0 < \alpha < 2$, whose ch.f. is given by (7.2)–(7.4). Then X is negatively associated if and only if the spectral measure Γ has no mass on S_d^+, i.e., $\Gamma(S_d^+) = 0$, where

$$S_d^+ = \{(s_1, \ldots, s_d) \in S_\alpha : s_i, s_j > 0 \text{ for some } i \neq j\}.$$

Remark 7.2 For the bivariate case the theorem implies that the spectral measure of X is concentrated on the second and the fourth quadrant. We will use this fact in Chapter 8 to test the association of bivariate α-stable returns.

Some other properties related to dependence concepts of stable random vectors have also been discussed in the statistical literature. Multiple regressions on stable random vectors have been considered by Wu and Cambanis (1991) and Samorodnitsky and Taqqu (1991). A version of Slepian-type inequalities, due to Fernique (1975), was extended to stable random vectors in terms of Lévy measures by Samorodnitsky and Taqqu (1990b).

We now look at some special cases of stable random vectors derived by products.

Let $Z = (Z_1, \ldots, Z_d)$ be an arbitrary symmetric α'-stable vector. Let T be a positive α/α'-stable random variable, $0 < \alpha < \alpha'$, independent of Z

and having Laplace transform $\mathbf{E}\exp(-\theta T) = \exp(-\theta^{\alpha/\alpha'})$, $\theta \geq 0$. Then the random vector defined by

$$X = T^{1/\alpha'}Z \tag{7.8}$$

is symmetric α-stable. They are sometimes referred to as product-type stable random vectors. In Section 5.1, we saw that these product-type stable random vectors can be obtained naturally from stable processes directed by an operational time stable process.

It is clear that components of the product-type stable vector X are conditionally independent. If one further assumes that $Z_1, \ldots, Z_d$ are i.i.d., then components of X are positively dependent by mixture as considered by Shaked (1977), Tong (1977,1980), and Shaked and Tong (1985). We note that components of the derived vectors X can be strongly dependent. This fact can be demonstrated by the following example.

Example 7.1 For any fixed positive integers $k_1 > 1$ and $k_2 > 1$, assume that $\{Z_i, i = 1, \ldots, d\}$ are d i.i.d. totally right skewed strictly $1/k_2$-stable random variables. Let T be a totally right skewed strictly $1/k_1$-stable variable, independent of $\{Z_i, i = 1, \ldots, d\}$. Then the derived vector $(X_1, \ldots, X_d) = T^{1/\alpha'}Z$, with $\alpha' = 1/k_1$, is $1/k_1k_2$ stable and its components are TP_2 in pairs. We will show that there are many cases where components of a product-type stable random vector are neither associated nor positive orthant dependent.

On the other hand, note that if $X = E^{1/\alpha'}Z$ where Z is a symmetric α'-stable random vector and if (i) E is independent of Z, (ii) E is an exponential random variable then X is a *geometric stable vector*, see further Section 7.1.

If E has arbitrary distribution on $\mathbf{R}_+$ then $X = E^{1/\alpha'}Z$ is called *Robbins mixture*: for applications of Robbins mixtures to reliability theory, queuing and finance modeling we refer to Szasz (1972), Szynal (1976), Korolev (1988), Rachev and Rüschendorf (1998b), Rachev and Samorodnitsky (1991).

When $Z = G = (G_1, \ldots, G_d)$ in (7.8) is a zero mean Gaussian vector in $\mathbf{R}^d$, independent of the positive α/α'-stable random vector T, then the derived vector $\mathbf{X} = T^{1/2}\mathbf{G}$ is called a *sub-Gaussian* $S\alpha S$ random vector, with governing Gaussian vector $\mathbf{G}$. Sub-Gaussian vectors form a special class of stable vectors which, unlike general stable vectors, can be characterized by finitely many parameters. Specifically, the sub-Gaussian vector $\mathbf{X}$ derived above has a ch.f. of the form

$$\phi_\alpha(\theta) = \exp\{-|\frac{1}{2}\sum_{i=1}^{d}\sum_{j=1}^{d}\theta_i\theta_j R_{ij}|^{\alpha/2}\},$$

where $R_{ij} := E(G_iG_j)$, $i, j = 1, \ldots, d$ are the covariances of the underlying Gaussian vector $G_1, \ldots, G_d$).[1]

---

[1] The results in the rest of this section are largely taken from Lee, Rachev and Samorodnitsky (1993).

Let Γ_0 be a uniform (i.e. rotationally invariant) finite Borel measure on S_d. Then for some $c \geq 0$

$$\int_{S_d} |\sum_{j=1}^{d} \theta_j s_j|^\alpha \Gamma_0(ds) = c[\frac{1}{2}\sum_{j=1}^{d} \theta_j^2]^{\alpha/2}.$$

Therefore, a symmetric α-stable random vector ($S\alpha S$ *random vector*), $\alpha < 2$, is sub-Gaussian with a governing Gaussian vector having i.i.d. components if and only if its spectral measure is uniform on the unit sphere S_d. A uniform spectral measure does not satisfy the required condition for association as was stated in Theorem 7.1. As a consequence, we have

Theorem 7.3 If a $S\alpha S$ random vector X is sub-Gaussian with a governing Gaussian vector having i.i.d. $N(0,\sigma^2)$ components, then components of X are positively dependent by mixture but they are neither associated nor positively orthant dependent.

In general, the spectral measure of a sub-Gaussian vector is a transform of the uniform measure Γ_0 on S_d. Hence we have

Theorem 7.4 A non-degenerate (i.e. having non-zero components) sub-Gaussian vector $T^{1/2}(G_1,\ldots,G_d)$ with governing Gaussian vector $\mathbf{G} = (G_1, \ldots,G_d)$ as defined in equation (7.8) is associated if and only if $G_1 = c_2 G_2 = \ldots = c_d G_d$ (with probability 1) for some $c_2 > 0,\ldots,c_d > 0$.
  Proof. Suppose $P(G_1 = c_2 G_2) = 0$ for any $c_2 \in \mathbf{R}$. Assume that the stable random vector $(T^{1/2}G_1,\ldots,T^{1/2}G_d)$ is associated. Then the sub-vector $(T^{1/2}G_1, T^{1/2}G_2)$ is also associated. Hence $(T^{1/2}G_1, T^{1/2}G_2)$ has a spectral measure which is concentrated on the first and third quadrant of the unit circle, see Theorem 7.1. On the other hand, any Gaussian vector can be written as a linear combination of i.i.d. standard normals. The condition $P(G_1 = c_2 G_2) = 0$ for any $c_2 \in \mathbf{R}$. implies that this linear transformation for the vector (G_1, G_2) is of full rank. Therefore the spectral measure of $(T^{1/2}G_1, T^{1/2}G_2)$ is a rigid transformation of the uniform measure on the unit sphere, and it maps the unit sphere onto the entire unit sphere. This leads to a contradiction. Similarly, the case $G_1 = c_2 G_2$ for some $c_2 < 0$ can be ruled out. $\square$
  Samorodnitsky and Taqqu (1991), (1994) derived regression equations for general stable random vectors. In particular, they show that when $(X_1, X_2) = (T^{1/2}G_1, T^{1/2}G_2)$ in (7.8) is a non-degenerate sub-Gaussian $S\alpha S$, (even when $\alpha \leq 1$), random vector with governing Gaussian vector G,

$$E(X_2|X_1 = x) = R_{12}R_{11}^{-1}x \quad \text{a.e.(almost everywhere)}$$

and $E(X_2^2|X_1 = x) < \infty$ a.e. if $1 < \alpha < 2$ (note that the unconditional second moment is infinite).

We can calculate the conditional variance as follows

$$
\begin{aligned}
E(G_2|G_1) &= R_{12}R_{11}^{-1}G_1, \\
\text{Var}(G_2|G_1) &= R_{22} - R_{12}^2R_{11}^{-1}, \\
E(X_2^2|X_1 = x) &= E(E(TG_2^2|T,G_1)|T^{1/2}G_1 = x) \\
&= E(T|X_1 = x)\text{Var}(G_2|G_1) + {R_{12}^2R_{11}^2}^{-1}x^2.
\end{aligned}
$$

Hence

$$
\text{Var}(X_2|X_1 = x) = E(T|X_1 = x)(R_{22} - R_{12}^2R_{11}^{-1}).
$$

We see that the conditional mean of X_2 given X_1 is completely determined by the Gaussian vector **G**. The above equation, however, demonstrates how the random variable T influences the variance of the conditional law of X_2 given X_1.

Wu and Cambanis (1991) show that

$$
\text{Var}(X_2|X_1 = x) = (\frac{1}{2})(R_{22} - R_{12}^2R - 11^{-1})f(x;\alpha)^{-1} \int\limits_{|x|}^{\infty} uF(u;\alpha)du,
$$

where $f(x;\alpha)$ is the density function of a $S_\alpha(1,0,0)$ random variable (i.e. having the ch.f. $\exp[-|t|^\alpha]$).

Moreover, if T in $\mathbf{X} = \sqrt{T}\mathbf{G}$ is standard exponentially distributed rather that positive stable distributed, then **X** has a *multivariate Laplace distribution*, that is, its ch.f. has the form

$$
\phi_\alpha(\theta) = \frac{1}{1 + \frac{1}{2}\sum_{i=1}^d \sum_{j=1}^d \theta_i\theta_j R_{ij}}.
$$

To characterize the dependence for sub-Gaussian vectors, we state a notion of *local correlation for sub-Gaussian random vectors*.

Bjerve and Doksum (1990) introduced a measure of local strength of dependence by combining ideas from nonparametric regression and of Galton (1988). They define the function

$$
\rho(x) = \frac{\sigma\beta(x)}{[\{\sigma\beta(x)\}^2 + \sigma_{X^2|X_1=x}^2]^{1/2}}
$$

where $\sigma^2 = \text{Var}(X_1)$, $\sigma_{X_2|X_1=x}^2 = \text{Var}(X_2|X_1 = x)$, and $\beta(x) = \frac{d}{dx}E(X_2|X_1 = x)$ is the slope of the nonparametric regression. More generally, they note that the conditional mean $E(X_2|X_1 = x)$ can be replaced by a location function. The variances $\sigma^2 = \text{Var}(X_1)$ and $\sigma_{X_2|X_1=x}^2 = \text{Var}(X_2|X_1 = x)$ can be replaced by squares of corresponding scale functions.

For an $S\alpha S$ random vector (X_1, X_2), Samorodnitsky and Taqqu (1991) show that in many cases the first, and when $1 < \alpha \le 2$, second conditional moments exist if a certain integrability condition holds. When $1 < \alpha \le 2$, the *covariation*[2] is designed to replace the covariance. It is a useful quantity and is appears naturally in the context of regression for stable random variables, see further Chapter 8 and 9.

Let X_1 and X_2 be jointly $S\alpha S$ with $\alpha > 1$ and let Γ be the spectral measure of the random vector (X_1, X_2). The *covariation* of X_1 and X_2 is defined to be the real number

$$[X_1, X_2]_\alpha = \int_{S_2} s_1 |s_2|^{\alpha-1} \text{sign}(s_2) \Gamma(ds).$$

As a result, we have

$$[X_1, X_2]_\alpha = \int_{s_2} |s_1|^\alpha \Gamma(ds) = \sigma_1^\alpha,$$

where σ_1 is the scale parameter of the $S\alpha S$ random variable X_1. Let $\mathcal{F}_\alpha$ be a linear space of jointly $S\alpha S$ random variables. Then when $\alpha > 1$, the covariation induces a norm[3] on $\mathcal{F}_\alpha$ such that

$$\|X\|_\alpha = ([X, X]_\alpha)^{1/\alpha}.$$

Convergence in $\|\cdot\|_\alpha$ is equivalent to convergence in probability and convergence in L^p for any $p < \alpha$. Moreover, for sub-Gaussian vector $(X_1, \ldots, X_d)$ with ch.f. defined by

$$\phi_\alpha(\theta) = \exp\left\{ -\|\frac{1}{2} \sum_{i=1}^{d} \sum_{j=1}^{d} \theta_i \theta_j R_{ij}\|^{\alpha/2} \right\},$$

we have

$$[X_i, X_j]_\alpha = 2^{-\alpha/2} R_{ij} R_{jj}^{(\alpha-2)/2}, \quad i, j = 1, \ldots, d, \text{and}$$
$$\|X_i\|_\alpha = 2^{-1/2} R_{ii}^{1/2}.$$

Note that when $\alpha = 2$, we have $[X_1, X_2]_2 = \frac{1}{2}\text{Cov}(X_1, X_2)$, and $[X_1, X_1]_2 = \frac{1}{2}\text{Var}(X_1) = \sigma_1^2$. For an $S\alpha S$ random variable X, $1 < \alpha < 2$, we use $k_\alpha \|X\|_\alpha$, with

$$k_\alpha = [\frac{\alpha \Gamma(1 - 1/\alpha)}{\Gamma(1/\alpha)}]^{1/2},$$

to replace the notion of $\{\text{Var}(X)\}^{1/2}$ in the calculation of a notion of local correlation function. Note that $k_2 = \sqrt{2}$ is consistent with the above computation.

---

[2] See Janicki and Weron (1994) and Samorodnitsky and Taqqu (1994), and the references therein.

[3] For an alternative notion – "dispersion of a stable vector" – we refer to Soltani and Moeanaddin (1994).

Hence we can define, for an $S\alpha S$ random vector (X_1, X_2), the local correlation curve as

$$\rho(x) = \frac{\beta(x) k_\alpha \|X_1\|_\alpha}{[\{\beta(x) k_\alpha \|X_1\|_\alpha\}^2 + \sigma^2_{X_2|X_1 = x}]^{\frac{1}{2}}}$$

whenever the conditional variance is finite a.e. Note that, for the special case when $\alpha = 2$, $\rho(x)$ is equal to the correlation coefficient of (X_1, X_2).

For $S\alpha S$ sub-Gaussian vector $(X_1, X_2) = (T^{1/2} G_1, T^{1/2} G_2)$ we have

$$\rho(x) = \frac{k_\alpha R_{12}}{[k_\alpha^2 R_{12}^2 + (R_{11} R_{22} - R_{12}^2) f(x; \alpha)^{-1} \int_{|x|}^\infty u f(u; \alpha) du]^{1/2}}.$$

It follows that $\rho(x)$ is an even function, and $\rho(0) = R_{12}/(R_{11} R_{22})^{1/2}$ is the correlation coefficient of G_1 and G_2. Moreover,

$$\rho(x) \sim \frac{k_\alpha}{\alpha(\alpha - 1)^{1/2}} R_{12}(R_{11} R_{22} - R_{12}^2)^{-1/2} |x|^{-1} \quad \text{as } |x| \to \infty.$$

Furthermore, $\rho(x) \equiv 0$ when G_1 and G_2 are independent; $\rho(x) \equiv 1$, when $G_1 = G_2$.

We next relate the product type stable random vector with the notion of subordination introduced in Chapter 5.

Let $\{X(t)\}$ be a Markov process with continuous transition probabilities and $\{T(t)\}$ a process with nonnegative independent increments, then $\{X(T(t))\}$ is again a Markovian process. The process $\{X(T(t))\}$ is said to be *subordinated to the parent process* $\{X(t)\}$ *using the operational time* $T(t)$, see Chapter 5. The process $\{T(t)\}$ is called the *directing process*. The role of the directing process is to inject some additional randomness into the parent process through its time parameter t. In equipment usage, for example, $\{X(t)\}$ may represent cumulative wear on a machine component after t hours of operation and $\{T(t)\}$ may represent the number of hours that the machine has operated after t hours of calendar time have passed. The process $\{T(t)\}$ thereby captures the random delays and accelerations of operational use of the machine over calendar time. The term *subordination* was first introduced by Bochner (1955). Various properties of derived processes were investigated by Stam (1965).

Whitmore and Lee (1991) considered statistical inferences for subordinated processes and applications.

Recall now that stochastic process $\{X(t)\}$ is called an α-*stable Lévy motion* with skewness parameter μ and scale parameter σ if

(1) $X(0) = 0$

(2) $\{X(t)\}$ has stationary independent increments.

(3) $X(t) - X(s)$ has the distribution $S_\alpha(\sigma(t-s)^{1/\alpha}, \eta, 0)$ (see (2.1.2)) for any $\sigma > 0$, $0 \leq s < t < \infty$, and for some $0 < \alpha \leq 2$, and $-1 \leq \eta \leq 1$.

When $\sigma = 1$, $\{X(t)\}$ is said to be a *standard α-stable Lévy motion.*

The following results was given in Lee and Whitmore (1991). Related results can also be found in Samorodnitsky and Taqqu (1994).

Theorem 7.5 Assume that $\{X(t)\}$ is a standard α-stable Lévy motion with $\alpha \neq 1$ and skewness parameter η, and that $\{T(t)\}$ is a standard β-stable Lévy motion with $0 < \beta < 1$ and the skewness parameter 1. Assume also that processes $\{X(t)\}$ and $\{T(t)\}$ are independent. Then

(a) If $\alpha\beta \neq 1$, then process $\{X(T(t))\}$ is an $\alpha\beta$-stable Lévy motion such that

$$X(T(t)) - X(T(s)) \stackrel{d}{=} S_{\alpha\beta}((\kappa(t-s))^{1/\alpha\beta}, \xi, 0), \qquad (7.9)$$

with $\xi = \tan(\zeta\beta)/(\tan \frac{\alpha\beta\pi}{2})$, $\kappa = (\cos\zeta\beta)(1+\eta^2\tan^2\frac{\pi\alpha}{2})^{\beta/2}(\cos\frac{\pi\alpha}{2})^{-1}$, and $\zeta = \arctan(\eta\tan\frac{\pi\alpha}{2})$.

(b) If $\alpha\beta = 1$ then the process $\{X(T(t))\}$ is of the form $\kappa(L(t) + t\tan\beta\zeta)$, where L is a standard symmetric 1-stable (Cauchy) motion, and κ and ζ are as in (a).

(c) The process $\{X(T(t))\}$ has the same one-dimensional distributions as that of the process $\{(T(t))^{1/\alpha}X(1)\}$.

As a special case of Theorem 7.5, consider k independent Brownian motions $\{X_j(t)\}$, $j = 1, 2, \ldots, k$, such that $X_j(0) = 0$ and $X_j(t) \stackrel{d}{=} N(0, t/c)$ for $j = 1, 2, \ldots, k$, where $c = (\cos\frac{\pi\alpha}{4})^{-1}$ and $\alpha < 2$. Assume that $\{T(t)\}$ is a standard totally right skewed $\alpha/2$ stable Lévy motion, independent of processes $\{X_j(t)\}$, $j = 1, 2, \ldots, k$. Then for any $t > 0$ fixed, the random vector $(X_1(T(t)), \ldots, X_k(T(t)))$ equals in distribution the symmetric α-stable random vector $(T(t)^{1/2}X_1(1), \ldots, T(t)^{1/2}X_k(1))$. The latter vector is a sub-Gaussian vector with governing Gaussian vector having i.i.d. $N(0, t/c)$ components.

Markov processes with TP_2 transition densities are useful in shock models. For example, inverse Gaussian processes, gamma processes and some right skewed stable processes have TP_2 transition densities, see Chapter 5. Lee and Whitemore (1991) show that if the transition densities of both the parent process and the operational time process are TP_2, then transition density of the derived subordinated process is also TP_2. They have the following results.

Theorem 7.6 Assume that the process $\{X_j(t)\}$ has a transition density function $f_{j,t}(x)$ which is TP_2 in t and x, for $j = 1, 2, \ldots, k$, and that $\{T(t)\}$ has a transition density function $u_t(s)$ which is TP_2 in t and s. If the process $\{T(t)\}$ is independent of processes $\{X_j(t)\}$, $j = 1, 2, \ldots, k$, then

(a) The transition density function $h_{j,t}(x)$ of the subordinated process $\{X_j(T(t))\}$ is TP_2 in t and x, for $j = 1, \ldots, k$.

(b) For any $t > 0$ fixed, the random vector $(X_1(T(t)), \ldots, X_k(T(t)))$ is TP_2 in pairs.

Theorem 7.7 For any two positive integers $k_1 > 1$, $k_2 > 1$ fixed, assume that $\{X_i(t)\}$ are n i.i.d. totally right skewed $1/k_2$-stable Lévy motions, $i = 1, \ldots, n$. Let $\{T(t)\}$ be a totally right skewed $1/k_1$-stable Lévy motion independent of $\{X_i(t)\}$, $i = 1, \ldots, n$. Then, for any $t > 0$ fixed, the vector $\langle X_1(T(t)), \ldots, X_n(T(t)) \rangle$ is $1/(k_1 k_2)$-stable and is TP_2 in pairs.

As a special case of subordination, consider an exponential time-change of α-stable Lévy motion $\{X(t)\}$. Let $Y(t) = X(Et)$, $t \geq 0$ where E is standard exponential random variable independent of X. Then by the self-similarity of Lévy motion, $Y \overset{d}{=} E^{1/\alpha} X$, unless $\alpha = 1$ and $\eta \neq 0$. The finite dimensional distributions of the process $\{Y(t)\}$ are geometric stable. In fact

$$E \exp(i\{(Y(t_1), \ldots, Y(t_k)), \theta\}) = \frac{1}{1 + \int_{S_k} |(\theta, s)|^\alpha \Gamma_{t_1, \ldots, t_k}(ds)},$$

where $m_{t_1, \ldots, t_k}$ is the spectral measure of $(X(t_1), \ldots, X(t_k))$. Rachev and Resnick (1991) derived similar results on max-stable processes, see also further Section 7.3.

Let us return now to the characterization properties of α-stable vectors. Obviously from (7.1) we have that a random vector X is α-stable if and only if for any $n \geq 2$, there is a vector $a_n \in R^d$ such that

$$X^{(1)} + X^{(2)} + \ldots + X^{(n)} \overset{d}{=} n^{1/\alpha} X + a_n,$$

where $X^{(1)}, X^{(2)}, \ldots, X^{(n)}$ are i.i.d. $X^{(i)} \overset{d}{=} X$. More generally we have the following:

Property 7.2 *(Domain of attraction of $(\alpha, +)$-stable distributions):* The α-stable distributions are weak limits of normalized sums of i.i.d. random vectors.

The multivariate d.f. F is said to be in the normal domain of attraction of the α-stable distribution H if for any sequence $Y^{(1)}, Y^{(2)}$ of i.i.d. random vectors with common d.f. F there is a sequence of vectors $\{a_n\}$ such that

$$n^{-1/\alpha}(Y^{(1)} + \ldots + Y^{(n)}) - a_n \overset{\omega}{\longrightarrow} X \tag{7.10}$$

where X has d.f. H.

The next property shows the precise rate of convergence of (7.10). Let ρ be the *uniform (Kolmogorov) metric* in the space of d-dimensional d.f.'s $F_X(x) = P\{X \leq x\}$, $x \in R^d$:

$$\rho(X', X'') := \rho(F_{X'}, F_{X''}) = \sup_{x \in \mathbf{R}^d} |F_{X'}(x) - F_{X''}(x)|. \tag{7.11}$$

Further, let ν_r be the *convolution metric*

$$\nu_r(X', X'') := \nu_r(F_{X'}, F_{X''}) := \sup_{h \in \mathbf{R}^d} |h|^r \nu(F_{X'} \circ F_{hS_\alpha}, F_{X''} \circ F_{hS_\alpha}), \tag{7.12}$$

where S_α is a symmetric α-stable distributed random vector, "$\circ$" denotes convolution, [4] and ν is the *total variation* metric

$$\nu(X', X'') := \text{var } (F_{X'}, F_{X''}) = \sup_{A(\text{Borel sets in } \mathbf{R}^d)} |P(X' \in A) - P(X'' \in A)|. \tag{7.13}$$

The metrics ν_r can be estimated in terms of the absolute pseudomoment of order τ,

$$\chi_\tau(X', X'') = \int_{-\infty}^{+\infty} \|x\|^r \|F_{X'} - F_{X''}\|(dx), \tag{7.14}$$

where $\|x\|$ is the Euclidean norm in $\mathbf{R}^d$, and $\|F_{X'} - F_{X''}\| = (F_{X'} - F_{X''})^+ + (F_{X'} - F_{X''})^-$ is the total variation based on the Jordan-Hahn decomposition of $(F_{X'} - F_{X''})(dx)$ (see, for example, Billingsley (1986), Rachev (1991)). For any $0 < r < 1$ we have

$$\nu_r(X', X'') \leq C_r \chi_r(X', X''). \tag{7.15}$$

In case of $r \in [1, 2)$ inequality (7.15) is still valid provided that $\mathbf{E}(X_i' - X_i'') = 0$ for all components of X' and X''.

Property 7.3 (See Rachev and Yukich (1989, 1991)): Let $0 < \alpha < 2$. Then, for all $\alpha < r < 2$ and i.i.d. random vectors $X, X^{(1)}, X^{(2)}$

$$\rho(n^{-1/\alpha}(X^{(1)} + \ldots + X^{(n)}), S_\alpha)$$
$$\leq C\nu_r(X, Y)n^{1-r/\alpha} + Cn^{-1/\alpha} \max\{\rho(X, Y), \nu_1(X, Y), \nu_r^{1/(r-\alpha)}(X, Y)\},$$

where C is an absolute constant.

The normalization $n^{-1/\alpha}$ for the sum of i.i.d. random vectors $X^{(1)}, \ldots, X^{(n)}$ in (7.16) leading an α-stable limiting random vector S_α, can be generalized to n^{-B}, where B is a linear operator. The possible limits for $n^{-B}(X^{(1)} + \ldots + X^{(n)})$ are called *operator-stable random vectors*.

We next give a short description of this class of generalized stable random vectors.[5]

---

[4] The convolution between F_X and F_Y is defined $F_X \circ F_Y(x) := \int_{\mathbf{R}^d} F_X(x - y) dF_Y(y), x \in \mathbf{R}^d$.

[5] The rest of the results in this section are due to Maejima and Rachev (1995).

A probability distribution μ on $\mathbf{R}^d$ is said to be full if μ is not concentrated on a proper hyperplane in $\mathbf{R}^d$. A full distribution μ on $\mathbf{R}^d$ is called *operator-stable* if there exist an invertible linear operator B on $\mathbf{R}^d$ and a function $b : (0, \infty) \to \mathbf{R}^d$ such that for all $t > 0$,

$$\hat{\mu}(z)^t = \hat{\mu}(t^{B^*}z)e^{ib(t)}, \quad \text{for all } z \in \mathbf{R}^d, \tag{7.16}$$

where $\hat{m}u$ is the characteristic function of μ, B^* is the adjoined operator of B and $t^A := \exp\{(\ln t)A\} := \sum_{k=0}^{\infty} (k!)^{-1}(\ln t)^k A^k$. The distribution μ is called *strictly operator-stable* if we can choose $b(t) \equiv 0$. We shall further assume that μ is a full strictly operator-stable distribution on $\mathbf{R}^d$. Sharpe (1969) showed that if 1 is not in the spectrum of B then the operator-stable law can be centered so as to become strictly operator-stable. Thus, the assumption of strict operator-stability is not so restrictive.

The invertible linear operator B in (7.16) is called an *exponent of* μ. When μ is operator-stable with an exponent B, μ may satisfy (7.16) for other B's. In this sense, the exponent of μ is not necessarily unique. however, throughout this paper, we fix the value of the exponent B, and denote by θ the random vector in $\mathbf{R}^d$ having the full strictly operator-stable distribution μ with this fixed B. It is known that every eigenvalue of B has its real part not less than $\frac{1}{2}$ (see Sharpe (1969)).

Let $X_1, X_2, \ldots$ be i.i.d. random vectors in $\mathbf{R}^d$. If

$$n^{-B} \sum_{i=1}^{n} X_i \overset{\omega}{\to} \theta, \tag{7.17}$$

then we say that $\{X_i\}$ belongs to the *domain of normal attraction of* μ.

We next state the an analog of Property 7.3 for operator stable random vectors.

Let $\| \cdot \|_0$ be the usual Euclidean norm of $\mathbf{R}^d$ and let $S(\mu)$ be the symmetry group associated with μ, that is, the group of all invertible linear operators A on $\mathbf{R}^d$ such that for some $a \in \mathbf{R}^d$, $\hat{\mu}(z) = \hat{\mu}(A^*z)e^{ia}$. Then since μ is full, $S(\mu)$ is compact and there exists a Haar probability measure H on the Borel subsets of $S(\mu)$. Define the following norm associated with B,

$$\|x\| \int_{S(\mu)} \int_0^1 \|g t^B x\|_0 \frac{dt}{t} dH(g); \tag{7.18}$$

$\|x\|$ was introduced by D. Weiner, (see Hudson, Veeh and Weiner (1988), also Hahn, Hudson and Veeh (1989). It has the following properties:

(i) $\| \cdot \|$ does not depend on the choice of the exponent B,

(ii) the map $t \mapsto \|t^B x\|$ is strictly increasing on $(0, \infty)$ for $x \neq 0$.

Define the norm of the linear operator A on $\mathbf{R}^d$ by $\|A\| = \sup_{\|x\|_1} \|Ax\|$. Then by property (ii) above,

(iii) the map $t \mapsto \|t^B\|$ is strictly increasing on $(0,\infty)$, (equivalently $t \mapsto$ $\|t^{-B}\| = \|(t^{-1})^B\|$ is strictly decreasing on $(0,\infty)$).

We now make a comment on the growth rate of $R(t) = \|t^B x\|$. Meerschaert (1989) showed that for every x the function $R_0(t) = \|t^B x\|_0$ varies regularly with index between λ_B and Λ_B, where λ_B and Λ_B are the minimum and the maximum of the real parts of the eigenvalues of B, respectively. On the other hand, since every norm $\|\cdot\|$ on $\mathbf{R}^d$ is equivalent to the Euclidean norm $\|\cdot\|_0$, the function $R(t) = \|t^B x\|$ is of the same order as the regularly varying function $R_0(t)$. Specifically, for any $\eta > 0$, there exists $t_0 > 0$ such that for any $t > t_0$

$$t^{\lambda_B - \eta}\|x\| < \|t^B x\| < t^{\Lambda_B + \eta}\|x\| \tag{7.19}$$

and

$$t^{-\Lambda_B - \eta}\|x\| < \|t^{-B} x\| < t^{-\lambda_B + \eta}\|x\| \tag{7.20}$$

Let $\mathcal{X}(\mathbf{R}^d)$ be the class of all random vectors in $\mathbf{R}^d$ and ρ the Kolmogorov metric in $\mathcal{X}(\mathbf{R}^d)$,

$$\rho(X,Y) := \sup_{x \in \mathbf{R}^d} |P(X \le x) - P(Y \le x)\|.$$

Here $x \le y$, or $x < y$, $x, y \in \mathbf{R}^d$, means component-wise inequality. Next we define a new uniform metric depending on the exponent B,

$$\rho^*(X,Y) := \sup_{t>0} \rho(t^B X, t^B Y).$$

Let Var be the total variation distance in $\mathcal{X}(\mathbf{R}^d)$,

$$\begin{aligned}
\operatorname{Var}(X,Y) \quad &:= \quad 2 \sup_{A \in \mathcal{B}(\mathbf{R}^d)} |P(X \in A) - P(Y \in A)| \\
&= \quad \int_{\mathbf{R}^d} |P_X - P_Y|(dx) \\
&= \quad \sup\{|\mathbf{E}f(X) - \mathbf{E}f(Y)| \; : \; f : \mathbf{R}^d \to \mathbf{R}, \text{ continuous }, \\
&\qquad\qquad |f(x)| \le 1 \text{ for all } x \in \mathbf{R}^d\}.
\end{aligned}$$

For $r > 0$, define a convolution type metric associated to Var:

$$\mu_r(X,Y) := \sup_{t>0} \|t^B\|^{-r}\operatorname{Var}(t^B X + \theta, t^B Y + \theta).$$

Here and in what follows, the notation $X_1 + X_2$ means the sum of two *independent* random vectors X_1 and X_2.

Our first result on the rate-of-convergence of normalized sum of i.i.d. vectors to operator-stable vector is the following.

Property 7.4 Let θ be a full strictly operator-stable random vector in $\mathbf{R}^d$ and B an exponent of θ. Let $r > \frac{\lambda_B}{\lambda_B} (\geq \frac{1}{\lambda_B})$ and take p such that $\frac{1}{\lambda_B} < pq\frac{\lambda_B}{\lambda_B}r$. Let $\{X_i\}_{i=1}^{\infty}$ be a sequence of i.i.d. random vectors in $\mathbf{R}^d$ with

$$\rho^* := \rho^*(X_1, \theta), \quad \mu_1 := \mu_1(X_1, \theta), \quad \mu_r := \mu_r(X_1, \theta), \qquad (7.21)$$

satisfying the moment type condition

$$\tau_r = \tau_r(X_1, \theta) := \max\left\{\rho^*, \mu_1, \mu_r^{\frac{1}{r-p}}\right\} < \infty. \qquad (7.22)$$

Then for some absolute constant $K = K(d, B, r, p) > 0$,

$$\rho\left(n^{-B}\sum_{i=1}^{n}, \theta\right) \leq \rho^*\left(n^{-B}\sum_{i=1}^{n}X_i, \theta\right) \qquad (7.23)$$

$$\leq K(n\|n^{-B}\|^r\mu_r + \|n^{-B}\|\tau_r) \quad \text{for all } n \geq 1.$$

Note that we did not explicitly assume that $\{X_i\}$ belongs to the domain of normal attraction of θ. However, since $\lambda_B > \frac{1}{2}$ and $r\lambda_B > 1$,

$$n\|n^{-B}\|^r\mu_r + \|n^{-B}\|\tau_r \to= \quad \text{as } n \to \infty,$$

because of (7.20). Consequently, conditions (7.21) and (7.22) are sufficient for $\{X_i\}$ to be in the domain of normal attraction of θ. As to the decreasing rate of $\|n^{-B}\|$, by (7.20), for every $\eta > 0$, there exists n_0 such that $\|n^{-B}\| \leq n^{-\lambda_B+\eta}$ for every $n \geq n_0$. Also, for any $\eta > 0$, we have the bound $\|n^{-B}\| \leq Mn^{-\lambda_B+\eta}$ for all $m \geq 1$, where $M = \sup_{t\geq 1}\|t^{-B+(\lambda_B-\eta)I}\| (< \infty)$.

Letting $B = \frac{1}{\alpha}I$, $0 < \alpha \leq 2$, we have the following analogue of Property 7.3.

Property 7.5 Let θ be a strictly α-stable random vector with index $0 < \alpha \leq 2$. Let $\alpha < p < r$ and $\{X_i\}$ be a sequence of i.i.d. random vectors in $\mathbf{R}^d$ satisfying $\tau_r < \infty$. Then for some absolute constant $K = K(d, \alpha, p) > 0$,

$$\rho^*\left(n^{-1/\alpha}\sum_{i=1}^{n}X_i, \theta\right) \leq K\left(n^{1-\frac{r}{\alpha}}\mu_r + n^{-\frac{1}{\alpha}}\tau_r\right) \quad \text{for all } n \geq 1. \qquad (7.24)$$

Resnick and Greenwood (1972) studied the limit theorem for $(\hat{\alpha}_1, \hat{\alpha}_2)$-stable laws[6] which corresponds to the operator-stable limit theorem with exponent

$$B = \begin{pmatrix} 1/\alpha_1 & 0 \\ 0 & 1/\alpha_2 \end{pmatrix}.$$

---

[6]We applied these laws in Chapter 8 in studying portfolios of stable returns with different indexes of stability.

Property 7.4 provides a bound for the rate-of-convergence in this particular case:

Property 7.6 Let $\theta = (\theta^{(1)}, \theta^{(2)})$ be a strictly (α_1, α_2)-stable bivariate vector (random pair), $0 < \alpha_1 \le \alpha_2 \le 2$. Let $r > \frac{\alpha_2^2}{\alpha_1}$ and take p such that $\alpha_2 < p < \frac{\alpha_1}{\alpha_2}r$. Let $\{X_i = (X_i^{(1)}, X_i^{(2)})\}_{i \ge 1}$ be a sequence of i.i.d. bivariate vectors satisfying $\tau_r < \infty$. Then for all $n \ge 1$,

$$\rho^* \left((n^{-1/\alpha_1} \sum_{i=1}^{n} X_i^{(1)}, n^{-1/\alpha_2} \sum_{i=1}^{n} X_i^{(2)}), \theta \right) \le K(n^{1-r/\alpha_1} \mu_r + n^{-1/\alpha_1} \tau_r).$$

In Properties 7.5 and 7.6 one can replace ρ^* with ρ on the left-hand side and in the definition of τ_r simultaneously. Moreover, in Property 7.5 we can assume that $\alpha \le p < r$; the case $p = \alpha$ is treated, in this particular case, in Rachev (1991), p.289.

The order on the right hand side of (7.24) is the correct order in the stable limit theorem; see Rachev (1991), Th.5.3.1.

We next state our results on the rates of convergence in the total variation distance Var. Let

$$r > \frac{1}{\lambda_B}, \quad b = \frac{5}{4} \|2^{-B}\|^r \|(\frac{2}{5})^{-B}\|^r, \quad c = \|2^B\|^r + \|3^B\|^r, \quad a = \frac{1}{bc} \|2^{-B}\|^r \tag{7.25}$$

and

$$M = \sup_{x \ge 1} \|x^{\frac{1}{r}I - B}\|^r \ (< \infty). \tag{7.26}$$

Property 7.7 Let $\{X_i\}_{i=1}^{\infty}$ be a sequence of i.i.d. random vectors in $\mathbf{R}^d$ satisfying

$$\nu_r = \nu_r(X_1, \theta) := \max\{\text{Var}(X_1, \theta), \mu_r\} \le \frac{a}{M}. \tag{7.27}$$

Then

$$\text{Var} \left(n^{-B} \sum_{i=1}^{n} X_i, \theta \right) \le cn \|n^{-B}\|^r \nu_r \le \frac{1}{bM} \|2^{-B}\|^r n \|n^{-B}\|^r \quad \text{for all } n \ge 1. \tag{7.28}$$

For the proofs of Properties 7.4-7.7 and further results we refer to Maejima and Rachev (1995).

7.2 Multivariate Max-stable and Min-stable Models. The Weibull-Marshall-Olkin distributions

As in the previous section, let $X = (X_1, \ldots, X_d), X^{(1)}, X^{(2)}$ be i.i.d. d-dimensional random vectors with common d.f. H, where $X^{(i)} = (X_1^{(i)}, \ldots, X_d^{(i)})$

represents the vector of returns of d dependent assets during the period $t = t_0 + i$.

Definition 7.3 The d.f. H is said to be *max-stable* if for all positive integers n there exist constants $a_n > 0$ and b_n such that

$$H^n(a_n^{-1}x - b_n) = H(x) \quad \text{for all } x \in \mathbf{R}^d. \tag{7.29}$$

Similarly, we say that X is *max-stable* if for all $n = 1,2,...$ there exists $a_n > 0$ and $b_n \in \mathbf{R}$ such that

$$a_n \bigvee_{j=1}^{n} X^{(j)} + b_n \stackrel{d}{=} X, \tag{7.30}$$

where $\bigvee$ denotes the max operator, i.e., $x \bigvee y := (x_1 \bigvee y_1, \ldots, x_d \bigvee y_d)$ and $ax = (ax_1, \ldots, ax_d)$ for any constant a and any vectors x and y with components x_i and y_i, respectively. If $a_n = n^{-1}$ and $b_n = 0$, H is said to be a *simple max-stable* d.f. (see de Haan and Resnick (1977)). A consequence of the definition of simple max-stable d.f. $H = F_X$ is that one dimensional marginal distributions are of the form $F_{X_j}(x) = \exp\{-c_j/x\}$, $x \geq 0$ (for some $c_j \geq 0$, $j = 1, \ldots, d$), i.e., there are of type ϕ_1, see de Haan and Rachev (1989).

Property 7.8 *(Explicit representation for simple max-stable multivariate distributions, see de Haan and Resnick, 1977)* H is simple max-stable d.f. on $\mathbf{R}$ if and only if H admits the representation

$$H(x_1, \ldots, x_d) = \exp\{- \int_S \left(\max_{1 \leq j \leq d} \frac{s_j}{x_j} \right) \lambda(ds_1, \ldots, ds_d)\},$$

where λ is a finite measure on

$$S := \{(s_1, \ldots, s_d) | s_j \geq 0, \ j = 1, \ldots, d; \sum_{j=1}^{d} s_j^2 = 1\}.$$

Simple max-stable distributions $H = F_X$ can be obtained as follows.

Property 7.9 *(Domain of attraction of simple max-stable distributions)* Let $Y^{(1)}, Y^{(2)}, \ldots$ be i.i.d. random vectors and $M_n = \bigvee_{i=1}^{n} Y^{(i)}$. If for some sequence a_n of positive constants $a_n M_n$ converges in distribution to a random vector $X = (X_1, \ldots, X_d)$, then for some $\alpha > 0$, the vector $(X_1^{1/\alpha}, \ldots, X_d^{1/\alpha})$ is simple max-stable.

Because max operations are invariant with respect to increasing monotone transformation, we can easily rewrite Properties 7.8 and 7.9 for general max-stable distributions. Here, in contrast to the multivariate stable case where the association of X depends on its spectral measure, we have the following property.

Property 7.10 *Any max-stable vector X is associated.*
 Proof: (see Definition 5.3 and Resnick, 1987a).

We can now reformulate the above results for the min-stable distributions and, especially, for multivariate Weibull distributions that arise as weak limits for minimum of i.i.d. random vectors.

Definition 7.4 The d.f. $W(x) = P(X \le x)$, $x \in \mathbf{R}^d$, is said to be *Weibull min-stable* if

$$\bar{W}^n(n^{-1/\alpha_1}x_1, n^{-1/\alpha_2}x_2, \ldots, n^{-1/\alpha_d}x_d) = \bar{W}(x) \quad \text{for all } x \in \mathbf{R}^d,$$

where $\bar{W}(x) = P(X > x) = P(X_1 > x_1, \ldots, X_d > x_d)$; the random variable X is called *Weibull min-stable*. If $\alpha_1 = \ldots = \alpha_d$ then X is called *simple min-stable*.

Each one-dimensional distribution F_{X_i} of X is Weibull, i.e.,

$$F_{X_i}(x) = \begin{cases} 0, & x \le 0 \\ 1 - \exp\{-\lambda_i x^{\alpha_i}\}, & x > 0 \end{cases}$$

for some $\lambda_i \ge 0$. If $\lambda_i = 0$, we have the degenerate case of $X_i = 0$.

Property 7.11 X is Weibull min-stable if and only if $\bar{W}(x) = P(X \ge x)$ admits the representation

$$W(X_1, \ldots, X_d) = \exp\{-\int_S \left(\max_{i \le j \le d} s_j x_j^{\alpha_j} \right) \lambda(ds_1, \ldots, ds_d)\}$$

where α_j are nonnegative constants and λ is a measure defined as in Property 7.8.

Clearly, the *bivariate Weibull-Marshall-Olkin* distribution $W_{x,\alpha}$, $\lambda = (\lambda_1, \lambda_2, \lambda_{12})$, $\alpha = (\alpha_1, \alpha_2)$, $\lambda_i > 0$, $\alpha_i > 0$,

$$\bar{W}_{\lambda,\alpha}(x,y) = \exp\{-\lambda_1 x^{\alpha_1} - \lambda_2 y^{\alpha_2} - \lambda_{12}\max(x^{\alpha_1}, y^{\alpha_2})\}, \quad x \ge 0, \ y \ge 0$$

is Weibull min-stable.[7]

Property 7.12 If X is Weibull min-stable then X is associated. In particular, if (X, Y) has a bivariate Weibull-Marshall-Olkin distribution, then (X, Y) is an associated pair of random variables.

---

[7]More facts about bivariate Weibull-Marshall-Olkin distribution will be given in the next section.

Since virtually any result concerning the max-scheme of random variables can be easily reformulated for the min-scheme we shall consider only results concerning maximum of i.i.d. random vectors and processes. The reason for studying the properties of max-stable processes is that we view asset returns as a stochastic process $Y(t)$, $t \in T$, i.e., as a random variable taking values in a certain function space B. In this setting we allow dependence of returns, $Y(t)$, $t \in T$. Let $B = B_r := (\ell_r(T), \| \cdot \|_r)$ $(1 \leq r < \infty)$ be the separable Banach space of all measurable functions $x : T \to \mathbf{R}$ (T is a Borel subset of $\mathbf{R}$) with finite norm $\|x\| = \|x\|_r := \{\int_T |x(t)|^r dt\}^{1/r}$. If $r = \infty$, we suppose that T is compact and $B_r := C(T)$ is the space of all continuous functions on T with supremum norm $\| \cdot \|_\infty$. For any a, b, x and $y \in B$ we define $x \bigvee y$ by $(x \bigvee y)(t) := x(t) \bigvee y(t)$ and $ax + b$ by $(ax + b)(t) = a(t)x(t) + b(t)$, for all $t \in T$. Let $\mathcal{X}(B)$ be the space of all B-valued r.v.'s X on a common probability space (Ω, A, P). In what follows, we assume that (Ω, A, P) has no atoms, and hence the space of all distributions $P_{X,Y}$ coincides with the space $L(B)^2)$ of all Borel probability measures on the Cartesian product $B^2 := B \times B$.

Definition 7.5 The B-valued r.v. Y is said to be *max-stable* (or a *max-stable process*), if for all $n = 1, 2, \ldots$ there exists $a_n > 0$ and b_n such that

$$a_n \bigvee_{k=1}^{n} Y_k + b_n \stackrel{d}{=} Y.$$

Y is said to be a *simple max-stable process*, if $a_n = n^{-1}$ (see de Haan and Rachev (1989) and the references therein).

Remark 7.3 *Max-stable random vectors* have been thoroughly discussed in de Haan and Resnick (1977), see also de Haan and Resnick (1994) and the references therein.

Property 7.13 *(Characterization of simple max-stable processes, see de Haan (1984)).* Let $Y = \{Y(t)\}_{t \in \mathbf{R}}$ be a continuous in probability simple max-stable process. Then there exists a finite measure ρ on $[0, 1]$ such that, if (X_k, T_k) is an enumeration of the points in the Poisson process on $\mathbf{R}_+ \times [0, 1]$ with intensity measure $(dx/x^2)\rho(ds)$, the random variables

$$Z_t = \max_{k \geq 1} f_t(T_k) X_k$$

with suitable functions $f_t \geq 0$, $\int_0^1 f_t(s)\rho(ds) < \infty$, have the same finite-dimensional distributions as Y.

From Property 7.13 one can easily obtain the formula for *Weibull-min processes* Y with "shape" parameter $\alpha > 0$, i.e.,

$$Y \stackrel{d}{=} n^{1/\alpha} \bigwedge_{i=1}^{n} Y^{(i)}$$

where $Y^{(i)}$'s are i.i.d. copies of Y, and $\bigwedge$ denotes the min operator.

Example 7.2 (*Weibull-min process Y*, see de Haan and Rachev (1989)). Consider a Poisson point process on $\mathbf{R}_+ \times [0,1]$ with intensity measure (dx^α) (dt). Let $\{X_k, T_k\}_{k=1}^\infty$ be an enumeration of the points in the process. Consider the family of nonnegative functions $\{f_t(\cdot)\}_{t \in T}$ defined on $[0,1]$. Suppose for any fixed $t \in T$ the function $f_t(\cdot)$ is measurable and

$$\int_0^1 f_t(x)^{-\alpha} dx < \infty, \quad \alpha > 0.$$

Then the family of random variables $(t \in T)$

$$Y_t := \inf_{k \geq 1} f_t(T_k) \cdot X_k$$

form a Weibull-min process. Clearly it is sufficient to show that for any $n = 1, 2, \ldots$ and $0 < t_1 < \ldots < t_n \in T$ the joint distribution of $(Y(t_1), \ldots, Y(t_n))$ satisfies

$$\left(P(r^{1/\alpha} Y(t_1) > y_1, \ldots, r^{1/\alpha} Y(t_n) > y_n) \right)^r = P(Y(t_1) > y_1, \ldots, Y(t_n) > y_n).$$

This equality holds, because

$$
\begin{aligned}
&P^r\{r^{1/\alpha} Y(t_1) > y_1, \ldots, r^{1/\alpha} Y(t_n) > y_n\} \\
&= P^r\{Y(t_1) > r^{-1/\alpha} y_1, \ldots, Y(t_n) > r^{-1/\alpha} y_n\} \\
&= P^r\{f_{t_i}(T_k) \cdot X_k > r^{-1/\alpha} y_i, \quad i = 1, \ldots, n, \quad k = 1, 2, \ldots\} \\
&\qquad \text{(because } Y(t) := \inf_{k \geq 1} f_t(T_k) \cdot X_k) \\
&= P^r\{X_k > r^{-1/\alpha} \max_{1 \leq i \leq n} y_i / f_{t_i}(T_k) \quad \text{for } k = 1, 2, \ldots\} \\
&= P^r\{\text{there are no points of the point process} \\
&\qquad \text{below the graph of function } g \colon [0,1] \to \mathbf{R}_+ \\
&\qquad \text{defined by } g(s) = r^{1/\alpha} \max_{1 \leq i \leq n} y_i / f_{t_i}(s)\} \\
&= \exp\left(-\int_0^1 \left[\int_{\mathbf{R}} I\{0 < x < r^{-1/\alpha} \max_{1 \leq i \leq n} y_i / f_{t_i}(s)\} dx^\alpha \right] ds \right)^r \\
&= \exp\left(-\int_0^1 r \max_{1 \leq i \leq n} y_i^\alpha / f_{t_i}^\alpha(s) ds \right)^r \\
&= \exp\left(-\int_0^1 r \max_{1 \leq i \leq n} y_i^\alpha / f_{t_i}^\alpha(s) ds \right) \\
&= P(Y(t_1) > y_1, \ldots, Y(t_n) > y_n).
\end{aligned}
$$

In the following, we shall consider only simple max-stable processes. In order to pass to the corresponding results for Weibull-min processes $\{Y(t)_{t \in T}\}$, one should use the fact that $X(t) = Y(t)^{-\alpha}$, $t \in T$ is a simple max-stable process.

Definition 7.6 A random process $X \in \mathcal{X}(\mathbb{B})$ belongs to the max-domain of attraction of a max-stable process Y if there exists constants $a_n > 0$ and b_n such that

$$a_n \bigvee_{i=1}^{n} X_i + b_n \overset{d}{\to} Y,$$

where X_i's are i.i.d. copies of X.

7.3   Weibull and Weibull-Marshall-Olkin Distributions: An Application to Stock Returns Distributions

In Section 7.2 we characterize Weibull-Marshall-Olkin laws as min-stable. In this section we will provide additional characterizations. Recall first the definitions of Weibull distribution function (d.f.):

$$W_{\lambda,\alpha}(x) = \begin{cases} 1 - e^{-\lambda x^\alpha}, & x \geq 0 \\ 0, & x < 0, \end{cases} \tag{7.31}$$

and the the bivariate Weibull-Marshall-Olkin d.f.

$$W_{\lambda,\alpha}(x,y) := \begin{cases} P(X \leq x, Y \leq y),, & x \geq 0, y \geq 0 \\ 0, & \text{otherwise}, \end{cases} \tag{7.32}$$

where $\lambda = (\lambda_1, \lambda_2, \lambda_{12})$, $\alpha = (\alpha_1, \alpha_2)$, $\lambda_i >$ and $\alpha_i > 0$, which is determined by the so-called "survivor" function

$$\bar{W}_{\lambda,\alpha}(x_1,y) := P(X > x, Y > y) = \exp\{-\lambda_1 x^{\alpha_1} - \lambda_2 y^{\alpha_2} - \lambda_{12} \max(x^{\alpha_1}, y^{\alpha_2})\}. \tag{7.33}$$

Here X and Y could represent the absolute returns of two *dependent* assets; or X could be the absolute return of an asset and Y the corresponding trading volume. Clearly, the marginal distributions of X and Y in (7.32) are both Weibull, $P(X > x) = \exp\{-(\lambda_1 + \lambda_{12})x^{\alpha_1}\}$, $x \geq 0$, and $P(Y > y) = \exp\{-(\lambda_2 + \lambda_{12})y^{\alpha_2}\}$, $y \geq 0$.

Without loss of generality, we may set case $\alpha = 1$ in (7.31). Since X possesses the Weibull distribution $W_{\lambda,\alpha}$ if and only if X^α has exponential distribution

$$E_\lambda(x) = P(X^\alpha < x) = \begin{cases} 1 - e^{-\lambda x}, & x \geq 0 \\ 0, & x < 0, \end{cases} \tag{7.34}$$

one can easily relate the properties of E_λ to the ones of the Weibull distribution $W_{\lambda,\alpha}$. Clearly, the vector (X,Y) has the joint Weibull-Marshall-Olkin distribution $W_{\lambda,\alpha}$ if and only if the vector $(X^{\alpha_1}, Y^{\alpha_2})$ has the joint Marshall-Olkin distribution

$$MO_\lambda(x,y) := P(X^{\alpha_1} > x, Y^{\alpha_2} > y) \qquad (7.35)$$

which is determined by

$$\bar{MO}_\lambda(x,y) := P(X^{\alpha_1} > x, Y^{\alpha_2} > y) = \exp\{-\lambda_1 x - \lambda_2 y - \lambda_{12}\max(x,y)\}. \qquad (7.36)$$

Thus having a characterization for the MO_λ-distribution, we can easily pass to the corresponding characterization of $W_{\lambda,\alpha}$.

We start with the univariate case-characterization of the Weibull distribution. By the property (7.34), it is enough to consider the case $\alpha = 1$, i.e. to deal with the exponential distribution only. Historically, the study of the exponential distribution within the framework of mathematical statistics began at a rather late date, only after a number of fundamental concepts of this discipline had been fully established. The theory of characterizations of the exponential distribution started even later. The book by Galambos and Kotz (1978) gives good collection of results of various kinds for the characterizations of the exponential distribution, also Obretanov and Rachev (1983) and Baxter and Rachev (1990).[8]

For illustrative purposes, we fitted the bivariate normal (BN), the bivariate exponential Marshall-Olkin (BEMO, see (7.36) and the bivariate Weibull-Marshall-Olkin (BWMO), see (7.33) distributions to daily stock return data of Chrysler and Ford covering the two-year period 1987-1988. The returns are measured by $r_t = lnp_t^* - lnp_{t-1}^*$, where p_t^* denotes the dividend-corrected price of a stock. The sample consists of 506 pairs of observations. Since both stocks are from the automobile sector, they are expected to be highly dependent. The chosen sample period is, from a statistical viewpoint, a difficult one, since it includes the stock market crash in October 1987 where both stocks experienced substantial price drops and a subsequent period of high volatility. As in the univariate case, we used the Kolmogorov distance (multiplied by 100) to measure the goodness of fit.

The means and standard deviations of the returns over the sample period are 5.693×10^{-4} and 2.599×10^{-2} for Chrysler and 1.556×10^{-3} and 2.112×10^{-2} for Ford; the correlation coefficient is 0.696. We measure the fit by examining the joint distribution $Pr(-x < X < x, -y < Y < y)$, which is of interest in a number of financial applications. The Kolmogorov distance for the BN distribution is $100\rho_{BN} = 8.86$.

When fitting the BEMO and BWMO distributions, one could estimate separate distributions for each of the four quadrants in $\mathbf{R}^2$ which would give rise to a total of 16 and 24 parameters, respectively. To reduce the parameter space to some extent, we assume symmetry, i.e., we impose the restriction

---

[8]See also Kakosyan, Klebanov and Melamed (1984) and Azlarov and Volodin (1986).

that the parameters are equal for all four quadrants, and, in addition, restrict λ_{12} to unity. This leaves us with three free parameters to estimate for the BEMO distribution and with five free parameters for the BWMO distribution. Since the specification of the BN requires five parameters, we are comparing the BN distribution with distributions that have less or the same number of free parameters.

Despite the restrictions imposed, both the BEMO and the BWMO distributions provide a better fit, namely $100\rho_{BEMO} = 7.40$ and $100\rho_{BWMO} = 4.40$, than the BN distribution. Table 7.1 reports the parameter estimates of the two distributions. Being specified by the same number of parameters the BWMO distribution yields a substantially better fit than the BN distribution. Even the three-parameter BEMO fits slightly better than the BN distribution.

Table 7.1   Estimates and Fit of BEMO and BWMO Distributions

Estimates	BEMO	BWMO	BN
α_1	n.a.	1.003	n.a.
α_2	n.a.	1.147	n.a.
λ_1	27.06	39.15	n.a.
λ_2	33.69	59.55	n.a.
k	1.807	27.42	n.a.
100ρ	7.396	4.398	8.858

7.4   Multivariate (α, M)-stable Distributions

The first example of a multivariate stable distribution with respect to multiplication scheme (shortly, multivariate (α, M)-stable distribution) is the (symmetric) multivariate log-normal distribution with density

$$
f_{\mathbf{X}}(\mathbf{x}) = \begin{cases} g(\ln x_1, \ldots, \ln x_d) \prod_{i=1}^{n} \dfrac{1}{x_i}, & \text{for } \mathbf{x} = (x_1, \ldots, x_d) \in \mathbf{R}_+^d \\ 0 & \text{otherwise} \end{cases} \tag{7.37}
$$

where g is the multivariate normal density

$$
g(\mathbf{x}) = \frac{1}{(2\pi)^{d/2}\sqrt{|A^{-1}|}} \exp[-\frac{1}{2}(\mathbf{x} - \mu)^{\mathrm{T}}A(\mathbf{x} - \mu)] \tag{7.38}
$$

with a mean-value vector μ and covariance matrix A^{-1}. In other words the vector $\mathbf{X} = (X_1, \ldots, X_d)$ has multivariate log-normal distribution if and only if

$$
X_i = e^{Y_i}, \quad i = 1, \ldots, d
$$

where $\mathbf{Y} = (Y_1, \ldots, Y_d)$ is a multivariate normal distribution.

For the general definition of a multivariate (α, M)-stable distribution we invoke the definition of multivariate $(\alpha, +)$-stable distribution (cf. Definition 7.1).

Definition 7.7 The random vector $\mathbf{X} = (X_1, \ldots, X_d)$ has an (α, M)-stable distribution if

$$X_i = \exp\{S_i\}, \quad i = 1, \ldots, d, \tag{7.39}$$

where $\mathbf{S} = (S_1, \ldots, S_d)$ has a ch.f. given by (7.3), (7.4).

Remark 7.4 Another plausible definition instead of (7.39) is

$$X_i = (\text{sign} S_i) \exp\{S_i\}. \tag{7.40}$$

The results regarding the domain of attraction for (α, M)-stable in both cases, (7.39), (7.40) are similar.

The stability property for multivariate (α, M)-stable random vector follows from (7.39): a non-negative random vector $\mathbf{X}$ is (α, M)-stable iff for any i.i.d. copies $\mathbf{X}^{(1)}, \ldots, \mathbf{X}^{(n)}$ of $\mathbf{X}$, there exist constants $A_n > 0$ such that

$$A_n (\mathbf{X}^{(1)} \cdots \mathbf{X}^{(n)})^{n^{-1/\alpha}} \overset{\mathrm{d}}{=} \mathbf{X}. \tag{7.41}$$

The multiplication in (7.40) is determined by $\mathbf{x} \cdot \mathbf{y} := (x_1 y_1, \ldots, x_d y_d)$. Further we shall consider the domain of attraction of a normalized product of random vectors to the multivariate log-normal distribution. Consider a sequence of independent identically distributed random vectors $\mathbf{X}^{(1)}, \mathbf{X}^{(2)}, \ldots$, with values in $\mathbf{R}_+^d$. Let $\mathbf{Y}^{(n)} := \ln \mathbf{X}^{(n)}$, i.e.,

$$Y_i^{(n)} = \ln\{X_i^{(n)}\}, \quad i = 1, \ldots, d, \tag{7.42}$$

and suppose that $\mathbf{E}\mathbf{Y}_1^{(1)} = 0$, $\mathbf{E}\|Y_1\|^{(2)} < \infty$, where $\|\cdot\|$ stands for the Euclidean norm in $\mathbf{R}^d$. We shall assume that the covariance operator of $\mathbf{Y}_1$ is the identity operator on $\mathbf{R}^d$. Let $\mathbf{Y}$ be a standard normal distributed vector with zero mean and identity covariance operator. Define $\mathbf{X} := \exp\{\mathbf{Y}\}$, i.e., $X_i = \exp\{Y_i\}$ for all $i = 1, \ldots, d$. We shall use the following metrics:

(i)
$$\rho(\mathbf{X}^*, \mathbf{Y}^*) = \sup\{|P(\mathbf{X}^* \in A) - P(\mathbf{Y}^* \in A)| A \in \mathbf{C}\},$$

where $\mathbf{C}$ is the set of all convex Borel subsets of $\mathbf{R}^d$ (ρ is called the *uniform metric over all convex subsets*);

(ii) *the total variation distance*

$$\nu(\mathbf{X}^*, \mathbf{Y}^*) = \sup_{A \in B(\mathbf{R}^d)} |P(\mathbf{X}^* \in A) - P(\mathbf{Y}^* \in A)|, \tag{7.43}$$

where $\mathcal{B}(\mathbf{R}^d)$ is the Borel σ-algebra in $\mathbf{R}^d$;

(iii) For any positive random vectors $\mathbf{X}^*$ and $\mathbf{Y}^*$ define

$$\xi_S(\mathbf{X}^*, \mathbf{Y}^*) = \sup_{f \in \mathcal{F}_S} |\mathbf{E}f(\ln \mathbf{X}^*) - \mathbf{E}f(\ln \mathbf{Y}^*)|, \qquad (7.44)$$

where $\mathcal{F}_S$, $S = m+\alpha$, $m = 0, 1, \ldots, \alpha \in (0,1]$, is the class of all bounded real functions on $\mathbf{R}^d$ such that

$$|f^{(m)}(x) - f^{(m)}(y)| \leq \|x - y\|^\alpha, \quad x, y \in \mathbf{R}^d.$$

(For $d = 1$, ξ_S was introduced by Grigorevski (1980). If $\mathbf{X}^*, \mathbf{Y}^* \in \mathbf{R}^d_+$, $\mathbf{E}\|\ln \mathbf{X}^*\|^{2+\delta} + \mathbf{E}\|\ln \mathbf{Y}^*\|^{2+\delta} < \infty$ for some $0 < \delta \leq 1$ and

$$\mathbf{E}\ln X_i^* = \mathbf{E}\ln Y_i^* \qquad (7.45)$$
$$\mathbf{E}(\ln X_i^*)(\ln X_j^*) = \mathbf{E}(\ln Y_i^*)(\ln Y_j^*), \qquad (7.46)$$

then

$$\xi_{2+\delta}(\mathbf{X}^*, \mathbf{Y}^*) \leq c \left(\mathbf{E}\|\ln \mathbf{X}^*\|^{2+\delta} + \mathbf{E}\|\ln \mathbf{Y}^*\|\right)^{2+\delta}. \qquad (7.47)$$

Here and below c denotes absolute constants which may be different in different places.

Theorem 7.8 *Let $\mathbf{X}^{(i)}$ and $\mathbf{Y}$ be defined as above. Then*

(a) for any $n \geq 1$

$$\rho\left((\mathbf{X}^{(1)} \cdots \mathbf{X}^{(n)})^{n^{-1/2}}, \mathbf{Y}\right) \leq c\xi_{2+\delta}(\mathbf{X}^{(1)}, \mathbf{Y})n^{-\delta/2}$$
$$+ c[\rho(\mathbf{X}^{(1)}, \mathbf{Y}) + \xi_1(\mathbf{X}^{(1)}, \mathbf{Y})$$
$$+ y_{2+\delta}^{1/\delta}(\mathbf{X}^{(1)}, \mathbf{Y})]n^{-1/2};$$

(b) there exists a constant $\alpha > 0$, such that if $\nu(\mathbf{X}^{(1)}, \mathbf{Y}) + \xi_3(\mathbf{X}^{(1)}, \mathbf{Y}) < \alpha$ then, for $n \geq 1$

$$\nu(\mathbf{X}^{(1)} \cdots \mathbf{X}^{(n)})^{n^{-1/2}}, \mathbf{Y}) \leq c(\alpha)[\nu(\mathbf{X}^{(1)}, \mathbf{Y}) + \xi_3(\mathbf{X}^{(1)}, \mathbf{Y})]n^{-1/2}.$$

The proof is similar to Senatov (1980, Theorems 1 and 3) and hence it is omitted.

7.5 Multivariate Geo-stable Distributions

The geo-stable model[9] for a vector of asset returns is defined similarly to the univariate case, see Section 2.2. The vector of returns of d assets during period

[9]The results of this section are due to Klebanov, Mittnik, Rachev, and Volkovich (1998).

i is denoted by $X^{(i)} = (X_1^{(i)}, \ldots, X_d^{(i)})$ with $\{X^{(i)}\}_{i \geq 1}$ being a sequence of i.i.d. random vectors. The cumulative returns up to a geometrically distributed random moment $T(p)$,

$$\mathbf{P}\{T(p) = k\} = (1 - p)^{k-1}p, \quad k = 1, 2, \ldots,$$

is given by the geometric sum

$$Y_p = \sum_{i=1}^{T(p)} X^{(i)}.$$

Here, $T(p)$ represents the moment at which the probabilistic structure governing the fundamentals of asset returns breaks down. Component k of vector $(Y_{p,1}, \ldots, Y_{p,d})$ denotes the cumulative return of asset k up to the moment of the 'crash' T_p, i.e.

$$Y_{p,k} = \sum_{i=1}^{T(p)} X_k^{(i)}, \quad k = 1, 2, \ldots, d.$$

Definition 7.8 The d-dimensional random vector Y is said to be multivariate strictly geometric stable (in short, strictly d-geo-stable, or simply, geo-stable) if there exists a sequence of i.i.d. random vectors $X^{(1)}, \ldots, X^{(n)}, \ldots$, a geometric random variable $T(p)$ independent of Y, and constants $a(p) > 0$, such that

$$a(p)Y_p \overset{w}{\to} Y, \text{ as } p \to 0.$$

Recall that $f_S(t) = \mathbf{E} \exp\{i(t, S)\}$ [10] is a characteristic function (ch.f.) of an α-stable d-dimensional random vector S if and only if there exist a finite measure Γ_S on the unit sphere $S^d = \{x : \|x\| = 1\}$ in $\mathbf{R}^d$ and a vector $\mu_S \in \mathbf{R}^d$ such that:

$$f_S(t) = \exp\left\{ -\int_{S^d} |(t,x)|^\alpha (1 - i \operatorname{sign}((t,x)) \tan \frac{\pi\alpha}{2}) \Gamma_S(dx) + i(t, \mu_S) \right\}$$

if $\alpha \neq 1$, and

$$f_S(t) = \exp\left\{ -\int_{S^d} |(t,x)|(1 + i\frac{\pi}{2} \operatorname{sign}((t,x)) \ln |(t,x)|\Gamma_S(dx) + i(t, \mu_S) \right\},$$

if $\alpha = 1$ (see 7.1). The pair (Γ_S, μ_S) is unique. Furthermore, S is a strictly α-stable vector if and only if

(i) in the case $\alpha \neq 1$,

$$\mu_S = 0,$$

---

[10] Here and what follows $(.,.)$ denotes the inner product, and $\|.\|$ is the L_2-norm.

(ii) in the case $\alpha = 1$,

$$\int_{S^d} (t, x) \Gamma_S(dx) = 0,$$

for all $t \in \mathbf{R}^d$, i.e. $\int_{S^d} x_k \Gamma(dx) = 0$ for all $k = 1, \ldots, d$.

The connection between strictly d-geo-stable random vectors and the strictly stable random vectors, see Section 7.1.

Proposition 7.1 A random vector G with ch.f. f_G is said to be strictly d-geo-stable if and only if its ch.f. is of the form

$$f_G(t) = \frac{1}{1 - \ln f_S(t)}, \quad t \in \mathbf{R}^d, \tag{7.48}$$

where f_S is the ch.f. of some strictly stable (d-dimensional) random vector S.

A major drawback in practical applications, such as risk assessment or estimation, has been the fact that the geo-stable distribution does not have an explicit representation and that there is no direct parametric description. In this section we present a new form of the ch.f. for the multivariate geo-stable distribution. It gives rise to a parametric description and permits the construction of straightforward estimators.

Theorem 7.9 Let G be a strictly geo-stable random vector in $\mathbf{R}^d$ with ch.f. $f_G(t)$, $t \in \mathbf{R}^d$, and let

$$\tau_G = \mathbf{C} + \mathbf{E} \ln \|G\|, \tag{7.49}$$

where the $\mathbf{C}$ denotes the Euler constant,

$$\mathbf{C} = \lim_{n \to \infty} \left(\sum_{i=1}^{n} \frac{1}{i} - \ln n \right) = -\Gamma'(1),$$

and $\Gamma(.)$ is the Gamma function. Then,

$$f_G(t) = \frac{1}{1 + \exp\left\{\alpha\tau_G + \alpha \int_{S^d} [\ln |(t, x)| - \frac{i\pi}{2} \operatorname{sign}(t, x)] d\sigma_G(x)\right\}}, \tag{7.50}$$

and

$$\sigma_G(A) = \mathbf{P}\left\{ \frac{G}{\|G\|} \in A \right\} \tag{7.51}$$

is a finite measure on the unit sphere S^d.

Proof. See Klebanov, Mittnik, Rachev, and Volkovich (1998). $\qquad \square$

The above leads to the following representation for the ch.f. of strictly geo-stable random variable Y:

$$f_Y(t) = \frac{1}{1 + \exp\left\{\alpha \ln |t| + \alpha \mathbf{E}\left(\ln |Y| - \frac{i\pi}{2} \operatorname{sign}(tY)\right) + \alpha\mathbf{C}\right\}} . \tag{7.52}$$

In the case of α-stable characteristic functions a similar representation is obtained in Lisitsky

Proposition 7.2 Suppose S is a strictly α-stable random vector with ch.f. $f_S(t)$. Then

$$f_S(t) = \exp\left\{ - \exp(\alpha \tau_S + \alpha \int_{S^d} (\ln |(y, x)| - \frac{i\pi}{2} \operatorname{sign}(y, x) \sigma_S(dx)) \right\},$$

where $\tau_S = \mathbf{C}\left(1 - \frac{1}{\alpha}\right) + \mathbf{E} \ln \|S\|$, and $\sigma_S(A) = \mathbf{P}\left\{ \frac{S}{\|S\|} \in A \right\}$.

Note that in Proposition 7.2, $\sigma_S \neq \sigma_G$ and $\tau_S \neq \tau_G$, and so, Theorem 7.9 is not a direct corollary of Propositions 7.1 and 7.2.

In case where the characteristic exponent α is known, Theorem 7.9 gives rise to straightforward construction of estimators for parameter τ_G and measure σ_G. If $\left(G^{(1)}, \ldots, G^{(n)}\right)$ is a sample from a population with strictly geo-stable d-dimensional distribution, then

$$\hat{\tau}_G = \mathbf{C} + \frac{1}{n} \sum_{i=1}^{n} \ln \|X^{(i)}\|$$

is a consistent estimator of τ ; and the empirical measure

$$\hat{\sigma}_G(A) = \frac{1}{n} \sum_{j=1}^{n} \mathbf{I}_{\left\{ \frac{G^j}{\|G^j\|} \in A \right\}}$$

is a consistent estimator for measure σ_G.

Similar estimators can be derived in case of multivariate α-stable distribution: if $\left(S^{(1)}, \ldots, S^{(n)}\right)$ is a sample from a population with a strictly α-stable distribution, then

$$\hat{\tau}_S = \mathbf{C}\left(1 - \frac{1}{\alpha}\right) + \frac{1}{n} \sum_{i=1}^{n} \ln \|S^{(i)}\|$$

is a consistent estimator of τ_S; and the empirical measure $\hat{\sigma}_S$ constructed from the normalized sample

$$\frac{S^{(1)}}{\|S^{(1)}\|}, \frac{S^{(2)}}{\|S^{(2)}\|}, \ldots, \frac{S^{(n)}}{\|S^{(n)}\|}$$

is a consistent estimator for measure σ_S.

Next we derive consistent estimators of α for

(i) d-geo-stable sample, and

(ii) α-stable sample.

(i) If $f_G(t)$, $t \in \mathbf{R}^d$ is the ch.f. of a strictly geo-stable random vector G, then, for all $p \in [0, 1]$

$$f_G(p^{1/\alpha}t) = \frac{f_G(t)}{p + (1 - p)f_G(t)}.$$

The function f is differentiable at any point t with non-zero coordinates. Setting $p = 1$ after the differentiating the previous relation with respect to p we obtain

$$\frac{i}{\alpha}\mathbf{E}(e^{i(t,G)}(G, t)) = -f_G(t)(1 - f_G(t)),$$

and thus

$$\alpha = -Im\frac{\mathbf{E}(e^{i(t,G)}(G, t))}{f_G(t)(1 - f_G(t))}. \tag{7.53}$$

Representation (7.53) holds for all t with non-zero coordinates, and in particular, for $t = \mathbf{1} = (1, \ldots, 1)^T$. To construct an consistent estimator for α it is sufficient to set $t = \mathbf{1}$ in (7.53) and replace the expectation and the ch.f. by their empirical counterparts. If now $(G^{(1)}, G^{(2)}, \ldots, G^{(n)})$ is a sample from a population with strictly geo-stable distribution, then

$$\hat{\alpha}_G = -Im\frac{\frac{1}{n}\sum_{j=1}^n u_j e^{iu_j}}{\frac{1}{n}\sum_{j=1}^n e^{iu_j}\left(1 - \frac{1}{n}\sum_{j=1}^n e^{iu_j}\right)}, \tag{7.54}$$

where $u_j = (G^{(j)}, \mathbf{1})$, is a *consistent estimator for* α.

(ii) In similar way we can construct a consistent estimator for the parameter α in case of strictly α-stable d-dimensional distribution. The ch.f. f_S of a strictly α-stable random vector S satisfies

$$f_S^b(t) = f_S(tb^{1/\alpha})$$

for all $b \geq 0$. Differentiating both sides of this equation with respect to b and setting $b = 1$ we find

$$f_S(t)\ln f_S(t) = (gradf_S(t), t)\frac{1}{\alpha}$$

or

$$\alpha = \frac{(gradf_S(t), t)}{f_S(t)\ln f_S(t)}. \tag{7.55}$$

Analogously to the arguments we used in (i) we obtain that if $(S^{(1)}, \ldots, S^{(n)})$ is a sample from a population with strictly α-stable d-dimensional distribution, then

$$\hat{\alpha}_S = Im\frac{\frac{1}{n}\sum_{j=1}^n v_j e^{iv_j}}{\frac{1}{n}\sum_{j=1}^n e^{iv_j}\ln(\frac{1}{n}\sum_{j=1}^n e^{iv_j})} \tag{7.56}$$

where $v_j = (S^{(j)}, \mathbf{1})$, is a *consistent estimator for* α.

The estimators (7.54) and (7.56) can be applied as initial estimators for one-step maximum likelihood estimation ("method of scoring", see, for example, Rao (1973, p. 366-368), in the case when the densities of these theoretical distributions are represented by fast convergent integrals (see Klebanov, Melamed, Mittnik and Rachev (1996)).

8

Estimation, Association, Risk, and Symmetry of Stable Portfolios

8.1 Overview

While much work has been devoted to investigate the distribution of individual asset return series, multivariate distributions of sets of assets have rarely been studied. Some results in this area can be found in Press (1972a, Chapter 12) and Mittnik and Rachev (1991). This surprises somewhat, given that modern portfolio management and asset– pricing theories involve distributional properties of sets of investment opportunities. In portfolio theory, for example, the Markowitz model assumes that returns of alternative investments have a joint multivariate distribution whose relevant properties are described by the mean and covariance matrix. In fact, and the optimal composition of an investor's portfolio depends crucially on the covariances between the individual returns. The issues of portfolio selection and asset pricing in the context of portfolios with multivariate stable distributions will be addressed in the next chapter. In this chapter we provide the necessary concepts to tackle these questions. In particular, we consider the questions of how to estimate the stability index of a stable Paretian portfolio; how to measure the association or dependence between two or more stable return series; how to specify the risk of a portfolio; and how test for multivariate symmetry.

Before dealing with these issues, it should be noted that returns need not obey a stable law for the results below to be useful. It suffices that they lie in the domain of attraction of a stable law, i.e., in the long run, the normalized sum of returns approximates closely that of the multivariate stable law specified below in (8.3). Equivalently, this means that the returns have distributions with Pareto-like tails, that is they have the same tail-behavior as the corresponding stable law they are "attracted to", see (8.5) below.

8.2   Estimation of the Index of Stability and the Spectral Measure

Recall that a d-dimensional random vector X (interpreted as the vector of returns) satisfies an *stable Paretian law* if its characteristic function has the form

$$\mathbf{E}e^{i(X,t)} \tag{8.1}$$

$$= \exp\left\{ -\int_{S_d} |(s,\mathbf{t})|^\alpha [1 - i\text{sign}(s,\mathbf{t})\phi(\alpha; s,\mathbf{t})]\Gamma(ds) + i(\mu_0,\mathbf{t}) \right\}, \quad \mathbf{t} \in \mathbf{R}^d,$$

where S_d is the unit hypersphere in $\mathbf{R}^d$; Γ is a finite Borel measure on S_d, $\mu_0 \in \mathbf{R}^d$; and

$$\phi(\alpha; s, t) = \begin{cases} \tan\frac{\pi\alpha}{2}, & \text{if } \alpha \neq 1, \\ -\frac{2}{\pi}\ln|(s,\mathbf{t})|, & \text{if } \alpha = 1. \end{cases}$$

Another way of stating this is that there exist a vector $\mathbf{b}_n \in \mathbf{R}^d$ such that the *summation–stability property*

$$n^{-\frac{1}{\alpha}} \sum_{i=1}^{n} X_i - \mathbf{b}_n \overset{d}{=} X$$

holds for all n, where the X_i are i.i.d. copies of X. Let Φ be the distribution of Γ. Passing to polar coordinates in (8.1), the characteristic function of X can be written in the form

$$\mathbf{E}e^{i(X,t)} = \exp\Big\{ -|\mathbf{t}|^\alpha \Big[\int_0^\pi \int_0^\pi \cdots$$

$$\cdots \int_0^{2\pi} |\cos(\mathbf{t},\theta)|^\alpha [1 - i\text{sign}(\cos(\mathbf{t},\theta))\tilde{\phi}(\alpha; \mathbf{t},\theta)]d\Phi(\theta)]$$

$$+i(\mathbf{t},\mu_0)\Big\}, \tag{8.2}$$

where

$$\tilde{\phi}(\alpha; \mathbf{t},\theta) := \begin{cases} \tan\frac{\pi\alpha}{2}, & \text{if } \alpha \neq 1, \\ -\frac{2}{\pi}\ln(\rho|\cos(\mathbf{t},\theta)), & \text{if } \alpha = 1, \end{cases}$$

with

$$\mathbf{t} = (\rho\sin\varphi_1 \ldots \sin\varphi_{d-1}, \rho\sin\varphi_1 \cdots \cos\varphi_{d-1}, \ldots, \rho\cos\varphi_1)'$$

and

$$\cos(\mathbf{t},\theta) = \left(\prod_{i=1}^{d} \sin\varphi_i \sin\theta_i\right) + \ldots + \cos\varphi_1\cos\theta_1.$$

Distribution function Φ has support on $\Omega_d = [0,\pi]^{d-2} \times [0,2\pi]$ and total mass $\Gamma(S_d)$.

Random vector $\mathbf{Z}$ is said to be in the *domain of attraction of* X, if there exist scalar $a_n > 0$ and vector $\mathbf{b_n} \in \mathbf{R^d}$, such that

$$\frac{1}{a_n} \sum_{i=1}^{n} \mathbf{Z_i} - b_n \xrightarrow{d} X, \tag{8.3}$$

with $\mathbf{Z_i}$ being i.i.d. copies of $\mathbf{Z}$.

The assumption that the $\mathbf{Z_i}$'s are i.i.d. is not overly restrictive. Under some regularity conditions (cf. Lipster and Shiryaev (1980); and Rachev and Rüschendorf (1998), Chapter 8), the Central Limit Theorem for convergence of martingales to a stable limit implies that the asymptotic results will be preserved even if $\mathbf{Z_i}$'s are martingale differences.[1]

Rewriting (8.3) in terms of the polar coordinates of $\mathbf{Z}$, denoted by $\rho = |\mathbf{Z}|$ and $\Theta = \theta(\mathbf{Z}), \Theta = (\theta_1, \ldots, \theta_{d-1}) \in \Omega_d$, we have

$$\lim_{n \to \infty} \frac{P(\rho > rx, \Theta_1 < \theta_1, \ldots, \Theta_{d-1} < \theta_{d-1})}{P(\rho > rx, \Theta_1 < \tilde{\theta}_1, \ldots, \Theta_{d-1} < \tilde{\theta}_{d-1})} = r^{-\alpha} \frac{\Phi(\theta_1, \ldots, \theta_{d-1})}{\Phi(\tilde{\theta}_1, \ldots, \tilde{\theta}_{d-1})}. \tag{8.4}$$

For $\alpha \in (0, 2)$, (8.4) is equivalent to

$$\lim_{n \to \infty} nP(\rho > ra_n, \Theta \leq \theta) = r^{-\alpha} \Phi(\theta) \tag{8.5}$$

(see Rvaceva (1962), pp. 196-197; de Haan and Resnick (1977); and Resnick and Greenwood (1979)). The interpretation of (8.5) is as follows: while the returns $\mathbf{X} = (X_1, \ldots, X_d)$ follow a multivariate stable distribution, our observations (say daily price changes) $\mathbf{Z}_i$ are in the domain of attraction of $\mathbf{X}$. Indeed, if $\mathbf{Z}_i \stackrel{d}{=} \mathbf{X}$ then $\mathbf{Z}_i$ are in the domain of attraction of $\mathbf{X}$. The aim of this section is the construction of tail-estimators for the index of stability α and the spectral-distribution function Φ.

Let $k = k_n$ be a sequence of integers satisfying $1 \leq k \leq n/2, n \in N, k \to \infty$ and $k/n \to 0$ as $n \to \infty$; and let (ρ_i, Θ_i) be the polar coordinates of $\mathbf{Z}_i$. We assume that ρ has a continuous characteristic function. We start with the definition of the *tail-estimator for the index of stability* α, namely we define

$$\alpha_n = \alpha_{n,k} := \frac{\ln 2}{\ln \rho_{n-k+1:n} - \ln \rho_{n-2k+1:n}}, \tag{8.6}$$

where $\rho_{k:n}$ denotes the k-th order statistics from $(\rho_1, \ldots, \rho_n)$. Next, we define the tail-estimator for the normalized spectral measure, $\varphi(\theta) = \Phi(\theta)/\Phi(\pi, \pi, \ldots, 2\pi)$:

$$\varphi_n(\theta) := \frac{1}{k} \sum_{i=1}^{n} \mathbf{1}_{(\Theta_i \leq \theta, \rho_i \geq \rho_{n-k+1:n})}, \qquad \theta = (\theta_1, \ldots, \theta_{d-1}). \tag{8.7}$$

---

[1] The reader is referred to Weron (1984), Janicki and Weron (1994) and Samorodnitsky and Taqqu (1994) for further details on multivariate stable Paretian laws. The results of this and the next section are due to Rachev and Xin (1991) and Cheng and Rachev (1995).

The asymptotic properties of the estimators are stated in the next four lemmas[2].

Lemma 8.1 *(Strong consistency of the estimators.)*

(A) If $k/\ln(\ln(n)) \to \infty$ as $n \to \infty$, then $\alpha_n \to \alpha$ a.s.

(B) If $k/\ln(n) \to \infty$ as $n \to \infty$, then $\varphi_n(\theta) \to \varphi(\theta)$, a.s. for all points $\theta \in \Omega_d$ of φ-continuity.

Lemma 8.1 specified some crude bounds for k — the number of last order statistics that can be used in practice. The "optimal" k depends on the value of the unknown α and φ, as it was shown by L. de Haan, P. Hall and their students (see the review in Mittnik and Rachev (1993a,b)). Certainly, there is a "trade-off" in the choice of α; on one hand α should be "small" to avoid unbiasness, on the other hand for small value of α, the variance of $\alpha_n = \alpha_{k,n}$ is exploding. In reality, one calculates the value of $\alpha_{n,k}$ for values $k = 1, \ldots, \frac{n}{2}$, and look at those values of $\alpha_{n,k}$ where the curve $k \to \alpha_{n,k}$ has a plato.

To construct confidence intervals for α and $\varphi(\theta)$ we need the following Lemma.

Lemma 8.2 If (8.5) holds at $r = 1$ uniformly for $\theta \in \Omega_d$, then $(W_{1n}(\theta), W_{2n}(r))$ converges weakly in $D|\Omega_d| \times D[0,3]$ to $(W_1(\theta), W_2(r))$, which is a mean zero Gaussian process with covariance structure

$$\mathbf{E}W_1(\theta')W_1(\theta'') = \varphi(\theta_1' \wedge \theta_1'', \ldots, \theta_{d-1}' \wedge \theta_{d-1}'') = \varphi(\theta' \wedge \theta''),$$

$$\mathbf{E}W_2(r_1)W_2(r_2) = r_1 \wedge r_2,$$

$$\mathbf{E}W_1(\theta)W_2(r) = (r \wedge 1)\varphi(\theta).$$

Lemma 8.3 *(Asymptotic normality of α_n)* Suppose

$$\lim_{n\to\infty} \sqrt{k}b(kn^{-1}) = 0. \tag{8.8}$$

holds.[3] Then,

$$\sqrt{k}(\alpha_n - \alpha) \overset{\omega}{\to} \frac{\alpha}{\ln 2}\left(W_2(1) - \frac{1}{2}W_2(2)\right),$$

where $\overset{\omega}{\to}$ stands for the weak convergence.

---

[2]The proofs of all lemmas in this section will be given at the end of this section.
[3]This is a stronger version of the domain of attraction condition (8.19) used in the proof if Lemma 8.2.

Next, we turn to the asymptotic normality of $\varphi(\theta)$. Let $S(x) = P(\rho > x)$ and S^- is the right continuous inverse of S. We can normalize ρ in (8.5) to get

$$\lim_{n\to\infty} nP(\rho > rS^-(n^{-1}), \Theta \le \theta) = \varphi(\theta)r^{-\alpha}. \qquad (8.9)$$

We now re-write the domain of attraction condition (see (8.3), (8.5), (8.9)): rescaling the radial component, we can write (with $R = S(\rho)$)

$$\lim_{n\to\infty} nP(R \le \frac{r}{n}, \Theta \le \theta) = r\varphi(\theta). \qquad (8.10)$$

Lemma 8.4 *(Asymptotic normality of the estimator for the normalized spectral measure)* Suppose (8.10 can be strengthened as follows: For some $\delta \in (0,1)$,

$$\lim_{n\to\infty} \sqrt{k} \sup_{\substack{0 < \theta \le 2\pi \\ 1-\delta \le r \le 1+\delta}} \left| \frac{n}{k} P(R \le \frac{kr}{n}, \Theta \le \theta) - r\varphi(\theta) \right| = 0. \qquad (8.11)$$

Then, the normalized process φ_n converges weakly in $D[\Omega_d]$ to a Gaussian process, i.e.,

$$\sqrt{k}(\varphi_n(\theta) - \varphi(\theta)) \overset{\omega}{\to} \Lambda(\theta), \qquad (8.12)$$

where $\Lambda(\theta) = W_1(\theta) - \varphi(\theta)W_2(1)$; and the Gaussian processes W_i's are defined as in Lemma 8.2.

Note that $W_2(r)$ and $\Lambda(\theta)$ are not correlated (cf. Lemma 8.2). Therefore, estimators α_n and $\varphi_n(\theta)$ are asymptotically independent. Moreover, again by Lemma 8.2, we have

$$\mathbf{E}\Lambda(\theta_1)\Lambda(\theta_2) = \varphi(\theta_1 \wedge \theta_2) - \varphi(\theta_1)\phi(\theta_2), \qquad \text{for all } \theta_i \in \Omega_d. \qquad (8.13)$$

Proofs of Lemmas 8.1 - 8.4

Proof of Lemma 8.1 First recall the definitions: $S(x) = P(\rho \ge x)$, $R = S(\rho)$. Next, define $R_i = S(\rho_i)$,[4]

$$F_n(\theta, r) = \frac{n}{k}P\left(\Theta \le \theta, R \le \frac{k}{n}r\right),$$

$$\mathbf{F}_n(\theta, r) = \frac{1}{k}\sum_{i=1}^{n} \mathbf{1}_{(\Theta_i \le \theta, R_i \le \frac{k}{n}r)},\,^{5} \qquad (8.14)$$

$$W_{1n}(\theta) = \sqrt{k}[\mathbf{F}_n(\theta, 1) - F_n(\theta, 1)], \qquad (8.15)$$

and

$$W_{2n}(r) = \sqrt{k}\left(\frac{1}{k}\sum_{i=1}^{n} \mathbf{1}_{(R_i \le \frac{k}{n}r)} - r\right).\,^{6} \qquad (8.16)$$

---

[4] R_i are i.i.d. uniformly distributed r.v.'s.

The domain of attraction condition (8.5) gives, for $\theta_1 = \theta_2 = \ldots = \theta_{d-2} = \pi$, $\theta_{d-1} = 2\pi$,

$$\lim_{n \to \infty} \frac{1}{a_n} S^- \left(\frac{t}{n} \right) = t^{-1/\alpha} \Phi^{1/\alpha}(2\pi), \tag{8.17}$$

recall that S^- is the right continuous inverse of S. The latter implies that, for all $x > 0$,

$$\lim_{u \downarrow 0}(\ln S^-(ux) - \ln S^-(u)) = -\frac{1}{\alpha} \ln x. \tag{8.18}$$

Therefore, for some positive function $b(t)$, $t > 0$,

$$\ln S^-(ux) - \ln S^-(u) = -\frac{1}{\alpha} \ln x + O(b(u)), \qquad \text{as } u \downarrow 0, \tag{8.19}$$

holds uniformly on $x \in [0.5, 2.5]$. Next we will need the following result of Wellner (1978).

Proposition 8.1 If $nb_n / \ln(\ln(n)) \to \infty$, $b_n \downarrow 0$, and F_n is the empirical distribution function based upon a sample of n i.i.d. observations, then, almost surely

$$\lim_{b_n \leq t \leq 1} \sup \frac{F_n(t)}{t} = \lim_{b_n \leq t \leq 1} \sup \frac{t}{F_n(t)} = 1.$$

From this proposition and the assumptions on $k = k_n$ and ρ, we have $R_{2k:n} = S(\rho_{2k:n}) \to 0$ and $R_{k:n}/R_{2k:n} \to 1/2$. Therefore, applying (8.18), we get

$$\ln \rho_{n-k+1:n} - \ln \rho_{n-2k+1:n} = \ln S^-(R_{k:n}) - \ln S^-(R_{2k:n}) \longrightarrow \frac{1}{\alpha} \ln(2).$$

This proves part (A) of Lemma 8.1.

To show (B)-part recall that $R_i = S(\rho_i)$, where (ρ_i, θ_i) are the polar coordinates of the random sample $\mathbf{Z_i} = (Z_{i1}, \ldots, Z_{id})$, $i = 1, \ldots, n$. Recall also the definition of $F_n(\theta, r) = \frac{n}{k} P(\Theta \leq \theta, R \leq \frac{k}{n} r)$ and its corresponding empirical counterpart $\mathbf{F}_n(\theta, r)$ (cf. (8.14)). Then, $\varphi_n(\theta) = \frac{1}{k} \sum_i^n \mathbf{1}_{(\Theta_i \leq \theta, R_i \leq R_{k:n})} = \mathbf{F}_n(\theta, \frac{n}{k} R_{k:n})$. Put $e_n = \frac{n}{k} R_{k:n}$, and let us show that $\mathbf{F}_n(\theta, e_n) \to \varphi(\theta) = \Phi(\theta)/\Phi(\pi, \pi, \ldots, 2\pi)$ a.s. It is enough to see that

$$D_{1,n} = \sup_{\substack{\theta \in \Omega_d \\ 0 \leq s \leq 2}} |\mathbf{F}_n(\theta, s) - F_n(\theta, s)|$$

and

$$D_{2,n} = |F_n(\theta, e_n) - \varphi(\theta)|$$

vanish as $n \to \infty$. To estimate $D_{1,n}$, apply the following multivariate analogue of the exponential bounds in Wellner (1978) and proved in Einmahl (1987) (see also Einmahl et al. (1993)):

Proposition 8.2 *(Einmahl (1987))* Let $(\mathbf{Z}_i)_{i=1,\ldots,n}$ be a random sample from a probability law C on $\mathbf{R}^d$, and C_n the empirical counterpart of C. Let $\mathcal{A}$ be the ring of rectangles $(a_1, b_1] \times \ldots \times (a_d, b_d] \subset \mathbf{R}^d$. Take $A \in \mathcal{A}$ with $0 < C(A) < 1/2$ and $0 < \delta < 1$. There exists a function $\Psi(\lambda) > 0$ *(e.g.,* $\Psi(\lambda) = 2\lambda^{-2}[(1+\lambda)\ln(1+\lambda) - \lambda])$ with $\Psi(\lambda) \uparrow 1$ as $\lambda \downarrow 0$, such that for all $\lambda > 0$,

$$P(\sup_{\tilde{A}\in\mathcal{A}} |n^{1/2}[C_n(\tilde{A}) - C(\tilde{A})]| \geq \lambda) \leq K(\delta)\exp\left\{\frac{-(1-\delta)\lambda^2}{2C(A)}\Psi\left(\frac{\lambda}{n^{1/2}C(A)}\right)\right\},$$

where $K(\delta)$ is an absolute positive constant.

It follows from Proposition 8.2 that for any $\epsilon > 0$,

$$P(D_{1,n} > \epsilon)$$

$$= P\left(\sup_{\substack{0 \leq \theta \leq 2\pi \\ 0 \leq s \leq 2}} \sqrt{n}\left|\frac{1}{n}\sum_{i=1}^{n} \mathbf{1}_{(\Theta_i \leq \theta, R_i < \frac{k}{n}s)} - \frac{1}{n}P(\Theta \leq \theta, R \leq \frac{k}{n}s)\right| \geq \epsilon\frac{k}{\sqrt{n}}\right)$$

$$\leq K(1/2)\exp\left\{\frac{-\epsilon^2\frac{k^2}{n}}{4P(A)}\Psi\left(\frac{\epsilon\frac{k}{\sqrt{n}}}{\sqrt{n}P(A)}\right)\right\}$$

$$= K(1/2)\exp\left\{-\frac{k\epsilon^2}{8}\Psi\left(\frac{\epsilon}{2}\right)\right\}$$

$$< n^{-1},$$

where $A = \{0 \leq \theta \leq 2\pi, R \leq 2k/n\}$. As for $D_{2,n}$, we use (8.9) and the fact that $e_n \to 1$ a.s. Hence, $D_{2,n} \to 0$ as $n \to \infty$. This completes the proof of part(B) of Lemma 8.1.   □

Proof of Lemma 8.2 First, we shall show that the finite dimensional distributions of the empirical processes $(W_{1n}(\theta), W_{2n}(r))$ converge in distribution. We apply the Cramér-Wald method (see Billingsley, (1968)) to check that the linear combination of the components of $W_{1n}(\theta)$ and $W_{2n}(r)$ converge in distribution. Take $u_1, \ldots, u_m, v_1, \ldots, v_q$ real, $\theta_1, \ldots, \theta_m$ from Ω_d and $r_1, \ldots, r_q$ from $[0,3]$. Set $\xi_i(\theta) = \mathbf{1}_{(\Theta_i \leq \theta, R_i \leq \frac{k}{n})} - P(\Theta \leq \theta, R \leq \frac{k}{n})$, $\eta_i(r) = \mathbf{1}_{(R_i \leq \frac{k}{n}r)} - \frac{k}{n}r$, $\Delta_i = \sum_{\alpha=1}^{m} u_\alpha \xi_i(\theta_\alpha) + \sum_{\alpha=1}^{q} v_\alpha \eta_i(r_\alpha)$, and $S_n = \frac{1}{\sqrt{k}}\sum_{i=1}^{n}\Delta_i$. Observe that the real-valued random variables $\Delta_i, i = 1, \ldots, n$, are identically distributed and independent of each other with zero mean and variance given by

$$\mathbf{E}\Delta_i^2 = \sum_{\alpha=1}^{m}\sum_{\beta=1}^{m} u_\alpha u_\beta P(\Theta \leq \theta_\alpha \wedge \theta_\beta, R \leq kn^{-1})$$

$$+ \sum_{\alpha=1}^{m}\sum_{\beta=1}^{q} P(\Theta \leq \theta_\alpha, R \leq \frac{k}{n}(r_\beta \wedge 1)) + O(k^2n^{-2})$$

$$= O(kn^{-1}).$$

In a similar manner, we compute the limiting form of the third absolute moment, namely $\mathbf{E}|\Delta_i|^3 = O(k/n)$. Then, the Lyapunov's condition holds;

$$\frac{\mathbf{E}|S_n|^3}{(\mathbf{E}S_n^2)^{3/2}} = O\left(\frac{\frac{n}{k^{3/2}}\mathbf{E}|\Delta_1|^3}{\frac{n}{k}\mathbf{E}|\Delta_1|)^{3/2}} \right) = O(k^{-1/2}) \to 0.$$

This limiting relation implies that the finite dimensional distribution of $(W_{1,n}, W_{2,n})$ converge to the corresponding laws of (W_1, W_2). Next, note that each sequence of the one-dimensional marginals $W_{1n}(\theta_1, \pi, \ldots, 2\pi), \ldots,$ $W_{1n}(\pi, \pi, \ldots, \theta_{d-1}), W_{2n}(r), n = 1, 2, \ldots$, is tight.[7]

This follows from the weak compactness criterion for distributions on the Skorokhod space $D[0, \pi]$ for the first $d - 1$ marginals and the weak compactness on $D[0, 2\pi]$ for the last marginal (see also Einmahl et al. (1991)). Therefore, $\{(W_{1n}, W_{2n})\}_{\mathbf{n} \geq 1}$ is a tight sequence, and by Prohorov's theorem (see Billingsley (1968), Section 6), Lemma is proved. $\qquad\square$

Proof of Lemma 8.3 Recall that $\alpha_n = \ln 2/(\ln \rho_{n-k+1:n} - \ln \rho_{n-2k+1:n})$ and $R_i = S(\rho_i)$. From (8.19)

$$\ln S^-(R_{kr:n}) - \ln S^-(kn^{-1}) = -\frac{1}{\alpha} \ln\left(\frac{rR_{kr:n}}{rkn^{-1}} \right) + O(k^{-1/2})$$

$$= -\frac{1}{\alpha} \ln r - \frac{1}{\alpha} \ln\left(\frac{R_{kr:n}}{rkn^{-1}} \right) + O(k^{-1/2}),$$

and, because $R_{rk:n}/(rkn^{-1}) \overset{\omega}{\to} 1,$[8]

$$\sqrt{k}\left(\ln S^-(R_{kr:n}) - \ln S^-(kn^{-1}) + \frac{1}{\alpha} \ln r \right) = -\sqrt{k}\frac{1}{\alpha} \ln\left(\frac{R_{kr:n}}{kr/n} \right) + O(1)$$

$$= \frac{1}{\alpha r} \sqrt{k}\left(\frac{n}{k} R_{kr:n} - r \right) + O(1)$$

$$\overset{\omega}{\to} \frac{1}{\alpha r}(-W_2(r)).$$

The last limiting relation follows from Lemma 8.2. In fact, from Lemma 8.2 and the Skorokhod-Dudley Theorem (cf. Dudley (1989), Theorem 11.7.1),

---

[7]Recall that a sequence $(\xi_n)_{n \geq 1}$ of random variables is *tight*, if for every $\epsilon > 0$, there exists an interval $[a_\epsilon, b_\epsilon]$ such that

$$\sup_n P(\xi_n \notin [a_\epsilon, b_\epsilon]) < \epsilon.$$

More generally, the sequence of processes $\xi_n : D[0, T] \to \mathbf{R}$ with trajectories in the Skorokhod space $D[0, T]$ is tight, if for every $\epsilon > 0$ there is compact $K_\epsilon \subset D[0, T]$ such that $\sup_n P(\xi_n \in D[0, T] \backslash K_\epsilon) < \epsilon$, see Billingsley (1968).

[8]The weak convergence '$\overset{\omega}{\to}$', here, implies the convergence in probability, i.e. for every $\epsilon > 0$, $P(|R_{rk:n} \backslash (rkn^{-1}) - 1| > \epsilon) \to 0$.

there exist a probability space $(\Omega, \tilde{P})$ and a sequence of processes $\tilde{W}_{2,n} \stackrel{d}{=}$ $W_{2,n}$, $\tilde{W}_{2n} \stackrel{d}{=} W_2$ $(\Omega, \tilde{P})$, such that $\sup_{0 \le r \le 3} |\tilde{W}_{2,n}(r) - \tilde{W}_2(r)| \to 0$ as $n \to \infty$ $\tilde{P}-$ a.s. Using the results of Vervaat (1972), the last limiting relation implies that $\sup_{0.5 \le r \le 2.5} |\sqrt{k}(\frac{n}{k} R_{kr:n} - r) - \tilde{W}_2| \to 0$ a.s. Combining the above bounds we obtain

$$\sqrt{k}\frac{\alpha}{a_n - 1} = \sqrt{k}\left(\alpha\frac{\ln S^-(R_{k:n}) - \ln S^-(R_{2k:n})}{\ln 2} - 1\right).$$

$$\stackrel{\omega}{\to} \frac{1}{\ln 2}\left(-W_2(1) + \frac{1}{2}W_2(2)\right). \quad\square$$

Proof of Lemma 8.4 Recall that

$$\varphi_n(\theta) = \mathbf{F}_n(\theta, e_n) = \frac{1}{k}\sum_{i=1}^{n} \mathbf{1}_{(\Theta_i \le \theta, R_i \le R_{k:n})}$$

(cf. (8.7) and (8.14)).
Claim: As $n \to \infty$, we have

$$\sqrt{k}\left[\varphi_n(\theta) - \frac{n}{k}P(\Theta \le \theta, R \le R_{k:n})\right] \stackrel{\omega}{\to} W_1(\theta)$$

in $D[\Omega_d]$.

To prove this claim, note that from Lemma 8.2, we have the weak convergence of the empirical processes $W_{1n} \stackrel{\omega}{\to} W_1$. Let us show that

$$\sup_{\theta \in \Omega_d} |\sqrt{k}(\mathbf{F_n}(\theta, r) - F_n(\theta, r)) - W_{1,n}(\theta)| \stackrel{p}{\to} 0, \qquad (8.20)$$

and

$$\sqrt{k}(e_n - 1) = O(1)(\text{hence, } P(k_n^{1/4}(e_n - 1) \ge 1) < \epsilon, \text{ for } n \text{ large}). \quad (8.21)$$

For (8.20), using Proposition 8.2 in the proof of Lemma 8.2, we obtain bound

$$P\left(\sup_{\substack{\theta \in \Omega_d \\ 1 - k^{-1/4} \le r \le 1 + k^{-1/4}}} \left|\sqrt{k}[\mathbf{F}_n(\theta, r) - F_n(\theta, r)] - W_{1n}(\theta)\right| > \epsilon\right)$$

$$\le P\left(\sup_{\substack{\theta \in \Omega_d \\ 1 \le r \le 1 + k^{-1/4}}} |\text{"same"}| > \epsilon) + P(\sup_{\substack{\theta \in \Omega_d \\ 1 - k^{-1/4} \le r \le 1}} |\text{"same"}| > \epsilon\right)$$

$$:= \Delta_1 + \Delta_2,$$

where, as $n \to \infty$, $\Delta_1 \le c_1 \exp\left\{-\epsilon^2 k_n^{1/4}\psi(\epsilon/c_2 k_n^{1/4})\right\} \to 0$ and, similarly, $\Delta_2 \to 0$. For (8.21), using Lemma 8.2 and Vervaat (1972) in a similar fashion as in the proof of Lemma 8.2, we obtain $\sqrt{k}(e_n - 1) = \sqrt{k}(\frac{n}{k}R_{k:n} - 1) \xrightarrow{\omega} W_2(1)$. This completes the proof of the claim.

From the claim and the fact that $e_n \to 1$ a.s., we have

$$
\begin{aligned}
\sqrt{k}[\varphi_n(\theta) - e_n\varphi(\theta)] &= \sqrt{k}\left(\varphi_n(\theta) - \frac{n}{k}P(\Theta \le \theta, R \le R_{k:n})\right) \\
&\quad + \sqrt{k}\left(\frac{n}{k}P(\Theta \le \theta, R \le \frac{n}{k}e_n) - e_n\varphi(\theta)\right) \\
&\xrightarrow{\omega} W_1(\theta)
\end{aligned}
$$

(the second term on the right hand side of the equation vanishes as $n \to \infty$ due to assumption (8.11)). Using Lemma 8.2, we now have

$$
\sqrt{k}[\varphi_n(\theta) - \varphi(\theta)] \xrightarrow{\omega} W_1(\theta) - \varphi(\theta)W_2(1).
$$

which completes the proof of Lemma 8.4.   □

8.3   A Test for Association

In this section we address the following problem: *are the returns in an d-dimensional stable portfolio dependent or not; how can one test the dependence?*

We shall construct a test for dependence (association) based on the tail-statistic φ_n for the spectral measure φ, studied in the previous section.

Recall that if $\mathbf{Z}$ has a stable Paretian distribution with $0 < \alpha < 2$, $\mathbf{Z}$ is positively associated if and only if the spectral measure Γ of $\mathbf{Z}$ satisfies condition

$$
\Gamma(S_d^-) = 0, \tag{8.22}
$$

where $S_d^- = \{(s_1, \ldots, s_d)\} \in S_d$, for some $i, j \in \{1, \ldots, d, s_is_j < 0\}$; $\mathbf{Z}$ is negatively associated if and only if

$$
\Gamma(S_d^+) = 0, \tag{8.23}
$$

where $S_d^+ = \{(s_1, \ldots, s_d) \in S_d$, for some $i \ne j, s_i, s_j > 0\}$ (see chapter 7).

Extending this result to the situation when $\mathbf{Z}$ is in the domain of attraction of stable Paretian random vectors leads to the tests for positive and negative association given in Theorems 8.1 and 8.2 below. The method we use resembles that developed by Einmahl et al. (1993) for estimating a multivariate extreme-value distribution. By assuming that returns $\mathbf{Z}$ lie in the domain of attraction of a stable Paretian law, we can conduct the test of association proposed below.

Let $\Lambda(\theta)$, $\theta \in \Omega_d = [0, \pi]^{d-2} \times [0, 2\pi]$ be defined as in Lemma 8.4, and define R_Λ to be the random measure generated by Λ. Given a distribution function φ on Ω_d, let R_φ be the probability measure with distribution function φ and let R_{φ_n} be its empirical counterpart.

Theorem 8.1 *(Test for positive association)* Suppose $\mathbf{Z}$ is in the domain of attraction of a stable Paretian random vector with spectral distribution function $\varphi(\theta) = \Phi(\theta)/\Phi(\pi, \ldots, \pi, 2\pi)$ (cf. (8.3) and (8.5)) and suppose that the $\mathbf{Z}$-components are positively associated. Then,

$$\text{(i)} \quad R_\varphi([0, \pi/2]^{d-1}) + R_\varphi([\pi/2, \pi]^{d-2} \times [\pi, 3\pi/2]) = 1, \qquad (8.24)$$

and, if (8.11) holds,

$$\text{(ii)} \quad \sqrt{k}(R_{\varphi_n}([0, \pi/2])^{d-1} + R_{\varphi_n}([\pi/2, \pi]^{d-2} \times [\pi, 3\pi/2]) - 1) \,\omega$$
$$\longrightarrow N(0, \sigma_\varphi^2), \qquad (8.25)$$

where

$$\sigma_\varphi^2 = \mathbf{E}\{R_\Lambda([0, \pi/2]^{d-1}) + R_\Lambda([\pi/2, \pi]^{d-2} \times [\pi, 3\pi/2])\}^2. \qquad (8.26)$$

The covariance structure of R_Λ is determined by (8.13). Moreover, (8.11) implies that

$$\sqrt{k}R_{\varphi_n}([0, \theta] \cap C_d) \xrightarrow{\omega} \Lambda([0, \theta] \cap C_d), \qquad (8.27)$$

where $[0, \theta] = [0, \theta_1] \times \ldots \times [0, \theta_{d-1}] \subset \Omega_d$ and

$$C_d = \Omega_d \backslash ([0, \pi/2]^{d-1} + [\pi/2, \pi]^{d-2} \times [\pi, 3\pi/2]).$$

The weak convergence in (8.27) is in $D[C_d]$. In particular,

$$\sqrt{k} \sup_{\theta \in C_d} R_{\varphi_n}([0, \theta] \cap C_d) \xrightarrow{\omega} \sup_{\theta \in C_d} \Lambda([0, \theta] \cap C_d). \qquad (8.28)$$

Proof: Under H_0, i.e., assuming that $\mathbf{Z}$ has positively associated components, the normalized spectral measure R_φ is concentrated on the complement of S_d^- (see (8.22)). Hence, (8.24) holds. Then, making use of (8.24) and applying Lemma 8.4, one can easily check (8.25); (8.27) follows immediately from Lemma 8.2; and taking the *sup* gives (8.28). $\qquad \square$

For the case $d = 2$, we can rewrite (8.24), (8.25), and (8.26) in a simpler form, namely, as in Rachev and Xin (1991),

$$\varphi(\pi) - \varphi(\pi/2) - \varphi(3\pi/2) + 1 = 0, \qquad (8.29)$$

$$\sqrt{k}(\varphi_n(\pi) - \varphi_n(\pi/2) - \varphi_n(3\pi/2) + 1) \xrightarrow{\omega} N(0, \sigma_\varphi^2), \qquad (8.30)$$

and

$$\sigma_\varphi^2 = 1 + \varphi(3\pi/2) - \varphi^2(3\pi/2) - \varphi(\pi) - \varphi^2(\pi) + \varphi(\pi/2) - \varphi^2(\pi/2)$$
$$+2\varphi(3\pi/2)\varphi(\pi) - 2\varphi(3\pi/2)\varphi(\pi/2) + 2\varphi(\pi)\varphi(\pi/2). \qquad (8.31)$$

In practice, one would replace σ_φ by its empirical counterpart σ_{φ_n}. Note that a stronger version of (8.25) can be derived from Lemma 8.4 as follows. Assuming (8.11),

$$\sqrt{k}[\varphi_n(\theta + \pi/2) - \varphi_n(\pi/2) + \varphi_n(\theta + 3\pi/2) - \varphi_n(3\pi/2)]$$
$$\xrightarrow{\omega} \Lambda(\theta + \pi/2) - \Lambda(\pi/2) + \Lambda(\theta + 3\pi/2) - \Lambda(3\pi/2) \qquad (8.32)$$

in $D(0, \pi/2]$. Note that this is the two-dimensional analogue of (8.27).

The following provides a test for negative association of $\mathbf{Z}$.[9]

Theorem 8.2 *(Test for negative association)* Suppose $\mathbf{Z}$ is in the domain of attraction of a stable Paretian random vector with spectral distribution function $\varphi(\theta)$; and suppose that the $\mathbf{Z}$-components are negatively associated. Then,

(i) $\varphi(\theta)$ is concentrated on the following set of dimension not greater than 2:

$$(S_d^+)^c = \{(0, \ldots, 0, s_i, 0, \ldots, 0, s_j, 0, \ldots, 0) : s_i s_j \leq 0\},$$

and

(ii) as $n \to \infty$,

$$\sqrt{k} R_{\varphi_n}(S_d^+) \xrightarrow{d} N(0, \tilde{\sigma}_\varphi^2). \tag{8.33}$$

where $\tilde{\sigma}_\varphi^2 = \mathbf{E} R_\Lambda^2 (S_d^+)$.

Cheng and Rachev (1995) apply this approach to test the association between daily returns of the D-Mark/USD and the Yen/USD exchange-rate series covering the period from 1980 to 1990. Their computation yields the value 1.67 for statistic α_n (see (8.6)). Furthermore, $\varphi_n(\pi) - \varphi_n(\pi/2) - \varphi_n(3\pi/2) + 1 = .72$ and $\sigma_{\varphi_n}/\sqrt{k} = .043$. These values imply that the two return series are positively associated at the 95% confidence level.

8.4   The Risk and Covariation Matrix of Stable Paretian Portfolios

In this section we study the risk of a portfolio of α-stable distributed returns. Our estimator r_n of the risk will be based on the tail-estimators α_n and $\varphi_n(\theta)$ defined in Section 8.2.

Let $\mathbf{X} = (X_1, \ldots, X_m)'$ denote the vector of individual returns of an m-asset portfolio and $\mathbf{c} = (c_1, \ldots, c_m)'$ the vector of weights indicating the portion with which each asset enters the portfolio. Press (1972a) considered the special case of a multivariate symmetric stable Paretian portfolio $\mathbf{X}$ with characteristic function given by

$$\mathbf{E} \exp i(\mathbf{t}, X) = \exp \left\{ -\frac{1}{2} \sum_{i=1}^{m} (\mathbf{t}' \Sigma_i \mathbf{t})^{\alpha/2} + i(\mathbf{t}, \mu_0) \right\}. \tag{8.34}$$

where the matrices Σ_i are positive definite. Press (1972a) defined the risk associated with portfolio $\mathbf{X}$ and weights $\mathbf{c} = (c_1, \ldots, c_m)' \in \mathbf{R}_+^m$ as the scale

---

[9]The proof is similar to that of preceding theorem and, hence, is omitted.

parameters of the portfolio stable distributed return:

$$r(\mathbf{c}) := \frac{1}{2} \sum_{j=1}^{m} (\mathbf{c}' \Sigma_j \mathbf{c})^{\alpha/2}. \tag{8.35}$$

This definition of portfolio risk arises naturally from the normal case: for $\alpha = 2$, $r(\mathbf{c})$ is an increasing function of the covariances. Assuming a general stable Paretian law of returns (cf. (8.1)), we define *the risk* as follows:

$$r(\mathbf{c}) := \int_{S_d} |(\mathbf{s}, \mathbf{c})|^\alpha \Gamma(d\mathbf{s}), \quad \mathbf{c} \in \mathbf{R}_+^d. \tag{8.36}$$

As (1972a, p. 344) indicated, in order to allow positive and negative price changes to be weighted in the same way, $\mathbf{X} - \mu_0$ should be "symmetric"; i.e. $\mathbf{X} - \mu_0$ should follow a (strictly) stable Paretian law with characteristic function

$$\mathbf{E}e^{i(\mathbf{t},\mathbf{X})} = \exp\left\{ -\int_{S_d} |(\mathbf{t}, s)|^\alpha \Gamma(ds) + i(\mathbf{t}, \mu_0) \right\}. \tag{8.37}$$

Then, for a scalar variable $v > 0$ and $\mathbf{t} = v\mathbf{c} \in \mathbf{R}_+^d$, the right-hand side of (8.37) becomes $\exp\{-|v|^\alpha r(\mathbf{c}) + iv(\mathbf{c}, \mu_0)\}$, which motivates the choice (8.36) of the notion of risk as the scalar parameter of the return distribution.[10]

To estimate $r(\mathbf{c})$ we need only an estimator for the spectral measure. To this end, assume that the i.i.d. observations (the returns) $\mathbf{Z}_1, \mathbf{Z}_2, \ldots$ are taken from the *normal* domain of attraction of stable Paretian vector $\mathbf{X}$, that is

$$\frac{1}{\lambda n^{1/\alpha}} \sum_{i=1}^{n} \mathbf{Z_i} - \mathbf{b_n} \xrightarrow{\omega} \mathbf{X}. \tag{8.38}$$

Without loss of generality, we assume that the scaling parameter $\lambda = 1$. Note that for $\mathbf{Z}$ being stable Paretian (*i.e.*, $\mathbf{Z} \overset{d}{=} \mathbf{X}$ with characteristic function (8.1)), limiting relation (8.38) holds with $\lambda = 1$. Using the same notations as in section 8.2, define

$$\Phi_n(\theta) := \varphi_n(\theta)\Phi_n(\Pi), \quad \Pi = (\pi, \ldots, \pi, 2\pi) \in \Omega_d. \tag{8.39}$$

as an estimator for the spectral measure $\Phi(\theta) = \varphi(\theta)\Omega(\Pi)$. In (8.39), φ_n is determined by (8.7). For $\Phi_n(\Pi)$ we invoke the stable Paretian estimator (8.6) and define

$$\Phi_n(\Pi) = \frac{k}{n}(\rho_{n-k:n})^{\alpha_n}. \tag{8.40}$$

The next lemma deals with the asymptotic normality of Φ_n. Recall first that from (8.5), $\lim_{n\to\infty} nS(rn^{1/\alpha}) = \Phi(\Pi)r^{-\alpha}$. Inversion yields the following

---

[10]For more facts about the motivation in choosing (8.37) as the measure of risk we refer to Section 9.1.

weak version of the domain of attraction condition (8.38)

$$\lim_{n\to\infty} \frac{k}{n} \frac{(S^-(kn^{-1}))^\alpha}{\Phi(\Pi)} = 1. \qquad (8.41)$$

Lemma 8.5 Suppose that assumptions (8.8) and (8.11) and a stronger version of (8.41), namely

$$\frac{k}{n} \frac{(S^-(kn^{-1}))^\alpha}{\Phi(\Pi)} = 1 + O(k^{-1/2}) \quad \text{as } n \to \infty, \qquad (8.42)$$

hold. Then, in $D[\Omega_d]$, the normalization of Φ_n converges weakly to a degenerate Gaussian process with zero mean; more precisely,

$$\frac{(\ln 2)\sqrt{k}}{\ln(n/k)} \left(\frac{\Phi_n(\theta)}{\Phi(\theta)} - 1 \right) \xrightarrow{d} N(0,1). \qquad (8.43)$$

Proof: We will show that Φ_n converges to Φ with a rate that is slower than that in $\varphi_n \xrightarrow{\omega} \varphi$. This, together with Lemma 8.4, leads to (8.43).

Claim: Assuming (8.8) and (8.42), then

$$\frac{\sqrt{k}}{\ln(nk^{-1})} \left(\frac{\Phi_n(\Pi)}{\Phi(\Pi)} - 1 \right) \xrightarrow{\omega} N(0,1). \qquad (8.44)$$

Proof of the claim: By (8.8) we have

$$\frac{\rho_{n-k:n}}{S^-(kn^{-1})} = \frac{S^-(R_{k:n})}{S^-(kn^{-1})} = 1 + O(k^{-\frac{1}{2}}).$$

By Lemma 8.3, $\sqrt{k}(\alpha_n - \alpha) \xrightarrow{\omega} \alpha N$, where $N \overset{d}{=} N(0,1)$. Combining these two limiting relations with (8.42), the asymptotic behavior of $\Phi_n(\Pi)$ is

$$
\begin{aligned}
\frac{\Phi_n(\Pi)}{\Phi(\Pi)} &= \frac{k}{n} \frac{(S^-(kn^{-1}))^\alpha}{\Phi(\Pi)} \left(\frac{\rho_{n-k:n}}{S^-(kn^{-1})} \right)^{\alpha_n} (S^-(kn^{-1})^{\alpha_n - \alpha} \\
&= \left[1 + O(k^{-1/2}) \right]^{\alpha_n} \left[1 + O(k^{-1/2}) \right] \exp\{(\alpha_n - \alpha) \ln S^-(kn^{-1})\} \\
&= \left[1 + O(k^{-1/2}) \right] \left[1 + \frac{\ln(nk^{-1}) + O(1)}{\sqrt{k}} \right].
\end{aligned}
$$

The last equality follows from $\ln S^-(kn^{-1}) = \ln(\frac{n}{k})^{1/\alpha} + \alpha^{-1} \ln \Phi(\Pi) + O(k^{-1/2})$, and $\alpha_n - \alpha = \frac{\alpha}{\sqrt{k}} N + O(1)$. This proves the claim.

Returning to the proof of Lemma 8.5 recall Lemma 8.4, which states that under (8.11) we have $\sqrt{k}(\varphi_n - \varphi) \xrightarrow{\omega} \Lambda$. The latter rate is faster than that in (8.43) and, therefore, the rate in $\Phi_n \xrightarrow{\omega} \varphi\Phi(\Pi)$ will be determined by that in (8.43). In fact, with $\Phi = \varphi\Phi(\Pi)$, we have $\Phi_n(\theta) = \varphi_n(\theta)\Phi_n(\Pi) =$

$\Phi(\theta) + \Phi(\theta)\frac{\ln(nk^{-1})}{\sqrt{k}}N + O\left(\frac{\ln(nk^{-1})}{\sqrt{k}}\right)$ which completes the proof of Lemma 8.5.

Lemma 8.5 implies the asymptotic normality of the *estimator for the risk* $r(\mathbf{c})$:

$$r_n(\mathbf{c}) = \int_{\Omega_d} (\xi(\mathbf{c},\theta))^{\alpha_n}\,d\Phi_n(\theta), \quad \mathbf{c} \in \mathbf{R}_+^d, \tag{8.45}$$

where $\xi(\mathbf{c},\theta) = |\mathbf{c}|\,|\cos(\mathbf{c},\theta)|$, (see (8.2)).

Theorem 8.3 Under regularity assumptions (8.8), (8.11) and (8.42) we have

$$\frac{(\ln 2)\sqrt{k}}{\ln(nk^{-1})}\left(\frac{r_n(\mathbf{c})}{r(\mathbf{c})} - 1\right) \xrightarrow{d} N, where N \stackrel{d}{=} N(0,1). \tag{8.46}$$

Proof: From Lemmas 8.3 and 8.5 we have $\sqrt{k}(\alpha_n - \alpha) \xrightarrow{\omega} \alpha\frac{(\omega(1)-\frac{1}{2}\omega(2))}{\ln 2}$ and $\frac{\sqrt{2}\sqrt{k}}{\ln(nk^{-1})}(\Phi_n - \Phi) \xrightarrow{\omega} \Phi N$. Because the second limit relation has a slower rate, it will play a dominant role in the convergence of $r_n(\mathbf{c})$ to $r(\mathbf{c})$. Indeed, as $n \to \infty$, we have

$$\begin{aligned}
r_n(\mathbf{c}) &= \int_{\Omega_d} \exp\{\alpha_n \ln \xi(\mathbf{c},\theta)\} d\Phi_n(\theta) \\
&= \int_{\Omega_d}\left(1 + \frac{1}{\sqrt{k}}(\alpha N)\ln\xi(\mathbf{c},\theta)\right)\xi(\mathbf{c},\theta)^\alpha d\Phi(\theta) \\
&\quad + \frac{\ln(nk^{-1})}{\sqrt{k}}\int_{\Omega_d}\left(1 + \frac{1}{\sqrt{k}}(\alpha N)\ln\xi(\mathbf{c},\theta)\right)\xi(\mathbf{c},\theta)^\alpha dN\Phi(\theta) \\
&\quad + O\left(\frac{\ln(nk^{-1})}{\sqrt{k}}\right).
\end{aligned}$$

Therefore, $r_n(\mathbf{c}) - r(\mathbf{c}) = \frac{\ln(nk^{-1})}{\sqrt{k}}Nr(\mathbf{c}) + O\left(\frac{\ln(nk^{-1})}{\sqrt{k}}\right)$.

Remark 8.1 The moment estimators for portfolio risk $r(c)$ (in form (8.35)) proposed by Press (1972a,b) have different structures based on the particular parametric form of the stable portfolio (cf. (8.34) and Press (1972a, Section 12.6.1)). They cannot be used in this general framework.

Remark 8.2 With estimates for index α and spectral distribution function $\Phi(\theta)$, the only parameter left to be estimated in (8.1) is the shift parameter μ_0. Because the assumption that $\alpha > 1$ is in general agreement with the empirical evidence , the vector of sample means $\mu_n = \frac{1}{n}\sum_{i=1}^{n}\mathbf{Z}_i$ (cf. (8.38)) is the most plausible estimator for the finite mean case.

Remark 8.3 Having estimated the portfolio risk (Theorem 8.3), the problem of determining the minimum–risk portfolio with stable Paretian distribution

amounts to finding the weight vector, $\mathbf{c} \in \mathbf{R}^d$ satisfying the constraints :
$\langle \mathbf{c}, \mu_0 \rangle = \sum_{j=1}^{y} c_j \mu_{0j} = r_p, \sum_{j=1}^{d} c_j = 1$, and such that $r_n(\mathbf{c})$ is minimal, where $\mu_0 \in \mathbf{R}^d$ is the vector of mean returns (the shift vector). The constraints come from the fact we would like to find the portfolio $\mathbf{c} = (c_1, \ldots, c_n)'$ with target mean return r_p and minimal risk. Note that $\mu_0 = (\mu_{01}, \ldots, \mu_{0d})'$ is the mean vector of returns only if $\alpha > 1$, for $0 < \alpha \leq 1$ it plays the role of a shift (centralizing) vector. Similar financial optimization problems will be addressed in the next chapter.

Remark 8.4 The risk of a stable α portfolio is closely related to the so-called *covariation* of a stable portfolio (see also the next Chapter 9). The notion of covariation $[R_1; R_2]_\alpha$ between stable returns R_1 and R_2 plays a role similar to that of the variation between normally distributed returns, and will be extensively used in CAPM for stable portfolios.

In the normal case ($\alpha = 2$) the risk of a stable portfolio is always an increasing functional on the space of covariance matrix

$$\Sigma_2 = \frac{1}{2} \|\text{cov}(X_i, X_j)\|_{1 \leq j \leq d}.$$

In the Paretian stable case ($0 < \alpha < 2$) a related concept is the *covariation matrix* Σ_α of random vector $X = (X_1, \ldots, X_\alpha)$ which follow a *symmetric stable distribution*. Recall X is symmetric stable vector if its characteristic function is of the form

$$\mathbf{E} \exp i(t, X) = \exp \left\{ -\int_{S_d} |(t, s)|^\alpha \Gamma(ds) \right\}, \tag{8.47}$$

where Γ is a symmetric finite measure on S_d. The covariation matrix of X is defined as

$$\Sigma_\alpha := \|[X_i, X_j]\|_{1 \leq j \leq d} := \left(\int_{S_d} s_i s_j^{\langle \alpha - 1 \rangle} \Gamma(ds) \right),$$

where $s^{\langle k \rangle} = (\text{sign} s)|s|^k$, and $s = (s_1, \ldots, s_d) \in S_d$. An estimator for $\sum_\alpha$ is given by the matrix $\sum_\alpha^{(n)}$ with entries:

$$[X_i, X_j]_\alpha^{(n)} := \int_{\Omega_d} s_i(\theta) s_j(\theta)^{\langle \alpha - 1 \rangle} d\Phi_n(\theta),$$

where $s_i(\theta)$ denotes the i-th-component of s in polar coordinates.

Theorem 8.4 Under the regularity conditions (8.41), (8.1), and (8.42) and assuming (8.47) we have

$$\frac{(\ln 2)\sqrt{k}}{\ln(n/k)} (\Sigma_\alpha^{(n)} - \Sigma_\alpha) \overset{\omega}{\longrightarrow} N(0, \Sigma_\alpha \cdot \Sigma_\alpha). \tag{8.48}$$

Here $\Sigma_\alpha \cdot \Sigma_\alpha$ signifies the dot product of two matrices. The proof is similar to that of Theorem 9.2, and hence will be omitted. Observe that when $\alpha = 2$, the covariation matrix is the covariance matrix of multivariate normal distributions. If X contains a shift factor μ_0 as in (8.37), then we can compute the covariation of $X - \mu_0$, so without loss of generality, we can assume that $\mu_0 = 0$. We list here some of the important properties of the covariation (see Samorodnitsky and Taqqu (1993) for their proofs and additional facts):[11]

(P1) $[X_1, X_2]_2 = \frac{1}{2}cov(X1, X2)$;

(P2) If (X_1, X_2, Y) are jointly symmetric α-stable, then $[X_1 + X_2, Y]_\alpha = [X_1, Y]_\alpha + [X_2, Y]_\alpha$; note, however, that the covariation is not additive in the second argument;

(P3) $[aX_1, bX_2]_\alpha = ab^{\langle \alpha-1 \rangle}[X_1, X_2]_\alpha$;

(P4) If X_1 and X_2 are independent, then $[X_1, X_2]_\alpha = 0$; however, for $1 < \alpha < 2$, it is possible that $[X_1, X_2]_\alpha = 0$ for dependent X_1 and X_2;

(P5) $[X_1, X_2]_\alpha = 0$ if and only if X_2 is *James orthogonal to* $X_1(X_1 \perp_J X_2)$, i.e. for every $\lambda > 0$,

$$[\lambda X_1 + X_2, \lambda X_1 + X_2]_\alpha \geq [X_2, X_2]_\alpha.$$

Furthermore, let us define the analogue of the correlation between the components of symmetric α-stable pair (X_1, X_2). The *covariation norm*[12] of an α-stable r.v. is defined by

$$\|X\|_\alpha := ([X, X]_\alpha)^{\frac{1}{\alpha}}.$$

Then for $1 < \alpha \leq 2$,

$$|[X_1, X_2]| \leq \|X_1\|_\alpha \|X_2\|_\alpha^{\alpha-1}.$$

Note that if X is symmetric α-stable with scale parameter σ, i.e., if

$$\mathbf{E}e^{itX} = e^{-|\sigma t|^\sigma},$$

then $\|X\|_\alpha = \sigma$ (cf. Samorodnitsky and Taqqu (1993)). This leads us the following definition of the α-*correlation* matrix

$$R_\alpha = \left(\frac{[X_i, X_j]_\alpha}{\|X_i\|_\alpha \|X_j\|_\alpha^{\alpha-1}} \right).$$

It is clear that if $\alpha = 2$, then R_α reduces to the standard correlation matrix.

---

[11]See also Chapter 9 for applications of Σ_α to CAPM with stable Paretian returns.
[12]Extensions of this notion will be given in Chapter 9.

Chen and Rachev (1995) apply the foregoing estimator to the yen and Deutschmark exchange rates; the data consist of 2853 pairs of observations of the successive differences of the logarithm of daily closing prices of the JY/USD and DM/USD exchange rates from 1/1/80 to 12/7/90. The value of the covariation is estimated to be .000116 and the α-correlation is determined to be .791. This is in accordance with the obtained positive association result, providing a measure of the strength of the association.

8.5   Testing Multivariate Symmetry

In this section we present a procedure for testing a general multivariate asset return distribution for symmetry and, also, a test for symmetry adapted to the special properties o f multivariate stable laws [13]. There is substantial literature on testing univariate random variables for symmetry.[14] Symmetry testing in the multivariate case has been considered by Aki (1993), Barminghaus and Henze (1991), Beran (1979), Blough (1989), and Kariya and Eaton (1977). Ghosh and Ruymgaart (1992) extend the methods based on the integrated empirical characteristic function of Feuerverger and Mureika (1977) to the multivariate case, but it is not clear that their procedure is convenient to use in practice. The literature is not extensive, although related characterization and inferential issues for general multivariate distributions are discussed by Fang and Anderson (1990), Fang, Kotz and Ng (1990), Johnson and Kotz (1972) and Press (1983).

In this section we discuss large sample procedures for testing the symmetry of multivariate random variables imposing minimal regularity and distributional conditions. Special focus will be on multivariate random variables whose distributions belong to the domain of attraction of a stable Paretian law. To do so, we consider first a general method of describing and testing multivariate symmetry and then a method that takes advantage of the special properties of multivariate stable Paretian laws. First, we treat univariate r.v.'s, making use of the empirical characteristic function by Csörgő and Heathcote (1982,1987). Then, we address the stable Paretian case using a tail estimator of the spectral measure, which asymptotic properties we studied in Section 8.2.

The definition of univariate symmetry used below is that a r.v. variable, X, is symmetric about the point μ if and only if the imaginary part of the characteristic function of the centered version of X vanishes identically. That is,

---

[13]The remainder of this section is based on Heathcote, Rachev and Chen (1995).
[14]See for example Aki (1987), Antille, Kersting and Zucchini (1982), Bhattacharya, Gastwirth and Wright (1982), Csörgő and Heathcote (1987), Doksum (1975), Doksum, Fenstad and Aaberge (1977), Hollander (1988), Konijn (1988), and Schuster and Barker (1987).

we are concerned with what may be called diagonal or ellipsoidal symmetry.[15] Let the characteristic function (ch.f.)of the random d-dimensional vector X be

$$c(t) = \mathbf{E}\exp i(X,t) = \mathbf{E}\exp i\sum_{k=1}^{d} X_k t_k \qquad (8.49)$$
$$= u(t) + iv(t) = r(t)\exp i\theta(t),$$

where $u(t) = \mathbf{E}\cos(X,t)$, $v(t) = \mathbf{E}\sin(X,t)$, $r(t) = [u^2(t) + v^2(t)]^{1/2}$, and $\tan\theta(t) = \frac{v(t)}{u(t)}$. Then, *symmetry of X about μ* means that

$$\mathbf{E}\sin(X - \mu, t) = v(t)\cos(\mu, t) - u(t)\sin(\mu, t) = 0, \qquad (8.50)$$

and thus

$$\frac{v(t)}{u(t)} = \tan(\mu, t), \qquad (\mu, t) \neq \pi(k + 1/2), \qquad k = \pm 1, \pm 2, \ldots$$

Hence, if r_0 denotes the root of $u(t)$ closest to the origin, then (using the principal value) symmetry about μ forces linearity of the argument $\theta(t)$ in the polar form of $c(t)$, $\theta(t) = \arctan[v(t)/u(t)] = (\mu, t)$, $|t| \leq |r_0|$. We shall refer to

$$\theta(t) = \arctan\frac{v(t)}{u(t)}, \qquad |t| < |r_0| \qquad (8.51)$$

as the *characteristic symmetry function* of X. The possible linearity of $\theta(t)$ and the possible vanishing of $\mathbf{E}\sin(X - \mu, t)$ provide a point of departure for testing symmetry via the characteristic function.

Inference will be based on (large) samples of independent random d-vectors $X_1, X_2, \ldots, X_n$, identically distributed as X. The real and imaginary parts of their empirical ch. f., $C_n(t)$, will be written as

$$U_n(t) := n^{-1}\sum_{j=1}^{n} \cos(X_j, t) \quad \text{and} \quad V_n(t) := n^{-1}\sum_{j=1}^{n} \sin(X_j, t), \quad (8.52)$$

respectively, where $C_n(t) = U_n(t) + iV_n(t)$, $t \in \mathcal{S}$, with $\mathcal{S}$ compact. For t in a compact set $\mathcal{S} \in R^d$, Csörgő (1981) gave detailed results on the covergence of $C_n(t)$ to $c(t)$. In particular Csörgő's Theorem 3.1 establishes the weak convergence of $n^{1/2}[C_n(t) - c(t)]$, $t \in \mathcal{S}$, to a Gaussian process under necessary and sufficient conditions ensuring essentially sample continuity of the limiting process. Without going into details, a sufficient condition is the existence of $E(\log^+ |X|)^{1+\delta}$, $\delta > 0$.[16] This is generally adequate for applications and

---

[15]This is the sort of symmetry we shall use in our approach to the CAPM with heavy-tailed distributed returns, see Chapter 9.
[16]Here, $\log^+(a) := \max(0, \log a)$, $a > 0$.

in particular is satisfied by stable Paretian laws. We will make use of the following condition.

Condition A: For $c(t)$ and $C_n(t)$, defined in (8.49) and (8.52), with $t \in \mathcal{S}$, $\mathcal{S}$ compact, $n^{1/2}[C_n(t) - c(t)]$ converges weakly to a zero mean Gaussian process, $\mathcal{C}$, whose covariance function is $\mathbf{E}[e^{i(X,s)} - c(s)][\overline{e^{i(X,t)} - c(t)}] = c(s - t) - c(s)\overline{c(t)}$, where $\overline{c(t)}$ denotes complex conjugate.

This condition will be generally assumed and usually applied to processes derived from $U_n(t)$ and $V_n(t)$.

The empirical version of the characteristic symmetry function (8.51) is a stochastic process that under symmetry estimates a plane. Studying symmetry via a stochastic process was initiated by Doksum (1975), who used the empirical distribution. This line of inquiry has been developed and extended by several authors, in particular, Aki (1987,1993). A different approach concerned mainly with odd central moments, as in for example Barminghaus and Henze (1991), also has a substantial literature. The third moment, in fact, appears as the first term after the linear in the Taylor expansion of $\theta(t)$ as $t \to 0$,

$$\theta(t) = (\mu, t) - \frac{t^3}{3!}\mathbf{E}(X - \mu, t)^3 + o(t^4), \qquad t \to 0,$$

where terms on the right, apart from (μ, t) vanish with odd central moments. An interpretation of the characteristic symmetry function is then that its departure from linearity depends on the full ch. f. of X and not only selected moments.

The above point was noted by Csörgő and Heathcote (1987) in the univariate case, where it was possible to find a convenient test statistic that did not depend on μ. Unfortunately, it does not seem possible to eliminate μ in the multivariate case without introducing undue complications. Further on, we present a test of symmetry in which μ must be estimated.

Before we do so, we consider some multivariate examples.

Example 8.1 The multivariate Laplace distribution is an example of a multivariate geometrically stable distribution as discussed in Chapter 7. Recall that the Laplace law plays the same role in the geometric-stable scheme, as the normal law plays in the summation scheme for independent returns. It has characteristic function $\mathbf{E}\exp i(X, t) = [i(\mu, t) + \frac{1}{2}(\Omega t, t)]^{-1}$. Then,

$$\theta(t) = \arctan \frac{(\mu, t)}{1 + \frac{1}{2}(\Omega t, t)}, \qquad |t| \leq |r_0|,$$

where r_0 is the first zero of the denominator. Clearly, X is symmetric if and only if $\mu = 0$, in which case $\theta(t)$ vanishes identically.

Example 8.2 Johnson and Kotz (1972, p. 299) discuss the so-called *Pierce-Dukstra-distribution* with the property that all marginal distributions are normal and, hence, symmetric, but which itself is not normal and not necessarily symmetric. The density is

$$f(x_1, x_2, \ldots, x_d) = \left[1 + x_1 x_2 \ldots x_d \exp\left\{-\frac{1}{2}\sum_{k=1}^{d} x_k^2\right\}\right](2\pi)^{-d/2} \exp\left\{-\frac{1}{2}\sum_{k=1}^{d} x_k^2\right\}$$

X is symmetric when d is even and asymmetric when d is odd. It is easy to check that $\theta(t)$ is either identically zero when d is even or else takes values significantly different from zero.

Example 8.3 A standard method of constructing bivariate distributions is to form $X = (X_1, X_2)$ with $X_1 = Y_1 + Y_3$ and $X_2 = Y_2 + Y_3$, where Y_1, Y_2 and Y_3 are three mutually independent random variables. Then, with $t = (t_1, t_2)$

$$\mathbf{E}e^{i(X,t)} = (\mathbf{E}e^{it_1 Y_1})(\mathbf{E}e^{it_2 Y_2})(\mathbf{E}e^{i(t_1+t_2)Y_3}).$$

McCulloch (1986)[17] considers the case when Y_j, $j = 1, 2, 3$, are stable Paretian with log-characteristic functions

$$\log \mathbf{E}e^{it_j Y_j} = \begin{cases} it_j\delta_j - c^\alpha|t_j|^\alpha[1 - i\beta_j \text{sign}(t_j)\tan(\alpha\frac{\pi}{2})], & \alpha \neq 1 \\ it_j\delta_j - c|t_j|[1 - i\beta_j \frac{2}{\pi}\ln|t_j|], & \alpha = 1. \end{cases}$$

One can show that for $\alpha \neq 1$

$$\theta(t) = t_1\delta_1 + t_2\delta_2 + (t_1 + t_2)\delta_3 \tag{8.53}$$
$$+[\beta_1|t_1|^\alpha\text{sign}t_1 + \beta_2|t_2|^\alpha\text{sign }t_2 + \beta_3|t_1 + t_2|^\alpha\text{sign}(t_1 + t_2)]c^\alpha \tan\left(\alpha\frac{\pi}{2}\right).$$

This is linear if and only if $\beta_1 = \beta_2 = \beta_3 = 0$, which is also easily seen to be the case when $\alpha = 1$.

We now start the descriptions of var test for symmetry. Given a sample $(X_1, \ldots, X_n)$, let us define the real and imaginary parts of the empirical characteristic function, denoted by $U_n(t)$ and $V_n(t)$, as in (8.52). If r_n is the first zero of $U_n(t)$, we define the empirical characteristic symmetry function by

$$\theta_n(t) := \arctan \frac{V_n(t)}{U_n(t)}, \qquad |t| \leq |r_n|. \tag{8.54}$$

Then,

$$\theta_n(t) - \theta(t) = \arctan \frac{\frac{V_n(t)}{U_n(t)} - \frac{v(t)}{u(t)}}{1 + \frac{V_n(t)}{U_n(t)}\frac{v(t)}{u(t)}}.$$

---

[17]McCulloch (1986) studied stable Paretian version of the Black-Scholes formula for European calls.

As $n \to \infty$, Condition A implies the uniform consistency of $V_n(t)$ and $U_n(t)$, $t \in S$. Expanding the inverse tangent we find

$$
\begin{aligned}
Z_n(t) &= n^{1/2}[\theta_n(t) - \theta(t)] \\
&= n^{-1/2} \sum_{j=1}^{n} \frac{u(t)\sin(X_j, t) - v(t)\cos(X_j, t)}{u(t)U_n(t) + v(t)V_n(t)} + o_p(1). \quad (8.55)
\end{aligned}
$$

Under Condition A the right hand side converges weakly to a zero mean Gaussian process with covariance

$$
\sigma(s, t) = \frac{g(s, t)}{2[u^2(s) + v^2(s)][u^2(t) + v^2(t)]}, \quad (8.56)
$$

where

$$
\begin{aligned}
g(s, t) &= [u(s)u(t) + v(s)v(t)]u(t - s) - [u(s)u(t) - v(s)v(t)]u(t + s) \\
&\quad + [u(s)v(t) - v(s)u(t)]v(t - s) - [u(s)v(t) + v(s)u(t)]v(t + s).
\end{aligned}
$$

When X is symmetric about μ, the covariance reduces to

$$
\sigma_0(s, t) = \frac{h(\mu; t - s) - h(\mu; t + s)}{2h(\mu; s)h(\mu; t)},
$$

where

$$
h(\mu; t) := \frac{u(t)}{\cos(\mu, t)} = \frac{v(t)}{\sin(\mu, t)}.
$$

Note that $\sigma_0(s, t)$ is the covariance function of $\sin(X - \mu, t)/\mathbf{E}\cos(X - \mu, t)$ and that under symmetry

$$
\begin{aligned}
\theta_n(t) - \theta(t) &= \frac{u(t)V_n(t) - v(t)U_n(t)}{u(t)U_n(t) + v(t)V_n(t)} + o_p(n^{-1/2}) \\
&= \frac{\cos(\mu, t)V_n(t) - \sin(\mu, t)U_n(t)}{\cos(\mu, t)U_n(t) + \sin(\mu, t)V_n(t)} + o_p(n^{-1/2}) \\
&= \frac{\sum_{j=1}^{n} \sin(X_j - \mu, t)}{\sum_{j=1}^{n} \cos(X_j - \mu, t)} + o_p(n^{-1/2}). \quad (8.57)
\end{aligned}
$$

Below the numerator of (8.57) the right hand side is shown to be asymptotically Gaussian, when the shift parameter μ is estimated from the sample.

Remark 8.5 Let S and $Z_n(t)$ be as in (8.55) and (8.56). To get an estimate for the covariance function of the limiting process, we shall show that the empirical process $Z_n(t)$ can be bootstrapped, see Remark 8.7 at the end of this section.

Remark 8.6 Set of S of t for which (8.55) holds is contained in a ball of radius $|r_n|$, where r_n is the first zero of $U_n(t)$. This defines the working region to which t must be confined when using $\theta_n(t)$ for purposes for inference. The distribution of r_n, when X is univariate, has been discussed by Heathcote and Hüsler (1990) but no results are available in the multivariate case. A rough bound can be obtained by approximating the cosine term in $U_n(t)$ by

$$U_n(t) \geq 1 - \frac{1}{2}\frac{1}{n}\sum_{j=1}^{n}(X_j, t)^2 = 1 - \frac{1}{2}(A_n t, t),$$

where A_n is the $d \times d$ matrix whose (i, ℓ) –element is $n^{-1}\sum_{j=1}^{n} X_{ij}X_{\ell j}$. Hence, r_n is greater in magnitude than the first t for which $(A_n t, t) = 2$. Heathcote, Cheng and Rachev (1995) report that their practical experience indicates that working from this level curve until numerical stability fails is a feasible practical procedure, at least for $d = 2, 3$.

Testing symmetry by examining departures of either $\theta_n(t)$ from linearity or of $\sum_{j=1}^{n} \sin(X_j - \mu, t)$ from zero yield asymptotically equivalent procedures (recall (8.50) and (8.57)). Both approaches suffer from the disadvantage that they depend on the unknown parameter μ. As noted previously, it does not seem possible to eliminate the parameter in the multivariate case without introducing undue complications. The following procedure is based on process $n^{-1/2}\sum_{j=1}^{n} \sin(X_j - \mu, t), t \in S$, which has zero expectation under symmetry. The covariance function is of the form

$$\text{Cov}\left(\sin(X - \mu, s), \sin(X - \mu, t)\right) = \frac{1}{2}[u_\mu(t - s) - u_\mu(t + s)] - v_\mu(s)v_\mu(t),$$

where $u_\mu(t) = \mathbf{E}\cos(X - \mu, t)$ and $v_\mu(t) = \mathbf{E}\sin(X - \mu, t)$. Quantity $v_\mu(t)$ is identically zero when symmetry about μ holds, see (8.50).

When μ is unknown and estimated by μ_n^* say, process

$$Y_n(t) = n^{-1/2}\sum_{j=1}^{n} \sin(X_j - \mu_n^*, t) \tag{8.58}$$

is useful only if $a_n(\mu_n^* - \mu)$ converges weakly with $a_n = n^{1/2}$. However, the choice of the sample mean or the maximum likelihood estimator may not be appropriate. Indeed, there are a number of location estimators, such as trimmed means and M estimators, which do not necessarily impose stringent tail conditions on X.

Consider then estimators of the form

$$\mu_n^* = n^{-1}\sum_{j=1}^{n} \ell(X_j), \tag{8.59}$$

which are assumed to be consistent and asymptotically normally distributed. Thus, suppose $n^{1/2}(\mu_n^* - \mu)$ converges weakly to a d-variate normally distributed random vector, Z, with zero mean and covariance matrix Σ_μ, i.e.,

$$n^{1/2}(\mu_n^* - \mu) \xrightarrow{\omega} Z, \qquad (8.60)$$

where Z is $N_d(O, \Sigma_\mu)$.

The following theorem gives rise to the symmetry test based on the empirical characteristic function described here.

Theorem 8.5 Suppose Condition A holds for $t \in S$, S compact. If X is symmetric about μ and if (8.60) holds, then $Y_n(t)$, $t \in S$, of (8.58) converges weakly to a zero mean Gaussian process with covariance function

$$
\begin{aligned}
\sigma(s, t) &= \frac{1}{2}[u_\mu(s - t) - u_\mu(s + t)] - u_\mu(t)\text{Cov}\left(\sin(X - \mu, s), (\ell(X) - \mu, t)\right) \\
&\quad -u_\mu(s)\text{Cov}\left(\sin(X - \mu, t), (\ell(X) - \mu, s)\right) \qquad (8.61) \\
&\quad +u_\mu(s)u_\mu(t)(\Sigma_\mu s, t). \qquad (8.62)
\end{aligned}
$$

If X is not symmetric about μ, then there is a nondegenerate set, S_0, such that $|Y_n(t)|$ diverges almost surely for $t \in S_0$.

Proof:

$$n^{-1/2}\sum_{j=1}^{n}\sin(X_j - \mu_n^*, t)$$

$$= n^{-1/2}\sum_{j=1}^{n}\sin\left((X_j - \mu) - (\mu_n^* - \mu), t\right)$$

$$= n^{-1/2}\sum_{j=1}^{n}\sin(X_j - \mu, t)\cos(\mu_n^* - \mu, t) - n^{-1/2}\sum_{j=1}^{n}\cos(X_j - \mu, t)\sin(\mu_n^* - \mu, t)$$

$$= \left[n^{-1/2}\sum_{j=1}^{n}\sin(X_j - \mu, t)\right][1 + o_p(n^{-1/2})] - u_\mu(t)\sin(\mu_n^* - \mu, t)$$

$$\quad - \left[n^{-1/2}\sum_{j=1}^{n}\cos(X_j - \mu, t) - u_\mu(t)\right]\sin(\mu_n^* - \mu, t)$$

$$= n^{-1/2}\sum_{j=1}^{n}\sin(X_j - \mu, t)u_\mu(t)\sin(\mu_n^* - \mu, t) + o_p(1).$$

Using (8.59), (8.60) and the Taylor expansion of $\sin(\mu_n^* - \mu, t)$, we obtain

$$n^{-1/2}\sum_{j=1}^{n}\sin(X_j - \mu_n^*, t)$$

$$= n^{-1/2}\sum_{j=1}^{n}[\sin(X_j - \mu, t) - u_\mu(t)(\ell(X_j) - \mu, t)] + o_p(1).$$

Brief calculation shows that $\sigma(s,t)$ of (8.62) is the covariance of the summand on the right hand side. Then, the theorem follows from Condition A.   □

The choice $l(X) = X$ gives the sample mean $\mu_n^* = \overline{X}$ and matrix Σ_μ is then the covariance matrix of X, provided second moments exist. In this case we also have, after rearranging terms,

$$\text{Cov}(\sin(X - \mu, t), (X - \mu, s)) = \mathbf{E}((X - \mu)\sin(X - \mu, t), s) = -\left(\frac{\partial}{\partial t}u_\mu(t), s\right),$$

simplifying the covariance $\sigma(s,t)$.

The major question is not so much the choice of μ_n^* but rather the detail of the procedure to be followed when testing the hypothesis of symmetry. It would be natural to base a test statistic on the supremum of $Y_n(t)$ over a working region as large as possible. However, little is known about the distribution of the supremum of a non-stationary Gaussian process (see Adler (1991) for a discussion). One possible strategy is to bootstrap; another is to use the approximation to the extreme tail of the distribution of the supremum by the tail of the normal distribution calculated at the point t_0 which maximizes the variance function over the region of interest, $\sigma^2(t_0) = \sigma(t_0, t_0) \geq \sigma(t, t)$, $t \in \mathcal{S}$. In this case, if $Y(t)$ is the weak limit of $Y_n(t)$ in Theorem 8.5, then for large x we have

$$P\left(\sup_{t \in \mathcal{S}}\left|\frac{Y(t)}{\sigma(t)}\right| > x\right) \cong P\left(\left|\frac{Y(t_0)}{\sigma(t_0)}\right| > x\right). \tag{8.63}$$

This is the procedure adopted by Csörgő and Heathcote (1987) in the univariate case.

Testing the null hypothesis of symmetry in this fashion route involves the following steps:

1. Select estimators μ_n^* and $\sigma_n^2(t)$ for μ and $\sigma^2(t) = \sigma(t, t)$, respectively, and working region $\mathcal{S}_n$.

2. Find the point t_{0_n} which maximizes $\sigma_n^2(t)$ over $\mathcal{S}_n$.

3. Reject the hypothesis of symmetry at significance level α if $|Y_n(t_{0_n})/\sigma_n (t_{0_n})| > z_{\alpha/2}$, where $z_{\alpha/2}$ is the $100(1 - \alpha/2)$ percentile of the standard normal distribution.

Set $\mathcal{S}_n$ will generally be strictly within the largest region over which the supremum can be taken and, in that sense, the procedure is conservative. Numerical instabilities can occur when $U_n^2(t) + V_n^2(t)$ is small.

If symmetry does not hold, the imaginary part of the centered characteristic function is not identically zero and process $Y_n(t)$ in (8.58) diverges almost surely.

Theorem 8.6 Suppose X is not symmetric and that μ_n^* is given by (8.59) with as $n \to \infty$, $\mu_n^* \xrightarrow{\omega} \mu_1$ and $n^{1/2}(\mu_n^* - \mu_1) \xrightarrow{\omega} Z_1$, where Z_1 is $N_d(0, \Sigma_1)$.

If

$$n^{-1} \sum_{j=1}^{n} \sin(X_j - \mu_1, t) \xrightarrow{p} v_{\mu_1}(t), \quad t \in \mathcal{S},$$

and Condition A holds, then $n^{-1/2} \sum_{j=1}^{n} [\sin(X_j - \mu_n^*, t) - v_{\mu_1}(t)] \xrightarrow{w} Y_1(t)$, where $Y_1(t)$, $t \in \mathcal{S}$, is a zero mean Gaussian process with covariance function

$$\begin{aligned}
\sigma_1(s,t) = {}& 1/2[u_{\mu_1}(s-t) - u_{\mu_1}(s+t) - 2v_{\mu_1}(s)v_{\mu_1}(t)] \\
& - u_{\mu_1}(s)\mathrm{Cov}\left(\sin(X - \mu_1, t), (\ell(X) - \mu_1, s)\right) \\
& - u_{\mu_1}(t)\mathrm{Cov}\left(\sin(X - \mu_1, s), (\ell, (X) - \mu_1, t)\right) + u_{\mu_1}(s)u_{\mu_1}(t)(\Sigma_1 s, t).
\end{aligned}$$

Proof: The argument is similar to the proof of Theorem 8.5 with the obvious modification that $v_{\mu_1}(t)$ is not identically zero. □

Power calculations are now possible for specified departures from symmetry with $\sup_{t \in \mathcal{S}} |v_{\mu_1}(t)|$ playing the role of a parameter asserted to be zero under the null hypothesis.

We now discuss briefly the estimation of μ. In the absence of further information it is prudent to select a robust estimator of μ, such as a trimmed mean. The $100\gamma\%$ trimmed mean, denoted by $\mu^*(\gamma)$, of random vector X with distribution function F is given by

$$\mu^*(\gamma) = \frac{1}{1-\gamma} \int_{\mathcal{S}(\gamma)} x F(dx),$$

where $\mathcal{S}(\gamma)$ is such that

$$1 - \gamma = \int_{\mathcal{S}(\gamma)} F(dx).$$

Typically $\mathcal{S}(\gamma)$ is an ellipsoid or sphere, with the latter being an appropriate choice in the case of symmetry. Alternatively one could adopt 'peeling' as described by Green (1981), for example.

Maller (1988) gives a general treatment of trimmed means in d dimensions and Berrkane (1987) discusses the bivariate case. For a sample size of n the trimming is with respect to sets $\mathcal{S}_n(\gamma)$ in the sense that $\mathcal{S}_n(\gamma)$ contains the proportion $1 - [n\gamma]/n \simeq 1 - \gamma$ of the sample $X_1, X_2, \ldots, X_n$. Under symmetry we choose $\mathcal{S}(\gamma)$ to be a sphere centered around the sample mean, $\overline{X}$, with radius equal to the $(n - [n\gamma])$th largest of the Euclidean distances $|X_j - \overline{X}|, j = 1, 2, \ldots, n$. The $100\gamma\%$ trimmed sample mean is the average of the sample members in $\mathcal{S}_n(\gamma)$. Together with this choice of μ_n^*, a variance estimator of $\sigma^2(t)$ is obtained by taking the empirical version of (8.62). Steps (2) and (3) of the test outlined above can then be implemented.

Asymptotic normality for trimmed means holds under the condition of the continuity of $F(x)$ on the boundary of $\mathcal{S}(\gamma)$, the generalization of the univariate requirement of continuity of the distribution function at the appropriate percentile. Theorems 8.5 and 8.6 are consistent with Maller's treatment provided that function ℓ is replaced by ℓ_n, depending on n, such that $\ell_n \to \ell$, $n \to \infty$, in the same way as the trimming region $\mathcal{S}_n(\gamma)$. To this end, take

$$\ell_n(x) = \begin{cases} x, & \text{if } x \in \mathcal{S}_n(\gamma) \\ 0, & \text{otherwise}. \end{cases}$$

With μ_n^* the γ trimmed mean and $u_\mu(t)$ estimated by

$$U_{n\mu_n}(t) = n^{-1} \sum_{j=1}^{n} \cos(X_j - \mu_n^*, t),$$

the estimate of $\sigma^2(t) = \sigma(t, t)$ is

$$\sigma_n^2(t) = \frac{1 - U_{n\mu_n}(2t)}{2} - \frac{2U_{n\mu_n}(t)}{(1 - \gamma)(n - [n\gamma])} \sum_{X_j \in \mathcal{S}_n(\gamma)} (X_j - \mu_n^*, t) \sin(X_j - \mu_n^*, t)$$

$$+ \frac{[U_{n\mu_n}(2t)]^2}{(1 - \gamma)^2} (\Sigma_n^* t, t). \tag{8.64}$$

Matrix Σ_n^* is the $d \times d$ sample covariance matrix of $X_j - \mu_n^*$ with entry (ℓ, m) given by

$$\Sigma_n^*(\ell, m) = \frac{1}{n - [n\gamma]} \sum_{X_j \in \mathcal{S}_n(\gamma)} (X_{\ell j} - \mu_{\ell n}^*)(X_{mj} - \mu_{mn}^*) - \gamma X_{\cdot \ell}(\gamma) X_{\cdot m}(\gamma).$$

Here, $X_{\cdot \ell}(\gamma)$ denotes the ℓth element of the vector $X_{\cdot}(\gamma)$ that lies on $\mathcal{S}(\gamma)$; that is, $X_{\cdot}(\gamma)$ has the $(n - [n\gamma])$th largest of the Euclidean distances $|X_j - \overline{X}|, j = 1, 2, \ldots, n$.

This estimate of the variance is then maximized over an appropriate region $\mathcal{S}_n$. The realized value of statistic

$$\frac{Y_n(t_{0n})}{\sigma(t_{0n})} = \frac{\sum_{j=1}^{n} \sin(X_j - \mu_n^*, t_{0n})}{n \sigma(t_{0n})} \tag{8.65}$$

can now be calculated. The hypothesis of symmetry is rejected at significance level α if $|Y_n(t_{0n})/\sigma(t_{0n})|$ exceeds the critical $\alpha/2$ point of the standard normal distribution.

Using this test Heathcote, Cheng and Rachev (1995) conclude that the bivariate daily return series of the D-Mark/USD and the Yen/USD daily exchange rates from 1980 to 1990 is symmetric.

In the rest of this section we propose a test for symmetry assuming that the observations are taken from the domain of attraction of an α-stable law. We use the notations of Section 8.2. The procedure is based on tail estimators of the normalized spectral measure ϕ_n (see Lemma 8.4). Again, as in

Section 8.2, we assume that while $\mathbf{X} = (X_1, \ldots, X_d)$ – the vector of returns – has an α-stable distribution given by its characteristic function (8.1) the real observations $\mathbf{Z}_1, \mathbf{Z}_2, \ldots$ of this portfolio belong to the domain of attraction of $\mathbf{X}$ only, they are not necessarily equal in distribution to $\mathbf{X}$. We want to test whether the law of $\mathbf{X}$ is symmetric given the data $\mathbf{Z}_1, \mathbf{Z}_2, \ldots$.

With all the preliminary results in Section 8.2 on estimation of the spectral measure of an α-stable law we are ready to construct the test for symmetry of an α-stable random vector.

A random vector X is called symmetric α-stable ($S\alpha S$) vector in R^d with $0 < \alpha < 2$ if X is stable and $X \stackrel{d}{=} -X$. The above condition is equivalent to saying an X is $S\alpha S$ if and only if in (8.1) $\mu = 0$ and Γ is symmetric, that is $\Gamma(A) = \Gamma(-A)$ for any Borel set A of S^d. X is called *shift-symmetric* (or symmetric about μ) α-stable vector if the spectral measure Γ of X is symmetric .

Let us restrict our attention initially to the case of bivariate $S\alpha S$ random vectors.

Theorem 8.7 Under the assumption (8.11) in Lemma 8.4

$$\sqrt{k} \sup_{0 \leq \theta \leq \pi} |\phi_n(\theta) - \phi_n(\theta + \pi) + \phi_n(\pi)| \stackrel{w}{\longrightarrow} \sup_{0 \leq \theta \leq \pi} |B(\theta)|,$$

where $B(\theta)$, $0 \leq \theta \leq \pi$, is a mean zero Gaussian process with

$$\mathbf{E} B(\theta_1) B(\theta_2) = 2\phi(\theta_1 \wedge \theta_2).$$

Observe that under the hypothesis that X is $S\alpha S$, we have

$$P\left(\sqrt{k} \sup_{0 \leq \theta \leq \pi} |\phi_n(\theta) - \phi_n(\theta + \pi) + \phi_n(\pi)| > c \right) \longrightarrow P(\sup_{0 \leq \theta \leq \pi} |B(\theta)| > c),$$

as $n \to \infty$. A bound for the limiting probability is given in Davies (1977),

$$P\left(\sup_{0 \leq \theta \leq \pi} |B(\theta)| > c \right) \leq 2\Phi(-c) + \frac{1}{\pi} e^{-c^2/2} \int_0^\pi (-\varrho(\theta))^{1/2} d\theta,$$

where Φ is the standard normal distribution function, and in our case,

$$\varrho(\theta) = \left[\frac{\partial^2}{\partial \theta_1^2} 2\phi(\theta_1 \wedge \theta) \right]_{\theta_1 = 0} = \left[\frac{\partial^2}{\partial \theta_1^2} 2\phi(\theta_1) \right]_{\theta_1 = 0} = 2\theta''(0).$$

Therefore, an asymptotic bound for the significance level of

$$P\left(\sqrt{k} \sup_{0 \leq \theta \leq \pi} |\phi_n(\theta) - \phi_n(\theta + \pi) + \phi_n(\pi)| > c \right)$$

is $2\Phi(-c) + e^{-c^2/2}(-2\phi''(0))^{1/2}$.

In the d-variate case, the symmetry condition for the spectral measure amounts to

$$P(0 < \theta_1 < t_1, \ldots, 0 < \theta_{d-1} < t_{d-1}) \tag{8.66}$$
$$= P(\pi - t_1 < \theta_1 < \pi, \ldots, \pi - t_{d-2} < \theta_{d-2} < \pi, \pi < \theta_{d-1} < \pi + t_{d-1}),$$

for all $0 < t_1 < \pi, \ldots, 0 < t_{d-2} \leq \pi, 0 < t_{d-1} \leq 2\pi$.

Let $\Lambda(\theta)$, $\theta \in \Omega_d$ be defined as in (8.11), that is, $\Lambda(\theta) = W_1(\theta) - \phi(\theta)W_2(1)$. We define the multivariate random measure generated by Λ: for any interval $[a, b] = \otimes_{i=1}^{n}[a_i, b_i] \subset \Omega_d$, set

$$\begin{aligned} \Lambda\{[a,b]\} = & \ \Lambda(b_1, \ldots, b_{d-1}) - \Lambda(b_1, \ldots, b_{d-2}, a_{d-1}) - \cdots \\ & - \Lambda(a_1, b_2, \ldots, b_{d-1}) + \cdots + (-1)^{d-1}\Lambda(a_1, \ldots, a_{d-1}). \end{aligned}$$

Given a distribution function ϕ on Ω_d, we denote by $\phi([\cdot])$ the probability measure defined by ϕ and let $\phi_n([\cdot])$ denote its empirical counterpart.

Theorem 8.8 *(Test for symmetry).* Suppose $\mathbf{Z}$ is in the domain of attraction of shift-symmetric α-stable random vector $\mathbf{X}$ satisfying the regularity condition (8.10). Then

$$\sqrt{k}(\phi_n(\theta) - \phi_n([\pi - \theta_1, \pi] \times \ldots \times [\pi - \theta_{d-2}, \pi] \times [\pi, \pi + \theta_{d-1}])) \xrightarrow{w} B(\theta),$$

where $\theta = (\theta_1, \ldots, \theta_{d-1}) \in \Omega_d$, the weak convergence is in $D(\Omega_d)$, and $B(\theta)$ is a zero mean Gaussian process on Ω_d with distribution given by

$$B(\theta) \overset{d}{=} \Lambda(\theta) - \Lambda([\pi - \theta, \pi] \times \ldots \times [\pi - \theta_{d-2}, \pi] \times [\pi, \pi + \theta_{d-1}]).$$

This is a general result. To obtain confidence intervals via the limiting process $B(\theta)$ one can rely on the bootstrap method based on tail estimators, see next Remark 8.7. The covariance structure of $B(\theta)$ depends on $\phi(\theta)$ only, and so, as a simplification, one can apply the tail estimator ϕ_n for ϕ to approximate the covariance function for $B(\theta)$.

In the case of an asymmetric distribution, it can be easily seen that the test statistic given in Theorem 8.8 grows unboundedly as n tends to infinity.

Heathcote, Cheng and Rachev (1995) consider a bivariate data set of 2853 daily exchange returns for two currencies DM and Yen (versus USD). The data is from January 1, 1980 to December 7, 1990. Theorem 8.7 was applied and the supremum of the normalized spectral measure $\phi(\theta)$ was estimated to be 1.07. This is less than the critical value of 1.96 and the hypothesis of symmetry is accepted.

Remark 8.7 *(Bootstrapping the empirical process)* As mentioned in Remark 8.5, an estimate of the limiting process of covariance function $\sigma(s, t)$, specified in (8.56), can be obtained by bootstrapping the empirical process. Bickel and Freedman (1981) (see also Shorack and Wellner (1986) Chapter 13) present a general approach for bootstrapping empirical processes, which will be used here.

As usual, the bootstrap result will be based on a certain "stability theorem" for empirical characteristic functions. With this in mind, consider two samples $\mathbf{X}_n = (X_1, \ldots, X_n)$ and $\tilde{\mathbf{X}}_n = (\tilde{X}_1, \ldots, \tilde{X}_n)$ of i.i.d. random vectors with characteristic functions $c = re^{i\theta}$, $\tilde{c} = \tilde{r}e^{i\tilde{\theta}}$, respectively. Let $\theta_n = \arctan(V_n/U_n)$ and $\tilde{\theta}_n = \arctan(\tilde{V}_n/\tilde{U}_n)$, be the corresponding empirical counterparts of $\theta = \arctan(v/u)$ and $\tilde{\theta} = \arctan(\tilde{v}/\tilde{u})$. The stability theorem we are looking for should be of the following form: If $Z_n = \sqrt{n}(\theta_n - \theta)$ and $\tilde{Z}_n = \sqrt{n}(\tilde{\theta}_n - \tilde{\theta})$, then

$$l(Z_n, \tilde{Z}_n) = O(\|u - \tilde{u}\| + \|v - \tilde{v}\|) + o_p(1). \qquad (8.67)$$

Here, $l(\xi, \eta) = l(P^\xi, P^\eta)$ is a metric in the space of probability laws on $(C(\mathcal{S}), \|\cdot\|)$, the space of continuous functions on the compact $\mathcal{S}$ equipped with the usual sup norm. The metric l should be chosen to metrize the weak convergence. We define l to be the Kantorovich-Dudley minimal metric (see, for example, Rachev (1991, p. 78)):

$$
\begin{aligned}
l(\xi, \eta) &= l(P^\xi, P^\eta) \\
&= \inf\{\mathbf{E}\|\tilde{\xi} - \tilde{\eta}\| \wedge 1 : \tilde{\xi} \overset{d}{=} \xi, \tilde{\eta} \overset{d}{=} \eta\} \\
&= \sup\{|\mathbf{E}f(\xi) - \mathbf{E}f(\eta)| : \text{over all bounded } f : C(\mathcal{S}) \to R, \\
&\quad \text{such that } |f(x) - f(y)| \le \|x - y\| \wedge 1, \ \forall x, y \in \mathcal{S}\}.
\end{aligned}
$$

Next, we verify (8.67). For any "coupling" of $\mathbf{X}_n$ and $\tilde{\mathbf{X}}_n$, i.e., for any joint distribution of $\mathbf{X}_n$ and $\tilde{\mathbf{X}}_n$ with fixed marginals, we let $\Delta_n := \|Z_n - \tilde{Z}_n\| \wedge 1$ be bounded by $const(1 + o_p(1))(\|u - \tilde{u}\| + \|v - \tilde{v}\| + o_p(1))$. Here, *const* stands for an absolute constant which can be different at different places but does not depend on n and the involved distribution law; indeed, *const* can be computed explicitly, but this is not necessary for our limiting results.

The proof is similar to that of the asymptotic normality for $Z_n(t)$. In fact, as in the proof of (8.55), we have

$$\Delta_n = \Delta_n^* \wedge 1 + O_p(n^{-1/2}),$$

where

$$\Delta_n^* = n^{1/2} \left\| \frac{uV_n - vU_n}{u^2 + v^2} - \frac{\tilde{u}\tilde{V}_n - \tilde{v}\tilde{U}_n}{\tilde{u}^2 + \tilde{v}^2} \right\|.$$

Define $\alpha = u/(u^2 + v^2)$, $\beta = v/(u^2 + v^2)$, $V_n^0 = V_n - v$, $U_N^0 = U_n - u$, and, in a similar way, $\tilde{V}_n^0$, $\tilde{U}_n^0$, $\tilde{\alpha}$, and $\tilde{\beta}$. By Condition A, $\sqrt{n}(U_n^0 + iV_n^0)$ and $\sqrt{n}(\tilde{U}_n^0 + i\tilde{V}_n^0)$ weakly tend to Gaussian process $\mathcal{C}$ and $\tilde{\mathcal{C}}$, respectively, so that

$$
\begin{aligned}
\Delta_n^* &= const(\|\alpha - \tilde{\alpha}\|\|\mathrm{Im}\beta\| + \|\tilde{\alpha}\|\sqrt{n}\|V_n^0 - \tilde{V}_n^0\| \\
&\quad + \|\beta - \tilde{\beta}\|\|\mathrm{Re}\,\mathcal{C}\| + \|\tilde{\beta}\|\sqrt{n}\|U_n^0 - \tilde{U}_n^0\|) + o_p(1)
\end{aligned}
$$

and implying that

$$\mathbf{E}\Delta_n = const(\|u - \tilde{u}\| + \|v - \tilde{v}\| + \mathbf{E}(\sqrt{n}(\|U_n^0 - \tilde{U}_n^0\| + \|V_n^0 - \tilde{V}_n^0\|) \wedge 1)) + o_p(1).$$

Passing to the minimum over all couplings of $\mathbf{X}_n$ and $\tilde{\mathbf{X}}_n$, we get

$$\mathbf{l}(Z_n, \tilde{Z}_n) = const(\|u - \tilde{u}\| + \|v - \tilde{v}\| + \mathbf{l}((\sqrt{n}U_n^0, \sqrt{n}V_n^0), (\sqrt{n}\tilde{U}_n^0, \sqrt{n}\tilde{V}_n^0))).$$

Here, the definition for $\mathbf{l}$ is extended to the space of laws on product $C(\mathcal{S}) \times C(\mathcal{S})$, namely

$$\mathbf{l}(\xi, \eta) = \sup |\mathbf{E}(f(\xi) - f(\eta))|$$

over all bounded $f : C\mathcal{S}) \times C(\mathcal{S}) \to R$ and such that for any $x_i, y_i \in C\mathcal{S})$; $|f(x_1, y_1) - f(x_2, y_2)| \le (\|x_1 - x_2\| + \|y_1 - y_2\|) \wedge 1$. Processes $(\sqrt{n}U_n^0, \sqrt{n}V_n^0)$ and $(\sqrt{n}\tilde{U}_n^0, \sqrt{n}\tilde{V}_n^0)$ converge weakly to $(\text{Re } \mathcal{C}, \text{Im } \tilde{C})$ and $(\text{Re } \tilde{C}, \text{Im } \tilde{C})$, respectively. Invoking the Skorokhod a.s. construction (see, for example Rachev (1991), p. 105) we can assume that, as $n \to \infty$, $\mathbf{l}((\sqrt{n}U_n^0, \sqrt{n}V_n^0), (\sqrt{n}\tilde{U}_n^0, \sqrt{n}\tilde{V}_n^0)) = O(\|u - \tilde{u}\| + \|v - \tilde{v}\|) + o_p(1)$. This completes the proof of stability bound (8.67).

Return now to the bootstrapping problem. Given sample $\mathbf{X}_n$ from a distribution with characteristic function $c(t) = u(t) + i\, v(t)$ let $\mathbf{X}_{m,n}^*$ be a bootstrap sample consisting of $\mathbf{X}_n$ conditionally independent vectors $X_{i,n}(i = 1, \ldots, m)$ with common characteristic function $c_n(t) = U_n(t) + iV_n(t)$. Denote the empirical ch. f. of $\mathbf{X}_{m,n}^*$ by $C_{m,n}(t) = U_{m,n}(t) + iV_{m,n}(t)$. Conditionally on $\mathbf{X}_n$ we have

$$\mathbf{l}\left(\sqrt{m}[\theta_{m,n} - \theta_n], \sqrt{m}[\theta_m - \theta]\right)$$
$$:= \ell\left(\sqrt{m}\left[\arctan\frac{V_{m,n}}{U_{m,n}} - \arctan\frac{V_n}{u_n}\right], \sqrt{m}\left[\arctan\frac{V_m}{U_m} - \arctan\frac{v}{u}\right]\right)$$
$$= O(\|U_n - u\| + \|V_n - v\|) + o_p(1);$$

here the argument rests on (8.67). The Glivenko-Cantelli theorem together with $\sqrt{m}[\theta_m - \theta] \xrightarrow{w} B$ implies the bootstrap result that, conditionally on X_n,

$$\sqrt{m}[\theta_{m,n} - \theta_n] \xrightarrow{w} B$$

as $m, n \to \infty$.

8.6   Test of dependence between two asset–return series

In this section we investigate the association (dependence) for asset return series and extend results in Section 8.3 and 8.4. For the sake of simplicity we consider here only the bivariate case. Let the respective observations of two asset returns denoted by $\mathbf{Z}_n = (\mathbf{Z}_n^{(1)}, \mathbf{Z}_n^{(2)})$, be in the domain of attraction of bivariate Paretian–stable (or geometric–stable) laws, ref. Chapter 7[18].

---

[18]The general case of d-dimensional vector of returns with the proof of the results in this section is given in Mittnik, Rachev and Rüschendorf (1995).

Treating $\{\mathbf{Z}_n\} = \{(\mathbf{Z}_n^{(1)}, \mathbf{Z}_n^{(2)})\}$ as a sample of i.i.d. random pairs we suppose that vectors $\mathbf{a}_n \in \mathbf{R}_+^2$ and $\mathbf{b}_n \in \mathbf{R}_+^2$ exist, such that

$$\left(\frac{1}{a_n^{(1)}} \sum_{j=1}^n Z_j^{(1)}, \frac{1}{a_n^{(2)}} \sum_{j=1}^n Z_j^{(2)} \right) - \mathbf{b}_n \xrightarrow{w} \mathbf{X}. \qquad (8.68)$$

To model the tail behavior of the returns jointly, we only assume that the observations $\{\mathbf{Z}_n\}$ are in the domain of attraction of a pair of random returns with heavy tails, denoted by $\mathbf{X} = (X^{(1)}, X^{(2)})$, i.e., the two components $X^{(1)}$ and $X^{(2)}$ are Paretian stable with index of stability α_1 and α_2, respectively. A more precise definition follows. (Note that in all previous sections of this chapter we considered the special case $\alpha_1 = \alpha_2$.)
Define

$$\mathbf{P}_n(t) = \left(\frac{1}{a_n^{(1)}} S_{[nt]}^{(1)} - t b_n^{(1)}, \frac{1}{a_n^{(2)}} S_{[nt]}^{(2)} - t b_n^{(2)} \right), \quad t \geq 0, \qquad (8.69)$$

to be a pair of processes with trajectories in the Skorokhod space $D(\mathbf{R}_+)^2$, where $\mathbf{S}_n = (S_n^{(1)}, S_n^{(2)})$ denotes the n-th partial sum of $\mathbf{Z}_n = (Z_n^{(1)}, Z_n^{(2)})$.[19] For details see Resnick and Greenwood (1979) and references therein. Next, if, for some $\mathbf{a}_n \in \mathbf{R}_+^2$ and $\mathbf{b}_n \in \mathbf{R}^2, \mathbf{P}_n(1) \xrightarrow{w} \mathbf{X}(1)$,[20] then $\mathbf{P}_n(\cdot) \xrightarrow{w} \mathbf{X}(\cdot)$ in $D(\mathbf{R}_+)^2$, where $\mathbf{X}$ is a Lévy process possessing the *self-similarity property*: for all $a > 0$,

$$\{\mathbf{X}(at), t \geq 0\} \stackrel{d}{=} \left\{ a^{1/\alpha_1} X^{(1)}(t) + t\beta_1(a), a^{1/\alpha_2} X^{(2)}(t) + t\beta_2(a), t \geq 0 \right\}, \qquad (8.70)$$

with $0 < \alpha_i \leq 2$ and $\beta = (\beta_1, \beta_2) \in \mathbf{R}^2$.

The ch. f. of $\mathbf{X}(t)$ is given by

$$E \exp\{i(\mathbf{X}(t), \tau)\} = e^{ih(\tau)}, \qquad (8.71)$$

where

$$h(\tau) = i(\mathbf{a}, \tau) + \frac{1}{2}(\mathbf{B}\tau, \tau) + \int_{\|s\|>1} \left(e^{i(\tau, s)} - 1 \right) \nu(ds)$$

$$+ \int_{0<\|s\|\leq 1} \left(e^{i(\tau, s)} - 1 - i(\tau, s) \right) \nu(ds), \qquad (8.72)$$

---

[19]More general normalization of $\mathbf{S}_{[nt]}$, namely, $Z_n(t) = \mathbf{A}_n S_{[nt]} - t b_n, \mathbf{A}_n \colon \mathbf{R}^2 \longrightarrow \mathbf{R}^2$— leads to *operator-stable* processes (see Sharp (1969); Hudson (1980), Hudson et al. (1986); Maejima and Rachev (1996)). A characterization of stable laws with respect to generalized (Urbanik-type) convolution operations, containing summation and maxima schemes as particular cases, is presented in Panorska (1992).
[20]$\mathbf{X}(t)$ can be interpreted as the process of vector asset returns having independent infinitely divisible components.

with $(\cdot, \cdot)$ denoting the usual inner product. In (8.72), $\mathbf{B} \in \mathbf{R}^{2 \times 2}$ is a symmetric, positive definite matrix representing the Gaussian part[21] in the distribution of $X(t)$; and ν represents the nonnegative Borel measure on $\mathbf{R}^2$ with $\int (s,s)/[1 + (s,s)]\nu(ds) < \infty, \nu(\{0\}) = 0$; i. e., ν is the so–called the Lévy spectral measure (see Gikhman and Skorokhod (1969), Ch. 5).

Components $(Z_n^{(1)})_{n \geq 1}$ and $(Z_n^{(2)})_{n \geq 1}$ (resp. $(X^{(1)})$ and $(X^{(2)})$) in (8.68) correspond to the observations (resp. returns) from Asset 1, and Asset 2 respectively. Then, five cases are to be considered:

(i) *The return observations Z_n of Assets 1 and 2 are in the domain of attraction of the normal law:* In this case, $\alpha_1 = \alpha_2 = 2$ and the continuous price process $\mathbf{X}(+)$ is a Brownian motion in $\mathbf{R}_+^2$.

(ii) *The return observations of Asset 1 have infinite variance and are in the domain of attraction of the α_1–Paretian stable law; and returns of Asset 2 are in the domain of attraction of the normal law :* In this case, $0 < \alpha_1 < \alpha_2 = 2$. The two components of $\mathbf{X}(+)$ will be *independent* (see Resnick and Greenwood (1979)). One component is an α_1-stable motion of the returns of Asset 1; the other is a Wiener process of returns of Asset 2.

(iii) *The return observations of Asset 2 have infinite variance and are in the domain of attraction of the α_2-Paretian stable law; and those of Asset 1 are in the domain of attraction of the normal law:* Here, $0 < \alpha_2 < \alpha_1 = 2$, which can be treated as case (ii).

(iv) *The return observations of both assets have heavy, stable–Paretian tails with one and the same index of stability:* In this case $0 < \alpha_1 = \alpha_2 = \alpha < 2$ and $\mathbf{X}(+)$ is a bivariate α-stable motion (see Ziemba (1974); de Haan and Resnick (1977); Resnick and Greenwood (1979); Samorodnitsky and Taqqu (1994)). This is the care we have treated in the previous sections. The process $\mathbf{X}(+)$ is determined by α-stable unit increments with characteristic function

$$Ee^{i(\mathbf{X}(1),\tau)} = \exp\left\{ -|\tau|^\alpha \int_0^{2\pi} |\cos(\tau,\theta)|^\alpha \right.$$

$$\left. \{(1 - i\text{sign}[\cos(\tau,\theta)]\phi(\alpha,\theta,\tau)\}d\Phi(\theta) \right\}, \quad (8.73)$$

where $\cos(\tau,\theta) := \cos\phi \cos\theta + \sin\phi \sin\theta$, for $\tau = (\rho\cos\phi\rho\sin\phi)$;

$$\phi(\alpha,\theta,\tau) := \begin{cases} \tan\frac{\pi\alpha}{2}, & \text{for } \alpha \neq 1 \\ -\frac{2}{\pi}\log(\rho \mid \cos(\tau,\theta) \mid), & \text{for } \alpha = 1; \end{cases}$$

[21]If $\mathbf{B} = 0$, then $\alpha < 2$.

and Φ is a distribution function on $[0, 2\pi]$ with positive total mass $\Phi(2\pi) > 0$. The fact that the two (real) return series $(Z_n^{(1)})_{n \geq 1}$ and $(Z_n^{(2)})_{n \geq 1}$ are in the domain of attraction of $\mathbf{X}(1)$ can be expressed as

$$\lim_{x \to \infty} \frac{P(\rho > rx, \Theta < \theta_1)}{P(\rho > x, \Theta < \theta_2)} = r^{-\alpha} \frac{\Phi(\theta_1)}{\Phi(\theta_2)}, \qquad (8.74)$$

where $\rho = |\mathbf{Z}|$ and $\Theta = \Theta(\mathbf{Z})$ are the polar coordinates of vector $\mathbf{Z} \stackrel{d}{=} (Z_1^{(1)}, Z_1^{(2)})$ (cf. 8.4). In other words, (8.74) is equivalent to the existence of $a_n > 0$ and $\mathbf{b}_n \in \mathbf{R}^2$ such that

$$\frac{1}{a_n} \sum_{i=1}^{n} \mathbf{Z}_i - \mathbf{b}_n \stackrel{w}{\to} \mathbf{X}(1). \qquad (8.75)$$

As we have noted in Section 8.2 the limit relation (8.75) is equivalent to the statement that the Z_i's are in the *domain of attraction of geometric-stable random pair* $\mathbf{X}^G(1)$ *with characteristic function*

$$E \exp\left\{i\left(\mathbf{X}^G(1), \tau\right)\right\} = \frac{1}{1 - \log E \exp\{i(\mathbf{X}^G(1), \tau)\}} \qquad (8.76)$$

in other words, (8.75) is equivalent to

$$a(p) \sum_{i=1}^{T(p)} (\mathbf{Z}_i - \mathbf{b}(p)) \stackrel{w}{\to} \mathbf{X}^G(1). \qquad (8.77)$$

(v) *Both return series have Paretian stable tails with different stability indexes:* Here, $0 < \alpha_i < 2$ with $\alpha_1 \neq \alpha_2$. This is the most interesting case and will be addressed in this section. The characteristic function of $\mathbf{X}(t)$ is now given by (8.71) and (8.72), with $\mathbf{B} = 0$. The domain–of–attraction condition for $\mathbf{Z}_n = (Z_n^{(1)}, Z_n^{(2)})_{n \geq 1}$, written, for example, in form

$$\mathbf{P}_n \stackrel{w}{\to} \mathbf{X} \text{ in } D(\mathbf{R}_+)^2, \qquad (8.78)$$

where $\mathbf{P}_n(t) = (S_{[nt]}^{(1)}/a_n^{(1)}, S_{[nt]}^{(2)}/a_n^{(2)}) - t\mathbf{b}_n$ (cf. (8.69)), is, in terms of the spectral measure ν, equivalent to the condition (cf. (8.72)) that for all Borel sets $A \subset \mathbf{R}^2 \setminus \{0\}$ with boundary ∂A with ν–mass zero and $\nu(A) < \infty$

$$\lim_{n \to \infty} nP\left(\left(\frac{Z_1^{(1)}}{a_n^{(1)}}, \frac{Z_1^{(2)}}{a_n^{(2)}}\right) \in A\right) \to \nu(A) \qquad (8.79)$$

(cf. Resnick and Greenwood (1979), p. 215). Analogous to the case $\alpha_1 = \alpha_2 = \alpha$ (cf. Section 8.3, the characterization of ν can be a starting point for constructing a test for association among components of $\mathbf{Z}_n$. However, the construction of such a test is an open problem (see Resnick (1987a); Lee et al. (1990)), which we shall attack further on this section.

However, before going into the detail description of the test for association, let us remark on the interplay between stable and geometric stable law for asset returns. To some extend this corresponds to a multivariate Gaussian process of asset returns with random covariance matrix.

We extend the idea in Chapter 7 for the case of $\alpha_1 = \alpha_2 = \alpha < 2$ that of $\alpha_1 \neq \alpha_2$. This leads to bivariate stable scheme for returns: Suppose that for any $n \geq 1, \mathbf{T}_n = (T_n^{(1)}, T_n^{(2)})$ is a pair of positive, integer–valued random variables independent of $(Y_n)_{n \geq 1}$ and, as $n \to \infty$,

$$\frac{1}{n}\mathbf{T}_n \overset{w}{\to} \mathbf{E} = (E^{(1)}, E^{(2)}), \tag{8.80}$$

and suppose that (8.78) holds. Then,[22]

$$\left(\frac{S^{(1)}_{[T_n^{(1)}t]}}{a_n^{(1)}} - b_n^{(1)}\frac{N_n^{(1)}}{n}t, \frac{S^{(2)}_{[T_n^{(2)}t]}}{a_n^{(2)}} - b_n^{(2)}\frac{N_n^{(2)}}{n}t\right)_{t \geq 0}$$
$$\xrightarrow[D(\mathbf{R}_+)^2]{w} \left(X^{(1)}(E^{(1)}t), X^{(2)}(E^{(2)}t)\right)_{t \geq 0}. \tag{8.81}$$

In Mittnik and Rachev (1991) the Marshall-Olkin (M–O) distribution was found to yield a good fit to a bivariate stock–return sample.[23] Pair $\mathbf{Z} = (Z^{(1)}, Z^{(2)})$ is M–O distributed if

$$P(Z_1 > t_1, Z_2 > t_2) = \exp\{-\lambda_1 t_1 - \lambda_2 t_2 - \lambda_{12}\max(t_1, t_2)\}, \quad t_i \geq 0. \tag{8.82}$$

In fact, the M–O law is one of the geometric–stable laws arising from limiting scheme (8.69)–(8.70). More precisely, suppose that $\mathbf{T} = (T^{(1)}, T^{(2)})$ follows the *general bivariate geometric* (GBG) *distribution*

$$P(T_1 = m, T_2 = n) = \begin{cases} p_{11}^{n-1}(p_{10} + p_{11})^{m-n-1}p_{10}(p_{01} + p_{00}), & \text{if } m > n \\ p_{11}^{m-1}p_{00}, & \text{if } m = n \\ p_{11}^{m-1}(p_{01} + p_{11})^{n-m-1}p_{01}(p_{10} + p_{00}), & \text{if } m < n. \end{cases}$$

Similar to (8.81), one obtains the following extension of the geometric scheme in Mittnik and Rachev (1991). Suppose that positive returns, denoted by $(Y_n^{+(1)})_{n \geq 1}$ and $(Y_n^{+(2)})_{n \geq 1}$, are such that $\mathbf{E}Y_n^{+(1)} = (\lambda_1 + \lambda_{12})^{-1}$ and $\mathbf{E}Y_n^{+(2)} = (\lambda_2 + \lambda_{12})^{-1}$. Moreover, suppose that stopping times (T_1, T_2)—representing moments of substantial changes in the fundamentals underlying $(Y_n^{+(1)})_{n \geq 1}$ and $(Y_n^{+(2)})_{n \geq 1}$, respectively—follow a GBG distribution with parameters

---

[22]For details see Rachev, Wu and Yakovlev (1995) as well as Resnick and Greenwood (1979, pp. 219-220), Rachev and Rüschendorf (1998), and Feldman and Rachev (1993).
[23]The sample consisted of daily returns (incl. dividends) on Chrysler and Ford common stocks over the two–year period 1987–88, a period that includes the October 1987 crash.

$(p_{00}, p_{01}, p_{10}, p_{11})$, such that $p_{01} = \lambda_1\theta, p_{10} = \lambda_2\theta, p_{00} = \lambda_{12}\theta$, with $\theta > 0$, and $p_{00} + p_{01} + p_{10} + p_{11} = 1$, $p_{10} + p_{11} < 1$, and $p_{01} + p_{11} < 1$. Then,

$$\left((p_{00} + p_{01}) \sum_{i=1}^{T_1} Y_i^{+(1)}, (p_{00} + p_{10}) \sum_{i=1}^{T_2} Y_i^{+(2)}\right) \overset{w}{\to} \mathbf{Z}, \quad \text{as } \theta \to 0, \quad (8.83)$$

where $\mathbf{Z}$ has M–O distribution (8.82).[24]

The Weibull–M–O distribution

$$P(Z_1^W > t_1, Z_2^W > t_2) = \exp\{-\lambda_1 t_1^{\alpha_2} - \lambda_2 t_2^{\alpha_2} - \lambda_{12}\max(t_1^{\alpha_1}, kt_2^{\alpha_2})\}, \quad t_i > 0, \quad (8.84)$$

with $\lambda_i > 0, \alpha_i > 0$ and $k > 0$, arises naturally from limit theorem (8.83) using componentwise, monotone transformations. In Mittnik and Rachev (1991) we also fit (8.84) and obtain favorable results.

After this remark on the random geometric summation scheme as a rational extension of the classical summation summation scheme for i.i.d. random vectors we go back to the bivariate case described in (8.68) -(8.72). We shall assume that the observations $(\mathbf{Z}_n)_{n\geq 1}$ satisfy (8.78), i.e. they are in the domain of attraction of a stable random pair $\mathbf{X}_c$ of asset returns.

The next lemma shows that we can test whether or not the components of $\mathbf{Z} \overset{d}{=} \mathbf{Z}_n$ are associated,[25] if we have an estimator for the spectral measure ν of $\mathbf{X}$. Recall here that, by (8.78) and (8.71)-(8.72), $\mathbf{X}$ is infinitely divisible, with no normal part, $B = 0$; i.e., its characteristic function is given by

$$\log \mathbf{E}e^{i(\theta,\mathbf{X})} = i(\mathbf{a}, \theta) + \int_{s>1} (e^{i(\theta,\mathbf{S})} - 1)\nu(ds) + \int_{0<s<1} [e^{i(\theta,\mathbf{S})} - 1 - i(\theta, \mathbf{S})]\nu(ds), \quad (8.85)$$

where $\mathbf{a}$ is the shift vector and ν is the spectral (Lévy) measure of $\mathbf{X}$. Setting $\tau(x_1, x_2) = (x_1^{<1/\alpha_1>}, x_2^{<1/\alpha_2>}), x^{<\alpha>} := |x|^\alpha \operatorname{sign} x$, the scaled measure

$$\tilde{\nu} = \nu \circ \tau \quad (8.86)$$

satisfies $a\tilde{\nu}(A) = \tilde{\nu}(a^{-1}A)$ for any positive a and $A \in \mathcal{B}(\mathbf{R}^2 \setminus \{0\})$ (see Resnick and Greenwood (1979)). For any A with polar representation

$$A = \{\mathbf{x} = (|\mathbf{x}|, \theta(\mathbf{x})): |x| > r, \theta(\mathbf{x}) \in H\}, r > 0, H \in \mathcal{B}([0, 2\pi]),$$

set $M(r, H) = \tilde{\nu}(A)$, so that

$$M(r, H) = r^{-1}S(H), \quad (8.87)$$

where $S(H) = M(1, H)$ is a finite measure on $[0, 2\pi]$.

---

[24]For details see the Wu (1992) and references therein.

[25]As we have argued at the beginning of Section 8.3 the notion of association is possibly the only reasonable way to measuring dependence, among heavy-tailed distributed returns.

The meaning of this transformation is to pass from returns with distribution tails $const \cdot \chi^{-\alpha_1}$ and $const \cdot \chi^{-\alpha_2}$ for χ large, to a transform pair with Pareto tail $const \cdot \chi^{-1}$ for both components. After the idea is to reduce the problem of association testing to the case of $\alpha_1 = \alpha_2 = 1$.

To facilitate proofs we assume continuous marginal d.f.'s for $\mathbf{Z} \overset{d}{=} \mathbf{Z_j}$, see (8.78).[26]

Lemma 8.6 Suppose that $\mathbf{Z}$ is in the domain of attraction of $\mathbf{X}$ and that $(Z^{(1)}, Z^{(2)})$ are either positively or negatively associated. Then, in the case of positive association, the spectral d.f. S is concentrated on the first and the third quadrant, while it is concentrated on the second and the fourth quadrant in the case of negative association.

With Lemma 8.6 we have reduced the problem of testing association among $\mathbf{Z}$–components to the problem of choosing appropriate estimators for $\tilde{\nu}$, the spectral measure generated by S (see (8.86)). Moreover, it is sufficient to obtain a "good" estimator of the *normalized dependence measure* μ induced by $\tilde{\nu}$. To define μ, set for $i = 1, 2$,

$$p_i = \lim_{x \to \infty} \frac{P(Z^{(i)} > x)}{P(|\, Z^{(i)} \,| > x)} \tag{8.88}$$

and $q_i = 1 - p_i$. Then, define μ on each quadrant of $\mathbf{R}^2 \setminus \{0\}$ as follows

$$\mu((0, x] \times (0, y]) := m(x, y) := \tilde{\nu}\left(\left[\frac{p_1}{x}, \infty\right), \left[\frac{p_2}{y}, \infty\right)\right), \text{ for } x > 0, y > 0,$$

$$\mu([x, 0) \times (0, y]) := m(x, y) := \tilde{\nu}\left(\left(-\infty, \frac{q_1}{x}\right] \times \left[\frac{p_2}{y}, \infty\right)\right), \text{ for } x < 0, y > 0$$

$$\mu((0, x] \times [y, 0)) := m(x, y) := \tilde{\nu}\left(\left[\frac{p_1}{x}, \infty\right) \times \left(-\infty, \frac{q_2}{y}\right]\right), \text{ for } x > 0, y < 0$$

$$\mu([x, 0) \times [y, 0)) := m(x, y) := \tilde{\nu}\left(\left(-\infty, \frac{q_1}{x}\right] \times \left(-\infty, \frac{q_2}{y}\right]\right), \text{ for } x < 0, y < 0.$$

$$\tag{8.89}$$

Function m is an analogue to the so–called dependence function in the tail (see Xin (1992)). The following lemma lists several properties of m.

(i) *Representation of m with spectral d.f. S:*

$$m(x, y) \;=\; \int_0^{\frac{\pi}{2}} \left(\frac{x \cos \theta}{p_1} \wedge \frac{y \sin \theta}{p_2}\right) S(d\theta), \text{ for } x > 0, y > 0;$$

---

[26] All proofs, which are rather technical, are provided in the multivariate case $d \geq 2$ in Mittnik, Rachev and Rüschendorf (1999).

$$m(x,y) = \int_{\frac{\pi}{2}}^{\pi} \left(\frac{x\cos\theta}{q_1} \wedge \frac{y\sin\theta}{p_2} \right) S(d\theta), \quad \text{for } x < 0, y > 0;$$

$$m(x,y) = \int_{\pi}^{3\pi/2} \left(\frac{x\cos\theta}{q_1} \wedge \frac{y\sin\theta}{q_2} \right) S(d\theta), \quad \text{for } x < 0, y < 0;$$

$$m(x,y) = \int_{3\pi/2}^{2\pi} \left(\frac{x\cos\theta}{p_1} \wedge \frac{y\sin\theta}{q_2} \right) S(d\theta), \quad \text{for } x > 0, y < 0. \quad (8.90)$$

(ii) *Marginal distributions:*

$$m(x,\infty) = m(\infty,x) = \mid x \mid, \quad x \in \mathbf{R} \setminus \{0\}. \quad (8.91)$$

(iii) *Homogeneity:* for all $u > 0, (x,y) \in \mathbf{R}^2 \setminus \{0\}$

$$m(ux, uy) = um(x,y). \quad (8.92)$$

All these properties follow from the domain-of-attraction condition (8.78), which can be re–written in term of the normalized Lévy measure $\tilde{\nu}$ (see 8.86) as follows. For all $\tilde{\nu}$–continuity sets $A \in \mathcal{B}(\mathbf{R}^2 \setminus \{0\})$ with $\tilde{\nu}(A) < \infty$, we have

$$\lim_{n\to\infty} nP((U_1(Z^{(1)}), U_2(Z^{(2)})) \in nA) = \tilde{\nu}(A), \quad (8.93)$$

where U_i are monotone functions equating the tails of $Z^{(i)}$, namely

$$U_i(x) = \frac{p_i}{P(Z^{(i)} > x)} I\{x > 0\} - \frac{q_i}{P(Z^{(i)} \le x)} I\{x \le 0\} \quad (8.94)$$

(see Resnick and Greenwood (1979)).

Remark 8.8 It follows from Lemma 8.6 that under $H_0 : (Z^{(1)}, Z^{(2)})$ *are positively associated*, $m(x,y)$ is concentrated on the first and third quadrant.

Next, define *tail estimator for* μ or, what is equivalent, a tail estimator for m. Let $(\mathbf{Z}_1, \ldots, \mathbf{Z}_n)$ be a sample from the $\mathbf{Z}$–distribution and $(Z^{(1)}_{k:n}, Z^{(2)}_{k:n}), k = 1, \ldots, n$, be the corresponding order statistics. Define the tail estimator $\hat{m}$ for m by

$$\hat{m}(x,y) = \frac{1}{k}\sum_{j=1}^{n} I\{Z^{(1)}_j > Z^{(1)}_{n-[kx]+1:n}, Z^{(2)}_j > Z^{(2)}_{n-[ky]+1:n}\}, \quad \text{for } x > 0, y > 0,$$

$$\hat{m}(x,y) = \frac{1}{k}\sum_{j=1}^{n} I\{Z^{(1)}_j \le Z^{(1)}_{[-kx]:n}, Z^{(2)}_j > Z^{(2)}_{n-[ky]+1:n}\}, \quad \text{for } x < 0, y > 0,$$

$$\hat{m}(x,y) = \frac{1}{k}\sum_{j=1}^{n} I\{Z^{(1)}_j \le Z^{(1)}_{[-kx]:n}, Z^{(2)}_j \le Z^{(2)}_{[-ky]:n}\}, \quad \text{for } x < 0, y < 0,$$

$$\hat{m}(x,y) = \frac{1}{k}\sum_{j=1}^{n} I\{Z^{(1)}_j \ge Z^{(1)}_{n-[kx]+1:n}, Z^{(2)}_j \le Z^{(2)}_{[-ky]:n}\}, \quad \text{for } x > 0, y < 0.$$

$$(8.95)$$

In the same way as in (8.89) we define the estimator $\hat{\mu}$ of μ generated by $\hat{m}$. To proceed, we require certain regularity conditions. In order to obtain asymptotic normality from $\hat{m}$, we need some second-order conditions on the tail of the $\mathbf{Z}$–law. Assuming that the components of $\mathbf{Z}$ have continuous d.f.'s F_1 and F_2, respectively, re–write the domain-of-attraction condition (8.93) as follows. For all $(x, y) \in \mathbf{R}^2 \setminus \{0\}$,

$$m(x, y) = \lim_{t \downarrow 0} \frac{1}{t} m^{(t)}(x, y), \qquad (8.96)$$

where, with $\overline{F}_i = 1 - F_i$,

$$
\begin{aligned}
m^{(t)}(x, y) :&= P(\overline{F}_1(Z^{(1)}) \le tx, \overline{F}_2(Z^{(2)}) \le ty), \text{ for } x > 0, y > 0, \\
&:= P(F_1(Z^{(1)}) \le -tx, \overline{F}_2(Z^{(2)}) \le ty), \text{ for } x < 0, y > 0, \\
&:= P(F_1(Z^{(1)}) \le -tx, F_2(Z^{(2)}) \le -ty), \text{ for } x < 0, y < 0, \\
&:= P(\overline{F}_1(Z^{(1)}) \le tx, F_2(Z^{(2)}) \le -ty), \text{ for } x > 0, y < 0. \qquad (8.97)
\end{aligned}
$$

For the dependence structure of the tail of the $\mathbf{Z}$–distribution we assume the following regularity conditions to hold:
RC 1: $m(x, y)$ has continuous first partial derivatives $m_1' = \frac{\partial m}{\partial x}$ and $m_2' = \frac{\partial m}{\partial y}$;
RC 2: as $t \downarrow 0$, uniformly on the unit circle $x^2 + y^2 = 1$,

$$m^t(x, y) = tm(x, y) + O(t^\delta), \text{ for some } \delta > 1.$$

To derive the limiting process B, let W be a continuous zero mean Gaussian process on $\mathbf{R}^2$ (Gaussian sheet) such that:

(i) the restrictions of W on each quadrant are independent;

(ii) the covariance function on each quadrant is given by

$$
\begin{aligned}
\mathbf{E}W(x_1, y_1)W(x_2, y_2) \ &= \ m(x_1 \wedge x_2, y_1 \wedge y_2), \text{ for } x_i \ge 0, y_i \ge 0, \\
&= \ m(x_1 \vee x_2, y_1 \wedge y_2), \text{ for } x_i < 0 \le y_i, \\
&= \ m(x_1 \vee x_2, y_1 \vee y_2), \text{ for } x_i < 0, y_i < 0, \\
&= \ m(x_1 \wedge x_2, y_1 \vee y_2), \text{ for } y_i < 0 \le x_i. \qquad (8.98)
\end{aligned}
$$

The sheet $W(x, y)$ generates a random measure $\mathbf{W}$ as follows,

$$
\begin{aligned}
W(x, y) \ &:= \ \mathbf{W}((0, x] \times (0, y]), \text{ for } x \ge 0, y \ge 0 \\
&:= \ \mathbf{W}([x, 0) \times (0, y]), \text{ for } x < 0 \le y, \\
&:= \ \mathbf{W}([x, 0) \times [y, 0)), \text{ for } x < 0, y < 0, \\
&:= \ \mathbf{W}((0, x] \times [y, 0)), \text{ for } x > 0, y < 0. \qquad (8.99)
\end{aligned}
$$

Define now the Gaussian sheet, B, by

$$B(x,y) = W(x,y) - (\text{sign}x)m_1'(x,y)W(x,\infty) - (\text{sign}y)m_2'(x,y)W(\infty,y).$$
(8.100)

The next theorem establishes convergence of $\hat{m}$. By "$\overset{D_\rho}{\to}$" we denote the convergence of random elements in $D(\mathbf{R}^2\backslash\{0\})$ under the uniform convergence on compacts with the metric

$$\rho(m,m^*) = \sum_{k\geq1} 2^{-k}\frac{\rho_k(m,m^*)}{1+\rho_k(m,m^*)},$$

where $\rho_k(m,m^*) = \sup_{|x|\leq k,|y|\leq k} |\, m(x,y) - m^*(x,y)\,|$.

Suppose **RC1** and **RC2** hold and let **RC3** $:k = O(n^{(2\delta-2)/(2\delta-1)})$. Then, as $n \to \infty$,

$$\sqrt{k}\{\hat{m} - m\} \overset{D_\rho}{\to} B.$$
(8.101)

While regularity conditions **RC1**, **RC2** and **RC3** imply asymptotic consistency of $\hat{m}$ less demanding conditions can be established.

Lemma 8.7 Suppose that the domain-of-attraction condition (8.96) holds, and for $k = k(n)$, $n \geq 1$, $1 \leq k \leq n$, $k(n) \to \infty$ assume that $\frac{k}{n} \to \infty$. Then,

$$\sup_{|x|\leq T}\sup_{|y|\leq T}[\hat{m}(x,y) - m(x,y)] \overset{p}{\to} 0$$

To test the homogeneity of $\hat{m}$, we require m to satisfy the homogeneity condition

$$m(ux,uy) = um(x,y),\text{for all }x,y \in \mathbf{R},\text{ and }u > 0.$$

While $\hat{m}$ is not a homogeneous function, it should be homogeneous in the limit.

Remark 8.9 : When testing for association it is desirable that m_n is homogeneous. In fact, if $m_n(t\cos\theta, t\sin\theta) = tm_n(\cos\theta,\sin\theta)$ and if $Z^{(1)}$ and $Z^{(2)}$ are positively associated (see Lemma 8.6), then

$$m_n(\cos\theta,\sin\theta) \approx 0 \text{ for } \theta \in \left(\frac{\pi}{2},\pi\right) \vee \left(\frac{3}{2}\pi,2\pi\right).$$

For $0 < T_1 < T_2$ let

$$h_n(T_1,T_2) := \sup_{0<\Theta<2\pi;T_1\leq t\leq T_2} \left| \frac{\hat{m}(t\cos\theta, t\sin\theta)}{\hat{m}(\cos\theta,\sin\theta)} - t \right|$$

be a test statistic for homogeneity. Then, under **RC1**, **RC2** and **RC3**,

$$\sqrt{k}h_n(T_1,T_2) \overset{w}{\to} h(T_1,T_2),$$
(8.102)

where

$$h(T_1, T_2) = \sup_{0 \leq \theta \leq 2\pi; T_1 \leq t \leq T_2} \frac{1}{m(\cos\theta, \sin\theta)} |B(t\cos\theta, t\sin\theta) - tB(\cos\theta, \sin\theta)|$$

and Gaussian process B defined by (8.100).

Suppose that after checking the homogeneity of $\hat{m}$ (via Lemma 8.9) we conclude that $\hat{m}$ is homogeneous, i.e., for all $t > 0$ and $0 \leq \theta \leq 2\pi$,

$$\hat{m}(t\cos\theta, t\sin\theta) \approx t\hat{m}(\cos\theta, \sin\theta). \tag{8.103}$$

Therefore, if m is concentrated on the first and the third quadrant only, we expect that $\hat{m}$ is almost zero on the second and the fourth quadrants. Letting, $I_i = (i\frac{\pi}{2}, (i+1)\frac{\pi}{2}]$ this observation leads us to the following test of associativeness.

Theorem 8.9 Suppose $\mathbf{Z} = (Z^{(1)}, Z^{(2)})$ is in domain-of-attraction of the bivariate stable r.v. $\mathbf{X}$ with characteristic function (8.84) and that

(i) $Z^{(1)}$ and $Z^{(2)}$ are positively associated, or

(ii) $Z^{(1)}$ and $Z^{(2)}$ are negatively associated.

Then, under regularity conditions **RC1**, **RC2** and **RC3** and if (i) holds,

$$\sqrt{k} \int_I d\hat{m}(\cos\theta, \sin\theta) \overset{w}{\to} \int_I dB(\cos\theta, \sin\theta) \tag{8.104}$$

for any interval $I \subset I_2 + I_4$. If (ii) holds, we have $I \subset I_1 + I_3$.

To obtain estimates for the probabilities of the right–hand sides of limit relations (8.91) and (8.104) we use a bootstap procedure. To obtain a bootstap estimator for the limiting process B in (8.104) on the first quadrant, we construct the bootstrap version of estimator $\hat{m}$ (see(8.100)). We shall outline the procedure (for details see Xin (1992)). Let $\rho(\theta) = 1/\mu((0, \cos\theta] \times (0, \infty)$ or $(0, \infty) \times (0, \sin\theta))$ for $0 < \theta < \frac{\pi}{2}$, where μ is defined by (8.89). With the help of estimator $\hat{m}$ (8.95) define

$$\hat{\rho}(\theta) = \left\{ \frac{[K\cos\theta]}{K} + \frac{[K\sin\theta]}{K} - \hat{m}(\cos\theta, \sin\theta) \right\},$$

then

$$\hat{\rho}_1(\theta) = \min\left\{ \hat{\rho}(\theta), \frac{1}{\cos\theta}, \frac{1}{\sin\theta} \right\}$$

and, finally, let $(\tilde{\rho}(\theta), \theta)_{0 \leq \theta \leq \frac{\pi}{2}}$ be the unique, minimal concave curve satisfying $\tilde{\rho}_1(\theta) \geq \hat{\rho}_1(\theta), 0 \leq \theta \leq \frac{\pi}{2}$. We define the bootstrap version of $\hat{m}$ in the first quadrant by setting, for $(x, y) \in \mathbf{R}_+^2$,

$$\tilde{m}(x, y) = x + y + \frac{\sqrt{x^2 + y^2}}{\tilde{\rho}(\arctan\frac{y}{x})}.$$

The attractive feature of $\tilde{m}$ is that

$$\tilde{m}_n(x,y) = \tilde{m}\left(x \wedge \frac{1}{\tilde{m}(1,1)}, y \wedge \frac{1}{\tilde{m}(1,1)}\right)$$

is a distribution function on $\mathbf{R}_+^2$. Then, we generate k replication $(\mathbf{Z}_j^* = (Z_j^{*(1)}, Z_j^{*(2)}))_{1 \geq j \leq k}$ of $\mathbf{Z}^*$ with d.f. $\tilde{m}_n$. Then, under some regularity conditions, bootstrap estimator

$$m^*(x,y) = \frac{1}{h}\sum_{j=1}^{k} I\left\{Z_j^{*(1)} \leq Z_{[hk]:k}^{*(1)}, Z_j^{*(2)} \leq Z_{[hy]:k}^{*(2)}\right\}$$

provides the required limit bootstrap result

$$\sqrt{h}(m^* - \hat{m}) \overset{w}{\to} B, \text{on } D([0,T]^2).$$

More precisely, the following holds.[27].

Theorem 8.10 *(Bootstrap estimation)* If $0 < h \leq k$, $h \to \infty$, $\frac{h^{3/2}}{k} \to 0$, as $n \to \infty$, $\frac{k^{\alpha+1}}{h^{1/\alpha}n^\alpha} \to 0$, and for each fixed $M > 0$, $\frac{k}{\sqrt{h}}\left\{\frac{h}{k}M - m(\frac{h}{k}M, 1)\right\} \to 0$, $\frac{k}{\sqrt{h}}\left\{\frac{h}{k}M - m(1, \frac{h}{k}M)\right\} \to 0$, then for each $\epsilon > 0$, there exists $N_\epsilon > 0$ and $A_n(\epsilon)$ with $P(A_n(\epsilon)) \geq 1-\epsilon$ such that, as $n \to \infty$, $\sqrt{h}(m^*(\cdot, w_n) - \hat{m}(\cdot, w_n)) \overset{w}{\to} B$ on $D([0,T]^2)$ for $w_n \in A_n(\epsilon)$.

Remark 8.10 The fact that the spectral measure is concentrated on the first and third quadrant only indicates that we may accept the hypothesis that the two returns $\mathbf{Z} = (Z^{(1)}, Z^{(2)})$ are positively associated. To measure the strength of positive association in this case, we define

$$U(Z^{(1)}, Z^{(2)}) = \frac{1}{R_1}\int_{I_1}(\theta - \theta_1)^2 dR(\theta) + \frac{1}{R_3}\int_{I_3}(\theta - \theta_3)^2 dR(\theta),$$

where $R(\theta) = m^+(\cos\theta, \sin\theta) + m^-(\cos\theta, \sin\theta)$ is the total variance of the signed measure $m(\cos\theta, \sin\theta) = m^+(\cos\theta, \sin\theta) - m^-(\cos\theta, \sin\theta)$; R_i is the total mass of $R(\theta)$ on I_i; and the θ_i's are corresponding means $\theta_i = \frac{1}{R_i}\int_{I_i}\theta dR(\theta)$.

Indeed, if $U(Z^{(1)}, Z^{(2)}) = 0$, then the measure R is concentrated on two points $\theta_i \in I_i$, and this shows that $Z^{(i)}$ are highly dependent. On the other hand if $Z^{(1)}$ and $Z^{(2)}$ are independent, then $R(\theta)$ is concentrated on the points $0, \frac{\pi}{2}, \pi, \frac{3\pi}{2}$ and $U(Z^{(1)}, Z^{(2)})$ has a maximal value.

---

[27]See Xin (1992), Theorem 5, for an analog of thus result to extreme value theory

9

Asset–Pricing and Portfolio Theory Under Stable Paretian Laws

In this chapter we investigate the implications on asset pricing and portfolio theory when asset returns have a multivariate stable Paretian distribution.[1] In asset pricing we focus on the Capital Asset Pricing Model (CAPM)— in particular the issue of computing the beta–coefficient– and the Arbitrage Pricing Theory (APT). We also address the question of testing the CAPM and APT. Subsequently, we extend the mean–variance portfolio theory of Markowitz (1952) and Sharpe (1964) for stable Paretian laws. We shall apply the tail-estimates for stable random vectors we obtained in Chapter 8.

9.1 Preliminaries to Stable CAPM and APT: Covariation, L_p Spaces and Risk

Recall that a random variable R is called *stable Paretian* if and only if for all $a > 0$ and $b > 0$ there exist $c > 0$ and $d \in \mathbf{R}$ such that

$$aR_1 + bR_2 \stackrel{d}{=} cR + d,$$

where R_1 and R_2 are independent copies of R. Alternatively stated, R is Paretian stable if and only if its characteristic function (ch.f.) is of the form

$$\Phi_R(\theta) = \mathbf{E}(\exp iR\theta) \tag{9.1}$$

---

[1] This chapter is based on Gamrowski and Rachev (1994a,b), (1995a,b,c), see Sections 9.1-9.5 and Ortobelli and Rachev (1999), see Sections 9.6-9.9.

$$= \left\{ \begin{array}{ll} \exp\left\{-\sigma^\alpha |\theta|^\alpha \left(1 - i\beta(\text{sign}\theta) \tan \frac{\pi\alpha}{2}\right) + i\mu\theta\right\} & if \alpha \neq 1, \\ \exp\left\{-\sigma|\theta| \left(1 + i\beta \frac{2}{\pi}(\text{sign}\theta) \ln \theta\right) + i\mu\theta\right\} & if \alpha = 1, \end{array} \right.$$

where α $(0 < \alpha \leq 2)$ is the index of stability, β $(-1 \leq \beta \leq 1)$ the skewness parameter, $\sigma > 0$ the scale parameter, and $\mu \in \mathbf{R}$ the location parameter.

We denote $R \overset{d}{=} S_\alpha(\sigma, \beta, \mu)$, see Samorodnitsky and Taqqu (1994) and Chapter 2. For the symmetric case, i.e., $\beta = 0$, the ch.f. of the stable Paretian distribution reduces to

$$\Phi_R(\theta) = \mathbf{E}(\exp\{iR\theta\}) = \exp\{-\sigma^\alpha |\theta|^\alpha + i\mu\theta\}. \tag{9.2}$$

We recall that for $\alpha = 2$ the stable Paretian distribution; reduces to the normal distribution; and as α decreases the stable Paretian distribution becomes increasingly *leptokurtic*, i.e., the distribution around the center becomes more peaked and the tails become fatter. The tails have the property that

$$\lim_{\lambda \to +\infty} \lambda^\alpha P(R > \lambda) = k_\alpha \frac{1+\beta}{2} \sigma^\alpha \tag{9.3}$$

and

$$\lim_{\lambda \to +\infty} \lambda^\alpha P(R < -\lambda) = k_\alpha \frac{1-\beta}{2} \sigma^\alpha, \tag{9.4}$$

where $k_1 = 2/\pi$ and if $\alpha \neq 1$

$$k_\alpha = \frac{1-\alpha}{\Gamma(2-\alpha)\cos(\pi\alpha/2)}, \tag{9.5}$$

with $\Gamma(\cdot)$ denoting the Gamma function. Parameter c in definition $aR_1 + bR_2 \overset{d}{=} cR + d$ satisfies

$$c = (a^\alpha + b^\alpha)^{1/\alpha}.$$

If $\alpha > 1$, the location parameter, μ, corresponds to the mean of the distribution; and the scale parameter, σ, can be regarded as a generalized version of the standard deviation. For $\alpha < 2$, the stable distribution has finite p-absolute moments for any $p < \alpha$. The property of the scale parameter gives rise to an explicit expression for the p-th (absolute) moment, namely

$$\|R\|_p = \mathbf{E}\left(|R - \mathbf{E}(R)|^p\right)^{1/p} = H(\alpha, \beta, p)\sigma, \tag{9.6}$$

with function H being given in Hardin (1984),[2] see also Samorodnitsky and Taqqu (1994) for a detailed exposition of the theory of stable laws.

---

[2] H is defined by

$$(H(\alpha, \beta, p))^p = \frac{2^{p-1}\Gamma(1 - \frac{p}{\alpha})}{p \int\limits_0^\infty u^{-p-1} \sin^2 u\, du} \left(1 + \beta^2 \tan^2 \frac{\alpha\pi}{2}\right)^{p/2\alpha} \cos(\frac{p}{\alpha} \arctan(\beta \tan \frac{2\pi}{2})),$$

see Hardin (1984), and Samorodnitsky and Taqqu (1994, p.18).

Analogous to the normal distribution, the stable Paretian distribution possesses an additivity property in the sense that a linear combination of stable Paretian r.v.'s with the same stability index, α, is again a stable Paretian r.v. with the same α value. This property provides a vector space structure for the set of all stable Paretian r.v.'s with the same stability index. Moreover, the existence of the scale parameter provides a norm for such a vector space. Apart from a multiplicative factor, the norm is the same as the L_p-norm ($p < \alpha$), provided that all r.v.'s have the same skewness, β.

The sum $R = R_1 + \ldots + R_n$ of n r.v.'s with the same stability index, $R_i \overset{\mathrm{d}}{=} S_\alpha(\sigma_i, \beta_i, \mu_i)$, has the stable Paretian distribution $R \overset{\mathrm{d}}{=} S_\alpha(\sigma, \beta, \mu)$, with parameters

$$\sigma = (\sigma_1^\alpha + \ldots + \sigma_n^\alpha)^{1/\alpha}, \tag{9.7}$$

$$\beta = \frac{\beta_1 \sigma_1^\alpha + \ldots + \beta_n \sigma_n^\alpha}{\sigma_1^\alpha + \ldots + \sigma_n^\alpha} \tag{9.8}$$

and

$$\mu = \mu_1 + \ldots + \mu_n. \tag{9.9}$$

We will make use of alternative parameterizations, namely that of, Feller (1971), who defines

$$\gamma = -\frac{2}{\pi} \arctan\left(\beta \tan\left(\frac{\pi\alpha}{2}\right)\right), \tag{9.10}$$

and that of Zolotarev (1983), who adopts

$$\theta = -\frac{\gamma}{\alpha} \quad \text{and} \quad \rho = \frac{1+\theta}{2}.$$

With very few exceptions, there are no analytic expressions for the density or distribution function of the stable Paretian distribution. However, Feller (1971) provides the following series expression for the density:

$$\varphi(x; \alpha, \beta) = \frac{1}{\pi} \sum_{k=0}^{\infty} c_k(\alpha, \gamma) x^k, \tag{9.11}$$

where, now,

$$\sigma = \left(\cos\left(\frac{\pi\gamma}{2}\right)\right)^{1/\alpha} = \left(1 + \beta^2 \tan^2 \frac{\pi\alpha}{2}\right)^{-1/2\alpha}, \tag{9.12}$$

and

$$c_k(\alpha, \gamma) = \frac{\Gamma\left(\frac{k+1}{\alpha} + 1\right)}{(k+1)!} \sin\left(\frac{(k+1)\pi}{2\alpha}(\alpha + \gamma)\right). \tag{9.13}$$

With this expression the distribution function can be written as

$$F(x) = \frac{\alpha + \gamma}{2\alpha} + \sum_{k=1}^{\infty} d_k x^k, \tag{9.14}$$

where

$$d_k = \frac{1}{\pi} \frac{c_{k-1}}{k} = \frac{1}{\pi} \frac{\Gamma\left(\frac{k}{\alpha} + 1\right)}{k(k!)} \sin \frac{k\pi}{2\pi}(\alpha + \gamma). \qquad (9.15)$$

9.1.1 Multivariate Stable Paretian Laws

An n-dimensional vector of random variables, denoted by R, is stable Paretian, if there exist for all positive a and b, a positive real number c and a vector $d \in \mathbf{R}^n$, such that

$$aR_1 + bR_2 \overset{d}{=} cR + d,$$

where R_1 and R_2 are independent copies of R, c.f. chapter 7.

Recall that the ch.f., $\Phi_R(\theta) = \mathbf{E}\left(e^{it\theta' R}\right)$, of a stable Paretian vector is given by

$$\Phi_R(\theta) = \exp\left\{-\int_{S_d} |\theta' s|^\alpha \left(1 - i\mathrm{sign}(\theta' s) \tan \frac{\pi\alpha}{2}\right) \Gamma(ds) + i\theta'\mu\right\}, \quad \text{if } \alpha \neq 1,$$

$$(9.16)$$

and

$$\Phi_R(\theta) = \exp\{-\int_{S_d} |\theta' s|(1 + i\mathrm{sign}(\theta' s) \ln |\theta' s|)\Gamma(ds) + i\theta'\mu\}, \quad \text{if } \alpha = 1,$$

where $\theta = (\theta_1, \cdots, \theta_d)'$; Γ represents a finite measure on the unit sphere $S_d \subset \mathbf{R}^d$. The spectral measure Γ of a symmetric (about μ) stable vector R is also symmetric; and the characteristic function is of the form

$$\Phi_R(\theta) = \exp\left\{-\int_{S_d} |\theta' s|^\alpha \Gamma(ds) + i\theta'\mu\right\}. \qquad (9.17)$$

For $\alpha = 2$ the characteristic function reduces to that of the multivariate normal distribution,

$$\Phi_R(\theta) = \exp\left\{-\theta'\Omega\theta + i\theta'\mu\right\}, \qquad (9.18)$$

where the covariance matrix Ω has entries

$$\Omega_{ij} = 2\int_{S_d} s_i s_j \Gamma(ds), \quad i, j = 1, \ldots, d. \qquad (9.19)$$

Letting $\sigma(\cdot)$ denote a function which assigns the scale parameter to a r.v., one can show that a linear combination of the elements of a stable Paretian vector satisfies

$$\sigma^\alpha(\theta' R) = \sigma^\alpha(\theta_1 R_1 + \ldots + \theta_d R_d) = \int_{S_d} |\theta' s|^\alpha \Gamma(ds). \qquad (9.20)$$

If stable Paretian laws have the same stability index, the same skewness parameter and the same location parameter, then they are first-order stochastically ordered according to their scale-parameter values. I.e., for the distribution function, $F(\cdot; \alpha, \beta, \sigma_i, \mu)$, which characteristic function is given by (9.1), we have $F(x; \alpha, \beta, \sigma_1, \mu) \geq F(x; \alpha, \beta, \sigma_2, \mu)$, for all x, if and only if $\sigma_1 \leq \sigma_2$, see for example, Samorodnitsky and Taqqu (1994). Given a concave utility function, the asset associated with σ_1, will be preferred, if $\sigma_1 \leq \sigma_2$. Hence, the scale parameter is a suitable measure for risk. The choice among assets with returns following stable Paretian laws with identical stability index, $\alpha > 1$, and skewness parameter, β, can be based on familiar mean-dispersion criteria but with dispersion being measured by the scale parameter.

Given that the scale parameter is directly related to existing moments, [3] the risk associated with stable Paretian assets can be estimated from their moments. Below, we will see that this gives rise to several ways of estimating risk.

An important aspect of risk management is diversification. For example, Fama (1965a) considers the case of n independent assets that follow a common stable law. In case of an equally weighted portfolio, i.e., $1/n$ of the wealth is invested in each asset, the portfolio risk, σ_p, will be

$$\sigma_p = n^{\frac{1-\alpha}{\alpha}} \sigma,$$

where σ is the risk of each of the n assets. The exponent of n is a decreasing function of α. This implies that the smaller α is the more difficult risk diversification becomes. In particular, if $\alpha = 1$, the inclusion of additional assets does not affect the portfolio risk. Matters are worse for $\alpha < 1$, because the portfolio risk will increase as the number of assets in the portfolio increases.

The statements above assume that all assets have the same α and β. If this is not the case, it is, in fact, impossible to find a preferential ordering independent of the utility function. Scale parameters (or the existing moments) are a rigorous risk measure, only if all assets have identical α's and identical β's. Thus, the approach will be only of practical use, if the assets under consideration have similar α's and β's. However, one should be aware that the concept of identical schemes underlies the Gaussian case as well, because for all assets we assume symmetry and $\alpha = 2$.

Given the similarities between the variance in the Gaussian case, and quantity σ^α (the so-called variation) in the non-Gaussian stable Paretian case, as measures of risk we next discuss the extension of the concept of covariance to that of covariation between two r.v.'s.

The *covariance* is a crucial component of theories and analysis involving the Gaussian law. (See Section 8.4 and also Cambanis and Miller (1981), Cambanis, Hardin and Weron (1988).) Samorodnitsky and Taqqu (1994) propose the concept of *covariation* as a corresponding tool for symmetric stable Paretian laws. Although covariation does not possess all the properties of covariance, it extends parts of the Gaussian theory to the symmetric α-stable Paretian case with $\alpha \in (1, 2]$.

---

[3] Recall that for an α-stable law all absolute moments of order $0 < p < \alpha$ exist, and are finite.

The *covariation* between two symmetric stable Paretian r.v.'s, say R_1 and R_2, with identical α's, denoted by $[R_1; R_2]_\alpha$, is defined by[4]

$$[R_1; R_2]_\alpha = \frac{1}{\alpha} \frac{\partial \sigma^\alpha (\theta_1 R_1 + \theta_2 R_2)}{\partial \theta_1} \bigg|_{\theta_1=0, \theta_2=1} = \int_{S_2} s_1 s_2^{<\alpha-1>} \Gamma(ds),$$

where $x^{<k>} = |x|^k \text{sign}(x)$. The covariation has the following properties. Let $1 < \alpha \le 2$. In the Gaussian case $\alpha = 2$,

$$[R_1; R_2]_\alpha = \frac{1}{2} \text{cov}(R_1; R_2).$$

Apart from this Gaussian case, the covariation is not symmetrically bilinear. It is linear with respect to the first argument, i.e.,

$$[\lambda R_1; R_2]_\alpha = \lambda [R_1; R_2]_\alpha$$

and

$$[R_1 + R_3; R_2]_\alpha = [R_1; R_2]_\alpha + [R_3; R_2]_\alpha,$$

but for the second argument we have

$$[R_1; \lambda R_2]_\alpha = \lambda^{<\alpha-1>} [R_1; R_2]_\alpha$$

and

$$[R_1; R_2 + R_3]_\alpha = [R_1; R_2]_\alpha + [R_2; R_3]_\alpha,$$

assuming that R_2 and R_3 are independent.

If R_1 and R_2 are independent, then their covariation is zero. However the converse is generally not true. Also, covariation is generally not symmetric, i.e., in general,

$$[R_1; R_2]_\alpha \ne [R_2; R_1]_\alpha.$$

Moreover, we have

$$[R_1; R_2]_\alpha \le \sigma(R_1) \sigma^{\alpha-1}(R_2)$$

and

$$\sigma(R) = [R; R]_\alpha^{1/\alpha} = v_\alpha(R)^{1/\alpha};$$

---

[4]For alternative measures of dependence we refer to Janicki and Weron (1994) and Samorodnitsky and Taqqu (1994) (see also Nowicka and Weron (1995). We mention only two if them:

(i) *dynamical functional* DF (Janicki and Weron (1994))

$$DF(R_1, R_2) = \mathbf{E} \exp\{i(R_1 - R_2)\}$$

(ii) *codifference* CD (Samorodnitsky and Taqqu (1994))

$$CD(R_1 - R_2) = \ln \mathbf{E} \exp\{i(R_1 - R_2)\} - \ln \mathbf{E} \exp\{iR_1\} - \ln \mathbf{E} \exp\{iR_2\}$$

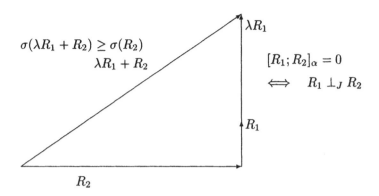

Fig. 9.1 Geometric Illustration of James–Orthogonality.

where $v_\alpha(R) = [R; R]_\alpha$ is the so-called *variation* of the r.v. α-stable R.

The fact that the concept of covariation can replace that of covariance is evident when considering the regression of one stable Paretian r.v. on another. Let $R = (R_1, R_2)$ be a symmetric stable Paretian vector, then Samorodnitsky and Taqqu (1994, p.241) show that for almost all $x \in \mathbf{R}$,

$$\mathbf{E}(R_2 | R_1 = x) = \frac{[R_1; R_2]_\alpha}{v_\alpha(R_2)} x.$$

The following three additional properties are important in the context of asset pricing modeling cf. Gamrowski and Rachev (1994a). The first concerns the notion of James-orthogonality. (For some facts on James-orthogonality see Section 9.5) Zero covariation does not correspond to the classical L_2-orthogonality, but to *James-orthogonality*, $(R_1 \perp_J R_2)$, which means that $[R_1; R_2]_\alpha = 0$ if and only if $\sigma(\lambda R_1 + R_2) \geq \sigma(R_2)$ for all real λ, see Samorodnitsky and Taqqu (1994, Section 2.9). Figure 9.1 illustrates geometrically the notion behind this property. The proof of the following three properties will be given in Section 9.5.

Property 9.1 Let R_1 and R_2 be two symmetric α-stable Paretian r.v.'s with $R_1 \neq 0$ and $[R_1; R_2]_\alpha = 0$. Then,

$$\sigma(R_1 + R_2) > \sigma(R_2).$$

The second property concerns the basis of the space spanned by a finite-dimensional stable Paretian vector, R. The *covariation matrix* of R (denoted by $\Omega(R)$) has entries $\Omega_{ij} = [R_i; R_j]_\alpha$. If the components of R form a linearly independent basis of the space they span, then the covariation matrix, $\Omega(R)$, will be diagonal. However, in a finite-dimensional space of stable Paretian random vectors bases with nondiagonal covariation matrices can be specified.

Property 9.2 *(cf. Lemma 9.1, in Section 9.5)* Every finite dimensional space of symmetric stable Paretian r.v.'s (called a symmetric stable Paretian space) can have a basis, whose covariation matrix is triangular and invertible.

The third property corresponds to the Riesz-theorem for α-stable r.v.'s. It is based on the fact that if $R = (R_1, \ldots, R_n)$ is a linearly independent family of symmetric stable Paretian r.v.'s (with identical α's), then the function measuring the variation of a linear combination of these r.v.'s,

$$r(\lambda) = \sigma^\alpha(\lambda' R), \quad \lambda \in \mathbf{R}^n,$$

is strictly convex.

Property 9.3 *(cf. Corollary 9.1, in Section 9.5)* Let Ψ be a linear functional on the symmetric stable Paretian space. Then, there exists a unique vector R_0 in this space, such that

$$\Psi(\cdot) \equiv [\,\cdot\,; R_0]_\alpha.$$

Covariation is concerned with symmetric r.v.'s. Next, we consider the asymmetric case. To do so, we consider the L_p-space, $p > 1$, of r.v.'s.

Given two p-integrable r.v.'s, i.e., their p-th absolute moments are finite, we define the so-called p-*product* by

$$\langle R_1; R_2 \rangle_p = \mathbf{E}\left\{ [R_1 - \mathbf{E}(R_1)][R_2 - \mathbf{E}(R_2)]^{<p-1>} \right\} = \int_{\mathbf{R}^2} x_1 x_2^{<p-1>} P^R(dx), \tag{9.21}$$

where P^R denotes the probability law of the pair of centered r.v.'s $R = (R_1 - \mathbf{E}(R_1), R_2 - \mathbf{E}(R_2))$.

It can be shown that the properties of the p-product are similar to those of covariation for α-stable r.v.'s and $1 < p < \alpha$. In the symmetric α-stable case, p-product and covariation are related by

$$\frac{[R_1; R_2]_\alpha}{\sigma^\alpha(R_2)} = \frac{\langle R_1; R_2 \rangle_p}{\|R_2\|_p^p}, \quad \text{for all} \quad p \in (1, \alpha), \tag{9.22}$$

where $\|R\|_p^p = \langle R, R \rangle_p$.

Next, we list properties of the p-product. First,

$$\langle R_1; R_2 \rangle_p = \frac{1}{p} \left. \frac{\partial \|\theta_1 R_1 + \theta_2 R_2\|_p^p}{\partial \theta_1} \right|_{\theta_1 = 0, \theta_2 = 1} = \int_{\mathbf{R}^2} x_1 x_2^{\langle p-1 \rangle} P^R(ds). \tag{9.23}$$

The p-product is linear in the first argument; for the second argument

$$\langle R_1; \lambda R_2 \rangle_p = \lambda^{\langle p-1 \rangle} \langle R_1; R_2 \rangle_p \tag{9.24}$$

holds. However, in contrast to covariation the p-product does not have the additivity property for the second argument. Based on Hölder's inequality the following inequality can be established:

$$\langle R_1; R_2 \rangle_p \le \|R_1\|_p \|R_2\|_p^{\langle p-1 \rangle}, \tag{9.25}$$

which helps us to show that a zero p-product corresponds to the James-orthogonality criterion, namely

$$\langle R_1; R_2 \rangle_p = 0 \quad \Longleftrightarrow \quad \|\lambda R_1 + R_2\|_p \geq \|R_2\|_p, \quad \text{for all real } \lambda. \quad (9.26)$$

Then, analogous to the symmetric stable case, (cf. Claim 9.3 in Section 9.5), we can establish that for $R_1 \neq R_2$, $\langle R_1 - R_2; R_2 \rangle_p = 0$ implies that $\|R_1\|_p > \|R_2\|_p$.

Every finite-dimensional space of p-integrable variables has a basis for which the matrix with entries $\langle R_i; R_j \rangle_p$ is triangular and invertible. If $R = (R_1, \ldots, R_d)'$ is a linearly independent set of random vectors, then $r_p(\lambda) := \|\lambda' R\|_p^p$ is strictly convex. Finally, we have an analogue to the Riesz-theorem which says that for every space of p-integrable variables there exists for any linear functions $\Psi(\cdot)$ a vector R_Ψ, (i.e. a p-integrable r.v), such that

$$\Psi(\cdot) = \langle \cdot \; ; R_\Psi \rangle_p.$$

The advantage of the p-product—apart from being applicable to all p-integrable r.v.'s—is that it provides a simple way of estimating covariation, which does not involve the estimation of spectral measures.

Multivariate risk analysis is a crucial aspect of portfolio theory. We now discuss three types of estimators for risk in multivariate settings. In Section 8.4, see (8.36), we defined the risk of the stable vector R as follows:

$$r(\theta) = \sigma^\alpha(\theta' R) = \int_{S_d} |\theta' s|^\alpha \Gamma(ds), \quad \theta \in \mathbf{R}^d. \quad (9.27)$$

It represents a direct generalization of the covariance matrix. The tail-estimator for $r(\theta)$ (see Section 8.4), has the advantage that it is strongly consistent and asymptotically normal. However, it turns out that the estimator requires large samples to guarantee reasonable precision, cf. Theorem 8.2.

A second type of estimator for $r(\theta)$ was presented by Lisitsky (1990), (see also Klebanov, Mittnik and Rachev (1998)), who uses the following alternative expression for the characteristic function of stable Paretian vectors,

$$\Phi_R(\theta) = \exp\left\{ -\exp\left[\alpha\tau + \alpha \int_{S_d} \left(\ln|\theta' s| - \frac{\pi i}{2}\text{sign}(\theta' s) \right) M(ds) \right] + i\theta'\mu \right\}, \quad (9.28)$$

where [5]

$$\tau = \mathbf{\Gamma}'(1)\left(\frac{1}{\alpha} - 1 \right) + \mathbf{E}(\ln(R)) \quad (9.29)$$

and

$$M(A) = P\left(\frac{R}{\|R\|} \in A \right), \quad \text{for all} \quad A \subset S_d. \quad (9.30)$$

---

[5] $\mathbf{\Gamma}'(1)$ is the derivative of Gamma-function at 1.

This form of the characteristic function leads to an alternative estimator for the stability index. Then an alternative expression for risk is

$$\tilde{r}(\theta) = \sigma^\alpha(\theta' R) = \exp\left\{\alpha\left(\tau + \int_{S_d} \ln|\theta' s| M(ds)\right)\right\}. \tag{9.31}$$

Given the expression for M, an estimator for the integral in $\int_{S_d} \ln|\theta' s| M(ds)$ is given by

$$\hat{I} = \frac{1}{N} \sum_{j=1}^{N} \ln j \left|\frac{\theta' R^{(j)}}{\|R^{(j)}\|}\right|, \tag{9.32}$$

where $R^{(j)}$ represents the j-th observation of the vector of α-stable returns, R. The properties of this estimator are not well known, but we refer to the discussion in Gamrowski and Rachev (1995a), who present some evidence based on Monte Carlo simulations.

The third type of estimator is a moment–based estimator. Here, the p-th absolute sample moment

$$\frac{1}{N} \sum_{j=1}^{N} |R^{(j)}|^p, \quad 0 < p < \alpha < 2 \tag{9.33}$$

is used to measure risk of α-stable portfolio $R = (R_1, \ldots, R_d)'$ with zero-mean. Various central limit theorems enable us to evaluate the asymptotic behavior of this risk estimator. If $p > \alpha/2$, we have, as $\lambda \to \infty$,

$$P\left(\left|R^{(j)}\right|^p > \lambda\right) \approx \frac{C}{\lambda^{\alpha/p}}. \tag{9.34}$$

Therefore, $|R^{(j)}|^p$ is the domain of attraction of the stable Paretian law with index α/p. The central limit theorem for α-stable laws (see for example, Feller, 1965) implies that

$$N^{(\alpha-p)/\alpha}\left(\frac{1}{N} \sum_{j=1}^{N} \left|R^{(j)}\right|^p - \mathrm{E}(|R|^p)\right) \xrightarrow{\omega} S_{\alpha/p}, \tag{9.35}$$

here $S_{\alpha/p}$ is stable r.v. with index $\frac{\alpha}{p}$, skewness 1, scale parameter $\frac{k_\alpha}{k_{\alpha/p}}\sigma^p$, and k_α is the constant defined in (9.5).

If $p \le \alpha/2$, then

$$\mathrm{var}\left(\left|R^{(j)}\right|\right) = \mathrm{E}\left(\left|R^{(j)}\right|^{2p}\right) \tag{9.36}$$

is finite, and thus $|R|^p$ is in the domain of attraction of a Gaussian law

$$N^{1/2}\left(\frac{1}{N} \sum_{j=1}^{N} \left|R^{(j)}\right|^p - \mathrm{E}(|R|^p)\right) \xrightarrow{w} N\left(0; H^p(\alpha; \beta; 2p)\sigma^p\right), \tag{9.37}$$

where H denotes the Hardin constant, see (9.6).

9.2 Stable Paretian Asset Pricing

9.2.1 The Asset–Pricing Problem

The *capital asset pricing model (CAPM)* was introduced by Sharpe (1964) and Lintner (1965). It states that, given certain market assumptions, the mean return of asset i is given by

$$\mathbf{E}(R_i) = \rho_0 + \beta_{im}(\mathbf{E}(R_m) - \rho_0), \qquad (9.38)$$

where ρ_0 represents the return of the riskless asset; R_m is the random return of the market portfolio (i.e., the portfolio of all marketed assets) and β_{im} — known as the "beta" of asset i—is $\text{cov}(R_i; R_m)/\text{var}(R_m)$.

The CAPM was the first attempt to explain the asset return behavior (with one factor) and has experienced considerable theoretical developments in the last thirty years. Merton (1973b) added a temporal dimension to CAPM by modeling asset returns by a diffusion process. Black (1972) in his "zero-beta" version widened assumptions on risk-free borrowing. And Chamberlain (1983) showed that the hypothesis of normality could be replaced with the weaker one of finite variance. But neither the CAPM nor its extensions seemed really satisfactory when empirically tested (see, for example, Affleck-Graves and Mac Donald, 1990; Blume and Friend, 1973; and Black et al. 1972). All these papers assume square integrability or, more strongly, normality of asset returns. If this is not the case, the statistical test may suffer from inconsistency.

The stable Paretian law was initially a widely accepted alternative to normality. Fama (1970) established a CAPM for symmetric stable Paretian[6] returns. It is of the form

$$R_i = \rho_i + b_i\delta + \epsilon_i, \qquad (9.39)$$

where δ and ϵ_i are independent and symmetric α-stable Paretian. Fama showed that in this case, the "beta" coefficient in (9.38) is given by

$$\beta_{im} = \frac{1}{\sigma(R_m)}\frac{\partial\sigma(R_m)}{\partial(\lambda_{im})}, \qquad (9.40)$$

where $R_m = \Sigma_i\lambda_{im}R_i$ ($\Sigma_i\lambda_{im} = 1$) represents the return of the market portfolio; and $\sigma(\cdot)$ is the scale parameter of the return under consideration. Ross (1978) also claimed that a CAPM-like formula would still hold for stable-distributed returns when restriction (9.39) for independence of δ and ϵ_i is not be satisfied. However, he does not provide an expression for beta analogous to (9.40) for this more general case. In fact, with stable Paretian returns it is not

---

[6]As Fama did, we assume $1 < \alpha < 2$ from now on. As we have pointed out $\alpha \leq 1$, does not seem to be encountered in financial return data.

possible to compute beta in this fashion or to conduct straightforward tests of the CAPM. Below, a computable expression for beta is given, enabling us to conduct empirical tests when asset returns follow symmetric stable Paretian laws, see further Section 9.2.2.

In response to the CAPM's empirical failures, Ross (1976) suggested a linear multi-factor pricing model, the so-called *Arbitrage Pricing Theory (APT)*. The APT implies that if the return of asset i, R_i, is of the form $\mathbf{E}(R_i) + \beta_{i1}\delta_1 + \cdots + \beta_{ik}\delta_k + \epsilon_i$ (here the δ_j's are the *factors* and the ϵ_i's are the *idiosyncratic risks*), then, under usual assumptions, the mean return, of the i-th asset is

$$\mathbf{E}(R_i) = \rho_0 + \beta_{il}\rho_1 + \cdots + \beta_{ik}\rho_k, \qquad (9.41)$$

where ρ_j is the *risk premium* linked to factor δ_j. The idea of the APT is that the mean return is not tied to its total variance, but only to that portion of the variance that is due to the market, because the idiosyncratic part can be diversified.

Two theories have evolved from Ross' work. The first is the so-called Asymptotic APT treated in Huberman (1982). It considers a sequence of economies with a growing number of assets. The second is the Equilibrium APT (see Chen and Ingersoll, 1983; Dybvig, 1983; and Grinblatt and Titman, 1983), where restrictions are placed on the returns or on agents' utility functions. Connor (1984) introduced a general theory encompassing the Equilibrium APT and the mutual fund separation theory. This represented already extension of the CAPM, but the returns were still in L_2. Milne (1988) further extended Connor's theory, assuming that returns only belong to any normed vector space, implying an stable Paretian Equilibrium APT. Nevertheless, a stable Paretian version of the APT has not yet been tested; tests so far usually assume returns to be normally distributed.

Next, we describe the derivation of the CAPM beta from the works of Fama (1970) and Ross (1991) as well as proofs of the CAPM and asymptotic APT for symmetric stable Paretian returns.

But before we do so, we should emphasize that these models assume symmetric return distribution, which may not hold in practice. Moreover, we assume that returns and idiosyncratic risks have the same index of stability. The fact that returns are not Gaussian does, of course, not imply that they have the same index of stability. Unfortunately, until we have an inner product on L_p, $0 \leq p < 2$ (or on the set of all stable distributions) with desirable properties we cannot expect to do better. However, when imposing normality, we also impose the same stability index for all returns[7], namely $\alpha = 2$. In other words, we keep the assumption that all returns have the same index, but we do not force it to be 2.

---

[7]In Section 8.6 we consider estimators for the normalized spectral measure for (α_1, α_2)-stable pairs $\alpha_1 \neq \alpha_2$. CAPM-test for this more general model is still an open problem.

9.2.2   Computation of Beta for Stable Paretian Laws

Under the assumption that (a) expected returns of asset i are described by (9.38), (b) there exists a riskless asset, and (c) all investors are risk–averse, Fama (1970) was the first to present a stable Paretian CAPM formula, namely

$$\mathbf{E}(R_i) = \rho_0 + \frac{1}{\sigma(\tilde{R}_m)} \frac{\partial \sigma(R_m)}{\partial \lambda_{im}} [\mathbf{E}(R_m) - \rho_0].$$

Here, $\sigma(\tilde{R}_m) = (\nu_\alpha(R_m))^{1/\alpha}$, where $\nu_\alpha(R) := [R, R;]_\alpha$ is the variation of the stable Paretian return under consideration (see Section 7.1 and 8.4). Hence,

$$\frac{1}{\sigma(R_m)} \frac{\partial \sigma(R_m)}{\partial \lambda_{im}} = \frac{1}{\alpha \nu_\alpha(R_m)} \frac{\partial \nu_\alpha(R_m)}{\partial \lambda_{im}}.$$

In addition, $\nu_\alpha(R_m) = \int_{S_n} |\Sigma_j \lambda_{jm} s_j|^\alpha \Gamma(ds)$, where Γ is the spectral measure of the α-stable vector of returns of all marketed assets $[R_1 \cdots R_n]$. This implies that

$$\frac{\partial \nu_\alpha(R_m)}{\partial \lambda_{im}} = \alpha \int_{S_n} s_i (\Sigma_j \lambda_{jm} s_j)^{\langle \alpha - 1 \rangle} \Gamma(ds) = \alpha [R_i, R_m]_\alpha.$$

Thus, the coefficient in Fama's CAPM can be rewritten as $\frac{[\tilde{R}_i; \tilde{R}_m]_\alpha}{\nu_\alpha(\tilde{R}_m)}$ and estimated as described in Section 8.4.

Next, we derive the same expression for the beta from Ross' (1978) mutual fund separation theory. According to Ross' Theorem 2 (Ross (1978, p. 267) and adding the assumption of the existence of a riskless asset, the return of the i-th asset is modeled by

$$R_i = \rho_i + b_i \delta + \epsilon_i, \quad i = 1, \dots, n, \tag{9.42}$$

where $\delta - \mathbf{E}(\delta)$ and the ϵ_i's are symmetric α-stable Paretian, satisfying $\mathbf{E}(\epsilon_i|\delta) = 0$, and the return of the market portfolio is modeled by $R_m = \rho_0 + \delta$. Following Kanter (1972) we have that

$$\mathbf{E}(\epsilon_i|\delta) = \frac{[\epsilon_i; \delta]_\alpha}{\nu_\alpha(\delta)} [\delta - \mathbf{E}(\delta)].$$

Therefore, $\mathbf{E}(\epsilon_i|\delta) = 0$ implies that $[\epsilon_i; \delta]_\alpha = 0$. Combining the above results we have $b_i = \frac{[R_i; R_m]_\alpha}{\nu_\alpha(R_m)}$. Ross (1978) also shows that $\mathbf{E}(R_i) - \rho_0 = b_i [\mathbf{E}(R_m) - \rho_0]$. Now Ross' mutual fund separation theory implies that under the following three assumptions:

(a) the preference of the agents have a von Neumann Morgenstern representation (with a monotone increasing concave function),

(b) there exists a riskless asset,

(c) the market portfolio has a non-zero variance,

the Sharpe-Lintner formula

$$\mathbf{E}(R_i) = \rho_0 + \beta_{im}[\mathbf{E}(R_m) - \rho_0] \tag{9.43}$$

holds with

$$\beta_{im} := \frac{[R_i; R_m]_\alpha}{\nu_\alpha(R_m)}. \tag{9.44}$$

Note that all symmetric α-stable vectors can be written in form (9.42) with $\mathbf{E}(\epsilon_i|\delta) = 0$. Fama's case is a restricted one, because it was obtained under the stronger assumption of independence of δ and the ϵ_i's.

Because variation and covariation in the space of α-stable symmetric r.v.'s play the roles of variance and covariance in L_2, respectively, $\frac{[R_i; R_m]_\alpha}{\nu_\alpha(R_m)}$ is the natural extension of the classical Beta= $\frac{\mathrm{cov}(R_i; R_m)}{\mathrm{var}(R_m)}$.

9.2.3   Proof of the Stable Paretian CAPM

In the previous section we have shown that β_{im} in the stable CAPM can be written as

$$\beta_{im} = \frac{1}{\sigma(R_m)} \frac{\partial \sigma(R_m)}{\partial \lambda_i} = \frac{[R_i; R_m]_\alpha}{\sigma^\alpha(R_m)}, \tag{9.45}$$

which is a computable expression, especially because we know (recall (9.22)) that for all p with $1 < p < \alpha$

$$\beta_{im} = \frac{[R_i; R_m]_\alpha}{\sigma^\alpha(R_m)} = \frac{\langle R_i; R_m \rangle_p}{\|R_m\|_p^p}. \tag{9.46}$$

We next give a direct proof of the stable Paretian CAPM. The proof corresponds to that of the square-integrable case (see Duffie (1988b) and the references therein). It can be generalized to L_p-spaces, if one assumes that investors measure risk with the p-th absolute moment.

The following definition and proposition are essential for the stable Paretian CAPM.

Definition 9.1 Given probability space $(\Omega; \mathcal{F}; P)$ we define *exchange economy*[8] $\mathcal{E}$ by $((S_\alpha; \succeq_i; \tilde{\omega}_i), i \in \mathcal{I})$, where S_α is the set of linear combinations of the constant 1 and all symmetric α-stable Paretian r.v.'s on $(\Omega; \mathcal{F}; P)$. For each agent $i \in \mathcal{I}$:

(i) S_α is the choice space,

(ii) $\succeq_i$ is the preference relation,

(iii) $\tilde{\omega}_i$ is the initial endowment.

---

[8]For the notion of exchange economy we refer to Duffie (1988b, p. 40).

Let $\mathcal{A} \subset S_\alpha$ be a set of assets for $\mathcal{E}$. We assume that $\mathcal{A}$ is such that the marketed space $\mathcal{M} = $ span $\mathcal{A}$ is finite-dimensional. Let $(\rho(x); x \in \mathcal{M})$ be a linear pricing functional on $\mathcal{M}$. We define stable Paretian return R_x by $\frac{x}{\rho(x)}$.[9] A preference relation $\succeq$ will be called α-*strictly variation averse*[10] if for every pair

$$x_1, x_2 \in S_\alpha \quad \text{such that} \quad \mathbf{E}(x_2) = 0 \quad \text{and} \quad \nu_\alpha(x_1 + x_2) > \nu_\alpha(x_1),$$

it follows that

$$x_1 \succ x_1 + x_2.$$

The proof of the next proposition follows step by step the proof of the classical L_2-case, and it is essentially given in Section 9.5, see Corollary 9.1.

Proposition 9.1 For any $x \in \mathcal{M}$,

$$\mathbf{E}(R_x - \rho_0) = \beta_{x\pi}\mathbf{E}(R_\pi - \rho_0), \tag{9.47}$$

where

$$\beta_{x\pi} = \frac{[R_x; R_\pi]_\alpha}{\nu_\alpha(R_\pi)},$$

and π with mean[11] $\mathbf{E}\pi = \frac{1}{\rho_0}$ is the unique asset[12] such that $p(\cdot) \equiv [\cdot; \pi]_\alpha$.

Theorem 9.1 *(CAPM for stable returns)* Let us consider an equilibrium for the exchange economy $(\mathcal{E}; \mathcal{A})$ defined above. Suppose that

(a) the preference relation of each agent is α-strictly variation averse;

(b) each agent's endowment, ω_i, is in the marketed space;

(c) the riskless asset 1_Ω has a non-zero market value; and

(d) the market portfolio $m = \Sigma_i \omega_i$ has non-zero variation.

Then, any asset $x \in \mathcal{M}$ with non-zero market value satisfies

$$\mathbf{E}(R_x) - \rho_0 = \beta_{xm}[\mathbf{E}(R_m) - \rho_0]. \tag{9.48}$$

---

[9] Here, we follow the standard approach to CAPM where the return R_x is defined by $\frac{x}{p(x)}$. In practice, we use "return" to denote the log-differences of consecutive level prices. On a real asset data both definitions give very close values, simply because the typical range of return r is between -0.04 and +0.04, see also the discussion in Kariya (1993), Chapter 7.

[10] Fama (1970) shows that any risk averse preference relation with von Neumann Morgenstern representation is α-*strictly* variation averse.

[11] This mean, in fact, defines the value ρ_0 in the formula (9.47).

[12] See Theorem 9.4 and Corollary 9.1 in Section 9.5.

Proof. It has to be shown that the market portfolio is in the span $\{1_\Omega; \pi\}$.

Let x be an equilibrium allocation. Set $x_0 = \mathbf{E}(x) + \lambda_x \pi_0$, where $\pi_0 = \pi - \mathbf{E}(\pi)$ and $\lambda_x = \frac{[x;\pi]_\alpha}{\nu_\alpha(\pi)}$. We have $\mathbf{E}(x) = \mathbf{E}(x_0)$ and $\rho(x) = \rho(x_0)$. Thus, because of (a), $\nu_\alpha(x_0) = \nu_\alpha(x)$. Moreover, $[x - x_0; x_0]_\alpha = 0$. Consequently, because of Claim 9.2 (see further, Section 9.5) we have $x = x_0$, implying that $m \in \text{span} \{1_\Omega; \pi_0\}$. Now we can deduce (9.48) from Proposition 9.1. □

9.2.4   The Stable Paretian APT

The Arbitrage Pricing Theory (APT) can be viewed as a multi-index gener-alization of the CAPM. Connor (1984) treats the APT for situations, where asset returns are defined in normed vector spaces. Without going into details, it should be noted that there are two versions of the APT for α-stable dis-tributed returns, a so-called equilibrium and an asymptotic version. Connors provides the proof for the former, while Gamrowski and Rachev (1994a) for the latter.

We briefly summarize the APT. It assumes that the returns of all assets are due to a finite number of common sources or risk factors, represented by random variables $\delta_1, \ldots, \delta_k$. The return of asset i, R_i, is assumed to be linearly related to the factors, namely

$$R_i = \mathbf{E}(R_i) + \beta_{i1}\delta_1 + \beta_{i2}\delta_2 + \ldots + \beta_{ik}\delta_k + \epsilon_i, \qquad (9.49)$$

where ϵ_i represents asset-specific risk. The ϵ_i's are assumed to be mutually independent and also independent of factors $\delta_1, \ldots, \delta_k$. Given some additional rather standard assumptions the APT shows that each risk, δ_j, has premium ρ_j associated with it, determining the expected return of asset i by

$$\mathbf{E}(R_i) = \rho_0 + \beta_{i1}\rho_1 + \beta_{i2}\rho_2 + \ldots + \beta_{ik}\rho_k. \qquad (9.50)$$

Remark 9.1 The difficulty in testing the APT empirically is the determi-nation of the risk factors. In the Gaussian case Joreskog's (1967) maximum likelihood based approach to multi—factor analysis can be adopted. Unfor-tunately, this approach cannot be generalized to stable Paretian laws. Gam-rowski and Rachev (1994a) (see further Section 9.3) developed a method for this case which is based on the fact that the subspace of $\mathbf{R}^n$ (n is the num-ber of assets under consideration) generated by the columns of the coefficient matrix

$$\beta = (\beta_{ij}), \quad 1 \le i \le n, \ 1 \le j \le k \qquad (9.51)$$

is the same as the subspace generated by $\{\nabla r(\lambda) : \lambda = (\lambda_1, \ldots, \lambda_n) \in \mathbf{R}^n\}$, where r is the portfolio risk, see (9.27).

The next two theorems provide proofs of the stable Asymptotic APT. The proofs are similar to those in Huberman (1982) for the L_2-case. They merely use the new notion of variation instead of variance.

Consider a sequence of economies, where the n-th economy has n assets, whose returns are modeled by r.v.'s $R_i^n (i = 1, \ldots, n)$ on a probability space

$(\Omega, \mathcal{F}, P)$. In a Paretian-stable setting we assume that R_i^n is generated by a linear k-factor model of the form

$$\rho_i^n + \beta_{i1}^n \delta_1^n + \cdots + \beta_{ik}^n \delta_k^n + \epsilon_i^n \tag{9.52}$$

with

$$\mathbf{E}(\delta_j^n) = 0 \tag{9.53}$$

$$\epsilon_i's \text{ are symmetric stable Paretian and independent,} \tag{9.54}$$

and the covariations of all δ_j^n are uniformly bounded:

$$\nu_\alpha(\epsilon_i^n) \leq V. \tag{9.55}$$

In matrix notation, we shall write $R^n = \rho^n + \beta^n \delta^n + \epsilon^n$.

Definition 9.2 An α–arbitrage $(1 < \alpha \leq 2)$ is a sequence of portfolios $\theta^n \in \mathbf{R}^n$, satisfying $\theta^{n'} 1^n = 0$ with $1^n = (1, \cdots, 1)'$ whose returns $\theta^{n'} R^n$ satisfy: $\lim_{n \to \infty}, \mathbf{E}(\theta^{n'} R^n) = +\infty$ and $\lim_{n \to \infty} \nu_\alpha(\theta^{n'} R^n) = 0$.

Theorem 9.2 *(Arbitrage Pricing Theory for Stable Paretian Returns: Model 1).* Suppose that risky returns R_i^n satisfy conditions (9.52) – (9.55) and that there in no α-arbitrage for any subsequence of R_i^n. Then, for any positive A and every n, there are constants $\rho_0^n, \gamma_1^n, \cdots, \gamma_k^n$

$$\sum_{i=1}^{n} \left| \rho_i^n - \rho_0^n - \sum_{j=1}^{k} \beta_{ij}^n \gamma_j^n \right|^\alpha \leq A.$$

Remark 9.2 Since under the assumptions (9.52)-(9.54), we have $\mathbf{E}(R_i^n) = \rho_i^n$, then, as $n \to \infty$, Theorem 9.2 represents an alternative version of the relation (9.50).

Proof. Project the vector of mean returns ρ^n on the subspace spanned by the unitvector 1^n and $\beta_j^n = (\beta_{1j}^n, \cdots, \beta_{nj}^n)'(j = 1, \cdots, k)$. Then there exists $\rho_0^n \in \mathbf{R}, \gamma^n \in \mathbf{R}^k$ and $\theta^n \in \mathbf{R}^n$ such that $\rho^n = \rho_0^n 1^n + \beta^n \gamma^n + \theta^n$ with $\theta^{n'} 1^n = 0$ and $\theta^{n'} \beta^n = 0$. Then, $\|\theta^n\|_\alpha^\alpha := \sum_i |\theta_i^n|^\alpha = \sum_i |\rho_i^n - \rho_0^n - \beta_i^{n'} \gamma^n|^\alpha$. Suppose that the theorem is false. Then there would exist a subsequence (still denoted by n) such that $\lim_{n \to \infty} \|\theta^n\|_\alpha = +\infty$. Let $p \in (-2, -1]$ and consider portfolio $\zeta^n = \lambda_n \theta^n$, where the multiplier $\lambda_n = \|\theta^n\|_\alpha^p$. The return of ζ^n is $\zeta^{n'} R^n = \zeta^{n'} \theta^n + \zeta^{n'} \epsilon^n = \|\theta^n\|_\alpha^p \|\theta^n\|_2^2 + \|\theta^n\|_\alpha^p \theta^{n'} \epsilon^n$.

Let us show that ζ_n is $\alpha-$ arbitrage portfolio. In fact, by (9.54), $\mathbf{E}(\zeta^{n'} R^n) = \|\theta^n\|_\alpha^p \|\theta^n\|_2^2 \geq \|\theta^n\|_\alpha^{p+2} \to +\infty$.
Furthermore, $\nu_\alpha(\zeta^{n'} R^n) = [\|\theta^n\|_\alpha^p \theta^n \epsilon^n; \|\theta^n\|_\alpha^p \theta^n \epsilon^n]_\alpha = \|\theta\|_\alpha^{p\alpha} \sum_i |\theta_i^n|^\alpha [\epsilon_i^n; \epsilon_i^n]_\alpha \leq \|\theta^n\|_\alpha^{(p+1)\alpha} V \to 0$. This contradicts the hypothesis of non-arbitrage. $\square$

Next, we consider a stationary model with (9.52) being replaced by

$$R^n = \theta^n + \beta \delta^n + \epsilon^n. \tag{9.56}$$

In the stationary case, we no longer consider a sequence of economies but one economy with an infinite number of assets.

Theorem 9.3 *(Arbitrage Pricing Theory for stable Paretian returns 2)* Suppose that the risky returns satisfy condition (9.56), (9.53)-(9.55), and that there is no α-arbitrage. Then, there exist constants $\theta_0, \gamma_1, \ldots, \gamma_k$ such that

$$\sum_{j=1}^{+\infty} \left| \theta_i - \theta_0 - \sum_{j=1}^{k} \beta_{ij} \gamma_j \right|^{\alpha} < +\infty.$$

Proof. The arguments are basically the same as in the normal case $\alpha = 2$ (see Huberman, 1982) with some modifications similar to those in Theorem 9.2. $\qquad\qquad\square$

9.3   Testing Stable Paretian Asset–Pricing Models

For both the CAPM and the APT model we are interested in examining whether the fact that $\alpha < 2$ affects empirical tests that are conducted under the (normal) L_2-assumption.

For testing the Paretian stable version of CAPM, one may apply the test-statistic for the covariation (see Section 8.4), and thus to obtain a tail-estimator for beta in (9.48). This allows to reproduce the initial test of the stable CAPM. For example $\Delta_x = \mathbf{E}(R_x) - \rho_0 - \beta_{xm}[\mathbf{E}(R_m) - \rho_0]$ tends to be positive when β_{xm} is high instead of zero as predicted by the standard (normal) CAPM, see Gamrowski and Rachev (1994a) and the references therein. Whether such a result holds with stable Paretian betas remain to be investigated.[13] The case of the APT's is more complicated, because it requires a multivariate methods such as factor analysis.

Before describing a testing procedure for a stable APT we provide necessary theoretical results. Without any restrictions on model (9.52)-(9.55) we assume that rank $(\beta) = k$ in (9.48)) and that $\{\delta_1, \cdots, \delta_k\}$ is an α-stable family of r.v.'s. Note that linear model (9.52) can be written as $R = \rho + (\beta P^{-1})(P\delta) + \epsilon$, where the exponent n is omitted and P is any invertible $k \times k$ matrix. Consequently, the goal is not to determine a particular β but span $\beta = \text{span } \beta P^{-1}$ (where span β designs the spanning of the columns β_j of β) that do not depend on P.

The following properties show that we can compute the factor loadings if we know the spectral measure of the α-stable vector $R^0 = \beta\delta$. Then the observations on R enables us to deduce the spectral measure of R^0. The procedure builds on the following two properties.

---

[13]Some results showing cases when the stable CAPM outperformed the normal CAPM are reported in Gamrowski and Rachev (1994b), (1995).

Property 9.4 We have
$$\text{span } \beta = \text{span } \nabla r^0$$

where span $\nabla r^0 = \text{span}\{\nabla r^0(\theta), \theta \in \mathbf{R}^n\}$ and $r^0(\theta)$ denotes the risk of portfolio θ on R^0.

Proof. By definition, $R^0 = \beta\delta$ and thus,
$$e^{-r^0(\theta)} = \mathbf{E}e^{i\theta' R^0} = \mathbf{E}e^{i\theta'\beta\delta} = \mathbf{E}e^{i(\beta'\theta)'\delta},$$

implying that $r^0(\theta) = \int_{S_k} |\theta'\beta s|^\alpha \Gamma_\delta(ds)$, where Γ_δ is the spectral measure of δ. Next

$$\frac{\partial r^0}{\partial \theta_i} = \alpha \sum_j \beta_{ij} \int_{S_k} s_j(\theta'\beta s)^{(\alpha-1)}\Gamma_\delta(ds), \quad i = 1,\dots,k$$

which by definition of $[\cdot, \cdot]_\alpha$ (see Section 9.1.1) implies that

$$\nabla r^0(\theta) = \alpha \sum_j [\delta_j; \theta'\beta\delta]_\alpha \beta_j,$$

where $\beta_j := (\beta_{1j}, \dots, \beta_{kj})'$. Therefore, span $\nabla r^0 \subset$ span β.

To show the reserve inclusion, we use Lemma 9.1 in Section 9.5 and let P denote an invertible matrix that transforms δ into $\delta^* = P\delta$ such that the covariation matrix $V_\alpha(\delta^*)$ with entries $[\delta_i^*, \delta_j^*]_\alpha$ is invertible. Because rank $(\beta) = k$, then for every $\ell \in \{1,\dots,k\}$ there exists a portfolio $\theta^\ell \in \mathbf{R}^k$ such that the ℓth-entry of δ^* equals

$$\delta_\ell^* = \theta^{\ell'}\beta\delta.$$

Thus from the formula we have obtained for $\nabla r^0(\theta)$ it follows that

$$\nabla r^0(\theta^\ell) = \alpha \sum_j [\delta_j; \delta_\ell^*]_\alpha \beta_j = \alpha\beta \begin{pmatrix} [\delta_1; \delta_\ell^*]_\alpha \\ \vdots \\ [\delta_k; \delta_\ell^*]_\alpha \end{pmatrix} = \alpha\beta P^{-1}P \begin{pmatrix} [\delta_1; \delta_\ell^*]_\alpha \\ \vdots \\ [\delta_k; \delta_\ell^*]_\alpha \end{pmatrix}.$$

In other words, $(\nabla r^0(\theta^1); \cdots; \nabla r^0(\theta^k)) = \alpha\beta P^{-1}V_\alpha(\delta')$, implying that

$$\beta = \frac{1}{\alpha}[\nabla r^0(\theta^1); \cdots; \nabla r^0(\theta^k)]V_\alpha(\delta')^{-1}P$$

Therefore, span $\beta \subset$ span ∇r^0 and, thus, span $\beta = $ span ∇r^0, as desired. $\square$

If $R^0 = \beta\delta$ was observable, one could compute ∇r^0 (recall that r^0 is the risk associated with R^0). Then examine whether vectors $\nabla r(\theta^1), \cdots, \nabla r(\theta^\eta)$ (with η large and $\theta^1, \cdots, \theta^\eta$ arbitrarily chosen) belongs to a linear subspace. Unfortunately, we do not observe R^0 but the actual return $R = \rho + R^0 + \epsilon$, so that we cannot directly estimate the spectral measure $\Gamma_0 = \Gamma_{R^0}$ and r^0, but only $\Gamma = \Gamma_R$ and $r(\theta) = \nu_\alpha(\theta' R)$. Nonetheless, we known that $\Gamma = \Gamma_0 + \Gamma_\epsilon$, where Γ_ϵ is the spectral measure of ϵ. Because ϵ is a vector of idiosyncratic risks, its spectral measure is composed of Dirac masses on the poles $(0; \cdots; 0; 1; 0; \cdots; 0)$ and $(0; \cdots; 0; -1; 0; \cdots; 0)$. Thus, idiosyncratic risks will appear in Γ only as Dirac masses on the poles. Our approach is to delete these Dirac masses in Γ. To this end we must check whether Γ_0 also has a Dirac mass on one of the poles. Property 9.5 addresses this problem.

Property 9.5 Assuming (9.52)–(9.55), R can be written as

$$R = \rho + \beta^* \delta^* + \epsilon^* \tag{9.57}$$

where $\delta^* = \delta_1^*, \ldots, \delta_{k^*}^*)'$, $(k^* < k)$, the ϵ_i's are idiosyncratic, span $\beta^* \subset$ span β; and the stable vector $R^{0*} = \beta^* \delta^*$ has no Dirac distribution on the poles of its spectral measure Γ_0.

Remark 9.3 Passing from (9.52) to (9.57) will in fact remove the idiosyncratic part of the β_i's and at the same time, the Dirac masses on the poles in Γ_0. Applying APT theorem to (9.52) and (9.57) is not a contradiction, but it just says that the risk premia in the "idiosyncratic directions" of the factors are null.

Proof. Suppose that Γ_0 has a Dirac mass $\lambda/2$ on $(1; 0; \cdots; 0)$. Then, $r^0(\theta) = \lambda|\theta_1|^\alpha + \int_{S_n} |\theta' s|^\alpha \bar{\Gamma}_0(ds)$, where $\bar{\Gamma}_0$ is still a spectral measure, $r^0(\theta) \geq \lambda|\theta_1|^\alpha$. On the other hand, $r^0(\theta) = \int_{S_k} |\theta' \beta_s|^\alpha \Gamma_\delta(ds)$. Let $\theta^1, \cdots, \theta^{N-k}$ be the directions of $(\text{span } \beta)^\perp$. Then $r^0(\theta^i) = 0$ implies that $\theta_1^i = 0$, for all $i = 1, \cdots, N - k$, and, thus, $e_1 = (1, 0, \ldots, 0)' \in$ span β. So, we can choose an invertible matrix P such that $\beta^* = \beta P^{-1}$, $\delta^* = P\delta$ and $\beta_1^* = e_1$. Consider $R^{0*} = R^0 - \nu e_1$, where ν is independent and $\nu \sim S_\alpha(\lambda^{1/\alpha})$. R^{0*} no longer has a Dirac mass on pole e_1. Writing $\beta_{11}^* \delta_1^* - \nu$ as δ_1^* and defining $\epsilon_1^* = \epsilon_1 + \nu$, $\epsilon_i^* = \epsilon_i (i > 1)$, we have $R = \rho + \beta^* \delta^* + \epsilon^*$, where ϵ^* is idiosyncratic, and the characteristic function of $R^{0*} = \beta^* \delta^*$ has no Dirac mass on the first pole. Property 9.5 is obtained by repeating the same argument for each pole.   □

This allows us to describe a test procedure for the APT test:

Step 1: Find the index of stability and the spectral measure of R from return data.

Step 2: Obtain the spectral measure of R^0 by "removing" the Dirac masses on the poles.

Step 3: Compute the gradient of r^0 for a large number of portfolios.

Step 4: Get span β by component analysis on the set of the gradients.

Step 5: Estimate the risk premia by regressing ρ on a constant and the β_j's.

9.4   Stable Paretian Portfolio Theory

The mean—variance portfolio theory of Markowitz (1952) and Sharpe (1964) can be extended to stable Paretian laws (see (9.16) by modifying the risk measure appropriately. Instead of the variance, the scale parameter σ, or the p-th moment $(1 \leq p < \alpha)$ may be chosen as risk measure, cf. (9.20), (9.23).

Given an n-asset portfolio let the return of asset i be R_i and the weight with which it enters the portfolio be λ_i, $i = 1, \ldots, n$. Then,

$$r(\lambda) = \sigma^\alpha(\lambda'R) = \int_{S_n} |\lambda's|^\alpha \Gamma(ds)$$

or, with $\|R\|_p^p = \langle R, R \rangle_p$, see (9.21),

$$r(\lambda) = \|\lambda'R\|_p^p, \quad 1 \leq p < \alpha,$$

where $R = (R_1, \ldots, R_n)'$ and $\lambda = (\lambda_1, \ldots, \lambda_n)'$ see (9.21), (9.23). In the absence of a risk-free asset the functions are strictly convex.

We next describe optimization algorithms for portfolio management in the case of α-stable returns. The optimization problem is of the following form:

$$\min_{\lambda \in \mathbf{R}^n} r(\lambda) \tag{9.58}$$

$$\text{subject to:} \quad \sum_{i=1}^{n} \lambda_i = 1,$$

$$\sum_{i=1}^{n} \lambda_i R_i = R^*,$$

where R^* represents the desired portfolio return. If no short-selling is allowed, the additional constraints $\lambda_i \geq 0$, $i = 1, \ldots, n$, need to be incorporated. If one wants to track a particular benchmark denoted by R^b, the following problem has to be solved:

$$\min_\lambda \sigma^\alpha(\lambda'R - R^b) \text{ or } \min \|\lambda'R - R^b\|_p^p \tag{9.59}$$

$$\text{subject to:} \quad \sum_{i=1}^{n} \lambda_i = 1$$

$$\sum_{i=1}^{n} \lambda_i \beta_i = 1,$$

where β_i denotes the beta coefficient of asset i with respect to the benchmark.

We now discuss two approaches to solving these problems. The first method (called "linear method"), is valid when the first moment is used as a risk measure and short-selling is not allowed. The second method (called "gradient method"), is applicable when the p-th moment $(1 < p < \alpha)$ is used as a risk measure.

(i) **Linear Method:**

Let $R_{i,t}$, $t = 1, \ldots, N$ be the set of N, i.i.d., observations of the return of asset i and $\overline{R}_i = \frac{1}{N} \sum_{t=1}^{N} R_{i,t}$. Let $X_{i,t}$ denote the deviation $R_{i,t} - \overline{R}_i$ of the return of asset i from its sample mean observed in period $t = 1, \ldots, N$. Then the portfolio risk, measured by the first central moment, $\mathbf{E}|\sum_{i=1}^{n} \lambda_i (R_i - \mathbf{E}R_i)|$ is estimated by

$$\hat{r}(\lambda) = \frac{1}{N} \sum_{t=1}^{N} \left| \sum_{i=1}^{n} \lambda_i X_{i,t} \right|.$$

To apply the simplex method for solving the minimization problem, we set it up as a linear programming problem. To do so, assume that $\overline{R}_n$ is the smallest mean return, $\overline{R}_n = \min_{1 \leq i \leq n} \overline{R}_i$ and $\overline{R}_1$ the largest $\overline{R}_1 = \max_{1 \leq i \leq n} \overline{R}_i$. Rewriting the "add-up" constraint, $\sum_{i=1}^{n} \lambda_i = 1$ as $\lambda_n = 1 - \sum_{i=1}^{n-1} \lambda_i$, consider the following empirical version of our minimization problem (9.58):

$$\min \frac{1}{N} \sum_{t=1}^{N} \left| \sum_{i=1}^{n-1} \lambda_i (X_{i,t} - X_{n,t}) + X_{n,t} \right| \tag{9.60}$$

$$\text{subject to:} \quad \sum_{i=1}^{n-1} \lambda_i \leq 1$$

$$\sum_{i=1}^{n-1} \lambda_i (\overline{R}_i - \overline{R}_n) = R^* - \overline{R}_n$$

$$\lambda_i \geq 0, \quad i = 1, \ldots, n.$$

Defining, for $i = 1, \ldots, n-1$,

$$Y_{i,t} = X_{i,t} - X_{n,t}, \tag{9.61}$$

$$c_i = \frac{\overline{R}_i - \overline{R}_n}{\overline{R}_1 - \overline{R}_n},$$

and

$$c_n = \frac{R^* - \overline{R}_n}{\overline{R}_1 - \overline{R}_n}$$

and the problem can be written as

$$\min \frac{1}{N} \sum_{t=1}^{N} \left| \sum_{i=2}^{n-1} \lambda_i (Y_{i,t} - c_i Y_{1,t}) + c_n Y_{1,t} + X_{n,t} \right| \tag{9.62}$$

$$\text{subject to:} \quad \sum_{i=1}^{n-1} \lambda_i \leq 1,$$

$$\sum_{i=1}^{n-1} \lambda_i c_i = c_n,$$

$$\lambda_i \geq 0, \quad i = 1, \ldots, n.$$

Denote the set of constraints concerning $\lambda = (\lambda_1, \ldots, \lambda_n)'$ in (9.62) as $\lambda \in K$. Assuming that K is non-empty, $\overline{R}_n \leq R^* \leq \overline{R}_1$, and by the way R_n and R_1 have been defined, it is guaranteed that both c_n and $1 - c_n$ are positive. Defining $a_{i,t} = Y_{i,t} - c_i Y_{1,t}$ and $b_t = c_n Y_{1,t} + X_{n,t}$, we introduce the variables ϵ_t^+ and ϵ_t^-, which satisfy

$$\epsilon_t^+ + \epsilon_t^- = \left| \sum_{i=2}^{n-1} a_{i,t} \lambda_i + b_t \right| \tag{9.63}$$

and

$$\epsilon_t^+ - \epsilon_t^- = \sum_i a_{i,t} \lambda_i + b_t, \tag{9.64}$$

so that the minimization problem becomes

$$\min \frac{1}{N} \sum_{t=1}^{N} (\epsilon_t^+ + \epsilon_t^-) \tag{9.65}$$

subject to: $\lambda \in K,$

$$\epsilon_t^+ - \epsilon_t^- = \sum_i a_{i,t} \lambda_i + b_t,$$

$$\epsilon_t^+, \epsilon_t^- \geq 0.$$

This is a standard linear programming formulation, with equality and inequality constraints. One can easily reformulate the set of constraints so that it will contain only inequality constraints. More important is, indeed the converges properties of this "randomized" mass-transportation problems—an issue we are not going to address here—for some standard references we refer to Rachev (1991).

(ii) Gradient Method:

The p-th moment, $1 < p < \alpha$, $r_p(\lambda) = \mathbf{E} |\sum_{i=1}^{n} \lambda_i (R_i - \mathbf{E}R_i)|^p$, $\lambda = (\lambda_1, \ldots, \lambda_n)'$, is used as a risk measure for the gradient method. We proceed iteratively as follows. Given a starting point we search the minimum along the direction of the gradient and project it onto the space of all constraints, to obtain the next point and repeat this procedure until convergence. The approach is applicable, because an expression for the gradient exists, the constraints are convex, the objective function is differentiable, and it is k-convex, i.e., it satisfies for all $x, y \in \mathbf{R}^n$,

$$r_p(y) \geq r_p(x) + \nabla r_p(x)'(y - x) + \frac{k}{2} \|y - x\|^2. \tag{9.66}$$

The proof of (9.66) needs some standard but cumbersome calculations, see Gamrowski and Rachev (1995a).

9.5   Lemmas on James–Orthogonality

The properties discussed above resemble Hilbert-space properties. Recall that in a vector space of symmetric α-stable r.v.'s (shortly, sas–$space$) James-orthogonality ($R_1 \perp_J R_2$) (shortly, sas–$space$) James-orthogonality ($R_1 \perp_J R_2$) means that

$$\sigma(\lambda R_1 + R_2) \geq \sigma(R_2) \quad \text{for all } \lambda \in \mathbf{R},$$

i.e. $\|\lambda R_1 + R_2\|_\alpha \geq \|R_2\|_\alpha$ for all $\lambda \in \mathbf{R}$, which is also equivalent to $[R_1; R_2]_\alpha = 0$. Further we consider only finite dimensional sas-spaces. The definition of James-orthogonality ensures that if

$$R_2 \perp_J R_1 - R_2 \quad \text{and} \quad R_2 \neq R_1, \tag{9.67}$$

then, $\|R_1\|_\alpha \geq \|R_2\|_\alpha$ moreover, Lemma 9.1 below shows that in the case of sas spaces, (9.67) implies $\|R_1\|_\alpha > \|R_2\|_\alpha$, see also Samorodnitsky and Taqqu (1994). Our main goal here is to show the main part of Propositon 9.1.

Claim 9.1 Let $\begin{pmatrix} R_1 \\ R_2 \end{pmatrix}$ be a sas vector and Γ its spectral measure. If

$$\int_{S_2} |s_1| |s_2|^{\alpha-1} \Gamma(ds) = \left(\int_{S_2} |s_1|^p \Gamma(ds) \right)^{\frac{1}{p}} \left(\int_{S_2} |s_2|^{(\alpha-1)q} \Gamma(ds) \right)^{\frac{1}{q}} \tag{9.68}$$

with p and q conjugate, $\frac{1}{p} + \frac{1}{q} = 1$, $p \geq 1$, $q \geq 1$), then R_1 and R_2 are proportional r.v.'s.

Proof. (9.68) with "$\leq$" follows from Hölder's inequality. Equality is possible only if Γ is concentrate on a set where $|s_1|$ and $|s_2|^{(\alpha-1)}$ are proportional, i.e., a set $\{\bar{s}; -\bar{s}\}$ containing two opposite points on the unit circle.

The characteristic function of $\begin{pmatrix} R_1 \\ R_2 \end{pmatrix}$ is $\mathbf{E}e^{i(\theta_1 R_1 + \theta_2 R_2)} = \exp\{-k|\theta_1 \bar{s}_1 + \theta_2 \bar{s}_2|^\alpha\}$. Without loss of generality, let $\bar{s}_1 \neq 0$. Then, $\mathbf{E}e^{i(\theta_1 R_1 + \theta_2 R_2)} = \exp\{-\sigma^\alpha |\theta_1 + \lambda\theta_2|^\alpha\}$ with $\lambda = \frac{\bar{s}_2}{\bar{s}_1}$ and $\sigma = k^{\frac{1}{\alpha}} |\bar{s}_1|$. Therefore, for all θ_1 and θ_2,

$$\mathbf{E}e^{i(\theta_1 R_1 + \theta_2 R_2)} = \mathbf{E}e^{i(\theta_1 + \lambda\theta_2)R} = \mathbf{E}e^{i(\theta_1 R + \theta_2(\lambda R))},$$

which implies that $R_2 = \lambda R_1$.   □

Claim 9.2 If R_1 and R_2 are two non-zero sas r.v.'s with $[R_1 - R_2; R_2]_\alpha = 0$, then the following implication holds

$$\nu_\alpha(R_1) = \nu_\alpha(R_2) \Rightarrow R_1 = R_2. \tag{9.69}$$

Proof. Let us suppose that $[R_1 - R_2; R_2]_\alpha = 0$ and $\nu_\alpha(R_1) = \nu_\alpha(R_2)$.

$$[R_1; R_2]_\alpha = [R_1 - R_2; R_2]_\alpha + [R_2; R_2]_\alpha = \nu_\alpha(R_2). \qquad (9.70)$$

From (9.70) we get $[R_1; R_2]_\alpha = \nu_\alpha(R_1)^{\frac{1}{\alpha}} \nu_\alpha(R_2)^{1-\frac{1}{\alpha}}$ which implies (9.68) (with $p = \alpha$). Thus, there exists $\lambda \in \mathbf{R}$ such that $R_1 = \lambda R_2$ implying that

$$\nu_\alpha(R_1) = |\lambda|^\alpha \nu_\alpha(R_2).$$

Since $\nu_\alpha(R_1) = \nu_\alpha(R_2)$ by assumption, we have $\lambda = \pm 1$. On the other hand, if $\lambda = -1$, then by (9.70), it follows that $R_2 = 0$. Thus, $R_1 = R_2$. □

Lemma 9.1 Any *sαs* space E_α can be endowed with a basis e such that the covariation matrix $V_\alpha(e)$ with entries $[e_i; e_j]_\alpha$ is is invertible and triangular.

Proof. Let R be a basis of E_α.
Step 1. $e_1 = R_1$.
Step i ($i > 1$). Set $f(\lambda_1; \cdots; \lambda_{i-1}) = f(\lambda) = R_i - \sum_{j=1}^{i-1} \lambda_j e_j$. Then

$$\nu_\alpha(f(\lambda)) = \int_{S_i} \left| s_i - \sum_{j=1}^{i-1} \lambda_j s_j \right|^\alpha \Gamma_i(ds),$$

where Γ_i is the spectral measure of $(e_1, \dots, e_{i-1}, R_i)'$. Observe that $\nu_\alpha(f(\cdot))$ is differentiable and positive. Moreover, $\lim_{\|\lambda\| \to +\infty} \nu_\alpha(f(\lambda)) = +\infty$, except in the case where the spectral measure is concentrate on a set of the form $\{s : \sum_{j=1}^{i-1} \bar{\lambda}_j s_j = 0\}$, which contradicts $\sum_{j=1}^{i-1} \bar{\lambda}_j e_j \neq 0$, and thus, that R be a basis. Therefore,

$$A_i = \arg\min_{\lambda \in \mathbf{R}^{i-1}} \nu_\alpha(f(\lambda)) \neq \emptyset.$$

Let $e_i = f(\lambda^*)$ with $\lambda^* \in A_i$. Next, $\frac{\partial}{\partial \lambda_k} \nu_\alpha(f(\lambda^*)) = 0$ implies that $\int_{S_i} s_k (s_i - \sum_j \lambda_j^* s_j)^{(a-1)} \Gamma_i(ds) = 0$, which leads to $[e_k; e_i]_\alpha = 0$, for all $k < i$. Thus, $V_\alpha(e)$ is invertible triangular and e is a basis. □

Claim 9.3 If e is a basis of a *sαs* space, then, $r\theta = \nu_\alpha(\theta'e)$ is strictly convex.

Proof. Let $r(\theta) = \int_{S_k} |\theta's|^\alpha \Gamma_e(ds)$. Since $|\cdot|^\alpha$ is strictly convex, r is convex. We can have equality of $r(\lambda\theta_1 + (1 - \lambda)\theta_2)$ and $\lambda r(\theta_1) + (1 - \lambda)r(\theta_2)$ only if the spectral measure of Γ_e is concentrate on a set such that $\theta_1's = \theta_2's$. This implies that $\nu_\alpha((\theta^1 - \theta^2)'e) = \int_{S_2} |(\theta^1 - \theta^2)'s|^\alpha \Gamma_e(ds) = 0$, and $(\theta^1 - \theta^2)'e = 0$, which contradicts the hypothesis that e is a basis. □

Theorem 9.4 Let E_α be a $s\alpha s$ space and E_α^* its dual space (i.e., the set of all linear forms on E_α). Then for any $p \in \mathrm{E}_\alpha^*$ there exists an unique $\pi_0 \in \mathrm{E}_\alpha$ such that $p(\cdot) \equiv [\cdot; \pi_0]_\alpha$.

Proof. Let $e = (e_1, \cdots, e_k)'$ be a basis of E_α. For any $\theta \in \mathbf{R}^k$ set $r(\theta) = r_e(\theta), q(\theta) = p(\theta'e)$ and $f(\theta) = \frac{1}{\alpha}r(\theta) - q(\theta)$. Since q is linear and r strictly convex differentiable, f is strictly convex and differentiable. Consider $\min\{f(\theta) : \theta \in \mathbf{R}^k\}$. Since $\lim_{\|\theta\|\to+\infty} f(\theta) = +\infty$ (because $\alpha > 1$ and e is a basis), and f is strictly convex, there exists an unique $\theta_0 \in \operatorname{argmin} f$. Then for all i

$$\frac{\partial f}{\partial \theta_i}(\theta_0) = 0 = \frac{\partial}{\partial \theta_i}\left(\frac{1}{\alpha}\int_{S_k} |\theta_0 s|^\alpha \Gamma_e(ds) - q(\theta_0)\right).$$

This implies that

$$p(e_i) = \int_{S_k} s_i (\theta_0's)^{\alpha-1} \Gamma_e(ds) = [e_i; \theta_0 e]_\alpha.$$

Letting $\pi_0 = \theta_0'e$, we have $p(\cdot) \equiv [\cdot; \pi_0]_\alpha$. $\square$

Corollary 9.1 Let M be the span of the constant 1 and an finite dimensional $s\alpha s$-space E_α, and M^* be the dual space. Then, for any "price" functional $p \in M^*$ there exists an unique $\pi \in \mathrm{E}_\alpha$ such that

$$p(\cdot) = [\cdot; \pi]_\alpha.$$

9.6   The Stable Paretian Approach to Safety-first Analysis and Portfolio Choice Theory

The theory of portfolio choice is based on the assumption that investors allocate their wealth across the available assets in order to maximize their expected utility of final wealth, see for example Ingersoll (1987) and Duffie (1996).

Markowitz (1959) and Tobin (1958) proposed for nonsatiable risk averse individuals the following mean variance selection rule for the portfolio selection problem: "From among a given set of investment alternatives (which includes the set of securities available in the market as well as all possible linear combinations of these basic securities), the admissible set of alternatives is obtained by discarding those investments with a lower mean and a higher variance than a member of the given set"[14].

The stochastic dominance rules play an increasingly prominent role in the literature on choice under uncertainty. Their essence is to provide an admissible set of choices under restrictions on the utility functions that follow

---

[14]The results in Sections 9.6 – 9.9 are due to Ortobelli and Rachev (1999).

from prevalent and appealing modes of economic behavior. The admissible sets generated are useful for a large group of individual decision makers and the optimal choice for an individual can then be obtained from among the smaller set of admissible choices. Relaxing the classical assumptions on the distributions of the returns, one can use the stochastic dominance rules to obtain the efficient frontiers for nonsatiable investors, for risk averse investors and for nonsatiable risk averse investors.

Safety-first rule introduced by Roy (1952) for decision making under uncertainty stands in a marked contrast. It stipulates choice of an alternative that minimizes the probability of the return falling below some threshold of disaster. Roy's safety-first rule is generalized by Bawa (1976-78) to n^{th} order safety-first rules using higher order lower partial moments of the probability distributions. The practical appeal of the generalized safety-first rules is demonstrated by Bawa (1979). He shows that for realistic portfolio choice problems where the distribution of portfolio returns is unknown, these rules can be used by applying them to the empirical distribution of portfolio returns used in lieu of the true, but unknown, distribution. However, assuming safety-first utility functions to justify safety-first analysis is not very appealing since in that case the class of investors is restricted. We shall consider a distributional approach to underline the efficiency of the safety-first principle instead, see Ortobelli and Rachev (1999).

Principal objective of Sections 9.6 – 9.9 is studying and extending stable Paretian approach and safety-first analysis in portfolio selection theory in coherence with the empirical evidence and stochastic dominance theory. We introduce single-period models with the assumption of elliptical or α stable distributions of the returns. In particular, we introduce a new stable Paretian version of the Markowitz financial optimization model in order to find an optimal frontier based on a more realistic model for the distribution of asset returns. As a generalization of the stable approach we shall see that when the gross returns belong to an α stable family (with $1 \leq \alpha < 2$), we can calculate the efficient frontier for nonsatiable investors, risk averse investors and nonsatiable risk averse investors. As a further generalization we shall consider portfolio selection for investors who wish to allocate their initial wealth among n investments with returns following general heavy-tailed distributions. In this case, the efficient frontier for nonsatiable investors and for nonsatiable risk averse investors can be calculated using some stochastic dominance results.

Pyle and Turnovsky (1970-71), Bawa (1976-78) and more recently Dave and Stahl (1997), and Ortobelli (1999) show that when the returns belong to an elliptical family of distributions, safety-first analysis gives us the efficient mean-dispersion frontier. We shall introduce the concept of stochastic bounds and give a modern interpretation of safety-first analysis in terms of Value-at-Risk (VAR), see also next Chapter 10, Safety-first portfolios always belong to the nonsatiable investors' efficient frontier without particular assumptions on the distributions of returns. Under some regularity conditions on the distributions of returns we have certain equivalence rules between the not stochastically dominated sets, the set of safety-first portfolios, and the k parameter efficient frontier. Moreover, we give some conditions on the set of safety-first portfolios to get other equivalence rules and we show how we can inductively generalize safety-first approach. Besides, these regularity conditions are the implicit distributional assumptions needed to justify safety-first analysis.

Finally, we present two direct methods to express the safety-first portfolios. In one of them, given a certain family of distributions for the returns, we derive an implicit analytical formulation. In the other, given the marginal distributions of the primary gross returns, we use a "better" conjoint distribution, in the sense of Levhari, Paroush and Peleg (1970), to express the safety-first portfolios.

In the rest ot this section we recall the stochastic dominance rules and safety-first rules. In Section 9.7 we shall present the portfolio choice problem and the assumptions we make. There we shall also study the efficient frontier in the case of elliptical or sub-Gaussian stable distributions of the returns. In Section 9.8 we shall analyze the elliptical return distribution case in a safety-first world and study the stable Paretian efficient frontier. In Section 9.9 we shall present the multiparameter safety-first analysis. We shall study the implicit distributional motivations to safety-first analysis and define the portfolio choice in a safety first world.

A commonly accepted theory of asset choice under uncertainty that provides the underpinnings for the analysis of asset demands uses the expected utility hypothesis. Under this hypothesis, an individual's preferences have an expected utility representation if there exists a function u such that random consumption X is preferred to random consumption Y if and only if $E(u(X)) \geq E(u(Y))$, where $E(.)$ is the expectation under the individual's probability belief, see for example Ingersoll (1987), and Duffie (1996). The main formal approach to a theory of choice under uncertainty was introduced by von Neumann and Morgenstern (1953) and the resulting function u is thus called the von Neumann Morgenstern utility function. Let $\pi(x)$ be the probability density for a particular lottery, and let $\psi(x)$ the cardinal utility function of a consumer. Then *von Neumann Morgenstern (1953) (vNM)* utility functional over lotteries is defined by

$$Q[\pi(x)] = E(\psi(x)) = \int \psi(x)\pi(x)dx.$$

Hence, preferences can be expressed using ordinal utility; however, the domain of the ordinal utility functional is the set of lotteries. A vNM utility function has the properties of any ordinal utility function, but, in addition, it is a "cardinal" measure. That is, unlike ordinal utility the numerical value of utility has a precise meaning (up to a scaling) beyond the simple rank of the numbers. This fact can be easily proved as follows. Suppose there is a single good. Now compare a lottery paying the units from 0 to 9 with equal probability to one giving 4 units for sure. Under the utility function $u(x) = x$, the former, with an expected utility of $E(u(x)) = \sum_{i=0}^{9} \frac{i}{10} = 4.5$, would be preferred. But if we apply the increasing transformation $v(x) = \sqrt{x}$ the lottery has an expected utility of $E(v(x)) = \sum_{i=0}^{9} \frac{\sqrt{i}}{10} \cong 1.93$, whereas the certain payoff's utility is 2. This proved that arbitrary monotone transformations of cardinal utility functions do not preserve ordering over lotteries. When all lottery payoffs come from some common family of distributions, it is often possible to express this ordinal functional for lotteries as an ordinal utility function defined over parameters of the distributions of the lotteries. For example, if there is a single good, the consumer's cardinal utility function is $\psi(x) = \log x$, and the payoff from each lottery is α-stable distributed $S_\alpha(\sigma, \beta, \mu)$, see Section 2.1.1, then $Q[\pi(x)] = E(\psi(x)) = G(\sigma, \beta, \mu)$ where μ, β and σ now are the "goods". Since this is an ordinal utility function, choices can be expressed equivalently using an increasing function of $G(\sigma, \beta, \mu)$ (see the example in Ingersoll (1987)). Utility functions like this are often called derived utility functions.

It is possible to construct other functionals which satisfy all the axioms except the independence one. Interesting research in this area has been done by Machina (1982), Schmeidler (1989) and Gilboa and Schmeidler (1989). Generally, such utility functionals preserve the first degree stochastic dominance and have most of the properties of the vNM utility functions.

Risk aversion theory was introduced and developed principally by Arrow (1971) and Pratt (1964). Its foundation is the mainstream von Neumann Morgenstern expected utility paradigm. A decision maker with a vNM utility function is said to be risk averse at a particular wealth level if she is unwilling to accept every actuarially fair and immediately resolved gamble with only wealth consequences, that is, one that leaves consumption good prices unchanged. If the decision maker with vNM utility function $u(W)$ is risk averse at all (relevant) wealth levels, she is globally risk averse. Practically, for state-independent utility of wealth, the *utility function is risk averse at W* if

$$u(W) > u(W + \varepsilon)$$

for all gambles with ε not constant and $E(\varepsilon) = 0$. If this relation holds at all levels of wealth, then the utility function is said to be *globally risk averse*.

Theorem 9.5 *(Ingersoll (1987)).* A decision maker is (globally) risk averse, as just defined, if and only if her vNM utility function of wealth is strictly concave at the relevant (all) wealth levels.

We note that by Theorem 9.5 risk averse individuals may have utility functions that are not monotonically increasing. For this reason we generally consider increasing utility functions. Equivalently, we say that an *individual is nonsatiable* if and only if his utility function is non-decreasing, non-constant and for every admissible portfolio X admits finite expected value $E(u(X))$.

Besides, we are interested in utility functions in situations involving risk and for this reason we consider the following function sets:

(i) for nonsatiable individuals: H_1, which represents the non-decreasing, non-constant utility functions u such that for every admissible portfolio X the expected value $E(u(X))$ is finite;

(ii) for nonsatiable, risk averse individuals: H_2, the concave utility functions u belonging to H_1.

A risky asset X dominates risky asset Y in the sense of *first degree stochastic dominance*, denoted $X\ FSD\ Y$, if all individuals having utility functions in H_1 prefer X to Y. If for every fixed level t, comparing the X and $Y's$ distributions, we observe that X maximizes the right asymmetry, (i.e. we get the following probability relation $P(X \geq t) \geq P(Y \geq t)$), then intuition suggests that any nonsatiable individual will prefer X to Y. It turns out that this condition is not only sufficient but also necessary. In fact, the following equivalence theorem holds.

Theorem 9.6 *(first stochastic dominance rule)* The following three statements are equivalent:

(i) $X\ FSD\ Y$, i.e. for every $u \in H_1$ we have $E(u(X)) \geq E(u(Y))$ with strict inequality for some u.

(ii) For every real t, $F_X(t) = P(X \leq t) \leq F_Y(t) = P(Y \leq t)$, with strict inequality for some t.

(iii) $X \overset{d}{=} Y + \alpha$ where the random variable $\alpha \geq 0$ and $P(\alpha > 0) > 0$.

The problem is studied by Quirk and Saposnik (1962), Fishburn (1964), Hadar and Russell (1969) , Hanoh and Levy (1969) and Kroll and Levy (1982), see also Huang and Litzenberger (1988). A risky asset X dominates a risky asset Y in the sense of it second degree stochastic dominance, denoted by $X\ SSD\ Y$, if all risk averse nonsatiable individuals having utility functions in H_2 prefer X to Y. The following equivalence theorem holds.

Theorem 9.7 *(second stochastic dominance rule)* The following three statements are equivalent:

(i) $X\ SSD\ Y$, i.e. for every $u \in H_2$ we have $E(u(X)) \geq E(u(Y))$ with strict inequality for some u.

(ii) For every real t $\int_{-\infty}^{t} F_X(p)dp \leq \int_{-\infty}^{t} F_Y(p)dp$, with strict inequality for some t.

(iii) $Y \overset{d}{=} X - \alpha + \varepsilon$ where the random variable $\alpha \geq 0$; $P(\varepsilon \neq 0) > 0$ and $E(\varepsilon|X - \alpha) = 0$.

By this theorem it follows $E(X) \geq E(Y)$ whenever $X\ SSD\ Y$. The second stochastic dominance rule is studied by Fishburn (1964), Hadar and Russell

(1969-71), Hanoh and Levy (1969), Rothschild and Stiglitz (1970), and Kroll and Levy (1982), see also Huang and Litzenberg (1988).

The main studies on the relationships between risk aversion behavior and stochastic dominance rules are due to Rothschild and Stiglitz (1970) who have established the following relations.

Theorem 9.8 *(Rothschild Stiglitz stochastic dominance rule)* The following three statements are equivalent:

(i) For every concave utility function u we have $E(u(X)) \geq E(u(Y))$ with strict inequality for some u.

(ii) $E(X) = E(Y)$ and for every real t $\int\limits_{-\infty}^{t} F_X(p)dp \leq \int\limits_{-\infty}^{t} F_Y(p)dp$, with strict inequality for some t.

(iii) $Y \overset{d}{=} X + \varepsilon$ where $P(\varepsilon \neq 0) > 0$ and $E(\varepsilon|X) = 0$.

We observe that in the Rothschild-Stiglitz case the dominating portfolio has smaller variance than dominated portfolios because $var(Y) = var(X) + var(\varepsilon)$, but if we cannot say that portfolios have finite variance, we need other assumptions on the distributions to find similar relations. Besides, the Rothschild-Stiglitz stochastic dominance implies the second degree stochastic dominance between portfolios with the same expected value. Hence, by the above stochastic relation the following scheme holds:

$$\begin{array}{ccc} FSD & \Longrightarrow & SSD \\ Rothschild - Stiglitz & \Longrightarrow & SSD \end{array} \qquad (9.71)$$

Less general but with more practical tractability are the safety first rules introduced by Roy (1952) and studied and extended by Bawa (1975), (1976), (1978) and other authors. Roy (1952) defines the principle of Safety First and postulates that maximization of probability of survival can be used as a decision criterion to determine an optimal portfolio.

Definition 9.3 *(first safety-first rule)* When the decision maker chooses one of the risky portfolios X satisfying

$$X \in \arg(\min_{Y \in C} F_Y(t))$$

with t belonging to the real line and for which there does not exist another Z belonging to $\arg(\min_{Y \in C} F_Y(t))$ such that $Z\, SSD\, X$ (where C is the set of all possible portfolios), we say that the decision maker follows the first safety-first rule with threshold t.

This is Roy's safety-first rule with threshold of disaster t. To the original safety-first rule we add that there does not exist another $Z \in \arg(\min_{Y \in C} F_Y(t))$

such that $Z\ SSD\ X$. This addition implies that the investor chooses portfolios that are not dominated. The safety-first principle fails to order risky assets which are unambiguously ordered by the principle of absolute preference (i.e. a distribution G is preferred to a distribution F if $G\ FSD\ F$). Hence, the first safety-first rule gives portfolios that we can obtain ordering portfolios with the first stochastic dominance rule (1978).

Many extensions followed Roy's work. Roy's safety-first rule is generalized by Bawa (1976), (1978) using higher order lower partial moments of the probability distributions. Safety-first rules are practically tractable and computationally feasible for general convex choice sets among arbitrary probability distributions (see Bawa (1979)). A relevant and interesting form of the safety-first principle was studied by Arzac and Bawa (1977). They introduced the following lexicographic form of the safety-first principle.

Definition 9.4 *(Arzac and Bawa's safety-first rule)* Agents choose portfolios under the following lexicographic rule:

$$\max_x(\pi_x, \mu_x),$$

where

$$\pi_x = \begin{cases} 1, & \text{if } p = P(Y_x \le s) \le \alpha \ , \\ 1 - p, & \text{otherwise} \end{cases}$$

and

$$\mu_x = E(Y_x),$$

where Y_x is the random value of final wealth in a single period choice situation, s is the critical level of wealth and α is the admissible probability of failure. In the lexicographic form of the safety-first principle a decision maker orders any two assets lexicographically according to π and μ, that is, the asset with higher π is the preferred one. If π is the same for both assets, the order is based upon μ. Two assets with the same π and μ are equally preferred.

This choice criterion is reasonable in that it implies desirable attitudes toward risk according to the Arrow (1971) and Pratt (1964) theory of risk aversion. The criterion is incompatible with the axiom of continuity (see Ingersoll (1987), p. 20-21) and when $\alpha > 0$, it is also incompatible with the axiom of independence (see Ingersoll (1987), p. 30-31). This means that safety-first lexicographic rule represents the preferences of investors other than expected utility maximizers. Arzac and Bawa (1977) have shown that the safety-first lexicographic approach implies attitudes toward risk, portfolio choices and market equilibrium which are comparable to those implied by the expected utility approach.

9.7   The Portfolio Choice Problem

Suppose we have a frictionless market without arbitrage opportunities where all investors act as price takers. Suppose that all investors have the same temporal horizon at a fixed date in the future. Given n risky securities, let r be the rate of return of the ith security and with $z_i = 1 + r_i$ the gross return; all random variables are defined in a probability space $(\Omega, \Im, P)$. The random vector of the gross returns is:

$$z = [z_1, ..., z_n]', \tag{9.72}$$

We define the following sets of portfolio weights:

$$S_t = \left\{ x \in R^n : \sum_i x_i = 1, \ x_i \geq t, \ i = 1, ..., n \right\},$$

where t is an extended non-positive real number and for $t > -\infty$ the sets S_t indicate limited short sale opportunities in the market. The justification of a compact market S_t can be given considering that the possible operations in an interval of time are finite in number and of a finite value. When $t > -\infty$ the sets S_t are compact without considering the extended portfolios and for this reason we call the market a *compact market*. We denote by S^* the set S_t, if there are no restrictions on t. So, all the results valid for S^* are valid for $S_t, t \in [\infty, 0)$ We also call portfolio or gross return the quantity $x'z$. We use the following notation $F_{x'z}(t) = P(x'z \leq t)$ to indicate the cumulative distribution of the gross return $x'z$ and for fixed t we call it risk of loss of factor t. In fact, in view of Value-at-Risk calculations (see next Chapter 10), $F_{x'z}(t_\alpha) = \alpha$, $\alpha = .01$ or $\alpha = .05$ indicates that t_α is lower bound for the possible portofolio-loss at $\alpha 100\%$-level. We say that a family of distributions (random variables) is translation invariant if whenever the distribution $F(t)$ (random variable X) belongs to the family, the distribution $G(t) = F(t+p)$ (random variable $X - p$) belongs to the family of distributions (random variables) as well. We assume that for every fixed λ there exist portfolio weights $x(\lambda)$ and $y(\lambda)$ belonging to S^* such that $x(\lambda)$ belongs to $\arg(\inf_{x \in S^*} P(x'z \leq \lambda))$ and $y(\lambda)$ belongs to $\arg(\sup_{x \in S^*} P(x'z \leq \lambda))$.

The investor with vNM utility function u wants to know which portfolio weight belonging to S^* maximizes the expected value of his utility function. Consequently, she is interested in the following portfolio weight sets (that for obvious reasons are called efficient sets):

$$W_i := W_{i,S^*} = \{x \in S^* | \ (x \in \arg(\sup_{p \in S^*} E(u(p'z))); u \in H_i) \wedge \text{(does not exist}$$

$y \in \arg(\sup_{p \in S^*} E(u(p'z)))$ such that $E(v(y'z)) \geq E(v(x'z))$ for all $v \in H_i$

and strictly for some v), with $i = 1, 2$.

We write for simplicity W_i $(i = 1, 2)$ because we assume that the space of definition S^* is known. W_1 represents the set of the not first degree dominated portfolio weights that maximize the expected utility of nonsatiable investors, while W_2 represents the set of the not second degree dominated portfolio weights that maximize the expected utility of nonsatiable risk averse investors.

$$\widetilde{W} := \widetilde{W}_{S^*} = \{x \in S^* | \ (x \in \arg(\sup_{p \in S^*} E(u(p'z))); \ u \text{ concave function })$$
$$\wedge(\text{does not exist} y \in \arg(\sup_{p \in S^*} E(u(p'z))) \text{ such that } E(v(y'z)) \geq E(v(x'z)),$$
$$\text{for all concave functions } v, \text{ and strictly ">" for some } v)\}.$$

Similarly, $\widetilde{W}$ represents the set of the not dominated portfolio weights in the sense of Rothschild-Stiglitz (see Theorem 9.8) that maximize the expected utility of risk averse investors. We observe that, with these definitions of efficient sets, we implicitly accept that an investor with utility function $u \in H_i$ (i=1,2) chooses the portfolio that maximizes the expected utility and that is not dominated (first or second degree) by another portfolio. For this reason we consider the following category of efficient sets:

$$T_i := T_{i,S^*} = \{x \in S^* | \text{ does not exist } y \in S^* \text{ such that } E(v(y'z))$$
$$\geq E(v(x'z)) \text{ for all } v \in H_i, \text{ and strictly ">" for some } v)\}, \text{ with } i = 1, 2.$$

T_1 represents the set of the not first degree stochastically dominated portfolio weights and T_2 represents the set of the not second degree stochastically dominated portfolio weights. Let

$$\widetilde{T} := \widetilde{T}_{S^*} = \{x \in S^* | \text{ does not exist } y \in S^* \text{ such that } E(v(y'z))$$
$$\geq E(v(x'z)) \text{ for all } \text{ concave utility function} v$$
$$\text{and strictly ">" for some } v)\}.$$

Thus, $\widetilde{T}$ represents the set of the not dominated portfolio weights in the sense of Rothschild-Stiglitz. We also define the sets often called "the worst world":

$$A_i := A_{i,S^*} = \{x \in S^* | \text{ does not exist } y \in S^* \text{ such that } E(v(x'z))$$
$$\geq E(v(y'z)) \text{ for all } v \in H_i \text{ and strictly ">" for some } v)\}, \text{ with } i = 1, 2.$$

Hence, A_1 represents the set of the not first degree dominating portfolio weights and A_2 represents the set of the not second degree dominating portfolio weights.

By these definitions and as a consequence of the stochastic dominance we have:

$$T_1 \supseteq T_2, \widetilde{T} \supseteq T_2, W_1 \supseteq W_2, \widetilde{W} \supseteq W_2, A_1 \supseteq A_2, \widetilde{T} \supseteq \widetilde{W}, T_i \supseteq W_i, \ i = 1, 2,$$
$$(9.73)$$

where the space S^* is known. Because of the relations above the following remark holds.

Remark 9.4 The following two properties are equivalent, with $i = 1, 2$:

(i) $T_i = W_i$

(ii) For every y belonging to T_i we get $\bigcap\limits_{x \in S^*} H_{x,y,i} \neq \emptyset$, where

$$H_{x,y,i} = \{u \in H_i / E(u(y'z)) \geq E(u(x'z))\}, \; i = 1, 2.$$

So far we have shown that when there exists a portfolio of assets that stochastically dominates in the sense of Rothschild-Stiglitz all the portfolios which have the same expected gross return, then this dominant portfolio must have the minimum variance among all the portfolios. This observation is one of the motivations for characterizing those portfolios with minimum variance for various levels of expected gross return. This consideration started the Markowitz mean variance analysis (1959) which considers the not dominated portfolios in the sense of Rothschild-Stiglitz with minimum variance for a fixed mean.

Next we shall study the case of heavy-tailed distributed returns. We shall consider elliptical distributions and as a special case of them the sub-Gaussian symmetric stable distributions, see Section 7.1 for the definition of sub-Gaussian random variable.

We consider the vector of gross returns $z = [z_1, ..., z_n]'$ without the riskless gross return and we suppose that all gross returns with risk belong to a particular elliptical family not necessarily with a finite variance but with a finite expected value in coherence with the empirical evidence. We recall that z is said to be distributed *elliptically* if and only if the characteristic function of z is of the form

$$\Phi_z(t) = E(e^{it'z}) = \Psi(t'Qt)e^{it'\mu}, \; t \in \mathbf{R}^n, \tag{9.74}$$

where Q is a positive definite matrix (called dispersion matrix), and $\Psi : \mathbf{R} \to \mathbf{R}$.

Without too much loss of generality we can assume that the distributions admit densities. In fact, Kelker (1970) shows that the existence of the density is only a minor restriction since most elliptical distributions possess densities. Owen and Rabinowitch (1983) show that if a random vector X admits a density, then X possesses a scale location parameter distribution if and only if X has an elliptical distribution. Then we say that the gross returns $x'z$ with (or similarly a *risky portfolio return*) risk belong to a family of elliptical distributions not necessarily with a finite variance (a family determined by the non-negative integrable function $g(y)$) if they have the following distribution:

$$P(x'z \leq \lambda) = \int\limits_{-\infty}^{\lambda} \frac{1}{|K| C_0 (x'Qx)^{1/2}} g\left(\frac{(t - x'\mu)^2}{K^2 x'Qx}\right) dt, \tag{9.75}$$

where μ is the mean gross return vector; Q is the finite, nonsingular dispersion matrix of the primary assets; K is a constant; and

$$C_0 := \int\limits_{-\infty}^{+\infty} \frac{1}{|K| (x'Qx)^{1/2}} g\left(\frac{(t - x'\mu)^2}{K^2 x'Qx}\right) dt. \tag{9.76}$$

Clearly, the elliptical distribution defined by (9.75) is symmetric around $x'\mu$.

Owen and Rabinowitch (1983) show that classic results of CAPM can be obtained assuming return distributions belong to an elliptical family of distributions not necessarily with a finite variance. In particular, the following dominance rules are verified under the assumption of elliptical distributions of the returns:

(i) *Elliptical stochastic order for nonsatiable investors.* Suppose portfolio $x'z$ has the same dispersion as $y'z$, and a lower expected value than $y'z$. Then for every λ, $\frac{\lambda - y'\mu}{(y'Qy)^{1/2}} \le \frac{\lambda - x'\mu}{(x'Qx)^{1/2}}$, and

$$P(y'z \le \lambda) = \int_{-\infty}^{\frac{\lambda - y'\mu}{(y'Qy)^{1/2}}} \frac{1}{|K|C_0} g\left(\frac{w^2}{K^2}\right) dt$$

$$\le \int_{-\infty}^{\frac{\lambda - x'\mu}{(x'Qx)^{1/2}}} \frac{1}{|K|C_0} g\left(\frac{w^2}{K^2}\right) dt = P(x'z \le \lambda), \forall \lambda \in R.$$

(9.77)

Thus, portfolio $y'z$ FSD $x'z$. If we maximize the expected return for a fixed dispersion we get portfolios not first degree stochastically dominated (hence belonging to T_1).

(ii) *Elliptical stochastic order for risk averse investors.* Given two gross returns $y'z$, and $x'z$ with the same mean $y'\mu = x'\mu = m$ and dispersion relation $x'Qx > y'Qy$, we have

$$\int_{-\infty}^{u} P(y'z \le \lambda) - P(x'z \le \lambda)d\lambda = \int_{-\infty}^{u} \left[\int_{\frac{\lambda - m}{(x'Qx)^{1/2}}}^{\frac{\lambda - m}{(y'Qy)^{1/2}}} \frac{1}{|K|C_0} g\left(\frac{w^2}{K^2}\right) dt \right] d\lambda \le 0,$$

(9.78)

for every real u with strict inequality for some u, because

$$p(\lambda) = \int_{\frac{\lambda - m}{(x'Qx)^{1/2}}}^{\frac{\lambda - m}{(y'Qy)^{1/2}}} \frac{1}{|K|C_0} g\left(\frac{w^2}{K^2}\right) dt = p(m + (\lambda - m)) = -p(m - (\lambda - m)).$$

Hence, $y'z$ dominates $x'z$ in the sense of Rothschild-Stiglitz (and also $y'z$ SSD $x'z$). If we minimize the dispersion for a fixed mean we get portfolios not dominated in the sense of Rothschild-Stiglitz (hence belonging to $\widetilde{T}$).

(iii) *Elliptical stochastic order for nonsatiable risk averse investors.* Given two gross returns $y'z$, and $x'z$ with mean relation $y'\mu \ge x'\mu$ and dispersion relation $x'Qx \ge y'Qy$ where at least one inequality is strict, we

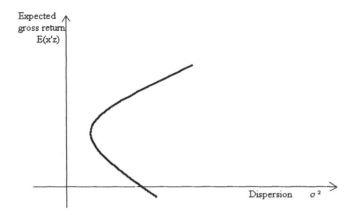

Fig. 9.2 Dispersion-Mean efficient frontier for risk averse investors. (Adapted from: Ortobelli, Rachev (1999))

deduce that

$$y'zSSDx'z \text{ and } x'z \overset{d}{=} y'z - (E(y'z) - E(x'z)) + \varepsilon, \text{ where } E(\varepsilon|y'z) = 0. \tag{9.79}$$

If we consider a random variable X, with $E(X) = E(x'z)$, having the same dispersion as $y'z$ and such that $X \overset{d}{=} y'z - E(y'z) + E(X)$, then X belongs to the same translation invariant family of elliptical distributions. By Theorem 9.8 and (9.78) we deduce that X dominates $x'z$ in the sense of Rothschild-Stiglitz (or equivalently $x'z \overset{d}{=} X + \varepsilon$ with $E(\varepsilon|X) = 0$) and by (9.77) it follows that $y'z$ FSD X SSD $x'z$. Hence, considering (9.71) and the transitivity property of stochastic dominance rules we get $y'z$ SSD $x'z$ and relation (9.79) follows. If we intersect the portfolios obtained by t(i) and (ii) we get portfolios not second degree stochastically dominated (hence belonging to T_2).

Under the elliptical assumption on the distribution we know that the dispersion $x'Qx$ of the portfolio with weight x is a measure of the risk. Hence, the portfolios in the following theorem and corollary are the not dominated portfolios in the sense of Rothschild-Stiglitz and belong to the classic extended Markowitz-Tobin mean-dispersion frontier.

Theorem 9.9 Suppose there are $n \geq 2$ risky assets traded in a frictionless economy where unlimited short selling is allowed and suppose the gross returns belong to the same elliptical family with nonsingular dispersion matrix Q. It is also assumed that the random gross return on any asset cannot be expressed as a linear combination of the gross returns on other assets. Then the solutions of the constrained problem:

$$
\begin{cases}
\min_{x \in S_{-\infty}} x'Qx \\
x'e = 1 \\
x'\mu = m
\end{cases}
$$

are all the portfolio weights x belonging to $S_{-\infty}$ satisfying the following analytical relation:

$$
x = \frac{(CQ^{-1}\mu - BQ^{-1}e)m + AQ^{-1}e - BQ^{-1}\mu}{AC - B^2}. \tag{9.80}
$$

Equivalently, in the mean-dispersion plane we have the relationship (Figure 9.2)

$$
\sigma^2(AC - B^2) - m^2C + 2mB - A = 0, \tag{9.81}
$$

where $\mu = E(z)$; $m = x'\mu$; $e = [1, ..., 1]'$; $A = \mu'Q^{-1}\mu$; $B = e'Q^{-1}\mu$; $C = e'Q^{-1}e$, and $\sigma^2 = x'Qx$.

Proof. The demonstration is the same as in the case of a finite variance (see Huang and Litzenberg (1988)). □

When we consider the presence of the riskless return we have the following corollary.

Corollary 9.2 Under the assumptions of the above theorem, the solutions of the following constrained problem

$$
\begin{cases}
\min_{x \in S_{-\infty}} x'Qx \\
x'\mu + (1 - x'e)z_0 = m
\end{cases}
$$

are all the portfolio weights x belonging to $S_{-\infty}$ satisfying the following analytical relation:

$$
x = Q^{-1}(\mu - z_0e)\frac{m - z_0}{A - 2Bz_0 + Cz_0^2}, \tag{9.82}
$$

or equivalently in the mean-standard deviation plane we have the relationship (Figure 9.3)

$$
\sigma = \begin{cases}
\frac{m - z_0}{\sqrt{A - 2Bz_0 + Cz_0^2}}, & \text{if } m \geq z_0, \\
-\frac{m - z_0}{A - 2Bz_0 + Cz_0^2}, & \text{if } m < z_0,
\end{cases}
$$

where $\mu = E(z)$; $m = x'\mu + x_0z_0$; x_0 is the quote of the riskless asset; $e = [1, ..., 1]'$; $A = \mu'Q^{-1}\mu$; $B = e'Q^{-1}\mu$; $C = e'Q^{-1}e$, and $\sigma^2 = x'Qx$.

Proof. See Huang and Litzenberg (1988). □

Similarly we can solve optimization problems to obtain the efficient frontiers for nonsatiable investors and for non satiable risk averse investors.

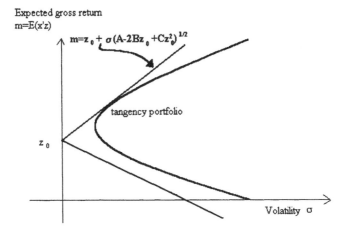

Fig. 9.3 Volatility-Mean efficient frontier for risk averse investors. (Adapted from: Ortobelli, Rachev (1999))

We observe that when the vector $z = [z_1, ..., z_n]'$ is sub-Gaussian symmetric (around its average μ) α-stable distributed $(1 < \alpha < 2)$, its characteristic function has the form

$$\Phi_z(t) = E(e^{it'z}) = e^{-(t'Qt)^{\alpha/2}+it'\mu}, \tag{9.83}$$

where Q is a positive definite matrix . Then a sub-Gaussian symmetric α-stable distribution is certainly elliptical. Moreover, since the density of a stable law always exists (see Samorodnitsky and Taqqu (1994)) a sub-Gaussian α-stable distribution, see Section 7.1, admits a representation (9.75). In particular, see Section 7.1, Press (1972c),(1982), and Ziemba (1974), we have that the dispersion matrix is given by $Q = \left[\frac{R_{i,j}}{2}\right]$. The terms $R_{i,j}$ are defined by

$$\frac{R_{i,j}}{2} = [z_i, z_j]_\alpha \, \|z_j\|_\alpha^{2-\alpha} \,,$$

where the covariation between two $(z_i$ and $z_j)$ jointly symmetric stable distributions is defined as

$$[z_i, z_j]_\alpha = \int_{S_2} s_i \, |s_j|^{\alpha-1} \, \text{sgn}(s_j)\Gamma(ds),$$

$$\text{in particular } \|z_i\|_\alpha = \left(\int_{S_2} |s_i|^\alpha \, \Gamma(ds)\right)^{\frac{1}{\alpha}} = ([z_i, z_i]_\alpha)^{1/\alpha} \,,$$

(here Γ is the spectral measure and its support is concentrated on the 2-dimensional unit sphere S_2, see Section 7.1).

All the portfolio weights from (9.80) or (9.82) are not dominated in the sense of Rothschild-Stiglitz. In fact, by the elliptical stochastic order rule for risk averse investors every not dominated portfolio in the sense of Rothschild-Stiglitz must have minimum dispersion for a fixed mean. Hence, the portfolio weights of (9.80) and (9.82) belong to $\widetilde{T}$. Markowitz (1959) and Tobin (1958) define the efficient frontier for nonsatiable risk averse investors whose portfolio distributions are univocally characterized by mean and variance that can be expressed now by the following generalized mean-dispersion dominance rule. We say that in the market the portfolios are ordered following the *mean-dispersion dominance rule* if for every couple of portfolios $x'z$ and $y'z$ with $E(y'z) \geq E(x'z)$ and $x'Qx \geq y'Qy$, where at least one inequality is strict, $y'z$ is preferable to $x'z$. Then we say that $y'z$ dominates $x'z$.

Clearly, the Markowitz-Tobin rule finds justification in the stochastic dominance rule (iii) (see (9.79)). By applying this rule to all admissible portfolios we get the Markowitz-Tobin efficient frontier, i.e. the second degree not stochastically dominated portfolios. The portfolios whose portfolio weights satisfy (9.80) or (9.82) are called *frontier portfolios* or *portfolios on the Markowitz-Tobin frontier*. We call *Markowitz-Tobin efficient frontier* the set of portfolios optimal in the sense of the mean-dispersion dominance rule, instead. Hence, the efficient frontier for portfolio weights without considering the riskless return is given by:

$$x = \frac{(CQ^{-1}\mu - BQ^{-1}e)m + AQ^{-1}e - BQ^{-1}\mu}{AC - B^2} \text{ with } m \geq \frac{B}{C}, \qquad (9.84)$$

and the efficient frontier for portfolio weights considering the riskless return is given by:

$$x = Q^{-1}(\mu - z_0 e)\frac{m - z_0}{A - 2Bz_0 + Cz_0^2} \text{ with } m \geq z_0. \qquad (9.85)$$

A preference for expected return and aversion to dispersion is implied by monotonicity and strict concavity of an individual's utility function. However, for arbitrary distributions and utility functions, expected utility cannot be defined just over the expected returns and dispersions.

Using Hanoh and Levy (1969), Bawa (1975), Rothschild and Stiglitz (1970), results (9.77), (9.78) and (9.79) explicitly show that when the gross returns belong to an elliptical family with a nonsingular dispersion matrix, the mean-dispersion dominance rule is equivalent to the second stochastic dominance rule. Equivalently, if the gross returns belong to an elliptical family, then

$$Markowitz\text{-}Tobin\ frontier = \widetilde{T}, \qquad (9.86)$$

$$Markowitz\text{-}Tobin\ efficient\ frontier = T_2. \qquad (9.87)$$

From Figure 9.2 and Figure 9.4 we can clearly see that the Markowitz-Tobin frontier strictly contains the Markowitz-Tobin efficient frontier. Besides, Bawa (1976) studies the nonsatiable efficient frontier for elliptical distributions of

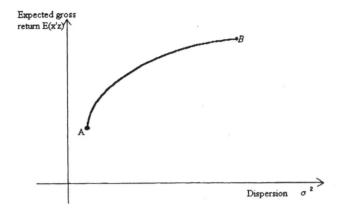

Fig. 9.4 Dispersion-Mean efficient frontier for non-satiable risk averse investors (Adapted from: Ortobelli, Rachev (1999))

the gross returns distinguishing the case of a compact market (for $t > -\infty$, the sets S_t are compact) from the unlimited short sale opportunity ($t = -\infty$). In fact, if unlimited short selling is allowed, then

$$\widetilde{T} = T_2 = Markowitz\text{-}Tobin \ efficient \ frontier. \qquad (9.88)$$

If the market is compact and the distributions of the returns are elliptical, the efficient frontier T_1 for nonsatiable investors (investors with utility function belonging to H_1) generally contains properly the efficient frontier T_2 for nonsatiable risk averse investors (that is an arch of the Markowitz-Tobin efficient frontier). In fact, Bawa (1976) described the mean-variance efficient frontier for nonsatiable investors and for a compact market without short sale opportunities identifying all admissible efficient portfolios as the mean-variance admissible portfolio plus a set of maximum variance portfolios. Here, we generalize the compact set of admissible portfolios and the mean-dispersion analysis (dispersion not necessarily variance). When we have a compact market with limited short sale opportunities (i.e. portfolio weights belonging to a compact set S_v), considering nonsatiable investors, the portfolio weight efficient frontier T_1 is compact, but it is not necessarily convex. This implies that under equilibrium conditions the market portfolio does not necessarily belong to the efficient frontier when we consider nonsatiable investors in a compact market. Convexity is guaranteed when the admissible portfolio with maximum dispersion σ^* is the admissible portfolio with maximum expected return $m^* = \dfrac{B + \left((C\sigma^* - 1)\left(AC - B^2\right)\right)^{1/2}}{C}$ and hence belongs to the Markowitz-Tobin efficient frontier. In this case, as shown in Bawa (1976), the efficient frontier for nonsatiable investors is coincident with the Markowitz-Tobin efficient frontier. Hence, in a compact market we can generally distinguish the

efficient frontier for nonsatiable risk averse investors from the efficient frontier
for nonsatiable investors where there can exist portfolios with the same mean
and different dispersion.

We observe that the Markowitz portfolio weights frontier (9.80) and (9.82)
is a closed convex set (in both cases) that can be generated by any two distinct frontier portfolio weights. Thus, if individuals prefer frontier portfolios
they can simply hold a linear combination of two frontier portfolios or mutual
funds. In that case, given any feasible portfolio, there exists a portfolio of
two mutual funds which individuals prefer at least as much as the original
portfolio. This phenomenon is termed *two fund separation*. Fund separation theory is introduced by Tobin (1958) and Markowitz (1959), important
improvements are given by Cass and Stiglitz (1970), and Ross (1978).

When returns have elliptical distributions and investors hold minimum dispersion portfolios, we have that two fund separation holds. So we can obtain
the classic equilibrium line of the capital asset pricing model for elliptical
distributions of the returns as shown by Owen and Rabinowitch (1983).

9.8   Stochastic Bounds and Two Parameter Safety-first Analysis

Assuming safety-first utility functions to justify safety-first analysis is not very
appealing, since in that case we consider only a restricted class of investors.
In fact, for every λ the *safety-first utility function* $u_\lambda(t) = I_{(\lambda,+\infty)}(x)$ (i.e. a
function equal to one for x in $(\lambda, +\infty)$, and zero otherwise) belongs to H_1 and

$$\arg\left(\sup_{x \in S^*} E(u_\lambda(x'z))\right) = \arg\left(\inf_{x \in S^*} P(x'z \leq \lambda)\right). \qquad (9.89)$$

Hence, we get the general property (proved by Bawa (1978)): "When there
exists a portfolio weight $x(\lambda) \in \arg\left(\inf_{x \in S^*} P(x'z \leq \lambda)\right)$, it belongs to W_1",
and

$$T_1 \supseteq W_1 \supseteq U. \qquad (9.90)$$

Starting from Bawa's (1976-78) and Roy's (1952) considerations we want
to see if by relaxing the hypothesis on the distributions of the returns, we
can get some relations among the efficient sets and the following safety-first
portfolio weights sets:

$$U := U_{S^*} = \left\{ x \in S^* \middle| \left(\exists \lambda \in R : x = x(\lambda) \in \arg\left(\inf_{x \in S^*} P(y'z \leq \lambda)\right)\right)\right.$$
$$\left. \wedge \left(\text{does not exist } w_1 \in \arg\left(\inf_{x \in S^*} P(x'z \leq \lambda)\right) \text{ such that } w'zSSDx'(\lambda)z\right)\right\}$$

(portfolio weights not dominated in the sense of the safety-first rule) and the set:

$$V := V_{S^*} = \left\{ y \in S^* | \left(\exists \lambda \in R : y = y(\lambda) \in \arg\left(\sup_{x \in S^*} P(x'z \le \lambda) \right) \right) \right.$$

$$\wedge \text{ does not exist } w_2 \in \arg\left(\sup_{x \in S^*} P(x'z \le \lambda) \right)$$

$$\left. \text{such that } y'(\lambda)z \; SSD \; w_2'(\lambda)z \right\}$$

(portfolio weights not dominating in the sense of the safety-first rule).

Firstly, we see that analogously to (9.90) the not dominating portfolio weights in the sense of safety-first rule $y(\lambda) \in \arg\left(\sup_{x \in S^*} P(x'z \le \lambda) \right)$ belong to the set of worst portfolio weights A_1.

Remark 9.5 Given a portfolio weight $y(\lambda)$ belonging to V, there does not exist a portfolio weight that is first degree stochastically dominated by $y(\lambda)$. Hence, $y(\lambda)$ belongs to A_1.

When for some λ_1, λ_2 we have $x(\lambda_1) = y(\lambda_2)$, then the portfolio weight belongs to $A_1 \cap W_1$. For example, as we can see below, if the distribution of the returns belongs to an elliptical family and we suppose that W_1 is a closed set, then the unique portfolio weight belonging to $A_1 \cap W_1$ is the global minimum dispersion portfolio:

$$x(-\infty) = y(+\infty) = \frac{Q^{-1}e}{C},$$

(where by $x(\infty)$ and $y(\infty)$ we mean the limit classes $\lim_{t \to \infty} x(t)$ or $\lim t \to \infty y(t)$, (see Figure 9.5).

As a consequence of (9.90) we can assume that U is the efficient set of the market that we want to study. In this case, we say that we are in a *safety first market (world)*. When for every λ there exist at most a portfolio weight $x(\lambda)$ belonging to $\arg(\min_x P(x'z \le \lambda))$, we usually call the safety first analysis (world) *one-dimensional safety-first analysis (world)*. In this case if for some distinct λ_i, λ_j the correspondent portfolio weights $x(\lambda_i) = \arg(\inf_x P(x'z \le \lambda_i))$ and $x(\lambda_j) = \arg(\inf_x P(x'z \le \lambda_j))$ are equal, then we have

$$\arg(\inf_x P(x'z \le \lambda_i)) = \arg(\inf_x P(x'z \le \lambda_j)) \tag{9.91}$$

As we could see below, typical example of one-dimensional safety-first market is when we have elliptical distributions of the returns.

In a market with limited short selling opportunities (a compact market) we can see that the gross returns are stochastically bounded. When we study a safety-first market, we can analytically express the distribution of the best bounds. Clearly, this bounds are related to the function $F(\lambda) = \inf_{y \in S^*} P(y'z \le$

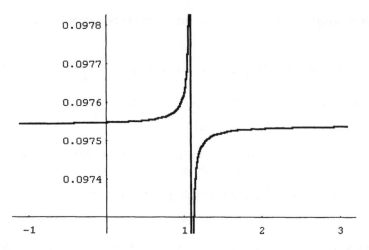

Fig. 9.5 VAR-mean frontier when the returns belong to an elliptical family of distributions. (Adapted from: Ortobelli, Rachev (1999))

λ), the respective portfolio weights $x(\lambda) \in \arg\left(\inf_{y \in S^*} P(y'z \le \lambda)\right)$, and the

function $G(\lambda) = Q(\lambda^+)$, where $Q(\lambda) = \sup_{y \in S^*} P(y'z \le \lambda)$ and the respective

portfolio weights $y(\lambda) \in \arg\left(\sup_{y \in S^*} P(y'z \le \lambda)\right)$. The next theorem is due to

Ortobelli (1999).

Theorem 9.10 Suppose there are $n \ge 2$ risky assets. The functions $F(\lambda) = \inf_{y \in S^*} P(y'z \le \lambda)$ and $G(\lambda) = Q(\lambda^+)$ are non-decreasing right continuous
functions. In particular, considering $a = \sup_x c(x)$, $b = \sup_x d(x)$, $\tilde{a} = \inf_x c(x)$,

and $\tilde{b} = \inf_x d(x)$, where

$$c(x) = \sup\left\{c \in \overline{R} | P(x'z \le c) = 0\right\}, \ d(x) = \inf\left\{d \in \overline{R} | P(x'z > d) = 0\right\},$$

we get

$$F(\lambda) = 0 \text{ for } \lambda < a; \ F(a) \ge 0; 0 < F(\lambda) < 1 \text{ for } \lambda \in (a, b), \qquad (9.92)$$

$$G(\tilde{a}) \ge 0; 0 < G(\lambda) < 1 \text{ for } \lambda \in (\tilde{a}, \tilde{b}); \text{ and } G(\lambda) = 1 \text{ for } \lambda \ge \tilde{b}. \qquad (9.93)$$

When we consider the riskless portfolio, we have $\tilde{a} \ge z_0$ and $\tilde{b} \le z_0$. Moreover,
if the portfolio weights belong to a compact set, then the function $F(\lambda)$ is the

first distribution first degree stochastically dominating all the gross returns and is defined in the domain :

$$F(\lambda) = 0 \text{ for } \lambda < a; \ F(a) \geq 0; \ 0 < F(\lambda) < 1$$
$$\text{for } \lambda \in (a,b); F(\lambda) = 1 \text{ for } \lambda \geq b. \tag{9.94}$$

Similarly, if the portfolio weights belong to a compact set, then the function $G(\lambda)$ is that is first degree stochastically dominated by all the gross returns and is defined in the domain:

$$G(\lambda) = 0 \text{ for } \lambda < \tilde{a}; \ G(\tilde{a}) \geq 0 \ ; \ 0 < G(\lambda) < 1$$
$$\text{for } \lambda \in (\tilde{a}, \tilde{b}) \ ; \text{ and } G(\lambda) = 1 \text{ for } \lambda \geq \tilde{b}. \tag{9.95}$$

When we consider portfolio weights belonging to a compact set we call $F(\lambda)$ the *stochastically dominating distribution* and $G(\lambda)$ the *stochastically dominated distribution*. We assume there exist two random variables Y_1 and Y_2 with respectively the stochastically dominating distribution $F(\lambda)$ and the stochastically dominated distribution $G(\lambda)$. We call the random variable Y_1

$$Y_1 : (\Omega, \Im, P) \longrightarrow \left(B_{[a,b]}, [a,b]\right) \tag{9.96}$$

preferential market growth and the random variable Y_2

$$Y_2 : (\Omega, \Im, P) \longrightarrow \left(B_{[\tilde{a},\tilde{b}]}, [\tilde{a}, \tilde{b}]\right) \tag{9.97}$$

the worst market growth (where $B_{[a^*,b^*]}$ is the Borel σ-field on the interval $[a^*, b^*]$). Generically, we call Y_1 and Y_2 stochastic bounds of the gross returns.

We consider the following sets of random variables:

$$B_1 = \{admissible \ random \ variables \ Y|$$
$$\forall u \in H_1, \forall x \in S^*, E(u(Y)) \geq E(u(x'z))\} \tag{9.98}$$

and

$$B_2 = \{admissible \ random \ variables \ Y|$$
$$\forall u \in H_1, \forall x \in S^*, E(u(x'z)) \geq E(u(Y)).\} \tag{9.99}$$

We see that Y_1 and Y_2 belong respectively to B_1 and B_2. Hence, Y_1 FSD $x'z$ Y_2 for every portfolio weight x belonging to S^*. In particular, we have that for every Y belonging to B_1, with distribution different from that of Y_1, Y FSD Y_1 and for every X belonging to B_2, with distribution different from that of Y_2, Y_2 FSD X. In this sense Y_1 and Y_2 are the stochastic bounds of the gross returns. Next we restrict our attention to a one-parameter safety-first world and we derive the functions $F(\lambda)$ and $G(\lambda)$ when the returns belong to an elliptical family of distributions that admit densities. Hence, if we consider the vector z of the gross returns without the riskless gross return and suppose that all gross returns with risk belong to a particular elliptical family not necessarily with a finite variance, then by transformation (9.77) we understand that

$$x(\lambda) = \arg(\inf P(x'z \leq \lambda)) = \arg(\inf(\frac{\lambda - x'\mu}{(x'Qx)^{1/2}})). \tag{9.100}$$

In the following theorem we express analytically the portfolios that minimize and maximize the risk of loss of value of factor λ when we have a return belonging to an elliptical family of distributions. The theorem was proved by Pyle and Turnovsky (1970-71) in the case of a normal distribution and generalized by Bawa (1976-78) to an elliptical family of distributions.

Theorem 9.11 Suppose there are $n \geq 2$ risky assets traded in a frictionless economy where unlimited short selling is allowed. If the gross returns belong to an elliptical family and the dispersion matrix is not singular, then for every real number λ all the portfolios satisfying the first order conditions of the constrained problem

$$\left\{ \begin{array}{l} \inf_{x \in S_{-\infty}} P(x'z \leq \lambda) \\ x'e = 1 \end{array} \right. \tag{9.101}$$

are portfolios of the mean-dispersion frontier

$$\sigma^2(AC - B^2) - m^2 C + 2mB - A = 0, \tag{9.102}$$

whose corresponding portfolio weights satisfy the following equivalent formulation of (9.80)

$$\begin{aligned} x &= \frac{(CQ^{-1}\mu - BQ^{-1}e)\sigma^2 + mQ^{-1}e - Q^{-1}\mu}{mC - B} = \\ &= \frac{(BQ^{-1}\mu - AQ^{-1}e)\sigma^2 + m^2 Q^{-1}e - mQ^{-1}\mu}{mB - A}, \end{aligned}$$

where $\mu = E(z)$; $m = x'\mu$; $e = [1, ..., 1]'$; $A = \mu' Q^{-1}\mu$; $B = e'Q^{-1}\mu$; $C = e'Q^{-1}e$, and $\sigma^2 = x'Qx$. Conversely, for every portfolio belonging to the mean-dispersion frontier (9.102) there exists an extended real number λ for which the portfolio satisfies the first order condition of (9.101). In particular, the global minimum dispersion portfolio weight $x = \frac{Q^{-1}e}{C}$ is the portfolio weight corresponding to the constrained problem (9.101) for $\lambda = \pm\infty$.

Proof. Solving the constrained problem $\inf(\frac{\lambda - x'\mu}{(x'Qx)^{1/2}})$, subject to $x'e = 1$, gives the results. See Bawa (1976), Pyle and Turnovsky (1970),(1971). $\square$

In the last years with the development of the concepts of Value at Risk the specialists interpret λ as an indicator of the tolerance at the level of risk, see also next Chapter 10. For this reason when mean-dispersion analysis is efficient we can rewrite one-parameter safety-first analysis as *VAR-mean analysis* or *VAR-dispersion analysis*.

The following result is a corollary from Theorem 9.11

Corollary 9.3 Under the assumptions of the above theorem we can express the portfolios satisfying the first order conditions of the constrained problem (9.101) in the following ways:

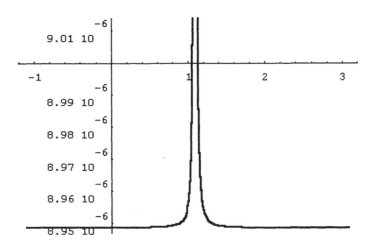

Fig. 9.6 VAR-dispersion frontier when the returns belong to an elliptical family of distributions. (Adapted from: Ortobelli, Rachev (1999))

(i) In the plane (λ, m) (see Figure 9.5):

$$m = \frac{\lambda B - A}{\lambda C - B};\tag{9.103}$$

(ii) In the plane (λ, σ) (see Figure 9.6):

$$\sigma^2 = \frac{\lambda^2 C - 2\lambda B + A}{(\lambda C - B)^2};\tag{9.104}$$

(iii) In the space (λ, σ, m):

$$\lambda = \frac{m^2 - \sigma^2 A}{m - \sigma^2 B} = \frac{m - \sigma^2 B}{1 - \sigma^2 C}.\tag{9.105}$$

Practically, with λ fixed, we can find the corresponding portfolio weights $x(\lambda)$, $y(\lambda)$ that minimize and maximize the risk of loss of value and calculate the corresponding risks of loss $F(\lambda) = \inf_{y \in S^*} P(y'z \leq \lambda)$ and $G(\lambda) = \sup_{y \in S^*} P(y'z \leq \lambda)$. In fact, the following corollary holds.

Corollary 9.4 Under the assumptions of Theorem 9.11 the solutions of the constrained problem (9.101) are given by the efficient portfolio weight of the Markowitz-Tobin efficient frontier and can be expressed as a function of the VAR λ:

$$x(\lambda) = \begin{cases} \frac{\lambda Q^{-1}e - Q^{-1}\mu}{\lambda C - B}, & \text{for } \lambda < \frac{B}{C}, \\ \lim_{t \to +\infty} \frac{(CQ^{-1}\mu - BQ^{-1}e)t + AQ^{-1}e - BQ^{-1}\mu}{AC - B^2}, & \text{for } \lambda \geq \frac{B}{C}, \end{cases}\tag{9.106}$$

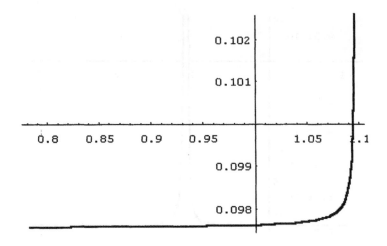

Fig. 9.7   VAR-mean efficient frontier. (Adapted from: Ortobelli, Rachev (1999))

in the (λ, m) plane Figure 9.7

$$m(\lambda) = \begin{cases} \frac{\lambda B - A}{\lambda C - B}, & \text{for } \lambda < \frac{B}{C}, \\ +\infty, & \text{for } \lambda \geq \frac{B}{C}, \end{cases} \qquad (9.107)$$

and in the (λ, σ) plane with the formula Figure 9.8

$$\sigma^2(\lambda) = \begin{cases} \frac{\lambda^2 C - 2\lambda B + A}{(\lambda C - B)^2}, & \text{for } \lambda < \frac{B}{C}, \\ +\infty, & \text{for } \lambda \geq \frac{B}{C}. \end{cases} \qquad (9.108)$$

Besides, we have that for every λ the corresponding minimum risk of loss of value is given by:

$$F(\lambda) = \begin{cases} \displaystyle\int\limits_{(-\infty,\lambda)} \frac{\lambda C - B}{|K|U(\lambda^2 C - 2\lambda B + A)^{1/2}} g\left(\frac{(t\lambda^2 C - -tB - \lambda B + A)^2}{K^2(\lambda^2 C - 2\lambda B + A)}\right) dt, \\ \qquad\qquad\qquad\qquad\qquad\qquad \text{for } \lambda < \frac{B}{C}, \\ \displaystyle\lim_{q \to \left(\frac{B}{C}\right)^-} \int\limits_{(-\infty,\lambda)} \frac{qC - B}{|K|U(q^2 C - 2qB + A)^{1/2}} g\left(\frac{(tq^2 C - -tB - qB + A)^2}{K^2(q^2 C - 2qB + A)}\right) dt, \\ \qquad\qquad\qquad\qquad\qquad\qquad \text{for } \lambda \geq \frac{B}{C}. \end{cases}$$
$$(9.109)$$

Proof. The results follow from Theorem 9.11.   □

Similarly, for the worst world we get the following theorem.

Theorem 9.12 Under the assumptions of Theorem 9.11 the solutions to the constrained problem

$$\begin{cases} \sup\limits_{x \in S_{-\infty}} P(x'z \leq \lambda) \\ x'e = 1 \end{cases} \qquad (9.110)$$

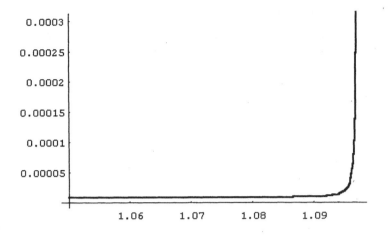

Fig. 9.8 VAR-dispersion efficient frontier. (Adapted from: Ortobelli, Rachev (1999))

are given by the inefficient portfolio weights of the Markowitz-Tobin frontier and can be expressed as a function of the VAR λ :

$$
y(\lambda) = \begin{cases} \lim\limits_{t \to -\infty} \dfrac{(CQ^{-1}\mu - BQ^{-1}e)t + AQ^{-1}e - BQ^{-1}\mu}{AC - B^2} , & \text{for } \lambda \le \frac{B}{C}, \\[2mm] \dfrac{\lambda Q^{-1}e - Q^{-1}\mu}{\lambda C - B} , & \text{for } \lambda > \frac{B}{C}. \end{cases} \tag{9.111}
$$

in the (λ, m) plane by

$$
m(\lambda) = \begin{cases} -\infty , & \text{for } \lambda \le \frac{B}{C}, \\[2mm] \dfrac{\lambda B - A}{\lambda C - B} , & \text{for } \lambda > \frac{B}{C}. \end{cases} \tag{9.112}
$$

and in the (λ, σ) plane with the formula

$$
\sigma^2(\lambda) = \begin{cases} +\infty , & \text{for } \lambda \le \frac{B}{C}, \\[2mm] \dfrac{\lambda^2 C - 2\lambda B + A}{(\lambda C - B)^2} , & \text{for } \lambda > \frac{B}{C}. \end{cases} \tag{9.113}
$$

Besides, we have that for every λ the corresponding maximum risk of loss of value is given by:

$$
G(\lambda) = \begin{cases} \lim\limits_{q \to \left(\frac{B}{C}\right)^+} \displaystyle\int_{(-\infty,\lambda]} \dfrac{qC - B}{|K|U(q^2C - 2qB + A)^{1/2}} g\left(\dfrac{(tq^2C - tB - qB + A)^2}{K^2(q^2C - 2qB + A)}\right) dt, \\[4mm] \hspace{6cm} \text{for } \lambda \le \frac{B}{C}, \\[3mm] \displaystyle\int_{(-\infty,\lambda]} \dfrac{\lambda C - B}{|K|U(\lambda^2C - 2\lambda B + A)^{1/2}} g\left(\dfrac{(t\lambda^2C - tB - \lambda B + A)^2}{K^2(\lambda^2C - 2\lambda B + A)}\right) dt, \\[4mm] \hspace{6cm} \text{for } \lambda > \frac{B}{C}. \end{cases} \tag{9.114}
$$

Proof. The proof is similar to the one of Theorem 9.11.   □

We know that increasing risk aversion preferences imply decreasing associated expected returns. In our graphics (Figure 9.5 and 9.7) we see that increasing λ implies increasing expected return. Besides, increasing the tolerance to risk increases the expected return but also the risk (dispersion) for optimal nonsatiable investors (Figure 9.8). This fact implicitly confirms the interpretation given to λ as an *indicator of tolerance at the level of risk* for nonsatiable investors.

We observe that when we have distributions of returns belonging to an elliptical family of distributions, for every λ greater than or equal to $\frac{B}{C}$ the portfolio weight $x(\lambda)$ that minimizes its distribution at point λ is the portfolio with mean equal to $+\infty$, hence the portfolio weight belongs to $S_{-\infty}$ and

$$x(\lambda) = \lim_{t \to \left(\frac{B}{C}\right)^-} x(t) = \lim_{t \to \left(\frac{B}{C}\right)^-} \frac{tQ^{-1}e - Q^{-1}\mu}{tC - B}.$$

Similarly, for every λ less than or equal to $\frac{B}{C}$ the portfolio weight $y(\lambda)$ that maximizes its distribution at point λ is the portfolio with mean $-\infty$; hence the portfolio weight belongs to $S_{-\infty}$ and

$$y(\lambda) = \lim_{t \to \left(\frac{B}{C}\right)^+} y(t) = \lim_{t \to \left(\frac{B}{C}\right)^+} \frac{tQ^{-1}e - Q^{-1}\mu}{tC - B}.$$

Clearly, by tabulating an elliptical distribution we can compare the Value at Risk of a given portfolio corresponding to a fixed probability with the equivalent VAR corresponding to the optimal portfolio at the same probability level. By this comparison we have an implicit measure of the efficiency of the portfolio for which we want to know the VAR. This is the starting point of other studies on implications connected with Risk Management theory.

Recall that in their work Markowitz and Tobin assumed that every return z_j has a finite variance. Next we shall assume that asset returns have a distribution with heavier tails than distributions with finite variance, i.e.,

$$P(|z_i| > x) \approx x^{-\alpha_i} L_i(x) \text{ as } x \to \infty, \tag{9.115}$$

where $0 < \alpha_i < 2$ and $L_i(x)$ is a slowly varying function at infinity, i.e.,

$$\lim_{x \to \infty} \frac{L_i(cx)}{L_i(x)} \to 1 \quad \text{for all} \quad c > 0,$$

The tail condition in (9.115) implies that the vector of returns $z = (z_1, z_2, \cdots, z_n)'$ is in the domain of attraction of an $(\alpha_1, \alpha_2, \cdots, \alpha_n)$-stable law (see (8.68) – (8.72) in Section 8.6). This is to say that having m i.i.d (independent and identically distributed) observations of z, namely

$$z^{(i)} = (z_1^{(i)}, z_2^{(i)}, \cdots, z_n^{(i)}) \ i = 1, 2, \cdots, m,$$

there exist normalizing constants

$$\underline{a}^{(m)} = (a_1^{(m)}, \cdots, a_n^{(m)}) \in R_+^n$$

and

$$\underline{b}^{(m)} = (b_1^{(m)}, \cdots, b_n^{(m)}) \in R_+^m,$$

such that

$$\frac{1}{\underline{a}^{(m)}} \sum_{i=1}^{m} \underline{z}^{(i)} + \underline{b}^{(m)} \overset{d}{\longmapsto} S(\alpha_1, \cdots, \alpha_n), \tag{9.116}$$

where $\frac{1}{\underline{a}^{(m)}} \sum_{i=1}^{m} \underline{z}^{(i)} + \underline{b}^{(m)} = \left(\sum_{i=1}^{m} \frac{z_1^{(i)}}{a_1^{(m)}} + b_1^{(m)}, \cdots, \sum_{i=1}^{m} \frac{z_n^{(i)}}{a_n^{(m)}} + b_n^{(m)} \right)$ and $S(\alpha_1, \cdots, \alpha_n)$ is an $(\alpha_1, \cdots, \alpha_n)$-stable random variable.

The constants $a_j^{(m)}$ have the form

$$a_j^{(m)} = m^{\frac{1}{\alpha_j}} L_j(m),$$

where $L_j(m)$ are slowly varying functions as $m \to \infty$.

Each component of $S(\alpha_1, \cdots, \alpha_n) = (s_1, \cdots, s_n)$ has a Pareto-Lévy stable distribution, i.e., its characteristic function is given by

$$\Phi_j(\theta) = E(e^{is_j\theta}) = \begin{cases} \exp\{-\sigma_j^{\alpha_j} |\theta|^{\alpha_j} (1 - i\beta_j(\operatorname{sgn}(\theta)) \\ \quad \times \tan(\frac{\pi\alpha_j}{2}) + i\mu_j\theta\}, & \text{if} \quad \alpha_j \ne 1, \\ \exp\{-\sigma_j|\theta|(1 + i\beta_j\frac{2}{\pi}(\operatorname{sgn}(\theta)) \\ \quad \times \log(\theta)) + i\mu_j\theta\}, & \text{if} \quad \alpha_j = 1, \end{cases} \tag{9.117}$$

where $\alpha_j \in (0, 2)$ is the so-called stable (tail) index of s_j.

The index of stability can be viewed as a measure of tail thickness. In fact, the asymptotic "power" behavior of the right tail is

$$\lim_{x \to \infty} x^{\alpha_j} P(s_j > x) = k_{\alpha_j} \frac{1 + \beta_j}{2} \sigma_j^{\alpha_j}, \tag{9.118}$$

and that of the left tail is

$$\lim_{x \to \infty} x^{\alpha_j} P(s_j < -x) = k_{\alpha_j} \frac{1 - \beta_j}{2} \sigma_j^{\alpha_j}, \tag{9.119}$$

where

$$k_{\alpha_j} = \begin{cases} \frac{1 - \alpha_j}{\Gamma(2 - \alpha_j)\cos(\pi\alpha_j/2)}, & \text{if} \quad \alpha_j \ne 1, \\ \frac{2}{\pi}, & \text{if} \quad \alpha_j = 1. \end{cases}$$

If $\beta_j = 0$, s_j has a symmetric distribution, and in this case

$$\Phi_j(\theta) = E(e^{i\theta s_j}) = e^{-\sigma_j^{\alpha_j} |\theta|^{\alpha_j} + i\mu\theta}.$$

If s_j is an α_j-stable random variable with parameters σ_j, β_j and μ_j, we denote $s_j \overset{d}{=} S_{\alpha_j}(\sigma_j, \beta_j, \mu_j)$, see Section 2.1.1.

Besides, we know that for every $p \in (0, \alpha_j)$ there exists the L_p-norm of $s_j - \mu$ and it is given by

$$(E|s_j - \mu_j|^p)^{1/p} = H(\alpha_j, \beta_j, p)\sigma_j, \qquad (9.120)$$

where

$$(H(\alpha, \beta, p))^{1/p} = \frac{2^{p-1}\Gamma(1 - p/\alpha)}{p \int_0^\infty u^{-p-1}(\sin u)^2 du} \times$$

$$\times(1 + \beta^2(\tan^2(\pi\alpha/2)))^{p/2\alpha} \cos(p/\alpha \arctan(\beta \tan(\pi\alpha/2))).$$

To estimate σ_j, one can use the empirical (sample) central moments,

$$\widehat{\mu}_{j,p} = \frac{1}{m} \sum_{i=1}^m \left| z_j^{(i)} - \mu_j \right|^p \text{ for } 1 < p < \alpha_j,$$

where $\left(z_j^{(i)} \right)_{1 \le i \le m}$ are i.i.d. observations of the jth gross return z_j and thus, by (9.120), σ_j admits the following estimator

$$\widehat{\sigma}_j = \frac{(\widehat{\mu}_{j,p})^{1/p}}{H(\widehat{\alpha}_j, \widehat{\beta}_j, p)}.$$

Here $\widehat{\alpha}_j$ and $\widehat{\beta}_j$ are estimators of α_j and β_j, and the constant $H(\widehat{\alpha}_j, \widehat{\beta}_j, p)$ is given in (9.120).

Suppose that the gross returns $z = (z_1, z_2, \cdots, z_n)'$ are jointly α-stable distributed with $1 < \alpha < 2$. Then every linear combination of the vector z is again α-stable. Hence, every gross return $x'z$ has an α-stable distribution $S_\alpha(\sigma_x, \beta_x, x'\mu)$ (see Samorodnitsky and Taqqu (1994)), where the scale parameter σ_x and the skewness parameter β_x are given by

$$\sigma_x = \left(\int_{S_n} |x's|^\alpha \, \Gamma(ds) \right)^{1/\alpha}, \beta_x = \frac{\int_{S_n} |x's|^\alpha \, sgn(x's)\Gamma(ds)}{\sigma_x^\alpha}.$$

and the mean is given by $E(x'z) = x'\mu$. The measure Γ is the spectral measure and its support is concentrated on the unit n–dimensional sphere, see Section 7.1. Under this assumption the following dominance rules are verified:

(i) *α -stable stochastic order for nonsatiable investors.*

Suppose the portfolio $x'z$ has the same σ and β as and a lower expected value than $y'z$,

$$y'z \overset{d}{=} x'z + E(y'z) - E(x'z). \qquad (9.121)$$

Thus, it follows that the portfolio $y'z$ FSD $x'z$. Hence, when unlimited short selling is allowed, we get portfolios not first degree dominated (hence belonging to T_1) by solving the following optimization problem varying the admissible σ^* and β^*:

$$\begin{cases} \max_x x'\mu \\ x'e = 1 \\ \sigma_x = \sigma^*, \beta_x = \beta^*. \end{cases} \tag{9.122}$$

A nonsatiable investor will choose the optimal portfolio among the portfolios of the above efficient frontier depending on the mean m, the scale parameter σ and the skewness parameter β.

(ii) α -stable stochastic order for risk averse investors.

Given two gross returns $y'z$ and $x'z$ with the same skewness parameter $\beta = \beta_x = \beta_y$ and mean $y'\mu = x'\mu = m$, dispersion relation $\sigma_x > \sigma_y$, and having $x'z \overset{d}{=} \sigma_x X + m$ and $y'z \overset{d}{=} \sigma_y X + m$, where $X \overset{d}{=} S_\alpha(1, \beta, 0)$, we obtain the following stochastic relation:

$$\begin{aligned} &\int_{-\infty}^{u} [P(y'z \le \lambda) - P(x'z \le \lambda)]d\lambda \wedge \\ &= \int_{-\infty}^{u} [P(X \le \tfrac{\lambda-m}{\sigma_y}) - P(X \le \tfrac{\lambda-m}{\sigma_x})]d\lambda \le 0 \end{aligned} \tag{9.123}$$

for every real u with strict inequality for some u. Hence, $y'z$ dominates $x'z$ in the sense of Rothschild-Stiglitz (and also $y'z$ SSD $x'z$). When unlimited short selling is allowed, we get portfolios not dominated in the sense of Rothschild-Stiglitz (hence belonging to $\tilde{T}$) by solving the following optimization problem varying the admissible m and β^*:

$$\begin{cases} \min_x \sigma_x \\ x'e = 1 \\ x'\mu = m, \beta_x = \beta^*. \end{cases} \tag{9.124}$$

A risk averse investor will choose the optimal portfolio among the portfolios of the above efficient frontier depending on the mean m, the scale parameter σ and the skewness parameter β.

(iii) α -stable stochastic order for non satiable risk averse investors.

Given two gross returns $y'z$ and $x'z$ with the same skewness parameter $\beta = \beta_x = \beta_y$, mean relation $y'\mu \ge x'\mu$, and the relation $\sigma_x \ge \sigma_y$ with at least one inequality being strict, we have

$$y'zSSDx'z \text{ and } x'z \overset{d}{=} y'z - (E(y'z) - E(x'z)) + \varepsilon \text{ where } E(\varepsilon/y'z) = 0. \tag{9.125}$$

If we consider the random variable Z with mean $E(Z) = E(x'z)$ and such that $Z \overset{d}{=} y'z - E(y'z) + E(Z)$, then Z belongs to the same translation invariant family of α-stable distributions and Z SSD $x'z$ by (9.123), thus (because by (9.121) $y'z$ FSD Z SSD $x'z$) it follows that $x'z \overset{d}{=} y'z - (E(y'z) - E(x'z)) + \varepsilon$ with $E(\varepsilon|y'z) = 0$. If we intersect the set of portfolios obtained by (i) and (ii), we get portfolios not second degree stochastically dominated (hence belonging to T_2).

Given two α-stable random variables X and Y with $0 < \alpha < 1$, and with the same σ and μ, if $\beta_X > \beta_Y$ then X FSD Y, see Samorodnitsky and Taqqu (1994). Suppose that the vector of gross returns $z = (z_1, z_2, \cdots, z_n)'$ is such that for every gross return $x'z$, the function $h(x'z) = (x'z)^2 \, sgn(x'z)$ belongs to the same $\alpha/2$-stable family of distributions $S_{\alpha/2}(\sigma, \beta, \mu)$ with $1 < \alpha < 2$. Under this assumption all the gross returns are in the domain of attraction of an α-stable law because for every positive t

$$P(|x'z|^2 > t) = P(|x'z| > t^{1/2}) \approx \left(t^{1/2}\right)^{-\alpha} L(t).$$

Now, if we maximize the skewness parameter $\beta_{h(x'z)}$ for fixed $\sigma_{h(x'z)}$ and $\mu_{h(x'z)}$ we get portfolios not first degree dominated because $P(h(x'z) \leq t) = P(x'z \leq \leq h^{-1}(t))$ and the function $h(.)$ preserves the first degree stochastic dominance.

As a further generalization, we assume that the portfolios are in the domain of attraction of an $(\alpha_1, \alpha_2, ..., \alpha_n)$-stable law. Hence, in order to express a multi-parameter choice in portfolio selection theory coherent with the empirical evidence and stochastic dominance rules, we need the following assumptions:

1) (*distributional assumption*). Portfolios $x'z$ belong to L^p with $1 \leq p < 2$ and are in the domain of attraction of an $(\alpha_1, \alpha_2, ..., \alpha_n)$-stable law.

2) (*stochastic dominance assumption*). There exists a differentiable strictly increasing function $h : R \rightarrow R$, such that for every portfolio $x'z$ we have that $h(x'z)$ belongs to L^k (where k is the number of parameters) and to a translation invariant family of random variables uniquely determined by the first k moments. Typically, it is logical to consider the function $h(y) = y^{r/d}$, where r and d are positive odd numbers and $r/d \leq p/k$.

If assumption 1) underlines the tail behavior of the gross returns' distribution, while assumption 2) guarantees the existence of the inverse strictly increasing function h^{-1} and for every couple of portfolios $y'z$ and $x'z$ we have that $h(y'z)$ FSD $h(x'z)$ if and only if $y'z$ FSD $x'z$ because

$$P(y'z \leq h^{-1}(t)) = P(h(y'z) \leq t) \leq P(h(x'z) \leq t) = P(x'z \leq h^{-1}(t)),$$

for every real t and strictly for some t. Then we can study the efficiency of the following portfolio weight sets:

$$F_{k,S^*}(h) = \left\{ x \in S^* \middle| x \in \arg \left(\max_{y \in S^* | E\left((h(y'z)-E(h(y'z)))^i\right)=\sigma_i; i=2,...,k} E(h(y'z)) \right) ; \right.$$
$$\left. (\sigma_2,...,\sigma_k) \in R^{k-1} \right\} \equiv F_k(h),$$

(9.126)

and

$$G_{k,S^*}(h) = \left\{ x \in S^* \middle| x \in \arg \left(\min_{y \in S^* | E\left((h(y'z)-E(h(y'z)))^i\right)=\sigma_i; i=2,...,k} E(h(y'z)) \right) ; \right.$$
$$\left. (\sigma_2,...,\sigma_k) \in R^{k-1} \right\} \equiv G_k(h),$$

(9.127)

because the following version of the fundamental theorem of moments analysis holds, see Ortobelli (1999).

Theorem 9.13 Suppose assumptions 1) and 2) hold. Then each gross return $x'z$, is first degree stochastically dominated by the existing gross returns $y'z$ (if they exist), whose functions $h(y'z)$ have strictly greater expected value and the same first k central moments as $h(x'z)$. Given the portfolio weight sets (9.126) and (9.127), we have that $F_k(h) \supseteq T_1$, $G_k(h) \supseteq A_1$ and the set of portfolio weights $x'z$ uniquely determined by the central moments associated with $h(x'z)$ $(F_k(h) \cap G_k(h))$, contains $T_1 \cap A_1$.

An immediate consequence is the following corollary, see Ortobelli (1999).

Corollary 9.5 Under the assumptions of Theorem 9.13, if we suppose that it is not possible to find a couple of portfolio weights x and y belonging to $F_k(h)$ such that $x'z$ SSD $y'z$, then:

$$T_1 = T_2 = F_k(h).$$

(9.128)

If it is not possible to find a couple of portfolio weights x and y belonging to $G_k(h)$ such that $x'z$ SSD $y'z$, then $A_1 = A_2 = G_k(h)$. We can limit these last hypotheses supposing it is not possible to find a couple of portfolio weights x and y belonging to $F_k(h)$ $(G_k(h))$ such that $x'z$ FSD $y'z$, then $T_1 = F_k(h)$ $(A_1 = G_k(h))$, see Figure 9.9.

In general, we cannot link $F_k(h)$ with the efficient sets when we don't have the previous conditions, but in some classical cases we can see that $T_1 = T_2 = F_k(h)$. In fact, the following corollary holds.

Corollary 9.6 Suppose assumptions 1) and 2) hold. If for every admissible $(\sigma_2,...,\sigma_k) \in R^{k-1}$ all the solutions to the constrained system

$$\max_{y \in S^* | E\left((h(y'z)-E(h(y'z)))^i\right)=\sigma_i; i=2,...,k} E(h(y'z))$$

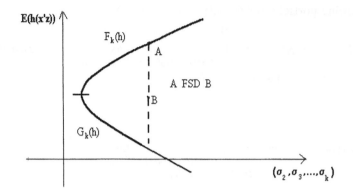

Fig. 9.9 Portfolios belonging to $F_k(h)$ and to $G_k(h)$. (Adapted from: Ortobelli, Rachev (1999))

belong to W_i, then $T_i = F_k(h) = W_i \supseteq T_1 \supseteq W_1$, i=1,2.

Consequence of the above corollary is that if $i = 2$ it follows that $T_1 = T_2 = F_k(h) = W_1 = W_2$. The theorem above gives us the efficient frontier depending on k parameters. Now, we introduce an equivalence relation "$\approx$" on the sets $F_k(h)$ and $G_k(h)$. We say that x is equivalent to y ($x \approx y$) if $x'z$ and $y'z$ have the same distribution. Then we obtain the following quotient spaces:

$$F'_{k,S^*}(h) = \left\{ \left[\arg \left(\max_{y \in S^* | E\left((h(y'z) - E(h(y'z)))^i\right) = \sigma_i; i = 2,\ldots,k} E(h(y'z)) \right) \right] ; \right.$$
$$\left. \left(\sigma_2, \ldots, \sigma_k\right) \in R^{k-1} \right\} \equiv F'_k(h)$$

(9.129)

and

$$G'_{k,S^*}(h) = \left\{ \left[\arg \left(\min_{y \in S^* | E\left((h(y'z) - E(h(y'z)))^i\right) = \sigma_i; i = 2,\ldots,k} E(h(y'z)) \right) \right] ; \right.$$
$$\left. \left(\sigma_2, \ldots, \sigma_k\right) \in R^{k-1} \right\} \equiv G'_k(h),$$

(9.130)

because every couple of portfolio weights x and y solutions of

$$\max_{y \in S^* | E\left((h(y'z) - E(h(y'z)))^i\right) = \sigma_i; i = 2,\ldots,k} E(h(y'z))$$

(with minimum in case we consider $G_k(h)$) for fixed parameters σ_i, $i = 2,\ldots,k$) admit portfolios $x'z$ and $y'z$ with the same distributions. On the sets $F'_k(h)$ and $G'_k(h)$ we can consider the partial order relations:

x weakly FSD y if and only if $F_{x'z}(t) \leq F_{y'z}(t)$, $\forall t \in R$,

x weakly SSD y if and only if $\int\limits_{-\infty}^{t} F_{x'z}(p)dp \leq \int\limits_{-\infty}^{t} F_{y'z}(p)dp$, $\forall t \in R$.

In particular, we see that weak SSD is well defined. In fact, if for some real t we have $F_{x'z}(t) < F_{y'z}(t)$, where $F_{x'z}(t)$ and $F_{y'z}(t)$ are non-decreasing and right continuous functions, there exists an interval (t,p) such that $F_{x'z}(u) < F_{y'z}(u)$ for every u belonging to (t,p). Thus, if for every t we get the equality $\int\limits_{-\infty}^{t} F_{x'z}(p)dp = \int\limits_{-\infty}^{t} F_{y'z}(p)dp$, then $F_{x'z}(t) = F_{y'z}(t)$ for every t. Therefore, simple consequence of Theorem 9.13 is the following corollary.

Corollary 9.7 Suppose assumptions 1) and 2) hold. The unions of the portfolio weights belonging to the maximal classes in $F'_k(h)$ under the partial order relations weak FSD and weak SSD are respectively equal to T_1 and T_2. The unions of the portfolio weights belonging to the minimal classes in $G'_k(h)$ under the partial order relations weak FSD and weak SSD are respectively equal to A_1 and A_2.

Throughout the above relations the central moments are considered in some sense parameters of asymmetry for which if it is not possible to compare stochastically (FSD or SSD) portfolios on $F'_k(h)$ with different parameters of asymmetry, then we get the unique efficient frontier $F'_k(h)$. The following proposition implicitly expresses the optimal portfolios for fixed parameters of asymmetry.

Proposition 9.2 Suppose assumptions 1) and 2) hold. Assuming that it is not possible to compare stochastically on $F_k(h)$ at i^{th} degree (i=1,2) portfolios with different asymmetry parameters, then all the portfolio weights, solutions of the following constrained problem:

$$
\begin{cases}
\max\limits_{y} E(h(y'z)) \\
y'e = 1 \\
E\left((h(y'z) - E(h(y'z)))^i \right) = \sigma_i; i = 2, ..., k
\end{cases}
\tag{9.131}
$$

belong to the efficient frontier T_i. Moreover, every portfolio weight x belonging to the efficient frontier T_1 that satisfies the first order conditions of the constrained system (9.131) is given by the following implicit formulation

$$E\left(h'(y'z)z\right) - \theta_1 e$$

$$-\sum_{i=2}^{k} i\theta_i E\left((h(y'z) - E\left(h(y'z)\right))^{i-1} (h'(y'z)z - E(h'(y'z)z)) \right)$$

$$= 0, \tag{9.132}$$

where θ_i are the coefficients of the Lagrangian.

Proof. The first part is a consequence of Theorem 9.13. We obtain (9.132) by the first order conditions of the constrained system (9.131).   □

By this proposition we get that under good regularity conditions the portfolio weights can be written as a function of k parameters: $x = x(\theta_1, ..., \theta_k)$ (where θ_i are the coefficients of the Lagrangian). If we consider the following system of k equations,

$$
\begin{cases}
m = E(h(y'z)) \\
y'e = 1 \\
E\left((h(y'z) - m)^i\right) = \sigma_i; i = 2, ..., k - 1
\end{cases}
\tag{9.133}
$$

we see that under a good condition of regularity we can obtain the portfolio weights belonging to T_1 only as a function of the $k - 1$ coordinates $(m, \sigma_2, ..., \sigma_{k-1})$

$$
x = x(m, \sigma_2, ..., \sigma_{k-1}).
\tag{9.134}
$$

A typical example is given by the mean-dispersion portfolio frontier when the returns belong to an elliptical family.

In the above considerations we study only the risky assets. If we add to the vector of gross returns the riskless gross return, then Theorem 9.13 gives us the equilibrium efficient frontier for nonsatiable investors under assumptions 1) and 2). In fact, considering the random vector of the gross returns:

$$
\widehat{z} = (z_0, z_1, \cdots, z_n)',
$$

where $z_i = 1 + r_i$ $(i=1,...,n)$ are the gross returns with risk and $z_0 = 1 + r_0$ is the riskless gross return, we have to assume that the portfolio weights belong to one of the following sets:

$$
\overline{S}_t = \left\{ x \in \overline{R}^{n+1} : \sum_i x_i = 1, x_i \geq t, i = 0, 1, ..., n \right\}.
$$

To simplify we denote by $\overline{S}^*$ the different cases of $\overline{S}_t$. Hence, as a consequence of Theorem 9.13 and Corollary 9.7 the following corollary holds.

Corollary 9.8 Suppose assumptions 1) and 2) hold (except for the riskless return that is a constant), then each gross return $x'\widehat{z}$ is first degree stochastically dominated by the existing gross returns $y'\widehat{z}$ (if they exist), whose functions $h(y'\widehat{z})$ have strictly greater expected value than and the same first k central moments as $h(x'\widehat{z})$. Let

$$
\overline{F}'_{k,\overline{S}^*}(h) = \{x^0\} \cup \left\{ \left[\arg \left(\max_{y \in \overline{S}^* | E((h(y'z) - E(h(y'z)))^i) = \sigma_i; i=2,...,k} E(h(y'z)) \right) \right] ;
$$
$$
(\sigma_2, ..., \sigma_k) \in R^{k-1} \right\} \equiv \overline{F}'_k(h),
$$

be the set of equivalent classes under the relation $\approx$, where $x^0 = (1, 0, ..., 0)'$ is the portfolio weight corresponding to the riskless return. The unions of the portfolio weights belonging to the maximal classes in $\overline{F}'_k(h)$ under the partial order relations weak FSD and weak SSD are respectively the efficient frontier for nonsatiable investors and the efficient frontier for nonsatiable risk averse investors.

In particular, when we have the gross returns belonging respectively to an elliptical family of distributions, or to k fund separating distributions, we find a linear valuation of capital asset pricing (see Ross (1978)).

9.9 Safety-first Analysis with More Parameters

In the last years, with the introduction of Value-at-Risk methodology, researchers have begun to interpret λ as an indicator of the risk tolerance, see also the next Chapter 10. For this reason when mean-dispersion analysis is efficient it can be interesting to rewrite one-dimensional safety-first analysis as mean-VAR analysis or dispersion-VAR analysis. Generally, there is no meaning using mean-VAR analysis if we live in a market depending on more asymmetry parameters. We have a typical example of a market depending on more asymmetry parameters under the assumptions 1) and 2) from the previous section. We see that under assumption 2 with $h : R \to R$ being a differentiable strictly increasing function for which $P(y'z \le h^{-1}(t)) = P(h(y'z) \le t)$, the following equivalence holds:

$$
\begin{aligned}
U := U_{S^*} = &\left\{ x \in S^* \,\Big|\, \left(\exists \lambda \in R : x = x(\lambda) \in \arg\left(\inf_y P(y'z \le \lambda) \right) \right) \right. \\
&\left. \wedge \left(\text{does not exist } w_1 \in \arg\left(\inf_x P(x'z \le \lambda) \right) \text{ such that } w_1' z SSD x'(\lambda)z \right) \right\} \\
= U(h) = &\left\{ x \in S^* \,\Big|\, \left(\exists \lambda \in R : x = x_h(\lambda) \in \arg\left(\inf_y P(h(y'z) \le \lambda) \right) \right) \right. \\
&\left. \wedge \left(\text{does not exist } w_h \in \arg\left(\inf_x P(h(x'z) \le \lambda) \right) \text{ such that } w_h' z SSD x_h'(\lambda)z \right) \right\}
\end{aligned}
$$

Besides, Theorem 9.13 tell us that the set $F_k(h)$ contains the set U because $F_k(h) \supseteq T_1 \supseteq U$. Under appropriate regularity conditions, we have the converse as a consequence of the following remark.

Remark 9.6 Suppose assumptions 1) and 2) hold and

$$
P(h(x'z) \le \lambda) = G(m(x), \sigma_2(x), ..., \sigma_k(x), \lambda),
$$

(where $m(x) = E(h(x'z))$, $\sigma_i(x) = E\left((h(x'z) - m(x))^i\right)$, $i = 2, ..., k$). If we can express every portfolio weight belonging to T_1 as $x = x(m, \sigma_2, ..., \sigma_{k-1})$ (like in (9.134)) and for every portfolio weight belonging to T_1 there exists a portfolio weight belonging to U such that

$$
x(m, \sigma_2, ..., \sigma_{k-1}) = x(m, \sigma_2, ..., \sigma_{k-2}, \lambda),
$$

then $T_1 = U = F_k(h) = W_1$.

It is important to observe that when assumptions 1) and 2) hold and $P(h(x'z) \leq \lambda) = G(m(x), \sigma_2(x), ..., \sigma_k(x), \lambda)$, the implicit portfolio weight satisfying the first order 4s of the constrained problem

$$\begin{cases} \inf_x P(h(x'z) \leq \lambda) \\ x'e = 1 \end{cases} \tag{9.135}$$

depends on $k + 1$ parameters. Since the portfolio weights that belong to the efficient frontier or to the worst frontier depend on k or $k - 1$ parameters, it appears logical to think that the hypothesis of the remark is verified and in this case, U is generally coincident with W_1. Besides, it is important to underline that the safety-first approach can be more general than moments analysis because if 2) is not verified, $F_k(h)$ can be different from the efficient sets W_i or T_i. Conversely, we know that every safety-first portfolio is efficient ($W_1 \supseteq U$). A consequence of the remark is the following corollary.

Corollary 9.9 Under the hypothesis of the above remark, suppose that for every fixed parameters λ and σ_{k-1} such that $x(m, \sigma_2, ..., \sigma_{k-2}, \sigma_{k-1}) = x(m, \sigma_2, ..., \sigma_{k-2}, \lambda)$ we have:

$\arg(\inf P(x'z \leq \lambda)) = \{x(\overline{m}, \overline{\sigma}_2, ..., \overline{\sigma}_{k-2}, \sigma_{k-1})/x(\overline{m}, \overline{\sigma}_2, ..., \overline{\sigma}_{k-2}, \lambda) =$
$= x(\overline{m}, \overline{\sigma}_2, ..., \overline{\sigma}_{k-2}, \sigma_{k-1})$ for every admissible $(\overline{m}, \overline{\sigma}_2, ..., \overline{\sigma}_{k-2}) \in R^{k-2}\}$.

If for some $\lambda_1 \neq \lambda_2$ we have $x(m, \sigma_2, ..., \sigma_{k-2}, \lambda_1) = x(m, \sigma_2, ..., \sigma_{k-2}, \lambda_2)$, then we get that

$$\arg(\inf P(x'z \leq \lambda_1)) = \arg(\inf P(x'z \leq \lambda_2)).$$

More generally we have the following definition.

Definition 9.5 Let for the real numbers λ_1 and λ_2 the portfolio weights
$\quad x(\lambda_1)$ belong to $\arg(\inf P(x'z \leq \lambda_1))$,
$\quad x(\lambda_2)$ belong to $\arg(\inf P(x'z \leq \lambda_2))$,
$\quad y(\lambda_1)$ belong to $\arg(\sup P(x'z \leq \lambda_1))$,
$\quad y(\lambda_2)$ belong to $\arg(\sup P(x'z \leq \lambda_2))$.

We say that the set of safety-first portfolio weights U admits the uniqueness property if the following relation is satisfied:
1) $x(\lambda_1) = x(\lambda_2)$ implies $\arg(\inf P(x'z \leq \lambda_1)) = \arg(\inf P(x'z \leq \lambda_2))$.

We say that the set of the worst-world portfolio weights A_1 admits the uniqueness property if the following relation is satisfied:
1') $y(\lambda_1) = y(\lambda_2)$ implies $\arg(\sup P(x'z \leq \lambda_1)) = \arg(\sup P(x'z \leq \lambda_2))$.

Practically, the uniqueness property allows us to partition U in distinct classes. In fact, when U admits the uniqueness property we call the portfolio weight set $\arg(\inf P(x'z \leq \lambda))$ class of λ tolerance at the risk. Clearly, under the hypothesis of the above corollary and in a one-parameter safety-first world we have always the uniqueness property. Another consequence of the uniqueness property is the following proposition.

Proposition 9.3 Let $L = \{p \in [0,1] \mid \exists \lambda : p = \inf P(x'z \leq \lambda)\}$ be the set of the possible risk of loss. For every fixed possible risk of loss l belonging to L we consider $C_l = \{v|l = \inf P(x'z \leq v)\}$. Then $\lambda_l = \inf C_l$ belongs to C_l. Moreover, if U admits the uniqueness property, then for every v belonging to C_l, the classes of λ_l and v tolerance at the risk contain the same portfolio weights, i.e.,

$$\arg\left(\inf P(x'z \leq \lambda_l)\right) = \arg\left(\inf P(x'z \leq v)\right). \tag{9.136}$$

If we compare the mean-variance approach with safety first approach in portfolio selection theory, we conclude:

1) For arbitrary distributions the mean-variance model can be motivated by assuming quadratic utility, while safety-first analysis is motivated by assuming safety-first utility functions. The economic conclusions in both cases are often counter intuitive.

2) For arbitrary preferences the mean-variance model can be motivated by assuming that gross returns on risky assets have a multivariate elliptical distribution, while safety-first analysis can be justified by some regularity conditions on the underlying distribution. Moreover, under the assumption of an elliptical distribution the approaches are equivalent and safety-first approach for its versatility can be more general than stable Paretian approach.

Furthermore, using the characterization of stochastic dominance (SSD and FSD) it is not difficult to find some rules to get $T_1 = U = W_1$ or $W_2 \subseteq T_2 \subseteq U \subseteq W_1$. The following propositions hold.

Proposition 9.4   (a) If for every portfolio weight x not belonging to U there exists a portfolio weight y such that $y'z \ FSD \ x'z$, then $T_1 = U = W_1$.

(b) If for every portfolio weight x not belonging to U there exists a portfolio weight y such that $y'zSSDx'z$, then $W_2 \subseteq T_2 \subseteq U \subseteq W_1$.

Proof. If every portfolio weight not belonging to U is stochastically dominated (first or second degree), then U contains the not dominated portfolio weights (first or second degree) and by (9.90) follows the thesis.   □

Another way to rewrite this result in terms of the distributional characterization of stochastic dominance is the following.

Proposition 9.5 Suppose that $\sup c(x) < +\infty$ and $\inf d(x) > -\infty$, where $c(x) = \sup\{c \in \overline{R}|P(x'z \leq c) = 0\}$, $d(x) = \inf\{d \in \overline{R}/P(x'z > d) = 0\}$.

Given $a = \sup c(x)$, $b = \inf d(x)$, if we consider a portfolio weight y not belonging to U and the set

$$B(y) = \{\alpha \in R | \exists \beta = \beta(\alpha) \in [a, b], \text{ such that } \forall t \le \alpha, F_{x'(\beta)z}(t) \le F_{y'z}(t)\}$$

(where $x(\beta) \in \arg(\inf P(x'z \le \beta)))$, then we get:

(a) If for each portfolio weight y not belonging to U we have $\sup B(y) \ge \ge b$, then $T_1 = U = W_1$.

(b) If for each portfolio weight y not belonging to U there exists a real number u belonging to $B(y)$ such that there exists a $\beta = \beta(u)$ belonging to $[a, b]$ for which for every λ belonging to $[u, +\infty)$ we get

$$\int_u^\lambda [F_{x'(\beta)z}(p) - F_{y'z}(p)]dp \le \int_{-\infty}^u [F_{y'z}(p) - F_{x'(\beta)z}(p)]dp, \qquad (9.137)$$

then $W_2 \subseteq T_2 \subseteq U \subseteq W_1$.

We can see that for every y not belonging to U, $B(y)$ is always different from the null set because $B(y)$ contains at least $a = \sup c(x)$. We have a simple application of this proposition when we consider the distribution of the risky returns belonging to an elliptical family. In that case for every portfolio weight y not belonging to U there exists a portfolio weight x such that $x'z$ FSD $y'z$, hence $T_1 = U = W_1$. Furthermore, we can see that for every portfolio weight y not belonging to U inequality (9.137) holds and when the markets are compact it can happen that U contains strictly W_2.

In the following theorem, see Ortobelli (1999), we note a "particular form of density" of the following set $\widetilde{U}$ in the efficient set W_1, where

$$\begin{aligned}\widetilde{U} := \widetilde{U}_{S^*} = \Big\{ &x \in S^* \Big| \Big(x \in \arg\Big(\max_y E\Big(\sum_{i=1}^m \alpha_i u_{\lambda_i}(y'z)\Big)\Big)\Big) \\ \wedge \Big(&\text{does not exist } w_1 \in \arg\Big(\max_y E\Big(\sum_{i=1}^m \alpha_i u_{\lambda_i}(y'z)\Big)\Big) \\ &\text{such that } w_1' zSSDx'(\lambda)z)\Big\} \end{aligned} \qquad (9.138)$$

set of not dominated portfolio weights that maximize convex combinations of the safety-first utility functions $u_\lambda(t) = I_{(\lambda, +\infty)}(t)$.

Theorem 9.14 If a bounded utility function $\widetilde{u}$ belongs to H_1, then for every ε greater than zero there exists a portfolio weight y belonging to $\widetilde{U}$ such that $\left| E(\widetilde{u}(y'z)) - \max_x E(\widetilde{u}(x'z)) \right| < \varepsilon$. Thus, if $U \supseteq \widetilde{U}$, then every investor with a bounded utility function in H_1 and an optimal solution in W_1 admits an approximate solution in U.

This result gives a sufficient condition for approximating the investor's optimal solution with an optimal portfolio weight belonging to U. Clearly by definition $\tilde{U} \supseteq U$, hence equivalently in the theorem we can require $\tilde{U}=U$ instead of $U \supseteq \tilde{U}$. Immediate consequences of Theorem 9.14 are the following corollaries.

Corollary 9.10 If for every integer m, and for every real number λ_i with i=1,...,m the portfolio weights, argument of the minimum of the following positive convex combination (i.e. $\sum_i \alpha_i = 1$; with $\alpha_i \in [0,1]$)

$$\sum_{i=1}^{m} \alpha_i P(x'z \leq \lambda_i), \tag{9.139}$$

belong to U, then every investor with a bounded utility function in H_1 and an optimal solution in W_1 admits an approximate solution in U.

Corollary 9.11 Let U be convex. If for every bounded functions f_1 and f_2 belonging to H_1 and for every $a \in [0,1]$ there exists a real number $b \in [0,1]$ such that

$$\arg\left(\max_x E\left(af_1(x'z) + (1-a)f_2(x'z)\right)\right) = b\arg\left(\max_x E\left(f_1(x'z)\right)\right)$$
$$+(1-b)\arg\left(\max_x E\left(f_2(x'z)\right),\right)$$

$$\tag{9.140}$$

then every investor with a bounded utility function in H_1 and an optimal solution in W_1 admits an approximate solution in U.

About this last result Dybvig and Ross (1982) gave some limits. They proved that in an incomplete market with finite economy the efficient set W_2 is closed, connected, but not convex and it is convex in a complete market or considering not too much assets or states. Besides, when the portfolio weights belong to a compact space and the distributions of returns belong to an elliptical family, we have not necessarily a convex efficient frontier for nonsatiable investors (cases analyzed in Bawa (1976), (1978)).

A natural generalization of a safety-first efficient set is given by these recursive definitions:

$$U_1 \equiv U,$$

$$\hat{H}_1 = \{u \in H_1 \mid \exists \text{ not } SSD \text{ dominated } x \in \arg(\max E(u(x'z)) \text{ and } x \in U_1\},$$

$$U_m \equiv U_{m,S^*} = \left\{x \in S^* \mid \left(x \in \arg(\max_y E\left(au(y'z) + (1-a)u_\lambda(y'z)\right)\right.\right.$$
$$u \in \hat{H}_{m-1}, a \in [0,1], \lambda \in R\right) \wedge \text{(does not exist another}$$
$$w_1 \in \arg(\max_y E\left(au(y'z) + (1-a)u_\lambda(y'z)\right) \text{ such that } w_1' z SSD y'z\left.\right)\right\},$$

$$\hat{H}_m = \{u \in H_1 \mid \exists \text{ not } SSD \text{ dominated } x \in \arg(\max E(u(x'z)) \text{ and } x \in U_m\}.$$

The extension suggests the following definition.

Definition 9.6 We call U_p the pth level safety-first optimal set. We call safety-first investors of the pth level all investors with utility functions in $\widehat{H}_p$. We say that the safety-first market is closed under convex sums at the pth level if p is the minimum integer for which $U_p = U_{p+1}$.

By these definitions, we see that $\widehat{H}_p \supseteq \widehat{H}_{p-1}$ and $U_p \supseteq U_{p-1}$, and as a consequence of Theorem 9.14 we get the following theorem.

Theorem 9.15 If $U_p = U_{p+1}$(or $\widehat{H}_p = \widehat{H}_{p+1}$), then every investor with a bounded utility function in H_1 and an optimal solution in W_1 admits an approximate solution in U.

The theorem above shows that when the safety-first market is closed under convex sums at the pth level every nonsatiable investor admits an approximate optimal solution in the pth level safety-first optimal set. In particular, when the distributions of the returns belong to an elliptical family, then $U = W_1$, $H_1 = \widehat{H}_1$ and the nonsatiable investors admit solutions in the first level safety-first optimal set. It is interesting to observe that Theorems 9.14 and 9.15 Corollaries 9.10 and 9.11 give us the implicit distributional assumption to justify safety-first analysis and we can say that for arbitrary preferences safety-first analysis can be justified by these implicit regularity conditions on the distributions .

Throughout this section we saw that the nonsatiable investors admit solutions in the first level safety-first optimal set under good regularity conditions on the distributions. We have not shown examples about the difference between U and W_1, and this question will be a subject of other studies.

To find the typical portfolio weight belonging to U we have the following three different situations:

> 1) We do not know the distributions of the returns. In this case we have to approximate the portfolio weights belonging to U. Bawa (1979) and Ortobelli (1999) study how to approximate indirectly the portfolio weights belonging to U.

> 2) We assume the distributions of the returns belong to a known family of distributions. Then under some assumptions on the distributions the portfolios belonging to U are expressed by the following proposition.

> 3) We know only the marginal distributions of the components in the gross return vector z. After the next proposition, we try to solve the problem assuming that the conjoint distribution is not dominated by other possible conjoint distributions.

Proposition 9.6 Suppose that every portfolio $x'z$ has a distribution dependent on a dispersion parameter $\sigma_2 = x'Qx$, where Q is a non-singular dispersion matrix. If we consider the distributions of the returns $\delta(x, \sigma_2(x), \lambda) =$

$P(x'z \leq \lambda)$ differentiable in x such that $\frac{\partial \delta}{\partial \sigma_2} \neq 0$, then a solution to the first order conditions of the constrained problem

$$\begin{cases} \inf_x P(x'z \leq \lambda) \\ x'e = 1 \end{cases} \tag{9.141}$$

is given by the portfolio weights implicitly specified by the following formulation

$$x = \frac{Q^{-1}\widetilde{\delta} - \left(x'\widetilde{\delta} + 2\frac{\partial \delta}{\partial \sigma_2}\sigma_2\right)Q^{-1}e}{2\frac{\partial \delta}{\partial \sigma_2}}, \tag{9.142}$$

where $\widetilde{\delta} = \frac{\partial \delta(x)}{\partial x} - 2\frac{\partial \delta}{\partial \sigma_2}Qx$.

Clearly, if we apply the proposition to a family of elliptical distributions we obtain the mean-dispersion efficient frontier. Other interesting examples with non-elliptical distributions can be built using stable distributions.

Definition 9.7 A subset V of R^n is comprehensive if for every $b \in V$ and $a \in R^n$ with $a_i \leq b_i$ (i=1, ..., n), $a \in V$. We say that a multivariate distribution G dominates another multivariate distribution F if for every non-decreasing function u on R^n (in the sense that $\forall x, y \in R^n$ such that $x_i \leq y_i$ (i=1, ..., n), $u(x) \leq u(y)$) we have $\int u dG \geq \int u dF$, with strict inequality for some non-decreasing function u. Equivalently, (equivalence proved by Levhari, Paroush and Peleg (1975)), G dominates F if and only if $\int_V dG \leq \int_V dF$ for every open comprehensive subset V of R^n and $F \neq G$.

Assuming that the returns joint distribution is not dominated by other possible joint distributions, the open question is "How can we find the portfolio weights belonging to U?". We know that given the marginal distributions $F_{z_i}(t)$, the function

$$\widetilde{F}(y_1, ..., y_n) = \min_i F_{z_i}(y_i) \tag{9.143}$$

is the Hoeffding distribution, see Rachev (1991), p.150. $\widetilde{F}$ can be viewed as the joint distribution of the random variables $Y_{z_i}(w) = \inf\{x/F_{z_i}(x) \geq w\}$ defined on the probability space $\left((0,1], B_{(0,1]}, \widetilde{P}\right)$, where $B_{(0,1]}$ is the Borel σ-field on the interval (0,1] and $\widetilde{P}$ is the Lebesgue measure induced on (0, 1]. Alternatively we can write

$$Y_{z_i} = F_{z_i}^{\leftarrow}(\widetilde{u}),$$

where $\widetilde{u}$ is uniformly distributed random variable on [0, 1), and $F_{z_i}^{\leftarrow}$ is the generlized inverse of the distribution function F_{z_i},

$$F_{z_i}(x) = \sup\{t : F_{z_i}(t) \leq x\},$$

see Rachev (1991), Theorem 7.3.2, see also Rachev and Rüschendorf (1998a), Chapter 1. We recall that another example of a pricing model that uses the distribution functions of the returns is Dybvig's payoff distribution pricing model (1988). We see that the joint distribution (9.143) maximizes the left asymmetry of the admissible conjoint distributions, because for every $\bar{y} \in R^n$ and for every admissible conjoint distribution $G(y_1, ..., y_n)$ we have

$$G(y_1, ..., y_n) = P(z_1 \leq y_1, ..., z_n \leq y_n) \leq \min_i F_{z_i}(y_i) = \tilde{F}(y_1, ..., y_n). \quad (9.144)$$

Hence, we can consider

$$F(y_1, ..., y_n) = \min_i F_{-z_i}(y_i) = 1 - \max_i F_{z_i}(-y_i^-) \quad (9.145)$$

as a joint distribution for the opposite asset vector $-z$. We know by Levhari, Paroush and Peleg (1975) that the maximum right asymmetry on this particular family of comprehensive sets is a necessary but not sufficient condition to guarantee the multivariate dominance in the sense of the above definition. The uniqueness of this distribution permits us to say that, given the distribution (9.145) to the opposite of z, the joint distribution associated with z is a stochastically not dominated conjoint distribution in the sense that it is the unique conjoint distribution that on this class of comprehensive sets is not dominated by other possible conjoint distributions and hence is not dominated. Then we can find the portfolio weights belonging to U in the usual way

$$x(\lambda) = \arg \left(\inf \int_{[x'y \geq -\lambda]} dF(y_1, ..., y_n) \right). \quad (9.146)$$

Therefore, given the marginal distributions, considering the maximal joint distribution (9.145), we can get the optimal portfolio weights (9.146).

10

Risk Management: Value at Risk for Heavy-Tailed Distributed Rating

10.1 Introduction: Value at Risk (VAR) and the New Bank Capital Requirements for Market Risk

One of the most important tasks of financial institutions is evaluation of exposure to market risks, which arise from variations in prices of equities, commodities, exchange rates, and interest rates [1]. The dependence on market risks can be measured by changes in the portfolio value, or profits and losses. A commonly used methodology for estimation of market risks is the *Value at Risk* (VAR).

Regulators and the financial industry advisory committees recommend VAR as a way of risk measuring. In July 1993, the Group of Thirty first advocated the VAR approaches in the study "Derivatives: Practices and Principles" (see Kupiec (1995); Simons (1996); Fallon (1996); Liu (1996)). In 1993, the European Union instructed setting capital reserves to balance market risks in the Capital Adequacy Directive "EEC 6-93", effective from January 1996 (see Liu (1996)). It was an improvement with respect to the 1988 Basle Capital Adequacy Accord of G10, which centered on credit risks and did not consider market risks in details (see Jackson, Maude, and Perraudin (1996, 1997)).

In 1994, the Bank for International Settlements in the Fisher report advised disclosure of VAR numbers (see Hendricks (1996, 1997)). In the April 1995 proposal "Supervisory Treatment of Market Risks", the Basle Commit-

---

[1] This chapter is based in the material included in Khindanova and Rachev (1999), Khindanova, Rachev and Schwartz (1999) and Gamrowski and Rachev (1996).

tee on Banking Supervision suggested that banks can use their internal models of VAR estimations as the basis for calculation of capital requirements (see Kupiec (1995); Jorion (1996a,b); Beder (1995)). In January 1996, the Basle Committee amended the 1988 Basle Capital Accord (see Basle Committee on Banking Supervision (1996)). The supplement suggested two approaches to calculate capital reserves for market risks: "standardized" and "internal models" (see Simons (1996); Jackson, Maude, and Perraudin (1997); Hopper (1996)). According to the in-house models approach, capital requirements are computed from multiplying the banks' VAR values by a factor between three and four. In August 1996, the US bank regulators endorsed the Basle Committee amendment (see Lopez (1996)). The Federal Reserve Bank allowed the two-year period for its implementation. The proposal is effective from January 1998 (see Hendricks and Hirtle (1997)). The US Securities and Exchange Commission suggested to apply VAR for enhancing transparency in derivatives activity. Derivatives Policy Group has also recommended VAR techniques for quantifying market risks (see Kupiec (1995)).

The use of VAR models is rapidly expanding. Financial institutions with significant trading and investment volumes employ the VAR methodology in their risk management operations (see Heron and Irving (1997); The Economist (1998)). In October 1994, JP Morgan unveiled its VAR estimation system (see JP Morgan (1995)), RiskMetrics™. Credit Swiss First of Boston developed proprietary Primerisk and PrimeClear (March 1997). Chase Manhattan's product is called Charisma. Bankers Trust introduced the RAROC in June 1996. Deutsche Bank uses the dbAnalyst 2.0 from January 1995. Corporations use VAR numbers for risk reporting to management, shareholders, and investors since VAR measures allow to aggregate exposures to market risks into one number in money terms. It is possible to calculate VAR for different market segments and to identify the most risky positions. The VAR estimations can complement allocation of capital resources, setting position limits, and performance evaluation (see Liu (1996); Jorion (1996a,b)). In many banks the evaluation and compensation of traders is derived from returns per unit VAR. Nonfinancial corporations employ the VAR technique to unveil their exposure to financial risks, to estimate riskiness of their cashflows, and to undertake hedging decisions. Primers of applying VAR analysis for estimating market risks by nonfinancial firms are two German conglomerates Veba and Siemens (see Priest (1997a and 1997b)). The Norwegian oil company Statoil implemented a system, which incorporates the VAR methodologies (see Hiemstra (1997)). Corporations hedge positions to "buy insurance" against market risks. An appealing implication of VAR is as an instrument for corporate self-insurance (see Shimko (1997a)). VAR can be explained as the amount of uninsured loss that a corporation accepts. If the self-insurance losses are greater than the cost of insuring by hedging, the corporation should buy external insurance. Investment analysts employ VAR techniques in project valuations (see Shimko (1997b)). Institutional investors, for instance, pension funds, use VAR for quantifying market risks.

The new market risk capital requirements become effective from January 1998. The US capital standards for market risks are imperative for banks with trading accounts (assets and liabilities) greater than $1 billion or 10 percent of total assets (see Hendricks and Hirtle (1997)). Though, the regulators can apply these standards to banks with smaller trading accounts. The market risk capital requirements allow to calculate capital reserves based either on "standardized" or "internal models" methods. The standardized method computes capital charges separately for each market (country) assigning percentage provisions for different exposures to equities, interest rate and currency risks (Example: The required capital reserves for positions in the US market recognize hedging by the US instruments but do not consider hedging by the UK instruments.). The total capital charge equals the sum of the market capital requirements. The main drawback of the "standardized" approach is that it does not take into consideration global diversification effects (In other words, the "standardized" method ignores correlations across markets in different countries. See Jackson, Maude and Perraudin (1997); Liu (1996)). The second approach determines capital reserves based on in-house VAR models. The VAR values should be computed with a 10-day time horizon at a 99 percent confidence level using at least one year data (For the exact definition of VAR see (1) with $\tau = 10$ and $\alpha = .99$ later in this section.).

The new capital requirements classify market risk on general market risk and specific risk. *The general risk* is the risk from changes in the overall level of equity and commodity prices, exchange rates and interest rates. *Specific risk* is the risk from changes in prices of a security because of reasons associated with the security's issuer.

The capital requirement for general market risk is equal to the maximum of:

(i) the *current VAR* (VAR_t) number and

(ii) the *average VAR* $\left(\frac{1}{60} \sum_{i=1}^{60} \text{VAR}_{t-i} \right)$ over the previous 60 days multiplied by a factor between three and four.

The capital charges for specific risk cover debt and equity positions. The specific risk estimates obtained from the VAR models should be multiplied by a factor of four. Thus, a market risk capital requirement at time t, C_t, is

$$C_t = A_t \, {}^*max \left\{ \frac{1}{60} \sum_{i=1}^{60} \text{VAR}_{t-i}, \text{VAR}_t \right\} + S_t \, ,$$

where A_t is a multiplication factor between three and four, S_t is the capital charge for specific risk.

The A_t values depend on accuracy of the VAR models in previous periods[2]. Denote by K the number of times when daily actual losses exceeded the pre-

---

[2]The regulators recommend to use the time horizon τ of 10 days (two weeks) in VAR estimations. For backtesting, the regulators use $\tau = 1$ day.

dicted VAR values over the last year, or the last 250 trading days[3]. Regulators split the range of values of K into three zones: the green zone ($K \leq 4$), the yellow zone ($5 \leq K \leq 9$), and the red zone ($K \geq 10$)[4]. If K is within the green zone, then $A_t = 3$. If K is within the yellow zone, $3 < A_t < 4$, in the red zone, $A_t = 4$.

A *VAR measure* is the highest possible loss over a certain period of time at a given confidence level. Formally, a VAR $= \text{VAR}_{t,\tau}$ is defined as the upper limit of the one-sided confidence interval:

$$P[\Delta P(\tau) < -VAR] = 1 - \alpha \qquad (10.1)$$

where α is the confidence level and $\Delta P(\tau) = \Delta P_t(\tau)$ is the *relative change (return)* in the portfolio value (*return*) in the portfolio value over the time horizon τ.

$$\Delta P_t(\tau) = P(t + \tau) - P(t),$$

where $P(t + \tau) = \log S(t + \tau)$ is the log-spot value at $t + \tau$, $P(t) = \log S(t)$, $S(t)$ is the portfolio value at t, the time period is $[t, T]$, with $T - t = \tau$, and t is the current time.

The time horizon, or the holding period, should be determined from the liquidity of assets and the trading activity. The confidence level should be chosen to provide a rarely exceeded VAR value.

The VAR measurements are widely used by financial entities, regulators, non-financial corporations, and institutional investors. Clearly, VAR is of importance for practitioners and academia alike. The aim of this chapter is to review the recent approaches to VAR and to outline the stable Paretian approach in evaluated VAR.

10.2 Computation of VAR

From the definition of VAR $= \text{VAR}_{t,\tau}$, (10.1), the VAR values are obtained from the probability distribution of portfolio value returns:

$$1 - \alpha = F_{\Delta P}(-\text{VAR}) = \int_{-\infty}^{-\text{VAR}} f_{\Delta P}(x) dx \ ,$$

where $F_{\Delta P}(x) = Pr(\Delta P \leq x)$ is the cumulative distribution function (cdf) of portfolio returns in one period, and $f_{\Delta P}(x)$ is the probability density function

---

[3]For more detailed explanation of the time horizon and the window length see also sections 3.3 and 3.4.

[4]Denote by $\hat{K}$ the fraction of days, when the observed losses exceeded the VAR estimate. If $K = 10$, then $\hat{K}$ is $10/250 = 0.04$. However, the 99% confidence level implies probability of 0.01 for exceeding the VAR estimate of daily losses.

(pdf) of ΔP[5]. The VAR methodologies mainly differ in ways of constructing $f_{\Delta P}(x)$.

The traditional techniques of approximating the distribution of ΔP are:

- the *parametric method* (analytic or models-based),

- *historical simulation* (nonparametric or empirical-based),

- *Monte Carlo simulation* (stochastic simulation), and

- *the stress-testing* (scenario analysis) (see JP Morgan (1995); Phelan (1995); Mahoney (1996); Jorion (1996a); Simons (1996); Fallon (1996); Linsmeier and Pearson (1996); Hopper (1996); Dave and Stahl (1997); Gamrowski and Rachev (1996); Duffie and Pan (1997); Fong and Vasicek (1997); Pritsker (1996)).

10.2.1 Parametric Method

If the changes in the portfolio value are characterized by a parametric distribution, VAR can be found as a function of distribution parameters. In this section we review:

- applications of two parametric distributions: normal and gamma,

- linear and quadratic approximations to price movements.

VAR for a Single Asset

Assume that a portfolio consists of a single asset, which depends only on one risk factor. Traditionally, in this setting, the distribution of asset return is assumed to be *the univariate normal distribution*, identified by two parameters: the mean, μ, and the standard deviation, σ. The problem of calculating VAR is then reduced to finding the $(1-\alpha)$th percentile of the standard normal distribution $z_{1-\alpha}$:

$$1 - \alpha = \int_{-\infty}^{X^*} g(x)dx = \int_{-\infty}^{z_{1-\alpha}} \Phi(z)dz = N(z_{1-\alpha}) , \quad \text{with} \quad X^* = z_{1-\alpha}\sigma + \mu ,$$

where $\phi(z)$ is the standard normal density function, N(z) is the cumulative normal distribution function, X is the portfolio return, $g(x)$ is the normal distribution function for returns with the mean μ and the standard deviation σ, and X^* is the lowest return at a given confidence level α.

Investors in many applications assume that the expected return μ equals 0. This assumption is based on the conjecture that the magnitude of μ is

---

[5]If $f_{\Delta P}(x)$ does not exist, then VAR can be obtained from cdf $F_{\Delta P}$.

substantially smaller than the magnitude of the standard deviation σ and, therefore, can be ignored. Then, it can be assumed:

$$X^* = z_{1-\alpha}\sigma \, ,$$

and, therefore,

$$\text{VAR} = -Y_0 X^* = -Y_0 z_{1-\alpha}\sigma \, ,$$

where Y_0 is the initial portfolio value.

Portfolio VAR

If a portfolio consists of many assets, the computation of VAR is performed in several steps. Portfolio assets are decomposed into "building blocks", which depend on a finite number of risk factors. Exposures of the portfolio securities are combined into risk categories. The total portfolio risk is constructed, based on aggregated risk factors and their correlations. We denote:

- X_p is the portfolio return in one period,

- N is the number of assets in the portfolio,

- X_i is the i-th asset return in one period $(\tau = 1), X_i = \Delta P(1) = P_i(1) - P_i(0)$, where P_i is the log-spot price of asset $i, i = 1, ..., N$. More generally, X_i can be the risk factor that enters linearly[6] in the portfolio return.

- w_i is the i-th asset's weight in the portfolio, $i = 1, \ldots, N$.

$$X_P = \sum_{i=1}^{N} w_i X_i \, .$$

In matrix notation,

$$X_P = w^T X \, ,$$

where $w = (w_1, w_2, \ldots, w_N)^T$, $X = (X_1, X_2, \ldots, X_N)^T$.
Then the portfolio variance is

$$V(X_p) = w^T \underline{\Sigma} w = \sum_{i=1}^{N} w_i^2 \sigma_{ii} + \sum_{i=1}^{N} \sum_{j=1, i \neq j}^{N} w_i w_j \rho_{ij} \sigma_i \sigma_j \, ,$$

where σ_{ii} is the variance of returns on the i-th asset, σ_i is the standard deviation of returns on the i-th asset, ρ_{ij} is the correlation between the returns

---

[6]If the risk does not enter linearly (as in a case of an option), then a linear approximation is used.

on the i-th and the j-th assets, $\underline{\Sigma}$ is the covariance matrix, $\underline{\Sigma} = [\sigma_{ij}], 1 \leq i \leq N, 1 \leq j \leq N$.

If all portfolio returns are *jointly normally distributed*, the portfolio return, as a linear combination of normal variables, is also *normally distributed*. The portfolio VAR based on the normal distribution assumption is

$$\text{VAR} = -Y_0 z_{1-\alpha}\sigma(X_p) \ ,$$

where $\sigma(X_p)$ is the portfolio standard deviation (the *portfolio volatility*),

$$\sigma(X_p) = \sqrt{V(X_p)} \ .$$

Thus, risk can be represented by a combination of linear exposures to normally distributed factors.

In this class of parametric models, to estimate risk, it is sufficient to evaluate the covariance matrix of portfolio risk factors (in the simplest case, individual asset returns).

The estimation of the covariance matrix is based on the *historical data* or on *implied data* from securities pricing models.

If portfolios contain zero-coupon bonds, stocks, commodities, and currencies, VAR can be computed from correlations of these basic risk factors and the asset weights. If portfolios include more complex securities, then the securities are decomposed into building blocks.

The portfolio returns are often assumed to be normally distributed (see JP Morgan (1995); Phelan (1995)). One of methods employing the normality assumption for returns is the *delta* method (the delta-normal or the variance-covariance method).

Delta Method

The *delta* method estimates changes in prices of securities using their "deltas" with respect to basic risk factors. The method involves a *linear* (also named as *delta* or *local*) *approximation* to (log) price movements:

$$P(X + U) \approx P(X) + P'(X)U,$$

or

$$\Delta P(X) = P(X + U) - P(X) \approx P'(X)U,$$

where X is the level of the basic risk factor (i.e., an equity, an exchange rate), U is the change in $X, P(X + U) = P(t + \tau, X + U), P(X) = P(t, X)$[7], $P(X)$ is the (log) price of the asset at the X level of the underlying risk factor,

---

[7]Because the time horizon (τ) is fixed and t is the present time, we shall omit the time argument and shall write $P(X + U)$ instead of underlying $P(t + \tau, X + U)$ and $P(X)$ instead of $P(t, X)$. We shall consider the dependency of P on the risk factor X only.

$P'(X) = \partial P/\partial X$ is the first derivative of $P(X)$, it is commonly called the *delta* ($\underline{\Delta} = \underline{\Delta}(X)$) of the asset.

Thus, the price movements of the securities approximately are

$$\Delta P(X) \approx P'(X)U = \underline{\Delta}U.$$

The *delta-normal* (the *variance-covariance*) method computes the portfolio VAR as

$$\text{VAR} = -Y_0 z_{1-\alpha}\sqrt{d^T \Sigma d},$$

where $d = d(X) = (\underline{\Delta}_1(X), \underline{\Delta}_2(X), \ldots, \underline{\Delta}_n(X))^T$ is a vector of the delta positions, $\underline{\Delta}_j(X)$ is the security's delta with respect to the j-th risk factor, $\underline{\Delta}_j = \partial P/\partial X_j$.

VAR Based on the Gamma Distribution Assumption

Since the normal model for factor distributions is overly simplistic, Fong and Vasicek (1997) suggest to estimate the probability distribution of the portfolio value changes ΔP by another type of the parametric distributions - *the gamma distribution*. They also assume that the basic risk factors X_i are jointly normally distributed with the zero mean and the covariance matrix Σ. However, Fong and Vasicek propose a *quadratic* (*gamma* or *delta-gamma*) *approximation* to the individual asset price changes:

$$\begin{aligned}\Delta P(X) &= P(X_1 + U_1, \ldots, X_n + U_n) - P(X_1, \ldots, X_n) \\ &\approx \sum_{j=1}^{n} \underline{\Delta}_j U_j + \frac{1}{2}\sum_{j=1}^{n}\Gamma_j U_j^2,\end{aligned}$$

where ΔP is a security price change, n is the number of basic risk factors, U_j is the change in the value of the j-th risk factor, $\underline{\Delta}_j = \underline{\Delta}_j(X)$ is the security's delta at the level X with respect to the j-th risk factor, $\underline{\Delta}_j = \partial P/\partial X_j, \Gamma_j$ is quadratic exposure (*the gamma*) at the level X to the j-th risk factor, $\Gamma_j = \Gamma_j(X) = \partial^2 P/\partial X_j^2$, $j = 1, \ldots, n$.

The delta-gamma approximation for the portfolio return in one period is defined by

$$\begin{aligned}\Delta P &= \Delta P(X) = P(X + U) - P(X) \\ &= \sum_{i=1}^{n} \underline{\Delta}_i w_i U_i + \frac{1}{2}\sum_{i=1}^{n}\sum_{j=1}^{n}\Gamma_{ij} w_i w_j U_i U_j,\end{aligned} \qquad (10.2)$$

where $X = (X_1, X_2, \ldots, X_n)^T$, X_i is i-th risk factor, U_i is the change in the risk factor X_i, w_i is the weight of the i-th risk factor, $\Gamma_{ij} = \Gamma_{ij}(X)$ is the *portfolio (i,j)-gamma*, $\Gamma_{ij}(X) = \partial^2 P(X)/\partial X_i \partial X_j$, $\Gamma_{jj} = \Gamma_j$, $i = 1, \ldots, n$, $j = 1, \ldots, n$. The variance of portfolio return can be estimated by

$$V(\Delta P(X)) = \sum_{i}\sum_{j}\underline{\Delta}_i\underline{\Delta}_j w_i w_j \text{cov}(X_i, X_j) +$$

$$\sum_i \sum_j \sum_k \underline{\Delta}_i \Gamma_{jk} w_i w_j w_k \mathrm{cov}(X_i, X_j X_k) +$$

$$\frac{1}{4} \sum_i \sum_j \sum_k \sum_l \Gamma_{ij} \Gamma_{kl} w_i w_j w_k w_l \mathrm{cov}(X_i X_j, X_k X_l) \ .$$

From (10.2), ΔP is a quadratic function of normal variates. This distribution of ΔP is, in general, non-symmetric. However, one can approximate the quantile by the skewness parameter and the standard deviation. In fact, Fong and Vasicek (1997) used the approximation for the portfolio VAR value, based on a generalized "*gamma*" distribution:

$$\mathrm{VAR} = -Y_0 k(\gamma, \alpha) \sigma(X_p) \ ,$$

where γ is the skewness of the distribution, $\gamma = \mu_3/\sigma^3$, μ_3 is the third moment of ΔP, $k(\gamma, \alpha)$ is the ordinate obtained from the generalized gamma distribution for the skewness γ at the confidence level α. Fong and Vasicek (1997) report the $k(\gamma, \alpha)$ values at $\alpha = 99\%$:

γ	$k(\gamma, \alpha)$	γ	$k(\gamma, \alpha)$
-2.83	3.99	0.50	1.96
-2.00	3.61	0.67	1.83
-1.00	3.03	1.00	1.59
-0.67	2.80	2.00	0.99
-0.50	2.69	2.83	0.71
0.0	2.33		

(Adapted from: Fong and Vasicek (1997))

The gamma distribution takes into consideration the skewness of the ΔP distribution, whereas the normal distribution is symmetric and does not reflect the skewness.

Historical Simulation

The *historical simulation* approach constructs the distribution of the portfolio value changes ΔP from historical data without imposing distribution assumptions and estimating parameters. Hence, sometimes the historical simulation method is called a *nonparametric* method. The method assumes that trends of past price changes will continue in the future. Hypothetical future prices for time t+s are obtained by applying historical price movements to the current (log) prices:

$$P_{i,t+s}^* = P_{i,t+s-1}^* + \Delta P_{i,t+s-\kappa} \ ,$$

where t is the current time, $s = 1, 2, \ldots, \kappa$, κ is the horizon length of going back in time, $P_{i,t+s}^*$ is the hypothetical (log) price of the i-th asset at time

$t+s$, $P_{i,t}^* = P_{i,t}$, $\Delta P_{i,t+s-\kappa} = P_{i,t+s-\kappa} - P_{i,t+s-1-\kappa}$, $P_{i,t}$ is the historical (log) price of the i-th asset at time t. Here we assumed that the time horizon $\tau = 1$.

A portfolio value $P_{p,t+s}^*$ is computed using the hypothetical (log) prices $P_{i,t+s}^*$ and the current portfolio composition. The portfolio return at time $t+s$ is defined as

$$P_{p,t+s}^* = P_{p,t+s}^* - P_{p,t} \,,$$

where $P_{p,t}$ is the current portfolio (log) price.

The portfolio VAR is obtained from the density function of computed hypothetical returns. Formally, VAR $= \text{VAR}_{t,\tau}$ is estimated by the negative of the $(1-\alpha)$th quantile, VAR*; namely, $F_{\kappa,\Delta P}(-\text{VAR}) = F_{\kappa,\Delta P}(\text{VAR}^*) = 1 - \alpha$, where $F_{\kappa,\Delta P}(x)$ is the empirical density function

$$F_{\kappa,\Delta P}(x) = \frac{1}{\kappa} \sum_{s=1}^{\kappa} 1\left\{R_{p,t+s}^* \leq x\right\}, \; x \in \mathbf{R} \,.$$

Monte Carlo Simulation

The *Monte Carlo* method specifies statistical models for basic risk factors and underlying assets. The method simulates the behavior of risk factors and asset prices by generating random price paths. Monte Carlo simulations provide possible portfolio values on a given date T after the present time $t, T > t$. The VAR (VAR$_T$) value can be determined from the distribution of simulated portfolio values. The Monte Carlo approach is performed according to the following algorithm:

1. Specify stochastic processes and process parameters for financial variables and correlations.

2. Simulate the hypothetical price trajectories for all variables of interest. Hypothetical price changes are obtained by simulations, draws from the specified distribution.

3. Obtain asset prices at time T, $P_{i,T}$, from the simulated price trajectories. Compute the portfolio value $P_{p,T} = \sum w_{i,T} P_{i,T}$.

4. Repeat steps 2 and 3 many times to form the distribution of the portfolio value $P_{p,T}$.

5. Measure VAR$_T$ as the negative of the $(1-\alpha)$th percentile of the simulated distribution for $P_{p,T}$.

Stress testing

The parametric, historical simulation, and Monte Carlo methods estimate the VAR (expected losses) depending on risk factors. The *stress testing* method examines the effects of large movements in key financial variables on the portfolio value. The price movements are simulated in line with the certain scenarios[8]. Portfolio assets are reevaluated under each scenario. The portfolio return is derived as

$$R_{p,s} = \sum w_{i,s} R_{i,s} \ ,$$

where $R_{i,s}$ is the hypothetical return on the i-th security under the new scenario s, $R_{p,s}$ is the hypothetical return on the portfolio under the new scenario s.

Estimating a probability for each scenario s allows to construct a distribution of portfolio returns, from which VAR can be derived.

10.3   Components of VAR Methodologies

Implementation of the VAR methodologies requires analysis of their components:

- distribution and correlation assumptions,

- volatility and covariance models,

- weighting schemes,

- the window length of data used for parameter estimations,

- the effect of the time horizon (holding period) on the VAR values, and

- incorporation of the mean of returns in the VAR analysis.

The parametric VAR methods assume that asset returns have parametric distributions. The parametric approaches are subject to "model risk": distribution assumptions might be incorrect. The frequent assumption is that asset returns have a multivariate normal distribution. Though, many financial time-series violate the normality assumption. Empirical data exhibit asymmetric, leptokurtic or platokurtic distributions with heavy tails. Fong and Vasicek (1997) suggest to use the gamma distribution. The historical simulation technique does not place the distribution assumptions, thus, it is free of model risk and "parameter estimation" risk. The Monte Carlo approach specifies the distributions of the underlying instruments.

The VAR methods apply diverse volatility and correlation models [9]:

- constant volatility (moving window),

---

[8]Scenarios include possible movements of the yield curve, changes in exchange rates, etc. together with estimates of the underlying probabilities.

[9]Duffie and Pan (1997); Jackson, Maude, and Perraudin (1997); JP Morgan (1995); Phelan (1995); Hopper (1996); Mahoney (1996); Hendricks (1996/1997).

- exponential weighting,
- GARCH,
- EGARCH (asymmetric volatility),
- cross-market GARCH,
- implied volatility,
- subjective views [10].

Constant Volatility Models

In the *constant volatility* (*equally weighted*) models, variances and covariances do not change over time. They are approximated by sample variances and covariances over the estimation "window":

$$\hat{\sigma}_{t,T}^2 = \frac{1}{T-t} \sum_{i=t+1}^{T} (R_i - \hat{\mu}_{t,T})^2 \ ,$$

where $\hat{\sigma}_{t,T}$ is the estimated variance of returns R_i over the time window $[t, T]$, $\hat{\mu}_{t,T}$ is the estimated mean of returns over the time window $[t, T]$,

$$\hat{\mu}_{t,T} = \frac{1}{T-t} \sum_{i=t+1}^{T} R_i.$$

If the mean return is assumed to be sufficiently small,

$$\hat{\sigma}_{t,T}^2 = \frac{1}{T-t} \sum_{i=t+1}^{T} R_i^2 \ .$$

Weighted Volatility Models

The empirical financial data do not exhibit constant volatility. The *exponential weighting* models take into account time-varying volatility and accentuate the recent observations:

$$\hat{\sigma}_{t,T}^2 = \sum_{i=t+1}^{T} \Theta_i (R_i - \hat{\mu}_{t,T})^2 \ ,$$

where θ_i are the weighting values:

$$0 < \Theta_i < 1, \ \sum_{i=t+1}^{T} \Theta_i = 1 \ . \tag{10.3}$$

---

[10]The method of "subjective views" means that analysts make predictions of volatility from own views of market conditions. See Hopper(1996/1997).

The weighting schemes are divided on *uniform* (see JP Morgan (1995); Jackson, Maude, and Perraudin (1997)) and *asset-specific* (see Lawrence and Robinson (1995)) schemes. The JP Morgan's RiskMetrics system adopted the *uniform weighting* approach:

$$\Theta_i = (1 - \lambda)\lambda^{T-i}c_{T-t} \ ,$$

where λ is the decay factor, $0 < \lambda < 1$, and $c_{T-t} > 0$ is chosen so that the constraints (10.3) are met. JP Morgan uses $\lambda = 0.94$ for a 1-day time horizon. Jackson, Maude and Perraudin (1997) demonstrate that the weighting schemes with lower values of λ in parametric models lead to higher tail probabilities, proportions of actual observations exceeding the VAR predictions (see Jackson, Maude, Perraudin (1997, table 4, p. 179)). They point out a trade-off between the degree of approximating time-varying volatilities and the performance of the parametric methods. Hendricks (1996/1997) found that decreasing λ accompanies with higher variability of the VAR measurements.

The CSFB's PrimeRisk employs *the asset-specific weighting schemes*. It develops specific volatility models (different weighting schemes) for different types of assets (i.e., equities, futures, OTC options).

ARCH Models

Popular models explaining time-varying volatility are *autoregressive conditional heteroskedasticity (ARCH)* models models, introduced by Engle index-AEngle, R. (1982). In the ARCH models the conditional variances follow autoregressive processes. The ARCH(q) model assumes the returns on the i-th asset $R_{i,1}$, $R_{i,2}$, ... are explained by the process:

$$R_{i,t} = \mu_i + \sigma_{i,t}u_{i,t} \ ,$$

$$\sigma_{i,t}^2 = \alpha_i + \sum_{j=1}^{q} \beta_{ij} \left(R_{i,t-j} - \mu_i\right)^2 \ ,$$

where μ_i is the expectation of R_i , $\sigma_{i,t}^2$ is the conditional variance of R_i at time t, $u_{i,t+1}$ is a random shock with the mean of zero and the variance of 1 (a common assumption is $(U_{i,t})_{t\geq 1} \sim$ iid $N(0,1)$), α_i and β_{ij} are constants, $\alpha_i > 0, \beta_{ij} \geq 0, j = 1, \ldots, q, i = 1, \ldots, n$ [11].

In the ARCH(1) model the conditional volatility at period t depends on the volatility at the previous period $t - 1$. If volatility at time $t - 1$ was large, the volatility at time t is expected to be large as well. Observations will exhibit clustered volatilities: one can distinguish periods with high volatilities and tranquil periods.

---

[11]The dependence structure of the returns $R_t = (R_{1,t}, R_{2,t}, \ldots, R_{n,t})$ needs additional specifications for each $t > 0$.

GARCH Models

Bollerslev (1986) suggested the *generalized ARCH (GARCH)* model (see also Bollerslev, Chou, and Kroner (1992)). In the GARCH models the conditional variance contains both autoregressive and moving average components (it follows an ARMA process). In the GARCH(p,q) model, the return on the i-th asset has the representation

$$R_{i,t} = \mu_i + \sigma_{i,t} u_{i,t} ,$$

the conditional variance is assumed to follow

$$\sigma_{i,t}^2 = \alpha_i + \sum_{j=1}^{q} \beta_{ij}(R_{i,t-j} - \mu_i)^2 + \sum_{k=1}^{p} \gamma_{jk}\sigma_{i,t-k}^2 ,$$

where $\alpha_i, \beta_{ij}, \gamma_{ik}$ are constants, $\alpha_i > 0, \beta_{ij} \geq 0, \gamma_{ik} \geq 0, j = 1, \ldots, q, k = 1, \ldots, p, i = 1, \ldots, n$.

The advantage of using the GARCH model ensues from the fact that an AR process of an high order might be represented by more parsimonious ARMA process. Thus, the GARCH model will have less parameters to be estimated than the corresponding ARCH model.

EGARCH Models

Nelson (1991) introduced the *exponential GARCH (EGARCH)* model. In the general EGARCH(p, q) model, the conditional variance follows (see Hamilton (1994)).

$$\log \sigma_t^2 = \alpha + \sum_{j=1}^{q} \beta_j \left\{ \left| \frac{R_{t-j} - \mu}{\sigma_{t-j}} \right| - E \left| \frac{R_{t-j} - \mu}{\sigma_{t-j}} \right| + \delta \frac{(R_{t-j} - \mu)}{\sigma_{t-j}} \right\}$$

$$+ \sum_{i=1}^{p} \gamma_i \log \sigma_{t-i}^2 .$$

The δ parameter helps explain asymmetric volatility. If $\beta_j > 0$ and $-1 < \delta < 0$, then negative deviations of R_t from the mean entail higher volatility than positive deviations do. If $\beta_j > 0$ and $\delta < -1$, then positive deviations lower volatility whereas negative deviations cause additional volatility.

The advantage of using the EGARCH model is that it does not impose positivity restrictions on coefficients, whereas the GARCH model requires coefficients to be positive.

Cross-market GARCH

The *cross-market GARCH* allows to estimate volatility in one market from volatilities in other markets. Duffie and Pan (1997) provide an example of cross-market GARCH, which employs the *bivariate GARCH* model:

$$
\begin{pmatrix} \sigma_{1,t}^2 \\ \sigma_{12,t} \\ \sigma_{2,t}^2 \end{pmatrix} = A + B \begin{pmatrix} R_{1,t}^2 \\ R_{1,t}\, R_{2,t} \\ R_{2,t}^2 \end{pmatrix} + \Gamma \begin{pmatrix} \sigma_{1,t-1}^2 \\ \sigma_{12,t-1} \\ \sigma_{2,t-1}^2 \end{pmatrix}
$$

where $\sigma_{1,t-1}$ is the conditional standard deviation of $R_{1,t}$, $\sigma_{2,t-1}$ is the conditional standard deviation of $R_{2,t}$, $\sigma_{12,t-1}$ is the conditional covariance between $R_{1,t}$ and $R_{2,t}$, $R_{1,t}$ is the return in the first market at time t, $R_{2,t}$ is the return in the second market at time t, A is a vector of three elements, B is a 3x3 matrix, Γ is a 3x3 matrix.

Implied Volatilities

Sometimes analysts use *implied volatilities* to estimate future volatilities. Implied volatilities are volatilities derived from pricing models. For instance, implied volatilities can be obtained from the Black-Scholes option pricing model (see also Chapter 11 and 12). Option prices calculated by the Black-Scholes formula $C_t = C(S_t, K, r, \sigma, \tau)$ are increasing in volatility σ. Hence, "inverting" the formula, one can obtain the implied volatility values $\sigma = \sigma(C_t, S_t, K, r, \tau)$. Here, C_t is the option price, S_t is the price of the underlying asset, K is the exercise price, r is the constant interest rate, and τ is the time to expiration.

The *implied tree* technique (see Derman and Kani (1994); Rubinstein (1994); Jackwerth and Rubinstein (1995 and 1996)) assumes implied volatilities change over time and computes them relating the modeled and observed option prices.

One of methods for estimating volatility is the method of *"subjective views"* (see Hopper (1996)). Analysts make predictions of volatility from own views of market conditions.

Besides the distribution assumptions and volatility models, the VAR computations also need specification of correlation assumptions on price changes and volatilities within and across markets (see Duffie and Pan (1997); Beder (1995); Liu (1996)). Beder (1995) illustrated the sensitivity of VAR results to correlation assumptions. She computed VAR using the Monte Carlo simulation method under different assumptions: (i) correlations across asset groups and (ii) correlations only within asset groups. The obtained VAR estimates were lower for the first type of correlation assumptions than for the second type.

Time horizon

The *time horizon* (the *holding period*) in the VAR computations can take any time value. In practice, it varies from one day to two weeks (10 trading days) and depends on liquidity of assets and frequency of trading transactions. It is assumed that the portfolio composition remains the same over the holding period. This assumption constrains dynamic trading strategies. The Basle Committee recommends to use the 10-day holding period. Users argue that the time horizon of 10 days is inadequate for frequently traded instruments and is restrictive for illiquid assets. Long holding periods are usually recommended for portfolios with illiquid instruments. Though, many model approximations are only valid within short periods of time.

Beder (1995) analyzed the impact of the time horizon on VAR estimations. She calculated VAR for three hypothetical portfolios applying four different approaches for the time horizons of 1-day and 10-day. For all VAR calculations, with the exception of one case, Beder reported larger VAR estimates for longer time horizons.

Window length

The *window length* is the length of the data subsample (the observation period) used for a VAR estimation. The window length choice is related to sampling issues and availability of databases. The regulators suggest to use the 250-day (one-year) window length.

Jackson, Maude, and Perraudin (1997) computed parametric and simulation VARs for the 1-day and 10-day time horizons using the window lengths from three to 24 months. They concluded that VAR forecasts based on longer data windows are more reliable (see Jackson, Maude, and Perraudin (1997, table 5, p. 180)). Beder (1995) estimated VAR applying the historical simulation method for the 100-day and 250-day window lengths. Beder shows that the VAR values increase with the expanded observation intervals. Hendricks (1996) calculated the VAR measures using the parametric approach with equally weighted volatility models and the historical simulation approach for window lengths of 50, 125, 250, 500, and 1250 days. He reports that the VAR measures become more stable for longer observation periods.

Incorporation of the mean of returns

In many cases the mean of returns is assumed to be zero. Jackson, Maude, and Perraudin (1997) analyze the effects of (i) inclusion of the mean in calculations and (ii) setting the mean to zero on VAR results. Their analysis did not lead to certain conclusions (see Jackson, Maude, and Perraudin (1997, table 6, p. 181)).

10.4 Evaluation of VAR Methods: Strength and Weaknesses

The VAR methods provide only estimated VAR values. The important problem is to evaluate accuracy of the VAR estimates. Researchers propose different performance measures.

Kupiec (1995) compares techniques for assessing the accuracy of the VAR methods. He describes daily monitoring tests based on: the time until the first failure, the time between additional failures, the number of failures; a test for infrequent monitoring schemes based on the sample proportion test statistics and the binomial distribution; tests based on historical simulation. Kupiec concludes: the tests based on observed data have low power; the critical values, obtained from historical simulations, are biased and subject to sampling errors. Lopez (1996), and Mahoney (1996) also investigate evaluations based on the binomial distribution. Hendricks and Hirtle (1997) explain back-testing of VAR results using the BIS red, yellow, and green frequency zones. Crnkovic and Drachman (1996) recommend to use the distribution forecast evaluation. Mahoney (1996) uses the chi-squared test to check the accuracy of the shape of the forecasted distribution. Fallon (1996) applies a root-mean square prediction error criteria and a standard regression test of efficiency. Lopez (1996) proposes the evaluation based on the probability forecasting framework. Christoffersen (1995) recommends the interval forecast evaluation. Dave and Stahl (1997) suggest the following performance measures: observed/predicted exceedence ratio against the confidence level, observed/predicted serial exceedence against confidence level, mean log-likelihood against confidence level, mean log-likelihood against volatility percentile.

Hendricks (1996) evaluates performance of the twelve VAR approaches for foreign exchange portfolios using nine criteria: mean relative bias, root mean squared relative bias, annualized percentage volatility, fraction of outcomes covered, multiple needed to attain desired coverage, average multiple of tail event to risk measure, maximum multiple of tail event to risk measure, correlation between risk measure and absolute value of outcome, and mean relative bias for risk measures scaled to desired level of coverage. Hendricks infers that almost all considered methodologies give the accurate VAR estimates at the 95 percent confidence level. At the 99 percent confidence level, the performance of the VAR methods is not sound. The historical simulation VAR estimates tend to be greater than the variance-covariance VAR estimates based on the normality assumptions. His results confirm that, in practice, extreme movements are more frequent than it is assumed by the normal distribution.

The trade-offs among accuracy, speed, and cost are considered by Pritsker (1996) and Robinson (1996).

The VAR methodologies are becoming necessary tools in risk management. It is important to be aware of *VAR strengths and weaknesses*[12].

Institutions use the VAR measurements to estimate exposure to market risks and assess expected losses. Application of different VAR methods provides different VAR estimates. The choice of methods should mostly depend

---

[12]Beder (1995); Mahoney (1996); Simons (1996); Jorion (1996a, 1996b/1997 and 1997); Hopper (1996); Shaw (1997); *Derivatives Strategy* (1998).

on the portfolio composition. If a portfolio contains instruments with linear dependence on basic risk factors, the *delta* method will be satisfactory. Strength of the delta approach is that computations of VAR are relatively easy. Drawbacks of the delta-normal method are: (i) empirical observations on returns of financial instruments do not exhibit the normal distribution and, thus, the delta-normal technique does not fit well data with heavy tails; (ii) accuracy of VAR estimates diminishes with nonlinear instruments: in their presence, VAR estimates are understated. For portfolios with option instruments, *historical* and *Monte Carlo simulations* are more suitable. The *historical simulation* method is easy to implement having a sufficient database. The advantage of using the historical simulation is that it does not impose distributional assumptions. Models based on historical data assume that the past trends will continue in the future. However, the future might encounter extreme events. The historical simulation technique is limited in forecasting the range of portfolio value changes. The *stress-testing* method can be applied to investigate effects of large movements in financial variables. A weakness of stress-testing is that it is subjective. The *Monte Carlo* method can incorporate nonlinear positions and non-normal distributions. It does not restrict the range of portfolio value changes. The Monte Carlo method can be used in conducting the sensitivity analysis. The main limitations in implementing the Monte Carlo methodology are: (i) it is affected by model risk; (ii) computations and software are complex; (iii) it is time consuming.

VAR methodologies are subject to *implementation risk*: implementation of the same model by different users produces different VAR estimates. Marshall and Siegel (1997) conducted an innovative study of implementation risk. They compared VAR results obtained by several risk management systems developers using one model, JP Morgan's RiskMetrics. Marshal and Siegel found that, indeed, different systems do not produce the same VAR estimates for the same model and identical portfolios. The varying estimates can be explained by the sensitivity of VAR models to users' assumptions. The degree of variation in VAR numbers was associated with the portfolio composition. Dependence of implementation risk on instrument complexity can be summarized in the following relative ascending ranking: foreign exchange forwards, money markets, forward rate agreements, government bonds, interest rate swaps, foreign exchange options, and interest rate options. Nonlinear securities entail larger discrepancy in VAR results than linear securities. In order to take into account implementation risk, it is advisable to accompany VAR computations for nonlinear portfolios with sensitivity analysis to underlying assumptions.

Other VAR weaknesses are:

- Existing VAR models reflect observed risks and they *are not useful in transition periods* characterized by structural changes, additional risks, contracted liquidity of assets, and broken correlations across assets and across markets.

- The trading positions change over time. Therefore, *extrapolation* of a VAR for a certain time horizon to longer time periods *might be problematic*. Duffie and Pan (1997) point out that if intra-period position size is stochastic, then the VAR measure obtained under the assumption of constant position sizes, should be multiplied by a certain factor[13].

- The VAR methodologies assume that necessary database is available. For certain securities, *data over a sufficient time interval may not exist*.

- If historical information on financial instruments is not available, the instruments are mapped into known instruments. Though, *mapping reduces precision of VAR estimations*.

- *Model risks* can occur if the chosen stochastic underlying processes for valuing securities are incorrect.

- Since true parameters are not observable, estimates of parameters are obtained from sample data. The *measurement error* rises with the number of parameters in a model.

- VAR is *not effective when strategic risks are significant*.

10.5   Testing VAR Measures

As we have seen in Section 10.2 most VaR models can be applied either to a single asset or to a multi-asset portfolio. Our tests will be based on a single asset - CAC240 French Stock Index. We present VAR estimation in the case of a single asset, that shall give brief explanation of what the extension is to several assets. We start first with the assumption that we have $N + n$ observations of returns of a given asset within a given time horizon:

$$R_{-n+1}, R_{-n+2}, \ldots, R_0, R_1, \ldots, R_N,$$

the return R_t being defined as the log-change of price of the asset between t and $t + 1$. VAR at date t with confidence interval p, with the same time horizon as the above observations and a unit amount of numeraire invested in the considered asset, is defined as the quantity VaR_t^1 [14] such that

$$P(R_t < -VAR_t) = p,$$

---

[13]Duffie and Pan (1997) provide an expression for the factor in the case of a single asset. If: (i) the underlying asset returns have constant volatility σ, (ii) the position size is a martingale and follows lognormal process with volatility s, then a multiplication factor is approximately of $(\exp(at) - 1)/(at)$, where $a = 2s^2 + 4\rho s\sigma$, ρ is the correlation of the position size with the asset.

[14]In fact, $VaR_t = VarR_t(p)$, but usually for shortness, one omits the index p.

(see 10.1) We assume that at each date t between 1 and N, VAR is estimated according to the latest n observations of the asset returns. That is:

$$\overline{VAR}_t = f(R_{t-1}, \ldots, R_{t-n}) \, .$$

Note that here R_{t-i} should be seen as an observation of the random change in value of the portfolio containing one unit of the asset. If one had to manage a multi-position portfolio, one could extend the single asset method in the following way. Suppose that P is the pricing function of a portfolio, depending on factors $1, \ldots, F$, with observed returns,

$$R^1_{-n+1}, R^1_{-n+2}, \ldots, R^1_0, R^1_1, \ldots, R^1_N, \ldots \quad ,$$
$$R^F_{-n+1}, R^F_{-n+2}, \ldots, R^F_0, R^F_1, \ldots, F^F_N \quad ,$$

and current levels at time t:

$$X^1_t, \ldots, X^F_t \, .$$

We denote the current value of the portfolio by

$$P_t = \mathbf{P}(X^1_t, \ldots, X^F_t) \, ,$$

Then VAR at confidence interval p is defined as:

$$P_t(\mathbf{P}(X^1_t(1 + R^1_t), \ldots, X^F_t(1 + R^F_t)) - P_t < -VAR_t) = p \, .$$

The estimator for VAR is defined by

$$\overline{VAR} = f(\Delta P^t_{t-1}, \ldots, \Delta P^t_{t-n}) \, ,$$

where [15]

$$\Delta P^t_{t-i} = \mathbf{P}(X^1_t(1 + R^1_{t-i}), \ldots, X^F_t(1 + R^F_{t-i})) - P_t) \, .$$

We shall evaluate the performance of the following methods:

- Non-parametric estimation: based on order statistics, the so-called "historical simulation method"

- Gaussian estimation,

- RiskMetrics™ method,

- Tail estimation using the Hill method, see section 3.6

We shall briefly recall these methods.

---

[15] The purpose of calculating ΔP^t_{t-i} is to generate observations of random changes of the portfolio.

Non-parametric estimation ("historical simulation" method)

Consider the last n observations of the asset returns $R_{t-1}, \ldots, R_{t-n}$ on which $\overline{VAR_t}$ is based and sort them by ascending order:

$$R_{(1)}, \ldots, R_{(n)} \, .$$

Assume that they are independent and identically distributed (i.i.d.) with density function f and distribution function F. Then, as $n \to \infty$, and if the ratio $p = k/n$ is kept constant, $R_{(k)}$ trends asymptotically to a normal lay with mean $\xi = F^{-1}(p)$ and standard deviation:

$$\frac{1}{f(\xi)} \sqrt{\frac{p(1-p)}{n}} \, .$$

In this framework, $R_{(k)}$ can be considered as an approximation of the $100 * p\%$ quantile.

The advantage of this method is that asset returns are only assumed to be i.i.d. The estimator is asymptotically normal for almost any distribution one uses in finance. The first main drawback is that the range of quantiles that one can estimate are limited: one can not expect to calculate properly a 0.5% quantile with a hundred observations! The second significant drawback stems from a more practical point of view; simulating the returns of a large and complex portfolio can be extremely computer-intensive.

The Gaussian Method

This procedure is simpler. Recent historical observations allow one to calculate the volatility of asset returns with the well-known least-square estimator:

$$\hat{\sigma}_t^2 = \frac{1}{n-1} \sum_{i=1}^{n} (R_{t-i} - \overline{R}_t)^2$$

where

$$\overline{R}_t = \frac{1}{n} \sum_{i=1}^{n} R_{t-i} \, .$$

Quantiles can be found easily by a numerical approximation of the distribution function. The typical assumption is the normality of the returns R_{t-i} and from there the name of the method (The Gaussian method). In this case, $\overline{VaR_t}$ is indeed equal to $\hat{\sigma}_t$ multiplied by the appropriate scalar determined by the quantile level.

RiskMetrics method

The RiskMetrics method is based on estimating the returns' volatility by the exponentially weighted average of square returns:

$$\hat{\sigma}_t^2 = \sum_{i=1}^{\infty} \omega_i (R_{t-i} - \overline{R_t})2 \,,$$

where

$$\omega_i = (1 - \lambda)\lambda^i \qquad (0 < \lambda < 1) \,,$$

The JP Morgan model assumes that the mean return of the asset is negligible and sets it to zero. With a short-term horizon, (e.g. one day), the volatility effect is indeed more important than the trend effect. The estimation formula of volatility leads us then to an easy recursive formula:

$$\hat{\sigma}_t^2 = \lambda\hat{\sigma}_{t-1}^2 + (1 - \lambda)R_{t-1}^2 \,.$$

Boudoukh, Richardson and Whitelaw (1995) showed that the method proposed by the JP Morgan model gives good results in terms of volatility prediction.

Tail Estimation Using Hill Method

We now replace the Gaussian (thin tail) hypothesis with the Pareto tail hypothesis (heavy tailed distributed returns) for stable returns:

$$F(x) \approx \frac{C}{|x|^a} \,, \text{as } x \to \infty \,,$$

or equivalently,

$$\ln F(x) \approx \ln C - \alpha \ln |x| \,.$$

consider the ordered latest n observations of returns $R_{(1)}, \ldots, R_{(m)}$, and define the Hill estimator,

$$\hat{\alpha}_{Hill} = \frac{1}{\frac{1}{m}\sum_{i=1}^{m} \ln |R_{(i)}| - \ln |R_{(m+1)}|} \,,$$

see Section 3.6. In this formula $m = n/10$ empirically seems to be a proper value. We define the sample distribution function as $\hat{F}(x) = \frac{1}{n}\sum_{i=1}^{n} \mathbf{1}_{\{R_{(i)-x}\}}$, $\ln \hat{C}$ can then be stimated as:

$$\ln \hat{C} = \frac{1}{m}\sum_{i=1}^{m} \ln \hat{F}(R_{(i)}) + \hat{\alpha}\frac{1}{m}\sum_{i=1}^{m} \ln |R_{(i)}| \,.$$

The estimator of VAR at $p\%$ confidence interval could then be derived from 16:

$$\overline{VaR} = \exp\left\{\frac{\ln \hat{C} - \ln p}{\hat{\alpha}}\right\}.$$

Our goal next is to test the null hypothesis that for any t:

$$P(R_t < -VAR_t) = p.$$

In order to derive a testing procedure, we first have to make the approximation that $P(R_t < \overline{VaR_t}) = \bar{p}$ is not too different from p. We have in fact:

$$\bar{p} = \int_{-\infty}^{\infty} Pr(R_t < -v)\varphi(v)dv$$

where φ is the density function of the estimator $\overline{VAR}$. We will have strict equality between p and $\bar{p}$ when $\varphi(v) = \delta_{v=VaR}$. Nonetheless, we will suppose that the precision of the estimator is "good enough" to confirm the approximation. We did some simple calculations in order to quantify the quality of the approximation. Assume again a Pareto-tail for the returns, i.e.:

$$P(R_t < -v) \approx \frac{C}{|v|^\alpha},$$

as well as a normal distribution of the VAR-estimator:

$$\varphi(v) = \frac{1}{\sigma\sqrt{2\pi}}\exp\left(-\frac{(v - VaR)^2}{\sigma^2}\right).$$

The following table gives us the ratio $\frac{\bar{p}-p}{p}$ according to the standard deviation of the VaR estimator and the value of the characteristic exponent α.

Characteristic exponent	1.5	1.5	3	3
Standard deviation	10%	20%	10%	20%
$\frac{\bar{p}-p}{p}$	1.6%	8.3%	5.96%	32.31%

If we accept this approximation, the hypothesis we want to test is now equivalent to the following:

$$
\begin{aligned}
\xi_t = \mathbf{1}_{\{R_t - VAR_t\}} \quad &= \quad 1 \text{ with probability } p, \text{ and} \\
&= \quad 0 \text{ with probability } 1 - p.
\end{aligned}
$$

---

[16] Under some regularity conditions similar to these for the Hill estimator, $\overline{VaR}$ is strongly consistent and asymptotically normal. Unfortunately, the use of tail estimator for $\overline{VaR}$ inherits the drawbacks of the Hill estimator, see section 3.6.

Thus $\frac{1}{\sqrt{n}}\left(\sum_{t=1}^{n}(\xi_t - p)\right)$ converges to a centered normal law with standard deviation $\sqrt{p(l-p)}$. If n is large enough, the fundamental hypothesis of VAR should therefore be rejected at $x\%$ confidence interval if $\sum_{t=1}^{n} \xi_t$ happens to be below $np - q_x\sqrt{p(l-p)}$ or above $np + q_x\sqrt{p(l-p)}$ where q_x is the corresponding normal quantile. Note that for very low quantiles (i.e. low values of p), convergence to the normal law happens to be slow. Thus, we considered $p = 0.5\%$ or $p = 1\%$ in the sequel and used the table for the binomial distribution of $\sum_{t=1}^{n} \xi_t$. Values S of this sum have been considered as contradictory with the hypothesis provided that they were such that:

$$1 - x \leq \sum_{s=0}^{S} C_N^s p^s (1-p)^{N-s} \leq x.$$

Table 10.1 gives the range of VaR exceedings as well as the range of exceeding frequencies $\frac{S}{N}$ in which the null hypothesis can not be rejected. These ranges are provided for $p = 0.5\%, 1\%, 5\%$ and $N = 500, 3000$.

Table 10.1 Number and frequency of exceedings.

| | 0.5% quantile | | | | | 0.5% quantile | | | |
	500 obs.		3000 obs.			500 obs.		3000 obs.	
95% c.i.	0	4	9	21	95% c.i.	0.0%	0.8%	0.3%	0.7%
99% c.i.	0	6	7	24	99% c.i.	0.0%	1.2%	0.2%	0.8%

| | 1% quantile | | | | | 1% quantile | | | |
	500 obs.		3000 obs.			500 obs.		3000 obs.	
95%c.i.	2	8	21	38	95% c.i.	0,4%	1,6%	0,7%	1.3%
99%c.i.	1	10	18	42	99% c.i.	0,2%	2,0%	0,6%	1,4%

| | 5% quantile | | | | | 5% quantile | | | |
	500 obs.		3000 obs.			500 obs.		3000 obs.	
95% c.i.	17	32	131	169	95% c.i.	3.4%	6.4%	4.4%	5.6%
99% c.i.	14	35	123	177	99% c.i.	2.8%	7.0%	4.1%	5.9%

VaR estimations at quantile levels $p = 0.5\%, 1\%, 5\%$ have been performed on a daily basis according to the diverse methodologies on CAC240 French Stock Index between 1976 and 1992. The testing procedure described above has been implemented on the whole sample (i.e. $N = 3000$) as well as for 6 consecutive sub- windows (i.e. $N = 500$). The number S of exceedings is displayed in Table 10.2 and 10.4 the frequency S/N of exceedings is given in Table 10.3 and 10.5

Table 10.2 Number of VaR exceedings on CAC240.

Method numb. of obs. c.i. of VAR	Hill method						Gaussian law								
	100 obs.			250 obs.			50 obs.			100 obs.			1000 obs.		
	0.5%	1%	5%	0.5%	1%	5%	0.5%	1%	5%	0.5%	1%	5%	0.5%	1%	5%
pass 3000	13	23	160	12	30	162	**37**	**53**	148	**35**	**42**	**127**	**38**	**46**	109
pass 500 (6 sub-per.)	2	3	22	1	1	17	4	4	21	3	4	20	2	3	**4**
	2	4	29	1	3	30	4	**11**	24	4	5	25	0	**1**	**9**
	4	5	**34**	**6**	**14**	**47**	**12**	**15**	**33**	**14**	**15**	30	**24**	**27**	**48**
	2	4	23	2	3	18	**5**	6	**15**	**6**	**6**	**13**	5	6	22
	2	4	28	2	4	26	**11**	**14**	**33**	5	7	23	4	4	**14**
	1	3	24	0	5	24	1	3	22	3	5	**16**	3	5	**12**

Method numb. of obs. c.i. of VAR	Historical simulation						RiskMetrics								
	100 obs.			1000 obs.			$\lambda = 0.85$			$\lambda = 0.9$			$\lambda = 0.95$		
	0.5%	1%	5%	0.5%	1%	5%	0.5%	1%	5%	0.5%	1%	5%	0.5%	1%	5%
pass 3000	x	29	153	17	35	143	**44**	**60**	160	**35**	**50**	150	**25**	**43**	134
pass 500 (6 sub-per.)	x	4	22	1	2	**12**	6	9	25	3	7	22	3	5	20
	x	5	28	0	0	22	8	**12**	27	6	**11**	26	4	7	23
	x	8	**35**	**16**	**25**	**59**	7	7	27	6	8	27	7	**10**	28
	x	4	20	0	1	24	8	8	22	6	6	19	4	6	**13**
	x	4	23	1	4	**14**	**12**	**17**	**37**	**10**	**14**	**33**	6	**11**	30
	x	4	25	0	3	**12**	4	7	22	4	4	23	1	4	20

Bold: Rejected at the 95% c.i.

Table 10.3 Frequency of VaR exceedings on CAC240. (in %)

Method numb. of obs. c.i. of VAR	Hill method						Gaussian law								
	100 obs.			250 obs.			50 obs.			100 obs.			1000 obs.		
	0.5%	1%	5%	0.5%	1%	5%	0.5%	1%	5%	0.5%	1%	5%	0.5%	1%	5%
pass 3000	0.43	0.77	5.33	0.40	1.00	5.40	**1.23**	**1.77**	4.93	**1.17**	**1.40**	**4.23**	**1.27**	**1.53**	3.63
pass 500 (6 sub-per.)	0.4	0.6	4.4	**0.2**	0.2	3.4	0.8	0.8	4.2	0.6	0.8	4.0	0.4	0.6	**0.8**
	0.4	0.8	5.8	0.2	0.6	6.0	0.8	**2.2**	4.8	0.8	1.0	5.0	0.0	**0.2**	**1.8**
	0.8	1.0	**6.8**	**1.2**	**2.5**	**9.4**	**2.4**	**3.0**	**6.6**	**2.8**	**3.0**	6.0	**4.8**	**5.4**	**9.6**
	0.4	0.8	4.6	0.4	0.6	3.6	**1.0**	1.2	**3.0**	**1.2**	1.2	**2.6**	**1.0**	1.2	4.4
	0.4	0.8	5.6	0.4	0.8	5.2	**2.2**	**2.8**	**6.6**	**1.0**	1.4	4.6	0.8	0.8	**2.8**
	0.2	0.6	4.8	0.0	1.0	4.8	0.2	0.6	4.4	0.6	1.0	**3.2**	0.6	1.0	**2.4**

Method numb. of obs. c.i. of VAR	Historical simulation						RiskMetrics								
	100 obs.			1000 obs.			$\lambda = 0.85$			$\lambda = 0.9$			$\lambda = 0.95$		
	0.5%	1%	5%	0.5%	1%	5%	0.5%	1%	5%	0.5%	1%	5%	0.5%	1%	5%
pass 3000	x	0.97	5.10	0.57	1.17	4.77	**1.47**	**2.00**	5.33	**1.17**	**1.67**	5.00	**0.83**	**1.43**	4.47
pass 500 (6 sub-per.)	x	0.8	4.4	0.2	0.4	**2.4**	**1.0**	**1.8**	5.0	0.6	1.4	4.4	0.6	1.0	4.0
	x	1.0	5.6	0.0	**0.0**	4.4	**1.6**	**2.4**	5.4	**1.2**	**2.2**	5.2	0.8	1.4	4.6
	x	1.6	**7.0**	**3.0**	**5.0**	**11.8**	1.4	1.4	5.4	**1.2**	1.6	5.4	**1.4**	**2.0**	5.6
	x	0.8	4.0	0.0	**0.2**	4.8	**1.6**	1.6	4.4	**1.2**	1.2	3.8	0.8	1.2	**2.6**
	x	0.8	4.6	0.2	0.8	**2.8**	**2.4**	**3.4**	**7.4**	**2.0**	**2.8**	**6.6**	**1.2**	**2.2**	6.0
	x	0.8	5.0	0.0	0.6	**2.4**	0.8	1.4	4.4	0.8	0.8	4.6	0.2	0.8	4.0

Bold: Rejected at the 95% c.i.

Table 10.4 Number of VaR exceedings on CAC240.

Method	Hill method						Gaussian law								
numb. of obs.	100 obs.			250 obs.			50 obs.			100 obs.			1000 obs.		
c.i. of VAR	0.5%	1%	5%	0.5%	1%	5%	0.5%	1%	5%	0.5%	1%	5%	0.5%	1%	5%
pass 3000	13	23	160	12	30	162	**37**	**53**	148	**35**	42	127	**38**	**46**	109
pass 500	2	3	22	1	1	17	4	4	21	3	4	20	2	3	**4**
(6 sub-per.)	2	4	29	1	3	30	4	**11**	24	4	5	25	0	1	**9**
	4	5	34	6	**14**	**47**	**12**	**15**	33	**14**	**15**	30	**24**	**27**	**48**
	2	4	23	2	3	18	5	6	15	6	6	**13**	5	6	22
	2	4	28	2	4	26	**11**	**14**	33	5	7	23	4	4	14
	1	3	24	0	5	24	1	3	22	3	5	16	3	5	**12**

Method	Historical simulation						RiskMetrics								
numb. of obs.	100 obs.			1000 obs.			$\lambda = 0.85$			$\lambda = 0.9$			$\lambda = 0.95$		
c.i. of VAR	0.5%	1%	5%	0.5%	1%	5%	0.5%	1%	5%	0.5%	1%	5%	0.5%	1%	5%
pass 3000	x	29	153	17	35	143	44	**60**	160	**35**	**50**	150	**25**	**43**	134
pass 500	x	4	22	1	2	**12**	6	9	25	3	7	22	3	5	20
(6 sub-per.)	x	5	28	0	0	22	**8**	**12**	27	6	**11**	26	4	7	23
	x	8	35	**16**	**25**	**59**	7	7	27	6	8	27	**7**	10	28
	x	4	20	0	**1**	24	**8**	8	22	6	6	19	4	6	**13**
	x	4	23	1	4	14	**12**	**17**	**37**	**10**	**14**	33	6	**11**	30
	x	4	25	0	3	12	4	7	22	4	4	23	1	4	20

Bold: Rejected at the 99% c.i.

Table 10.5 Frequency of VaR exceedings on CAC240. (**in %**)

Method	Hill method						Gaussian law								
numb. of obs.	100 obs.			250 obs.			50 obs.			100 obs.			1000 obs.		
c.i. of VAR	0.5%	1%	5%	0.5%	1%	5%	0.5%	1%	5%	0.5%	1%	5%	0.5%	1%	5%
pass 3000	0.43	0.77	5.33	0.40%	1.00	5.40	**1.23**	**1.77**	4.93	**1.17**	1..40	4.23	**1.27**	**1.53**	**3.63**
pass 500	0.4	0.6	4.4	0.2	0.2	3.4	0.8	0.8	4.2	0.6	0.8	4.0	0.4	0.6	**0.8**
(6 sub-per.)	0.4	0.8	5.8	0.2	0.6	6.0	0.8	**2.2**	4.8	0.8	1.0	5.0	0.0	0.2	**1.8**
	0.8	1.0	6.8	1.2	**2.5**	**9.4**	**2.4**	**3.0**	6.6	**2.8**	**3.0**	6.0	**4.8**	**5.4**	**9.6**
	0.4	0.8	4.6	0.4	0.6	3.6	1.0	1.2	3.0	1.2	1.2	**2.6**	1.0	1.2	4.4
	0.4	0.8	5.6	0.4	0.8	5.2	**2.2**	**2.8**	6.6	1.0	1.4	4.6	0.8	0.8	2.8
	0.2	0.6	4.8	0.0	1.0	4.8	0.2	0.6	4.4	0.6	1.0	3.2	0.6	1.0	**2.4**

Method	Historical simulation						RiskMetrics								
numb. of obs.	100 obs.			1000 obs.			$\lambda = 0.85$			$\lambda = 0.9$			$\lambda = 0.95$		
c.i. of VAR	0.5%	1%	5%	0.5%	1%	5%	0.5%	1%	5%	0.5%	1%	5%	0.5%	1%	5%
pass 3000	x	0.97	5.10	0.57	1.17	4.77	**1.47**	**2.00**	5.33	**1.17**	**1.67**	5.00	**0.83**	**1.43**	4.47
pass 500	x	0.8	4.4	0.2	0.4	**2.4**	1.0	1.8	5.0	0.6	1.4	4.4	0.6	1.0	4.0
(6 sub-per.)	x	1.0	5.6	0.0	**0.0**	4.4	**1.6**	**2.4**	5.4	1.2	**2.2**	5.2	0.8	1.4	4.6
	x	1.6	7.0	**3.0**	**5.0**	**11.8**	**1.4**	1.4	5.4	1.2	1.6	5.4	**1.4**	2.0	5.6
	x	0.8	4.0	0.0	**0.2**	4.8	**1.6**	1.6	4.4	1.2	1.2	3.8	0.8	1.2	**2.6**
	x	0.8	4.6	0.2	0.8	2.8	**2.4**	**3.4**	7.4	**2.0**	**2.8**	6.6	1.2	**2.2**	6.0
	x	0.8	5.0	0.0	0.6	2.4	0.8	1.4	4.4	0.8	0.8	4.6	0.2	0.8	4.0

Bold: Rejected at the 99% c.i.

The bold-typed quantities in in the the four tables indicate the cases when we reject the null hypothesis.

The conclusions of this text-procedural are as follows:

- The use of too many data depreciates the quality of the prediction. This is simply due to natural heteroskedasticity of financial data. Note that our test is not a test of the precision of the estimator. Further comments will therefore concentrate on methods based on 100 observations.

- For 5% quantile level, RiskMetrics and historical simulation provide good results. They both pass the test on the whole period. One rejection out of 6 sub-periods can still be considered "acceptable".

- For 1% quantile level, only historical simulation and the Hill method provide good results.

- For 0.5% quantile level, historical simulation can hardly be applied. A quantile estimator based on order statistics would require a lot of data, which would diminish the predictive power. Only the Hill method provides satisfactory results.

- 5% quantile levels are more easily handled than 1% or 0.5% quantiles. Precision of estimation is much better at the 5events are not properly taken into account under Gaussian hypothesis is also less sensitive at 5% than at 1%.

- RiskMetrics' exponential weighting seems to improve calculations compared with traditional Gaussian estimators.

Additional remarks can be made.

- At the 95% confidence interval, figures obtained with the three methods are not too different. At the 99% c.i., they would be more divergent. Historical simulation and Hill methods allow variations of the ratio between 1% and 5% $VaR's$ whereas it is fixed to 2.33/1.64 in other methods.

- RiskMetrics data are not as reliable. A sharp change in the factor has more impact on the measure. On the other hand, this impact will fade away smoothly as time goes by. With the Gaussian or historical simulation method, the sharp change will have another impact when it goes out of the observation window.

In a conclusion the above test shows clearly that non-traditional hypothesis for financial returns, i.e. not based on the Gaussian Law, dramatically increase the quality of VAR estimations. Whereas, the gain in quality is not always detectable in the case of "average" relations (see e.g. Gamrowski and Rachev (1999)). Hits gain is undeniable when one tries to model extreme events like in a VAR approach.

10.6   Stable Modeling of VAR

In this section we propose the use of stable distributions in VAR modeling. We shall describe the stable VAR approach with the existing methodologies[17].

Estimation of stable parameters[18]

We start with examining the methods of estimating the stable parameters and their applicability in VAR computations, where the primary concern is the tail behavior of distributions. It has been proposed that it is more useful to evaluate directly the tail index (the index of stability) instead of fitting the whole distribution. The latter method is claimed to negatively affect the estimation of the tail behavior by its use of "center" observations. We shall briefly recall both approaches: tail estimation and entire-distribution modeling. We suggest a method, which combines the two techniques: it is designed for fitting the overall distribution with greater emphasis on the tails.

Tail estimators for the index of stability α are based on the asymptotic Pareto tail behavior of stable distributions[19]. We shall consider the following estimators of tail thickness: the Hill, the Pickands, and the modified unconditional Pickands[20]. The Hill estimator[21] is described by

$$\hat{\alpha}_{\text{Hill}} = \frac{1}{\frac{1}{k} \sum_{j=1}^{k} \ln(X_{n+1-j:n}) - \ln X_{n-k:n}},$$

where $X_{j:n}$ denotes the j-th order statistic of sample $X_1, \ldots, X_n$ [22]; the integer k points where the tail area "starts". The selection of k is complicated by a tradeoff: it must be adequately small so that $X_{n-k:n}$ is in the tail of the distribution; but if it is too small, the estimator is not accurate. The disadvantage of the estimator is the condition to explicitly determine the order statistic $X_{n-k:n}$. It is proved that, for stable Paretian distributions, the

---

[17]The results of this setions are due to Khindanova, Rachev and Schwartz (1999).

[18]For additional references on estimation of four parameters of stable univariate laws, see Chobanov, Mateev, Mittnik, and Rachev (1996), Gamrowski and Rachev (1994, 1995a, and 1995b), Klebanov, Melamed, and Rachev (1994), Kozubowski and Rachev (1994), McCulloch (1996), Mittnik and Rachev (1991), Rachev and SenGupta (1993). For the multivariate case estimation of: the spectral measure, the index of stability, the covariation and tests for dependence of stable distributed returns, see Cheng and Rachev (1995), Gamrowski and Rachev (1994, 1995a, 1995b, and 1996), Heathcote, Cheng, and Rachev (1995), Mittnik and Rachev (1993b), Rachev and Xin (1993).

[19]See section 3.1.

[20]For details on the Hill, Pickands, and the modified unconditional Pickands estimators, see Mittnik, Paolella, Rachev (1998b) and references therein.

[21]Hill (1975).

[22]Given a sample of observations $X_1, \ldots, X_n$, we rearrange the sample in increasing order $X_{1:n} \leq \cdots \leq X_{n:n}$, then the j-th order statistic is equal to $X_{j:n}$.

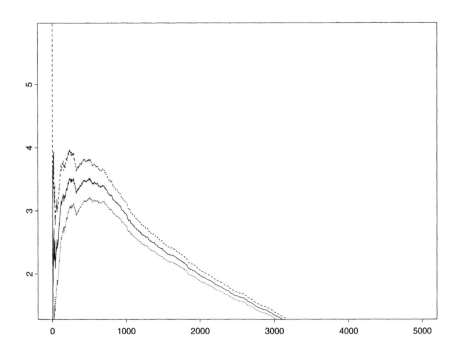

Fig. 10.1   Hill estimator for 10,000 standard stable observations with index $\alpha = 1.9$. (Adapted from: Khindanova, Rachev and Schwartz (1999))

Hill estimator is consistent and asymptotically normal. Mittnik, Paolella, and Rachev (1998b), see Section 3.6, found that, the small sample performance of $\hat{\alpha}_{\text{Hill}}$ does not resemble its asymptotic behavior, even for $n > 10,000$ (see Figure 10.1 [23]).

It is necessary to have enormous data series in order to obtain unbiased estimates of α, for example, with $\alpha = 1.9$, reasonable estimates are produced only for $n > 100,000$ (see Figure 10.2 [24]). Alternatives to the Hill estimator are the Pickands and the modified unconditional Pickands estimators. The "original" Pickands estimator[25] takes the form

---

[23]In Figure 10.1, the true value of α is 1.9, the sample size is $n{=}10,000$; the x-axis shows values of k from 1 to $n/2 = 5000$. Notice that the estimator for $\hat{\alpha} = \hat{\alpha}(k(n), n)$ is unbiased when $\lim_{n\to\infty}(k(n)/n) \to 0$. So, unbiasedness of the estimator requires very small values of k. However, for a small value of k, the variance of the estimator is large. A close look at the estimator $\hat{\alpha}(k, n)$ suggests a value of $\hat{\alpha}$ around 2.2, whereas $\alpha{=}1.9$.
[24]In Figure 10.2, the true α is again 1.9, the sample size is $n = 500,000$, $k = 1, \ldots, n/2 = 250,000$. One can see that, for very small values of k, $\alpha \approx 1.9$.
[25]Pickands (1975).

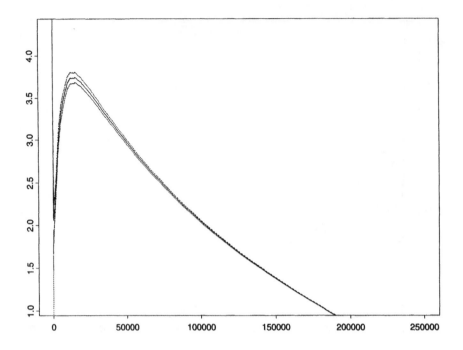

Fig. 10.2 Hill estimator for 500,000 standard stable observations with index $\alpha = 1.9$.
(Adapted from: Khindanova, Rachev and Schwartz (1999))

$$\hat{\alpha}_{Pick} = \frac{\ln 2}{\ln(X_{n-k+1:n} - X_{n-2k+1:n}) - \ln(X_{n-2k+1:n} - X_{n-4k+1:n})}, 4k < n.$$

The Pickands estimator requires choice of the optimal k, which depends on the true unknown α. Mittnik and Rachev (1996a) proposed a new tail estimator named "the modified unconditional Pickands (MUP) estimator", $\hat{\alpha}_{MUP}$. An estimate of α is obtained by applying the nonlinear least squares method to the following system:

$$k_2 \approx X_2 X_1^{-1} k_1 + \varepsilon,$$

where

$$X_1 = \left[\begin{array}{cc} X_{n-k+1:n}^{-\alpha} & X_{n-k+1:n}^{-2\alpha} \\ X_{n-2k+1:n}^{-\alpha} & X_{n-2k+1:n}^{-2\alpha} \end{array} \right], X_2 = \left[\begin{array}{cc} X_{n-3k+1:n}^{-\alpha} & X_{n-3k+1:n}^{-2\alpha} \\ X_{n-4k+1:n}^{-\alpha} & X_{n-4k+1:n}^{-2\alpha} \end{array} \right],$$

$$k_1 = \left[\begin{array}{c} k-1 \\ 2k-1 \end{array} \right], \text{and } k_2 = \left[\begin{array}{c} 3k-1 \\ 4k-1 \end{array} \right].$$

Mittnik, Paolella, and Rachev (1998c) found that the optimal k for $\hat{\alpha}_{MUP}$ is far less dependent on α than in the case of either the Hill or Pickands estimators. Studies demonstrated that $\hat{\alpha}_{MUP}$ is approximately unbiased for $\alpha \in [1.00, 1.95)$ and nearly normally distributed for large sample sizes. The MUP estimator appears to be useful in empirical analysis, see Section 3.6.

Next we shall describe the following methods of estimating stable parameters with fitting the entire distribution: quantile approaches, characteristic function (CF) techniques, and maximum likelihood (ML) methods.

Fama and Roll (1971) suggested the first quantile approach based on observed properties of stable quantiles. Their method was designed for evaluating parameters of symmetric stable distributions with index of stability $\alpha > 1$. The estimators exhibited a small asymptotic bias. McCulloch (1986) offered a modified quantile technique, which provided consistent and asymptotically normal estimators of all four stable parameters, for $\alpha \in [0.6, 2.0]$ and $\beta \in [-1, 1]$. The estimators are derived using functions of five sample quantiles: the 5%, 25%, 50%, 75%, and 95% quantiles. Since the estimators do not consider observations in the tails (below the 5% quantile and above the 95% quantile), the McCulloch method does not appear to be suitable for estimating parameters in VAR modeling.

Characteristic function techniques are built on fitting the sample CF to the theoretical CF. Press (1972b and 1972c) proposed several CF methods: the minimum distance, the minimum r-th mean distance, and the method of moments. Koutrouvelis (1980, 1981) developed the iterative regression procedure. Kogon and Williams (1998) modified the Koutrouvelis method by eliminating iterations and limiting the estimation to a common frequency interval[26]. CF estimators are consistent and under certain conditions are asymptotically normal[27].

Maximum likelihood methods for estimating stable parameters differ in a way of computing the stable density. DuMouchel (1971) evaluated the density by grouping data and applying the fast Fourier transform to "center" values and asymptotic expansions - in the tails. Mittnik, Rachev, and Paolella (1998) calculated the density at equally spaced grid points via an fast Fourier transform of the characteristic function and at intermediate points - by linear interpolation. Nolan (1998a) computed the density using numerical approximation of integrals in the Zolotarev integral formulas for the stable density[28]. DuMouchel (1973) proved that the ML estimator is consistent and asymptotically normal. In Section 4 we analyze applicability of the ML method in VAR estimations.

---

[26] For additional references, see Arad (1980); Feuerverger and McDunnough (1981); Mittnik, Rachev, and Paolella (1998); Paulson, Holcomb, and Leitch (1975).

[27] Heathcote, Cheng, and Rachev (1995).

[28] For additional references, see Mittnik, Rachev, Doganoglu, and Chenyao (1997).

Tail estimation using the Fourier Transform (FT) method is based on fitting the characteristic function in a neighborhood of the origin t=0. Here we use the bounds:

$$P(X \leq -\frac{1}{a}) \leq P(|X| \geq \frac{1}{a}) \leq \frac{K}{a} \int_0^a |(1 - f_X(t)|dt^{29}, \text{ for all } a > 0,$$

where $f_X(t)$ is the characteristic function of a random variable X. Precise estimation of the characteristic function guarantees accurate tail estimation, which leads to an adequate evaluation of VAR.

Suppose that the distribution of returns r is symmetric-α-stable[30] , that is: the *characteristic function* of r is given by $f_r(t) = Ee^{irt} = e^{it\mu - |ct|^\alpha}$. If $\alpha > 1$[31], then, given observations $r_1, \ldots, r_n$, we estimate μ by the sample mean $\bar{\mu} = \bar{r} = \frac{1}{n}\sum_{i=1}^n r_i$. For large values of n , the characteristic function of observations $R_i = r_i - \bar{r}$ approaches $f_R(t) = e^{-|ct|^\alpha}$. Consider the *empirical characteristic function* of the centered observations: $\hat{f}_{R,n}(t) = \frac{1}{n}\sum_{i=1}^n e^{iR_k t}$. Because the theoretical characteristic function, $f_R(t)$, is real and positive, we have that $\hat{f}_{R,n}(t) = Re\left(\frac{1}{n}\sum_{i=1}^n e^{iR_k t}\right) = \frac{1}{n}\sum_{i=1}^n \cos(R_k t)$.

Now the problem of estimating α and c is reduced to determining $\hat{\alpha}$ and $\hat{c}$ such that $\int_0^M |\frac{1}{n}\sum_{k=1}^n \cos(R_k t) - e^{-(\hat{c}t)^{\hat{\alpha}}}|dt$ is minimal, where M is a sufficiently large value.

The realization of the FT method is performed in the following steps:

Step 1. Given the asset returns $r_1, \ldots, r_n$, compute the centered returns $R_i = r_i - \bar{r}, i = 1, \ldots, n$, where $\bar{r} = \frac{1}{n}\sum_{k=1}^n r_i$.

Step 2. Construct the sample characteristic function

$$\hat{f}(t_j) = \frac{1}{n}\sum_{k=1}^n \cos(R_k t_j),$$

where $t_j = j\frac{\kappa\pi}{\tau}, j = 1, \ldots, \tau, \kappa\pi$ is the maximal value of t, τ is the number of grid points on $(0, \kappa\pi]$[32].

Step 3. Do the search for best $\hat{\alpha}$ and $\hat{c}$ such that $\sum_{j=1}^\tau |\frac{1}{n}\sum_{k=1}^n \cos(R_k t_j) -e^{-(\hat{c}t_j)^{\hat{\alpha}}}|$ is minimal.

---

[29]The last inequality is by Lemma 3 on p.321 in Shiryayev, 1984.

[30]Empirical evidence suggests that β does not play a significant role for VAR estimation.

[31] As we have already observed, in all financial return data, fitting an α-stable model results in $\alpha > 1$, which implies existence of the first moment.

[32]For computation purposes, we have chosen $\kappa = 20$ and $\tau = 10000$. In the realization of the FT method we selected the following grid steps ht: if $0 \leq t \leq 1$, $ht = 20\pi/50000$; if $t > 1$, $ht = 20\pi/1000$. In order to emphasize the tail behavior, we refined the mesh near $t = 0$ and named that approach *FT-Tail* (FTT): if $0 \leq t \leq 0.1$, $ht = 20\pi/100000$; if $0.1 \leq t \leq 1.0$, $ht = 20\pi/10000$; if $t > 1$, $ht = 20\pi/1000$. The numerical results are reported in section 10.6.

Table 10.6 Financial data series.

Series	Source	Number of observations	Time period	Frequency
Yen/BP	Datastream	6285	1.02.74-1.30.98	Daily (D)
BP/US$	D. Hindanov	6157	1.03.74-1.30.98	D
DM/BP	Datastream	6285	1.02.74-1.30.98	D
S&P 500	Datastream	7327	1.01.70-1.30.98	D
DAX30	Datastream	8630	1.04.65-1.30.98	D
CAC40	Datastream	2756	7.10.87-1.30.98	D
Nikkei 225	Datastream	4718	1.02.80-1.30.98	D
DJCPI	Datastream	5761	1.02.76-1.30.98	D

(Adapted from: Khindanova, Rachev and Schwartz (1999))

Using the above estimation procedure we next consider a stable VAR model, which assumes that the portfolio return distribution follows a stable law. We derive "stable" VAR estimates and analyze their properties applying in-sample and forecast evaluations. We use "normal" VAR measurements as benchmarks for investigating characteristics of "stable" VAR measurements. We conduct analysis for various financial data sets:

- the Yen/British Pound (BP) exchange rate,

- the BP/US$ exchange rate,

- the Deutsche Mark (DM)/BP exchange rate,

- the S&P 500 index,

- the DAX30 index,

- the CAC40 index,

- the Nikkei 225 index,

- the Dow Jones Commodities Price Index (DJCPI).

A short description of the data is given in Table 10.6.

In this part we evaluate stable and normal VAR models by examining distances between the VAR estimates and the empirical VAR measures.

By a formal definition of VAR, VAR estimates, $\overline{VAR}_{t,\tau}$, are such that

$$P\left[\Delta P_t(\tau) < -\overline{VAR}_{t,\tau}\right] \approx 1 - c, \qquad (10.4)$$

where c is the confidence level, $\Delta P_t(\tau)$ is the relative change in the portfolio value over the time horizon τ, i.e., $\Delta P_t(\tau) = R_{t,\tau}$, is the portfolio return at moment t over the time horizon τ, and t is the current time.

For the purpose of testing VAR models financial regulators advise to choose a time horizon of one day, so we take $\tau = 1$. In the text below, if the time horizon is not stated explicitly, it is assumed to equal one day. At each time t, an estimate $\overline{\text{VAR}}_t$ is obtained using lw recent observations of portfolio returns $R_{t-1}, R_{t-2}, \ldots, R_{t-lw}$:

$$\overline{\text{VAR}}_t = \text{VAR}(R_{t-1}, R_{t-2}, \ldots, R_{t-lw}) , \qquad (10.5)$$

see Section 10.5. The lw parameter is called the *window length*. In this subsection, VAR is estimated employing the entire sample of observations, i.e., $lw = N$, where N is the sample size. Hence, we do not point out the present time t.

We obtain "stable" ("normal") VAR measurements at the confidence level c in two steps:

(i) fitting empirical data by a stable (normal) distribution,

(ii) calculating a VAR as the negative of the (1-c)th quantile of a fitted stable (normal) distribution.

"Stable" fitting is implemented using three methods: maximum likelihood (ML), Fourier Transform (FT), and Fourier Transform-Tail (FTT)[33]. Estimated parameters of densities and corresponding confidence intervals are presented in Table 10.7. In the FT and FTT fitting we assume that distributions of returns are symmetric, i.e., the skewness parameter β is equal to zero. Since the index of stability $\alpha > 1$ for our data series, the location parameter μ is approximated by the sample mean. The ML estimates were computed applying the STABLE program by J.P. Nolan[34]. The confidence intervals (CI) for the FT and FTT parameter estimates were derived using a bootstrap method with 1000 replications[35]. Empirical analysis showed that a set of 1000 replications is: (i) satisfactory for constructing 95% CI; (ii) insufficient for obtaining reliable 99% CI. In our experiments, sets of 1000 replications generated: (i) 95% CI for α and σ whose bounds coincided up to two decimal points; 95% CI for μ with slightly varying bounds; (ii) varying 99% CI, with insignificant variation of left limits.

VAR measurements were calculated at confidence levels $c = 99\%$ and $c = 95\%$. The 99% (95%) VAR was determined as the negative of the 1% (5%) quantile. For calculating stable quantiles we used our program, built on the Zolotarev integral representation form of the cumulative distribution function. The 99% and 95% VAR estimates are reported in Tables 10.8 and 10.9,

---

[33]Evaluation of parameters of stable distributions is provided in Khindanova, Rachev and Schwartz (1999). 10.6

[34]The STABLE program is described in Nolan (1997b).

[35]For references on bootstrapping, see Heathcote, Cheng, and Rachev (1995); for discussion on CI based on ML parameter estimates, see Nolan (1998a).

respectively. Biases of stable and normal VAR measurements are provided in Table 10.10[36].

Table 10.7 Parameters of stable and normal densities*

Series	Normal			Stable			
	Mean	Standard deviation	Method	α	β	μ	σ
Yen/BP	-0.012	0.649	ML	1.647	-0.170	-0.023	0.361
			FT	1.61		-0.018	0.34
				[1.57, 1.66]		[-0.095, 0.015]	[0.33, 0.36]
				[1.55, 1.68]		[-0.178, 0.025]	[0.33, 0.37]
			FTT	1.50		-0.018	0.32
				[1.46, 1.55]		[-0.131, 0.034]	[0.31, 0.34]
				[1.44, 1.64]		[-0.261, 0.070]	[0.31, 0.39]
BP/US	0.006	0.658	ML	1.582	0.038	0.007	0.349
			FT	1.57		0.006	0.33
				[1.53, 1.65]		[-0.096, 0.045]	[0.32, 0.36]
				[1.51,1.75]		[-0.393, 0.065]	[0.32, 0.47]
			FTT	1.45		0.006	0.31
				[1.41, 1.51]		[-0.134, 0.070]	[0.30, 0.33]
				[1.40, 1.62]		[-0.388, 0.097]	[0.30, 0.47]
DM/BP	-0.012	0.489	ML	1.590	-0.195	0.018	0.256
			FT	1.60		-0.012	0.24
				[1.54, 1.75]		[-0.064, 0.013]	[0.23, 0.26]
				[1.53, 1.75]		[-0.165, 0.022]	[0.23, 0.27]
			FTT	1.45		-0.012	0.23
				[1.41, 1.55]		[-0.114, 0.038]	[0.22, 0.26]
				[1.40, 1.77]		[-0.402, 0.061]	[0.22, 0.40]
S&P 500	0.032	0.930	ML	1.708	0.004	0.036	0.512
			FT	1.82		0.032	0.54
				[1.78, 1.84]		[-0.013, 0.057]	[0.53, 0.54]
				[1.77, 1.84]		[-0.062, 0.067]	[0.53, 0.55]
			FTT	1.60		0.032	0.48
				[1.56, 1.65]		[-0.066, 0.078]	[0.47, 0.49]
				[1.54, 1.66]		[-0.120, 0.095]	[0.46, 0.50]

(Continuation next page)

*The CIs right below the estimates are the 95% CIs, the next CIs are the 99% CIs.

---

[36]Biases are computed by subtracting the empirical VAR from the model VAR estimates.

Parameters of stable and normal densities (continued)

Series	Normal			Stable			
	Mean	Standard deviation	Method	α	β	μ	σ
DAX30	0.026	1.002	ML	1.823	-0.084	0.027	0.592
			FT	1.84		0.026	0.60
				[1.81, 1.88]		[-0.015, 0.050]	[0.59, 0.60]
				[1.80, 1.89]		[-0.050, 0.057]	[0.58, 0.62]
			FTT	1.73		0.026	0.57
				[1.69, 1.77]		[-0.031, 0.061]	[0.56, 0.58]
				[1.68, 1.79]		[-0.124, 0.073]	[0.56, 0.59]
CAC40	0.028	1.198	ML	1.784	-0.153	0.027	0.698
			FT	1.79		0.028	0.70
				[1.73, 1.85]		[-0.050, 0.088]	[0.68, 0.73]
				[1.71, 1.87]		[-0.174, 0.103]	[0.67, 0.74]
			FTT	1.76		0.028	0.69
				[1.71, 1.84]		[-0.053, 0.091]	[0.67, 0.72]
				[1.69, 1.87]		[-0.394, 0.101]	[0.66, 0.77]
Nikkei 225	0.020	1.185	ML	1.444	-0.093	-0.002	0.524
			FT	1.58		0.02	0.59
				[1.53, 1.64]		[-0.127, 0.102]	[0.57, 0.62]
				[1.52, 1.67]		[-0.421, 0.130]	[0.57, 0.69]
			FTT	1.30		0.02	0.49
				[1.26, 1.47]		[-0.451, 0.316]	[0.47, 0.69]
				[1.05, 1.67]		[-1.448, 0.860]	[0.47, 1.10]
DJCPI	0.006	0.778	ML	1.569	-0.060	0.003	0.355
			FT	1.58		0.006	0.35
				[1.53, 1.66]		[-0.026, 0.100]	[0.34, 0.37]
				[1.52, 1.67]		[-0.140, 0.120]	[0.33, 0.39]
			FTT	1.49		0.006	0.33
				[1.44, 1.55]		[-0.160, 0.062]	[0.32, 0.36]
				[1.44, 1.69]		[-0.396, 0.100]	[0.32, 0.46]

Source: Khindanova, Rachev and Schwartz (1999)

We accompany our computations with plots of:

- daily price levels,

- daily returns,

- fitted empirical, normal, and stable densities with the ML, FT, and FTT estimated parameters,

- daily empirical, normal, and stable VAR* estimates at the 99% and 95% confidence levels[37].

In general, the stable modeling (ML, FT, and FTT) provided evaluations of the 99% VAR greater than the empirical 99% VAR (see Tables 10.8 and

---

[37]The VAR* numbers are the negative values of the VAR estimates, VAR* = -VAR.

10.10). It underestimated the sample 99% VAR in the applications of two methods: FT - for the CAC40, S&P 500, and DAX30 indices, and ML - for the DAX30 index. Biased downwards stable VAR estimates were closer to the true VAR than the normal estimates (see Table 10.10). Among the methods of stable approximation, the FT method provided more accurate VAR estimates for 7 data sets (see Table 10.10). For all analyzed data sets, the normal modeling underestimated the empirical 99% VAR. Stable modeling provided more accurate 99% VAR estimates: mean absolute bias [38] under the stable (FT) method is 42% smaller than under the normal method.

At 95% confidence level, the stable VAR estimates were lower than the empirical VAR for all data sets. The normal VAR measurements exceeded the true VAR, except the Yen/BP exchange rate series (see Table 10.11). For the exchange rate series (Yen/BP, BP/US$, and DM/BP), the normal method resulted in more exact VAR estimates. For the S&P 500, DAX30, CAC40, and DJCPI indices, stable methods underestimated VAR, though the estimates were closer to the true VAR than the normal estimates. Mean absolute biases under stable and normal modeling are of comparable magnitudes.

In-sample examination of VAR models showed:

- the stable modeling generally results in conservative and accurate 99% VAR estimates, which is preferred by financial institutions and regulators[39],

- the normal approach leads to overly optimistic forecasts of losses in the 99% VAR estimation,

- from a conservative point of view, the normal modeling is acceptable for the 95% VAR estimation,

- the stable models underestimate the 95% VAR. In fact, the stable 95% VAR measurements are closer to the empirical VAR than the normal 95% VAR measurements.

The next step in evaluating VAR models is analysis of their forecasting characteristics.

Forecast-evaluation of VAR estimates

In this section we investigate the forecasting properties of stable and normal VAR modeling by comparing predicted VAR with observed returns.

---

[38]Let $b_{m,s}$ be a bias of a VAR estimate: $b_{m,s} = \text{VAR}_{m,s} - \text{VAR}_{Empirical,s}$. The mean absolute bias equals $MAB_m = (\sum_{s=1}^{8} |b_{m,s}|)/8$, where m denotes normal, stable-ML, stable-FT, and stable-FTT methods, and $s - a$ series.

[39]In the 99% VAR estimation for data series from Table 10.6, mean absolute bias under the stable modeling was 42% smaller than under the normal modeling.

Table 10.8 Empirical, Normal, and Stable 99% VAR estimates.*

	99% VAR				
Series	Empirical	Normal	Stable		
			ML	FT	FTT
Yen/BP	1.979	1.528	2.247	2.212	2.494
				[1.968, 2.252]	[2.276, 2.736]
				[1.919, 2.415]	[2.230, 2.836]
BP/US$	1.774	1.526	2.221	2.200	2.668
				[2.014, 2.412]	[2.436, 2.925]
				[1.956, 2.593]	[2.358, 3.029]
DM/BP	1.489	1.149	1.819	1.520	1.996
				[1.190, 1.712]	[1.792, 2.211]
				[1.179, 1.742]	[1.700, 2.329]
S&P 500	2.293	2.131	2.559	2.200	2.984
				[2.117, 2.258]	[2.757, 3.243]
				[2.106, 2.470]	[2.700, 3.336]
DAX 30	2.564	2.306	2.464	2.375	2.746
				[2.260, 2.502]	[2.557, 2.949]
				[2.240, 2.569]	[2.523, 2.997]
CAC 40	3.068	2.760	3.195	3.019	3.144
				[2.753, 3.364]	[2.788, 3.504]
				[2.682, 3.520]	[2.700, 3.841]
Nikkei 225	3.428	2.737	4.836	3.842	6.013
				[3.477, 4.254]	[5.190, 6.701]
				[3.367, 4.453]	[4.658, 19.950]
DJCPI	2.053	1.804	2.446	2.285	2.603
				[1.955, 2.423]	[2.382, 2.870]
				[1.916, 2.474]	[2.288, 3.035]

*The CIs right below the estimates are the 95% CIs, the next CIs are the 99% CIs.
(Adapted from: Khindanova, Rachev and Schwartz (1999))

We test the null hypothesis that equation (10.1) for a time horizon of 1 day ($\tau=1$) holds at any time t:

$$P[\Delta P_t < -\text{VAR}_t] = 1 - c, \qquad (10.6)$$

where ΔP_t is the relative change (return) in the portfolio value, i.e. $\Delta P_t = R_t$ is the portfolio return at moment t, VAR_t is the VAR measure at time t, c is the VAR confidence level, t is the current time, $t \in [1, T]$, and T is the length of the testing interval. The test is performed by checking whether $P[R_t < -\overline{\text{VAR}}_t]$ is reasonably close to 1 - c, where $\overline{\text{VAR}}_t$ is the estimate of VAR_t. Recall that $\overline{\text{VAR}}_t$ is computed using the last lw observations[40].

---

[40]See equation 10.5

Table 10.9 Empirical, Normal, and Stable 95% VAR estimates.*

Series	Empirical	Normal	95% VAR		
				Stable	
			ML	FT	FTT
Yen/BP	1.103	1.086	1.033	0.968 [0.926, 1.047] [0.911, 1.186]	0.995 [0.937, 1.132] [0.911, 1.329]
BP/US$	1.038	1.077	0.981	0.944 [0.898, 1.072] [0.876, 1.599]	0.986 [0.917, 1.158] [0.895, 1.588]
DM/BP	0.806	0.816	0.772	0.687 [0.652, 0.749] [0.641, 0.894]	0.748 [0.695, 0.894] [0.678, 1.418]
S&P 500	1.384	1.497	1.309	1.308 [1.275, 1.361] [1.265, 1.411]	1.319 [1.265, 1.423] [1.246, 1.503]
DAX 30	1.508	1.623	1.449	1.451 [1.415, 1.500] [1.402, 1.533]	1.452 [1.405, 1.521] [1.395, 1.650]
CAC 40	1.819	1.943	1.756	1.734 [1.653, 1.837] [1.621, 1.944]	1.734 [1.647, 1.845] [1.616, 2.288]
Nikkei 225	1.856	1.929	1.731	1.666 [1.570, 1.839] [1.558, 2.280]	1.840 [1.582, 2.512] [1.500, 5.022]
DJCPI	1.066	1.274	1.031	0.994 [0.888, 1.047] [0.870, 1.200]	1.011 [0.944, 1.188] [0.915, 1.615]

*The CIs right below the estimates are the 95% CIs, the next CIs are the 99% CIs.
(Adapted from: Khindanova, Rachev and Schwartz (1999))

Let b_t be the indicator function $\mathbf{1}\{R_t < -\text{VAR}_t\}, 1 \leq t \leq T$. If the equation (10.6) holds, then

$$b_t = \mathbf{1}\{R_t < -\overline{\text{VAR}}_t\} = \begin{cases} 1, & \text{probability} = 1 - c \\ 0, & \text{probaility} = c. \end{cases}$$

Let us denote by E the number of exceedings $(R_t < -\overline{\text{VAR}}_t)$[41] over the testing interval $[1, T]$. If equation (10.6) is valid, then the variable $E =$

---

[41] In nominal levels, an exceeding implies a case when actual losses exceeded the predicted losses.

Table 10.10 Biases of Normal and Stable 99% VAR estimates.

	99% VAR_m-99% $\text{VAR}^*_{Emprirical}$			
		Stable		
Series	Normal	ML	FT	FTT
Yen/BP	-0.451	0.268	0.133	0.515
BP/US$	-0.248	0.447	0.426	0.894
DM/BP	-0.340	0.330	0.031	0.507
S&P 500	-0.162	0.266	-0.093	0.691
DAX30	-0.258	-0.100	-0.189	0.182
CAC40	-0.308	0.127	-0.049	0.076
Nikkei 225	-0.691	1.408	0.414	2.585
DJCPI	-0.249	0.393	0.232	0.550
Mean absolute bias	0.338	0.416	0.196	0.750

*m denotes normal, stable-ML, stable-FT, and stable-FTT methods.
(Adapted from: Khindanova, Rachev and Schwartz (1999))

$\sum_{t=1}^{T} b_t$ has a binomial distribution. We can formulate a testing rule: reject the null hypothesis at level of significance x if

$$\sum_{t=0}^{E} \binom{T}{t} (1-c)^t c^{T-t} \leq \frac{x}{2} \text{ or } \sum_{t=0}^{E} \binom{T}{t} (1-c)^t c^{T-t} \geq 1 - \frac{x}{2}.$$

For large T and sufficiently high VAR confidence levels, the binomial distribution can be approximated by the normal distribution. Hence, the testing rule for large T is: reject the null hypothesis at level of significance x if

$$E < T(1-c) - z_{1-x/2}\sqrt{T(1-c)c} \text{ or } E > T(1-c) + z_{1-x/2}\sqrt{T(1-c)c},$$

where z_p is the p% standard normal quantile. The bounds of admissible VAR exceedings E and exceedings frequencies, $\frac{E}{T}$, for testing at level of sigificance 5% and 1% are provided in Table 10.12.

We examined forecasting properties of stable and VAR models for data series described in Table 10.6. In testing procedures we considered the following parameters:

- window lengths $lw = 260$ observations (data over 1year) and $lw = 1560$ observations (data over 6 years),
- lengths of testing intervals T= 500 days and T=1500 days.

Evaluation results are reported in Tables 10.13 and 10.14. We indicate by the bold font the numbers, which are outside of acceptable ranges.

Table 10.11   Biases of Normal and Stable 95% VAR estimates.

| | | 95% VAR_m-95% $VAR^*_{Emprirical}$ | | |
| | | | Stable | |
Series	Normal	ML	FT	FTT
Yen/BP	-0.017	-0.070	-0.135	-0.108
BP/US	0.039	-0.057	-0.094	-0.052
DM/BP	0.010	-0.034	-0.119	-0.058
S&P 500	0.113	-0.075	-0.076	-0.065
DAX30	0.115	-0.059	-0.057	-0.056
CAC40	0.124	-0.063	-0.085	-0.085
Nikkei 225	0.073	-0.125	-0.190	-0.016
DJCPI	0.208	-0.035	-0.072	-0.055
Mean absolute bias	0.087	0.065	0.104	0.070

*m denotes normal, stable-ML, stable-FT, and stable-FTT methods.
(Adapted from: Khindanova, Rachev and Schwartz (1999))

Table 10.12   Admissible VAR exceedings and exceeding frequencies.

| VAR confidence level, c | Length of a testing interval, T | Admissible VAR exceedings, E | | Admissible VAR frequencies, E/T | |
| | | Significance level, x | | Significance level, x | |
		5%	1%	5%	1%
95%	500	[17,33]	[14,36]	[3.40%, 6.60%]	[2.80%, 7.20%]
	1500	[61,89]	[56,94]	[4.07%, 5.93%]	[3.73%, 6.27%]
99%	500	[2,8]	[0,10]	[0.40%, 1.60%]	[0.00%, 2.00%]
	1500	[9,21]	[6,23]	[0.60%, 1.40%]	[0.40%, 1.53%]

(Adapted from: Khindanova, Rachev and Schwartz (1999))

From Table 10.13 we can see that normal models for the 99% VAR computations commonly produce numbers of exceedings above the acceptable range, which implies that normal modeling significantly underestimates VAR (losses). At window length of 260 observations, stable modeling is not satisfactory. It provided permissible number of exceptions only for the BP/US$ and DJCPI series. At sample size of 1560 and testing interval of 500 observations, exceedings by the stable-FT method are outside of the admissible interval for the S&P 500, DAX30, and CAC40 indices. Testing on the longer interval

Table 10.13   99% VAR exceedings.

Series	Length of a testing interval, T	99% VAR exceedings							
		Window length = 260 obs.				Window length = 1560 obs.			
		Normal		FT		Normal		FT	
		E	E/T	E	E/T	E	E/T	E	E/T
Yen/BP	500	**15**	**3.00%**	**13**	**2.60%**	10	2.00%	2	0.40%
	1500	**40**	**1.67**	**34**	**2.27**	45	3.00	21	1.40
BP/US$	500	10	2.00	5	1.00	1	0.20	0	0.00
	1.500	**26**	**1.73**	13	0.86	17	1.33	**5**	**0.33**
DM/BP	500	**18**	**3.60**	**14**	**2.80**	**17**	**3.40**	8	1.60
	1500	**45**	**3.00**	**33**	**2.20**	**50**	**3.33**	19	1.27
S&P 500	500	**17**	**3.40**	**13**	**2.60**	**25**	**5.00**	**13**	**2.60**
	1500	**35**	**2.33**	**27**	**1.80**	**28**	**1.87**	14	0.93
DAX30	500	**21**	**4.20**	**14**	**2.80**	**19**	**3.80**	**18**	**3.60**
	1500	**41**	**2.73**	**29**	**1.93**	**25**	**1.67**	20	1.33
CAC40	500	**16**	**3.20**	**14**	**2.80**	**14**	**2.80**	**13**	**2.60**
	1500	**34**	**2.27**	**29**	**1.93**	17	1.63	19	1.27
Nikkei 225	500	**15**	**3.00**	**14**	**2.80**	**13**	**2.60**	7	1.40
	1500	**31**	**2.07**	23	1.53	**26**	**1.73**	10	0.67
DJCPI	500	**12**	**2.40**	7	1.40	**15**	**3.00**	10	2.00
	1500	**29**	**1.93**	15	1.00	**28**	**1.87**	17	1.13

(Adapted from: Khindanova, Rachev and Schwartz (1999))

with T=1500 showed that numbers of "stable" exceptions are within permissible range. Table 10.13 demonstrates that increasing the window length from 260 observations to 1560 observations reduces the number of stable-FT exceedings. In contrast, extending the window length for normal models does not decrease E, in some cases, even elevates it. Results illustrate that stable modeling outperforms normal modeling in the 99% VAR estimations.

The 95% VAR normal estimates (except the DAX30 series), obtained using 260 observations, are within the permissible range. Increasing the window length generally worsens the normal VAR measurements. The stable-FT method provided sufficient 95% VAR estimates for the Yen/BP and BP/US$ exchange rates and the CAC40 and Nikkei 225 indices. A study of the predictive power of VAR models suggests that:

• the normal modeling significantly underestimates 99% VAR,

Table 10.14 95% VAR exceedings.

Series	Length of a testing interval, T	95% VAR exceedings							
		Window length = 260 obs.				Window length = 1560 obs.			
		Normal		FT		Normal		FT	
		E	E/T	E	E/T	E	E/T	E	E/T
Yen/BP	500	35	7.00%	**38**	**7.60%**	27	5.40%	31	6.2%
	1500	94	6.27	**104**	**6.93**	109	7.27	122	8.13
BP/US$ 5	500	33	6.60	**45**	**9.00**	**10**	**2.00**	17	3.40
	1.500	73	4.87	**96**	**6.40**	**46**	**3.07**	57	3.80
DM/BP	500	32	6.40	**38**	**7.60**	29	5.80	**37**	**7.40**
	1500	89	5.93	**114**	**7.60**	105	7.00	**139**	**9.27**
S&P 500	500	34	6.80	**39**	**7.80**	43	8.60	**47**	**9.40**
	1500	79	5.27	**98**	**6.53**	62	4.13	69	4.60
DAX30	500	**47**	**9.40**	50	10	42	8.40	45	9.00
	1500	**98**	**6.53**	109	7.27	62	4.13	79	5.27
CAC40	500	32	6.40	34	6.80	31	6.20	32	6.40
	1500	81	5.40	87	5.80	**51**	**4.90**	82	5.47
Nikkei 225	500	**37**	**7.40**	40	8.00	28	5.60	33	6.60
	1500	85	5.67	90	6.00	68	5.43	87	5.80
DJCPI	500	29	5.80	35	7.00	**37**	**7.40**	**46**	**9.20**
	1500	70	4.67	93	6.20	77	5.13	**108**	**7.20**

(Adapted from: Khindanova, Rachev and Schwartz (1999))

- the stable method results in reasonable 99% VAR estimates,

- 95% normal measurements are in the admissible range for the window length of 260 observations. Increasing lw to 1560 observations might deteriorate the precision of the estimates.

Conclusions

The Value-at-Risk (VAR) measurements are widely applied to estimate the exposure to market risks. The traditional approaches to VAR computations - the delta method, historical simulation, Monte Carlo simulation, and stress-testing - do not provide satisfactory evaluation of possible losses. The delta-normal methods do not describe well financial data with heavy tails. Hence, they underestimate VAR measurements in the tails. The historical simulation does not produce robust VAR estimates since it is not reliable in approximating low quantiles with a small number of observations in the tails. The stress-testing VAR estimates are subjective. The Monte Carlo VAR numbers might be affected by model misspecification.

We suggest to apply stable processes in VAR estimation. The in-sample- and forecast-evaluation shows that stable VAR modeling outperforms the normal modeling for high values of the VAR confidence level:

- the stable modeling generally produces conservative and accurate 99% VAR estimates, which is preferred by financial institutions and regulators,

- the normal method leads to overly optimistic forecasts of losses in the 99% VAR estimation,

- the normal modeling is acceptable for the 95% VAR estimation.

Future work is this direction will be construction of models that capture the features of financial empirical data such as heavy tails, time-varying volatility, and short and long range dependence[42].

---

[42]For some preliminary results see Liu and Brorsen (1995), Mittnik, Rachev, and Paolella (1998), Mittnik, Paolella, and Rachev (1997, 1998a, and 1998b), Panorska, Mittnik, and Rachev (1995).

11

Option Pricing Under Alternative Stable Models

11.1 The Option-Pricing Problem

During the last 25 years options have become an important financial instrument. For example, the Chicago Board of Option Exchange (CBOE) was opened on April 26, 1973; and 911 option contracts were made on that day. One year later about 20,000 contracts were made per day; and in 1987 the average number of contracts on the 550 stocks and various stock indexes reached 770,000 per day.[1]

There are many types of option contracts. First, we distinguish between *call options* and *put options*.

A *call option* gives the holder the right to *purchase* a certain quantity of a particular asset (such as a common stake, stock index, foreign currency, precious metal, agricultural commodity, etc.) for a specified expiration date, the so-called strike or exercise price. The holder of a *put option* has the right to *sell* the asset on or before the expiration date. In both cases the holder has the right but not the obligation to buy or sell.

Second, we distinguish between *American options* and *European options*. With a *European option* the right to sell (put) or buy (call) can only be exercised on the specified expiration date, whereas an *American option* can be exercised on or before the expiration date.

Throughout this chapter we will use the following notation:

C : current option value

---

[1] See Hull (1997), Willmott, Dewynne and Howison (1993) and the review of Shiryaev (1994) and the references therein.

S_t : price of the underlying asset at time t

K : exercise or strike price

τ : time to maturity or expiration of option

R : one plus the risk-free interest rate

In the remainder of this introductory section we briefly discuss the option-pricing problem in discrete- and continuous-time as well as for stable returns.

We provide a short review of: (1) Discrete-time option pricing; (2) Continuous-time option pricing in complete and incomplete markets; and (3) Mandelbrot's Paretian-stable Mandelbrot's Paretian-stable and its application to option pricing. For details on the material in this chapter we refer to Karandikar and Rachev (1995), Rachev and Samorodnitsky (1993) and Rachev and Rüschendorf (1994).

11.1.1 Discrete-time Option Pricing: Binomial Option Pricing formulae

Black and Scholes (1973) made a major breakthrough by deriving a formula for the valuation of an European call option for nondivident-paying stocks. We motivate the Black-Scholes formula by considering the situation where asset price movements are described by a multiplicative binomial process over discrete time. This "binomial" approach to option pricing seems to have been proposed independently by Sharpe (1978), by Cox, Ross and Rubinstein (1979)—whose line we shall follow—and by Rendleman and Barter (1979).

Let the current asset price be $S = S_0$ (the known price at $t_0 = 0$) and τ the length of calendar time until expiration of the call (the terminal time). In the binomial model, the elapsed time between successive stock price changes is discrete and equals $h = \tau/N$, where N is the number of periods prior to expiration. At the end of the period $(kh, (k+1)h)$, the price is assumed to be either $S_{k+1} = US_k$ with probability q or DS_k with probability $1 - q$. Letting R be one plus the interest rate over one period, we assume $U > R > 1 > D$. Therefore, successive price movements are given recursively by $S_{k+1} = S_k[\xi_{k+1}U + (1 - \xi_{k+1})D]$, where ξ_k are i.i.d. Bernoulli random variables with success probability q and define $C_U := (US - K)^+$ with probability q and $C_D = (DS - K)^+$ with probability $1 - q$. One can easily check that if there are to be no riskless arbitrage opportunities, the current value of the call must be equal to the current value of an equivalent portfolio $S\Delta + B$ containing Δ shares of the stock and an amount B in riskless bonds;[2] the Δ and B are chosen to equate the end of the period values of the call for each possible outcome, that is, $C_U = US\Delta + RB$ with probability q and $C_D = DS\Delta + RB$ with probability $1 - q$. With these values for Δ and B

---

[2]For the discrete-time markets with two securities "riskless bond" and "risky stock", Harrison and Pliska (1981) and Willinger and Taqqu (1987) showed that it is necessary for the derivation of a fair price for options, to have that over any time period $[kh, (k+1)/h]$ the stock has at most only two possible price values.

the call value $C = S\Delta + B$ equals $C = (pC_U + (1-p)C_D)/R$, where p is the riskless interest rate, satisfying $pUS + (1-p)DS = RS$. Using the same recursive arguments for any $N \in \mathbf{N}$ we obtain the general *binomial option pricing formula*

$$C = C(N) = R^{-N} \sum_{j=0}^{N} \binom{N}{j} p^j (1-p)^{N-j} (U^j D^{N-j} S - K)^+ \quad (11.1)$$

$$= SBi(a_N; n, p') - KR^{-N} Bi(a_N; n, p)$$

with $Bi(a_N; n, p) = \sum_{j=a_N}^{N} \binom{N}{j} p^j (1-p)^{N-j}$, where $p = (R-D)/(U-D)$ and $p' = (U/R)p$, and a_N is the smallest nonnegative integer exceeding $\log(K/SD^N)/\log(U/D)$. If $a^N > N$, then $\mathbf{C} = 0$.

Formula (11.1) assumes non-dividend-paying stocks. Various kinds of generalizations, such as the impact of dividends, dependence of up's and down's from asset-price levels, multinomial versions, etc., are considered in Cox and Rubinstein (1985), Jarrow and Rudd (1983), Ritchken (1987), Hull (1997), Duffie (1992), and references therein.

Moreover, it has been assumed that we deal with European options. Merton (1973a)[3] has shown that if the stock pays no dividends, European and the American call options are valued equally, because in this case the American option will not be exercised before the expiration date. Consequently, the Black-Scholes formula can be used to value the American call options on non-dividend paying stocks. In the presence of dividends, the American call option can be worth more than the European since there is a positive probability for an early exercise. For further details on American options, see Schwartz (1977), Roll (1977), Parkinson (1977), Geske and Johnson (1984), and Shiryaev et al. (1994).

11.1.2   *Continuous-time Option Pricing*

As continuous trading is approached the elapsed time, $h = \tau/N$, goes to zero and the N-dependent quantities of U, D, R, and q need to be adjusted, to obtain a meaningful limiting valuation of a call option. Cox, Ross and Rubinstein (1979) chose $U = \exp(\sigma\sqrt{\tau/N})$, $D = \exp(-\sigma\sqrt{\tau/N})$, $q = \frac{1}{2}(1 + (\mu/\sigma)\sqrt{\tau/N})$, $R^N = R_0$, in the binomial option pricing formula (11.1) for $C = C(N)$. Then, as N goes to infinity the limiting value of the call, $C = \lim_{N\to\infty} C(N)$, equals the *Black-Scholes formula*

$$C = S\Phi(x) - KR_0^{-\tau}\Phi(x - \sigma\sqrt{\tau}),$$

where $x = \frac{\log(S/KR^{-\tau})}{\sigma\sqrt{\tau}} + \frac{1}{2}\sigma\sqrt{\tau}$ and $\Phi(\cdot)$ is the standard normal distribution function.

---

[3]See also Smith's (1976) review of this work.

The alternative derivation of the continuous-trading call valuation obtained in the work of Black and Scholes was based on the assumption that asset prices follow the log-normal diffusion process $dS(t) = S(t)[\mu dt + \sigma dW(t)]$, $S(0) = s$, where $S(t)$ is the asset value at time t, μ is the drift term, $\sigma > 0$ is the volatility coefficient, and $W(t)$ is a Brownian motion in $\mathbf{R}$. W is defined on the complete probability space $(\Omega, \mathbf{F}, P)$, where $\{\mathbf{F}_t\}$ stands for the P-augmentation of the natural filtration generated by W. The price of the risk-free asset, $B(t)$, is given by $dB(t) = B(t)r(t)dt, B(0) = 1$.

More generally, one could treat r, μ and σ as time-dependent variables.[4] In this case, we assume the following regularity conditions: $r(t)$, $\mu(t)$ and $\sigma(t)$ are progressively measurable with respect to $\{\mathbf{F}_t\}$ and bounded uniformly in $\mathbf{R} \times \Omega$; and $\sigma(t)$ is strictly positive (greater than some $\epsilon > 0$) for all t; see Karatzas, 1989, and Cvitanić and Karatzas, 1992.

The European option contract is equivalent to a payment of $(S(\tau) - K)^+$ at the expiration date τ. Black and Scholes (1973) asserted that—in the case of constant μ, σ and r—there is a unique rational value for the option independent of the investor's risk attitude. It is of the form

$$f(x,t) = x\Phi(g(x,t)) - Ke^{-rt}\Phi(h(x,t))$$

with $g(x,t) = \{\ln(x/K) + (r + \frac{1}{2}\sigma)t\}/\sigma\sqrt{t}$, and $h(x,t) = g(x/t) - \sigma\sqrt{t}$. The unique rational value is $f(S(0), \tau)$. It is easy to verify that $f(x,t)$ satisfies

$$\frac{\partial}{\partial t}f(x,t) = \frac{1}{2}\sigma^2 x^2 \frac{\partial}{\partial^2 x^2}f(x,t) + rx\frac{\partial}{\partial x}f(x,t) - rf(x,t), \ f(x,0) = (x - K)^+.$$

Black and Scholes (1973) derived their option pricing formula by solving this partial differential equation. In fact, their method is one of at least four methods that can be used to obtain their formula (see Duffie, 1988b). The arbitrage arguments used by Black and Scholes (1973) and Merton (1973a) have become the starting point for option pricing valuation in deterministic bond price.

Further research in option pricing include the following directions:

- Cox and Ross (1976) developed the risk-neutral approach to option pricing—the Black and Scholes theory was viewed as an analogue of Modigliani-Miller (1958) theory,

- Harrison and Kreps (1979), Harrison and Pliska (1981), (1983), Kreps (1981) used the martingale theory to show that a price process is arbitrage free if it is, after renormalization, a martingale with respect to some equivalent probability measure,

---

[4]Models with time-arying σ were analyzed in Hull and White (1987), Scott (1987), Wiggins (1987), Stein and Stein (1991), Heston (1993), Kallsen and Taqqu (1995), see also the references therein.

- Duffie (1988a) explored an indirect solution of the Black-Scholes differential equation via Feynman-Kac formula to extend the Merton (1973a) continuous-time asset pricing model,

- The arbitrage arguments for option pricing with stochastic interest rate environment were extended in Kopp and Elliott (1989), Turnbull and Milne (1991), Cheng (1991), and Hofmann et al. (1992), see also Duffie (1996). In the vast literature on the "term structure of the interest rate" the bond price is determined by a Markovian instantaneous interest rate; see, for example, the reviews by Duffie (1992) and Shiryaev (1994).[5]

- Different types of options such exotic, Boston, look–back, Asian, Russian option, α-percentile option etc.; see Shiryaev et al. (1994), Shepp and Shiryaev (1993), Miura (1992), Akahori (1995) and references therein.

A slightly more general notion than European option is that of *European contingent claim (EEC)*, which is a financial instrument consisting of payment B at terminal time t; we assume that B is a nonnegative $\mathbf{F}_\tau$-measurable random variable with finite moments of order greater than 1 (see Karatzas, 1989). To define a hedging strategy against any EEC, let $X(t)$ be the wealth of an investor at time t, $\pi(t)$ the amount to be invested in an asset stock and $c(t)$ is the process of the consumption rate.[6] The wealth process $X(t)$ is then determined by

$$dX(t) = \pi(t)\{\mu(t)dt + \sigma(t)dW(t)\} - c(t)dt + \{X(t) - \pi(t)\}r(t)dt.$$

The non-degeneracy condition $(\sigma(t) > \epsilon > 0)$ in Karatzas' approach implies the existence of the equivalent measure to P, namely the "risk-neutral" measure $P^*(A) = E\{Z(\tau)\mathbf{1}_A\}$, where Z is the exponential martingale

$$Z(t) = \exp\left\{ - \int_0^t \theta(s)dW(s) - \frac{1}{2}\int_0^t |\theta(s)|^2 ds \right\}, \quad \theta(s) = \frac{\mu(t) - r(t)}{\sigma(t)}.$$

Pair (π, c) is now called *admissible* for the initial capital $s \geq 0$ if the wealth process, $X(t)$, satisfies almost surely $X(t) > 0$ for $0 < t < \tau$.

A *hedging strategy* against an EEC is an admissible pair (π, c) (with initial wealth $s > 0$), which has at terminal time the same value as the EEC, i.e., $X(t) = B$ almost surely. The *fair price*, v, at the time $t = 0$ for the EEC is then the smallest value of s for which a hedging strategy exists; its explicit value is, in fact, given by $v = E^*[B\exp(-\int_0^\tau r(u)du)]$. Moreover, there exists a hedging strategy with consumption rate $c = 0$ and wealth process

$$X(t) = E^*\left[B\exp\left(-\int_t^\tau \tau(u)du\right) |\mathbf{F}_t \right], \quad X(0) = v,$$

---

[5] Some related work on term-structure models are Brennan and Schwartz (1979), Hogan (1993), Duffie, Ma and Yong (1995).
[6] Here the regularity conditions are: (i) $\pi(t)$ is progressively measurable with respect to $\{\mathbf{F}_t\}$ and square integrable on $[0, \tau]$ almost everywhere; (ii) $\int_0^T c(t)dt < \infty$ almost everywhere.

(see Karatzas, 1989). Further extensions of this approach are in Ocone and Karatzas (1991) and Cvitanić and Karatzas (1992).

The models above assume frictionless markets. Hedging strategies in the presence of transaction costs were studied in:

- Gilster and Lee (1984) and Leland (1985), who derived formulae for call options, that are revised at finite number of times, see also Avellaneda, and Parás (1994) for some extensions.

- Dybvig and Ross (1986), Prisman (1986) and Ross (1987), who considered multiperiod market models in the presence of taxes.

- Bensaid et al. (1991) developed a hedging strategy for the binomial model with proportional transaction costs, see also Bensaid et al. (1992), Boyle and Vorst (1992), Edirisinghe, Naik and Uppal (1993) and Boyle and Tan (1994).

- Jouini and Kallal (1992) computed arbitrage bounds for contingent claims valuations for markets with transaction costs using the martingale approach.

- Figlewski (1989) investigated the numerically effects of transaction costs on hedging, for continuous-time model with some relaxation of the hedging, see Davis and Clark (1994) and Soner, Shreve and Cvitanić (1995). Related works on option pricing with transaction costs are Gilster and Lee (1984), Hodges and Neuberger (1989), Merton (1989b), Shen (1990), Davis, Panas and Zariphopoulou (1993), Davis and Zariphopoulou (1994), Flesaker and Hughston (1994), Hodges and Clewlow (1993), Henrotte (1992), Panas (1993), Pliska and Selby (1993), Toft (1993) and Dewynne, Whalley and Willmott (1994), Korn (1998).[7]

The above contingent claim valuation model assumes that financial markets are *complete*. This means that any claim is *redundant*; i.e., it can be replicated by a self-financing strategy based only on the asset-price process, $\{S(t)\}_{0 \le t \le \tau}$, defined on $(\Omega, \mathbf{F}, P)$. In other words, any contingent claim can be represented as a stochastic integral with respect to semimartingale S. If markets are *incomplete*, a contingent claim is not necessarily a stochastic integral of S; i.e., there exist non-redundant claims carrying an intrinsic risk. Föllmer and Sondermann (1986) introduced the notion of a risk-minimizing strategy and, making use of the projection technique of Kunita and Watanabe (1967), showed that, in the martingale case there exists such a strategy and that it is unique. Extensions to a more general model for incomplete markets, where S is only a semimartingale with respect P, were studied in Schweizer (1988), who defined a risk-minimizing strategy in a local sense, and in Föllmer and Schweizer (1989), who assumed S is a semimartingale with

---

[7]For an extensive survey on option pricing with transaction costs we refer to Safarian (1996).

continuous paths.[8] For further generalizations of the notion of incomplete market see Cvitanić and Karatzas (1992). For a general approach to contingent claim pricing in incomplete markets based on a diffusion model for asset returns with stochastic and path–dependent volatilities we refer to Hofmann et al. (1992).[9]

11.1.3 Stable Models for Asset Returns and Option Pricing

Empirical validations of the Black-Scholes formula have produced mixed results. One possible explanation is that, asset-price processes do *not* satisfy the conditions of the Black-Scholes model.[10] The form of the distribution of asset-price changes represents a controversial issue in modeling functionals of prices. A basic assumption in viewing the Black-Scholes formula as the limiting case of the binomial option pricing formula was that price changes were in domain of attraction of the normal law. As has been discussed earlier in this book, empirical studies typically reject normality for a wide range of financial assets. This holds especially for short-term returns, which are particularly relevant for the limiting case.

The remainder of this section briefly discusses option valuation under the assumption that asset prices follow the stable Paretian model of Mandelbrot and Taylor (1967). Details are given in an appendix at the end of this chapter.

The crucial feature of the Mandelbrot–Taylor Model is that the return process $(W(T))_{T \geq 0}$, is measured in relation to the transaction volume and not physical or calendar time. Transaction volume is assumed to follow Brownian motion with zero drift and variance v^2. The cumulative volume $(T(t))_{t \geq 0}$, i.e., the number of transactions up to calendar time t is assumed to follow a

---

[8]Eberlein and Jacod (1995) considered option valuation for stock price processes with discontinuous paths (typically these models are incomplete). They showed that the set of values of an European call option with strike K and expiration λ are τ, using all possible equivalent martingale measures for the call-valuation, is dense in interval $[(S_0 - e^{-r\tau}K)_t, S_0]$ In this framework the choice of an equivalent martingale measure for option valuation leads to different approaches in arguing what is "a fair price of an option" for price process with discontinuous paths. For one such approach based on Esscher transform we refer to Eberlein and Keller (1995a,b). Other approaches will be discussed later in this chapter and in Chapter 12.

[9]Kallsen and Taqqu (1995) showed that market's completeness holds for a class of ARCH-models redefined in a suitable continuous-time position. For option valuation for ARCH and GARCH price return process we refer to Engle and Mustafa (1992), Duan (1995), Kallsen and Taqqu (1995).

[10]For an alternative approach, based on a microeconomic equilibrium model, see Platen and Schweizer (1994).

positive $\frac{\alpha}{2}$-stable process[11] with characteristic function

$$\mathbf{E}e^{i\theta T(t)} = \exp\left\{-\nu t|\theta|^{\frac{\alpha}{2}}(1 - i(\theta/|\theta|)\tan(\pi\alpha/4))\right\} \quad 1 < \alpha < 2, \ \nu > 0. \quad (11.2)$$

The subordinated process $Z(t) = W(T(t))$ representing the return process with respect to calendar time is then an α-stable Lévy motion with characteristic function (ch.f.)

$$\mathbf{E}e^{i\theta Z(t)} = e^{-t|\sigma\theta|^{\alpha}}, \quad (11.3)$$

where $\sigma^{\alpha} = \nu(v^2/2)^{\alpha/2}/\cos(\frac{\pi\alpha}{4})$ (see Example 5.2 in Section 5.1). As returns are defined as the consecutive differences of the logarithms of the prices, $S(t) = \exp\{Z(t)\}$ represents the price process in the Mandelbrot-Taylor model.

A discrete version of the Mandelbrot-Taylor model is considered in Rachev and Samorodnitsky (1993). There, similar to the price tree in the binomial option pricing formula, consecutive price movements are determined by

$$S_k \stackrel{d}{=} S \prod_{i=1}^{k} U_i^{\delta_i} D_i^{(1-\delta_i)},$$

where δ_i's are i.i.d. Bernoulli $(\frac{1}{2})$-random variables which are assumed to be independent of U_i and D_i. In contrast to the standard binomial option pricing model, where $U_i = U = \text{const}$, $D_i = D = \text{const}$, it is assumed that U_i and D_i are random, namely $U_i = \exp\{\sigma|X_i^{(n)}|\}$, $D_i = U_i^{-1}$, where n represents the number of movements until the expiration date, τ, and $\{X_i^{(n)}, i = 1,\ldots,n\}$ are i.i.d. symmetric Pareto r.v.'s with $P(|X_i^{(n)}| > x) = n^{-1}x^{-\alpha}$, for $x \geq n^{-1/\alpha}$, and $1 < \alpha < 2$. For the discrete-time price process $(S_k)_{k\geq 0}$, $S_0 = S$, we write $\log(S_k/S) \stackrel{d}{=} \sigma \sum_{i=1}^{k} X_i^{(n)}$, so that the process $Z_n(t) = \log(S_k/S)$, $\tau\frac{k-1}{n} < t \leq \tau\frac{k}{n}$, $k = 1,\ldots,n$, $Z_n(0) = 0$, converges weakly to a symmetric α-stable Lévy motion $Z(t)$ on $D[0,\tau]$ with ch.f. given by (11.3). The random "riskless" interest rate in period i is defined by

$$R_i := \frac{1}{2}(U_i + D_i). \quad (11.4)$$

Formula (11.4) ensures the martingale property of the sequence $S_k^* = S_k/(R_1 \cdots R_k)$ with respect to the filtration generated by the random up's and down's:

$$E(S_k^*|\sigma(U_1,\ldots,U_{k-1},D_1,\ldots,D_{k-1})) = S_{k-1}^* \frac{1}{2}E(U_k + D_k)/R_k = S_{k-1}^*.$$

---

[11]In Appendix 11.6 at the end of this chapter we discuss valuation of options based on Clark's (1973) subordinated price process as an alternative to the Mandelbrot–Taylor model. It assumes $T(t)$ to be log–normal process, see also Example 5.5 in Section 5, and Theorem 11.3.

Therefore, (11.4) provides a riskless measure and the option price can be defined as:

$$C_n := \mathrm{E}c^{(n)} = \mathrm{E}\frac{(S_n - K)^+}{R_1 \ldots R_n},$$

where

$$
\begin{aligned}
c^{(n)} \quad := \quad & \frac{1}{2^n R_1 \cdots R_n}\{(U_1 \cdots U_n S - K)^+ + \ldots \\
& + \left[(U_1 \ldots U_{n-1} D_n S - K)^+ + \cdots \right. \\
& + \left.(D_1 U_2 \ldots U_n S - K)_+\right]^+ \ldots \\
& + (D_1 \ldots D_n S - K)^+\}.
\end{aligned}
$$

Rachev and Samorodnitsky (1992) (see the appendix, Section 11.5) show that $R_1 \cdots R_n$ does not converge to a constant in contrast to the classical Black-Scholes formula, where $R_1 \cdots R_n$ is set to be $R^n = R_0^{-\tau}$, with τ being the expiration date.

To derive an expression for the limit $C = \lim_{n \to \infty} C^{(n)}$, suppose that the ξ_i's are i.i.d. uniforms on $(0, 1)$ and the ϵ_i's are independent of ξ_i's $\{-1, 1\}$–valued r.v.'s. Then, $X_i^{(n)} \stackrel{d}{=} \epsilon_i n^{-1/\alpha}\xi_i^{-1/\alpha}$ and rearranging $(X_1^{(n)}, \ldots, X_n^{(n)})$ in an increasing absolute order, say $(X_{1,n}^{(n)}, \ldots, X_{n,n}^{(n)})$, we observe that the latter order statistics have the same joint distribution as $\left[\frac{\Gamma_{n+1}}{n}\right]^{1/\alpha}(\epsilon_1\Gamma_1^{-1/\alpha}, \ldots, \epsilon_n\Gamma_n^{-1/\alpha})$, where $\Gamma_1, \Gamma_2, \ldots$ form a standard Poisson process independent of the ϵ_i's. We can rewrite $C^{(n)}$ as

$$C^{(n)} = \mathrm{E}\frac{(Se^{\sigma(X_1^{(n)}+\ldots+X_n^{(n)})} - K)^+}{2^{-n}\prod_{i=1}^{n}(e^{\sigma|X_i^{(n)}|} + e^{-\sigma|X_i^{(n)}|})},$$

Theorem 11.1 *(Rachev and Samorodnitsky, 1993)*. Letting $n \to \infty$ the "discretized" Mandelbrot-Taylor model implies $C^{(n)} \to C$, where

$$C = \mathrm{E}\frac{(S\exp(\sum_{i=1}^{\infty}\sigma\epsilon_i\Gamma_i^{-1/\alpha}) - K)^+}{\mathrm{E}_{(\epsilon_1,\epsilon_2,\ldots)}[\exp\{\sum_{i=1}^{\infty}\sigma\epsilon_i\Gamma_i^{-1/\alpha}\}]}.$$

Proof. See Appendix 11.5

Rachev and Samorodnitsky (1992) point out that, unlike in the classical Black-Scholes model, it appears impossible to use the hedging argument throughout the whole computation. This is due to the fact that the average is taken only with respect to the *magnitudes* of the jumps of the underlying Lévy motion and, using a hedging argument, with respect to the *directions* of the jumps. This partial averaging will reduce the uncertainty and risk associated with any pricing by taking average.

Below, in Sections 11.2, 11.3 and 11.4, we present an alternative option–pricing formula based on the Mandelbrot–Taylor price process.

11.2   Option Pricing for Generalized Binomial Model

Let us assume that asset-price movements of a particular asset follows

$$S_{n+1} = \begin{cases} S_n U_{n+1} & \text{if } \xi_{n+1} = 1, \\ S_n D_{n+1} & \text{if } \xi_{n+1} = 0, \end{cases}$$

that is, for $n \geq 0$,

$$S_{n+1} = S_n(\xi_{n+1}U_{n+1} + (1 - \xi_{n+1})D_{n+1}), \tag{11.5}$$

where
(i) S_0 is the current market price of the underlying asset;
(ii) $U_N = (U_1, \ldots, U_N)$, $D_N = (D_1, \ldots, D_N)$ are random sequences with finite mean describing the values of up and down moves;
(iii) the vector $\xi_N = (\xi_1, \ldots, \xi_N)$,

$$P(\xi_i = 0 \text{ or } 1) = 1, \tag{11.6}$$

describes the probability for ups and downs;
(iv) it is assumed that

$$P(0 < D_i < R_i < U_i < \infty) = 1, \qquad R_i = 1 + r_i; \tag{11.7}$$

here r_i is the rate of interest on a default-free loan over the ith period, i.e., an amount x in secure bonds on $(i - 1)$th day fetches an interest $r_i x$ on ith day;
(v) N stands for the number of periods until expiration time τ.

Our problem is to obtain a notion of a fair price of a (European) option contract with strike price K and expiration day N.

Note that in model (11.5), the distribution of the triple (U_N, D_N, ξ_N) is quite arbitrary. The only assumption in addition to (11.6) and (11.7) is

$$P(\xi_n = 1|(U_N, D_N)) = P(\xi_n = 1|(U_n, D_n)), \qquad \text{for } n < N, \tag{11.8}$$

that is, having observed vectors $U_n = (U_1, \ldots, U_n)$ and $D_n = (D_1, \ldots, D_n)$, ξ_n does not contain any additional information on $U_{n+1}, D_{n+1}, U_{n+2}, D_{n+2}, \ldots$, U_N, D_N.

We assume that random variables U_{n+1} and D_{n+1} are observed on the nth day and thus can be used to decide the amount π_{n+1} an investor may want to invest in the asset on the nth day. Thus, an investment strategy is given by $\{f_n\}$, where f_n is a function of $U_n = (U_1, \ldots, U_n) \in R_+^n$, $D_n = (D_1, \ldots, D_n) \in R_+^n$, $\epsilon_{n-1} = (\epsilon_1, \ldots, \epsilon_{n-1}) \in \{0, 1\}^{n-1}$. Having observed U_n, D_n and ξ_{n-1} the investor invests $\pi_n = f_n(U_n, D_n, \epsilon_{n-1})$ on the $(n-1)$st day.

Suppose an investor with initial wealth x chooses investment strategy $\{f_n\}$. If there is no inflow or outflow of funds, any excess (shortfall) of funds after investing in the asset are lent (put in the bank) at the appropriate rate of interest (r_i on day i), the worth X_n of the "portfolio" at time n satisfies

$$
\begin{aligned}
X_n &= \pi_n \frac{S_n}{S_{n-1}} + (X_{n-1} - \pi_n)R_n \\
&= R_1 \cdots R_n \left\{ x + \sum_{j=0}^{n-1} \frac{\pi_{j+1}}{R_0 \cdots R_j} \left[\frac{S_{j+1}}{S_j R_{j+1}} - 1 \right] \right\}, \quad R_0 = 1. (11.9)
\end{aligned}
$$

To define what will be a "fair" or "rational price" x^* for an option, set, for $u_n, d_n, \epsilon_n \in R_+^n \times R_+^n \times \{0,1\}^n$,

$$
h_n(u_n, d_n, \epsilon_n) = S_0 \prod_{j=1}^{n} (\epsilon_j u_j + (1 - \epsilon_j)d_j)
$$

$$
v_n(u_n, d_n, \epsilon_n) = (h_n(u_n, d_n, \epsilon_n) - K)^+
$$

and, given investment strategy $\{f_n\}$, let

$$
\begin{aligned}
g_n(x, u_n, d_n, \epsilon_n) = R_1 \cdots R_n \Big\{ x + \sum_{j=0}^{n-1} (R_0 \ldots R_j)^{-1} f_{j+1}(u_{j+1}, d_{j+1}, \epsilon_j) \\
\times \left[\epsilon_{j+1} \frac{u_{j+1}}{R_{j+1}} + (1 - \epsilon_{j+1}) \frac{d_{j+1}}{R_{j+1}} - 1 \right] \Big\}.
\end{aligned}
$$

Then, $S_n = h_n(U_n, D_n, \epsilon_n)$ is the price at time n and, with initial wealth x and investment strategy $\{f_n\}$, the worth of the portfolio at time n is given by $X_n = g_n(x, U_n, D_n, \epsilon_n)$.

In analogy with the binomial case[12] one would like to define the price of the option to be x^* if there exists an investment strategy $\{f_j\}$ such that

$$
Eg_N(x^*, U_N, D_N, \eta_N) = Ev_N(U_N, D_N, \eta_N) \tag{11.10}
$$

for all $\{0,1\}$-valued random variables $\{\eta_i\}$ with

$$
P(\eta_n = 1 | (U_N, D_N)) = P(\eta_n = 1 | (U_n, D_n)). \tag{11.11}
$$

In particular, taking η_i to be degenerate, i.e., $\eta_i = \epsilon_i \in \{0,1\}$ for all i,

$$
Eg_N(x^*, U_N, D_N, \epsilon_N) = Ev_N(U_N, D_N, \epsilon_N) \tag{11.12}
$$

for all $\epsilon_i \in \{0,1\}$. When $\{U_i, D_i\}$ are constant, (11.12) means that $\{f_i\}$ is a hedging strategy.

---

[12]Recall that the Cox-Ross-Rubinstein model assumes that U_n and D_n are constants and that ξ_n's are i.i.d.; moreover, U_n, D_n and ξ_n depend on n only.

We will prove below that (11.10) uniquely determines x^*, for which there exists a strategy $\{f_j\}$ which ensures (11.10). We will also obtain a formula for x^* and argue, as in binomial case, that x^* must be the fair price of the option.[13]

Lemma 11.1   (i) Suppose that there exists a strategy $\{f_j\}$ such that 11.10) holds. Then,

$$x^* = \frac{Ev_N(U_N, D_N, \xi_N^*)}{R_1 \cdots R_N},\tag{11.13}$$

where ξ_i^* are $\{0, 1\}$-valued random variables such that

$$P(\xi_i^* = \epsilon_i, i \le N | (U_N, D_N)) = \prod_{i=1}^{N} p_i^{\epsilon_i}(1 - p_i)^{1 - \epsilon_i}$$

with (p_i) determining the "riskless measure"

$$p_i = \frac{R_i - D_i}{U_i - D_i}.$$

(ii) There exists an explicit strategy $\{f_j\}$ which yields (11.10).

Proof. (i) Clearly, $\{\xi_i^*\}$ satisfies (11.11). Hence, (11.10) holds for $\eta_i = \xi_i^*$. Also, by the "riskless" choice of p_i,

$$E[\xi_{j+1}^* U_{j+1} + (1 - \xi_{j+1}^*) D_{j+1} | (U_{j+1}, D_{j+1})] = p_{j+1} U_{j+1} + (1 - p_{j+1}) D_{j+1}$$
$$= R_{j+1},$$

implying that

$$Eg_N(x^*, U_N, D_N, \xi_N^*) = R_1 \cdots R_N x^*.$$

Then, the required formula, (11.13), follows from (11.10). Finally, note that letting $S_n^* = S_0 \prod_{j=1}^{n}(\xi_j^* U_j + (1 - \xi_j^*) D_j)$ be the asset–price process under the new "riskless measure," we can rewrite (11.13) as

$$x^* = (R_1 \ldots R_N)^{-1} E(S_N^* - K)^+.\tag{11.14}$$

(ii) Next we construct an explicit investment strategy, $\{f_j\}$, yielding (11.10). It is obtained by taking suitable conditional form of the hedging strategy similar to that in the binomial pricing formula. We define $\{f_j\}$ by backward induction. To do so, we introduce the following notation.

Let $F_{n-1}(x, y; u_{n-1}, d_{n-1}) = P(U_n \le x, D_n \le y | U_{n-1} = u_{n-1}, D_{n-1} = d_{n-1})$ be the joint conditional distributions of U_n and D_n.

---

[13]The results of this and the next section are due to Karandikar and Rachev (1995).

Next, define $\{w_n^1, w_n^0, v_n^*, \ f_n, v_{n-1}\}$, $n = N, N-1, \ldots, 1$, by following backward induction (note v_N has been defined earlier as the call–option price given the tree of price movements):

1. $w_n^1(u_n, d_n, \epsilon_{n-1}) = v_n(u_n, d_n, (\epsilon_{n-1}, 1))$,
   (w_n^1 represents the call value if the asset price is "up" at the end of interval nth);

2. $w_n^0(u_n, d_n, \epsilon_{n-1}) = v_n(u_n, d_n, (\epsilon_{n-1}, 0))$,
   (w_n^0 represents the call value if the asset price is "down" at the end of interval n);

3.
$$f_n(u_n, d_n, \epsilon_{n-1}) = \frac{w_n^1(u_n, d_n, \epsilon_{n-1}) - w_n^0(u_n, d_n, \epsilon_{n-1})}{u_n - d_n}$$

(f_n represents for the neutral hedge ratio);

4.
$$v_n^*(u_n, d_n, \epsilon_{n-1}) = w_n^1(u_n, d_n, \epsilon) \frac{R_n - d_n}{u_n - d_n} + w_n^0(u_n, d_n, \epsilon_{n-1}) \frac{u_n - R_n}{u_n - d_n}$$

(v_n^* stands for the conditional mean of the call given the up's and down's at the end of interval n),

$$v_{n-1}(u_{n-1}, d_{n-1}, \epsilon_{n-1})$$
$$= \int \frac{1}{R_n} v_n^*((u_{n-1}, x), (d_{n-1}, y), \epsilon_{n-1}) F_{n-1}(dx, dy; u_{n-1}, d_{n-1})$$

(representing call value at the end of interval $(n-1)$).

Let $\{\eta_n\}$ be a sequence of random variables satisfying (11.10). Writing $\eta_n = (\eta_1, \eta_2, \ldots, \eta_n)$ and recalling that $X_n = g_N(x, U_n, D_n, \epsilon_n) = \pi_n \frac{S_n}{S_{n-1}} + X_{n-1}R_n - R_n\pi_n$ it follows that

$$\hat{\pi}_n(\eta_n U_n + (1 - \eta_n)D_n) + v_n^*(U_n, D_n, \eta_{n-1}) - R_n\hat{\pi}_n = v_n(U_n, D_n, \eta_n),$$

where $\hat{\pi}_n = f_n(U_n, D_n, \eta_{n-1})$. Taking expectation and noting that

$$Ev_n^*(U_n, D_n, \eta_{n-1}) = R_n Ev_{n-1}(U_{n-1}, D_{n-1}, \eta_{n-1})$$

we get, in view of (11.11),

$$E[\hat{\pi}_n(\eta_n U_n + (1 - \eta_n)D_n) + R_n v_{n-1}(U_{n-1}, D_{n-1}, \eta_{n-1}) - \hat{\pi}_n R_n]$$
$$= E\, v_n(U_n, D_n, \eta_n)$$

or, equivalently, writing $\hat{v}_n = v_n(U_n,D_n,\eta_n)$

$$E\hat{\pi}_n\left[\frac{1}{R_n}(\eta_n U_n + (1-\eta_n)D_n) - 1\right] = E\left[\frac{\hat{v}_n}{R_n} - \hat{v}_{n-1}\right].$$

Thus, $E\sum_{n=1}^{N} \frac{\hat{\pi}_n}{R_1\dots R_{n-1}}[(\eta_n U_n + (1-\eta_n)D_n)/R_n - 1] = E\left[\frac{\hat{v}_n}{R_1\dots R_N} - v_0\right]$,
or $Eg_N(v_0,U_n,D_n,\eta_n) = Ev_N(U_N,D_N,\eta_N)$. Therefore, the strategy given by
functions $\{f_N\}$ defined via (1-4) satisfies (11.10).   □

By Lemma 11.1, v_0 must be equal to x^*. It is a direct consequence of the
definitions that

$$v_{n-1}(U_{n-1},D_{n-1},\eta_{n-1}^*) = \frac{1}{R_n}E[v_n(U_n,D_n,\eta_n^*)|(U_{n-1},D_{n-1},\eta_{n-1})]$$

and hence $v_0 = (R_1\cdots R_N)^{-1}E[v_n(\ U_N,D_N,\eta_N^*] = (R_1\cdots R_N)^{-1}\ E(S_N^* - K)^+$. In view of the preceding discussion, we can define x^* given by (11.13)
(or (11.14)) as the rational price of the option. We call S_n^* the *risk-free* asset–
price process associated with S_n.

11.3   Option Pricing for the Generalized Mandelbrot-Taylor Model

We now consider a generalized version of the Mandelbrot-Taylor model for
asset returns and obtain an option-valuation formula. Let $(W(t))_{t\geq 0}$ be a
standard Brownian motion defined on $(\Omega_1,\mathcal{F}_1,\mathcal{P}_1)$ and let $(T(t))_{t\geq 0}$ be a
positive $\alpha/2$-stable motion with $0 < \alpha < 2$ defined on $(\Omega_0,\mathcal{F}_0,\mathcal{P}_l)$ with
characteristic function (11.2). We consider the product space $(\Omega,\mathcal{F},\mathcal{P}) = (\Omega_0,\mathcal{F}_0,\mathcal{P}_0) \otimes (\Omega_1,\mathcal{F}_1,\mathcal{P}_1)$ and assume $((W(t))_{t\geq 0},(T(t))_{t\geq 0})$ are independent processes on $(\Omega,\mathcal{F},\mathcal{P})$. Let $r(s)$ be the risk-free rate at time s. This
means that lending one unit at time u in bonds yields $\exp\left\{\int_u^t r(s)ds\right\}$ units
at time t.

Let the asset price be modeled by

$$S_t = S_0\exp\left\{\int_0^t r(s)ds + W(T(t)) + \int_0^t \mu(s)dT(s)\right\}, \qquad (11.15)$$

where $\mu(s)$ is a continuous function.[14] When $\mu = 0$, $\log S_t$ becomes a stable
motion, as desired, in the Mandelbrot model (11.2) – (11.3). Thus, $\mu(u)$ can
be interpreted as a "drift". We want to determine the price of an option
on this asset with terminal time τ (non-random) and strike price K. Let

---

[14]In a similar way we can treat a slightly more general case, namely

$$S_t = S_0\exp\left\{\int_0^t r(s)ds + \int_0^t \sigma(s)dW(T(s)) + \int_0^t \mu(s)dT(s)\right\}.$$

$Z(t) = W(T(t)) + \int_0^t \mu(s)dT(s)$ and introduce an auxiliary process

$$S_t^* = S_0 R(t) \exp \{W_0(T(t))\}, \tag{11.16}$$

where $W_0(s) = W(s) - s/2$ and $R(t) = \exp \left\{\int_0^t r(s)ds\right\}$.

Theorem 11.2 The price of the option on $\{S(t)\}_{0 \leq t \leq \tau}$ with expiration time τ and strike price K is

$$x^* = E\left[\frac{1}{R_\tau}(S_\tau^* - K)^+\right].$$

Proof Let us first remark that we cannot interpret the price as in the Black-Scholes formula, that is, we cannot demand or postulate existence of a continuous–time hedging strategy. Instead, here the interpretation is via discrete approximation of the S-process. To be precise, we construct approximations $(S_t(n, m))_{t \geq 0}$ to the price process $(S_t)_{t \geq 0}$, such that the price, x_{nm}^*, of the option on $(S_t(n, m))_{t \geq 0}$ with expiration time τ and strike price K converges to x^*.

To construct $[S_t(n, m))_{t \geq 0}]$, divide interval $[0, \tau]$ into nm subintervals, and define, for t in the interval $\frac{i-1}{n} + \frac{j-1}{nm} \leq \frac{t}{\tau} < \frac{i-1}{n} + \frac{j}{nm}$, $(1 \leq i \leq n, 1 \leq i \leq m)$,

$$
\begin{aligned}
S_t(n, m) &= S_0 \prod_{l=1}^{i-1} \prod_{k=1}^{m} \{\xi_{lk}U_{lk} + (1 - \xi_{lk})D_{lk}\} \\
&\quad \prod_{k=1}^{j-1} \{\xi_{ik}U_{ik} + (1 - \xi_{ik})D_{ik}\}, \tag{11.17}
\end{aligned}
$$

$$S_\tau(n, m) = S_{\tau^-}(n, m) := \lim_{t \uparrow \tau} S_t(n, m), \tag{11.18}$$

where

$$U_{lk} = U_{lk}(n, m) = \left[1 + [\theta_l^n \frac{1}{\sqrt{m}}] \wedge \frac{1}{2}\right]e^{r_{lk}(n,m)}, \tag{11.19}$$

$$D_{lk} = D_{lk}(n, m) = \left[1 - [\theta_l^n \frac{1}{\sqrt{m}}] \wedge \frac{1}{2}\right]e^{r_{lk}(n,m)},$$

$$\theta_l^n = \{T[\frac{l-1}{n}] - T[\frac{l-2}{n} \vee 0]\}^{1/2},$$

One can check that if we start with price process

$$S_t = S_0 \exp\left\{\int_0^t \alpha(s)ds + \int_0^t \beta(s)W(s) + \int_0^t \sigma(s)dW(T(s)) + \int_0^t \mu(s)dT(s)\right\},$$

then the only case for which one can meaningfully define the price x^*, of the option on S_t, is when $\alpha(s) = r(s)$ and $\beta(s) = 0$, for more details, we refer to Hurst, Platen and Rachev (1995a, 1995b).

and

$$r_{lk} = r_{lk}(n,m) = \int_0^{\tau/nm} r\left(\tau\left(\frac{l-1}{n} + \frac{k-1}{nm} + u\right)\right) du.$$

Furthermore, $\{\xi_{ik} = \xi_{ik}(n,m)\}$ are $\{0,1\}$-valued random variables satisfying $P\left[\xi_{lk} = 1\right]$
$T\left[\frac{\tau i}{n} : 0 \le i \le n\right] = q_{lk}$; where

$$q_{lk}(n,m) = \frac{1}{2} + \frac{1}{2}\left[\theta_l^n \frac{1}{\sqrt{m}} \mu\left[\tau\left(\frac{i-1}{n} + \frac{j-1}{nm}\right)\right]\right] \wedge 1.$$

and $\{\xi_{lk} : 1 \le l \le n, 1 \le k \le m\}$ are conditionally independent given $\{T\left[\frac{\tau i}{n}\right] : 0 \le i \le n\}$.

First let us show that $(S_t(n,m))_{t\ge 0}$ weakly converges to $S(t)_{t\ge 0}$ in $D[0,\infty)$. Next, write, for $\tau\left[\frac{i-1}{n} + \frac{j-1}{nm}\right] \le t < \left[\frac{i-1}{n} + \frac{j}{nm}\right]\tau$, $\hat{t} := \left[\frac{i-1}{n} + \frac{j-1}{nm}\right]\tau$, $\log S_t(n,m) = \int_0^{\hat{t}} r(u)du + X(t)$, where

$$X_t = X_t(n,m) = \sum_{l=1}^{i-1}\sum_{k=1}^{m}[\xi_{lk}\log(1+v_{lk}) + (1-\xi_{lk})\log(1-v_{lk})]$$

$$+ \sum_{k=1}^{j-1}[\xi_{ik}\log(1+v_{ik}) + (1-\xi_{ik})\log(1-v_{ik})]$$

and $v_{lk}(n,m) = \left[\theta_l^n \frac{1}{\sqrt{m}}\right] \wedge \frac{1}{2}$. Conditioned on the $(T(s))_{s\le\tau}$-process, $\{\xi_{lk} : 1 \le l \le n, l \le k \le m\}$ are independent random variables and v_{lk} are constants. Thus, using the Lindberg-Feller theorem for triangular arrays, (it is easy to verify the Lyapunov condition, see for example, Shiryaev (1984), p. 331). It follows that conditioned on $\mathcal{A}_\tau = \{T(t): t \le \tau\}$, the finite dimensional distributions of the process $(X_t)_{t\ge 0}$ converges to the corresponding distribution of a Gaussian process with independent increments. Mean and variance functions of the Gaussian process are given by

$$\lim_{n,m\to\infty} \sum_{l,k:\tau\left[\frac{l-1}{n} + \frac{k-1}{nm}\right]\le t} E[\xi_{lk}|\mathcal{A}_\tau]$$

and

$$\lim_{n,m\to\infty} \sum_{l,k:\tau\left[\frac{l-1}{n} + \frac{k-1}{nm}\right]\le t} E\left(\left[\xi_{lk} - E(\xi_{lk}|\mathcal{A}_\tau)\right]^2 |\mathcal{A}_\tau\right),$$

respectively. Explicit computations show that these two limits are $\int_0^t \mu(s)$ $dT(s)$ and $T(t)$, respectively. Thus, as $n,m \to \infty$, the conditional distribution of $\left[X_{t_1},\ldots,X_{t_p}\right]$ given $(T(s))_{s\le\tau}$ converges to the conditional distribution $\{Z(t_1),\ldots,Z(t_p)\}$ given $(T(s))_{s\le\tau}$. Under the conditional measure, tightness of the laws of $\{(X_t = X_t(n,m))_{t\ge 0} : n,m \ge 1\}$ can be proved in the same fashion as the Donsker invariance principle. Thus, we can conclude that conditional on $(T(s))_{s\le\tau}$ the process $(X_t)_{t\ge 0}$ weakly converges to $(Z_t)_{t\ge 0}$ in the

Skorohod topology $D[0, \infty]$. Thus, $(S_t(n, m))_{t \geq 0} \overset{\omega}{\to} (S_t)_{t \geq 0}$. Using (11.14) the price x^*_{nm} of an option on $S_t(n, m)$ is,

$$x^*_{nm} = R_\tau^{-1} E(S^*_\tau(n, m) - K)^+, \tag{11.20}$$

with $R_t = \exp\left[\int_0^t r(s) ds\right]$. In deducing (11.20), we have assumed that the interest rate over period $\left[\tau \left[\frac{i-1}{n} + \frac{j-1}{nm}\right], \tau \left[\frac{i-1}{n} + \frac{j}{nm}\right]\right]$ is $\exp\left[\int_0^{\frac{\tau}{nm}} r \left(\left(\frac{i-1}{n}\right.\right.\right.$ $\left.\left.+ \frac{j-1}{nm}\right) \tau + s\right) ds\right] - 1$ and that the portfolio altered only at multiples of τ/nm; that at time $t = \left[\frac{i-1}{n} + \frac{j-1}{nm}\right] \tau$ one has observed $(T(s)_{s \leq t})$; and that this information can be used to decide the investment strategy.

It remains to evaluate the limit of x^*_{nm}. Let us recall that $S^*_t(n, m)$ is given by the same expression as (11.17) with ξ^*_{lk}, here,

$$P\left[\xi^*_{lk}(n, m) = 1 | T(\frac{\tau i}{n}) : 0 \leq i \leq n\right] = p_{lk}(n, m)$$

and, again, $\{\xi^*_{lk}\}$ are independent given $\left\{T\left(\frac{\tau i}{n}\right) : i \leq n\right\}$. Given the choice of U's and D's, it can be verified that

$$p_{lk}(n, m) = 1/2. \tag{11.21}$$

Now, taking $\mu = 1/2$ in the previous convergence argument, it follows that $(S^*_t(n, m))_{t \geq 0} \overset{\omega}{\to} (S^*_t)_{t \geq 0}$. Using (11.21), it follows that $ES^*_t(n, m) = S_0 R_t$ for all t, n, m. Similarly, using conditioning with respect to $\{T(s) : s \leq \tau\}$, it follows that $ES^*_t = S_0 R_t$. Thus, $S^*_\tau(n, m) \to S^*_\tau$ [15] weakly and $ES^*_\tau(n, m) \to ES^*_\tau$. Hence, $Eg(S^*_\tau(n, m) \to Eg(S^*_\tau)$ for all continuous functions g on $\mathbf{R}_+$ with $\limsup_{x \to \infty} g(x)/x < \infty$. Taking $g(x) = (x - K)^+$, we get $E(S^*_\tau(n, m) - K)^+ \to E(S^*_\tau - K)^+$, i.e., $x^*_{nm} \to x^* = E\left[R_\tau^{-1}[S^*_\tau - K]^+\right]$. Thus, the price of the option on $(S_t)_{t \geq 0}$ with expiration time τ and strike price K is $x^* = E\left[R_\tau^{-1}(S^*_\tau - K]^+\right)$. $\qquad \square$

Theorem 11.2 does not establish the existence of a hedging strategy, but that with initial endowment x^* one can choose a strategy, adapted to observations $(S(t), T(t))$ at time t, which generates "on the average" same return as the option, as long as the price movements conforms to model (11.15), irrespective of drift $\mu(s)$.

---

[15] In fact, we have convergence in the Kantorovich metric,

$$\kappa(S^*_\tau(n, m), S^*_\tau) \to 0 \quad \text{as } n, m \to 0,$$

where

$$\kappa(X, Y) = \sup\{Eg(X) - Eg(Y) : g : \mathbf{R} \to \mathbf{R},$$
$$E|g(X)| + E|g(Y)| < \infty, |g(x) - g(y)| \leq |x - y|, \text{ for all } x, y \in \mathbf{R}\},$$

see Rachev (1991).

It is important to note is that we have used arguments involving conditioning on $\{T(t) : 0 \le t \le \tau\}$ only in the convergence proofs. When it came to defining a strategy in the discretized version, at time t, only $\{T(s) : s \le t\}$ were assumed to have been observed.[16]

Next, we present a simpler expression for x^*. For $a > 0, \sigma > 0$, let $\psi(a, \sigma^2) = E\left[\exp\left[\sigma Z - \frac{1}{2}\sigma^2\right] - a\right]^+$, where Z is standard normal. It is easy to see that $\psi(a, \sigma) = \phi(-\frac{\log a}{\sigma} + \frac{1}{2}\sigma) - a\phi(-\frac{\log a}{\sigma} - \frac{1}{2}\sigma)$ with $\phi(u)$ being the standard normal distribution function. For the option value x^* we now obtain

$$
\begin{aligned}
x^* &= R_\tau^{-1}E(S_\tau^* - K)^+ = S_0 E\left(\exp\left\{W(T(\tau)) - \frac{1}{2}T(\tau)\right\} - KR_\tau^{-1}S_0^{-1}\right)^+ \\
&= S_0 E v(T(\tau)), \qquad\qquad\qquad\qquad\qquad\qquad\qquad\qquad (11.22)
\end{aligned}
$$

where $v(\sigma) = \phi(KR_\tau^{-1}S_0^{-1}, \sigma^2)$. Here, $v(\sigma)$ can be interpreted as the value of the option if the asset price was modeled as $\hat{S}_t^\sigma = \sigma W(t) + \int_0^t r_s ds$. Thus, to compute x^*, we only need to estimate parameters of $\frac{\alpha}{2}$-stable r.v. $\{T(\tau)\}$ (cf. (11.2)), because K, R_τ and S_0 are given, see Janicki and Weron (1994).

11.4 Option valuation for subordinated asset pricing model

In this section we generalize the model we had in Section 11.3 assuming a more general subordinated price process. We model the *asset price* process $S = \{S(t), t \ge 0\}$ by a stochastic equation of the type

$$
S(t) = S(t_0)\exp\left\{\int_{t_0}^t \mu(s)ds + \int_{t_0}^t \rho(s)dT(s) + \int_{t_0}^t \sigma(s)dW(T(s))\right\} \quad (11.23)
$$

for $0 \le t_0 \le t \le \infty$.[17] The stochastic process $T = \{T(t), t \ge 0\}$, as already mentioned in Section 5.1, is called the *intrinsic time process* and has non-negative stationary independent increments. As it was suggested in Mandelbrot and Taylor (1967) $T(t)$ can be thought of as the cumulative trading volume process which measures the cumulative volume of all the transactions up to physical time t. The intrinsic time process T is defined on the probability space. $(\Omega_0, \mathcal{F}_0, \mathcal{P}_0)$ and generates the filtration $\mathcal{F}^T = \{\mathcal{F}_t^T\} = \sigma\{T(s), 0 \le s \le t\}, t \ge 0\}$. The stochastic process $W = \{W(u), u \ge 0\}$ represents the *noise (shot) process* which is introduced on the *intrinsic* time

---

[16]In the discrete case, one can use similar arguments to define the option value, x^*, for price process

$$
S_t = S_0 \exp\left\{\int_0^t \alpha(s)ds + \int_0^t \sigma(s)dW(T(s)) + \int_0^t \mu(s)dT(s)\right\},
$$

see Hurst, Platen and Rachev (1995a,b) for details, and the next two sections.

[17]The results of this section are due to Hurst, Platen and Rachev (1995a, 1995b).

scale. It is assumed to be a standard Wiener process defined on another probability space $(\Omega_1, \mathcal{F}_1, \mathcal{P}_1)$ and thus independent of T. It generates the filtration $\mathcal{F}^W = \{\mathcal{F}_u^W = \sigma\{W(v), 0 \le v \le u\}, u \ge 0\}$. The process denoted by $Z = \{Z(t) = W(T(t)), t \ge 0\}$. It is used as the *driving process* in equation (11.23) and is defined on the product probability space $(\Omega, \mathcal{F}, \mathcal{P}) = (\Omega_0, \mathcal{F}_0, \mathcal{P}_0 \otimes (\Omega_1, \mathcal{F}_1, \mathcal{P}_1)$. Furthermore it is adapted to the joint filtration $\mathcal{F}^Z = \{\mathcal{F}_t^Z = \mathcal{F}_t^T \otimes \mathcal{F}_{T(t)}^W, t \ge 0\}$. We note that the process T plays the role of a stochastic internal time that is independent from the noise process W. In equation (11.23), the *drift in the physical time scale* $\mu = \{\mu(t), t \ge 0\}$, the *drift in the intinsic time scale* $\rho = \{\rho(t), t \ge 0\}$ and the *volatility* $\sigma = \{\sigma(t), t \ge 0\}$ are assumed to be right continuous functions having limits from the left. The stochastic integrals in equation (11.23) is understood in a standard way, see for example Protter (1990).

We introduce the *short term interest rate* $r = \{r(t), t \ge 0\}$ as a right continuous with left-hand limits time-dependent function.[18] The *money account* is then defined by

$$B = \left\{ B(t) = \exp\left(\int_0^t r(s)ds \right), \ t \ge 0 \right\}. \tag{11.24}$$

Now the *discounted asset price* is

$$\bar{S}(t) = S(t)\frac{B(t_0)}{B(t)} = S(t)\exp\left\{ \int_{t_0}^t r(s)ds \right\} \tag{11.25}$$

for $0 \le t_0 \le t < \infty$, which by equation (11.23) can be written as

$$\bar{S}(t) = S(t_0)\exp\left\{ \int_{t_0}^t (\mu(s) - r(s))ds + \int_{t_0}^t \rho(s)dT(s) + \int_{t_0}^t \sigma(s)dW(T(s)) \right\}. \tag{11.26}$$

The continuous time subordinated asset price model introduced above will be further interpreted as an idealization of the naturally discrete price. By keeping the drift and diffusion coefficients piecewise constant we shall investigate a range of well-known discrete time asset price models, see Section 5.1. To his end, we introduce a time discretization of the interval $[t_0, \mathcal{T}]$ in the form

$$t_0 = \tau_0 < \tau_1 < \ldots < \tau_N = \mathcal{T} \tag{11.27}$$

with $N \in \{1, 2, \ldots\}$ and $0 \le t_0 \le \mathcal{T} < \infty$. The discretization points (τ_i) may be random, and we define for a given $t \ge t_0$,

$$k_t := \max\{k \in \{0, 1, \ldots\}, \tau_k \le t\}. \tag{11.28}$$

---

[18]In a more general set-up one could choose the functions μ, ρ, σ and r to be stochastic processes which would also require appropriate measurability assumptions. To assume that they are given time dependent functions will allow us to avoid certain technical complexity and to concentrate on our aim of contingent claim pricing.

We assume for all $t \geq t_0$ that the r.v. τ_{k_t} is $\mathcal{F}_t^T$-measurable.

From now on throughout the rest of this section we assume that μ, ρ, σ and r represent time dependent functions which are piecewise constant (right continuous with left-hand limits) between the discretization points of our given time discretization. Then we obtain from equation (11.26) the following recursive relation for the discounted asset price process

$$\begin{aligned}
\bar{S}(\tau_k) = {} & \bar{S}(\tau_{k-1}) \exp\{(\mu(\tau_{k-1}) - r(\tau_{k-1}) + \rho(\tau_{k-1})(T(\tau_k) - T(\tau_{k-1})) \\
& + \sigma(\tau_{k_t})(W(T(t)) - W(T(\tau_{k_t})))\}
\end{aligned} \tag{11.29}$$

for all $k \in \{1, \ldots, N\}$ with $\bar{S}(\tau_0) = S(t_0)$. For times t which do not coincide with any discretization point, the value of the discounted asset price $\bar{S}(t)$ given in equation (11.26) appears as a natural interpolation of the values given by equation (11.29) in the form

$$\begin{aligned}
\bar{S}(t) = {} & \bar{S}(\tau_{k_t}) \exp\{(\mu(\tau_{k_t}) - r(\tau_{k_t}))(t - \tau_{k_t}) + \rho(\tau_{k_t})(T(t) - T(\tau_{k_t})) \\
& + \sigma(\tau_{k_t})(W(T(t)) - W(T(\tau_{k_t})))\}, \tau_k < t \leq \tau_{k+1}, \tag{11.30}
\end{aligned}$$

for all $t \in [t_0, T]$.

We further assume that there exists an equivalent probability product measure $\tilde{P} = P_0 \otimes \tilde{P}_1$ such that the discounted asset price process $\bar{S}\{\bar{S}(t), t \in [t_0, T]\}$ represents a $(\tilde{P}, \mathcal{F}^Z)$-martingale. Thus $\tilde{P}$ represents the risk neutral pricing measure. It will be characterized by a measure transformation with Radon-Nikodym derivative

$$\Psi = \frac{d\tilde{P}_1}{dP_1} \tag{11.31}$$

such that the process $\tilde{W} = \{\tilde{W}(u), u \geq 0\}$ with

$$\tilde{W}(u) = W(u) - \int_0^u \psi(v)dv \tag{11.32}$$

becomes a $\tilde{P}_1$-Wiener process. It then follows that

$$\bar{S}(t) = \bar{S}(s) \left\{ \int_s^t \sigma(u)d\tilde{W}(T(u)) - \frac{1}{2} \int_s^t \sigma^2(u)dT(u) \right\} \tag{11.33}$$

for all $t_0 \leq s \leq t \leq T$.

Let $\hat{\mathcal{F}}^Z$ be the joint filtration $\{\hat{\mathcal{F}}_t^Z = \mathcal{F}_T^T \otimes \mathcal{F}_{T(t)}^W, t \in [t_0, T]\}$. Note that this filtration is generated by the σ-algebra $\mathcal{F}_T^T$ and the family of σ-algebras $\mathcal{F}_{T(\cdot)}^W$ and therefore contains more information than the filtration $\mathcal{F}^Z$ (see the paragraph below equation (11.23)), that is

$$\mathcal{F}_t^Z \subset \hat{\mathcal{F}}_t^Z. \tag{11.34}$$

Then with $\tilde{E}$ being the expectation with respect to the probability measure $\tilde{P}$, we have for the discounted asset price (see 11.25) the martingale property

$$\tilde{E}(\bar{S}(t)|\mathcal{F}_s^Z)$$

$$= \tilde{E}(\tilde{E}(\bar{S}(t)|\hat{\mathcal{F}}_s^Z)|\mathcal{F}_s^Z)$$

$$= \bar{S}(s)\tilde{E}\left(\tilde{E}\left(\exp\left\{\int_s^t \sigma(u)d\tilde{W}(T(u)) - \frac{1}{2}\int_s^t \sigma^2(u)dT(u)\right\}\middle|\hat{\mathcal{F}}_s^Z\right)\middle|\mathcal{F}_s^Z\right)$$

$$= \bar{S}(s)\tilde{E}(1|\mathcal{F}_s^Z)$$

$$= \bar{S}(s) \tag{11.35}$$

for all $t_0 \le t \le \mathcal{T}$.

To determine the Radon-Nikodyn derivative Ψ which provides us with this martingale property, we must identify a piece-wise constant function ψ, that is

$$\int_{T(\tau_{k-1})}^{T(\tau_k)} \psi(v)dv = \psi(\tau_{k-1})(T(\tau_k) - T(\tau_{k-1})), \tag{11.36}$$

which fulfills relations (11.32) and (11.33). Thus equating the right-hand sides of (11.29) and (11.33) with $s = \tau_{k-1}$ and $t = \tau_k$ we have

$$(\mu(\tau_{k-1}) - r(\tau_{k-1}))(\tau_k - \tau_{k-1}) + \rho(\tau_{k-1})(T(\tau_k) - T(\tau_{k-1}))$$
$$+\sigma(\tau_{k-1})(W(T(\tau_k)) - W(T(\tau_{k-1}))) \tag{11.37}$$

$$= \sigma(\tau_{k-1})(\tilde{W}(T(\tau_k)) - \tilde{W}(T(\tau_{k-1}))) - \frac{1}{2}\sigma^2(\tau_{k-1})(T(\tau_k) - T(\tau_{k-1}))$$

and by equations (11.32) and (11.36) we obtain

$$(\mu(\tau_{k-1}) - r(\tau_{k-1}))(\tau_k - \tau_{k-1}) + \rho(\tau_{k-1})(T(\tau_k) - T(\tau_{k-1}))$$
$$+\sigma(\tau_{k-1})(W(T(\tau_k)) - W(T(\tau_{k-1})))$$

$$= \sigma(\tau_{k-1})(W(T(\tau_k)) - W(T(\tau_{k-1}))) - \sigma(\tau_{k-1})\psi(\tau_{k-1})(T(\tau_k) - T(\tau_{k-1}))$$
$$-\frac{1}{2}\sigma^2(\tau_{k-1})(T(\tau_k) - T(\tau_{k-1})) \tag{11.38}$$

Solving this relation for *the market price for risk* ψ we get

$$\psi(\tau_{k-1}) = \left(\frac{r(\tau_{k-1}) - \mu(\tau_{k-1})}{\sigma(\tau_{k-1})}\right)\frac{\tau_k - \tau_{k-1}}{T(\tau_k) - T(\tau_{k-1})} - \frac{\rho(\tau_{k-1}) + \frac{1}{2}\sigma^2(\tau_{k-1})}{\sigma(\tau_{k-1})}. \tag{11.39}$$

Let us discuss the asymptotic behavior of ψ for finer time discretizations. We observe that for $t \in [t_0, \mathcal{T}]$ the random ratio $(\tau_{k_t} - \tau_{k_t-1})/(T(\tau_{k_t}) - T(\tau_{k_t-1}))$ does not in general approach a well defined limit as $\max_{t \in [t_0, \mathcal{T}]}\{\tau_{k_t} - \tau_{k_t-1}\} \to 0$. For example, this is the case when T is a maximal positively skewed $\frac{\alpha}{2}$-stable Lévy process with $\alpha \in (1, 2)$. In fact, with the notation in Section 5.1, the Laplace transform of the increment $T(\tau_k) - T(\tau_{k-1})$ is given by

$$L_{T,s}(\gamma) = Ee^{-(T(\tau_k)-T(\tau_{k-1}))\gamma}$$

$$= \exp\left\{-\frac{(c\gamma)^{\alpha/2}s}{\cos\left(\frac{\pi\alpha}{2}\right)}\right\}, \quad 1 < \alpha < 2,$$

with $s = \tau_k - \tau_{k-1}$. Thus the Laplace transform of the ratio $(T(\tau_k) - T(\tau_{k-1}))/s$ converges to 0 as $s = \tau_k - \tau_{k-1} \to 0$. In other words, as $s \to 0$,

$$\frac{s}{T(\tau_k) - T(\tau_{k-1})} \xrightarrow{p} \infty.$$

Consequently when $\mu \neq r$ the market price for risk ψ may blow to ∞ as the time discretization is taken finer. Therefore, in view of (11.39), when $\mu \neq r$ we cannot expect existence of an equivalent martingale measure in the continuous time limit of finer and finer time discretizations. We shall then assume that $\mu = r$ and derive an equivalent martingale measure as described by equation (11.40). In this case the continuous time martingale measure $\tilde{P} = P_0 \otimes \tilde{P}_1$ is defined by

$$\Psi(t) = \frac{d\tilde{P}_1}{dP_1}(t) = \exp\left\{\int_{t_0}^{t} \psi(u)dW(u) - \frac{1}{2}\int_{t_0}^{t} \psi^2(u)du\right\} \qquad (11.40)$$

where

$$\psi(t) = -\frac{\rho(t) + \frac{1}{2}\sigma^2(t)}{\sigma(t)} \qquad (11.41)$$

for $t \in [t_0, T]$.

We are now going to consider the problem of pricing derivatives on the subordinated asset price model and concentrate for simplicity on the example of a European call option with exercise price K and time to maturity T. Let

$$K_{r,t,T} = K\frac{B(t)}{B(T)} = K\exp\left\{-\int_{t}^{T} r(u)du\right\} \qquad (11.42)$$

be the discounted exercise price of the option.

The value of the European call option C_t at time t is the discounted expected payoff at the time to maturity T, where the expectation is taken with respect to the risk neutral pricing measure $\tilde{P}$, i.e.

$$C_t = \tilde{E}\left(\exp\left\{-\int_{t}^{T} r(s)ds\right\}(S(T) - K)^+ \bigg| \mathcal{F}_t^Z\right). \qquad (11.43)$$

Using equations (11.25), (11.33) and (11.43) this can be written as

$$C_t = \tilde{E}\left(\left(S(t)\exp\left\{\int_{t}^{T} \sigma(s)d\tilde{W}(T(s)) - \frac{1}{2}\int_{t}^{T} \sigma^2(s)dT(s)\right\} - K_{r,t,T}\right)^+ \bigg| \mathcal{F}_t^Z\right). \qquad (11.44)$$

By conditioning with respect to the intrinsic time process T first or equivalently with respect to the filtration $\hat{\mathcal{F}}_Z$ (see (11.34)), we get

$$C_t = \tilde{E}(\hat{C}_t | \mathcal{F}_t^Z). \qquad (11.45)$$

We observe that in the above formula

$$\hat{C}_t = \tilde{E}\left(\left(\left(S(t)\exp\left\{\int_t^T \sigma(s)d\tilde{W}(T(s)) - \frac{1}{2}\int_t^T \sigma^2 dT(s)\right\} - K_{r,t\mathcal{T}}\right)^+ \Big| \hat{\mathcal{F}}_t^Z\right)\right)$$

(11.46)

is the value of the European call option conditioned on the intrinsic time process T, where the asset price process in this conditional European call option $\hat{C}_t$ has the form of a lognormal process. Consequently, by the Black and Scholes European call option pricing formula for time dependent functions we have

$$\hat{C}_t = S(t)\Phi\left(\frac{\log\left\{\frac{S(t)}{K_{r,t,\mathcal{T}}}\right\} + \frac{1}{2}\int_t^T \sigma^2(s)dT(s)}{\sqrt{\int_t^T \sigma^2(s)dT(s)}}\right)$$

$$- K_{r,t,\mathcal{T}}\Phi\left(\frac{\log\left\{\frac{S(t)}{K_{r,t,\mathcal{T}}}\right\} - \frac{1}{2}\int_t^T \sigma^2(s)dT(s)}{\sqrt{\int_t^T \sigma^2(s)dT(s)}}\right)$$

(11.47)

where Φ denotes the standard normal distribution function.[19]

Moreover, since $\hat{C}_t$ only involves the dependence on the intrinsic time process T from physical time t to $\mathcal{T}$, the expectation in equation (11.45) remains to be taken with respect to the probability measure P_0, i.e.

$$C_t = E_0(\hat{C}_t | \mathcal{F}_t^Z).$$

(11.48)

By (11.47), and (11.48), we have

$$C_t = S(t)E_0\left(\Phi\left(\frac{\log\left\{\frac{S(t)}{K_{r,t,\mathcal{T}}}\right\} + \frac{1}{2}\int_t^T \sigma^2(s)dT(s)}{\sqrt{\int_t^T \sigma^2(s)dT(s)}}\right)\Big| \mathcal{F}_t^Z\right)$$

$$- K_{r,t,\mathcal{T}}E_0\left(\Phi\left(\frac{\log\left\{\frac{S(t)}{K_{r,t,\mathcal{T}}}\right\} + \frac{1}{2}\int_t^T \sigma^2(s)dT(s)}{\sqrt{\int_t^T \sigma^2(s)dT(s)}}\right)\Big| \mathcal{F}_t^Z\right)$$

(11.49)

Then the value of the European call option is

$$C_t = S(t)\int_0^\infty \Phi\left(\frac{\log\left\{\frac{S(t)}{K_{r,t,\mathcal{T}}}\right\} + \frac{1}{2}y}{\sqrt{y}}\right)dF_Y(y)$$

$$- K_{r,t,\mathcal{T}}\int_0^\infty \Phi\left(\frac{\log\left\{\frac{S(t)}{K_{r,t,\mathcal{T}}}\right\} - \frac{1}{2}y}{\sqrt{y}}\right)dF_Y(y),$$

(11.50)

---

[19] We emphasize that the conditional European call option price $\hat{C}_t$ is depending on the trajectory of our intrinsic time process T and thus is a random variable which is measurable with respect to the filtration $\hat{\mathcal{F}}_t^Z$ but not the filtration $\mathcal{F}_t^Z$.

where Y is the random variable $\int_t^{\mathcal{T}} \sigma^2(s)dT(s)$. For convenient notation we introduce the functions

$$F_{\pm}(x) = \int_0^{\infty} \Phi\left(\frac{x \mp \frac{1}{2}y}{\sqrt{y}}\right) dF_Y(y); \qquad (11.51)$$

Here $F_{\pm}(\cdot)$ may be viewed as the distribution functions of the distributions subordinated to the normal distributions, with means $\pm\frac{1}{2}Y$ and variance Y.

Proposition 11.1 The value at time t of a European call option with exercise price K and time to maturity $\mathcal{T}$ is

$$C_t = S(t)F_-\left(\log\left\{\frac{S(t)}{K_{r,t,\mathcal{T}}}\right\}\right) - K_{r,t,\mathcal{T}}F_+\left(\log\left\{\frac{S(t)}{K_{r,t,\mathcal{T}}}\right\}\right). \qquad (11.52)$$

Here $K_{r,t,\mathcal{T}}$ is the discounted exercise price in equation (11.42) and $F_{\pm}(\cdot)$ are given above in (11.51). Thus the European call option price at time t is a function of the asset price $S(t)$, the exercise price K, the time to maturity $\mathcal{T}$, the time dependent interest rate r and the time dependent volatility σ.[20]

As we have mentioned before, if we would model the money account evolving in intrinsic time, that is $B = \{B(t) = \exp(\int_0^t r(s)dT(s)), t \geq 0\}$, the European call option price would be formulated by equations (11.47) and (11.48) where $K_{r,t,\mathcal{T}}$ is the appropriate discounted exercise price in equation (11.42). In this case the European call option price can also be simplified but involves other distribution functions. This pricing formula is also a generalization of the Black and Scholes pricing formula where we again average with respect to a random intrinsic time scale.

We next use the European call option pricing formula (11.52) to numerically calculate option prices for the Mandelbrot and Taylor logstable asset price model. In Sections 5.1 and 5.2 we compared various asset price models for the Standard & Poor 500 index (S & P 500) and showed that in terms of tail probabilities this model was the best. Below we summarize this model, see also Example 5.2, Section 5.1.

The subordinated process $Z = \{Z(t) = \hat{W}(T(t)), t \geq 0\}$ is a standard symmetric α-stable Lévy process. The intrinsic process T is a maximal skewed $\alpha/2$-stable Lévy process, T have stationary independent increments

$$T(t+s) - T(t) \overset{\mathrm{d}}{=} S_{\frac{\alpha}{2}}(cs^{\frac{2}{\alpha}}, 1, 0) \qquad (11.53)$$

for all $s, t \geq 0$ and $\alpha \in (0,2)$, $c > 0$ in the notation of Section 5.1.

---

[20]Clearly, we have a pricing formula that is a generalization of the celebrated Black and Scholes pricing formula, where we average with respect to a random intrinsic time scale. In the case that the intrinsic time is just deterministic physical time we have exactly the Black and Scholes pricing formula. We emphasize that the result of the proposition can be easily generalized for more general contingent claims.

The relationship between the intrinsic time process T and the subordinated process Z is formulated in the following proposition, which proof follows immediately from the discussion in Section 5.1.[21]

Proposition 11.2 The increments $Z(t + s) - Z(t)$, where $s, t \geq 0$, of the subordinated process $Z = \{Z(t) = \hat{W}(T(t)), t \geq 0\}$ have distribution function

$$F_{Z,s}(x) = \int_0^\infty \Phi\left(\frac{x}{\sqrt{u}}\right) dF_{T,s}(u) \tag{11.54}$$

where Φ is the standard normal d.f., probability density function

$$f_{Z,s}(x) = \frac{1}{\sqrt{2\pi}} \int_0^\infty \frac{1}{\sqrt{u}} \exp\left\{-\frac{x^2}{2u}\right\} dF_{T,s}(u) \tag{11.55}$$

if it exists, and ch.f.

$$\phi_{Z,s}(\theta) = L_{T,s}\left(\frac{1}{2}\theta^2\right), \tag{11.56}$$

where $L_{T,s}$ is defined by (5.13) in Section 5.1.

By Proposition 11.2 the ch.f. of the increment of Z is

$$\phi_{Z,s}(\theta) = \exp\{-\varsigma^\alpha s|\theta|^\alpha\}, \tag{11.57}$$

where

$$\varsigma = \frac{\sqrt{\frac{1}{2}c}}{\cos\left(\frac{\pi\alpha}{4}\right)^{\frac{1}{\alpha}}}, \tag{11.58}$$

(see also Example 5.2), and

$$c = 2\cos\left(\frac{\pi\alpha}{4}\right)^{\frac{2}{\alpha}}. \tag{11.59}$$

We note that for the characterization of the intrinsic time process in the logstable model we only need to specify the index of stability $\alpha \in (0, 2)$. Thus we need one additional parameter in comparison to the classical lognormal model. Furthermore it can be shown that for $\alpha \to 2$ the intrinsic time process T asymptotically approaches physical time which leads us to the classical lognormal model.

We set $\alpha = 1.714$ as the index of stability for the standard Wiener process $\hat{W}$ and the standard symmetric α-stable Lévy process Z which is subordinated to the standard Wiener process $\hat{W}$ by the intrinsic time process T. This is the value that was estimated for the S & P 500 index in Section 5.2.

---

[21] We use the notations $F_{Z,s}, F_{T,s}, \phi_{Z,s}, L_{T,s}$ as defined in Section 5.1.

We let the volatility σ be constant to simplify calculations. Now by using Proposition 11.1, the random variable Y in equation (11.50) is

$$\begin{aligned} Y &= \sigma^2 \{ T(\mathcal{T} - T(t)) \} \\ &= \lambda V, \end{aligned} \tag{11.60}$$

where

$$\lambda = 2\sigma^2 \cos\left(\frac{\pi\alpha}{4}\right)^{\frac{2}{\alpha}} (\mathcal{T} - t)^{\frac{2}{\alpha}} \tag{11.61}$$

and V is an $\alpha/2$-stable random variable with both the skewness parameter and scale parameter equal to one, that is

$$V \overset{\mathrm{d}}{=} S_{\frac{\alpha}{2}}(1,1,0). \tag{11.62}$$

In terms of the probability density function $f_V(\cdot)$ of the $\alpha/2$-stable random variable V, the distribution functions $F_{\pm}(\cdot)$ given by equation (11.51) can be written as

$$F_{\pm}(x) = \int_0^\infty \Phi\left(\frac{x \mp \frac{1}{2}\lambda v}{\sqrt{\lambda v}}\right) f_V(v)dv. \tag{11.63}$$

Now we apply the transformation $v = u(1-u)^{-3}$ so that the integrand becomes a sufficiently smooth function to be integrated over the now finite interval $[0,1]$. That is

$$F_{\pm}(x) = \int_0^1 \Phi\left(\frac{x \mp \frac{1}{2}\lambda \frac{u}{(1-u)^3}}{\sqrt{\lambda \frac{u}{(1-u)^3}}}\right) f_V\left(\frac{u}{(1-u)^3}\right) \frac{1+2u}{(1-u)^4} du. \tag{11.64}$$

This can also be re-written as

$$F_{\pm}(x) = \int_0^1 g_{\pm}(x, \alpha, \sigma, u) H(\alpha, u) du, \tag{11.65}$$

where

$$g_{\pm}(x, \alpha, \sigma, u) = \Phi\left(\frac{x \mp \frac{1}{2}\lambda \frac{u}{(1-u)^3}}{\sqrt{\lambda \frac{u}{(1-u)^3}}}\right) \tag{11.66}$$

and

$$h(\alpha, u) = f_V\left(\frac{u}{(1-u)^3}\right) \frac{1+2u}{(1-u)^4}. \tag{11.67}$$

We numerically integrate this integral using the extended midpoint rule (see Press et al. (1992), Chapter 4). Therefore, $F_{\pm}(x)$ is approximately equal to

$$F_{\pm}(x) \approx h \sum_{i=0}^{k-1} g_{\pm}(x, \alpha, \sigma, u_i) h(\alpha, u_i), \tag{11.68}$$

where $h = 1/k$ with $k \in \{1, 2, 3, \ldots\}$ and $u_i = h(i + \frac{1}{2})$. The distribution functions $F_{\pm}(x)$ involve a term $h(\alpha, u)$ that is dependent on the index of stability α and the integrating variable u and terms $g_{\pm}(x, \alpha, \sigma, u)$ that are dependent on α, u but also on the quantile x and the volatility σ. Therefore for a given number of integral subdivisions k and a fixed index of stability α the function $h(\alpha, u_i)$, which involves the computation of the $\alpha/2$-stable probability density function, needs only to be calculated once and then can be used repeatedly in the calculation of any option price on the given asset.

In Hurst, Platen and Rachev (1995a,b) we illustrated how the European call option price is dependent on the index of stability α, the volatility σ, the strike price K, the time to maturity $\mathcal{T}$ and the interest rate r. To compare option prices for different indexes of stability one needs to have a relationship involving the corresponding volatilities for these different distributions. We obtain this by making the distributions have the same lower and upper quartiles (see either McCulloch (1986) and Samorodnitsky and Taqqu (1994)).

The Black and Schole European call option pricing formula uses the normal distributions whereas our European call option pricing formula (11.52) uses the symmetric α-stable distributions. The difference between the European call option prices (11.52) and the Black and Scholes prices for these distributions, where the time to maturity is six months and the interest rate is zero was analyzed in Hurst, Platen and Rachev (1995a,b) [22]. The main results are:

(i) as the index of stability decreases the European call option price (11.52) increases;

(ii) as the index of stability decreases the level and curvature of the volatility smile both increase;

The *implied volatility* of a given European call option price is the volatility that equates the Black and Scholes European call option price to that price (see for example Hull (1997)). If the market prices for European call options would be consistent with the Black and Scholes option pricing model, then the implied volatility would be the same for all the option prices with different maturities and exercise prices at a certain time. As is well-known in practice this is not the case. Deep in-the-money and deep out-of-the-money options have higher implied volatilities than at-the-money options. This phenomenon is called the *volatility smile* as for instance discussed in Derman and Kani (1994), Platen and Schweizer (1994) and references within. This indicates that the assumptions of the Black and Scholes option pricing model are not fulfilled.

The Black and Scholes formula can not be analytically inverted to make the implied volatility an explicit function of the asset price S, the exercise

---

[22]Similar analysis on the DAX-option data was done in Rieken, Mittnik and Rachev (1998), see also Chapter 13.

price K, the time to maturity $\mathcal{T}$, the interest rate r and the option price C. This does not cause a problem because the implied volatility can be calculated numerically by efficient root finding procedures (see Press et al. (1992), Chapter 9).

Hurst, Platen and Rachev (1995a,b) use equation (11.68) in the European call option pricing formula (11.52) given in Proposition 11.1 to numerically calculate option prices for the logstable model. European call option prices (11.52) for the S & P 500 daily returns are calculated using the maximum likelihood estimates for the logstable model given in Section 5.2, namely $\hat{\alpha} = 1.714$ and $\hat{\sigma} = 0.004950$, which can be converted to an annual volatility by $\hat{\sigma}_{ann.} = \hat{\sigma} \times 365^{1/\hat{\alpha}} = 0.1547$. The implied volatilities of the option prices (11.58) were calculated which graphically appeared as a volatility smile [23]. Moreover, the time to maturity shortens the curvature of the volatility smile increases and level of the volatility smile at-the-money decreases. These properties of the volatility smile implied by the European call option prices (11.52) are consistent with observations in the market, for example as shown for the S & P 500 by Derman and Kani (1994).

11.5 Appendix: Option Pricing with Heavy-Tailed Distributed Returns

Proof[24] **of Theorem 11.1.** Recall the main ingredients of the Mandelbrot and Taylor (1967) model. Let $\{W(T), T \geq 0\}$ be a Brownian motion with zero drift and variance ν^2, which is viewed as the process of stock log prices on the time scale measured in volume of transactions. Let $\{T(t), t \geq 0\}$ be a positive $\frac{\alpha}{2}$-stable stochastic process with characteristic function (11.2) Then $Z(t) = W(T(t))$ is a subordinated process to $W(t)$ with a directing process $T(t)$, and $Z(t)$ represent the (log) price of the stock at time t. The resulting process $Z(t)$ is now α-stable Lévy motion with ch.f. (11.3) To model a stock price process whose logarithm is $\xi(t)$ we assume that if the current price of a stock is $S = S_0$, the stock price S_1 at the end of the first period is described by

$$S_1 = \begin{cases} U_1 S_0 & \text{with probability } \frac{1}{2} \\ D_1 S_0 & \text{with probability } \frac{1}{2}, (U_1 \geq 1 \geq D_1) \end{cases} \quad (11.69)$$

Continuing as in (11.69), the consecutive movements of the stock are given by

$$S_k \stackrel{d}{=} S \prod_{i=1}^{k} U_i^{\delta_i} D_i^{(1-\delta_i)}, \quad (11.70)$$

or

$$\log(S_k/S) \stackrel{d}{=} \sum_{i=1}^{k} (U_i \delta_i + D_i (1 - \delta_i)), \quad (11.71)$$

[23] For a similar analysis see 13

[24] The results in Appendix 11.5 and 11.6 are due to Rachev and Samorodnitsky (1993).

where $U_i := \log U_i, D_i := \log D_i$, and δ_i's are *i.i.d.* Bernoulli($\frac{1}{2}$)-independent of U_i's and D_i's. We assume that the log-increments of our stock price process are symmetrically distributed,

$$U_i = \sigma|X_i^{(n)}|, D_i = -U_i, \tag{11.72}$$

where n represents the number of movements until the terminal time T of a call and $\{X_i^{(n)}, i = 1, \ldots, n\}$ are i.i.d. symmetric[25] Pareto r.v.'s with

$$P(|X_i^{(n)}| > x) = n^{-1}x^{-\alpha}, x \geq n^{-1/\alpha}, 1 < \alpha < 2. \tag{11.73}$$

In other words $Y_i = n^{1/\alpha}X_i^{(n)}$, $i = 1, 2, \ldots$ are in the domain of attraction of a symmetric α-stable r.v. We write

$$\log(S_k/S) \stackrel{d}{=} \sigma \sum_{i=1}^{k} X_k^{(n)}, \tag{11.74}$$

and thus the process

$$Z_n(t) = \log(S_k/S), \tag{11.75}$$

for all t in the interval $\tau\frac{k-1}{n} < t \leq \tau\frac{k}{n}$, $k = 1, \ldots, n$, $(Z_n(0) = 0)$, converges weakly to a symmetric α-stable Lévy motion $Z(t)$ in $D[0, t]$. Let R_i denote the "riskless interest rate" at the ith period,

$$R_i = \frac{1}{2}(U_i + D_i). \tag{11.76}$$

In contrast with the classical Cox-Ross-Rubinstein model $R_i = R_i(\omega)$ is now random. With this in mind we continue to follow the usual arguments leading to the binomial option pricing formulae. For fixed ω, in order to have an "equivalent portfolio" and "no riskless arbitrary opportunities", the value $c = c^{(n)}$ of the call — with expiration date τ which is just n periods away and striking price K — equals

$$c^{(n)} = \frac{2^{-n}}{R_1 \cdots R_n}\{(U_1 \cdots U_nS - K)^+ + [(U_1 \cdots U_{n-1}D_nS - K)^+ \tag{11.77}$$
$$+ \cdots + (D_1U_2 \cdots U_nS - K)^+] + \cdots + (D_1 \cdots D_nS - K)^+\}.$$

Formula (11.77) represent the random value $c^{(n)}$ of the call. In contrast with the classical binomial pricing formula, $c^{(n)}$ gives us a unique rational value for fixed ω. Now, how much would be willing to pay for the call at time 0? It is quite reasonable, in the absence of a unique deterministic solution, to

---

[25] For most of commodities and for some stocks it is not a serious restriction to assume that the log-price changes are symmetrically distributed.

look at the mean value $C^{(n)} = \mathrm{E}c^{(n)}$. Our goal is an expression for the limit $C = \lim_{n\to\infty} C^{(n)}$.

Suppose ξ_i's are i.i.d uniforms on $(0,1)$ and ϵ_i's are independent of ξ_i's Rademacher random signs.[26] Then $X_i^{(n)} \stackrel{d}{=} \epsilon_i n^{-1/\alpha}\xi_i^{-1/\alpha}$ and rearranging in $(X_1^{(n)},\ldots,X_n^{(n)})$ in an increasing absolute order, say $(X_{1,n}^{(n)},\ldots,X_{n,n}^{(n)})$, we observe that the latter order statistics have the same joint distribution as

$$\left(\frac{\Gamma_{n+1}}{n}\right)^{1/\alpha}\left(\epsilon_1\Gamma_1^{-1/\alpha},\ldots,\epsilon_n\Gamma_n^{-1/\alpha}\right)$$

where $\Gamma_1,\Gamma_2,\ldots$ are Poisson arrivals with intensity 1, independent of ϵ_i's.

Lemma 11.2 *(Binomial option pricing formula for heavy tailed distributed stock returns).* If the stock movements are described by the "discretized" Mandelbrot-Taylor model (11.73)–(11.75) then for any $n \geq 1$

$$C^{(n)} = \mathrm{E}\frac{(S\exp(\sigma(\frac{\Gamma_{n+1}}{n})^{1/\alpha}\sum_{i=1}^{n}\epsilon_i\Gamma_i^{-1/\alpha}) - K)^+}{2^{-n}\prod_{i=1}^{n}\exp(\sigma(\frac{\Gamma_{n+1}}{n})^{1/\alpha}\Gamma_i^{-1/\alpha}) + \exp(-\sigma(\frac{\Gamma_{n+1}}{n})^{1/\alpha}\Gamma_i^{-1/\alpha})}$$
(11.78)

or, equivalently,

$$C^{(n)} = \mathrm{E}\frac{(S\exp(\sigma(\frac{\Gamma_{n+1}}{n})^{1/\alpha}\sum_{i=1}^{n}\epsilon_i\Gamma_i^{-1/\alpha}) - K)^+}{\mathrm{E}_{(\epsilon_1,\ldots,\epsilon_n)}\exp(\sigma(\frac{\Gamma_{n+1}}{n})^{1/\alpha}\sum_{i=1}^{n}\epsilon_i\Gamma_i^{-1/\alpha})},$$
(11.79)

where we use the standard notation $\mathrm{E}_{(\epsilon_1,\ldots,\epsilon_n)}$ to denote the expectation taken with respect to $\epsilon_1,\ldots,\epsilon_n$.

Proof. Recall that $R_i = \frac{1}{2}(U_i+D_i)$, then by the formula for $C^{(n)}$ (cf. (11.77), (11.72), (11.76)) we can rewrite $C^{(n)}$ as

$$C^{(n)} = \mathrm{E}\frac{(Se^{\sigma(X_1^{(n)}+\cdots+X_n^{(n)})} - K)^+}{2^{-n}\prod_{i=1}^{n}(e^{\sigma|X_i^{(n)}|} + e^{-\sigma|X_i^{(n)}|})},$$
(11.80)

which implies (11.78) and (11.79).   □

To prove Theorem 11.1 we need to show that $C^{(n)} \to C$, where

$$C = \mathrm{E}\frac{(S\exp(\sum_{i=1}^{\infty}\sigma\epsilon_i\Gamma_i^{-1/\alpha}) - K)^+}{\mathrm{E}_{(\epsilon_1,\epsilon_2,\ldots)}\exp\{\sum_{i=1}^{\infty}\sigma\epsilon_i\Gamma_i^{-1/\alpha}\}}.$$
(11.81)

Indeed, it is sufficient to consider the case $\sigma = 1$ only. Using the representation (11.79) for $C^{(n)}$ we let $n \to \infty$, then clearly $\left(\frac{\Gamma_{n+1}}{n}\right)^{1/\alpha}\sum_{i=1}^{n}\epsilon_i\Gamma_i^{-1/\alpha} \to$

---

[26] $(\epsilon_i)_{i\geq 1}$ is a sequence of Rademacher random signs, if ϵ_i's are mutually independent and $P(\epsilon_i = +1) = P(\epsilon_i = -1) = 1/2$.

$\sum_{i=1}^{\infty} \epsilon_i \Gamma_i^{-1/\alpha}$ a.s., and thus the numerator of (11.79) converges to the numerator in (11.81). Our next step is to show that the denominator in (11.79) converges to the denominator in (11.81). Using the above limit relationship it is enough to show the following claim.

Claim. Suppose that $a_1, a_2, \ldots$ is a sequence of real numbers such that, as $n \to \infty$,

$$\sum_{i=1}^{n} a_i \epsilon_i \to \sum_{i=1}^{\infty} a_i \epsilon_i \text{ a.s.}, \tag{11.82}$$

which is equivalent to $\sum_{i=1}^{\infty} a_i^2 < \infty$. Suppose $R_n \to 1$ as $n \to \infty$, then

$$\mathrm{E} \exp \left(R_n \sum_{i=1}^{n} a_i \epsilon_i \right) \to \mathrm{E} \exp \left(\sum_{i=1}^{\infty} a_i \epsilon_i \right). \tag{11.83}$$

Proof of the claim. By Hölder's inequality

$$|\mathrm{E} \exp(R_n \sum_{i=1}^{n} a_i \epsilon_i) - \mathrm{E} \exp(\sum_{i=1}^{n} a_i \epsilon_i)|^2$$

$$\leq [\mathrm{E} \exp(2 \sum_{i=1}^{\infty} a_i \epsilon_i)][\mathrm{E}(-1 + \exp(R_n - 1) \sum_{i=1}^{n} a_i \epsilon_i)^2]$$

$$=: T_1 T_2.$$

The term T_1 in the above product is finite by hypothesis. As $R_n \to 1$, the second term T_1 is bounded by

$$
\begin{aligned}
T_2 &= \int_0^{\infty} \mathrm{P}((-1 + \exp(R_n - 1) \sum_{i=1}^{n} a_i \epsilon_i)^2 > t) dt \\
&\leq \int_0^{\infty} \mathrm{P}(|R_n - 1|| \sum_{i=1}^{n} a_i \epsilon_i| > \log(1 + \sqrt{t})) dt \\
&\quad + \int_0^1 \mathrm{P}(|R_n - 1|| \sum_{i=1}^{n} a_i \epsilon_i| < \log(1 - \sqrt{t})) dt \\
&\leq 2 \int_0^{\infty} \exp(-\frac{(\log(1 + \sqrt{t}))^2}{2(R_n - 1)^2 \sum_{i=1}^{n} a_i^2}) dt \\
&\quad + 2 \int_0^1 \exp(-\frac{(\log \frac{1}{1 - \sqrt{t}})^2}{2(R_n - 1)^2 \sum_{i=1}^{2} a_i^2}) dt.
\end{aligned}
$$

The last inequality follows from the exponential bound for $\sum_{i=1}^{\infty} b_i^2 < \infty$,

$$\mathrm{P}(| \sum_{i=1}^{\infty} b_i \epsilon_i| > t) \leq 2 \exp \left(-\frac{t^2}{2 \sum_{i=1}^{\infty} b_i^2} \right), \tag{11.84}$$

see, e.g. Ledoux and Talagrand (1991). The two integrals in the right-hand-side of the bound for T_2 vanish as $n \to \infty$, since $R_n \to 1$ and $\sum_{i=1}^{\infty} a_i^2 < \infty$, and thus

$$E \exp(R_n \sum_{i=1}^{n} a_i \epsilon_i) - E \exp(\sum_{i=1}^{n} a_i \epsilon_i) \to 0. \tag{11.85}$$

To show that

$$E \exp(\sum_{i=1}^{n} a_i \epsilon_i) \to E \exp(\sum_{i=1}^{\infty} a_i \epsilon_i) \tag{11.86}$$

we use the same argument as before. Using the exponential bound (11.78) and $\sum_{i=1}^{\infty} a_i^2 < \infty$,

$$|E \exp(\sum_{i=1}^{n} a_i \epsilon_i) - E \exp(\sum_{i=1}^{\infty} a_i \epsilon_i)|^2$$
$$\leq \text{ const. } E(e^{-\sum_{i=n+1}^{\infty} a_i \epsilon_i} - 1)^2$$
$$\leq \text{ const. } \int_0^{\infty} \exp(-\frac{(\log(1+\sqrt{t}))^2}{2 \sum_{i=n+1}^{\infty} a_i^2}) dt$$
$$+ \text{ const. } \int_0^1 \exp(-\frac{(1-\sqrt{t}))^2}{2 \sum_{i=n+1}^{\infty} a_i^2}) dt,$$

and the latter bound vanishes at $n \to \infty$. Combining (11.85) and (11.86) completes the proof of the claim and, by the bounded convergence theorem, of Theorem 11.2 as well. □

Remark 11.1 The construction of our "discrete" version of the Mandelbrot-Taylor model suggests that the option pricing formula (11.81) may remain unchanged even if the price changes are dependent. To see that, suppose the rate of return over ith period of time can have two possible values — each of them with probability $1/2$:

$$U_i^* - 1 = \exp(\Gamma_i^{-1/\alpha} W_i) - 1 \tag{11.87}$$

and

$$D_i^* - 1 = \exp(-\Gamma_i^{-1/\alpha} W_i) - 1. \tag{11.88}$$

In (11.87) and (11.88), $\alpha \in (0,2), W_i$'s are i.i.d. nonnegative r.v.'s, with $EW_1^{\alpha} < \infty, \Gamma_i$'s are independent of W_i's and represent a sequence of arrival times of a Poisson process with unit rate. The stock price after n periods of time equals

$$S_n^* = S \exp \sum_{i=1}^{n} (\epsilon_i U_i^* + (1 - \epsilon_i) D_i^*) \tag{11.89}$$

with ϵ_i's being Bernoulli $(\frac{1}{2})$r.v.'s independent of (Γ_i, W_i) and, as before, $U_i^* = \log U_i^*, D_i^* = \log D_i^*$. In other words, (11.89) reads

$$\log(S_n^*/S) = \sum_{i=1}^{n} \epsilon_i \Gamma_i^{-1/\alpha} W_i. \tag{11.90}$$

Then, as $n \to \infty$, we have

$$\log(S_n^*/S) \to \sum_{i=1}^{\infty} \epsilon_i \Gamma_i^{-1/\alpha} W_i \overset{d}{=} S_\alpha(\sigma_\alpha, 0, 0). \qquad (11.91)$$

Here $S_\alpha(\sigma_\alpha, 0, 0)$ stands for a symmetric α- stable law with scaling parameter $\sigma_\alpha \geq 0$, given by

$$\sigma_\alpha^\alpha = \frac{1}{c_\alpha} EW_1^\alpha, c_\alpha := \left(\int_0^\infty x^{-\alpha} \sin x dx \right)^{-1} = \begin{cases} \frac{1-\alpha}{\Gamma(2-\alpha)\cos(\pi\alpha 2)} & \text{if } \alpha \neq 1 \\ 2/\pi & \text{if } \alpha = 1 \end{cases}, \qquad (11.92)$$

see, e.g. Samorodnitsky and Taqqu (1994). The limit relation (11.91) shows that at the terminal time the distribution of the stock price is the same as in the Mandelbrot-Taylor model. We now use the assumption of "riskless interest rate", $R_i = \frac{1}{2}(U_i + D_i)$, and "no riskless arbitrage opportunities" arguments, to conclude that the mean-value $C^{*(n)}$ of the call $c^{*(n)}$ n-periods before the expiration rate equals

$$C^{*(n)} = Ec^{*(n)} \qquad (11.93)$$

$$= E\frac{2^{-n}}{R_1 R_2 \cdots R_n} ((e^{U_1 + \cdots + U_n} S - K)_+ + [(e^{U_1 + \cdots + U_{n-1} + D_n} S - K)^+ + \cdots$$

$$+ (e^{D_1 + U_2 + \cdots + U_n} S - K)^+] + \cdots + (e^{D_1 + \cdots + D_n} S - K)^+).$$

Corollary 11.1 If the stock price after n moves is determined by (11.87)–(11.89) then

$$C^{*(n)} \to C^*, \qquad (11.94)$$

where

$$C^* = E\frac{(Se^{\sum_{i=1}^{\infty} \epsilon_i \Gamma_i^{-1/\alpha} W_i} - K)^+}{E_{(\epsilon_1, \epsilon_2, \ldots)} e^{\sum_{i=1}^{\infty} \epsilon_i \Gamma_i^{-1/\alpha} W_i}}. \qquad (11.95)$$

The proof is similar to that of Theorem 11.1 and thus omitted.

Remark 11.2 From (11.91), (11.92) the limiting distribution for S_n^* depends on the distribution of W_i's through the mean EW_1^α. So, one should expect that C^* depend on the distribution of W_i's only through EW_1^α. To see that, we rewrite C^* in (11.95) as follows

$$C^* = E\frac{(e^{\sum_{i=1}^{\infty} \epsilon_i \Gamma_i^{-1/\alpha} W_i} S - K)_+}{\prod_{i=1}^{\infty} \frac{1}{2}[e^{\Gamma_i^{-1/\alpha} W_i} + e^{-\Gamma_i^{-1/\alpha} W_i}]}.$$

Thus, it is enough to prove that the distribution of the point process $\mathcal{N} = \{\Gamma_i^{-1/\alpha} W_i, i = 1, 2, \ldots\}$ depends only on EW_1^α. First it is easy to see that $\mathcal{N}$

is a Poisson process. The next step is to show that its intensity measure μ depends on the distribution of W_i's only through EW_1^α. In fact, for any $\lambda > 0$

$$
\begin{aligned}
\mu((\lambda, \infty)) &= \sum_{i=1}^{\infty} P(\Gamma_i^{-1/\alpha} W_i > \lambda) \\
&= \sum_{i=1}^{\infty} \int_0^\infty \frac{x^{i-1}}{(i-1)!} e^{-x} P(W_i^\alpha > x\lambda^\alpha) dx \\
&= \lambda^{-\alpha} \int_0^\infty P(W_1^\alpha > x) dx = \lambda^{-\alpha} EW_1^\alpha.
\end{aligned}
$$

11.6   Appendix: Option Pricing with Returns in the Domain of Attraction of the Normal Law

While Mandelbrot (1963a,b) set out to explain the non-normality in price changes by assuming that they are α-stable with $\alpha < 2$, Clark (1973) presented the opposite hypothesis assuming that the price change is subordinate to Brownian motion with directing process having finite variance. Clark (1973) modelled the process of stock changes by

$$Z(t) = W(T(t)), \tag{11.96}$$

that is Z subordinated to $W(t)$ with directing process $T(t) \geq 0, ET(t)^2 < \infty$. If W and T have stationary independent increments, $EW(t) = 0$, and $VarW(t) = v^2 t$, and $ET(t) = \beta t$ then $Z(t)$ has stationary independent increments, $EZ(t) = 0$ and $VarZ(t) = \beta v^2 t$. The special case considered in Clark's paper is W being a Wiener process with zero mean and $VarW(t) = \sigma_2^2 t$ and $T(t)$ a log-normal, that is density of $\tau(1)$ is

$$f(x, \mu, \sigma_1^2) = \frac{1}{2\pi\sigma_1^2 x} \exp\left(-\frac{(\log x - \mu)^2}{2\sigma_1^2}\right), x > 0. \tag{11.97}$$

The random process Z has unit increments with density

$$f_{Z(1)}(y) = \frac{1}{2\pi\sigma_1^2\sigma_2^2} \int_0^\infty v^{-3/2} \exp\left(\frac{-(\log v - \mu)^2}{2\sigma_1^2}\right) \exp\left(\frac{-y^2}{2v\sigma_2^2}\right) dv. \tag{11.98}$$

Since the choice of a log-normal directed process is not completely justified in the Clark (1973) paper we shall only assume that $T(t)$ has a finite first moment.

To model a stock price process whose logarithm is $Z(t)$ in (11.96) we assume the same "discretized" model of stock price as in Section 11.5, (see (11.70) and (11.71)), but this time the log-increments of our stock price process are taken to be in the domain of attraction of the normal distribution. Specifically, we define the random up's ($\tilde{U}_i$'s) and down's ($\tilde{D}_i$'s) by

$$\log \tilde{U}_i := \tilde{\mathrm{U}}_i := \sigma\tau^{1/2} |n^{-1/2} X_1|, \tilde{\mathrm{D}}_i := \log \tilde{D}_i := -\tilde{\mathrm{U}}_i, \tag{11.99}$$

where $X_1, \ldots, X_n$ are i.i.d. symmetric r.v.'s with unit variance, and thus the "discretized" Clark's model of stock price is given by

$$\{\tilde{S}_k\}_{k=1,\ldots,n} \overset{d}{=} \{S \exp \sum_{i=1}^{k} (\epsilon_i \tilde{U}_i + (1 - \epsilon_i)\tilde{D}_i)\}_{k=1,\ldots,n}, \qquad (11.100)$$

when ϵ_i's are Bernoulli $(\frac{1}{2})$ independent of $\tilde{U}_i$'s.

The same arguments as in Appendix 11.5 yield a binomial option pricing formula — the random value $(\tilde{c}_n)$ of a call n periods prior to the expiration date.

$$\tilde{c}_n = \frac{2^{-n}}{\tilde{R}_1 \cdots \tilde{R}_n} \{(\tilde{U}_1 \cdots \tilde{U}_n S - K)_+$$
$$+ [(\tilde{U}_1 \cdots \tilde{U}_{n-1} \tilde{D}_{n-1} S - K)^+ + \cdots + (\tilde{D}_1 \tilde{U}_2 \cdots \tilde{U}_n S - K)^+] + \cdots$$
$$+ (\tilde{D}_1 \cdots \tilde{D}_n S - K)^+\}.$$

where $\tilde{R}_i$ is the "riskless interest rate"

$$\tilde{R}_i = \frac{1}{2}(\tilde{U}_i + \tilde{D}_i). \qquad (11.101)$$

In contrast to the Mandelbrot-Taylor model, in the "discretized" Clark's model, the product of the interest rate does converge to a constant.

Lemma 11.3 If τ is the expiration date corresponding to n movements in the discretized Clark's model, then $\tilde{R}_1 \cdots \tilde{R}_n$ converges in probability (in distribution) to a constant;

$$\tilde{R}_1 \cdots \tilde{R}_n \to e^{\frac{1}{2}\sigma^2 \tau}. \qquad (11.102)$$

Proof. The above limit relation follows immediately from the following claim.
Claim. Let $X_1, X_2, \cdots$ be a sequence of *i.i.d.* zero mean random variables with a finite variance $\sigma^2 = EX_1^2$. Then

$$\lim_{n \to \infty} \prod_{i=1}^{n} \left(\frac{1}{2} e^{X_i n^{-1/2}} + \frac{1}{2} e^{X_i n^{-1/2}} \right) = e^{\sigma^2/2} \text{ a.s.}$$

Proof of the claim. By the Strong Law of Large Numbers,

$$\frac{X_1^2 + \cdots + X_n^2}{n} \to \sigma^2 \text{a.s., as} n \to \infty, \qquad (11.103)$$

and thus, as $n \to \infty$,

$$n^{-1/2} X_n \to 0 \text{ a.s.} \qquad (11.104)$$

In particular, it follows from (11.104) that

$$\lim_{n \to \infty} n^{-1/2} \max_{i \leq n} |X_i| = 0 \text{ a.s.} \qquad (11.105)$$

Fix any ω for which both (11.103) and (11.105) hold. Clearly,

$$\lim_{a \to 0} \frac{\log \frac{(e^a + e^{-a})}{2}}{a^2/2} = 1. \tag{11.106}$$

It follows then from (11.105) and (11.106) that for any $0 < \epsilon < 1$ there is an $N = N(\omega, \epsilon)$ such that for every $n > N$, and every $i \le n$,

$$\log \left(\frac{e^{X_i n^{-1/2}} + e^{-X_i n^{-1/2}}}{2} \right) \in \left((1-\epsilon)\frac{X_i^2}{2n}, (1+\epsilon)\frac{X_i^2}{2n} \right). \tag{11.107}$$

It follows now that for every $n > N$

$$\sum_{i=1}^{n} \left(\log \frac{e^{X_i n^{-1/2}} + e^{-X_i n^{-1/2}}}{2} \right) \in \left((1-\epsilon)\frac{X_1^2 + \cdots + X_n^2}{2n}, \right.$$
$$\left. (1+\epsilon)\frac{X_1^2 + \cdots + X_n^2}{2n} \right) \tag{11.108}$$

Thus by (11.103)

$$(1-\epsilon)\frac{\sigma^2}{2} \le \liminf_{n \to \infty} \sum_{i=1}^{n} \left(\log \frac{e^{X_i n^{-1/2}} + e^{-X_i n^{-1/2}}}{2} \right)$$
$$\le \limsup_{n \to \infty} \sum_{i=1}^{n} \left(\log \frac{e^{X_i n^{-1/2}} + e^{-X_i n^{-1/2}}}{2} \right) \le (1+\epsilon)\frac{\sigma^2}{2}.$$

Since this is true for any $1 > \epsilon > 0$, we conclude that

$$\lim_{n \to \infty} \sum_{i=1}^{n} \left(\log \frac{e^{X_i n^{-1/2}} + e^{-X_i n^{-1/2}}}{2} \right) = \frac{\sigma^2}{2}. \tag{11.109}$$

The claim now follows from (11.109). This proves the lemma as well. $\square$

The next theorem gives us the option pricing formula for the mean value $C = \lim_{n \to \infty} E\tilde{c}^n$ of the call under Clark's model.

Theorem 11.3 *(Pricing formula for stock returns governed by the subordinated process $Z(t) = W(T(t))$. Letting $n \to \infty$ in the "discretized" Clark model (11.101)–(11.101) implies*

$$\tilde{C} = \lim_{n \to \infty} E\tilde{c}^n \stackrel{d}{=} e^{-1/2\sigma^2 \tau} E(Se^{\sigma \sqrt{\tau} N} - K)^+, \tag{11.110}$$

where N has standard normal distribution.
Proof. From (11.101) and (11.99) a simple conditioning argument implies that

$$C^{(n)} = E\tilde{c}^{(n)} = E\frac{(Se^{\sigma \tau^{1/2} n^{-1/2}(X_1 + \cdots + X_n)} - K)^+}{R_1 \cdots R_n}. \tag{11.111}$$

It is sufficient to show (11.110) for $\tau = 1$. In other words, we need to prove that if $X_1, X_2, \cdots$ are i.i.d. symmetric r.v. with a finite variance $\sigma^2 = EX_1^2$, then

$$E\frac{(Se^{n^{-1/2}(X_1+\cdots+X_n)} - K)^+}{\prod_{i=1}^n(\frac{1}{2}e^{X_i n^{-1/2}} + \frac{1}{2}e^{-X_i n^{-1/2}})} \to e^{-(1/2)\sigma^2}E(Se^{\sigma N} - K)^+. \quad (11.112)$$

Let $\epsilon_1, \epsilon_2, \ldots$ be a sequence of i.i.d. Rademacher random variables, independent of $X_1, X_2, \ldots$ Then

$$E\frac{(Se^{n^{-1/2}(X_1+\cdots+X_n)} - K)^+}{\prod_{i=1}^n(\frac{1}{2}e^{X_i n-(1/2)} + \frac{1}{2}e^{-X_i^{-1/2}})}$$

$$= E\frac{(Se^{2n^{-1/2}}(X_1 + \cdots + X_n) - K)^+}{E_{(\epsilon_1,\ldots,\epsilon_n)}e^{n^{-1/2}(\epsilon_1 X_1+\cdots+\epsilon_n X_n)}}$$

$$= E\frac{E_{(\epsilon_1,\ldots,\epsilon_n)}(Se^{n^{-1/2}(\epsilon_1 X_1+\cdots+\epsilon_n X_n)} - K)^+}{E_{(\epsilon_1,\ldots,\epsilon_n)}e^{n^{-1/2}(\epsilon_1 X_1+\cdots+\epsilon_n X_n)}} := EV_n.$$

Observe that $V_n \le S$ a.s. for all n. Therefore, bounded convergence theorem would apply (11.112) once we prove that

$$V_n \to e^{-\frac{1}{2}\sigma^2}E(Se^{\sigma N} - K)^+ \text{ a.s.} \quad (11.113)$$

Since we have already proved that the denominator in V_n converges a.s. to $e^{\frac{1}{2}\sigma^2}$, it remains to show that

$$E_{(\epsilon_1,\ldots,\epsilon_n)}(Se^{n^{-1/2}(\epsilon_1 X_1+\cdots \epsilon_n X_n)} - K)^+ \to E(Se^{\sigma N} - K)^+ \text{ a.s.} \quad (11.114)$$

As before, it is enough to prove convergence in (11.114) for ω's for which both (11.103) and (11.105) hold. For the simplicity of notation, we will assume that $\epsilon_1, \epsilon_2, \ldots$ live on some other probability space $(\Omega_1, \mathcal{F}_1, P_1)$. Denote

$$a_1^{(n)} := n^{-1/2}X_i(\omega), i = 1, \ldots, n, n = 1, 2, \ldots \quad (11.115)$$

The first step is to show that the sequence $\sum_{i=1}^n \epsilon_i a_i^{(n)}, n = 1, 2, \ldots$ converges in distribution to σN, as $n \to \infty$. For the corresponding characteristic functions we get

$$E_{(\Omega_1, \mathcal{F}_1, P_1)} \exp(i\theta \sum_{j=1}^n \epsilon_j a_j^{(n)}) = \prod_{j=1}^n E_1 e^{i\theta\epsilon_j a_j^{(n)}}$$

$$= \prod_{j=1}^n(\frac{1}{2}e^{i\theta a_j^{(n)}} + \frac{1}{2}e^{-i\theta a_j^{(n)}})$$

$$= \prod_{j=1}^n(\frac{1}{2}e^{i\theta X_j n^{-1/2}} + \frac{1}{2}e^{-i\theta X_j n^{-1/2}})$$

$$= \prod_{j=1}^n \cos(\theta X_j n^{-1/2}),$$

and the same argument as in the proof of the lemma above shows that

$$E_{(\Omega_1,\mathcal{F}_1,P_1)}e^{i\theta\sum_{j=1}^n \epsilon_j a_j^{(n)}} \to e^{\frac{-\sigma^2\theta^2}{2}}. \tag{11.116}$$

Now, (11.116) will imply (11.114) if we show that the sequence

$$(Se^{\sum_{j=1}^n \epsilon_j a_1^{(n)}} - K)^+, n = 1, 2, \ldots, \tag{11.117}$$

is uniformly integrable. To this end we show that

$$\sup_{n\geq 1}[E_{(\Omega_1,\mathcal{F}_1,P_1)}(Se^{\sum_{j=1}^n \epsilon_j a_j^{(n)}} - K)^+]^2 < \infty. \tag{11.118}$$

In fact,

$$E_{(\Omega_1,\mathcal{F}_1,P_1)}(Se^{\sum_{j=1}^n \epsilon_j a_j^{(n)}} - K)_+^2 \leq S^2 E_{(\Omega_1,\mathcal{F}_1,P_1)}e^{2\sum_{j=1}^n \epsilon_j a_j^{(n)}} \tag{11.119}$$

$$= S^2 E_{(\Omega_1,\mathcal{F}_1,P_1)}e^{2n^{-1/2}\sum_{j=1}^n \epsilon_j X_j} = S^2 \prod_{i=1}^n \left(\frac{1}{2}e^{2n^{-1/2}X_j} + \frac{1}{2}e^{-2n^{-1/2}X_j}\right).$$

Clearly, this is an expression of the same form as in the claim of Lemma 11.3 and so by the same argument, it converges to a finite limit as $n \to \infty$. This proves (11.118) and Theorem 11.3 as well.   □

11.7   Appendix: Term Structure of Interest Rates Driven by Stable Motion

The usual way of pricing products contingent on interest rate is to assume that interest rate follows some Brownian motion type process and then use the Ito formula for the derivative processes. This implies normal distribution of returns, which as we have shown is unrealistic. In sections 11.2 - 11.4 we are trying to draw attention to alternative stable processes: instead of the Gaussian law we use Lévy stable law to describe the increments of the log-price process.

Although technically more demanding, there are immediate benefits in such an approach: the models allow for fat tails and there are four parameters that can be used to fit data. As a result, in several examples stable models for the term structure perform better than lognormal.[27]

The usual approach to pricing bonds and their derivatives is to assume that the short-term interest rate $r(t)$ follows a process of the form

$$dr = a(t, r)dt + b(t, r)dB(t), \tag{11.120}$$

---

[27]The results in this section are due to Dostoglou and Rachev (1995).

where B is a Wiener process. The coefficients a and b are chosen to allow for mean reversion and to fit the current structure, see chapter 15 of Hull (1993).

Based on the model for options on stock (see Section 11.4) we examine a model where the term structure follows a subordinate process directed by an α-stable motion:

$$dr = m(r)dt + a(r)d\tau + b(r)dB(\tau),$$

where $\tau(t)$ is an α-stable motion for some value of α in $(1,2)$. That is,

$$\tau(t) - \tau(t') \sim (t - t')^{\frac{1}{\alpha}} S_\alpha(1,0,0),$$

where $S_\alpha(\sigma,\beta,\mu)$ denotes the α-stable distribution, see (2.2) in Section 2.1.

As an example, we set $m = 0$, $a(r) = ar$ and $b(r) = br$ for constants a and b, so that the process becomes

$$dr = ard\tau + brdB(\tau),$$

which is process (11.120) with physical time replaced by the randomized time $\tau(t)$.

The price $P(t,T)$ at time t of a discount bond that pays 1 dollar at time T is contingent on r and therefore it would follow the process

$$dP = mPd\tau + sPdB(\tau)$$

for m and s given by Ito's Lemma. Then P would satisfy the Black and Scholes type equation

$$\frac{\partial P}{\partial \tau} + Mr\frac{\partial P}{\partial r} + \sigma^2 r^2 \frac{\partial^2 P}{\partial r^2} = rP,$$

with physical time replaced by randomized time and with boundary condition $P(\tau(T)) = 1$.

The standard Black and Scholes argument would then formally give

$$P(t,T) = \hat{\mathbf{E}}(e^{-\bar{r}(T-t)})$$

for $\bar{r}$ the τ-average of r in the relevant interval and $\hat{\mathbf{E}}$ the risk-free expected value.

In reality the argument why $P(t,T)$ is the fair price of the bond is more technical, it involves the existence of equivalent martingale measure for a semi-martingale. For this we use Melnikov and Shiryaev (1996).

With this granted,

$$\hat{\mathbf{E}}(P_T/B_T) = \hat{\mathbf{E}}(P_t/B_t).$$

For $t = t_0$, this gives $\hat{\mathbf{E}}(P_T/B_T) = P_t/B_t$. By taking the current bank account to be $B_t = 1$, we calculate the current value

$$P_t = \hat{\mathbf{E}}(B_T^{-1}) = \hat{\mathbf{E}}\left(\exp\left(-\int_t^T r(s)ds\right)\right) = \hat{\mathbf{E}}(\exp(-\bar{r}(T-t))).$$

If $R(t,T)$ is the (known) interest rate for the same period, then the bond price $P(t,T)$ can also be calculated as

$$P(t,T) = e^{-R(t,T)(T-t)}.$$

Then

$$-\frac{1}{T-t}\ln(\hat{E}(e^{-\bar{r}(T-t)})) = R(t,T).$$

The procedure then is to start with some value of α and improve on it by calculating the error

$$-\frac{1}{T-t}\ln(\hat{E}(e^{-\bar{r}(T-t)})) - R(t,T)$$

and iterating back.

In preliminary computer simulations so far the stable model produces smaller error than the Gaussian with the same drift and volatility.

12

Option Pricing for Infinitely Divisible Return Models

12.1 The Problem

The stable Paretian model is only one in the class of distributions used to describe the law of asset returns. Distributions like Student–t, mixture of normals and, especially, the Weibull law provide in many instances models with better statistical fit than the stable Paretian law, see Mittnik and Rachev (1993a,b). To derive option–pricing formulae for alternative stable models— covering, in particular these alternatives—we depart from the stable Paretian law and consider *infinitely divisible return processes.*[1]

In this chapter we proceed in three steps, to develop option pricing models for infinitely divisible return processes.

We consider first the class of all infinite divisible distributions as possible return distributions and check which member of this class can be approximated by the simple binomial model, so that, as a result the option price appears as a limit of the binomial corresponding model. As it turns out, the only cases attainable in this way are the normal, the Poisson and the degenerate case. Then, in a second step, we modify the binomial model by allowing the number of price changes in the binomial model to be random. This leads to a much richer class of limiting distributions, including the stable distribution, t–distribution and mixture of normals. Here, we discuss several examples and also derive the corresponding functional limit theorems for discrete-time option models. Finally, a second kind of randomization is introduced over the

---

[1] The results in this chapter are due to Rachev and Rüschendorf (1994a) with the exception of the last section 12.8 which is due to Rejman, Weron and Weron (1997).

parameters governing the up and down movements in the binomial model. This randomization allows us to model a broad class of distributions, among them the Weibull law.

Both types of randomizations can be introduced directly in the continuous-time limiting models. The first randomization is then closely related to the idea of random time transformation (subordinated processes) suggested by Mandelbrot (1967) and Clark (1973) which we already discussed in Chapter 11. Both randomizations together allow us, by some simple modifications of the Cox, Ross and Rubinstein (1979) model, to derive pricing formulas of the Black-Scholes type for a large class of possible asset-price distributions.

12.2   Limits of the Binomial Option Pricing Model

Let $S = S_0$ be the known asset price at time $t_0 = 0$ and, as before, τ the length of calendar time representing the expiration of a call. Following the binomial option pricing model (see the discussion at the beginning of Chapter 11), assume that $\tau = nh, n \in \mathbf{N}$, and let at the end of each period $(k, k+1)$ the value S_{k+1} be equal to US_k with probability p and to DS_k with probability $q = 1 - p$, where $0 < D \leq 1 \leq R \leq U$. Therefore, defining $\mathrm{U} = \log U, \mathrm{D} = \log D$, we have

$$\log(S_n/S) = \sum_{k=1}^{n} X_{n,k},\qquad(12.1)$$

where

$$X_{n,k} = \zeta_{n,k}\mathrm{U} + (1 - \zeta_{n,k})\mathrm{D}\qquad(12.2)$$

and $\zeta_{n,k}$ are i.i.d. Bernoulli with success probability p [2]. We assume that U, D and p are functions of n (or h) and consider the class of possible limits of (12.1) in the all *infinite divisible (ID) distributions*, assuming that[3]

$$\lim_{n\to\infty} \mathrm{U} = \lambda, \ \lim_{n\to\infty} \mathrm{D} = -\mu, \lambda \geq 0, \ \mu \geq 0.\qquad(12.3)$$

Cox et al. (1979) (see (11.1) in Section 11.1.1) considered the special case of $\mathrm{U} = \sigma\sqrt{\tau/n} = \sigma\sqrt{h}$, and $\mathrm{D} = -\sigma\sqrt{h}$, to obtain normal limits, and $\mathrm{U}(n) = \mathrm{U}(0) = \text{const}$ and $\mathrm{D} = -\sigma h$, to obtain Poisson limit for (12.1). In this section we allow for a general scenario by considering the following nine different cases:

Case 1: $\lambda = \mu = 0$;
Case 2: $0 < \lambda < \infty, \mu = 0$;
Case 3: $0 < \lambda < \infty, 0 < \mu < \infty$;
Case 4: $\lambda = 0, 0 < \mu < \infty$;

---

[2]This is clearly a simpler version of (11.5), see Section 11.2.
[3]We omit the index n in $\mathrm{U} = \mathrm{U}(n)$, $\mathrm{D} = \mathrm{D}(n)$ and $p = p(n)$, if there is no ambiguity.

Case 5: $0 < \lambda < \infty, \mu = \infty$;
Case 6: $\lambda = \infty, 0 < \mu < \infty$;
Case 7: $\lambda = 0, \mu = \infty$;
Case 8: $\lambda = \infty, \mu = 0$;
Case 9: $\lambda = \infty, \mu = \infty$.

To investigate the limit distributions of (12.1), we assume that the $X_{n,k}$'s satisfy the uniform asymptotic negligibility (UAN) condition, stating that as $n \to \infty$ (i.e., $h = \frac{T}{n} \to 0$)

$$(C.1) \qquad \max_{1 \le k \le n} P(|X_{n,k}| \ge \epsilon) \to 0 \text{ for all } \epsilon > 0.$$

It turns out that in the case of normal limits the UAN condition is automatically satisfied in the binomial model (12.1); hence, (C.1) does not impose a restriction in this case.

Lemma 12.1 (a) In Case 1 ($\lambda = \mu = 0$) (C.1) is satisfied.

(b) In Cases 2 and 8 ($0 < \lambda \le \infty, \mu = 0$)

$$(C.1) \Leftrightarrow p \to 0. \qquad (12.4)$$

(c) In Cases 4 and 7 ($\lambda = 0, 0 < \mu \le \infty$):

$$(C.1) \Leftrightarrow q \to 0. \qquad (12.5)$$

(d) In the other cases ($0 < \lambda \le \infty, 0 \le \mu \le \infty$) (C.1) does not hold.

Proof.

(a) This follows from the equivalent form of the UAN-condition (C.1), namely

$$\max_{1 \le k \le n} \int \frac{x^2}{1 + x^2} dF_{n,k} \to 0, \qquad (12.6)$$

where $F_{n,k}$ denotes the d.f. of $X_{n,k}$.

(b) – (d) Use (12.6) or, equivalently,

$$p \frac{U^2}{1 + U^2} + q \frac{D^2}{1 + D^2} \to 0, \qquad \text{as } n \to \infty. \qquad (12.7)$$

$\square$

Next, we invoke the formulation of the Central Limit Theorem (CLT) for triangular arrays of independent r.v.'s subject to the UAN-condition (cf. for example, Loeve, 1977, Section 23).

Lemma 12.2 Suppose that $(X_{n,k})$ is any independent triangular array of UAN r.v.'s.

a) The family of weak limits of $\mathcal{L}(\sum_{k=1}^{n} X_{n,k})$,[4] $n \in \mathbf{N}$, coincides with the family of infinitely divisible (ID) laws or, equivalently, with the family of laws of r.v.'s X with ch.f.

$$\phi_X(u) = \mathrm{E}e^{iuX} = \exp\left\{ iu\alpha + \int_{-\infty}^{\infty} \left(e^{iux} - 1 - \frac{iux}{1+x^2} \right) \frac{1+x^2}{x^2} d\psi(x) \right\},$$
(12.8)

where $\alpha \in \mathbf{R}$; and ψ is a d.f. up to a multiplicative constant.

b) $\sum_{k=1}^{n} X_{n,k}$ converges to X with ch.f. (12.8) if

$$(C.2) \qquad\qquad \alpha_n \to \alpha$$

and

$$(C.3) \qquad\qquad \psi_n \xrightarrow{w} \psi \ \text{(weak convergence)},$$

where

$$\alpha_n := \sum_{k=1}^{n} \left[a_{n,k} + \int_{-\infty}^{\infty} \frac{x}{1+x^2} d\bar{F}_{n,k}(x) \right];$$
(12.9)

$$\psi_n := \sum_{k=1}^{n} \int_{-\infty}^{x} \frac{y^2}{1+y^2} d\bar{F}_{n,k}(y);$$
(12.10)

$a_{n,k} := \int xI\{|x| < \tau\}dF_{n,k}(x)$; $F_{n,k}$ is the d.f. of $X_{n,k}$; $\bar{F}_{n,k} = F_{n,k}(x + a_{n,k})$ and $t \in (0,\infty) > \tau > 0$ is arbitrarily fixed.

To check conditions (C.2) and (C.3) for the binomial process (12.1), denote $R:=U - D$ and, without loss of generality, choose τ small enough.

Lemma 12.3   (a) In Case 1 ($\lambda = \mu = 0$):

$$(C.2) \Leftrightarrow n\left(qD + pU - \frac{pqR}{1+p^2R^2} + \frac{pqR}{1+q^2R^2} \right) \to \alpha$$
(12.11)

and

$$(C.3) \Leftrightarrow n\left(q\frac{R^2p^2}{1+R^2p^2} + p\frac{R^2q^2}{1+R^2q^2} \right) \to \sigma^2,$$
(12.12)

[4]Here, $\mathcal{L}(X)$ stands for the probability law (distribution) of random variable X.

where α and σ^2 are nonnegative constants depending only on expiration date τ.

(b) In Case 2 $(0 < \lambda < \infty, \mu = 0)$ for $0 < \tau < \lambda$:

$$(\text{C.2}) \Leftrightarrow n\left(qD + \frac{pqD}{1 + p^2D^2} + p\frac{U - qD}{1 + (U - qD)^2}\right) \to \alpha \qquad (12.13)$$

and

$$(\text{C.3}) \Leftrightarrow \lim_{n \to \infty} np \text{ exists.} \qquad (12.14)$$

(c) In Case 8 $(\lambda = \infty, \mu = 0)$ (12.13) holds again, while (12.14) is replaced by

$$(\text{C.3}) \Leftrightarrow \lim_{n \to \infty} nqp^2D^2 \text{ exists.} \qquad (12.15)$$

(d) In Case 4 $(\lambda = 0, 0 < \mu < \infty)$ for $\tau < \mu$:

$$(\text{C.2}) \quad \Leftrightarrow \quad n\left(pU + \frac{pqU}{1 + q^2U^2} + q\frac{D - pU}{1 + (D - pU)^2}\right) \to \alpha, \quad (12.16)$$

$$(\text{C.3}) \quad \Leftrightarrow \quad \lim_{n \to \infty} nq \text{ exists.} \qquad (12.17)$$

(e) In Case 7 $(\lambda = 0, \mu = \infty)$ (12.16) holds and (C.3)$\Leftrightarrow \lim_{n \to \infty} nq = 0$.

Proof.

(a) Case 1 $(\lambda = \mu = 0)$: For large enough

$$a_{n,k} = pUI\{|U| < \tau\} + qDI\{|D| < \tau\} = pU + qD = EX_{n,k} \qquad (12.18)$$

and

$$\int \frac{x}{1 + x^2} d\bar{F}_{n,k}(x) = q\frac{-pR}{1 + p^2R^2} + p\frac{qR}{1 + q^2R^2},$$

which implies (12.11). Furthermore, by (12.10),

$$\psi_n(x) = n\int_{-\infty}^{(x/R)+p} \frac{R^2(y - p)^2}{1 + R^2(y - p)^2} dF_{n,1}(y)$$

$$= \begin{cases} 0, & \text{if } x < -pR, \\ nq\frac{R^2p^2}{1 + R^2p^2}, & \text{if } -pR \le x < qR, \\ nq\frac{R^2p^2}{1 + R^2p^2} + np\frac{R^2p^2}{1 + R^2q^2}, & \text{if } x \ge qR. \end{cases}$$

Because $\lambda = \mu = 0$ and, thus, R=U - D$\to 0$, we obtain

$$\psi_n(x) \to \psi(x) = \begin{cases} 0, & \text{if } x < 0, \\ \lim_{n \to \infty} n\left(q\frac{R^2p^2}{1 + R^2p^2} + p\frac{R^2q^2}{1 + R^2q^2}\right), & \text{if } x \ge 0, \end{cases}$$

$$(12.19)$$

if the limit on the right-hand-side exists.

(b) Case 2 $(0 < \lambda < \infty, \mu = 0)$: For $\tilde{\tau} < \lambda$ and n large enough, $a_{n,k} = qD$ and

$$\int \frac{x}{1+x^2} d\bar{F}_{nk} = q\frac{pD}{1+p^2D^2} + p\frac{U-qD}{1+(U-qD)^2} \,. \qquad (12.20)$$

Similarly,

$$\psi_n(x) = n \int_{-\infty}^{\frac{x-pD}{R}} \frac{(yR+pD)^2}{1+(yR+pD)^2} dF_{n,1}(y) \qquad (12.21)$$

and, thus,

$$(C.3) \Leftrightarrow \psi(x) = \begin{cases} 0, & \text{if } x < 0, \\ \lim_{n\to\infty} nq\frac{p^2D^2}{1+p^2D^2}, & \text{if } 0 \le x < \lambda, \\ \lim_{n\to\infty} \left[nq\frac{p^2D^2}{1+p^2D^2} + np\frac{(U-qD)^2}{1+(U-qD)^2} \right], & \text{if } x > \lambda. \end{cases}$$
$$(12.22)$$

Because $1 + p^2D^2 \to 1$, it follows that $\lim np^2qD^2$ exists. Furthermore,

$$\lim_{n\to\infty} np\frac{(U-qD)^2}{1+(U-qD)^2} = \lim_{n\to\infty} np\frac{\lambda^2}{1+\lambda^2}$$

and, thus,

$$\lim_{n\to\infty} np^2qD^2 = \lim_{n\to\infty} nq\frac{p^2D^2}{1+p^2D^2} = 0.$$

Summarizing the above relations we have

$$\psi_n(x) \xrightarrow{w} \psi(x) = \begin{cases} 0, & \text{if } x < \lambda, \\ \frac{\lambda^2}{1+\lambda^2} \lim_{n\to\infty}(np), & \text{if } x \ge \lambda. \end{cases} \qquad (12.23)$$

(c) Case 8 $(\lambda = \infty, \mu = 0)$: In this case we readily have

$$\psi(x) = \lim_{n\to\infty} \psi_n(x) = \begin{cases} 0, & \text{if } x < 0, \\ \lim_{n\to\infty} nqp^2D^2, & \text{if } x > 0. \end{cases} \qquad (12.24)$$

(d) Case 4 $(\lambda = 0, 0 < \mu < \infty)$ is quite similar to the Case 2. We obtain

$$\psi_n(x) \xrightarrow{w} \psi(x) = \begin{cases} 0, & \text{if } x < -\mu, \\ \lim_{n\to\infty} nq\frac{(D-pU)^2}{1+(D-pU)^2}, & \text{if } -\mu < x < 0, \\ \lim_{n\to\infty} \left[nq\frac{(D-pU)^2}{1+(D-pU)^2} + np\frac{q^2U^2}{1+q^2U^2} \right], & \text{if } x > 0. \end{cases}$$
$$(12.25)$$

With $\lim_{n\to\infty} nq\frac{(D-pU)^2}{1+(D-pU)^2} = \lim_{n\to\infty} nq\frac{\mu^2}{1+\mu^2}$, we have

$\lim_{n\to\infty} np\frac{q^2 U^2}{1+q^2 U^2} = 0$ and, thus,

$$\psi_n(x) \xrightarrow{w} \psi(x) = \begin{cases} 0, & \text{if } x < -\mu, \\ \lim_{n\to\infty} nq\frac{\mu^2}{1+\mu^2}, & \text{if } x \geq -\mu. \end{cases} \tag{12.26}$$

(e) In Case 7 ($\lambda = 0, \mu = \infty$) the limiting relation (12.16) is easily verified. Analogous to (12.26) we have $\psi_n \xrightarrow{w} \psi(x) = \lim_{n\to\infty} nq$ for all x. Because ψ is a d.f. of a nonnegative measure, it follows that $\psi(x) = 0$. □

Lemmas 12.1, 12.2, and 12.3 imply that the class of possible ID limits of the binomial model is restricted to the normal, the Poisson and the degenerate case. This is summarized in the following theorems.

Theorem 12.1   (a) In Case 1 ($\lambda = \mu = 0$), (12.11) and (12.12) are necessary and sufficient for asymptotic normality of $\log(S_n/S)$. We have

$$\mathcal{L}(\log(S_n/S) \xrightarrow{w} N(\alpha, \sigma^2). \tag{12.27}$$

(b) In Case 2 ($0 < \lambda < \infty, \mu = 0$) conditions (C.1), (C.2) and (C.3) are equivalent to the existence of the limits

$$a = \lim np \quad \text{and} \quad b = \lim nD. \tag{12.28}$$

In this case the limit

$$\mathcal{L}(\log S_n/S) \xrightarrow{w} b + \lambda\text{Poisson}(a) \tag{12.29}$$

is a scaled and shifted Poisson distribution. Moreover, (12.29) and the UAN condition ($p \to 0$) are equivalent to (12.28).

(c) In Case 8 ($\lambda = \infty, \mu = 0$) conditions (C.1), (C.2) and (C.3) are equivalent to

$$\alpha = \lim_{n\to\infty} (nD + \frac{np}{U}) \text{ and } p \to 0. \tag{12.30}$$

Thus, we have the degenerate convergence

$$\mathcal{L}(\log(S_n/S)) \xrightarrow{w} \alpha \tag{12.31}$$

and, again, (12.31) and UAN imply (12.30).

(d) In Case 4 ($\lambda = 0, 0 < \mu < \infty$), (C.1), (C.2) and (C.3) are equivalent to $q \to 0$ and the existence of limits $a = \lim nq$ and $b = \lim nU$. In this case

$$\mathcal{L}(\log(S_n/S)) \xrightarrow{w} b - \mu\text{Poisson}(a). \tag{12.32}$$

(e) In Case 7 ($\lambda = 0, \mu = \infty$), (C.1), (C.2) and (C.3) are equivalent to the conditions,

$$\lim nU = \alpha \quad \text{and} \quad \lim nq = 0, \tag{12.33}$$

implying the degenerate limit,

$$\mathcal{L}(\log(S_n/S)) \xrightarrow{w} \alpha. \tag{12.34}$$

Moreover, (12.34) and $q \to 0$ imply (12.33).

Proof. This is a consequence of Lemmas 12.1, 12.2 and 12.3. □

By making use of Theorem 12.1 we can easily derive all possible limiting distributions of the binomial model. We give three examples.

Example 12.1 Let $U = \tilde\sigma\sqrt{h}, D = -\tilde\sigma\sqrt{h} = -\tilde\sigma\sqrt{\tau/n}, p = p(n) = \frac{R(n)-D(n)}{U(n)-D(n)}$, $R(n) = R_0^{\tau/n}$, then, $p \approx \frac{1}{2} + \frac{1}{2}\frac{\alpha}{\tilde\sigma}\sqrt{\tau/n}$ and $E(\log S_n/S) = n(qD + pU) \to (\log R_0 - \frac{1}{2}\tilde\sigma^2)\tau$. This correspondents to Case 1. Hence, by (12.1),

$$(\text{C.2}) \Leftrightarrow n(qD + pU) + n\frac{pq(q-p)R^3}{(1 + q^2R^2)(1 + p^2R^2)} \to \alpha,$$

with $\alpha = \log R_0 - \frac{1}{2}\tilde\sigma^2)\tau$. Further, by (12.12)

$$(\text{C.3}) \Leftrightarrow nq\frac{4\tilde\sigma^2 hp^2}{1 + 4\tilde\sigma^2 hp^2} + np\frac{4\tilde\sigma^2 hq^2}{1 + 4\tilde\sigma^2 hq^2} \to \frac{1}{8}4\tilde\sigma^2\tau + \frac{1}{8}4\tilde\sigma^2\tau = \tilde\sigma^2\tau = \sigma^2.$$

This choice of U, D and p has been considered in Cox et al. (1979).

Example 12.2 Let $U = \lambda, D = -\bar\mu h = -\bar\mu\tau/n$, $\lambda > 0$, $\bar\mu > 0$, and $p = vh$. This is Case 2. By (12.28), $a = \lim np = v\tau$, $\alpha = \lim nD + a\frac{\lambda}{1+\lambda^2} = -\bar\mu\tau + v\tau\frac{\lambda}{1+\lambda^2}$. We obtain the shifted and scaled Poissonian case $\mathcal{L}(\log S_n/S) \xrightarrow{w} -\bar\mu\tau + \lambda$ *Poisson* $(v\tau)$, i.e., there are instantaneous asset price movements (see Cox and Ross, 1975, Cox and Rubinstein, 1985).

Example 12.3 Let $U \to \lambda = \infty, D = -v\frac{\tau}{n}, v > 0, \frac{p}{U} = c\frac{\tau}{n}$, then, by (12.30), $S_n \xrightarrow{w} Se^{(v+c)\tau}$.

In the next step we establish the functional CLT's corresponding to Theorem 12.1. In other words, we will be interested in the limiting distribution of the return process defined by (12.2). Recall that $X_{n,k} = \xi_{n,k}U + (1 - \xi_{n,k})D$, where $(\xi_{n,k})$ is an i.i.d. sequence of binomials $\mathcal{B}(1,p)$. Define

$$\bar X_{n,k} = X_{n,k} - a_{n,k} \stackrel{d}{=} X_{n,1} - a_{n,1}, \tag{12.35}$$

where $a_{n,k} = \int_{-\infty}^{\infty} xI\{|x| < \tau\}dF_{n,k}(x)$, for $\tau > 0$ suitably chosen, and define

$$\bar S_{n,k} = \bar X_{n,1} + \ldots + \bar X_{n,k}. \tag{12.36}$$

Consider the $D[0, \tau]$-valued random process

$$\bar{X}_n(u) = \bar{S}_{n,k}, \quad \text{for} \quad \frac{k-1}{n} \le \frac{u}{\tau} < \frac{k}{n}, \ 1 \le k \le n, \ \bar{X}_n(t) = \bar{S}_{n,n}, \quad (12.37)$$

where τ is the fixed expiration time. Write

$$v_n := n \int_{-\infty}^{\infty} \frac{x}{1+x^2} d\bar{F}_{n,1}(x), \bar{F}_{n,1}(x) = F_{n,1}(x + a_{n,1}) \quad (12.38)$$

and

$$\psi_n(x) = n \int_{-\infty}^{x} \frac{y^2}{1+y^2} d\bar{F}_{n,1}(y) \quad (12.39)$$

and consider conditions

$$(\overline{\text{C.2}}) \quad v_n \to v$$

and, as before,

$$(\text{C.3}) \psi_n \xrightarrow{w} \psi$$

to apply the following convergence theorem (cf. Gikhman and Skorokhod, 1969, Theorem 2, p. 480) to the Cases 1, 2 and 8.

Theorem 12.2 Under conditions $(\overline{\text{C.2}})$ and (C.3) process $\bar{X}_n$ converges weakly in $D[0, t]$ to a homogeneous process, $\bar{X}$, with independent increments and characteristic function

$$Ee^{i\vartheta \bar{X}(u)} = \exp\left\{ \frac{u}{\tau}\left[i\vartheta v + \int_{-\infty}^{\infty}\left(e^{i\vartheta x} - 1 - \frac{i\vartheta x}{1+x^2}\right)\frac{1+x^2}{x^2}d\psi(x)\right]\right\},$$

$$0 \le u \le \tau. \quad (12.40)$$

Case 1 ($\lambda = \mu = 0$): By (12.18) $a_{n,k} = pU + qD = EX_{n,k}$, for n large enough. Furthermore,

$$
\begin{aligned}
v_n &= n \int \frac{x}{1+x^2} d\bar{F}_{n,1}(x) \\
&= npqR\left[\frac{1}{1+q^2R^2} - \frac{1}{1+p^2R^2}\right] \\
&= npqR\frac{1+p^2R^2 \, 1 - q^2R^2}{(1+q^2R^2)(1+p^2R^2)} \\
&= npqR^3\frac{p-q}{(1+p^2R^2)(1+q^2R^2)},
\end{aligned}
$$

i.e., $v = \lim_n npqR^3 \frac{p-q}{(1+p^2R^2)(1+q^2R^2)}$. On the other hand, by (12.19)

$$\psi(x) = \begin{cases} 0, & \text{if } x < 0, \\ \sigma^2, & \text{if } x \ge 0, \end{cases}$$

where

$$\sigma^2 = \lim_n n(q\frac{p^2R^2}{1+p^2R^2} + p\frac{q^2R^2}{1+q^2R^2}) = \lim_n \frac{npqR^2}{(q+p^2R^2)(1+q^2R^2)}.$$

Thus, $\bar{X}$ is a Wiener process with

$$\mathbf{E}\bar{X}(u) = v\frac{u}{\tau}, \quad \text{Var}\bar{X}(u) = \sigma^2\frac{u}{\tau}. \tag{12.41}$$

If, as in Cox et al. (1979), $U = \tilde{\sigma}\sqrt{\tau/n}, D = -\tilde{\sigma}\sqrt{\tau/n}, a_{n,k} = EX_{n,k} = qD + pU \approx \frac{\alpha}{n}$, we have $p \approx \frac{1}{2} + \frac{1}{2}\frac{\alpha}{\tilde{\sigma}}\sqrt{\tau/n}$ and $v = 0, \sigma^2 = \tilde{\sigma}^2\tau$. Therefore, with $na_{n,1} \to \alpha, \alpha = (\log R_0 - \frac{\tilde{\sigma}}{2})\tau$ and

$$X_n(u) = \bar{X}_n(u) + \frac{[\frac{nu}{\tau}]}{n}na_{n,1} = \begin{cases} \sum_{j=1}^{k} X_{n,j}, & \frac{k-1}{n} \leq \frac{u}{\tau} < \frac{k}{n}, \\ \log S_n/S, & u = \tau, \end{cases} \tag{12.42}$$

it follows from Theorem 12.2 that

$$X_n \xrightarrow{w} X, \tag{12.43}$$

where X is a Wiener process with

$$EX(u) = \frac{\alpha u}{\tau}, \alpha = \left(\log R_0 - \frac{1}{2}\tilde{\sigma}^2\right)t, \quad \text{Var}X(u) = \tilde{\sigma}^2 u. \tag{12.44}$$

Case 2 $(0 < \lambda < \infty, \mu = 0)$: Here, for $\tau < \lambda$, $a_{n,k} = qD, v_n = nq\frac{pD}{1+p^2D^2}$ $+ np\frac{U-qD}{1+(U-qD)^2} \to a\frac{\lambda}{1+\lambda^2} = v$, where $a = \lim_{n\to\infty} np$, and

$$\psi_n(x) \to \psi(x) = \begin{cases} 0, & \text{if } x < \lambda, \\ \frac{\lambda^2}{1+\lambda^2}, & \text{if } x > \lambda. \end{cases}$$

Thus, we have

$$\bar{X}_n \xrightarrow{w} \bar{X}, \tag{12.45}$$

where $\bar{X}$ is a homogeneous Poisson process with

$$\log Ee^{i\vartheta\bar{X}(u)} = \frac{u}{\tau}\left[i\vartheta a\frac{\lambda}{1+\lambda^2} + a\left(e^{iu\lambda} - 1\right)\right]. \tag{12.46}$$

In the Cox and Ross (1975) model with $U = \lambda$, $D = -\bar{\mu}\frac{\tau}{n}$ and $p = v\frac{\tau}{n}$, we have $a_{n,k} = qD \approx -\bar{\mu}\frac{\tau}{n}$ and $a = \lim(np) = v\tau$. Thus, $\bar{X}$ has the characteristic function

$$\log Ee^{i\vartheta\bar{X}(u)} = vu\left[i\vartheta\frac{\lambda}{1+\lambda^2} + \left(e^{iu\lambda} - 1\right)\right]. \tag{12.47}$$

Case 8 $(\lambda = \infty, \mu = 0)$: $a_{n,k} = qD$ and

$$\bar{X}_n(u) \to \bar{X}(u) \stackrel{d}{=} \alpha\frac{u}{\tau}, \tag{12.48}$$

where $\alpha = \lim \left[nD + \frac{np}{U} \right]$ (see (12.30)). Then, recalling Example 12.3, $U \rightarrow \lambda = \infty$, $\frac{p}{U} = c\frac{\tau}{n}$, $D = -v\frac{\tau}{n}$, and $\alpha = -v\tau + c\tau$ so that

$$\bar{X}(u) = (c - v)u, 0 \le u \le \tau. \tag{12.49}$$

I.e., we have the degenerate case.

Remark 12.1 Let $W = (W(u), 0 \le u \le \tau)$ be a standard Wiener process and suppose that in Case 1 ($\lambda = \mu = 0$) $\sum_{k=1}^{n} a_{n,k} = n a_{n,1} \rightarrow a(a_{n,1} = EX_{n,1})$. Then,

$$X_n(u) = \bar{X}_n(u) + \frac{\left[\frac{un}{\tau}\right]}{n} n a_{n,1} \xrightarrow{w} X(u) = a\frac{u}{\tau} + \sigma\frac{u}{\tau}W(u) =: \tilde{a}u + \tilde{\sigma}W(u),$$

$$\tag{12.50}$$

where $\tilde{a} = \frac{a}{\tau}$ and $\tilde{\sigma} = \frac{\sigma u}{\tau}$. In other words, the limiting asset price at time u is given by

$$S_n(u) = Se^{X_n(u)} \xrightarrow{w} S(u) = Se^{X(u)} \overset{d}{=} Se^{\tilde{a}u + \sigma \tilde{W}(u)}. \tag{12.51}$$

By Ito's formula $S(u)$ satisfies the stochastic differential equation

$$dS(u) = S(u) \left[\left(\tilde{a} + \frac{\tilde{\sigma}^2}{2} \right) du + \tilde{\sigma} dW(u) \right]. \tag{12.52}$$

In Cox et al. (1979) we have $\tilde{a} = \log R_0 - \frac{1}{2}\tilde{\sigma}^2$ and $\tilde{\sigma} = \sigma$ so that

$$dS(u) = S(u) \left[(\log R_0) \, du + \tilde{\sigma} dW(u) \right]. \tag{12.53}$$

12.3   A Random Number of Price Changes

Now we consider the case where the number of price movements per unit of calendar time is random. Let S^* be the price at the expiration time τ and $\{N_n\}$ a sequence of integer-valued random times, which are independent of the returns $(X_{n,k}; n, k \in N)$,

$$X_{nk} = \xi_{n,k}U + (1 - \xi_{n,k})D, \quad \xi_{n,k} \overset{d}{=} B(1, p), \tag{12.54}$$

with, typically, $EN_n = n$ and let

$$S^* = S_{N_n} \quad \text{or} \quad \log(S^*/S) = \sum_{k=1}^{N_n} X_{n,k}. \tag{12.55}$$

I.e., we consider a random number of jumps in interval $[0, \tau]$, with each jump being of the simple Bernoulli type. The jumps could be uniformly distributed over $[0, t]$, so that we obtain random intervals of equal length $h = t/N_n$. Alternatively, and more realistically, we may model the times of price movements by a point process on $[0, \tau]$ with N_n points, such that we can identify our price change model with a marked point process (with independent marks). Because formula both models lead to the same option pricing formula, we prefer the simpler of these two, that, with constant inter-arrival times $h = \tau/N_n$.

The next lemma, the so-called "transfer theorem", is due to Robbins (1948), Rényi (1967) and Gnedenko (1970, 1983a,b).

Lemma 12.4 Let $(X_{n,k})_{k \in \mathbb{N}}$ be an i.i.d. sequence of real r.v.'s and let N_n be an integer-valued r.v. independent of $X_{n,k}, n \in \mathbb{N}$. If, as $n \to \infty$,

$$\sum_{k=1}^{n} X_{n,k} \xrightarrow{w} X, \tag{12.56}$$

and

$$\frac{N_n}{n} \xrightarrow{w} Y, \tag{12.57}$$

then

$$\sum_{k=1}^{N_n} X_{n,k} \xrightarrow{w} Z. \tag{12.58}$$

The ch.f. of Z is given by

$$\varphi_Z(u) = \int_0^\infty (\varphi_X(u))^z dF_Y(z), \tag{12.59}$$

where φ_X is the ch.f. of X and F_Y the d.f. of Y.

If Y is an infinitely divisible (ID) r.v., then, by Feller (1966), Z is also ID.

Example 12.4 (a) Let N_n be a geometric r.v. with mean n, i.e.,

$$P(N_n = k) = \frac{1}{n}\left(1 - \frac{1}{n}\right)^{k-1}, \quad k = 1, 2, \dots . \tag{12.60}$$

Then, Y is exponential with mean 1 and

$$\varphi_Z(u) = \frac{1}{1 - \log \varphi_X(u)}. \tag{12.61}$$

Because, from (12.56), X is ID, the distribution of Z is a geometric infinite divisible distribution (cf. Klebanov et al., 1984).

(b) If N_n is uniformly distributed on $(1, \dots, 2n - 1)$, we have

$$P(N_n = k) = \frac{1}{2n - 1}, \quad 1 \le k \le 2n - 1. \tag{12.62}$$

Then,

$$\varphi_Z(u) = \frac{1}{2}\int_0^2 (\varphi_X(u))^z dz = \frac{1}{2 \ln \varphi_X(u)}(\varphi_X(u)^2 - 1). \tag{12.63}$$

(c) If N_n is Poisson distributed with mean n, then $N_n/n \xrightarrow{\text{a.s.}} 1$, and, therefore, $\varphi_Z = \varphi_X$.

(d) If X is normally distributed, then, by a result of Gnedenko (1983a,b), Z is again normal if and only if F_Y is a one-point measure. $\qquad\square$

As in Section 11.2 we shall consider the limit behavior of $\log(S_{N_n}/S)$, where constants $U = U(n) = \log U$ and $D = D(n) = \log D$ are independent of n and

$$\lim_{n \to \infty} U(n) = \lambda \quad \text{and} \quad \lim_{n \to \infty} D(n) = -\mu. \tag{12.64}$$

In each case we shall assume that (12.56) and (12.57) hold.

Theorem 12.3 Suppose that $\frac{N_n}{n} \xrightarrow{w} Y$.
(a) In Case 1 ($\lambda = \mu = 0$)

$$\log(S_{N_n}/S) \xrightarrow{w} Z \tag{12.65}$$

holds, where the distribution of Z is a mixture of normals,

$$\varphi_Z(u) = \int_0^\infty e^{i\alpha z u - \frac{\sigma^2}{2} z u^2} dF_Y(z), \tag{12.66}$$

with α and σ^2 being determined by (12.11) and (12.12).
(b) In Case 2 ($0 < \lambda < \infty, \mu = 0$) (12.65) holds, where Z is a mixture of Poisson distributions with

$$\varphi_Z(u) = \int_0^\infty \exp\left\{ iubz + za\left(e^{iu\lambda} - 1\right)\right\} dF_Y(z) \tag{12.67}$$

and $a = \lim(np)$, $b = \lim(nD)$ and $\alpha = b + a\frac{\lambda}{a+\lambda^2}$.
(c) In Case 8 ($\lambda = \infty, \mu = 0$) (12.65) holds with

$$\varphi_Z(u) = \int_0^\infty e^{i\alpha u z} dF_Y(z) \quad \text{and} \quad \alpha = \lim_{n \to \infty} nD. \tag{12.68}$$

Proof. Follows from Theorem 12.1 and Lemma 12.4. $\qquad\square$
Cases 4 ($\lambda = 0, 0 < \mu < \infty$) and 7 ($\lambda = 0, \mu = \infty$) are symmetric and can be treated similarly.

Example 12.5 (Geometric case) We consider again Example 12.4 (a).
(a) In Case 1 ($\lambda = \mu = 0$) we have, by straightforward calculation,

$$Z \stackrel{d}{=} Z_1 - Z_2, \tag{12.69}$$

where Z_1 and Z_2 are independent exponentials with means

$$a_1 = \frac{\alpha + \sqrt{\alpha^2 + 2\sigma^2}}{2} \quad \text{and} \quad a_2 = \frac{-\alpha + \sqrt{\alpha^2 + 2\sigma^2}}{2}, \tag{12.70}$$

respectively where α and σ^2 are as in (12.11) and (12.12).

Recall that X is an stable with parameters $\alpha \in (0,2)$, $\sigma \geq 0$, $-1 \leq \beta \leq 1$, and $\mu \in \mathbb{R}$, if its ch.f. $\varphi_X(u)$ has the form:

$$\log \varphi_X(u) = \begin{cases} -\sigma^\alpha |u|^\alpha (1 - i\beta(\operatorname{sign}\vartheta)\tan\frac{\pi\alpha}{2}) + i\mu u, & \text{if } \alpha \neq 1, \\ -\sigma|u|(1 + i\beta\frac{2}{\pi}(\operatorname{sign}u)\ln|u|) + i\mu u, & \text{if } \alpha = 1. \end{cases} \quad (12.71)$$

Then, Z with ch.f. $\varphi_Z(u) = \frac{1}{1-\log\varphi_X(u)}$ is indeed a geometric stable r.v. In our particular case (12.70) Z is a geometric stable r.v. having a Laplace distribution.

(b) In Case 2 $(0 < \lambda < \infty, \mu = 0)$ the limiting distribution has ch.f.

$$\varphi_Z(u) = \frac{1}{1 - iub - (e^{iu\lambda} - 1)a}. \quad (12.72)$$

(c) In Case 8 $(\lambda = \infty, \mu = 0)$ the limiting distribution is exponential with parameter α (cf. (12.68)).

Remark 12.2 (a) Note that (12.66) is equivalent to

$$Z \overset{d}{=} \alpha Y + N_{0,\sigma^2}\sqrt{Y}, \quad (12.73)$$

where N_{0,σ^2} is a normal r.v. with zero mean and variance σ^2 independent of Y. So the density of Z is given by

$$f_Z(x) = \frac{1}{\sqrt{2\pi\sigma^2}} \int_0^\infty e^{-\frac{(x-ay)^2}{2y\sigma^2}} y^{-1/2} dF_Y(y). \quad (12.74)$$

(b) Differentiating (12.59) one easily gets

$$\mathbf{E}Z = \mathbf{E}X\,\mathbf{E}Y \quad \text{and} \quad \frac{\operatorname{Var}Z}{\mathbf{E}Z} = \frac{\operatorname{Var}X}{\mathbf{E}X} + \mathbf{E}X\frac{\operatorname{Var}Y}{\mathbf{E}Y}, \quad (12.75)$$

provided that $\mathbf{E}X \neq 0$, $\mathbf{E}X^2 < \infty$ and $\mathbf{E}Y^2 < \infty$ (see Keilson and Steutel, 1972).

Corresponding to Theorem 12.2, we next establish the functional CLT in the randomized model for the binomial case. Define

$$\bar{X}_{n,k} = X_{n,k} - a_{n,k}, \quad (12.76)$$

where $X_{n,k}$ is defined as in (12.2), $X_{n,k} = \xi_{n,k}U + (1 - \xi_{n,k})D$ and assume, as in $(\overline{\text{C}.2})$ and (C.3) (see also 12.38) and (12.39)), that

$$v_n := n \int \frac{x}{1+x^2} d\bar{F}_{n,1}(x) \to \nu \quad (12.77)$$

and

$$\psi_n(x) = n \int_{-\infty}^x \frac{y^2}{1+y^2} d\bar{F}_{n,1}(y) \to \psi(x). \quad (12.78)$$

So, by Theorem 12.2,

$$\bar{X}_n \xrightarrow{w} \bar{X}, \quad \text{where} \quad \bar{X}_n(u) = \sum_{j=1}^{[\frac{u}{\tau}n]} \bar{X}_{n,j}, \tag{12.79}$$

and $\bar{X}(u)$ is a homogeneous process with independent increments and ch.f.[5]

$$\mathrm{E}e^{i\vartheta\bar{X}(u)} = \exp\left\{\frac{u}{\tau}\left[i\vartheta v + \int_{-\infty}^{\infty}\left(e^{i\vartheta x} - 1 - \frac{i\vartheta x}{1+x^2}\right)\frac{1+x^2}{x^2}d\psi(x)\right]\right\}, 0 \le u < \infty \tag{12.80}$$

Define for an integer-valued random sequence $\{N_n\}$ the randomized process

$$\bar{Z}_n := \sum_{j=1}^{[N_n\frac{u}{\tau}]} \bar{X}_{n,j}, \quad 0 \le u \le \tau. \tag{12.81}$$

Theorem 12.4 Assuming that (12.77), (12.78) and $\frac{N_n}{n} \xrightarrow{w} Y$ hold the sequence of processes $\bar{Z}_n$ converges weakly in $D[0,\infty)$ to

$$\bar{Z}(u) = \bar{X}(Yu), \quad 0 \le u \le \tau. \tag{12.82}$$

Proof. Note that $\bar{Z}_n(u) = \bar{X}_n\left(\frac{N_n}{n}u\right), 0 \le u \le \tau$. I.e., $\bar{Z}_n$ is a random time transformation of $\bar{X}_n$. Because (N_n) is independent of $(\bar{X}_n)$, we have the weak convergence for the bivariate process, i.e., $\left(\frac{N_n}{n}, \bar{X}_n\right) \xrightarrow{w} (Y, \bar{X})$. Assume, without loss of generality, that Y and $\bar{X}$ are also independent. By Skorohod's a.s. (almost sure) representation theorem, there exist (possibly on a different probability space) versions (K_n, U_n) and (K, U) of the processes converging a.s., i.e. $(K_n, U_n) \overset{d}{=} \left(\frac{N_n}{n}, \bar{X}_n\right), (K, U) \overset{d}{=} (Y, \bar{X})$ and $(K_n, U_n) \xrightarrow{\text{a.s.}} (K, U)$ (see, for example, Dudley, 1989). Next, observe that $U_n(\omega) \in D[0,\infty)$ and $(K_n(\omega)u)_{u\ge0} \in D[0,\infty)$ is non-decreasing for $n \ge 0$ and $(K(\omega)u)_{n\ge0}$ is continuous. Consequently, we have (cf. Resnick, 1987, p. 221)

$$d(U_n(K_t)_{t\ge0}, U(K_t)_{tgeq0}) \xrightarrow{\text{a.s.}} 0, \tag{12.83}$$

where "$\xrightarrow{\text{a.s.}}$" stands for "almost sure convergence", i.e. "convergence with probability 1", and d is the Skorohod metric on $D[0,\infty)$. Thus, in $D[0,\infty)$, we have the required weak convergence

$$\bar{Z}_n = \bar{X}_n\left(\frac{N_n}{n}t\right)_{t\ge0} \xrightarrow{w} \bar{Z} = \bar{X}(Y_t)_{t\ge0}. \tag{12.84}$$

$\square$

---

[5]In (12.80) the convergence is in the Skorokhod space $D[0,\infty)$; for some basic properties of $D[0,\infty)$ we refer to Resnick (1987a) Section 4.4.

Corollary 12.1 Under the assumptions of Theorem 12.4 and the additional assumption that

$$na_{n,1} \to a \tag{12.85}$$

we have

$$Z_n \xrightarrow{w} Z \quad \text{on} \quad D[0,\infty), \tag{12.86}$$

where $Z_n(u) = \sum_{j=1}^{[N_n \frac{u}{\tau}]} X_{n,j}$ and $Z(u) = \bar{X}(Yu) + a\frac{u}{\tau}Y$.

Proof. The proof is similar to that of Theorem 12.4. □

We apply Theorem 12.4 and Corollary 12.1 to the normal case (Case 1, $\lambda = \mu = 0$). Then, by (12.41), $X_n \xrightarrow{w} X$, where $X(u) \overset{d}{=} \alpha\frac{u}{\tau} + \frac{\sigma}{\sqrt{\tau}}W(u)$, $\alpha = v + a$, and $W(u)$ is a standard Wiener process. Therefore, $Z_n \xrightarrow{w} Z$, where

$$Z(u) \overset{d}{=} \frac{\alpha}{\tau}Yu + \frac{\sigma}{\sqrt{\tau}}\sqrt{Y}W(u), \tag{12.87}$$

Using that $(W(Yu))_{u\geq 0} \overset{d}{=} (\sqrt{Y}W(u))_{u\geq 0}$, we obtain the following result:

Theorem 12.5 (Case 1, $\lambda = \mu = 0$) Assume that, as $n \to \infty$, $\frac{N_n}{n} \xrightarrow{w} Y$, $na_{n,1} = n(pU + qD) \to a$, $n\left(q\frac{R^2 p^2}{1+R^2 p^2} + p\frac{R^2 q^2}{1+R^2 q^2}\right) \to \sigma^2$ and $npqR^3 \frac{p-q}{(1+p^2R^2)(1+q^2R^2)} \to v$. Then,

$$Z_n \xrightarrow{w} Z, \tag{12.88}$$

where $(Z(u))_{0\leq u\leq \infty} \overset{d}{=} \left(\frac{\alpha}{\tau}Yu + \frac{\sigma}{\sqrt{\tau}}\sqrt{Y}W(u)\right)_{0\leq u<\infty}$, $\alpha = v\zeta + a$, and W is a Wiener process independent of Y. □

Remark 12.3 (a) In the Cox-Ross-Rubinstein model are sets $U = \tilde{\sigma}\sqrt{\tau/n}$, $D = -\tilde{\sigma}\sqrt{\tau/n}, r^n = R_0^\tau, \alpha/\tau = \log R_0 - \frac{1}{2}\tilde{\sigma}^2$ and $\frac{\sigma}{\sqrt{\tau}} = \tilde{\sigma}$. Thus, for Z in (12.88) we have the representation

$$(Z(u))_{u\geq 0} \overset{d}{=} \left(\left(\log R_0 - \frac{1}{2}\tilde{\sigma}^2\right)uY + \tilde{\sigma}\sqrt{Y}W(u)\right)_{u\geq 0}, \tag{12.89}$$

i.e. Z is a Brownian motion with random mean and variance both determined by Y, R_0 and $\tilde{\sigma}$. Subsequent examples address the following cases:

1. Y is Exp(1). Then, Z has Laplace-distributed marginals $Z(u)$.

2. Y is a positive $\alpha/2$-stable r.v. $(0 < \alpha < 2)$. Then, $\sqrt{Y}W(u)$ is symmetric stable and therefore $Z(u)$ is heavy tailed.

3. Y is Gamma distributed. Then, $\sqrt{Y}W$ is a convolution of Gamma distributions.

4. Y is discrete. Then, Z is a mixture of Wiener processes and $Z(u)$ is a mixture of normals.

5. $1/Y$ is χ^2-distributed. Then, $\sqrt{Y}W(u)$ has a t-Distribution.

(b) In the random Cox-Ross-Rubinstein model the limiting asset price is given by (12.89). Applying Ito's formula it is seen that the price process satisfies the stochastic differential equation

$$dS(u) = S(u)\left[\tilde{\sigma}\sqrt{Y}dW(u) + (\log R_0)\,Y\,du\right], \qquad (12.90)$$

where $Z(u) = \log(S(u)/S)$ or

$$S(u) = Se^{\tilde{\sigma}\sqrt{Y}W(u)+aYu}, \quad a = \log R_0 - \frac{1}{2}\tilde{\sigma}^2. \qquad (12.91)$$

In fact, $S(u) = f(u, \xi(u))$, where $f(u,x) = Se^x$ and $\xi(u) = \tilde{\sigma}\sqrt{Y}W(u) + aYu := BW(u) + A(u)$. Thus

$$
\begin{aligned}
dS(u) &= \left[f'_u(u,\xi(u)) + f'_x(u,\xi(u))A(u) + \frac{1}{2}f''_{xx}(u,\xi(u))B^2\right]du \\
&\quad + f'_x(u,\xi(u))BdW(u) \\
&= \left[S(u)aYu + \frac{1}{2}S(u)\tilde{\sigma}^2 Y\right]du + S(u)\tilde{\sigma}\sqrt{Y}dW(u) \\
&= S(u)\left[\tilde{\sigma}\sqrt{Y}dW(u) + \log R_0 Y\,du\right].
\end{aligned}
$$

12.4   Convergence of the Binomial Pricing Formula

Recalling formula (11.1) in Section (11.1.1), the value, C, of a call option is given by

$$C_n = S\phi(a_n, n, p') - KR^{-n}\phi(a_n, n, p), \qquad (12.92)$$

where $\phi(a_n, n, p) = P\left(\sum_{k=1}^n \xi_{n,k} \geq a_n\right)$, $(\xi_{n,k})$ are i.i.d. Bernoulli r.v.'s with success probability p (in short, $B(1,p)$), $a_n := \left[\frac{\log(K/d^n S)}{\log(u/d)}\right]_+$, $[\,]_+$ denotes the positive Gauss bracket, $[a]_+ := n+1$ if $a \in (n, n+1]$, $n \in \mathbf{N}$, and R is one plus the risk-free interest rate over one period of the length h. Recall also that "riskless" meant that

$$pU + (1-p)D = R, \qquad (12.93)$$

or

$$p = \frac{R-D}{U-D} \quad \text{and} \quad p' = \frac{U}{R}p. \qquad (12.94)$$

If R_0 denotes one plus the interest rate over the full time period τ, then

$$R^n = R_0^\tau \quad \text{or} \quad R = R_0^h. \qquad (12.95)$$

Expression (12.94) is, in fact, a transition to a new "riskless" measure, P^*, in the sense that $(R^{-k}S_k)$ becomes a martingale sequence (see Section 11.1.1). The option pricing formula is given by

$$C_n = E^*(BR_0^\tau) = E^*(BR^{-n}). \qquad (12.96)$$

Cox et al. (1979) derived the Black-Scholes formula for the normal case as the limiting case of (12.92) choosing $U = \log U = \tilde{\omega}\sqrt{h}$ and $D = \log D = -\tilde{\sigma}\sqrt{h}$, i.e.,

$$p = \frac{R - D}{U - D} = \frac{R_0^h - e^{-\tilde{\sigma}\sqrt{h}}}{e^{\tilde{\sigma}\sqrt{h}} - e^{-\tilde{\sigma}\sqrt{h}}} \approx \frac{1}{2} + \frac{1}{2}\frac{\log R_0 - \frac{1}{2}\tilde{\sigma}}{\tilde{\sigma}}\sqrt{h}. \qquad (12.97)$$

Then, in the limit they obtained the Black-Scholes formula

$$C = S\phi(x) - Kr_0^{-\tau}\phi(x - \tilde{\sigma}\sqrt{\tau}), \qquad (12.98)$$

where

$$x = \frac{\log(S/Kr_0^{-\tau})}{\tilde{\sigma}\sqrt{\tau}} + \frac{1}{2}\tilde{\sigma}\sqrt{t} \qquad (12.99)$$

and $\phi(\cdot)$ the standard normal distribution function.

Using results in Section 12.2 we now determine all possible limiting cases for the binomial option pricing formula assuming, again, that $U \to \lambda$ and $D \to -\mu$. Replacing (12.95) by the somewhat weaker assumption

$$\lim_{n\to\infty} R^n = R_0^\tau \qquad (12.100)$$

we obtain the following result.

Theorem 12.6 (Case 1, $\lambda = \mu = 0$) Suppose the existence of limits α, α', σ^2 and σ'^2, where

$$\alpha = \lim_{n\to\infty} n\left(qD + pU - \frac{pqR}{1 + p^2R^2} + \frac{pqR}{1 + q^2R^2}\right), R := U - D; \qquad (12.101)$$

α' is analogous to (12.101) with p and q being replaced by

$$p' = p\frac{u}{r} \quad \text{and} \quad q' = 1 - p' = q\frac{d}{r}; \qquad (12.102)$$

$$\sigma^2 = \lim_{n\to\infty} n\left(q\frac{p^2R^2}{1 + p^2R^2} + p\frac{q^2R^2}{1 + q^2R^2}\right); \qquad (12.103)$$

and σ'^2 is analogous to σ^2 with p and q being replaced, again, by p' and q'. Then,

$$C_n \to C := C_\tau := S\phi(x') - KR_0^{-t}\phi(x), \qquad (12.104)$$

where

$$x = \frac{\log(S/K) + \alpha}{\sigma} \quad \text{and} \quad x' = \frac{\log(S/K) + \alpha'}{\sigma'}. \qquad (12.105)$$

Proof. With $\log(S_n/S) = (\sum_{k=1}^{n} \xi_{n,k})\mathrm{R} + n\mathrm{D}$ we have $\phi(a, n, p) = P(\log(S_n /S) \geq a\mathrm{R} + n\mathrm{D})$. From Theorem 12.1 (a) we obtain

$$\mathcal{L}(\log(S_n/S)) \xrightarrow{w} N(\alpha, \sigma^2).$$

For some $\epsilon \in (0,1), a_n\mathrm{R} + n\mathrm{D} = \log(K/SD^n) + \epsilon\mathrm{R} + n\mathrm{D} = \log(K/S) + \epsilon\mathrm{R} \to \log(K/S)$. So, by the uniform convergence above, we have $\phi(a_n, n, p) \to P(N_{0,1} \geq \frac{\log(K/S) - \alpha}{\sigma}) = \phi(x)$, where $N_{0,1}$ is a r.v. with standard normal distribution. The same arguments apply to obtain $\phi(a_n, n, p') \to \phi(x')$. $\quad\square$

Note that, by Theorem 12.1, conditions (12.101) and (12.103) are necessary to obtain normal limits.

Example 12.6 Let $\mathrm{U} = \log U = \tilde{\sigma}\sqrt{h}$, $\mathrm{D} = \log D = -\tilde{\sigma}\sqrt{h}$ and $p = \frac{R-D}{U-D}$. Then,

$$
\begin{aligned}
\alpha &= \lim_{n\to\infty} n\left(q\mathrm{D} + p\mathrm{U} + qp(q - p)\frac{\mathrm{R}^3}{(1 + p^2\mathrm{R}^2)(1 + q^2\mathrm{R}^2)}\right) \\
&= \lim_{n\to\infty} n\left[\left(\frac{1}{2} - \frac{1}{2}\frac{\log R_0 - \frac{1}{2}\tilde{\sigma}^2}{\tilde{\sigma}^2}\right)\sqrt{h}\left(-\tilde{\sigma}\sqrt{h}\right) + \left(\frac{1}{2} + \frac{1}{2}\frac{\log R_0 - \frac{1}{2}\tilde{\sigma}}{\tilde{\sigma}^2}\right)\right. \\
&\qquad \left. \sqrt{h}\left(\tilde{\sigma}\sqrt{h}\right)\right] \\
&= \tau\left(\log R_0 - \frac{1}{2}\tilde{\sigma}^2\right).
\end{aligned}
$$

Similarly, from (12.103), $\sigma^2 = \tilde{\sigma}^2\tau$ and $\alpha' = \tau\left(\log R_0 + \frac{1}{2}\tilde{\sigma}^2\right)$ and $\sigma'^2 = \tilde{\sigma}^2$ showing that (12.104) coincides with the Black-Scholes formula (12.98). $\quad\square$

Next, we describe the cases leading to a Poissonian Black-Scholes formula.

Theorem 12.7 (Case 2, $0 < \lambda < \infty, \mu = 0$) Under the assumptions of Theorem 12.1 for $\mathrm{U}, \mathrm{D}, p$, and $p' = p\frac{U}{R} < 1$, i.e., $a = \lim np, b = \lim n\mathrm{D}$ and $a' = \lim np'$, we have

$$C_n \to C := C_\tau = SP'(x) - KR_0^{-\tau}P(x). \tag{12.106}$$

where

$$P(x) = P(Poisson(a) \geq x),$$

(*Poisson* (a) stands for a r.v. with Poisson distribution with parameter a.)

$$P'(x) = \mathbf{P}\left(Poisson(a') \geq x\right), \tag{12.107}$$

$$x := \left[\frac{\log(K/S) - b}{\lambda}\right]_+,$$

provided that $\frac{\log(K/S)-b}{\lambda}$ is not an integer.

Proof. With $R = U - D$, $a_n = [\log(K/Sd^n)/R]_+$, $\phi(a_n, n, p) = P(\sum_k \xi_{n,k} \geq a) = P(\log(S_n/S) \geq a_n R + nD) = P(\log(S_n/S) \geq \log(K/S) + \epsilon_n R)$, where $\epsilon_n = a_n - \frac{1}{R}\log(K/Sd^n) \geq 0$. From Theorem 12.1(b), $\log(S_n/S) \xrightarrow{w} b + \lambda$ *Poisson*(a) and, thus, $\phi(a_n, n, p) = \mathbf{P}\left(\frac{\log(S_n/S)-b}{\lambda} \geq \frac{\log(K/S)+\epsilon_n R-b}{\lambda}\right) \rightarrow$

$\mathbf{P}(Poisson(a) \geq x) = P(x)$, if $x = \left[\frac{\log(K/S)-b}{\lambda}\right]_+$ is not an integer. In a similar way one can handle $\phi(a_n, n, p')$, to obtain (12.106) from (12.92). $\square$

Remark 12.4 (a) If $x = \frac{\log(K/S)-b}{\lambda}$ is an integer and $R > 0$, $\epsilon > 0$ for all n, then, in the limit we obtain

$$C = SP'(x+1) - Kr_0^{-t}P(x+1). \tag{12.108}$$

If $R < 0$, then (12.107) remains valid.

(b) Let $U = \lambda$, $D = -\bar{\mu}h$ and $p = vh$ (as in Example 12.2) and suppose that $v(e^\lambda - 1) - \bar{\mu} > 0$, then, $R^n = (pe^U + qe^D)^n \rightarrow R_0^t$, where $\log R_0 = v(e^\lambda - 1) - \bar{\mu} > 0$. Moreover,

$$a = \lim np = vt, \; b = \lim nD = -\bar{\mu}\tau, \; a' = v\tau e^\lambda. \tag{12.109}$$

So, from (12.106),

$$C = SP'(x) - KR_0^{-\tau}P(x) \tag{12.110}$$

with a , a' and b as in (12.109). Expression (12.110) is given in , J. and Rubinstein (1985, p.366) They omitted, however, condition $x \notin \mathbf{N}$.

(c) Note that in (12.92) $C = 0$, if $a_n > n$. Equivalently, $\frac{\log(K/S)-nD}{U-D} > n$ or $\log(K/S) > nU$ imply that $C = 0$. Therefore, for the analogue of Theorem 12.7 in Case 4 ($\lambda = 0, 0 < \mu < \infty$) one should require

$$\log(K/S) < b := \lim nU, \tag{12.111}$$

to avoid the degenerate case $C = 0$.

12.5   Black-Scholes Formulas when the Number of Price Movements is Random

As in Section 12.3 we consider a random number, N_n, of price changes in interval $[0, \tau]$. Let $p = p(n)$ be the probability of an upturn and, as in (12.93),

$$R := pU + qD \tag{12.112}$$

be one plus the riskless discounting factor, where $q = 1 - p$. We assume $U > R > 1 > D > 0$ and recall (see (12.94)) the definitions

$$p' := p\frac{U}{R} \quad \text{and} \quad q' = 1 - p' = p\frac{D}{R}. \tag{12.113}$$

At the terminal time, τ, we have

$$R^{N_n} = R_0^\tau \quad \text{or} \quad R_0 = R^{N_n/\tau} \tag{12.114}$$

are random. The resulting option pricing formula is

$$C(N_n) := \mathrm{E}\, C_{N_n} = \sum_{k=1}^{\infty} C_k \mathrm{P}(N_n = k). \tag{12.115}$$

Remark 12.5 In an editorial comment in Rachev and Rüschendorf (1994, p.72) A.N. Shiryaev pointed out the connection of formula (12.115) for $C(N_n)$ and the general notion of a hedging strategy described in Shiryaev et al. (1994a,b). Shiryaev described scenario to motivate for model (12.115) by assuming additional randomness (N_n) in the market behavior. At first the random variable N_n is "tossed", if the result is $N_n = k$, the agent selects a hedging strategy π_k (depending on k). In this case, the rational value of the call is $C_k = \inf x(\pi_k)$, where $x(\pi_k)$ is the premium, payable to the call-seller and the infimum is taken over all hedging strategies. Let π be a family of strategies $(\pi_k)_{k\geq 0}$ (π_k is chosen when $N_n = k$). Define the *rational value of the call* $C(N_n)$ as the minimal value $E\inf x(\pi_{N_n})$ where the infimum is taken over all families $\pi = (\pi_k)$ of hedging strategies. Consequently,

$$
\begin{aligned}
C(N_n) &= \mathrm{E} \inf x(\pi_{N_n}) \\
&= \sum_k C_k \mathrm{P}(N_n = k), \tag{12.116}
\end{aligned}
$$

as in (12.115). As Shiryaev argued, $C(N_n)$ describes the *fair mean value of the option* – the price which the call-buyer should pay to the call-seller under this scenario.

Remark 12.6 An alternative derivation is obtained by considering R_0 to be a fixed discount rate per time unit, implying that $R = R_0^{\tau/N_n} = R_{N_n}$ is the random discount rate per unit period. Therefore, the risk neutral probabilities $p = \frac{R-D}{U-D} = p_{N_n}$ also are random. From (12.92), by conditioning on N_n, we obtain

$$C(N_n) = \mathrm{E}C_{N_n} = \mathrm{S}\mathrm{E}\phi(a_{N_n}, N_n, p'_{N_n}) - K R_0^{-\tau} \mathrm{E}\phi(a_{N_n}, N_n, p_{N_n}) \tag{12.117}$$

with $p' = \frac{U}{R}p$. $\qquad\qquad\square$

Next, we derive some asymptotic formulas for pricing formula (12.115). Let

$$\Omega_n := \mathrm{E}R^{-N_n} \tag{12.118}$$

and define r.v.'s N_n^* independent of $(\xi_{n,1})$ with distribution

$$\mathrm{P}(N_n^* = k) = \frac{1}{\Omega_n} R^{-k} \mathrm{P}(N_n = k). \tag{12.119}$$

From (12.92) we obtain representation

$$C(N_n) = SE\phi(a_{N_n}, N_n, p') - K\Omega_n E\phi(a_{N_n^*}, N_n^*, p), \qquad (12.120)$$

$$a_n = \left[\frac{\log(K/S) - nD}{R}\right]_+, \quad n \in \mathbb{N}, R := U - D.$$

If $a_{N_n} > N_n$, i.e., if $UN_n < \log(K/S)$, then $C(N_n) = 0$. For the following we assume that

$$\liminf_{n\to\infty} U(n)N_n > \log(K/S) \text{ a.s.}, \qquad (12.121)$$

$$\liminf_{n\to\infty} U(n)N_n^* > \log(K/S) \text{ a.s.},$$

and, as before, $U(n) \to \lambda, D(n) \to -\mu$.

Lemma 12.5 Assume that $\frac{N_n}{n} \xrightarrow{w} Y$ with Laplace-transform $\psi_Y(\vartheta)$ $= Ee^{-\vartheta Y}$ and $R^n \to \bar{R}_0^\tau$. Then, $\frac{N_n^*}{n} \xrightarrow{w} Y^*$ with Laplace transform

$$\psi_{Y^*}(\vartheta) = \frac{E[\bar{R}_0^{-\tau} e^{-Y\theta}]}{E\bar{R}_0^{-\tau Y}}. \qquad (12.122)$$

Proof. $Ee^{-\vartheta \frac{N_n^*}{n}} = \sum_{k=1}^\infty e^{-\vartheta \frac{k}{n}} P(N_n = k) R^{-k} \frac{1}{\Omega_n} = \frac{1}{ER^{-N_n}} \sum_{n=1}^\infty P(N_n = k)$ $e^{-\frac{k}{n}(\theta + \tau \log \bar{R}_0 + \epsilon_n)}$ with $\epsilon_n \to 0$. In fact, since $ER^{-N_n} = ER^{-n\frac{N_n}{n}} \to ER_0^{-\tau Y}$, then, by the continuity of the Laplace transform, we have $Ee^{-\theta N_n^*/n} \to \frac{Ee^{-Y(\theta + \tau \log \bar{R}_0)}}{E\bar{R}_0^{-\tau Y}}$. $\qquad \square$

Theorem 12.8 (Case 1, $\lambda = \mu = 0$) Assume the existence of the limits α, α', σ^2 and σ'^2 as specified in (12.101) and (12.103) and that

$$\frac{N_n}{n} \xrightarrow{w} Y \text{ and } R^n \to \bar{R}_0^\tau. \qquad (12.123)$$

Then,

$$C(N_n) \to C := S\phi_{Z'}(x) - K(E\bar{R}_0^{-\tau Y})\phi_{Z^*}(x), \qquad (12.124)$$

where $x = \log(K/S)$; $\phi_{Z^*}(x) = P(Z^* \geq x)$; Z^* has the ch.f. of a mixture of normals,

$$\varphi_Z^*(u) = \int_0^\infty e^{i\alpha z u - \frac{\sigma^2}{2} z u^2} dF_{Y^*}(z), \qquad (12.125)$$

with Y^* as in (12.122); and $\phi_{Z'}$ is defined analogous to ϕ_{Z^*} in (12.125) but with α', σ' and Y instead of α, σ and Y^*.

Proof. Recall that

$$E\phi(a_{N_n}, N_n, p') = P(\log(S_{N_n}/S) - a_{N_n}R - N_nD \geq 0), \qquad (12.126)$$

where $p' = p\frac{U}{R}$. With $\log(S_n/S) = \sum_i X_{ni}$, $X_{ni} = \xi_{ni}R + (1 - \zeta_{ni})D$, the ch.f. of the right-hand-side of (12.126) is

$$\sum_{k=1}^{\infty} P(N_n = k)e^{-(a_k R + kD)iu}\mathrm{E}\exp\{\log(S_k/S)\} \tag{12.127}$$

$$= \int_0^{\infty} e^{-(a_x R + xD)iu}\left(\phi_{X_{n,1}}(u)\right)^x dP^{N_n}(x)$$

$$= \int_0^{\infty} e^{-(a_{nz}R + nzD)iu}\left(\phi_{X_{n,1}}^n(u)\right)^z dP^{N_n/n}(z)$$

$$\longrightarrow \int_0^{\infty} e^{-\log(K/S)iu}\left(\phi_X(u)\right)^z dP^Y(z),$$

where $X \overset{d}{=} N(\alpha', \sigma'^2)$. The last step follows from Theorem 12.1(a), implying that $\varphi_{X_{n,1}}^n(u) \to \varphi_X(u)$ and the fact that, because $R = R(n) \to 0$, $a_{nz}R + nzD \to \log(K/S)$. From (12.127) we have $\log(S_{N_n}/S) - a_{N_n}R - N_nD \overset{w}{\longrightarrow} Z' - \log(K/S)$, implying

$$\mathrm{E}\phi(a_{N_n}, N_n, p') \to P(Z' \geq \log(K/S)). \tag{12.128}$$

By Lemma 12.5 and Theorem 12.3(a), a similar argument applies to $\mathrm{E}\phi(a_{N_n^*}, N_n^*, p)$. So we obtain (12.124) from (12.120) and observe that, by (12.123),

$$\Omega_n \to \mathrm{E}\bar{R}_0^{-\tau Y}. \tag{12.129}$$

Example 12.7 Let, as in Example 12.6, $U = \tilde{\sigma}\sqrt{\tau/n}$, $D = -\tilde{\sigma}\sqrt{\tau/n}$, $R = R_0^{\tau/n}$, $p = \frac{R-D}{U-D} \approx \frac{1}{2} + \frac{1}{2}\frac{\log R_0 - \frac{1}{2}\tilde{\sigma}^2}{\tilde{\sigma}}\sqrt{\tau/n}$ and consider the geometric case (cf. Example 12.5) $P(N_n = k) = \frac{1}{n}(1 - \frac{1}{n})^{k-1}, k \geq 1$. The "random" Black-Scholes-type formula (12.124) has the form

$$C = S\phi_{Z'}(x) - \frac{K}{1 + \tau \log R_0}\phi_{Z^*}(x), \tag{12.130}$$

where $Z' \overset{d}{=} Z'_1 - Z'_2$; Z'_i are independent exponentials with means $a_{1,2} = \frac{1}{2}(\pm\alpha' + \sqrt{\alpha' + 2\sigma'^2})$; and $Z^* \overset{d}{=} Z_1^* - Z_2^*$ are independent exponentials with means

$$a_{1,2}^* = \frac{1}{2}\left(\pm\alpha' + \sqrt{\alpha^{*2} + 2\sigma^{*2}}\right), \quad \alpha^* = \frac{\alpha}{1 + \tau \log R_0}, \quad \sigma^{*2} = \frac{\sigma^2}{1 + \tau \log R_0}.$$

In fact, $\mathrm{E}R_0^{-\tau Y} = \frac{1}{1 + \tau \log R_0}$ and $\mathrm{E}R_0^{-\tau Y}e^{-Y\vartheta} = \frac{1}{1 + \vartheta + \tau \log R_0}$ and, thus, by Lemma 12.5,

$$\psi_{Y^*}(\vartheta) = \frac{1 + \tau \log R_0}{1 + \vartheta + \tau \log R_0} = \frac{1}{1 + \frac{\vartheta}{1 + \tau \log R_0}}.$$

Furthermore, by (12.125),

$$\varphi_{Z^*}(t) = \int_0^\infty e^{i\alpha z u - \frac{\sigma^2}{2} z u^2} dF_{Y/1 + \tau \log R_0}(u) = \int_0^\infty e^{i\alpha^* w u - \frac{\sigma^{*2}}{2} w u^2} dF_Y(w).$$

By Example 12.6, $\alpha = \tau(\log R_0 - \frac{1}{2}\tilde{\sigma}^2)$, $\sigma^2 = \tilde{\sigma}^2 \tau$, $\alpha' = \tau(\log R_0 + \frac{1}{2}\tilde{\sigma}^2)$ and $\sigma'^2 = \tilde{\sigma}^2 \tau$. Further,

$$a'_{1,2} = \frac{1}{2}\left(\pm(\log R_0 + \frac{1}{2}\tilde{\sigma}^2) + \sqrt{\tau^2(\log R_0 + \frac{1}{2}\tilde{\sigma}^2) + 2\tilde{\sigma}\tau}\right),$$

$$a^*_{1,2} = \frac{1}{2}\left(\pm\frac{\tau(\log R_0 - \frac{1}{2}\tilde{\sigma}^2)}{1 + \tau \log R_0} + \sqrt{\frac{\tau^2(\log R_0 - \frac{1}{2}\tilde{\sigma}^2)^2}{(1 + \tau \log R_0)^2} + 2\frac{\tilde{\sigma}^2 \tau}{(1 + \tau \log R_0)}}\right)$$

and, thus, $\phi_{Z^*}(x) = P(Z^* \geq x) = P(Z_1^* - Z_2^* \geq x), \phi_{Z'}(x) = P(Z' \geq x) = P(Z'_1 - Z'_2 \geq x)$, where Z_i^* and Z'_i are independent exponentials with means a_i^* and a'_i, respectively. □

Next, we consider the case of mixtures of Poissons and the degenerate case.

Theorem 12.9   (a) (Case 2, $0 < \lambda < \infty, \mu = 0$) Assume limits

$$a = \lim np, \quad b = \lim nD, \quad a' = \lim np', \quad p' = \frac{pU}{R} < 1 \qquad (12.131)$$

exist and that

$$\frac{N_n}{n} \xrightarrow{w} Y \quad \text{and} \quad R^n \to \bar{R}_0^\tau. \qquad (12.132)$$

Then,

$$C(N_n) \to C := S\phi_{Z'}(0) - K(E\bar{r}_0^{-\tau Y})\phi_{Z'}(0), \qquad (12.133)$$

where the law of Z' is a Poisson mixture with ch.f.

$$\varphi_{Z'}(u) = \int_0^\infty e^{-\left[\frac{\log(K/S) - zb'}{\lambda}\right]_+ \lambda i \tau + a' z (e^{i\lambda u} - 1)} dP^Y(z), \qquad (12.134)$$

and where Z^* is defined as in (12.134) with a', b' and Y being replaced by a, b and Y^* from (12.122).

(b) (Case 8, $\lambda = \infty, \mu = 0$) Suppose that limits

$$b = \lim nD, \quad c = \lim \frac{np}{U}, \quad c' = \lim \frac{np'}{U}, \quad p' = \frac{pU}{R} \qquad (12.135)$$

exist and let

$$\frac{N_n}{n} \xrightarrow{w} Y, R^n \to \bar{R}_0^\tau. \qquad (12.136)$$

Then,

$$C(N_n) \to C := S\phi_{Z'}(0) - K(\mathrm{E}\bar{R}_0^{-\tau Y})\phi_{Z*}(0), \tag{12.137}$$

where

$$\varphi_{Z'}(u) = \int_0^\infty e^{-\left[\frac{\log(K/S)-zb}{\lambda}\right]_+ \lambda iu + zc'iu} d\mathrm{P}^Y(z) \tag{12.138}$$

and

$$\varphi_{Z*}(u) = \int_0^\infty e^{\left[\frac{\log(K/S)-zb}{\lambda}\right]_+ \lambda iu + ciu} d\mathrm{P}^{Y*}(z), \tag{12.139}$$

with Y^* from (12.122).

Proof. The proof of Theorem 12.9 is similar to that of Theorem 12.8. □

Remark 12.7 (a) Returns that follow a mixture of normals of the type $\alpha Y + \sigma\sqrt{Y}N$, where N denotes the standard normal, can, by Theorem 12.8 or Theorem 12.3, be modeled with a random number of movements, N_n, where $\frac{N_n}{n} \xrightarrow{w} Y$, allowing us to calculate the generalized Black-Scholes option price. Because location and scale mixtures of normals are generally not identifiable, there are possibly different sequences $\frac{N'_n}{n} \to Y'$, which, by Theorem 12.8, lead to the same Black-Scholes value.

(b) In contrast to the "nonrandom" case $N_n \equiv n$, where Case 8 ($\lambda = \infty$, $\mu = 0$) leads to the degenerate convergence $\log(S_n/S) \to \alpha = \lim_{n\to\infty}\left[nD + \frac{np}{U}\right]$ one obtains in the "random case" $\log(S_{N_n}/S) \to \alpha Y$.

Example 12.8 (Mixtures of Gamma Distributions) Define for $m \in \mathbf{N}$ the generalized geometric distribution

$$P(N_n^{(m)} = 1 + km) = \begin{cases} \left(\frac{1}{n}\right)^{1/m}, & \text{for } k = 0, \\ \frac{\prod_{j=0}^{k-1}\left(\frac{1}{m}+j\right)}{k!}\left(\frac{1}{n}\right)^{1/m}\left(1-\frac{1}{n}\right)^k, & \text{for } k = 1,2,\dots, \end{cases} \tag{12.140}$$

(cf. Klebanov, Manija and Melamed, 1984; Melamed, 1988; and the references therein). For $m = 1$, $N_n^{(1)}$ is geometrically distributed with mean n. Then,

$$\frac{N_n^{(m)}}{n} \xrightarrow{w} Y \tag{12.141}$$

holds, where Y is a Gamma $(\frac{1}{m}, m)$ distributed r.v. with Laplace transform

$$\psi_Y(\theta) = \mathrm{E}e^{-\theta Y} = \left(\frac{1}{a+m\theta}\right)^{1/m} \tag{12.142}$$

and density

$$f_Y(x) = \begin{cases} 0, & \text{for } x < 0, \\ \frac{1}{\Gamma(\frac{1}{m})m^{1/m}} x^{(1/m)-1} e^{-x/m}, & \text{for } x > 0. \end{cases} \qquad (12.143)$$

Given $N_n := N_n^m$ and $\mathrm{P}(N_n^* = k) = \frac{1}{\Omega_n} R^{-k} \mathrm{P}(N_n = k)$, where $R = R_0^{\tau/n}$, and $\Omega_n = \mathrm{E} R^{-N_n^m}$ Lemma 12.5 implies that $\Omega_n R^n \to \mathrm{E} R_0^{\tau Y} = \left(\frac{1}{1+m\tau \log R_0}\right)^{1/m}$ and $\frac{N_n^*}{n} \xrightarrow{w} Y^*$ with

$$\psi_{Y^*}(\vartheta) = \frac{\mathrm{E} e^{-(\vartheta + \tau \log R_0)Y}}{\mathrm{E} R_0^{-\tau Y}} = \left(1 + \frac{m}{1 + m\tau \log R_0}\vartheta\right)^{-1/m}. \qquad (12.144)$$

I.e., Y^* is again Gamma distributed with density

$$f_{Y^*}(x) = \begin{cases} \frac{1}{\Gamma(1/m)(m\Delta)^{(1/m)+1}} x^{(1/m)-1} e^{-x/m\Delta}, & \text{if } x > 0, \\ 0, & \text{if } x < 0, \end{cases} \qquad (12.145)$$

where $\Delta = (1 + m\tau \log R_0)^{-1}$, i.e., $Y^* \stackrel{d}{=} \Gamma(\frac{1}{m}, m\Delta)$. Therefore, the ch.f. of Z^* (cf. (12.125)) is given by

$$\varphi_{Z^*}(u) = \int_0^\infty e^{\alpha z i u - \frac{\sigma^2}{2} z u^2} dF_{Y^*}(z) = \int_0^\infty e^{\alpha^* z i u - \frac{\sigma^{*2}}{2} z u^2} dF_Y(z), \qquad (12.146)$$

where $\alpha^* = \Delta\alpha$, $\sigma^{*2} = \Delta\sigma^2$; and α and σ^2 are given by (12.101) and (12.103). Recall that in the classical case we have $\mathrm{U}(n) = \tilde{\sigma}\sqrt{\tau/n}$, $\mathrm{D}(n) = -\tilde{\sigma}\sqrt{\tau/n}$, $R = R_0^{\tau/n}$, $\alpha = \tau(\log R_0 - \frac{1}{2}\tilde{\sigma}^2)$, and $\sigma^2 = \tilde{\sigma}^2\tau$.

Observe that for $\sigma^2 = 0$, as in Case 8 ($\lambda = \infty$, $\mu = 0$)

$$\int_0^\infty e^{\alpha^* z i u} dF_Y(z) = (1 - \alpha^* i u m)^{-1/m} \qquad (12.147)$$

and, if $\alpha^* = 0$,

$$\int_0^\infty e^{-\frac{\sigma^{*2}}{2} z u^2} dF_Y(z) = \left(1 + m\frac{\sigma^{*2}}{2} u^2\right)^{-1/m} \qquad (12.148)$$

$$= \left(1 - i\sqrt{m}\frac{\sigma^*}{\sqrt{2}} u\right)^{-1/m} \left(1 + i\sqrt{m}\frac{\sigma^*}{\sqrt{2}} u\right)^{-1/m},$$

i.e., in the first case Z^* has Gamma-distribution

$$Z^* \stackrel{d}{=} \Gamma\left(\frac{1}{m}, \alpha^* m\right) \qquad (12.149)$$

and in the second case

$$Z^* \stackrel{d}{=} \Gamma\left(\frac{1}{m}, \sqrt{m}\frac{\sigma^*}{\sqrt{2}}\right) \Gamma\left(\frac{1}{m}, -\sqrt{m}\frac{\sigma^*}{\sqrt{2}}\right). \qquad (12.150)$$

In the same way

$$\varphi_{Z'}(u) = \int_0^\infty e^{\alpha' ziu - \frac{\sigma'^2}{2}zu^2} dF_Y(z), \qquad (12.151)$$

where α' and σ' are determined by Theorem 12.8. Recall that in the classical case $U(n) = \tilde{\sigma}\sqrt{\tau/n}$, $D(u) = -\tilde{\sigma}\sqrt{\tau/n}$, $\alpha' = \tau(\log R_0 + \frac{1}{2}\tilde{\sigma}^2)$, and $\sigma'^2 = \sigma^2 = \tilde{\sigma}^2 \tau$. The "randomized" Black-Scholes formula corresponds, by Theorem 12.3 (a), to a limiting Gamma mixture of the asset price $\log(S_{N_n}(m)/S) \xrightarrow{w}$ Z with $\varphi_Z(u) = \int_0^\infty e^{\alpha ziu - \frac{\sigma^2}{2}zu^2} dF_Y(z)$ and α and σ being determined by Theorem 12.3.

Example 12.9 (*$\tilde{\alpha}$-stable laws*) Let $\frac{N_n}{n} \xrightarrow{w} Y$, where Y is a positive $\tilde{\alpha}/2$-stable random variable with Laplace transform

$$Ee^{-\vartheta Y} = e^{-|\vartheta|^{\tilde{\alpha}}/2}. \qquad (12.152)$$

(a) The limiting price, S^*, has, by Theorem 12.3, a distribution determined by the ch.f. of the return, $\log(S^*/S)$,

$$\varphi_{\log(S^*/S)}(u) = \int_0^\infty e^{\alpha ziu - \frac{\sigma^2}{2}zu^2} dF_Y(z), \qquad (12.153)$$

where α and σ are determined by (12.11) and (12.12).

From the definition of Y we have

$$\varphi_{\log(S^*/S)}(u) = \int_0^\infty e^{-z\left(\frac{\sigma^2}{2}u^2 - in\alpha\right)} dF_Y(z) \qquad (12.154)$$

$$= e^{-\left|\frac{\sigma^2}{2}u^2 - iu\alpha\right|^{\frac{\tilde{\alpha}}{2}}}$$

$$= e^{-\left(\frac{\sigma^4}{4}u^4 + u^2\alpha^2\right)^{\frac{\tilde{\alpha}}{4}}}.$$

If $\alpha = 0$, then

$$\varphi_{\log(S^*/S)}(u) = e^{-\left|\frac{\sigma u}{\sqrt{2}}\right|^{\tilde{\alpha}}}, \qquad (12.155)$$

i.e., the total return, $\log(S^*/S)$, has a symmetric $\tilde{\alpha}$-stable distribution. Note that for $\alpha \neq 0$, $1 < \tilde{\alpha} < 2$ and $E|\log(S^*/S)| = \infty$. Moreover, because $Z = \log(S^*/S) \overset{d}{=} \alpha Y + N_{0,\sigma^2}\sqrt{Y}$ it follows that for a series of independent copies $(Y_i)_{i\geq 1}$ of Y and N_i of N_{0,σ^2}

$$\frac{Z_1 + \cdots + Z_n}{n^{2/\tilde{\alpha}}} \overset{d}{=} \alpha \frac{Y_1 + \cdots + Y_n}{n^{2/\tilde{\alpha}}} + \frac{N_1\sqrt{Y_1} + \cdots + N_n\sqrt{Y_n}}{n^{2/\tilde{\alpha}}} \to Y; \quad (12.156)$$

so Z is in the domain of attraction of a symmetric $\tilde{\alpha}/2$-stable law Y.

In the Black-Scholes formula (12.124) we have $ER_0^{-\tau Y} = e^{-|\tau \log R_0|^{\tilde{\alpha}/2}}$, $ER_0^{-\tau Y}e^{-Y\vartheta} = e^{-|\vartheta + \tau \log R_0|^{\tilde{\alpha}/2}}$ and, therefore, by Lemma 12.5

$$\psi_{Y^*}(\vartheta) = e^{-|\vartheta + \tau \log R_0|^{\tilde{\alpha}/2} + \tau \log R_0|^{\tilde{\alpha}/2}}. \qquad (12.157)$$

Remark 12.8 The Black-Scholes formulas simplify, if $R = R(n) = 1$. Recall that, from (12.112), $R(n) = p(n)U(n) + q(n)D(n)$ and $U(n) > R(n) > 1 > D(n)$. Defining $D^*(n) := \frac{D(n)}{R(n)} < 1$ and $U^*(n) = \frac{U(n)}{R(n)} > 1$ the riskless rate is now $R(n) \equiv 1$. For this reason it is sometimes assumed that, without loss of generality, $R(n) \equiv 1$. We demonstrate the effect of this assumption by considering, again, Example 12.6 with $U(n) = \tilde{\sigma}\sqrt{\tau/n}$, $D(n) = -\tilde{\sigma}\sqrt{\tau/n}$, $R = R_0^{\tau/n}$, and $p = \frac{R-D}{U-D} \approx \frac{1}{2} + \frac{1}{2}\frac{\log R_0 - \frac{1}{2}\tilde{\sigma}^2}{\tilde{\sigma}}\sqrt{\tau/n}$. Define

$$\mathbf{U^*} := \log U^* = \log\frac{U}{R} = U - \log R = \tilde{\sigma}\sqrt{\tau/n} - \frac{\tau}{n}\log R_0,$$

$$\mathbf{D^*} := \log D^* = \log D/R = D - \log R = -\tilde{\sigma}\sqrt{\tau/n} - \frac{\tau}{n}\log R_0;$$

and let $\tilde{\lambda} = \lim U^*(n)$ and $\tilde{\mu} = \lim D^*(n)$. In our case $\tilde{\lambda} = \tilde{\mu} = 0$ and, after some calculation, the characteristics $\bar{\alpha}, \bar{\sigma}$ in this new model (cf. Example 12.6) can be shown

$$\bar{\alpha} = \tau\left(\log R_0 - \frac{1}{2}\tilde{\sigma}^2\right) - (\log R_0)\tau = -\frac{\tau}{2}\tilde{\sigma}^2, \bar{\alpha}' = \frac{\tau}{2}\tilde{\sigma}^2 \qquad (12.158)$$

and $\sigma = \bar{\sigma} = \tilde{\sigma}\sqrt{\tau} = \sigma' = \bar{\sigma}'(p' = p\frac{U}{R} = pU^*)$. Note that R_0 cancels in the formulas for $\bar{\alpha}$, $\bar{\alpha}'$, σ, and $\bar{\sigma}$. In this case (12.104) becomes

$$C = S\phi(x') - K\phi(x), \qquad (12.159)$$

where

$$x = \frac{\log(S/K) - \frac{\tau}{2}\tilde{\sigma}^2}{\tilde{\sigma}\sqrt{\tau}} \quad \text{and} \quad x\prime = \frac{\log(S/K) + \frac{\pi}{2}\tilde{\sigma}}{\tilde{\sigma}\sqrt{\tau}}.$$

This coincides with the classical Black-Scholes formula with $R \equiv 1$, but not with the correct pricing formula in the riskless model. For this reason the suggestion to assume $R = 1$ does not seem to be justified.

Calculations simplify in the random binomial model with $R \equiv 1$. If $\frac{N_n}{n} \xrightarrow{w} Y$, then (12.124) becomes

$$C = S\phi_{\tilde{Z}'}(x) - K\phi_{\tilde{Z}^*}(x), \qquad (12.160)$$

where $x = \log(K/S)$,

$$\varphi_{\tilde{Z}^*}(u) = \int_0^\infty e^{-\frac{\tilde{\sigma}^2}{2}\tau z i u - \frac{\tilde{\sigma}^2}{2}\tau z u^2}dF_{Y^*}(u) = \int_0^\infty e^{-\frac{\tilde{\sigma}^2}{2}\tau z(iu+u^2)}dF_{Y^*}(u) \qquad (12.161)$$

and

$$\varphi_{\tilde{Z}'}(u) = \int_0^\infty e^{\frac{\tilde{\sigma}^2}{2}\tau z(iu-u^2)}dF_Y(u). \qquad (12.162)$$

If $P(N_n = k) = \frac{1}{n}\left(1 - \frac{1}{n}\right)^{k-1}$ with $k \in \mathbf{N}$ holds, we have $Y \stackrel{d}{=} \mathrm{Exp}(1)$, $\tilde{Z}^* \stackrel{d}{=} \tilde{Z}_1 - \tilde{Z}_2$, where $\tilde{Z}_i$ independent exponentials, $\tilde{a}_1 = E\tilde{Z}_1 = \frac{1}{2}\left(\tilde{\alpha} + \sqrt{\tilde{\alpha}^2 + 2\tilde{\sigma}^2}\right)$

$$= -\tfrac{\tau}{4}\tilde{\sigma}^2 + \tilde{\sigma}\sqrt{\tfrac{\tau^2}{4} + 2\tau}, \; \tilde{a}_2 = E\tilde{Z}_2 = \tfrac{\tau\tilde{\sigma}^2}{4} + \tilde{\sigma}\sqrt{\tfrac{\tau^2}{4} + 2\tau};$$ and, analogously, $\tilde{Z}' \overset{d}{=} \tilde{Z}'_1 - \tilde{Z}'_2$ where $\tilde{Z}'_i$ are independent exponentials with $E\tilde{Z}'_1 = \tilde{a}_1 = \tfrac{\tau}{4}\tilde{\sigma}^2 + \sqrt{\tfrac{\tau^2}{4} + 2\tau}$ and $E\tilde{Z}'_2 = \tilde{a}'_2 = -\tfrac{\tau}{4}\sigma^2 + \sqrt{\tfrac{\tau^2}{4} + 2\tau}.$

12.6 Some Examples

In this section we present three examples of the random pricing model for heavy-tailed distributed asset returns.

12.6.1 Paretian Stable Y

Let Y be a positive Paretian stable r.v. with Laplace transform

$$\psi_Y(\vartheta) = Ee^{-\vartheta Y} = e^{-\vartheta^{\alpha/2}}, \; \vartheta > 0, \; 0 < \alpha < 2. \tag{12.163}$$

If, for example,

$$P(N_n = k) := P(k - 1 < nY \le k), k \in \mathbf{N}, \tag{12.164}$$

then $P(\tfrac{N_n}{n} > x) = P(N_n > xn) = P(N_n > [xn]) = P(nY > [xn]) = P(Y > \tfrac{[xn]}{n}) = \to P(Y > x)$, for all $x \ge 0$, i.e.,

$$\frac{N_n}{n} \overset{w}{\longrightarrow} Y. \tag{12.165}$$

If $U = -D = \tilde{\sigma}\sqrt{\tau/n}$ and $\tilde{\sigma} > 0$, then $R = R(n) = \tfrac{1}{2}\left(e^{\tilde{\sigma}\sqrt{\tau/n}} + e^{-\tilde{\sigma}\sqrt{\tau/n}}\right)$ and $R^n \to e^{\tfrac{1}{2}\tilde{\sigma}^2\tau}$, i.e., $R_0 = e^{\tfrac{1}{2}\tilde{\sigma}^2}$. By Theorem 12.3,

$$\log\left(S_{N_n}/S\right) \overset{w}{\longrightarrow} Z = \log(S^*/S), \tag{12.166}$$

where

$$Z \overset{d}{=} N_{0,\sigma^2}\sqrt{Y}, \quad \sigma^2 = \tilde{\sigma}^2\tau, \tag{12.167}$$

and, therefore,

$$Ee^{i\vartheta Z} = \int_{-\infty}^{\infty} e^{-\tfrac{\vartheta^2 y\sigma^2}{2}} dP^Y(y) = e^{-\left(\tfrac{\vartheta\sigma}{\sqrt{2}}\right)^{\alpha}}. \tag{12.168}$$

In this case Z has a symmetric α-stable distribution with scale parameter $\tfrac{\sigma}{\sqrt{2}}$. The Black-Scholes formula, given by Theorem 12.8, is

$$C = S\phi_{Z'}(x) - K\left(ER_0^{-\tau Y}\right)\phi_{Z^*}(x), \tag{12.169}$$

where, by (12.125),

$$\varphi_{Z^*}(u) = \int_0^{\infty} e^{-\tfrac{\sigma^2}{2}zu^2} dP^{Y^*}(z) = Ee^{-\tfrac{\sigma^2}{2}u^2 Y^*}. \tag{12.170}$$

By Lemma 12.5,

$$\psi_{Y^*}(\vartheta) = \frac{ER_0^{-\tau Y} e^{-Y\vartheta}}{Er_0^{-\tau Y}} = \frac{Ee^{-\left(\frac{\tau}{2}\tilde{\sigma}^2 + \vartheta\right)Y}}{Ee^{-\frac{\tau}{2}\tilde{\sigma}^2 Y}} = \frac{e^{-\left(\frac{\tau}{2}\tilde{\sigma}^2 + \vartheta\right)^{\alpha/2}}}{e^{-\left(\frac{\tau}{2}\tilde{\sigma}^2\right)^{\alpha/2}}}. \tag{12.171}$$

Therefore,

$$
\begin{aligned}
\varphi_{Z^*}(u) &= e^{-\left(\frac{\tau}{2}\tilde{\sigma}^2 + \frac{\tilde{\sigma}^2}{2}u^2\right)^{\alpha/2} + \left(\frac{\tau}{2}\tilde{\sigma}^2\right)^{\alpha/2}} \\
&= \exp\left\{-\left(\frac{\tilde{\sigma}}{\sqrt{2}}\right)^\alpha \left[(\tau + u^2)^{\alpha/2} - \tau^{\alpha/2}\right]\right\}. \tag{12.172}
\end{aligned}
$$

If $1 < \alpha < 2$, it follows that $EZ^* = 0$, but indeed Z^* does not have a second moment. Regarding Z' in (12.169) we have

$$Z' \stackrel{d}{=} \alpha'Y + N_{0,\sigma'^2}\sqrt{Y} \tag{12.173}$$

and

$$\varphi_{Z'}(u) = \int_0^\infty e^{\alpha' z i u - \frac{\sigma'^2}{2} z u^2} dP^Y(z),$$

where, by Theorem 12.6, $\alpha' = \lim_{n\to\infty} n(p' + q')\tilde{\sigma}\sqrt{\tau/n}$, $p' = p\frac{U}{R}$ $= \frac{e^{\tilde{\sigma}\sqrt{\tau/n}}}{e^{\tilde{\sigma}\sqrt{\tau/n}} + e^{-\tilde{\sigma}\sqrt{\tau/n}}}$, and $q' = q\frac{D}{R} = \frac{e^{-\tilde{\sigma}\sqrt{\tau/n}}}{e^{\tilde{\sigma}\sqrt{\tau/n}} + e^{-\tilde{\sigma}\sqrt{\tau/n}}}$. Thus,

$$\alpha' = \tilde{\sigma}^2 \tau, \quad \sigma'^2 = \sigma^2 = \tilde{\sigma}^2 \tau \tag{12.174}$$

and

$$Z' \stackrel{d}{=} \tilde{\sigma}^2 \tau Y + N_{0,\tilde{\sigma}^2 \tau}\sqrt{Y}. \tag{12.175}$$

Because $ER_0^{-\tau Y} = e^{-\left(\frac{\tau}{2}\tilde{\sigma}^2\right)^{\alpha/2}}$, we finally obtain

$$C = S\phi_{Z'}(x) - Ke^{-\left(\frac{\tau}{2}\tilde{\sigma}^2\right)^{\alpha/2}}\phi_{Z^*}(x), \tag{12.176}$$

with $x = \log(K/S)$ and Z' and Z^* given by (12.172) and (12.175), respectively.

12.6.2   Finite Normal Mixtures

Boness et al. (1974) suggest that the observed kurtosis in the distribution of asset returns may be caused by the fact that returns follow a finite mixture of normal distributions; i.e., for return $Z = \log(S^*/S)$ we have

$$\varphi_Z(u) = \sum_{j=1}^k \vartheta_j e^{i a_j u - \frac{\sigma_j^2}{2} u^2} = \int_0^\infty e^{\alpha z i u - \frac{\sigma_z^2}{2} u^2} dF_Y(z), \tag{12.177}$$

where $P(Y = z_j) = \vartheta_j = a_j$ and $\frac{\sigma^2 z_j}{2} = \sigma_j^2, 1 \leq j \leq k$, assuming that $\frac{\alpha_i}{\alpha} = \frac{2\sigma_j^2}{\sigma^2}, j = 1, \ldots, k$.

Consider k Poisson r.v.'s, $N_n^{(j)} = Poisson(nz_j)$, and define N_n by the mixture $P(N_n = i) = \sum_{j=1}^k \vartheta_j P(N_n^{(j)} = i)$. Then, $\frac{N_n}{n} \xrightarrow{w} Y$ and, by Theorem 12.3, $\log(S_{N_n}/S) \xrightarrow{w} Z$ with ch.f. (12.177) and α and σ being determined by (12.11) and (12.12), respectively.

Option pricing formula (12.124) holds with

$$\mathrm{E}\bar{R}_0^{-\tau Y} = \sum_{j=1}^k \vartheta_j \bar{R}_0^{-\tau z_j}, \tag{12.178}$$

$$\varphi_{Z'}(u) = \int_0^\infty e^{i\alpha' z u - \frac{\sigma'^2}{2} z u^2} dF_Y(z) = \sum_{j=1}^k \vartheta_j e^{i\alpha' z_j u - \frac{\sigma'^2}{2} z_j u^2}, \tag{12.179}$$

with α' and σ' given by (12.101) and (12.103), respectively, and

$$\phi_{Z'}(x) = \sum_{j=1}^k \vartheta_j \phi_{N(\alpha' z_j, \sigma'^2)}(x). \tag{12.180}$$

Furthermore, by Lemma 12.5,

$$\psi_{Y^*}(u) = \frac{\mathrm{E}\bar{R}_0^{-\tau Y} e^{-Yu}}{\mathrm{E}\bar{R}_0^{-tY}} = \sum_{j=1}^n \vartheta_j^* e^{-z_j u}, \quad \vartheta_j^* = \frac{\vartheta_j \bar{R}_0^{-\tau z_j}}{\sum \vartheta_i \bar{R}_0^{-\tau z_i}}, \tag{12.181}$$

with Y^* being a discrete distribution, and, by (12.125),

$$\phi_{Z^*}(x) = \sum_{j=1}^k \vartheta_j^* \phi_{N(\alpha z_j, \sigma^2)}(x), x = \log(K/S). \tag{12.182}$$

12.6.3   Asset Price Changes With Student's Distributions

If $1/Y$ is χ_n^2-distributed, then $Z \overset{d}{=} N_{0,\sigma^2}\sqrt{Y}$ is t_n-distributed. Blattberg and Gonedes (1979) suggested that security returns may follow a Student t-distribution. Again, we can apply Theorem 12.8, to obtain a Black-Scholes formula when $\log(S^*/S)$ is t-distributed.

Note that, by Keilson and Steutel (1972), the class $\mathcal{L}$ of all r.v.'s Z with a representation of the form $N_{0,1}Y^{1/2}$ coincides with the class of all Z with ch.f. φ_Z, such that $\varphi_Z(|t|^{1/2})$ is a distribution function on $[0,\infty)$. $\mathcal{L}$ contains all r.v.'s with symmetric densities that are distribution functions in x^2; $\mathcal{L}$ is closed under mixing and convolution.

12.7   An Alternative Randomization and Continuous Trading

In Section 12.3 we modified the original binomial option model by randomizing the number of price changes. Now we introduce a randomization of the up and down movements of asset prices in the context of a modified version of the standard model of Cox et al. (1979).

Consider the binomial model with

$$U = \tilde{\sigma}\sqrt{\tau/n}, \; D = -\sigma^*\sqrt{\tau/n}, \; p = p(n) = \frac{R(n) - D(n)}{U(n) - D(n)}, \; R(n) = R_0^{\tau/n}.$$

$$(12.183)$$

After some calculation we obtain

$$p(n) = \frac{\sigma^*}{\tilde{\sigma} + \sigma^*} + \frac{\log R_0 - \frac{\sigma^* \tilde{\sigma}}{2}}{\tilde{\sigma} + \sigma^* \sqrt{\tau/n}} + O(\tau/n), \tag{12.184}$$

$$\alpha = \lim_{n \to \infty} n(qD + pU) + n \frac{pq(q-p)R^3}{(1 + q^2 R^2)(1 + p^2 R^2)} = \left(\log R_o - \frac{\sigma^* \tilde{\sigma}}{2}\right)\tau, \tag{12.185}$$

$$R = U - D,$$

and

$$\sigma^2 = \lim_{n \to \infty} n\left((1-p)\frac{R^2 p^2}{1 + R^2 p^2} + p\frac{R^2 q^2}{1 + R^2 q^2}\right) = \tilde{\sigma}\sigma^*\tau, \tag{12.186}$$

so that conditions C.2 and C.3 of Lemma 12.2 are satisfied, and

$$\log(S_n/S) \xrightarrow{w} N(\alpha, \sigma^2). \tag{12.187}$$

Furthermore,

$$p' = p\frac{U}{R} = \frac{\sigma^*}{\tilde{\sigma} + \sigma^*} + \frac{\log \bar{R}_0 + \sigma^* \tilde{\sigma} 2}{\tilde{\sigma} + \tilde{\tau}}\sqrt{\tau/n} + O(\tau/n), \tag{12.188}$$

$$\alpha' = \lim n(q'D + p'U) = \log R_0 + \frac{\tilde{\sigma}\sigma^*}{2}\tau, \tag{12.189}$$

$$\sigma' = \sigma \tag{12.190}$$

The binomial pricing formula (12.92) implies

$$C_n = C_n(\tilde{\sigma}, \sigma^*) = S\phi(a_n, n, p') - KR^{-n}\phi(a_n, n, p), \tag{12.191}$$

where $\phi(a_n, n, p) = P(\sum \xi_{n,k} \geq a_n)$, $a_n = \left\lceil \frac{\log(K/S) - nD}{R} \right\rceil$. By Theorem 12.6,

$$C_n \to C = C(\tilde{\sigma}, \sigma^*) = S\phi(x') - KR_0^{-\tau}\phi(x), \tag{12.192}$$

$$x = \frac{\log(S/K) + \alpha}{\sigma}, \quad x' = \frac{\log(S/K) + \alpha'}{\sigma'}.$$

The limiting process of X_n is, by Theorem 12.2,

$$X(u) = \left(\log R_0 - \frac{\sigma^* \tilde{\sigma}}{2}\right)u + \sqrt{\tilde{\sigma}\sigma^*}W(u). \tag{12.193}$$

Let Σ and T be nonnegative r.v. independent of $(\xi_{n,k})$ and consider the randomized version of the binomial model with random up and down movements specified by

$$U = \Sigma\sqrt{\tau/n}, \quad D = -T\sqrt{\tau/n}, \tag{12.194}$$

$$\log(S_n/S) = \sum_{k=1}^{n} X_{n,k}, \, X_{n,k} + \xi_{n,k}U + (1 - \xi_{n,k})D. \tag{12.195}$$

By (12.187), the conditional distribution of $\log(S_n/S)$ given that the "up volatility" $\Sigma = \tilde{\sigma}$ and the "down volatility" $T = \sigma^*$ is asymptotically normal, i.e. $P^{\log(S_n/S)|\Sigma=\tilde{\sigma},T=\sigma^*} \xrightarrow{w} N(\alpha, \sigma^2)$, where $\alpha = \alpha(\tilde{\sigma}, \sigma^*)$ and $\sigma^2 = \tilde{\sigma}\sigma^*\tau$ (cf. (12.185) and (12.186)). Therefore,

$$P^{\log(S_n/S)} \xrightarrow{w} \int N(\alpha(\tilde{\sigma}, \sigma^*), \tilde{\sigma}\sigma^*\tau)dP^{\Sigma,T}(\tilde{\sigma}, \sigma^*). \tag{12.196}$$

The pricing formula for the modified binomial model is

$$C_n = \int C_n(\tilde{\sigma}, \sigma^*)dP^{(\Sigma,T)}(\tilde{\sigma}, \sigma^*). \tag{12.197}$$

To motivate (12.197), observe that $P^* = \int P^*_{\tilde{\sigma},\sigma^*}dP^{\Sigma,T}(\tilde{\sigma}, \sigma^*)$ is the riskless measure for the model (12.195), such that $(R^{-k}S_k)$ becomes a martingale, where $P^*_{\tilde{\sigma},\sigma^*}$ are the riskless measures in the conditional model. Therefore, the Black-Scholes value of a call, $B = (S_n - K)^+$, is given by $C_n = \int BR_0^{-\tau}dP^* = \int C_n(\tilde{\sigma}, \sigma^*)dP^{(\Sigma,T)}(\tilde{\sigma}, \sigma^*)$. Using the dominated convergence theorem we obtain from (12.192) the limiting Black-Scholes formula

$$C = S \int \phi\left(\frac{\log(K/S) + \log R_0 + \frac{\tilde{\sigma}\sigma^*}{2}\tau}{\tilde{\sigma}\sigma^*\tau}\right) dP^{\Sigma,T}(\tilde{\sigma}, \sigma^*) \tag{12.198}$$

$$- Kr_0^{-\tau} \int \phi\left(\frac{\log(K/S) + \log R_0 - \frac{\sigma^*\tilde{\sigma}}{2}\tau}{\tilde{\sigma}\sigma^*\tau}\right) dP^{\Sigma,T}(\tilde{\sigma}, \sigma^*).$$

The expression simplifies if $\Sigma = T$. The limiting process for the randomized model is given by

$$X^{(2)}(u) = \left(\log R_0 - \frac{T\Sigma}{2}\right)u + \sqrt{T\Sigma}W(u) \tag{12.199}$$

(cf. (12.193)). In comparison, the model with a random number of price changes has the limiting (riskless) process

$$X^{(1)}(u) = \left(\log R_0 - \frac{\sigma^*\tilde{\sigma}}{2}\right)Yu + \sqrt{\sigma^*\tilde{\sigma}}\sqrt{Y}W(u). \tag{12.200}$$

The differential equation corresponding to return process (12.195) is given by

$$dS^{(2)}(u) = S^{(2)}(u)\left((\log R_0)du + \sqrt{T\Sigma}dW(u)\right) \tag{12.201}$$

(cf. (12.90)).

Remark 12.9 The idea of randomizing the parameters can also be carried out in continuous time option models. Taking, for example, the classical diffusion model (in its riskless version, cf. Harrison and Pliska, (1981), or Karatzas, (1989)

$$dS(u) = S(u)\left((\log R_0)du + \sigma dW(u)\right) \qquad (12.202)$$

and considering a random volatility, σ, we can directly analyze the continuous model leading to a Black-Scholes formula as in (12.198).

The idea of random time changes in Gaussian models for stock price changes has been suggested by Mandelbrot and Taylor (1967) and Clark (1973). This idea is closely related to our first randomization model, leading in the limit to the random time transformed Wiener process

$$Z(u) = \log\frac{S(u)}{S} = \frac{\alpha}{\tau}Yu + \frac{\sigma}{\sqrt{\tau}}W(Yu). \qquad (12.203)$$

If, for example, Y is a positive stable r.v. with index of stability less than 1, then $W(Y_u)$ is a Lévy motion as in Mandelbrot and Taylor (1967).   □

12.8   An Example of the Difference Between Continuous and Discrete Option Valuation; the Hyperbolic Model

In this section we consider two special cases of our general valuation scheme for options. Employing Theorem 12.6 we generalize to Cox, Ross and Rubinstein (1979) binomial model and find the option price formula for the limiting model with hyperbolic distributions. It turns out that the results in the continuous (see Section 5.1, Example 5.3) and discrete models lead to markedly different fair prices.[6]

Eberlein and Keller (1994, 1995) show that the hyperbolic law fits daily German stock market data return much better than the Gaussian law and apply a hyperbolic Lévy motion as return model. We shall use hyperbolic distributions in the model we proposed in Section 12.5.

The name *hyperbolic distribution* comes from the fact that its log density forms a hyperbola, contrasting the normal distribution, whose log density forms a parabola. It was pointed out by Barndorff-Nielsen (1977) that this law can be represented as a normal variance-mean mixture where the mixing distribution is one of the generalized inverse Gaussian laws. Using our results in Section 5.1 (see Example 5.3), 11.4, 12.3 and 12.5 we present option valuation based on both the continuous and discrete hyperbolic models.

---

[6]The results of Sections 12.8 – 12.12 are due to Rejman, Weron and Weron (1997).

First, recall the generalized inverse Gaussian and the hyperbolic laws. A random variable Y has the generalized inverse Gaussian distribution, i.e., $Y \sim GIG(\lambda, \chi, \psi)$, if its density is of the following form

$$f_Y(x) = \frac{(\psi/\chi)^{\lambda/2}}{2K_\lambda\left(\sqrt{\chi\psi}\right)} x^{\lambda-1} \exp\left\{-\frac{1}{2}[\chi x^{-1} + \psi x]\right\}, \quad x \geq 0,$$

where the normalizing constant $K_\lambda(\cdot)$ is a modified Bessel function of the third kind with index λ. The generalized inverse Gaussian law is often defined by its Laplace transform

$$\mathbf{E}\exp(-\theta Y) = \frac{\psi^{\lambda/2}}{(\psi + 2\theta)^{\lambda/2}} \frac{K_\lambda\left(\sqrt{\chi(\psi + 2\theta)}\right)}{K_\lambda\left(\sqrt{\chi(\psi)}\right)} \tag{12.204}$$

Next, we define the hyperbolic distribution as a normal variance-mean mixture with the generalized inverse Gaussian mixing distribution $GIG(1, \chi, \psi)$. A random variable Z has the hyperbolic distribution, if

$$(Z|Y) \sim N(\mu + \alpha Y, Y),$$

where $Y \sim GIG(1, \chi, \psi)$. This means that $Z \sim Hyp(\chi, \psi, \alpha, \mu)$ can be represented as $Z = \mu + \alpha Y + \sqrt{Y} N(0, 1)$ with ch.f.

$$\Phi_z(u) = e^{iy\mu} \int_0^\infty e^{\{i\alpha z u - \frac{1}{2}z u^2\}} dF_Y(z). \tag{12.205}$$

Density function $f(x) = f(x; \chi, \psi, \alpha, \mu)$ can be written as

$$\begin{aligned} f(x) \quad = \quad & \frac{(\psi/\chi)^{1/2}}{2K_1(\sqrt{\chi\psi})}(\psi + \alpha^2)^{-1/2} \\ & \exp\left\{-\sqrt{(\psi + \alpha^2)}(\chi + (x - \mu)^2) + \alpha(x - \mu)\right\}. \end{aligned}$$

Theorem 12.3 implies that if $\mu = 0$ then the hyperbolic distribution is a limit law of sums with a random number of components. Now we need to find the corresponding N_n and sequence $(X_{n,k})$. Recall that N_n has to be such that

$$\frac{N_n}{n} \xrightarrow{d} Y \sim GIG(1, \chi, \psi)$$

when $n \to \infty$. One device for the law of N_n is the "discrete hyperbolic distribution"

$$P(N_n = k) = P(k - 1 < nY \leq k)$$

Further, we shall find $(X_{n,k})$ such that $\sum_{k=1}^n X_{n,k} \to X$ with $X \sim N(\alpha, \sigma^2)$. Then, we will have convergence

$$\log S_{N_n}/S_0 = \sum_{k=1}^{N_n} X_{n,k} \xrightarrow{d} Z$$

where the ch.f. of Z is given by

$$\begin{aligned}\phi_Z(u) &= \int_0^\infty \exp\left\{iazu - \tfrac{1}{2}z\sigma^2u^2\right\}dF_Y(z) \\ &= \int_0^\infty \exp\left\{i\tfrac{a}{\sigma^2}zu - \tfrac{1}{2}zu^2\right\}dF_{\sigma^2 Y}(z).\end{aligned}$$

To find the parameters of Z for the hyperbolic model, note that if $Y \sim GIG(1;\chi,\psi)$, then $aY \sim GIG(1;\chi,\psi/a)$ and, therefore, $Z \sim Hyp(\sigma^2\chi,\psi/\sigma^2, \alpha/\sigma^2,0)$. This gives rise to

Corollary 12.2 Under the assumption of Corollary 12.1 and $N_n/n \overset{d}{\to} GIG(1; \chi,\psi)$ the series $\sum_{k=1}^{N_n} X_{n,k}$ converges weakly to

$$Z \sim Hyp\left(\sigma^2\chi, \frac{\psi}{\sigma^{2\prime}} \frac{\alpha}{\sigma^{2\prime}},0\right).$$

Next, we apply Theorem 12.8, to obtain the binomial option pricing formula for asset returns with hyperbolic distribution.

In fact by Theorem 12.4 we have the following version of Gnedenko's transfer theorem (see, for example, Rachev and Rüschendorf, (1994a)).

Corollary 12.3 Let $(X_{n,k})_{k\geq 1}$ be sequences of iid r.v.'s (in each series), $n \geq 1$; and let (N_n) be a sequence of positive integral-valued r.v.'s independent of $(X_{n,k})$. If

$$\sum_{k=1}^n X_{n,k} \overset{d}{\to} N(\alpha,\sigma^2), \quad \frac{N_n}{n} \overset{w}{\to} Y,$$

then, $\sum_{k=1}^{N_n} X_{n,k} \overset{d}{\to} Z$, where the ch.f. of Z is

$$\phi_Z(u) = \int_0^\infty \exp\left\{iazu - \frac{\sigma^2 z}{2}u^2\right\}dF_Y(z). \tag{12.206}$$

Next, we consider the special version of Theorem 12.8, in which Z has a hyperbolic distribution.

Corollary 12.4 Let α,α',σ and σ' be the parameters of the Gaussian laws obtained as limit distributions of $\log S_n/S_0$ as specified in Theorem 12.8; and let N_n be a positive integer-valued r.v. independent of sequence $\log S_n/S_0$, such that

$$\frac{N_n}{n} \overset{d}{\to} Y \quad \text{and } R^n \to R_0^{-\tau},$$

where Y has the generalized inverse Gaussian distribution $GIG(1,\chi,\psi)$. Then, the fair price of the call is given by

$$\begin{aligned}C &= lim_{n\to\infty}C(N_n) \tag{12.207} \\ &= S_0 \int_{\log K/S_0}^\infty f\left(x;\sigma'^2\chi, \frac{\psi}{\sigma'^2}, \frac{\alpha'}{\sigma'^2},0\right)dx \\ &\quad -K\left(\mathbf{E}\bar{R}_0^{-\tau y}\right)\int_{\log K/S_0}^\infty f\left(x;\sigma'^2\chi, \frac{\psi + 2t\log r_0}{\sigma'^2}, \frac{\alpha'}{\sigma^2},0\right)dx,\end{aligned}$$

where $f(\cdot)$ denotes the density of the hyperbolic distribution.

The proof is similar to that of Theorem 12.8; for details we refer to Rejman, Weron and Weron (1997).

Consider the following example. Let $\log S_n/S_0$ be a random walk on the interval $[0, \tau]$ with

$$U = \tilde{\sigma}\sqrt{\frac{t}{n}}, D = -U = -\tilde{\sigma}\sqrt{\frac{t}{n}}, \quad R^n = \bar{R}_0^t, \quad p = \frac{1}{2} + \frac{1}{2}\frac{m}{\sigma}\sqrt{\frac{t}{n}}.$$

Such a process converges to a Brownian motion with drift and then $\log S_t/S_0 \overset{d}{=} N(\alpha, \sigma^2)$, where $\alpha = E\log S_t/S_0 = t(m - \tilde{\sigma}^2/2)$ and $\sigma^2 = Var(\log S_t/S_0) = t\tilde{\sigma}^2$. Here, however, we consider the random walk with a stochastic number of components driven by N_n, such that $N_n/n \overset{d}{\to} Y \sim GIG(1, \chi, \psi)$. With n tending to infinity we have a new limit distribution, namely

$$\begin{aligned} Z &= \log S_t/S_0 = Y\alpha + \sqrt{Y}\sigma N(0,1) \qquad (12.208) \\ &= Hyp(\hat{\chi}, \hat{\psi}, \hat{m}, \hat{\mu},) = Hyp\left(\sigma^2\chi, \frac{\psi}{\sigma^2}, \frac{m}{\sigma^2}, \hat{\mu}\right), \end{aligned}$$

which is similar to what we have observed in (12.200.)

Eberlein and Keller (1995) assume that returns, S_t, have a hyperbolic distribution and, therefore, can be written as

$$\log S_1/S_0 = \mu + \hat{m}\hat{Y} + \sqrt{\hat{Y}}N(0,1)$$

with $\hat{Y} \sim GIG(1, \hat{\chi}, \hat{\psi})$. Together with the hypothesis of independent increments they obtain the Lévy motion process whose daily increments follow the hyperbolic law. In the hyperbolic CRR model, see (12.207), all cumulative returns are hyperbolic in contrast to the model of Eberlein and Keller (1995).

To compute the option price, see Corollary 12.4, we define the densities of Z' and Z^* as follows

$$\begin{aligned} Z' &\sim Hyp\left(\sigma^2\chi, \frac{\psi}{\sigma^{2'}}\frac{\alpha + \sigma^2}{\sigma^2}, 0\right) \qquad (12.209) \\ Z^* &\sim Hyp\left(\sigma^2\chi, \frac{\psi + 2t\log r_0}{\sigma^2}, \frac{\alpha}{\sigma^2}, 0\right), \end{aligned}$$

where $\alpha = t(\log r_0 - \tilde{\sigma}^2/2)$. Eberlein and Keller (1995) approximate the parameters of the hyperbolic law of daily returns of stocks in the German stock market and for the Deutsche Bank they receive

$$\hat{\chi} = 910^{-6}, \quad \hat{\psi} = 11794.12, \quad \hat{m} = 0.3972, \quad \hat{\mu} = 0.$$

They establish also $t = 10, S_0 = 700\text{DM}$ and the annual interest rate $r = 0.08$. Notice that in (12.207)-(12.208) we have an additional parameter σ which

	$\sigma = 2.0$	$\sigma = 1.0$	$\sigma = 0.5$	$\sigma = 0.1$	$\sigma = 0.05$
K = 680	24.0118	24.0118	24.0119	24.0308	24.0553
K = 700	10.7714	10.7718	10.7717	10.7734	10.8259
K = 720	4.2417	4.2418	4.2419	4.2475	4.2641

can not be computed from the other parameters and therefore we calculate the option price for different σ's and the parameters given above

Since in our case the parameter σ does not have a large influence on the price of the call, we set $\sigma = 1$. The table below presents prices of the call for different models: the Black-Scholes model (BS), the hyperbolic model of Eberlein and Keller (1995), and the CRR hyperbolic model (see Corollary 12.4)

strike K	BS price	hyperbolic EK price	hyperbolic CRR price
680	25.462	25.444	24.011
700	12.666	12.579	10.771
720	5.015	4.995	4.241

Rejman, Weron and Weron (1997) made the observation that the hyperbolic CRR prices are different from the hyperbolic EK prices. In the classical Black-Scholes model the price for a European call in continuous time coincides with the limit of the binomial option prices as the number of periods to the terminal time goes to infinity. As soon as one moves away from the normal assumption for the asset returns, it is not clear that both approaches (continuous and discrete) will lead to the same price. Eberlein and Keller (1995), and Küchler et al. (1994) report that the hyperbolic distributions provide better fit to German stock return data than the normal distribution. Thus it is natural to consider Black-Scholes-type formula for asset returns following hyperbolic law. The above example demonstrates clearly the sharp difference in obtained prices. As Rejman, Weron and Weron (1997) argued, the observed difference between the Black-Scholes and the hyperbolic CRR prices is an expected feature as we move away from the normal assumption [7].

Distributional assumptions concerning security returns play a key role in option pricing. Beginning with the work of Mandelbrot (1963a,b,c), evidence indicates that empirical distributions of daily stock returns differ significantly from the traditional Gaussian model, see e.g. Mittnik and Rachev (1993a,b) and references therein. In a search for satisfactory descriptive models of financial data, large numbers of distributions have been tried and many further distributions have been proposed recently. Küchler et al. (1994) and Eberlein and Keller (1995) show that the hyperbolic law fits data from the German

---

[7]We shall examine again the hyperbolic model in the next chapter.

stock market much better than the Gaussian one. Moreover, Eberlein and Keller (1995) apply a hyperbolic Lévy motion process as a model of stock returns. Barndorff–Nielsen (1995) proposed the normal inverse Gaussian (NIG) Lévy process for modeling stock returns. Such distributions have heavier tails than the hyperbolic ones. Hurst, Platen and Rachev (1997) performed tests on the Dow Jones and Nikkei 225 indexes to determine which of a number of subordinated models best captures the typical tail behavior of these indexes. They found that the three parameter log Student t model, which is a special case of the generalized hyperbolic model, gave the best fit.

In Sections 12.9 – 12.13 we will use generalized hyperbolic distributions in the framework proposed by Rachev and Rüschendorf (1994a) (denoted herein by RR), see Sections 12.1 – 12.6. Following Section 12.5 we find option prices for the generalized hyperbolic RR model. We compare these prices with prices determined by exponential tilting for the hyperbolic Lévy model of Eberlein and Keller (1995), the NIG Lévy model of Barndorff–Nielsen (1995) and the NIG subordinated model studied by Hurst, Platen and Rachev (1997). None of the pricing formulas presented in this paper is "canonical", because the market is incomplete under the considered models.

12.9   The Rachev-Rüschendorf approach

In this section we start by recalling basic ideas of the Cox, Ross and Rubinstein (1979) option pricing model and its extensions. Assume that the stock price $S = (S_k)$ follows a multiplicative binomial process over discrete periods which divide the time interval $[0, t]$ into n parts of length h

$$S_{k+1} = \begin{cases} uS_k & \text{with probability} \quad q \\ dS_k & \text{with probability} \quad 1 - q \end{cases}$$

where $S_0 > 0$ and $u > 1 > d$ are real constants.

Define $U = \log u$ and $D = \log d$. Let $\epsilon_{n,i}$ be a sequence of independent random variables with $\mathbf{P}(\epsilon_{n,i} = 1) = q$ and $\mathbf{P}(\epsilon_{n,i} = 0) = 1 - q$. The cumulative return process can be defined as

$$\log \frac{S_k}{S_0} = \sum_{i=1}^{k} (\epsilon_{n,i} U + (1 - \epsilon_{n,i})D) = \sum_{i=1}^{k} X_{n,i}, \quad k = 1, \ldots, n. \quad (12.210)$$

Furthermore, assume that $\rho \in (d, u)$ is one plus the riskless interest rate over one period, i.e. $B_{k+1} = \rho B_k$, where B_k is the currency (e.g. USD) amount in riskless bonds. Under such assumptions Cox, Ross and Rubinstein determined the fair price of a European call option with strike K and maturity n (or equivalently t)

$$C_n = S_0 \Psi(a, n, p') - K\rho^{-n}\Psi(a, n, p), \quad (12.211)$$

where

$$p = \frac{\rho - d}{u - d}, \quad p' = \frac{u}{\rho} p, \quad a = 1 + \left\lfloor \log \frac{K}{S_0 d^n} \Big/ \log \frac{u}{d} \right\rfloor,$$

$$\Psi(a, n, p) = \mathbf{P}(\sum_{i=1}^{n} \epsilon_{n,i}^{\star} \geq a),$$

and $\epsilon_{n,i}^{\star}$ is a sequence of independent random variables with distribution $\mathbf{P}(\epsilon_{n,i}^{\star} = 1) = p$ and $\mathbf{P}(\epsilon_{n,i}^{\star} = 0) = 1 - p$. Here $\lfloor x \rfloor$ denotes the integer part of x.

Now, assume that the number of changes n of the underlying asset in the interval $[0, t]$ increases to infinity. Note that the random walk $\log(S_n/S_0)$ depends on $U = U(n)$, $D = D(n)$, $q = q(n)$ and $\rho = \rho(n)$. In Theorem 12.1 we found necessary and sufficient conditions for the convergence of the sums $\sum_{k=1}^{n} X_{n,k}$ to the Gaussian law. In what follows we assume that for some m and σ^2

$$\sum_{k=1}^{n} X_{n,k} \xrightarrow{d} N(m, \sigma^2).$$

Moreover, we assume that we obtain Gaussian limits with parameters β, σ^2 and β', σ'^2 for probability measures for which the random walk $\log(S_n/S_0)$ exhibits upward movements with probabilities p and p', respectively.

In order to obtain the Black-Scholes formula as a limit of (12.211) it is necessary to assume that $\lim \rho^n(n) = e^{rt}$, where r denotes the riskless interest rate. Then

$$C_n \to C_t = S_0 \Phi(x') - K e^{-rt} \Phi(x), \tag{12.212}$$

where $x = (\log(S_0/K) + \beta)/\sigma$, $x' = (\log(S_0/K) + \beta')/\sigma'$ and $\Phi(x)$ is the standard normal distribution function.

Rachev and Rüschendorf (1994a) propose a model with a random number of components (RR), see Section 12.3. Introducing N_n, a positive integer valued random variable independent of the sequence $(X_{n,k})$, they define the stock price that exhibits a random number of jumps $X_{n,k}$ in the interval $[0, t]$ and then let

$$\log \frac{S_t}{S_0} = \log \frac{S_{N_n}}{S_0} = \sum_{k=1}^{N_n} X_{n,k}. \tag{12.213}$$

The following general framework can be applied here.

Theorem 12.10 Let $(X_{n,k})_{k \geq 1}$ be sequences of independent and identically distributed random variables (in each series), $n \geq 1$, and let (N_n) be a sequence of positive integer valued random variables independent of $(X_{n,k})$. If

$$\sum_{k=1}^{n} X_{n,k} \xrightarrow{d} N(\beta, \sigma^2) \quad \text{and} \quad \frac{N_n}{n} \xrightarrow{w} Y,$$

then $\sum_{k=1}^{N_n} X_{n,k} \xrightarrow{d} Z$, where the characteristic function of Z is

$$\phi_Z(u) = \mathbf{E} e^{iuZ} = \int_0^\infty \exp\left\{i\beta zu - \frac{\sigma^2 z}{2} u^2\right\} dF_Y(z). \qquad (12.214)$$

See Section 12.3 and Gnedenko (1983a,b) or Rachev and Rüschendorf (1994a) for the proof.

The above formula (12.214) shows that all normal variance–mean mixtures can be obtained as a limiting distribution of sums of independent binomial random variables with a random number of components.

12.10   Generalized Hyperbolic Distributions

Let us start by recalling the generalized inverse Gaussian distribution. A random variable Y has the generalized inverse Gaussian distribution $GIG(\lambda, \chi, \psi)$ if its density has the form

$$f_Y(x) = \frac{(\psi/\chi)^{\lambda/2}}{2K_\lambda(\sqrt{\chi\psi})}\, x^{\lambda-1} \exp\left\{-\frac{1}{2}[\chi\,x^{-1} + \psi\,x]\right\}, \quad x > 0,$$

where the normalizing constant $K_\lambda(\cdot)$ is a modified Bessel function of the third kind with index λ. The GIG distribution is often characterized by its Laplace transform

$$\mathbf{E}\exp(-\theta\,Y) = \frac{\psi^{\lambda/2}}{(\psi + 2\theta)^{\lambda/2}}\, \frac{K_\lambda\left(\sqrt{\chi(\psi + 2\theta)}\right)}{K_\lambda\left(\sqrt{\chi\psi}\right)}. \qquad (12.215)$$

The generalized hyperbolic distribution is defined as a normal variance-mean mixture where GIG is the mixing distribution. More precisely, a random variable Z has the generalized hyperbolic distribution if

$$(Z|Y) \sim \mathrm{N}\left(\mu + \beta Y, Y\right),$$

where $Y \sim GIG(\lambda, \chi, \psi)$. This means that $Z \sim GHyp(\lambda, \chi, \psi, \beta, \mu)$ can be represented in the form $Z = \mu + \beta Y + \sqrt{Y} N(0,1)$ with the characteristic function

$$\phi_Z(u) = \exp(iu\mu) \int_0^\infty \exp\left\{i\beta zu - \frac{1}{2}zu^2\right\} dF_Y(z). \qquad (12.216)$$

For $\lambda = 1$ we obtain the hyperbolic distribution itself and its density function is given in the form

$$\begin{aligned}
f(x) &= f(x; \lambda = 1, \chi, \psi, \beta, \mu) \\
&= \frac{(\psi/\chi)^{1/2}}{2K_1(\sqrt{\chi\psi})}(\psi + \beta^2)^{-\frac{1}{2}} \times \\
&\quad \exp\left[-\sqrt{(\psi + \beta^2)(\chi + (x-\mu)^2)} + \beta(x - \mu)\right]. \quad (12.217)
\end{aligned}$$

See Barndorff–Nielsen (1977) for details. Küchler et al. (1994) and Eberlein and Keller (1995) find that the hyperbolic distribution provides an excellent fit to the distributions of daily returns, measured on the log scale, of stocks from a number of leading German enterprises. However, one desirable feature that the class of hyperbolic distributions lacks is that of being closed under convolution.

For $\lambda = -\frac{1}{2}$ we obtain the normal inverse Gaussian distribution (NIG) introduced by Barndorff–Nielsen (1995) with density $f(x) = f(x; \lambda = -\frac{1}{2}, \chi, \psi, \beta, \mu)$ in the form

$$
\begin{aligned}
f(x) &= \frac{1}{\pi} \sqrt{\chi} e^{\sqrt{\chi \psi}} \sqrt{\frac{\psi + \beta^2}{(x - \mu)^2 + \chi}} \times \\
&\quad K_1 \left(\sqrt{((x - \mu)^2 + \chi)(\psi + \beta^2)} \right) e^{\beta(x - \mu)}.
\end{aligned} \tag{12.218}
$$

This law is represented as a normal variance-mean mixture where the mixing distribution is the classical inverse Gaussian law, hence its name. In contrast to the hyperbolic distribution the NIG is closed under convolution.

Comparison of (12.214) and (12.216) implies that if $\mu = 0$ then the generalized hyperbolic distribution is a limiting law of sums with a random number of components. It is sufficient to find N_n and the sequence $(X_{n,k})$. Recall that we need N_n such that

$$
\frac{N_n}{n} \overset{d}{\to} Y \sim,
$$

when $n \to \infty$. A possible choice for N_n is

$$
\mathbf{P}(N_n = k) = \mathbf{P}(k - 1 < nY \le k).
$$

Further, let $(X_{n,k})$ be such that $\sum_{k=1}^{n} X_{n,k} \overset{d}{\to} X \sim N(\beta, \sigma^2)$. Then $\log(S_{N_n}/S_0) = \sum_{k=1}^{N_n} X_{n,k} \overset{d}{\to} Z$, where the characteristic function of Z is given by

$$
\begin{aligned}
\phi_Z(u) &= \int_0^\infty \exp \left\{ i\beta z u - \frac{1}{2} z \sigma^2 u^2 \right\} dF_Y(z) \\
&= \int_0^\infty \exp \left\{ i \frac{\beta}{\sigma^2} z u - \frac{1}{2} z u^2 \right\} dF_{\sigma^2 Y}(z).
\end{aligned}
$$

To find the parameters of the distribution notice that if

$$
Y \sim GIG(\lambda, \chi, \psi) \quad \text{then} \quad aY \sim GIG(\lambda, a\chi, \psi/a),
$$

and therefore $Z \sim GHyp(\lambda, \sigma^2 \chi, \psi/\sigma^2, \beta/\sigma^2, 0)$.
Consequently we have

Corollary 12.5 Under the assumptions of Theorem 12.10, if $\sum_{k=1}^{n} X_{n,k} \overset{d}{\to} N(\beta, \sigma^2)$ and $N_n/n \overset{d}{\to} GIG(\lambda, \chi, \psi)$, then the series $\sum_{k=1}^{N_n} X_{n,k}$ converges weakly to

$$Z \sim GHyp\left(\lambda,\ \sigma^2\chi,\ \frac{\psi}{\sigma^2},\ \frac{\beta}{\sigma^2},\ 0\right).$$

This result will be applied in the option pricing in the next section.

12.11 Option Pricing in Discrete Models

The CRR formula (12.211) gives the fair price of a call with the expiration time t and a fixed number of jumps in the interval $[0, t]$. Rachev and Rüschendorf (1994a) propose a "rational" price of a call when the number of jumps in the interval is the random variable N_n as follows. Let $C(k)$ denote the fair price of a call option for the underlying asset with k movements $X_{n,i}$ until time t, and $C(N_n)$ denote the "rational" price of a call option for the underlying asset with a random number of jumps. It is natural to define $C(N_n)$ as the mean value of the option prices $C(k)$

$$C(N_n) = \sum_{k=1}^{\infty} C(k)\mathbf{P}(N_n = k). \tag{12.219}$$

Following the Editor's comments on page 172 of Rachev and Rüschendorf (1994a) we assume the following scenario. At the beginning the quantity N_n is chosen by the market. If $N_n = k$, then the seller of the option has an opportunity to choose his hedging strategy π_k, dependent on k. In this case the value $C(k)$ is set equal to $\inf x(\pi_k)$, where $x(\pi_k)$ is the premium paid to the seller of the option, and inf is taken with respect to all hedging strategies. If we take $C(N_n) = \mathbf{E} \inf x(\pi_{N_n})$ then

$$C(N_n) = \mathbf{E} \inf x(\pi_{N_n}) = \sum_{k} C(k)\mathbf{P}(N_n = k).$$

The quantity $C(N_n)$ reflects the average value, which the buyer of the option should pay for its purchase. We will refer to this value as the RR price.

From equation (12.219) we obtain the counterpart of equation (12.211)

$$
\begin{aligned}
C(N_n) &= \sum_{k=1}^{\infty} \left(S_0\Psi(a_k, k, p') - K\rho^{-k}\Psi(a_k, k, p)\right)\mathbf{P}(N_n = k) \\
&= S_0\mathbf{E}\Psi(a_{N_n}, N_n, p') - K\mathbf{E}\rho^{-N_n}\Psi(a_{N_n}, N_n, p), \tag{12.220}
\end{aligned}
$$

where $p = p(n)$, $p' = p'(n)$,

$$a_k = 1 + \left\lfloor \log\frac{K}{S_0 d(n)^k} \middle/ \log\frac{u(n)}{d(n)} \right\rfloor,$$

$$\Psi(a_k, k, p) = \mathbf{P}(\textstyle\sum_{i=1}^{k} \epsilon_{n,i} \geq a_k)$$

with $\mathbf{P}(\epsilon_{n,i} = 1) = p$ and $\mathbf{P}(\epsilon_{n,i} = 0) = 1 - p$, the expectation $\mathbf{E}$ is taken with respect to N_n.

Formula (12.220) is complicated from the computational point of view. For this reason it is natural to look for its limiting case. We will find the option pricing formulas in the Rachev–Rüschendorf framework when the log price of a stock is driven by the generalized hyperbolic distribution.

Theorem 12.11 Let $\beta, \beta', \sigma, \sigma'$ be the parameters of the Gaussian laws obtained as limiting distributions of $\log(S_n/S_0)$ for the different probability measures considered in Section 12.9, and let N_n be a positive integer valued random variable independent of the sequence $\log(S_n/S_0)$ such that

$$\frac{N_n}{n} \xrightarrow{d} Y \quad \text{and} \quad \rho^n \to e^{rt},$$

where Y has the generalized inverse Gaussian distribution. Then the limiting RR price of a call option, where the underlying asset has a random number of jumps, is given by

$$
\begin{aligned}
C \;=\; & \lim_{n\to\infty} C(N_n) = S_0 \int_{\log(K/S_0)}^{\infty} f\left(x; \lambda, \sigma'^2 \chi, \frac{\psi}{\sigma'^2}, \frac{\beta'}{\sigma'^2}, 0\right)\, dx \\
& - \; K\, \mathbf{E} e^{-rtY} \int_{\log(K/S_0)}^{\infty} f\left(x; \lambda, \sigma^2 \chi, \frac{\psi + 2rt}{\sigma^2}, \frac{\beta}{\sigma^2}, 0\right)\, dx, \quad (12.221)
\end{aligned}
$$

where $f(\cdot)$ denotes the density of the generalized hyperbolic distribution with the given parameters.

Proof. To prove the theorem we have to find the limits of the expectations in (12.220). From the definition of $\Psi(a_{N_n}, N_n, p')$ and $X_{n,k}$ we have

$$
\begin{aligned}
\mathbf{E}\Psi(a_{N_n}, N_n, p') \;&=\; \sum_{k=1}^{\infty} \mathbf{P}\left(\sum_{i=1}^{k} \tilde{X}(k) \geq 0\right) \mathbf{P}(N_n = k) \\
&=\; \mathbf{P}\left(\sum_{i=1}^{N_n} \tilde{X}(N_n) \geq 0\right),
\end{aligned}
$$

where $\tilde{X}(k) = \sum_{i=1}^{k} X_{n,i} - a_k R - kD$. Observe that the characteristic function of $\tilde{X}(N_n)$ has the form

$$
\mathbf{E} \exp\left(i\, u \tilde{X}(N_n)\right) = \int_0^{\infty} e^{i\, u(-a_{nx} R - nx D)} \left(\phi_{X_{n,1}}^n(u)\right)^x d\mathbf{P}^{\frac{N_n}{n}}(x).
$$

Since $\phi_{X_{n,1}}^n(u) \to \phi_{N(\beta',\sigma'^2)}(u)$, $R = R(n) = U(n) - D(n) \to 0$ and consequently $a_{nx} R + nx D \to \log(K/S_0)$ (see (12.221)), we have the following form of the limiting characteristic function

$$
\mathbf{E} \exp\left(iu\tilde{X}(N_n)\right) \to \int_0^{\infty} e^{i\, u(-\log(K/S_0))} \left(\phi_{N(\beta',\sigma'^2)}(u)\right)^x d\mathbf{P}^{Y}(x),
$$

where we have used the fact that $\frac{N_n}{n} \overset{d}{\to} Y$. Now, it is clear that

$$\tilde{X}(N_n) \overset{d}{\to} Z' - \log \frac{K}{S_0},$$

where $Z' \sim GHyp(\lambda, \sigma'^2\chi, \psi/\sigma'^2, \beta'/\sigma'^2, 0)$. Finally, we deduce that

$$\mathbf{E}\Psi(a_{N_n}, N_n, p') \quad \to \quad \mathbf{P}\left(Z' \geq \log \frac{K}{S_0}\right) \tag{12.222}$$

$$= \int_{\log(K/S_0)}^{\infty} f\left(x; \lambda, \sigma'^2\chi, \frac{\psi}{\sigma'^2}, \frac{\beta'}{\sigma'^2}, 0\right) dx.$$

Similarly we compute the second integral in (12.220)

$$\mathbf{E}\rho^{-N_n}\Psi(a_{N_n}, N_n, p) = \sum_{k=1}^{\infty} \mathbf{P}\left(\sum_{i=1}^{k} \epsilon_{n,i} \geq a_k\right) \rho^{-k}\mathbf{P}(N_n = k)$$

$$= \mathbf{E}\rho^{-N_n} \sum_{k=1}^{\infty} \mathbf{P}\left(\tilde{X}(k) \geq 0\right) \frac{\rho^{-k}\mathbf{P}(N_n = k)}{\mathbf{E}\rho^{-N_n}}$$

$$= \mathbf{E}\rho^{-N_n} \mathbf{P}\left(\tilde{X}(N_n^\star) \geq 0\right),$$

where $N_n^\star$ has the distribution $\mathbf{P}(N_n^\star = k) = \rho^{-k}\mathbf{P}(N_n = k)/\mathbf{E}\rho^{-N_n}$. Since $\lim \rho^n = e^{rt}$, we have

$$\mathbf{E}\rho^{-N_n} \to \mathbf{E}e^{-rtY} \quad \text{with} \quad Y \sim GIG(\lambda, \chi, \psi).$$

Further, we get

$$\tilde{X}(N_n^\star) \overset{d}{\to} Z^\star - \log \frac{K}{S_0},$$

where $\text{Law}(Z^\star)$ is the limiting distribution of

$$\sum_{k=1}^{N_n^\star} X_{n,k},$$

with $N_n^\star/n \overset{d}{\to} Y^\star$. To identify the mixing distribution $\text{Law}(Y^\star)$ we first compute the Laplace transform of $\frac{N_n^\star}{n}$ by Lemma 5.1 of Rachev–Rüschendorf (1994)

$$\mathbf{E}e^{-\theta \frac{N_n^\star}{n}} = \frac{\mathbf{E}\exp\left(-\frac{N_n}{n}(\theta + tr + \delta_n)\right)}{\mathbf{E}\rho^{-N_n}},$$

with $\delta_n \to 0$. When n tends to infinity we obtain the Laplace transform of $Y^\star$

$$\mathbf{E}e^{-\theta \frac{N_n^\star}{n}} \to \frac{\mathbf{E}e^{-Y(\theta+rt)}}{\mathbf{E}e^{-rtY}}. \tag{12.223}$$

The above limit is a quotient of two Laplace transforms of the generalized inverse Gaussian distribution at the points $\theta + tr$ and tr. From (12.215) we have

$$\frac{\mathbf{E}e^{-Y(\theta+tr)}}{\mathbf{E}e^{-rtY}} = \frac{(\psi + 2tr)^{\lambda/2}}{(\psi + 2\theta + 2tr)^{\lambda/2}} \frac{K_\lambda\left(\sqrt{\chi(\psi + 2\theta + 2tr)}\right)}{K_\lambda\left(\sqrt{\chi(\psi + 2tr)}\right)}.$$

Hence, Y^* has the generalized inverse Gaussian distribution $GIG(\lambda, \chi, \psi+2tr)$ and therefore

$$Z^* \sim GHyp\left(\lambda, \sigma^2\chi, \frac{\psi + 2tr}{\sigma^2}, \frac{\beta}{\sigma^2}, 0\right).$$

Moreover

$$\mathbf{E}\rho^{-N_n} \Psi(a_{N_n}, N_n, p) \to \mathbf{E}e^{-rtY} P\left(Z^* \geq \log \frac{K}{S_0}\right) \qquad (12.224)$$

$$= \mathbf{E}e^{-rtY} \int_{\log(K/S_0)}^{\infty} f\left(x; \lambda, \sigma^2\chi, \frac{\psi + 2tr}{\sigma^2}, \frac{\beta}{\sigma^2}, 0\right) dx.$$

Collecting the results (12.220), (12.222), and (12.224) we complete the proof.

□

Finally, we obtain the RR price of a call option for the generalized hyperbolic model.

Corollary 12.6 Let $\log(S_n/S_0)$ be the random walk on the interval $[0, t]$ defined in Section 12.9 with

$$U = \hat{\sigma}\sqrt{\frac{t}{n}}, \quad D = -U = -\hat{\sigma}\sqrt{\frac{t}{n}}, \quad \rho^n = e^{rt}, \quad q = \frac{1}{2} + \frac{1}{2}\frac{m}{\hat{\sigma}}\sqrt{\frac{t}{n}},$$

such that $\log(S_n/S_0) \overset{d}{\to} N(mt, \hat{\sigma}^2 t)$ and let $N_n/n \to Y \sim GIG(\lambda, \chi, \psi)$. Then

$$\log(S_{N_n}/S_0) \overset{d}{\to} GHyp\left(\lambda, \hat{\sigma}^2 t\chi, \frac{\psi}{\hat{\sigma}^2 t}, \frac{m}{\hat{\sigma}^2}, 0\right),$$

and

$$C = \lim_{n\to\infty} C(N_n) = S_0 \int_{\log(K/S_0)}^{\infty} f\left(x; \lambda, \hat{\sigma}^2 t\chi, \frac{\psi}{\hat{\sigma}^2 t}, \frac{r}{\hat{\sigma}^2} + \frac{1}{2}, 0\right) dx$$

$$- K\, \mathbf{E}e^{-rtY} \int_{\log(K/S_0)}^{\infty} f\left(x; \lambda, \hat{\sigma}^2 t\chi, \frac{\psi + 2rt}{\hat{\sigma}^2 t}, \frac{r}{\hat{\sigma}^2} - \frac{1}{2}, 0\right) dx. (12.225)$$

12.12   Option Pricing in Continuous Time Models

In this section we present an overview of recent development in the continuous time generalized hyperbolic models for stock prices. For some of these models we derive the potential option prices determined by the technique of exponential tilting proposed by Gerber and Shiu (1994).

12.12.1 The hyperbolic and NIG Lévy models

The model of stock prices which produces exactly hyperbolic returns along time intervals of length 1 is the process

$$S_t = S_0 \exp(Z_t), \tag{12.226}$$

where $(Z_t)_{t \geq 0}$ is a hyperbolic Lévy process, i.e. $(Z_t)_{t \geq 0}$ is a process with stationary and independent increments and $Z_1 \sim GHyp(1, \chi, \psi, \beta, \mu)$. Following the idea of Gerber and Shiu (1994) Eberlein and Keller (1995) compute a possible option price using the Esscher transform. Let $f_t(x)$ be the density of Law(Z_t). For some real number θ define a new density

$$f_t(x; \theta) = \frac{e^{\theta x} f_t(x)}{\int_{-\infty}^{\infty} e^{\theta x} f_t(x)\, dx}. \tag{12.227}$$

One seeks θ so that the discounted stock process $(e^{-rt} S_t)_{t \geq 0}$ is a martingale with respect to the probability measure corresponding to θ. In particular

$$S_0 = e^{-rt} \mathbf{E}^\theta S_t.$$

Finally, if the derivative security is a European call option with exercise price K and time to expiration t, and the underlying asset price is given by (12.226), then the Gerber–Shiu (GS) value of this option is

$$
\begin{aligned}
C &= e^{-rt} \mathbf{E}^{\theta^*} [S_t - K]_+ \\
&= S_0 \int_{\log(K/S_0)}^{\infty} f_t(x; \theta^* + 1)\, dx \\
&\quad - e^{-rt} K \int_{\log(K/S_0)}^{\infty} f_t(x; \theta^*)\, dx,
\end{aligned} \tag{12.228}
$$

where θ^* is the solution of

$$
\ln \frac{K_1\left(\sqrt{\chi (\psi + \beta^2 - (\beta + \theta^* + 1)^2)}\right)}{K_1\left(\sqrt{\chi (\psi + \beta^2 - (\beta + \theta^*)^2)}\right)} - \frac{1}{2} \ln \frac{\psi + \beta^2 - (\beta + \theta^* + 1)^2}{\psi + \beta^2 - (\beta + \theta^*)^2} = r. \tag{12.229}
$$

A simpler formula was obtained by Barndorff–Nielsen (1995) when $(Z_t)_{t \geq 0}$ is the NIG Lévy motion. Then the GS value of the call option is

$$
\begin{aligned}
C &= S_0 \int_{\log(K/S_0)}^{\infty} f\left(z; -\frac{1}{2}, t^2 \chi, \psi + \beta - (\beta + \theta^* + 1)^2, \beta + (\theta^* + 1), 0\right) dz \\
&\quad - K e^{-rt} \int_{\log(K/S_0)}^{\infty} f\left(z; -\frac{1}{2}, t^2 \chi, \psi + \beta - (\beta + \theta^*)^2, \beta + \theta^*, 0\right) dz, \tag{12.230}
\end{aligned}
$$

where θ^* satisfies the equation

$$\sqrt{\psi + \beta^2 - (\beta + \theta^*)^2} - \sqrt{\psi + \beta^2 - (\beta + \theta^* + 1)^2} = \frac{r}{\sqrt{\chi}}, \qquad (12.231)$$

and $f(\cdot)$ denotes the density of the generalized hyperbolic distribution.

12.12.2   The generalized hyperbolic subordinated model

The method of modeling stock prices by subordinated processes generalizes the classical lognormal asset price model in continuous time. The physical time is substituted by an intrinsic time which provides a long tail effect observed in the market. Suppose that $W = \{W_t, t \geq 0\}$ is a Wiener process and $T = \{T_t, t \geq 0\}$ is a non-negative stochastic process. Then the new process $\{W_{T_t}, t \geq 0\}$ is said to be subordinated to W by the intrinsic time process T.

Hurst, Platen and Rachev (1997) compare a number of subordinated processes as possible models of asset returns and among them analyze an NIG model closely related to that of Barndorff–Nielsen (1995), the Student t model of Praetz (1972) and Blattberg and Gonedes (1974), and the variance gamma model of Madan and Seneta (1990). They model the asset price $S = \{S_t, t \geq 0\}$ by a stochastic equation of the type

$$S_t = S_0 \exp\left\{ \int_0^t \mu(s)\, ds + \int_0^t \rho(s)\, dT_s + \int_0^t \sigma(s)\, dW_{T_s} \right\}, \qquad (12.232)$$

and the riskless bond $B = \{B_t, t \geq 0\}$ as

$$B_t = \exp\left\{ \int_0^t r_s\, ds \right\}, \qquad (12.233)$$

where μ - the drift in the physical time scale, ρ - the drift in the intrinsic time scale, σ - the volatility, r- the riskless interest rate, are real and piecewise constant functions. In the generalized hyperbolic model the intrinsic time process is the generalized inverse Gaussian process with stationary and independent increments such that

$$T_{t+1} - T_t = \text{GIG}(\lambda, \chi, \psi). \qquad (12.234)$$

On the assumption that the asset price follows (12.232) Hurst, Platen and Rachev (1997) proposed to price a European call option with strike price K and time to maturity t as

$$C = S_0 F_-\left(\log\left\{\frac{S_0}{K/B_t}\right\}\right) - \frac{K}{B_t} F_+\left(\log\left\{\frac{S_0}{K/B_t}\right\}\right), \qquad (12.235)$$

where

$$F_\pm(x) = \int_0^\infty \Phi\left(\frac{x \mp \frac{1}{2} y}{\sqrt{y}}\right) dF_Y(y),$$

F_Y is the distribution function of the random variable $Y = \int_0^t \sigma^2(s)\,dT_s$ and Φ denotes the standard normal distribution function. This price, which we will refer to as the HPR price, is determined via a change to an equivalent (but non-unique) martingale measure.

In the case of the NIG subordinated model, obtained by letting $\lambda = -1/2$ in (12.234), the HPR price of a call option for the stock described by the subordinated process (12.232) is

$$
\begin{aligned}
C = \; & S_0 \int_{\log(K/S_0)}^{\infty} f(z; -\frac{1}{2}, \sigma^2 t^2 \chi, \frac{\psi}{\sigma^2}, +\frac{1}{2}, rt)\,dz \qquad (12.236) \\
& - Ke^{-rt} \int_{\log(K/S_0)}^{\infty} f(z; -\frac{1}{2}, \sigma^2 t^2 \chi, \frac{\psi}{\sigma^2}, -\frac{1}{2}, rt)\,dz,
\end{aligned}
$$

provided ρ, σ, r are constant and $\mu = 0$.

12.13   Empirical Analysis

In this section we compare the RR, GS and HPR option prices. To do this consider the price of Dresdner Bank stocks listed on the German Stock Exchange with the current price $S_0 = 40\text{DM}$. The maximum likelihood estimates of the approximating hyperbolic distribution of daily returns are

$$
\psi = 1.3847 \cdot 10^4, \quad \chi = 1.6 \cdot 10^{-5}, \quad \beta = 8.8, \quad \mu = 0,
$$

see Küchler et al. (1994). For the approximating NIG density the parameter values are as follows

$$
\psi = 1.1102 \cdot 10^4, \quad \chi = 4 \cdot 10^{-4}, \quad \beta = 8.8, \quad \mu = 0,
$$

see Barndorff–Nielsen (1995). Note that the variances of the above distributions are not equal. This will result in different Black-Scholes (BS) prices for these models, see Tables 12.1 and 12.2. Suppose that the annual interest rate is 8%, *i.e.* the daily interest rate $r = 0.08/365$. The free parameters $\hat{\sigma}$ and σ in the option pricing formulas (12.225) and (12.236) are equal $\hat{\sigma} = \sigma = 1$, and the option price is computed for $t = 1, 2, 5, 10, 20, 50, 100$ days.

In Figures 12.1 and 12.2 we plot the differences between the option prices of the considered models and the Black-Scholes prices. We start with the NIG Lévy model with GS pricing. Figure 12.1 shows that if the GS method gave the accurate price the Black-Scholes prices would be over-valued at-the-money and under-valued in-the-money and out-of-the-money for small t. For large t the Black-Scholes prices would be always over-valued. This is demonstrated on two different vertical scales. The same conclusions can be drawn for the NIG subordinated model with HPR pricing.

In Figure 12.2 we study the difference between the NIG RR and the Black-Scholes prices. Again, if the RR method gave the accurate price the Black-Scholes prices would be over-valued at-the-money and in-the-money, and

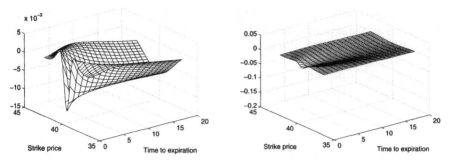

Fig. 12.1 The GS price under the NIG Lévy model minus the BS price with the annual interest rate 8% presented on two different vertical scales. (Adapted from: Rejman, Weron and Weron (1997))

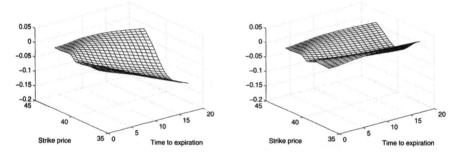

Fig. 12.2 The RR price under the NIG RR model minus the BS price with the annual interest rate (a) 8%, (b) 0%.(Adapted from: Rejman, Weron and Weron (1997))

under-valued deep out-of-the-money. We consider here two different values of the annual interest rate: 8% and 0%.

Figure 12.3 shows differences between the discrete model – the NIG RR and two continuous models – the GS and HPR under the NIG Lévy model with the annual interest rate 8%. In contrast to the classical case, where the CRR model converges to the BS model, here we discover a marked difference. The discrete model does not approximate the continuous in the NIG case!

Summarizing the results we conclude that the difference between the option prices increases as the time to maturity increases. The NIG prices are generally smaller than the Black-Scholes prices. Such a result for hyperbolic prices has been observed by Rejman, Weron and Weron (1997).

Tables 12.1 and 12.2 show that the hyperbolic prices are smaller than the NIG prices for all models. This result is caused by the fact that for the parameters given by Barndorff–Nielsen (1995) and Küchler et al. (1994) the NIG distribution has a higher volatility (standard deviation) than the hyperbolic distribution:

$$\sigma_{NIG} = 0.01387, \quad \sigma_{Hyp} = 0.01283.$$

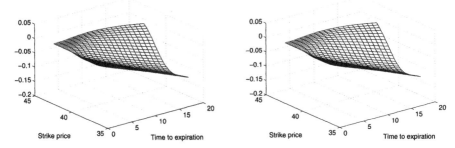

Fig. 12.3   (a) The RR price under the NIG RR model minus the GS price under the NIG Lévy model, (b) the RR price under the NIG RR model minus the HPR price under the NIG Lévy model with the annual interest rate 8%. (Adapted from: Rejman, Weron and Weron (1997))

For this reason we must consider two Gaussian models. In Tables 12.1 and 12.2 we present the Black-Scholes prices with two volatilities for the NIG and the hyperbolic model, separately. Obviously the Black-Scholes prices with σ_{NIG} volatilities are higher than those with σ_{Hyp}.

Eberlein and Keller (1995), Küchler et al. (1994) and Barndorff–Nielsen (1995) show that the hyperbolic and NIG distributions provide a much better fit to stock return data than the normal distribution.

Table 12.1 Option prices – under the NIG and hyperbolic hypotheses with annual interest rate 8%.

Time	K	NIG				hyperbolic		
		BS	GS	HPR	RR	BS	GS	RR
1	38	2.0083	2.0087	2.0088	2.0005	2.0083	2.0088	2.0005
	39	1.0156	1.0191	1.0194	1.0111	1.0130	1.0177	1.0099
	40	0.2258	0.2140	0.2143	0.2099	0.2092	0.1856	0.1855
	41	0.0088	0.0128	0.0127	0.0123	0.0056	0.0113	0.0109
	42	0.0000	0.0007	0.0007	0.0006	0.0000	0.0007	0.0007
2	38	2.0177	2.0191	2.0192	2.0040	2.0171	2.0186	2.0038
	39	1.0514	1.0527	1.0533	1.0392	1.0423	1.0454	1.0333
	40	0.3219	0.3120	0.3125	0.2969	0.2984	0.2823	0.2623
	41	0.0414	0.0429	0.0428	0.0425	0.0309	0.0348	0.0360
	42	0.0018	0.0039	0.0038	0.0052	0.0009	0.0033	0.0050
5	38	2.0643	2.0658	2.0663	2.0329	2.0566	2.0591	2.0289
	39	1.1771	1.1738	1.1748	1.1367	1.1522	1.1482	1.1132
	40	0.5170	0.5088	0.5097	0.4694	0.4798	0.4661	0.4147
	41	0.1617	0.1585	0.1586	0.1448	0.1342	0.1302	0.1199
	42	0.0342	0.0360	0.0359	0.0398	0.0236	0.0271	0.0346
10	38	2.1754	2.1741	2.1751	2.1063	2.1524	2.1517	2.0894
	39	1.3647	1.3594	1.3607	1.2832	1.3228	1.3152	1.2349
	40	0.7440	0.7363	0.7375	0.6638	0.6915	0.6793	0.5865
	41	0.3440	0.3386	0.3392	0.2969	0.2979	0.2901	0.2464
	42	0.1328	0.1315	0.1317	0.1229	0.1035	0.1030	0.1031
20	38	2.4098	2.4056	2.4071	2.2652	2.3629	2.3579	2.2197
	39	1.6704	1.6636	1.6654	1.5193	1.6057	1.5959	1.4347
	40	1.0778	1.0697	1.0714	0.9386	1.0037	0.9917	0.8293
	41	0.6429	0.6358	0.6371	0.5406	0.5720	0.5618	0.4529
	42	0.3530	0.3483	0.3491	0.2977	0.2953	0.2897	0.2464
50	38	3.0201	3.0124	3.0149	2.6798	2.9285	2.9183	2.5650
	39	2.3534	2.3442	2.3469	2.0244	2.2462	2.2334	1.8704
	40	1.7841	1.7742	1.7768	1.4837	1.6680	1.6539	1.3109
	41	1.3146	1.3048	1.3073	1.0600	1.1975	1.1839	0.9014
	42	0.9410	0.9322	0.9343	0.7433	0.8305	0.8187	0.6186
100	38	3.8359	3.8251	3.8286	3.2127	3.6982	3.6839	3.0184
	39	3.2078	3.1959	3.1996	2.6131	3.0555	3.0393	2.3842
	40	2.6491	2.6365	2.6402	2.0972	2.4870	2.4697	1.8530
	41	2.1602	2.1475	2.1511	1.6645	1.9940	1.9765	1.4293
	42	1.7395	1.7271	1.7305	1.3096	1.5746	1.5578	1.1016

(Adapted from: Rejman, Weron and Weron) (1997))

Table 12.2 Option prices – under the NIG and hyperbolic hypotheses with annual interest rate 0%.

Time	K	NIG BS	GS	HPR	RR	hyperbolic BS	GS	RR
1	38	2.0000	2.0004	2.0004	2.0004	2.0000	2.0005	2.0005
	39	1.0073	1.0110	1.0111	1.0111	1.0046	1.0099	1.0099
	40	0.2214	0.2096	0.2099	0.2099	0.2048	0.1850	0.1855
	41	0.0084	0.0122	0.0123	0.0123	0.0054	0.0108	0.0109
	42	0.0000	0.0006	0.0006	0.0006	0.0000	0.0006	0.0007
2	38	2.0011	2.0026	2.0026	2.0040	2.0005	2.0022	2.0038
	39	1.0360	1.0375	1.0377	1.0392	1.0266	1.0301	1.0333
	40	0.3131	0.3032	0.3037	0.2969	0.2896	0.2736	0.2623
	41	0.0395	0.0408	0.0410	0.0425	0.0294	0.0328	0.0360
	42	0.0017	0.0036	0.0036	0.0052	0.0008	0.0030	0.0050
5	38	2.0248	2.0264	2.0266	2.0329	2.0165	2.0194	2.0289
	39	1.1432	1.1401	1.1407	1.1367	1.1175	1.1142	1.1132
	40	0.4951	0.4869	0.4877	0.4694	0.4578	0.4453	0.4147
	41	0.1521	0.1487	0.1494	0.1448	0.1254	0.1216	0.1199
	42	0.0315	0.0331	0.0333	0.0398	0.0215	0.0244	0.0346
10	38	2.1022	2.1011	2.1017	2.1063	2.0777	2.0773	2.0894
	39	1.3033	1.2980	1.2990	1.2832	1.2599	1.2528	1.2349
	40	0.7001	0.6924	0.6936	0.6638	0.6475	0.6360	0.5865
	41	0.3182	0.3127	0.3137	0.2969	0.2733	0.2659	0.2464
	42	0.1205	0.1190	0.1197	0.1229	0.0928	0.0919	0.1031
20	38	2.2773	2.2731	2.2743	2.2652	2.2272	2.2215	2.2197
	39	1.5579	1.5509	1.5525	1.5193	1.4907	1.4822	1.4347
	40	0.9900	0.9819	0.9836	0.9386	0.9156	0.9016	0.8293
	41	0.5807	0.5735	0.5751	0.5406	0.5115	0.5027	0.4529
	42	0.3131	0.3083	0.3096	0.2977	0.2585	0.2521	0.2464
50	38	2.7295	2.7214	2.7237	2.6797	2.6307	2.6190	2.5650
	39	2.0965	2.0870	2.0896	2.0243	1.9845	1.9713	1.8704
	40	1.5649	1.5549	1.5576	1.4836	1.4474	1.4330	1.3109
	41	1.1344	1.1246	1.1273	1.0600	1.0194	1.0057	0.9014
	42	0.7982	0.7895	0.7920	0.7433	0.6929	0.6813	0.6186
100	38	3.3024	3.2908	3.2943	3.2126	3.1521	3.1365	3.0184
	39	2.7208	2.7083	2.7120	2.6130	2.5598	2.5426	2.3842
	40	2.2123	2.1993	2.2032	2.0971	2.0462	2.0282	1.8530
	41	1.7752	1.7624	1.7662	1.6644	1.6100	1.5923	1.4293
	42	1.4061	1.3938	1.3975	1.3096	1.2470	1.2304	1.1016

(Adapted from: Rejman, Weron and Weron (1997))

13

Numerical Results on Option Pricing: Modeling and Forecasting

13.1 Overview

Since its publication, the Black and Scholes (BS, 1973) option pricing model has been subject to a large number of empirical tests [1]. Despite marginal differences in their conclusions, there is overwhelming agreement that the BS model misprices options in a systematic way.[2] One indicator of a systematic mispricing of options is the smile–effect, i.e., the implied volatility (IV), obtained by setting the BS model price equal to the market price and solving for the volatility parameter, is typically higher for options that trade away from the money than for options trading at–the–money (AM).[3] For options on the S&P 500 index Rubinstein (1994)shows that before the crash in October 1987, a plot of IVs against the strike price typically had a U-Form with higher IVs for in– and out–of– than for at–the–money options. For the post–crash period, however, the stylized IV curve is typically asymmetric with higher IVs for calls having low than for calls having high strike prices, see Dumas et al. (1996).The smile-effect is most pronounced for short maturity options whereas the smiles typically flatten down as the time to maturity increases.

The empirical evidence of a smile–effect can be interpreted as evidence against the validity of the BS model. In particular, the Gaussian assump-

---

[1]The results in this chapter are due to Rieken, Mittnik and Rachev (1998), Hurst, Platen and Rachev (1997, 1999) and Schumacher (1997).

[2]See Black and Scholes, (1972) and MacBeth and Merville, (1979) for some early evidence.

[3]See, for example, the studies of Rubinstein (1985, 1994,)Sheikh (1991),Derman and Kani (1994),Heynen (1994)and Dumas et al. (1996)for stock and stock index options and Taylor and Xu (1994)for currency options.

tion for asset returns with constant variance seems to be violated. Empirical distribution of asset and index returns are typically "fat tailed" with large asset price movements having higher probability than predicted by normality. Alternative option pricing models, based on non–normal, more realistic distributional assumptions, have been developed. One possible explanation for fat tails in asset returns is stochastic volatility. The so-called "stochastic volatility" models extend the Gaussian diffusion process governing returns by a second diffusion equation governing the return variance. Bivariate diffusion models in this line with different specifications of both differential equations have been developed by Hull and White (1987), Johnson and Shanno (1987), Scott (1987), Wiggins (1987), Melino and Turnbull (1990), Stein and Stein (1991), and Heston (1993). Discrete time models of time varying volatility are the GARCH–type models.[4] Duan (1995) developed an option pricing model under the assumption that the stock price follows a GARCH process. All these models generate heavy–tailed return distributions and are compatible with the smile–effect.

In this chapter, two alternative approaches to modeling asset prices and their implications for option pricing are analyzed. The first approach is based on the subordination principle introduced by Bochner (1955).The option pricing theory based on a subordinated return process was developed by Hurst *et al.* (1997),see . The second approach is based on a simple generalization of the binomial option price model of Cox, Ross, and Rubinstein (1979), henceforth CRR), see 12 and Schumacher (1997).We shall analyze the empirical performance of each six specifications of the subordinated and ID option pricing model for the pricing of options on the German Stock Index (DAX), which are traded on the Deutsche Terminbörse (DTB). The DAX is constructed as a performance index, i.e., dividends are assumed to be reinvested in the stocks going ex-dividend. Therefore, dividends can be ignored for DAX options pricing and the ambiguity in other studies from from estimating future dividends over the options' time to maturity can be avoided. Also, DAX options are European–type, which further simplifies valuation. By considering DAX options we can therefore focus on the systematic mispricing behavior generated by the different option pricing models that can be attributed to the the specification of the stochastic process generating index returns. considered here are suitable for DAX–options in this respect. The BS model, assuming Gaussian returns, is considered to be the benchmark model for comparison. The characteristics of the different model candidates are analyzed in– and out–of–sample. Before we present the empirical results, the generalizations of the BS and the CRR model are summarized in Section 13.2. A description of the data and estimation and forecasting methodology as well as a discussion of the empirical results follows in Sections 13.3, 13.4 and 13.5.

---

[4]The GARCH model, developed by Bollerslev (1986), is a generalization of the autoregressive conditional heteroskedasticity model introduced by Engle (1982) .

13.2   Description of the Models

13.2.1   The General Subordinated Stock Price Model

The general version of the subordinated stock price model is given by:

$$S_{t+s} = S_t \exp\left\{\mu s + \sigma[W(T(t+s)) - W(T(t))]\right\}, \quad t,s \geq 0, \qquad (13.1)$$

where $W(t)$ is a Wiener process, which is subordinated to the intrinsic time process, $T(t)$, see Section 5.1.1 and Chapter 13.1. Taking the natural logarithm, the process can be written in the equivalent form:

$$\Delta L_{t,s} = L_{t+s} - L_t = \mu s + \sigma[W(T(t+s)) - W(T(t))]. \qquad (13.2)$$

By using a stochastic time scale, the subordinated model allows for time periods of high and low volatility (measured in the physical time scale), depending on the specification of the directing process $\{T(t), t \geq 0\}$. For example, on could specify the intrinsic time process such that the intrinsic time process is equal to physical time, on average, i.e., $E[\Delta T_{t,s}] = s$. Calm periods of low volatility with a slow information flow and low trading volume in the markets would occur if $\Delta T_{t,s} < s$, i.e., intrinsic time passes more slowly than physical time. On the other hand, periods where unexpected information arrives with a high rate combined with high volume and volatility are compatible with $\Delta T_{t,s} > s$, i.e., operational time passes more quickly than physical time. Subordinated processes of the form in (13.1) can therefore be interpreted as stochastic volatility processes. We assume that $\{T(t), t \geq 0\}$ is a process with stationary independent increments.

The probabilistic features of the returns can be studied by combining the constant volatility parameter σ with the subordinated process $W(T(t))$ to get the new process:

$$Z = \widetilde{W}(T(t)) = \sigma W(T(t)), \qquad (13.3)$$

where $\widetilde{W}(t)$ is a Wiener process having stationary independent increments

$$\Delta \widetilde{W}_{t,s} = \widetilde{W}(t+s) - \widetilde{W}(t) \sim N(0, \sigma^2 s), \quad s,t \geq 0. \qquad (13.4)$$

The expected value, variance, and the kurtosis of the increments $\Delta Z_{t,s} = Z_{t+s} - Z_t$, $s,t \geq 0$, are:

$$\mu_{Z,s} = E(\Delta Z_{t,s}) = 0, \qquad (13.5)$$

$$\sigma_{Z,s}^2 = E(\Delta Z_{t,s} - \mu_{Z,s})^2 = \sigma^2 \mu_{T,s}, \qquad (13.6)$$

see Clark (1973). In 13.5 and 13.6 $\mu_{T,s} = E(\Delta T_{t,s})$ is the expected value of an intrinsic time increment in the physical time interval $[t; t+s]$ of length s,

$$\kappa_{Z,s} = \frac{E\left[(\Delta Z_{t,s} - \mu_{Z,s})^4\right]}{\sigma_{Z,s}^4} = 3\left(1 + \frac{\sigma_{T,s}^2}{\mu_{T,s}^2}\right) \qquad (13.7)$$

with $\sigma_{T,s}^2 = E\left[(\Delta T_{t,s} - \mu_{T,s})^2\right]$, and furthermore the skewness of the distribution of $\Delta Z_{t,s}$ is

$$\beta_{Z,s} = \frac{E\left[(\Delta Z_{t,s} - \mu_{Z,s})^3\right]}{\sigma_{Z,s}^3} = 0. \qquad (13.8)$$

Hence, the model is symmetric around the expected value of zero. As can be seen from (13.6), the increments of Z have finite variance if the expected value $\mu_{T,s}$ of the intrinsic time increments is finite. Assuming that the expected value and variance of the intrinsic time increments are finite and the intrinsic time process is non-deterministic, the kurtosis in (13.7) is always higher than 3, which is the kurtosis of the normal distributions. Therefore, the use of an intrinsic time scale as the directing process for the Wiener process as in (13.1) leads to leptokurtic return processes with probability density function probability density functions (if they exist) which are heavy-tailed and higher around the mode, compared to the normal distribution. The probability density function of the increments $\Delta Z_{t,s}$ is given by:

$$\begin{aligned} f_{Z,s}(x) &= \int_0^\infty \frac{1}{\sqrt{2\pi\sigma^2 u}} \exp\left(-\frac{x^2}{2\sigma^2 u}\right) dF_{T,s}(u) \\ &= \frac{1}{\sqrt{2\pi\sigma^2}} \int_0^\infty \frac{1}{\sqrt{u}} \exp\left(-\frac{x^2}{2\sigma^2 u}\right) dF_{T,s}(u) \qquad (13.9) \end{aligned}$$

with $f_{T,s}(u) = \frac{d}{du} F_{T,s}(u)$ denoting the probability density function and $F_{T,s}(u)$ denoting the density function of $\Delta T_{t,s}$. Hence, the distribution of the returns is an infinite mixture of normals with randomized variance $\sigma^2 \Delta T_{t,s}$. Equivalently, the density function and the characteristic function are defined by:

$$F_{Z,s}(x) = \int_0^\infty \Phi\left(\frac{x}{\sigma\sqrt{u}}\right) dF_{T,s}(u) \qquad (13.10)$$

and

$$\phi_{Z,s}(\theta) = E(e^{-\theta z}) = \int_0^\infty \exp\left(-\frac{1}{2}\theta^2 \sigma^2 u\right) dF_{T,s}(u), \qquad (13.11)$$

respectively. The characteristic function can be represented in terms of the Laplace transform, which is defined by:

$$\mathcal{L}_{T,s}(\gamma) = \int_0^\infty \exp(-\gamma x) dF_{T,s}(x). \qquad (13.12)$$

In terms of the Laplace transform, the characteristic function can be written as:

$$\phi_{Z,s}(\theta) = \mathcal{L}_{T,s}(\frac{1}{2}\theta^2 \sigma^2). \qquad (13.13)$$

Therefore, the subordinated returns are uniquely defined by the probabilistic characteristics of the intrinsic time process.

We shall recall now the six alternative distributional assumptions for the increments of the intrinsic time process, considered in Hurst, Platen and Rachev

(1997, 1999) (HPR), see Chapter 5 and Chapter 11. All these distributions belong to family of the so–called *infinitely divisible (ID) distributions*.. Due to their ID property the distributional characteristics of the returns belonging to an arbitrary physical time increment of length $s' \geq 0$ are uniquely determined by the returns belonging to a time increment of length $s \geq 0$. This is a consequence of the following property of the characteristic function for processes having stationary independent increments:

$$\phi_{X,s'}(\theta) = \{\phi_{X,s}(\theta)\}^{\frac{s'}{s}}. \tag{13.14}$$

The property (13.14) is a desirable property for any model for asset returns, because it states that returns are close under aggregation, i.e., returns considered over different time horizons belong to the same family of distributions. This is not always true. For example, a mixture of normal distributions does not share this property.

(a) The Classical Lognormal Model (Samuelson (1955), Osborne (1959))

Let $T(t) = t, t \geq 0$, i.e., the intrinsic time process is deterministic and identical to physical time. In this case the general subordinated stock price model (13.1) reduces to

$$S_{t+s} = S_t \exp\{\mu s + \sigma[W_{t+s} - W_t]\}. \tag{13.15}$$

The model in (13.15) is the lognormal stock price process assumed by Black and Scholes (1973).In this model the increments of Z are normally distributed with mean $\mu_{Z,s} = 0$ and $\sigma_{Z,s}^2 = \sigma^2 s$. The probability density function is therefore given by:

$$f_{Z,s}(x) = \frac{1}{\sqrt{2\pi\sigma^2 s}} \exp\left(-\frac{x^2}{2\sigma^2 s}\right). \tag{13.16}$$

Hence, the transition from the intrinsic to the physical time scale leads to the lognormal asset price process assumed in the BS model. The lognormal price model has also been proposed by Samuelson(1955) and Osborne (1959).

(b) The Log–Stable Model (Mandelbrot (1963b, 1967), Fama (1963b, 1965))

In the Mandelbrot (1963) model asset returns follow a symmetric α-stable Lévy process, i.e. the increments $\Delta T_{t,s}$ of the intrinsic time process are distributed stable with characteristic exponent $\alpha/2$,

$$\Delta T_{t,s} \sim S_{\alpha/2}(cs^{2/\alpha}, 1, 0), \quad 0 < \alpha < 2, \quad c > 0. \tag{13.17}$$

The characteristic function of the increments $\Delta Z_{t,s}$ of the subordinated process Z can be obtained by substituting the Laplace transform of $\Delta T_{t,s}$, defined by

$$\mathcal{L}_{T,s}(\gamma) = \exp\left\{\frac{-(c\gamma)^{\alpha/2}s}{\cos\left(\frac{\pi\alpha}{4}\right)}\right\}, \qquad (13.18)$$

into (13.12). The characteristic function of $\Delta Z_{t,s}$ becomes:

$$
\begin{aligned}
\phi_{Z,s}(\theta) &= \exp\left\{-\left(\frac{\sigma\sqrt{\frac{1}{2}c}}{\cos\left(\frac{\pi\alpha}{4}\right)^{1/\alpha}}\right)^{\alpha}|\theta|^{\alpha}s\right\} \\
&= \exp\left(-\tilde{c}^{\alpha}s\,|\theta|^{\alpha}\right) \qquad (13.19)
\end{aligned}
$$

$$\text{with}\ \tilde{c} = \frac{\sigma\sqrt{c/2}}{\cos\left(\frac{\pi\alpha}{4}\right)^{1/\alpha}}. \qquad (13.20)$$

Since the characteristic function of a symmetric α-stable random variable X with location parameter equal to zero is defined by

$$\phi_X(\theta) = \exp\left(-c_X^{\alpha}\,|\theta|^{\alpha}\right), \qquad (13.21)$$

it follows that the increments $\Delta Z_{t,s}$ are α-stable distributed with scale parameter $\tilde{c}s^{1/\alpha}$ and scale and location parameter equal to zero:

$$\Delta Z_{t,s} \sim S_{\alpha}(\tilde{c}s^{1/\alpha}, 0, 0). \qquad (13.22)$$

Hence, the process Z is a symmetric α-stable Lévy process. It can be shown that if $\alpha \to 2$, then the intrinsic time process converges to the deterministic physical time. Therefore, this model contains the classical lognormal model in (13.15) as a special case.

(c) The Barndorff-Nielsen Model (Barndorff-Nielsen (1994))

has applied the *Gaussian\\Inverse Gaussian* (GIG) model for asset returns, in which the Wiener process is directed by an intrinsic time process with increments following an inverse–Gaussian (IG) distribution,

$$\Delta T_{t,s} \sim IG(\alpha, \delta s), \qquad \alpha, \delta, t, s \geq 0, \qquad (13.23)$$

see also Eberlein and Keller (1995). Here, the density of the intrinsic time increments is given by

$$f_{T,s}(x) = \frac{\delta s}{\sqrt{2\pi x^3}}\exp\left(\frac{-(\alpha x - \delta s)^2}{2x}\right), \qquad x > 0, \qquad (13.24)$$

with expected value $E(\Delta T_{t,s}) = \frac{\delta s}{\alpha}$. The Laplace transform (cf. 13.12) has the form:

$$\mathcal{L}_{T,s}(\gamma) = \exp\left\{\alpha\delta s\left(1 - \sqrt{1 + \frac{2\gamma}{\alpha^2}}\right)\right\}. \qquad (13.25)$$

The probability density function of the increments $\Delta Z_{t,s}$ can be derived by substituting (13.24) into (13.9). Using the reparameterization

$$\tilde{\alpha} := \frac{\alpha}{\sigma}, \quad \tilde{\delta} := \sigma\delta, \tag{13.26}$$

the probability density function can be written as:

$$f_{Z,s}(x) = \frac{\tilde{\alpha}\tilde{\delta}s \exp(\tilde{\alpha}\tilde{\delta}s)}{\pi\sqrt{x^2 + (\tilde{\delta}s)^2}} K_1\left(\tilde{\alpha}\sqrt{x^2 + (\tilde{\delta}s)^2}\right), \quad x \in \mathbf{R}, \tag{13.27}$$

where $K_1(\omega)$ stands for the modified Bessel function of the third kind with index 1,

$$K_1(\omega) = \frac{1}{2}\int_0^\infty \exp\left\{-\frac{1}{2}\omega\left(x + \frac{1}{x}\right)\right\} dx, \quad \omega > 0; \tag{13.28}$$

see Barndorff-Nielsen (1977).Then applying (13.25) and (13.10) we derive the density function for the increments of Z:

$$F_{Z,s}(x) = \frac{\tilde{\delta}s}{\sqrt{2\pi}}\int_0^\infty u^{-\frac{3}{2}}\exp\left\{-\frac{(\tilde{\alpha}u - \tilde{\delta}s)^2}{2u}\right\}\Phi\left(\frac{x}{\sqrt{u}}\right) du. \tag{13.29}$$

The characteristic function of the increments of Z can be obtained by substituting (13.24) into (13.11):

$$\phi_{Z,s}(\theta) = \exp\left\{\tilde{\alpha}\tilde{\delta}s\left(1 - \sqrt{1 + \frac{1}{\tilde{\alpha}^2}\theta^2}\right)\right\}. \tag{13.30}$$

The distribution of the increments of Z belongs to the family of the generalized hyperbolic distribution with, according to the parameterization in Barndorff-Nielsen (1978), $\lambda = -\frac{1}{2}, \alpha = \tilde{\alpha}, \beta = 0, \mu = 0$ and $\delta = \tilde{\delta}s$. It can be shown that the intrinsic time process with $IG(\alpha, \delta s)$-distributed increments approaches the deterministic physical time process as $\alpha, \delta \to \infty$. Hence, the classical lognormal model with probability density function of the increments of Z in (13.16) is nested in this model.

While for the models discussed above a relatively simple representation of the distributional characteristics of the increments of the intrinsic time process and the subordinated returns for any $s > 0$, the general representation is far more complex for the models left. For the case $s = 1$, however, a description in a compact form is possible. Therefore, without loss of generality, we discuss only this special case. The distributional characteristics for the general case $s > 0$ are uniquely and completely defined by (13.14).

(d) The Log–Laplace Model (Mittnik and Rachev (1993a,b))

The symmetric Laplace distribution belongs to the family of the symmetric geometric summation–stable distributions, as defined in 2.2. In the subordinated model the symmetric Laplace process follows from the requirement that the (unit) increments of the intrinsic time process are distributed negative-exponential, i.e.,

$$\Delta T_{t,1} \sim Exp(\lambda), \quad t \geq 0, \tag{13.31}$$

for some $\lambda > 0$. The probability density function of the unit increments $\Delta T_{t,1}$ is therefore

$$f_{T,1}(x) = \lambda \exp(-\lambda x), \quad x > 0. \tag{13.32}$$

By substitution of (13.32) into (13.9) the probability density function of the unit increments $\Delta Z_{t,1}$ of Z can be written as follows:

$$f_{Z,1}(x) = \frac{\sqrt{\lambda}}{\sigma\sqrt{2}} \exp\left(-\frac{\sqrt{2\lambda}\,|x|}{\sigma}\right), \quad x \in \mathbf{R}, \tag{13.33}$$

or with $\tilde{\sigma} = \frac{\sigma}{\sqrt{2\lambda}}$,

$$f_{Z,1}(x) = \frac{1}{2\tilde{\sigma}} \exp\left(-\frac{|x|}{\tilde{\sigma}}\right), \quad x \in \mathbf{R}. \tag{13.34}$$

The density function in (13.34) is the density of a symmetric Laplace–distributed random variable with expected value equal to zero, i.e.,

$$\Delta Z_{t,1} \sim L(0, \tilde{\sigma}) \tag{13.35}$$

with $\mu_{Z,1} = 0$ and $\sigma_{Z,1}^2 = 2\tilde{\sigma}^2 = \frac{\sigma^2}{\lambda^2}$.

(e) The log–Student–t Model (Praetz (1972), Blattberg and Gonedes (1974))

In this model the unit time increments are governed by an "inverse" Chi-square distribution, i.e.

$$\Delta T_{t,1} \sim \frac{\nu}{\chi_\nu^2}, \quad \nu > 0, \tag{13.36}$$

where χ_ν^2 denotes a Chi-square distribution with ν degrees of freedom. The probability density function of $\Delta T_{t,1}$ is given by

$$f_{T,1}(x) = \frac{\tilde{\nu}^{\tilde{\nu}}}{\Gamma(\tilde{\nu})} x^{-\tilde{\nu}-1} \exp\left(-\frac{\tilde{\nu}}{x}\right), \quad \tilde{\nu} = \frac{\nu}{2}, \quad x > 0, \tag{13.37}$$

where $\Gamma(u) = \int_0^\infty x^{u-1} e^{-x} dx$ denotes the Gamma function. The expected value of a unit time increment is then

$$\mu_{T,1} = \frac{\nu}{\nu - 2} \quad \text{for } \nu > 2. \tag{13.38}$$

If $\nu \leq 2$, the mean does not exist.

By substitution of (13.37) into (13.9) the probability density function of the increments $\Delta Z_{t,1}$ of Z has the following form:

$$f_{Z,1}(x) = \frac{1}{\sigma} f_\nu \left(\frac{x}{\sigma}\right), \quad x \in \mathbf{R}. \tag{13.39}$$

Here, $f_\nu(u)$ denotes the probability density function of a Student-t distributed random variable with ν degrees of freedom:

$$f_\nu(u) = \frac{\Gamma(\frac{\nu+1}{2})}{\Gamma(\frac{\nu}{2})} \frac{\left(1 + \frac{u^2}{\nu}\right)^{-\frac{\nu+1}{2}}}{\sqrt{\nu\pi}}, \quad u \in \mathbf{R}. \tag{13.40}$$

Hence, the unit increment $\Delta Z_{t,1}$ follows a scaled t-distribution, i.e.

$$\Delta Z_{t,1} \sim \sigma t_\nu, \quad \nu > 0, \tag{13.41}$$

where t_ν denotes a t-distributed random variable with ν degrees of freedom. The mean and the variance of the increments of Z are therefore $\mu_{Z,1} = 0$ for $\nu > 1$ and $\sigma_{Z,1}^2 = \sigma^2 \frac{\nu}{\nu-2}$ for $\nu > 2$. As the degrees of freedom increase $(\nu \to \infty)$, the inner time process converges asymptotically to the deterministic physical time process, so that this model nests the Gaussian model as a special case. In particular, for $\nu \to \infty$ the increments $\Delta Z_{t,1}$ converge to a normal distribution with variance σ^2.

(f) The Clark Model

Clark (1973) has proposed an asset price model, in which the Wiener process $W(t)$ is subordinated to a directing process $T(t)$ with lognormal stationary independent increments. HPR modified this assumption by assuming the log-price process instead of the price process itself to be driven by a subordinated Wiener process $Z = \widehat{W}(T(t))$ with intrinsic time process having lognormal increments:

$$\Delta T_{t,1} \sim \log N(\mu, \varphi^2), \quad \mu \in \mathbf{R}, \ \varphi > 0, \tag{13.42}$$

with $\mu_{T,1} = \mu + \frac{1}{2}\varphi^2$. The probability density function of the unit intrinsic time increments $\Delta T_{t,1}$, is therefore:

$$f_{T,1}(x) = \frac{1}{x\sqrt{2\pi\varphi^2}} \exp\left[-\frac{1}{2}\left(\frac{\ln x - \mu}{\varphi}\right)^2\right], \quad x > 0. \tag{13.43}$$

The probability density function of the unit returns $\Delta Z_{t,1}$ can be obtained by substituting (13.43) into (13.9):

$$f_{Z,1}(x) = \frac{1}{2\pi\varphi} \int_0^\infty y^{-\frac{3}{2}} \exp\left\{-\frac{1}{2}\left[\frac{x^2}{y} + \left(\frac{\ln y - \mu - \ln \sigma^2}{\varphi}\right)^2\right]\right\} dy, \quad x \in \mathbf{R}, \tag{13.44}$$

where $y = \sigma^2 u$. Defining

$$\tilde{\mu} := \mu + \ln \sigma^2 \qquad (13.45)$$

this density can be written as:

$$f_{Z,1}(x) = \frac{1}{2\pi\varphi} \int_0^\infty u^{-\frac{3}{2}} \exp\left\{-\frac{1}{2}\left[\frac{x^2}{u} + \left(\frac{\ln u - \tilde{\mu}}{\varphi}\right)^2\right]\right\} du, \quad x \in \mathbf{R}.$$
$$(13.46)$$

Hence, the distribution of the increments of Z can be characterized as the product

$$\Delta Z_{t,1} \sim \sqrt{\mathcal{L}}\mathcal{Z}, \qquad (13.47)$$

where $\mathcal{L}$ and $\mathcal{Z}$ are independent random variables, $\mathcal{L} \sim \log N(\mu, \varphi^2)$ and $\mathcal{Z} \sim N(0, \sigma^2)$ or equivalently, using the reparameterization in (13.45), $\mathcal{L} \sim \log N(\tilde{\mu}, \varphi^2)$ and $\mathcal{Z} \sim N(0, 1)$.

The variance of the increments of the intrinsic time process following a lognormal distribution with parameters μ and φ^2 is:

$$\sigma_{T,1}^2 = \exp(2\mu + 2\varphi^2) - \exp(2\mu + \varphi^2). \qquad (13.48)$$

This variance converges to zeros as $\varphi \to 0$ so that the intrinsic time process asymptotically approaches physical time. Hence, the classical lognormal model is obtained for the special case as $\varphi \to 0$.

We now recall some of the facts we shall need in option pricing for subordinated asset return processes. In the chapter following the results in HPR, we derived the fair option value for the case that the asset price is driven by a subordinated process of the general form in (13.1). However, the fair option value resulting from the assumed subordinated process cannot be interpreted in the same way as in the BS model, because no hedge–portfolio exists that eliminates all the risk—stock price and volatility risk [5].

Assume that the option to be priced is a European call option on a non–dividend paying stock, where the stock price S is driven by the subordinated process in (13.1). Denoting the strike price of the call by K and its time to

---

[5] Consequently, the option price cannot be derived using a no–arbitrage argument, as in the BS model. The non-existence of a hedge portfolio is equivalent to the non-existence of an equivalent martingale measure in continuous time which could be used to derive a fair option value which is independent of risk preferences; see Hurst et al. (1999). The non-existence of an equivalent martingale measure is a consequence of the fact that the return on the asset and on the risk–free asset evolve in different time scales. HPR note that an equivalent measure would exist if one would assume that the return on the risk-free security evolves in the intrinsic time scale. Because this assumption is unrealistic, assumptions concerning the investors' utility function are necessary to obtain a fair option value. HPR assume that investors are indifferent towards the risk arising from the random operational time or, equivalently, towards the stochastic volatility, measured in the physical time scale.[6] Under the assumption that $\mu = r$ in (13.1), where r denotes the instantaneous continuously compounded return on a risk–free asset (risk–free rate), HPR show that a call option pricing formula exists, that extends the BS option pricing formula to the subordination setting.

maturity (measured in the physical time scale) by $T - t$, where t is current time and T is the time the option expires, the option's payoff at maturity time T is $(S_T - K)^+$ with $(\cdot)^+ = \max(0, \cdot)$. The variance of the stock return over the option's time to maturity, $\log \frac{S_T}{S_t}$, measured in the physical time scale, is given by:

$$Y = \sigma^2 [T(T) - T(t)]. \tag{13.49}$$

Conditional on the inner time process, the log-price process is normal, and the conditional fair option value at current time t can be computed via the BS formula [7]

$$\hat{C}^{BS}[S, K, T - t, r, \sigma \,|\, T(T) - T(t)] = S\Phi\left(\frac{m + \frac{1}{2}\sigma^2(T(T) - T(t))}{\sigma\sqrt{T(T) - T(t)}}\right)$$

$$- K_{r,t,T}\Phi\left(\frac{m - \frac{1}{2}\sigma^2(T(T) - T(t))}{\sigma\sqrt{T(T) - T(t)}}\right), \tag{13.50}$$

where $K_{r,t,T} = K\exp\{-r(T - t)\}$ denotes the discounted strike price of the option, $m = \log \frac{S}{K_{r,t,T}}$ denotes the moneyness, and $\Phi(x)$ denotes the density function of the standard normal distribution with argument x . Denoting the density function of Y by $F_Y(y)$, the fair option value in the subordinated model can be written as:

$$C^{sub} = \int_0^\infty \hat{C}^{BS}(S, K, T - t, r \,|\, y)\, dF_Y(y) \tag{13.51}$$

$$= S\int_0^\infty \Phi\left(\frac{m + \frac{1}{2}y}{\sqrt{y}}\right) dF_Y(y) - K_{r,t,T}\int_0^\infty \Phi\left(\frac{m - \frac{1}{2}y}{\sqrt{y}}\right) dF_Y(y) \tag{13.52}$$

Defining

$$F_\pm^{sub}(x) = \int_0^\infty \Phi\left(\frac{x \pm \frac{1}{2}y}{\sqrt{y}}\right) dF_Y, \tag{13.53}$$

the fair option value in the subordinated model can be written in the compact form:

$$C^{sub} = SF_+^{sub}(m) - K_{r,t,T}F_-^{sub}(m). \tag{13.54}$$

The pricing formula (13.54) is a generalization of the BS formula. For the special case that the inner time process equals physical time, the random variance Y in (13.49) reduces to the deterministic variance

$$\tilde{y} = \sigma^2(T - t). \tag{13.55}$$

Consequently, the functions (13.53) reduce to

$$F_\pm^{BS}(x) = \Phi\left(\frac{x \pm \frac{1}{2}\tilde{y}}{\sqrt{\tilde{y}}}\right), \tag{13.56}$$

---

[7] To simplify notation, the subscript t for the option price C is disposed here and in the subsequent discussion.

and the valuation formula (13.54) reduces to the BS formula

$$C^{BS}(S, K, \mathcal{T} - t, r, \sigma) = SF_+^{BS}(m) - K_{r,t,\mathcal{T}}F_-^{BS}(m). \tag{13.57}$$

13.3   The Binomial Model with Non–identically Distributed Jumps

In Chapter 12, following Cox, Ross and Rubinstein (1979), we analyzed a stock price model (in short, CRR model) in a discrete time lattice framework. The time interval $[t, \mathcal{T}]$ of length $\tau = \mathcal{T} - t$ is divided into n non–overlapping periods of equal length $h = \tau/n$. As before, t is current time and $\mathcal{T}$ is the time the option expires. All stock price movements occur at the end of the periods. Denoting the stock price at the end of the kth period by S_k, the stock price satisfies the recursive equation

$$S_{k+1} = \xi_{n,k}S_k, \quad k = 1, \ldots, n, \tag{13.58}$$

where $S_0 = S_t$ is the current stock price and $\xi_1, \ldots \xi_n$ are $i.i.d.$ Bernoulli random variables with $P(\xi_k = U) = q$ and $P(\xi_k = D) = 1 - q$. Hence, within a given period, the stock can either go upward from S_k to $S_{k+1} = US_k$ ("up–tick") or downward to $S_{k+1} = DS_k$ ("down–tick").

The stock price at expiration, S_n, is uniquely determined by the random variables $\xi_{n,k}$, describing stock price changes within periods $1, \ldots, n$. From recursion formula (13.58) the terminal stock price is:

$$S_n = S \prod_{k=1}^{n} \xi_{n,k}. \tag{13.59}$$

The continuously compounded return on the stock within the time interval $[t, \mathcal{T}]$, $\log \frac{S_n}{S}$, can therefore be expressed as:

$$\log \frac{S_n}{S} = \sum_{k=1}^{n} X_{n,k}, \tag{13.60}$$

where $X_{n,k} = \log U := u$ with probability q and $X_{n,k} = \log D := d$ with probability $1 - q$. Equivalently, $X_{n,k}$ can be expressed as:

$$X_{n,k} = \zeta_{n,k}u + (1 - \zeta_{n,k}d), \tag{13.61}$$

where $\zeta_{n,k}$ is a sequence of $i.i.d.$ Bernoulli random variables with success probability p, i.e., $P(\zeta_{n,k} = 1) = p$ and $P(\zeta_{n,k} = 0) = 1 - p$.

In Chapter 12 we investigated all possible limiting distributions of $i.i.d.$ binomial stock prices changes[8]. Under the assumption that the $X_{n,k}$'s in (13.61) satisfy the uniform asymptotic negligible (UAN) condition:

$$\max_{k=1,\ldots,n} P(|X_{n,k}| \geq \varepsilon) \longrightarrow 0 \quad \forall \varepsilon > 0, \tag{13.62}$$

---

[8]See also Rachev and Rüschendorf (1991, 1994a).

as $n \to \infty$, they show that all possible limits of the multiplicative binomial process with *i.i.d.* stock price changes are exhausted by the lognormal, the log–Poisson and the degenerate distributions.

The restricted possible limit laws of the multiplicative binomial process in the standard CRR model results from binomial returns being independent *identically* distributed. However, the "identically" part of the *i.i.d.* assumption in the standard model can be disposed of without destroying the arbitrage argument. This was done by Schumacher (1997), who models the terminal stock price, $S_T = S_n$, according to (13.60), where now the $X_{n,k}$'s are allowed to be non-identically distributed:

$$X_{n,k} = \zeta_{n,k} u_{n,k} + (1 - \zeta_{n,k}) d_{n,k} + \frac{r}{n} \qquad (13.63)$$

with $\zeta_{n,k}$, $k = 1, \ldots, n$, denoting Bernoulli random variables with success probabilities $q_{n,k}$.[9] Under the UAN condition (13.62), the weak limits of $\log \frac{S_n}{S} = \sum_{k=1}^{n} X_{n,k}$ span the family of infinitely divisible (ID) distributions. The ID family is defined as follows.[10]

Definition 13.1 *(Infinitely Divisible)* A distribution function F is called ID if for every integer $n \geq 1$ there exists a distribution function F_n such that F is the n-fold convolution of F_n, i.e., $F = F_n * F_n * \ldots * F_n = (F_n)^{n*}$ or equivalently if its characteristic function ϕ (also called ID) is the n-th power of a characteristic function ϕ_n for every integer $n \geq 1$.

The ID law is uniquely defined by the Lévy–Khintchine representation of its characteristic function:

$$\phi_{\log \frac{S_n}{S}}(u) = \exp\left\{ iu\alpha + \int_{\mathbf{R}} \left(e^{iux} - 1 - \frac{iux}{1+x^2} \right) \frac{1+x^2}{x^2} d\Psi(x) \right\}, \qquad (13.64)$$

where $\alpha \in \mathbf{R}$ and $\Psi(x)$ is a left–continuous, non-decreasing function with $G(-\infty) = 0$ and $G(\infty) = 1$. This characteristic function describes the return distribution over the option's time to maturity in the *natural* world. Hence, α and $\Psi(x)$ in (13.64) can be estimated from observed stock price data. In the case of a finite variance of $\frac{S_n}{S}$ (13.64) simplifies to:

$$\phi_{\log \frac{S_n}{S}}(u) = \exp\left\{ iu\alpha + \int_{\mathbf{R}} \left(e^{iux} - 1 - iux \right) \frac{1}{x^2} d\Psi(x) \right\}. \qquad (13.65)$$

The finite variance ID model with characteristic function (13.65) contains the Normal and the Poisson distributions as special cases. Suppose that

$$\Psi(x) = \sigma I_{[0,\infty)}(x) \qquad (13.66)$$

$$= \begin{cases} 0, & x < 0, \\ \sigma, & x \geq 0. \end{cases} \qquad (13.67)$$

---

[9] As in the CRR model, to find the no–arbitrage solution for the European call option, we pass to risk–neutral probabilities $p_{n,k}$.

[10] Additional properties of ID distributions not discussed here can be found in Feller (1966, §§VI.3 and VI.4.),Patel *et al.* (1976, p.102)and Chow and Teicher (1988, p. 425).

In this case the integral in (13.65) becomes $-\sigma^2 t^2/2$ and the characteristic function in (13.65) reduces to:

$$\phi_{\log \frac{S_n}{S}}(u) = \exp\left\{iu\alpha - \sigma^2 t^2/2\right\}, \qquad (13.68)$$

which is the characteristic function of a normal random variable with mean α and variance σ^2. The Poisson distribution is obtained from (13.65) by setting $\Psi(x) = \lambda K^2 I_{[K,\infty)}$ for $K \neq 0$. In this case the characteristic function (13.65) becomes

$$\phi_{\log \frac{S_n}{S}}(u) = \exp \lambda(e^{itx} - 1 - itx). \qquad (13.69)$$

This is the characteristic function of a scaled and shifted Poisson random variable of the form $K(Z_\lambda - \lambda)$, where Z_λ denotes a Poisson random variable with parameter λ, i.e.,

$$P(Z_\lambda = k) = \frac{\lambda^k}{k!}e^{-\lambda}, \quad k \geq 0. \qquad (13.70)$$

Hence, the ID return distribution with characteristic function (13.65) can be interpreted as an infinite mixture of independent Poisson random variables and one independent normal random variable.

Since the terminal stock price distribution was decomposed into binomial jumps, the arbitrage argument can be applied in a similar manner as in the standard CRR model. In general, however, the decomposition of $\log \frac{S_n}{S} = \sum_{k=1}^{n} X_{n,k}$ is not unique. And, more important, several decompositions which are equivalent in distributions, may lead to different option prices. In the limit, as the length of the binomial time steps gets finer ($h \to 0$), the fair value of the call was shown by Schumacher (1997) to be:

$$C = e^{-r\tau} \int_{\mathbf{R}} (Se^{r\tau+y} - K)^+ dF_Y(y). \qquad (13.71)$$

The characteristic function of Y in (13.71) is given by

$$\begin{aligned}
\phi_Y(u) = {}& \exp\bigg\{iur + \int_{-\infty}^{\infty} (e^{iux} - 1 - iux)x^{-2} d\Psi(x) \\
& -iu \int_{-\infty}^{\infty} (e^x - 1 - x)x^{-2} d\Psi(x)\bigg\},
\end{aligned} \qquad (13.72)$$

where Y is the risk–neutral distribution of the return at the terminal time $\mathcal{T}$.

As was already noted, the ID model contains the normal and the Poisson distribution as special cases. This generalization carries over to option pricing. The BS formula is obtained by selecting $\Psi(x) = \sigma I_{[0,\infty)}(x)$. If $\Psi(x) = \lambda I_{[K,\infty)}(x)$, where $K \neq 0$, the ID formula is equivalent to the pure jump option pricing formula of Cox et al. (1979).

13.4 Empirical Analysis: the DAX–Options Market

The analysis of the pricing performance of the alternative option pricing model candidates is based on European–type DAX–index options. The pricing performance of the different models is studied in– and out–of–sample. In the in–sample (ex–post) analysis the models are estimated from transaction data observed on a certain day t and the fit of the models is determined by comparing the model to the market prices. The out–of–sample (ex–ante) pricing performance is measured by estimating the models on day t and using the estimated parameters to price options on the next trading day $t + 1$. The ex-ante analysis is important for detecting a possible "overfitting" of the models. In addition to their *absolute* (total) pricing performance for a cross–section of options the models will also be judged by their *relative* pricing performance. Before we present the empirical results, we describe the data set below.

(a) The Data

European–type options on the DAX started trading on the Deutsche Terminbörse (DTB) in August 1991. Since then the DAX option has become a highly liquid instrument, which now exceeds the combined trading volume of all stock options currently traded on the DTB. Option prices are in index points rather than in Deutsch mark (DEM), as is usual for index options. The contract value is DEM10 per index point, i.e., the payoff at the expiration date $\mathcal{T}$, where the index value is $S_{\mathcal{T}}$, is DEM10$\times(S_{\mathcal{T}} - K)^+$ for an index call and DEM10$\times(K - S_{\mathcal{T}})^+$ for an index put. Since the tick size is 0.1, one tick equals DEM1. Expiration dates are in the next three months and the two months from the cycle March, June, September, and December. The maximum time to maturity is nine months. The options expire on the third Friday of the expiration month. Option series are introduced with five different strike prices, each of which is a multiple of 25 index points. If, for options with at least 10 days to expiration, on two consecutive days the closing index value falls below (rises above) the average of the second– and third–lowest (–highest) exercise price, a new series with a lower (higher) exercise price is introduced.

The DAX is a capital–weighted performance index comprised of 30 major stocks. As a performance index the DAX is adjusted for dividends, stock splits and capital changes. In contrast to other stock indices, reflecting exclusively price movements of the underlying stocks, dividends on the 30 component stocks are assumed to be reinvested into the share going ex–dividend, such that the index value remains unaffected. Therefore, dividends paid until the expiration date of the option need not be considered when pricing DAX options. The index is computed every minute during the time of floor trading (10:30 am to 01:30 pm) by the German Stock Exchange at an accuracy of 0.01 index points.

The options data we used consists of all transactions in the period from February 3, 1992 to September 29, 1995. Each record is time–stamped up to centiseconds and contains the strike price, expiration month, transaction price, and contract size. All options transactions are paired with the most recent update of the DAX. Only options traded between 10:30 am to 1:30 pm, i.e., when floor trading of stocks takes place, are included.[11]

As a proxy for the risk free rate daily data for Frankfurt interbank bid and offer rates[12] for overnight, 1–, 3– and 6–months maturities were used. The mean of the bid–ask spread was used for simplicity. This spread was typically very narrow. Interest rates matching the time to maturity of the options were obtained by simple linear interpolation [13]. Since no interest rates for maturities longer than 6 months were available, options with more than 6 months to expiration were excluded from the sample, making the longest term to expiration 182 days. This left us with 323,074 transactions for calls and 309,796 for puts, matched with the contemporaneous index and interest rate.

The options data set was screened for data errors due to mistrades. According to the so–called "mistrade rule" the DTB compares the transaction price of every trade to the fair value, as implied by the Black and Scholes (1973)option pricing model using an implied volatility. If the price of a transaction deviates substantially from the fair option value, the trade is defined to be a mistrade.[14] In case of a mistrade both contract partners are informed by the exchange, and the position must be closed by an opposite transaction. Unfortunately, the DTB data do not indicate such mistrades and the off–setting counter trade. Applying the DTB's mispricing criteria (see Footnote 14) we identified mistrades by checking for an off–setting transaction within the next 10 trading days and excluded this pair of trade from our analysis. The number of mistrades found in the data set was 862 for calls and 7521 for puts. Aside from mistrades options having more than 60 and less than 10 days to expiration were discarded. This is because very–short–term implied volatilities (IVs) typically show an erratic behavior due to expiration day effects, and the smile usually flattens down for longer term options. Furthermore, options far away from the money ($|m| > 0.1$) were deleted from the sample for two reasons. First, options away from the money are only thinly traded. Second, for these options the option price is quite insensitive with respect to volatility changes, making IV estimates unreliable.[15] Also excluded from

---

[11]Trading hours at the DTB are from 9:30 am to 4:00 pm.

[12]These can be regarded as analogues to the T–Bill rates, which are typically used in empirical studies for U.S. options markets.

[13]The potential bias induced by this approximation should be negligible, since the sensitivity of options prices with respect to the interest rate is quite low for options with less than one year to maturity; see, e.g., Cox and Rubinstein (1985, p.275).

[14]The DTB defines a trade to be a mistrade, if the absolute deviation either exceeds (a) DEM15 or (b) 1.5 times the maximum spread, provided the mispricing exceeds 30% of the fair option value.

[15]See Latané and Rendleman(1976).The BS Vega, i.e., the partial derivative of the BS price with respect to the volatility, is highest for m close to zero; see, for example, Rubinstein (1985).

consideration were low–priced options with prices lower than 0.5 index points (5 German marks), because the effect of the minimum tick size (0.5 index points) on IVs is substantial for these options. Finally, options violating the lower boundary[16]

$$(S - K_{r,t,\mathcal{T}})^+ \leq C^M(S, t, K, \mathcal{T}, r) \tag{13.73}$$

with C^M denoting the market price were excluded, because they are not compatible with the assumptions of the BS model. Consequently, for these options no IV exists. After applying all filter criteria we were left with 387,263 option transactions, 195,158 for calls and 192,105 for puts.

The daily DAX closing values for the 922 trading days in the sample period and the corresponding returns are plotted in Figure 13.1. The daily returns were computed as:

$$R_t = \ln \frac{S_t}{S_{t-1}} \cdot 100, \quad t = 2, \ldots, 922, \tag{13.74}$$

with S_t as index close on trading day t. Hence, the returns can be interpreted as daily percentage returns. The index value varied between 1420.30 and 2317.01 points in this period with daily returns in the range -4.08 and 4.31 percent. Descriptive statistics of the daily returns are contained in Table 13.1. The daily variance of 0.8502 corresponds to an annualized historical volatility of $\left(\frac{0.8502}{10000} \times 252\right)^{0.5} = 0.1464$ for the returns, based on 252 trading days per year. The negative skewness coefficient shows that the daily returns are skewed to the left with fatter lower and thinner upper tails as compared to the normal distribution. The estimated coefficient of kurtosis is higher than 3, the kurtosis of the normal distribution. Hence, the daily returns are leptokurtic.

Table 13.1 Descriptive Statistics of DAX Daily Percentage Returns (Feb. 2, 1992 – Sep. 29, 1995).

Min.	Max.	Mean	Variance	Skewness	Kurtosis
-4.0757	4.3070	0.0281	0.8502	-0.1201	4.5238

(Adapted from: Rieken, Mittnik, and Rachev (1998))

The information from the descriptive statistics in the table about the overall distributional characteristics of the daily returns is rather limited. For that reason the empirical return density was estimated using a kernal density estimator of the form:[17]

$$\hat{f}(x) = \frac{1}{nh} \sum_{i=1}^{n} K\left(\frac{x - X_i}{h}\right), \quad K(y) = \frac{1}{\sqrt{2\pi}} e^{-\frac{y^2}{2}} \tag{13.75}$$

---

[16]See, for example, Hull (1997, p.242).
[17]See, for example, Silverman(1986, p.15).

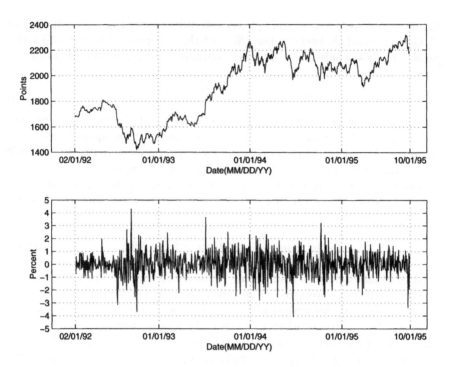

Fig. 13.1 DAX Daily Index Points and Percentage Returns, February 3, 1992 to September 29, 1995.(Adapted from: Rieken, Mittnik, and Rachev (1998))

Here, $\widehat{f}(x)$ denotes the estimated probability density function value at argument x, $n = 10000$ is the number of replications, X_i, $i = 1, \ldots, 10000$, and h is the smoothing parameter or window width, which was set to $h = 0.1$. The estimated density of standardized returns is shown in Figure 13.2 which also contains the standard normal density for comparison. The estimated density is bimodal and has humps at standardized returns of about -2 and 2.5. Moreover, both tails are fatter than those of the normal distribution. The negative skewness is only slight and therefore not visible from the shape of the empirical density.

In Table 13.2 we compare the observed frequency distribution of the percentage returns R_t to the theoretical frequencies, obtained from the normal distribution with the same mean and variance. The leptokurtosis of daily DAX returns results in observed frequencies higher than those implied by the normal distribution for values close to the mean, whereas extreme returns are observed much more often than is consistent with normality. Consider, for example, daily returns that are higher than 4 percent in the absolute sense. According to the observed frequency of two in the sample, such an extreme event should, on the average, occur every 460.5 trading days or equivalently

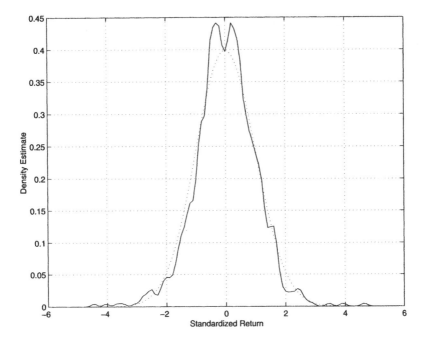

Fig. 13.2 Estimated Density of Standardized DAX Daily Returns, February 3, 1992 to September 29, 1995.(Adapted from: Rieken, Mittnik, and Rachev (1998))

(based on 252 trading days per year) 1.83 years. Based on the normal distribution such extreme observations are extremely unlikely and should, on the average, occur every 74878.05 trading days or 297.13 years only.

We test for normality of the daily returns by applying the Jarque–Bera test, (see Jarque and Bera (1980)). The test statistic is based on the third and fourth moments of the observations. It is given by:

$$\chi^2_{JB} = \frac{1}{6N}\left(\sum_{i=1}^{N} x_i^3\right)^2 + \frac{1}{24N}\left[\sum_{i=1}^{N}(x_i^4 - 3)\right]^2 \qquad (13.76)$$

where $N = 921$ is the number of observation and x_i stands for the daily standardized returns, $x_i = (R_i - \bar{R})/s(R_i)$ with $\bar{R}$ and $s(R_i)$ denoting the sample mean and standard deviation, respectively. Under normality, the test statistic is asymptotically distributed χ^2 with 2 degrees of freedom. The empirical value of the test statistic is $\chi^2_{JB} = 91.31$. The critical values form the $\chi^2(2)$ distribution corresponding to significance levels of 5, 1, and 0.1%

Table 13.2   Observed versus Theoretical Frequency Distribution of DAX Daily Percentage Returns (Feb. 2, 1992 – Sep. 29, 1995).

Interval for R_t		Relative Frequency		Absolute Frequency	
From	To under	Observed	Theoretical	Observed	Theoretical
$-\infty$	-4.0	0.0011	0.0000	1	0.0053
-4.0	-3.5	0.0011	0.0001	1	0.0542
-3.5	-3.0	0.0022	0.0004	2	0.4114
-3.0	-2.0	0.0163	0.0134	15	12.3513
-2.0	-1.0	0.0966	0.1185	89	109.1516
-1.0	0.0	0.3692	0.3554	340	327.3473
0.0	1.0	0.3822	0.3662	352	337.2852
1.0	2.0	0.1140	0.1297	105	119.4420
2.0	3.0	0.0141	0.0156	13	14.3674
3.0	3.5	0.0011	0.0006	1	0.5073
3.5	4.0	0.0011	0.0001	1	0.0690
4.0	∞	0.0011	0.0000	1	0.0070
	$\sum$	1.0000	1.0000	921	921

(Adapted from: Rieken, Mittnik, and Rachev (1998))

are 5.99, 9.21, and 13.82, respectively. Therefore the hypothesis of Gaussian daily DAX returns can be safely rejected.[18]

(b) Model Specification and Implementation

The subordinated stock price processes are specified as described in Section 5.1.1. Depending on the specification of the inner time process as in the log–Laplace, the log–Student–t, the Clark, the Barndorff–Nielsen, and the log–Stable model, the resulting subordinated stock price and the option pricing model are both denoted by the LBS, tBS, CBS, BNBS, and SBS model, respectively. In order to make all the subordinated models comparable, a restriction concerning the average length of a unit increment of the intrinsic time process must be applied. A natural assumption is that, on average, one unit of physical time equals one unit of operational time. Therefore, the mean length of a unit operational time increment was set to $\mu_{T,1} = 1$ if this expectation exists. In this case the expected unannualized variance Y in (13.49) over the time left to expiration becomes:

$$E(Y) = \sigma^2 E(T(\mathcal{T}) - T(t)) = \sigma^2(\mathcal{T}) - t)\mu_{T,1} = \sigma^2(\mathcal{T} - t) = \widetilde{y}. \quad (13.77)$$

---

[18]The p-value associated with the empirical value of the test statistic is lower than 10^{-16}.

Hence, on average, the (unannualized) conditional variance over the time remaining to expiration is the same, if measured in the physical or in the intrinsic time scale. The requirement of intrinsic and physical time increments having equal length, on average, leads to the parameter restrictions $\lambda = 1$ in the LBS, $\alpha = \delta$ in the BNBS and $\mu = 1 - \frac{\varphi^2}{2}$ in the CBS model. In the tBS model we have $\mu_{T,1} = \frac{\nu}{\nu-2}$ for $\nu > 2$. In this case the restriction $\mu_{T,1} = 1$ can be imposed using the transformation:

$$\Delta \widetilde{T}_{t,1}(i) = \frac{\Delta T_{t,1}(i)}{\mu_{T,1}} = (1 - \frac{2}{\nu})\Delta T_{t,1}(i). \tag{13.78}$$

Note that $\mu_{T,1}$ does not exists for $\nu \leq 2$. However, the case $\nu \leq 2$ is not relevant in practical applications, an thus without a significant loss of generality we restrict ν to $\nu > 2$ in the subsequent analysis.

In the SBS the expected value $\mu_{T,1}$ is infinite over the whole parameter space $\alpha \in (0,2)$ of the characteristic exponent. Several alternatives for fixing the location of the unit time increments and, equivalently, the scale parameter of the corresponding return distribution, are possible. For example, one could require the return distribution to have the same quartiles as the normal distribution as done in Hurst *et al.*(1999).Alternatively, a trimmed mean could be used. Since the standardization of the intrinsic time increments for all the other models is done via the expected value, a trimmed mean standardization is used in the SBS model to facilitate a comparison of all models. For a given characteristic exponent α the truncation level is set equal to the 99.99 percentage point. The trimmed mean is then given by:

$$\mu_{T,1}^* = \int_0^{x_{0.9999}} x dF_{T,1}(x) \tag{13.79}$$

with $x_{0.9999}$ denoting the 99.99 percentage point of the unit time increment $\Delta T_{t,1}$. The trimmed means of $S_{\frac{\alpha}{2}}(1,1,0)$ distributed random variables were estimated via simulation. The simulations were carried out for $\alpha = 1.0001$, $1.01, 1.02, \ldots, 1.99, 1.9999$ using $n = 1,000,000$ replications each. For a given α the sample estimator for the trimmed mean is then:

$$\widehat{\mu_{T,1}^*} = \frac{1}{999900} \sum_{i=1}^{999900} X_{[i]}, \tag{13.80}$$

where $X_{[i]}$, $i = 1, \ldots, 999900$, is the ith order statistics of the simulated intrinsic time increments X_i. After applying the parameter restrictions discussed above, the LBS stock price3 model contains just one parameter, the volatility parameter σ, whereas the remaining models are two–parameter models.

Note that, using the parameter restrictions discussed above, the LBS model is the only one–parameter model among the subordinated model, because after setting $\lambda = 1$ the only remaining parameter in this model is the volatility parameter σ. This is a property that the LBS model shares with the BS model.

On the other hand, the LBS model is the only model that does not include the BS model as a special case. In addition to the volatility parameter σ, the remaining four subordinated models tBS, CBS, BNBS, and SBS contain one more parameter, a shape parameter controlling the leptokurtosis and therefore the tail–thickness of the returns.

The ID model is specified as the sum of a (scaled) ID random variable Z, and three independent (scaled) Poisson random variables:

$$X = \sigma Z + a_1 Y_1 + a_2 Y_2 + a_3 Y_3 + \mu, \qquad (13.81)$$

where Y_i, $i = 1, \ldots, 3$, are independent Poisson random variables with parameters λ_i, Z is an independent ID random variable, and $\mu \in \mathbf{R}$ is a shift parameter. In the different ID models the ID random variable Z is, in addition to a standard normal random variable, specified as in the subordinated models LBS, tBS, CBS, BNBS, and SBS models. In the different ID models the same restrictions for the subordinated part Z as for the corresponding subordinated models are applied to standardize the (truncated) mean to 1. In order to reduce the complexity and number of parameters of the models we use the following parameter restrictions in each of the models: $a_2 = -a_1$, $a_1 > 0$, and $\lambda_1 = \lambda_2$. The model with Gaussian Z is denoted by IDN3r, where "N" stands for the Normal subordinated random variable and "3r" stands for the three Poissons in (13.81), using the above restrictions. Similarly, in case that Z is a non-normal subordinated random variable, which is specified as in the LBS, tBS, CBS, BNBS, or SBS model, the model is denoted as the IDL3r, IDt3r, IDC3r, IDBN3r, or IDS3r model, respectively. The restricted models therefore contain five to six parameters: the four parameters of the Poissonian part, $a_1, a_3, \lambda_1, \lambda_3$, and, depending on the subordinated model underlying Z, one or two parameters of the subordinated part, i.e., the scaling parameter σ and the parameter ν, φ^2, γ, or α in the IDt3r, IDC3r, IDBN3r, or IDS3r, respectively.

The model (13.81) is an attempt to specify the stock price process in a parsimonious way, but in accordance with the smile effect typically found in the option markets. The first two, restricted, Poissons in (13.81) allow the IDN3r model to generate leptokurtic returns, which is consistent with the smile effect. The third, unrestricted, Poisson in (13.81) is capable to model a possible skewness–effect in the smile, which is consistent with a skewed implied risk–neutral terminal return distribution.[19] The additional specifications of Z as in the non-normal subordinated models are applied in order to check whether this additional source of kurtosis can further improve the pricing performance.

Option model prices are computed via Monte–Carlo simulation. The Monte–Carlo simulations for the subordinated models are based on the subordinated pricing formula (13.52) for European calls. For computing subordinated model prices $n = 10,000$ realizations y_i, $i = 1, \ldots, n$, of the random variable

---

[19]See, for example, Hull(1997, pp.492ff).

Y in (13.49) were generated:

$$y_i = \sigma^2(\mathcal{T} - t)\Delta T_{t,1}(i), \quad i = 1, \ldots, n, \qquad (13.82)$$

with $\Delta T_{t,1}(i)$ denoting the i-th replication of the unit intrinsic time increment $\Delta T_{t,1}$ having the distribution assumed in the corresponding model. Given the realized values of Y, an estimator of the subordinated option price is given by the arithmetic mean of the conditional BS prices:

$$\widehat{C}^{sub} = \frac{1}{n}\sum_{i=1}^{n}\widehat{C}^{BS}(S, K, \mathcal{T} - t, r|y_i) \qquad (13.83)$$

with

$$\widehat{C}^{BS}(S, K, \mathcal{T} - t, r|y_i) = S\Phi\left(\frac{m + \frac{1}{2}y_i}{\sqrt{y_i}}\right) - K_{r,t,\mathcal{T}}\Phi\left(\frac{m - \frac{1}{2}y_i}{\sqrt{y_i}}\right). \qquad (13.84)$$

Since the ID models, incorporating discrete Poisson jumps, exhibit a high variance of the estimated option price, the antithetic variable technique was applied to increase the efficiency of the price estimator.[20] The ID model option prices are computed as:

$$C = e^{-r\tau}\frac{1}{N}\sum_{j=1}^{N}C_j, \qquad (13.85)$$

$$\text{where } C_j = \frac{(Se^{r\tau + X_{j,\tau}} - K)^+ + (Se^{r\tau + X^*_{j,\tau}} - K)^+}{2} \qquad (13.86)$$

denotes the option price for simulation trial j, $j = 1, \ldots, N$ and $X_{j,\tau}$ and $X^*_{j,\tau}$ denote the ith realization of the continuously compounded excess stock return over the risk–free rate until expiration time T and its antithetic counterpart, respectively. Due to the ID property of the (excess) returns, option prices for different maturities can be valued using simulated annualized returns $X_j, j = 1, \ldots, N$. For each maturity τ, these annualized returns are then rescaled and shifted to have the appropriate mean and variance. For a given setting of the parameters in the ID model, option prices for different maturities (and strike prices) can therefore be calculated from a given set of simulated annualized returns. The variance of X in (13.81) is equal to $\sigma_X^2 = \sigma^2 + \sum_{i=1}^{3}a_i^2\lambda_i$.[21] In accordance with (13.71), for given values of σ, a_i, and λ_i, $i = 1, \ldots, 3$, the shift parameter μ for the annualized returns in (13.81) is set to $\mu = -\frac{\sigma_X^2}{2}$.

---

[20] The general method is described in Ross (1991, pp.114ff).For an application in the framework of option pricing via Monte–Carlo simulation see Hull (1997, pp.364f), Hull and White (1987)and Leippold (1997).

[21] Because we used a truncated mean of the intrinsic time increments in the log–stable model, the variance of Z is a truncated variance in this model. If Z is specified as an α–stable model, σ_X^2 is therefore the truncated variance of X.

(c) Estimation

Often in practice, the model parameters are estimated using historical return data. One drawback of this method is the large sample of historical data needed to make the variance of the estimator sufficiently small. For estimating the volatility parameters this is problematic since volatility typically changes over time. From this point of view, using less historical data may be more convenient, but in this case the variance of the estimated parameters increases. Furthermore, applying historical data, the comparison of models will depend on the chosen estimation method. Alternatively, the model parameters can be "implied" from market data by seeking for the parameterizations of the models which fit observed market prices best. This method, known as "calibration", is just an extension of the IV method to a more–parameter setting.[22] This restricts the amount of data needed for estimation to a cross–section of options observed at one point in time or within a short time period, e.g., one day. A second advantage of the implied approach is that the models can be better compared in terms of their pricing performance, because the models which best fit observed option prices instead of past returns are compared [23].

The BS IVs of otherwise identical calls and puts have been found to differ in a systematic way. Therefore, the estimation is done for calls and puts separately. The put prices are translated into call prices using the put–call parity condition:

$$C - P = S - Ke^{-rr}. \tag{13.87}$$

Let θ denote the parameter vector to be estimated. Further, let C_i be the observed price of call option (converted put option, via put–call parity) $i, i = 1, \ldots, n$, and $\hat{C}_i(\theta)$ its model price. The objective function is defined as the sum of squared pricing errors with an adjustment to include the trading volume. The implied parameter vector $\hat{\theta}$ is then given by the solution to the following optimization problem:

$$OF(\theta) = \sum_{i=1}^{n} \frac{V_i}{\sum_{i=1}^{n} V_i} \left[C_i - \hat{C}_i(\theta) \right]^2. \tag{13.88}$$

The inclusion of the relative transaction volume in the objective function punishes an option's mispricing on a given day with a factor proportional to its trading volume.

For solving the minimization problem in (13.88), a Sequential Quadratic Programming (SQP) routine was implemented. In each iteration step the Hessian estimator is updated using the formula of Broydon (1970), Fletcher

---

[22]This method was used by Engle and Mustafa (1992) to "imply" the parameters of a GARCH option pricing model and by Bakshi *et al.* (1997)to empirical compare the performance of several option pricing models.

[23]The numerical results in this section and the rest of this chapter are due to Rieken, Mittnik and Rachev (1998).

(1970), Goldfarb (1970), and Shanno (1970) (BFGS–formula). The sample is restricted to trading days with maturities 10, 30, and 60 days. There are 43, 40 and 42 trading days in the sample period February 1992 to November 1995 with these maturities traded, respectively. In Table 13.3 the total trading volume is given for calls and puts having 10, 30 or 60 days to expiration. The volume is classified according to the options' moneyness and days to maturity. The Table 13.3 shows that for both calls and puts market depth is highest for 10 days–to–maturity options trading AM, with $|m| \leq 0.02$. For the different maturity classes in the table the portion of AM options transactions ranges from 33 to 61%. This percentage decreases as time to expiration increases. For options traded outside this AM range, market depth is higher for calls and puts trading OM, i.e., where $m < 0$ and $m > 0$, respectively. For both option types and all three maturities, only a very small portion of transactions (up to 5%) correspond to DIM options with $|m| > 0.1$.

Table 13.3 Total Trading Volume of 10–, 30–, and 60–Days–to–Maturity Calls and Puts, Classified by Moneyness and Time to Expiration.

	Calls				Puts			
	Days to Maturity				Days to Maturity			
Moneyness m	10	30	60	10–60	10	30	60	10–60
$-\infty < m < -0.1$	0.40^a	0.30	1.78	2.48	5.89	1.16	0.29	7.34
	$(0.00)^b$	(0.00)	(0.01)	(0.00)	(0.02)	(0.00)	(0.00)	(0.01)
$-0.1 \leq m \leq -0.05$	8.43	19.22	12.03	39.68	6.52	10.21	1.80	18.53
	(0.02)	(0.06)	(0.10)	(0.05)	(0.02)	(0.03)	(0.01)	(0.02)
$-0.05 < m \leq -0.02$	103.48	76.40	37.28	217.16	23.70	11.21	7.77	42.68
	(0.25)	(0.24)	(0.30)	(0.26)	(0.07)	(0.04)	(0.06)	(0.05)
$-0.02 < m \leq 0.02$	246.89	175.41	49.54	471.84	210.10	135.15	44.45	389.70
	(0.61)	(0.56)	(0.40)	(0.56)	(0.60)	(0.44)	(0.33)	(0.49)
$0.02 < m \leq 0.05$	33.69	26.61	14.10	74.41	76.65	97.18	34.07	207.89
	(0.08)	(0.08)	(0.12)	(0.09)	(0.22)	(0.32)	(0.25)	(0.26)
$0.05 < m \leq 0.1$	11.58	15.09	5.21	31.88	27.85	43.00	39.73	110.58
	(0.03)	(0.05)	(0.04)	(0.04)	(0.08)	(0.14)	(0.29)	(0.14)
$0.1 < m < \infty$	3.20	1.50	2.54	7.24	1.61	6.68	7.27	15.56
	(0.01)	(0.00)	(0.02)	(0.01)	(0.00)	(0.02)	(0.05)	(0.02)
$-\infty < m < \infty$	407.67	314.54	122.48	844.69	352.31	304.59	135.38	792.28
	(1.00)	(1.00)	(1.00)	(1.00)	(1.00)	(1.00)	(1.00)	(1.00)

[a] Total trading volume in the moneyness/maturity class (in 1000).
[b] Total trading volume in the moneyness/maturity class, divided by the total trading volume for all options with the specified maturity.
(Adapted from: Rieken, Mittnik, and Rachev (1998))

A certain amount of data for different strikes in one point of time is needed for estimation. For the DAX options considered here, there are only about two transactions per minute, on the average. Thus, we use options traded within one day for estimation. One problem occurring in this context is the violation of arbitrage restrictions, which are inconsistent with any option pricing model. As was shown by Merton (1973a), at a fixed point in time, the no–arbitrage condition leads to the following restrictions on the first and second partial derivative of the call price function $C(K)$ with respect to the strike price K:

$$\frac{\partial C}{\partial K} \leq 0, \tag{13.89}$$

and

$$\frac{\partial^2 C}{\partial K^2} \geq 0, \tag{13.90}$$

If either (13.89) or (13.90) is violated, an instant risk–free profit can be obtained[24].

To eliminate violations of conditions (13.89) and (13.90) by using a smoothing technique proposed by Shimko(1993). The smoothing procedure consists of the following steps. First, for a given trading day and options' maturity, the BS IVs are computed. For a given call option having strike price K, maturity τ, which is traded at the market price C^M at time t, the BS IV is defined as the volatility parameter that equates the BS model price to that market price, i.e.,

$$v(S_t, m, \tau, r, C^M) = \left(C^{BS}\right)^{\leftarrow}(S_t, m, \tau, r, C^M). \tag{13.91}$$

Second, a smile model is fitted to the daily smile. Typically, a parabolic smile of the form:

$$v(m) = a_0 + a_1 m + a_2 m^2 + u, \tag{13.92}$$

where u is an error term, fits the smile reasonably well. Therefore, this smile model is used. Finally, the estimated smile $\hat{v}(m) = \hat{a}_0 + \hat{a}_1 m + \hat{a}_2 m^2$, estimated using OLS, is used to translate the smoothed IVs into smoothed market prices by substituting $\hat{v}(m)$ for σ in the BS formula (13.57).

For each day and maturity a total of 20 smoothed market prices is used as input into objective function (13.88). These prices are obtained by computing the smoothed market prices for 20 different values of the moneyness, which are equally spaced between the minimum and the maximum moneyness value observed. The smoothed market prices, smoothed via Shimko (1993)'s method, can be regarded as a summary of the market's pricing behavior on a given day. A further advantage of using smoothed instead of raw market prices for estimating the model parameters is that smoothed market prices reduce the probability of overfitting the market data, resulting in a reduced out–of–sample (ex-ante pricing) performance of the model; see Dumas *et al.* (1996).To overcome the problem of changing index values on a given trading day, all option transactions are standardized to an index value of $S_0 = 1,000$.[25]

---

[24]For a discussion of arbitrage trading strategies that convert violations of either condition into riskless profits see, for example, Cox and Rubinstein (1985).
[25]As shown by Merton (1973a) every rational option pricing model is homogeneous of degree one in the strike and underlying spot price, i.e., a doubling of the strike and spot price leads

For all trading days with 10–, 30– or 60 days–to–maturity options traded, the estimation procedure was implemented by adapting the following steps:

Step 1: For a given trading day t collect all options with 10, 30 or 60 days to expiration and estimate the parabolic smile model in (13.92) for the BS IVs via OLS.

Step 2: Divide the range of observed strike prices, $[K_{\min}, K_{\max}]$, into $h = 19$ subintervals of equal length $d_K = (K_{\max} - K_{\min})/h$ and compute the IVs $v_i(K_i)$ for the 20 equally spaced strike prices $K_i = K_{\min} + (i-1)d_K$, $i = 1, \ldots, h + 1$, using the estimated smile model.

Step 3: Compute the smoothed market prices $C_i(K_i, S_i)$ for strike prices K_i by substituting the estimated (smoothed) IVs $v_i(K_i, S_i)$ into the BS formula. Compute the standardized smoothed market prices $C_i(K_i, S_0) = C_i/S_iS_0$. Use the total trading volume occurring in the interval $[K_i \pm \frac{d_K}{2}]$ as input for V_i in (13.88).

Step 4: Solve the optimization problem in (13.88) to find the implied parameter $\hat{\theta}$ vector for each of the models.

The Steps 1 to 4 are repeated for each trading day in the sample.

In Table 13.4 we report the results of the implied parameter estimation for the six subordinated models. The estimation results are summarized by the medians and the lower and upper quartiles of each of the parameters.

As is evident from Table 13.4, the (median) volatility parameter of all the models is higher for puts than for calls. This is true for all three maturities. From the one–parameter models BS and LBS it can therefore be concluded that put options were relatively overpriced as compared to call options. This conclusion follows from the fact that the model price is an increasing function of the volatility parameter. As compared to the BS model, the estimated volatility parameters tend to be somewhat higher in the subordinated models with the highest estimates in the SBS model.

The wide interquartile ranges of the estimated shape parameters indicate that the point estimators vary over a wide range in the sample.[26] However, the lower and upper quartiles of the shape parameters of the models tBS, CBS, BNBS, and SBS suggest, that these models are far from Gaussian, in general. Comparing the results for calls and puts, it can be observed that these models are closer to the BS model for calls than for puts. The estimated parameters of the six ID models IDN3r, IDL3r, IDt3r, IDC3r, IDBN3r, and IDS3r are summarized in the Tables 13.5 to 13.10. In addition, the contribution of the Poissonian part to the mean of the returns is summarized by $a_1\lambda_1$ and $a_3\lambda_3$,

---

to a doubling of the option price. This property is exploited here to make daily options corresponding to different spot prices comparable.

[26]For the tBS model the minimum parameter estimate for ν is $\hat{\nu} = 3.22$. The restriction $\nu > 2$ in the tBS model is therefore always non-binding.

Table 13.4 Parameter Estimates for Subordinated Models.

		Calls			Puts		
		Days to Maturity			Days to Maturity		
		10	30	60	10	30	60
Para-meter		Number of Days			Number of Days		
		43[a]	40	38	42	40	32
Model ↓		(43)[b]	(40)	(42)	(43)	(40)	(42)
BS	$\hat{\sigma}$	0.1507[c]	0.1453	0.1481	0.1618	0.1636	0.1657
		[0.1180;0.1739][d]	[0.1250;0.1720]	[0.1310;0.1772]	[0.1435;0.1810]	[0.1410;0.1869]	[0.1445;0.2025]
y LBS	$\hat{\sigma}$	0.1626	0.1591	0.1678	0.1769	0.1801	0.1835
		[0.1285;0.1890]	[0.1373;0.1920]	[0.1461;0.1973]	[0.1562;0.1995]	[0.1547;0.2068]	[0.1601;0.2213]
tBS	$\hat{\nu}$	16.7343	23.8288	24.9738	7.8954	7.9553	10.6607
		[7.8954;23.9383]	[15.8880;42.4840]	[23.2204;25.1169]	[6.2851;10.6607]	[6.8238;10.6803]	[7.8954;10.6807]
	$\hat{\sigma}$	0.1515	0.1464	0.1500	0.1670	0.1737	0.1678
		[0.1229;0.1764]	[0.1291;0.1735]	[0.1349;0.1801]	[0.1462;0.1950]	[0.1457;0.1890]	[0.1465;0.2065]
CBS	$\hat{\varphi}^2$	0.1686	0.0008	0.0007	0.8760	0.8838	1.0187
		[0.0018;0.9493]	[0.0001;0.1754]	[0.0001;0.0648]	[0.5226;1.1966]	[0.7147;1.2757]	[0.6096;1.3350]
	$\hat{\sigma}$	0.1595	0.1481	0.1550	0.1801	0.1851	0.1834
		[0.1303;0.1907]	[0.1294;0.1827]	[0.1352;0.1802]	[0.1620;0.2039]	[0.1584;0.2160]	[0.1694;0.2276]
BNBS	$\hat{\eta}$	2.9026	17.4518	27.6510	1.4973	1.4384	1.4277
		[1.4586;5.5583]	[3.7375;24.3488]	[4.4760;45.5689]	[1.1095;2.1725]	[0.9624;1.6204]	[0.9391;2.8814]
	$\hat{\sigma}$	0.1531	0.1453	0.1485	0.1681	0.1723	0.1735
		[0.1214;0.1762]	[0.1274;0.1745]	[0.1335;0.1801]	[0.1497;0.1885]	[0.1457;0.1941]	[0.1545;0.2118]
SBS	$\hat{\alpha}$	1.9102	1.9300	1.9409	1.7835	1.7670	1.7310
		[1.7459;1.9509]	[1.8710;1.9735]	[1.9100;1.9798]	[1.7367;1.8365]	[1.7118;1.7905]	[1.6462;1.8115]
	$\hat{\sigma}$	0.2426	0.1844	0.1828	0.3426	0.3551	0.3779
		[0.1915;0.2980]	[0.1527;0.2348]	[0.1484;0.2562]	[0.2519;0.4333]	[0.2870;0.4703]	[0.3038;0.6535]

[a] Number of days with given options' maturity in the sample that satisfy the exclusion criteria; see text. Only these days were used for implying the model parameters.
[b] Total number of days with given options' maturity in the sample.
[c] Median of daily parameter estimates.
[d] Lower and upper quartiles of daily parameter estimates.
(Adapted from: Rieken, Mittnik, and Rachev (1998))

which are close to zero and therefore multiplied by 100 in the tables. Note that, due to the restrictions $a_2 = -a_1$ and $\lambda_1 = \lambda_2$ imposed on the scaling factors and parameters of the first two Poissonian random variables, their total contribution to the mean of the returns is equal to zero. The contribution to the mean return attributed to the third Poisson random variable is $a_3\lambda_3$. This unrestricted Poisson random variable is the only possible source of skewness in the return distribution. If $\lambda_3 \neq 0$ and $a_3 > 0$ $(a_3 < 0)$, the return distribution is skewed to the right (left). Moreover, the estimated contribution of the Poissonian part, $\hat{\sigma}^2_{Poi}$, to the total variance of the returns, $\hat{\sigma}^2_{tot}$, measured by the ratio

$$\frac{\hat{\sigma}^2_{Poi}}{\hat{\sigma}^2_{tot}} = \frac{2\hat{a}_1^2\hat{\lambda}_1 + \hat{a}_3^2\hat{\lambda}_3}{\hat{\sigma}^2 + 2\hat{a}_1^2\hat{\lambda}_1 + \hat{a}_3^2\hat{\lambda}_3}, \tag{13.93}$$

is also given. As for the subordinated models, the summary statistics presented are the median, as well as the lower and upper quartiles.

For a given option type and maturity the daily estimates of most parameters are characterized by a considerable variation, as is indicated by the quartiles in the tables. In comparison to the corresponding subordinated models, i.e., the subordinated models having the same distribution of Z in (13.81), for the ID models the medians of the estimated shape and scale parameters tend to be somewhat different; cf. Table 13.4. For example, the estimated scaling parameters $\hat{\sigma}$ for the subordinated part in (13.81) tend to to be lower than in the corresponding subordinated models. An exception is the IDS3r model with substantially higher estimates of σ than for the SBS for the puts. The median estimates of the average size of the symmetric jumps (of different

Table 13.5 Parameter Estimates for the IDN3r Model

Para-meter	Calls Days to Maturity			Puts Days to Maturity		
	10	30	60	10	30	60
	Number of Days			Number of Days		
	43^a	40	38	42	40	32
	$(43)^b$	(40)	(42)	(43)	(40)	(42)
$\hat{\sigma}$	0.1403^c	0.1465	0.1491	0.1527	0.1591	0.1580
	$[0.1179;0.1765]^d$	[0.1260 ;0.1722]	[0.1310 ;0.1814]	[0.1181 ;0.1710]	[0.1326 ;0.1808]	[0.1362 ;0.1987]
$\hat{a}_1$	0.1130	0.1077	0.1099	0.1002	0.0999	0.1043
	[0.1009 ;0.5851]	[0.1000 ;0.2401]	[0.1008 ;0.2009]	[0.0994 ;0.1355]	[0.0979 ;0.2460]	[0.0985 ;0.2251]
$\hat{a}_3$	0.1000	0.1007	0.0969	0.0998	0.0987	0.0984
	[0.0389 ;0.1192]	[0.0962 ;0.1190]	[0.0439 ;0.1028]	[0.0583 ;0.1023]	[0.0401 ;0.1001]	[0.0859 ;0.1097]
$\hat{\lambda}_1$	0.0092	0.0084	0.0072	0.0100	0.0091	0.0066
	[0.0054 ;0.0111]	[0.0069 ;0.0111]	[0.0052 ;0.0094]	[0.0093 ;0.0222]	[0.0086 ;0.0126]	[0.0022 ;0.0087]
$\hat{\lambda}_3$	0.0042	0.0004	0.0047	0.0084	0.0024	0.0000
	[0.0000 ;0.0230]	[0.0000 ;0.0119]	[0.0000 ;0.0155]	[0.0000 ;0.0329]	[0.0000 ;0.0153]	[0.0000 ;0.0083]
$\hat{a}_1\hat{\lambda}_1$ (×100)	0.1202	0.1086	0.0932	0.1014	0.0926	0.0827
	[0.0925 ;0.4776]	[0.0824 ;0.1740]	[0.0746 ;0.1444]	[0.0948 ;0.3791]	[0.0858 ;0.3805]	[0.0281 ;0.1447]
$\hat{a}_3\hat{\lambda}_3$ (×100)	0.0021	0.0001	0.0004	0.0001	0.0000	0.0000
	[0.0000 ;0.1905]	[0.0000 ;0.1037]	[0.0000 ;0.0580]	[0.0000 ;0.2245]	[0.0000 ;0.1326]	[0.0000 ;0.0004]
$\dfrac{\hat{\sigma}^2_{Poi}}{\hat{\sigma}^2_{tot}}$	0.0385	0.0176	0.0142	0.0256	0.0269	0.0107
	[0.0112 ;0.3068]	[0.0092 ;0.0652]	[0.0068 ;0.0282]	[0.0111 ;0.4371]	[0.0063 ;0.3162]	[0.0057 ;0.0812]

^{a} Number of days with given options' maturity in the sample that satisfy the exclusion criteria. Only these days were used for implying the model parameters.
^{b} Total number of days with given options' maturity in the sample.
^{c} Median of daily parameter estimates.
^{d} Lower and upper quartiles of daily parameter estimates.
(Adapted from: Rieken, Mittnik, and Rachev (1998))

Table 13.6 Parameter Estimates for the IDL3r Model^a

Para-meter	Calls Days to Maturity			Puts Days to Maturity		
	10	30	60	10	30	60
	Number of Days			Number of Days		
	43	40	38	42	40	32
	(43)	(40)	(42)	(43)	(40)	(42)
$\hat{\sigma}$	0.1467	0.1561	0.1581	0.1578	0.1619	0.1622
	[0.1178 ;0.1835]	[0.1251 ;0.1833]	[0.1312 ;0.1858]	[0.1309 ;0.1780]	[0.1300 ;0.1914]	[0.1380 ;0.2074]
$\hat{a}_1$	0.1310	0.1338	0.1186	0.1160	0.1610	0.1594
	[0.1002 ;0.5314]	[0.0998 ;0.2188]	[0.1007 ;0.2108]	[0.1008 ;0.1609]	[0.0996 ;0.2490]	[0.1029 ;0.2151]
$\hat{a}_3$	0.1037	0.1011	0.1025	0.0998	0.0992	0.1004
	[0.0577 ;0.1264]	[0.0836 ;0.1257]	[0.0875 ;0.1211]	[0.0646 ;0.1235]	[0.0580 ;0.1132]	[0.0905 ;0.1378]
$\hat{\lambda}_1$	0.0086	0.0077	0.0047	0.0103	0.0091	0.0041
	[0.0045 ;0.0115]	[0.0000 ;0.0155]	[0.0001 ;0.0114]	[0.0079 ;0.0204]	[0.0048 ;0.0175]	[0.0000 ;0.0160]
$\hat{\lambda}_3$	0.0023	0.0013	0.0011	0.0014	0.0008	0.0007
	[0.0001 ;0.0394]	[0.0000 ;0.0294]	[0.0001 ;0.0323]	[0.0001 ;0.0579]	[0.0000 ;0.0535]	[0.0000 ;0.0119]
$\hat{a}_1\hat{\lambda}_1$ (×100)	0.1013	0.1122	0.0870	0.1248	0.1167	0.0286
	[0.0743 ;0.5634]	[0.0000 ;0.3075]	[0.0017 ;0.1916]	[0.0931 ;0.3784]	[0.0388 ;0.4270]	[0.0000 ;0.2903]
$\hat{a}_3\hat{\lambda}_3$ (×100)	0.0007	0.0006	0.0007	0.0008	0.0000	0.0000
	[0.0000 ;0.2310]	[0.0000 ;0.1095]	[0.0000 ;0.0124]	[0.0000 ;0.6634]	[0.0000 ;0.2007]	[0.0000 ;0.0139]
$\dfrac{\hat{\sigma}^2_{Poi}}{\hat{\sigma}^2_{tot}}$	0.0348	0.0280	0.0224	0.0555	0.0536	0.0381
	[0.0081 ;0.3416]	[0.0006 ;0.0916]	[0.0006 ;0.0624]	[0.0122 ;0.2404]	[0.0081 ;0.2511]	[0.0003 ;0.1459]

^{a} Notes: See Table 13.5.
(Adapted from: Rieken, Mittnik, and Rachev (1998))

sign) from the first two Poisson random variables, $a_1\lambda_1$ and $a_2\lambda_2$, is about 0.001 and -0.001 for the IDN3r and the IDL3r models. Since these values are annualized, the (individual) contribution from the two symmetric Poissons to the return is rather low for these models. For the other models, however, these values are typically about ten times as high and much higher in some cases. The median estimates of the average contribution to the mean return generated by the unrestricted Poisson process, $\hat{a}_3\hat{\lambda}_3$, tends to be much lower for all models. As can be seen from the lower quartiles, the sign of α_3 corresponding to each of the models tends to be positive in most cases. This is somewhat surprising, given the typical BS smile shape indicating a negative skewness of the implied risk–neutral return distribution, at least for options

Table 13.7 Parameter Estimates for the IDt3r Model[a]

Para-meter	Calls			Puts		
	Days to Maturity			Days to Maturity		
	10	30	60	10	30	60
	Number of Days			Number of Days		
	43	40	38	42	40	32
	(43)	(40)	(42)	(43)	(40)	(42)
$\bar{\nu}$	17.7285	24.7112	25.1951	11.5922	9.1288	14.0863
	[7.7967 ;24.7863]	[15.2618 ;41.1477]	[21.4933 ;32.3944]	[7.0290 ;19.0260]	[6.9987 ;21.8264]	[6.9629 ;25.0578]
$\hat{\sigma}$	0.1384	0.1402	0.1425	0.1529	0.1512	0.1508
	[0.0999 ;0.1681]	[0.1157 ;0.1612]	[0.1194 ;0.1660]	[0.1130 ;0.1706]	[0.1166 ;0.1770]	[0.1333 ;0.1929]
$\hat{a}_1$	0.1084	0.1184	0.1123	0.1105	0.1126	0.1536
	[0.0997 ;0.1571]	[0.0595 ;0.1581]	[0.0771 ;0.1737]	[0.0863 ;0.1766]	[0.0860 ;0.1896]	[0.0637 ;0.2027]
$\hat{a}_3$	0.1000	0.0883	0.0548	0.0855	0.0736	0.0675
	[0.0840 ;0.1218]	[0.0586 ;0.1141]	[0.0196 ;0.0953]	[0.0693 ;0.1256]	[0.0538 ;0.0987]	[0.0101 ;0.0880]
$\hat{\lambda}_1$	0.1005	0.1003	0.1007	0.0994	0.0946	0.0913
	[0.0981 ;0.1064]	[0.0927 ;0.1068]	[0.0903 ;0.1067]	[0.0910 ;0.1019]	[0.0774 ;0.0994]	[0.0711 ;0.0974]
$\hat{\lambda}_3$	0.0726	0.0775	0.0797	0.0465	0.0161	0.0112
	[0.0159 ;0.1000]	[0.0297 ;0.1469]	[0.0139 ;0.1276]	[0.0026 ;0.1265]	[0.0008 ;0.0769]	[0.0003 ;0.0824]
$\hat{a}_1\hat{\lambda}_1$ (×100)	1.1178	1.1470	1.1517	1.1239	1.1030	1.1808
	[0.9971 ;1.5997]	[0.6727 ;1.7151]	[0.7911 ;1.7148]	[0.8699 ;1.7007]	[0.8554 ;1.6529]	[0.6622 ;1.7431]
$\hat{a}_3\hat{\lambda}_3$ (×100)	0.6575	0.6309	0.1624	0.3763	0.0271	0.0060
	[0.1582 ;0.9997]	[0.0374 ;0.9878]	[0.0064 ;0.7196]	[0.0189 ;1.0791]	[0.0009 ;0.3076]	[0.0000 ;0.0815]
$\dfrac{\hat{\sigma}^2_{Poi}}{\hat{\sigma}^2_{tot}}$	0.1605	0.1573	0.1406	0.1469	0.1133	0.1546
	[0.1123 ;0.3452]	[0.0918 ;0.2547]	[0.0668 ;0.2626]	[0.0601 ;0.3599]	[0.0731 ;0.2907]	[0.0408 ;0.2336]

[a] Notes: See Table 13.5.
(Adapted from: Rieken, Mittnik, and Rachev (1998))

Table 13.8 Parameter Estimates for the IDC3r Model[a]

Para-meter	Calls			Puts		
	Days to Maturity			Days to Maturity		
	10	30	60	10	30	60
	Number of Days			Number of Days		
	43	40	38	42	40	32
	(43)	(40)	(42)	(43)	(40)	(42)
φ^2	0.1565	0.0194	0.0043	0.8761	0.8895	1.0106
	[0.0237 ;0.9410]	[0.0008 ;0.1585]	[0.0001 ;0.0178]	[0.5099 ;1.1958]	[0.6758 ;1.2571]	[0.6329 ;1.2989]
$\hat{\sigma}$	0.1346	0.1357	0.1385	0.1650	0.1635	0.1681
	[0.1058 ;0.1584]	[0.1129 ;0.1478]	[0.1179 ;0.1572]	[0.1348 ;0.1884]	[0.1432 ;0.2006]	[0.1457 ;0.2105]
$\hat{a}_1$	0.1125	0.1144	0.1098	0.1151	0.1330	0.1092
	[0.0473 ;0.1712]	[0.0729 ;0.1807]	[0.0673 ;0.1842]	[0.0704 ;0.1425]	[0.0751 ;0.1906]	[0.0517 ;0.1754]
$\hat{a}_3$	0.0975	0.0736	0.0559	0.0973	0.1114	0.0360
	[0.0600 ;0.1195]	[-0.0097 ;0.0980]	[0.0078 ;0.0900]	[0.0707 ;0.1163]	[0.0772 ;0.1405]	[-0.1311 ;0.1032]
$\hat{\lambda}_1$	0.1001	0.0999	0.1082	0.0996	0.0932	0.0884
	[0.0973 ;0.1061]	[0.0914 ;0.1159]	[0.0905 ;0.1213]	[0.0973 ;0.1022]	[0.0859 ;0.0993]	[0.0818 ;0.0970]
$\hat{\lambda}_3$	0.1060	0.0970	0.0923	0.0837	0.0060	0.0865
	[0.0216 ;0.1772]	[0.0244 ;0.2028]	[0.0420 ;0.3033]	[0.0011 ;0.1701]	[0.0000 ;0.0603]	[0.0004 ;0.1297]
$\hat{a}_1\hat{\lambda}_1$ (×100)	1.1238	1.3504	1.1752	1.1294	1.2613	1.0755
	[0.4698 ;1.7190]	[0.7603 ;1.9503]	[0.5985 ;1.7082]	[0.7601 ;1.5167]	[0.7703 ;1.6884]	[0.3117 ;1.4930]
$\hat{a}_3\hat{\lambda}_3$ (×100)	0.7077	0.2709	0.2523	0.6132	0.0451	0.0001
	[0.0028 ;1.3620]	[0.0000 ;0.9386]	[0.0002 ;0.5750]	[0.0086 ;1.7439]	[0.0000 ;0.3451]	[-1.2927 ;0.0581]
$\dfrac{\hat{\sigma}^2_{Poi}}{\hat{\sigma}^2_{tot}}$	0.2051	0.2493	0.2067	0.1253	0.1218	0.1153
	[0.0825 ;0.3290]	[0.1091 ;0.3189]	[0.0817 ;0.2857]	[0.0730 ;0.2370]	[0.0846 ;0.1990]	[0.0390 ;0.1920]

[a] Notes: See Table 13.5.
(Adapted from: Rieken, Mittnik, and Rachev (1998))

having longer term to maturity. However, this result should not be overvalued, because options which are sensitive to jumps are options far away from the money, and the volume of such options is very low; cf. Table 13.3. Hence, such options play a minor role when maximizing objective function (13.88).

The variance ratio, defined in (13.93), indicates that the portion of the total variance that can be attributed to the Poissonian part is typically quite low (with medians of about one to five percent) for the IDN3r and the IDL3r models, while it is substantially higher for the other models. In the models IDt3r, IDC3r, IDBN3r, and IDS3r the median values are of orders 11 to 16%, 11 to 25%, 18 to 25%, and 4 to 13%, respectively. In the latter model this ratio is extremely low (about 4%) only for puts. This is because the estimates of the volatility parameter σ corresponding to the subordinated part of the return

Table 13.9 Parameter Estimates for the IDBN3r Model[a]

Para-meter	Calls — Days to Maturity / Number of Days			Puts — Days to Maturity / Number of Days		
	10 / 43 (43)	30 / 40 (40)	60 / 38 (42)	10 / 42 (43)	30 / 40 (40)	60 / 32 (42)
$\hat\gamma$	2.8914	17.4624	27.1516	1.3952	1.2815	1.3799
	[1.4402 ;5.5248]	[3.6624 ;24.6130]	[4.3907 ;45.5703]	[0.8618 ;2.1722]	[0.8821 ;1.5823]	[0.9196 ;2.8941]
$\hat\sigma$	0.1387	0.1291	0.1416	0.1516	0.1549	0.1599
	[0.1023 ;0.1702]	[0.1074 ;0.1561]	[0.1196 ;0.1594]	[0.1230 ;0.1875]	[0.1270 ;0.1821]	[0.1334 ;0.1985]
$\hat a_1$	0.1052	0.1144	0.1565	0.1383	0.1954	0.2643
	[0.0991 ;0.1804]	[0.0741 ;0.2034]	[0.0856 ;0.2100]	[0.0959 ;0.2057]	[0.1038 ;0.3214]	[0.1559 ;0.3068]
$\hat a_3$	0.1012	0.0924	0.0712	0.0952	0.1039	0.0884
	[0.0930 ;0.1291]	[0.0345 ;0.1203]	[0.0044 ;0.1039]	[0.0861 ;0.1227]	[0.0764 ;0.1348]	[0.0692 ;0.1334]
$\hat\lambda_1$	0.0898	0.0904	0.0903	0.0859	0.0763	0.0628
	[0.0855 ;0.0941]	[0.0669 ;0.1022]	[0.0843 ;0.0961]	[0.0826 ;0.0923]	[0.0653 ;0.0885]	[0.0516 ;0.0761]
$\hat\lambda_3$	0.0749	0.0638	0.0497	0.0051	0.0062	0.0021
	[0.0069 ;0.0976]	[0.0056 ;0.1364]	[0.0290 ;0.1170]	[0.0011 ;0.1458]	[0.0001 ;0.0674]	[0.0001 ;0.0565]
$\hat a_1\hat\lambda_1$ (×100)	0.9754	1.1716	1.4048	1.2280	1.4883	1.4053
	[0.8789 ;1.6085]	[0.6710 ;1.6183]	[0.8438 ;1.7707]	[0.8335 ;1.7770]	[0.8940 ;1.9945]	[0.9993 ;1.6807]
$\hat a_3\hat\lambda_3$ (×100)	0.7235	0.1531	0.1580	0.0401	0.0214	0.0069
	[0.0292 ;0.9696]	[0.0032 ;1.1006]	[0.0105 ;0.5837]	[0.0019 ;1.1818]	[0.0004 ;0.4262]	[0.0001 ;0.3113]
$\dfrac{\hat\sigma^2_{Poi}}{\hat\sigma^2_{tot}}$	0.1584	0.2091	0.2340	0.1805	0.2510	0.1988
	[0.1040 ;0.3586]	[0.1091 ;0.2644]	[0.0865 ;0.2836]	[0.0754 ;0.3418]	[0.0846 ;0.3789]	[0.1415 ;0.3278]

[a] Notes: See Table 13.5.
(Adapted from: Rieken, Mittnik, and Rachev (1998))

Table 13.10 Parameter Estimates for the IDS3r Model[a]

Para-meter	Calls — Days to Maturity / Number of Days			Puts — Days to Maturity / Number of Days		
	10 / 43 (43)	30 / 40 (40)	60 / 38 (42)	10 / 42 (43)	30 / 40 (40)	60 / 32 (42)
$\hat\alpha$	1.8311	1.8933	1.9226	1.7131	1.6668	1.6484
	[1.6955 ;1.9425]	[1.8240 ;1.9816]	[1.8434 ;1.9704]	[1.6554 ;1.7884]	[1.6225 ;1.7176]	[1.6021 ;1.7713]
$\hat\sigma$	0.2334	0.1857	0.1823	0.3997	0.4505	0.4290
	[0.1863 ;0.3229]	[0.1524 ;0.2295]	[0.1510 ;0.2581]	[0.2591 ;0.5293]	[0.3645 ;0.5972]	[0.3266 ;0.7238]
$\hat a_1$	0.1794	0.1822	0.1492	0.1323	0.2250	0.2372
	[0.1036 ;0.2289]	[0.1034 ;0.2194]	[0.0899 ;0.1958]	[0.0885 ;0.2551]	[0.1232 ;0.2831]	[0.1951 ;0.2950]
$\hat a_3$	0.0952	0.0695	0.0665	0.0600	0.0628	0.0412
	[0.0694 ;0.1274]	[0.0270 ;0.1013]	[0.0386 ;0.0944]	[0.0224 ;0.1090]	[0.0210 ;0.1268]	[-0.0004 ;0.0912]
$\hat\lambda_1$	0.0999	0.1000	0.0997	0.0985	0.0978	0.0976
	[0.0979 ;0.1001]	[0.0977 ;0.1002]	[0.0974 ;0.1001]	[0.0958 ;0.1008]	[0.0931 ;0.1001]	[0.0875 ;0.1000]
$\hat\lambda_3$	0.0170	0.0397	0.0571	0.0657	0.0041	0.0097
	[0.0011 ;0.1045]	[0.0060 ;0.1080]	[0.0161 ;0.1062]	[0.0011 ;0.1871]	[0.0001 ;0.0721]	[0.0011 ;0.0752]
$\hat a_1\hat\lambda_1$ (×100)	1.5735	1.6948	1.3835	1.2426	2.1888	2.2624
	[1.0445 ;2.2338]	[1.0310 ;2.2208]	[0.9010 ;1.9101]	[0.8611 ;2.3860]	[1.1780 ;2.8270]	[1.7168 ;2.7376]
$\hat a_3\hat\lambda_3$ (×100)	0.1447	0.1479	0.3032	0.0304	0.0036	0.0057
	[0.0060 ;1.4878]	[0.0149 ;1.0123]	[0.0388 ;0.8321]	[0.0000 ;1.5861]	[0.0000 ;0.4276]	[-0.0004 ;0.0553]
$\dfrac{\hat\sigma^2_{Poi}}{\hat\sigma^2_{tot}}$	0.0889	0.1299	0.1040	0.0477	0.0407	0.0395
	[0.0576 ;0.1579]	[0.0848 ;0.1985]	[0.0402 ;0.1925]	[0.0366 ;0.0679]	[0.0320 ;0.0523]	[0.0300 ;0.0633]

[a] Notes: See Table 13.5.
(Adapted from: Rieken, Mittnik, and Rachev (1998))

model tends to be much higher for puts than for calls, while the jump–related parameters are comparable in size for both option types.

13.4.1 Ex–Post Analysis of the Pricing Performance

(a) Comparison of the Pricing Fit

In Table 13.11 we compare the pricing performance of the different models by the objective function in (13.88), averaged across the days used for estimation. In order to simplify the comparison with the BS as the benchmark model, Table 13.11 also contains a standardized performance measure for each of the models, which is given in brackets. This standardized measure of pricing performance is obtained by dividing all mean objective functions by the mean objective function corresponding to the BS model and multiplying by 100.

As can be seen from Table 13.11, the subordinated models outperform the BS model, in general. An exception is the LBS model which fits the data worse than the BS model for calls, though better for puts. The other models fit the market data at least as well as does the BS model. This is to be expected, because these models include the BS model as a special case. In general, the passage from the BS model to the subordinated models leads to a much higher pricing improvement (which is negative for calls priced via the LBS model) for puts than for calls. Consider, for example, the SBS model, which improves the pricing performance, relative to the BS model, by about 13 to 41% for calls, but by about 47 to 66% for puts.

In Table 13.12 the models are ranked according to their mean objective function. Surprisingly, the ranking of the models does not vary much across maturity and option type. The best–fitting models are always the CBS and the SBS models with a mean objective function reduced by between 13% (using the SBS model for 30-day calls) and 66% (using the SBS model for 10-day puts), relative to the BS model. In most cases the difference between both models is rather small. For both calls and puts, the SBS model outperforms the CBS model for short maturity (10-day) options, whereas the CBS model is somewhat better for longer maturities. Although the CBS and SBS are the best models in terms of in–sample fit, also the other subordinated models often lead to a substantial pricing improvement as well. The BNBS model ranks third, irrespective of maturity and option type.

In Table 13.13 we provide summary statistics of the pricing fit for the six ID models, measured by the objective function (13.88). To facilitate a comparison with the corresponding subordinated models, the statistics reported for each option class in the table are the same as in Table 13.11. Again, the BS model is considered to be the benchmark model. Thus, the standardization of the daily means of the objective functions is done with respect to the fit of the BS model in Table 13.11, which was standardized to 100.

As is obvious from a comparison of the Tables 13.13 and 13.11, allowing for discrete jumps in the asset price process improves the fit substantially. These lower means of the objective function go together with lower standard deviations. This is true for all models and option categories. Even in the Gaussian model, superimposing Poisson jumps to the geometric Brownian motion results in a considerably better pricing performance. In comparison to the BS model, the IDN3r model reduces the average objective function by more than 40% for the calls and even more for the puts. For both option types combined, the average pricing improvement amounts to about 50%. The relatively pricing performance for calls, relative to puts, which was much in favor of the puts for the subordinate models, becomes more similar when allowing for jumps. Consider, for example, the performance of the CBS and the IDC3r models for 10-day options. While the for the CBS model the mean

Table 13.11 Mean Objective Functions for Subordinated Models[a]

Model	Calls				Puts				Calls and Puts			
	Days to Maturity				Days to Maturity				Days to Maturity			
	10	30	60	All	10	30	60	All	10	30	60	All
BS	19.90 (31.99) [100.00}	43.45 (65.00) [100.00}	57.25 (66.21) [100.00}	39.41 (57.67) [100.00}	21.82 (15.44) [100.00]	58.76 (49.04) [100.00]	114.62 (92.60) [100.00]	60.83 (68.23) [100.00]	20.85 (25.08) [100.00]	51.10 (57.72) [100.00]	83.47 (83.86) [100.00]	49.80 (63.78) [100.00]
LBS	28.62 (28.61) [143.85]	85.11 (76.18) [195.89]	145.23 (115.77) [253.67]	83.92 (92.69) [212.91]	13.12 (14.97) [60.12]	31.37 (48.31) [53.38]	78.81 (115.13) [68.76]	37.96 (72.39) [62.41]	20.96 (24.07) [100.55]	58.24 (68.91) [113.96]	114.87 (119.38) [137.61]	61.62 (86.41) [123.74]
tBS	16.30 (27.74) [81.91]	39.53 (58.62) [90.97]	52.52 (56.44) [91.74]	35.35 (50.97) [89.69]	10.67 (9.94) [48.89]	35.54 (38.58) [60.48]	86.34 (92.92) [75.33]	40.63 (62.07) [66.80]	13.51 (21.00) [64.83]	37.53 (49.35) [73.44]	67.98 (76.65) [81.44]	37.91 (56.56) [76.13]
CBS	13.75 (22.80) [69.12]	37.76 (55.99) [86.91]	47.64 (56.33) [83.21]	32.33 (48.85) [82.03]	8.26 (8.86) [37.86]	23.07 (36.84) [39.26]	59.01 (90.59) [51.48]	27.70 (56.34) [45.54]	11.04 (17.49) [52.95]	30.41 (47.67) [59.52]	52.84 (73.63) [63.30]	30.09 (52.56) [60.41]
BNBS	15.80 (26.78) [79.42]	39.02 (55.71) [89.81]	49.77 (55.35) [86.93]	34.14 (49.09) [86.63]	10.34 (9.23) [47.38]	28.58 (37.79) [48.65]	73.41 (89.07) [64.05]	34.45 (57.95) [56.63]	13.10 (20.19) [62.85]	33.80 (47.59) [66.14]	60.58 (73.13) [72.57]	34.29 (53.46) [68.85]
SBS	11.66 (19.17) [58.58]	37.95 (55.61) [87.35]	49.02 (56.08) [85.63]	32.08 (48.53) [81.40]	7.33 (8.11) [33.61]	24.61 (36.82) [41.88]	60.93 (90.05) [53.16]	28.44 (56.45) [46.75]	9.52 (14.85) [45.67]	31.28 (47.34) [61.20]	54.47 (73.25) [65.25]	30.32 (52.44) [60.87]

[a] Notes: Daily means of objective functions computed over all days in the sample with 10–, 30– or 60–days to maturity options traded; in parentheses: standard deviations; in brackets: standardized means when setting the mean objective function for the BS model equal to 100. The daily objective function is the (relative) volume–weighted sum of squared market–model price differences, $OF_i = \sum_{i=1}^{n} \frac{V_i}{\sum_{i=1}^{n} V_i} (C_i - \hat{C}_i)^2$ with V_i denoting the (interpolated) Volume, C_i the (smoothed) transaction price and $\hat{C}_i$ the model price.
(Adapted from: Rieken, Mittnik, and Rachev (1998))

Table 13.12 Ranking of Subordinated Models According to their Mean Objective
Function

Model	Calls Days to Maturity 10	30	60	All	Puts Days to Maturity 10	30	60	All	Calls and Puts Days to Maturity 10	30	60	All
BS	5	5	5	5	6	6	6	6	5	5	5	5
LBS	6	6	6	6	5	4	4	4	6	6	6	6
tBS	4	4	4	4	4	5	5	5	6	6	6	6
CBS	2	1	1	2	2	1	1	1	2	1	1	1
BNBS	3	3	3	3	3	3	3	3	3	3	3	3
SBS	1	2	2	1	1	2	2	2	1	2	2	2

(Adapted from: Rieken, Mittnik, and Rachev (1998))

objective function is 13.75 for calls and 8.26 for puts, the average pricing fit
of the IDC3r model (4.44 for calls and 4.69 for puts) is roughly equal for both
option types.

In Table 13.14 we compare the ranking of the six models. The IDS3r model
always ranks first or second, irrespective of the option class considered. As
compared to the BS model, this model reduces the objective function by about
70% for calls and 80% for puts, on the average. The IDS3r model performs
best for puts within all maturity classes and for both option types combined,
with the exception of 10-day options, where the IDC3r model performs slightly
better. The results for IDC3r and the IDBN3r models are less clear cut than
for their respective counterparts CBS and BNBS, which always ranked first
or second and third, respectively, in the no-jump scenario.

(b) Tests of Pricing Biases Related to the Moneyness

If a model is correctly specified, the pricing error, defined as

$$PE_i = C_i - \hat{C}_i, \qquad (13.94)$$

with C_i denoting the (smoothed) market and $\hat{C}_i$ the model price, should not
vary with the moneyness m. We performed two tests of this hypothesis. Both
tests are conducted for options classified into five subgroups, according to their
moneyness. The first test is the conventional t-test of the (null) hypothesis
that a given theoretical option pricing model yields an unbiased estimate of
the market price, i.e., that the expected pricing error is zero. The t-statistic
is given by

$$t = \sqrt{n}\frac{\overline{PE}}{s(PE)}. \qquad (13.95)$$

Here, n is the number of options in the subgroup considered, and $\overline{PE}$ and
$s(PE)$ denote the sample mean and the (bias–corrected) sample standard deviation in the subgroup, respectively, i.e., $\overline{PE} = 1/n \sum_{i=1}^{n} PE_i$ and $s(PE) =$
$[1/(n-1)\sum_{i=1}^{n}(PE_i - \overline{PE})^2]^{0.5}$. Under the null hypothesis that the population mean is zero, the statistic in (13.95) is distributed Student-t with $n-1$

Table 13.13 Mean Objective Functions for ID Models[a]

Model	Calls				Puts				Calls and Puts			
	Days to Maturity				Days to Maturity				Days to Maturity			
	10	30	60	All	10	30	60	All	10	30	60	All
IDN3r	10.70 (18.28) [53.79]	25.57 (52.83) [58.86]	31.28 (54.95) [54.63]	22.08 (45.08) [56.02]	8.93 (7.52) [40.91]	27.49 (33.28) [46.78]	50.67 (45.13) [44.21]	27.16 (35.24) [44.64]	9.82 (13.98) [47.13]	26.53 (43.88) [51.91]	40.14 (51.27) [48.09]	24.54 (40.60) [49.28]
IDL3r	20.57 (20.54) [103.37]	62.95 (66.43) [144.88]	99.85 (108.33) [174.41]	59.48 (79.14) [150.91]	8.70 (8.28) [39.87]	23.54 (27.39) [40.06]	63.87 (87.06) [55.73]	29.39 (53.58) [48.32]	14.70 (16.74) [70.52]	43.24 (54.24) [84.62]	83.40 (100.12) [99.91]	44.88 (69.46) [90.12]
IDt3r	7.33 (15.88) [36.83]	18.29 (35.12) [42.10]	21.80 (28.08) [38.08]	15.50 (27.77) [39.32]	5.23 (6.58) [23.96]	12.40 (19.15) [21.10]	40.48 (69.72) [35.32]	17.64 (41.11) [29.00]	6.29 (12.18) [30.17]	15.35 (28.26) [30.03]	30.34 (51.91) [36.35]	16.54 (34.83) [33.20]
IDC3r	4.44 (6.63) [22.33]	16.93 (28.03) [38.96]	14.74 (18.19) [25.74]	11.80 (20.09) [29.94]	4.69 (6.52) [21.49]	11.39 (19.56) [19.38]	30.48 (67.11) [26.60]	14.28 (38.66) [23.47]	4.56 (6.54) [21.89]	14.16 (24.18) [27.70]	21.94 (47.57) [26.28]	13.00 (30.50) [26.11]
IDBN3r	7.85 (19.37) [39.46]	12.57 (17.58) [28.94]	17.12 (22.09) [29.91]	12.32 (19.92) [31.27]	4.56 (5.54) [20.90]	13.22 (21.64) [22.50]	43.37 (65.05) [37.84]	18.49 (39.89) [30.40]	6.22 (14.33) [29.86]	12.90 (19.60) [25.24]	29.12 (48.34) [34.89]	15.32 (31.33) [30.75]
IDS3r	6.15 (16.94) [30.92]	12.95 (22.95) [29.81]	16.02 (19.62) [27.98]	11.50 (20.19) [29.18]	4.29 (5.42) [19.64]	9.90 (17.28) [16.84]	24.52 (47.76) [21.39]	11.93 (28.41) [19.62]	5.23 (12.60) [25.08]	11.43 (20.24) [22.36]	19.90 (35.34) [23.85]	11.71 (24.48) [23.51]

[a]*Notes*: Daily means of objective functions computed over all days in the sample with 10–, 30– or 60–days to maturity options traded; in parentheses: standard deviations; in brackets: standardized means when setting the mean objective function for the BS model equal to 100. The daily objective function is the (relative) volume–weighted sum of squared market–model price differences, $OF_i = \sum_{i=1}^{n} \frac{V_i}{\sum_{i=1}^{n} V_i} (C_i - \hat{C}_i)^2$ with V_i denoting the (interpolated) Volume, C_i the (smoothed) transaction price and $\hat{C}_i$ the model price.
(Adapted from: Rieken, Mittnik, and Rachev (1998))

Table 13.14 Ranking of ID Models According to their Mean Objective Function

	Calls				Puts				Calls and Puts			
	Days to Maturity				Days to Maturity				Days to Maturity			
Model	10	30	60	All	10	30	60	All	10	30	60	All
IDN3r	5	5	5	5	6	6	5	5	5	5	5	5
IDL3r	6	6	6	6	5	5	6	6	6	6	6	6
IDt3r	3	4	4	4	4	3	3	3	4	4	4	4
IDC3r	1	3	1	2	3	2	2	2	1	3	2	2
IDBN3r	4	1	3	3	2	4	4	4	3	2	3	3
IDS3r	2	2	2	1	1	1	1	1	2	1	1	1

(Adapted from: Rieken, Mittnik, and Rachev (1998))

degrees of freedom. The t-test was used before by Hansson *et al.* (1995) for testing the unbiasedness of the BS model for Swedish index–options.[27] Rubinstein (1985) has proposed a non-parametric test, which is based on the signs of the pricing errors.[28] Under the null hypothesis that a theoretical option pricing model is unbiased, the probability of observing a negative PE should be 0.5. Hence, the number of negative PEs in a sample of size n, denoted by n^-, is distributed Binomial with parameters n and success probability 0.5. For large n, the corresponding test statistic can be approximated by

$$z = \frac{n^- + c - n/2}{\sqrt{\frac{n}{4}}}, \qquad c = \begin{cases} +0.5 & \text{if } n^- < n/2 \\ 0 & \text{if } n^- = n/2 \\ -0.5 & \text{else,} \end{cases} \qquad (13.96)$$

with c as a correction for approximating a discrete random variable by the normal distribution. If the null hypothesis is true, the test statistic in (13.96) is asymptotically a standard normal variate.

The results of the t-tests for the six subordinated models, separated by option type, maturity and moneyness subgroup, are exhibited in the Table 13.15. As can be seen from the Table 13.15, there are more insignificant[29] mean pricing errors for short– than for longer–term options. This is to be expected, as the time value, i.e., the part of the option price to be explained by a theoretical valuation model, increases as the time to expiration increases. No single option pricing model is capable of eliminating the moneyness–bias. Especially for short–term options, there are some insignificant biases. However, if a theoretical valuation model is correctly specified, such pricing errors should be random and insignificantly different from zero. Therefore, the re-

---

[27] Note the error in equation (4.5) of Hansson *et al.* (1995), who (in the notation used here) have $t = \frac{\overline{PE}}{s(\overline{PE})/\sqrt{n}}$. Since $s(\overline{PE}) = s(PE)/\sqrt{n}$, the term $\sqrt{n}$ should be omitted in their formula (4.5).

[28] Rubinstein (1985) has conducted this test for testing the unbiasedness of IVs instead of PEs.

[29] In the following discussion the significance level is set to 5%, if not otherwise stated.

Table 13.15 t-Tests of the Ex–post Moneyness Pricing Bias, Subordinated Model

Days[b]	Model	Moneyness Class Calls[a]					Moneyness Class Puts[a]				
		DOM	OM	AM	IM	DIM	DIM	IM	AM	OM	DOM
	N^c	27	153	376	184	120	72	143	357	186	82
	BS	1.50^d	-0.06	0.17	7.55	10.01	9.83	2.90	-0.78	5.04	6.97
		$(0.11)^e$	(75.73)	(41.10)	(0.00)	(0.00)	(0.00)	(0.00)	(0.02)	(0.00)	(0.00)
	LBS	-8.56	-5.84	1.09	2.56	7.21	2.69	-3.02	-0.05	-0.72	0.70
		(0.00)	(0.00)	(0.00)	(0.00)	(0.00)	(0.44)	(0.00)	(79.26)	(0.01)	(2.41)
	tBS	0.57	-0.92	0.46	6.19	8.90	5.86	0.34	-0.16	2.65	3.19
10		(17.40)	(0.00)	(2.06)	(0.00)	(0.00)	(0.00)	(53.88)	(39.43)	(0.00)	(0.00)
	CBS	1.23	-1.45	0.23	4.74	7.45	4.72	-1.29	-0.15	0.47	1.52
		(0.55)	(0.00)	(26.65)	(0.00)	(0.00)	(0.00)	(1.64)	(41.81)	(0.02)	(0.00)
	BNBS	1.23	-0.95	0.44	5.94	8.57	6.06	0.18	-0.17	2.20	3.07
		(0.42)	(0.00)	(2.44)	(0.00)	(0.00)	(0.00)	(76.01)	(36.79)	(0.00)	(0.00)
	SBS	0.39	-1.85	0.35	3.86	4.45	2.09	-1.40	-0.08	0.27	-0.62
		(35.14)	(0.00)	(8.54)	(0.00)	(0.00)	(0.94)	(0.43)	(65.29)	(5.31)	(0.01)
	N	83	161	287	178	91	64	109	253	186	188
	BS	-3.92	-3.80	1.46	7.52	12.78	-1.53	-7.73	-4.68	5.66	10.20
		(0.00)	(0.00)	(0.00)	(0.00)	(0.00)	(41.43)	(0.00)	(0.00)	(0.00)	(0.00)
	LBS	-15.78	-9.23	5.43	1.52	2.29	-14.75	-12.45	0.19	-0.02	-0.89
		(0.00)	(0.00)	(0.00)	(4.86)	(2.29)	(0.00)	(0.00)	(54.51)	(93.63)	(0.03)
	tBS	-4.90	-4.30	1.83	6.78	11.02	-5.66	-8.04	-2.47	4.44	5.77
30		(0.00)	(0.00)	(0.00)	(0.00)	(0.00)	(0.26)	(0.00)	(0.00)	(0.00)	(0.00)
	CBS	-5.28	-4.43	2.11	6.24	9.42	-9.39	-10.35	-0.95	1.54	-0.02
		(0.00)	(0.00)	(0.00)	(0.00)	(0.00)	(0.00)	(0.00)	(0.05)	(0.00)	(92.43)
	BNBS	-5.20	-4.04	1.97	7.20	11.40	-7.00	-9.11	-2.26	3.28	3.38
		(0.00)	(0.00)	(0.00)	(0.00)	(0.00)	(0.04)	(0.00)	(0.00)	(0.00)	(0.00)
	SBS	-6.15	-4.67	2.25	6.09	8.10	-10.53	-9.60	-1.40	2.48	-1.54
		(0.00)	(0.00)	(0.00)	(0.00)	(0.00)	(0.00)	(0.00)	(0.00)	(0.00)	(0.00)
	N	77	130	256	137	80	41	76	204	144	155
	BS	-8.71	-5.15	1.96	7.57	11.94	-18.09	-15.67	-6.91	5.77	11.97
		(0.00)	(0.00)	(0.00)	(0.00)	(0.00)	(0.00)	(0.00)	(0.00)	(0.00)	(0.00)
	LBS	-23.92	-9.27	8.44	3.27	-2.61	-33.37	-16.18	2.54	3.89	-0.75
		(0.00)	(0.00)	(0.00)	(0.05)	(3.21)	(0.00)	(0.00)	(0.00)	(0.00)	(6.48)
	tBS	-9.39	-5.32	2.48	7.13	9.24	-20.13	-14.58	-4.02	6.33	8.53
60		(0.00)	(0.00)	(0.00)	(0.00)	(0.00)	(0.00)	(0.00)	(0.00)	(0.00)	(0.00)
	CBS	-8.89	-5.11	2.84	6.68	6.67	-26.45	-15.00	0.02	4.64	1.91
		(0.00)	(0.00)	(0.00)	(0.00)	(0.00)	(0.00)	(0.00)	(96.70)	(0.00)	(0.00)
	BNBS	-8.79	-5.09	2.43	7.34	9.18	-23.02	-14.85	-2.47	5.90	5.25
		(0.00)	(0.00)	(0.00)	(0.00)	(0.00)	(0.00)	(0.00)	(0.00)	(0.00)	(0.00)
	SBS	-9.50	-5.19	2.91	6.72	5.48	-26.45	-14.60	-0.84	5.55	1.69
		(0.00)	(0.00)	(0.00)	(0.00)	(0.01)	(0.00)	(0.00)	(3.18)	(0.00)	(0.03)

[a] Moneyness classes: DIM calls/DOM puts: $m > 0.05$; IM calls/OM puts: $0.02 < m \leq 0.05$; AM calls/puts: $-0.02 \leq m \leq 0.02$; OM calls/IM puts: $-0.05 \leq m < -0.02$; DOM calls/DIM puts: $m < -0.05$.

[b] Days to expiration.

[c] Number of options within the class.

[d] Mean pricing error in the class, measured in DEM, standardized to an index value of 1000. The pricing error is defined as $PE_i = C_i - \hat{C}_i$, where C_i ($\hat{C}_i$) denotes the market (model) price of option i.

[e] p-value (in %) associated with a two–sided test of the hypothesis that the population mean pricing error is zero.

(Adapted from: Rieken, Mittnik, and Rachev (1998))

sults for each of the six subordinated models are quite unsatisfactory. For any model (including the BS model) considered here, the mean PE is significantly different from zero (even at the 10%–level) at least in three out of five moneyness subgroups. This is true for both option types and all three maturities. In general, it cannot even be stated that the subordinated models are better than the BS model with respect to producing significant biases in less moneyness subgroups.

The results from the parametric tests presented above are supported by the sign tests, which are summarized in Table 13.16. Typically, a significant pricing bias for a certain option class found from the t-test is confirmed by the sign test. The highly significant pricing bias of the BS model for AM put contracts with a fraction of about 86% being overpriced is insignificant for the models CBS and SBS. For these models mispricings in both directions roughly balance each other. Similar results can be observed for DIM calls and DOM puts, where the percentage of contacts underpriced by the BS model amounts to about 81% (DIM calls) and 100% (DOM puts). The CBS and the SBS models do much better for these options by generating portions of mispricings of either sign that are consistent with the hypothesis that both signs of pricing errors are equally likely.

We also performed the t and the sign–test for the ID models. The results of the parametric and the non-parametric tests are displayed in the Tables 13.17 and 13.18, respectively. First, look at the results from the t-test in Table 13.17. In general, the mean PEs in the table are substantially lower than for the corresponding subordinated models, supporting the evidence of less pronounced pricing biases from the graphical analysis of the mispricing. However, as compared to the results for the subordinated model in Table 13.15, the global picture with respect to the significance of the moneyness bias does not change substantially. As was the case for the subordinated models, irrespective of the option type, maturity and pricing model considered, an insignificance of the pricing bias is the exception rather than the rule. Hence, it can concluded that none of the ID models considered here is correctly specified. The classes of options and moneyness subgroups, where, for certain ID models, no significant pricing bias can be found, are often the same as for the corresponding subordinated models.

The above results are confirmed by the results from the sign–tests; cf. the Table 13.18. Similar to the outcomes of both tests for the subordinated models, there are only minor changes between the results of both tests. In most cases, insignificant (at common significance levels) pricing biases indicated by the t-test are also indicated by the sign test. With respect to the number of insignificant pricing biases at the 1% level found in the five moneyness subgroups, the "best models" are: the IDS3r model for 10-day calls (3 insignificant biases), the IDL3r model for 10-day puts (3), the IDN3r model for 30-day calls (2), the IDC3r model for 30-day puts (4), and the IDC3r model for 60-day puts. For 60-day calls there is (at the same significance level of 1%)

Table 13.16 Nonparametric Sign–Tests of the Ex–post Moneyness Pricing Bias, Subordinated Models

Days[b]	Model	Moneyness Class Calls[a]					Moneyness Class Puts[a]				
		DOM	OM	AM	IM	DIM	DIM	IM	AM	OM	DOM
	N[c]	27	153	376	184	120	72	143	357	186	82
	BS	18.52[d]	52.29	52.39	8.15	0.00	8.33	39.16	66.95	3.76	0.00
		(0.21)[e]	(62.76)	(38.06)	(0.00)	(0.00)	(0.00)	(1.21)	(0.00)	(0.00)	(0.00)
	LBS	96.30	98.04	35.90	28.26	10.00	36.11	70.63	44.26	63.44	39.02
		(0.00)	(0.00)	(0.00)	(0.00)	(0.00)	(2.51)	(0.00)	(3.43)	(0.03)	(6.05)
	tBS	48.15	71.24	43.09	8.70	1.67	16.67	60.14	56.30	10.75	4.88
10		(100.00)	(0.00)	(0.85)	(0.00)	(0.00)	(0.00)	(1.92)	(1.99)	(0.00)	(0.00)
	CBS	22.22	71.24	44.15	21.20	2.50	31.94	69.93	46.78	34.41	19.51
		(0.71)	(0.00)	(2.66)	(0.00)	(0.00)	(0.32)	(0.00)	(24.43)	(0.00)	(0.00)
	BNBS	22.22	64.05	44.95	15.22	2.50	23.61	61.54	54.62	13.44	3.66
		(0.71)	(0.07)	(5.64)	(0.00)	(0.00)	(0.00)	(0.75)	(9.03)	(0.00)	(0.00)
	SBS	51.85	84.31	42.82	24.46	14.17	41.67	68.53	51.26	38.71	76.83
		(100.00)	(0.00)	(0.63)	(0.00)	(0.00)	(19.49)	(0.00)	(67.20)	(0.26)	(0.00)
	N	83	161	287	178	91	64	109	253	186	188
	BS	80.72	80.12	35.54	30.34	16.48	59.38	81.65	85.77	8.60	0.00
		(0.00)	(0.00)	(0.00)	(0.00)	(0.00)	(16.91)	(0.00)	(0.00)	(0.00)	(0.00)
	LBS	100.00	95.65	19.51	42.13	38.46	81.25	84.40	39.13	50.54	62.77
		(0.00)	(0.00)	(0.00)	(4.30)	(3.60)	(0.00)	(0.00)	(0.07)	(94.15)	(0.06)
	tBS	85.54	83.23	32.06	30.34	16.48	71.88	80.73	72.33	9.14	3.72
30		(0.00)	(0.00)	(0.00)	(0.00)	(0.00)	(0.07)	(0.00)	(0.00)	(0.00)	(0.00)
	CBS	85.54	81.37	28.92	30.34	16.48	71.88	80.73	49.41	29.57	50.53
		(0.00)	(0.00)	(0.00)	(0.00)	(0.00)	(0.07)	(0.00)	(89.99)	(0.00)	(94.19)
	BNBS	83.13	81.37	31.01	30.34	16.48	70.31	80.73	69.57	10.22	13.83
		(0.00)	(0.00)	(0.00)	(0.00)	(0.00)	(0.18)	(0.00)	(0.00)	(0.00)	(0.00)
	SBS	93.98	85.71	28.22	31.46	25.27	76.56	80.73	59.68	18.28	75.53
		(0.00)	(0.00)	(0.00)	(0.00)	(0.00)	(0.00)	(0.00)	(0.25)	(0.00)	(0.00)
	N	77	130	256	137	80	41	76	204	144	155
	BS	98.70	89.23	33.59	17.52	18.75	90.24	94.74	85.78	18.75	0.00
		(0.00)	(0.00)	(0.00)	(0.00)	(0.00)	(0.00)	(0.00)	(0.00)	(0.00)	(0.00)
	LBS	100.00	89.23	12.50	33.58	60.00	100.00	97.37	29.41	18.06	67.74
		(0.00)	(0.00)	(0.00)	(0.02)	(9.35)	(0.00)	(0.00)	(0.00)	(0.00)	(0.00)
	tBS	100.00	90.00	30.86	18.98	27.50	100.00	94.74	76.96	9.72	0.00
60		(0.00)	(0.00)	(0.00)	(0.00)	(0.01)	(0.00)	(0.00)	(0.00)	(0.00)	(0.00)
	CBS	98.70	89.23	26.17	20.44	45.00	100.00	100.00	45.59	10.42	45.81
		(0.00)	(0.00)	(0.00)	(0.00)	(43.38)	(0.00)	(0.00)	(23.40)	(0.00)	(33.51)
	BNBS	98.70	89.23	30.47	17.52	30.00	95.12	93.42	67.16	10.42	13.55
		(0.00)	(0.00)	(0.00)	(0.00)	(0.05)	(0.00)	(0.00)	(0.00)	(0.00)	(0.00)
	SBS	100.00	89.23	26.56	21.17	51.25	100.00	100.00	56.37	2.08	45.16
		(0.00)	(0.00)	(0.00)	(0.00)	(91.10)	(0.00)	(0.00)	(8.01)	(0.00)	(26.08)

[a] Moneyness classes: DIM calls/DOM puts: $m > 0.05$; IM calls/OM puts: $0.02 < m \leq 0.05$; AM calls/puts: $-0.02 \leq m \leq 0.02$; OM calls/IM puts: $-0.05 \leq m < -0.02$; DOM calls/DIM puts: $m < -0.05$.
[b] Days to expiration.
[c] Number of options within the class.
[d] Percentage of negative pricing errors in the class. The pricing error is defined as $PE_{i,t} = C_{i,t} - \hat{C}_{i,t}$, where $C_{i,t}$ denotes the market price of option i, observed on day t, and $\hat{C}_{i,t}$ denotes the fair option price, using the option pricing model with parameters estimated from price data observed on the same trading day, t.
[e] p-value (in %) associated with a two–sided test of the hypothesis that the probability of a negative pricing errors in the class is equal to 0.5.
(Adapted from: Rieken, Mittnik, and Rachev (1998))

Table 13.17 *t*–Tests of the Ex–post Moneyness Pricing Bias, Inifinitely Divisible Models

Days[b]	Model	Moneyness Class Calls[a]					Moneyness Class Puts[a]				
		DOM	OM	AM	IM	DIM	DIM	IM	AM	OM	DOM
	N[c]	27	152	376	184	120	72	143	357	186	82
	IDN3r	3.04[d]	0.81	0.06	5.31	8.57	5.73	2.29	-0.58	3.04	3.84
		(0.00)[e]	(0.00)	(66.75)	(0.00)	(0.00)	(0.00)	(0.00)	(0.00)	(0.00)	(0.00)
	IDL3r	-6.32	-5.31	0.93	1.80	5.17	-0.35	-3.82	-0.27	-1.22	-1.06
		(0.00)	(0.00)	(0.00)	(0.00)	(0.00)	(63.56)	(0.00)	(9.66)	(0.00)	(0.58)
	IDt3r	2.06	-0.34	0.14	4.10	7.27	3.66	0.38	-0.21	1.50	2.80
10		(0.00)	(3.31)	(26.83)	(0.00)	(0.00)	(0.00)	(34.22)	(8.05)	(0.00)	(0.00)
	IDC3r	1.89	-0.92	0.13	2.03	2.83	6.89	0.23	-0.21	0.67	1.91
		(0.00)	(0.00)	(26.59)	(0.00)	(0.00)	(0.00)	(57.30)	(7.81)	(0.00)	(0.00)
	IDBN3r	2.60	-0.40	0.02	3.12	6.50	4.07	0.43	-0.21	1.56	2.85
		(0.00)	(4.76)	(91.55)	(0.00)	(0.00)	(0.00)	(28.65)	(9.15)	(0.00)	(0.00)
	IDS3r	1.96	-0.25	-0.04	2.76	4.87	6.78	1.52	-0.13	1.54	2.13
		(0.00)	(7.40)	(76.94)	(0.00)	(0.00)	(0.00)	(0.00)	(27.60)	(0.00)	(0.00)
	N	83	161	287	178	91	64	109	253	186	188
	IDN3r	-0.17	-1.17	0.64	4.74	11.02	0.58	-4.18	-3.17	2.95	6.44
		(61.23)	(0.01)	(0.50)	(0.00)	(0.00)	(68.85)	(0.00)	(0.00)	(0.00)	(0.00)
	IDL3r	-13.37	-7.93	4.38	1.69	3.18	-13.54	-11.43	-0.08	-0.94	-1.91
		(0.00)	(0.00)	(0.00)	(1.37)	(0.20)	(0.00)	(0.00)	(78.75)	(0.02)	(0.00)
	IDt3r	-3.65	-3.05	1.29	3.75	7.29	-5.38	-5.67	-1.12	1.45	3.07
30		(0.00)	(0.00)	(0.00)	(0.00)	(0.00)	(0.00)	(0.00)	(0.00)	(0.00)	(0.00)
	IDC3r	-4.09	-2.93	1.33	3.17	5.50	-2.61	-7.21	-0.71	0.65	0.66
		(0.00)	(0.00)	(0.00)	(0.00)	(0.00)	(8.06)	(0.00)	(0.02)	(0.08)	(0.00)
	IDBN3r	-3.63	-2.74	1.24	3.44	4.56	-5.84	-6.86	-1.25	1.78	1.47
		(0.00)	(0.00)	(0.00)	(0.00)	(0.00)	(0.09)	(0.00)	(0.00)	(0.00)	(0.00)
	IDS3r	-3.63	-2.30	1.10	2.58	4.20	-2.36	-4.83	-0.89	1.58	1.18
		(0.00)	(0.00)	(0.00)	(0.00)	(0.00)	(7.12)	(0.00)	(0.00)	(0.00)	(0.00)
	N	77	130	256	137	80	41	76	204	144	155
	IDN3r	-3.01	-2.17	0.38	4.82	9.21	-11.79	-9.72	-4.70	3.94	6.66
		(0.00)	(0.00)	(17.73)	(0.00)	(0.00)	(0.00)	(0.00)	(0.00)	(0.00)	(0.00)
	IDL3r	-19.20	-6.02	6.22	2.57	-1.52	-30.48	-13.99	2.16	2.95	-2.71
		(0.00)	(0.00)	(0.00)	(0.21)	(17.93)	(0.00)	(0.00)	(0.00)	(0.00)	(0.00)
	IDt3r	-6.14	-2.96	1.71	3.71	4.26	-16.52	-10.07	-1.90	3.53	4.08
60		(0.00)	(0.00)	(0.00)	(0.00)	(0.00)	(0.00)	(0.00)	(0.00)	(0.00)	(0.00)
	IDC3r	-5.58	-2.26	1.55	2.40	1.30	-18.32	-9.78	0.28	2.73	1.01
		(0.00)	(0.00)	(0.00)	(0.00)	(6.44)	(0.00)	(0.00)	(36.44)	(0.00)	(0.14)
	IDBN3r	-5.32	-2.60	1.49	3.31	2.76	-18.74	-11.17	-1.48	4.40	2.48
		(0.00)	(0.00)	(0.00)	(0.00)	(0.02)	(0.00)	(0.00)	(0.00)	(0.00)	(0.00)
	IDS3r	-5.22	-2.38	1.49	2.78	1.54	-11.31	-7.35	-1.06	3.21	1.49
		(0.00)	(0.00)	(0.00)	(0.00)	(3.82)	(0.00)	(0.00)	(0.01)	(0.00)	(0.00)

[a] Moneyness classes: DIM calls/DOM puts: $m > 0.05$; IM calls/OM puts: $0.02 < m \leq 0.05$; AM calls/puts: $-0.02 \leq m \leq 0.02$; OM calls/IM puts: $-0.05 \leq m < -0.02$; DOM calls/DIM puts: $m < -0.05$.

[b] Days to expiration.

[c] Number of options within the class.

[d] Mean pricing error in the class, measured in DEM, standardized to an index value of 1000. The pricing error is defined as $PE_i = C_i - \hat{C}_i$, where C_i ($\hat{C}_i$) denotes the market (model) price of option i.

[e] p-value (in %) associated with a two–sided test of the hypothesis that the population mean pricing error is zero.

(Adapted from: Rieken, Mittnik, and Rachev (1998))

no insignificant pricing bias for the IDBN3r model, and the other five models do equally "well" with one insignificant bias each.

The results from the significance tests suggest that all ID models exhibit statistically significant pricing biases. Though leading to a less severe mispricing of options, as compared to the "pure" subordinated model, the Poisson jumps incorporated in the ID models cannot capture the moneyness–related mispricing found for the subordinated models.

(c) Analysis of the Smile–Effect

As was discussed above, the smile–effect in the BS model can be interpreted as direct evidence against the distributional assumption of geometric Brownian motion for asset returns. To facilitate a comparison of the smiles generated by the different models, we therefore analyze implied volatility ratios (IVRs), i.e., relative IVs, instead of absolute IVs. On a given trading day t the IVR of an option having moneyness m and maturity τ is defined as the IV $v_t(m, \tau)$ of that option, divided by IV of the at-the-money (AM) option, $v_t(0, \tau)$, on that day, i.e.,

$$V_t^{\text{rel}}(m, \tau) = \frac{v_t(m, \tau)}{v_t(0, \tau)}, \tag{13.97}$$

where $v_t(0, \tau)$ denotes the estimated AM IV for the same maturity on that day. If a model is correctly specified, the model's IVs should not differ strikes, i.e., the IVRs, defined in (13.97), should all be equal to 1. For the LBS model the IV can be defined in an analogous way to the IV for the BS model, because the volatility σ is the only (volatility) parameter in this model; see equation (13.91). The other subordinated models contain two parameters: a structural parameter (ν, φ^2, γ and α in the tBS, CBS, BNBS and SBS model, respectively), determining the shape of the return distribution, and a volatility parameter, σ. In these models the IV corresponding to a market price C_i observed on day t can be defined as a conditional IV, given the structural parameter. Holding the structural parameter fix, the (conditional) IV can be computed numerically by solving for the volatility parameter, v, that equates the model price to the market price:

$$v(S, t, K, \mathcal{T}, r, C; \hat{\theta}) = \left(C^{\text{Model}} \right) \leftarrow (S, t, K, \mathcal{T}, r, C^M; \theta). \tag{13.98}$$

Here, θ denotes the shape parameter corresponding to a given model. To numerically solve for the IVs of the different models, a Sequential Quadratic Programming (SQP) routine was implemented. For an option belonging to a specific subsample containing options of the same type (puts or calls) and maturity (10, 30 or 60 days), the volatility parameter estimated for the whole subsample of options was used as the starting value.

After all IVs are computed the IVRs can be computed. Since typically no observation for $m = 0$ is available, the AM IV was computed using linear interpolation from the two options around $m = 0$. The IVRs are then classified

Table 13.18 Nonparametric Sign–Tests of the Ex–post Moneyness Pricing Bias, Inifinitely Divisible Models

		Moneyness Class Calls[a]					Moneyness Class Puts[a]				
Days[b]	Model	DOM	OM	AM	IM	DIM	DIM	IM	AM	OM	DOM
	N[c]	27	152	376	184	120	72	143	357	186	82
	IDN3r	18.52[d]	40.13	55.05	18.48	10.00	26.39	35.66	61.06	7.53	14.63
		(0.21)[e]	(1.87)	(5.64)	(0.00)	(0.00)	(0.01)	(0.08)	(0.00)	(0.00)	(0.00)
	IDL3r	96.30	96.71	41.76	30.43	16.67	45.83	79.72	47.06	74.73	53.66
		(0.00)	(0.00)	(0.17)	(0.00)	(0.00)	(55.57)	(0.00)	(28.98)	(0.00)	(58.08)
	IDt3r	11.11	55.26	47.34	17.39	1.67	30.56	53.15	52.38	16.13	10.98
10		(0.01)	(22.37)	(32.72)	(0.00)	(0.00)	(0.15)	(50.35)	(39.71)	(0.00)	(0.00)
	IDC3r	11.11	71.71	48.14	22.28	11.67	12.50	58.74	52.66	37.63	13.41
		(0.01)	(0.00)	(50.26)	(0.00)	(0.00)	(0.00)	(4.48)	(34.08)	(0.10)	(0.00)
	IDBN3r	11.11	52.63	52.39	15.22	0.83	20.83	47.55	55.18	11.29	6.10
		(0.01)	(57.02)	(38.06)	(0.00)	(0.00)	(0.00)	(61.58)	(5.67)	(0.00)	(0.00)
	IDS3r	25.93	54.61	52.66	12.50	0.00	0.00	34.27	54.06	12.90	19.51
		(2.09)	(29.17)	(32.72)	(0.00)	(0.00)	(0.00)	(0.02)	(13.84)	(0.00)	(0.00)
	N	83	161	287	178	91	64	109	253	186	188
	IDN3r	33.73	55.90	51.57	37.08	14.29	45.31	65.14	81.82	11.83	7.98
		(0.43)	(15.60)	(63.68)	(0.07)	(0.00)	(53.20)	(0.22)	(0.00)	(0.00)	(0.00)
	IDL3r	100.00	95.65	21.25	47.75	31.87	85.94	88.99	41.50	62.37	73.40
		(0.00)	(0.00)	(0.00)	(59.98)	(0.08)	(0.00)	(0.00)	(0.83)	(0.10)	(0.00)
	IDt3r	78.31	90.06	34.15	32.02	10.99	64.06	78.90	61.66	20.43	5.32
30		(0.00)	(0.00)	(0.00)	(0.00)	(0.00)	(3.36)	(0.00)	(0.03)	(0.00)	(0.00)
	IDC3r	79.52	84.47	35.19	34.83	14.29	51.56	88.99	49.80	55.91	41.49
		(0.00)	(0.00)	(0.00)	(0.01)	(0.00)	(90.05)	(0.00)	(100.00)	(12.36)	(2.38)
	IDBN3r	63.86	85.09	36.24	29.21	16.48	64.06	68.81	60.87	24.19	22.87
		(1.57)	(0.00)	(0.00)	(0.00)	(0.00)	(3.36)	(0.01)	(0.07)	(0.00)	(0.00)
	IDS3r	78.31	79.50	34.84	36.52	21.98	53.12	74.31	62.85	25.27	30.85
		(0.00)	(0.00)	(0.00)	(0.04)	(0.00)	(70.77)	(0.00)	(0.01)	(0.00)	(0.00)
	N	77	130	256	137	80	41	76	204	144	155
	IDN3r	66.23	73.08	46.88	26.28	26.25	75.61	93.42	81.37	16.67	3.87
		(0.62)	(0.00)	(34.85)	(0.00)	(0.00)	(0.18)	(0.00)	(0.00)	(0.00)	(0.00)
	IDL3r	100.00	81.54	16.02	37.23	57.50	100.00	96.05	32.84	20.14	79.35
		(0.00)	(0.00)	(0.00)	(0.37)	(21.88)	(0.00)	(0.00)	(0.00)	(0.00)	(0.00)
	IDt3r	93.51	83.08	30.08	26.28	35.00	95.12	92.11	63.73	20.83	9.03
60		(0.00)	(0.00)	(0.00)	(0.00)	(1.01)	(0.00)	(0.00)	(0.01)	(0.00)	(0.00)
	IDC3r	93.51	76.92	28.12	31.39	42.50	100.00	98.68	46.57	22.22	43.23
		(0.00)	(0.00)	(0.00)	(0.00)	(21.88)	(0.00)	(0.00)	(36.27)	(0.00)	(10.82)
	IDBN3r	83.12	84.62	32.03	21.90	30.00	75.61	85.53	64.22	11.81	23.23
		(0.00)	(0.00)	(0.00)	(0.00)	(0.05)	(0.18)	(0.00)	(0.01)	(0.00)	(0.00)
	IDS3r	84.42	86.15	29.69	27.74	51.25	80.49	82.89	62.75	4.86	41.94
		(0.00)	(0.00)	(0.00)	(0.00)	(91.10)	(0.02)	(0.00)	(0.04)	(0.00)	(5.39)

[a] Moneyness classes: DIM calls/DOM puts: $m > 0.05$; IM calls/OM puts: $0.02 < m \leq 0.05$; AM calls/puts: $-0.02 \leq m \leq 0.02$; OM calls/IM puts: $-0.05 \leq m < -0.02$; DOM calls/DIM puts: $m < -0.05$.
[b] Days to expiration.
[c] Number of options within the class.
[d] Percentage of negative pricing errors in the class. The pricing error is defined as $PE_{i,t} = C_{i,t} - \hat{C}_{i,t}$, where $C_{i,t}$ denotes the market price of option i, observed on day t, and $\hat{C}_{i,t}$ denotes the fair option price, using the option pricing model with parameters estimated from price data observed on the same trading day, t.
[e] p-value (in %) associated with a two–sided test of the hypothesis that the probability of a negative pricing errors in the class is equal to 0.5.
(Adapted from: Rieken, Mittnik, and Rachev (1998))

by the moneyness. The moneyness classes used divide the moneyness range $m \in [-0.1, 0.1]$ into eight non-overlapping subintervals of equal length. For each moneyness class all IVRs in the sample are then gathered and the mean IVR is computed. In Figure 13.3 these means are plotted against the means of the corresponding moneyness class.

The (mean) relative smiles in Figure 13.3 exhibit an asymmetric shape, composed of a linear and a quadratic moneyness–effect. The quadratic effect decreases as the time to maturity increases. For 10-day calls having negative moneyness, the BS smile is almost flat and very similar to the smiles produced by the subordinated models. The differences between the smiles generated by the models become more apparent in the positive moneyness range, where the BS model produces the highest IVRs of all models with IVs for DIM options that are, on the average, more than twice as high as the AM IVs. All subordinated models are able to smoothen the smile to a considerable degree in this moneyness range. The SBS does best for DIM, 10-days–to–maturity calls, where the IVRs are, relative to the BS model, reduced from more than two to about 1.3. The CBS model does somewhat worse for this option category, followed by the BNBS and the tBS model. For calls having longer maturity, the results depends on the moneyness–side. The subordinated models do somewhat worse than the BS model in the OM range, while they do better in the IM range. For calls having 30 and 60 days to maturity the highest reduction of the BS smile–effect in the positive moneyness range is obtained by the SBS model, followed by the CBS, the BNBS and the tBS model. However, for calls having 30 days to maturity the models that produce smoother smiles for positive moneyness tend to produce more pronounced (negative) smiles for negative moneyness. For 60-days–to–maturity OM calls this adverse performance of the models, relative to IM calls, is less pronounced. Here, the IVRs of all the models are very similar for OM calls, while the SBS and the CBS generate almost flat smiles for IM calls.

The BS smile for 10-day puts is about symmetric with higher IVs for options away from the money than for AM options. Hence, for this option category the gain obtained by the subordinated models can be expected to better than for a skewed BS smile, because the BS smile–effect is consistent with the implications of the subordinated models generating heavy–tailed, symmetric returns. As is evident from Figure 13.3, all subordinated models lead to a reduction of the smile–effect on either side of the AM point ($m = 0$). This is to be expected, because the trade–off between a better pricing of IM *and* OM does not exist in this situation of a U-shaped, symmetric smile. The relative smiles generated by the different subordinated models are very similar. The tBS and the BNBS tend to produce somewhat more pronounced smiles than the LBS, the CBS and the SBS model. The latter models generate almost flat smile in the OM range ($m > 0$). While on the average the SBS model tends to produce IVs for DOM 10-day puts that are lower than the AM IVs, this bias is the opposite for the other models.

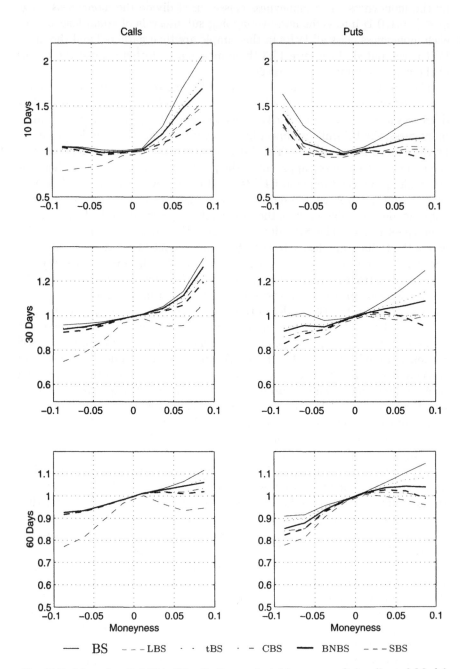

Fig. 13.3 Mean Implied Volatility Ratios against Moneyness, Subordinated Models (Adapted from: Rieken, Mittnik, and Rachev (1998))

In order to analyze the smile–effect of implied volatilities for the ID models, the two–step procedure for computing IVs, when conditioning on the estimated structural parameter $\hat{\theta}$ in (13.98), as described for the subordinated models above, is adopted with the following changes. First, the vector of estimated structural parameters, $\hat{\theta}$, containing the shape parameter of the subordinated model, is extended for the estimates of the six parameters of the Poissonian part. For each option i from a subgroup traded on day t, the volatility parameter σ corresponding to a given model that equates the model to the market price is then computed by conditioning on the estimated parameter vector $\hat{\theta}$ for the whole option subgroup on that day. This implied volatility parameter is denoted by $v_{i,\text{sub}}$. The IV for the ID models is defined as the square root of the implied total variance:

$$v_i = \sqrt{v_{i,\text{sub}}^2 + \sum_{j=1}^{3} \hat{a}_j^2 \hat{\lambda}_j}. \tag{13.99}$$

Again, an SQP method is applied to numerically solve for the IVs. The volatility parameter σ estimated for the whole subgroup of options on a certain day was used as a starting value. In contrast to the subordinated models, where an IV could always be found, an IV could not be found in a few cases for the ID models. The existence of an IV is determined by the jump–related parameters and the actual realization of the Poisson process. Holding the remaining parameters constant, the option price in the ID models is an increasing function of the volatility parameter σ. Whether an IV exists can therefore be checked by computing the fair option values of a given model for a minimum allowed and a maximum allowed value of the volatility parameter. These values are denoted by $\sigma_{\min}$ and $\sigma_{\max}$ respectively. Then the pricing error in (13.94) is determined for both fair option values:

$$PE_{i,\min} = C_i - \hat{C}_i(\hat{\theta}, \sigma_{\min}) \tag{13.100}$$

and

$$PE_{i,\max} = C_i - \hat{C}_i(\hat{\theta}, \sigma_{\max}) \tag{13.101}$$

If $PE_{i,\min} < 0$, the model price is higher than the market price for all values of the volatility parameter in the allowed region; hence, an IV does not exist. If, on the other hand, $PE_{i,\min} > 0$ and $PE_{i,\max} > 0$, a solution does not exist in the allowed IV space $v_i \in [\sigma_{\min}, \sigma_{\max}]$, although a solution might exist for $\sigma > \sigma_{\max}$. A solution in the allowed IV space is therefore indicated by a switch of the sign of the PE between $\sigma_{\min}$ and $\sigma_{\max}$, i.e., $PE_{i,\min} > 0$ and $PE_{i,\max} < 0$. Before the SQP procedure was applied to solve for the IV corresponding to a given option and model, its existence was checked using the procedure described above with $\sigma_{\min}^2 = 10^{-25}$ and $\sigma_{\max}^2 = 400$. Note that these values correspond to an allowed range for $v_i \in [0.00001, 20]$, which is quite conservative, when compared to values that are typically realized in the option markets.

The number and the percentage among all 4700 options within the 235 daily subsamples, for which no IV exists, is 104 (2.21%) for the IDN3r, 341 (7.26%) for the IDL3r, 97 (2.06%) for the IDt3r, 106 (2.26%) for the IDC3r, 209 (4.45%) for the IDBN3r, and 93 (1.98%) for the IDS3r model. The case that $PE_{i,\min} > 0$ and $PE_{i,\max} > 0$ did not occur. Hence, the possibility of an upper bound for the IV that is too low can be excluded. As for the subordinated models, we plot the smile in relative instead of absolute form, i.e., as each IV is divided by the AM IV observed on the same day. As for the subordinated models, the AM IV is computed using linear interpolation from the two options having negative and positive moneyness closest to zero.

In Figure 13.4 we compare the conditional means of the IVR, when conditioning on the moneyness class. The same moneyness intervals as for the subordinated models were used. For the purpose of comparison between the six ID models, an option was disregarded in the conditional mean computation if no IV could be computed for any of the models. In total 817 such options (17.38% of the sample) were excluded from the mean comparison.

Consider first the smiles for the IDN3r model. Obviously, the (mean) IVRs are far from flat and typically exhibit very similar patterns as for the BS model; cf. Figure 13.3. It can therefore be hypothesized that allowing for Poissonian jumps in the Gaussian model does not reduce the smile–effect notably. When comparing the average relative smiles for the other ID models with those for the corresponding subordinated models in Figure 13.3, it can be seen that this similarity carries over to the models with non–Gaussian subordinated part. It appears that, for certain values of the moneyness, some ID–smiles are somewhat closer to unity than the corresponding subordinated smiles; but at the cost of more pronounced smile–effects for other moneyness values. The comparison of the Figures 13.3 and 13.4 seems to indicate that the generalization of the subordinated models to allow for three restricted discrete jumps is not sufficient to capture the pricing biases remaining in the subordinated models. However, the comparison of both figures may be misleading, since the IVRs may be influenced by the "missing values", i.e., options for which no IVR can be computed, in the ID models. Aside from this point, a comparison of each subordinated model with the corresponding ID model is difficult from these plots. Therefore, we recompute the mean IVRs for the subordinated models based on the subsample of options for which an IV could be computed for any ID model and display the resulting relative smile together with that of the corresponding ID model in the same plot. The plots for each of the subordinated (and corresponding ID) models are contained in the Figures 13.5 to 13.10.

The conclusion that the smile patterns do not change substantially due to the Poisson jumps is supported by these plots. The question whether or not the discrete jumps help to smoothen the smile depends on the particular model and subsample considered.

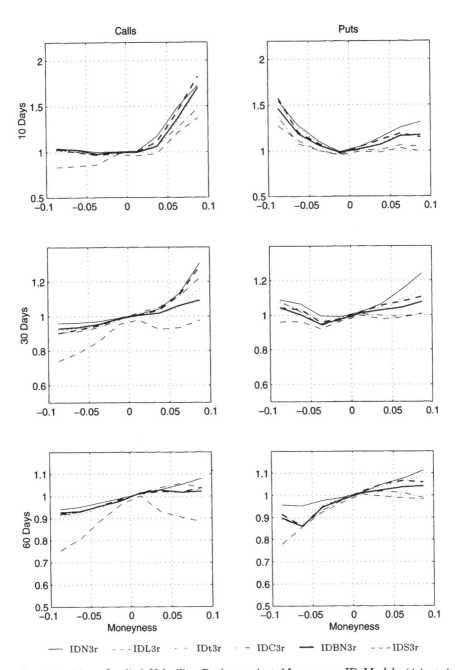

Fig. 13.4 Mean Implied Volatility Ratios against Moneyness, ID Models (Adapted from: Rieken, Mittnik, and Rachev (1998))

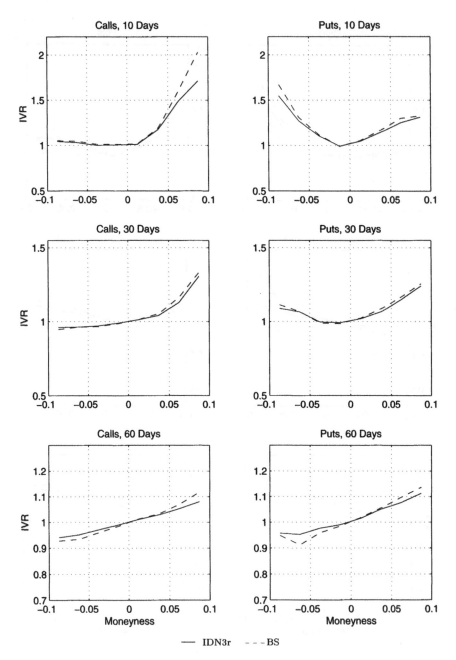

Fig. 13.5 Mean Implied Volatility Ratios against Moneyness, BS and IDN3r Model
(Adapted from: Rieken, Mittnik, and Rachev (1998))

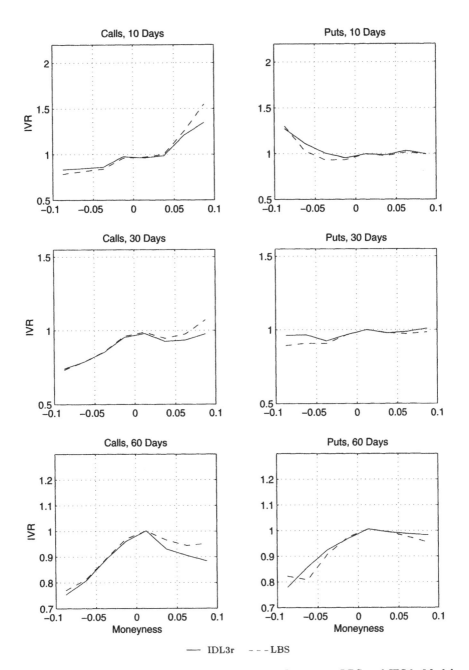

Fig. 13.6 Mean Implied Volatility Ratios against Moneyness, LBS and IDL3r Model (Adapted from: Rieken, Mittnik, and Rachev (1998))

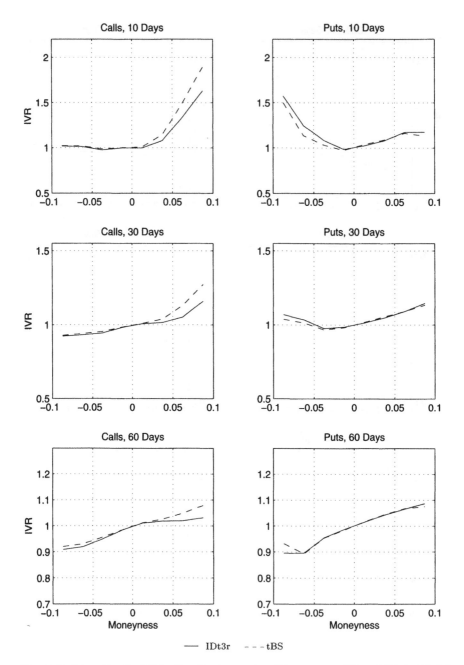

Fig. 13.7 Mean Implied Volatility Ratios against Moneyness, tBS and IDt3r Model
(Adapted from: Rieken, Mittnik, and Rachev (1998))

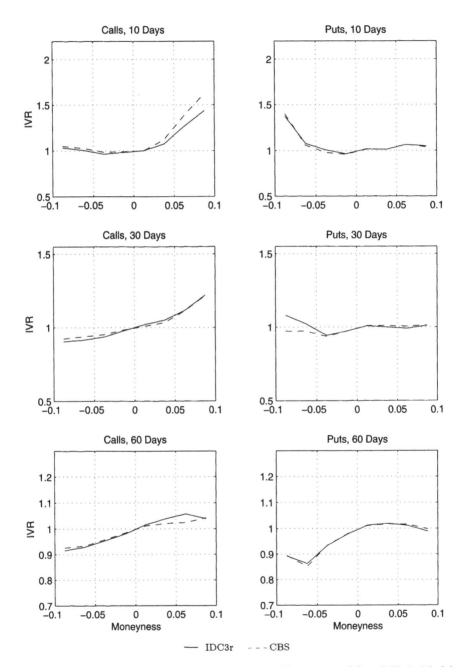

Fig. 13.8 Mean Implied Volatility Ratios against Moneyness, tBS and IDt3r Model
(Adapted from: Rieken, Mittnik, and Rachev (1998))

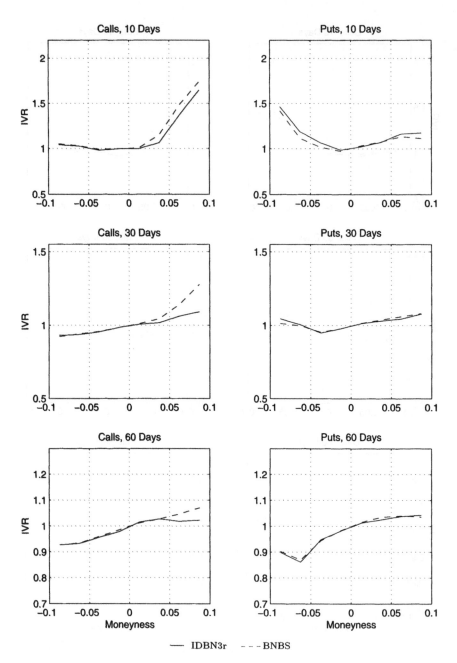

Fig. 13.9 Mean Implied Volatility Ratios against Moneyness, BNBS and IDBN3r Model (Adapted from: Rieken, Mittnik, and Rachev (1998))

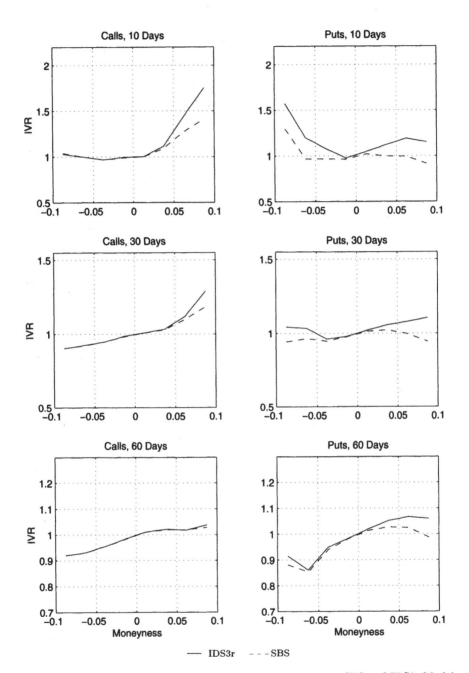

Fig. 13.10 Mean Implied Volatility Ratios against Moneyness, SBS and IDS3r Model
(Adapted from: Rieken, Mittnik, and Rachev (1998))

13.4.2   Analysis of the Forecasting Performance

In this section the prediction performance of the 12 model alternatives is compared. The parameter estimates in Table 13.4 for the subordinated and in the Tables 13.5 to 13.10 for the ID models, estimated from subsamples of option transactions on day t_0, are used to value options, of the same type and maturity, on the next trading day t_1.[30] Three of the four exclusion criteria corresponding to moneyness and trading days used for estimation are also applied to the options used for assessing the prediction errors. The moneyness criterion is somewhat modified to avoid a prediction of prices for options having moneyness outside the moneyness–interval used for estimation. With the same reasoning as in the estimation procedure, we do not compare the predicted to the "raw" data directly. Instead, we again apply the method of Shimko (1993)to back out 20 smoothed market prices, equally space between the minimum and maximum moneyness–value (after applying the moneyness criterion specified above), from each ex–ante subsample of raw market prices. For ease of comparison, all ex–ante market prices were again standardized to an index value of 1000. After the option price and moneyness–criteria, excluding low–priced and far-away-from-the-money options, were applied, five daily option subsamples with less than the required 20 option transactions were excluded. Hence, the number of ex–post and corresponding ex–ante subsamples decreases from 235 to 230. Typically, the ex–ante subsample corresponds to the next calendar day. There is never a weekend between an ex–post and the corresponding ex–ante sample. In 4 out of the 230 subsamples (each 2 for calls and puts) there is one exchange holiday between the observation of the ex–post and the corresponding ex–ante subsample. After applying the above exclusion criteria, all daily ex–ante subsamples of smoothed market prices satisfy the no–arbitrage conditions (13.89) and (13.90).

In Table 13.19 we compare the prediction performance of all subordinated models for subsamples of options in terms of the average of the absolute prediction errors (APEs). The APE for an option i is defined as:

$$\text{APE}_{i,t_0,t_1} = \left| C_{i,t_1} - \hat{C}_{i,t_0,t_1} \right|, \tag{13.102}$$

APE_{i,t_0,t_1} indicates that the APE corresponds to a forecast on day t_0 of the price of option i, which is observed on day t_1. Further, $\hat{C}_{i,t_0,t_1}$ stands for the predicted price of option i for day t_1, which is computed using the parameters estimated on day t_0 and C_{i,t_1} denotes the realized price of option i at time t_1. For each pricing model and option subgroup Table 13.19 also contains the standard error of the APEs, as well as a standardized average

---

[30]The maturity, of course, is not really the same, because it is reduced by the number of days to the next trading day. Since the next day's interest rate is unknown at time t_0, the maturity specific interest rate at the day of estimation, time t_0 was used as input to the models.

APE, obtained by dividing each model's average APE by that of the BS model and multiplying by 100. Hence, again the BS model is considered to be the benchmark of comparison.

As can be seen from Table 13.19, the standard deviations of the APEs are relatively high with values comparable in size to the means. The variability of the APEs tends to be somewhat higher for put than for call options. Moreover, it tends to increase with increasing term to maturity. The mean APEs range from 0.53 to 1.23 index points, or equivalently DEM5.30 to DEM12.30. The mean APEs are lowest for the SBS model predicting 10-day options and the CBS model predicting 10-day puts. The highest mean APE is obtained by the LBS model for 60-day call options. With respect to the time to maturity it can be seen that the models have a tendency to produce higher mean APEs for longer than for shorter maturities. This is to be expected, because—under equal conditions—longer–maturity options have higher time values. Because the part of the option price (as the sum of the inner and the time value) explained by a theoretical valuation model is the time value, the effects of possible model misspecifications on the pricing error are more severe for higher time values. Systematic differences with respect to the option type are also evident from the table. With the exception of the LBS model, for short maturities the models tend to generate lower mean APEs for puts than for calls, whereas for longer maturities the model prices tend to be closer to market prices for calls.

For a given subsample of options, the relative performance of the models is very similar—in a qualitative manner—to the ex–post performance, in terms of the objective function (13.88); see Table 13.11. For the subgroups of options aggregated over calls and puts, i.e., classified by maturity only, the SBS model is the best model for 10-day options, whereas the CBS model is the best model for longer maturities. For the subgroup of all options, aggregated over both option type and maturity, these two models do about equally well by reducing the APE of the BS model by about 14.5%, on the average.

In Table 13.20 we compare the subsample averages of the absolute ex-ante pricing errors (APEs) for the six ID models. As before, the numbers given in parentheses and in brackets are, respectively, the standard deviations and the standardized APEs, when setting the APE of the BS model equal to 100. To facilitate a comparison with the results for the subordinated models in Table 13.19, one more entry is contained in the table for each model and option subsample. This number, given in braces, is the percentage loss of prediction performance when allowing for jumps, measured as

$$\frac{\overline{APE}_{\text{ID},j} - \overline{APE}_{\text{sub},j}}{\overline{APE}_{\text{sub},j}} \times 100\%, \qquad (13.103)$$

where $\overline{APE}_{\text{ID},j}$ is the average APE in subsample j for a given ID model, and $\overline{APE}_{\text{sub},j}$ is the corresponding value for the subordinated model with the same subordinated distribution as in the ID model.

Table 13.19 Mean Absolute Ex-ante Pricing Errors for Subordinated Models[a]

Model	Calls				Puts				Calls and Puts			
	Days to Maturity				Days to Maturity				Days to Maturity			
	10 (43)	30 (40)	60 (34)	All (117)	10 (42)	30 (40)	60 (31)	All (113)	10 (85)	30 (80)	60 (65)	All (230)
BS	0.64 (0.55) [100.00]	0.77 (0.68) [100.00]	0.85 (0.76) [100.00]	0.75 (0.67) [100.00]	0.63 (0.57) [100.00]	0.94 (0.70) [100.00]	1.12 (0.94) [100.00]	0.87 (0.76) [100.00]	0.64 (0.56) [100.00]	0.86 (0.70) [100.00]	0.98 (0.86) [100.00]	0.81 (0.72) [100.00]
LBS	0.65 (0.50) [101.17]	0.91 (0.67) [118.41]	1.23 (0.97) [144.28]	0.91 (0.76) [121.51]	0.58 (0.62) [92.14]	0.72 (0.74) [76.62]	0.99 (1.11) [88.37]	0.74 (0.84) [84.91]	0.62 (0.56) [96.75]	0.82 (0.71) [95.47]	1.11 (1.05) [113.79]	0.83 (0.80) [102.09]
tBS	0.61 (0.53) [94.86]	0.76 (0.66) [98.94]	0.85 (0.75) [100.33]	0.73 (0.65) [98.11]	0.55 (0.55) [87.71]	0.78 (0.70) [82.89]	1.01 (0.96) [90.27]	0.76 (0.76) [86.77]	0.58 (0.54) [91.35]	0.77 (0.68) [90.13]	0.93 (0.86) [94.84]	0.75 (0.71) [92.10]
CBS	0.57 (0.51) [88.57]	0.74 (0.67) [95.30]	0.86 (0.75) [100.96]	0.71 (0.66) [95.04]	0.53 (0.57) [83.28]	0.66 (0.73) [69.79]	0.90 (1.05) [80.56]	0.68 (0.79) [77.19]	0.55 (0.54) [85.98]	0.70 (0.70) [81.30]	0.88 (0.90) [89.84]	0.69 (0.73) [85.57]
BNBS	0.61 (0.52) [94.09]	0.76 (0.68) [98.52]	0.85 (0.76) [100.00]	0.73 (0.66) [97.61]	0.55 (0.55) [86.47]	0.72 (0.71) [76.87]	0.93 (1.00) [83.08]	0.71 (0.77) [81.63]	0.58 (0.54) [90.36]	0.74 (0.69) [86.64]	0.89 (0.88) [90.77]	0.72 (0.71) [89.13]
SBS	0.53 (0.49) [82.85]	0.73 (0.66) [94.84]	0.87 (0.76) [101.99]	0.70 (0.65) [93.41]	0.53 (0.56) [83.15]	0.67 (0.70) [71.67]	0.93 (1.04) [82.93]	0.69 (0.78) [78.70]	0.53 (0.52) [82.99]	0.70 (0.68) [82.12]	0.90 (0.90) [91.59]	0.69 (0.72) [85.61]

[a] *Notes:* Daily means of absolute ex-ante pricing errors; in parentheses: standard errors (below the options' maturities: number of days in the sample); in brackets: standardized means when setting the mean of the absolute ex-ante pricing error for the BS model equal to 100. The ex-ante pricing error is defined as the ex-ante (smoothed) market price minus the predicted model price of an option.

(Adapted from: Rieken, Mittnik, and Rachev (1998))

Table 13.20 Mean Absolute Ex-ante Pricing Errors for ID Models[a]

Model	Calls 10	Calls 30	Calls 60	Calls All	Puts 10	Puts 30	Puts 60	Puts All	Calls and Puts 10	Calls and Puts 30	Calls and Puts 60	Calls and Puts All
IDN3r	0.64 (0.48) [99.76] {-0.24}	0.74 (0.57) [96.19] {-3.81}	1.02 (0.76) [120.56] {+20.56}	0.79 (0.62) [105.38] {+5.38}	0.62 (0.52) [98.48] {-1.52}	1.00 (0.72) [106.08] {+6.08}	1.19 (0.84) [106.83] {+6.83}	0.91 (0.73) [104.30] {+4.30}	0.63 (0.50) [99.14] {-0.86}	0.87 (0.66) [101.62] {+1.62}	1.11 (0.80) [113.07] {+13.07}	0.85 (0.68) [104.81] {+4.81}
IDL3r	0.69 (0.52) [107.39] {+6.15}	0.88 (0.69) [114.30] {-3.47}	1.30 (1.05) [152.72] {+5.85}	0.93 (0.80) [124.81] {+2.72}	0.57 (0.59) [89.72] {-2.63}	0.76 (0.76) [80.57] {+5.16}	1.19 (1.05) [106.23] {+20.21}	0.80 (0.83) [92.04] {+8.40}	0.63 (0.56) [98.73] {+2.05}	0.82 (0.73) [95.79] {+0.34}	1.25 (1.05) [127.37] {+11.93}	0.87 (0.82) [107.43] {+5.23}
IDt3r	0.76 (0.64) [118.04] {+24.44}	0.95 (0.82) [123.44] {+24.76}	1.05 (0.82) [123.64] {+23.23}	0.91 (0.77) [121.80] {+24.15}	0.55 (0.49) [87.53] {-0.21}	0.92 (0.84) [97.52] {+17.65}	1.22 (1.12) [109.46] {+21.26}	0.87 (0.87) [99.03] {+14.13}	0.66 (0.58) [103.09] {+12.85}	0.94 (0.83) [109.22] {+21.18}	1.13 (0.98) [115.91] {+22.22}	0.89 (0.82) [109.72] {+19.13}
IDC3r	0.74 (0.65) [115.11] {+29.96}	0.96 (0.86) [124.32] {+30.45}	1.04 (0.90) [122.01] {+20.85}	0.90 (0.81) [120.64] {+26.94}	0.68 (0.67) [107.08] {+28.58}	1.04 (1.05) [110.17] {+57.86}	1.40 (1.48) [124.72] {+54.82}	1.00 (1.11) [114.45] {+48.27}	0.71 (0.66) [111.18] {+29.31}	1.00 (0.96) [116.55] {+43.36}	1.21 (1.23) [123.49] {+37.46}	0.95 (0.97) [117.36] {+37.15}
IDBN3r	0.75 (0.63) [116.36] {+23.67}	0.95 (0.87) [122.84] {+24.69}	1.04 (0.85) [122.76] {+22.76}	0.90 (0.79) [120.77] {+23.73}	0.57 (0.57) [90.46] {+4.61}	0.93 (0.97) [99.43] {+29.35}	1.05 (1.12) [94.13] {+13.30}	0.85 (0.92) [95.16] {+16.57}	0.66 (0.61) [103.67] {+14.73}	0.94 (0.92) [109.99] {+26.95}	1.05 (0.99) [107.15] {+18.05}	0.87 (0.86) [107.18] {+20.25}
IDS3r	0.82 (0.66) [126.89] {+53.16}	1.03 (0.91) [132.88] {+40.11}	1.13 (0.96) [133.27] {+30.67}	0.98 (0.85) [131.11] {+40.36}	0.60 (0.56) [94.15] {+13.23}	0.87 (0.90) [93.02] {+29.79}	1.16 (1.38) [103.45] {+24.74}	0.85 (0.99) [96.98] {+23.23}	0.71 (0.62) [110.85] {+33.57}	0.95 (0.91) [111.00] {+35.17}	1.14 (1.18) [117.01] {+27.75}	0.92 (0.92) [113.01] {+32.01}

[a] *Notes:* Daily means of absolute ex-ante pricing errors; in parentheses: standard errors; in brackets: standardized means of the ID model when setting the mean ex-ante pricing error for the BS model equal to 100; in braces: increase of the absolute ex-ante pricing error, relative to the corresponding subordinated model. The ex-ante pricing error is defined as the ex-ante (smoothed) market price minus the predicted model price of an option. (Adapted from: Rieken, Mittnik, and Rachev (1998))

For the calls, the mean APEs in the Table 13.20 range from DEM6.40 to DEM13.00. Irrespective of the model considered, the (average) ex-ante prediction errors increase in magnitude with increasing maturity. This can be explained by the higher time value and therefore higher option prices as the maturity increases. For all maturities, the IDN3r model is the best model for the calls. This result is quite surprising, given the bad in-sample fit of this model. As compared to the BS model, the IDN3r model leads to rather slight reductions of the ex-ante mean APE for 10- and 30-day calls, whereas for 60 days to maturity the average APE increases by more than 20%. Except for the BS model predicting 10- and 30-day calls and the LBS model predicting 30-day calls, the ex-ante fit deteriorates by the jumps for all other models and maturities. It appears that the loss of prediction accuracy by adding jumps is highest for those subordinated models that already fit the market prices relatively well (without discrete jumps) in–sample.

Let us summarize our findings:

- In–sample, most subordinated models fit observed option prices substantially better than the BS model. The only subordinated model that does not fit observed market prices better than the BS model is the LBS model when used to price DAX calls.

- The gain of switching from the BS to a subordinated model is higher for puts than for calls and can even be improved in many cases by allowing for discrete jumps.

- The best models among the subordinated models are the CBS and the SBS models. The ranking of the models is similar when allowing for Poissonian jumps. The corresponding ID counterparts of these to models, the IDC3r and the IDS3r model, share this good performance with the IDBN3r model. The exact ranking of the models typically depends on the subsample of options considered.

- The pattern of the models' IV as a function of the moneyness suggest that all models are still misspecified. However, though both the subordinated and the ID models are far from complete, these patterns are typically less pronounced than the patterns implied by the BS model.

- The tests for statistical significance of the pricing bias indicate that, for all models considered, most biases generated by the models are significant.

- The ranking of the subordinated models with respect to their ability to forecast next day's option prices is similar to the in–sample performance. In particular, the gain obtained by using a subordinated instead of the BS model, is higher for puts than for calls. For calls this gain is, depending on the option subsample considered and particular model used, often low or even negative.

- When allowing for discrete jumps in the price process by adding a Poisson part to the subordinated Wiener process, the predictive ability of all models deteriorates in most subsamples.

14
Stable Models in Econometrics

As we pointed out in Chapter 1, stable non-Gaussian models have recently attracted the attention of economists, econometricians, probabilists, statisticians and time series analysts. Economists formulate hypotheses in unspecified functional forms to explain economic processes, while econometricians try to specify economic relationships in the form of regressions to test whether the economic hypotheses in a given model can be accepted empirically. While econometricians base their work on economic theories in specifying their models, time series analysts follow purely statistical principles. Both of them, however, use statistical models for the analysis of their data. To explain an economic variable in a statistical model fully, the dimension of the exogenous variables or the order of lag of the endogenous variable must be infinite, because in an economic system all variables depend on each other, and almost all of them are nonstationary. In practice the final model consists of a combination of identified exogenous variables and unspecified disturbances based on distributional assumptions.

The innovation processes for econometric models can, therefore, be viewed as sums of a very large number of variables, each of which by itself is insufficiently important to be included in the model. The distribution of innovation processes is possibly the most important premise in econometric and time series models. Statistical inference, the consistency and limiting distribution of estimators, as well as the formulation of statistical hypotheses depend crucially on the distributional assumptions in the underlying model. The oldest and most dominant such assumption has been Gaussian. The strongest statistical argument for it is based on the Central Limit Theorem (CLT), which states that the sum of a large number of independently distributed variables from a finite-variance distribution will tend to be normally distributed. In this case, the innovation processes will have normally distributed marginals so that one can make use of the t, χ^2 and F tests with sampling distributions based on Gaussian variables.

However, many empirical observations and studies provide evidence against the Gaussian assumption:

Discordant values and asymmetric samples are often observed in empirical economic time series. Student (1927) was already aware of a long-tailed distribution, which he viewed as a contaminated Gaussian distribution. Mandelbrot (1963b), put forward the Paretian hypothesis for the distribution of financial returns, requiring a power law for the decay of its density function. In his empirical works, Mandelbrot found clear evidence that some asset returns data are heavy-tailed and excessively peaked around zero.

Since Keynes (1936), observed the asymmetric phenomenon in the Real Business Cycle, the significance of this so-called Real Business Cycle Hypothesis for both theoretical and empirical work has been stressed by many authors. Using a nonparametric test, Neftci (1984), found asymmetric behavior in differenced US unemployment rates. DeLong and Summers (1986), adopted the standard skewness statistic to measure an alternative concept of asymmetry. Teräsvirta and Anderson (1992), found asymmetric behavior in the transmission mechanism (in the form of smooth transition nonlinear dynamics) for many of the macroeconomic variables for 13 OECD countries.

Phenomena such as heavy-tailedness and asymmetry in economic variables and their relationships, which cannot be captured by a linear model with constant parameters under the Gaussian assumption, have been analyzed as outlier problems, structural breaks, ARCH structures and/or nonlinear dynamics.

Our discussion on modeling economic relationships with infinite–variance error processes will encompass the following issues [1]:

1. We investigate the empirical evidence for heavy-tailedness and skewness in economic variables and their relationships.

2. We provide sampling distributions based on stable non-Gaussian (or Paretian) random variables (r.v.'s).

3. We study econometric issues such as outliers, structural breaks, ARCH processes, and nonlinearities from the viewpoint of the stable non-Gaussian assumption. We generalize or modify estimators and statistics for hypothesis testing, and investigate their asymptotic properties.

4. We build up econometric models with stable non-Gaussian distributed variables and discuss the implications for various econometric issues.

---

[1]The results of this and the next chapter are due to Rachev, Kim and Mittnik (1997), (1999), Paulauskas and Rachev (1998) and Mittnik, Rachev and Samorodnitsky (1998).

14.1 Empirical Evidence for the Stable Paretian Against the Gaussian Assumption

In Teräsvirta and Anderson (1992), we found evidence for the Paretian hypothesis in certain macroeconomic variables, such as the unemployment rates of some industrial countries, as well as financial index data, such as the S&P500 and DAX (the German stock index). Figure 14.1 shows the heavy-tailedness of some financial and macroeconomic variables.

Other empirical evidence for the Paretian hypothesis is the asymmetry of innovation processes for economic variables which cannot be captured by the

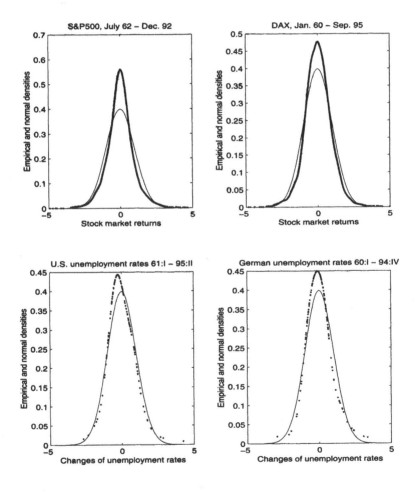

Fig. 14.1 Sample densities of stock market returns, unemployment rates and the corresponding fitted normal densities.(Adapted from: Rachev, Kim and Mittnik (1999))

Gaussian hypothesis. Until now, the asymmetry phenomenon in the Real Business Cycle has been modeled by some nonlinear transmission mechanism and Gaussian innovation processes. Typically, in econometric literature, smooth transition models (STMs) have been used for the modeling of the Real Business Cycle, see Teräsvirta (1994), for more discussion on the STMs.

We claim that the evidence for asymmetry can result not only from a nonlinear transmission mechanism under the normality assumption for innovation processes, but also from a linear transmission mechanism under the assumption of a non-Gaussian asymmetric stable distribution. Kim (1996b), found indications for asymmetric innovation processes from linearly prewhitened macroeconomic data. The gross national product series and unemployment rates series for most industrial countries turned out to be asymmetrical, and to have heavier tails than that of the normal law. Table 14.1 shows the results of testing the symmetry of German and US unemployment rates. The null hypothesis of symmetry for both series cannot be accepted at a significance level of 5%.

Table 14.1 Some evidence for asymmetric innovations.

	Germany (60:I-94:IV)	US (61:I-95:II)
BIC[a]	-13.2489(2)	-2.4612(1)
α[b]	1.6706	1.8337
β[c]	0.3950	0.7082
DeLong/Summer[d]	1.6523	3.0650
	(0.0492)	(0.0022)
HRC[e]	2.3534	2.5584
	(0.0186)	(0.0105)

[a] Akaike's Information Criterion.
[b] Index of stability.
[c] Index of skewness.
[d] Symmetry test based on ordinary skewness statistic, see DeLong and Summers (1986).
[e] Multivariate symmetry test based on spectral measure, see Heathcote, Rachev, and Cheng (1995).
(Adapted from: Rachev, Kim and Mittnik (1999))

Applying various tests in Kim, Mittnik, and Rachev (1997), we investigated detecting asymmetries in observations processes using linear transmission and the non-Gaussian stable innovation process. From these empirical studies, we conclude that for many time series and/or their innovation processes, the Gaussian distributional assumption is clearly violated; the α-stable assumption is an attractive alternative supported by the empirical analysis.

We next survey the results on sampling distributions based on stable innovations.

A. χ^2-type distribution $(_\alpha\chi^2)$

In Mittnik and Kim (1996) and Rachev, Kim and Mittnik (1997), we study the distribution of sums of squared r.v.'s with heavy-tailed distributions. Considering r.v.'s in the DA of a stable Paretian law, we derive the limiting distribution as the degrees of freedom approach infinity. The limiting distribution of sums of squared standard α-stable r.v.'s is, after a suitable normalization,[2] an $\alpha/2$-stable *subordinator*.

Theorem 14.1 If $\{X_i\}_{i=1}^{\infty}$ are in the DA of an α-stable law with $0 < \alpha < 2$, then there exist constants $A_\nu > 0$ and $B_\nu \in \mathbf{R}$, such that, as $\nu \to \infty$,

$$A_\nu^{-1}\,_\alpha\chi^2(\nu) - B_\nu \overset{w}{\Longrightarrow} Z, \tag{14.1}$$

where Z is an $\frac{\alpha}{2}$-stable r.v.

The following two remarks characterize constants A_ν and B_ν and the distributional form of Z.

Remark 14.1 *(Choice of constants A_ν and B_ν in (14.1)):* The choice of A_ν and B_ν is not unique. However, for any selected A_ν we have $A_\nu = \nu^{2/\alpha}\ell(\nu)$, with $\ell(\nu)$ a slowly varying function. One choice of A_ν and B_ν is as follows (cf. Feller (1971), p. 304). Define the truncated moment function $m_\delta(x) = \mathrm{E}[X_1^\delta]\mathrm{I}_{\{X_1^2 < x\}}$, $x > 0$, $\delta > 0$, and choose A_ν to be a solution of

$$m_4(A_\nu) = \frac{A_\nu^2}{\nu}. \tag{14.2}$$

In fact, any A_ν satisfying

$$\frac{\nu}{A_\nu^2} m_4(A_\nu) \longrightarrow 1, \quad \text{as} \quad \nu \to \infty, \tag{14.3}$$

will suffice. A constant B_ν is chosen to be the truncated second moment $B_\nu := \nu A_\nu^{-1} m_2(A_\nu)$. Because $\alpha/2 < 1$, B_ν has a limit as $\nu \to \infty$, $\lim_{\nu\to\infty} B_\nu = B$. Therefore, $A_\nu^{-1}\,_\alpha\chi^2(\nu)$ converges to a stable limit and, without loss of generality, one can set $B \equiv 0$.

Corollary 14.1 Under the assumption of Theorem 1, we have

$$A_\nu^{-1}\,_\alpha\chi^2(\nu) \overset{w}{\Longrightarrow} Z, \quad \text{as} \quad \nu \to \infty, \tag{14.4}$$

where A_ν is chosen to satisfy (14.2) or, more generally, (14.3); and Z is an $\frac{\alpha}{2}$-stable r.v.

---

[2]In fact, we study all possible normalizations and their rate of convergence leading to a non-degenerate limit, cf. also Davis and Resnick (1986).

Remark 14.2 *(Distribution of Z in (14.4))* Because Z is $\alpha/2$-stable distributed with $0 < \alpha < 2$, its first absolute moment is infinite. Moreover, the tails of the distribution of Z satisfy

$$\lim_{x \to \infty} x^{\frac{\alpha}{2}} P(Z > x) = \frac{4 - \alpha}{\alpha}, \tag{14.5}$$

and

$$\lim_{x \to \infty} x^{\frac{\alpha}{2}} P(Z < -x) = 0. \tag{14.6}$$

In other words, Z is an $\alpha/2$-*stable subordinator*, i.e., a positive r.v. with Laplace transform $E e^{-\theta Z} = \exp\{-a^{\alpha/2} \theta^{\alpha/2}\}, \theta > 0$, where

$$a^{\frac{\alpha}{2}} := \frac{\sigma^{\frac{\alpha}{2}}}{\cos(\pi\alpha/4)} = \frac{4 - \alpha}{\alpha} \Gamma\left(1 - \frac{\alpha}{2}\right).$$

Thus, Z is a stable r.v. with distribution $S(x; \frac{\alpha}{2}, 1, \sigma, \nu)$. From (14.1) we have (see also Samorodnitsky and Taqqu (1994), Property 1.2.15):

$$\lim_{x \to \infty} x^{\frac{\alpha}{2}} P(Z > x) = \frac{4 - \alpha}{\alpha} = C_{\frac{\alpha}{2}} \sigma^{\frac{\alpha}{2}},$$

where $C_a = [\Gamma(1 - a) \cos(\pi a/2)]^{-1}$, for $0 < a < 1$. Thus,

$$\sigma = \left[\frac{4 - \alpha}{\alpha} \Gamma\left(1 - \frac{\alpha}{2}\right) \cos\left(\pi\frac{\alpha}{4}\right)\right]^{\frac{2}{\alpha}}.$$

Finally, because the normalization in Corollary 14.1 is self-centering, we have $\mu = 0$.

Corollary 14.2 The limiting distribution in (14.1) is α-stable with support on $[0, \infty)$ and Laplace transform

$$E e^{-\theta Z} = \exp\left\{-\frac{4 - \alpha}{\alpha} \Gamma\left(1 - \frac{\alpha}{2}\right) \theta^{\frac{\alpha}{2}}\right\}, \quad \theta \geq 0.$$

Corollaries 14.1 and 14.2 emphasize the crucial difference between the limiting distribution of the usual χ^2 sum, $_2\chi^2(\nu)$, where the X_i are Gaussian, and that of $_\alpha\chi^2(\nu)$, where the X_i are in the DA of an α-stable law. For the Gaussian case the CLT implies that there exist constants $C_\nu > 0$ and $D_\nu \in \mathbf{R}$, such that $C_\nu^{-1}\chi^2(\nu) - D_\nu \overset{w}{\Longrightarrow} N(0, 1)$. In the non-Gaussian case Corollaries 1 and 2 show that the normalized sum $_\alpha\chi^2(\nu)$ has an $\alpha/2$-stable limit, totally concentrated on the positive half-line with a heavy-tailed distribution and no finite mean.

B. Student t-type distribution $(_\alpha t)$

In Kim, Mittnik, and Rachev (1996b), we introduced a Student's t-type distribution as the ratio of a standard symmetric α-stable r.v. to the square root of an independently distributed sum of squared standard α-stable r.v.'s. The limiting distribution as the number of degrees of freedom approaches infinity is obtained. This distribution is, after a suitable normalisation, the ratio of an α-stable r.v. and an independent $\alpha/2$-stable positive r.v.

Theorem 14.2 Let $X, X_1, X_2, \cdots$ be iid r.v.'s in the DA of an α-stable law with $0 < \alpha < 2$, and the Student's t-type r.v. $t(\nu) = t^{\alpha,p}(\nu)$ is defined by

$$t(\nu) := t^{\alpha,p}(\nu) := \frac{X}{\left(\frac{1}{\nu} \sum_{i=1}^{\nu} |X_i|^p\right)^{min(1,1/p)}}. \tag{14.7}$$

Then, as $\nu \to \infty$,

  (i) if $0 < p < \alpha$ and X is α-stable distributed,

$$t(\nu) \xrightarrow{a.s.} \frac{X}{(E|X|^p)^{min(1,1/(p)}}, \tag{14.8}$$

  and

(ii) if $p > \alpha$

$$\left(\nu^{\frac{p}{\alpha}-1} L(\nu)\right)^{min(1,1/p)} t(\nu) \xrightarrow{w} \frac{X}{Z^{min(1,1/p)}}, \tag{14.9}$$

where X and Z are independent r.v's. and the slowly varying function $L(\nu)$ and the distribution of Z are specified as in Corollary 1 and Corollary 2.

In the "classical" case $p = 2$, we have for the stable version of Student's t-type r.v.

$$t^{\alpha,2}(\nu) = \frac{X}{\sqrt{\frac{1}{\nu} \sum_{i=1}^{\nu} X_i^2}}, \quad 0 < \alpha < 2, \tag{14.10}$$

the following limiting result.

Corollary 14.3 Let $0 < \alpha < 2$. Then, as $\nu \to \infty$,

$$\nu^{\frac{1}{\alpha}-\frac{1}{2}} \ell(\nu) t^{\alpha,2}(\nu) \xrightarrow{w} \frac{X}{\sqrt{Z}}, \tag{14.11}$$

where X and Z are independent, Z is an $\frac{\alpha}{2}$-stable positive r.v. with Laplace transform

$$Ee^{-\theta Z} = e^{-\frac{4-\alpha}{\alpha}\Gamma\left(1-\frac{\alpha}{2}\right)\theta^{\frac{\alpha}{p}}},$$

and $\ell(\nu)$ is a slowly varying function as $\nu \to \infty$.

We next study the uniform rate of convergence in Theorem 14.2 (ii). We shall use a variety of probability metrics and their properties. For an account of the theory of probability metrics we refer to Rachev (1991), and the references therein. Our result is in terms of tail-closeness between the p-th absolute value of the α-stable r.v. X and the $\frac{\alpha}{p}$-stable r.v. Z. More precisely, define the $\zeta_{m,\lambda}$ metric in the space of distribution functions on $[0, \infty)$:

$$\zeta_{m,\lambda}(\xi_1, \xi_2) = \left[\int_0^\infty \left| \int_x^\infty \frac{(t-x)^m}{m!} d\left(F_{\xi_1}(t) - F_{\xi_2}(t) \right) \right|^\lambda dx \right]^{\frac{1}{\lambda}},$$

where $m = 0, 1, \cdots$, and $1 \leq \lambda < \infty$ (see Rachev (1991), Ch. 14). Metric $\zeta_{m,\lambda}$ is called *ideal of order* $r = m + \frac{1}{\lambda} > 0$. This means that for every choice of independent r.v.'s $\xi_1, \cdots \xi_\nu$ and $\eta_1, \cdots \eta_\nu$, and for all positive constants $C_1, \cdots, C_\nu$ we have (see Rachev (1991), p. 302)

$$\zeta_{m,\lambda}\left(\sum_{i=1}^\nu C_i \xi_i, \sum_{i=1}^\nu C_i \eta_i \right) \leq \sum_{i=1}^\nu |C_i|^r \zeta_{m,\lambda}(\xi_i, \eta_i).$$

The condition

$$\delta_r(X) := \zeta_{m,\lambda}(|X|^p, Z) < \infty, \tag{14.12}$$

where X and Z are defined in Theorem 14.2, merely measures the closeness of the tails of $F_{|X|^p}(x)$ and $F_Z(x)$. The higher $r = m + \frac{1}{\lambda} > 0$ is, the faster the uniform convergence of $F_{t(\nu)}$ to F_U. Here, U is the limiting r.v. in Theorem 14.2 (ii):

$$U := \frac{X}{Z^{p^*}}, \quad p^* = \min(1, 1/p), \quad p > 0, \tag{14.13}$$

and uniform convergence means convergence in terms of the uniform (Kolmogorov) metric:

$$\rho(\xi_1, \xi_2) = \sup_{x \in \mathbf{R}} |F_{\xi_1}(x) - F_{\xi_2}(x)|.$$

We are now ready to state our rate of convergence result.

Theorem 14.3 Let the r.v.'s $X, X_1, X_2, \cdots$ and Z be defined as in Theorem 2. Let U and p^* be determined as in (14.13), and suppose that (14.12) holds for some $\nu = m + \frac{1}{\lambda} > 0$. Then,

$$\rho\left(\nu^{(\frac{p}{\alpha}-1)p^*} t^{\alpha,p}(\nu), U \right) \leq \left(1 + \sup_{x \in \mathbf{R}} p_z(x) \right) \delta_r(X)^{\frac{1}{1+r}} C_{m,\lambda}^{\frac{1}{1+r}} \nu^{\frac{1-\frac{rp}{\alpha}}{1+r}}, \tag{14.14}$$

where

$$C_{m,\lambda} = \frac{(2m+2)!(2m+3)^{\frac{1}{2}}}{(m+1)!(3-\frac{2}{\lambda})^{\frac{1}{2}}}, \tag{14.15}$$

and $p_z(x)$ is the density of the $\alpha/2$-stable subordinator Z.

14.2   Stable Paretian Econometrics: Modifications of Test Statistics

If we choose the class of Paretian distributions to model economic relationships, so that we are dealing with *Stable Paretian Econometrics*, many aspects of the *Gaussian Econometrics* must be re-considered. A number of asymptotic results for estimators and model-checking statistics must be newly developed. Phillips and Loretan (1991), studied the properties of the von Neumann ratio for time series and regression residuals with infinite variance. They also studied the cumulated sum of squares testing methods for "constant-over-time" unconditional variance of time series under the stable Paretian assumption. Runde (1996), investigated the asymptotic distribution of the Box-Pierce statistic for r.v. with infinite variance.

Important aspects of the generalization to stable r.v.'s of Gaussian econometrics dealing with outliers, structural breaks, ARCH-effects and nonlinear dynamics, must also be re-interpreted from the viewpoint of Paretian econometrics. We shall briefly discuss these issues.

A. Outliers under the Paretian hypothesis

In Rachev, Mittnik, and Kim (1996b), we modified tests for outliers and analyzed the relevant observations assuming α-stable distributions. These include outlier-resistant distributions and outlier-prone distributions indicating that the degree of outlier-proneness (or outlier-resistance) can be measured by the tail-thickness parameter α. This section surveys three points: Firstly, we provide the limiting distribution of the standardized maximum (or minimum) based test in Grubbs (1969), the standardized sample range based test in David, Hartley, and Pearson (1954), and the standardized absolute maximum value based test. Secondly, we modify these test statistics for the α-stable assumption and analyze the corresponding limiting distributions. Thirdly, using simulation, we extend the critical values under the Gaussian assumption in Grubbs and Beck (1972), to the α-stable assumption in response surface regression for finite samples.

In what follows, our focus will be on the asymptotic distributions and the rates of convergence of our modified and generalized statistics. Grubbs in Grubbs (1969), proposed a test statistic based on the standardized maximum value from

$$M_n = \frac{\max_{1 \le i \le n} X_i - \bar{X}}{S_x}, \qquad (14.16)$$

and the standardized minimum value

$$m_n = \frac{\bar{X} - \min_{1 \le i \le n} X_i}{S_x} \qquad (14.17)$$

from a set of observations; here, $\bar{X} = n^{-1} \sum_{i=1}^{n} X_i$ is the sample mean and $S_x = \sqrt{\frac{1}{n} \sum_{i=1}^{n} (X_i - \bar{X})^2}$ is the consistent sample standard deviation. In practice one typically uses a modified version of (14.16) and (14.17), namely

$$\bar{M}_n = \frac{\max_{1 \le i \le n} |X_i| - \bar{X}}{S_x}. \tag{14.18}$$

The next two theorems underline the drastic change in the asymptotic behavior of the statistics (14.16) – (14.18) when the normality assumption is replaced with the non-normal stable assumption.

Theorem 14.4 *(The normal case)* Suppose that $\{X_i\}_{i \ge 1}$, are iid standard normal r.v.'s. Then

$$\sqrt{2 \log n} \, M_n - B_n \overset{w}{\Longrightarrow} \Lambda, \tag{14.19}$$

$$\sqrt{2 \log n} \, m_n - B_n \overset{w}{\Longrightarrow} \Lambda, \tag{14.20}$$

and

$$\sqrt{2 \log n} \, \bar{M}_n - B_n - \log 2 \overset{w}{\Longrightarrow} \Lambda, \tag{14.21}$$

where $B_n = 2 \log n - \frac{1}{2} \log \log n - \frac{1}{2} \log 4\pi$ and Λ has the extreme-value distribution of type Λ:

$$F_\Lambda(x) = P(\Lambda < x) = \exp\left\{-e^{-x}\right\}, \quad -\infty < x < \infty.$$

Proof. For iid standard normal X_i's, it is well-known that

$$Z_n := a_n(\max_{1 \le x \le n} X_i - b_n) \overset{w}{\Longrightarrow} \Lambda, \tag{14.22}$$

where $a_n = (2 \log n)^{\frac{1}{2}}$ and $b_n = (2 \log n)^{\frac{1}{2}} - \frac{1}{2}(2 \log n)^{-\frac{1}{2}}(\log \log n + \log 4\pi)$ (see, for example, Leadbetter, Lingren, and Rootzen (1980), Theorem 1.5.3). Furthermore, as $n \to \infty$,

$$a_n M_n = \frac{Z_n + a_n b_n - a_n \bar{X}}{S_x} \approx \frac{Z_n + a_n b_n - a_n(O_p(\frac{1}{\sqrt{n}}))}{1 + O_p(\frac{1}{\sqrt{n}})}. \tag{14.23}$$

The last asymptotic relation follows from combining the CLT with the method of a particular probability space, see, for example, Rachev (1991), p. 105 and the references therein. Combining (14.22) and (14.23) we have

$$a_n M_n - a_n b_n \overset{w}{\Longrightarrow} \Lambda,$$

which completes the proof of (14.19). By the symmetry, the limiting relationship (14.20) is an immediate consequence of (14.19).

To prove (14.21) we use a slight modification of (14.23). Namely, if a_n and b_n are given as in (14.22), then a straightforward repetition of the arguments leading to (14.23) yields

$$a_n(\bar{M}_n - b_n) - \log 2 \overset{w}{\Longrightarrow} \Lambda.$$

Then, as for M_n, we conclude that (14.21) also holds, completing the proof of the theorem. $\qquad\qquad\qquad\qquad\qquad\qquad\qquad\qquad\qquad\qquad\qquad\qquad$ □

We now examine the stable (non-Gaussian) case, with $1 < \alpha < 2$. Note that if $0 < \alpha \leq 1$ we cannot center our statistics using $\bar{X}$, because $\bar{X}$ increases to ∞ as $n \to \infty$, so that one would have to replace $\bar{X}$ with the empirical median or trimmed mean, when defining M_n, m_n and $\bar{M}_n$. Since the infinite mean case $0 < \alpha \leq 1$ does not seem to be of practical importance, we assume in the following that $\alpha > 1$.

Next, we assume that observations $(X_i)_{i \geq 1}$ are in the DA of an α-stable law with index $\alpha \in (1, 2)$, i.e., there exist constants $a_n \geq 0$ and $b_n \in \mathbf{R}$ such that

$$a_n^{-1} S_n - b_n \overset{w}{\Longrightarrow} S_\alpha, \qquad (14.24)$$

where $S_n = X_1 + \ldots + X_n$, and S_α is an α-stable r.v. In particular, when the X_i's are α-stable, (14.24) holds with

$$a_n = n^{\frac{1}{\alpha}} \quad \text{and} \quad b_n = \mu(n^{1-\frac{1}{\alpha}} - 1),$$

and, moreover, we have $a_n^{-1} S_n - b_n \overset{d}{=} X_1$.

The assumption that observations are only in the DA of an α-stable law is a relaxation of the assumption that the observations are α-stable distributed, requiring only conditions on the tails of the distribution. Indeed, the DA condition (14.24) is equivalent to the assumption that the tail behavior of X_1, is of Pareto-Lévy form (cf. Feller (1971), p. 303):

$$P(|X_1| > t) = t^{-\alpha} L(t), \quad t > 0,[3] \qquad (14.25)$$

where $L(t)$ is a slowly varying function as $t \to \infty$, and

$$\lim_{t \to \infty} \frac{P(X_1 > t)}{P(|X_1| < t)} = p, \quad \lim_{t \to \infty} \frac{P(X_1 < -t)}{P(|X_1| < t)} = q, \qquad (14.26)$$

for some $p \geq 0$, $q \geq 0$, $p + q = 1$.

From (14.25), it follows that the mean $\mu = EX_1$ exists for $1 < \alpha \leq 2$, and, thus, we can assume $\mu = 0$ without loss of generality. However, $E[X_1^2] = \infty$, and so the sample variance

$$S_x^2 = S_{x,n}^2 = \frac{1}{n} \sum_{i=1}^n (X_i - \bar{X})^2,$$

which plays the role of a normalizing factor in (14.16) – (14.18), tends to infinity as $n \to \infty$. Thus, in the stable case we need another normalization

---

[3]When $0 < \alpha < 2$, X is in the DA of an α-stable law and when $\alpha \geq 2$, X is in the DA of a normal distribution.

to obtain a proper limit. To this end define the truncated moment function $m_\delta(x) = Ex_1^\delta I_{\{X_1^2 < x\}}$, $x > 0$, $\delta > 0$, and choose A_n to be a solution of

$$m_4(A_n) = \frac{A_n^2}{n}. \qquad (14.27)$$

We can relax (14.27) by assuming that an A_n satisfying the limiting relation

$$\frac{n}{A_n^2} m_4(A_n) \longrightarrow 1, \quad \text{as} \quad n \to \infty \qquad (14.28)$$

suffices (cf. (5),(6)). For any choice of A_n in (14.28), $A_n = n^{2/\alpha}\ell(n)$, where $\ell(n)$ is a slowly varying function, as $n \to \infty$.

Lemma 14.1 Suppose that $\{X_i\}_{i \geq 1}$ are in the DA of an α-stable law with $1 < \alpha < 2$ and the sequence $(A_n)_{n \geq 1}$ is chosen to satisfy (14.28). Then,

$$nA_n^{-1}S_{x,n}^2 \overset{w}{\Longrightarrow} Z,$$

where $Z = Z^{(\alpha)}$ is an $\alpha/2$-stable nonnegative r.v. with Laplace transform

$$Ee^{-\gamma Z} = \exp\left\{ -\frac{4-\alpha}{\alpha} \Gamma\left(1 - \frac{\alpha}{2}\right) \gamma^{\alpha/2} \right\}, \quad \gamma \geq 0.$$

Proof. First note that

$$A_n^{-1} \sum_{i=1}^{n} X_i^2 \overset{w}{\Longrightarrow} Z^{(\alpha)}. \qquad (14.29)$$

In fact, $P(X_1^2 > t) = t^{-\alpha/2}L(x)$; so $\{X_i^2\}_{i \geq 1}$ are in the DA of an $\alpha/2$-stable law. Moreover, $Z = Z^{(\alpha)}$ is totally skewed to the right, i.e., $P(Z < t) = 0$ for all $t < 0$, see Samorodnitsky and Taqqu (1994), p. 17-18. In other words, Z in Lemma 14.11 is an $\alpha/2$-stable subordinator, i.e., a positive r.v. with Laplace transform $Ee^{-\gamma Z} = \exp\{-\alpha^{\alpha/2}\gamma^{\alpha/2}\}$, $\gamma > 0$, with $\alpha^{\alpha/2} = \frac{\sigma^{\alpha/2}}{\cos(\pi\alpha/4)} = \frac{4-\alpha}{\alpha}\Gamma\left(1 - \frac{\alpha}{2}\right)$. Therefore, the distribution of Z is $S(x; \alpha/2, 1, \sigma, \mu)$. By (14.24), see also Property 1.2.15 of Samorodnitsky and Taqqu (1994),

$$\lim_{x \to \infty} x^{\frac{\alpha}{2}} P(Z > x) = \frac{4-\alpha}{\alpha} = C_{\frac{\alpha}{2}} \sigma^{\frac{\alpha}{2}},$$

where $C_\alpha = [\Gamma(1-\alpha)\cos(\pi\alpha/2)]^{-1}$. This determines

$$\sigma = \left(\frac{4-\alpha}{\alpha}\Gamma\left(1 - \frac{\alpha}{2}\right) \cos\left(\pi\frac{\alpha}{4}\right) \right)^{\frac{2}{\alpha}}.$$

Because the normalization in (14.29) is "self-centering", we have $\mu = 0$ (see, for example, Feller (1971), p. 304-305). This is equivalent to saying that

Z satisfies the stable property $Z_1 + \cdots + Z_n \overset{d}{=} n^{2/\alpha} Z$, where the Z_i's are iid copies of Z. This proves (14.29). Finally, by (14.29), the Law of Large Numbers (LLN) and the fact that $A_n = n^{2/\alpha} \ell(n)$ we obtain the desired result

$$A_n^{-1} \sum_{i=1}^{n} (X_i - \bar{X})^2 = A_n^{-1} \sum_{i=1}^{n} X_i^2 - A_n^{-1} n \bar{X}^2 \overset{w}{\Longrightarrow} Z. \qquad \square$$

Next, we investigate the natural normalization of the numerators in statistics M_n, m_n and $\bar{M}_n$ in (14.16) – (14.18), when the X_i's are stable r.v.'s.

Lemma 14.2 Suppose that $\{X_i\}_{i \geq 1}$ are in the DA of an α-stable law with $1 < \alpha < 2$. Then for some slowly varying functions $L_+(n)$, $L_-(n)$ and $L(n)$ we have

$$n^{-\frac{1}{\alpha}} L_+(n) \left(\max_{1 \leq i \leq 2} X_i - \bar{X} \right) \overset{w}{\Longrightarrow} Y, \tag{14.30}$$

$$n^{-\frac{1}{\alpha}} L_-(n) \left(\bar{X} - \min_{1 \leq i \leq 2} |X_i| \right) \overset{w}{\Longrightarrow} Y, \tag{14.31}$$

and

$$n^{-\frac{1}{\alpha}} L(n) \left(\max_{1 \leq i \leq 2} |X_i| - \bar{X} \right) \overset{w}{\Longrightarrow} Y, \tag{14.32}$$

where $Y = Y^{(\alpha)}$ is a r.v. with the extreme-value distribution function

$$F_Y(x) = \begin{cases} \exp(-x^{-\alpha}), & x \geq 0 \\ 0, & x < 0. \end{cases} \tag{14.33}$$

Proof. We shall outline the proof of (14.30) only. Since X_1 is in the domain of an α-stable law, then by (14.25) and (14.26), the right tail $P(X_1 > x)$, $x > 0$, has the form $x^{-\alpha} L(x)$ for some slowly varying function $L(x)$. Choose γ_n to be the solution of $\bar{F}^{\leftarrow}(\gamma_n) = 1/n$ where $\bar{F}(x) = P(X_1 > x)$ and $\bar{F}^{\leftarrow}$ is the generalized inverse of $\bar{F}$. Then, $\gamma_n = n^{-\frac{1}{\alpha}} L_+(n)$ for some slowly varying function L_+. This and the LLN lead us to limit (14.30). $\qquad \square$

Combining Lemmas 14.1 and 14.2 we obtain a characterization of the limiting behavior of the statistics, M_n, m_n and $\bar{M}_n$, for heavy-tailed variables.

Theorem 14.5 *(The stable case)* Suppose that $(X_i)_{i \geq 1}$ are in the DA of an α-stable law with $1 < \alpha < 2$. Then, for any $\epsilon > 0$,

$$n^{-\frac{1}{2}+\epsilon} M_n \overset{p}{\longrightarrow} \infty, \quad n^{-\frac{1}{2}+\epsilon} m_n \overset{p}{\longrightarrow} \infty, \quad n^{-\frac{1}{2}+\epsilon} \bar{M}_n \overset{p}{\longrightarrow} \infty$$

and

$$n^{-\frac{1}{2}-\epsilon} M_n \overset{p}{\longrightarrow} 0, \quad n^{-\frac{1}{2}-\epsilon} m_n \overset{p}{\longrightarrow} 0, \quad n^{-\frac{1}{2}-\epsilon} \bar{M}_n \overset{p}{\longrightarrow} 0.$$

Theorems 14.4 and 14.5 demonstrate the crucial difference in the limiting behavior of the statistics M_n, m_n and $\bar{M}_n$ for the normal and the stable (non-normal) case. This "discontinuity" in behavior for $1 < \alpha < 2$ and $\alpha = 2$ is due to the choice of $S_x = \sqrt{\frac{1}{n}\sum(X_i - \bar{X})^2}$ as the normalization for the deviation measures $\max_{1\leq i\leq n} X_i - \bar{X}$, $\bar{X} - \min_{1\leq i\leq n}|X_i|$, and $\max_{1\leq i\leq n}|X_i| - \bar{X}$. Recall that in the normal case $S_x \to 1$ and in the stable case $(1 < \alpha < 2)$ $S_x \overset{a.s.}{\to} \infty$, and, moreover, by Lemma 14.1,

$$n^{\frac{1}{2}-\frac{1}{\alpha}} L(n) S_{x,n} \overset{w}{\Longrightarrow} \sqrt{Z},$$

where Z is a positive $\alpha/2$-stable r.v. We now propose modified versions of the statistics (14.16) – (14.18), using the empirical central L_1-moment

$$L_x = L_{x,n} = n^{-1} \sum_{i=1}^{n} |X_i - \bar{X}|,$$

instead of the sample standard deviation, S_x. With $1 < \alpha < 2$ and X_1 an α-stable r.v., we have by the LLN,

$$L_{x,n} \overset{p}{\longrightarrow} \mu_\alpha, \tag{14.34}$$

with $\mu_\alpha := E|X_1|$. In the normal case, $X_1 \sim N(0,\sigma^2)$, we have

$$L_{x,n} \overset{p}{\longrightarrow} \mu_2,$$

with $\mu_2 = \sqrt{2/\pi}\sigma$. If, on the other hand, X_1 is symmetric α-stable, i.e., its characteristic function is $f(t) = Ee^{itX_1} = e^{-|\sigma t|^\alpha}$, then (see, for example, Nikias and Shao (1995),p. 35)

$$\mu_\alpha = \frac{2}{\pi}\Gamma\left(1 - \frac{1}{\alpha}\right)\sigma.$$

We now define *the modified tests of outliers*

$$M_n^* = \frac{\max_{1\leq i\leq n} X_i - \bar{X}}{L_x}, \tag{14.35}$$

$$m_n^* = \frac{\bar{X} - \min_{1\leq i\leq n} X_i}{L_x} \tag{14.36}$$

and

$$\bar{M}_n^* = \frac{\max_{1\leq i\leq n} |X_i| - \bar{X}}{L_x}. \tag{14.37}$$

The next two theorems follow immediately from Theorem 14.4, Lemma 14.2 and (14.34).

Theorem 14.6 *(The normal case)* Suppose that $(X_i)_{i\geq 1}$ are iid standard normal. Then

$$\sqrt{\pi \log n}\, M_n^* - B_n \overset{w}{\Longrightarrow} \Lambda,$$

$$\sqrt{\pi \log n} \ \mathrm{m}_n^* - B_n \overset{w}{\Longrightarrow} \Lambda$$

and

$$\sqrt{\pi \log n} \ \bar{\mathrm{M}}_n^* - B_n - \log 2 \overset{w}{\Longrightarrow} \Lambda,$$

where B_n and the law of Λ are defined in Theorem 14.4.

Theorem 14.7 *(The stable case)* Suppose that $(X_i)_{i \geq 1}$ are α-stable r.v.'s with $1 < \alpha < 2$. Then, for some slowly varying functions $L_+(n)$, $L_-(n)$ and $L(n)$ we have

$$n^{-\frac{1}{\alpha}} L_+(n) \mathrm{M}_n^* \overset{w}{\Longrightarrow} Y,$$

$$n^{-\frac{1}{\alpha}} L_-(n) \mathrm{m}_n^* \overset{w}{\Longrightarrow} Y,$$

and

$$n^{-\frac{1}{\alpha}} L(n) \bar{\mathrm{M}}_n^* \overset{w}{\Longrightarrow} Y,$$

where the distribution of Y is given in Lemma 14.2.

Finally, consider the alternative tail-statistic

$$U_n = \frac{\max_{1 \leq i \leq n} X_i - \min_{1 \leq i \leq n} X_i}{S_x}$$

and its modification

$$U_n^* = \frac{\max_{1 \leq i \leq n} X_i - \min_{1 \leq i \leq n} X_i}{L_x}.$$

We note that both statistics admit the alternative representations

$$U_n = \frac{M_n - m_n}{S_x} = \frac{\max_{i,j}(x_i - x_j)}{S_x} \tag{14.38}$$

and

$$U_n^* = \frac{M_n^* - m_n^*}{L_x} = \frac{\max_{i,j}(x_i - x_j)}{L_x}. \tag{14.39}$$

The statistics (14.38) and (14.39) and application of Theorems 14.4, 14.5, 14.6, and 14.7 again show the contrast between the normal and the (non-normal) stable case. In the normal case the correct normalization for U_n and U_n^* is $\sqrt{2 \log n}$ (cf. Theorem 4 and 6); in the stable case, the appropriate normalization for U_n is $n^{-\frac{1}{2}}$ (cf. Theorem 14.5) and $n^{-\frac{1}{\alpha}}$ for U_n^* (cf. Theorem14.7).

Next, we analyze numerically the finite-sample behavior of test statistic $\bar{M}_n$ in (14.18) with r.v.'s from symmetric standard α-stable distributions. The index of stability α takes the values 1.99, 1.95, 1.9, 1.8, 1.7, 1.6, 1.5, 1.4, 1.3, 1.2, 1.1, 1.0, and the value 2 (the standard normal distribution). For each value of α we take samples of size $n = 20$, 30, 50, 75, 100, 150, 200, 300, 500, 1,000, 2,000, and 3,000. For each of the 156 possible (α, n)-combinations 30,000 replications were generated.

Rather than tabulating results for selected sample sizes and α values, we use response surface techniques to present our simulation results in a compact fashion. Response surface methodology has been used in various statistical and econometric applications. Specifically, we focused on the $\epsilon = .05$ quantiles. For the surfaces of quantiles $cv(\alpha, n)$ for a given (α, n)-pair, the functional form in (14.40) was specified as a polynomial in $(2 - \alpha)$, n and their products for $1 < \alpha < 2$, while the functional form in (14.41) was a polynomial in n in (14.41) for $\alpha = 2$:[4]

$$cv(\alpha, n) = \sum_{i=0}^{3} \sum_{j=1}^{3} \phi_{ij}(2 - \alpha)^{\frac{i}{8}} n^{\frac{j}{8}}, \quad 1 < \alpha < 2, \tag{14.40}$$

$$cv(\alpha, n) = \sum_{i=0}^{8} \theta_i n^{\frac{i}{16}}, \quad \alpha = 2. \tag{14.41}$$

For the estimation of the response surface regression, generalized least squares was used. The estimation was based on the 144 (α, n)-combinations for (14.40) and 12 (α, n)-combinations for (14.41). To derive the approximate response surface, we selected the subset of regressors which maximized the adjusted-R^2 value. The estimation results for $1 < \alpha < 2$ and $\alpha = 2$, respectively, were

$$
\begin{aligned}
cv(\alpha, n) = \ & 1.8452 n^{\frac{1}{8}} + 88.8864(2 - \alpha)^{\frac{1}{8}} n^{\frac{1}{8}} - 70.8006(2 - \alpha)^{\frac{1}{8}} n^{\frac{2}{8}} \\
& + 6.3680(2 - \alpha)^{\frac{1}{8}} n^{\frac{3}{8}} - 187.6700(2 - \alpha)^{\frac{2}{8}} n^{\frac{1}{8}} \\
& + 130.1192(2 - \alpha)^{\frac{2}{8}} n^{\frac{2}{8}} \\
& + 106.2692(2 - \alpha)^{\frac{3}{8}} n^{\frac{1}{8}} - 72.7327(2 - \alpha)^{\frac{3}{8}} n^{\frac{2}{8}}, \tag{14.42}
\end{aligned}
$$

$$cv(\alpha, n) = 2.3127 n^{\frac{1}{8}} - 0.1649 n^{\frac{5}{16}}. \tag{14.43}$$

Next we shall generalize Theorem 14.5. We assume that the sample $(X_1, \ldots, X_n)$ of i.i.d. observations is *in the domain of attraction of an α-stable law* with index $\alpha \in (1, 2)$, that is there exist constants $a_n \geq 0$ and $b_n \in \mathbf{R}$ such that

$$a_n^{-1} S_n - b_n \overset{w}{\Rightarrow} S_\alpha, \tag{14.44}$$

where $S_n = X_1 + \cdots + X_n$, S_α is an α-stable random variable.

Indeed, the domain–of–attraction condition (14.44) is equivalent to the assumption that the tail behavior of X_1 is of the Pareto–Lévy form (cf. Feller, 1966, p. 303)

$$P(|X_1| > t) = t^{-\alpha} L(t), \quad t > 0, [5] \tag{14.45}$$

---

[4]These functional forms were specified after various trial.
[5]When in (14.61) $0 < \alpha < 2$, X is in the domain of attraction of an α-stable law and when $\alpha \geq 2$, X is in the domain of attraction of a normal distribution.

where $L(t)$ is a slowly varying as $t \to \infty$,[6] and

$$\lim_{t \to \infty} \frac{P(X_1 > t)}{P(|X_1| < t)} = p, \quad \lim_{t \to \infty} \frac{P(X_1 < -t)}{P(|X_1| < t)} = q, \qquad (14.46)$$

for some $p \geq 0$, $q \geq 0$, $p + q = 1$. Further, we shall assume that X_i are in *the domain of normal attraction of an α-stable law*, that is, $b_n = 0$ in (14.44), or equivalently, for some $c > 0$,

$$P(|X_1| > t) \sim ct^{-\alpha} \quad \text{as } t \to \infty,$$

and furthermore (14.46) holds.

Next we recall the definitions of M_n and m_n, see (14.16) and (14.17). Consider the symmetrized test-for-outlier statistic

$$O_n = M_n + m_n = \frac{\max_{1 \leq i \leq n} X_i - \min_{1 \leq i \leq n} X_i}{S_x}. \qquad (14.47)$$

Suppose that the observations $(X_i)_{i \geq 1}$ are i.i.d. random variables in the domain of attraction of α-stable law with index $\alpha \in (1, 2)$, that is the relations (14.60) – (14.46) hold. Given the tail mass p and q defined by (14.46), consider the random variable N with a geometric type distribution:

$$P(N = k) = pq^{k-1} + qp^{k-1}, \ k \geq 2. \qquad (14.48)$$

Next let $(\Gamma_i)_{i \geq 1}$ be the sequence of arrivals of a standard Poisson process, that is,

$$\Gamma_i = e_1 + \ldots + e_i,$$

where $(e_j)_{j \geq 1}$, are i.i.d. exponential random variables with mean 1.

We assume that $(\Gamma_i)_{i \geq 1}$ is independent of N, and then introduce the random variable

$$U^* := \frac{\Gamma_1^{-1/\alpha} + \Gamma_N^{-1/\alpha}}{(\sum_{i=1}^{\infty} \Gamma_i^{-2/\alpha})^{1/2}} \qquad (14.49)$$

Now we formulate our main result.

Theorem 14.8 Suppose that $(X_i)_{i \geq 1}$ are in the domain of normal attraction of α-stable law with $1 < \alpha < 2$. Then, as $n \to \infty$,

$$n^{-1/2} O_n \overset{w}{\Rightarrow} U^*. \qquad (14.50)$$

Remark 14.3 An alternative representation of the limiting distribution for the test statistic O_n is given by

$$U^* \overset{d}{=} \frac{p^{1/\alpha}(\Gamma_1^{(1)})^{-1/\alpha} + q^{1/\alpha}(\Gamma_1^{(2)})^{-1/\alpha}}{\left(p^{2/\alpha} \sum_{i=1}^{\infty}(\Gamma_i^{(1)})^{-2/\alpha} + q^{2/\alpha} \sum_{i=1}^{\infty}(\Gamma_i^{(2)})^{-2/\alpha}\right)^{1/2}} \qquad (14.51)$$

---

[6] $L(x)$ is also a slowly varying as $x \to \infty$, if for every constant $c > 0$, $\lim_{x \to \infty} L(cx)/L(x)$ exists and is equal to 1. Here and in follows we always use L or l to denote some slowly varying function.

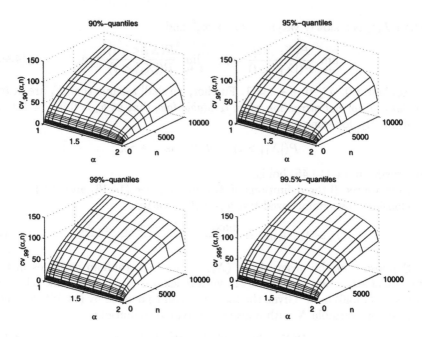

Fig. 14.2 Simulated Critical Values for Outlier Statistic O_n. (Adapted from: Mittnik, Rachev and Samorodnitsky (1999a))

where $(\Gamma_i^{(1)})_{i\geq 1}$ and $(\Gamma_i^{(2)})_{i\geq 1}$ are two independent sequences of standard Poisson arrivals.

Proof. See Section 14.4.   □

In Mittnik, Rachev and Samorodnitsky (1999a) we simulated test statistic O_n in (14.47) finite samples with random variables from symmetric standard α-stable distributions with the index of stability, α, assuming values 1.01, 1.05, 1.1, 1.2, ..., 1.8, 1.9, 1.95, 1.99 for sample sizes n = 10, 20, 30, 40, 50, 75, 100, 200, 300, 400, 500, 750, 1,000, 2,000, 3,000, 4,000, 5,000, 7,500, and 10,000. For each of the 247 (α, n)-combinations we generated 30,000 replication.[7] The simulated critical values for the $100q\%$ points with $q = .90$, .95, .99, .995 are shown in Figure 14.2.

Rather than tabulating results for selected sample sizes and α values, we employ response surface techniques to summarize our simulation results in a compact fashion.[8] By doing so, we obtain close approximations as was to

---

[7]The pseudo random variates for the α-stable distributions were generated with the algorithm of Weron (1996).

[8]Response surface methodology has been used in various statistical and econometric applications; see, for example, Myers et al. (1989).

Table 14.2 Response Surface Estimates for $1 < \alpha < 2^a$.

Coefficient	.90	.95	q .975	.99	.995
$c_{q,00}$	0.0099	-0.0002	0.0071	-0.0247	-0.0538
$c_{q,01}$	1.2252	1.2717	1.3125	1.3598	1.3875
$c_{q,10}$	0.1131	-0.0179	0.0542	0.0769	0.0805
$c_{q,11}$	0.1936	0.1574	0.1377	0.1309	0.1279
$c_{q,20}$	0.1202	0.1241	0.1200	0.0992	0.0841
$c_{q,21}$	-0.0047	-0.0098	-0.0102	-0.0057	-0.0021
$\bar{R}^2$	.99976	.99992	.99988	.99992	.99997

[a]The entries are the least squares estimates of coefficients c_{ij} in (14.52). $\bar{R}^2$ is the adusted R^2-value.
(Adapted from: Mittnik, Rachev and Samorodnitsky (1999a))

be expected given the smoothness of the simulated critical values shown in Figure 14.2. Specifically, we considered the $100q\%$ points for $q = .90, .95, .975, .99, .995$. For the responses surfaces the functional form

$$cv_q(\alpha, n) \approx \sum_{i=0}^{2} \sum_{j=0}^{1} c_{q,ij} \bar{\alpha}^i n^{j/2}, \qquad 1.01 \leq \alpha \leq 1.99, \qquad (14.52)$$

was specified, where $cv_q(\alpha, n)$ denotes the approximate quantiles for a given (α, n)–pair; and

$$\bar{\alpha} = \ln(2 - \alpha).$$

For each q–value, the estimation is based on 247 simulated data points. The estimation results for the coefficients $c_{q,ij}$ are given in Table 14.2. The $\bar{R}^2$–values reported in Table 14.2 indicate that the response surface approximations based on only six coefficients yield rather close fits to the simulated values.

We also simulated the range statistic O_n for the random variables from a standard normal distribution (i.e., $\alpha = 2$) and obtain close matches to the critical values reported in David, Hartley and Pearson (1954).[9] The critical values for $\alpha < 2$, behave quite differently from those for $\alpha = 2$, in that they increase rather slowly as n increases. Fitting the response suface

$$cv_q(2, n) \approx d_0 + d_1 \ln n + d_2 \ln \ln n \qquad (14.53)$$

to the simulated quantiles, we obtain the OLS estimates reported in Table 14.3. As the $\bar{R}^2$–values indicate, the fit of (14.53) is extremely close. If at all

---

[9]They report all the quantiles we consider, but their sample sizes range from $n = 3$ to $n = 1,000$.

Table 14.3 Response Surface Estimates for $\alpha = 2^a$.

Coefficient	.90	.95	q .975	.99	.995
d_0	1.1135	1.0859	1.0381	0.9225	0.8115
d_1	0.2063	0.1507	0.0976	0.0202	-0.0380
d_2	2.3675	2.6988	3.0224	3.4937	3.8564
$\bar{R}^2$	.999998	.999999	.999999	.999997	.999996

[a]The entries are the least squares estimates of coefficients d_i in (14.53). $\bar{R}^2$ is the adusted R^2-value.

(Adapted from: Mittnik, Rachev and Samorodnitsky (1999a))

necessary, approximate critical values for $1.99 < \alpha < 2$ could be obtained via linear interpolation between $cv_q(1.99, n)$ and $cv_q(2, n)$.

B. Structural breaks under the Paretian hypothesis

Tests for stability over time of the parameters of a linear regression model can be carried out through the cumulative sum (CUSUM) test. Brown, Durbin and Evans (1975), proposed the CUSUM and CUSUM of squares tests based on recursive residuals. MacNeill (1978) considered the CUSUM test based on ordinary least squares (OLS) residuals while McCabe and Harrison (1980), used the CUSUM of squares residuals. Both modifications are based on the assumption of iid disturbances. Ploberger and Krämer (1992), modified the CUSUM tests for correlated and heteroskedastic OLS residuals. For all these tests the innovation processes, u_t, are assumed to have finite variance. In Kim, Mittnik, and Rachev (1996c), we have considered the non-Gaussian stable assumption for the CUSUM test based on OLS residuals. The CUSUM squares test for the infinite variance assumption was investigated by Loretan and Phillips.

We consider the *stable* linear regression model

$$y_t = x_t'\beta + u_t, \qquad t = 1, \cdots, T, \qquad (14.54)$$

where y_t is the observation on the dependent variable at time t, $x_t = [1, x_{1t}, \cdots, x_{tK}]'$ is a $K \times 1$ vector of nonstochastic independent variables, with first component equal to unity, and β is a vector of regression coefficients. Further, we assume that the u_t are iid disturbances in the normal DA of a symmetric α-stable r.v. X with characteristic function

$$Ee^{i\theta X} = e^{-|\sigma\theta|^\alpha}, \quad 0 < \alpha \le 2. \qquad (14.55)$$

The coefficients in (14.54) are estimated consistently by the OLS regression irrespective of the tail-thickness parameter α, see Kanter and Steiger (1974) and Hannan and Kanter (1977).

Consider next the OLS residuals

$$\hat{u}_t^{(T)} = y_t - x_t'\hat{\beta}^{(T)},$$

where the estimates of the $K \times 1$ vector of regression coefficients is given by

$$\hat{\beta}^{(T)} = \frac{\Sigma_{t=1}^T x_t y_t}{\Sigma_{t=1}^T x_t x_t'}.$$

Define the random process[10]

$$B^T(z) = \frac{1}{\sigma T^{\frac{1}{\alpha}}} \sum_{t=1}^{[Tz]} \hat{u}_t^{(T)}, \qquad 0 \le z \le 1$$

with trajectories in the Skorokhod space $D[0,1]$.[11] The next lemma shows that B^T converges weakly to a (standard) α-stable Lévy Bridge LB_α. Here the distribution of LB_α is defined in the usual way. First we introduce the (standard) Lévy motion L_α: a process with stationary independent increments, starting at 0, (i.e., $L_\alpha(0) = 0$) and having standard α-stable distributed unit increments, with

$$E \exp\{i\theta L_\alpha(1)\} = e^{-|\theta|^\alpha}, \quad \theta \in \mathbf{R}.$$

The distribution of the Lévy Bridge LB_α can be defined in terms of the Lévy motion L_α:

$$(LB_\alpha(z))_{0 \le z \le 1} \overset{d}{=} (L_\alpha(z) - zL_\alpha(1))_{0 \le z \le 1}. \qquad (14.56)$$

Next we introduce the main assumption leading to weak convergence of the normalized sum-of-residuals process B^T.

Assumption 1(cf. Ploberger and Krämer (1992)).

$$\frac{1}{T} \sum_{t=1}^T x_t x_t' \overset{w}{\Longrightarrow} R,$$

where R is a $K \times K$ deterministic matrix R, which may without loss of generality be reparametrized to

$$R = \begin{bmatrix} 1 & 0 \\ 0 & R^* \end{bmatrix}.$$

---

[10]Hereafter, $[a]$ denotes the integer part of a.
[11]See Rachev (1991) for various metrizations of $D[0,1]$.

Theorem 14.9 Suppose that the regressors x_t satisfy Assumption 1. Then under the hypothesis H_0 that the vector of regression coefficients β does not change over time, we have

$$\left(B^T(z)\right)_{0 \le z < 1} \overset{w}{\Longrightarrow}_{D[0,1]} \left(LB_\alpha(z)\right)_{0 < z \le 1}.$$

Proof:[12] By definition, for any $0 \le z \le 1$

$$
\begin{aligned}
B^T(z) &= \sigma^{-1} T^{-\frac{1}{\alpha}} \sum_{t=1}^{[Tz]} \hat{u}_t^{(T)} \\
&= \sigma^{-1} T^{-\frac{1}{\alpha}} \sum_{t=1}^{[Tz]} u_t - \sigma^{-1} T^{-\frac{1}{\alpha}} \sum_{t=1}^{[Tz]} x_t'(\hat{\beta}^{(T)} - \beta) \\
&=: A^{(T)}(z) - B^{(T)}(z).
\end{aligned}
$$

Consider first the difference

$$\sigma\left(A^{(T)}(z) - a^{(T)}(z)\right) := T^{-\frac{1}{\alpha}} \sum_{t=1}^{[Tz]} u_t - T^{-\frac{1}{\alpha}} z \sum_{t=1}^{T} u_t.$$

Because of the independence of the $\{u_t\}_{t \ge 1}$, we can split $A(z) - a(z)$ into two independent quantities. In fact,

$$
\begin{aligned}
\sigma(A^{(T)}(z) - a^{(T)}(z)) &= T^{-\frac{1}{\alpha}}(1-z) \sum_{t=1}^{[Tz]} u_t - z T^{-1/\alpha} \sum_{t=[Tz]+1}^{T} u_t \\
&= \frac{[Tz]^{\frac{1}{\alpha}}}{T^{\frac{1}{\alpha}}} (1-z)[Tz]^{-\frac{1}{\alpha}} \sum_{t=1}^{[Tz]} u_t \\
&\quad - z \frac{(T - [Tz] - 1)^{\frac{1}{\alpha}}}{T^{\frac{1}{\alpha}}} (T - [Tz] - 1)^{-\frac{1}{\alpha}} \sum_{t=[Tz]+1}^{T} u_t \\
&=: A_1^{(T)}(z) - A_2^{(T)}(z).
\end{aligned}
$$

Applying the Donsker-Prohorov invariance principle and recalling the independence of the processes $A_1^{(T)}$ and $A_2^{(T)}$, we obtain the weak convergence of the difference

$$\left(A_1^{(T)}(z) - A_2^{(T)}(z)\right)_{0 \le z < 1} \overset{w}{\Longrightarrow} (\ell(z))_{0 \le z \le 1}.$$

Here, $\ell(z)$ is a process with independent and stationary increments, and $\ell(z) = z^{\frac{1}{\alpha}}(1-z)L_\alpha(1) - z(1-z)^{\frac{1}{\alpha}} \tilde{L}_\alpha(1)$, where $L_\alpha(1)$ and $\tilde{L}_\alpha(1)$ are iid standard

---

[12]The proof follows the main arguments provided in Ploberger and Krämer (1992) for the Gaussian case, i.e., $\alpha = 2$.

symmetric α-stable r.v.'s. Therefore, $\ell(\alpha) = L_\alpha(z) - zL_\alpha(z) - z\tilde{L}_\alpha(1 - z)$, where L_α and $\tilde{L}_\alpha$ are two independent α-stable Lévy motions. This leads us to $\ell(z) \stackrel{d}{=} L_\alpha(z) - z\, L_\alpha(1) \stackrel{d}{=} LB_\alpha(z)$. Summarizing, we have that

$$\left(A^{(T)}(z) - a^{(T)}(z)\right)_{0 \le z \le 1} \stackrel{w}{\Longrightarrow} (LB_\alpha(z))_{0 \le z \le 1}.$$

Consider now,

$$B^{(T)}(z) - a^{(T)}(z) = \sigma^{-1}T^{-\frac{1}{\alpha}} \sum_{t=1}^{[Tz]} x_t'(\hat{\beta}^T - \beta) - \sigma^{-1}T^{-\frac{1}{\alpha}}z \sum_{t=1}^{T} u_t.$$

By Assumption 1,

$$\frac{1}{T} \sum_{t=1}^{T} x_t \stackrel{p}{\longrightarrow} [1, 0, \cdots, 0]'.$$

Moreover, again by Assumption 1 and the definition of $\hat{\beta}^{(T)}$ we have[13]

$$T^{1-\frac{1}{\alpha}}\left(\hat{\beta}^{(T)} - \beta\right) = T^{-\frac{1}{\alpha}} \begin{bmatrix} 1 & 0 \\ 0 & R^* \end{bmatrix}^{-1} \begin{bmatrix} \sum_{t=1}^{T} u_t \\ \sum_{t=1}^{T} \tilde{x}_t u_t \end{bmatrix} + o_p^{(T)}(1).$$

Summarizing, we get

$$\begin{aligned} \sigma\left(B^{(T)}(z) - a^{(T)}(z)\right) &= [z, 0, \cdots, 0]'T^{-\frac{1}{\alpha}} \begin{bmatrix} 1 & 0 \\ 0 & P^* \end{bmatrix}^{-1} \begin{bmatrix} \sum_{t=1}^{T} u_t \\ \sum_{t=1}^{T} \tilde{x}_t u_t \end{bmatrix} \\ &\quad - T^{-\frac{1}{\alpha}}z \sum_{t=1}^{T} u_t + o_p^{(T)}(1) = o_p^{(T)}(1). \end{aligned}$$

Finally,

$$\begin{aligned} \left(A^{(T)}(z) - B^{(T)}(z)\right)_{0 \le z \le 1} &= \left(A^{(T)}(z) - a^{(T)}(z)\right)_{0 \le z \le 1} \\ &\quad - \left(B^{(T)}(z) - a^{(T)}(z)\right)_{0 \le z \le 1} \\ &\stackrel{w}{\Longrightarrow} (LB(z))_{0 \le z < 1} \end{aligned}$$

as required.   □

If we also assume that the u_i are symmetric α-stable r.v.'s with characteristic function as in (14.55), we can replace the unknown σ in the definition of $B^{(T)}(z)$ by a strongly consistent moment estimator $\hat{\sigma}_p, 0 < p < \alpha$. Recall that if the u_t has an α-stable law, then all absolute moments $E|u_t|^p$ of order

---

[13]Hereafter $o_p^{(T)}(1)$ denotes a random quantity which converges to zero in probability as $T \to \infty$.

$0 < p < \alpha$ exist. Moreover, we have the following lemma; see, for example, Samorodnitsky and Taqqu (1994) and Nikias and Shao (1995).

Lemma 14.3 Let X be a symmetric r.v. with characteristic function $E\,e^{i\theta X} = e^{-|\sigma\theta|^{\alpha}}$, $0 < \alpha < 2$. Then $E(|X|^p) = C(p,\alpha)\sigma^p, 0 < p < \alpha$, where

$$C(p,\alpha) = 2^{p+1}\Gamma\left(\frac{p+1}{2}\right)\Gamma\left(\frac{-p}{\alpha}\right) \Big/ \alpha\sqrt{\pi}\,\Gamma\left(\frac{-p}{2}\right),$$

and $\Gamma(\cdot)$ is the Gamma function $\Gamma(x) = \int_0^\infty t^{x-1}e^{-t}dt$.

Given Lemma 14.3, we are now ready to define $\hat{\sigma}_p$ in the special case when the residuals are assumed to be α-stable with the characteristic function (14.55). For $0 < p < \alpha$ we define the estimator $\hat{\sigma}_p$ for σ as

$$\hat{\sigma}_p := \left(\frac{\hat{m}_p}{C(p,\alpha)}\right)^{\frac{1}{p}},$$

where $\hat{m}_p$ is the p-th sample absolute moment

$$\hat{m}_p = \frac{1}{T}\sum_{i=K}^{T}|\hat{u}_i|^p.$$

From Lemma 14.3, we then conclude that $\hat{\sigma}_p \xrightarrow{p} \sigma$. Combining Theorem 14.9 and Lemma 14.3, we have the following corollary.[14]

Corollary 14.4 Suppose that the conditions in Theorem 8 are satisfied, $0 < p < \alpha$, and $\hat{u}_t^{(T)}$ are α-stable r.v.'s with the characteristic function (14.55). Set

$$\hat{B}^{(T)}(z) := \frac{1}{\hat{\sigma}_p T^{\frac{1}{\alpha}}}\sum_{t=1}^{[Tz]}\hat{u}_t^{(T)}, \qquad 0 \le z \le 1. \tag{14.57}$$

Then, in $D[0,1]$, we have the weak convergence

$$\left(\hat{B}^{(T)}(z)\right)_{0\le z < 1} \xRightarrow{w} (LB_\alpha(z))_{0\le z \le 1},$$

---

[14]Loretan and Phillips (1994) studied the CUSUM squares test in the presence of infinite variance errors. Basically they chose the L_2-norm of the errors for the test normalization, while we prefer to use the L_1-norm. In their setting, if the tail-index α of u_t is less than 4, then u_t^2 will be attracted to an $\alpha/2$-stable law and consequently a functional limit theorem similar to our Theorem 8 holds, see Proposition 3, p. 221 in Loretan and Phillips (1994). If $\alpha > 4$ then u_t^2 is in the DA of the normal law and their functional limit theorem is analogous to that of Ploberger and Krämer (1992). Note that for $\alpha < 2$ our result is preferable, since the CUSUM squares test will lead to an $\alpha/2(< 1)$-stable bridge, and the corresponding confidence intervals will be based on a process with marginal distributions having infinite means.

where LB_α is an α-stable Lévy Bridge.

Figure 14.3 presents simulated 95%-quantiles for the Lévy Bridge LB_α with $\alpha = 1.1, 1.5$ and 1.9.

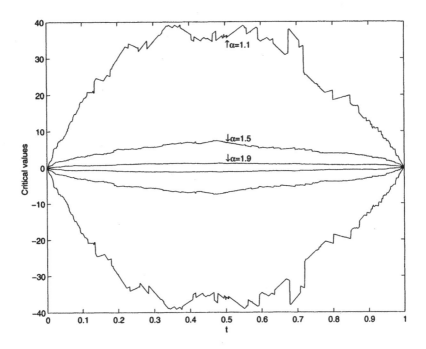

Fig. 14.3 95%-quantiles for the Lévy Bridge LB_α with $\alpha = 1.1, 1.5$ and 1.9.(Adapted from: Rachev, Kim, and Mittnik (1999).

Test statistics:
In the Gaussian case, $\alpha = 2$, the test statistic is merely the supremum of

$$\frac{1}{\hat{\sigma}_z \sqrt{T}} \sum_{t=1}^{[Tz]} \hat{u}_t^{(T)},$$

and therefore its limiting distribution is the maximum of the standard Brownian bridge (see Ploberger and Krämer (1992)). For $0 < \alpha < 2$, the trajectories of LB_α are discontinuous; they are the only elements of the space $D[0,1]$ endowed with the Skorokhod metric d. Recall that d does not have an explicit representation,

$$d(x,y) := \inf\{\epsilon > 0 \quad : \quad \text{there exists a strictly increasing continuous transformation}$$

$$\Lambda_\epsilon : [0,1] \longrightarrow [0,1] \text{ with } \Lambda_\epsilon(0) = 0,$$

$$\Lambda_\epsilon(1) = 1, \text{ such that } \sup_{0 \le t \le 1} |\Lambda_\epsilon(t) - t| \le \epsilon,$$

$$\text{and } \sup_{0 \le t \le 1} |x(\Lambda_\epsilon(t)) - y(t)| \le \epsilon \text{ }\}.$$

Corollary 14.5 Under the assumption of Corollary 14.4, there exists a probability space such that

$$d\left(\hat{B}^{(T)}(\cdot), \; LB_\alpha(\cdot)\right) \xrightarrow{a.s.} 0,$$

where $\hat{B}^{(T)}$ and LB_α are here defined on the above probability space, and have distributions defined by (14.56) and (14.57), respectively.

The standard Lévy Bridge LB_α can be simulated using the technique proposed in Janicki and Weron (Janicki and Weron (1994), Section 6.4) with described confidence intervals. Corollary 14.5 claims that under H_0, $\hat{B}^{(T)}(z), 0 < z \le 1$ should stay in a small d-neighbourhood of LB_α.

Since d is difficult to visualize we use a slightly weaker metric, d_H, the so-called Hausdorff metric between $\hat{B}^{(T)}$ and the simulated version $LB_\alpha^{(s)}$ of the stable Bridge LB_α. The Hausdorff distance $d_H(x,y)$[15] between two functions x and y on $D[0,1]$ is defined as follows: Let $\bar{x}$ and $\bar{y}$ be the completed graphs of x and y. Define $d_H(x,y) := r(\bar{x}, \bar{y})$, where r is the Hausdorff distance between closed sets A, B in the plane $r(A,B) := \inf \{\epsilon > 0 : A^\epsilon \supseteq B, B^\epsilon \supseteq A\}$; here $A^\epsilon = \{x : \| x - A \| < \epsilon\}$ is the open-ϵ-neighborhood of A, and $\| \cdot \|$ is the Euclidean norm in $\mathbf{R}^2$, that is,

$$r(\bar{x}, \bar{y}) = \max \left\{ \sup_{u \in \bar{x}} \inf_{v \in \bar{y}} \| u - v \|, \; \sup_{v \in \bar{y}} \inf_{u \in \bar{x}} \| u - v \| \right\}.$$

One can perform our test in the following two-step procedure:

Step 1. Simulate a sufficient number of trajectories of a standard α-stable Bridge,

$$LB_\alpha(z) = L_\alpha(z) - zL_\alpha(1),$$

where $L_\alpha(z), 0 \in z \le 1$, is a standard Lévy motion, and construct 95%-quantiles.

Step 2. Reject H_0 for a given $\hat{B}^{(T)}(z), 0 \le z \le 1$ if

$$d_H\left(\bar{B}^{(T)}, \mathbf{B}^{95\%}\right) > .05,$$

where $\bar{B}^{(T)}$ is the completed graph of $\left(\hat{B}^{(T)}(z)\right)_{0 \le z \le 1}$, and $\mathbf{B}^{95\%}$ is the band within which 95% of the simulated trajectories of $LB_\alpha(z)$, $0 \le z \le 1$ lie.

---

[15]For all relevant facts about metrics on the space of probability measures, or on various functional spaces, we refer to Rachev (1991) and the references therein.

Disturbances u_t were drawn from symmetric standard stable Paretian distributions (i.e., $c = 1$ and $\delta = 0$) with the tail-thickness parameter α assuming values 1.1, 1.2, 1.3, 1.4, 1.5, 1.6, 1.7, 1.8, 1.9. 30,000 samples of size 1,000 were generated. For practical convenience, we summarize the critical values at significance level 95% in a response surface regression. For the estimation of a response surface regression we chose sample quantiles $z = 0$, .05, .1, .15, .2, .25, .3, .35, .4, .45, .5.[16] For each α, 30,000 replications were generated, that is, the response surface regression was estimated from the 99 (α, ξ)–combinations in the following functional form

$$cv(\alpha, z) = \sum_{j=0}^{3} \sum_{i=0}^{4} a_{ij}(2 - \alpha)^{\frac{i}{4}} \xi^{\frac{j}{4}} + u_{\alpha,z}, \quad 0 < \alpha < 2. \qquad (14.58)$$

On estimating (14.58) with generalized least squares, it turned out that only a subset of regressors was needed to fit the simulated quantiles. We selected the subset by maximizing the adjusted-R^2 value. The estimated coefficients are presented in Table 14.4; the adjusted-R^2 value was 0.9929.

Table 14.4 Parameter estimates a_{ij} of fitted response surface.[a]

j	i 0	1	2	3	4
0	–	–	–	-44.96 (-2.38)	76.20 (3.19)
1	–	–	–	393.53 (2.43)	-677.25 (-3.32)
2	6.42 (6.17)	-99.29 (-7.41)	510.93 (9.65)	-1812.97 (-4.89)	2106.29 (4.61)
3	–	–	–	555.87 (2.32)	-964.50 (-3.21)

[a] t-values are given in brackets.

(Adapted from: Rachev, Kim and Mittnik (1999))

We shall next generalize Theorem 14.6, see also Mittnik, Rachev and Samorodnitsky (1998).

Recall first that if the logarithm of ch.f.,$f(\theta) = Ee^{i\theta X}$, of α–stable r.v. X, can be written as

$$\ln f(\theta) = \begin{cases} -\sigma^\alpha |\theta|^\alpha [1 - i\beta \, \text{sign}(\theta) \tan \frac{\pi\alpha}{2}] + i\mu\theta, & \text{for } \alpha \neq 1, \\ -\sigma|\theta|[1 + i\beta \frac{\pi}{2} \text{sign}(\theta) \ln|\theta|] + i\mu\theta, & \text{for } \alpha = 1, \end{cases} \qquad (14.59)$$

[16]Using the property that the power of the CUSUM test based on OLS residuals is asymptotically symmetric about the midpoint of the sample, one may use the second half of sample quantiles.

then we write $X \stackrel{d}{=} S_\alpha(\beta, \sigma, \mu)$. Recall also that a sample $U_1, U_2, \ldots$ of i.i.d. observations is said to be *in the domain of attraction of an α-stable law* with index $\alpha \in (0, 2]$ if there exist constants $a_n \geq 0$ and $b_n \in \mathbf{R}$ such that

$$a_n^{-1} S_n - b_n \stackrel{w}{\Rightarrow} X, \tag{14.60}$$

where $S_n = U_1 + \cdots + U_n$, X is a non–degenerate α–stable random variable, and "$\stackrel{w}{\Rightarrow}$" stands for weak convergence.

For $\alpha < 2$ the domain–of–attraction condition (14.60) is equivalent to the assumption that the tail behavior of U_i is of the Pareto–Lévy form (cf. Feller (1971), p. 303):

$$P(|U_i| > t) = t^{-\alpha} L(t), \quad t > 0, \tag{14.61}$$

where $L(t)$ is a slowly varying function as $t \to \infty$,[17] and

$$\lim_{t \to \infty} \frac{P(U_i > t)}{P(|U_i| < t)} = p, \quad \lim_{t \to \infty} \frac{P(U_i < -t)}{P(|U_i| < t)} = q, \tag{14.62}$$

for some $p \geq 0$ and $q \geq 0$ with $p + q = 1$.

We shall further assume that U_i are in the *domain of normal attraction of an α-stable law*, that is, for some $c > 0$,

$$P(|U_i| > t) \sim ct^{-\alpha} \quad \text{as } t \to \infty, \tag{14.63}$$

and furthermore the limiting relationships (14.62) hold.[18]

Let $g(x) = 1/P(|U_i| > x)$ and consider the generalized inverse of $g(x)$:

$$g^{\leftarrow}(y) := \sup\{x : g(x) \leq y\}.$$

Set

$$a_n := g^{\leftarrow}(n), \quad n \geq 1, \tag{14.64}$$

then, as $n \to \infty$, $a_n \sim cn^{1/\alpha}$.[19]

Next, we need some basic definitions and results on Poisson random measures (see Resnick (1987a)). Let E be a locally compact topological space with a countable base and let $\mathcal{E}$ be the Borel σ-algebra of subsets of E. A *point measure* m on $\mathcal{E}$ with support $\{x_i, i \geq 1\} \subset E$ is defined by

$$m = \sum_{i=1}^{\infty} \epsilon_{x_i}, \tag{14.65}$$

---

[17]$L(t)$ is a slowly varying function as $t \to \infty$, if for every constant $c > 0$, $\lim_{t \to \infty} L(ct)/L(t)$ exists and is equal to 1. Here and in what follows we always use L or l to denote a slowly varying function.

[18]U_i are in the domain of normal attraction of an α-stable law, if (14.60) holds with $a_n = c_0 n^{1/\alpha}$ for some positive constant c_0. Note that when U_i are in the *general* domain of attraction, then in (14.60) $a_n = n^{1/\alpha} L(n)$, for some slowly varying function $L(n)$, as $n \to \infty$.

[19]Here, and in what follows, c stands for a generic constant, that can be different in different places.

where

$$\epsilon_{x_i}(A) = \begin{cases} 1, & \text{if } x_i \in A, \\ 0, & \text{if } x_i \notin A, \end{cases} \quad A \in \mathcal{E}. \tag{14.66}$$

A *point process* N on E is a random element,

$$N : (\Omega, \mathcal{A}, P) \to (M_P(E), \mathcal{M}_p(E)),$$

on the original probability space $(\Omega, \mathcal{A}, P)$ with values in the space $M_P(E)$ of all point measures on E with the σ-algebra $\mathcal{M}_P(E)$ generated by the sets $\{m \in M_P(E) : m(F) \in B\}$, $F \in \mathcal{E}$, and B a Borel set in $[0, \infty]$, i.e. $B \in \mathcal{B}([0, \infty])$.

Let μ be a Radon measure on $(E, \mathcal{E})$, that is, μ is finite on all compact subsets of E. A point process N is called *Poisson random measure (PRM)* with mean measure μ if,

(i) for every $F \in \mathcal{E}$, and every $k \in \mathbf{N} := \{1, 2, \ldots\}$,

$$P(N(F) = k) = \begin{cases} \frac{\mu(F)^k}{k!} e^{-\mu(F)}, & \text{if } \mu(F) < \infty, \\ 0, & \text{if } \mu(F) = \infty; \end{cases}$$

and

(ii) if $F_1, \ldots, F_k$ (for every $k \in \mathbf{N}$) are mutually disjoint sets in $\mathcal{E}$, then $N(F_1), \ldots, N(F_k)$ are independent random variables.

Consider next an array of random variables $(U_{n,j}, j \geq 1, n \geq 1)$ with values in $(E, \mathcal{E})$, and assume that for each n, $(U_{n,j})_{j \geq 1}$ are i.i.d. r.v.'s.. Suppose that the sequence of finite measures defined by

$$\mu_n(A) := nP(U_{n,1} \in A), \quad A \in \mathcal{E}, \tag{14.67}$$

converges vaguely to a Radon measure μ on $(E, \mathcal{E})$. (Recall that $(\mu_n)_{n \geq 1}$ *converges vaguely* to μ $(\mu_n \overset{v}{\to} \mu)$ if $\limsup_{n \to \infty} \mu_n(K) \leq \mu(K)$ for all compact sets $K \subset E$ and $\liminf_{n \to \infty} \mu_n(G) \geq \mu(G)$ for all open relatively compact sets $G \subset E$.)

Proposition 14.1 *(see Resnick (1987a), Proposition 3.21).* Let

$$\xi_n = \sum_{k \geq 1} \varepsilon_{(\frac{k}{n}, U_{k,n})}$$

and ξ be a PRM on $[0, \infty) \times E$ with mean measure $dt \times d\mu$. Then

$$\mu_n \overset{v}{\to} \mu \tag{14.68}$$

if and only if [20]

$$\xi_n \overset{w}{\Rightarrow} \xi. \tag{14.69}$$

---

[20] Here $\overset{w}{\Rightarrow}$ in (14.69) stands for the weak convergence of stochastic point processes, in this case the weak convergence in the space $M_P([0, \infty) \times E)$.

We now apply the above proposition to the sequence $(U_i)_{i\geq 1}$ of i.i.d. random variables in the domain of normal attraction of an α-stable law. Namely, we take $E := [-\infty, \infty] \setminus \{(0)\}$), (i.e. relatively compact sets are those bounded away from the origin) and set in Proposition 14.1, $U_{k,n} = \frac{U_k}{a_n}$, where a_n was defined as $g^{\leftarrow}(n)$, see (14.64). Then, as $n \to \infty$,

$$\mathbf{X}_n^* := \sum_{k=1}^{\infty} \varepsilon_{\left(\frac{k}{n}, \frac{U_k}{a_n}\right)} \overset{w}{\Rightarrow} \sum_i \varepsilon_{(t_i, j_i)} =: \mathbf{X}^* \tag{14.70}$$

in $M_p([0, \infty) \times E)$, where the limit in (14.70) is a PRM with mean measure $dt \times d\nu$, and

$$\nu(dx) = \alpha p x^{-(1+\alpha)} dx \mathbf{1}(\{x > 0\}) + \alpha q |x|^{-(1+\alpha)} dx \mathbf{1}(\{x > 0\}) \tag{14.71}$$

(see formula (4.70) in Resnick (1987a), p. 226). Furthermore, the points of $\mathbf{X}^*$ on $\{t \leq 1\}$ arranged in the non–increasing order by the magnitude of the "jumps" j_i's can be represented in distribution as

$$\left(U_j^0 \delta_j, \Gamma_j^{-1/\alpha}\right)_{j \geq 1}, \tag{14.72}$$

where $(U_j^0)_{j\geq 1}, (\delta_j)_{j\geq 1}$ and $(\Gamma_j)_{j\geq 1}$ are three independent sequences of random variables; $(U_j^0)_{j\geq 1}$ are i.i.d. r.v.'s uniformly distributed on $[0,1]$, $(\delta_j)_{j\geq 1}$ are i.i.d. random signs, $P(\delta_j = 1) = 1 - P(\delta_j = -1) = p$, and $(\Gamma_j)_{j\geq 1}$ are the standard Poisson arrivals, i.e. $\Gamma_j = e_1 + \ldots + e_j$ where $(e_j)_{j\geq 1}$ is a sequence of i.i.d. exponential r.v.'s with mean 1.

Consider now the regression model:

$$Y_i = X_i'\beta + U_i, \ 1 \leq i \leq n, \tag{14.73}$$

where $\beta = (\beta_0, \ \beta_1)'$,

$$X_i = \begin{pmatrix} 1 \\ Z_i \end{pmatrix}, \ 1 \leq i \leq n, \tag{14.74}$$

with

$$\frac{1}{n}\sum_{i=1}^{n} Z_i \to_{n\to\infty} 0, \tag{14.75}$$

$$\frac{1}{n}\sum_{i=1}^{n} Z_i^2 \to_{n\to\infty} R > 0, \tag{14.76}$$

and $U_1, U_2, \ldots$ are i.i.d. r.v.'s in the domain of normal attraction of an α–stable law.

Define the normalizing constants a_n by (14.64), and so, $a_n \sim cn^{1/\alpha}$ as $n \to \infty$.

We assume, in addition, the following:

(**A1**) $If 1 < \alpha < 2$, then $E(U_1) = 0$.

(**A2**) $If \alpha = 1$, then $\displaystyle\int_{-n}^{n} x dF_{U_1}(x) \to_{n\to\infty} 0$,   (14.77)

where $F_{U_1}(x)$ is the distribution function of U_1.[21]
No additional assumptions are imposed for the case $0 < \alpha < 1$.
Let

$$\hat{\beta}^{(n)} := \left(\sum_{i=1}^{n} X_i X_i'\right)^{-1} \sum_{j=1}^{n} Y_j X_j \qquad (14.78)$$

be the OLS estimator for β, and let

$$U_i^{(n)} := Y_i - X_i' \hat{\beta}^{(n)}, \quad 1 \le i \le n, \qquad (14.79)$$

be the OLS residuals.

Our main result is Theorem 14.10 below; it provides a functional limit theorem for the cumulative sum process based on self–normalized OLS residuals. We shall examine the weak limit in the Skorokhod space $D[0,1]$ of the following sequence of processes: for $\xi \in [0,1]$, and $n \ge 1$ let

$$X_n(\xi) := \frac{\sum_{i=1}^{[n\xi]} U_i^{(n)}}{\left(\sum_{i=1}^{n} \left(U_i^{(n)}\right)^2\right)^{1/2}} = \frac{a_n^{-1} \sum_{i=1}^{[n\xi]} U_i^{(n)}}{\left(a_n^{-2} \sum_{i=1}^{n} \left(U_i^{(n)}\right)^2\right)^{1/2}}. \qquad (14.80)$$

Next, let

$$X_\infty(\xi) := \frac{\sum_{j=1}^{\infty} \delta_j \Gamma_j^{-1/\alpha} \left(\mathbf{1}_{\{V_j \le \xi\}} - \xi\right)}{\left(\sum_{j=1}^{\infty} \Gamma_j^{-2/\alpha}\right)^{1/2}}, \quad 0 \le \xi \le 1, \qquad (14.81)$$

where the sequences $(V_j)_{j\ge1}$, $(\delta_j)_{j\ge1}$ and $(\Gamma_j)_{j\ge1}$, are independent; $(V_j)_{j\ge1}$ are "random signs", that is, i.i.d. r.v.'s, with uniformly distributed on $[0,1]$, $V_j \stackrel{d}{=} U(0,1)$; $(\delta_j)_{j\ge1}$ are "random signs", that is i.i.d. r.v.'s, with $P(\delta_j = 1) = 1 - P(\delta_j = -1) = p$, where p is defined in (14.62) and $(\Gamma_j)_{j\ge1}$ are the arrivals of a standard Poisson process.

Theorem 14.10 *Under the assumption* **A1** *if* $1 < \alpha < 2$ *and the assumption* **A2** *if* $\alpha = 1$, *the sequence of processes* $(X_n(\xi))_{0\le\xi\le1}$ *converges weakly in the Skorokhod* $J1$ *topology in* $D[0,1]$ *to the process* $(X_\infty(\xi))_{0\le\xi\le1}$:

$$\mathbf{X}_n \stackrel{w}{\Rightarrow} \mathbf{X}_\infty. \qquad (14.82)$$

---

[21]Note that the Assumption **A2** implies, in particular, that $U_1, U_2, \ldots$ are attracted to a symmetric 1–stable (Cauchy) law. No symmetry assumptions are made in the case $\alpha \ne 1$.

Proof: See Section 14.3.   □

It is the usual statistical practice to approximate the finite–sample distributions of a test statistic by its limiting distribution. The functional limit theorem proved in the last section allows us to construct different tests for constancy of the regression coefficient β in (14.73) by focusing on various aspects of possible departure of the distribution of the estimated residuals $U_i^{(n)}$ from what is should be if the regression coefficient was constant. The only requirement our test statistic has to satisfy is that it should be a functional of $(X_n(\xi), 0 \leq \xi \leq 1)$ that is continuous in the Skorokhod topology on $D[0,1]$, at least with probability 1 with respect to the law of the limiting process $(X_\infty(\xi), 0 \leq \xi \leq 1)$. One then derives the distribution of the same test statistic functional evaluated on the limiting process. In our situation of heavy tailed innovations the limiting process $(X_\infty(\xi), 0 \leq \xi \leq 1)$ is not a standard one, and because of its complicated probabilistic structure one has to resort to simulations to tabulate the distribution, density and critical values of most test statistics. In this section we concentrate on the marginal distributions of the limiting process. We also present initial evidence that already for sample sizes of $n = 100$ the finite–sample distributions are reasonably well approximated by the limiting distributions.

We simulated 10,000 replications of $X_\infty(\xi)$ for $\xi = .01, .02, \ldots, .99$, truncating the infinite sums in (14.81) at 1000. The inclusion of additional summands had no noticeable impact on the approximations. For the corresponding finite–sample distributions of $X_n(\xi)$ we also simulated 10,000 replications with $n = 100$. For $\alpha = 1.5$, Figure 14.4 shows the estimated density of the the finite–sample distributions (top graph) and the approximate limit distributions (bottom graph) as a function of ξ [22] [23].

To derive critical values we simulated the finite-sample distribution with U_i is drawn from symmetric α-stable distributions with $\alpha \in \{1.0, 1.1, \ldots, 1.9, 2.0\}$. Given the closeness of finite-sample and limiting distributions, we simulated $\mathbf{X}_n(\xi)$ (see (14.80)) with sample size $n = 100$ in order to keep the computational burden manageable. Because $\mathbf{X}_n(\xi) \stackrel{d}{=} \mathbf{X}_n(1-\xi)$, $\xi \in [0,1]$, we can restrict ourselves to $\xi \in [0,1/2]$. Specifically, we considered values $\xi \in \{0, 0.01, \ldots, 0.49, 0.5\}$. For each of the 561 (α, ξ)-combinations we simulated 20,000 replications of $\mathbf{X}_n(\xi)$.[24]

Instead of tabulating the critical values for selected values of α and ξ, we use the response surface technique to compactly summarize the simulation re-

---

[22] The distributions become highly peaked as ξ approaches 0 and 1. This is especially highly pronounced for small α.

[23] We have restricted our simulation studies to this α range, because it covers the α estimates reported in empirical work.

[24] As simulations show, the choice of sample size n has no relevant impact on the simulated critical values.

Simulated Pre–Limit Density, a=1.5

Simulated Limit Density, a=1.5

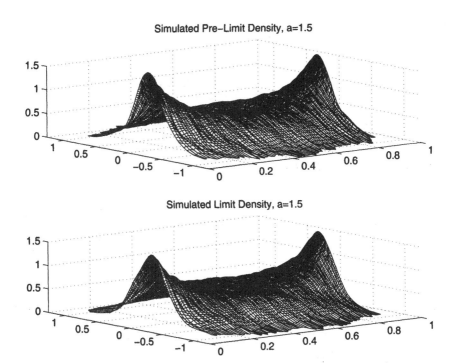

Fig. 14.4 Simulated Finite-sample and Limit Distributions for $\alpha = 1.5$.(Adapted from: Mittnik, Rachev and Samorodnitsky (1998))

sults.[25] Another advantage of this approach is that it allows us to approximate critical values for intermediate α- and ξ-values. We consider the significance levels $1 - \gamma$, with $\gamma = .01, .05, .10$, and fit to each of the three sets of 561 (α, ξ)-combinations a function of the form

$$cv_\gamma(\alpha_*, \xi_*) = \sum_{i=0}^{I_\gamma} \sum_{j=1}^{J_\gamma} c_{\gamma,i,j} \alpha_*^i \xi_*^j, \qquad (14.83)$$

where

$$\begin{aligned} \alpha_* &= (\ln \alpha)^{1.15}, \\ \xi_* &= (\ln(1 + \xi))^{1/P_\gamma}, \end{aligned}$$

with

$$P_\gamma = \begin{cases} 2, & \text{if } \gamma = .10, \\ 3, & \text{if } \gamma = .01, .05, \end{cases}$$

[25]See Hendry (1984) and Myers, Khuri and Carter (1989) for details of the response surface methodology.

and

$$I_\gamma = \begin{cases} 1, & \text{if } \gamma = .05, .10, \\ 2, & \text{if } \gamma = .01, \end{cases}$$

$$J_\gamma = \begin{cases} 5, & \text{if } \gamma = .05, .10, \\ 2, & \text{if } \gamma = .01. \end{cases}$$

The least-squares estimates of coefficients $c_{\gamma,i,j}$ are reported in Table 14.5.

Table 14.5 Coefficients of Response Surface Estimates $c_{\gamma,i,j}$ in Eqn. (14.83).

γ	i	1	2	j 3	4	5
	0	-2.929	21.90	-26.64	-7.519	18.53
.10	1	5.483	-31.77	41.77	13.83	-34.20
	2	—	—	—	—	—
	0	-8.926	87.85	-248.5	295.0	-127.6
.05	1	15.22	-137.9	404.7	-487.4	210.3
	2	—	—	—	—	—
	0	6.754	-19.46	27.11	-13.93	—
.01	1	-1.240	10.74	-24.64	18.33	—
	2	-11.71	33.28	-19.85	-5.538	—

(Adapted from: Mittnik, Rachev, and Samorodnitsky (1998))

C. Nonlinear dynamics under the Paretian hypothesis

Finally, in Mittnik, Kim, and Rachev (1996b), we generalized the Lagrange-multiplier-type (LM) test for linearity under the α-stable assumption, and showed with some empirical examples that the test conclusion depends crucially on the distribution of the innovation processes. Teräsvirta (1994), investigated smooth transition autoregression (STAR) models which encompass threshold autoregression models and the exponential autoregression as special cases. Consider the following STAR model of order p

$$y_t = a_0 + \sum_{i=1}^{p} a_i y_{t-i} + \left(b_0 + \sum_{i=1}^{p} b_i y_{t-i} \right) F(y_{t-d}) + w_t, \qquad (14.84)$$

where w_t are iid $N(0,\sigma^2)$ and $F(\cdot)$ is a transition function with transition variable y_{t-d}. Luukkonen (see Luukkonen Saikkonen, and Teräsvirta (1988)) studied testing under the null hypothesis $H_0 : b_j = 0, \quad j = 0, \cdots p$. Since the b_i's are not identified under the null hypothesis, they use a third-order Taylor expansion approximation

Table 14.6 Lagrange-multiplier test for linearity for normal u_t's.

T	1.9	1.8	1.7	1.6	α 1.5	1.4	1.3	1.2	1.1
50	52.7	47.2	40.5	34.0	29.0	23.9	19.5	17.3	12.7
100	52.3	42.1	40.9	29.2	27.1	21.3	17.2	13.0	11.5
200	48.2	40.7	33.5	26.4	23.3	14.6	14.5	9.7	7.8
500	48.6	40.3	31.7	24.3	20.5	15.2	14.8	10.5	9.0
1000	47.2	36.5	29.3	20.4	18.5	11.7	11.2	8.1	6.9

(Adapted from: Rachev, Kim and Mittnik (1999))

$$\hat{u}_t = a_0 + \sum_{i=1}^{p} a_i y_{t-i} + \sum_{i=1}^{p}\sum_{j=i}^{p} \alpha_{ij} y_{t-i} y_{t-j}$$
$$+ \sum_{i=1}^{p}\sum_{j=1}^{p} \beta_{ij} y_{t-i} y_{t-j}^2$$
$$+ \sum_{i=1}^{p}\sum_{j=1}^{p} \gamma_{ij} y_{t-i} y_{t-j}^3 + v_t. \tag{14.85}$$

Using (14.85) the LM-type test for linearity, with the null hypothesis

$$H_0 : \alpha_{ij} = 0, \quad i = 1, \cdots, p, j = i, \cdots p, \text{ and } \beta_{ij} = \gamma_{i,j} = 0, \quad i, j = 1, \cdots p,$$

we proceed with the following steps:

1. Regress y_t on $\{1, y_{t-i}; i = 1, \cdots p\}$ and compute the residual sum of squares $SSE_0 = \sum \hat{u}_i^2$;

2. Regress $\hat{u}_t$ on $\{1, y_{t-i}, y_{t-i}y_{t-j}; i = 1, \cdots, p; j = i, \cdots, p, \ y_{t-i}y_{t-j}^h; i, j = 1, \cdots p;$
   $h = 2, 3\}$ and compute the residual sum of squares $SSE_1 = \sum \hat{v}_i^2$;

3. Compute the test statistic $LM = T(SSE_0 - SSE_1)/SSE_0$, where T denotes the sample size.

If the u_t's are normal, the test statistic is asymptotically χ^2 distributed with $\frac{1}{2}p(p+1) + (h-1)p^2$ degrees of freedom. To examine the consequences of wrongly assumed normal errors, we generated 1,000 samples of size $T = 50$, 100, 200, 500 and 1000 from standard symmetric α-stable distributions. The entries in Table 14.6 represent the percentage of cases of (correctly) accepting the null hypothesis of linearity.

If we relax the normal assumption on $\hat{u}_t$ and allow for a non-normal α-stable distribution or, more generally, if the u_t's are in the DA of an α-stable law, then the usual LM statistic is no longer asymptotically χ^2-distributed. Davis and Resnick in Davis and Resnick (1986) have shown that it converges in distribution to the ratio of two independent stable r.v.'s with indices α and $\alpha/2$, respectively. Hannan and Kanter (1977) proved the convergence of least squares estimators of a stationary linear autoregressive model with infinite-variance errors.

Assume that the u_t are in the DA of symmetric α-stable r.v. X with $1 < \alpha < 2$, i.e.,

$$\frac{1}{T^{\frac{1}{\alpha}}\ell_\alpha(T)} \sum_{i=1}^{T} \hat{u}_i \stackrel{w}{\Longrightarrow} X, \quad \text{as} \quad T \to \infty, \tag{14.86}$$

where ℓ_α is a slowly varying function, and X has the characteristic function

$$\mathrm{E}e^{itX} = e^{-|ct|^\alpha}, \quad c > 0, \quad 1 < \alpha < 2. \tag{14.87}$$

Then there exists a slowly varying function $L_u(T)$ such that

$$\frac{1}{A_{T,n}} \sum_{i=1}^{T} \hat{u}_i^2 \stackrel{w}{\Longrightarrow} Z, \tag{14.88}$$

where $A_{T,n} = \frac{T^{2/\alpha}}{L_u(T)}$, and $Z = Z^{(\alpha)}$ is $\alpha/2$-stable subordinator, i.e., $Z^{(\alpha)}$ is a nonnegative r.v. with Laplace transform

$$\mathrm{E}e^{-\gamma Z} = \exp\left\{ -\frac{4-\alpha}{\alpha}\Gamma\left(1 - \frac{\alpha}{2}\right)\gamma^{\frac{\alpha}{2}} \right\}, \quad \gamma \geq 0. \tag{14.89}$$

The normalization constants $A_{T,n}$ in (14.88) are chosen to satisfy

$$\frac{T}{A_{T,n}^2}\mathrm{E}\left(\hat{u}_1^4 \mathrm{I}_{\{\hat{u}_1^2 < A_{T,n}\}} \right) \to 1, \quad \text{as} \quad T \to \infty. \tag{14.90}$$

Any choice of $L_u(T)$ satisfying (14.90) will imply the limiting relation (14.88). Similarly assume that the v_i are in the domain of a symmetric α'-stable r.v. with $1 < \alpha' < 2$. Then there exists a slowly varying function $L_v(T)$ such that

$$T^{-\frac{2}{\alpha}}L_v(T) \sum_{i=1}^{T} \hat{v}_i^2 \stackrel{w}{\Longrightarrow} Z', \tag{14.91}$$

where $Z' = Z^{(\alpha')}$ is an $\alpha'/2$-stable subordinator, see Section 14.2.

Consider the modified statistic

$$_{\alpha,\alpha'}LM_T(k) := c_{\alpha,\alpha'}(T) \frac{\sum_{i=1}^{T} \hat{u}_i^2 - \sum_{i=1}^{T-k} \hat{v}_i^2}{\left(\sum_{i=1}^{T} |\hat{u}_i| \right)^2}, \tag{14.92}$$

where $c_{\alpha,\alpha'}(T) := \min\left(T^{2-2/\alpha}L_u(T), \ T^{2-2/\alpha'}L_v(T) \right).$[26]

----

[26]Because the first absolute moment of $\hat{u}_t$ exists for $\alpha > 1$, the modified statistic in (14.92) is valid for $\alpha \in (1,2)$. The case $\alpha = 2$ calls for a different normalization in (14.92) and (14.93).

Note that if the $\hat{u}_t$ are α-stable r.v.'s, then

$$\frac{1}{T} \sum_{i=1}^{T} |\hat{u}_i| \xrightarrow{a.s.} E|X|,$$

by the strong LLN. Under the null hypothesis, as $T \to \infty$, the $\hat{u}_t$ and $\hat{v}_t$ are equal.[27]

If we assume that $\hat{u}_t$ and $\hat{v}_t$ are symmetric α-stable and finally $\hat{u}_t \approx \hat{v}_t$, as $T \to \infty$, then

$$\left[\frac{2}{\pi} \Gamma \left(1 - \frac{1}{\alpha} \right) \right]^2 {}_{\alpha\alpha'} LM_T(k) \xrightarrow{w}{}_{\alpha} \chi^2(k), \tag{14.93}$$

where ${}_\alpha \chi^2$ is χ^2-type distribution with k degrees of freedom.

In deriving (14.93), we used the representation of Zolotarev (see Zolotarev (1986a)) for the absolute moments of an α-stable law:

$$E|X|^p = \frac{2}{\pi} \Gamma \left(1 - \frac{p}{\alpha} \right) \Gamma(p) \sin(\frac{\pi}{2}p) \, c^p, \quad 0 < p < \alpha.$$

If, more generally, the $\hat{u}_t$ are in the DA of X, then ${}_\alpha LM_T(k)$ is an asymptotically $\alpha/2$-stable subordinator, as T and k approach ∞.

Under the alternative hypothesis, the sequences $\hat{u}_t$ and $\hat{v}_t$ may exhibit various degrees of dependence and may exhibit different limiting behavior as $T \to \infty$; in particular it may be that $\alpha = \alpha'$.

According to the limits in (14.88) and (14.91), if $\alpha > \alpha'$

$$c_{\alpha,\alpha'}(T) {}_{\alpha,\alpha'} L_T(k) \xrightarrow{w} \frac{-Z'}{(E|X|)^2}, \tag{14.94}$$

where Z' is the $\alpha'/2$-stable subordinator in (14.91). Alternatively if $\alpha' > \alpha$,

$$c_{\alpha,\alpha'}(T) {}_{\alpha,\alpha'} L_T(k) \xrightarrow{w} \frac{Z}{(E|X|)^2}, \tag{14.95}$$

where Z is the $\alpha/2$-stable subordinator defined by (14.89). If $\alpha' = \alpha$, consider the ratio

$$\ell_{\alpha,\alpha'}(T) = \frac{L_u(T)}{L_v(T)}.$$

Should $\liminf_{T\to\infty} \ell_{\alpha,\alpha'}(T)$ be ∞, we have once again the limiting case (14.94). If, on the otherhand, $\limsup_{T\to\infty} \ell_{\alpha,\alpha'}(T)$ is 0 we are in the situation (14.95). The other possible cases can be analyzed in a similar fashion.

---

[27]Therefore, assuming $\hat{u}_t = \hat{v}_t$, the modified statistic has the form $LM_T(k) = T^2 \dfrac{\sum_{i=T-k+1}^{T} \hat{u}_i^2}{\left(\sum_{i=1}^{T} |\hat{u}_i| \right)^2}$.

Table 14.7 Lagrange-multiplier test for linearity for stable u_t's.

T	1.9	1.8	1.7	1.6	α 1.5	1.4	1.3	1.2	1.1
50	81.4	89.6	91.8	92.2	93.8	94.0	95.5	95.5	96.3
100	80.6	87.8	90.1	91.2	92.6	93.0	93.3	94.8	94.8
200	76.9	85.8	89.3	90.7	91.2	92.7	92.8	94.1	94.3
500	76.3	85.4	87.5	90.1	90.2	91.8	91.8	93.1	93.4
1000	73.6	84.3	86.5	89.2	89.6	91.1	91.4	92.6	92.9

For example, if $\ell_{\alpha,\alpha'}(T) \to 1$, as $T \to \infty$, then

$$_{\alpha,\alpha'}LM_T(k) \overset{w}{\Longrightarrow} \frac{Z - Z'}{(E|X|)^2},$$

where Z and Z' are two independent $\alpha/2$-stable subordinators.

To illustrate the properties of the modified LM test, we specify an auxiliary regression in (14.85) with $p = 2$ and $h = 2$, i.e.,

$$\hat{u}_t = a_0 + \sum_{i=1}^{2} a_i y_{t-i} + \sum_{i=1}^{2}\sum_{j=i}^{2} \alpha_{ij} y_{t-i} y_{t-j} + \sum_{i=1}^{2}\sum_{j=1}^{2} \beta_{ij} y_{t-i} y_{t-j}^2 + v_t.$$

The modified LM statistic is then $_\alpha\chi^2(7)$ distributed when the u_t are in the DA of an α-stable law. 1,000 samples of $\hat{u}_t$ were generated from an iid symmetric α-stable distribution with $\alpha = 1.9, 1.8, 1.7, 1.6, 1.5, 1.4, 1.3, 1.2,$ and 1.1 with sample sizes $T = 50, 100, 200, 500$ and 1,000.

The results of the simulation are reported in Table 14.7. The entries represent the percentage of cases of (correctly) accepting of the null hypothesis of linearity.

Here, we used critical values from the $_\alpha\chi^2$ distribution.[28] Comparing with Table 14.6, we note that the type-I error was reduced by the modified statistic, and the correct use of its limiting distribution.

Next, we study an empirical example. Figure 14.5 shows the quarterly US unemployment rate for the period from 1961:I - 1995:II. This series is nonstationary, after testing by the Augmented Dickey-Fuller test in Dickey and Fuller (1979), with a t-value of -2.1514 in the test regression with a constant term. Figure 4b shows the differenced series. After stationarization, we specify an AR(1) model after Bayesian Information Criterion (BIC) (-2.4612). Figures 4c and 4d show its residual process with AR(1)-prewhitening and empirical density, respectively.

---

[28]We use the test statistic: $\left[\frac{2}{\pi}\Gamma(1 - \frac{1}{\alpha})\right]^2 T^2 \frac{\sum_{i=1}^{T} \hat{u}_i^2 - \sum_{i=1}^{T-k} \hat{v}_i^2}{(\sum_i^{T} |\hat{u}_i|)^2}$ in our simulation.

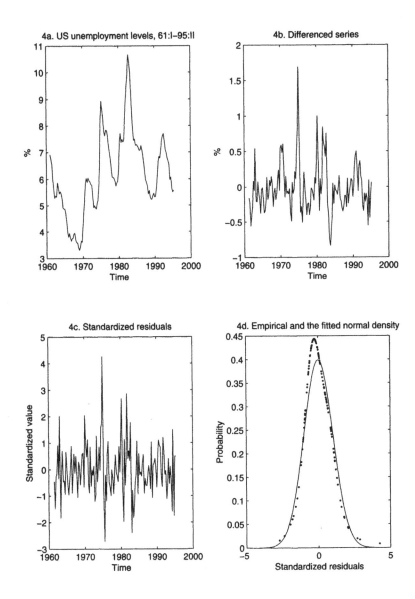

Fig. 14.5 US unemployment rate, its differences and residuals.(Adapted from: Rachev, Kim and Mittnik (1999))

The LM statistic, based on the auxiliary regression (14.85), ignoring the heavy-tailed residual distribution is 18.0553, with a p-value 0.0117, so that the null hypothesis of linearity cannot be accepted even at a marginal significance level of 95%, with a critical value 18.5 from the (usual) χ^2 distribution. The maximum likelihood estimation of Chen in Chen (1991) gives an estimated α of 1.7786. If our modified LM statistic is employed with $\alpha = 1.7786$, we have a statistic of 31.9816 and a corresponding critical value $_{1.7786}\chi^2_{.9490}(7) = 32.1367$ from the $_{\alpha}\chi^2$ distribution in Section 14.1 Thus, the null hypothesis of linearity cannot be rejected at a significance level of 5%.

14.3 Testing for Structural Breaks

In this section we shall prove the Theorem 14.10[29]. Recall the notations (14.59) – (14.82).

Proof of Theorem 14.10. Observe that the OLS estimator $\hat{\beta}^{(n)} = (\hat{\beta}_0^{(n)}, \hat{\beta}_1^{(n)})'$ has the form

$$
\begin{pmatrix} \hat{\beta}_0^{(n)} \\ \hat{\beta}_1^{(n)} \end{pmatrix} = \begin{pmatrix} n & \sum_{i=1}^{n} Z_i \\ \sum_{i=1}^{n} Z_i & \sum_{i=1}^{n} Z_i^2 \end{pmatrix}^{-1} \begin{pmatrix} \sum_{j=1}^{n}(\beta_0 + \beta_1 Z_j + U_j) \\ \sum_{j=1}^{n}(\beta_0 Z_j + \beta_1 Z_j^2 + U_j Z_j) \end{pmatrix}
$$

$$
= \frac{1}{n\sum_{i=1}^{n} Z_i^2 - (\sum_{i=1}^{n} Z_i)^2} \begin{pmatrix} \sum_{i=1}^{n} Z_i^2 & -\sum_{i=1}^{n} Z_i \\ -\sum_{i=1}^{n} Z_i & n \end{pmatrix}
$$

$$
\times \begin{pmatrix} \sum_{j=1}^{n}(\beta_0 + \beta_1 Z_j + U_j) \\ \sum_{j=1}^{n}(\beta_0 Z_j + \beta_1 Z_j^2 + U_j Z_j) \end{pmatrix}. \tag{14.96}
$$

Therefore,

$$
\hat{\beta}_0^{(n)} = \beta_0 + \frac{\sum_{i=1}^{n} Z_i^2 \sum_{j=1}^{n} U_j - \sum_{i=1}^{n} Z_i \sum_{j=1}^{n} U_j Z_j}{n\sum_{i=1}^{n} Z_i^2 - (\sum_{i=1}^{n} Z_i)^2}, \tag{14.97}
$$

and

$$
\hat{\beta}_1^{(n)} = \beta_1 + \frac{n\sum_{i=1}^{n} U_i Z_i - \sum_{i=1}^{n} U_i \sum_{j=1}^{n} Z_j}{n\sum_{i=1}^{n} Z_i^2 - (\sum_{i=1}^{n} Z_i)^2}. \tag{14.98}
$$

From (14.97) and (14.98), we conclude

$$
U_i^{(n)} = \beta_0 + \beta_1 Z_i + U_i - (1, Z_i)\left(\hat{\beta}_0^{(n)}, \hat{\beta}_1^{(n)}\right)'
$$

$$
= U_i - \frac{\sum_{k=1}^{n} Z_k^2 \sum_{j=1}^{n} U_j - \sum_{k=1}^{n} Z_k \sum_{j=1}^{n} U_j Z_j}{n\sum_{j=1}^{n} Z_j^2 - (\sum_{j=1}^{n} Z_j)^2} \tag{14.99}
$$

$$
- Z_i \frac{n\sum_{k=1}^{n} U_k Z_k - \sum_{k=1}^{n} U_k \sum_{j=1}^{n} Z_j}{n\sum_{j=1}^{n} Z_j^2 - (\sum_{j=1}^{n} Z_j)^2}, \quad i = 1, \dots, n.
$$

Therefore, for $0 \leq \xi \leq 1$,

$$
\sum_{i=1}^{[n\xi]} U_i^{(n)} = \sum_{i=1}^{[n\xi]} U_i - [n\xi]\frac{\sum_{k=1}^{n} Z_k^2 \sum_{j=1}^{n} U_j - \sum_{k=1}^{n} Z_k \sum_{j=1}^{n} U_j Z_j}{n\sum_{j=1}^{n} Z_j^2 - (\sum_{j=1}^{n} Z_j)^2}
$$

[29]The results of this section are due to Mittnik, Rachev, Samorodnitsky (1999b).

$$-\sum_{i=1}^{[n\xi]} Z_i \frac{n\sum_{k=1}^{n} U_k Z_k - \sum_{k=1}^{n} U_k \sum_{j=1}^{n} Z_j}{n\sum_{j=1}^{n} Z_j^2 - (\sum_{j=1}^{n} Z_j)^2}$$

$$= \left(\sum_{i=1}^{[n\xi]} U_i - \frac{[n\xi]}{n}\sum_{i=1}^{n} U_i\right)$$

$$+ \frac{[n\xi]\sum_{k=1}^{n} Z_k \sum_{j=1}^{n} U_j Z_j - n\sum_{i=1}^{[n\xi]} Z_i \sum_{k=1}^{n} U_k Z_k}{n\sum_{j=1}^{n} Z_j^2 - (\sum_{j=1}^{n} Z_j)^2}$$

$$+ \frac{\sum_{i=1}^{[n\xi]} Z_i \sum_{j=1}^{n} Z_j \sum_{k=1}^{n} U_k - \frac{[n\xi]}{n}\sum_{k=1}^{n} U_k (\sum_{j=1}^{n} Z_j)^2}{n\sum_{j=1}^{n} Z_j^2 - (\sum_{j=1}^{n} Z_j)^2}$$

$$=: \left(\sum_{i=1}^{[n\xi]} U_i - \frac{[n\xi]}{n}\sum_{i=1}^{n} U_i\right) + I_1^{(n)}(\xi) + I_2^{(n)}(\xi). \qquad (14.100)$$

We rewrite the process defined in (14.80) as

$$X_n(\xi) = \frac{a_n^{-1}\sum_{i=1}^{[n\xi]} U_i^{(n)}}{\left(a_n^{-2}\sum_{i=1}^{n} U_i^{(n)2}\right)^{1/2}}, \qquad 0 \le \xi \le 1, \, n \ge 1, \qquad (14.101)$$

where $(a_n, n \ge 1)$ are given by (14.64). By (14.100), the numerator of (14.101) has the representation

$$\frac{1}{a_n}\sum_{i=1}^{[n\xi]} U_i^{(n)} = \left(\frac{1}{a_n}\sum_{i=1}^{[n\xi]} U_i - \frac{1}{a_n}\xi\sum_{i=1}^{n} U_i\right) \qquad (14.102)$$

$$+ \frac{1}{a_n}\left(\xi - \frac{[n\xi]}{n}\right)\sum_{i=1}^{n} U_i + \frac{1}{a_n}I_1^{(n)}(\xi) + \frac{1}{a_n}I_2^{(n)}(\xi)$$

$$= (I_\xi(\mathbf{X}_n^*) - \xi I_1(\mathbf{X}_n^*)) + \frac{1}{a_n}\left(\xi - \frac{[n\xi]}{n}\right)\sum_{i=1}^{n} U_i$$

$$+ \frac{1}{a_n}I_1^{(n)}(\xi) + \frac{1}{a_n}I_2^{(n)}(\xi),$$

where $(\mathbf{X}_n^*)$ is given by the right–hand side of (14.70), and

$$I_\xi(\mathbf{X}) := \int_{t \le \xi} j \, d\mathbf{X}, \qquad 0 \le \xi \le 1, \qquad (14.103)$$

for all measures $\mathbf{X}$ on $[0, \infty) \times E$ for which the integral is well defined. Observe that for every fixed $\xi \in [0, 1]$, $\xi - \frac{[n\xi]}{n} \to_{n\to\infty} 0$. Furthermore, the sequence $(\frac{1}{a_n}\sum_{i=1}^{n} U_i)_{n\ge 1}$ is tight,[30] which follows from Lemma 14.4 below. Therefore,

---

[30] A sequence of r.v.'s $(\eta_i, \, i \ge 1)$, is tight, if for every $\epsilon > 0$ there exists a constant $K_\epsilon > 0$, such that $\sup_{i\ge 1} P(|\eta_i| > K_\epsilon) < \epsilon$ (see, for example, Billingsley (1968)).

$$\frac{1}{a_n}\left(\xi - \frac{[n\xi]}{n}\right)\sum_{i=1}^{n}U_i \xrightarrow{p}_{n\to\infty} 0, \tag{14.104}$$

where $\xrightarrow{p}$ stands for convergence in probability.

Considering the denominator in (14.101), we have

$$
\begin{aligned}
\sum_{i=1}^{n}(U_i^{(n)})^2 &= \sum_{i=1}^{n}U_i^2 + \frac{n(\sum_{k=1}^{n}Z_k^2\sum_{j=1}^{n}U_j - \sum_{k=1}^{n}Z_k\sum_{j=1}^{n}U_jZ_j)^2}{n(\sum_{j=1}^{n}Z_j^2 - (\sum_{j=1}^{n}Z_j)^2)^2} \\
&+ \frac{\sum_{i=1}^{n}Z_i^2(n\sum_{k=1}^{n}U_kZ_k - \sum_{k=1}^{n}U_k\sum_{j=1}^{n}Z_j)^2}{(n\sum_{j=1}^{n}Z_j^2 - (\sum_{j=1}^{n}Z_j)^2)^2} \\
&- \frac{2\sum_{i=1}^{n}U_i(\sum_{k=1}^{n}Z_k^2\sum_{j=1}^{n}U_j - \sum_{k=1}^{n}Z_k\sum_{j=1}^{n}U_jZ_j)}{n\sum_{j=1}^{n}Z_j^2 - (\sum_{j=1}^{n}Z_j)^2} \\
&- \frac{2\sum_{i=1}^{n}U_iZ_i(n\sum_{k=1}^{n}U_kZ_k - \sum_{k=1}^{n}U_k\sum_{j=1}^{n}Z_j)}{n\sum_{j=1}^{n}Z_j^2 - (\sum_{j=1}^{n}Z_j)^2} \\
&+ \frac{2\sum_{i=1}^{n}Z_i(\sum_{k=1}^{n}Z_k^2\sum_{j=1}^{n}U_j - \sum_{k=1}^{n}Z_k\sum_{j=1}^{n}U_jZ_j)}{n\sum_{j=1}^{n}Z_j^2 - (\sum_{j=1}^{n}Z_j)^2} \\
&\times \frac{n\sum_{u=1}^{n}U_kZ_k - \sum_{k=1}^{n}U_k\sum_{j=1}^{n}Z_j}{n\sum_{j=1}^{n}Z_j^2 - (\sum_{j=1}^{n}Z_j)^2} \\
&=: \sum_{i=1}^{n}U_i^2 + \sum_{j=1}^{5}R_j(n). \tag{14.105}
\end{aligned}
$$

To continue the analysis of $\sum_{i=1}^{n}(U_i^{(n)})^2$ we need the following lemma, whose the proof is given in the appendix of this section.

Lemma 14.4 Let $(V_i)_{i\geq 1}$ be i.i.d. r.v.'s such that for some $0 < \alpha < 2$ and $c > 0$

$$P(|V_i| > \lambda) \leq c\lambda^{-\alpha}, \quad \lambda > 0, \tag{14.106}$$

for all $i \geq 1$. Let $(\xi_i)_{i\geq 1}$ be a sequence of real numbers such that

$$\overline{\lim}_{n\to\infty}\frac{1}{n}\sum_{j=1}^{n}|\xi_j|^2 < \infty. \tag{14.107}$$

(i) If $0 < \alpha < 1$, then

the sequence $(n^{-1/\alpha}\sum_{j=1}^{n}V_j\xi_j), n \geq 1$, is tight. \qquad (14.108)

(ii) If $\alpha = 1$, and

$$\int_{-n}^{n}xdF_{V_n}(x) \to_{n\to\infty} 0,$$

then (14.108) holds.

(iii) If $1 < \alpha < 2$ and $E(V_j) = 0$, then (14.108) holds.

For $0 \leq \xi \leq 1$ let

$$T_n(\xi) := \frac{a_n^{-1} \sum_{i=1}^{[n\xi]} U_i^{(n)}}{(a_n^{-2} \sum_{i=1}^n U_i^2)^{1/2}}. \tag{14.109}$$

Then, by the decomposition (14.102),

$$
\begin{aligned}
T_n(\xi) &= \frac{I_\xi(\mathbf{X}_n^*) - \xi I_1(\mathbf{X}_n^*)}{(a_n^{-2} \sum_{i=1}^n U_i^2)^{1/2}} + \frac{\frac{1}{a_n}(\xi - \frac{[n\xi]}{n}) \sum_{i=1}^n U_i}{(a_n^{-2} \sum_{i=1}^n U_i^2)^{1/2}} \\
&\quad + \frac{\frac{1}{a_n} I_1^{(n)}(\xi)}{(a_n^{-2} \sum_{i=1}^n U_i^2)^{1/2}} + \frac{\frac{1}{a_n} I_2^{(n)}(\xi)}{(a_n^{-2} \sum_{i=1}^n U_i^2)^{1/2}} \tag{14.110} \\
&=: H_n(\xi) + R_1^{(n)}(\xi) + R_2^{(n)}(\xi) + R_3^{(n)}(\xi).
\end{aligned}
$$

Lemma 14.5 As $n \to \infty$,

$$R_i^{(n)}(\xi) \xrightarrow{p}_{n \to \infty} 0, \tag{14.111}$$

for all $i = 1, 2, 3$ and for all $0 \leq \xi \leq 1$.

The proof is given in the appendix of this section.

For any $0 < a < b < \infty$, let $I_{a,b}^{(2)}(\mathbf{X})$ be defined on $M_p([0, \infty] \times ([-\infty, \infty] \setminus \{0\}))$ as

$$I_{a,b}^{(2)}(\mathbf{X}) := \int_{t \leq 1} j^2 \mathbf{1}_{\{a \leq |j| \leq b\}} \, d\mathbf{X}, \tag{14.112}$$

and let $I^{(2)}(\mathbf{X} = \lim_{a \to 0, b \to \infty} I_{a,b}^{(2)}(\mathbf{X})$. Define, similarly, for $0 \leq \xi \leq 1$,

$$I_{a,b;\xi}^{(1)}(\mathbf{X}) := \int_{t \leq \xi} j \mathbf{1}_{\{a \leq |j| \leq b\}} \, d\mathbf{X}. \tag{14.113}$$

It is well known (Resnick, 1987a) that $I_{a,b;\xi}^{(1)}$ is a map $M_p([0, \infty] \times ([-\infty, \infty] \setminus \{0\})) \to \mathbf{R}$ that is almost surely continuous with respect to the law of $\mathbf{X}^*$ (see (14.66)). Fix now a small $\gamma > 0$, and let

$$H_{a,b;\xi;\gamma}(\mathbf{X}) = \frac{I_{a,b;\xi}^{(1)}(\mathbf{X}) - \xi I_{a,b;1}^{(1)}(\mathbf{X})}{(I_{a,b}^{(2)}(\mathbf{X}))^{1/2} + \gamma}. \tag{14.114}$$

Then, $H_{a,b;\xi;\gamma}$ is a functional $M_p([0, \infty] \times ([-\infty, \infty] \setminus \{0\}))$ which is almost surely continuous with respect to the law of $\mathbf{X}^*$. For arbitrary $0 \leq \xi_1 < \ldots < \xi_k \leq 1$, the functional

$$
\begin{aligned}
H_{a,b;\gamma}^{(k)}&(\xi_1, \ldots, \xi_k; \mathbf{X}) \\
&:= (H_{a,b;\xi;\gamma}(\xi_1), \ldots, H_{a,b;\xi;\gamma}(\xi_k)) : M_p([0, \infty] \times ([-\infty, \infty] \setminus \{0\})) \to \mathbf{R}^k
\end{aligned}
\tag{14.115}
$$

is almost surely continuous. By the Continuous Mapping Theorem, we have

$$\left(H_n^{a,b;\gamma}(\xi_1), \ldots, H_n^{a,b;\gamma}(\xi_k)\right)$$

$$\overset{w}{\Rightarrow}_{n\to\infty} \left(\frac{I_{a,b;\xi_1}^{(1)}(\mathbf{X}^*) - \xi_1 I_{a,b;1}^{(1)}(\mathbf{X}^*)}{(I_{a,b}^{(2)}(\mathbf{X}^*))^{1/2} + \gamma}, \ldots, \frac{I_{a,b;\xi_k}^{(1)}(\mathbf{X}^*) - \xi_k I_{a,b;1}^{(1)}(\mathbf{X}^*)}{(I_{a,b}^{(2)}(\mathbf{X}^*))^{1/2} + \gamma}\right)$$

$$(14.116)$$

in $\mathbf{R}^k$, where for $0 \le \xi \le 1$,

$$H_n^{a,b;\gamma}(\xi) := H_{a,b;\xi;\gamma}(\mathbf{X}_n^*) \qquad (14.117)$$

and $\mathbf{X}_n^*$ is defined in (14.70).

It turns out that a, b and γ can be set to $a = 0$, $b = \infty$ and $\gamma = 0$ (and, thus, we can replace $H_n^{a,b;\gamma}(\xi)$ by $H_n(\xi)$ defined in (14.110)). This is shown in the following lemma.

Lemma 14.6 As $n \to \infty$,

$$\left(H_n(\xi_1), \ldots, H_n(\xi_k)\right) \overset{w}{\Rightarrow}_{n\to\infty} \left(\frac{I_{\xi_1}(\mathbf{X}^*)}{(I^{(2)}(\mathbf{X}^*))^{1/2}}, \ldots, \frac{I_{\xi_k}(\mathbf{X}^*)}{(I^{(2)}(\mathbf{X}^*))^{1/2}}\right) \quad (14.118)$$

in $\mathbf{R}^k$, where

$$I_\xi(\mathbf{X}^*) := \sum_{j=1}^{\infty} \delta_j \Gamma_j^{-1/\alpha} (\mathbf{1}_{\{U_j^{(0)} \le \xi\}} - \xi), \ 0 \le \xi \le 1, \qquad (14.119)$$

and the sequences $(\delta_j)_{j\ge1}, (\Gamma_j)_{j\ge1}$ and $(U_j^{(0)})_{j\ge1}$ are defined in (14.81).

The proof is given in the appendix of this section.

From (14.110), Lemma 14.5 and Lemma 14.6 it follows that

$$\left(T_n(\xi_1), \ldots, T_n(\xi_k)\right) \overset{w}{\Rightarrow}_{n\to\infty} \left(\frac{I_{\xi_1}(\mathbf{X}^*)}{I^{(2)}(\mathbf{X}^*)^{1/2}}, \ldots, \frac{I_{\xi_k}(\mathbf{X}^*)}{I^{(2)}(\mathbf{X}^*)^{1/2}}\right). \quad (14.120)$$

Since the coordinates of the vector in the right–hand side of (14.120) are almost surely non-zero, we also have

$$\left(\frac{1}{T_n(\xi_1)}, \ldots, \frac{1}{T_n(\xi_k)}\right) \overset{w}{\Rightarrow}_{n\to\infty} \left(\frac{I^{(2)}(\mathbf{X}^*)^{1/2}}{I_{\xi_1}(\mathbf{X}^*)}, \ldots, \frac{I^{(2)}(\mathbf{X}^*)^{1/2}}{I_{\xi_k}(\mathbf{X}^*)}\right). \quad (14.121)$$

Next, we replace in the above limiting relation $T_n(\xi_i)$ by $X_n(\xi_i)$ as given in (14.101). Arguments similar to those used in the appendix of this section to prove Lemma 14.5 imply that

$$a_n^{-2} R_j(n) \overset{p}{\to}_{n\to\infty} 0, \text{ for all } j = 1, \ldots, 5, \qquad (14.122)$$

with $R_j(n)$ as in (14.105). Therefore,

$$\left\|\left(\frac{1}{X_n(\xi_1)}, \ldots, \frac{1}{X_n(\xi_k)}\right)\left(\frac{1}{T_n(\xi_1)}, \ldots, \frac{1}{T_n(\xi_k)}\right)\right\|^2 \tag{14.123}$$

$$\leq \sum_{j=1}^{5} |a_n^{-2} R_j(n)| \sum_{m=1}^{k} \frac{1}{|a_n^{-1} \sum_{i=1}^{[n\xi_m]} U_i^{(n)}|^2} \xrightarrow{p}_{n\to\infty} 0,$$

because, for each $m = 1, \ldots, k$, $|\sum_{i=1}^{[n\xi_m]} U_i^{(n)}/a_n|$ converges weakly to an almost surely positive limit.

We conclude from (14.121) and (14.123) that

$$\left(\frac{1}{X_n(\xi_1)}, \ldots, \frac{1}{X_n(\xi_k)}\right) \xrightarrow{w}_{n\to\infty} \left(\frac{(I^{(2)}(\mathbf{X}^*))^{1/2}}{I_{\xi_1}(\mathbf{X}^*)}, \ldots, \frac{I^{(2)}(\mathbf{X}^*)^{1/2}}{I_{\xi_k}(\mathbf{X}^*)}\right),$$
$$\tag{14.124}$$

which implies, as above, that

$$(X_n(\xi_1), \ldots, X_n(\xi_k)) \xrightarrow{w}_{n\to\infty} \left(\frac{I_{\xi_1}(\mathbf{X}^*)}{I^{(2)}(\mathbf{X}^*)^{1/2}}, \ldots, \frac{I_{\xi_k}(\mathbf{X}^*)}{I^{(2)}(\mathbf{X}^*)^{1/2}}\right). \tag{14.125}$$

We have now established that

$$(X_n(\xi))_{0\leq\xi\leq1} \xrightarrow{w}_{n\to\infty} \left(\frac{I_\xi(\mathbf{X}^*)}{I^{(2)}(\mathbf{X}^*)^{1/2}}\right)_{0\leq\xi\leq1} \tag{14.126}$$

in the sense of convergence of the finite-dimensional distributions. Recalling representation (14.72) of the the points of $\mathbf{X}^*$, we immediately see that

$$\left(\frac{I_\xi(\mathbf{X}^*)}{I^{(2)}(\mathbf{X}^*)^{1/2}}\right)_{0\leq\xi\leq1} \stackrel{d}{=} (X_\infty(\xi))_{0\leq\xi\leq1}, \tag{14.127}$$

with $X_\infty(\xi)$ defined in (14.81). Therefore, it remains to prove that (14.126) also holds in the sense of weak convergence in the J_1-topology in $D([0,1])$. Since we have already proved the convergence of finite-dimensional distributions, it remains only to prove tightness. This follows from Lemma 14.7, which is proved in the appendix of this section.

Lemma 14.7 The sequence $(\{X_n(\xi), 0 \leq \xi \leq 1\}, n \geq 1)$, is tight in $D([0,1])$.

Lemma 14.7 completes the proof of Theorem 14.10 □

Appendix

Proof of Lemma 14.4. *The case $0 < \alpha < 1$:* It follows from (14.106) that there are constants $a, b \in (0, \infty)$ such that

$$|V_j| \stackrel{st}{\leq} aS_j + b, \tag{14.128}$$

where $S_j \overset{d}{=} S_\alpha(1,1,0)$.[31] Therefore,

$$
n^{-1/\alpha} |\sum_{j=1}^{n} V_j \xi_j| \leq n^{-1/\alpha} \sum_{j=1}^{n} |V_j||\xi_j|
$$

$$
\overset{st}{\leq} n^{-1/\alpha} \sum_{j=1}^{n} (aS_j + b)|\xi_j| \tag{14.129}
$$

$$
= an^{-1/\alpha} \sum_{j=1}^{n} S_j|\xi_j| + bn^{-1/\alpha} \sum_{j=1}^{n} |\xi_j|.
$$

Now, by (14.107),

$$
n^{-1/\alpha} \sum_{j=1}^{n} |\xi_j| \to_{n\to\infty} 0, \tag{14.130}
$$

whereas

$$
n^{-1/\alpha} \sum_{j=1}^{n} S_j|\xi_j| \overset{d}{=} S_\alpha \left(\left(\frac{1}{n} \sum_{j=1}^{n} |\xi_j|^\alpha \right)^{1/\alpha}, 1, 0 \right). \tag{14.131}
$$

Since the scale parameter in the right hand side of (14.131) is bounded, we conclude that both terms on the right hand side of (14.129) are tight, and so the sequence $(n^{-1/\alpha} \sum_{j=1}^{n} V_j \xi_j, \; n \geq 1)$ is itself tight.

The case $1 < \alpha < 2$: Write

$$
X_n^{(1)} := n^{-1/\alpha} \sum_{i=1}^{n} \xi_i V_i \mathbf{1}(|V_i| \leq n^{1/\alpha}), \; X_n^{(2)} := n^{-1/\alpha} \sum_{i=1}^{n} \xi_i V_i \mathbf{1}(|V_i| > n^{1/\alpha}).
$$
$$\tag{14.132}$$

We have

$$
E(X_n^{(1)})^2 = n^{-2/\alpha} E(V_1^2 \mathbf{1}(|V_1| \leq n^{1/\alpha})) \sum_{i=1}^{n} \xi_i^2
$$

$$
+ n^{-2/\alpha} E(V_1 \mathbf{1}(|V_1| \leq n^{1/\alpha}))^2 \sum_{1 \leq i \leq n, 1 \leq j \leq n, i \neq j} \xi_i \xi_j \tag{14.133}
$$

$$
\leq n^{-2/\alpha} E(V_1^2 \mathbf{1}(|V_1| \leq n^{1/\alpha})) \sum_{i=1}^{n} \xi_i^2
$$

$$
+ n^{-2/\alpha} E(V_1 \mathbf{1}(|V_1| \leq n^{1/\alpha}))^2 (\sum_{i=1}^{n} |\xi_i|)^2.
$$

---

[31] We say that a r.v. X is stochastically smaller than a r.v. Y (denoted $X \overset{st}{\leq} Y$) if $P(X \geq x) \leq P(Y \geq x)$ for all $x \in \mathbf{R}$.

Now, by (14.106),

$$
\begin{aligned}
E(V_1^2 \mathbf{1}(|V_1| \le n^{1/\alpha})) &= \int_0^\infty P(V_1^2 \mathbf{1}(|V_1| \le n^{1/\alpha}) > \lambda) d\lambda \\
&= \int_0^{n^{2/\alpha}} P(\lambda^{1/2} \le |V_1| \le n^{1/\alpha}) \, d\lambda \\
&\le c \int_0^{n^{2/\alpha}} \lambda^{-\alpha/2} \, d\lambda \\
&= c n^{-1+2/\alpha}.
\end{aligned}
$$

Here and in the sequel c is some finite positive constant that may change from line to line. We conclude that there exists a constant $D_1 < \infty$, such that for all $n \ge 1$,

$$
n^{-2/\alpha} E(V_1^2 \mathbf{1}(|V_1| \le n^{1/\alpha})) \sum_{i=1}^n \xi_i^2 \le c \frac{1}{n} \sum_{i=1}^n \xi_i^2 \le D_1. \tag{14.134}
$$

Furthermore, because $EV_1 = 0$,

$$
\begin{aligned}
|E(V_1 \mathbf{1}(|V_1| \le n^{1/\alpha}))| &= |E(V_1 \mathbf{1}(|V_1| > n^{1/\alpha}))| \\
&\le E(|V_1| \mathbf{1}(|V_1| > n^{1/\alpha})) \\
&= \int_0^\infty P(|V_1| \mathbf{1}_{\{|V_1| > n^{1/\alpha}\}} > \lambda) \, d\lambda \tag{14.135} \\
&= n^{1/\alpha} P(|V_1| > n^{1/\alpha}) + \int_{n^{1/\alpha}}^\infty P(|V_1| > \lambda) \, d\lambda \\
&\le c n^{-1+1/\alpha} + c \int_{n^{1/\alpha}}^\infty \lambda^{-\alpha} \, d\lambda \\
&= c n^{-1+1/\alpha}.
\end{aligned}
$$

Therefore, by (14.107),

$$
n^{-2/\alpha} \left(E(V_1 \mathbf{1}(|V_1| \le n^{1/\alpha})) \right)^2 \left(\sum_{i=1}^n |\xi_i| \right)^2 \le c \left(\frac{1}{n} \sum_{i=1}^n |\xi_i| \right)^2 \le D_2 < \infty \tag{14.136}
$$

for some absolute constant D_2.

It follows now from (14.133), (14.134) and (14.136) that $(E(X_n^{(1)})^2)_{n \ge 1}$ is a uniformly bounded sequence, and so

$$
(X_n^{(1)})_{n \ge 1} \text{ is tight.} \tag{14.137}
$$

Finally, by (14.135) we have for an absolute constant D_3,

$$
E|X_n^{(2)}| \le n^{-1/\alpha} \left(E(V_1 \mathbf{1}(|V_1| \le n^{1/\alpha})) \right) \sum_{i=1}^n |\xi_i| \le c \frac{1}{n} \sum_{i=1}^n |\xi_i| \le D_3 < \infty. \tag{14.138}
$$

This implies that

$$(X_n^{(2)}, \ n \geq 1) \text{ is tight;} \qquad (14.139)$$

and our statement follows in the case $1 < \alpha < 2$ from (14.132), (14.137) and (14.139).

The case $\alpha = 1$: We still use the decomposition (14.132). The same argument as in the case $1 < \alpha < 2$ shows that the sequence $(X_n^{(1)}, \ n \geq 1)$ is tight. Further, take any $0 < \theta < 1$, and choose a constant $b > 0$, so large that

$$P(|V_i| > bn \text{ for some } i = 1, \ldots, n) \leq \frac{\theta}{2}, \ \text{ for all } n \geq 1. \qquad (14.140)$$

Then, for every $M > 0$

$$P(|X_n^{(2)}| \geq M) \leq \frac{\theta}{2} + P\left(n^{-1} \sum_{i=1}^{n} \xi_i V_i \mathbf{1}(n < |V_i| < bn) > M\right).$$

Now,

$$E\left|\frac{1}{n} \sum_{i=1}^{n} \xi_i V_i \mathbf{1}(n < |V_i| < bn)\right| \leq \frac{1}{n} \sum_{i=1}^{n} |\xi_i| E(|V_1| \mathbf{1}(n < |V_1| < bn))$$

$$= \frac{1}{n} \sum_{i=1}^{n} |\xi_i| \int_{n}^{bn} x \, dF_{|V_1|}(x)$$

$$\leq \frac{1}{n} \sum_{i=1}^{n} |\xi_i| \left(nP(|V_1| > n)\right.$$

$$\left. + \int_{n}^{bn} P(|V_1| > y) \, dy\right)$$

$$\leq \frac{1}{n} \sum_{i=1}^{n} |\xi_i| \left(c + c \int_{n}^{bn} \frac{dy}{y}\right)$$

$$= c\frac{1}{n} \sum_{i=1}^{n} |\xi_i|(1 + \log b) \leq c(b) < \infty.$$

Choosing $M \geq \frac{2c(b)}{\theta}$, we have

$$P(|X_n^{(2)}| > M) \leq \theta, \text{ for all } n \geq 1.$$

Hence, the tightness property of $(X_n^{(2)}, \ n \geq 1)$ is established. $\square$

Proof of Lemma 14.5 In our notation, $a_n^{-2} \sum_{i=1}^{n} U_i^2 = I^{(2)}(\mathbf{X}_n^*)$. It converges weakly to a positive r.v.. Therefore, $(I^{(2)}(\mathbf{X}_n^*)^{-1/2}, \ n \geq 1)$ is a tight sequence and, by (14.104),

$$R_1^{(n)}(\xi) \xrightarrow{P}_{n \to \infty} 0, \text{ for all } 0 \leq \xi \leq 1.$$

The remaining part of the lemma will follow once we prove that

$$\frac{1}{a_n} I_i^{(n)}(\xi) \xrightarrow{p}_{n\to\infty} 0 \text{ for } i = 1, 2 \text{ and all } 0 \leq \xi \leq 1.$$ (14.141)

We have by (14.75) and Lemma 14.4, that

$$\left| \frac{[n\xi] \sum_{k=1}^{n} Z_k \sum_{j=1}^{n} U_j Z_j}{n^2 n^{1/\alpha}} \right| \leq \frac{1}{n} \left| \sum_{k=1}^{n} Z_k \right| \left| n^{-1/\alpha} \sum_{j=1}^{n} U_j Z_j \right| \xrightarrow{p}_{n\to\infty} 0.$$ (14.142)

Similarly,

$$\left| \frac{n \sum_{i=1}^{[n\xi]} Z_i \sum_{k=1}^{n} U_k Z_k}{n^2 n^{1/\alpha}} \right| \leq \frac{1}{[n\xi]} \left| \sum_{i=1}^{[n\xi]} Z_i \right| \left| n^{-1/\alpha} \sum_{k=1}^{n} U_k Z_k \right| \xrightarrow{p}_{n\to\infty} 0.$$ (14.143)

Moreover, by (14.75) and (14.76),

$$\frac{1}{n^2} \left| n \sum_{j=1}^{n} Z_j^2 - \left(\sum_{j=1}^{n} Z_j \right)^2 \right| \to_{n\to\infty} R > 0.$$ (14.144)

Now, (14.141) with $i = 1$ follows from (14.142) – (14.144). Furthermore,

$$\left| \frac{\sum_{i=1}^{[n\xi]} Z_i \sum_{j=1}^{n} Z_j \sum_{k=1}^{n} U_k}{n^2 n^{1/\alpha}} \right| \leq \frac{1}{[n\xi]} \left| \sum_{i=1}^{[n\xi]} Z_i \right| \frac{1}{n} \left| \sum_{j=1}^{n} Z_j \right| \left| n^{-1/\alpha} \sum_{k=1}^{n} U_k \right| \xrightarrow{p}_{n\to\infty} 0$$

(14.145)

by (14.75) and because the sequence $(n^{-1/\alpha} \sum_{k=1}^{n} U_k)_{n\geq 1}$ is tight.
Similarly,

$$\left| \frac{\frac{[n\xi]}{n} (\sum_{j=1}^{n} Z_j)^2 \sum_{k=1}^{n} U_k}{n^2 n^{1/\alpha}} \right| \leq \left(\frac{1}{n} \sum_{j=1}^{n} Z_j \right)^2 \left| n^{-1/\alpha} \sum_{k=1}^{n} U_k \right| \xrightarrow{p}_{n\to\infty} 0.$$

(14.146)

Therefore, we have (14.141) with $i = 2$ by (14.144) – (14.146). □

Proof of Lemma 14.6. Observe that $I_\xi(\mathbf{X}^*)$ is well defined, and

$$I^{(1)}_{a,a^{-1},\xi}(\mathbf{X}^*) - \xi I^{(1)}_{a,a^{-1},1}(\mathbf{X}^*) \to_{a\to 0} I_\xi(\mathbf{X}^*) \quad \text{almost surely.} \quad (14.147)$$

To prove the lemma we will use Theorem 4.2 of Billingsley (1968). The first step is to show that for any $\gamma > 0$

$$\left(\frac{\frac{1}{a_n}\sum_{i=1}^{[n\xi_j]} U_i - \xi_j \frac{1}{a_n}\sum_{i=1}^{n} U_i}{(a_n^{-2}\sum_{i=1}^{n} U_i^2)^{1/2} + \gamma}, \ j = 1,\ldots,k \right)$$

$$\overset{w}{\Rightarrow}_{n\to\infty} \left(\frac{I_{\xi_j}(\mathbf{X}^*)}{(I^{(2)}(\mathbf{X}^*))^{1/2} + \gamma}, \ j = 1,\ldots,k \right). \quad (14.148)$$

To this end it is enough to show that for every $0 \le \xi \le 1$,

$$\lim_{a\to 0} \overline{\lim}_{n\to\infty} P(|\Delta_n(\xi)| \ge \varepsilon) = 0 \text{ for every } 0 < \varepsilon < 1, \quad (14.149)$$

where

$$\Delta_n(\xi) = \frac{\frac{1}{a_n}\sum_{i=1}^{[n\xi]} U_i \mathbf{1}(a_n a < |U_i| < a_n a^{-1})}{(a_n^{-2}\sum_{i=1}^{n} U_i^2 \mathbf{1}(a_n a < |U_i| < a_n a^{-1})^{1/2} + \gamma}$$

$$- \frac{\xi\frac{1}{a_n}\sum_{i=1}^{n} U_i \mathbf{1}(a_n a < |U_i| < a_n a^{-1})}{(a_n^{-2}\sum_{i=1}^{n} U_i^2 \mathbf{1}(a_n a < |U_i| < a_n a^{-1})^{1/2} + \gamma}$$

$$- \frac{\frac{1}{a_n}\sum_{i=1}^{[n\xi]} U_i - \xi\frac{1}{a_n}\sum_{i=1}^{n} U_i}{(a_n^{-2}\sum_{i=1}^{n} U_i^2)^{1/2} + \gamma}. \quad (14.150)$$

We have

$$P(|\Delta(\xi)| \ge \varepsilon) \le P\left(\left| \frac{\frac{1}{a_n}\sum_{i=1}^{[n\xi]} U_i \left(\mathbf{1}(|U_i| < a_n a) + \mathbf{1}(|U_i| > a_n a^{-1}) \right)}{(a_n^{-2}\sum_{i=1}^{n} U_i^2 \mathbf{1}(a_n a < |U_i| < a_n a^{-1}))^{1/2} + \gamma} \right. \right.$$

$$\left. \left. - \frac{\xi\frac{1}{a_n}\sum_{i=1}^{n} U_i \left(\mathbf{1}(|U_i| < a_n a) + \mathbf{1}(|U_i| \ge a_n a^{-1}) \right)}{(a_n^{-2}\sum_{i=1}^{n} U_i^2 \mathbf{1}(a_n a < |U_i| < a_n a^{-1}))^{1/2} + \gamma} \ge \frac{\varepsilon}{2} \right| \right)$$

$$+ P\left(\left| \frac{1}{a_n}\sum_{i=1}^{[n\xi]} U_i - \xi\frac{1}{a_n}\sum_{i=1}^{n} U_i \right| \left| \frac{1}{(a_n^{-2}\sum_{i=1}^{n} U_i^2)^{1/2} + \gamma} \right. \right.$$

$$\left. \left. - \frac{1}{(a_n^{-2}\sum_{i=1}^{n} U_i^2 \mathbf{1}(a_n a < |U_i| < a_n a^{-1}))^{1/2} + \gamma} \right| \ge \frac{\varepsilon}{2} \right)$$

$$=: q_n^{(1)}(a,\varepsilon) + q_n^{(2)}(a,\varepsilon). \quad (14.151)$$

Furthermore,

$$
\begin{aligned}
q_n^{(1)}(a,\varepsilon) &\leq P\left(\frac{1}{a_n}\left|\sum_{i=1}^{[n\xi]} U_i \mathbf{1}(|U_i| < aa_n)\right| > \frac{\varepsilon\gamma}{8}\right) \\
&+ P\left(\frac{1}{a_n}\left|\sum_{i=1}^{[n\xi]} U_i \mathbf{1}(|U_i| > a^{-1}a_n)\right| > \frac{\varepsilon\gamma}{8}\right) \\
&+ P\left(\frac{1}{a_n}\left|\sum_{i=1}^{n} U_i \mathbf{1}(|U_i| < aa_n)\right| > \frac{\varepsilon\gamma}{8}\right) \\
&+ P\left(\frac{1}{a_n}\left|\sum_{i=1}^{n} U_i \mathbf{1}(|U_i| > a^{-1}a_n)\right| > \frac{\varepsilon\gamma}{8}\right) \qquad (14.152) \\
&:= q_n^{(1,1)}\left(a,\frac{\varepsilon\gamma}{8}\right) + q_n^{(1,2)}\left(a,\frac{\varepsilon\gamma}{8}\right) + q_n^{(1,3)}\left(a,\frac{\varepsilon\gamma}{8}\right) + q_n^{(1,4)}\left(a,\frac{\varepsilon\gamma}{8}\right).
\end{aligned}
$$

We claim that

$$
\lim_{a\to 0} \overline{\lim}_{n\to\infty} q_n^{(1,i)}(a,\varepsilon) = 0, \text{ for } i = 1,\dots,4. \qquad (14.153)
$$

Clearly, (14.153) and (14.152) will imply that

$$
\lim_{a\to 0} \overline{\lim}_{n\to\infty} q_n^{(1)}(a,\varepsilon) = 0. \qquad (14.154)
$$

We prove (14.153) only for $i = 3, 4$, as the other two cases are similar. The proof of (14.153) for $i = 4$ follows from the following inequalities: for some constant $c > 0$,

$$
\begin{aligned}
q_n^{(1,4)}(a,\epsilon) &\leq P\left(\text{at least one } U_i, i = 1,\dots,n, \text{ satisfies } |U_i| > a^{-1}a_n\right) \\
&= 1 - \left(1 - P(|U_i| > a^{-1}n^{1/\alpha})\right)^n \\
&\leq 1 - (1 - ca^\alpha n^{-1})^n \to_{n\to\infty} 1 - e^{-ca^\alpha}.
\end{aligned}
$$

We turn now to the proof of (14.153) with $i = 3$. For the case $0 < \alpha < 1$ we use the inequalities

$$
\begin{aligned}
q_n^{(1,3)}(a,\epsilon) &\leq c\epsilon^{-1}n^{-1/\alpha} nE(|U_1|\mathbf{1}(|U_1| < aa_n)) \\
&\leq c\epsilon^{-1}n^{-1/\alpha+1}\int_0^{an^{1/\alpha}} P(|U_1| > y)\, dy \\
&\leq c\epsilon^{-1}n^{-1/\alpha+1}\int_0^{an^{1/\alpha}} y^{-\alpha}\, dy \\
&= c\epsilon^{-1}a^{1-\alpha}.
\end{aligned}
$$

Thus, (14.153) holds for $i = 3$.

Consider now the case $1 < \alpha < 2$. Repeating the computation used in the proof of Lemma 14.4, we have

$$
E\left(\frac{1}{n^{1/\alpha}}\left|\sum_{i=1}^{n} U_i \mathbf{1}(|U_i| < an^{1/\alpha})\right|\right)^2
$$

$$
\leq n^{1-2/\alpha}\left[E\left(U_1^2 \mathbf{1}(|U_i| < an^{1/\alpha})\right) + n\left(E(U_1 \mathbf{1}(|U_i| \leq an^{1/\alpha}))\right)^2\right]
$$

$$
\leq cn^{1-2/\alpha}\left[a^{2-\alpha}n^{-1+2/\alpha} + n(a^{\alpha-1}n^{-1+1/\alpha})^2\right] \tag{14.155}
$$

$$
\leq c\left(a^{2-\alpha} + a^{2\alpha-2}\right),
$$

for some $0 < c < \infty$. Therefore,

$$
\lim_{a\to 0}\overline{\lim}_{n\to\infty} E\left(\frac{1}{n^{1/\alpha}}\left|\sum_{i=1}^{n} U_i \mathbf{1}(|U_i| < an^{1/\alpha})\right|\right)^2 = 0, \tag{14.156}
$$

implying (14.153) with $i = 3$.

The case $\alpha = 1$ remains. Here, we use assumption **(A2)** and repeat the computation in (14.155) above to obtain

$$
E\left(\frac{1}{n}\left|\sum_{i=1}^{n} U_i \mathbf{1}(|U_i| \leq an)|\right)^2
$$

$$
\leq cn^{-1}\left(an + n\left(E(U_1 \mathbf{1}(|U_i| \leq an))\right)^2\right) \to_{n\to\infty} ca. \tag{14.157}
$$

Hence, (14.156) still holds and (14.153) has been proved for all cases.

If we show that

$$
\lim_{a\to 0}\overline{\lim}_{n\to\infty} q_n^{(2)}(\epsilon, i) = 0, \tag{14.158}
$$

then (14.151), (14.153) and (14.158) imply (14.149), and (14.148) will follow.

To this end, observe that, by Lemma 14.4, the sequence

$$
\left(\left|\frac{1}{a_n}\sum_{i=1}^{[n\xi]} U_i - \xi\frac{1}{a_n}\sum_{i=1}^{n} U_i\right|\right)_{n\geq 1}
$$

is tight. Therefore, (14.158) will follow once we prove that

$$
\lim_{a\to 0}\overline{\lim}_{n\to\infty} P(|\tilde{\Delta}_n| > \epsilon) = 0, \tag{14.159}
$$

where

$$
\tilde{\Delta}_n := \frac{1}{\left(a_n^{-2}\sum_{i=1}^{n} U_i^2\right)^{1/2} + \gamma} - \frac{1}{\left(a_n^{-2}\sum_{i=1}^{n} U_i^2 \mathbf{1}(aa_n < |U_i| < a^{-1}a_n)\right)^{1/2} + \gamma}.
$$

However,

$$|\tilde{\Delta}_n| \le \gamma^{-2} \left(a_n^{-2} \sum_{i=1}^{n} U_i^2 \left(\mathbf{1}(|U_i| < aa_n) + \mathbf{1}(|U_i| > a^{-1}a_n) \right) \right),$$

and so (14.159) follows from the same arguments we used in proving (14.153) for $i = 3, 4$. Therefore, (14.148) follows.

We now turn to the proof of (14.118). Using once again Theorem 4.2 of Billingsley (1968) and (14.148), we conclude that it is enough to show that for every $0 < \xi < 1$, and for every $0 < \varepsilon < 1$, we have

$$\lim_{\gamma \to 0} \overline{\lim}_{n \to \infty} P \left(\left| \frac{(a_n^{-2} \sum_{i=1}^{n} U_i^2)^{1/2} + \gamma}{\frac{1}{a_n} \sum_{i=1}^{[n\xi]} U_i - \xi \frac{1}{a_n} \sum_{i=1}^{n} U_i} \right. \right.$$
$$\left. \left. - \frac{(a_n^{-2} \sum_{i=1}^{n} U_i^2)^{1/2}}{\frac{1}{a_n} \sum_{i=1}^{[n\xi]} U_i - \xi \frac{1}{a_n} \sum_{i=1}^{n} U_i} \right| > \varepsilon \right) = 0. \qquad (14.160)$$

However, (14.160) follows from the fact that $|a_n^{-1} \sum_{i=1}^{[n\xi]} U_i - \xi a_n^{-1} \sum_{i=1}^{n} U_i|$ converges weakly, as $n \to \infty$, to an almost surely positive limit. This completes the proof of Lemma 14.6. $\square$

Proof of Lemma 14.7. Observe that the denominator in (14.101) converges weakly to an almost surely positive limit. Therefore, it is enough to prove that the sequence of processes

$$Y_n(\xi) = \left\{ \frac{1}{a_n} \sum_{i=1}^{[n\xi]} U_i^{(n)}, 0 \le \xi \le 1 \right\} \qquad (14.161)$$

is tight.

To this end we turn to (14.100). Taking (14.75) and (14.76), into account the tightness in (14.161) will follow once we prove the following statements:

$$\text{Sequence} \left\{ a_n^{-1} \sum_{i=1}^{[n\xi]} U_i, \ 0 \le \xi \le 1 \right\} \quad \text{is tight;} \qquad (14.162)$$

$$\text{Sequence} \left\{ \left(a_n^{-1} \sum_{i=1}^{n} U_i \right) \frac{[n\xi]}{n}, \ 0 \le \xi \le 1 \right\} \text{is tight;} \qquad (14.163)$$

$$\text{Sequence} \left\{ a_n^{-1} \frac{[n\xi] \sum_{k=1}^{n} Z_k \sum_{j=1}^{n} U_j Z_j - n \sum_{i=1}^{[n\xi]} Z_i \sum_{k=1}^{n} U_k Z_k}{n^2}, 0 \le \xi \le 1 \right\}$$

$$(14.164)$$

is tight;

$$\text{Sequence} \left\{ a_n^{-1} \frac{\sum_{i=1}^{[n\xi]} Z_i \sum_{j=1}^{n} Z_j \sum_{k=1}^{n} U_k - \frac{[n\xi]}{n} \left(\sum_{j=1}^{n} Z_j \right)^2 \sum_{k=1}^{n} U_k}{n^2}, 0 \le \xi \le 1 \right\}$$

(14.165)

is tight.

Now, by the invariance principle, the sequence in (14.162) actually converges weakly in $D([0,1])$ and is, therefore, tight. Furthermore, $\{ \frac{[n\xi]}{n}, 0 \le \xi \le 1 \} \to \{ \xi, 0 \le \xi \le 1 \}$ in $D([0,1])$. Since $(a_n^{-1} \sum_{i=1}^{n} U_i, n \ge 1)$ is tight, (14.163) follows. An identical argument shows that the sequence

$$\left\{ a_n^{-1} \frac{[n\xi] \sum_{k=1}^{n} Z_k \sum_{j=1}^{n} U_j Z_j}{n^2}, 0 \le \xi \le 1 \right\} \text{ is tight.}$$

(14.166)

Moreover, it follows from (14.75) that

$$\sup_{0 \le \xi \le 1} \frac{1}{n} \left| \sum_{i=1}^{[n\xi]} Z_i \right| \to_{n \to \infty} 0.$$

(14.167)

Therefore, the sequence

$$\left\{ n \sum_{i=1}^{[n\xi]} Z_i \sum_{k=1}^{n} U_k Z_k, 0 \le \xi \le 1 \right\}$$

(14.168)

is tight. Now, (14.164) follows from (14.166) and (14.168). The proof of (14.165) uses the same arguments as the proof of (14.164). This proves Lemma 14.7. □

14.4 Test for Outlier in Heavy-tailed Samples; Proof of the Main Theorem

In this section we prove Theorem 14.8[32].

Proof of Theorem 14.8. Recall the notations (14.63) – (14.72). Let $g(x) = 1/P(|X_i| > x)$ and recall the form of the generalized inverse of $g(x)$:

$$g^{\leftarrow}(y) = sup\{x : g(x) \leq y\}.$$

Set $a_n = g^{\leftarrow}(n)$, $n \geq 1$, then, as $n \to \infty$, $a_n \sim cn^{-1/\alpha}$.[33]

Observe that, for $\mathbf{X} \in M_P([0,\infty] \times E)$,

$$M_+(\mathbf{X}) = \max\{j : (t,j) \in \mathbf{X}, t \leq 1\} \tag{14.169}$$

is a functional that is continuous except on a set with measure 0 with respect to the law of the PRN in the right–hand–side of (14.70). A similar argument is valid for

$$M_-(\mathbf{X}) = \min\{j : (t,j) \in \mathbf{X}, t \leq 1\}. \tag{14.170}$$

The continuity of M_+ is stated and proved in Resnick (1987a, pp. 211, 214). The situation with respect to M_- is analogous. The above continuity is established in Resnick (1987a) for M_+ when $p > 0$, and, thus, for M_- when $q > 0$. This leaves only the case of, say, M_- with $q = 0$ to be considered. In this case, we interpret M_- as $M_-(m) = 0$ for every $m \in M_P([0,\infty] \times E$, and that $m([0,\infty) \times [-\infty,0)) = 0$ and $m((0,1) \times (0,\varepsilon]) = \infty$ for all $\varepsilon > 0$. Observe that, for $q = 0$,

$$\mathbf{X}^* := \sum_i \varepsilon_{(t_i,j_i)} \tag{14.171}$$

(see (14.70)) has the above properties a.s., and if $m_n \in M_P([0,\infty) \times E)$, $n \geq 1$, such that $m_n \xrightarrow{v} m$, then, m_n will eventually have points arbitrarily close to 0, and no points below a given positive distance from 0, implying that $M_-(m_n) \xrightarrow{w} M_-(m)$. Therefore, M_+ and M_- are a.s. continuous.

Furthermore, for $0 < a < b < \infty$, let

$$I_{a,b}^{(2)}(\mathbf{X}) = \int_{t \leq 1} j^2 \mathbf{1}(a \leq |j| \leq b)d\mathbf{X}. \tag{14.172}$$

It follows from Resnick (1987a, Exercise 4.4.2.8 (c)) that $I_{a,b}^{(2)}$ is a map

$$I_{a,b}^{(2)}(\mathbf{X}) : M_P([0,\infty) \times E) \to \mathbf{R}_+,$$

---

[32]This section follows the results in Mittnik, Rachev and Samorodnitsky (1999a).
[33]Here, and in what follows, c stands for a generic constant which can be different in different contexts.

that is, a.s. continuous with respect to the law of $\mathbf{X}^*$. Therefore, for every $0 < a < b < \infty$,

$$\frac{M_+(\mathbf{X}) - M_-(\mathbf{X})}{(I_{a,b}^{(2)}(\mathbf{X}))^{1/2}} \tag{14.173}$$

is a.s. continuous, $M_P([0, \infty) \times E) \to \mathbf{R}$, and so by the Continuous Mapping Theorem, as $n \to \infty$, relationship (14.70) implies

$$\frac{M_+(X_n) - M_-(X_n)}{(I_{a,b}^{(2)}(X_n))^{1/2}} \overset{w}{\Rightarrow} \frac{M_+(\mathbf{X}^*) - M_-(\mathbf{X}^*)}{I_{a,b}^{(2)}(\mathbf{X}^*))^{1/2}}, \tag{14.174}$$

where $X_n = \sum_{k \geq 1} \varepsilon_{(\frac{k}{n}, \frac{x_k}{a_n})}$. Now,

$$M_+(\mathbf{X}_n) = \frac{1}{a_n} \max_{i \leq n} X_i, \quad M_-(\mathbf{X}_n) = \frac{1}{a_n} \min_{i \leq n} X_i, \tag{14.175}$$

and

$$I_{a,b}^{(2)}(\mathbf{X}_n) = \frac{1}{a_n^2} \sum_{i=1}^{n} X_i^2 \mathbf{1}(aa_n \leq |X_i| \leq ba_n). \tag{14.176}$$

Furthermore, the points of $\mathbf{X}^*$ on $\{t \leq 1\}$ arranged in the non–increasing order by the magnitude of the "jumps" j_i's can be represented in distribution as $(U_j^o \delta_j \Gamma_j^{-1/\alpha})$, $j \geq 1$, where $(U_j^o, j \geq 1), (\delta_j, j \geq 1)$ and $(\Gamma_j, j \geq 1)$ are three independent sequences of random variables; $(U_j^0, j \geq 1)$ are i.i.d. uniformly distributed on $[0, 1]$, i.e., $U_j^0 \overset{d}{=} U(0, 1), (\delta_j, j \geq 1)$ are i.i.d. Bernoulli r.v.'s, $P(\delta_j = 1) = 1 - P(\delta_j = -1) = p$, and finally $(\Gamma_j, j > 1)$ are the standard Poisson arrivals. Therefore, by (14.175),

$$\frac{\max_{i \leq n} X_i - \min_{i \leq n} X_i}{\left(\sum_{i=1}^{n} X_i^2 \mathbf{1}(aa_n \leq |X_i| \leq ba_n)\right)^{1/2}}$$
$$\overset{w}{\Rightarrow} \frac{\Gamma_1^{-1/\alpha} + \Gamma_N^{-1/\alpha}}{\left(\sum_{i=1}^{\infty} \Gamma_i^{-2/\alpha} \mathbf{1}(a \leq \Gamma_i^{-2/\alpha} \leq b)\right)^{1/2}} := U^*(a, b), \tag{14.177}$$

where $P(N = k) = p(1-p)^{k-1} + (1-p)p^{k-1}$, $k = 2, 3, \ldots$ (in particular, $N = +\infty$, a.s., implies $\Gamma_N^{-1/\alpha} = 0$ if p or $(1-p) = 0$).

Also, recall that N is assumed to be independent of $(\Gamma_j, j \geq 1)$. Our goal is to prove that

$$\frac{\max_{i \leq n} X_i - \min_{i \leq n} X_i}{(\sum_{i=1}^{n} X_i^2)^{1/2}} \overset{w}{\Rightarrow} \frac{\Gamma_1^{-1/\alpha} + \Gamma_N^{-1/\alpha}}{\left(\sum_{i=1}^{\infty} \Gamma_i^{-2/\alpha}\right)^{1/2}} := U^*. \tag{14.178}$$

To this end, it is enough to show that

$$\frac{\sum_{i=1}^{n} X_i^2}{(\max_{i \leq n} X_i - \min_{i \leq n} X_i)^2} \overset{w}{\Rightarrow} (U^*)^{-2}. \tag{14.179}$$

It follows from (14.177) that, for $0 < a < 1$,

$$\frac{\sum_{i=1}^n X_i^2 \mathbf{1}\left(aa_n \leq |X_i| \leq a^{-1}a_n\right)}{(\max_{i\leq n} X_i - \min_{i\leq n} X_i)^2} \overset{w}{\Rightarrow} (U^*(a, a^{-1}))^{-2} \qquad (14.180)$$

and that $U^*(a, a^{-1}) \overset{w}{\Rightarrow} U^*$, as $a \to 0$. Therefore, limiting relationship (14.179) will follow from the continuity Theorem 4.2 of Billingsley (1968), once we prove that

$$\lim_{a \to 0} \limsup_{n \to \infty} P(|\Delta_n(a)| \geq \varepsilon) = 0 \qquad (14.181)$$

for all $\varepsilon \in (0, 1)$, where

$$\Delta_n(a) = \frac{\sum_{i=1}^n X_i^2}{(\max_{i\leq n} X_i - \min_{i\leq n} X_i)^2} - \frac{\sum_{i=1}^n X_i^2 \mathbf{1}(aa_n \leq |X_i| \leq a^{-1}a_n)}{(\max_{i\leq n} X_i - \min_{i\leq n} X_i)^2}. \qquad (14.182)$$

We have

$$
\begin{aligned}
P(|\Delta_n(a)| \geq \varepsilon) \quad &\leq P\left(\left(\frac{1}{a_n}(\max_{i\leq n} X_i - \min_{i\leq n} X)\right)^{-1} \geq \varepsilon^{-1/4}\right) \\
&+ P\left(\frac{1}{a_n^2}\sum_{i=1}^n X_i^2 \mathbf{1}(|X_i| < aa_n) \geq \frac{1}{2}\varepsilon^{3/2}\right) \qquad (14.183) \\
&+ P\left(\frac{1}{a_n^2}\sum_{i=1}^n X_i^2 \mathbf{1}\left(|X_i| > a^{-1}a_n\right) \geq \frac{1}{2}\varepsilon^{3/2}\right) \\
&:= P_1^{(n)}(\varepsilon) + P_2^{(n)}(a, \varepsilon) + P_3^{(n)}(a, \varepsilon)
\end{aligned}
$$

Now,

$$\frac{1}{a_n}(\max_{i\leq n} X_i - \min_{i\leq n} X_i) \text{ converges weakly to an a.s. positive random variable.} \qquad (14.184)$$

Therefore,

$$\lim_{n\to\infty} P_1^{(n)}(\varepsilon) = 0, \text{ for all } 0 < \varepsilon < 1. \qquad (14.185)$$

Furthermore,

$$
\begin{aligned}
E(a_n^{-2})\sum_{i=1}^n X_i^2 \mathbf{1}(|X_i| < aa_n) \quad &\leq cn^{-2/\alpha}nE(X_1^2 \mathbf{1}(|X_1| < an^{1/\alpha})) \\
&= cn^{-2/\alpha+1}\int_0^{an^{1/\alpha}} x^2 F_{|X_1|}(dx) \\
&= cn^{-2/\alpha+1}\int_0^{an^{1/\alpha}} 2yP(y < |X_i| \leq an^{1/\alpha})\,dy
\end{aligned}
$$

$$\leq 2cn^{-2/\alpha+1} \int_0^{an^{1/\alpha}} P(|X_1| > y)y\, dy$$

$$\leq c_1 n^{-2/\alpha+1} \int_0^{an^{1/\alpha}} y^{-\alpha+1}\, dy = c_2 a^{2-\alpha}.$$

Therefore,

$$P_2^{(n)}(a,\varepsilon) \leq \frac{c_2 a^{2-\alpha}}{\frac{1}{2}\varepsilon^{3/2}}, \quad \text{for all } a \text{ and } n,$$

and so

$$\lim_{a \to 0} \limsup_{n \to \infty} P_2^{(n)}(a,\varepsilon) = 0. \tag{14.186}$$

Furthermore, as $n \to \infty$,

$$
\begin{aligned}
P_3^{(n)}(a,\varepsilon) &\leq P(\text{at least one of } X_i's,\ i = 1,\dots,n \text{ satisfies } |X_i| > a^{-1}a_n) \\
&= 1 - (P(|X_i| \leq ca^{-1}n^{1/\alpha}))^n \\
&= 1 - (1 - P(|X_i| > ca^{-1}n^{1/\alpha}))^n \\
&\leq 1 - (1 - c_1 a^\alpha n^{-1})^n \\
&\to 1 - e^{-c_1 a^\alpha}.
\end{aligned}
$$

Therefore,

$$\lim_{a \to 0} \limsup_{n \to \infty} P_3^{(n)}(a,\varepsilon) = 0. \tag{14.187}$$

Then, (14.181) follows from (14.185), (14.186) and (14.187). Hence, (14.179) and, thus, (14.178) have been proved.

Alternatively, thinning the Poisson proceed we can represent U^* as

$$U^* = \frac{p^{1/\alpha}(\Gamma_1^{(1)})^{-1/\alpha} + (1-p)^{1/\alpha}(\Gamma_1^{(2)})^{-1/\alpha}}{(p^{2/\alpha}\sum_{i=1}^\infty (\Gamma_i^{(1)})^{-2/\alpha} + (1-p)^{2/\alpha}\sum_{i=1}^\infty (\Gamma_i^{(2)})^{-1/\alpha})^{1/2}}, \tag{14.188}$$

where $(\Gamma_j^{(1)}\ j \geq 1)$ and $(\Gamma_j^{(2)}\ j \geq 1)$ are independent sequences of standard Poisson arrivals.

We conclude that the limiting relation (14.179) holds. Next,

$$\left(n^{1/\alpha}\frac{S_x}{\max_{i \leq n} X_i - \min_{i \leq n} X_i}\right)^2 = \frac{(\sum_{i=1}^n X_i^2)}{(\max_{i \leq n} X_i - \min_{i \leq n} X_i)^2} \tag{14.189}$$
$$- \frac{n(\bar{X})^2}{(\max_{i \leq n} X_i - \min_{i \leq n} X_i)^2}.$$

Since $\bar{X} \to_{n \to \infty} E(X)$ a.s. and

$$a_n^{-1}(\max_{i \leq n} X_i - \min_{i \leq n} X_i) \overset{w}{\Rightarrow} W_1, \tag{14.190}$$

where W_1 is a non-degenerate a.s. positive r.v., it follows that

$$\frac{n(\bar{X})^2}{(\max_{i \le n} X_i - \min_{i \le n} X_i)^2}$$

$$= (\bar{X})^2 \frac{1}{(a_n^{-1}(\max_{i \le n} X_i - \min_{i \le n} X_i))^2} \frac{n}{a_n^2} \to_{n \to \infty} 0 \quad (14.191)$$

in probability, because $a_n \sim n^{-1/\alpha} L_n$, as $n \to \infty$, where L_n is a slowly varying function and $\alpha < 2$. It follows from (14.179) and (14.189) – (14.191) that

$$\left(n^{1/2} \frac{S_x}{\max_{i \le n} X_i - \min_{i \le n} X_i} \right)^2 \overset{w}{\Rightarrow} (U^*)^{-2}.$$

implying that $n^{-1/2} \dfrac{\max_{i \le n} X_i - \min_{i \le n} X_i}{S_x} \overset{w}{\Rightarrow} U^*$, as desired. $\qquad \square$

It is important to compare the test–statistic O_n with its L_1–version

$$O_n^* := \frac{\max_{1 \le i \le n} X_i - \min_{1 \le i \le n} X_i}{\frac{1}{n} \sum_{i=1}^n |X_i|} \quad (14.192)$$

when $1 < \alpha < 2$. From (14.184) we see that there exists a slowly varying function $L(n)$ such that

$$n^{-1/\alpha} L(n) O_n^* \overset{w}{\Rightarrow} \frac{W_1}{E|X_1|}. \quad (14.193)$$

Comparing the limiting results for O_n and O_n^* (cf. (14.50) and (14.193)) we conclude that the self–normalization of O_n avoid the use of slowly varying function $L(n)$, which can only be determined by examining the tails of the unknown distribution for X_1.

Remark 14.4 An argument identical to the one used in the proof of Theorem 14.8 at the begin of this section gives limiting distributions of the statistics M_n, m_n and $\bar{M}_n$, see (14.16), (14.17) and (14.18). In fact,

$$n^{-1/2} M_n \overset{w}{\Rightarrow} U_+^*, \quad (14.194)$$

with

$$U_+^* := \frac{\Gamma_{N_1}^{-1/\alpha}}{(\sum_{i=1}^{\infty} \Gamma_i^{-2/\alpha})^{1/2}}, \quad (14.195)$$

where N_1 is a geometric random variable

$$P(N_1 = k) = p(1-p)^{k-1}, \quad k = 1, 2, \ldots,$$

independent of the Poisson process $(\Gamma_i)_{i \ge 1}$,

$$n^{-1/2} m_n \overset{w}{\Rightarrow} U_-^*, \quad (14.196)$$

with

$$U_-^* := \frac{\Gamma_{N_2}^{-1/\alpha}}{(\sum_{i=1}^{\infty} \Gamma_i^{-2/\alpha})^{1/2}}, \qquad (14.197)$$

where N_2 is a geometric random variable

$$P(N_2 = k) = q(1-q)^{k-1}, \ k = 1, 2, \ldots,$$

independent of the Poisson process $(\Gamma_i)_{i \geq 1}$, and

$$n^{-1/2} \bar{M}_n \overset{w}{\Rightarrow} U_{\pm}^*, \qquad (14.198)$$

with

$$U_{\pm}^* := \frac{\Gamma_1^{-1/\alpha}}{(\sum_{i=1}^{\infty} \Gamma_i^{-2/\alpha})^{1/2}}. \qquad (14.199)$$

Furthermore, alternative representations of the type (14.51) are available for both U_+^* and U_-^*.

15

Stable Paretian Econometrics: Unit-Root Theory and Cointegrated Models

15.1 Statistical Inference in Time Series with Unit-Root:

Granger in Granger (1981) analyzed the integrated processes of economic time series and Nelson and Plosser in Nelson and Plosser (1982) reported strong evidence for nonstationarity in U.S. macroeconomic time series. We study the stochastic trends in economic time series under the Paretian assumption. In Rachev, Mittnik and Kim(1996b), we analyzed the asymptotic distributions of t-statistics of unit-root tests (cf. Chan and Tran (1989) and Phillips (1990)) and provided the generalized Dickey-Fuller tables. Table 15.1 summarizes test statistics, where we consider below Case I and Case II.

Table 15.1 Data generating processes (DGPs) and estimated regressions for standard Dickey–Fuller tests

Case	DGP[a]	Estimated Regression	t-statistic
I	$y_t = y_{t-1} + u_t$	$\Delta y_t = \beta y_{t-1} + u_t$	t_β
II	$y_t = y_{t-1} + u_t$	$\Delta y_t = \mu + \beta y_{t-1} + u_t$	$t_{\beta,\mu}$
III	$y_t = \mu + y_{t-1} + u_t$	$\Delta y_t = \mu + \tau t + \beta y_{t-1} + u_t$	$t_{\beta,\mu,\tau}$

[a] All $u_t \overset{iid}{\sim} N(0, \sigma^2)$

(Adapted from: Rachev, Kim and Mittnik (1999))

In this section we derive the asymptotic distributions of estimators $\hat{\mu}$ and $\hat{\beta}$ and the t-statistics t_β and $t_{\beta,\mu}$. We go beyond the work of Chan and

Tran (1989) and Phillips (1990) by considering regression Case II for the test regression $\Delta y_t = \mu + \beta y_{t-1} + u_t$, which is the more relevant case in applied work.[1]

Suppose that the u_t are iid random variables (r.v.'s) in the DA of a strictly stable r.v. $L_\alpha(1)$ with index $0 < \alpha < 2$ and that, if $\alpha = 1$, $L_1(1)$ is a symmetric (Cauchy) stable r.v. Then, there exists a positive constant a_n such that

$$\frac{1}{a_n} \sum_{t=1}^{[nt]} u_t \xrightarrow{w} L_\alpha(t) \quad \text{in} \quad D[0,1], \tag{15.1}$$

where $a_n = n^{1/\alpha} l(n)$, with $l(n)$ a slowly varying function as $n \to \infty$, and $L_\alpha(t)$ is a Lévy process with strictly stable increments.

Lemma 15.1 As $n \to \infty$,

$$\left(\frac{1}{a_n} \sum_{t=1}^{[nt]} u_t, \frac{1}{a_n^2} \sum_{t=1}^{[nt]} u_t^2 \right) \xrightarrow{w} (L_\alpha(t), [L_\alpha](t)) \quad \text{in} \quad D[0,1]^2, \tag{15.2}$$

where $[L_\alpha]$ is defined for the Lévy process L_α, $t \geq 0$ as

$$
\begin{aligned}
[L_\alpha](t) \quad &:= \quad L_\alpha^2(t) - 2 \int_0^t L_\alpha(s-) dL_\alpha(s), \quad t \geq 0, \\
&\overset{d}{=} \quad \sum_i \left(L_\alpha^2(t_i) - L_\alpha^2(t_i-) - L_\alpha(t_i)[L_\alpha(t_i) - L_\alpha(t_i-)] \right),
\end{aligned}
$$

with (t_i) being the jump points of $L_\alpha(t)$ on $[0,t]$.

In the next two theorems we study the asymptotic behavior of $\hat{\beta}$ and the t-statistics under the null hypothesis $\beta = 1$. Almost all of the results can be easily extended to the case $0 < \alpha \leq 1$, but we shall restrict ourselves to the case $1 < \alpha < 2$.

Theorem 15.1 Consider the first-order autoregressive process $y_t = \beta y_{t-1} + u_t$, $y_0 = 0$, where the u_t are iid r.v.'s. Assume that the u_t are in the DA of a strictly α-stable law $L_\alpha(1)$, $\alpha \in (1,2)$.

(a) Then, under the null hypothesis $\beta = 1$, we have for the OLS estimator

$$\hat{\beta} = \frac{\sum_{t=1}^n y_t y_{t-1}}{\sum_{t=1}^n y_{t-1}^2},$$

the asymptotic result

$$n(\hat{\beta} - 1) \xrightarrow{w} \frac{\int_0^1 L_\alpha(s-) dL_\alpha(s)}{\int_0^1 L_\alpha^2(s) ds},$$

---

[1]The proofs are given in Rachev, Mittnik and Kim (1998), see also the references there.

where the Lévy process $L_\alpha(s)$ is defined in (15.1).

(b) Moreover, the t-statistic

$$t_\beta = \frac{\hat{\beta} - 1}{s_{\hat{\beta}}},$$

where

$$s_{\hat{\beta}}^2 = \frac{n^{-1} \sum_{t=1}^n (y_t - \hat{\beta} y_{t-1})^2}{\sum_{t=1}^n y_{t-1}^2},$$

admits the weak limit

$$t_\beta \xrightarrow{w} \frac{\int_0^1 L_\alpha(s-)dL_\alpha(s)}{\sqrt{[L_\alpha](1) \int_0^1 L_\alpha^2(s)ds}}.$$

Remark 15.1 In the normal case, $\alpha = 2$ (see Chan and Tran (1989) and Phillips (1990)), Theorem 15.1 leads to $n(\hat{\beta} - 1) \xrightarrow{w} \int_0^1 W(s)dW(s)/\int_0^1 W^2(s)ds$, where W is a Brownian motion, and

$$t_\beta = \frac{\hat{\beta} - 1}{s_\beta} \xrightarrow{w} \frac{\int_0^1 W(s)dW(s)}{\sqrt{\int_0^1 W^2(s)ds}}.$$

Theorem 15.2 Consider the first-order autoregressive process with drift, $y_t = \mu + \beta y_{t-1} + u_t$, and assume that the u_t are defined as in Theorem 1. Let $\hat{\beta}$ be the OLS estimator for β:

$$\hat{\beta} = \frac{\sum_{t=1}^n y_t y_{t-1} - \frac{1}{n} \left(\sum_{t=1}^n y_{t-1} \right) \left(\sum_{t=1}^n y_t \right)}{\sum_{t=1}^n y_{t-1}^2 - \frac{1}{n} \left(\sum_{t=1}^n y_{t-1} \right)^2}.$$

Then, under the null hypothesis $\mu = 0$, $\beta = 1$, $n(\hat{\beta} - 1) \xrightarrow{w} N_\alpha$, where

$$N_\alpha := \frac{\int_0^1 L_\alpha(s-)dL_\alpha(s) - L_\alpha(1) \int_0^1 L_\alpha(s)ds}{\int_0^1 L_\alpha^2(s)ds - (\int_0^1 L_\alpha(s)ds)^2}.$$

Lemma 15.2 Suppose that the assumptions of Theorem 15.2 hold. Then, under the null hypothesis $\mu = 0$, $\beta = 1$, the OLS estimator for μ,

$$\hat{\mu} = \frac{\sum_{t=1}^n y_t \sum_{t=1}^n y_{t-1}^2 - \sum_{t=1}^n y_{t-1} \sum_{t=1}^n y_t y_{t-1}}{n \sum_{t=1}^n y_{t-1}^2 - \left(\sum_{t=1}^n y_{t-1} \right)^2}$$

has the limiting behavior $\frac{n}{a_n}\hat{\mu} \overset{w}{\Longrightarrow} M_\alpha$, where

$$M_\alpha = \frac{L_\alpha(1)\int_0^1 L_\alpha^2(s)ds - \int_0^1 L_\alpha(s)ds\int_0^1 L_\alpha(s-)dL_\alpha(s)}{\int_0^1 L_\alpha^2(s)ds - \left(\int_0^1 L_\alpha(s)ds\right)^2}.$$

Corollary 15.1 Suppose that the assumptions of Theorem 15.2 hold. Then, under the null hypothesis $\mu = 0$, $\beta = 1$, the t-statistic $t_{\beta,\mu} = (\hat{\beta}-1)/s_{\hat{\beta}}$, with

$$s_{\hat{\beta}}^2 = \frac{\frac{1}{n}\sum_{t=1}^n (y_t - \hat{\mu} - \hat{\beta}y_{t-1})^2}{\sum_{t=1}^n y_{t-1}^2 - \frac{1}{n}\left(\sum_{t=1}^n y_{t-1}\right)^2},$$

converges weakly, as $n \to \infty$, to

$$\frac{\int_0^1 L_\alpha^- dL_\alpha - L_\alpha(1)\int_0^1 L_\alpha ds}{\sqrt{\int_0^1 L_\alpha^2 ds - \left(\int_0^1 L_\alpha ds\right)^2}}\sqrt{\frac{\int_0^1 L_\alpha^2 ds}{[L_\alpha](1)}}.$$

To illustrate the limiting distribution we present the following simulation procedure:

1. Generate a sample $X_1, \cdots, X_n$, of n iid standard symmetric α-stable random variables with $\alpha = 1.1$, 1.5 and 1.9.

2. Compute $S_k := \sum_{i=1}^k X_i$, $k = 1, \cdots, n$, and set $S_0 := 0$.

3. Compute the simulated values of the integrals

$$D_1 := \int_0^1 L_\alpha(s-)dL_\alpha(s) \approx \sum_{i=1}^n \frac{S_{i-1}}{n^{1/\alpha}}\frac{X_i}{n^{1/\alpha}};$$

$$D_2 := [L_\alpha](1) \approx \left(\frac{S_n}{n^{1/\alpha}}\right)^2 - 2\sum_{i=1}^n \frac{S_{i-1}}{n^{1/\alpha}}\frac{X_i}{n^{1/\alpha}};$$

$$D_3 := \int_0^1 L_\alpha^2(s)ds \approx \sum_{i=1}^n \left(\frac{S_n}{n^{1/\alpha}}\right)^2\frac{1}{n}.$$

4. Compute the estimate for t_β

$$t_\beta \overset{w}{\Longrightarrow} \frac{\int_0^1 L_\alpha(s-)dL_\alpha(s)}{\sqrt{[L_\alpha]_1\int_0^1 L_\alpha^2(s)ds}} \approx \frac{D_1}{\sqrt{D_2 D_3}}.$$

5. Compute

$$D_4 := \int_0^1 L_\alpha(s)ds \approx \sum_{i=1}^{n} \left(\frac{S_i}{n^{1/\alpha}}\right)\frac{1}{n}.$$

6. Compute the estimate for $t_{\mu,\beta}$

$$t_{\mu,\beta} \approx \frac{D_1 - \left(\frac{S_n}{n^{1/\alpha}}\right)D_4}{\sqrt{D_3 - D_4^2}}\sqrt{\frac{D_3}{D_2}}.$$

We set $n = 500$ and perform 60,000 replications. Figure 15.1 shows the simulated limiting distribution of the t-statistics, t_β and $t_{\beta,\mu}$ for $\alpha = 2.0$, and 1.5. Table 15.2 gives the empirical and simulated limiting values of the t-statistics for the unit root; it shows the 90%-, 95%- and 99%-quantiles of the empirical limiting distribution. The critical values from the empirical and simulated distributions are approximately equal except for $t_{\beta,\mu}$ at 1%. It is clear that the quantiles from the limiting distributions depend on the value of α, and also on whether there is a constant term in the test regression or not.

Table 15.2 Empirical and simulated limiting values of t-statistics for the unit root test[a].

α	t_β			$t_{\beta,\mu}$		
	1%	5%	10%	1%	5%	10%
1.9	-2.54	-1.92	-1.60	-3.50	-2.86	-2.56
	(-2.56)	(-1.93)	(-1.60)	(-3.53)	(-2.87)	(-2.57)
1.5	-2.46	-1.83	-1.50	-3.99	-2.94	-2.56
	(-2.49)	(-1.84)	(-1.51)	(-4.05)	(-2.96)	(-2.58)
1.1	-2.43	-1.72	-1.38	-4.82	-3.12	-2.61
	(-2.42)	(-1.72)	(-1.38)	(-5.01)	(-3.13)	(-2.62)

[a]Simulated values are given in brackets.

(Adapted from: Rachev, Kim and Mittnik (1999))

15.2 Statistical Inference in Regression with Integrated Variables under Stable Assumption:

This subsection discusses a particular class of vector unit root processes known as cointegrated processes which formally developed by Engle and Granger (1987). The basic idea of the cointegrated processes is that each of the processes is stochastically trended (i.e., nonstationary) but some linear combination of the processes reduces the order of integratedness and produces a stationary error processes. Economically interpreted, even though most of macroeconomic variables, like GNP, money stock themselves are trended but the difference between them is in the long-run constant. We may regard these

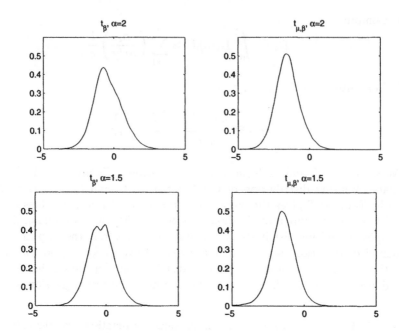

Fig. 15.1 Simulated limiting distributions of t_β and $t_{\mu,\beta}$ for $\alpha = 2$ and $\alpha = 1.5$.(Adapted from Rachev, Kim and Mittnik (1999))

series as defining a long-run equilibrium relationship and, as the difference between them is stationary. Moreover, the representation theorem (see Engle and Granger, 1987) states that if a set of variables are cointegrated, then there exists a valid error-correction representation of the data. A convenient representation for a cointegrated processes was introduced by Phillips (1991) [2] and by Park and Phillips (1988) is given by

$$Y_k = AX_k + u_k, \qquad k = 1, 2, \ldots, n \qquad (15.3)$$

where Y_k is p-dimensional random vector, $A = \{a_{ij}\}$ is $p \times q$ matrix of coefficients and the q-dimensional vectors X_k, $k \geq 0$, are generated by a random-walk process

$$X_k = X_{k-1} + v_k. \qquad (15.4)$$

We need some notation for the coordinates of the introduced vectors

---

[2]The so-called triangular error-correction model presents only long-run relation parametrically – in the form of multiple regression and short-run dynamics in the (cointegrating) disturbances which follow a moving average process (see, for details Phillips (1991). The results in this section are due to Paulauskas and Rachev (1998).

$$Y_k = \left(y_{k1}, \ldots, y_{kp}\right)', \qquad X_k = \left(x_{k1}, \ldots, x_{kq}\right)',$$

$$u_k = \left(u_{k1}, \ldots, u_{kp}\right)', \qquad v_k = \left(v_{k1}, \ldots, v_{kq}\right)'.$$

All vectors are vector-columns and the sign $'$ stands for transposition. Our limiting results do not depend on the initial value X_0 of the process (15.4), so we shall assume that X_0 is an arbitrary random variable.

Let $r = p + q$ and $w_k = \left(w_{k1}, \ldots, w_{kr}\right)'$, where $w_{ki} = u_{ki}$ if $i = 1, \ldots, p$ and $w_{k,p+j} = v_{kj}$ for $j = 1, \ldots, q$.

Our assumptions on the sequence $\{w_k, \ k \geq 1\}$ generating the cointegrated model are as follows. Let $\alpha = (\alpha_1, \alpha_2, \ldots, \alpha_r)$ be an multiindex, satisfying $1 < \alpha_i \leq 2$, $i = 1, \ldots, r$, $S_n = D_n \sum_{i=1}^{n} w_i$, where $D_n = \text{diag}\left(n^{-1/\alpha_1}, \ldots, n^{-1/\alpha_r}\right)$ and $\text{diag}(d_1, \ldots, d_k)$ stands for a diagonal $k \times k$ matrix with entries d_i in the diagonal. As all $\alpha_i > 1$, then without loss of generality we may assume that $E w_k = 0$, $k \geq 1$. Here it is worth mentioning that this assumption is made only because in practice it is difficult to interpret innovations having infinite mean values.

Assumption (A) Here w_k, $k \geq 1$ is a sequence of i.i.d. random vectors belonging to the domain of normal attraction (DNA) of an $\bar{\alpha}$-stable r-dimensional vector $\xi(1)$, that is,

$$S_n \Rightarrow \xi(1) \quad \text{in} \quad R^r, \tag{15.5}$$

where $\Rightarrow$ stands for the weak convergence of distributions (or random elements).

Let $D_r \equiv D\left([0,1], R^r\right)$ be the space of R^r-valued cadlag functions defined on $[0,1]$ and equipped with the Skorokhod topology. Let

$$Z_n(t) = S_{[nt]}, \qquad 0 \leq t \leq 1$$

and let $\xi(t)$, $0 \leq t \leq 1$, be r-dimensional Lévy stable process, determined by the α-stable random vector $\xi(1)$, appearing in Assumption (A). In the Appendix it is shown that 15.5 is equivalent to the following relation

$$Z_n \Rightarrow \xi \quad \text{in} \quad D_r. \tag{15.6}$$

In assumption (A), instead of DNA we can use the domain of attraction (DA); only the cumbersome calculations arising when dealing with slowly varying functions have forced us to state our results in the framework of DNA [3]. Note that we do not exclude the case where some exponents, α_j with $j = i_m$, $1 \leq i_1 < \ldots < i_k \leq r$ are equal 2. Then the vector

$$\left(\xi_{i_1}(t), \ldots, \xi_{i_k}(t)\right)$$

---

[3] More information about relations (15.5) and (15.6), some facts about Lévy stable processes, and relations between spaces D_r and $(D_1)^r$ will be given in Appendix (see also Samorodnitsky and Taqqu (1994), Gikhman and Skorokhod (1969), Jacod and Shiryaev (1987)).

will be the k-dimensional Brownian motion and will be independent of the vector of the remaining coordinates $(\xi_i(t),\ i \neq i_j,\ j = 1, \ldots, k)$.

The vector w_k consists of two parts of lengths p and q, and when dealing with $r \times r$ matrices $(r = p + q)$ it will be convenient to denote corresponding blocks of the matrix in the following way: if $B = \{b_{ij}\}_{i,j=1,\ldots,r}$ then

$$B = \begin{bmatrix} [B]_{11} & [B]_{12} \\ [B]_{21} & [B]_{22} \end{bmatrix},$$

e.g. $[B]_{11} = \{b_{ij}\}_{i,j=1,\ldots,p}$, $[B]_{21} = \{b_{ij}\}_{i=p+1,\ldots,r}^{j=1,\ldots,p}$.

We consider the ordinary least-squares (OLS) regression estimator of the matrix A, which will be denoted by $\hat{A}_n$. Where it will not cause misunderstanding, we suppress the subscript n and will simply write $\hat{A}$; the same remark will be applied to other variables as well. Denote

$$\begin{aligned}
\mathbf{X}' &= \mathbf{X}'_n = (X_1, X_2, \ldots, X_n), \\
\mathbf{Y}' &= \mathbf{Y}'_n = (Y_1, Y_2, \ldots, Y_n), \\
\mathbf{U}' &= \mathbf{U}'_n = (u_1, u_2, \ldots, u_n), \\
\mathbf{V}' &= \mathbf{V}'_n = (v_1, v_2, \ldots, v_n).
\end{aligned}$$

Here $\mathbf{X}'$ and $\mathbf{V}'$ are $q \times n$ matrices and $\mathbf{Y}'$ and $\mathbf{U}'$ are $p \times n$ matrices. Then (see, for example Park and Phillips (1988) or Phillips and Durlauf (1986)),

$$\hat{A} = \mathbf{Y}'\mathbf{X}(\mathbf{X}'\mathbf{X})^{-1} \tag{15.7}$$

and

$$\hat{A} - A = \mathbf{U}'\mathbf{X}(\mathbf{X}'\mathbf{X})^{-1}. \tag{15.8}$$

In the case where the innovations u_k and v_k have finite variances (all $\alpha_i = 2$) the normalization of the quantity (15.8) is simple $(n(\hat{A}_n - A))$; in contrast, here for each entry of the matrix $\hat{A}_n - A$ a different normalization is needed. To this end we introduce the diagonal matrices

$$\begin{aligned}
\mathbf{T}_1 &= \mathbf{T}_{1,n} = \operatorname{diag}(n^{-1/\alpha_1}, \ldots, n^{-1/\alpha_p}) \\
\mathbf{T}_2 &= \mathbf{T}_{2,n} = \operatorname{diag}(n^{-1/\alpha_{p+1}}, \ldots, n^{-1/\alpha_{p+q}}). \tag{15.9}
\end{aligned}$$

It is not difficult to see that the proper normalizations for $\mathbf{U}'\mathbf{X}$ and $\mathbf{X}'\mathbf{X}$ are $\mathbf{T}_1\mathbf{U}'\mathbf{X}\mathbf{T}_2$ and $n^{-1}(\mathbf{T}_2\mathbf{X}'\mathbf{X}\mathbf{T}_2)$, respectively. Therefore the proper normalization for the quantity (15.8) is

$$n(\mathbf{T}_1(\hat{A} - A)\mathbf{T}_2^{-1}). \tag{15.10}$$

It remains to introduce some notation describing the limit distribution of (15.10). We recall that $\xi(\cdot)$ is a limiting process in (15.6), $\xi_i(\cdot)$, $i = 1, 2, \ldots, r$ being its coordinates. The notation

$$\int_0^t \xi_i^-(s)\, d\xi_j(s)$$

will stand for the Ito stochastic integral. Here $x^-(s)$ denotes the left-limit of the function $x \in D[0,1]$ at point $0 < s \leq 1$. For simplicity of writing we shall suppress this upper script and will write $\int_0^t \xi_i(s)\, d\xi_j(s)$ or simply $\int_0^t \xi_i\, d\xi_j$ when there is no ambiguity in such notation. Then $\int_0^t \xi(s)\, d\big(\xi(s)\big)'$, or simply, $\int_0^t \xi\, d\xi'$ stands for the matrix with elements $\int_0^t \xi_i\, d\xi_j$, $i,j = 1,\ldots,r$. Next we denote

$$\big[\xi_i, \xi_j\big]_t = \xi_i(t)\xi_j(t) - \int_0^t \xi_j\, d\xi_i - \int_0^t \xi_i\, d\xi_j,$$

$$[\xi,\xi]_t = \left\{\big[\xi_i,\xi_j\big]_t\right\}_{i,j=1,\ldots,r}.$$

Several monographs and textbooks are devoted to the theory of stochastic integration, as, for example, Protter (1990), Elliott (1982), Kopp (1984).

Our main result follows.

Theorem 15.3 Suppose that in the cointegrated processes model (15.3) and (15.4) the sequence of innovations $\{w_k, k \geq 1\}$ satisfies the assumption (A), and therefore the invariance principle (15.4) holds. Then for the estimated matrix $\hat{A}_n$, given by (15.7), the following limit relation (weak convergence in $R^{p \times q}$) holds,

$$n\left(\mathbf{T}_1(\hat{A}_n - A)\mathbf{T}_2^{-1}\right)$$
$$\Rightarrow \left[\xi(1)\big(\xi(1)\big)' - \int_0^1 \xi(s)\, d\big(\xi(s)\big)'\right]_{12} \left\{\left[\int_0^1 \xi(s)\big(\xi(s)\big)'\, ds\right]_{22}\right\}^{-1}, \quad (15.11)$$

as $n \to \infty$, where the diagonal matrices $\mathbf{T}_i$, $i = 1, 2$ are defined in (15.9).

Remark 15.2 It is easy to see that the limit distribution in (15.11) can be written in a different, but equivalent form, namely as

$$\left[\left(\int_0^1 \xi(s)\, d\big(\xi(s)\big)'\right)' + [\xi,\xi]_1\right]_{12} \left\{\left[\int_0^1 \xi(s)\big(\xi(s)\big)'\, ds\right]_{22}\right\}^{-1}.$$

Remark 15.3 The univariate model (15.3) with Y_{k-1} instead of X_k and with $p = 1$ and $A = 1$ was considered earlier by Chan and Tran (1989) (see also Phillips (1990)). Caner (1995) studied the model (15.1) with $A = I$, $X_k = Y_{k-1}$, $p \geq 1$, assuming a more complicated structure of the innovations u_t. One of the goals of the paper is to provide a mathematically rigorous proof of the main asymptotic result in cointegration theory when the innovations are i.i.d. and are in the domain of attraction of $(\alpha_1, \ldots, \alpha_r)$-stable law. The novelty of our approach is the use of general results for the convergence of stochastic integrals for semimartingales, proved by Jakubowski, Memin and

Pages (1989) and Kurtz and Protter (1991a,b), (1996a,b). This approach is new even in the Gaussian case, and it promises to weaken the i.i.d. assumption and allow the investigation of weakly dependent and nonidentically distributed innovations. We believe that limit theorems based on verification of the UT condition (using results from the above cited papers and references therein) may lead to simpler proofs of some existing limiting results in econometrics as well as to provide approaches to new results, such as asymptotic analysis of the Johansen's cointegration model with stable innovations (see Johansen (1991)).

Remark 15.4 There is another possible approach to our limiting problem; namely, instead of using limit theorems for partial sums one can apply convergence results for point processes generated by the innovations. Although the functionals arising in this approach are also discontinuous, there are various ways to deal with these type of obstacles, see Davis and Resnick (1985) and Resnick (1987).

Proof of Theorem 15.3 We can write

$$n\big(\mathbf{T}_1(\hat{A} - A)\mathbf{T}_2^{-1}\big) = \big(\mathbf{T}_1\mathbf{U}'\mathbf{X}\mathbf{T}_2\big)\big(n^{-1}(\mathbf{T}_2\mathbf{X}'\mathbf{X}\mathbf{T}_2)\big)^{-1},$$

therefore it is clear, that the main step in the proof of the theorem is the following lemma.

Lemma 15.3 Under the assumption (A), we have as $n \to \infty$,

$$\big(\mathbf{T}_1\mathbf{U}'\mathbf{X}\mathbf{T}_2, n^{-1}(\mathbf{T}_2\mathbf{X}'\mathbf{X}\mathbf{T}_2)\big)$$

$$\Rightarrow \left[\xi(1)\big(\xi(1)\big)' - \int_0^1 \xi(s)\, d\big(\xi(s)\big)'\right]_{12}, \left\{\left[\int_0^1 \xi(s)\big(\xi(s)\big)'ds\right]_{22}\right\}^{-1}, (15.12)$$

in R^{qr}.

By the continuous mapping theorem and (15.11), taking into account that

$$P\left\{\det\left[\int_0^1 \xi(s)\big(\xi(s)\big)'ds\right]_{22} = 0\right\} = 0,$$

we obtain (15.11). Before proving (15.12) we make the following comments. Without mentioning it we shall use repeatedly the following well-known result (see, for example, Billingsley (1968), Th. 4.4): if $X_n \Rightarrow X_0$, $Y_n \xrightarrow{p} a$, then $(X_n, Y_n) \Rightarrow (X_0, a)$ and, in particular, if addition is defined and is continuous operation, then $X_n + Y_n \Rightarrow X_0 + a$. Here random elements X_n and Y_n are with values in a separable metric space, and we shall use this result in the case of multidimensional spaces and $a = 0$.

The next comment concerns the idea of the proof of (15.11). This relation is of the form

$$W_n \Rightarrow W_0,$$

where W_n and W_0 are qr-dimensional random vectors. Since W_n is some function of the process Z_n and we have (15.6), one may get the impression that the continuous mapping theorem gives us (15.12) without difficulties. Unfortunately, it is not the case for the following reason. The part of coordinates of the right-hand side vector in (15.12) are of the form of stochastic integrals

$$\int_0^1 \xi_i(t) \, d\xi_j(t)$$

and generally we cannot prove the limit relation using the continuous mapping theorem, unless the integrals under consideration can be understood as path-by-path Stieltjes integrals. In order for the last situation to hold at least one of the processes ξ_i or ξ_j must be of finite variation with probability one. It is known (unfortunately, we did not find relevant reference for this fact; on the other hand it is not difficult to prove it) that Lévy stable processes with index $\alpha > 1$ are of unbounded variation on every bounded interval a.s., therefore the limit relation (15.12) can not be obtained using the continuous mapping theorem only. There were earlier papers dealing with such a problem (see, for example, Chan and Wei (1988), Jeganathan (1991)). Here we propose the following approach to overcome the above difficulty, and we explain the idea (which is a simple one and send a message: use the powerful results from stochastic analysis) in a simple two-dimensional situation. Suppose that we have a sequence (X_n, Y_n) of two-dimensional processes and $(X_n, Y_n) \Rightarrow (X_0, Y_0)$ in D_2. Let $f \colon D_2 \to R^2$, $f = (f_1, f_2)$, $Z_n = f(X_n, Y_n)$, $Z_0 = f(X_0, Y_0)$. We want to prove that $Z_n \Rightarrow Z_0$, but we know that the relation

$$f_1(X_n, Y_n) \Rightarrow f_1(X_0, Y_0)$$

cannot be obtained by the continuous mapping theorem (one reason for this can be that f_1 is not continuous on the support of (X_0, Y_0)). Let us denote $U_n = f_1(X_n, Y_n)$, $U_0 = f_1(X_0, Y_0)$. Suppose that we can prove the relation

$$(X_n, Y_n, U_n) \Rightarrow (X_0, Y_0, U_0) \quad \text{in} \quad D_2 \times R. \tag{15.13}$$

When the functional f_1 is a stochastic Ito integral (and this case is of interest to us) there is a vast literature devoted to limit theorems of such a type (see, for example Kurtz and Protter (1991a),(1996a,b), Stricker (1985), Jakubowski, Memin and Pages (1989)). Now we take

$$g \colon D_2 \times R \to R^2, \quad g(x, y, u) = \big(u, f_2(x, y)\big) \qquad (x, y) \in D_2, \ u \in R. \tag{15.14}$$

If f_2 is a continuous functional on D_2, then g is the continuous mapping on $D_2 \times R$. Now (15.12), (15.13) and continuous mapping theorem gives us

$$g(X_n, Y_n, U_n) \Rightarrow g(X_0, Y_0, U_0)$$

and since $g(X_n, Y_n, U_n) = Z_n$ and $g(X_0, Y_0, U_0) = Z_0$ we have the wanted relation.

Now we can start with a proof of (15.12).

Proof of Lemma (15.3) Firstly we consider separately the matrices on the left-hand side of (15.12). If $A = \{a_{ij}\}$ then $(A)_{ij}$ will stand for a_{ij}. We have for $i = 1, \ldots, p$, $j = 1, \ldots, q$

$$
\begin{aligned}
(\mathbf{T_1 U'XT_2})_{ij} &= n^{-(1/\alpha_i + 1/\alpha_{p+j})} \sum_{k=1}^{n} u_{ki} x_{kj} \\
&= n^{-(1/\alpha_i + 1/\alpha_{p+j})} \sum_{k=1}^{n} u_{ki} \left(x_{0j} + \sum_{m=1}^{k} v_{mj} \right) \\
&= \left(n^{-1/\alpha_i} \sum_{k=1}^{n} u_{ki} \right) \left(n^{-1/\alpha_{p+j}} \sum_{k=1}^{n} v_{kj} \right) \\
&\quad - \sum_{k=1}^{n} n^{-1/\alpha_{p+j}} v_{kj} \left(n^{-1/\alpha_i} \sum_{m=1}^{k-1} u_{mi} \right) \\
&\quad + n^{-1/\alpha_{p+j}} x_{0j} n^{-1/\alpha_i} \sum_{k=1}^{n} u_{ki},
\end{aligned}
$$

where $\sum_{i=1}^{0} a_i = 0$. Since

$$
n^{-1/\alpha_i} \sum_{k=1}^{t} u_{ki} = Z_{ni}\left(\frac{t}{n}\right), \quad n^{-1/\alpha_{p+j}} \sum_{k=1}^{t} v_{kj} = Z_{n,p+j}\left(\frac{t}{n}\right),
$$

then we can write

$$
(\mathbf{T_1 U'XT_2})_{ij} = Z_{ni}(1) Z_{n,p+j}(1) - \int_0^1 Z_{ni}(t)\, dZ_{n,p+j}(t) + o_p(1). \quad (15.15)
$$

Now, for $i, j = 1, \ldots, q$,

$$
n^{-1}(\mathbf{T_2 X'XT_2})_{ij} = n^{-\left(1 + 1/\alpha_{p+i} + 1/\alpha_{p+j}\right)} \sum_{k=1}^{n} x_{ki} x_{kj}.
$$

Since $x_{ki} = x_{0i} + \sum_{j=1}^{k} v_{ji}$, we obtain after simple calculations

$$
n^{-1}(\mathbf{T_2 X'XT_2})_{ij} = \int_0^1 Z_{n,p+i}(s) Z_{n,p+j}(s)\, ds + o_p(1). \quad (15.16)
$$

From 15.15 and 15.16 we see that the only terms for which we can not apply the continuous mapping theorem are the stochastic integrals

$$
\int_0^1 Z_{n,i}(s)\, dZ_{n,p+j}(s), \qquad i = 1, \ldots, p, \ j = 1, \ldots, q.
$$

Therefore, according to our plan (see 15.12), we need the following result.

Lemma 15.4 Under assumption (A) we have the relation

$$\left(Z_n, \int_0^t Z_{ni}(u)\, dZ_{n,p+j}(u), \quad i=1,\ldots,p, \; j=1,\ldots,q\right)$$

$$\Rightarrow \left(\xi, \int_0^t \xi_i(u)\, d\xi_{p+j}(u), \quad i=1,\ldots,p, \; j=1,\ldots,q\right) \quad \text{in } D_s, \quad (15.17)$$

as $n \to \infty$, where $s = p + q + pq$.

Proof of Lemma 15.4 There is a large number of papers, devoted to convergence of stochastic integrals, only a small part of which was mentioned above. The problem can be formulated as follows. We have two sequences of (real or vector-valued) stochastic processes X_n and Y_n and we know that $(X_n, Y_n) \Rightarrow (X_0, Y_0)$ in an appropriate space. Then we look at what conditions ensure that

$$\left(X_n, Y_n, \int X_n\, dY_n\right) \Rightarrow \left(X_0, Y_0, \int X_0\, dY_0\right).$$

It turns out that in a very general situation, when processes X_n and Y_n are semimartingales, the last relation holds if the so-called UT (uniform tightness) condition for the sequence Y_n is satisfied. This condition was introduced in Stricker (1985), and a general result was proved in Jakubowski, Memin and Pages (1989). In Kurtz and Protter (1991a) another condition was given and it was proved (see Kurtz and Protter (1991a), (1991b), Memin and Slominski (1991)) that both conditions are equivalent and, furthermore, they are necessary in some sense.

Let X_n be a sequence of random processes with sample paths in $D([0, \infty), \mathbf{M}^{k,m})$, where $\mathbf{M}^{k,m}$ stands for real-valued $k \times m$ matrices, and let Y_n be another sequence of random processes from $D([0, \infty), R^m)$. For a process $A(t)$ with sample paths of finite variation on bounded time intervals, let

$$Var_t(A) := \sup_i \sum \|A(t_{i+1}) - A(t_i)\|,$$

where the supremum is taken over finite partitions of $[0, t]$. Here and in what follows $\|x\| := \left(\sum_{i=1}^n x_i^2\right)^{1/2}$, $\|x\|_\infty := \max_{1 \le i \le m} |x_i|$.

Lemma 15.5 *(see Th.2.7 in Kurtz and Protter (1991a)).* For each n let (X_n, Y_n) be an $\mathcal{F}_t^n$-adapted process with sample paths in $D([0, \infty), \mathbf{M}^{k,m} \times R^m)$ and let Y_n be an $\mathcal{F}_t^n$-semimartingale. Suppose that $Y_n = M_n + A_n + \tilde{Y}_n$ where M_n is a local $\mathcal{F}_t^n$-martingale, A_n is an $\mathcal{F}_t^n$-adapted, finite variation process and $\tilde{Y}_n$ is constant except for finitely many discontinuities in any finite time interval. Let $N_n(t)$ denote the number of discontinuities of $\tilde{Y}_n$ in the interval $[0, t]$. Suppose $\{N_n(t)\}$ is stochastically bounded for each $t > 0$ and (UT) for each $r > 0$ there exist stopping times τ_n^r such that $P\{\tau_n^r \le r\} \le \frac{1}{r}$ and

$$\sup_n E\left\{[M_n]_{t \wedge \tau_n^r} + \text{Var}_{t \wedge \tau_n^r}(A_n)\right\} < \infty. \quad (15.18)$$

If $(X_n, Y_n, \tilde{Y}_n) \Rightarrow (X_0, Y_0, \tilde{Y}_0)$ in the Skorokhod topology on $D([0, \infty), \mathbf{M}^{k,m} \times R^m \times R^m)$, then Y_0 is a semimartingale with respect to a filtration to which X_0 and Y_0 are adapted and

$$\left(X_n, Y_n, \int_0^t X_n \, dY_n \right) \Rightarrow \left(X_0, Y_0, \int_0^t X_0 \, dY_0 \right)$$

in the Skorokhod topology on $D([0, \infty), \mathbf{M}^{k,m} \times R^m \times R^k)$. If $(X_n, Y_n, \tilde{Y}_n) \to (X_0, Y_0, \tilde{Y}_0)$ in probability, then the triple converges in probability.

The setting which we are interested in is a little bit different from the result formulated above; in our case X_n will be not a matrix-valued but rather a vector-valued random process and we deal with interval the $[0, 1]$ instead of $[0, \infty))$. However, it is not difficult to see that minor changes allow us to consider our setting and essentially the only thing we need to do is to verify a UT-type condition for the sequence of processes $\{Z_{n, p+j}, \ j = 1, \dots, q\}$ ($\{Z_{n,i}, \ i = 1, \dots, p\}$ in our case will be as $\{X_n\}$). In order not to write $p+j$ every time , we "rename" the second part of S_n, Z_n and ξ in the following way

$$\bar{Z}_n = (\bar{Z}_{n1}, \dots, \bar{Z}_{nq}), \qquad \bar{S}_n = (\bar{S}_{n1}, \dots, \bar{S}_{nq}), \qquad \bar{\xi} = (\bar{\xi}_1, \dots, \bar{\xi}_q),$$

where $\bar{Z}_{nj} = Z_{n,p+j}$, $\bar{S}_{nj} = S_{n,p+j}$, $\bar{\xi}_j = \xi_{p+j}$. If $a_{nj} = n^{1/\alpha_{p+j}}$, $j = 1, \dots, q$, then

$$\bar{S}_{nj} = a_{nj}^{-1} \sum_{k=1}^n v_{kj},$$

$$\bar{Z}_{nj}(t) = \bar{S}_{[nt],j}, \qquad 0 \le t \le 1,$$

and, under assumption A,

$$\bar{Z}_n \Rightarrow \bar{\xi} \quad \text{in} \quad D_q.$$

We remind that we have assumed $E v_{1j} = 0$ and that Assumption (A) implies

$$\Lambda_k = \sup_{t>0} t^{\alpha_{p+k}} P\{|v_{1k}| > t\} < \infty, \qquad k = 1, \dots, q.$$

As a first step in proving the UT condition, we separate large jumps of the process $\bar{Z}_n$ from small ones. Let $b > 0$ be some fixed number and

$$v_i^{(n)} = (v_{i,1}^{(n)}, \dots, v_{i,q}^{(n)}), \qquad v_{i,j}^{(n)} = a_{nj}^{-1} v_{i,j},$$

$$B(b) = \{x \in R^q \colon \|x\|_\infty \le b\},$$

$$a_n(b) = E v_1^{(n)} \mathbf{1}\{v_1^{(n)} \in B(b)\},$$

$$\tilde{v}_i^{(n)}(b) = v_i^{(n)} \mathbf{1}\{v_i^{(n)} \in B(b)\} - a_n(b),$$

$$\tilde{\tilde{v}}_i^{(n)}(b) = v_i^{(n)} \mathbf{1}\{v_i^{(n)} \in (B(b))^c\}.$$

Now we can write

$$\bar{Z}_n(t) = Y_n^{(1)}(t) + A_n(t) + Y_n^{(2)}(t),$$

where

$$Y_n^{(1)}(t) = \sum_{i=1}^{[nt]} \tilde{v}_i^{(n)}(b), \qquad Y_n^{(2)}(t) = \sum_{i=1}^{[nt]} \tilde{\tilde{v}}_i^{(n)}(b) \qquad A_n(t) = [nt]a_n(b).$$

Lemma 15.6 For any fixed $0 < b < \infty$ the function $A_n(t)$ is of finite variation, the process $Y_n^{(2)}$ is of finite variation a.s. and there exist a constant C, depending on b and on parameters of distribution v_1 such that

$$\sup_n \mathrm{Var}_1(A_n) \leq \sup_n E\mathrm{Var}_1(Y_n^{(2)}) \leq C.$$

If $N_n(t)$ denotes the number of discontinuities of $Y_n^{(2)})$ in the interval $[0,t]$, then $\{N_n(t), n \geq 1\}$ is stochastically bounded for each t.

Proof of Lemma 15.6 From the definition of variation it is easy to see that due to the relation $a_n(b) = -E\tilde{\tilde{v}}_1^{(n)}(b)$, we have to prove that

$$\sup_n nE\|\tilde{\tilde{v}}_1^{(n)}(b)\| \leq C. \tag{15.19}$$

Let F_n stand for the distribution of $\|v_1^{(n)}\|_\infty$. Then

$$E\|\tilde{\tilde{v}}_1^{(n)}(b)\| \leq CE\|\tilde{\tilde{v}}_1^{(n)}(b)\|_\infty \leq C\int_b^\infty x\,dF_n(x).$$

But

$$bP\{\|v_1^{(n)}\|_\infty > b\} \leq \sum_{i=1}^q bP\{|v_{1i}| > ba_{ni}\} \leq \frac{1}{n}\sum_{i=1}^q \Lambda_i.$$

In a similar way we can estimate the term

$$\int_b^\infty P\{\|v_1^{(n)}\|_\infty > x\}dx \leq \sum_{i=1}^q \int_b^\infty P\{|v_{1i}| > xa_{ni}\}dx \leq \frac{1}{n}\sum_{i=1}^q C_i\Lambda_i,$$

where $C_i = \int_b^\infty x^{-\alpha_p+i}dx$. From these estimates (2.8) follows. Now since $N_n(t) = \sum_{i=1}^{[nt]} \mathbf{1}\{v_i^{(n)} \in (B(b))^c\}$ and

$$P\{N_n(t) > c\} \leq c^{-1}EN_n(t) = c^{-1}[nt]P\{v_1^{(n)} \in (B(b))^c\},$$

the same inequalities prove the stochastic boundedness of $\{N_n(t)\}$ for all t and Lemma 15.6 is proved.

As Lemma 15.6 shows that the part of our process Z_n which is of finite variation can be controlled uniformly with respect to n without using stopping times, we construct stopping times based on $Y_n^{(1)}$ only. Noting that the process $Y_n^{(1)}$ is a martingale with respect to the natural filtration

$$\mathcal{F}_t^n = \sigma\big(v_1, \ldots, v_{[nt]}\big), \qquad 0 \le t \le 1$$

and that it is a jump process with jumps at the points $t = \frac{k}{n}$, $k = 1, \ldots, n$, we need to consider the triangular array

$$\left\{\tilde{S}_n^k = \sum_{i=1}^k \tilde{v}_i^{(n)}(b), \ \ k = 0, 1, \ldots, n\right\}, \qquad n \ge 1,$$

with its natural filtration $\mathcal{F}_k^n = \sigma(v_1, \ldots, v_k)$. We also need to construct stopping times τ_n^d such that for each d

$$\sup_n E\|\tilde{S}_n^{k \wedge \tau_n^d}\|^2 \le C, \tag{15.20}$$

and for each k there exists $d = d(k)$ such that

$$P\{\tau_n^d > k\} \ge 1 - \frac{1}{k}. \tag{15.21}$$

For any $d > 0$ let us define

$$\tau_n^d = \min\big\{k\colon \|S_n^j\| \le d, \ j = 1, \ldots, k-1, \ \|\tilde{S}_n^k\| t > d\big\}$$

with the agreement that $\min\{\text{empty set}\} = +\infty$. It is a stopping time, since it is the hitting time of an open set $\big\{x \in R^q\colon \|x\| > d\big\}$ for the random process $Y_n^{(1)}$, see Protter (1990). Now, if $\tau_n^d > k$ then $\|\tilde{S}_n^k\| \le d$ and if $\tau_n^d \le k$, then

$$\|\tilde{S}_n^{\tau_n^d}\| = \|\tilde{S}_n^{\tau_n^d - 1} + \tilde{v}_{\tau_n^d}(b)\| \le d + \|\tilde{v}_{\tau_n^d}(b)\| \le d + c\|\tilde{v}_{\tau_n^d}(b)\|_\infty \le d + c \cdot b.$$

Therefore

$$E\|\tilde{S}_n^{k \wedge \tau_n^d}\|^2 \le (d + cb)^2$$

and we have (15.20). It is interesting to note, that if we were able somehow to control the "size" of the jumps at a time of hitting the set $\big\{x\colon \|x\| > d\big\}$, there would be no need to separate large jumps. But if we multiply $\tilde{\tau}_n^d$ (constructed in the same way, only with $\bar{S}_n$ instead of $\tilde{S}_n$) by the indicator function of the event $\big\{\|v_{\tilde{\tau}_n^d}^{(n)}\| \le b\big\}$, the multiplied random variable is no longer a stopping time. In order to get (15.21) we note that for $0 < \alpha \le 1$

$$P\{\tau_n^d > n\alpha\} = P\big\{\max_{j \le n\alpha} \|\tilde{S}_n^j\| \le d\big\}.$$

As $n \to \infty$ this probability approaches the probability

$$P\big\{\sup_{0 \le t \le \alpha} \|\xi^{(1)}(t)\| \le d\big\},$$

and this probability can be made arbitrary close to 1 taking sufficiently large d. Here $\xi^{(1)}$ is a stable Lévy process obtained as a limit for the sequence $Y_n^{(1)}$. That the latter sequence is convergent,as well as the convergence $(Z_n, Y_n^{(2)}) \Rightarrow (\xi, \xi^{(2)})$, which is required in Theorem A (we remind that here Z_n stands for both X_n and Y_n, $\bar{Z}_n$ playing the role of Y_n),can be proved in a way similar to Gikhman and Skorokhod (1969), th. 9.6.1 and 9.6.2, where truncation of summands in a triangular array is used, or by the point processes technique, as in Davis and Resnick (1985). Lemma (15.4) is proved.

Having (15.17) and taking the appropriate mapping h: $D_s \to R^{qr}$ we get (15.12). Therefore Lemma (15.3), as well as the theorem is proved.

15.3   Appendix. Some Facts on Lévy Processes

We collect here some known facts about relations (15.5) and (15.6), Lévy processes and Skorokhod spaces.

Although we shall deal with relations (15.5) and (15.6), we introduce new notation, independent of the notations of the previous section. Thus let $X_i = (X_{i1}, \ldots, X_{id})$, $i \geq 1$ be i.i.d. random vectors in R^d. In order not to deal with centering we assume that $EX_{1j} = 0$ for those j, for which the expectations exist.

Denote

$$S_n = (S_{n1}, \ldots, S_{nd}), \qquad S_{nj} = a_{nj}^{-1} \sum_{i=1}^{n} X_{ij},$$

$$Z_n(t) = \big(Z_{n1}(t), \ldots, Z_{nd}(t)\big), \quad Z_{nj} = S_{[nt],j}, \quad 0 \leq t \leq 1. \quad (15.22)$$

Although it is possible to state results with general norming vectors $a_n = (a_{n1}, \ldots, a_{nd})$, for simplicity of writing and clarity of understanding we take the special case where

$$a_{nj} = n^{1/\alpha_j}, \qquad 1 \leq j \leq d, \qquad (15.23)$$

and $\bar{\alpha} = (\alpha_1, \alpha_2, \ldots, \alpha_d)$ is a multiindex with $0 < \alpha_i \leq 2$, $i = 1, 2, \ldots, d$. This setting can be reformulated as follows: we consider sums of i.i.d. d-dimensional vectors in the DNA of operator-stable random vector, restricting normalization only to diagonal matrices and thus, we assume that marginal distributions of summands belong to the DNA of some stable univariate law, including the Gaussian one.

When dealing with stochastic process Z_n, two spaces are appropriate. One is $D\big([0,1], R^d\big)$ and which was already introduced earlier. Another one is $\big(D[0,1]\big)^d = D[0,1] \times \cdots \times D[0,1]$ – the usual product of Skorokhod spaces $D[0,1]$ with product topology. For the first one we shall use the introduced notation D_d and for the second one we use the notation D^d. The relations between these spaces are following (see, for example, Jacod and Shiryaev

(1987)). As "abstract" sets they coincide, σ-fields of Borel sets on both spaces coincide, too, but as topological spaces they are different – the topology of D_d is strictly finer than product topology on D^d. Therefore, from the weak convergence of measures in space D_d there follows the weak convergence of these measures in D^d, but it is possible to give examples, showing that the converse statement is not true.

Let $\{Y(t),\ t \geq 0\}$ be the Lévy process with values in R^d, that is, a stochastically continuous process with independent and strictly stationary increments. Then it is well-known (see, for example, Protter (1990) or Gikhmann and Skorokhod (1969)) that there exist a vector $a \in R^d$, a symmetric non-negative defined matrix Γ and a measure ν on R^d satisfying

$$\nu\{0\} = 0, \qquad \int_{R^d} \|x\|^2 \left(1 + \|x\|^2\right)^{-1} \nu(dx) < \infty,$$

such that for any $z \in R^d$

$$
\begin{aligned}
\mathrm{E}\, exp\left\{i\left(z, Y(t)\right)\right\} \;=\; & \exp\left\{t\left[i(z,a) - \frac{1}{2}\left(\Gamma z, z\right)\right.\right. \\
& + \int_{\|x\| \leq 1} \left(e^{i(x,z)} - 1 - (z,x)\right) \nu(dx) \\
& \left.\left. + \int_{\|x\| > 1} \left(e^{i(x,z)} - 1\right) \nu(dx)\right]\right\}. \quad (15.24)
\end{aligned}
$$

The measure ν is called the Lévy measure for the process Y. Matrix Γ corresponds to the Gaussian part of the Lévy process Y.

Lévy processes have cadlag sample paths, all are semimartingales, and they have good integrability properties. For example, we use in the main text the fact that one-dimensional α-stable Lévy processes on a finite interval are in L_p for any $p > 0$, (see Samorodnitsky and Taqqu (1994), p. 510 for this fact).

We are interested in the following statements

$$
\begin{aligned}
S_n &\;\Rightarrow\; Y(1) &&\text{in}\quad R^d, & (15.25) \\
Z_n(\cdot) &\;\Rightarrow\; Y(\cdot) &&\text{in}\quad D^d, & (15.26) \\
Z_n(\cdot) &\;\Rightarrow\; Y(\cdot) &&\text{in}\quad D_d. & (15.27)
\end{aligned}
$$

Here for the multiindex $\bar{\alpha}$ we shall assume that $0 < \alpha_i \leq \alpha_{i+1} \leq 2$ for all i (although in the main text such an assumption generally is not acceptable, since we cannot rearrange the coordinates of innovation vectors).

Let us consider two cases
a) $0 < \alpha_1 \leq \alpha_2 \leq \ldots \leq \alpha_d < 2$

Proposition 15.1 Let S_n, Z_n be defined by (15.22) and (15.23) and let Y be a Lévy process with Lévy spectral measure ν and $\Gamma \equiv 0$ in (15.24). Then all statements (15.25)–(15.27) are equivalent and each of them is equivalent to the following statement

$$\lim nP\{X_1^{(n)} \in A\} = \nu(A) \qquad (15.28)$$

for all $A \in \mathcal{B}(R^d \setminus \{0\})$ such that $\nu(\partial A) = 0$, $\nu(A) < \infty$, here ∂A denotes the boundary of a set A and

$$X_1^{(n)} = (n^{-1/\alpha_1} X_{11}, \ldots, n^{-1/\alpha_d} X_{1d}). \qquad (15.29)$$

Remark 15.5 The Lévy measure ν of the process Y can be described as follows. Let $\tau\colon R^d \to R^d$ $\tau(x) = (\mathrm{sgn}x_1|x_1|^{1/\alpha_1}, \ldots, \mathrm{sgn}x_d|x|^{1/\alpha_d})$ and $\tilde\nu = \nu \circ \tau$. Then

$$\tilde\nu\left\{x\colon \|x\| \geq r, \frac{x}{\|x\|} \in B\right\} = r^{-1} H(B), \qquad (15.30)$$

where H is some finite measure on the unit sphere of R^d, $S^d = \{x\colon \|x\| = 1\}$ and $B \in \mathcal{B}(S^d)$. It is easy to see that in the case $\alpha_1 = \alpha_2 = \ldots = \alpha_d = \alpha$ we get the usual result about the DNA and in this case

$$\nu\left\{x\colon \|x\| > r, \frac{x}{\|x\|} \in B\right\} = r^{-\alpha} H(B).$$

Remark 15.6 Components of the limiting process Y (and of $Y(1)$, in particular) will be independent if the measure H in (15.30) is discrete and concentrated at points $\pm e_k$, $k = 1, 2, \ldots, d$, where e_k is the k-th element of the standard orthonormal basis in R^d. This happens if the coordinates of X_1 are independent, but this is not a necessary condition for independence of the coordinates of Y.

Now let us consider the second case:

b) $0 < \alpha_1 \leq \ldots \leq \alpha_k < \alpha_{k+1} = \ldots = \alpha_d = 2$, $1 \leq k < d$.

In this case it is convenient to divide all vectors under consideration into two parts, therefore we shall write

$$\begin{aligned}
S_n &= (S_n^{(1)}, S_n^{(2)}), & Z_n &= (Z_n^{(1)}, Z_n^{(2)}), \\
Y_n &= (Y^{(1)}, Y^{(2)}), & Y(1) &= (Y^{(1)}(1), Y^{(2)}(1)), \\
X_1^{(n)} &= (X_1^{(n,1)}, X_1^{(n,2)}),
\end{aligned}$$

where, for example,

$$\begin{aligned}
Y^{(1)}(t) &= (Y_1(t), \ldots, Y_k(t)), \\
Y^{(2)}(t) &= (Y_{k+1}(t), \ldots, Y_d(t)), \\
X_1^{(n,1)} &= (n^{-1/\alpha_1} X_{11}, \ldots, n^{-1/\alpha_k} X_{1k}).
\end{aligned}$$

Here $Y^{(1)}$ is a Lévy process in R^k and $Y^{(2)}$ is Brownian motion in R^{d-k}, namely, for $z \in R^{d-k}$

$$Ee^{i(z, Y^{(2)}(t))} = \exp\left\{ -\frac{1}{2} t (\Gamma z, z) \right\},$$

where Γ is a symmetric non-negative definite $(d-k) \times (d-k)$ matrix. The processes $Y^{(1)}$ and $Y^{(2)}$ are independent, see Sharpe (1969). Let us consider one more relation

$$S_n^{(1)} \Rightarrow Y^{(1)}(1) \text{ in } R^k, \qquad S_n^{(2)} \Rightarrow N(0,\Gamma) \text{ in } R^{d-k}, \tag{15.31}$$

where as usual $N(0,\Gamma)$ stands for normal distribution with mean zero and covariance matrix Γ.

Proposition 15.2 Let Γ be some symmetric non-negative definite $(d-k) \times (d-k)$ matrix and let ν be a Lévy measure on R^k, defined in the same way as in Proposition 1 $\left(\nu \circ \tau = \tilde{\nu}, \tilde{\nu}\{x \in R^k : \|x\| > r, \frac{x}{\|x\|} \in B\} = r^{-1}H(B), B \in \mathcal{B}(S^k)\right)$. Then the statements (15.25)–(15.27) and (15.31) are equivalent and each of them is equivalent to the following condition:

for every $A \in \mathcal{B}(R^k \setminus \{0\})$ such that $\nu(\partial A) = 0$, $\nu(A) < \infty$ we have

$$\lim n P\{X_1^{n,1} \in A\} = \nu(A)$$

and for $\forall z \in R^{d-k}$ and for $\forall \epsilon > 0$

$$\lim n \quad \left\{ E\big|(z, X_1^{(n,2)})\big|^2 \mathbf{1}\{\|X_1^{(n,2)}\| \le \epsilon\} \right.$$
$$\left. - \big(E(z, X_1^{(n,2)})\mathbf{1}\{\|X_1^{(n,2)}\| \le \epsilon\}\big)^2 \right\} = (\Gamma z, z).$$

Proof of Propositions 15.1 and 15.2 The case $d = 2$ (but without the statement (15.27) was considered in Resnick and Greenwood (1979). (Here it is necessary to mention that in order to apply the UT condition (see Theorem A in Section 2) (15.26) is not sufficient and we need (15.27). Certainly, Propositions 15.1 and 15.2 should be credited to Skorokhod (1957); in fact, in Skorokhod (1957), where essentially one-dimensional case was considered, it is written: "…we wish to point that all results of §§1 − 3 can be carried over to the case of a finite-dimensional Banach space." Thus the following several lines can be considered as the explanation how this can be done.

Convergence of finite-dimensional distributions of Z_n to the corresponding finite-dimensional distributions of Y follows in a standard way, thus it remains to prove the tightness of the sequence of distributions of Z_n. In contrast to the proof of implication (15.25)→(15.26), when tightness of $\{Z_n, n \ge 1\}$ in D^d is simply implied by the tightness of coordinates $\{Z_{ni}, n \ge 1\}$ $i = 1, \ldots, d$, generally the tightness of coordinates does not imply the tightness in D_d. The straightforward approach in proving the tightness of Z_n in D_d would be as follows. Since the modulus of continuity in the space D_d is defined in the same way as in D except that the absolute value sign is changed by the norm, one can repeat all steps (with necessary changes) in obtaining the bound for this modulus of continuity for Z_n. We can propose the following approach, which seems to be a little bit simpler (at least, notationally). We can use the following fact (see Problem 22 on p. 153 of Ethier and Kurtz (1986)):

$\{(X_n^1, X_n^2, \ldots, X_n^d),\ n \geq 1\}$ is relatively compact in $D([0,\infty]R^d)$ if and only if $\{X_n^k,\ n \geq 1\}$ and $\{X_n^k + X_n^l,\ n \geq 1\}$ are relatively compact in $D[0,\infty)$ for all $k, l = 1, \ldots, d$. Since we have the tightness of coordinates of the process Z_n, we need to establish the tightness of processes $\{Z_{nk} + Z_{nl},\ n \geq 1\}$ for all possible combinations of $k, l = 1, \ldots, d$. (Here it is appropriate to note that addition is not continuous operation in D spaces, therefore we cannot apply the continuous mapping theorem.) Let us fix k and l, $1 \leq k \neq l \leq d$, and let us denote

$$\zeta_{ni} = a_{nk}^{-1} X_{ik} + a_{nl}^{-1} X_{il}, \qquad V_n = \sum_{i=1}^{n} \zeta_{ni},$$

$$U_n(t) = V_{[nt]}, \qquad 0 \leq t \leq 1.$$

Thus we have triangular array $\{\zeta_{ni},\ i = 1, \ldots, n\}$, $n \geq 1$, and for each n random variables $\zeta_{ni}, i = 1, \ldots, n$ are independent and identically distributed. From (15.28), taking a special set $A_x = \{z \in R^d \colon |z_k + z_l| > x\}$ we get a measure ν_{kl} on line, defined by the relation

$$\nu_{kl}(y \colon |y| > x) = \int_{A_x} \nu(dz).$$

For this measure we have

$$\lim nP\{|\zeta_{n1}| > x\} = \nu_{kl}\{y \colon |y| > x\}. \tag{15.32}$$

Having (15.32), we can easily check that the conditions of Theorem 9.6.1 from Gikhman and Skorokhod (1969) are satisfied, thus we get the tightness of the sequence $\{U_n,\ n \geq 1\}$, which is exactly the sequence $\{Z_{nk} + Z_{nl},\ n \geq 1\}$. Applying the above mentioned fact we get the tightness of Z_n, $n \geq 1$ in $D([0,1], R^d)$. Then the relation (15.27) follows and we have completed the proof of Propositions 15.1 and 15.2.

Remark 15.7 There is substantial evidence that many economic time series, especially financial data, are better described by general stable Paretian distribution than the normal distribution. Here, in the last two chapters of our work, we have provided an overview over several recent advances in economic modeling under the stable Paretian hypothesis. We believe that the methods developed in this book constitute valuable building blocks for the emerging field of *stable Paretian finance and econometrics*.

References

1. Aaronson, J. and Denker, M. (1998). Characteristic functions of random variables attracted to 1-stable laws. *Annals of Probability*, 26, 399-415.

2. Abramowitz, M. and Stegun, I. A. (1972). *Handbook of Mathematical Functions*, 8th. Dover Publ., New York.

3. Adler, R. (1981). *The Geometry of Random Fields*. Wiley, New York.

4. Adler, R. J. (1989). Fluctuation Theory for Systems of Signed and Unsigned Particles with Interaction Mechanisms Based on Interaction Local Times. *Adv. in. Appl. Probab.*, 21, 331-356.

5. Adler, R. J. (1990). The Net Charge Process for Interacting, Signed Diffusions. *Ann. Probab.*, 18, 602-625.

6. Adler, R. J. (1991). An Introduction to Continuity, Extrema, and Related Topics for General Gaussian Processes. *IMS Lecture Notes-Monograph Series*, IMS, Hayward, California.

7. Adler, R. J. and Eppstein, R. (1987). A Central Limit Theorem for Markov Paths and some Properties of Gaussian Random Fields. *Stochastic Process. Appl.*, 25, 157-202.

8. Adler, R. J., Feldman, R. and Lewin M. (1991). Intersection Local Times for Infinite Systems of Planar Brownian Motios and the Brownian Density Processes. *Ann. Probab.*, 19, 192-220.

9. Adler, R. J., Feldman, R. and Taqqu, M. (1998). *A Practical Guide to Heavy Tails: Statistical Techniques and Applications.* Birkhäuser, Boston, Basel, Berlin.

10. Affleck-Graves, J. and Mac Donald, B. (1990). Multivariate Tests of Asset Pricing: The Comparative Power of Alternative Statistics. *Journal of Financial and Quantitative Analysis*, 25, 163-185.

11. Ait-Sahalia, Y. and Lo, A. (1995). Nonparametric Estimation of State-Price Densities Implicit in Financial Asset Prices. *Working Paper*, 5351, NBER Working Paper Series. (1998. *Journal of Finance*, 53, 499-548).

12. Ait-Sahalia, Y. and Lo, A. (1997). Nonparametric Risk Management and Implied Risk Aversion. *Working Paper*, 6130, NBER Working Paper Series. (1998 "http://gsbwww.uchicago.edu/fac/~finance/papers /risk.pdf").

13. Akahori, J. (1995). Some Formulae for a New Type of Path-Dependent Option. *Annals of Appl. Probab.*, 5, 383-388.

14. Akgiray, V. and Booth, G. G. (1988). The Stable-Law Model of Stock Returns. *Journal of Business and Economic Statistics*, 6, 51-57.

15. Akgiray V., Booth G. G. and Seifert B. (1988). Distribution properties of Latin American black market exchange rates. *J. of International Money and Finance*, 7, 37-48.

16. Akgiray, V. and Lamoureux, C. G. (1989). Estimation of Stable-law Parameters: A Comparative Study. *Journal of Business and Economic Statistics*, 7, 85-93.

17. Aki, S. (1987). On Nonparametric Tests for Symmetry. *Ann. Inst. Statist. Math.*, 39, 457-472.

18. Aki, S. (1993). On Nonparametric Tests for Symmetry in R^m. *Ann. Inst. Statist. Math.*, 45, 787-800.

19. Alam, K. and Saxena, K. M. L. (1982). Positive Dependence in Multivariate Distributions. *Comm. Statist.*, A10, 1183-1186.

20. An, H. Z. and Chen, Z. G. (1982). On Convergence of LAD Estimates in Autoregression with Infinite Variance. *J. Multivariate Anal.*, 12, 335-345.

21. Anderson, T. W. (1993). Goodness of Fit Tests for Spectral Distributions. *Ann. Statist.*, 21, 830-347.

22. Anderson, T. W. and Darling, D. A. (1952). Asymptotic Theory of Certain "Goodness of Fit" Criteria Based on Stochastic Processes. *Annals of Mathematical Statistics*, 23, 193-212.

23. Andrews, C. (1995). An Analysis of Currency Options and Exchange Rate Distributions. "http://lib.stat.cmu.edu/www/cmu-stats/tr/tr629/tr629.html", Carnegie Melon University.

24. Annis, A. A. and Lloyd, E. H. (1976). The expected value of the adjusted rescaled Hurst range of independent normal summands. *Biometrika*, 73, 111-116.

25. Antille, A., Kersting, G. and Zucchini, W. (1982). Testing Symmetry. *Journal of the American Statistical Association*, 77, 639-646.

26. Arad, R. W. (1980). Parameter Estimation for Symmetric Stable Distributions. *International Economic Review*, 21, 209-220.

27. Arak, T. V. and Zaitsev, A. Yu (1988). *Uniform Limit Theorems for Sums of Independent Random Variables*, Proc. Steklov Institute of Math., AMS, Providence, Rhode Island.

28. Aram, K. and Saxena, K. M. L. (1981). Positive Dependence in Multivariate Distributions. *Comm. Statist. - Theor. Meth.*, A10, 1183-1186.

29. Araujo, A. and Giné, E. (1980). *The Central Limit Theorem for Real and Banach Valued Random Variables*. Wiley, New York.

30. Arnold, B.C. (1983). *Pareto Distributions*. I. C. Publ. House, Fairland, MD.

31. Arrow, K. J. (1971). *Essay in the theory of risk bearing*. Markham, Chicago.

32. Arzac, E. R. and Bawa, V. S. (1977). Portfolio choice and equilibrium in capital markets with safety firstInvestors. *J. Finan. Econ.*, 4, 277-288.

33. Avellaneda, M. and Parás, A. (1994). Dynamic Hedging Portfolios for Derative Securities in the Presence of Large Transaction Costs. *Applied Mathematical Finance*, 1.

34. Avram, F. and Taqqu, M. S. (1986). Convergence of Moving Averages with Infinite Variance, (E. Eberlein and M.S. Taqqu, editors). *Dependence in Probability and Statistics*, 399-415. Birkhäuser, Boston.

35. Azlarov, T. A., Dzhamirzaev, A. A. and Sultanov, M. M. (1972). Characterizing Properties of the Exponential Distribution and Their Stability. *Random Processes and Statistical Conclusions* (in Russian), 10-19, 2nd ed., Tashkent.

36. Azlarov, T. A. and Volodin, N. A. (1986). *Characterization Problems Associated with the Exponential Distribution*. Springer, Berlin.

37. Bachelier, L. (1900). Théorie de la Spéculation. *Annales de Ecole Normale Superieure Series*, 3, 17, 21-86. (1964, English Transl., (Coonter, P.H., editor). *The Random Character of Stock Market Prices*. MIT Press, Cambridge, MA.)

38. Baillie, B. T. (1996). Long memory processes and fractional integration in econometrics. *Journal of Econometrics*, 73, 5-59.

39. Baillie, R. T. and Bollerslev, T. (1989). The Message in Daily Exchange Rates: A Conditional-Variance Tale. *Journal of Business and Economic Statistics*, 7(3), 297-305.

40. Baillie, R. T. and Bollerslev, T. (1992). Prediction in Dynamic Models with Time Dependent Conditional Variances. *Journal of Econometrics*, 52, 91-113.

41. Baillie, R. T., Bollerslev, T. and Mikkelsen, H. O. (1996). Fractionally Integrated Generalized Autoregressive Conditional Heteroskedasticity. *Journal of Econometrics*, 74, 3-30.

42. Baillie, R. T., Chung, C.-F. and Tieslau, M. A. (1996). Analyzing Inflation by the Fractionally Integrated ARFIMA-GARCH Model. *Journal of Applied Econometrics*, 11, 23-40.

43. Baillie, B. T. and King, M. L. (1996). Fractional differencing and long memory processes. *Journal of Econometrics*, 73. Special issue.

44. Bakshi, G., Cao, C., Chen, Z. (1997). Empirical Performance of Alternative Option Pricing Models. *Journal of Finance*, 52, 2003-2049.

45. Banz, R. W. and Miller, M. H. (1978). Prices for State-contingent Claims: Some Estimates and Applications. *Journal of Business*, 51(4), 653-672.

46. Barlow, R. E. and Proschan, F. (1965). *Mathematical Theory of Reliability*. Wiley, New York.

47. Barlow, R. E. and Proschan, F. (1975). *Statistical Theory of Reliability and Life Testing: Probability Models*. Holt, Rinehart & Winston, New York.

48. Barlow, R. E. and Proschan, F. (1981). *Statistical Theory of Reliability and Life Testing*. Holt, Rinehart & Winston, New York.

49. Barminghaus, L. and Henze, N. (1991). Limit Distributions for Measures of Skewness and Kurtosis Based on Projections. *Journal of Multivariate Analysis*, 38, 51-69.

50. Barndorff-Nielsen, O. E. (1977). Exponentially Decreasing Distributions for the Logarithm of Particle Size. *Proceedings of the Royal Society of London*, Series A 353, 401-419.

51. Barndorff-Nielsen, O. E. (1978). Hyperbolic Distributions and Distributions on Hyperbolae. *Scandinavian Journal of Statistics*, 5, 151-157.

52. Barndorff-Nielsen, O. E. (1994). Gaussian Inverse Gaussian Processes and the Modeling of Stock Returns. *Technical Report*, Aarhus University.

53. Barndorff-Nielsen, O. E. (1995). Normal inverse Gaussian processes and the modeling of stock returns. *Research Report*, Aarhus University.

54. Barnea, A. and Downes, D. H. (1973). A Reexamination of the Empirical Distribution of Stock Price Changes. *Journal of the American Statistical Association*, 68, 348-350.

55. Bartlett, M. S. (1954). Problemes de l'Aanalyse Spectrale des Séries temporelles stationnaires. *Publ. Inst. Statist.*, 3, 119-134, Univ. Paris III.

56. Bartlett, M. S. (1955). *An Introduction to Stochastic Processes with Special Reference to Methods and Applications.* Cambridge University Press, Cambridge.

57. Basle Committee on Banking Supervision (1996). *Amendment to the Capital Accord to Incorporate Market Risks.*

58. Bassi F., Embrechts P. and Kafetzaki M. (1997). Risk Management and Quantile Estimation, (Adler, R. et al., editors). *A Practical Guide to Heavy Tails, Statistical Techniques for Analyzing Heavy Tailed Distributions.* Birkhäuser, Boston.

59. Basu, A. P. (1965). On some tests of hypotheses relating to the exponential distribution when some outliers are present. *Journal of the American Statistical Association*, 60, 548-559.

60. Bawa, V. S. (1975). Optimal rules for ordering uncertain prospects. *J. Finan. Econ.*, 2, 95-121.

61. Bawa, V. S. (1976). Admissible portfolio for all individuals, *J. Finance*, 31, 1169-1183.

62. Bawa, V. S. (1978). Safety-first stochastic dominance and optimal portfolio choice. *J. Finan. and Quantit. Anal.*, 255-271.

63. Bawa, V. S. (1979). Portfolio choice and capital market equilibrium with unknown distributions. *Estimation Risk and Optimal Portfolio Choice.* Bawa, Brown and Klein, North-Holland.

64. Bawa, V. C., Elton, E. L. and Gruber, M. J. (1979). Simple Rules for Optimal Portfolio Selection in Stable Paretian Markets. *Journal of Finance*, 34, 1041-1047.

65. Baxter, L., Rachev, S. T. (1990). A note on the stability of the estimation of the distribution. *Probability and Statistics Letters*, 10, 37-41.

66. Beckstrom, R. and Campbell, A. (1995). *An Introduction to VAR.* CATS Software, Inc, Palo Alto, CA.

67. Beder, T. (1995). VAR: Seductive But Dangerous. *Financial Analysts Journal*, (September/October), 12-24. (1997, (Grayling, S., editor). *VAR: Understanding and applying Value at risk*, 113-122. Risk, London).

68. Beirlant, J., Vynckier, P., and Teugels, J. L. (1996). Tail Index Estimation, Pareto Quantile Plots, and Regression Diagnostics. *Journal of the American Statistical Association*, 91(436), 1659-1667.

69. Bensaid, B., Lesne, J. P., Pages, H. and Scheinkman, J. (1992). Derivate Asset Pricing with Transaction Costs. *Mathematical Finance*, 2, 63-86.

70. Bentkus, V. Yu. and Rachkaukas, A. (1985). Estimates of the Distance Between Sums of Independent Random Elements in Banach spaces. *Theory Prob. Appl.*, 29, 50-65.

71. Bera, A. K., Higgins, M. L. and Lee, S. (1992). Interaction Between Autocorrelation and Conditional Heteroskedasticity: A Random Coefficient Approach. *Journal of Business and Economic Statistics* , 10, 133-142.

72. Beran, R. (1979). Testing for Elliptical Symmetry of a Multivariate Density. *Ann. Statist.*, 7, 150-162.

73. Beran, R. (1994). *Statistics for Long-Memory Processes.* Chapman and Hall, New York, London.

74. Bergström, H. (1952). On Some Expansions of Stable Distributions. *Arkiv för Mathematik II*, 18, 375-378.

75. Berkane, M. (1987). The Bivariate Trimmed and Winsorised Means and Their Asymptotic Properties. *American Statistical Association: Proceedings of the Social Statistics Section*, 172-174.

76. Berkes, I. and Phillip, W. (1979). Approximation Theorems for Independent and Weakly Dependent Random Vectors. *Ann. Probab.*, 7, 29-54.

77. Bertoin, J. (1998). Lévy Processes. *Cambridge Tracts in Mathematics*, 121. Cambridge UP.

78. Bhansali, R. J. (1984). Order Determination for Processes with Infinite Variance, Robust and Nonlinear Time Series Analysis. *J. Franke, W. Hardle and D. Martin*, 17-25. Springer, New York.

79. Bhansali, R. J. (1988). Consistent Order Determination for Processes with Infinite Variance. *J. Roy. Statist. Soc. Ser. B*, 50, 46-60.

80. Bhansali, R. J. (1993). Estimation of the Impulse Response Coefficients of a Linear Process with Infinite Variance. *J. Multiv. Anal.*, 45, 274-290.

81. Bhattacharya, R. M. and Ranga Rao, R. (1976). *Normal Approximation and Asymptotic Expansions*. Wiley, New York.

82. Bhattacharya, P. K., Gastwirth, J. L. and Wright, A. L. (1982). Two Modified Wilcoxon Tests for Symmetry About an Unknown Location Parameter. *Biometrica*, 69, 377-382.

83. Bickel, P. J. and Freedman, D. A. (1981). Some Asymptotic Theory for the Bootstrap. *Ann. Statistic.*, 9, 1196-1217.

84. Bidarkota, P. and McCulloch, J. H. (1996). State-Space Modeling of Economic Time Series with Stable Shocks. *Tech. Rep. Dept. of Economics*, Institution Ohio State University.

85. Billingsley, P. (1968). *Convergence of Probability Measures*. Wiley, New York.

86. Billingsley, P. (1986). *Probability and Measure*. Wiley, New York.

87. Bingham, N. H. and Goldie, C. M. and Teugels, J. L. (1987). *Regular Variation*, Cambridge University Press.

88. Bjerve, S. and Doksum, K. (1990). Correlation Curves: Measures of Association as Functions of Covariate Values. *Preprint*.

89. Black, F. and Scholes, M. (1972). The Valuation of Option Contracts and a Test of Market Efficiency. *Journal of Finance*, 27, 399-417.

90. Black, F. and Scholes, M. (1973). The Pricing of Options and Corporate Liabilities. *Journal of Political Economy*, 81, 637-659.

91. Blattberg, R. C. and Gonedes, N. J. (1974). A Comparison of the Stable and Student Distributions as Statistical Models for Stock Prices. *Journal of Business*, 47, 244-280.

92. Blattberg, R., and Sargent, T. (1971). Regression with Non-Gaussian Stable Disturbances: Some Sampling Results. *Econometrica* , 39(3), 501-510.

93. Blough, D. K. (1989). Multivariate Symmetry via Projection Pursuit. *Ann. Inst. Statist. Math.*, 41, 461-475.

94. Blume, M. and Friend, I. (1973). A New Look at the Capital Asset Pricing Model. *Journal of Finance*, 28, 19-33.

95. Bochner, S. (1955). *Harmonic Analysis and the Theory of Probability.* University of California Press, Berkeley.

96. Bollerslev, T. (1986). Generalized Autoregressive Conditional Heteroskedasticity. *Journal of Econometrics*, 31, 307-327.

97. Bollerslev, T. (1987). A Conditional Heteroskedastic Time Series Model for Speculative Prices and Rates of Return. *Review of Economics and Statistics*, 69, 542-547.

98. Bollerslev, T., Chou, R. Y. and Kroner, K. F. (1992). ARCH modeling in finance. A review of the theory and empirical evidence. *Journal of Econometrics* , 52, 5-59.

99. Bollerslev, T., Engle, R. F. and Nelson, D. B. (1994). ARCH Models, (Engle, R. and McFadden, D., editors). *Handbook of Econometrics*, 4, chapter 49. Elsevier Science B.V., Amsterdam, The Netherlands.

100. Boness, A., Chen, A. and Jatusipitak, S. (1974). Investigations of Nonstationary Prices. *Journal of Business*, 47, 518-537.

101. Boothe, P. and Glassman, D. (1987). Statistical Distribution of Exchange Rates. *Journal of International Economics*, 22, 297-319.

102. Borodin, A. N. and Ibragimov, I. A. (1995). Limit Theorems for Functionals of Random Walks. *Proceedings of the Steklov Institute of Mathematics*, 195, American Mathematical Society.

103. Borovkov, A. A. (1983). Limit Problems, the Invariance Principle, Large Deviations. *Usp. Mat. Nauk*, 28, 227-254.

104. Bouchaud, J. P., Sornette, D., Walter, C. and Aguilar, J. P. (1995). Taming large events; optimal portfolio theory for strongly fluctuating assets. *Working Paper*, Stern School of Business, New York University.

105. Boudoukh, J., Richardson, M. and Whitelaw, R. (1995). The stochastic behavior of interest rates. *Working Paper*, Stem School of Business, New York University.

106. Boudoukh, J., Richardson, M. and Whitelaw, R. (1997). (Expect the Worst, Grayling, S., editor). *VAR: Understanding and applying Value at risk*, 79-81. Risk, London.

107. Boudoukh, J., Richardson, M. and Whitelaw, R. (1998). The Best of Both Worlds: A Hybrid Approach to Calculating Value at Risk. *Social Science Research Network Electronic Library, Financial Economics Network*. ("http://papers.ssrn.com/toptens/topten20360.html" and *Risk*, 11 (May), 64-67).

108. Bougerol, P. and Picard, N. (1992a). Stationarity of GARCH Processes and some Nonnegative Time Series. *Journal of Econometrics*, 52, 115-127.

109. Bougerol, P. and Picard, N. (1992b). Strict Stationarity of Generalized Autoregressive Processes. *Annals of Probability*, 20, 1714-1730.

110. Bouleau, N. and Lépingle, D. (1994). *Numerical Methods for Stochastic Processes*. Wiley, New York.

111. Box, G. E. P. and Jenkins, G. M. (1976). *Time Series Analysis: Forecasting and Control, 2nd ed.*. Holden-Day, San Francisco.

112. Box, G. E. P. and Tiao, G. C. (1962). A Further Look At Robustness Via Bayes Theorem. *Biometrika*, 49, 419-432.

113. Box, G. E. P. and Tiao, G. C. (1973). Bayesian Inference In Statistical Analysis. Addison-Wesley, Reading, Massachusetts.

114. Box, G. E. P. and Tiao, G. C. (1975). Intervention analysis with applications to economic and environmental problems. *Journal of the American Statistical Association* 70, 70-79.

115. Boyle, P. P. and Tan, K. S. (1994). Lure of the Linear. *Risk*, 7, 43-46.

116. Boyle, P. P. and Vorst, T. (1992). Option Replication in Discrete Time with Transaction Costs. *Journal of Finance*, 47, 272-293.

117. Brachet, M., Taflin, E., and Tcheou, J. M. (1997). Scaling transformation and probability distributions for financial time series. *Technical Report*, Laboratoire de Physique Statistique, CNRS URA 1306, France.

118. Brada, J. E. and Van Tassel, J. (1966). The Distribution of Stock-Price Differences: Gaussian After All? *Operations Research*, 14, 332-340.

119. Braglia, M. (1990). On the Variance of Stock Price Distributions. *Economic Letters*, 33, 171-173.

120. Breeden, D. T. and Litzenberger, R. H. (1978). Prices of State-contingent Claims Implicit in Option Prices. *Journal of Business*, 51(4), 621-651.

121. Breiman, L. (1968). *Probability*. Addison-Wesley, Reading, MA.

122. Brennan, M. and Schwartz, E. (1979). Acontinous Time Approach to the Pricing of Bonds. *J. Banking Finance*, 3, 133-155.

123. Brindley, J. E. C. and Thompson, J. W. A. (1972). Dependence and Aging Aspects of Multivariate Survival. *J. Amer. Statist. Assoc.*, 67, 821-829.

124. Brockwell, P. J. and Davis, R. A. (1991). *Time Series: Theory and Methods, 2nd. ed.* Springer, New York.

125. Brorsen, W.B., and Preckel, P.V. (1993). Linear Regression with Stably Distributed Residuals. *Communications in Statistics-Theory and Methods*, 22(3), 659-667.

126. Brorsen, W. B. and Yang, S. R. (1990). Maximum Likelihood Estimates of Symmetric Stable Distribution Parameters. *Communications in Statistics-Simulation*, 19(4), 1459-1464.

127. Brown, M. (1990). Error Bounds for Exponential Approximation of Geometric Convolutions. *Ann. Probab.*, 18, 1388-1402.

128. Brown, A. (1997). The Next 10 VAR Disasters. *Derivatives Strategy*, 2 (March), 68-70.

129. Brown, R. L., Durbin, J. and Evans, J. M. (1975). Techniques for testing the constancy of regression relationships over time. *Journal of the Royal Statistical Society*, Series B 37, 149-163.

130. Brown, G. and Toft, K. B. (1997). Constructing Binomial Trees From Multiple Implied Probability Distributions. *Working Paper*, Department of Finance, University of Texas, Austin.

131. Broydon, C. G. (1970). The Convergence of a Class of Double-rank Minimization Algorithms. *Journal of the Institute of Mathematics and its Applications*, 6, 76-90.

132. Buckle, D. J. (1995). Bayesian Inference for Stable Distribution. *Journal of the American Statistical Association*, 90, 605-613.

133. Bunde, A. and Havlin, S. (1991). *Fractals and Disordered Systems*. Springer, Berlin.

134. Bunge, J. (1996). Composition semigroups and random stability, *Ann. of Probab.*, 24, 1476-1489.

135. Butler, R. J., McDonald, J. B., Nelson, R. D. and White, S. B. (1990). Robust and Partially Adaptive Estimation of Regression Models. *The Review of Economics and Statistics*, 72, 321-327.

136. Butler, J. S. and Schachter, B. (1996). Improving Value-at-Risk Estimates by Combining Kernel Estimation with Historical Simulation. Working Paper, 96-1, Office of the Comptroller of the Currency, Economic & Policy Analysis.

137. Calder, M., and R. Davis (1998). Inference for Linear Processes with Stable Noise, (Adler, R. et al., editors). *A Practical Guide to Heavy Tails*, 159-177. Birkhäuser, Boston.

138. Calderson-Ressel, J. and Ben-Horim, M. (1982). The Behaviour of Foreign Exchange Rates. *Journal of International Business*, 99-111.

139. Cambanis, S., Simons, G. and Stout, W. (1976). Inequalities for Ek(X,Y) When the Marginals are Fixed. *Z. Wahrsch. Verw. Geb.*, 36, 285-294.

140. Cambanis, S. and Miller, G. (1981a). Linear Problems in pth Order and Stable Processes. *SIAM J. Appl. Math.*, 41, 43-69.

141. Cambanis, S. and Miller, G. (1981b). Some Path Properties of pth Order and Symmetric Stable Processes. *Ann. Prob.*, 8, 1148-1156.

142. Cambanis, S. and Hardin, C. D., Jr. and Weron, A. (1988). Innovations and Wold Decomposition of Stable Sequences. *Probab. Theor. Rel. Fields*, 79, 1-27.

143. Cambanis, S. and Simons, G. and Stout, W. (1976). Inequalities for Ek(X,Y) When the Marginals are Fixed. *Z. Wahrsch. Verw. Geb.*, 36, 285-294.

144. Campa,J. M., Chang, P. H. K. and Reider, R. L. (1997). Implied Exchange rate Distributions:Evidence From OTC Option Markets. *Technical Report*, Stern School of Business, New York University.

145. Campbell, J. Y., Lo, A. W. and MacKinley, A. C. (1997). *The Econometrics of Financial Markets*. Princeton University Press, Princeton, NJ.

146. Canani, L. and Figlewski, S. (1993). The Information Content of Implied Volatility. *Review of Financial Studies*, 6, 659-681.

147. Caner, M. (1995). Tests for Cointegration with Infinite Variance Errors. *Preprint.*

148. Caner, M. (1996). Tests for cointegration with infinite variance errors. *Discussion Paper*, Department of Economics, Brown University.

149. Canina, L. and Figlewski, S. (1993). The information content of implied volatility. *Review of Financial Studies*, 6, 659-681.

150. Cass, D. and Stiglitz, J. E. (1970). The structure of investor preferences and asset returns and separability portfolio allocation: A contribution to the pure theory of mutual funds. *J. Econ. Theory*, 2, 122-160.

151. Chamberlain, G. (1983). A Characterization of the Distributions that Imply Mean Variance Utility Functions. *Journal of Economic Theory* , 29, 985-988.

152. Chamberlain, T. W., Cheung, C. S. and Kwan, C. C.(1990). Optimal Portfolio Selection Using the General Multi-Index Model: a Stable-Paretian Framework. *Decision Sciences*, 21, 563-571

153. Chambers, J., Mallows, C. and Stuck, B. (1976). A Method for Simulating Stable Random Variables. *Journal of the American Statistical Association*, 71, 340-344.

154. Chan, N. M. and Tran, L. T. (1989). On the First-Order Autoregressive Process with Infinite Variance. *Econometric Theory*, 5, 354-362.

155. Chan, N. H. and Wei C. Z. (1988). Limiting distribution of least squares estimates of unstable autoregressive processes. *Ann. Stat.*, 16, 1, 367-401.

156. Chan, G. and Wood, A. T. A. (1998). Simulation of Multifractional Brownian Motion. *Technical report*, Department of Statistics, University of New South Wales.

157. Chen, Y. (1991). Distributions for Asset Returns. *Unpublished Ph. D. Dissertation*, SUNY-Stony Brook, Department of Economics.

158. Chen, N. F. and Ingersoll, J. (1983). Exact Pricing in Linear Factor Models with Many Assets: A Note., *Journal of Finance*, 38, 985-988.

159. Chen, C. and Liu, L. M. (1993). Joint estimation of model parameters and outlier effects in time series. *Journal of the American Statistical Association*, 88, 284-297.

160. Cheng, S. T. (1991). On the Feasibility of Arbitrage-Based Option Pricing When Stochastic Bond Price Processes Are Involved. *J. Econ. Theory*, 53, 185-198.

161. Cheng, B. N. and Rachev, S. T. (1993). Multivariate Stable Securities in Financial Markets. *Technical Report*, Department of Statistics and applied probability, University of California, Santa Barbara, CA 93106-3110.

162. Cheng, B. N. and Rachev, S. T. (1994). The Stable Fit to Asset Returns. *Technical Report*, 273, Department of Statistics and Applied Probability, UCSSB.

163. Cheng, B. N. and Rachev, S. T. (1995). Multivariate Stable Future Prices. *Mathematical Finance*, 5, 133-153.

164. Chobanov, G. (1999). Modeling Financial Asset Returns with Shot Noise Processes. *Mathematical and Computer Modelling*, 29, 17-21.

165. Chobanov, G., Mateev, P., Mittnik, S. and Rachev, S. T. (1996). Modeling the Distribution of Highly Volatile Exchange-Rate Time Series,

(Robinson, P. and Rosenblatt, M., editors). *Time Series Analysis*, 130-144, Athens Conference on Applied Probability and Time Series, II. Springer, New York.

166. Chover, J., Ney, P. and Wainger, S. (1973). Functions of Probability Measures. *J. Analyse Math.*, 26, 255-302.

167. Chow, Y. S. and Teicher, H. (1988). *Probability Theory: Independence, Interchangeability, Martingales*, 2nd ed. Springer, New York.

168. Christensen, B. and Prabhala, N. (1994). On Dynamics and Information Content of Implied Volatility: A Bivariate Time Series Perspective. *Preprint.*

169. Christoffersen, P. (1995). Evaluating Interval Forecasts, Manuscript, Department of Economics, University of Pennsylvania.

170. Christoffersen, P. and Diebold, F. X. (1997). How Relevant is Volatility Forecasting for Financial Risk Management. *Working Paper*, 97-45, Wharton Financial Institutions Center Working Paper Series.

171. Cioczek-Georges, R. and Mandelbrot, B. B. (1994a). A Class of Micropulses and Antipersistent Fractional Brownian Motion. *Preprint.*

172. Cioczek-Georges, R. and Mandelbrot, B. B. (1994b). Alternative Micropulses and Fractional Brownian Motion. *Preprint.*

173. Cioczek-Georges, R. and Mandelbrot, B. B. (1995a). Stable Fractal Sums of Pulses: The Conical Case. *Preprint.*

174. Cioczek-Georges, R. and Mandelbrot, B. B. (1995b). A class of micropulses and antipersistent fractional Brownian motion. *Stochastic Processes and their applications*, 60, 1-18.

175. Cioczek-Georges, R. and Mandelbrot, B. B. (1996). *Stable Fractal Sums of Pulses: The General Case.*

176. Cioczek-Georges, R., Mandelbrot, B. B., Samorodnitsky, G. and Taqqu, M. (1995). Stable Fractal Sums of Pulses: The Cylindrical Case *Bernoulli*, 1, 201-216.

177. Clark, P. K. (1973). A Subordinated Stochastic Process Model with Finite Variance for Speculative Prices. *Econometrica*, 41, 135-155.

178. Cline, D. B. H. (1983). Estimation and Linear Prediction for Regression, Autoregression and ARMA with Infinite Variance Data, Colorado State University.

179. Cline, D. B. H. (1987). Convolutions of Distributions with Exponential and Subexponential Tails, *J. Austral. Math. Soc. A*, 43, 347-365.

180. Cline, D. B. H. and Brockwell, P. J. (1985). Linear prediction of ARMA processes with infinite variance. *Stoch. Proc. Appl.*, 19, 281-296.

181. Cohen, A. C. and Whitten, B. J. (1988). *Parameter Estimation in Reliability and Life Span Models*. Marcel Dekker, Inc, New York.

182. Cohen, J. W. (1973). Derived Markov Chains. *Proc. Kon. Ned. Ak. van Wetensch.*, A65, 55-92.

183. Connor, G. (1984). A Unified Beta Pricing Theory. *J. Econ. Theory*, 34, 13-31.

184. Conover, W. J. (1980). Practical Nonparametric Statistics, 2nd edition. *Wiley Series in Probability and Mathematical Statistics*. Wiley, New York.

185. Cont, R. (1997). Scaling and correlation in financial time series. *Science and Finance Working Paper*, 97-01. Laboratoire de Physique de la Mati'ere ndensée, Université de Nice, France.

186. Cont, R., Potters M. and Bouchaud, J.-P. (1997). Scaling in stock market data: stable laws and beyon. *Lecture Notes*, 14. Laboratoire de Physique de Mati'ere Condensée, Université de Nice, France.

187. Cootner, P. H. (1964). *The Random Character of Stock Market Prices*. The M.I.T. Press, Cambridge, Massachusetts.

188. Cox, J. C. and Ross, S. A. (1975). The Pricing of Options for Jump Processes. *White Center Working Paper*, 2-75, Univ. of Pennsylvania, Philadelphia.

189. Cox, J. C. and Ross, S. A. (1976). The Valuation of Options for Alternative Processes. *J. Financial Economics*, 3, 145-166.

190. Cox, J. C., Ross, S. A. and Rubinstein, M. (1979). Option Pricing: A Simplified Approach. *J. Financial Economics*, 7, 229-264.

191. Cox, J. C. and Rubinstein, M. (1985). *Options Markets*. Prentice-Hall, Englewood Cliffs, N.J.

192. Coy, P. (1997). Taking the Angst out of Taking a Gamble. *Business Week*, (July 14), 52-53.

193. Cramér, H. (1963). On Asymptotic Expansions for Sums of Independent Random Variables with a Limiting Stable Distribution. *Sankhya*, Series A, 25, 13-24.

194. Crnkovic, C. and Drachman, J. (1996). Quality Control, 9 (September), 138-143. (1997, (Grayling, S., editor). *VAR: Understanding and applying Value at risk*, 47-54. Risk, London).

195. Csörgő, S. (1981). Multivariate Empirical Characteristic Functions. *Z: Wahr. verw. Geb.*, 55, 203-229.

196. Csörgő, S. and Heathcote, C. R. (1982). Some Results Concerning Symmetric Distributions. *Bulletin Austral. Math. Soc.*, 25, 327-335.

197. Csörgő, S. and Heathcote, C. R. (1987). Testing for Symmetry. *Biometrica*, 74, 177-184.

198. Cutland, N. J., Kopp, P. E., and Willinger, W. (1995). Stock price returns and the Joseph effect: a fractional version of the Black-Scholes model, Bolthausen, (E., Dozzi, M., and Russo, F., editors). *Seminar on Stochastic Analysis, Random Fields, and Applications*, 327-351. Birkhäuser, Boston.

199. Cvitanić, J. and Karatzas, I. (1992). Convex Duality in Constrained Portfolio Optimization. *Annals of Appl. Probability*, 2, 767-818.

200. D'Agostino, R. and Stephens, M. (1986). *Goodness of Fit Techniques.* Marcel Dekker, New York.

201. Dahlhaus, R. (1985). Asymptotic Normality of Spectral Estimates. *J. Multivariate Anal.*, 16, 412-431.

202. Dahlhaus, R. (1988). Empirical Spectral Processes and their Application to Time Series Analysis. *Stoch. Proc. Appl.*, 30, 69-83.

203. Dahlhaus, R. (1989). Efficient Parameter Estimation for Self Similar Processes. *Annals of Statistic*, 17(4), 1749-1766.

204. Danielsson, J. and de Vries, C. G. (1997a). *Beyond the Sample: Extreme Quantile and Probability Estimation.* "http://www.hag.hi.is/~joind /research".

205. Danielsson, J. and de Vries, C. G. (1997b). *Value-at-Risk and Extreme Returns.* "http://www.hag.hi.is/~joind/research".

206. Danielsson, J. and de Vries, C. G. (1997c). Tail index and quantile estimation with very high frequency data. *Journal of Empirical Finance*, 4, 241-257.

207. Danielsson, J., Hartmann, P. and de Vries, C. G. (1998). The Cost of Conservatism: Extreme Returns, Value-at-Risk, and the Basle 'Multiplication Factor'. *Risk*, 11 (January) and "http://cep.lse.ac.uk/~joind".

208. Danielsson, J., Jansen, D. W. and de Vries, C. G. (1996). The Method of Moments Ratio Estimator for the Tail Shape Parameter. *Communications in Statistics - Theory and Methods*, 25(4), 711-720.

209. D'Aristotile, A., Diaconis, P. and Freedman, D. (1988). On Merging of Probabilities. *Technical Report*, 301, Dept. of Statistics, Stanford University.

210. Dave, R. D. and Stahl, G. (1997). On the Accuracy of VAR Estimates Based on the Variance-Covariance Approach. *Working Paper.*

211. David, H. A., Hartley, H. O. and Pearson, E. S. (1954). The distribution of the ratio, in a single normal sample, of range to standard deviation. *Biometrika*, 41, 482-493.

212. Davies, R. B. (1977). Hypothesis Testing when a Nuisance Parameter is Present Only Under the Alternative. *Biometrica*, 64, 247-254.

213. Davis, M. H. A. and Clark, J. M. C. (1994). A Note on Super- Replicating Strategies. *Philos. Trans. Roy. Soc. London*, Serie A 347, 485-494.

214. Davis, M. H. A. and Norman, A. (1990). Portfolio Selection with Transaction Costs. *Math. Oper. Res.*, 15, 676-713.

215. Davis, M. H. A., Panas, V. G. and Zariphopoulou, T. (1993). European Option Pricing with Transaction Costs. *SIAM J. Contol Optim.*, 31, 470-493.

216. Davis, M. H. A. and Zariphopoulou, T. (1994). American Options and Transaction Fees. *Proc. IMA Workshop on Math. Finance.* Springer, New York.

217. Davis, R. (1996). Gauss-Newton and M-Estimation for ARMA Processes with Infinite Variance. *Stoch. Proc. Appl.*, 63, 75-95.

218. Davis, R. A., Knight, K. and Liu, J. (1992). M-Estimation for Autoregressions with Infinite Variance. *Stochastic Process. Appl.*, 40, 145-180.

219. Davis, R. A. and Resnick, S. I. (1984). Tail Estimates Motivated by Extreme Value Theory. *Ann. Statist.*, 12, 1467-1487.

220. Davis, R. A. and Resnick S. I. (1985). Limit theorems for moving averages of random variables with regularly varying tail probabilities. *Ann. Probab.*, 13,1, 179-195.

221. Davis, R. A. and Resnick, S. I. (1986). Limit theory for the Sample Covariance and Correlation Functions of Moving Averages. *Annals of Statistics* , 14, 533-558.

222. Davis, R. A. and Wu, W. (1994). Bootstrapping M-Estimates in Regression and Autoregression with Infinite Variance. *Preprint*, Colorado State University, Dept. of Statistics.

223. Day, T. and Lewis, C. (1992). Stock market volatility and the information content of stock index options. *Journal of Econometrics*, 52, 267-287.

224. Deb, P. and Sefton, M. (1996). The Distribution of a Lagrange Multiplier Test of Normality. *Economics Letters*, 51, 123-130.

225. Debreu, G. (1959). *Theory of Value*. Wiley, New York.

226. DeGroot, M. H.(1986). *Probability and Statistics*, 2nd ed. Addison-Wesley, Reading, MA.

227. de Haan, L. and Rachev, S. T. (1989). Estimates of the Rate of Convergence for Max-stable Processes. *Annals of Probability*, 17, 651-677.

228. de Haan, L. and Resnick, S. I. (1994). Random Transformation for Poisson Processes. *Comm. Statist.-Stochastic Models*, 10(1), 205-221.

229. de Haan, L. and Resnick, S. I. (1977). Limit Theorems for Multivariate Samples Extremes. *Z. Wahrsch. verw. Geb.*, 40, 317-333.

230. de Haan, L. and Resnick, S. I. (1993). Estimating the Limit Distributions of Multivariate Extremes. *Commun. Statist.- Stochastic Models*, 9, 275-309.

231. de Haan, L., Resnick, S. I., Rootzen, H. and Vries, C. G. (1989). Extremal Behavior of Solutions to a Stochastic Difference Equation with Applications to ARCH Processes. *Stochastic Processes and Applications*, 32, 213-224.

232. Deheuvels, P. and Tiago de Oliveira, J. (1989). On the Non-Parametric Estimation of the Bivariate Extreme Value Distributions. *Statist. and Prob. Letters*, 8, 315-323.

233. Dekkers, A. L. M. and de Haan, L. (1993). Optimal Choice of Sample Fraction in Extreme-Value Estimation. *Journal of Multivariate Analysis*, 47, 173-195.

234. Dekkers, A., Einmahl, J. and de Haan, L. (1989). A Moment Estimator for the Index of an Extreme Value Distribution. *The Annals of Statistics*, 17(4), 1833-1855.

235. Dellacherie, C. and Meyer, P. A. (1982). *Probabilities and Potentials.*, B, Amsterdam, North-Holland.

236. DeLong, J. B. and Summers, L. H. (1986). Are business cycle asymmetric? (Gordon, R. J., editor). *The American Business Cycle: Continuity and Change*. Chicago University Press, Chicago.

237. Derivatives Strategy (1998). Roundtable. *The Limits of VAR*, (April), 3(4), 14-22.

238. Derman, E. and Kani, I. (1994). Riding on a Smile. *Risk*, 7, 32-39.

239. Derman, E., Kani, I. and Chriss, N. (1996). Implied Trinomial Trees of the Volatility Smile. *The Journal of Derivatives*, Summer 1996, 7-22.

240. de Vries, C. G. (1991). On the Relation Between GARCH and Stable Processes. *Journal of Econometrics*, 48, 313-324.

241. Devroye, L. (1986). *Non-Uniform Random Variate Generation.* Springer, New York.

242. Dewachter, H. and Gielens, G. (1994). A Note on the Sum-Stability of Speculative Returns. *Economic Notes by Monte dei Paschi di Siena*, 23(1), 116-124.

243. Dewynne, J. N., Whalley, A. E. and Wilmott, P. (1994). Path Dependent Options. *Philos. Trans. Roy. Soc. London*, Series A 347, 517-529.

244. Dhrymes, P. J. (1989). *Topics in Advanced Econometrics.* Springer, New York.

245. Dickey, D. A. and Fuller, W. A. (1979). Distribution of the estimators for autoregressive time series with a unit root. *J. Amer. Statist. Soc.*, 74, 427-431.

246. Diebold, F. X. (1988). *Empirical Model of Exchange Rate Dynamics.* Springer, Berlin.

247. Diebold, F. (1986). Testing for Serial Correlation in the Presence of ARCH, Proceedings of the Business and Economic Statistics Section, American Statistical Association, 323-328.

248. Diebold, F. and Schuermann, T. (1992). Exact Maximum Likelihood Estimation of ARCH Models. *Unpublished Manuscript*, University of Pennsylvania.

249. Dobrushin, P. L. (1955). A Lemma on the Limit of a Complex Random Function. *Uspekhi Math. Nauk.*, 10, No. 2, 157-159.

250. Doganoglu, T. and Mittnik, S. (1998). An Approximation Procedure for Asymmetric Stable Paretian Densities. *Computational Statistics*, 13, 463-475.

251. Doksum, K. A. (1975). Measures of Locationi and Asymmetry. *Scandinavian Journal of Statistics*, 2, 11-22.

252. Doksum, K. A., Fenstad, G. and Aaberge, R. (1977). Plots and Tests for Symmetry. *Biometrika*, 64, 473-487.

253. Domowitz, I. and Hakkio, C. S. (1985). Conditional Variance and the Risk Premium in the Foreign Exchange Market. *Journal of International Economics*, 19, 47-66.

254. Dostoglou, S. and Rachev, S. T. (1995). *A Stable Model for the Term Structure of Interest Rates.*

255. Dostoglou, S. A. and Rachev, S. T. (1999). Stable Distributions and the Term Structure of Interest Rates. *Mathematical and Computer Modelling*, 29, 57-60.

256. Drees, H. (1996). Refined Pickands Estimators with Bias Correction. *Communications in Statistics - Theory and Methods*, 25(4), 837-851.

257. Duan, J.-C. (1995). The GARCH Option Pricing Model. *Mathematical Finance*, 5, 13-32.

258. Dudley, R. M. (1989). *Real Analysis and Probability.* Wadsworth and Brooks/Cole, Pacific Grove, California.

259. Duffie, J. D. (1988a). An Extension of the Black-Scholes Model of Security Valuation. *J. Econ. Theory*, 46, 194-204.

260. Duffie, J. D. (1988b). *Security Markets. Stochastic Models*, Academic Press, London.

261. Duffie, J. D. (1996). *Dynamic Asset Pricing Theory.* University Press, Princeton.

262. Duffie, J. D. and Lions, P.-L. (1993). PDE Solutions of Efficient Differential Utility. *J. Math. Econom.*, 21, 577-606.

263. Duffie, J. D., Geoffard, P. Y. and Skiadas, C. (1994). Efficient and Equilibrium Allocations with Stochastic Differential Utility. *J. Math. Econom.*, 23, 133-146.

264. Duffie, J. D., Ma, J. and Yong, J. (1995). Blacks Consol Rate Conjecture. *The Annals of Applied Probability*, 5, 356-382.

265. Duffie, J. D. and Pan, J. (1997). An Overview of Value at Risk. *Journal of Derivatives*, 4 (Spring), 7-49.

266. Dumas, B., Fleming, J. and Whaley, R. E. (1996). Implied Volatility Functions: Empirical Tests. *Working Paper*, 5500, NBER Working Paper Series, National Bureau of Economic Research.

267. DuMouchel, W. (1971). Stable Distributions in Statistical Inference. *Ph. D. Thesis*, University of Ann Arbor, Ml.

268. DuMouchel, W. (1973a). Stable Distributions in Statistical Inference: 1. Symmetric Stable Distribution Compared to Other Symmetric Long-tailed Distributions. *Journal of the American Statistical Association*, 68, 469-477.

269. DuMouchel, W. (1973b). On the Asymptotic Normality of the Maximum-Likelihood Estimate when Sampling from a Stable Distribution. *Annals of Statistics*, 3, 948-957.

270. DuMouchel, W. H. (1975). Stable Distributions in Statistical Inference 2: Information From Stably Distributed Samples. *Journal of the American Statistical Association*, 70, 386-393.

271. DuMouchel, W. (1983). Estimating the Stable Index α in Order to Measure Tail Thickness: A Critique. *Annals of Statistics*, 11, 1019-1031.

272. Dusak, K. (1973). Futures Trading and Investors Return: An Investigation of Commodity Market Risk Premiums. *Journal of Political Economy*, 81, 1387-1406.

273. Dybvig, P. (1983). An explicit bound on individual assets' deviations from APT pricing in a finite economy. *Journal of Financial Economics*, 12, 483-496.

274. Dybvig, P. (1988). Distributional analysis of portfolio choice. *J. Business* , 61, 369-393.

275. Dybvig, P. (1989). Bond and Option Pricing Based on the Current Term Structures. *Technical Report*, Washington University, St. Louis.

276. Dybvig, P. and Ross, S. (1982). Portfolio efficient sets. *Econometrica*, 50, 1525-1546.

277. Dybvig, P. and Ross, S. (1986). Tax Clienteles and Asset Pricing. *Journal of Finance*, 41, 751-762.

278. Dynkin, E. B. and Mandelbaum, A. (1983). Symmetric Statistics, Poisson Point Processes and Multiple Wiener Integrals. *Ann. Statist.*, 11, 739-745.

279. Dzhaparidze, K. (1986). *Parameter Estimation and Hypothesis Testing in Spectral Analysis of Stationary Time Series*. Springer, Berlin, New York.

280. Eades, S. (1992). *Option Hedging and Arbitrage*. Probus, Chicago.

281. Eberlein, E. (1992). On Modeling Questions in Security Valuations. *Mathematical Finance*, 2, 17-32.

282. Eberlein, E. and Jacod, J. (1995). On the Range of Options Prices. *Technical Report*, Institut für Mathematische Stochastik, Universität Freiburg.

283. Eberlein, E. and Keller, K. (1995). Hyperbolic Distributions in Finance. *Bernoulli*, 1, 281-299.

284. Economist, The (1998). *Model Behavior*, (February 28), p. 80.

285. Edirisinghe, C., Naik, V. and Uppal, R. (1993). Optimal Replications of Options with Transaction Costs and Trading Restrictions. *Journal of Finance and Quantitative Analysis*, 28, 117-138.

286. Einmahl, J. H. J. (1987). Multivariate Empirical Processes. *CWI Tract*, 32, Mathematisch Centrum Amsterdam.

287. Einmahl, J. H. J., de Haan, L. and Xin, H. (1993). Estimating a Multi Dimensional Extreme-Value Distribution. *J. Mult. Anal.*, 47, 35-47.

288. Elliott, R. J. (1982). *Stochastic Calculus and Applications*. Springer, New York, Heidelberg, Berlin.

289. Embrechts, P. and Goldie, C. M. and Veraverbeke, N. (1979). Subexponentiality and Infinite Divisibility. *Z. Wahr. verw. Geb.*, 49, 335-347.

290. Embrechts, P., Klüppelberg, C. and Mikosch, T. (1997). *Modelling Extremal Events for insurance and finance*. Springer, Berlin, Heidelberg, New York.

291. Embrechts, P. and Schmidlitt (1994). Modeling of Extremal Events in Insurance and Finance. *Mathematical Methods of Operations Research*, 39, 1-34.

292. Enders, W. (1995). *Applied Econometric Time Series*, High Frequency Data in Finance. Wiley, New York.

293. Engle, R. F. (1982). Autoregressive Conditional Heteroskedasticity With Estimates of the Variance of U.K. Inflation. *Econometrica*, 50, 987-1008.

294. Engle, R. F. and Bollerslev, T. (1986). Modeling the Persistence of the Variance of U. K. Inflation. *Econometrica*, 50, 987-1008.

295. Engle, R. F. and Granger, C. W. J. (1987). Cointegration and Error Correction Representation, Estimation and Testing. *Econometrica* , 55, 251-276.

296. Engle, R. and Mezrich, J. (1995). Grappling with GARCH. *Risk Magazine*, (September), 112-117.

297. Engle, R. F. and Mustafa, C. (1992). Implied ARCH Models from Options Prices. *Journal of Econometrics*, 52, 289-311.

298. Engle, R.F. and Yoo, S.B. (1987). Forecasting and testing in Cointegrated Systems. *J. Econometrics*, 35, 143-159.

299. Epstein, L. (1987). The Global Stability of Efficient Intertemporal Allocations. *Econometrica*, 55,329-355.

300. Epstein, R. (1989). Some Limit Theorems for Functionals of the Brownian Sheet. *Ann. Probab.*, 17, 538-558.

301. Epstein-Feldman, R. and Rachev, S. T. (1993). U-Statistics of Random-Size Samples and Limit Theorems for Systems of Markovian Particles with Non-Poisson Initial Distributions. *Annals of Probabililty*, 21, 1927-1945.

302. Esary, J., Proschan F. and Walkup D. (1967). Association of Random Variables, with Applications. *Ann. Math. Statist.*

303. Estrella, A. (1996). Taylor, Black and Scholes: Series Approximations and Risk Management Pitfalls. *Risk Measurement and Systemic Risk*, 359-379, Proceedings of a Joint Central Bank Research Conference Board of Governors of the Federal Reserve System, Washington, DC.

304. Estrella, A., Hendricks, D., Kambhu, J., Shin, S. and Walter, S. (1994). The Price Risk of Options Positions: Measurement and Capital Requirements. *Federal Reserve Bank of New York Quarterly Review*, 19, 12 (Summer-Fall), 27.

305. Ethier, S. N. and Kurtz, T. G. (1986). *Markov processes. Characterization and Convergence.* Wiley, New York.

306. Evertsz, C. J. G. and Mandelbrot, B. B. (1992). Multifractal Measures. *Appendix B, in Chaos and Fractals by H.-O. Peitgen, H. Jürgens and Saupe, D..* Springer, New York.

307. Evertsz, C. J. G. (1995a). Fractal geometry of financial time series. *Fractals*, 3, 609-616.

308. Evertsz, C. J. G. (1995b). Self-similarity of High Frequency USD-DEM Exchange Rates. *Proceedings of First International Conference on High Frequency Data in Finance*

309. Falconer, K. J. (1990). *Fractal Geometry: Mathematical Foundations and Applications.* Wiley, New York.

310. Falkenstein, E. (1997). Value at Risk and Derivatives Risk. *Derivatives Quarterly*, 4 (1), 42-50.

311. Fallon, W. (1996). Calculating Value at Risk. *Working Paper*, 96-49, Wharton Financial Institutions Center Working Paper Series.

312. Fama, E. (1963a). The Distribution of Daily Differences of Stock Prices: a Test of Mandelbrots Stable Paretian Hypothesis. *Doctoral Dissertation*, Graduate School of Business, University of Chicago.

313. Fama, E. (1963b). Mandelbrot and the Stable Paretian Hypothesis. *Journal of Business*, 36, 420-429.

314. Fama, E. (1963c). Mandelbrot and the Stable Paretian Hypothesis. *Journal of Business*, 36, 420-429. (Reprinted, (Cootner, P.H., editor). *The Random Character of Stock Market Prices'*, 297-306, Cambridge (MA)).

315. Fama, E. (1965a). The Behavior of Stock Market Prices. *Journal of Business*, 38, 34-105.

316. Fama, E. F. (1965b). Portfolio Analysis in a Stable Paretian market. *Management Science*, 11, 404-419.

317. Fama, E. (1970). Risk, Return and Equilibrium. *Journal of Political Economy*, 78, 30-55.

318. Fama, E. and French, K. R. (1988). Permanent and Temporary Components of Stock Prices. *Journal of Political Economy*, 96, 246-273.

319. Fama, E. and Roll, R. (1968). Some Properties of Symmetric Stable Distributions. *Journal of the American Statistical Association*, 63, 817-836.

320. Fama, E. and Roll, R. (1971). Parameter Estimates for Symmetric Stable Distributions. *Journal of the American Statistical Association*, 66, 331-338.

321. Fang, K.-T. and Anderson, T. W (1990). *Statistical Inference in Elliptically Contoured and Related Distributions*. Allerton Press, New York.

322. Fang, K.-T., Kotz, S. and Ng, K.-W. (1990). *Symmetric Multivariate and Related Distributions*. Chapman and Hall, London.

323. Feigin, P. and Resnick, S. I. (1992). Estimation for autoregressive Processes with Positive Innovations. *Comm. Statist. Stochastic Models*, 8, 479-498.

324. Feigin, P. and Resnick, S. I. (1994). Distributions for Linear Programming Time Series Estimators. *Stochastic Process. Appl*, 51, 135-166.

325. Feldman, R. and Rachev, S. T. (1993). U-Statistics of Random-Size Samples and Limit Theorems for Systems of Markovian Particles with Non-Poisson Initial Distributions. *Ann. of Probability*, 21, 1927-1945.

326. Feller, W. (1966). *An Introduction to Probability Theory and Its Application*, II. Wiley, New York.

327. Feller, W. (1971). *An Introduction to Probability Theory and Its Applications*, II, 2nd ed. Wiley, New York.

328. Fernique, X. (1975). Regularitfse des Trajectoires des Fonctions aléatoires Gaussiennes. *In Lecture Notes in Mathematics*, 480, 1-96. Springer, New York.

329. Feuerverger, A. and Mureika, R. A. (1977). The Empirical Characteristic Function and its Applications. *Ann. Statist.*, 5, 88-97.

330. Feuerverger, A. and McDunnough, P. (1981). On Efficient Inference in Symmetric Stable Laws and Processes, (Csörgö, M. et al., editors). *Statistics and Related Topics*, Amsterdam, North-Holland.

331. Findley, M., Chapman and Whitmore, G. A. (1978). *Stochastic dominance*. Lexington Books.

332. Fielitz, B. D. and Roselle, J. P. (1981). Method-of-moments estimators for stable distribution parameters. *Appl. Math. and Comput.*, 8, 4, 303-320.

333. Figlewski, S. (1989). Options Arbitrage in Imperfect Markets. *Journal of Business*, 38, 34-105.

334. Fishburn, P. C. (1964). *Decision and value theory*. Wiley, New York.

335. Flesaker, B. and Hughston, L. P. (1994). Contingent Claim Replication in Continuous Time with Transaction Costs. *Roc. Derivative Securities Conference.*, Cornell University.

336. Fletcher, R. (1970). A New Approach to Variable Metric Algorithms. *Computer Journal*, 13, 317-322.

337. Föllmer, H. (1991). Probabilistic Aspect of Options. *Disscusion Paper*, B202, SFB 303. Univ.

338. Föllmer, H. and Schweizer, M. (1989). Hedging Contingent Claims Under Incomplete Information. *Technical Report*. Institut für Angewandte Mathematik, Universität Bonn.

339. Föllmer, H. and Schweizer, M. (1990). *Hedging of Contingent Claims under Incomplete Information*.

340. Föllmer, H. and Schweizer, M. (1991). Hedging of Contingent Claims under Incomplete Information, (Davis, M. H. A. and Elliot, R. J., editors). *Applied stochastic analysis. Stochsatic Monographs*, 5, 389-414. Gordon and Breach, London-New York.

341. Föllmer, H. and Schweitzer, M. (1993). Microeconomic Approach to Diffusion Models for Stock Prices. *Math. Finance*, 3, 1-23.

342. Föllmer, H. and Sondermann, D. (1986). Hedging of Non-Redundant Contingent Claims, (Hildenbrand, W. and Mas Aollell, A., editors). *Contributions to Mathematical Economics*, 205-223.

343. Fofack, H. and Nolan, J. P. (1998). Tail Behavior, Modes and Other Characteristics of Stable Distributions. *Preprint.*

344. Fong, G. and Vasicek, O. A. (1997). A Multidimensional Framework for Risk Analysis. *Financial Analysts Journal*, (July/August), 51-58.

345. Fortuin, C. Kastelyn, P. and Ginibre, J. (1971). Correlation Inequalities on some Partially Ordered Sets. *Comm. Math. Phys.*, 22, 89-103.

346. Fox, R. and Taqqu, M. S. (1986). Large-Sample Properties of Parameter Estimates for Strongly Dependent Stationary Gaussian Time Series. *The Annals of Statistics*, 14, 517-532.

347. Frankfurter, G. M. and Lamoureux, C. G. (1987). The Relevance of the Distributional Form of Common Stock Returns to the Construction of Optimal Portfolios. *Journal of Financial and Quantitative Analysis*, 22, 505-511.

348. Franses, P. H., and van Dijk, D. (1996). Forecasting Stock Market Volatility Using (Non-Linear) GARCH Models. *Journal of Forecasting*, 15, 229-235.

349. French, K. R. (1980). Stock Returns and the Weekend Effect. *Journal of Financial Economics*, 8, 55-69.

350. Frye, J. (1997). Principals of Risk: Finding Value-at-Risk Through Factor-Based Interest Rate Scenarios, (Grayling, S., editor). *VAR: Understanding and Applying Value-at-Risk*, 275-287. Risk, London.

351. Fuller, W. A. (1976). *Introduction to Statistical Time Series.* Wiley, New York.

352. Gadrich, T. (1993) Parameter Estimation for ARMA Processes with Symmmetric Stable Innovations, *D. Sc. Thesis*, Technion, Haifa.

353. Galambos, T. (1978). *The Asymptotic Theory of Extreme Order Statistics.* Wiley, New York.

354. Galambos, J., Kotz, S. (1978). *Characterizations of probability distributions : a unified approach with an emphasis on exponential and related models.* Springer-Verlag, Berlin, Heidelberg.

355. Gallant, A. R. and Tauchen, G. (1989). Seminonparametric Estimation of Conditionally Constrained Heterogeneous Processes: Asset Pricing Applications. *Econometrica*, 57, 1091-1120.

356. Gallant, A. R., Hsieh, D., and Tauchen, G.E. (1989). On Fitting a Recalcitrant Series: The Pound/Dollar Exchange Rate, (Barnett, W. et al., editors). *Nonparametric and Semiparametric Methods in Econometrics and Statistics*. Cambridge University Press, Cambridge.

357. Galton, F. (1888). Co-Relations and Their Measurement , Chiefly from Anthropometric Data. *Proc. Roy. Soc. London*, 45, 135-145.

358. Gamrowski, B. and Rachev, S. T. (1993). Stable Laws in Testable Asset Pricing. *Technical Report*, Department of Statistics and Applied Probability, University of California, Santa Barbara, CA 93106-3110.

359. Gamrowski, B. and Rachev, S. T. (1994a). Stable Models in Testable Asset Pricing. *Approximation, Probability and Related fields*, 223-235. Plenum Press, New York.

360. Gamrowski, B. and Rachev, S. T. (1994b). The Implementation of Stable Laws in Financial Models: A Practical Approach. *Technical Report*, Dept. of Statistics and Applied Probability, University of California at Santa Barbara, Santa Barbara, USA.

361. Gamrowski, B. and Rachev, S. T. (1995a). Stable Paretian Laws in Testable CAPT and APT. *Technical Report*, Laboratoire DEconométrie de lEcole Polytechnique.

362. Gamrowski, B. and Rachev, S. T. (1995b). Financial Models Using Stable Laws, (Prohorov, Yu. V., editor). *Probability Theory and Its Applications, Surveys in Applied and Industrial Mathematics*, 2, 556-604.

363. Gamrowski, B., and Rachev, S. T. (1996). Testing the Validity of Value-at-Risk Measures, (Heyde, C. C., et al., editors). *Applied Probability* . Springer, 307-320.

364. Gamrowski, B. and Rachev, S. T. (1999). A Testable Version of the Pareto-stable CAPM. *Mathematical and Computer Modelling*, 29, 61-81.

365. Gardiner, C. W. (1983). *Handbook of stochastic methods*. Springer, New York.

366. Garman, M. B. (1996a). Improving on VAR. *Risk*, 9, (May), 61-63. (1997, (Grayling, S., editor). *VAR: Understanding and Applying Value-at-Risk*, 89-93. Risk, London).

367. Garman, M. B. (1996b). Making VAR More Flexible. *Derivatives Strategy*, (April), 52-53.

368. Garman, M. B. (1996c). *Making VAR Proactive*, (September). Financial Engineering Associates, Inc.

369. Garman, M. B. (1997). *Ending the Search for Component VAR*, (March). Financial Engineering Associates, Inc.

370. Gelbrich, M., (1989). L^p-Wasserstein-Metriken und Approximationen stochastischer Differentialgleichungen. *Dissertation*, Sektion Mathematik, Humboldt-Universitat zu Berlin.

371. Gelbrich, M. (1990). On a Formula for the L^p Wasserstein Metric between Measures on Euclidean and Hilbert Spaces. *Math. Nachr.*, 147, 185-203.

372. Gelbrich, M. (1995). Simultaneous Time and Chance Discretization for Stochastic Differential Equations. *J. Computational and Appl. Math.*, 58(3), 255-290.

373. Gelbrich, M. and Rachev, S. T. (1995). Discretization for Stochastic Differential Equations, L^p-Wasserstein Metrics, and Econometrical Models, Distributions with Fixed Marginals. *American Mathematical Society, Providence, R.I.*, 28, 98-119.

374. Geman, H. and Ané, T. (1996). Stochastic Subordination. *Risk*, 9, 146-149.

375. Gerber, H. U. and Shiu, E. S. W. (1994). Option pricing by Esscher transforms. *Trans. Soc. Actuaries*, 46, 51-92.

376. Geske, R. (1979). The Valuation of Compund Options. *Journal of Financial Economics*, 7, 63-81.

377. Geske, R. and Johnson, H. (1984). The American Put Option Valued Analytically. *Journal of Finance*, 39, 1511-1524.

378. Ghashgaie, S., Breymann, W., Peinke, J., Talkner, P., and Dodge, Y. (1996). Turbulent cascades in foreign exchange markets. *Nature*, 381, 767-770.

379. Ghosh, S. and Ruymgaart, F. H. (1992). Applications of Empirical Characteristic Functions in some Multivariate Problems. *Canadian J. Statist.*, 20, 429-440.

380. Ghysels, E., Gouriéroux, C. and Jasiak, J. (1995). Market Time and Asset Price Movements: Theory and Estimation. *Technical report*, CIRANO and CREST.

381. Gikhman, I. I. and Skorokhod, A. V. (1969). *Introduction to the Theory of Stochastic Processes*. Sanders Co.

382. Gikhman, I. I. and Skorokhod, A. W. (1979). *The Theory of Stochastic Processes*, III (in Russian). Springer, Berlin.

383. Gilboa, I. and Schmeidler (1989). Maxmin expected utility with non-unique prior. *J. Math. Econ*, 18, 141-153.

384. Gilster, J. and Lee, W. (1984). The Effect of Transaction Costs and Different Borrowing and Lending Rates on the Option Pricing Model: A Note. *Journal of Finance*, 39, 1215-1222.

385. Giné, E. and Leon, J.R. (1990). On the Central Limit Theorem in Hilbert Space. *Stochastica*, 4, 43-71.

386. Giraitis, L. and Leipus, R. (1990). A Functional Central Limit Theorem for Non-parametric Estimates of Spectra and the Change-Point Problem for Spectral Functions. *Lith. Math. Trans. (Lit. Mat. Sb.)*, 30, 674-697.

387. Giraitis, L. and Leipus, R. (1992). Testing and Estimating in the Change-Point Problem of the Spectral Function. *Lith. Math. Trans. (Lit. Mat. Sb.)*, 32, 20-38.

388. Giraitis, L., Leipus, R. and Surgailis, D. (1996). The Change-Point Problem for Dependent Observations. *J. Statist. Plan. Inf.*, 53(3), 297-310.

389. Giraitis, L. and Surgailis, D. (1990). A Central Limit Theorem for Quadratic Forms in Strongly Dependent Linear Variables and Application to Asymptotical Normality of Whittle's Estimarte. *Probability Theory and Related Fields*.

390. Giraitis, L. and Surgailis, D. (1994). A Central Limit Theorem for the Empirical Process of a long Memory Linear Sequence. *Preprint*.

391. Girsanov, I. V. (1960). On Transforming a Certain Class of Stochastic Processes by Absolutely Continuous Substitution of Measures. *Theory Probab. Appl.*, 5, 285-301.

392. Givens, C. R. and Shortt, R. M. (1984). A Class of Wasserstein Metrics for Probability Distributions, *Michigan Math. J.*, 31, 231-240.

393. Gnedenko, B. V. (1938). On Convergence of Laws of a Distribution of Sums of Independent Summands. *Doklady Akad. Nauk SSSR*, 18, 4-5, 231-234.

394. Gnedenko, B. V. (1943). Sur la Distribution Limite du Terme Maximum d'une Serie Aleatoire. *Ann. Math.*, 44, 423-453.

395. Gnedenko, B. V. (1967). The Connection Between the Theory of Summation of Independent Random Variables and the Problems of Queueing Theory and Reliability Theory. *Rev. Roumaine Math. Pure Appl.*, 12, 9, 1243-1253.

396. Gnedenko, B. V. (1970). Limit Theorems for Sums of a Random Number of Positive Independent Random Variables. *Proc. 6th Berkeley Symp. Math. Statist. Prob.*, 2, 537-549.

397. Gnedenko, B. V. (1983a). On Some Stability Theorems. *Lecture Notes in Math.*, 982, 24-31. Springer, Berlin.

398. Gnedenko, B. V. (1983b). On Limit Theorems for a Random Number of Random Variables. *Lecture Notes in Math.*, 1021, 167-176. Springer.

399. Gnedenko, B. V. (1983c). *Mathematical Aspects of Reliability Theory.* Nauka (in Russian), Moskow.

400. Gnedenko, B. V. and Fahim H. (1969). A Certain Transfer Theorem, *Dokl. Akad. Nauk USSR*, 187, 1, 15-17.

401. Gnedenko, B. V. and Fahim H. (1969). On a Transfer Theorem. *Dokl. Akad. Nauk USSR*, 187, 1, 15-17.

402. Gnedenko, B. V. and Fraier, B. (1969). Several Remarks on a Paper by I. N. Kovalenko. *Litovsk. Math. Sb.*, 9, 1, 181-187.

403. Gnedenko, B. V. and Kolmogorov, A. N. (1954). *Limit Distributions for Sums of Independent Random Variables.* Addison-Wesley, Reading, MA.

404. Gnedenko, B. V. and Korolev, V. Yu. (1996). *Random Summation. Limit Theorems and Applications.* CRC Press, Boca Raton.

405. Grenander, V. and Rosenblatt, M. (1984). *Statistical Analysis of Stationary Time Series*, 2nd. Chelsea Publishing Co, New York.

406. Goldie, C. M., and Smith, R. L. (1987). Slow Variation with Remainder: Theory and Applications. *Quarterly Journal of Mathematics*, 2nd Ser, 38, 45-71, Oxford.

407. Goldfarb, D. (1970). A Family of Variable Metric Updates Derived by Variational Means. *Mathematics of Computing*, 24, 23-26.

408. González-Rivera, G. (1997). *A Note on Adaptation in GARCH Models, Econometric Reviews*, 16(1), 55-68.

409. Gouriéroux, C. (1997). *ARCH Models and Financial Applications.* Springer, New York.

410. Gourieroux, C. and Monfort, A. (1992). Qualitative threshold ARCH Models. *Journal of Econometrics*, 52, 159-199.

411. Granger, C. W. J. (1981). Some Properties of Time Series Data and Their Use in Econometric Model Specification. *Journal of Econometrics*, 16, 121-130.

412. Granger, C. W. J. (1992). Forecasting Stock Market Prices. *Journal of Forecasting*, 8, 3-13.

413. Granger, C. W. J. and Morgenstern, O. (1970). *Predictability of Stock Market Prices*. D.C. Heath and Co., Lexington, Mass.

414. Granger, C. and Ding, Z. (1995). *Some Properties of Absolute Return, An Alternative Measure of Risk, Annales D'economie et de Statistique*, 40, 67-91.

415. Grayling, S. (1997). *VAR: Understanding and Applying Value-at-Risk*. Risk, London.

416. Green, R. F. (1976). Outlier-prone and outlier-resistant distributions. *Journal of the American Statistical Association*, 71, 502-505.

417. Green, P. J. (1981). Peeling Bivariate Data, (Barnett, V., editor). *Interpreting Multivariate Data*. Wiley, Chichester.

418. Grigorevski, N. B. (1980). Ideal Metrics and Multiplication of Independent Random Variables. *Stability Problems for Stochastic Models* (in Russian), 18-32, Proceedings, VNIISI, Moscow. (English Transl. *J. Soviet Math.*, 32, 1, 1986).

419. Grinblatt, M. and Titman, S. (1983). Factor pricing in a finite economy. *Journal of Financial Economics*, 12, 497-508.

420. Grubbs, F. E. (1969). Procedures for detecting outlying observations in samples. *Technomet.*, 11, 1-21.

421. Grubbs, F. E. and Beck, G. (1972). Extension of sample sizes and percentage points for significance tests of outlying observations. *Technomet.*, 14, 847-854.

422. Guillaume, D. M., Dagorodna, M. M., Davé, R. R., Müller, V. A., Olsen, R. B. and Pictet, O. V. (1994). From the Bird's Eye to the Microscope: A Survey of New Stylized Facts of Intra-Daily Foreign Exchange Markets. *Discussion Paper*. Olson and Associates, Zurich, Switzerland.

423. Guillaume, D. M., Dacorogna, M. M., Davé, R. R., Müller, U. A., Olsen, R. B., and Pictet, O. V. (1997). From the bird's eye to the

microscope: A survey of new stylized fact of the intra-daily foreign exchange markets. *Finance and Stochastics*, 1, 95-129.

424. Hadar, J. and Russel, W. (1969). Rules of ordering uncertain prospects. *Am. Econ. Rev.*, 59, 25-34.

425. Hadar, J. and Russel, W. (1971). Stochastic dominance and diversification. *J. Econ. Theory*, 3, 288-305.

426. Hagerman, R. L. (1978). More Evidence on the Distribution of Security Returns. *Journal of Finance*, 23, 1213-1221.

427. Hahn, M. G., Hudson, W. N. and Veeh, J. A. (1989). Operator Stable Laws: Series Representations and Domains of Normal Attraction. *Journal Theoretical. Probability*, 2, 3-35.

428. Hahn, M. G. and Klass, M. J. (1997). Approximation of partial sums of arbitrary i.i.d. random variables and the precision of the usual exponential upper bound. *Ann. of Probab.*, 25, 1451-1470.

429. Hahn, M. G. and Weiner, D. C. (1991). On Joint Estimation of an Exponent of Regular Variation and an Asymmetry Parameter for Tail Distributions, Sums, Trimmed Sums and Extremes, (M.G. Hahn, D.M. Mason and D.C. Weiner, editor). *Progress in Probability*, 23. Birkhäuser, Boston.

430. Hannan, E. J. (1973). The Asymptotic Theory of Linear Time Series Models. *Journal of Applied Probability*, 10, 130-145.

431. Hannan, E. J. (1982). Recursive Estimation of ARMA order. *Biometrika*, 69, 81-94.

432. Hanoh, G. and Levy, H. (1969). The efficiency analysis of choices involving risk. *Rev. Econ. Studies* , 36, 35-46.

433. Hall, P. (1982). On Simple Estimates of an Exponent of Regular Variation. *Journal of the Royal Statistical Society*, Series B, 44, 37-42.

434. Hall, P. and Welsh, A. H. (1984). Best Attainable Rates of Convergence for Estimates of Regular Variation. *Annals of Statistics*, 12, 1079-1083.

435. Hamilton, J. D. (1994). *Time Series Analysis*. Princeton University Press, Princeton, New Jersey.

436. Hannan, E. J. and Kanter, M. (1977). Autoregressive processes with infinite variance. *J. Appl. Prob.* 14, 411-415.

437. Hansen, L. (1982). Large Sample Properties of Generalized Method of Moments Estimators. *Econometrica*, 50, 1029-1054.

438. Hansson, B., Hörndahl, P. and Nordén, L. (1995). Empirical Evidence of Biases in the Black-Scholes Option Pricing Formula. A Transaction Data Analysis of Swedish OMX-Index Call and Put Options. *Working Paper*, 57, Department of Economics, School of Economics and Management, Lund, Sweden.

439. Hardin Jr., C.D. (1984). Skewed stable variables and processes. *Technical Report*, 79. Center for Stochastic Processes at the University of North Carolina, Chapel Hill.

440. Harris, T. E. (1963). *The Theory of Branching Processes*. Springer, Berlin.

441. Harrison, J. M. and Kreps, D. M. (1979). Martingales and Arbitrage in Multiperiod Security Markets. *J. Econ. Theory*, 20, 381-408.

442. Harrison, J. M. and Pliska, S. R. (1981). Martingales and Stochastic Integrals in the Theory of Continuous Trading. *Stochastic Processes Appl.*, 2, 215-260.

443. Harrison, J. M. and Pliska, S. R. (1983). A Stochastic Calculus Model of Continuous Trading; Complete Markets. *Stochastic Processes and Their Applications*, 15, 313-316.

444. Harvey, C. and Whaley, R. (1991). S & P 100 index option volatility. *Journal of Finance*, 46, 1551-1561.

445. Harvey, C. and Whaley, R. (1992). Market volatility prediction and the efficiency of the S & P 100 index option market. *Journal of Financial Economics*, 31, 43-74.

446. Haslett, J. and Raftery, A. E. (1989). Space-time modelling with long-memory dependence: assessing Ireland's wind power resource. *Applied Statistics*, 38, 1-50.

447. Heath, D. R., Jarrow, R. and Morton, A. (1989). Bond Pricing and the Term Structure of Interest Rates: A New Methodology. *Technical Report*, Cornell University, Ithaca.

448. Heathcote, C. R. and Hüsler, J. (1990). The First Zero of an Empirical Characteristic Function. *Stoch. Proc. Appl.*, 35, 347-360.

449. Heathcote, C. R., Cheng, B. and Rachev, S. T. (1995). Testing Multivariate Symmetry. *Journal of Multivariate Analysis*, 54, 91-112.

450. Helson, H. (1993). Smoothed Periodogram Asymptotics and Estimation for Processes and Fields with Possible Long-Range Dependence. *Stochastic Processes and their Applications*, 45, 169-182.

451. Hendricks, D. (1996). Evaluation of Value-at-Risk Models Using Historical Data. *Federal Reserve Bank of New York Economic Policy Review*, 2 (April), 39-70. (1996, *Risk Measurement and Systemic Risk*, 323-357, Proceedings of a Joint Central Bank Research Conference, Board of Governors of the Federal Reserve System, Washington DC and 1997, (Grayling, S. editor), *VAR: Understanding and Applying Value-at-Risk*, 151-171. Risk, London).

452. Hendricks, D. and Hirtle, B. (1997). Bank Capital Requirements for Market Risk: The Internal Models Approach. *Federal Reserve Bank of New York Economic Policy Review*, 3 (December), 1-12.

453. Hendry, D. A. (1984). Monte Carlo experimentation in econometrics, (Griliches, Z. and Intrilligator, M. D., editors). *Handbook of Econometrics*, 2, Ch.16, Amsterdam.

454. Hengartner, W. and Theodorescu, R. (1973). *Concentration Functions*. Academic Press, New York-London.

455. Henrotte, P. (1992). Transaction Costs and Duplication Strategies. *Preprint*, Graduate School of Business, Stanford University.

456. Heron, D. and Irving, R. (1997). Banks Grasp the VAR Nettle, (Grayling, S., editor). em VAR: Understanding and Applying Value-at-Risk, 35-39. Risk, London.

457. Heston, S. (1993). A Closed Form Solution for Options with Stochastic Volatilities with Applications to Bond and Currency Options. *Review of Financial Studies*, 6, 327-343.

458. Heynen, R. (1994). An Empirical Investigation of Observed Smile Patterns. *Working Paper*, Tinbergen Institute, Erasmus University Rotterdam.

459. Hida, T. (1980). *Brownian Motion*. Springer, Berlin, New York.

460. Hiemstra, M. (1997). VAR with Muscles, (Grayling, S. editor). *VAR: Understanding and Applying Value-at-Risk*, 359-361. Risk, London.

461. Higuchi, T. (1988). Approach to an irregular time series on the basis of the fractal theory. *Physica D*, 31, 277-283.

462. Hill, B. M. (1975). A Simple Approach to Inference about the Tail of a Distribution. *Annals of Statistics*, 3, 1163-1174.

463. Hirose, H. (1991). Percentile Point Estimation in the Three-Parameter Weibull Distribution by the Extended Maximum Likelihood Estimate. *Computational Statistics & Data Analysis*, 11, 309-331.

464. Ho, T., Chen, M. and Eng, F. (1996). VAR Analytics: Portfolio Structure, Key Rate Convexities and VAR Betas. *Journal of Portfolio Management*, 23 (Fall), 89-98. (1997, (Grayling, S., editor). *VAR: Understanding and Applying Value-at-Risk*, 225-231. Risk, London).

465. Hodges, S. D. and Clewlow, L. J. (1993). Optimal Delta-Hedging under Transaction Costs. *Preprint*, Financial Options Research Center, Univ. Warwick.

466. Hodges, S. D. and Neuberger, A. (1989). Optimal Replication of Contingent Claims under Transaction Costs. *Review of Future Markets*, 8, 222-239.

467. Höpfner, R. and Rüschendorf, L. (1999). Comparison of Estimators in Stable Models. *Mathematical and Computer Modelling*, 29, 145-160.

468. Hofmann, N., Platen, E. and Schweizer, M. (1982). *Option Pricing under Incompleteness and Stochsatic Volatility*. Department of Mathematics, University of Bonn.

469. Hogan, M. (1993). Problems in Certain Two Factor Term Structure Models. *Ann. Appl. Probab.*, 3, 576-581.

470. Hollander, M. (1988). Testing for Symmetry, (Johnson, N.L. and Kotz, S., editors). *Encyclopedia Statist. Sci.*, 9, 211-216.

471. Hols, M. C., and de Vries, C. G. (1991). The Limiting Distribution of Extremal Exchange Rate Returns, *Journal of Applied Econometrics*, 6, 287-302.

472. Holt, D. R. and Crow, E. L. (1973). Tables and Graphs of the Stable Probability Density Functions. *Journal of Research of the National Bureau of Standards*, 77B, 143-198.

473. Holtsmark, J. (1919). Über die Verbreiterung von Spektrallinien. *Annalen der Physik*, 58, 577-630.

474. Hopper, G. (1996). Value at Risk: A New Methodology For Measuring Portfolio Risk. *Federal Reserve Bank of Philadelphia Business Review*, (July/August), 19-30. (1997, (Grayling, S., editor). *VAR: Understanding and Applying Value-at-Risk*, 141-149. Risk, London).

475. Horvath, L. and Kokoszka, P. (1995). The Effect of Long-Range Dependence on Change-Point Estimators. *Preprint*.

476. Hougaard, P. (1986). Survival Models for Heterogenous Populations Derived from Stable Distributions. *Biometrika*, 73, 387-396.

477. Hsieh, D. A. (1988). The Statistical Properties of Daily Foreign Exchange Rates: 1974-1983. *Journal of International Economics*, 24, 129-145.

478. Hsieh, D. A. (1989). Modeling Heteroscedasticity in Daily Foreign-Exchange Rates. *Journal of Business and Economic Statistics*, 7(3), 307-317.

479. Hsing, T. (1991). On Tail Index Estimation Using Dependent Data. *Ann. Statist.*, 19, 1547-1569.

480. Hsing, T. (1993). On Some Estimates Based on Sample Behaviour Near High Level Excursions. *Theory Related Fields*, 95, 331-356.

481. Hsu, D. A., Miller, R. and Wichern, D. (1974). On the Stable Behavior of Stock Market Prices. *Journal of the American Statistical Association*, 69, 108-113.

482. Huang, C., Litzenberger, R. (1988). *Foundations for financial economics*, North-Holland, N.Y.

483. Huberman, G. (1982). A Simple Approach to Arbitrage Pricing Theory. *J. Econ. Theory*, 28, 183-191.

484. Hudson, W. N. (1980). Operator-Stable Distributions and Stable Marginals. *Journal Multivr. Anal.*, 10, 26-37.

485. Hudson, W. N., Jurek, Z. J. and Veeh, J. A. (1986). The Symmetry Group and Exponents of Operator Stable Probability Measures. *Ann. Probab.*, 14, 1014-1023.

486. Hudson, W. N. and Mason, J. D. (1981). Operator-Stable Laws. *Multivar. Anal.*, 11, 434-447.

487. Hudson, W. N., Veeh, J. A. and Weiner, D. C. (1988). Moments of Distributions Attracted to Operator-Stable Laws. *J. Multivar. Anal.*, 24, 1-10.

488. Hull, J. C. (1991). *Futures and Option Markets*. Prentice-Hall, Englewood Cliffs, N.J.

489. Hull, J. C. (1993). *Options, Futures, and Other Derivative Securities*, 2nd. ed. Prentice Hall.

490. Hull, J. C. (1997). *Options, Futures, and Other Derivatives*, 3rd ed. Prentice Hall, Upper Saddle River, NJ.

491. Hull, J. C. and White, A. (1987). The Pricing of Options on Assets with Stochastic Volatilities. *Journal of Finance*, 42, 281-300.

492. Hull, J. C. and White, A. (1998). Value at Risk When Daily Changes in Market Variables Are Not Normally Distributed. *Journal of Derivatives*, 5 (Spring), 9-19.

493. Hurst, H. E. (1951). Long-term storage capacity of reservoirs. *Transactions of the American Society of Civil Engineers*, 116, 770-808.

494. Hurst, S. R., Platen, E. and Rachev, S. T. (1995a). A Comparison of Subordinated Asset Pricing Models. *Technical Report of Statistics and Applied Probability*, UCSB, Santa Barbara, CA 93106, USA.

495. Hurst, S. R., Platen, E. and Rachev, S. T. (1995b). Option Pricing for Asset Returns Driven by Subordinated Process. *Technical Report*, 81, Dept. of Statistics and Applied Probability, UCSB, Santa Barbara, CA 93106, USA.

496. Hurst, S. H., Platen, E. and Rachev, S. T. (1997). Subordinated Market Index Models: A Comparison. *Financial Engineering and the Japanese Markets*, 4, 97-124.

497. Hurst, S. H., Platen, E. and Rachev, S. T. (1999). Option Pricing for a Logstable Asset Price Model. *Mathematical and Computer Modelling*, 29, 105-119

498. Ibragimov, I. A. and Khasminskii, R. Z. (1979). Asymptotic Theory of Estimation. *Nauka* (in Russian), Moscow.

499. Iglehart, D. L. and Shedler, G. S. (1980). *Regenerative Simulation of Response Time in Networks of Queues*. Springer, Berlin.

500. Ikeda, N. and Watanabe, S. (1981). *Stochastic Differential Equations and Diffusion Processes*, Amsterdam, North-Holland.

501. Ingersoll jr., J. E. (1987). *Theory of financial decision making*. Rowman & Littlefield, Totowa.

502. It'o, K. (1969). *Stochastic Processes*, 16, Aarhus University Lecture Notes Series.

503. It'o, K. (1983). Distribution Valued Processes Arising from Independent Brownian Motions. *Math. Z.*, 182, 17- 33.

504. It'o, K. and McKean, H. P., Jr. (1965). *Diffusion Processes and Their Sample Paths*. Springer, New York.

505. Jackson, P., Maude, D. and Perraudin, W. (1996). Value-at-Risk Techniques: An Empirical Study. *Risk Measurement and Systemic Risk*, 295-322, Proceedings of a Joint Central Bank Research Conference, Board of Governors of the Federal Reserve System, Washington DC.

506. Jackson, P., Maude, D. and Perraudin, W. (1997). Bank Capital and Value-at-Risk. *Journal of Derivatives*, 4 (Spring), 73-90. (1997, (Grayling, S., editor). *VAR: Understanding and Applying Value-at-Risk*, 173-185. Risk, London).

507. Jackwerth, J. C. and Rubinstein, M. (1995). Implied Probability Distributions: Empirical Analysis. *Finance Working Paper*, 250, Research Program in Finance Working Paper Series, Institute of Business and Economic Research, University of California at Berkeley.

508. Jackwerth, J. C. and Rubinstein, M. (1996). Recovering Probability Distributions from Option Prices. *The Journal of Finance*, LI(5), 1611-1631.

509. Jacod, J. (1979). Calcul Stochastique et Problémes de Martingales. *Lecture Notes in Mathematics*, 714, Springer, Berlin.

510. Jacod, J. and Shiryaev, A. N. (1987). *Limit Theorems for Stochastic Processes*. Springer, Berlin, Heidelberg, New York.

511. Jakubowski, A., Memin, J. and Pages, G. (1989). Convergence en loi des suites d'integrales stochastiques sur l'espace D^1 de Skorokhod. *Probab. Th. Rel. Fields*, 81, 111-37.

512. Janicki, A. and Weron, A. (1994). *Simulation and Chaotic Behavior of α-stable Stochastic Processes*. Marcel Dekker, New York.

513. Janicki, A., Popova, I., Ritchken, R. and Woyczynski W. (1997). Option Pricing Bounds in an α-stable Security Market. *Communication in Statistics - Stochastic Models*, 13, 817-839.

514. Jansen, D. W. and de Vries, C. G. (1983). On the Frequency of Large Stock Returns: Putting Booms and Busts into Perspective. *Review of Economics and Statistics*, 73, 18-24.

515. Janssen, R. (1984). Discretization of the Wiener-Process in Difference-Methods for Stochastic Differential Equations. *Stoch. Processes and their Appl.*, 18, 361-369.

516. Jarque, C. M. and Bera, A. K. (1980). Efficient Tests for Normality, Homoscedasticity and Sertian Independence of Regression Residuals of Observations and Regression Residuals. *Economics Letters*, 6, 255-259.

517. Jarque, C. M. and Bera, A. K. (1987). A Test for Normality of Observations and Regression Residuals. *International Statistical Review*, 55(2), 163-172.

518. Jarrow, R. A. and Rudd, A. (1982). Approximate Option Valuation for Arbitrary Stochastic Processes. *Journal of Financial Economics*, 10, 347-369.

519. Jarrow, R. A. and Rudd, A. (1983). *Option Pricing*. Richard D. Irwin, Inc. Homewood, IL.

520. Jeganathan, P. (1991). On the asymptotic behavior of least-squares estimators in AR time series with roots near the unit circle. *Econometric Theory*, 7, 269-306.

521. Joag-Dev, K., Perlman, M. D. and Pitt, L. D. (1983). Association of normal random variables and Slepian's inequality. *The Annals of Probability*, 11, 451-455.

522. Joag-Dev, K. and Proschan, F. (1983). Negative Association of Random Variables with Applications. *Ann. Statist.*, 11, 286-295.

523. Johansen, S. (1988). Statistical analysis of cointegration vectors. *J. Econ. Dynamics and Control*, 12, 231-254.

524. Johansen, S. (1991). Estimation and hypothesis testing of cointegration vectors in Gaussian vector autoregressive models. *Econometrica*, 59, 6, 1551-1580.

525. Johnson, H. and Shanno, D. (1987). Option Pricing When the Variance is Changing. *Journal for Financial and Quantitative Analysis*, 22, 143-151.

526. Johnson, N. L. and Kotz, S. (1972). *Distributions in Statistics: Continuous Multivariate Distributions*. Wiley, New York.

527. Johnston, J. (1984). *Econometric Methods*, 3rd. ed. Mc-Graw Hill Book Company, Singapore.

528. Joreskog, K. G. (1967). Some contributions to maximum likelihood factor analysis. *Psychometrika*, 32, 443-482.

529. Jorion, P. (1995). Predicting volatility in the foreign exchange market. *Journal of Finance*, 50(2), 507-528.

530. Jorion, P. (1996a). *Value at Risk: The New Benchmark for Controlling Market Risk*. Irwin Professional.

531. Jorion, P. (1996b). Risk^2: Measuring the Risk in Value At Risk. *Financial Analysts Journal*, 52 (November/December). (1997, (Grayling, S., editor). *VAR: Understanding and Applying Value-at-Risk*, 187-193. Risk, London).

532. Jorion, P. (1997). In Defense of VAR. *Derivatives Strategy*, 2 (April), 20-23.

533. JP Morgan (1995). *Risk Metrics*, 3rd ed. JP Morgan.

534. JPMorgan &Co (1996). *Risk Metric:Technical Document*, Global Research Department, JP Morgan&Co.

535. Jouini, E. and Kallal, H. (1992). Martingales, Arbitrage and Equilibrium in Securities Markets with Transaction Costs. *Technical Report*, Laboratoire d'Econometrie de l'Ecole Polytechnique, Paris.

536. Jurlewicz, A., Weron, A. and Weron, K. (1996). Asymptotic behavior of stochastic systems with conditionally exponential decay property. *Applicationes Mathematicae*, 23, 379-394.

537. Kac, M. (1951). On Some Connections Between Probability Theory and Differential and Integral Equations. *roc Second Berekeley Symp. Math. Statist. Probab.*, 189-215. Univ. California Press, Berkeley.

538. Kadlec, G. B. and Patterson, D. M. (1998). A Transactions Data Analysis of Nonsynchronous Trading. *Technical report*, Pamplin College of Business, Virginia Polytechnic Institute.

539. Kagan, A. M. (1976). Fisher information contained in a finite dimensional linear space and the correct version of the method of moments (in Russian). *Problemy Peredaci Informacii*, 12, 2, 20-42.

540. Kakosyan, A. V., Klebanov, L. B. and Melamed, I. A. (1984). Characterization of Distributions by the Method of Intensively Monotone Operators. *Lecture Notes in Math.*, 1088. Springer, Berlin.

541. Kakosyan, A. V., Klebanov, L. B. and Rachev, S. T. (1988). *Quantitative Criteria for the Convergence of Probability Measures* (in Russian). Aiastan, Erevan.

542. Kalashnikov, V. V. (1989). Analytical and Simulation Estimates of Reliability for Regenerative Models. *Syst. Anal. Model. Simul.*, 6, 833-851.

543. Kalashnikov, V. V. (1997). *Geometric Sums: Bounds for Rare Events with Applications*. Kluwer Acad. Publ., Dordrecht.

544. Kalashnikov, V. V. and Rachev, S. T. (1990). *Mathematical Methods for Construction of Queuing Models*. Wadsworth & Brooks/Cole, Pacific Grive, California.

545. Kalashnikov, V. V. and Vsekhsvyatskii, A. Yu. (1985). Metric Estimates of the First Occurrence Time in Regenerative Processes, (Kalashnikov, V.V. and Zolotarev, V.M., editors). *Stability Problems for Stochastic Models*, 102-130. Springer, Berlin.

546. Kalashnikov, V. V. and Vsekhsvyatskii, A. Yu. (1989). On the Connection of Renyi's Theorem and Renewal Theory. *Stability Problems for Stochastic Models*. Proceedings. *Lecture Notes in Mathematics*, 1412. Springer, 83-109.

547. Kalbfleisch, J. D. and Prentice, R. L. (1980). *The Statistical Analysis of Failure Time Data*. Wiley, New York.

548. Kallsen, J. and Taqqu, M. (1994). On Strong Solutions, Birgit Operators, and Filtrations in Girsanov̀s Theorem. *Preprint.*

549. Kallsen, J. and Taqqu, M. (1998). Option Pricing in ARCH-Type Models. *Mathematical Finance,* 8(1,2), 13-26.

550. Kanagawa, S. (1986). The Rate of Convergence for Approximation Solutions of Stochastic Differential Equations. *Tokyo J. Math.,* 12, 33-48.

551. Kanter, M. (1972). Linear sample spaces and stable processes. *Journal of Functional Analysis,* 9, 441-459.

552. Kanter, M. and Steiger, W. L. (1974). Regression and autoregression with infinite variance. *Adv. Appl. Prob.* 6, 768-783.

553. Karandikar, R. L. and Rachev, S. T. (1995). A Generalized Binomial Model and Option Formulae for Subordinated Stock-Price Processes. *Probability and Mathematical Statistics,* 15, 427-446.

554. Karandikar, R. L. and Rachev, S. T. (1997). A Generalized Binomial Model and Option Formulae for Subordinated Stock Price Processes. *Probability and Mathematical Statistics,* 15, 427-446.

555. Karatzas, I. (1989). Optimization Problems in the Theory of Continuous Trading. *SIAM J. Control and Optimization,* 27, 1221-1259.

556. Karatzas, I. and Shreve, S. E. (1984). Connections Between Optimal Stopping and Singular Stochastic Control I. Monotone Follower Problems. *SIAM J. Control Optim.,* 22, 856-877.

557. Karatzas, I. and Shreve, S. E. (1988). *Brownian Motion and Stochastic Calculus..* Springer, Berlin.

558. Karatzas, I. and Shreve, S. E. (1991). *Brownian Motion and Stochastic Calculus,* 2nd ed. Springer, New York.

559. Kariya, T. (1993). Quantitative Methods for Portfolio Analysis. *MTV Model Approach,* Kluver Head. Publ., Dordrecht.

560. Kariya, T. and Eaton, M. L. (1977). Robust Tests for Spherical Symmetry. *Ann. Statist.,* 1, 206-215.

561. Kariya, T., Tsukuda, Y., Maru, J., Matsue, Y. and Omaki, K. (1995). An Extensive Analysis on the Japanese Markets vis S. Taylor's Model. *Financial Engineering and the Japanese Markets,* 2, 15-86.

562. Karlin, S. (1968). *Total Positivity,* 1. Stanford University Press, Stanford, CA.

563. Karr, A. F. (1991). *Point Processes and Their Statistical Inference.* Dekker, New York.

564. Kawata, T. (1972). *Fourier Analysis in Probability Theory.* Academic Press, New York.

565. Keilson, J. and Steutel, F. W. (1972). Families of Infinitely Divisible Distributions Closed under Mixing and Convolution. *Ann. Math. Statist. 43*, 242-250.

566. Kelker, D. (1970). *Distribution theory of spherical distributions and a location scale parameter generalization,* Sankjya A32, 419-30.

567. Kesten, H. and Spitzer, F. (1984). Convergence in Distribution for Products of Random Matrices. *Zeitschrift für Wahrscheinlichkeitstheorie und Verwandte Gebiete,* 67, 363-386.

568. Keynes, J. M. (1936). *The General Theory of Employment, Interest and Money.* Macmillan, London.

569. Khalfin, L. A. (1958). Contribution to the decay theory of a quasi-stationary state. *J. of Experimental and Theoretical Physics,* 6, 1053-1063.

570. Khinchin, A. Y. (1938). *Limit Laws for Sums of Independent Random Variables.* ONTI, Moscow.

571. Khindanova, I. and Rachev, S. T. (1999). Value-at-Risk: Recent Advances. *Problems in Risk Analysis.*

572. Khindanova, I., Rachev, S. T. and Schwartz, E. (1999). Stable Modeling of Value-at-Risk. *Stabel Models in Finance,* Pergamon Press.

573. Kim, J.-R. (1994). Analyse kointegrierter Modelle *Dissertation.* Haag und Herchen, Frankfurt.

574. Kim, J.-R. (1996a). Stable non-Gaussian economic variables. *Unpublished Manuscript,* Institute of Statistics and Econometrics, Christian Albrechts University, Kiel, Germany.

575. Kim, J.-R. (1996b). Asymmetry in economic variables. *Unpublished Manuscript,* Institute of Statistics and Econometrics, Christian Albrechts University at Kiel.

576. Kim, J.-R. (1999). Testing for Bivariate Symmetry: An Empirical Application. *Mathematical and Computer Modelling,* 29, 197-201.

577. Kim, J.-R., Mittnik, S. and Rachev, S. T. (1996a). Detecting Asymmetries in Observed Time Series and Disturbances. *Studies in Nonlinear Dynamics and Econometrics,* 1, 131-138.

578. Kim, J.-R., Mittnik, S. and Rachev, S. T. (1996b). Student's t-type Distributions for Heavy-tailed Variates. *Unpublished Manuscript*, Institute of Statistics and Econometrics, Christian Albrechts University. Kiel.

579. Kim, J.-R., Mittnik, S. and Rachev, S. T. (1996c). The CUSUM Test Based on OLS-residuals When Disturbances are Heavy-tailed. *Unpublished Manuscript*, Institute of Statistics and Econometrics, Christian Albrechts University. Kiel.

580. Kim, J.-R., Mittnik, S., and Rachev, S. T. (1997). Econometric Modelling in the presence of heavy-tailed innovations. *Communications in Statistics - Stochastic Models*, 13, 841-886.

581. Klebanov, L. B., Manija, G. M. and Melamed, I. A. (1984). A Problem of Zolotarev and Analogs of Infinitely Divisible and Stable Distributions in a Scheme for Summing a Random Number of Random Variables. *Theory of Probability and Its Applications*, 29, 791-794.

582. Klebanov, L. B., Manija, G. M. and Melamed, I. A. (1985). Analogs of Infinitely Divisible and Stable Laws for Sums of Random Number of Random Variables. *Fourth International Vilnius Conference on the Theory of Probability and Mathematical Statistics* (in Russian), 2, 40-41.

583. Klebanov, L. B., Manija, G. M. and Melamed, I. A. (1986). Non-Strictly Stable Laws and Estimation of Their Parameters, (Kalashnikov, V.U. et al., editors). *Stability Problems for Stochastic Models*, 23-31. Springer, Berlin.

584. Klebanov, L. B., Manija, G. M., and Melamed, I. A. (1987). ν_p-Strictly Stable Laws and Their Estimation of Their Parameters. *Lecture Notes in Math.*, 1223, 21-31. Springer, Berlin.

585. Klebanov, L. B. and Melamed, I. A. (1984). On stable estimation of parameters by the modified method of scoring. *Proc. Third Prague Symp. on Asymptotic Statistics*, 347-354.

586. Klebanov, L. B., Melamed, I. A. and Rachev, S. T. (1988). On the Products of a Random Number of Random Variables in Connection with a Problem from Mathematical Economics. *Lecture Notes in Math.*, 1412, 103-109. Springer, Berlin.

587. Klebanov, L. B., Melamed, I. A. and Rachev, S. T. (1994). On the Joint Estimation of Stable Law Parameters, (Anastassion, G. and Rachev, S. T., editors). *Approximation, Probability and Related Fields*, 315-320. Plenum Press, New York.

588. Klebanov, L. B., Melamed, I. A., Mittnik, S. and Rachev, S. T. (1996). Integral and Assymptotic Representation of Geo-Stable Densities. *Applied Mathematical Letters*, 9, 37-40.

589. Klebanov, L. B., Mittnik, S., Rachev, S. T., and Volkovich, V. E. (1998). A New Representation for the Characteristic Function of the Strictly Geo-stable Vectors. *Technical Report*, Department of Statistics and Mathematical Economics, University of Karlsruhe.

590. Klebanov, L. B. and Rachev, S. T. (1996). Sums of a Random Number of Random Variables and Their Approximations with ν -Accompanying Infinitely Divisible Laws. *Serdica*, 22, 471-498.

591. Klebanov, L. B. and Rachev, S. T. (1996b). Integral and asymptotic representations of geo-stable densities. *Applied Mathematics Letters*, 9 37-40.

592. Klebanov, L. B., Rachev, S. T., Safarian, M. (1999). Local *Pre*-limit Theorems and Their Applications to Finance. *Appl. Math. Letters*, to appear.

593. Klebanov, L. B., Rachev, S. T., Szekely, G. (1998). The Central *Pre*-limit Theorem and Its Applications. *Technical Report*, Department of Statistics and Applied Probability, University of California, Santa Barbara.

594. Kloeden, P. E. and Platen, E. (1992). *Numerical Solution of Stochastic Differential Equations*. Springer, Berlin.

595. Klüppelberg, C. and Mikosch, T. (1993). Spectral Estimates and Stable Processes. *Stoch. Proc. Appl.*, 47, 323-344.

596. Klüppelberg, C. and Mikosch, T. (1994). Some Limit Theory for the Selfnormalised Periodogram of p-stable Processes. *Scand. J. Statist.*, 21, 485-491.

597. Klüppelberg, C. and Mikosch, T. (1995a). Explosive Poisson Shot Noise Processes with Applications to risk Reserves. *Bernoulli*, 1, 125-147.

598. Klüppelberg, C. and Mikosch, T. (1995b). Modelling Delay in Claim Settlement. *Scand. Actuar. Journal*, 2, 154-168.

599. Klüppelberg, C. and Mikosch, T. (1996a). The Integrated Periodogram for Stable Periodogram. *Ann. Statist.*, 24, 1855-1877.

600. Klüppelberg, C. and Mikosch, T. (1996b). Gaussian Limit Fields for the Integrated Periodogram. *Annals of Applied Probability*, 6, 969-991.

601. Knight, K. (1987). Rate of convergence of centered estimates of autoregressive parameters for infinite variance autoregressions. *Journal of Time Series Analysis*, 8, 51-60.

602. Knight, K. (1989). Consistency of Akaike's Information Criterion for Infinite Autoregressive Processes. *Ann. Statist.*, 17, 824-840.

603. Koedijk, K. G. and Kool, C. J. (1992). Tail Estimates of East European Exchange Rates. *Journal of Business and Economic Statistics*, 10(1), 83-96.

604. Koedijk, K. G., Schafgans, M. M. and de Vries, C. G. (1990). The Tail Index of Exchange Rate Returns. *Journal of International Economics*, 29, 93-116.

605. Koedijk, K. G., Stork, P. A. and de Vries, C. G. (1992). Differences Between Foreign Exchange Rate Regimes: The View from the Tails. *Journal of International Money and Finance*, 11, 462-473.

606. Kogon, S. M. and Williams, D. B. (1998). Characteristic Function Based Estimation of Stable Distribution Parameters, (Adler, R. et al. (editors). *A Practical Guide to Heavy Tails: Statistical Techniques and Applications*, 311-335. Birkhäuser, Boston.

607. Kokoszka, P. S. and Mikosch, T. (1997). The integrated periodogram for long-memory processes with finite or infinite variance. *Stoch. Proc. Appl.*, 66, 55-78.

608. Kokoszka, P. S. and Taqqu, M. S. (1994). Infinite Variance Stable ARMA Processes. *Journal of Time Series Analysis*, 15, 203-220.

609. Kokoszka, P. S. and Taqqu, M. S. (1995). The Integrated Periodogram for Long-Memory Processes with Finite or Infinite Variance. *Technical Report*, Univ. of Groningen, Dept. of Math., POBox 800, Groningen.

610. Kokoszka, P. S. and Taqqu, M. S. (1996). Parameter Estimation for Infinite Variance Fractional ARIMA. *Ann. Statist.*, 24, 1880-1913.

611. Kokoszka, P. S. and Taqqu, M. S. (1999). Discrete Time Parametric Models with Long Momory and Infinite Variance. *Mathematical and Computer Modelling*, 29, 203-215.

612. Kolmogorov, A. N. (1953). Some latest works on limit theorems in probability theory (In Russian). *Vestnik MGU*, 10, 28-39.

613. Komlós, J., Major, P. and Tusnáddy, G. (1975). An Approximation of Partial Sums of Independent RV's, and the Sample DF, II. *Z. Wahrscheinlichkeitstheorie verw. Geb.*, 34, 33-58.

614. Kon, S. (1984). Models of Stock Returns - a Comparison. *Journal of Finance*, 39, 147-165.

615. Konijn, H. (1988). Symmetry Tests, Pure and Combined, (Johnson, N.L. and Kotz, S., editors). *Encyclopedia Statist. Sci.*, 9, 139-142.

616. K'ono, N. and Maejima, M. (1991). Self-Similar Stable Processes with Stationary Increments, (Cambanis, S., Samorodnitsky, G. and Taqqu, M. S., editors). *Progress in Probability*, 25, 275-295. Birkhäuser, Boston.

617. Kopp, P. E. (1984). *Martingales and stochastic integrals*. Cambridge Univ. Press, Cambridge.

618. Kopp, P. E. and Elliott, R. J. (1989). Option Pricing with the Brownian Bridge. *Technical Report*, University of Alberta.

619. Korn, R. (1998). Portfolio Optimization with strictly positive transaction costs and impulse control. *Journal of Finance and Stochsatics*, 85-114.

620. Korolev, V. Y. (1988). The Asymptotic Distributions of Random Sums. *Lecture Notes Math.*, 1412, 110-123. Springer, New York.

621. Korolev, V. Y. (1989). Approximations of Distributions of Random Sums of Independent Random Variables by Mixtures of Normal Laws. *Theory Prob. Appl.*, 34, 523-531.

622. Kotz, S., Ostrovskii, I. V. and Hayfavi, A. (1995). Analytic and Asymptotic Properties of Linniks Probability Densities I. *Journ. Math. Analysis and Appl.* , 193, 353-371.

623. Koutrouvelis, I. A. (1980). Regression-type Estimation of the Parameters of Stable Laws. *Journal of the American Statistical Association*, 75, 918-928.

624. Koutrouvelis, I. A. (1981). An Iterative Procedure for the Estimation of the Parameters of the Stable Law. *Communication in Statistics-Simulation and Computation*, 10, 17-28.

625. Kozubowski, T. J. (1992). The Theory of Geometric Stable Laws and Its Use in Modeling Financial Data. *Ph. D. Dissertation*, Department of Statistics and Applied Probability, University of California, Santa Barbara, CA 93106-3110.

626. Kozubowski, T. J. (1994a). Representation and Properties of Geometric-Stable Laws, (Anastassiou, G. and Rachev, S.T., editors). *Approximation, Probability and related Fields*, 321-327. Plenum, New York.

627. Kozubowski, T. J. (1994b). The inner characterization of geometric stable laws. *Statist. Decisions*, 12, 307-327.

628. Kozubowski, T. J. (1999). Geometric Stable Laws: Estimation and Applicatiion. *Mathematical and Computer Modelling*, 29, 241-263.

629. Kozubowski, T. J. and Panorska, A. K. (1999a). Simulation of geometric stable and other limiting multivariate distributions arising in random summation scheme. *Mathematical and Computer Modelling*, 29, 255-262.

630. Kozubowski, T. J. and Panorska, A. K. (1999b). Multivariate Geometric Stable Distributions in Financial Applications. *Mathematical and Computer Modelling*, 29, 83-92.

631. Kozubowski, T. J. and Rachev, S. T. (1994). The Theory of Geometric Stable Laws and its Use in Modeling Financial Data. *European Journal of Operations Research: Financial Modeling*, 74, 310-324.

632. Kozubowski, T. J. and Rachev, S. T. (1999a). Univariate geometric stable laws. *J. Comput. Anal. Appl.*, 1(2), 177-217.

633. Kozubowski, T. J. and Rachev, S. T. (1999b). Multivariate geometric stable laws. *J. Comput. Anal. Appl.*, to appear.

634. Krämer, W. and Runde, R. (1996). Stochastic Properties of German Stock Returns, *Empirical Economics*, 21, 281-306.

635. Kratz, M. and Resnick, S. I. (1996). The QQ-Estimator and Heavy Tails. *Communications in Statistics - Stochastic Models*, 12(4), 699-724.

636. Kreps, D. (1981). Arbitrage and Equilibrium in Economics with Infinitely many Commodities. *Journal of Mathematical Economics*, 8, 15-35.

637. Kroll, Y. and Levy, H. (1982). Stochastic dominance: A note. *J. Finance*, 37, 871-875.

638. Kruglov, V. M. and Korolev, V. Yu. (1990). *Limit Theorems for Random Sums* (in Russian). Izdat. Moskov. Gos. Univ, Moscow.

639. Küchler, U., Neumann, K., Sørensen, M. and Streller, A. (1999). Stock returns and hyperbolic distributions. *Mathematical and Computer Modelling*, 29, 1-15.

640. Küelbs, J. (1973). A representation theorem for symmetric stable processes and stable measures on H. *Zeitschrift für Wahrscheinlichkeitstheorie und verwandte Gebiete*, 26, 259-271.

641. Kunita, H. and Watanabe, S. (1967). On Square Integrable Martingales. *Nagoya Mathematical Journal*, 30, 209-245.

642. Kupiec, P. (1995). Techniques for Verifying the Accuracy of Risk Measurement Models. *Journal of Derivatives*, 3 (Winter), 73-84. (1996, *Risk*

Measurement and Systemic Risk, 381-401, Proceedings of a Joint Central Bank Research Conference, Board of Governors of the Federal Reserve System, Washington DC and 1997, (Grayling, S., editor), VAR: Understanding and Applying Value-at-Risk, 195-204, Risk, London).

643. Kurtz, T. G. and Protter, P. (1991a). Weak limit theorems for stochastic integrals and stochastic differential equations. *Ann. Probab.*, 19, 3, 1035-1070.

644. Kurtz, T. G. and Protter, P. (1991b). Characterization the weak convergence of stochastic integrals. *Math. Soc. Lecture*, 167, Cambridge Univ. Press. London.

645. Kurtz, T. G. and Protter, P. (1996a). Weak convergence of stochastic integrals and differential equations, (Talay, D. and Tubaro, L., editors). *Lect. Notes Math.*, 1627. Springer.

646. Kurtz, T. G. and Protter, P. (1996b). Weak convergence of stochastic integrals and differential equations II: Infinite dimensional case, (Talay, D. and Tubaro, L., editors). *Lect. Notes Math.*, 1627. Springer.

647. Kwapien, S. and Woyczynski, W. A. (1992). Random Series and Stochastic Integrals: Single and Multiple. Birkhäuser, Basel.

648. Lange, K. L., Little, R. J. and Taylor, J. M. G. (1989). Robust Statistical Modeling Using the t Distribution. *Journal of the American Statistical Association*, 84(408), 881-896.

649. Lassner, F. (1974a). Sommes de Produits de Variables Alleatoires Independantes. *Thesis*, Universite de Paris VI.

650. Lassner, F. (1974b). Sur Certain Types de Mecanismes Additifs en Economie Stochastique. *C.R.Acad. Sci. Paris A*, 279, 33-36.

651. Latané, H. A. and Rendleman, R. J. (1976). Standard Deviations of Stock Price Ratios Implied in Option Prices. *Journal of Finance*, 31, 369-381.

652. Lau, A. H.-L., Lau, H.-S. and Wingender, J. R. (1990). The Distribution of Stock Returns: New Evidence Against the Stable Model. *Journal of Business and Economic Statistics*, 8, 217-223.

653. Lawrence, C. (1997). Working Liquidity Into Your VAR. *Derivatives Strategy*, 2 (February), 45-47.

654. Lawrence, C. and Robinson, G. (1995). How Safe Is RiskMetrics? *Risk*, 8 (January), 26-29. (1997, (Grayling, S., editor). *VAR: Understanding and Applying Value-at-Risk*, 65-69. Risk, London).

655. Leadbetter, M. R., Lindgren, G. and Rootzen, M. (1983). *Extremes and Related Properties of Random Sequences and Processes.* Springer, New York.

656. Ledoux, M. and Talagrand, M. (1991). *Isoperimetry and Processes in Probabilities in Banach Spaces.* Springer, New York.

657. Lee, A. J. (1990). *U-Statistics: Theory and Practice.* Dekker, New York.

658. Lee, M.-L. T., Rachev, S. T. and Samorodnitsky, G. (1990). Association of Stable Random Variables. *Ann. Probability,* 18, 1759-1764

659. Lee, M.-L. T., Rachev, S. T. and Samorodnitsky, G. (1993). Dependence of Stable Random Variables. *Stochastic Inequalities,* 22, 219-234, IMS Lecture Notes-Monograph Series.

660. Lehmann, E. L. (1966). Some Concepts of Dependence. *Ann. Math. Statist.,* 37, 1137-1153.

661. Leippold, M. (1997). Numerische Methoden in der Optionspreis-theorie: Monte Carlo und Quasi-Monte Carlo Methoden. *Finanzmarkt und Portfoliomanagement,* 11, 179-196.

662. Leland, H. (1985). Option Pricing and Replication with Transaction Costs. *Journal of Finance,* 40, 1283-1301.

663. Le Page, R. (1980). Multidimensional Infinitely Divisible Variables and Processes. Part I: Stable case. *Lecture Notes in Math.,* 1391, 153-163.

664. Levhari, D., Paroush J. and Peleg, B.(1975). Efficiency analysis for multivariate distributions. *Rev. Econ. Studies* , 42, 87-91.

665. Lévy, P. (1937). *Théorie de L'Addition des Variables Aléatoires,* 2nd ed. Paris: Gauthier-Villars.

666. Lévy-Vehel, J. (1995). Fractal Approaches in Signal Processing. *Fractals,* 3, 755-775.

667. Lewis, P. A. (1964). A Branching Poisson Process Model for the Analysis of Computer Failure Pattern. *Journal Royal Stat. Soc.,* Ser. B, 26, 398-456.

668. Linde, W. (1983). *Infinitely Divisible and Stable Measures on Banach Spaces.* Wiley-Intersience, Chicester.

669. Linnik, Yu. V. (1960). *Decomposition of Probability Laws* (in Russian). Leningrad University.

670. Linsmeier, T. and Pearson, N. (1996). *Risk Measurement: An Introduction to Value at Risk,* Department of Accountancy and Department of Finance, University of Illinois at Urbana-Champaign.

671. Lintner, J. (1965). The Valuation of Risk Assets, and the Selection of Risky Investments in Stock-Portfolios and Capital Budgets. *Review of Economics and Statistics*, 47, 13-37.

672. Lipster, R. and Shiryayev, A. (1980). A Functional Central Limit Theorem for SemiMartingales. *Theory Probability*, 25, 667-688.

673. Lisitsky A. D. (1990). New expression for characteristic function of multidimentional strict stable law. *Problems of Stability for Stochastic Models* (in Russian), 49-53, VNIISI, Moscow.

674. Litterman, R. (1996). Hot Spots™ and Hedges. *The Journal of Portfolio Management*, Special Issue 1996, 52-75.

675. Liu, R. (1996). VAR and VAR Derivatives. *Capital Market Strategies*, 5 (September), 23-33.

676. Liu, S. M. and Brorsen, B. W. (1995). Maximum Likelihood Estimation of a GARCH-stable Model. *Journal of Applied Econometrics*, 10, 273-285.

677. Lo, A. (1991). Long-term memory in stock market prices. *Econometrica*, 59, 1279-1313.

678. Lo, A. W. and MacKinlay, A. C. (1988). Stock Market Prices Do Not Follow Random Walks: Evidence from a Simple Specification Test. *Review of Financial Studies*, 1, 41-66.

679. Loeve, M. (1963). *Probability Theory*, Princeton.

680. Logan, B. F., Mallows, C. L., Rice, S. O. and Shepp, L. A. (1973). Limit distributions of self-normalized sums. *The Annals of Probability*, 1, 788-809.

681. Longerstaey, J. and Zangari, P. (1997). A Transparent Tool, (Grayling, S., editor). *VAR: Understanding and Applying Value-at-Risk*. Risk, 71-73, London.

682. Longin, F. M. (1996). The Asymptotic Distribution of Extreme Stock Market Returns. *Journal of Business*, 69(3), 383-408.

683. Lopez, J. A. (1996). Regulatory Evaluation of Value-at-Risk Models. *Working Paper*, 96-51, Wharton Financial Institutions Center Working Paper Series.

684. Lorden, G. (1971). Procedures for reacting to a change in distribution. *The Annals of Mathematical Statistics*, 42, 1897-1908.

685. Loretan, M. and Phillips, P. B. C. (1994). Testing the Covariance Stationarity of Heavy-Tailed Time Series. *Journal of Empirical Finance*, 1, 211-248.

686. Lucas, A. (1997). A Note on Optimal Estimation from a Risk Management Perspective under Possibly Mis-specified Tail Behavior, University Amsterdam Research Memorandum Series. *Research Memorandum* 1997-56 (November).

687. Lucas, A. and Klaasen, P. (1997). The Effect of Fat Tails on Optimal Asset Allocations and Downside Risk. *Working Paper*, (March 1997).

688. Lüdecke, T. (1997). The Karlsruher Kapitalmarktdatenbank. *Technical Report*, 190, Institut für Entscheidungstheorie und Unternehmensforschung, Universität Karlsruhe.

689. Lukacs E. (1970). *Characteristic Functions*, 2nd ed. Griffin, London.

690. Lumsdaine, R. L. (1995). Finite-Sample Properties of the Maximum Likelihood Estimator in GARCH(1,1) and IGARCH(1,1) Models: A Monte Carlo Investigation. *Journal of Business and Economic Statistics*, 13(1), 1-10.

691. Luukkonen, R., Saikkonen, P. and Teräsvirta, T. (1988). Testing linearity against smooth transition autoregressive model. *Biometrika* 75, 491-499.

692. Lux, T. (1995). The Stable Paretian Hypothesis and the Frequency of Large Returns: An Examination of Major German Stocks. *Volkswirtschaftliche Diskussionsbeiträge*, 72, University of Bamberg, Germany.

693. MacBeth, J. D. and Merville, L. J. (1979). An Empirical Examination of the Black-Scholes Call Option Pricing Model. *Journal of Finance*, 34, 1173-1186.

694. MacBeth, J. D. and Merville, L. J. (1980). Tests of the Black-Scholes and Cox Call Option Valuation Models. *The Journal of Finance*, 35, 285-303.

695. Machina, M. J. (1982). Expected utility analysis without the independence axiom. *Econometrica*, 50, 277-323.

696. MacNeill, I. B. (1978). Properties of sequences of partial sums of polynomial regression residuals with applications to tests for change of regression at unknown times. *Ann. Statist.*, 6, 422-433.

697. Madan, D. B. and Seneta, E. (1990). The variance gamma model for share market returns. *J. Business*, 63, 511-524.

698. Maddala, G. S. and Rao, C. R. (1996). Statistical Methods in Finance. *Handbook of Statistics*,14. Elsevier Science B.V., Amsterdam.

699. Maejima, M. (1983). On a class of self-similar processes. *Zeitschrift für Wahrscheinlichkeitstheorie und verwandte Gebiete*, 62, 235-245.

700. Maejima, M. and Rachev, S. T. (1987). An Ideal Metric and the Rate of Convergence to a Self-similar Process. *Annals of Probability*, 15, 702-727.

701. Maejima, M. and Rachev, S. T. (1996). Rates of Convergence in the Operator-Stable Limit Theorem. *Journal of Theoretical Probability*, 37-85.

702. Mahoney, J. (1996). Empirical-Based Versus Model-Based Approaches to Value-at-Risk: An Examination of Foreign Exchange and Global Equity Portfolios. *Risk Measurement and Systemic Risk*, 199-217, Proceedings of a Joint Central Bank Research Conference, Board of Governors of the Federal Reserve System, Washington DC.

703. Maller, R. A. (1988). Asymptotic Normality of Trimmed Means in Higher Dimensions. *Ann. Prob.*, 16, 1608-1622.

704. Mandelbaum, A. and Taqqu, M. S. (1967). Invariance Principle for Symmetric Statistics. *Ann. Statist.*, 12, 483-496.

705. Mandelbrot, B. (1959). Variables et processus stochastiques de Pareto-Levy, et la repartition des revenus. *C.R. Acad. Sc. Paris*, 23, 2153-2155.

706. Mandelbrot, B. (1960). The Pareto-Levy law and the distribution of income. *Internat. Econ. Rev.*, 1, 79-106.

707. Mandelbrot, B. B. (1961). Stable Paretian random functions and the multiplicative variation of income. *Econometrica*, 29, 517-543.

708. Mandelbrot, B. B. (1962a). Paretian distributions and income maximization. *Quarterly Journal of Economics*, 76, 57-85.

709. Mandelbrot, B. B. (1962b). The Variation of Certain Speculative Prices. *IBM Research Report NC-87*, (March).

710. Mandelbrot, B. B. (1962c). Sur Certain Prix Spéculatifs: Faits Empiriques et Modèle Basé sur les Processes Stables Additifs de Paul Lévy. *Comptes Rendus*, 254, 3968-3970.

711. Mandelbrot, B. B. (1963a). New Methods in Statistical Economics. *Journal of Political Economy*, 71, 421-440.

712. Mandelbrot, B. B. (1963b). The Variation of Certain Speculative Prices. *Journal of Business*, 36, 394-419.

713. Mandelbrot, B. B. (1963c). New methods in statistical economics. *Journal of Political Economy*, 71, 421-440.

714. Mandelbrot, B. B. (1967). The Variation of some Other Speculative Prices. *Journal of Business*, 40, 393-413.

715. Mandelbrot, B. B. (1968). Some aspects of the random walk model of Stock Market prices: comment. *International Economic Review*, 9, 258.

716. Mandelbrot, B. B. (1970a). Statistical dependence and prices and interest rates. *Papers of the Second World Congress of the Economteric Society*, Cambridge, England.

717. Mandelbrot, B. B. (1970b). Analysis of long-run dependence in time-series: the *R/S* technique. *Fiftieth Annual Report of the National Bureau of Economic Research*, 107-108.

718. Mandelbrot, B. B. (1971a). When can price be arbitraged efficiently? A limit to the validity of the random walk and martingale model. *Review of Economics and Statistics*, 53, 225-236.

719. Mandelbrot, B. B. (1971b). Statistical dependence and prices and interest rates. *Fifty-first Annual Report of the National Bureau of Economic Research*, 141-142.

720. Mandelbrot, B. B. (1971c). Analysis of long-run dependence in time-series: the *R/S* technique. *Econometrica*, 39, (July Supplement), 68-69.

721. Mandelbrot, B. B. (1972). Correction of an error in "The variation of certain speculative prices" (1963). *Journal of Business*, 40, 542-543.

722. Mandelbrot, B. B. (1973). Comments on "A subordinated stochastic process with finite variance for speculative prices", by Peter K. Clark. *Econometrica*, 41, 157-160.

723. Mandelbrot, B. B. (1977). *The Fractal Geometry of Nature*. Freeman, New York.

724. Mandelbrot, B. B. (1982a). *The Fractal Geometry of Nature*. Freeman, New York.

725. Mandelbrot, B. B. (1982b). The variation of certain speculative prices. *current contents*, 14, 20.

726. Mandelbrot, B. B. (1995a). Introduction to Fractal Sums of Pulses. Lévy Flights and Related Phenomena in Physics (Nice, 1994), (Zaslawsky, G., Schlesinger, M.F. and Frisch, U., editors). *Lecture Notes in Physics*. Springer, New York.

727. Mandelbrot, B. B. (1995b). Fractal Sums of Pulses: Self-Affine Global Dependence and Lateral Limit Theorems. *Preprint*.

728. Mandelbrot, B. B. (1995c). The Paul Lévy I knew. *Lévy Flights and Related Phenomena in Physics* (Nice, 1994), (Schlesinger, M. F., Zaslawsky, G. and Frisch, U., editors). *Lecture Notes in Physics.* Springer, New York.

729. Mandelbrot, B. B. (1997a). *Fractal and Scaling in Finance Discontinuity, Concentration, Risk.* Springer, New York, Berlin, Heidelberg.

730. Mandelbrot, B. B. (1997b). *Fractals, hasard et finance.* Flammarion, Paris.

731. Mandelbrot, B. B. and Taqqu, M. S. (1979). Robust R/S analysis of long-run serial correlation. *Bulletin of the International Statistical Institute*, 48, 69-104.

732. Mandelbrot, B. B. and Taylor, M. (1967). On the Distribution of Stock Price Differences. *Operations Research*, 15, 1057-1062.

733. Mandelbrot, B. B. and Van Ness, J. W. (1968). Fractional Brownian Motions, Fractal Noises and Applications. *SIAM Review*, 10, 422-437.

734. Mandelbrot, B. B. and van Ness, J. W. (1968). Fractional Brownian motions, fractional noises and applications. *SIAM Review*, 10, 422-437.

735. Mandelbrot, B. B. and Wallis, J. R. (1969). Robustness of the rescaled range R/S in the measurement of noncyclic long-run statistical dependence. *Water Resources Res.*, 5, 967-988.

736. Mantegna, R. N. (1991). Lévy Walks and Enhanced Diffusion of Milan Stock Exchange. *Physica*, 179,232-242.

737. Mantegna, R. N. and Stanley, H. E. (1995). Scaling behavior in the dynamics of an economic index. *Nature*, 376, 46-49.

738. Marcus, D.J. (1983). Non Stable laws with all projections stable. *Zeitschrift für Wahrscheinlichkeitstheorie und verwandte Gebiete*, 64, 139-156.

739. Marinelli, C., Rachev, S. T. and Roll, R. (1999). Subordinated Exchange Rate Models: Evidence for Heavy Tailed Distributions and Long-Range Dependence, (Mittnik, S. and Rachev S. T., editors). *Stable Models in Finance*, to appear. Pergamon Press.

740. Marinelli, C., Rachev, S. T., Roll, R. and Göppl, H. (1999). Subordinated Stock Price Models: Heavy Tails and Long-Range Dependence in the High-frequency Deutsche Bank Price Record . *Technical Report*, Department of Statistics and Mathematical Economics, University of Karlsruhe.

741. Markowitz, H. M. (1952). Portfolio selection. *Journal of Finance*, 7, 77-91.

742. Markowitz, H. (1959). *Portfolio selection; efficient diversification of investment.* Wiley, New York.

743. Marshall, C. and Siegel, M. (1997). Value at Risk: Implementing A Risk Management Standard. *Journal of Derivatives*, 4 (Spring), 91-110. (1997, (Grayling, S., editor). *VaR: Understanding and Applying Value-at-Risk.* Risk, 257-273, London).

744. Martin-Löf, A. (1976). Limit Theorems for the Motion of a Poisson System of Independent Markovian Particles with the High Density. *Z. Wahrsch. Verw. Gebiete*, 34, 205-223.

745. Maruyama, G. (1955). Continuous Markov Processes and Stochastic Equations. *Rend. Circolo Math. Palermo*, 4, 48-90.

746. Mason, D. M. (1982). Laws of Large Numbers for Sums of Extreme Values. *The Annals of Probability*, 10, 754-764.

747. McCabe, B. P. M. and Harrison, M. J. (1980). Testing the Constancy of Regression Relationships Over Time Using Least Squares Residuals. *J. R. Statist. Soc.*, C, 29, 142-148.

748. McConnell, T. R. and Taqqu, M. S. (1986). Decoupling Inequalities for Multilinear Forms in Independent Symmetric Random Variables. *Ann. Probab.*, 14, 943-954.

749. McCulloch, J. H. (1985). Interest-Free Deposit Insurance Premia. Stable ARCH Estimates. *Journal of Banking and Finance*, 9, 137-156.

750. McCulloch, J. H. (1986). Simple Consistent Estimators of Stable Distribution Parameters. *Communications in Statistics-Computation and Simulation*, 15, 1109-1136.

751. McCulloch, J. H. (1994a). Measuring Tail Thickness in Order to Estimate the Stable Index α: A Critique. *Preprint.*

752. McCulloch, J. H. (1994b). Time Series Analysis of State-Space Models with Symmetric Stable Errors by Posterior Mode Estimation. *The Ohio State University Working Paper*, 94-01, Ohio State University.

753. McCulloch, J. H. (1994c). Numerical Approximation of the Symmetric Stable Distribution and Density. *The Ohio State University Working Paper*, Ohio State University.

754. McCulloch, J. H. (1996a). Financial Applications of Stable Distributions, (Maddala, G. S. and Rao, C. R., editors). *Handbook of Statistics*

- *Statistical Methods in Finance*, 14, 393-425. Elsevier Science B.V, Amsterdam.

755. McCulloch, J. H. (1996b). Toward Numerical Approximation of the Skew-Stable Distributions and Densities. *Working Paper*, 96-33, Department of Economics, The Ohio State University.

756. McCulloch, J. H. (1996c). On the parametrization of the afocal stable distribution. *Bulletin of the London Mathematical Society*, 28, 651-655.

757. McCulloch, J. H. (1997a). Financial Applications of Stable Distributions. (Maddala, G. and Rao, C., editors). *Handbook of Statistics*, 14. Elsevier Science.

758. McCulloch, J. H. (1997b). Measuring Tail Thickness in Order to Estimate the Stable Index α: A Critique. *Journal of Business and Economic Statistics*, 15(1), 74-81.

759. McCulloch, J. H. (1997c). Linear regression with stable disturbances, (Adler, R., Feldman, R. and Taqqu, M., editors). *A Practical Guide to Heavy Tails*, 359-376. Birkhäuser, Boston.

760. McDonald, J. B. and Newey, W. K. (1988). Partially Adaptive Estimation of Regression Models Via the Generalized t Distribution. *Econometric Theory*, 4, 428-457.

761. McFarland, J. W., Pettit, R. R. and Sung, S. K. (1982a). The Distribution of Foreign Exchange Price Changes: Trading Day Effects and Risk Measurement. *Journal of Finance*, 37, 693-715.

762. McFarland, J. W., Pettit, R. R. and Sung, S. K. (1982b). Distribution of Exchange Rates: Trading Day Effects and Risk Measurement. *Journal of Finance*, 37, 693-715.

763. McFarland, J. W., Pettit, R. R. and Sung, S. K. (1982c). Distribution of Exchange Rates - A Reply. *Journal of Finance*, 37, 693-715.

764. McFarland, J. W., Pettit, R. R. and Sung, S. K. (1987). The Distribution of Foreign Exchange Price Changes: Trading Day Effects and Risk Measurement - A Reply. *Journal of Finance*, 42, 189-194.

765. McGuirk, A., Robertson, J. and Spanos, A. (1993). Modeling Exchange Rate Dynamics: Nonlinear Dependence and Thick Tails. *Econometric Reviews*, 12(3), 261-330.

766. Meerschaert, M. M. (1989). Moments of Random Vectors which Belong to some Domain of Normal Attraction. *Ann. Probab.*, 18, 870-876.

767. Melamed, J. A. (1988). Limit Theorems in the Set-Up of Summation of a Random Number of Independent Identically Distributed Random

Variables, (Kalashnikov, V.V. and Zolotarev, V.M., editors). *Stability Problems for Stochastic Models*, LNM 1412, 194-228. Springer, Berlin.

768. Melino, A. and Turnbull, S. (1990). Pricing Foreign Currency Options with Stochastic Volatility. *Journal of Econometrics*, 45, 239-265.

769. Melnikov, A. V. and Shiryaev, A. N. (1996). Criteria for the Absence of Arbitrage in the Financial Market, (Shiryaev, A. N. et al., editor). *Progress in the Theory of Probability and its Applications*, II, TVB, Moscow, 121-134.

770. Memin, J. and Slominski, L. (1991). Condition UT et stabilité en loi des solutions d'equations differentielles stochastiques, Sém. de Probab. XXV. *Lecture Notes in Math.*, 1485, 162-177. Springer, Berlin.

771. Menezes, C., Geiss, C. and Tressler, J. (1980). Increasing downside risk. *Am. Econ. Rev.*, 7, 921-932.

772. Merton, R. C. (1973a). Theory of Rational Option Pricing. *Bell J. Econ. Management Sci.*, 4, 141-183.

773. Merton, R. C. (1973b). An Intertemporal Capital Asset Pricing Model. *Econometrica*, 41, 967-986.

774. Merton, R. C. (1976). Option Pricing When the Underlying Sock Returns are Discontinuous. *Journal of Financial Economics*, 3, 125-144.

775. Merton, R. C. (1989a). On the Application of the Continuous Time Theory of Finance to Financial Intermediation and Insurance. *The Geneva Papers on Risk and Insurance*, 225-261.

776. Merton, R. C. (1989b). *Continuous Time Finance*. Blackwell, Cambridge, MA.

777. Métivier, M. (1982). *Semimartingales*. de Gruyter, Berlin.

778. Métivier, M. and Pellaumail, J. (1980). *Stochastic Integration*. Academic Press, New York.

779. Meyer, P. A. (1976). Séminaire Probabilités X. *Lecture Notes in Math.*, 511. Springer, New York.

780. Mijnheer, J. L. (1975). *Sample path properties of Stable Processes. Mathematical Centre Tracts.* Mathematical Centrum, Amsterdam.

781. Mikosch, T. (1991). Functional Limit Theorems for Random Quadratic Forms. *Stoch. Proc. Appl.*, 37, 81-98.

782. Mikosch, T., Gadrich, T., Klüppelberg, C. and Adler, R. J. (1995). Parameter Estimation for ARMA Models with Infinite Variance Innovations. *The Annals of Statistics*, 23(1), 305-326.

783. Miller, G. (1978). Properties of Certain Symmetric Stable Distributions. *J. Multivariate Anal.*, 8, 346-360.

784. Milne, F. (1988). Arbitrage and diversification in a general equilibrium asset economy. *Econometrica*, 56, 815-840.

785. Mittnik, S., Doganoglu, T. and Chenyao, D. (1999). Computing the Probability Density Function of the Stable Paretian Distribution. *Mathematical and Computer Modelling*, 29, 235-240.

786. Mittnik, S. and Kim, J.-R. (1996). Unit-root inference in the presence of finite-variance disturbances. *Discussion Paper*, 86, Institute of Statistics and Econometrics, Christian Albrechts University, Kiel.

787. Mittnik, S., Kim, J.-R. and Rachev, S. T. (1996). *Testing Linearity when Disturbances are Heavy-tailed , Unpublished Manuscript ,* Institute of Statistics and Econometrics, Christian Albrechts University at Kiel.

788. Mittnik, S. and Mizrach, B. (1992). Parametric and Semiparametric Analysis of Nonlinear Time Series. *Unpublished manuscript.*

789. Mittnik, S. and Niu, Z. (1993). Asymmetries in business cycles: Econometric techniques and empirical evidence, (Semmler, W., editor). *Business Cycles: Theory and Empirical Methods.* Kluwer Academic Publishers, Dordrecht.

790. Mittnik, S., and Paolella, M. S. (1999). A Simple Estimator for the Characteristic Exponent of the Stable Paretian Distribution. *Mathematical and Computer Modelling*, 29, 161-176.

791. Mittnik, S., Paolella, M. S. and Rachev, S. T. (1997). Modeling the Persistence of Conditional Volatilities with GARCH-stable Processes. *Technical Report*, University of California, Santa Barbara.

792. Mittnik, S., Paolella, M. S. and Rachev, S. T. (1998a). Unconditional and Conditional Distributional Models for the Nikkei's Index. *Asia-Pacific Financial Markets*, 5, 99-128.

793. Mittnik, S., Paolella, M. S. and Rachev, S. T. (1998b). A tail estimator for the index of the stable Paretian distribution. *Communications in Statistics-Theory and Methods.* 27, 1239-1262.

794. Mittnik, S., Paolella, M. S. and Rachev, S. T. (1998c). The Prediction of Down-Side Risk with GARCH-stable Models. *Technical Report*, Institute of Statistics and Econometrics, University of Kiel, Germany.

795. Mittnik, S., Paulauskas, V. and Rachev, S. T. (1998). Statistical inference in regression with heavy-tailed integrated variables. *Technical Report*, 346, University of California at Santa Barbara.

796. Mittnik, S. and Rachev, S. T. (1989). Stable Distributions for Asset Returns. *Applied Mathematics Letters*, 2, 301-304.

797. Mittnik, S. and Rachev, S. T. (1991). Alternative Multivariate Stable Distributions and Their Applications to Financial Modeling, (Cambanis, S. et al., editors). *Stable Processes and Related Topics*. Birkhäuser, Boston, 107-119.

798. Mittnik, S. and Rachev, S. T. (1993a). Modeling Asset Returns with Alternative Stable Distributions. *Econometric Reviews*, 12, 261-330.

799. Mittnik, S. and Rachev, S. T. (1993b). Reply to Comments on Modeling Asset Returns with Alternative Stable Distributions and some extensions. *Econometric Review*, 12, 347-389.

800. Mittnik, S. and Rachev, S. T. (1996a). Tail Estimation of the Stable Index α. *Applied Mathematics Letters*, 9, 53-56.

801. Mittnik, S. and Rachev, S. T. (1999). Option Pricing for Stable and Infinitely Divisible Asset Returns. *Mathematical and Computer Modelling*, 29, 93-104.

802. Mittnik, S., Rachev, S. T. and Chenyao, D. (1996). Distribution of Exchange Rates: A Geometric Summation-Stable Model. *Proceedings of the Seminar on Data Analysis*, (September), 12-17, Sozopol, Bulgaria.

803. Mittnik, S., Rachev, S. T. and Chenyao, D. (1997). Distribution of Exchange Rates: A Geometric Summation-stable Model. *Proceeding of the 1996 International Conference on Data Analysis*, Bulgarian Academy of Science, Sofia.

804. Mittnik, S., Rachev, S. T., Doganoglu, T. and Chenyao, D. (1999). Maximum Likelihood Estimation of Stable Paretian Models. *Mathematical and Computer Modeling*, 29, 275-293.

805. Mittnik, S., Rachev, S. T. and Kim, J.-R. (1996). Testing for Unit-roots in the Presence of Finite-variance Disturbances. *Unpublished Manuscript*, Institute of Statistics and Econometrics, Christian Albrechts University, Kiel.

806. Mittnik, S., S.T. Rachev, J.-R. Kim and (1998). Chi-square-type distributions for heavy-tailed variates. *Econometric Theory*, 14, 339-354

807. Mittnik, S., Rachev, S. T. and Kim, J.-R. (1999). Time series with unit roots when disturbances are heavy-tailed. *J. Econ. Theory*, to appear.

808. Mittnik, S., Rachev, S. T. and Paolella, M. S. (1996). Integrated Stable GARCH Processes. *Unpublished Manuscript*, Institute of Statistics and Econometrics, Christian Albrechts University at Kiel.

809. Mittnik, S., Rachev, S. T. and Paolella, M. S. (1998). Stable Paretian Modeling in Finance: Some Empirical and Theoretical Aspects, (Adler, R. et al., editors). *A Practical Guide to Heavy Tails: Statistical Techniques and Applications*, 79-110. Birkhäuser, Boston.

810. Mittnik, S., Rachev, S. T. and Rüschendorf, L. (1999). Test of Association Between Multivariate Stable Vectors. *Mathematical and Computer Modeling*, 29, 181-195.

811. Mittnik, S., Rachev, S. T., and Samorodnitsky, G. (1998). Testing for Structural Breaks in Time Series Regressions with Heavy-tailed Disturbances. *Technical Report*, Department of Statistics and Mathematical Economics, University of Karlsruhe.

812. Mittnik, S., Rachev, S. T., and Samorodnitsky, G. (1999a). The Distribution of Test Statistics for Outlier Detection in Heavy-tailed Samples. *Technical Report*, Department of Statistics and Mathematical Economics, University of Karlsruhe.

813. Mittnik, S., Rachev, S. T., and Samorodnitsky, G. (1999b) Testing for Structural Breaks in Time Series Regressions with Heavy-tailed Disturbances. *Technical Report*, Department of Statistics and Mathematical Economics, University of Karlsruhe.

814. Miura, R. (1992). A Note on Look-Back Options Based on Order Statistics. *Hitotsubashi Journal of Commerce and Management*, 27, 15-28.

815. Modigliani, F. and Miller, M. H. (1958). The Cost of Capital, Corporate Finance, and the Theory of Investment. *American Economic Review*, 48, 261-297.

816. Mood, A., Graybill, F. and Boes, D. (1974). *Introduction to the Theory of Statistics*, 3rd ed. McGraw-Hill, Tokyo.

817. Montanari, A., Taqqu, M. S. and Teverowski, V. (1999). Estimating Long-Range Dependence in the Presence of Periodicity. An Empitical Study. *Mathematical and Computer Modelling*, 29, 217-228.

818. Mori, T. and Sato, Y. (1994). Construction and Asymptotic Behavior of a Class of Self-Similar Stable Processes. *Preprint*.

819. Mori, A., Ohsawa M. and Shimizu, T. (1996). A Framework for More Effective Stress Testing. *Risk Measurement and Systemic Risk*, 403-430, Proceedings of a Joint Central Bank Research Conference, Board of Governors of the Federal Reserve System, Washington DC.

820. Müller, U. A., Dacorogna, M. M. and Picet, O. V. (1997). Heavy Tails in High-Frequency Financial Data, (Adler, R. et al., editors). *A Practical*

Guide to Heavy Tails, Statistical Techniques for Analyzing Heavy Tailed Distributions. Birkhäuser, Boston.

821. Myers, R. H., Khuri, I. and Carter, W.-H., Jr. (1989). Response surface methodology: 1966-1988. *Technometrics*, 31, 137-157.

822. Neftci, S. N. (1984). Are economic time series asymmetric over the business cycle? *J. Polit. Econom.*, 92, 307-328.

823. Neftci, S. N. (1996). *An Introduction to the Mathematics of Financial Derivatives.* Academic Press.

824. Nelson, D. B. (1990). Stationarity and Persistence in GARCH(1,1) Model. *Econometric Theory*, 6, 318-334.

825. Nelson, D. B. (1991), Conditional Heteroskedasticity in Asset Returns: A New Approach. *Econometrica*, 59, 347-370.

826. Nelson, D. B. and Cao, C. Q. (1992). Inequality Constraints in the Univariate GARCH Model. *Journal of Business and Economic Statistics*, 10(2), 229-235.

827. Nelson, D. B. and Foster, D. B. (1994). Asymptotic Filtering Theory For Univariate ARCH Models. *Econometrica*, 62, 1-41.

828. Nelson, C. R. and Plosser, C. I. (1982). Trends and Random Walks in Macroeconomic Time Series. *Journal of Monetary Economics*, 10, 139-162.

829. Neyman, J. and Scott, E. L. (1971). Outlier proneness of phenomena and of related distributions, (Rustagi, J. S., editor). *Optimizing Methods in Statistics.* Academic Press, New York.

830. Niederreiter, H. (1992). *Random Number Generation and Quasi-Monte Carlo Methods.* Society for Industrial and Applied Mathematics, Philadelphia, Pennsylvania.

831. Nikias, C. L. and Shao, M. (1995). *Signal Processing with Alpha-Stable Distributions and Applications.* Wiley, New York.

832. Nikias, C. L. and Shao, M. (1996). *Signal Processing with Alpha-Stable Distributions.* Wiley.

833. Nikol'skii, S. M. (1977). Approximation of the Functions of Several Variables and Embedding Theorems. *Nauka*, Moscow.

834. Nolan, J. P. (1996). An Algorithm for evaluating stable densities in Zolotarev's (M) parametrization. *Preprint*, Amerikan University, Washington.

835. Nolan, J. P. (1997a). Maximum Likelihood Estimation of Stable Parameters. *Unpublished manuskript.*

836. Nolan, J. P. (1997b). Numerical Computation of Stable Densities and Distribution Functions, Communications in Statistics. *Stochastic Models*, 13(4), 759-774.

837. Nolan, J. P. (1998a). Maximum Likelihood Estimation and Diagnostics for Stable Distributions. *Working Paper*, Department of Mathematics and Statistics, American University.

838. Nolan, J. P. (1998b). Parameterizations of Stable Distributions. *Statistics and Probability Letters*, 38, 187-195.

839. Nolan, J. P. (1999). An Algorithm for Evaluating Stable Densities in Zolotarev's *(M)* Parametrization. *Mathematical and Computer Modelling*, 29, 229-233.

840. Nowicka, J. and Weron, A. (1995). Numerical Approximation of Dependence Structure for Symmetric Stable AR(2) Processes. *Technical Report*, 294, Dept. of Statistics and Applied Probab., Univ. of California, Santa Barbara.

841. Obretanov, A., Rachev, S. T. (1983). Stability of some characterization properties of the exponential distribution. *Stability Problems for Stochastic Models, Proceedings*, VNIISI, Moscow, 79-87 (in Russian); (1986) *J. Soviet Math.*, 32, No.6, 643-651 (English transl.).

842. Ocone, D. L. and Karatzas, I. (1991). A Generalized Clark Representation Formula, with Application to Optimal Portfolios. *Stochastics*, 39, 187-220.

843. Officer, R. R. (1972). The Distribution of Stock Returns. *Journal of the American Statistical Association*, 76, 807-812.

844. Officer, R. (1973). The Variability of the Market Factor of the New York Stock Exchange. *Journal of Business*, 46, 434-453.

845. Omey, E. (1988). Rates of Convergence for Densities in Extreme Value Theory. *Annals of Probability*, 16, 479-486.

846. Omey, E. and Rachev, S. T. (1988). On the Rate of Convergence in Extreme Value Theory. *Theory of Probability and Its Applications*, 33, 601-607.

847. Ortobelli, S. L. (1999). Portfolio selection: moments analysis and safety-first analysis. *Ph. D. Dissertation*, Bergamo.

848. Ortobelli, S. L. and Rachev, S. T. (1999). Safety-first Analysis and Stable Paretian Approach to Portfolio Choice Theory. *Technical Report*, University of Bergamo and University of Karlsruhe.

849. Osborne, M. F. M. (1959). Brownian Motion in the Stock Market. *Operations Research*, 7, 145-173. (Reprinted, (Cootner, P.H., editor). *The Random Character of Stock Market Prices*, 100-128, Cambridge (MA)).

850. Owen, A. and Tavella, D. (1997). Scrambled Nets for Value-at-Risk Calculations, (S. Grayling, S., editor). *VAR: Understanding and Applying Value-at-Risk*, 289-297. Risk, Lodon.

851. Owen, J. and Rabinovitch, R. (1983). On the class of elliptical distributions and their applications to the theory of portfolio choice. *J. Finance*, 38, 745-752.

852. Page, E. S. (1954). Continuous inspection schemes. *Biometrika*, 41, 100-115.

853. Page, M. and Costa, D. (1997). The Value-at-Risk of a Portfolio of Currency Derivatives Under Worst-Case Distributional Assumptions, (Grayling, S., editor). *VAR: Understanding and Applying Value-at-Risk*, 317-324. Risk, London.

854. Panas, V. G. (1993). Option Pricing with Transaction Costs. *Ph. D. Thesis*, Imperial College, London.

855. Panorska, A. (1992). Generalized Convolutions. *Ph. D. Dissertation*, Department of Statistics and Applied Probability, University of California, Santa Barbara, CA 93106-3110.

856. Panorska, A. (1999). Generalized Convolutions on R with Applications to Financial Modeling. *Mathematical and Computer Modelling*, 29, 263-274.

857. Panorska, A., Mittnik, S. and Rachev, S. T. (1995). Stable GARCH Models for Financial Time Series. *Applied Mathematics Letters*, 815, 33-37.

858. Pareto, V. (1897). *Cours d'Economie Politique*. F. Rouge, Lausanne, Switzerland.

859. Park, J. Y. and Phillips, P. C. B. (1988). Statistical inference in regressions with integrated processes: Part I. *Econometric Theory*, 4, 468-498.

860. Parkinson, M. (1977). Option Pricing; the American Put. *Journal of Business*, 50, 21-36.

861. Paskov, S. H. and Traub, J. F. (1995). Faster Valuation of Financial Derivatives. *The Journal of Portfolio Management*, (Fall), 113-120.

862. Patel, J. K., Kapadia, C. H. and Owen, D.B. (1976). Handbook of Statistical Distributions. *Dekker Series Statistics: Textbooks and Monographs*, 20, New York.

863. Paulauskas, V. and Rachev, S. T. (1998). Cointegrated processes with infinite variance innovations. *Ann. Appl. Prob.*, 8, 775-792.

864. Paulson, A. S., Holcomb, E. W. and Leitch, R. A. (1975). The Estimation of the Parameters of the Stable Law. *Biometrika*, 62, 163-170.

865. Paxson, V. (1997). Fast, Approximate Synthesis of Fractional Gaussian Noise for Generating Self-Similar Network Traffic. *Computer Communication Review*, 27, 5-18.

866. Perrakis, S. and Henin, C. (1974). Evaluation of Risky Investments with Random Timing of Cash Returns. *Management Science*, 21, 79-86.

867. Peters, E. E. (1991). *Chaos and Order in the Capital Markets.* Wiley, New York.

868. Peters, E. E. (1994). *Fractal market analysis.* Wiley, New York.

869. Petersen, M. A. and Fialkowski, D. (1994). Posted versus effective spreads, good prices or bad quotes? *Journal of Financial Economics*, 35(3), 269-292.

870. Petrosky, T., Prigogine, I. (1997). *Advances in Chemical Physics*, XCIX, 1-120. Wiley, Chichester, New York.

871. Petrov, V. V. (1975). *Sums of Independent Random Variables.* Springer, Berlin, New York.

872. Petrov, V. V. (1995). *Limit Theorems of Probability Theory.* Oxford UP, Oxford.

873. Phelan, M. J. (1995). Probability and Statistics Applied to the Practice of Financial Risk Management: The Case of JP Morgan's Riskmetrics™. *Working Paper*, 95-19, Wharton Financial Institutions Center Working Paper Series.

874. Phillips, P. C. B. (1987). Time series regression with a unit root. *Econometrica*, 55, 277-301.

875. Phillips, P. C. B. (1990). Time Series Regression with a Unit Root and Infinite-Variance Errors. *Econometric Theory*, 6, 44-62.

876. Phillips, P. C. B. (1991). Optimal inference in cointegrated systems. *Econometrica*, 59, 283-306.

877. Phillips, P. C. B. (1993). Comment on "Modeling Asset Returns with Alternative Stable Models" and Some Extensions. *Econometric Reviews*, 12, 331-338.

878. Phillips, P. C. B. and Durlauf, S. N. (1986). Multiple time series regression with integrated processes. *Rev. Econom. Stud.*, 53, 473-495.

879. Phillips, P. C. B. and Loretan, M. (1991). The Durbin-Watson ratio under infinite-variance errors. *J. Economet.*, 47, 85-114.

880. Phillips, P. C. B. and Perron, P. (1988). Testing for a unit root in time series regression. *Biometrika*, 75, 335-346.

881. Pickands III, J. (1975). Statistical Inference Using Extreme Order Statistics. *The Annals of Statistics*, 3(1), 119-131.

882. Pictet, O. V., Dacorogna, M. M. and Müller, U. A. (1996). *Behavior of Tail Estimators Under Various Distributions*. Presented at the Satellite Meeting to the 4th World Congress of the Bernoulli Society on "Stable Processes and Other Heavy-tailed Models for Highly Volatile Phenomena", (August 23-25). Wroclaw, Poland.

883. Pitt, L. (1982). Positively Correlated Normal Variables Are Associated. *Ann. Prob.*, 10, 496-499.

884. Platen, E. (1981). An Approximation Method for a Class of Itô Processes. *Lictuvos Math. Rink. XXI*, 1, 121-133.

885. Platen, E. and Schweizer, M. (1994). On Smile and Skewness. *Statistic Research Report SRR 027-94*, The Australian National University, School of Mathematical Sciences, Centre for Mathematics and its Applications.

886. Pliska, S. R. and Selby, M. J. P. (1993). On a Free Boundary Problem that Arises in Portfolio Management. *Preprint*, Dept. Finance, Univ. Illinois, Chicago.

887. Ploberger, W. and Krämer, W. (1992). The CUSUM test with OLS residuals. *Econometrica*, 60, 271-285.

888. Poincaré, H. (1890). Sur une Classe Nouvelle de Transcendantes Uniformes. *J. Math. Pures Appl. 4ᵉ Sér.*, 6, 313-365, Oeuvres, IV, 537-582.

889. Pollard, D. (1984). *Convergence of Stochastic Processes*. Springer, New York.

890. Poterba, J. M. and Summers, L. H. (1988). Mean Reversion in Stock Prices. *Journal of Financial Economics*, 22, 27-59.

891. Praetz, P. (1972). The Distribution of Share Price Changes. *Journal of Business*, 45, 49-55.

892. Pratt, J. W. (1964). Risk-Aversion in the small and in the large. *Econometrica*, 32, 122-136.

893. Press, S. J. (1967). A Compound Events Model for Security Prices. *Journal of business*, 40, 317-335.

894. Press, S. J. (1972a). Multivariate Stable Distributions. *Journal of Multivariate Analysis*, 2, 444-462.

895. Press, S. J. (1972b). Estimation of Univariate and Multivariate Stable Distributions. *Journal of the American Statistical Association*, 67, 842-846.

896. Press, S. J. (1972c). *Applied Multivariate Analysis.* Holt, Rinehart and Winston, Inc., New York.

897. Press, S. J. (1982). *Applied Multivariate Analysis*, 2nd ed. Robert E. Krieger, Malabar.

898. Press, S. J. (1983). *Applied Multivariate Analysis*, 2nd ed. Holt. Rinehart and Winston, New York.

899. Press, W. H., Teukolsky, S. A., Vetterling, W. T. and Flannery, B. P. (1991). *Numerical Recipes in Fortran: The Art of Scientific Computing*, 2nd ed. Cambridge University Press, New York.

900. Press, W. H., Teukolsky, S. A., Vetterling, W. T. and Flannery, B. P. (1992). *Numerical Recipes in C: The Art of Scientific Computing*, 2nd ed. Cambridge University Press, New York.

901. Priest, A. (1997a). Veba's Way with VAR, (Grayling, S., editor). *VAR: Understanding and Applying Value-at-Risk*, 355-357. Risk, London.

902. Priest, A. (1997b). Not So Simple for Siemens, (Grayling, S. editor). *VAR: Understanding and Applying Value-at-Risk*, 363-365. Risk, London.

903. Priestley, M. B. (1981). *Spectral Analysis and Time Series*. Academic Press, London.

904. Prisman, E. (1986). Valuation of Risky Assets in Arbitrage Free Economies with Frictions. *Journal of Finance*, 41, 545-560.

905. Pritsker, M. (1996). Evaluating Value at Risk Methodologies: Accuracy Versus Computational Time. *Working Paper*, 96-48, Wharton Financial Institutions Center Working Paper Series. (1997, (Grayling, S., editor). *VAR: Understanding and Applying Value-at-Risk*, 233-255, Risk, London).

906. Protter, P. (1990). Stochastic Integration and Differential Equations. *Applications of Mathematics*, 21. Springer, Berlin.

907. Pyle, D. H. and Turnovsky (1970). Safety-first and expected utility maximization in mean standard deviation portfolio selection. *Rev. Econ. Stat.*, 52, 75-81.

908. Pyle, D. H. and Turnovsky (1971). Risk aversion in change-constrained portfolio selection. *Management Science*, 18, 218-225.

909. Quirk, J. P. and Saposnik, R. (1962). Admissibility and measurable utility function. *Rev. Econ. Studies*, 29, 140-146.

910. Rachev, S. T. (1981). On the Hausdorff Metric Structure in the Space of Probability Measures. *J. Sov. Math.*, 17(6).

911. Rachev, S. T. (1986). Probability Metrics and Their Applications to the Problems of Stability for Stochastic Models. *Doctor of Science Dissertation*, Steklov Mathematical Institute, Moscow.

912. Rachev, S. T. (1991). *Probability Metrics and the Stability of Stochastic Models*. Wiley, Chichester, New York.

913. Rachev, S. T. (1993). Rate of Convergence for Maxima of Random Arrays with Applications to Stock Returns. *Statistics & Decisions*, 11, 279-288.

914. Rachev, S. T. and Han, S. (1999). Optimization problems in mathematical finance. *Technical Report*.

915. Rachev, S. T. and Karandikar, R. L. (1995). A Generalized Binomial Model and Option Formulae for Subordinated Stock Price Processes. *Probability and Mathematical Statistics*, 15, 427-447.

916. Rachev, S. T. and Kim, J.-R. (1996). Statistical inference in regression with heavy-tailed integrated variables. *Unpublished Manuscript*, Institute of Statistics and Econometrics, Christian Albrechts University, Kiel, Germany.

917. Rachev, S. T., Kim, J.-R. and Mittnik, S. (1996a). Statistical inference in regressions with integrated processes in the presence of heavy-tailed residuals. *Unpublished Manuscript*, Institute of Statistics and Econometrics, Christian Albrechts University, Kiel.

918. Rachev, S. T., Kim, J.-R. and Mittnik, S. (1996b). Testing symmetry when observations are heavy-tailed. *Unpublished Manuscript*, Institute of Statistics and Econometrics, Christian Albrechts University, Kiel.

919. Rachev, S. T., Mittnik, S. and Kim, J.-R. (1996a). Modeling Economics Relationships Driven by Heavy-tailed Innovation Processes: A Survey of Some Recent Results. *Unpublished Manuscript* Institute of Statistics and Econometrics, Christian Albrechts University, Kiel.

920. Rachev, S. T., Mittnik, S. and Kim, J.-R. (1996b). Testing Outliers when Observations are Heavy-tailed. *Unpublished Manuscript*, Institute of Statistics and Econometrics, Christian Albrechts University, Kiel.

921. Rachev, S. T., Mittnik, S. and Kim, J.-R. (1996c). Statistical Inference in Time Series with Unit Roots in the Presence of Heavy-tailed Error Processes. *Unpublished Manuscript*, Institute of Statistics and Econometrics, Christian Albrechts University, Kiel.

922. Rachev, S. T., Kim, J.-R. and Mittnik, S. (1997). Econometric Modeling in the Presence of Heavy-tailed Innovations: A Survey of Some Recent Advances. *Stochastic Models*, 13, 841-866.

923. Rachev, S. T., Mittnik, S. and Kim, J.-R. (1998a). Time series with unit roots and infinite-variance disturbances. *Appl. Math. Lett.*, 11, 69-74.

924. Rachev, S. T., Mittnik, S. and Kim, J.-R. (1999). Stable Paretian Models in Econometrics. *Math. Scientist*, 24, 24-55.

925. Rachev, S. T., Kim, J.-R. and Mittnik, S. (1999). Stable Paretian Models in Econometrics, Part 1 and Part 2. *Mathematical Scientists*, 24, 24-55 .

926. Rachev, S. T., Mittnik, S. and Paolella, M. S. (1997). Modeling the Persistence of Conditional Volatilities with GARCH-stable Processes. *Technical Report*, Institute of Statistics and Econometrics, Christian Albrechts University, Kiel, Germany.

927. Rachev, S. T., Mittnik, S. and Paolella, M. S. (1998). Stable Paretian Modeling in Finance, (Adler, R. J., Feldman, R. E. and Taqqu, M. S., editors). *A Practical Guide to Heavy Tails: Statistical Techniques for Analyzing Heavy Tailed Distributions*, 79-110. Birkhäuser, Boston.

928. Rachev, S. T. and Resnick, S. I. (1991). Max-Geometric Infinite Divisibility and Stability. *Stochastic Models*, 2, 191-218.

929. Rachev, S. T. and Rüschendorf, L. (1994a). Models for option prices. *Theory of Applied Probability*, 39, 120-152.

930. Rachev, S. T. and Rüschendorf, L. (1994b). On the Cox-Ross and Rubinstein Model for Option Pricing. *Theory of Probability Applied*, 39, 150-190.

931. Rachev, S. T. and Rüschendorf, L. (1998a). *Mass Transportation Problems, Volume I: Theory.* Springer, New York.

932. Rachev, S. T. and Rüschendorf, L. (1998b). *Mass Transportation Problems, Volume II: Applications.* Springer, New York.

933. Rachev, S. T. and Samorodnitsky, G. (1993). Option Pricing Formulae for Speculative Prices Modelled by Subordinated Stochastic Processes. *Pliska*, 19, 175-190.

934. Rachev, S. T. and Samorodnitsky, G. (1994). Geometric Stable Distributions in Banach Spaces. *Journal of Theoretical Probability*, 7, 351-373.

935. Rachev, S. T. and Samorodnitsky, G. (1995). Limit Laws for a Stochastic Process and Random Recursion Arising in Probabilistic Modeling. *Advances in Applied Probability*, 27, 185-202.

936. Rachev, S. T. and SenGupta, A. (1992). Geometric Stable Distributions and Laplace-Weibull Mixtures. *Statistics & Decisions*, 10, 251-271.

937. Rachev, S. T. and SenGupta, A. (1993). Laplace-Weibull Mixtures for Modeling Price Changes. *Management Science*, 1029-1038.

938. Rachev, S. T. and Todorovich, P. (1990). On the Rate of Convergence of some Functionals of a Stochastic Process. *J. Appl. Probab.*, 27, 805-814.

939. Rachev, S. T., Weron, A. and Weron, R. (1997). Conditional Exponential Dependence Model for Asset Returns. *Applied Mathematics Letters*, 10, 5-9.

940. Rachev, S. T., Weron, A. and Weron, R. (1999). CED Model for Asset Returns and Fractal Market Hypothesis. *Mathematical and Computer Modelling*, 29, 23-36.

941. Rachev, S. T., Wu, C and Yakovlev, A. Yu. (1995). A bivariate limiting distribution of tumor latency time. *Mathematical Biosciences*, 127, 127-147.

942. Rachev, S. T. and Xin, H. (1993). Test on Association of Random Variables in the Domain of Attraction of Multivariate Stable Law. *Probability and Math. Statist.*, 14, 125-141.

943. Rachev, S. T. and Yukich, J. (1989). Rates for CLT via New Ideal Metrics. *Annals of Probability*, 17, 775-788.

944. Rachev, S. T. and Yukich, J. (1991). Rates of Convergence of α-stable Random Motions. *Journal of Theoretical Probability*, 4, 333-352.

945. Rady, S. (1994). State Prices Implicit in Valuation Formulae for Derivative Securities: A Martingale Approach. *Discussion Paper*, 0181, Financial Markets Group Discussion Papers, London School of Economics.

946. Rahman, M. and Gokhale, D. (1996). On Estimation of Parameters of the Exponential Power Family of Distributions. *Communication in Statistics - Simulation and Computation*, 25(2), 291-299.

947. Ralston, M. L. and Jennrich, R. I. (1978). DUD, A Derivative-Free Algorithm for Nonlinear Least Squares. *Technometrics*, 1, 7-14.

948. Ramachandran, B. (1969). On Characteristic Functions and Moments. *Sankhya*, Series A, 31, 1-12.

949. Rao, C. R. (1973). *Linear Statistical inference and Its Applications.* J.Wiley & Sons, New York.

950. Rao, M. M. and Ren, Z. D. (1991). *Theory of Orlicz Spaces.* Marcel Dekker, New York.

951. Ravacea, E. L. (1962). On Domains of Attraction of Multi-Dimensional Distribution. Selected Translations in Probability Theory and Mathematical Statistics 2. *American Mathematical Society*, Providence, 183-205.

952. Reiss, R. D. (1989). *Approximate Distributions of Order Statistics.* Springer, New York.

953. Rejman, A. and Weron, A. (1996). Option pricing for hyperbolic CRR model. *Lect. Notes Stat.*, 114, 321-331, Springer.

954. Rejman, A., Weron, A. and Weron, R. (1997). Option Pricing Proposals under the Generalized Hyperbolic Model. *Commun. Statist. - Stochastic Models*, 13, 377-390.

955. Rendleman, R. J., Jr. and Barter, B. J. (1979). Two-State Option Pricing. *Journal of Finance*, 34, 519-525.

956. Rényi, A. (1956). Poisson-folymat egy Jemllemzese. *Magyar Tud. Akad. Mat. Kutatò Int. Közl.*, 4, 519-527.

957. Rényi, A. (1967). On the Asymptotic Distribution of the Sum of Random Number of Independent Random Variables. *Acta Math. Acad. Sci. Hung.*, 8, 193-199.

958. Resnick, S. I. (1986), Point processes regular variation and weak convergence. *Adv. Appl. Prob.*, 18, 66-138.

959. Resnick, S. I. (1987a). *Extreme Values, Regular Variation and Point Processes.* Springer, New York.

960. Resnick, S. I. (1987b). Uniform Rates of Convergence to Extreme-value Distributions, (Srivastava, T., editor). *Probability in Statistics: Essays in Honor of Franklin A. Graybill.* North-Holland, Amsterdam.

961. Resnick, S. I. (1988). Association and Multivariate Extreme Value Distributions, (Heyde, C. C., editor). *Gani Festschrift: Studies in Statistical Modeling and Statistical Science*, 261-271, Statistical Society of Australia.

962. Resnick, S. I. and Greenwood, P. (1972). A Bivariate Stable Characterization and Domains of Attraction. *J. Mult. Anal.*, 9, 206-221.

963. Resnick, S. I. and Greenwood, P. (1979). A Bivariate Stable Characterization and Domains of Attraction. *Journal Mult. Anal.*, 10, 206-221.

964. Revuz, D. and Yor, M. (1987). *Continuous Martingales and Brownian Motion.* Springer, Berlin.

965. Rieken, S., Mittnik, S. and Rachev, S. T. (1998). Modeling and Forecasting the DAX-Option Market. *Technical Report*, University of Karlsruhe.

966. Ritchken, P. (1987). *Option.* Scott, Foresman and Co., Glenview IL.

967. Robinson, G. (1996). More Haste, Less Precision. *Risk*, 9 (September), 117-121. (1997, (Grayling, S. editor). *VAR: Understanding and Applying Value-at-Risk*, 95-101. Risk, London).

968. Robbins, H. E. (1948). The asymptotic distribution of the sum of a random number of variables. *Bull. Amer. Math. Soc.*, 54, 1151-1161.

969. Rockette, H., Antle, C. E. and Klimko, L. A. (1974). Maximum Likelihood Estimation with the Weibull Model. *Journal of the American Statistical Association*, 69, 246-249.

970. Rogers, L. C. G. (1997). Arbitrage with fractional Brownian motion. *Mathematical Finance*, 7, 95-105.

971. Rogers, L. and Williams, D. (1987). *Diffusions , Markov Processes, and Martingales 2, Chap 4.* Wiley, New York.

972. Roll, R. (1970). *The Behavior of Interest Rates: An Application of the Efficient Market Model to U.S. Treasury Bills.* Basic Books, New York.

973. Roll, R. (1977). An Analytic Valuation Formula for Unprotected American Call Options on Stocks with Known Dividends. *Journal of Financial Economics*, 5, 251-258.

974. Rosen, O. and Weissman, I. (1996). Comparison of Estimation Methods in Extreme Value Theory. *Communications in Statistics - Theory and Methods*, 25(4), 759-773.

975. Rosinski, J. (1976). Weak Compactness of Laws of Random Sums of Identically Distributed Random Vectors in Banach Spaces. *Coll. Math.*, 35, 313-325.

976. Rosinski, J. (1989). Remarks on Banach Spaces of stable Type. *Probab. Math. Statist.*, 1, 67-71.

977. Rosinski, J. and Woyczynski, W. A. (1987). Multilinear Forms in Pareto-like Random Variables and Product Random Measures. *Coll. Math.*, 51, 303-313.

978. Ross, S. A. (1976). The Arbitrage Theory of Capital Asset Pricing. *J. Econ. Theory*, 13, 341-360.

979. Ross, S. A. (1978). Mutual Fund Separation in Financial Theory - The Separating Distributions. *Journal of Economic Theory*, 17, 254-286.

980. Ross, S. A. (1987). Arbitrage and Martingales with Taxation. *Journal of Political Economy*, 95, 371-393.

981. Ross, S. M. (1991). A Course in Simulation. *Mathematics and Statistics.* Macmillan Publishing Company, New York.

982. Rossi, P. E. (1996). *Modelling Stock Market Volatility - Bridging the Gap to Continuous Time.* Academic Press, New York.

983. Rotar, V. I. (1975). An Extension of the Lindberg-Feller Theorem. *Math. Notes*, 18, 660-663.

984. Rothschild, M. and Stiglitz, J. E. (1970). Increasing risk: I. definition. *J. Econ. Theory*, 2, 225-243.

985. Rozelle, J. and Fielitz, B. (1980). Skewness in Common Stock Returns. *Financial Review*, 15,1-23.

986. Roy, A. D. (1952). Safety-first and the holding of assets. *Econometrica*, 20, 431-449.

987. Rubinstein, M. (1983). Displaced Diffusion Option Pricing. *Journal of Finance*, 38, 213-217.

988. Rubinstein, M. (1985). Nonparametric Tests of Alternative Option Pricing Models Using All Reported Trades and Quotes on the 30 Most Active CBOE Option Classes from August 23, 1976 through August 31, 1978. *Journal of Finance*, 40, 455-480.

989. Rubinstein, M. (1994). Implied Binomial Trees. *Journal of Finance*, 69, 771-818.

990. Runde, R. (1993). A Note on the Asymptotic Distribution of the F-statistic for Random Variables with Infinite Variance. *Statistics & Probability Letters*, 18, 9-12.

991. Runde, R. (1996). The Asymptotic Null Distribution of the Box-Pierce Q-statistic for Random Variables with Infinite Variance - With an Application to German Stock Returns. *Unpublished Manuscript*, Department of Statistics, University of Dortmund.

992. Rvaceva, E. L. (1962). On domains of attraction of multidimensional distributions. *Select. Transl. Math. Statist. Prob. Theory*, 2, 183-205.

993. Safarian, M. (1996). Option Pricing and Hedging in the Presence of Transaction Costs. *Ph.D. Thesis*, Humboldt Univ., Berlin.

994. Sakalauskas, B. (1985). On the Limit Behaviour of the Sum of Random Number of Random Variables. *Lit. Mat. Journal*, 25, 164-175.

995. Samorodnitsky, G. (1995). Infinitely Divisible Processes in Financial Modeling. *Technical Report.*

996. Samorodnitsky, G. (1996). A Class of shot noise model for financial applications, (Heyde, C. C., Prohorov, Yu. V., Pyke, R. and Rachev, S.T., editors). *Proceeding of Athens International Conference on Applied Probability and Time Series.*, 1: Applied Probability, 332-353, Springer.

997. Samorodnitsky, G. and Taqqu, M. S. (1990a). *Stable Random Processes..* Wadsworth and Brooks, Cole, Pacific Grove, CA.

998. Samorodnitsky, G. and Taqqu, M. S. (1990b). Stochastic Monotonicity and Slepian-Type Inequalities for Infinitely Divisible and Stable Random Vectors. *Preprint*

999. Samorodnitsky, G. and Taqqu, M. S. (1991). Conditional Moments for Stable Random Variables. *Stochastic Processes and their Applications*, 39, 183-199.

1000. Samorodnitsky, G. and Taqqu, M. S. (1994). *Stable Non-Gaussian Random Processes*, Stochastic Models with Infinite Variance. Chapman and Hall, New York, London.

1001. Samorodnitsky, G. and Taqqu, M. S. (1995). A Class of Shot Noise Models for Financial Applications, Heyde. *Applied Probability.* Springer, New York.

1002. Samuelson, P. A. (1955). Brownian Motion in Stock Market. *Unpublished manuscript.*

1003. Samuelson, P. A. (1965). Rational Theory of Warrant Pricing. *Industrial Management Review*, 6, 13-32

1004. Sapogov, N. A. (1974). On a Uniqueness Problem for Finite Measures in Euclidean Spaces. *Zap. Nauch. Sem. Leningrad. Otdel. Math. Inst. Steklov.*, 41, 3-13.

1005. Sato, Y. (1991). Distributions of Stable Random Fields of Chentsov Type. *Nagoya Mathematical Journal*, 123, 119-139.

1006. Schachter, B. (1997). The Lay Person's Introduction to Value at Risk. *Financial Engineering News*, 1 (August).

1007. Scheffler, H. P. (1999). On estimation of the spectral measure of certain nonnormal operator stable laws. *Stat. and Prob. Lett.*, 43, 385-392.

1008. Schmeidler, D. (1989). Subjective probability and expected utility without additivity. *Econometrica*, 57, 571-587.

1009. Schumacher, M. (1999). Binomial Option Pricing with Nonindentically Distributed Returns and its Implications. *Mathematical and Computer Modelling*, 29, 121-143.

1010. Scott, L.O. (1987). Option Pricing When the Variance Changes Randomly: Theory, Estimation, and an Application. *Journal of Financial and Quantitative Analysis*, 22, 419-438.

1011. Schröder, M. (1997). The Value-at-Risk Approach: Proposals on a Generalization, (Grayling, S., editor). *VAR: Understanding and Applying Value-at-Risk*, 299-305, Risk, London.

1012. Schuster, E. F. and Barker, R. C. (1987). Using the Bootstrap in Testing Symmetry and Asymmetry. *Comm. Statist. Simul. Comp.*, 16, 69-84.

1013. Schwartz, E. S. (1977). The Valuation of Warrants: Implementing a New Approach. *Journal of Financial Economics*, 4, 407-425.

1014. Schweizer, M. (1988). Hedging of Options in a General Semimartingale Model. *Doctor of Mathematics Dissertation*, ETHZ, 8615, Swiss Federal Institute of Technology, Zürich.

1015. Schumacher, N. (1997). Option Pricing With Infinitely Divisible Returns. *Unpublished Dissertation*, UCSB.

1016. Schwert, W. G. (1989). Why Does Stock Market Volatility Change Over Time? *Journal of Finance*, 44, 1115-1153.

1017. Scott, L. (1987). Option Pricing When the Variance Changes Randomly. *Journal of Financial and Quantitative Analysis*, 22, 419-438.

1018. Senatov, V. V. (1977). On Certain Properties of Metrics on the Set of Distribution Functions. *Mat. Sb.*, 102(144), 3, 425-434.

1019. Senatov, V. V. (1980). Uniform Estimates of the Rate of Convergence in the Multidimensional Central Limit Theorem. *Theory Prob. Appl.*, 25, 745-759.

1020. Senatov, V. V. (1981). Some Lower Estimates for the Rate of Convergence in the Central Limit Theorem on Hilbert Space. *Sov. Math. Dokl.*, 23, 188-192.

1021. Shaked, M. (1977). A Concept of Positive Dependence for Exchangeable Variables. *Ann. Statist.*, 5, 505-515.

1022. Shaked, M. and Tong, Y. L. (1985). Some Partial Orderings of Exchangeable Random Variables by Positive Dependence. *J. Multivariate Anal.*, 17, 339-349.

1023. Shanno, D. F. (1970). Conditioning of Quasi-Newton Methods for Functional Minimization. *Mathematics of Computing*, 24, 647-656.

1024. Shao, M. and Nikias, C. L. (1993). Signal Processing with fractional lower order moments: stable processes and applications. *Proceedings of the IEEE*, 81, 984-1010.

1025. Sharpe, M. (1969). Operator-Stable Probability Distributions on Vector Groups. *Trans. Amer. Math. Soc.*, 136, 51-65.

1026. Sharpe, W. F. (1963). A Simplified Model for Portfolio Analysis. *Management Science*, 9, 277-93.

1027. Sharpe, W. F. (1964). Capital Asset Prices: A Theory of Market Equilibrium under Conditions of Risk. *J. Finance*, 19, 425-442.

1028. Sharpe, W. F. (1978). *Investment.* Prentice Hall, Englewood Cliffs, N.J.

1029. Shaw, J. (1997). Beyond VAR and Stress Testing, (Grayling, S., editor). *VAR: Understanding and Applying Value-at-Risk*, 211-223. Risk, London.

1030. Shefi, H. (1996). A Checklist for VAR Systems. *Derivatives Strategy*, 1 (November), 52-53.

1031. Sheikh, A. M. (1991). Transaction Data Tests of S&P 100 Call Option Pricing. *Journal of Financial and Quantitative Analysis*, 26, 459-475.

1032. Shen, Q. (1990). Bid-Ask Prices for Call Options with Transaction Costs. *Working paper*, The Warton School, Uni. Pennsylvania.

1033. Shepp, L. and Shiryaev, A. N. (1993). The Russian Option: Reduced Regret. *Annals of Applied Probability*, 3, 631-640.

1034. Shimko, D. (1993). Bounds of Probability. *Risk*, 6, 33-37.

1035. Shimko, D. (1996). What is VAR? *Risk*, 9 (January). (1997, (Grayling, S. editor). *VAR: Understanding and Applying Value-at-Risk*, 331-332. Risk, London).

1036. Shimko, D. (1997a). VAR for Corporates, (Grayling, S., editor). *VAR: Understanding and Applying Value-at-Risk*, 345-347. Risk, London.

1037. Shimko, D. (1997b). Investors' Return on VAR, (Grayling, S., editor). *VAR: Understanding and Applying Value-at-Risk*, 349. Risk, London.

1038. Shiraga, T. and Tanaka, H. (1985). Central Limit Theorem for a System of Markovian Particles with Mean Field Interactions. *Z. Wahrsch. Verw. Gebiete*, 69, 439-459.

1039. Shiryaev, A. N. (1984). *Probability*. Springer, New York.

1040. Shiryaev, A. N. (1994). On some basic concepts and stochastic models in financial mathematics. *Teor. Veroyatnost. i Primenen.*, 39, 5-22.

1041. Shiryaev, A. N., Kabanov, Yu. M., Kramkov, D. O. and Melnikov, A. V. (1994a). On the Theory of Evaluation European and American Options, I, II. *Theory of Probability Applied*, 39, 27-129.

1042. Shiryaev, A. N., Kabanov, Yu. M., Kramkov, D. O. and Melnikov, A. V. (1994b). Towards the Theory of Pricing of Options of both European and American Types. I. Discrete Time. *Teor. Veroyatnost. i Primenen.*, 39, 23-79.

1043. Shorack, G. and Wellner, J. A. (1986). *Empirical Processes with Applications to Statistics*. Wiley, New York.

1044. Shreve, S. E. and Soner, H. M. (1994). Optimal Investment and Consumption with Transaction Costs. *Ann. Appl. Probab.*, 4, 609-692.

1045. Silverman, B. W. (1986). *Density Estimation for Statistics and Data Analysis*. Chapman and Hall, London.

1046. Simkowitz, M. and Beedles, W. (1980). Asymmetric Stable Distributed Security Returns. *Journal of the American Statistical Association*, 75, 306-312.

1047. Simons, K. (1996). Value at Risk - New Approaches to Risk Management. *Federal Reserve Bank of Boston New England Economic Review*, (Sept/Oct), 3-13. (1997, (Grayling, S., editor). em VAR: Understanding and Applying Value-at-Risk, 133-139. Risk, London).

1048. Singh, R. S. (1988). Estimation of Error Variance in Linear Regression Models With errors Having a Multivariate Student-t Distribution With Unknown Degrees of Freedom. *Economics Letters*, 27, 47-53.

1049. Singh, M. (1997). Value at Risk Using Principal Components Analysis. *Journal of Portfolio Management*, 24 (Fall), 101-110.

1050. Skorokhod, A. V. (1957). Limit theorems for stochastic processes with independent increments. *Theory Probab. Appl.*, 2, 138-171.

1051. Slominski, L. (1989). Stability of strong solutions of stochastic differential equations. *Stoch. Process. Appl.*, 31, 173-202.

1052. Smirnov, N. V. (1948). Table for Estimating the Goodness of Fit of Empirical Distributions. *Ann. Math. Statist.*, 19, 279-281.

1053. Smith, C. W. Jr. (1976). Option Pricing: A Review. *Journal of Financial Economics*, 3, 3-51.

1054. Smith, R. L. (1982). Uniform Rates of Convergence in Extreme-value Theory. *Advances in Applied Probability*, 14, 600-622.

1055. Smith, R. L. (1987). Estimating Tails of Probability Distributions. *Annals of Statistics*, 15, 1174-1207,

1056. Smith, W. L. (1958). Renewal Theory and its Ramifications (with Discussions). *Roy, J. Statist. Soc.*, 20, 243-302.

1057. Smithson, C. W., Smith C. W. Jr. and Wilford, D. S. (1995). *Managing Financial Risk: A Guide to Derivative Products, Financial Engineering, and Value Maximization.* Irwin Professional Publishing, New York.

1058. Snitzman, A. S. (1984). Nonlinear Reflecting Diffusion Process, and the Propagation of Chaos and Fluctuations Associated. *J. Funct. Anal.*, 56, 311-336.

1059. So, J. C. (1987a). The Distribution of Foreign Exchange Price Changes: Trading Day Effects and Risk Measurement. *Journal of Finance*, 42, 181-188.

1060. So, J. C. (1987b). Distribution of Exchange Rates: A Comment. *Journal of Finance*, 42, 181-188.

1061. Sobol, I. M. (1973). Numerical Monte Carlo Methods. *Nauka* (in Russian), Moscow.

1062. Soderlind, P. and Svensson, L. E. O. (1997). New Techniques To Extract Market Expectations From Financial Instruments. *Working Paper*, 5877, NBER Working Paper Series.

1063. Soltani, A. R. and Moeanaddin, R. (1994). On Dipersion of Stable Random Sectors and its Application in the Prediction of Multivariate Stable Processes. *J. Appl. Probab.*, 31, 691-699.

1064. Soner, H. M., Shreve, S. E. and Cvitanić J. (1995). There is No Nontrivial Hedging Portfolio for Option Pricing with Transaction Costs. *Ann. Appl. Probability*, 5, 327-355.

1065. Spanos, A. (1993). On Modeling Speculative Prices: Student's t Autoregressive Model with Dynamic Heteroskedasticity. *Technical Report*, University of Cyprus.

1066. Spinner, K. (1996). Adapting VAR to the Corporate Jungle. *Derivatives Strategy*, 1 (April).

1067. Stam, A. J. (1965). Derived Stochastic Processes. *Composito Math.*, 17, 102-140.

1068. Stein, E. and Stein, J. (1991). Stock Price Distributions with Stochastic Volatility: an Analytic Approach. *Review of Financial Studies*, 4, 727-752.

1069. Steutel, F. W. (1970). Preservation of Infinite Divisibility Under Mixing and Related Topics. *MCT*, Amsterdam.

1070. Stock, J. (1988). Estimating Continuous Time Processes subject to Time Deformation. *Journal of the American Statistical Association*, 83, 77-84.

1071. Stock, J. H. and Watson, W. W. (1988). Testing for common trends. *J. Amer. Statist. Assoc.*, 83, 1097-1107.

1072. St. Pierre, E. F. (1993). The Importance of Skewness and Kurtosis in the Time- Series of Security Returns. *Ph. D. Thesis*, The Florida State University College of Business.

1073. Stricker, C. (1985). Lois de semimartingales et criteres de compacite, Sem. de Probab., XIX. *Lecture Notes in Math.*, 1123. Springer, Berlin.

1074. Stroock, D. and Yor, M. (1980). On Extremal Solutions of Martingale Problems. *Annales Scientifiques e lÉcole Normale Superieure*, 13, 95-164.

1075. Student [W.S. Gosset], (1927). Errors of routine analysis. *Biometrika*, 19, 151-164.

1076. Studer, G. and Luthi, H.-J. (1997). Quadratic Maximum Loss, (Grayling, S., editor). *VAR: Understanding and Applying Value-at-Risk*, 307-315. Risk, London.

1077. Szász, D. (1972). Limit Theorems for the Distributions of the Sums of a Random Number of Random Variables. *Ann. Math. Stat.*, 43, 1902-1913.

1078. Szynal, D. (1976). On Limit Distribution Theorems for Sums of a Random Number of Random Variables appearing in the study of rarefaction of a recurrent process. *Zasfosowania matematyki*, 15,277-288.

1079. Takenaka, S. (1991). Integral-Geometric Construction of Self-Similar Stable Processes. *Nagoya Mathematical Journal*, 123, 1-12.

1080. Tanaka, K. (1996). *Time Series Analysis, Nonstationary and Noninvertible Distribution Theory.* Wiley, New York.

1081. Tapia, R. A. and Thompson, J. R. (1978). *Nonparametric Probability Density Estimation.* Johns Hopkins UP.

1082. Tapia, R. A. and Thompson, J. R. (1990). *Nonparametric Function Estimation, Modelling, and Simulation.* SIAM, Philadelphia.

1083. Taqqu, M. S. and Teverovsky, V. (1997). Robustness of Whittle - type estimates for time series with long-range dependence. *Stochastic Models,* 13, 723-757.

1084. Taqqu, M. S. and Teverovsky, V. (1998). On Estimating the Intensity of Long-Range Dependence in Finite and Infinite Variance Time Series, (Adler, R. J., Feldman, R. E., and Taqqu, M. S., editors). *A Practical Guide to Heavy Tails.* Birkäuser, Boston.

1085. Taylor, S. (1986). *Modelling Financial Time Series.* Wiley, Chichester.

1086. Taylor, S. and Xu, X. (1994). The Magnitude of Implied Volatility Smiles: Theory and Empirical Evidence for Exchange Rates. *Review of Futures Markets,* 13, 355-380.

1087. Taylor, S. and Xu, X. (1995). The Incremental Volatility Information in One Million Foreign Exchange Quotations, 4. *Proceedings of HFDF-1 Conference,* (March), 29-31, Zürich.

1088. Teichmoeller, J. (1971). A Note on the Distribution of Stock Price Changes. *Journal of the American Statistical Association,* 66, 282-284.

1089. Teräsvirta, T. (1994). Specification, estimation and evaluation of smooth transition autoregressive models. *J. Amer. Statist. Soc.,* 89, 208-218.

1090. Teräsvirta, T. (1996). Two Stylized Facts and the GARCH(1,1) Model. *Working Paper,* 96, Stockholm School of Economics.

1091. Teräsvirta T. and Anderson, H. M. (1992). Characterizing nonlinearities in business cycles using smooth transition autoregressive models. *J. Appl. Economet.* 7, 119-136.

1092. Thavaneswaran, A. and Peiris, S. (1999). Estimation for Regression with Infinite Variance Errors. *Mathematical and Computer Modelling,* 29, 177-180.

1093. Thisted, R. A. (1988). *Elements of Statistical Computing.* Chapman and Hall, New York.

1094. Thompson, C. M. (1941). Table of percentage points of the χ^2 distribution. *Biometrika* 32, 187-191.

1095. Tobin, J. (1958). Liquidity preference as behavior toward risk. *Rev. Econ. Stud.*, 25, 65-86.

1096. Toft, K. B. (1993). Exact Formulas for Expected Hedging Error and Transaction Costs in Option Replication. *Preprint*, Uni. California, Berkeley.

1097. Tong, Y. L. (1977). An Ordering Theorem for Conditionally Indentically Distributed Random Variables. *Ann. Statist.*, 5, 505-515.

1098. Tong, Y. L. (1980). *Probability Inequalities in Multivariate Distributions.* Academic Press, New York.

1099. Tong, Y. L. (1990). *The Multivariate Normal Distribution.* Springer, New York.

1100. Tsay, R. (1986). Time series model specification in the presence of outliers. *Journal of the American Statistical Association* 81, 132-141.

1101. Tucker, A. L. (1992). A Reexamination of Finite-Variance and Infinite-Variance Distributions as Models of Daily Stock Returns. *Journal of Business and Economic Statistics*, 10, 73-81.

1102. Turnbull, S. T. and Miln, F. (1991). A Simple Approach to Interest-Rate Option Pricing. *The Review of Financial Studies*, 4, 87-120.

1103. Turner, C. (1996). VAR as an Industrial Tool. *Risk*, 9 (March), 38-40. (1997, (Grayling, S., editor). *VaR: Understanding and Applying Value-at-Risk*, 341-343. Risk, London).

1104. Vandev, D., Ignatov, Zv. and Rachev, S. T. (1982). Metrics That are Invariant Relative to Monotone Transformations. *Stability Problems for Stochastic Models* (in Russian), 25-36, Proceedings, UNIISI, Moscow. (English Transl. *J. Soviet. Math.*, 35(3), 2466-2478).

1105. Venkataraman, S. (1997). Value at Risk for a Mixture of Normal Distributions: The Use of Quasi-Bayesian Estimation Techniques. *Economic Perspectives*, (March/April), 3-13, Federal Reserve Bank of Chicago.

1106. Vere-Jones, D. (1970)., Stochastic Models for Earthquake Occurencies. *Journal Royal Stat. Soc.*, Ser. B, 532, 1-42.

1107. Vervaat, W. (1972). Functional Central Limit Theorems for Processes with Positive Drift and Their Inverses. *Zeitschrift für Wahrsch. Verw. Gebiete.*, 10, 73-81.

1108. Von Neumann, J. and Morgenstern, O. (1953). *Theory of games and economic behavior*, Princeton University Press, Princeton, N.J.

1109. Walsh, J. B. (1986). An Introduction to Stochastic Partial Differential Equations. *Ecole d' Eté de Probabilités de Saint-Flour XIV. Lecture Notes in Math.*, 1180, 265-439. Springer, Berlin.

1110. Walter, C. (1989). Les Risque de Marché et les Distributions de Lévy. *Analyse Financière*, 78, 40-50.

1111. Walter, C. (1990). Mise en Évidence de Distributions Lévy-stables et d'une Structure Fractale Sur le Marché de Paris. *Actes du Premier Colloque International de lAFIR*, 3, 241-259.

1112. Walter, C. (1991). L'Utilisation des Lois Lévy-stable en Finance: une Solution Possible au Problème Posé par les Discontinuité des Trajectoires Boursiéres. *Bulletin de l'Institut des Actuaires Francais*, 349,3-32 and 350, 3-23.

1113. Walter, C. (1999). Lévy-Stability-Under-Addition and Fractal Structure of Markets: Implications for the Investment Management Industry and Emphasized Examination of MATIF Notional Contract. *Mathematical and Computer Modelling*, 29, 37-56.

1114. Watanabe, S. (1993). Generalized Arc-Sine Laws for One Dimensional Diffusion Processes and Random Walks. *Preprint*, Kyoto Univ.

1115. Wei, W. S. (1990). em Time Series Analysis: Univariate and Multivariate Methods. Addison-Wesley, Reading, MA.

1116. Wellner, J. A. (1978). Limit Theorems for the Ration of the Empirical Distribution Function to the Distribution Function. *Z. Wahr. verw. Geb.*, 45, 73-88.

1117. Weron, A. (1984). Stable Processes and Measures: A Survey. *Probability Theory on Vector Spaces III, Lecture Notes in Math*, 1080, 306-364.

1118. Weron, R. (1996). On the Chambers-Mallows-Stuck method for simulating skewed stable random variables. *Statistics and Probability Letters*, 28, 165-171.

1119. Weron, K. and Jurlewicz, A. (1993). Two forms of self-similarity as a fundamental feature of the power-law dielectric relaxation. *Journal of Physics A: Mathematical and General*, 26, 395-410.

1120. Weron, A. and Weron, K. (1985). Stable Measures and Processes in Statistical Physics. *Lecture Notes in Mathematics*, 1143, 440-452, Proceedings, Probability in Banach Spaces. Springer.

1121. Westerfield, R. (1977a). The Distribution of Common Stock Price Changes: An Application of Transaction Time and Subordinated Stochastic Models. *Journal of Financial and Quantitative Analysis*, 12, 743-765.

1122. Westerfield, R. (1977b). Foreign Exchange Risk Under Fixed and Floating Rate Regimes. *Journal of International Economics*, 7, 181-200.

1123. Whitmore, G. A. and Lee, M.- L. T. (1991). Inferences for Poisson Hougaard Processes. *Preprint*.

1124. Whittle, P. (1953). Estimation and Information in Stationary Time Series. *Ark. Mat.*, 2, 423-434.

1125. Wichura, M. J. (1987). An accurate algorithm for computing quantiles of the normal distribution. *Unpublished Manuscript*, Department of Statistics, University of Chicago.

1126. Widder, D. V. (1946). *The Laplace Transform.*, Princeton Univ. Press.

1127. Wiggins, J. (1987). Option Values Under Stochastic Volatility: Theory and Empirical Estimates. *Journal of Financial Economics*, 19, 351-372.

1128. Wilkinson, S. R., Bharucha, C. F., Fisher, M. C., et al, (1997). Experimental evidence for non-exponential decay in quantum tunnelling. *Nature*, 387, 575-577.

1129. Willinger, W. and Taqqu, M. (1987). The Analysis of Finite Securities Markets Using Martingales. *Advances in Applied Probability*, 19, 1-25.

1130. Willinger, W., Taqqu, M. S., and Teverovsky, V. (1999). Stock market prices and long-range dependence. *Finance and Stochastics*, 3, 1-13.

1131. Willmott, P., Dewynne, J. and Howison, S. (1993). *Option Pricing, mathematical models and computation.* Oxford Financial Press, Oxford.

1132. Wilson, E. B. and Hilferty, M. M. (1931). The distribution of chi-square. *Proceedings of the National Academy of Science*, 17, 684-688.

1133. Wilson, T. (1994). Plugging the GAP. *Risk*, 7, 10 (October), 74-80.

1134. Winter, R. G. (1961). Evolution of a quasi-stationary state. *Phys. Rev.*, 123, 1503-1507.

1135. Wintner, A. (1936). On a class of Fourier transforms. *American Journal of Mathematics*, 58, 45-90.

1136. Woysczynski, W. A. (1980). On Marcinkiewicz-Zygmund Laws of Large Numbers in Banach Spaces and Related Rates of Convergence. *Probab. Math. Stat.*, 1, 117-131.

1137. Wu, W. and Cambanis, S. (1991). Conditional Variance of Symmetric Stable Variables, (Cambanis, S. Samorodnitsky, G. and Taqqu, M. S., editors). *Stable Processes and Related Topics*, 85-100, A selection of papers from MSI workshop 1990. Birkhäuser, Boston, MA.

1138. Xin, H. (1992). Statistics of Bivariate Extreme Values. *Ph. D Thesis*, Tinbergen Institute Research Series, Erasmus University, Rotterdam, The Netherlands.

1139. Yamazato, M. (1978). Unimodality of infinitely divisible distributions of class *l*. *Annals of Probability*, 6, 523-531.

1140. Zangari, P. (1996). How Accurate is the Delta-Gamma Methodology? *RiskMetrics Monitor*, (Third Quarter 1996), 12-29.

1141. Zellner, A. (1971). *An Introduction to Bayesian Inference in Econometrics* . Wiley, New York.

1142. Zellner, A. (1976). Bayesian and Non-Bayesian Analysis of the Regression Model With Multivariate Student-t Error Terms. *Journal of the American Statistical Association*, 71(354), 400-405.

1143. Zenios, S. A. (1993). *Financial Optimization*, Cambridge University Press.

1144. Ziemba, W. T. (1974). Choosing Investment Portfolios When the Returns Have Stable Distributions, (Hammer, P. L. and Zoulendijl, G., editors). *Mathematical Programming in Theory and Practice*, 443-482, North-Holland.

1145. Ziemba, W. T. and Vickson, R. G. (1975). *Stochastic Optimization Models in Finance*. Academic Press, New York.

1146. Zolotarev, V. M. (1964). On the Representation of Stable Laws by Integrals. *Selected Translations in Mathematical Statistics and Probability*, 4, 84-88.

1147. Zolotarev, V. M. (1966). On Representation of the Stable Laws by Integrals. *Selected Translations in Mathematical Statistics and Probability*, 6, 84-88. American Mathematical Society, Providence, Rhode Island.

1148. Zolotarev, V. M. (1976). Metric Distances in Spaces of Random Variables and of Their Distributions. *Mat. Sb.*, 101 (143), 3 (11), 416-454.

1149. Zolotarev, V. M. (1978). On Pseudomoments. *Theory Prob. Appl.*, 23, 269-278.

1150. Zolotarev, V. M. (1981). On the Properties and the Relations of Certain Types of Metrics. *J. Sov. Math.*, 17, 6.

1151. Zolotarev, V. M. (1983a). Goodness of Fit Section) Uniform quadratic metric. *Theor. Verojat. Primenen.*, 28, 810.

1152. Zolotarev, V. M. (1983b). Probability Metrics. *Theory of Probability and Its Applications*, 28, 278-302.

1153. Zolotarev, V. M. (1983c). One-Dimensional Stable Distributions. *Nauka* (in Russian), Moscow. (1986, English translation, *American Mathematical Society*, Provindence, R.I.).

1154. Zolotarev, V. M. (1986a). One-dimensional Stable Distributions. *Translations of Mathematical Monographs*, 65, American Mathematical Society, Providence.

1155. Zolotarev, V. M. (1986b). Contemporary Theory of Summation of Independent Random Variables. *Nauka* (in Russian), Moscow.

1156. Zolotarev, V. M. and Senatov, V. V. (1975). Two-Side Estimates of the Lévy Metric. *Theory of Probability and Its Applications*, 20, 239-250.

1157. Zygmund, A. (1988). *Trigonometric Series*, First Paperback. Cambridge University Press, Cambridge.

Indexes

Author-Index

Kim, J., xvii, 664–668, 671, 682, 687, 689, 696, 697, 723, 724, 727, 728
King, M., 222
Klüppelberg, C., 32, 197, 200, 212, 215
Klebanov, L., xvii, 35, 42, 52, 54, 55, 77, 80, 92, 98, 273, 348, 351, 353, 356, 407, 492, 560, 573
Kloeden, P., 294
Koedijk, K., 106, 111
Kogon, S., 495
Kokoszka, P., 197, 205, 207, 208, 211–213, 269
Komlós, J., 320
Kono, N., 194
Kool, C., 111
Kopp, P., 513, 731
Korn, R., 514
Korolev, V., 331
Kotz, S., 42, 348, 374, 376
Koutrouvelis, I., 84, 495
Kozubowski, T., xvii, 35, 39, 492
Krämer, W., 682–684, 686, 687
Kreps, D., 512
Kroll, Y., 428, 429
Kroner, K., 14, 172, 182, 305, 310, 478
Kunita, H., 514
Kupiec, P., 465, 466, 481
Kurtz, T., 732, 733, 735, 742

L

Lüdecke, T., 253
Lévy, P., xvi
Lange, K., 159
Latané, H., 618
Lawrence, C., 477
Leadbetter, M., 672
Ledoux, M., 540
Lee, M., 328, 330, 331, 335, 336
Lee, S., 10, 170
Lee, W., 514
Leippold, M., 625
Leitch, R., 495
Leland, H., 514
Levhari, D., 426, 463, 464
Levy, H., 428, 429, 438
Lingren, G., 672
Linnik, Yu. V., 42

Linsmeier, T., 469
Lintner, J., 409
Lipster, R., 359
Lisitsky, A., 354, 407
Litzenberg, R., 436
Litzenberger, R., 428, 429
Liu, R., 465–467, 479
Liu, S., 284, 508
Lloyd, E., 222
Lo, A., 222, 224
Loeve, M., 551
Lopez, J., 466, 481
Loretan, M., 108, 304, 671, 686
Luukkonen, R., 696
Lux, T., 108

M

Ma, J., 513
Mac Donald, B., 23, 409
MacBeth, J., 603
Machina, M., 427
MacNeill, I., 682
Madan, D., 596
Maejima, M., 194–196, 338, 342, 388
Mahoney, J., 469, 475, 481
Major, P., 320
Maller, R., 382
Mandelbrot, B., xvi, 1, 19, 26, 77, 182, 185, 194, 219, 221, 222, 236, 304, 305, 515, 526, 542, 550, 582, 607, 664
Manija, G., 54, 98, 573
Marinelli, C., xvii, 216, 219, 220, 226, 227, 233, 250, 252, 261, 268
Markowitz, H., 399, 419, 424, 438, 440
Marshall, C., 482
Maruyama, G., 294
Mason, D., 106
Mateev, P., 149, 492
Maude, D., 465–467, 475, 477, 480
McCabe, B., 682
McCulloch, J., 27, 83, 84, 120, 130, 132, 147, 193, 225, 226, 305, 377, 492, 495, 535
McDunnough, P., 495
Meerschaert, M., 340
Melamed, I., 42, 54, 55, 92, 98, 348, 356, 492, 573

Subject-Index

Printed and bound by CPI Group (UK) Ltd, Croydon, CR0 4YY

23/04/2025

14660955-0003